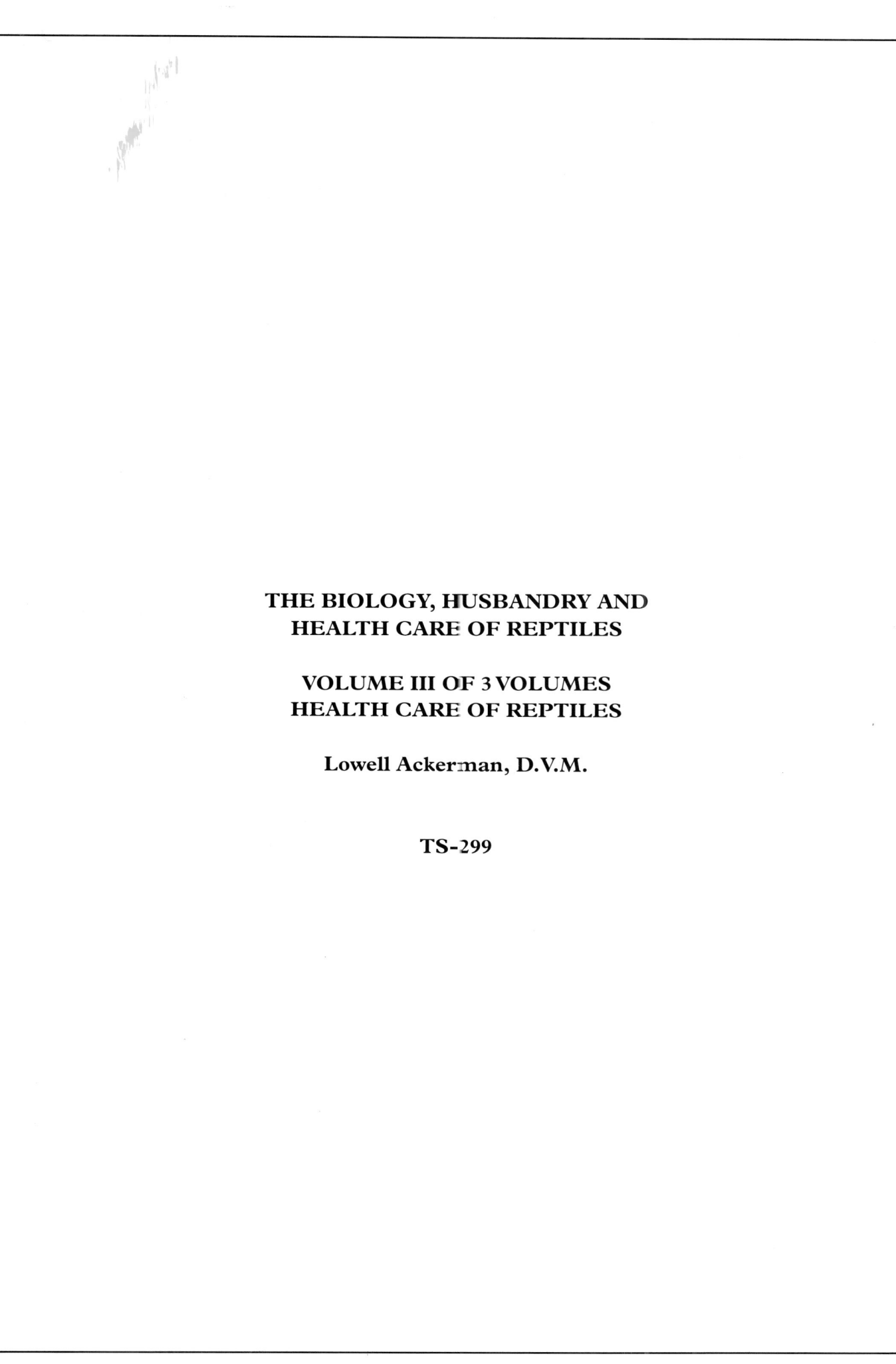

THE BIOLOGY, HUSBANDRY AND HEALTH CARE OF REPTILES

VOLUME III OF 3 VOLUMES
HEALTH CARE OF REPTILES

Lowell Ackerman, D.V.M.

TS-299

NOTICE

The authors and editors have exerted every effort to ensure that medical information mentioned in this book is in accord with current recommendations and practice at the time of publication. However, in view of the ongoing advances in veterinary medicine, readers are urged to consult with their veterinarian regarding individual health issues.

Distributed in the UNITED STATES to the Pet Trade by T.F.H. Publications, Inc., One T.F.H. Plaza, Neptune City, NJ 07753; distributed in the UNITED STATES to the Bookstore and Library Trade by National Book Network, Inc. 4720 Boston Way, Lanham MD 20706; in CANADA to the Pet Trade by H & L Pet Supplies Inc., 27 Kingston Crescent, Kitchener, Ontario N2B 2T6; Rolf C. Hagen Inc., 3225 Sartelon St. Laurent-Montreal Quebec H4R 1E8; in CANADA to the Book Trade by Vanwell Publishing Ltd., 1 Northrup Crescent, St. Catharines, Ontario L2M 6P5; in ENGLAND by T.F.H. Publications, PO Box 15, Waterlooville PO7 6BQ; in AUSTRALIA AND THE SOUTH PACIFIC by T.F.H. (Australia), Pty. Ltd., Box 149, Brookvale 2100 N.S.W., Australia; in NEW ZEALAND by Brooklands Aquarium Ltd. 5 McGiven Drive, New Plymouth, RD1 New Zealand; in Japan by T.F.H. Publications, Japan—Jiro Tsuda, 10-12-3 Ohjidai, Sakura, Chiba 285, Japan; in SOUTH AFRICA by Lopis (Pty) Ltd., P.O. Box 39127, Booysens, 2016, Johannesburg, South Africa. Published by T.F.H. Publications, Inc.

MANUFACTURED IN THE
UNITED STATES OF AMERICA
BY T.F.H. PUBLICATIONS, INC.

THE BIOLOGY, HUSBANDRY AND HEALTH CARE OF REPTILES

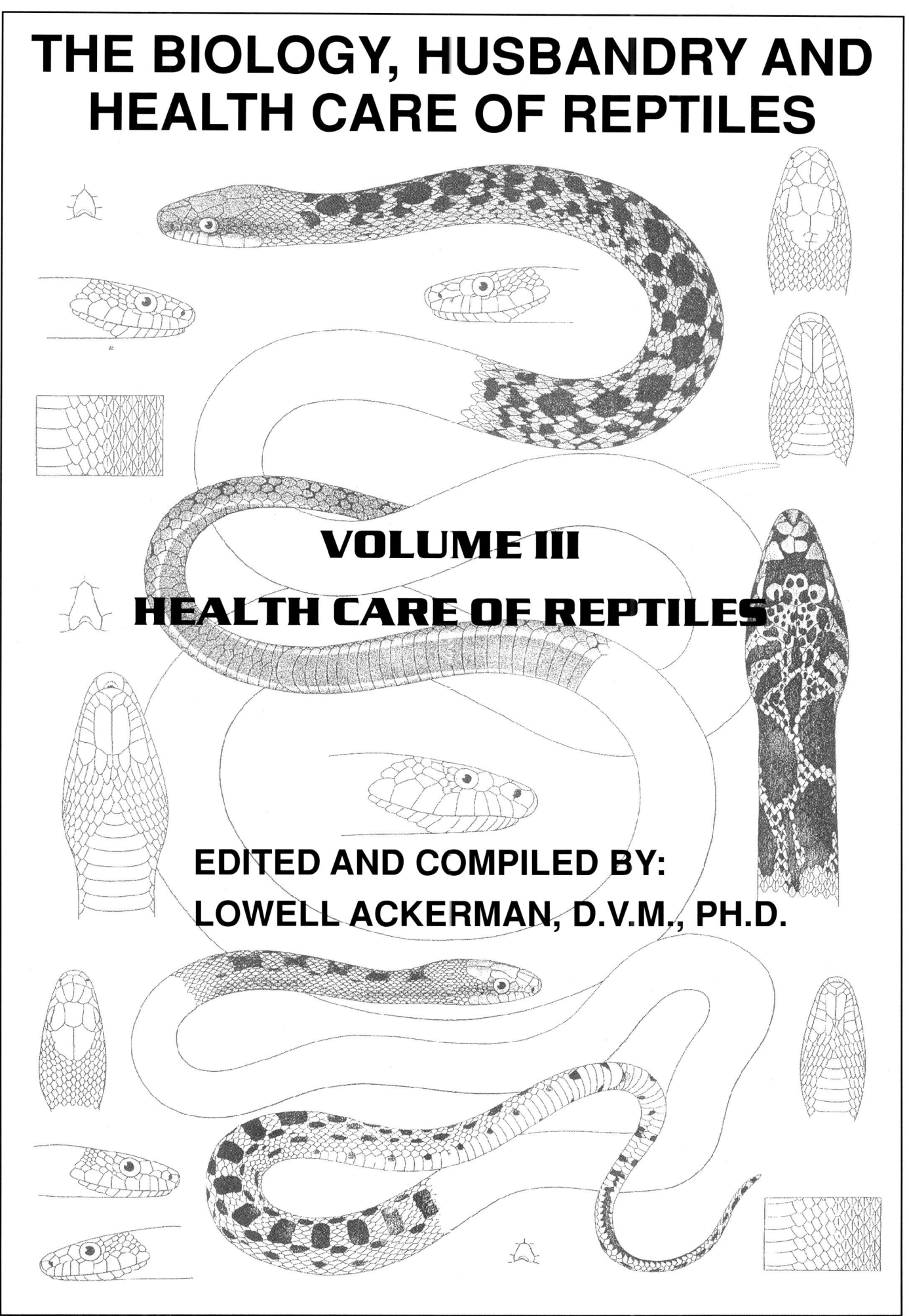

VOLUME III

HEALTH CARE OF REPTILES

EDITED AND COMPILED BY:
LOWELL ACKERMAN, D.V.M., PH.D.

In addition to being available separately as individual volumes, the three books that constitute *The Biology, Husbandry and Health Care of Reptiles* are available also as a set under that title.

Volume I, *The Biology of Reptiles*

T.F.H. Publications, Inc. style number TS-297
ISBN 0-7938-0501-5

Volume II, *The Husbandry of Reptiles*

T.F.H. Publications, Inc. style number TS-298
ISBN 0-7938-0502-3

Volume III, *The Health Care of Reptiles*

T.F.H. Publications, Inc. style number TS-299
ISBN 0-7938-0503-1

The Biology, Husbandry and Health Care of Reptiles, a three-volume set comprising all three of the above-listed books:

T.F.H. Publications, Inc. style number TS-300
ISBN 0-7938-0504-X

Please Note: The following pages include the Tables of Contents of all 3 volumes.

TABLE OF CONTENTS
VOLUME I - BIOLOGY OF REPTILES

TABLE OF CONTENTS
VOLUME II – HUSBANDRY OF REPTILES

TABLE OF CONTENTS
VOLUME III - HEALTH CARE OF REPTILES

TECHNICAL EDITORS
Tara K. Harper
Lowell Ackerman DVM, PhD
Herbert R. Axelrod, Ph.D., DSC

LIST OF CONTRIBUTING AUTHORS
Lowell Ackerman DVM PhD
Pet Health Initiative, Scottsdale, Arizona

Frank Austin DVM, PhD
College of Veterinary Medicine, Mississippi
State University

Michael J. Balsai, BA
University of Pennsylvania

Sean J. Barry, MS
Section of Evolution and Ecology, University
of California, Davis

Brad Bolon, DVM, MS, PhD, Diplomate,
American College of Veterinary Pathologists
Pathology Associates International Corpora-
tion, Jefferson Arkansas

Shelley Burgin, Bsc, Msc, PhD
Faculty of Science and Technology, University
of Western Sydney-Hawkesbury, Australia

John Coborn
P.O. Box 344, Nanango, Queensland 4615,
Australia

James C. Cokendolpher AAS, BS, MS
Department of Biology, Midwestern State
University, Wichita Falls, Texas

Todd Driggers, DVM
Foothills Mobile Exotic DVM, Phoenix Arizona

Chantal Dupont, DVM MS
School of Veterinary Medicine, University of
Wisconsin-Madison

Robert E. Espinoza BS, MS
University of Nevada, Reno

Luette Forrest DVM
University Laboratory Animal Resources, University of California, Irvine

Mark F. Gerber
Boise State University

P. Gopalakrishnakone
Venom and Toxin Research Group, Faculty of
Medicine, National University of Singapore

Michael S. Grace PhD
Department of Biology, University of Virginia,
Charlottesville, Virginia

Ellis C. Greiner PhD
College of Veterinary Medicine, University of
Florida, Gainesville, Florida

Steve Grenard RT
Staten Island University Hospital, New York

Janice S. Grumbles, DVM
Statesboro Animal Hospital, Statesboro, Georgia

Trudy Hagstrom, MA
Pathology Associates International Corporation, Jefferson Arkansas

Dr. Chris J. Harvey-Clark
University Director of Animal Care, Dalhousie
University, Halifax Nova Scotia, Canada

Craig Hassapakis BS
Amphibian and Reptile Conservation, Provo,
Utah

Sun Huh, MD PhD
College of Medicine, Hallym University,
Chunchon, Korea

James L. Jarchow, DVM
Sonora Animal Hospital, Tucson Arizona

Melissa Kaplan
RepEnvirEd, Rohnert Park California

Gretchen E. Kaufman, DVM
Tufts Wildlife Clinic, Tufts University School
of Veterinary Medicine, North Grafton Massachusetts

Michael Kiedrowski DVM
Mountain View Animal Hospital, Phoenix Arizona

David T. Kirkpatrick, PhD
Department of Biology, University of North
Carolina-Chapel Hill

Michael Kreger, MS
Animal Welfare Information Center, Beltsville, Maryland

Khursheed Mama, DVM, Diplomate, American College of Veterinary Anesthesia

Department of Clinical Sciences Veterinary Medicine, Colorado State University, Ft. Collins, CO

Kathy Massie
Laboratory of Reproductive Ecology, Ohio University

Mark Miller
Herpetology On-line Network; President, Philadelphia Herpetological Society

Christopher J. Murphy DVM PhD
School of Veterinary Medicine, University of Wisconsin-Madison

Willard Nelson, DVM
Exotic Pet and Bird Clinic, Kirkland Washington

Kevin A. Nunan
City University of New York- College of Staten Island

Brent D. Palmer, PhD
Laboratory of Reproductive Ecology, Ohio University

M. Jane Perkins
Laboratory of Reproductive Ecology, Ohio University

Sharon Pickavance Bsc (Hons) B Vet Med, MRCVS
Royal (Dick) School of Veterinary Studies, Edinburgh, Scotland

Adrian Renshaw, B.App.Sc.
Faculty of Science and Technology, University of Western Sydney-Hawkesbury, Australia

B. J. Richardson BSc, PhD
Faculty of Science and Technology, University of Western Sydney-Hawkesbury, Australia

David C. Rostal, PhD
Department of Biology, Georgia Southern University, Statesboro, Georgia

Juergen Schumacher, Dr. med. vet
Wildlife and Zoological Medicine Service, College of Veterinary Medicine, University of Florida, Gainesville Florida

Sue Simon
Laboratory of Reproductive Ecology, Ohio University

Craig W. Stevens PhD
Department of Pharmacology and Physiology, Oklahoma State University, College of Osteopathic Medicine

Jennifer Swofford, BS
Highland Park, Illinois

M.C.A. Uribe, PhD
Lab. Biologia de la Reproduccion, Universidad Nacional Autonoma de Mexico

Craig Smith Bsc, PhD
Centre for Hormone Research, University of Melbourne, Australia

Michael B. Thompson, PhD
School of Biological Sciences, University of Sydney, Australia

C. Richard Tracy PhD
Biological Resources Research Center, University of Nevada, Reno

Stuart K. Ware, PhD
Deparment of Clinical Sciences, University of Kentucky, Lexington Kentucky

James Watson BVSc (hons) MACVSc
Animal Health Laboratory, Depatment of Primary Industries and Fisheries, Tasmania Australia

Stan Willenbring, PhD
Department of Pharmacology and Physiology, Oklahoma State University, College of Osteopathic Medicine

Bruce Young,
Department of Biology, Lafayette College, Easton , PA.

PREFACE

Reptile biology, husbandry and health care are dynamic disciplines that involve the input of various professionals, paraprofessionals and hobbyists. Until recently, these factions have been working separately, but with a similar goal - to expand the knowledge base for reptiles and their care. This book is the first to try to assimilate, in a comprehensive fashion, the diverse information collected by biologists, herpetologists, herpetoculturists and veterinarians. I believe you'll find that this makes for very interesting reading. It also provides a single source for identifying many of the fascinating aspects of reptiles and their care that aren't available in other books.

This book provides a wealth of information on many different levels. Although it is impossible to be all things to all people, there are sections in this book to address the needs of herpetoculturists, herpetologists, veterinarians, biologists, conservationists and hobbyists. The goal was to bring together experts on reptiles, but from very different backgrounds and areas of expertise. By incorporating the work of experts from different facets of reptile care, everyone benefits from the exposure. This is not an easy task, and I would especially like to thank my senior technical editor, Tara Harper, for her diligent work on this project.

Because reptile care is far from a standardized science, you will find some differences in approaches and opinions amongst the different authors. Far from being a problem, this is a wonderful forum to express different views and explore different ideas. Controversy in science is a good thing - it stops us from being complacent and keeps us searching for the real answers. Keep this in mind while reading this book and discussing the contents with others. I hope this book keeps you asking important questions and searching for the truth.

Lowell Ackerman, DVM PhD

HISTORY AND CLINICAL EXAMINATION

James L. Jarchow, DVM*
Sonora Animal Hospital
410 W. Simmons Rd.
Tucson AZ 85705

Lowell J. Ackerman, DVM PhD
P.O. Box 12093
Scottsdale, AZ 85267-2093

* Address correspondence to Dr. James Jarchow, Sonora Animal Hospital, 410 W. Simmons Rd., Tucson, AZ 85705

Dr. James Jarchow is an adjunct associate professor of Veterinary Science at the University of Arizona and a consulting veterinarian to both the Arizona-Sonora Desert Museum and the Research Branch of the Arizona Game and Fish Department. He is also employed by Sonora Animal Hospital where he accepts referrals in exotic animal medicine and surgery.

Dr. Lowell Ackerman is a practicing veterinarian, consultant, author, lecturer and radio personality. To date he has written 34 books and over 150 book chapters and articles dealing with animal health care issues.

INTRODUCTION

The Class Reptilia presents an astonishing array of diversity, reflecting a broad spectrum of ecological adaptation. Thus, it is not surprising that an accurate diagnosis of the reptile patient is sometimes difficult to discern and successful treatment may be elusive. The first steps in the diagnostic process must therefore be to gather relevant information about the animal's past and then thoroughly examine that animal. This will direct the rest of the process and ultimately regulate the outcome of the problem.

PATIENT HISTORY

Inappropriate husbandry procedures are responsible for most problems seen in veterinary practices. Reptiles are, in general, acutely dependent on the physical features of their environments to provide security and promote their well-being. Enclosure size and construction, temperature regulation and lighting regimes, method of watering, shelter availability, ventilation, substrate composition, cage furnishings, cleaning and disinfection practices, and handling

Sinaloan milksnake (*Lampropeltis triangulum sinaloae*) with prefrontal fibrosis resulting from frequent nose pushing. Photo courtesy of Dr. James Jarchow.

procedures should be evaluated and recorded for every reptile presented.

In community enclosures, the number, sex, age and species of cagemates should be noted. Feeding frequency and diet are obviously important and must be documented. The clinician or reptile keeper must familiarize themselves with individual species' requirements. This is best accomplished by maintaining a comprehensive library (including this book) and communicating with zoo keepers, professional and amateur herpetologists and veterinarians with a specific interest in reptile medicine and husbandry. In some cases in which rare species are kept, there may be little or no information available for their care in domesticated settings. Sometimes it is necessary to search the research literature for information gleaned from free-ranging populations.

Superficial rostral abrasion, Burmese python (*Python molurus bivittatus*). Photo by Bernard Mangone.

THE MEDICAL HISTORY

Careful, deliberate questioning is critical for compiling a reliable patient history and this, in turn, is extremely important in suggesting likely causes for problems and how they can best be solved. Reptile owners, like anyone else, may give misleading responses on occasion in an attempt to demonstrate their own knowledge, please the interviewer or absolve themselves of blame. However, truth is the only thing likely to benefit the reptile; blame has no role and makes many cases more confusing than they are already. An accurate diagnosis and effective treatment largely depend on the accuracy of the information provided.

Questions that need to be answered

Question	Reason for asking
How long have you owned this particular reptile?	When a reptile is moved from one environment to another, it will exhibit a period of acclimation which is typically characterized by anorexia, nervousness, torpor or hyperactivity and repeated escape attempts. Often there is increased susceptibility to opportunistic infections (immunosuppression).
Where did you acquire this particular reptile?	Wild-caught animals may take three weeks or longer to acclimate to captivity and they may host a greater variety of parasites, including those with complex life cycles. Captive-reared individuals generally acclimate more quickly. Reptiles purchased from pet stores or animal dealers usually have origins and histories that are unknown, and may have had a greater opportunity for exposure to dangerous infections and parasites.
Does this reptile have a history of medical problems?	Some diseases, such as mycoplasmosis and entamebiasis are chronic or recurrent by nature. Reptiles previously treated with antibiotics may be host to antibiotic-resistant bacterial colonization. Some drugs have delayed side effects, such as sterile abscess formation from injections of vitamin A-in-oil suspensions.
How is this reptile housed?	Outdoor enclosures are preferred for chelonians, crocodilians and many lizard species in milder climates. Iguanas and terrestrial chelonians may have difficulty maintaining optimal body temperatures if they roam free in the house. Secretive animals that are easily stressed may not do well in busy areas of the house.

How is the enclosure constructed?	Abrasive surfaces may result in rostral trauma to snakes and lizards. Adequate ventilation is important even in species requiring high relative humidity.
How is heat provided?	Diurnal reptiles generally bask to warm themselves and many, especially lizards and chelonians, respond best to an overhead radiant heat source such as an incandescent lamp. Lizards and snakes frequently sustain burns from lying on or too near their heat source.
What is the temperature regime?	Because reptiles are ectotherms, they must be furnished with an ambient temperature which will optimize physiological function. This range of temperature is referred to as the Preferred Body Temperature (PBT) or the Preferred Optimal Temperature Zone (POTZ) and it varies amongst and between species. Most reptiles benefit from having a variety of surface temperatures provided in their enclosure and will exhibit thermoregulatory behavior, moving from site to site. Species originating from temperate climates may require seasonal as well as circadian temperature change to function normally.
How is light provided?	Many chelonian and lizard species require direct sunlight or specific artificial lighting systems providing adequate UVB output to maintain normal calcium metabolism (due to UV activation of vitamin D, which in turn affects calcium metabolism). Changing photoperiod may initiate reproductive cycles in some species.
How is water provided?	The manner in which water is offered is critical to maintaining hydration; many species won't simply drink from a water bowl. Some lizard species (e.g., chameleons, geckoes, anoles) require dripping water or sprinkled droplets to drink. Chuckwallas (*Sauromalus* spp.) generally don't drink at all but they do require 70% water content in their forage. Many tortoise species must be soaked or rained upon (natural or simulated) to stimulate drinking. Reptile owners may mistakenly prevent desert species from having free access to water; these species are proficient at reducing water loss through the skin by behavioral adaptation and microhabitat selection. The captive environment may interfere with these adaptations. Unless water bowls are frequently cleaned, they may harbor opportunistic microbes such as *Pseudomonas*.

Gopher snake (*Pituophis melanoleucus*) exhibiting severe rostral abrasion, stenotic nares and resulting gular inflation on exhalation, and scarring of spectacles all resulting from persistent nose rubbing. Photo by Bernard Mangone.

Mucous nasal discharge in a desert tortoise (*Gopherus agassizi*). Photo by Bernard Mangone.

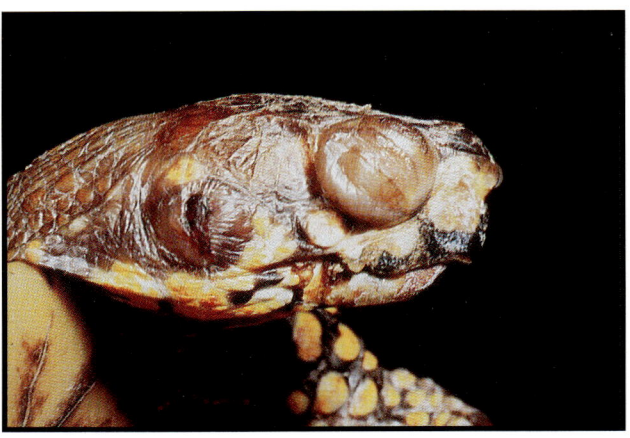

Bacterial (*Pasteurella*) conjunctivitis and otitis media in an eastern box turtle (*Terrapene carolina*). Photo courtesy of Dr. James Jarchow.

Are humidity levels appropriate for the species of reptile?	Those species originating in moist habitats such as tropical forests generally possess a more permeable epithelium and increased vulnerability to dehydration by evaporative water loss; if water consumption rate isn't sufficient to maintain hydration, the enclosure must be humidified to reduce the rate of evaporative loss. Desert species may be subject to opportunistic bacterial and parasitic diseases if relative humidity is too high.
What substrate is used in the enclosure?	Floor coverings should allow easy and effective cleaning and disinfection or be disposable. Wood shavings having sharp splintered fragments may be accidentally ingested and result in intestinal perforation. Cedar shavings are toxic to reptiles. Sand and ground nutshell bedding may be ingested resulting in intestinal impactions. Herbivorous species may attempt to ingest carpet fibers. Burrowing species should be provided with a substrate conducive to their natural behavior.
How is the enclosure furnished?	To minimize stress of captivity, shelter sites should simulate those utilized by the species in nature. Those species which retreat to mammal burrows will readily accept hiding boxes; crevice dwellers may require snug spaces between flat rocks or boards. Arboreal species should be provided with branches or perches upon which to climb and rest.
What are the cleaning and disinfection practices?	*Pseudomonas* is a common opportunistic bacterial pathogen in reptiles. Thus, disinfectants should be effective against this organism. Phenols are toxic to reptiles and should be avoided in all circumstances.

Drooping upper eyelid (ptosis) in a hypocalcemic iguana (*Iguana iguana*). Photo courtesy of Dr. James Jarchow.

Caseous exudate obstructing outflow from nasolacrimal duct in the Burmese python (Page 8). Photo courtesy of Dr. James Jarchow.

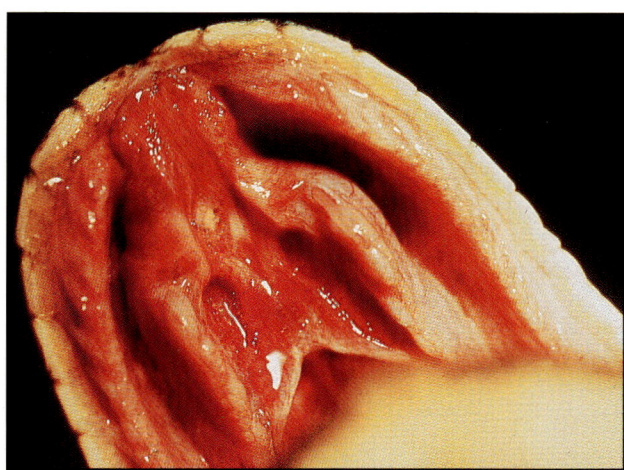

What is the diet being fed?	A great deal of misinformation permeates the pet trade and herpetological communities regarding feeding practices, especially of herbivorous lizards and chelonians. Unfortunately, nutritional studies of reptiles have rarely been conducted or reported; the diets of free-ranging animals should be reviewed to evaluate the appropriateness of the captive diet. In nature, green iguanas (*Iguana iguana*) are strict herbivores which rarely consume fruits; box turtles (*Terrapene* spp.) are omnivores while most tortoises are strict herbivores. Frequency and amounts fed should be noted.
How often, when and how is the reptile being handled?	Recently-acquired reptiles should, in general, not be handled until they have acclimated to their captive environment, or until they are exhibiting normal behavior patterns such as basking and feeding. Naive owners may misinterpret some stressful reactions, such as passivity and closed eyelids, as pleasurable responses to handling. Snakes may regurgitate if handled too soon after eating.
Is the reptile allowed to hibernate?	Many species from temperate regions have reproductive cycles initiated by emergence from hibernation. Chilling tropical species below the ambient temperatures they experience in nature is more likely to suppress their immune systems than to stimulate reproduction.
Is there any reproductive history?	Infertility, egg retention, embryonic death and stillbirths are commonly reported problems in breeding colonies and may be indications of a variety of pathological conditions. Nutritional and hydration status, temperature regimes, nesting site availability and infectious disease are all frequently associated with reproductive success or failure.
Any exposure to other animals?	Newly-acquired reptiles should be quarantined in a separate room for at least 60 days and examined for parasites and infectious diseases before introduction into a collection. Animals on breeding loan may be exposed to bacterial pathogens or parasites and should also be quarantined. Most reptiles are territorial and will establish a hierarchy if housed with members of their own species. Subordinate animals may languish.
Any behavioral changes?	Reptile keepers that maintain records of feeding and shedding frequency, reproductive activity and weight can provide information of tremendous diagnostic value. Torpor as well as hyperactivity and repeated escape attempts may be indications of disease and/or inappropriate husbandry practices. Anorexia, regurgitation or vomiting (emesis), diarrhea, abnormal movements, labored breathing and difficulty or increased shedding are obvious signs of disease and should be noted accordingly.

Otitis media in a red-eared slider (*Trachemys scripta*). Photo courtesy of Dr. James Jarchow.

PHYSICAL EXAMINATION

Physical examination requires a patient that is properly restrained. In many cases this can be done with effective handling, but sometimes, drugs are required. The examination must be thorough and complete while ensuring the safety of all present, including the patient.

Some lizard species, particularly chameleons and anoles, may exhibit a stress-induced color change during handling and examination and this reaction should be regarded as a significant indicator that handling should cease or the procedure modified. Venomous snakes, large monitors (*Varanus* spp.), crocodilians and reticent tortoises may require chemical restraint to allow hands-on evaluation.

The patient should be examined in a thorough, methodical manner. Often, the tendency is to focus on the apparent problem (the reason the reptile was brought to the clinic) while the rest of the patient receives only cursory examination. This is a mistake and may lead to inappropriate or incomplete diagnosis of the problem. A step-by-step examination proceeding from nose to tail is warranted in most cases. In small patients, a hand lens is a useful tool in helping to ensure a complete examination.

Prior to performing the physical examination, the clinician will want to determine dimensions and weights. In snakes and lizards, the length is taken from rostrum to cloaca. In those lizards species that store fat in the base of their tails, the diameter of this site should also be noted. In chelonians, the carapace length is measured and in certain genera such as *Testudo* spp., calculations can be made based on body weight and carapace length which give an indication of whether the animal is underweight, overweight or right on target. All reptiles should be weighed at regular intervals or at least with every physical examination. Weight losses may indicate dehydration or catabolic processes. Young animals should exhibit continuous gains with growth.

ROSTRUM

The surface should be smooth and intact. Abrasions may result from repeated escape attempts (e.g., nose rubbing) and/or abrasive surfaces in the enclosure, especially in maladapted lizards and snakes. Swelling of the rostrum, which may extend to prefrontal and frontal areas of the head may be edematous (swollen) or fibrous (scarred), also resulting from repeated escape attempts (nose pushing), especially in maladapted lizards and snakes. Swelling, discoloration and/or ulceration may be the result of bacterial infections.

Mucous discharge from the glottis of a Burmese python (*Python molurus bivittatus*), a sign of tracheitis or pneumonia. Photo courtesy of Dr. James Jarchow.

Necrotic ulcerations of the carapace resulting from opportunistic bacterial infection in a map turtle (*Graptemys kohni*). Photo courtesy of Dr. James Jarchow.

NARES

The nares (nose openings) should be equal in size, patent (open) and free of debris. Stenosis (narrowing) often results from rostral trauma. Unshed skin or dried mucous crust may result in occlusion and should be gently removed with forceps after saturation with water. the patient will often exhibit gular (throat) inflation on exhalation or open-mouth breathing.

Serous (watery), mucous or caseous (cheesy) exudates are indications of bacterial infections. Many lizards have nasal salt glands which actively secrete sodium and potassium salts. Salt encrustations around the nares and associated sneezing may be normal in these animals.

JAWS, LABIAL SCALES, BEAK (CHELONIANS)

Malocclusions may result from metabolic bone disease, infections or trauma. These animals are especially vulnerable to increased evaporative water loss and dehydration as well as exposure gingivitis and secondary bacterial infection.

Chelonian beaks should be examined for cracks or fissures. Early beak repair may prevent severe fractures and malocclusions. In most cases, swelling,

discoloration and erosion of mucocutaneous junctions are indications of bacterial infection. Labial pits of pythons may harbor parasitic mites and ticks. Look for them!

MOUTH

The snake's mouth may be opened by inserting a smooth rod or rubber spatula between its jaws. Lizards will often gape threateningly if the rostrum is touched; in others, gentle but steady ventral traction on the intermandibular skin will open the jaws. The mouth of chelonians may be opened with downward pressure on the mentum (chin) while restraining the head, or pried open with a dull curved dental scaler. Examination of the chelonian head and mouth often requires a great deal of patience and persistence; avoid using brute force as injuries are likely to occur. The gingivae (gums) should be light pink in color, moist and free of exudates and inflammation.

Gingival inflammation, caseous exudation or ulcerations (most often at the base of the teeth or the lip margins) are typically due to bacterial infection, often opportunistic microbes causing problems in an immune-compromised animal. Thickened, ropy saliva may be noted in dehydrated animals as well as those with bacterial stomatitis.

The choanae or internal nares should be examined also. Inflammation, mucus or caseous exudate may occur with viral or bacterial infections. The glottis should be exposed and visualized during several respirations. Lizards and snakes with pneumonia will often discharge a mucoid exudate. In many chelonians the glottis is more difficult to examine; those with congested breathing sounds resulting from pneumonia or tracheitis will continue making these abnormal sounds even when the mouth is opened.

Gingival petecchiae (pinpoint hemorrhage or bruising on the gums) often occurs with *Pseudomonas* or *Aeromonas* infections. Areas of swelling, nodules or other raised masses should be noted and may indicate infection, trauma or neoplasia (cancer). Some metazoan parasites, including trematodes (flukes) and pentastomids may occasionally be seen moving freely in the oral cavity.

For all patients with suspected infections of the nose (rhinitis), mouth (stomatitis), trachea (tracheitis) or lungs (pneumonia) due to immune compromise, samples should be collected for bacterial culture and sensitivity. Most pathogens are Gram-negative bacilli (rods) and smears can be taken from exudates and examined microscopically. Occasionally these smears also reveal ova or larvae of pulmonary parasites.

EYES AND ADNEXAE

Snakes and some lizards lack eyelids but have a clear ocular scale or spectacle covering the eye. Several days prior to shedding, this scale becomes milky or opaque in coloration. Unlike lizards and snakes, chelonians lack a nasolacrimal duct and may occasionally appear to tear excessively. both eyes and their lids should have the same appearance. Spectacles, corneas and lenses should be clear. both pupils should be the same size and shape; shining a light into the eyes should elicit proper pupillary light reflexes.

Enophthalmia (sunken eyes) may result from end-stage ocular scarring (phthisis), dehydration and/or inanition in lizards and chelonians. Exophthalmia (bulging eyes) may result from panophthalmitis (infection in the eye), retrobulbar abscesses (abscesses behind the eye), hypertension (high blood pressure), or obstructed venous drainage from the orbital sinus. Snakes with nasolacrimal duct obstruction exhibit a "pseudoexophthalmia" resulting from an increased volume of tears and spectacle distention.

In lizards and chelonians, white or tan caseous plaques may cover corneal ulcers. These corneal ulcers may be highlighted and visualized with the aid of fluoroscein strips which stain the ulcer surface green.

Mucoid or caseous ocular exudates (visible through the spectacle in snakes) often indicate bacterial conjunctivitis (infection of the lining of the eye). Conjunctivitis, keratitis (infection of the cornea), anterior uveitis (infection of the uveal tract) and panophthalmitis of reptiles appear as they do in other species and may be associated with bacterial infection and septic conditions.

Inflammation or encrustation of the free lid margins occurs in bacterial blepharitis and requires aggressive treatment to prevent lid margin ulceration, fibrosis (scarring) and secondary keratitis. Snakes burrowing in abrasive substrates often exhibit spectacle abrasions and opacities.

Squamous metaplasia of the conjunctiva in vitamin A-deficient chelonians is well known and probably over-diagnosed. Hopefully, most people are aware of the vitamin requirements of their chelonians and are providing them with a reasonable diet. Many turtles with caseous ocular exudates yield large numbers of Gram-negative bacilli when cultured and respond to antibiotic therapy alone.

TYMPANAE

The tympanae (eardrums) of most lizards are nearly transparent structures as they are in mammals. In chelonians, the tympanic membrane is unspecialized epithelium. Snakes lack a tympanum.

Otitis media (infection of the middle ear) is manifested by the appearance of mucous, caseous or blood-tinged exudate visible through the tympanum in lizards. Chelonians and lizards often exhibit lateral cephalic swelling, distending or bulging the tympanum.

HEAD

The temporal regions and the mandible should be bilaterally symmetrical and the temporal musculature should appear full and "fleshy" in most species. The rostral skull may be pliant and the mandible bilaterally enlarged in lizards and chelonians experiencing metabolic bone disease. Dehydration or inanition may result in a bony, angular appearance. Asymmetry may result from skull fractures, muscular injury or underlying infections. Some skull fractures are most obvious during oral examination.

TRUNK

The trunk of lizards and snakes and the lateral fossae of chelonians should be palpated. Anesthesia may be required to effectively palpate large boids and tortoises. Anatomical diagrams and cadavers provide reference points for the neophyte reptile clinician.

Nephropathies (kidney diseases) in lizards and snakes may result in swollen, painful kidneys which

Subadult desert tortoise (*Gopherus agassizi*) exhibiting metabolic bone disease. Photo courtesy of Dr. James Jarchow.

Juvenile bolson tortoise (*Gopherus flavomarginatus*) exhibiting dietary protein deficiency. Note that carapace scutes are thin and collapsing inwards, resulting from diminished shell osteoid. Photo courtesy of Dr. James Jarchow.

Carpal joint swelling in a veiled chameleon (*Chamaeleo calyptratus*). Differential diagnoses include septic arthritis, articular gout, and trauma. Note the dark coloration, an acute stress-induced color change. Photo courtesy of Dr. James Jarchow.

are detectable on palpation. Intestinal foreign bodies, visceral abscesses, cystic calculi (bladder stone) and other abnormal masses may be detected by this method. Mature ovarian follicles, eggs, developing embryos and testes in spermatogenesis are all palpable in most cases.

HEART

The heart is readily auscultated (heard with a stethoscope) in lizards and snakes and palpable in snakes. Heart location varies amongst species. In most lizards, it is found at the level of the pectoral girdle, but is more caudal in monitors (*Varanus* spp.). In arboreal snakes it is usually found at the caudal extent of the cranial one-fourth of the body but may be found as far caudal as midbody in terrestrial species. Chelonians require electrocardiography (EKG) or laparoscopy to evaluate cardiac function.

Cardiomegaly (enlarged heart) and pericardial effusions (fluid collected in the pericardial sac) are often palpable through the ventral body wall of snakes. Arteriosclerosis and stenosis (narrowing) of aortic arches may be detectable, causing ejection murmurs on auscultation.

LUNGS

Reptilian lungs are relatively large, hollow organs. The lung fields of tortoises are easily percussed through the carapace by resting the ani-mal on one hand while tapping with the other. the same region of each lung field should produce equally hollow tones. Dull sounds on percussion may indicate pneumonia, thickened lung tissue or regions of previous carapce injury. The diagnosis can often be confirmed by radiography (x-rays). Because pneumonia rarely affects both lungs equally, aquatic turtles will exhibit a diagnostic loss of normal buoyancy in water, listing to one side.

Snakes and lizards with pneumonia often keep their lung fields expanded to an exaggerated extent. Snakes may keep the forward portion of their trunk elevated, pooling fluid in the lung caudally, allowing more efficient oxygenation of blood. Reptiles will exhibit cyanosis (blue-tinged coloration) of mucous membranes and dyspnea (abnormal breathing), as other vertebrates do if airway obstruction, atelectasis (incomplete expansion of the lungs) or severe pneumonia occurs.

THE CHELONIAN SHELL

The turtle's shell consists of an expanded, fused rib cage (endochondral bone) covered by dermal bone plates and a superficial layer of keratin. Shell injuries heal from deeper endochondral layers. Ischemia (interference with blood supply) of dermal bone plates usually follows shell trauma, with eventual sloughing of ischemic dermal bone fragments once deeper healing is completed.

Soft shells of young chelonians may result from metabolic bone disease, dietary protein deficiency, or both. A distinguishing characteristic of protein deficiency is thinning of the shell osteoid; plastron osteoid may become so thin that it is translucent, allowing visualization of viscera.

VERTEBRAL COLUMN AND PELVIS

The spine and pelvis of lizards should be palpated and visualized. Back and pelvic musculature should be full and "fleshy". The back should have normal curvature and no detectable instabilities.

Metabolic bone disease commonly results in kyphosis or scoliosis in lizards, chelonians and crocodilians. Fractures and luxations can often be detected by careful palpation. Dehydration and/or inanition will result in a bony appearance of the pelvis and spine in lizards and the spine in snakes.

Bony masses associated with vertebrae or ribs may be palpable in snakes and lizards. Fracture calluses can be differentiated from osteomyelitis radiographically.

LIMBS

The limbs of lizards, chelonians and crocodilians should be visualized and palpated. Opposite limbs should be symmetrical in appearance, and in tortoises, show equal wear of toenails. Areas of swelling, atrophy, discoloration and other conformational changes should be noted. Be aware that hyperplastic fibrous osteodystrophy is common in lizards with metabolic bone disease.

Most fractures can be detected by careful palpation. Radiography is used to confirm the diagnosis. Swollen joints, especially tarsal and carpal joints, may occur from septic arthritis, articular gout or trauma. Arthrocentesis and synovial fluid examination and culture, blood chemistries and radiography may be necessary to provide an accurate diagnosis.

INTEGUMENT (SKIN)

The entire epithelial surface of the patient, including the keratin scutes of the chelonian shell, should be carefully examined. Areas of abrasion, ulceration, wounds, swelling, encrustation, discoloration and incomplete shedding should receive careful attention. External parasites, especially mites and ticks, may prove difficult to find because they attach beneath overlapping scales, or around tympanae and in skin folds in lizards. the skin should exhibit normal turgor. Dehydrated snakes will often exhibit "tenting" or raised skin folds on the inner surfaces of curves or coils. Retained, unshed skin and crusts should be moistened and carefully removed to examine underlying tissue.

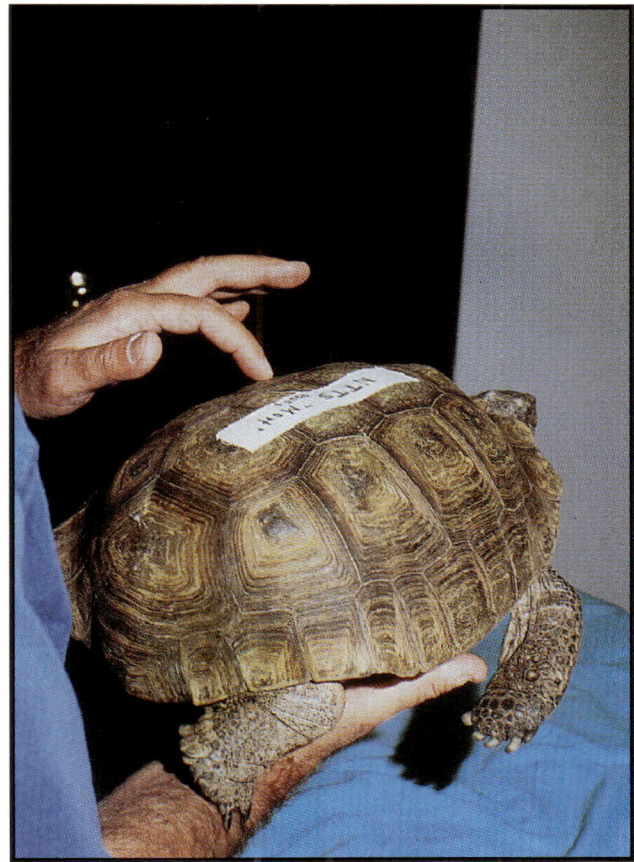

Technique for percussing the lung fields of a desert tortoise (*Gopherus agassizi*). Photo courtesy of Dr. James Jarchow.

VENT

Cloacal mucosa may be visualized by manually everting the vent or inserting and viewing through an otoscope. The vent should be examined for signs of inflammation, hemorrhage, ulceration, encrustation and swelling.

Bacterial and parasitic cloacal infections are commonly encountered in clinical practice. Cloacal swabs should be taken for wet mounts and cytological evaluation. Flagellated protozoan parasites are frequently found in large numbers, as are opportunistic bacteria.

Urate encrustations and obstruction of ureteral flow may result from severe dehydration. Blood chemistries, including uric acid, are indicated. Cloacal saline flushes and soaking in tepid water may prove effective and should be instituted immediately.

Prolapses of the cloaca, colon, urinary bladder and oviducts can and do occur in reptiles. Prolapsed tissue should be handled carefully, kept moist with isotonic or hypertonic solutions, and anatomically identified before reduction surgery so that the tissue is replaced correctly.

TAIL

The tail should have a uniform surface and

Ataxia in a gartersnake (*Thamnophis* sp) resulting from thiamin deficiency. This snake was fed a steady diet of thiaminase-rich goldfish. Photo courtesy of Dr. James Jarchow.

gradual taper. Snakes and lizards may exhibit distal ischemia and necrosis of the tail resulting from trauma, infection or embolism. Snakes and lizards have musk glands located ventrolaterally at the base of the tail. Swelling or discoloration in this area may result from musk inspissation or glandular infection. Male snakes and lizards may accumulate exudate in hemipenile sulci, resulting in a similar appearance. Gentle, manual expression will usually discharge either exudate through the vent.

OBSERVATION

POSTURE AND LOCOMOTION

The patient should be released, preferably into its own enclosure, and observed to evaluate behavior, neuromuscular function and ambulation. Although many chelonians will withdraw into their shells in a defensive posture, most normal patients should be alert; eyelids of lizards and chelonians should be open; snakes and monitors (*Varanus* spp.) should exhibit actively flicking tongues, and nearly all species should raise their heads off the floor, the exception being frightened individuals relying on their hiding for defense. Tortoises, box turtles (*Terrapene* spp.) and some lizards (e.g., monitors, green iguanas, leopard geckoes) should raise their bodies well off the ground when walking. Lameness should be noted, as should ataxia or incoordination.

Hypocalcemic and/or hyperphosphatemic lizards often exhibit decreased tonus of skeletal muscles, evidenced by drooping upper eyelids (ptosis), inability to raise the head above the ground and generalized muscular flaccidity and weakness. Some individuals display muscle fasciculation, especially of the limb muscles.

Polymyopathies and generalized muscular weakness resulting from chronic disease or malnutrition are commonly found in tortoises and lizards which drag their bodies over the ground while ambulating.

Uremic and/or dehydrated individuals often move stiffly. Blood chemistries and hematology, including uric acid, albumin, and packed cell volume (PCV; Hematocrit) are indicated in animals suspected of being dehydrated or uremic.

Hind limb paresis or paralysis and flaccid body wall musculature are often found resulting from spinal cord trauma and/or vertebral osteomalacia secondary to metabolic bone disease. head tilting and circling may indicate otitis media or vestibular disease. Snakes which rest in loose, relaxed coils may be experiencing discomfort or may be anemic. Labored breathing may be observed in chelonians characterized by open-mouthed breathing with head and neck extended and forelimb movements in and out with each respiratory cycle. Lizards and snakes may also exhibit open-mouthed breathing. Dyspneic lizards often display bellows-like breathing with exaggerated rib movements.

Righting and toe-and-tail-pinch reflexes are well developed in reptiles and should be included in neurological evaluations. Corneal and palpebral reflexes may be used in lizards, chelonians and crocodilians to monitor depth of anesthesia.

An iguana (*Iguana iguana*) exhibiting dehydration and renal failure. Note the sunken eye (enophthalmia) and stiff posture. Photo courtesy of Dr. James Jarchow.

FECAL EXAMINATION

Fecal examination for enteric parasites should be included in every physical examination. Fresh fecal specimens should be examined by flotation as well as wet mount smear techniques. Fecal specimens can usually be collected from snakes by stroking the snake's ventral body wall repeatedly, starting a few inches cranial to the vent and working caudally.

ADDITIONAL ROUTINE TESTS

Additional diagnostic steps are often necessary to arrive at a definitive diagnosis. Inflammatory exudates should be routinely submitted for bacterial culture and sensitivity. Hematology and blood chemistry analyses are often critical to patient evaluation, and even captive-reared reptiles should be examined for external, pulmonary, enteric, and hematogenous parasites. Tissue biopsy, radiography, laparoscopy and endoscopy have proven diagnostic utility in selected cases.

RECOMMENDED READING

—**Cowan, DF:**
Adaptation, maladaptation and Disease. In, Reproductive Biology and Diseases of Captive Reptiles, JB Murphy and JT Collins (Eds). Society for the Study of Amphibians and Reptiles, Lawrence, KS, 1980.

—**Fowler, ME:**
Disinfectant and insecticide usage around birds and reptiles. In, Current Veterinary Therapy VII - Small Animal Practice, RW Kirk (Ed). Saunders Publishing, Philadelphia, 1983, pp 606-608.

—**Frye, FL (Ed).**
Biomedical and Surgival Aspects of Captive Reptile Husbandry, 2nd ed, Vols I and II. Krieger, Melbourne, FL, 1991.

—**Jacobson, ER:**
Evaluation of the reptile patient. In, Contemporary Issues in Small Animal Practice, Vol. 9: Exotic Animals, ER Jacobson and GV Kollias, Jr. (Eds). Churchill-Livingstone, New York, 1988.

—**Jarchow, JL:**
Hospital Care of the Reptile Patient. In, Contemporary Issues in Small Animal Practice, Vol. 9: Exotic Animals, ER Jacobson and GV Kollias, Jr. (Eds). Churchill-Livingstone, New York, 1988, pp. 19-34.

—**Licht, P:**
Environmental physiology of reptilian breeding cycles. *Gen Comp Endocrinol*, suppl., 1972; 3: 477-488.

—**Mader, DR (Ed).**
Reptile Medicine and Surgery. W.B. Saunders, Philadelphia, 1996.

—**Murphy, JB; Adler, K; Collins, JT (Eds).**
Captive Management and Conservation of Amphibians and Reptiles. Society for the Study of Amphibians and Reptiles, Lawrence, KS, 1994.

—**Peaker, M: Linzell, JL:**
Salt Glands in Birds and Reptiles. Cambridge University Press, Cambridge, 1975.

MICROCHIP IDENTIFICATION

Willard Nelson DVM
Exotic Pet and Bird Clinic
903 Fifth Avenue, Suite 101*D*
Kirkland, WA 98033

Dr. Willard Nelson is a graduate of the University of Illinois College of Veterinary Medicine and operates the Exotic Pet and Bird Clinic in Kirkland Washington. He has spent 28 years treating domestic and non-domestic pets, zoo animals and wildlife.

INTRODUCTION

A tiny implantable transponder, a microchip, less than 1/16 inch square (the size of a pencil lead) can provide a safe and sophisticated means of positive identification for many herps. A quick surgical implantation in the appropriate location on the body permanently identifies an individual with a unique and unalterable code for safety against lost identity. Owners will be able to positively identify recovered pets as their very own through the use of these silicon chip "burglar alarms". Pets need only be "Scanned" with a multi frequency Scanner and the single, unique alpha-numeric code number will appear on the Scanner's readout screen. An unmarked pet, when scanned, will show no ID number code. (Instead of an ID number, the Scanner screen will say "NO ID FOUND").

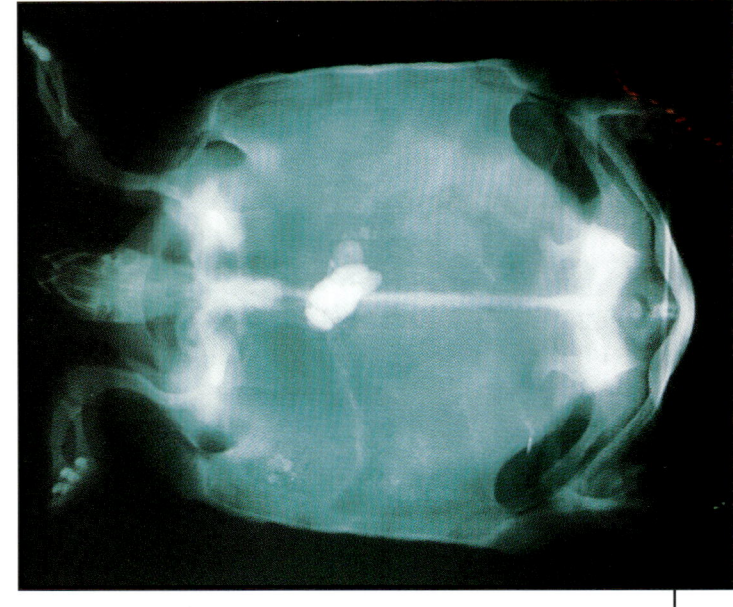

Above: Radiograph of a tortoise with an ID transponder in the subcutaneous tissue of the left rear flank. Note the incidental smooth intestinal mineralizations (rocks) in the more remote view.

Left: ID transponder scanner and its associated 110 volt charger

Scanning an iguana for a microchip in the dorsal midline.

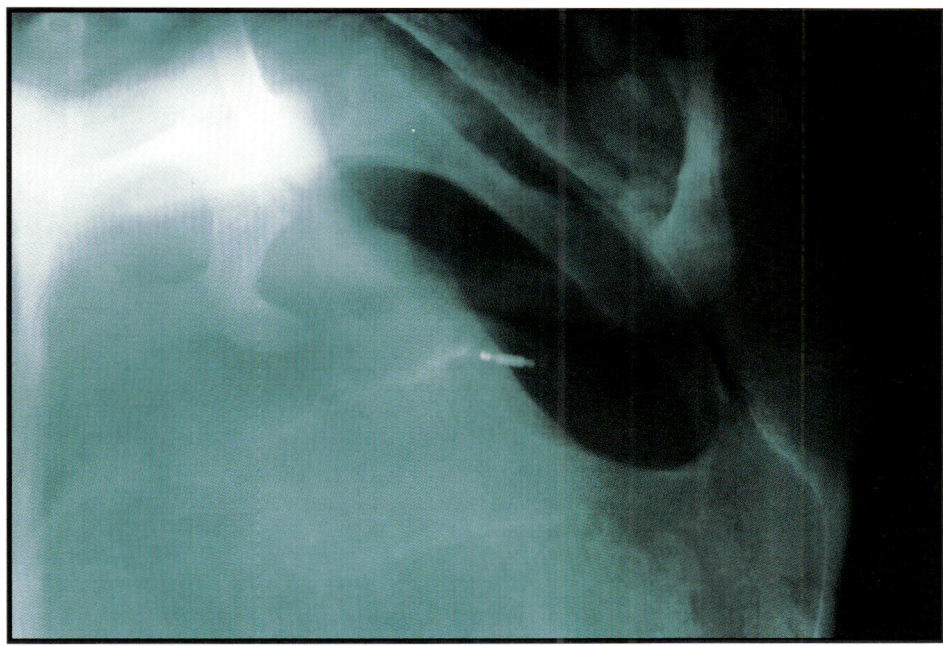

Close-up of radiograph of an ID transponder in tissue of left rear flank of a tortoise.

IMPLANTATION & ACCESS

Implantation is a brief procedure, very much like an injection. The site in the dorsal midline somewhere between the neck and shoulders is usually selected. Alternate sites are under consideration for species in which the neck is not well suited.

A 10 digit alphanumeric identification code is assigned to each and every animal entered into the system. The code can be read in an instant by the "Scanner". Thirty four billion codes are possible. The device in the pet cannot be lost, altered or removed without difficult microsurgery. The Scanner even has an output port to enable the operator to input the ID code directly into a computer for finding owners of lost pets.

If a pet is lost (or stolen), owners can provide the transponder ID number to veterinarians, police, humane societies, animal control officers and pet shops in the area to assist in recovery. It is expected that veterinarians, pet shops, law enforcement and animal control agencies will have Scanners available in the not too distant future.

REGISTRIES

Data bases for domestic pets have been established nation wide. These include 800 numbers which can be accessed 24 hours a day. Adding herps to the data bases is easy and the data base managers don't even notice that the species is not the dog, cat, horse etc. which they expect.

INTERNAL MEDICINE

Todd Driggers, DVM
Foothills Mobile Exotic DVM
3301 E. Hiddenview Dr.
Phoenix, Arizona 85044

Dr. Todd Driggers is the exotic animal veterinarian of Foothills Mobile Exotic DVM in Phoenix, Arizona and a 1994 graduate of Purdue University. He places special emphasis on diseases and disease prevention of reptiles. He is a member of The Association of Reptilian and Amphibian Veterinarians, American Federation of Herpetoculturists, Association of Avian Veterinarians, and the Association of Zoological Veterinarians.

INTRODUCTION

Reptile internal medicine is in its infancy when compared to human and small animal medicine. Research is conducted, for the most part, on marketable products (drugs) or procedures to prevent, manage, or to cure disease. Research, drug dosages, treatment protocols, etc. must be extrapolated from small animal and human medicine and literature.

This chapter will focus on clinical herpetological medicine as seen in captive animal populations and on the impact that husbandry has on disease-related processes. Internal medicine is a field in veterinary medicine that encompasses every organ system in the body. Ideally, all the medicine mentioned in this chapter should apply to all reptile. This will not be the case as a tortoise is no more related to a snake than a dog is related to a goat. There are approximately 6000 species of reptiles including: 252 species of turtles, 21 crocodiles, one tuatara, and 5726 species of lizards and snakes (Jacobson, 1992). Big differences exist between reptiles and amphibians of different geographical areas and microhabitats that affect the way they are treated medically. Dietary differences are also evident as: all snakes are carnivorous; turtles are carnivorous and omnivorous; tortoises are herbivorous, and; lizards can be carnivorous, omnivorous, or herbivorous. The assumptions made with drug dosing alone are truly astounding, but a necessary extrapolation exists for practicality sake. Few studies (literally) have been done with respect to drug dosing in reptiles. Veterinarians are forced to make these assumptions due to the cost of research and licensing of drugs through the FDA.

Husbandry-related problems account for more than 95% of the health-related problems seen in reptile medicine. Due the lack of knowledge of disease in wild populations, separating spontaneous disease from husbandry-related disease in a clinical or subclinical sense is therefore impossible at the current level of knowledge in this field . Though husbandry is discussed elsewhere in this book, a few points are worth mentioning twice. Reptiles are ectothermic (rely on external sources for temperature regulation). Being ectothermic in a captive environment lends itself to problems for both beginning and advanced reptile owners. Reptiles must be kept within a temperature range specific for each individual species. The temperature range is often called the Preferred Optimal Temperature Zone (POTZ).

The POTZ can be reached by establishing thermal gradients with any number of heat-producing products. Heat tapes, heating pads, incandescent bulbs, and infrared heat emitters are a few of the products on the market. This equipment should be used to set up both vertical and horizontal thermal gradients. Both types of thermal gradients are established because temperatures are highest near the source and drop with distance from the source. Cage branching, hide boxes, plants, and other cage decor should be optimally placed based on the natural history of the individual reptile being housed. This should be done in order to optimize the widest temperature gradient possible and to simulate the natural environment. Reptiles generally utilize the thermal gradients and heat sources very efficiently. They should spend approximately 50% of their time near the heat source and 50% of their time away from their heat source if the temperature range is in the POTZ. The heat sources that are most effective for larger reptiles are those that radiate from above the reptile. Top radiating heat sources (incandescent or full spectrum bulbs and infrared heat emitters) produce efficiently absorbed heat for the reptile. Reptiles generally are darker (have more melanophores) on their dorsal surface. Darker surfaces absorb heat more efficiently, as anyone with black interior in their car can attest. A reptile's ventrum (underside) is usually much lighter or white (less pigmented). The undertank type heat sources (heat pads and heat tapes) are most efficient for thinner-bodied smaller reptiles. The warmth produced by the undertank heat sources can warm thin bodied reptiles efficiently. Reptiles get burned when they are thicker-bodied specimens kept in a cooler cage kept with under-the-tank type heat source (hot rocks, heat tape, and heating pads). Older hot rocks are the classic culprits in heat burns because only one heating element is used per rock and core temperatures typically exceed 140-150°F. In order to reach their POTZ, reptiles will bask on the heat source until they get 3rd degree burns. Reptiles will attempt to attain their POTZ in order to carry out necessary metabolic functions intimately associated with temperature regulation, such as digestion and efficient immune system activity. Reptiles are not stupid, just instinctual. They will attempt to utilize whatever heat source is offered to them.

The POTZ requirement must be met for each specific reptile species. A Desert Iguana needs it warmer (hotter) than does a Green Iguana because the area that it evolved in over centuries was hotter. Green iguanas need a higher humidity due to their tropical rainforest habitat. Green Iguanas are also arboreal (tree dwelling). Desert Iguanas are ground dwellers. The main point here is that reptiles cannot be classed simply as "reptiles", and one cage set up is not efficient for all reptiles. Each individual reptile occupies a very specific niche, on a very specific diet, with very specific habits. Some "herps" are nocturnal, some diurnal. Some are insectivorous, some herbivorous. Diets for snakes in captivity compared to snakes in the wild are amazingly different. A specific wild prey item is not a domestic mouse, is not a bird, is not a goldfish, is not a vole, is not a gerbil, is not a spiny mouse, is not a hamster, is not a guinea pig, is not a rat, is not a rabbit, is not a capybara, etc. Though most of these prey type items have an adequate balance of macrominerals (calcium and phosphorus), their fat type (brown vs. normal) and quantity, and also their vitamin and protein content variance, may differ tremendously from the wild diet of the individual reptile.

All of the natural history influences should be taken into account when designing a cage and a husbandry protocol for the specific reptile. Green Iguanas do best if kept in a large, taller enclosure with a vertical heat gradient, UV light, and a totally herbivorous diet (NO DOG FOOD/MONKEY CHOW/TROUT CHOW). Ultraviolet lights must be provided for iguanas and other herbivores to allow the skin production of vitamin D-3 (necessary for dietary absorption of calcium). Reptilian diet, temperature, and cleanliness all affect their immune systems. Immune suppression due to any of these aspects will make reptiles and amphibians more susceptible to bacterial infections, abscesses, parasites, viruses, cancer etc.

The following discussion of topics is hardly conclusive of all of the medical happenings inside reptiles. It is however, a monologue of the more commonly recognized diseases and syndromes happening in reptile medicine in the author's practice and experience. The author's intent is to give basic background information for better understanding for veterinarians and for herpetoculturists to know what to look for in a sick reptile. Common things do happen commonly. Knowledge and diagnosis of the common diseases should not replace a thorough physical examination and routine diagnostic testing. Similarly, the author realizes that there is more than one way to treat most conditions. Diagnosing and treating diseases in reptiles requires that we have an open mind, common sense, and the ability to adapt knowledge from mammals to cold blooded, scaly creatures.

REPRODUCTIVE DISORDERS

PRE-OVULATORY EGG BINDING

Reproductive problems are common in captive reptiles. Egg binding (pre-ovulatory) is a common problem in monitors, iguanas, turtles, and tortoises. The presenting clinical signs usually include anorexia, vomiting, muscle tremors, seizures, distended caudal (sometimes fluid-filled) coelomes, sunken eyes, cachexia, decreased stool output, or death. The incidence of egg binding in the wild is unknown but is assumed to be low. In captivity many hormonal cues are absent or irregular resulting in **suspected** low levels of luteinizing hormone (LH) which controls ovulation. The author is unsure why reproductive hormones of ovulation are low, but **suspects** it is a combination of poor diet, improper lighting and/or photoperiod, temperatures outside the preferred optimum for the particular species, restriction of normal behavior, and/or lack of exposure of the female to identical male species. When pre-ovulatory egg binding occurs, the author tries to rule out other medical conditions for surgical prognostication and for assessing overall health. A systemic bacterial infection may be presen,t affecting both ovarian and uterine function. Other common conditions that may affect the reptiles general health are subclinical Metabolic Bone Disease (MBD), visceral gout, chronic entertis, renal disease, fatty liver, and hypoproteinemia. The underlying disease must be diagnosed by routine diagnostics such as blood chemistry profiles, complete blood counts, radiographs, urinalysis, etc.

Normal mammalian and avian reproductive cycles consist of a combination of hormones to cause follicle maturation, ovulation, and gestation/egg laying. The first spring after sexual maturity most birds begin the egg laying process (i.e. increasing photoperiod is a significant cue for egg laying in birds). This simplified process is dependent on increasing photoperiod. The pituitary gland and the hypothalamus regulate the level and the release of the gonadatropic hormones. Release of the gonadatropic hormones stimulates the hypothalamus to release follicle stimulating hormone (FSH), which begins stimulating the ovary to pro-

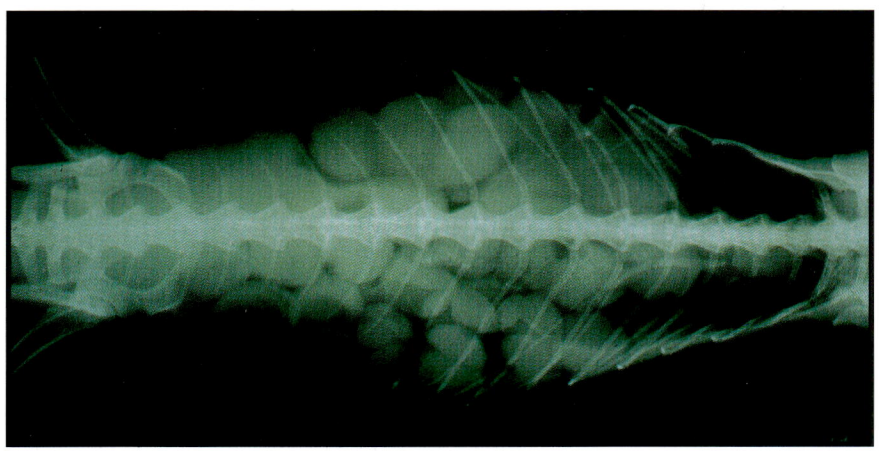

This radiographic technique uses air introduced into the coelomic cavity through a syringe. The injection site is on either side behind the last rib. The ovoid shapes of the eggs indicate these are post-ovulatory. More rounded masses indicate pre-ovulatory follicles. Photo courtesy of Dr. Todd Driggers.

duce follicles and estrogen. When the estrogen reaches a certain level (presumably species specific), luteinizing hormone (LH) is released causing ovulation. The post-ovulatory follicle is most often caught by the infundibulum (the first part of the oviduct). When the post-ovulatory follicle (ovum) is not caught by the infundibulum, it is released into the abdomen (coelomic cavity in reptiles) (King and McLelland, 1977). Here the follicle can either be absorbed or cause inflammation. Reproductive cycles in reptiles have not been extensively written about but are thought to observe the same basic principles as thise found in mammal and avian species.

The primary way the author diagnoses pre-ovulatory egg binding in iguanas is by contrast radiography. A pneumocoelogram (taking a radiograph with air injected in the coelomic cavity) will allow air contrast of the soft tissues to diagnose the pre-ovulatory egg follicles (60ml air/kg BW). The individual follicles are round, approximately 2-3cm in size, and clustered. Pre-ovulatory follicles can be resorbed if they are not too large. If the reptile is anorectic related to the pre-ovulatory follicles then they are probably too large to be resorbed. An oophoractory may be indicated (surgerical removal of the overies).

If the reptile (iguana) is bright, alert, and responsive the author recommends hyper-supplementing with liquid calcium orally at 500 mg/kg twice daily and force feeding baby (vegetable) food 15 ml/kg twice daily for up to 10 days. The reptile owner can try to introduce the female to a male of the same species and should already have a nesting area in the animals enclosure. If

the reptile is/becomes lethargic or the CBC shows an inflammatory picture the author recommends an oophorectomy.

POST-OVULATORY EGG BINDING AND EGG YOLK PERITONITIS

Post-ovulatory egg binding is a condition seen frequently in snakes, tortoises, turtles, and various lizards. It occurs for many reasons but is usually husbandry related. In this condition, the ovulated follicles are found partially or fully shelled in the uterus (oviduct). Causes for post ovulatory egg binding are hypocalcemia, uterine malformation (previous egg laying trauma or congenital anomalies), lack of proper nesting substrate or environment, stress, cage temperature too high or low, abnormal egg shape, and/or two eggs in the pelvic canal. The clinical signs are the same as pre-ovulatory egg binding.

Egg Yolk Peritonitis (EYP) is frequently associated with post-ovulatory egg binding. The author is not exactly sure why this occurs. EYP complicates egg binding and exacerbates the anorexia due to the associated inflammatory response of the coelomic cavity. If the yolks are ovulated in front of the vestigial diaphragm (iguanas), the lung can be irritated.

As with pre-ovulatory egg binding, radiology and clinical signs are the best methods of diagnosis. If the eggs are well mineralized, sometimes they will bulge the skin out and are very evident radiographically. Treatment can be managed conservatively by giving arginine vasotocin or oxytocin. If

This radiograph demonstrates egg yolk peritonitis (coelomitis) as evidenced by multiple coalescing soft tissue densities in the "thoracic" area. Photo courtesy of Dr. Todd Driggers.

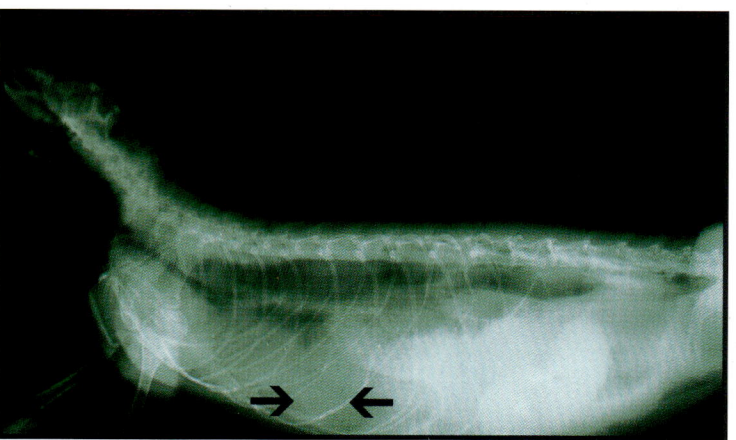

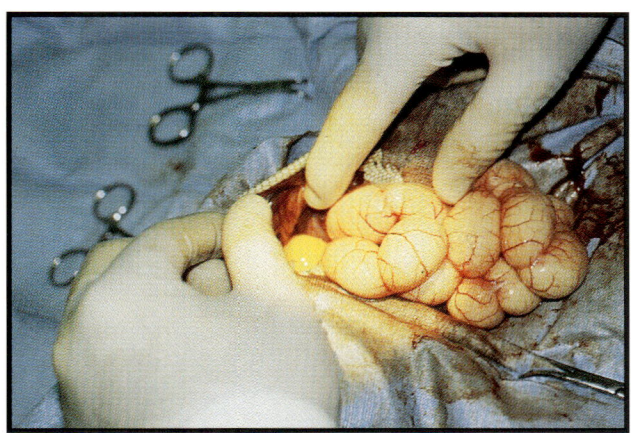

This is an *Iguana iguana*. Note the post-ovulatory eggs in the oviduct and the free floating yolk in the coelomic cavity. Photo courtesy of Dr. Todd Driggers.

the eggs are undercalcified, it is clinically difficult to distinguish from pre & post ovulatory egg binding. Radiographs will aid in the differentiation. The pneumocoelogram is recommended. Adding air to the coelomic cavity causes contrast of the soft tissues away from the body wall. Oblong, egg shaped masses will be apparent. Egg yolk peritonitis should be suspected if there is opacity ventral to the lung on a lateral radiograph where the machine is in the lateral position.

Unless she is systemically ill, the treatment of choice for a pet iguana with undercalcified eggs is administration of oral calcium, force feed, maintain hydration, and make sure she has adequate nesting areas. If she is depressed, anorectic, initial treatment is unsuccessful after 5 days, or she has a possible associated egg yolk peritonitis; an oopherosatory is the treatment of choice . Frye suggests that spayed iguanas live longer than intact iguanas. This fact is due to the lack of seasonal fluctuation and associated metabolic demand of egg laying (Frye, 1994). When egg yolk peritonitis is evident the coelomic cavity must be thoroughly lavaged and suctioned. The author gives post operative antibiotics when egg yolk peritonitis is associated with egg binding. Egg yolk provides an excellent medium for bacterial infections.

RESPIRATORY DISORDERS

Respiratory diseases plague many reptiles in captivity. Anatomically, respiratory diseases can arise from the upper, lower, or both respiratory tracts. Snakes, turtles, tortoises, and lizards are all susceptible to respiratory diseases. Reptiles have primitive respiratory defense systems compared to mammals. Mammals have a mucociliary apparatus that aids in bringing respiratory secretions to be coughed out and swallowed. Reptiles do not have this defense mechanism. Reptiles also lack a true diaphragm that enables mammals' the ability to cough. Therefore, whatever goes into a reptiles trachea stays in the respiratory system until it can be removed by the immune system. The immune systems of reptiles must deal with the pathogen while it is in the lungs. Alveolar macrophages are generally the key cell responsible for phagocytosis of bacteria. When reptiles are kept below their preferred optimal temperature zone, their immune systems are ineffective at bacterial removal. If the bacterial infection in the lung or airsac is not dealt with by the immune system an abscess may form as their bodies try to put a scar tissue wall around the affected area.

This ball python (*Python regius*) presented in severe respiratory distress. Note the open mouth breathing. Photo courtesy of Dr. Michael Kiedrowski.

LOWER AND UPPER RESPIRATORY DISEASE IN SNAKES

Boids (boas and pythons) are by far the most commonly affected reptiles with respiratory disease in captivity. Snakes are prone to respiratory disease due to their anatomy and overall size. Snakes usually have one functional lung and one lung that is considered vestigial or nonfunctional. The lung is composed of a cranial part where gaseous exchange takes place and a caudal aspect that is a functional air sac. The large boids particularly, are very hard to keep properly in captivity. Most large pythons do not live to eight years in a lifespan that should be at least 15 years. They commonly outgrow their cages in length and spend most of their time trying to escape, or are curled up, confined, with restricted activity. Snakes are the longest, shortest animals on the earth, i.e., they may be 12 feet long but are only four inches tall. Because of their long size and the lack of ability to move around in most captive situations Most large snakes breath in, crawl through, and eat from the area in which bodily wastes are or have been deposited. Proper cage cleaning goes a long way toward snake health and reduces the incidence of respiratory disease (but does not eliminate it). Proper cage design is also very important. Snakes kept in small cages with screen sides or for lids abrade their rostrum while trying to move about or escape the confines. Snakes should be able to at least stretch out to their full length in the cage. Cage branching is also very important. When snakes have respiratory disease, they often produce excessive mucous. Cage branches give them the ability to climb and to hang their necks over to allow gravity to expel the mucous in small quantities.

Clinical signs of lower respiratory disease (LRD) in snakes are excess mucous production coming from the mouth or trachea, open mouth breathing, frequent gaping (yawning), mouth infections, (stomatitis) and head and upper body resting in a vertical position on the side of the cage. Upper respiratory diseased (URD) snakes may make hissing noises as air rushes though stenotic, inflamed, or encrusted nares. URD in snakes can cause and occur simultaneously with LRD. Therefore, some clinical signs will overlap. Respiratory disease in tortoises is discussed in the infectious diseases chapter.

Diagnosis of respiratory disease is based upon husbandry, history, and the clinical signs. Diagnosing the specific pathogen (if bacterial) is important and should be based on a culture and sensitivity. A culture can be done either by placing a culturette in the snake's trachea or mouth (if stomatitis) or by performing a transtracheal wash (through the glottis). A complete blood count with a high number of azurophils (reptile monocyte equivalent) suggests chronicity or severity. *Aeromonas*, *Pseudomonas*, *Klebsiella*, *E. coli*, and *Proteus* are commonly isolated pathogens in the author's practice. A gram stain should be done to find out the immediate group of antibiotics to put the reptile on. A complete fecal exam and a swab of the glottis should also be done to decide if the underlying pathogen is parasitic. Rhabdias (lung worms) and pentastomes cause recurring respiratory disease.

Treatment must be focused at correcting the husbandry. As previously stated large boids are difficult to keep in a captive situation due to their size. A room or a large closet that the snake can completely stretch out is appropriate. During treatment the temperature should be increased 5 degrees above the preferred optimal temperature zone (POTZ) which is species specific. Depending on the antibiotic used and its frequency, intracoelomic fluids may be required. Daily soaking in warm water baths will also assist in maintaining hydration status as well as to help break up mucous in the lungs. Acetylcysteine (at the mammalian dose) may also be used along with coupage therapy to break up inspissated mucous. Common traditional antibiotics used are enrofloxacin at 5 mg/kg q48 hours (Young et al, 1994) and amikacin at 2.5-5 mg/kg q72 hours (Frye, 1991). New antibiotics such as second and third generation cephalosporins are being used to augment treatment with aminoglycosides to spare the kidneys. Ceftazidime is used by the author at 20 mg/kg q72 hours starting on day two, alternating with amikacin. If internal parasite eggs or larvae are present on respiratory swabs or in the fecal, the appropriate anthelmintic should be used along with the antibiotic (to clear up the secondary bacterial infections).

DIGESTIVE DISORDERS

Many diseases plague the G.I. tract of reptiles. Most commonly implicated problems are related to parasites, acute or chronic bacterial infections, protozoa, foreign bodies, fatty liver, gout, metastatic calcification, and ileus. The clinical signs for these problems range from inapparent to vomiting, diarrhea, anorexia, pathologic fractures, poor doers, bloating, prolapse, and joint swelling. Getting a good husbandry history, doing a good physical exam and doing routine diagnostics are paramount. Fecal exams, fecal cultures, CBC's, blood chemistry profiles, plain and positive contrast radiographs (X-rays) will aid in diagnosing the problem.

MOUTH ROT

Mouth rot is not a disease nor a diagnosis - it is a clinical description. As such, it is impossible to initiate treatment without getting additional information and making a more specific diagnosis. Table 1 list conditions that should be considered when someone believes their reptile has "mouth rot".

PARASITES

Internal parasites are common in reptiles in captivity. Most captive reptiles have been wild-caught or farm-raised. This fact makes internal parasites very common in a captive situation. Though many wild caught reptiles harbor internal parasites with relatively no problems, captive conspecifics are not so lucky. Wild caught reptiles forage, photoregulate, hide, flee danger, thermoregulate, and copulate according to the environment in which they adapted (i.e. they are perfectly adapted to their environment). The inability of captive reptiles to do the aforementioned reptile rights causes them stress. Stress causes immunesuppression, abscesses, septicemia, and bacterial parasitic and

Examining a crocodile throat. This photo was taken at time of necropsy. Photo courtesy of Dr. Willard Nelson.

Using a fiberoptic device to examine an Iguana throat to search for esophageal lesions. Photo courtesy of Dr. Willard Nelson.

Culturing a snake's glottis/trachea. The technique here is to position the micro-tipped culture swab near the snake's normally closed glottis and to wait for the patient to inhale. As soon as the snake inhales, the tip can be inserted carefully to swab the inside of the trachea. Photo courtesy of Dr. Willard Nelson.

Table 1: Conditions to be considered in the Differential Diagnosis of Mouth rot*

Condition	Description
Ulcerative/necrotic stomatitis	Caused mostly by bacteria, most notably *Pseudomonas aeruginosa* and *Aeromonas hydrophila*. The signs include debris accumulating on the lips, sometimes seeming to seal the mouth shut as it dries on the outside of the lips. The oral cavity is often coated in mucus, and when the mucus is removed with the aid of a cotton tip applicator, ulcers and necrotic areas of the oral mucosa are often visible. Teeth can be seen to fall out in severe cases.
Traumatic stomatitis	From rubbing on cage screen wires or other rough portions of the quarters
Stomatitis/enteritis complex	The oral disease is the most visible part of the disease but represents the proverbial "tip of the iceberg"
Upper respiratory inflammation	Pneumonia, caused mostly by *Aeromonas* and *Pseudomonas* infections as well as *Klebsiella pneumoniae*. Snake mites, *Ophionyssus natricis* are a principal cause of spread of these bacteria; pentastomid parasites can be a predisposing factor. The oral lesions are often caused by the appearance of exudate from the glottis accumulating in the mouth
Septicemia	Caused by *Pseudomonas* and *Salmonella*; can include oral disease signs as a part of the total disease process.
Metabolic Bone Disease	Distortions of the mandible in metabolic bone disease (nutritional secondary hyperparathyroidism etc.) are common, and some affected individuals show debris accumulating on the lips and even mucus dried inside the mouth.
Keratinization Disorders	Most commonly associated with relative deficiency of vitamin A.
Malocclusion	Overgrowth of mouthparts, especially in chelonians can sometimes be confused with mouth rot. Treatment includes surgically paring back the excess tissue to achieve normal occlusion.
Trauma	Damage from electrical, chemical and caustic sources can traumatically alter the mouth and result in necrosis and sloughing.

*Information provided by Dr. Willard Nelson

protozoal overgrowth. Thus, the stress of captivity plays a role in most, if not all, diseases of reptile medicine.

Parasites are, by definition, metabolically-dependent organisms that are detrimental to the host. Nematodes (roundworms), cestodes (tapeworms), trematodes (flukes), various protozoa (flagellates, ciliates, coccidia, amoebae), arachnids (mites and ticks), fly larvae, mosquitos, and leeches are examples of the variety seen in or on various reptiles. Parasites can be external (on the skin) or internal (within the body). They can have direct life cycles (where they can directly reinfect the host). They also have indirect life cycles (where the parasites are dependent on a vector such as an insect for the maturing and transmission of the parasite). In captivity parasites that have direct life cycles are most detrimental due to cage confinement and constant contact with their own feces or parasites. Auto-superinfection occurs when reptiles eat their own stool (coprophagy) or their prey eats their stools. The direct acting parasites of concern are the mites, ticks, coccidia, amoebas, strongyloids, rhabdias, and pinworms. Once a reptile has been deparasitized with the appropriate anthelmintic, indirect parasites are not a problem (Klingerburg, 1994). To eliminate them from the captive environment one must eliminate feeding the vector to the host.

Much is known about parasites and their effects on mammalian species. This same knowledge can be applied to their cold blooded counterparts as well. Parasites cause many types of clinical disease in reptiles including weight loss, anorexia, diarrhea, vomiting, and respiratory disease. Subclinical diseases such as slow growth stunting, and lack of reproduction are also evident in parasitized reptile populations. Internal parasitism is very common in most wild caught species of reptiles (Mader, 1994). There are several factors to keep in mind before you treat a reptile species. Species must be treated in categories based upon their dietary differences (herbivores vs. carnivores vs. insectivores). Protozoa are very common in most herbivorous reptiles and are thought to aid in the digestive process (much the same as with cattle). Some intestinal protozoa are considered more pathogenic in reptiles such as *Hexamita* (Barnard, 1986). Aggressive fluid therapy, force feeding, and antiprotozoal drugs maybe necessary to save these patients. In carnivorous and insectivorous reptiles, protozoa either cause disease or be an indicator of a more significant disease process. The author recommends treating any flagellated protozoa in insectivores and carnivores. Pinworms are very common in iguanids and tortoises but, rarely cause problems. Annual fecal exams and dewormings will eliminate or keep pinworms and other internal parasites to a minimum levels. In snakes, pinworms are pseudoparasites from rodent prey and therefore do not require treatment. The author treats all other nematodes in all other reptiles. Dosages of anthelmintics are listed elsewhere, but Ivomec® warrants special attention. Chelonians (turtles and tortoises) will exhibit paralysis, anorexia, bloating, and

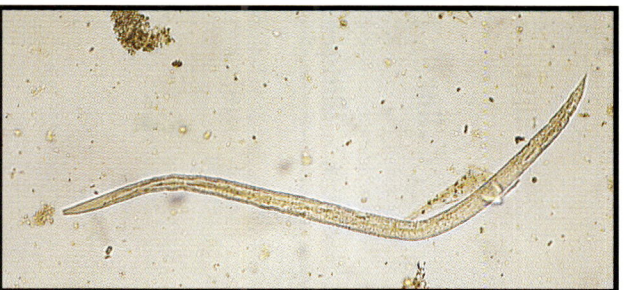

Strongyloides are intestinal parasites that undergo a migration through the lungs. Their presence in large numbers in the stool is indicative of superinfections and possible immunosuppression. Photo courtesy of Dr. Todd Driggers.

death when treated with ivermectin. One report of a Solomon Islands Skink also indicated an idiosyncratic reaction to the drug.

Diagnosis of parasites is based on a thorough physical exam looking for external parasites (mites, ticks, leeches, fly larvae) and on a fecal examination. Both direct smear and fecal flotation should be done on all reptiles both initially and yearly. Swamp-dwelling reptiles and all freshwater turtles should have a sediment run on their stool to look for fluke eggs. If a fecal sample is not saved or presented with the reptile, an appropriately sized red rubber catheter can be introduced into the colon and lavaged with saline (colonic wash).

Treatment should be based upon the clinical signs and the results of the fecal exam. The appropriate anthelmintic must be administered. If there are clinical signs of dehydration, anorexia, vomiting, cachexia, blood in the stool, etc., further diagnostic testing and treatment are warranted.

STOMATITIS

Stomatitis occurs in snakes most frequently, but turtles and lizards are affected as well. This disease

These are adult pinworms in an asymptomatic iguana. The iguana died of seizures related to MBD. Photo courtesy of Dr. Todd Driggers.

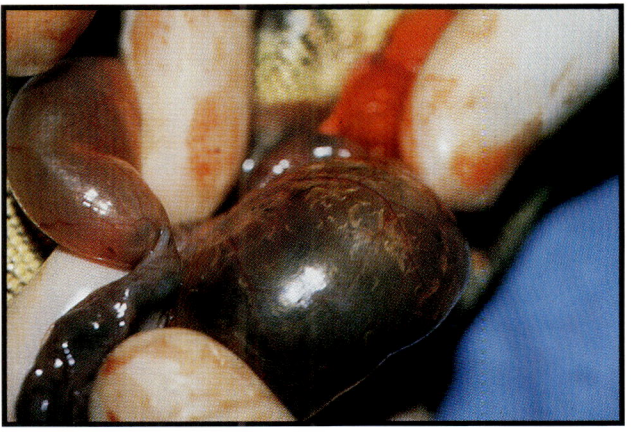

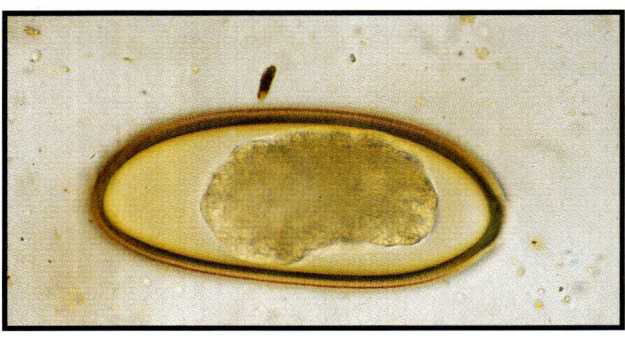

Pinworm egg. Photo courtesy of Dr. Todd Driggers.

is common due to the immune suppressions effect of stress from the captive envirement. Partial sheds (in snakes), feeding extruded pellets (dog food and other commercial products) in iguanas, and internal and external parasites also act as stressors, increasing the incidence of stomatitis. The clinical signs can include anorexia, increased amounts of mucus or purulent exudate (pus) from the mouth, inability to close the mouth completely, and swelling or reddening of the mouth.

Diagnosis is based upon observance of the clinical signs. Diagnostics should include a complete blood count and a culture of the mucous or purulent exudate. Treatment be similar to respiratory diseases with the addition of localized flushing of the affected area. If abscesses are apparent, they should be lanced and flushed with dilute Betadine® solution. The author flushes, cleanses, and packs the wound with silvadene creme twice daily for a minimum of seven days. Correcting husbandry problems is the most important aspect of treating this disease.

BACTERIAL INFECTIONS

Most of the time bacterial infections in reptiles are associated with the host immune systems. As previously discussed, reptile immune systems are dependent their ability to thermoregulate. Decreased immunity associated with temperature, poor sanitation, diet, lighting, lack of exercise, parasites and bacteria to multiply within the intestines to be shed in the stool or absorbed through the intestinal wall into the bloodstream. Once absorbed into bloodstream through the intestinal wall bacteria can be distributed anywhere in the body including the skin, lungs, and liver. Shedding of excessive bacteria is associated with anorexia, vomiting, diarrhea, blood in the stool, straining to defecate and other gastrointestinal signs. Most bacterial associated with intestinal disease are Gram-negative (G-) and include *Salmonella, Pseudomonas, E.cachexia coli, Klebsiella,* and *Aeromonas* (Mader 1993). Reptiles may shed these bacteria in low numbers and be clinically healthy as well.

Salmonella sp. bacteria are of particular concern due to their zoonotic potential (Frye, 1995).

A culture is the most reliable way to diagnose bacterial infections. A sensitivity will give you a list of antimicrobials with which the particular organism that is cultured can be treated with. A culture and sensitivity is recommended anytime gastrointestinal signs are presen,t or if the reptileis kept around a child or is immuno-compromised. A fecal parasite exam and a complete blood count is always warranted in sick reptiles.

The sensitivity will give valuable information about the treatment of the cultured bacteria. If *Salmonella* is cultured from the reptile in question, the question is if to treat at all (Mader, 1993). There is growing concern about the treatment of Salmonella in many animals including reptiles. The concern is due to the resistant strains of this bacteria developing because of ineffective treatment. When resistant strains of this bacteria develop, human contact could result in a life threatening situation.

A positive culture of most other types of bacteria along with clinical signs of disease warrants treatment with antibiotics. Supportive treatment with fluids, proper thermoregulation, forced feeding, and proper lighting should be considered for best chance of recovery.

OBESITY

Obesity in reptiles is very common. This condition occurs for a combination of reasons depending on the reptile, diet, cage space, and decor. Reptiles are generally overfed. After all, it is fun to watch a small creature blossom into a beautiful large specimen. Some owners take delight to see how long it takes a hatchling Burmese python to reach 20 feet. While it is fun to watch, it is harmful to the reptile for many reasons.

First, herbivorous lizards and tortoises are often fed animal-based protein to grow to a certain size quickly. Nutritionally, young reptiles cannot metabolically process high levels of protein without overworking their kidneys, liver, and intestines. Intestinal bloat is associated with the intake of large quantities of easily digestible proteins and carbohydrates (Frye, 1991). The more animal based protein herbivorous reptiles ingest, the more water they must drink to keep their kidneys diuresed. In young tortoises, excessive water intake and high dietary protein are associated with doming of the scutes. This is why many captive tortoises have "pyramiding" bumps all over their carapace. Young herbivorous lizards are predisposed to gout, nutritional secondary hyperparathyroidism, renal disease, and early deaths.

Secondly, many foods are too high in fat. Commercial rat breeders feed their rats at least 27% fat. Most mice are fed diets around 14% fat. Most juvenile snakes are fed small prey items 1-2 times weekly.

This is a Savannah monitor (*Varanus exanthematicus*) that was fed a mouse daily for two years straight. This monitor was severly depressed and very painful on abdominal palpation. Photo courtesy of Dr. Todd Driggers.

As snakes increase in size and age, they are fed larger prey (like rats). If rats have a diet higher in fat, logical minds would argue that the potential energy they produce as prey compared to mice is concomitantly higher. Most snake owners in quest of attaining rapid growth will maintain the same feeding schedule despite the large relative increase in fat in the diet. As the snake gets to large for the cage, its activity and ability to exercise decreases. Therefore, large snakes can be likened to "couch potatoes". Their relative large size to a small cage predisposes them to respiratory disease as previously discussed. Obese reptiles are also less efficient reproductively in production of libido, ovum production, and delivering the eggs or young. Their fatty diet and lack of opportunity to exercise predisposes them to developing fatty liver disease and steatitis (fat inflammation). With fatty liver syndrome, snakes, lizards, tortoises, crocodiles, and turtles lose the ability to dilute toxins, to break down and to synthesize proteins (important for the immune response), to produce vitamins etc. General immuo-suppression is the result. Insectivorous lizards fed diets high in mealworms; monitors fed like snakes (excessive mice and rats); and tortoises fed bulky vegetables (instead of green leafy and grass hays) may also suffer from fatty liver disease.

Presumptive diagnosis is made by the physical examination, history of the diet, and husbandry (including exercise history). A definitive diagnosis can be made by ultrasound or liver biopsy. Blood chemistries with elevated liver enzymes, high cholesterol, and triglycerides suggest fatty liver diseases.

The primary way to treat obesity and fatty liver disease is to adjust the diet and feeding regimen. Dietary quantity and quality must be considered along with frequency and ability to exercise. Large animals need proportionately larger spaces. If the reptile is clinically ill from fatty liver disease, rule out other contributing diseases, then treat appropriately. Fatty liver disease can be medically-treated by giving injectable glucocorticoids (stimulation of gluconeogenesis). Oral gavaging with corn syrup (no protein and no fat) 1:2 with water at 15 ml/kg is beneficial to maintain serum glucose levels. Antibiotics are also warranted to prevent bacterial infections secondary to steroid use and/or immune suppression from fatty liver disease itself.

CLOACAL/INTESTINAL PROLAPSE

Prolapse occurs for many reasons including trauma, foreign bodies, back fractures, stenosis of the spinal canal, hypocalcemia, dehydration, intestinal parasites, bacterial and protozoal irritation,

This is a hemipenal prolapse of unknown origin in a Savannah Monitor (*Varanus exanthematicus*). Photo courtesy of Dr. Todd Driggers.

preferred treatment is to insert an appropriately sized tubular structure (endotracheal tubes with cuffs) about 2/3 to 3/4 the size of the cloaca through the cloaca and into the rectum. The taped tube should be left in place for 1-3 weeks depending on the severity and amount of tissue necrosis. A colonic enema should be done before taping the tube to the tail to prevent formed feces from plugging the tube. The author does not feed iguanas for the first three days. Then he begins feeding a psyllium based product such as Metamucil® orally at 15 ml/kg. Lactulose syrup is also given to soften the stool at mammalian dose. The theory behind tube placement is to bypass the cloaca with the tube to allow contraction and fibrosis of the inflamed compromised tissue. Alternative measures have been discussed in other literature.

colitis, cloacitis, uroliths, renomegaly, and improper diet (protein and fiber content). The anatomical organ that prolapses must be identified. In reptiles, cloacal and intestinal prolapses are the most common. Hemipenes, hemipenis, and oviducts (uterus) rarely prolapse compared to the intestine and cloaca. A thorough history must be taken and routine diagnostics must be done to decide the exact cause. Once the cause and anatomical organ have been determined, treatment plan can be chosen.

The prolapse may need to be corrected first, before the primary cause is determined, in order to reduce the avascular necrosis of the prolapsed tissue. The prolapse should be dealt with quickly in lizards and tortoises due to the possibility of puncturing, tearing, or stepping on the prolapse. The best first aid is to push the cloaca back into the body if possible as a reptile owner. The second best is to moisten a small piece of cloth or gauze sponge with saline or water around the prelapse and transport the animal to the veterinarian.

If the prolapsed tissue is viable, it can be soaked in a saturated sugar solution to decrease the swelling. Snakes, small lizards, turtles, and tortoises can be treated by placing simple interrupted or pursestring-type sutures on both sides of the cloacal opening. The hole between the sutures should be large enough for some stool to be able to pass if possible. Anti-hemorrhoidal medication can be applied to further decrease swelling. The suture can be left in for months if the reptile is defecating and urinating properly. If the intestines are prolapsed and necrotic, external resection and anastomosis can be done. The cloaca can never be excised and resected due to the important urinary tract anatomy. Larger lizards and chronically prolapsed reptiles should have other surgical procedures performed to prevent continual prolapse including colonopexy. The author's

METABOLIC DISORDERS

METABOLIC BONE DISEASE
Metabolic Bone Disease (MBD) plagues many

A cloacal prolapse in an Emerald Tree Boa (*Corallus caninus*) with a chronic distal fracture of the back. The snake had a cloacal pursestring placed for 4 days and was given anti-hemorrhoidal suppositories to decrease the inflammation. Photo courtesy of Dr. Todd Driggers.

adult herbivores and insectivores and nearly all juveniles (herbivore, insectivore, and carnivore). MBD has many different names that mean slightly different things. MBD itself refers to any problem that causes bone weakening. Nutritional secondary hyperparathyroidism (NSHP), rickets and fibrous osteodystrophy (FOD) are commonly used as synonyms for MBD when each points toward a specific cause. Many things induce MBD including calcium and/or vitamin D3 deficient diets, high

This is a typical Green Iguana with classic Metabolic Bone Disease. The herbivorous Green Iguana is the poster child for this disease. This lizard is a complex specimen to keep properly and often is underestimated by the novice reptile owner because it is relatively inexpensive. Photo courtesy of Dr. Todd Driggers.

phosphorus diets, lack of exposure to ultraviolet light, and kidney disease.

A brief discussion of reptile calcium metabolism is necessary to understand this complex disease. Calcium is necessary for mineralization of the skeleton, muscle contraction, nerve stabilization and for the clotting cascade. Blood calcium is maintained relatively constant by the interplay of calcium intake and lysis of the bone when intake is inadequate or unbalanced with phosphorus. When blood calcium is low, seizures may occur. These small seizures will occur until the parathyroid gland senses the low calcium and secretes parathyroid hormone (PTH). PTH effectively weakens the bone by releasing calcium to the bloodstream to meet perceived needs. When the bone calcium is released into blood, the tetanic seizures stop until the new calcium is utilized. When the parathyroid gland is constantly stimulated to produce its hormone, MBD results from Nutritional Secondary Hyperparathyroidism (NSHP). The parathyroid gland is also stimulated when dietary phosphorus is relatively high with respect to the calcium (this happens when feeding herbivores a carnivore diet, in kidney disease, and by feeding carnivores calcium-deficient diets). A calcium-to-phosphorus ratio between 1.5:1 to 2:1 is the ideal maintenance ratio. Chronic NSHP results in Fibrous Osteodystrophy (FOD) where strong bones are gradually replaced by fibrous connective tissue (cartilage). Low blood calcium (hypocalcemia) may also be caused from a lack of Vitamin D3 which in turn is caused by a lack of exposure to unfiltered ultraviolet UV-B rays or lack of dietary supplementation.

MBD manifests itself by many clinical signs ranging from lethargy, anorexia, paresis to paralysis (rear legs affected by fracture of lower back or spinal cord swelling), fine intention tremors of the muscles (noticed in nonweight-bearing phalanges first), pathologic fractures of any bone, FOD (cartilaginous tissue replacing bone), soft facial bones (particularly the lower jaw), intestinal prolapses, renal disease, and even full blown tetanic seizures. MBD has multifactorial causes and is not simply a lack of calcium in the diet. Prevention of MBD depends on the owner's ability to provide proper feeding, heating and lighting requirements.

Nutritional aspects are covered in depth elsewhere in this book. Here is a quick summary. Herbivores need high quality plant material. Green leafy vegetables such as kale, collard greens, mustard greens, turnip greens and dandelion greens fit this category. Please note that none of these staples include lettuce. Head lettuce is particularly bad for young herbivores due to its high water content and overall low nutritive value. Do not feed head lettuce. Small amounts (less than 10% by weight) of a mixed assortment of carrots, peas, green beans, corn, squash, etc.. can also be added to the diet but are not as important and should not replace the greens. Flowers can be added to spice up the diet. Hibiscus flowers and leaves seem to be enjoyed particularly. Carnivorous reptiles also need special dietary attention.

Small snakes and various insectivores commonly suffer from MBD related to calcium-deficient food consumption. Pinky mice and improperly fed insect prey (crickets, mealworms, etc.) are nearly always calcium-deficient. When these prey items are not supplemented properly, stunting and clinical MBD result. Insects should be gut loaded with dog food and vegetables when fed to insectivores. Powdered supplements can be used to coat the

This is an omnivorous Mexican spiny-tailed Iguana (*Ctenosaurus* sp) with severe fibrous osteodystrophy in both legs. The normal bony matrix is being utilized for its calcium stores and replaced with cartilaginous connective tissue. Photo courtesy of Dr. Todd Driggers.

insects using the "shake and bake" method in a plastic bag. Pinkie mice should be allowed to nurse for 3 days before feeding in order to obtain a better calcium to phosphorus ratio.

The important aspects of nutrition which many reptile owners overlook is not about the food that is offered. The real determinants of risk are the quantity of food offered and which foods are actually eaten. If reptiles are fed so many vegetables, fruits, flowers etc. that they cannot eat the entire amount, they often will eat only their favorite foods. If these foods are nutritionally incorrect (too much phosphorus, too little calcium) gradual weakening of the bones will take place. In young iguanas with little to no calcium reserves in the bone, the clinical signs will be lethargy, paresis, and mild to moderate tetanic spasms. Neonate iguanas require a near perfect calcium to phosphorus ratio in their diets due to their lack of bony reserve. It is hard to oversupplement calcium in the diet of young growing iguanas. Supplementation of phosphorus-free calcium is critical to the typical captive iguana where light, food, and the ability to thermoregulate is suboptimal (compared to the wild).

The ability for every reptile to thermoregulate is imperative to nutrition. Most reptiles exist in a state of homeostasis when their temperatures are kept within a preferred range known as the preferred optimal temperature zone (POTZ). This zone is species specific. Having the ability to thermoregulate entails being able to behaviorally decide where one chooses to be within the defined area of the cage to control one's own temperature. Reptiles digest food more efficiently when kept in conditions conducive to thermoregulating in their POTZ. Iguanas, in fact, can not efficiently absorb dietary calcium at temperatures below 80° F. Kept at a temperature below the minimum of 85° F, most iguanas will suffer from MBD.

Lack of exposure to unfiltered ultraviolet light also will cause MBD. The exact mechanism of action of Vitamin D3 production is not known in reptiles but is assumed to be the same as in birds and mammals. The author feels that temperature regulation is at least as important than exposure to UV light with respect to the prevention of MBD in iguanas. Other species of reptiles seem to require more UV light to prevent MBD. UVa lights, such as Vitalites, do have positive behavioral reproductive and feeding effects on reptiles. Increased feeding response will cause more calcium to be eaten due to sheer increase in food intake (assuming the diet is balanced). Recent manufacturing of other commercial lights with more UVb

This is a carnivorous black and gold Tegu (_Tupinambis teguixens_) fed a calcium-deficient diet of mealworms and nutritionally-deficient, non-supplemented crickets. Simply feeding the crickets properly with a carnivore-based diet (i.e., dog food or cricket food) and biweekly calcium dusting the crickets will prevent softened bones from developing. Photo courtesy of Dr. Todd Driggers.

This omnivorous Eastern box turtle (*Terrapene carolinensis*) requires special attention to avoid MBD when born in captivity. This particular specimen was raised predominantly on mealworms fed in a free-choice format. The high phosphorus and low calcium content of mealworms halts the growing of the bony shell while the external keratin continues to grow. Photo courtesy of Dr. Todd Driggers.

spectrum have more direct impact upon calcium absorption than do the UVa producing lights. Vitamin D3, the desired beneficial product from exposure to UVb light is essential to dietary absorption of calcium. Vitamin D3 is also available in some oral calcium supplements. Recent investigations, however, in oral supplementation of Vitamin D3 suggest than diurnal (day active) lizards can become toxic (Allen, 1995) resulting in kidney disease). Oral vitamin D3 can be oversupplemented in the adult resulting in metastatic mineralization of some soft tissues including the stomach, intestines, kidneys, skin, etc...One must keep in mind the vitamin D3 is the active ingredient in rodent poisoning. Their is a fine line between supplementation and overdosing. The author therefore recommends routine sunbathing during adequate climatic conditions through outside caging and/or walks, The more diurnal reptiles are exposed to natural sunlight or black lights, the less keepers must worry about exactness of calcium supplementation. Sunbathing is appropriate anytime the temperature is about 70° F. Outside caging is very good so long as the reptile is not in direct sunlight and can be cooled (setting up a drip system is a good idea). When exposure to the sun is impossible, oral supplementing with vitamin D3 is essential. Juvenile iguanas (<1.5 years) or egg-laying females can be supplemented up to four times weekly. Older iguanas (>1.5 years) should be supplemented only once or twice weekly. Cherry flavored Tums tablets can be used as a calcium supplement that does not have vitamin D3. Older lizards do fine on Tums and also enjoy the taste.

Renal disease also can cause MBD. Phosphorus is excreted by the kidneys. If the kidneys are not functioning adequately, elevated phosphorus levels stimulate the parathyroid gland similar to dietary phosphorus. If the kidney disease is chronic, clinical signs of kidney failure are yellow urates, pale mucous membranes, straining to defecate, and constipation.

Egg-bound females will often present in muscle fasciculations or acute tetany related to hypocalcemia. The blood calcium is utilized to calcify the eggs. A salpingectomy/oophorectomy may be a necessary treatment once the patient's calcium level is stabilized.

Most reptiles are solitary animals that will try to minimize social interaction with owners as well as cage mates. Cage paired iguanas nearly always have subclinical to clinical metabolic bone disease. One reptile is nearly always more aggressive. The more dominant iguana has first access to the food, and the better basking place. The second place subordinate iguana will often be much smaller as a result and have MBD. Stress plays a large part in this disease. Secondary bacterial infections are common with MBD. The suggested clinical workup for iguanas with MBD includes a blood chemistry profile, hematocrit, total protein, and radiographs.

Treatment for clinical MBD depends on the severity of the disease and may take as long as 6 months to resolve. Mild cases respond quicker. Some reptiles lose the ability to eat due to softening jaw bones. Treatment consists of heavily supplementing with calcium at 200-500 mg calcium twice daily (BID) by mouth or by intracoelomic or intramuscular injections for at least 2 weeks. If the reptile is still eating, daily oral calcium on the food is usually sufficient. Force feeding with an appropriate carnivore/herbivore baby food diet is simple and effective. The dose the author uses is 15 mL per kg twice daily (BID) until the reptile is self feeding. Injectable vitamin D3 should also be given. Exposure to unfiltered ultraviolet light and temperature regulation are also very important. The author recommends removing all cage perching and other decor in the cage to prevent fractures from occuring.

Pathologic fractures are common with MBD. Long bone limb fracture as well as back fracture complicate the treatment of MBD. Tape splinting or simply leaving the reptile alone are options that are based upon the veterinarian's personal judgment and level of expertise. Tape splinting will do harm if not properly placed or if the reptile is allowed too much free roam time. General small animal splint application knowledge should be applied. Internal fixation should not be utilized due to the inherent weakness of the bone. Back fractures carry a guarded prognosis for full return to rear leg function. If the rectal tissue is flaccid, and/or the reptile cannot urinate properly then euthanasia is often recommended.

GOUT

Gout is a disease by which uric acid (a normal by product of protein metabolism) builds up to toxic levels in the body and deposits in the soft tissues. There is a tremendous genetic predisposition for this to occur in human medicine. In reptile medicine, gout occurs for many different reasons.

Reptiles are a diverse group of ectotherms that require various specific diets in order to prosper. There are herbivores, carnivores, insectivores, and omnivores in the reptile class. Each should be fed according to the diet which they would eat in the wild. Carnivores should be fed an animal-based protein and herbivores a plant based protein. In general, most herbivores require a much lower percentage basis of protein in their diets. Plant proteins are also metabolically different with respect to their metobolic by-products. The plant based proteins are metabolized down to excretable by-products (carbon dioxide and ammonia) in herbivores. Animal-based proteins in herbivores are broken down into not easily excretable by products such as uric acid as the end product (Mader, 1995). Herbivorous lizards and tortoises are therefore most commonly afflicted with gout. Misinformation about their dietary "needs" for animal based proteins is repeated constantly in lay magazines and by uninformed veterinarians. As proteins are broken down and turned into amino acids by the liver, the by products are transported by the blood to the kidneys (where they are excreted or resorbed). Uric acid is excreted entirely, unless the amount of uric acid in the blood overwhelms the kidney's ability to remove uric acid resulting in hyperuricemia. Hyperuricemia occurs if there is excessive animal-based proteins fed, the animal is dehydrated, has existing renal disease, or is kept chronically at temperatures below the preferred optimum. Uric acids begin depositing in the soft tissues such as the kidneys, liver, pericardial sac, and in the joints.

Gout in its early stages is rarely diagnosed. A good reptilian veterinarian should have a high index of suspicion with any herbivore being fed a regular diet of animal based protein. MBD herbivores with pathologic fractures should always arouse suspicion as also having gout for other dietary reasons. It is established that carnivore diets have a higher level of protein in them than herbivore diets. It is also known that carnivore based diets have a relatively high amount of phosphorus as compared to calcium. The unbalanced calcium to phosphorus ratio stimulates parathyroid hormone production. This causes lytic bone lesions and therefore pathologic fractures, NSHP. A good physical exam and reptile blood chemistry profiles are essential. The mouth should be examined dorsally as sometimes the translucent choana will show gout crystals (tophi). All the joints should be palpated for pain while flexed and extended. Decreased range of motion and excessive discomfort should prompt radiographs to be taken. If joint lesions are radiographically apparent severe joint damage has been sustained. Blood chemistries should also be drawn and the kidney values thoroughly evaluated. Uric acid levels can vary between 5-15mg/dl for many herbivores. Phosphorus levels should be in check with a calcium to phosphorus ratio of 1.5-2:1. Elevated phosphorus can indicate either NSHP, renal dysfunction, or both.

Most treatment is modified from human gout recommendations. Humans are treated in cases of acute

This insectivorous Leopard gecko (*Eublepharis macularis*) was fed calcium and nutritionally-*deficient* insect prey resulting in softening facial bones. Photo courtesy of Jeff Wines.

gout by NSAIDS and colchicine. In cases of chronic gout, allopurinol is used (Mader, 1995). These drugs are experimental at best in reptiles. Correcting the diet is of the utmost importance in reptiles. Some reptiles will be reluctant to eat a new diet once hooked on meat based food. Force feeding vegetable baby food from a syringe at 15-20 ml/kg twice daily works well to get them to begin eating again. If the reptile is resistant to move or shows intense pain in a specific joint, this will also be manifested by anorexia. Maintaining and diuresing them with fluids is also important. This can be achieved by giving intracoelomic fluids or by placing a catheter in the ventral abdominal vein in lizards and jugular catheters in tortoises. If the temperature is below the preferred optimum, increasing the temperature and daily warm water soaks may all be needed to lower the hyperuricemia. In cases of severe gout, the affected joints may have to be surgically lavaged.

RENAL DISORDERS

Renal disease occurs commonly in captive reptiles for many different reasons. It occurs due to improper nutrition, dehydration, excessive mineral supplementation, improper usage of antibiotics, spontaneous tumors, etc. Chronic renal failure and urolithiasis are the most common syndromes seen in the author's practice.

Iguanas are the poster child for nutritionally related renal diseases due to the feeding of animal based protein packed foods such as dog food, trout chow, monkey chow, etc. Feeding of animal-based protein to the herbivore causes the liver and kidneys to have to work hard to process the by products of protein metabolism. Animal-based proteins will cause increased need for water intake in the herbivore, coupled with excessive uric acid formation that must be excreted by the kidneys. If water is present, most iguanas will drink enough to offset clinical disease initially. Over time, the excessive animal protein intake overrides the iguana's ability to dilute and excrete the uric acid in the blood stream with concomitant renal dysfunction; resulting in hyperuricemia, visceral gout, renal gout, nutritional/renal secondary hyperparathyroidism, and possible urolithiasis. Iguanas that are not heavily supplemented with calcium during the time they are being fed animal based proteins will also have elevated dietary phosphorus. If the phosphorus level is higher than or equal to the level of phosphorus (Ca:Phos less than a 1:1 ratio) NSHP will occur before clinical renal disease does. If calcium is supplemented heavily during the time in which animal-based proteins are being fed, and the calcium to phosphorus ratio is 1.5-2:1 or greater, renal disease and renal secondary hyperparathyroidism may occur first. The result will be a MBD iguana with compromised renal function, possible gout, and metastatic mineralization.

Urates from a Green Iguana with obstruction of the intestines due to renomegaly. Photo courtesy of Dr. Todd Driggers.

Clinical signs of renal disease in iguanas are general malaise, anorexia, pale mucous membranes, lameness, paresis, pathologic fractures, straining to defecate, prolapsed cloaca, slimy white/tan/yellow urates with scant to no fecal material, skin/mouth ulcerations, bloating, and vomiting.

The author can palpate enlarged kidneys cranial to the pelvis in renal diseased herbivores about 60 percent of the time when disease is present. Diagnostic tests that can aid in the diagnosis include a CBC, blood chemistry profiles, urinalysis, radiographs, and ultrasound guided or surgical renal biopsy. A non-regenerative anemia with radiographic evidence of enlarged kidneys or bowel obstructive patterns is consistent with renal disease. Bladder stones are generally radiodense and are uric acid concretions. The chemistry panel should guide treatment with respect to the calcium/phosphorus regulation and should result in suggestions about major husbandry changes. Phosphorus elevated above 15-20mg/dl carries a guarded prognosis with other signs of renal disease. Renal disease (lack of phosphorus excretion) should be differentiated from nutritional hyperphosphatemia (elevated phosphorus from animal proteins) by discontinuing animal based protein in the diet, aggressive fluid treatment, and calcium/phosphorus values done at two weeks, six weeks, and 18 weeks post treatment. Hematocrits (PCVs) and the degree of polychromasia (regeneration of red blood cells) should be assessed if the iguana is initially anemic.

The degree of treatment depends upon the stage of the disease and the clinical signs being exhibited. If the kidney disease is severe with major protein loss through the kidneys, moderate to severe anemia, elevated phosphorus, and obstructive bowel patterns - the prognosis is poor. The author has kept several patients alive for as long as three months with very aggressive management. The author places a catheter in the ventral abdominal vein and diuresis for 3-4 days at 60 ml/kg/day LRS + dehydration deficit (four boluses unless patient allows constant infusion) administration of aluminum hydroxide (Amphogel) at 2ml/kg BID; and a warm soapy enema (if obstipated); calcium 500 mg/kg BID; and injectable iron dextran, vitamin B complex, and vitamin A/D3 are therapeutic. If the white blood cell count from the CBC is elevated or cellular toxicity is evident antibiotics are administered.

Diseases of the urinary tract in non-herbivorous reptiles have infectious, iatrogenic, or spontaneous etiologies (tumors). Snakes can present being asymptomatic, obstipated, constipated, egg bound, with caudal coelomic swelling, dehydrated, anorectic, with discolored urates etc. Renal adenocarcinomas occur periodically in older snakes and renal styphalodorias (Kazocos, Fisher, 1977) is reported. Systemic bacterial infections, gout, and trauma also cause renal dysfunction. Chelonians, particularly tortoises, are known to get large uroliths. Tortoises can show signs of runny noses, decreased caudal limb function, anorexia, egg binding, obstipation, or present clinically normal. A diagnosis should be based on physical exam (palpated in inguinal areas) and or radiographs. Blood chemistries are helpful to determine if the animal is hyperuricemic. Treatment of urolithiasis is surgical removal of the urolith. Feeding peelings from citrus fruits may decrease the size of the urolith prior to surgery. Surgery can be performed months later if no clinical signs or problems are noted from the urolith. Surgery should be referred unless the veterinarian is adequately skilled and equipped.

REFERENCES AND RECOMMENDED READING

—**Allen, M.E.; Oftedal, O.T.; Horst, R.L.:**
Biologic Effects of Light 1995; Symposum. 1995. Gruyter & Company, Berlin • New York. pp 13-35.
—**Barnard, S.M. :**
Color Atlas of Reptilian Parasites; Part I: Protozoans. *Compendium on Continuing Education for the Practicing Veterinarian,* 1986 8(3): 145-148.
—**Barnard, S.M. :**
Color Atlas of Reptilian Parasites; Part II: Flatworms and Roundworms. *Compendium on Continuing Education for the Practicing Veterinarian,* 1986 8(4): 259-262.
—**Barnard, S.M. :**
Color Atlas of Reptilian Parasites; Part III: Miscellaneous Endoparasites and Ectoparasites. *Compendium on Continuing Education for the Practicing Veterinarian,* 1986 8(5): 287-290.
—**Boyer, T.H.:**
Common Problems and Treatment of Green Iguanas. *Bulletin of the Association of Reptilian and Amphibian Veterinarians,* 1991 1(1): 8-11.
—**Driggers, T.E.:**
Metabolic Bone Disease. *Captive Breeding,* July 1994 2(4):10-15.

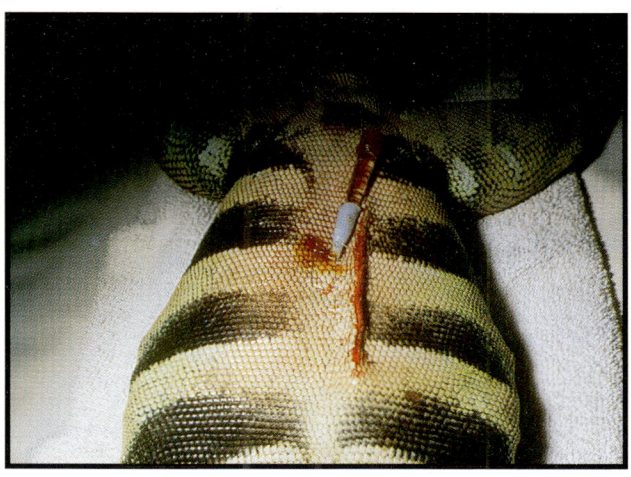

An IV catheter was placed in the ventral abdominal vein to diurese this obtunded iguana. Renal biopsy was performed and hardened feces was removed from the intestines. Photo courtesy of Dr. Todd Driggers.

—**Frye, F.L.:**
Salmonellosis. *Reptiles,* May 1995: 26-40.
—**Frye, F.L:**
Biomedical and Surgical Aspects of Captive Reptile Husbandry. Kreiger Pub., Malabar FL, 1991.
—**Frye, F.L.; Townsend, W.:**
Reproduction. Iguanas: A Guide to their Biology and Captive Care. Kreiger Pub., Malabar FL, 1994, pp. 59-62.
—**Jacobson, E.R.:**
The Desert Tortoise and Upper Respiratory Tract Disease. *Bulletin of the Association of Reptilian and Amphibian Veterinarians,* 1994 4(1): 6-7.
—**Kazocos, K. R.; Fisher, L.F.:**
Renal Styphlodoriases in a Boa Constrictor. *JAVMA,* 1977 171(9):876-878.

This is a renal adenocarcinoma in a Brazilian Rainbow Boa (*Epicrates cenchria*). The tumor was removed and the boa is asymptomatic for metastatic disease. Photo courtesy of Dr. Todd Driggers.

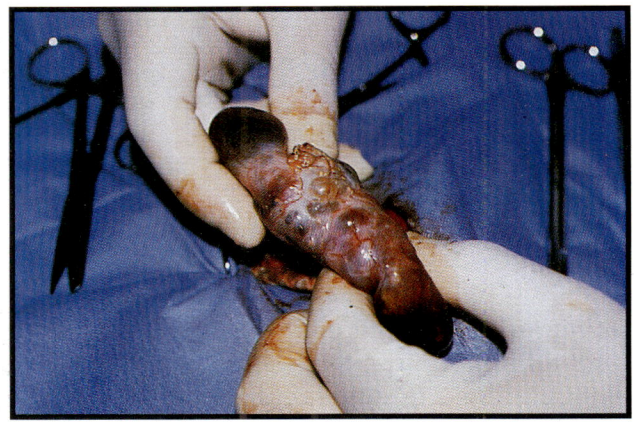

—**King, A.S.; McLelland, J.:**
Female Reproductive System. Birds/Their Structure and Function. Bailliere Tindall Pub., London England 1977, pp. 145-165.

—**Klingenburg, R. J.:**
Understanding Reptile Parasites. Advanced Vivarium Systems Lakeside, CA 1994:

—**Mader, D.R.:**
My Reptile Won't Eat. *Reptiles*, Aug. 1994: 38-43.

—**Mader, D.R.:**
Reptilian Anatomy. *Reptiles*, June 1995: 84-93.

—**Mader, D.R.:**
Obesity in Reptiles. *Reptiles*, Dec. 1993: 33-35.

—**Mader, D.R.:**
Reptile Endoparasites. *Reptiles*, Apr. 1994: 64-71.

—**Mader, D.R.:**
Reptilian Gout. *Reptiles*, Feb. 1995: 40-46.

—**Mader, D.R.:**
Egg Binding in Reptiles. *Reptiles*, Oct. 1995: 88-91.

—**Mader, D.R.;DeRemer, K:**
Salmonellosis in Reptiles. *Vivarium*, 1993; 4 (4): 12,13,22.

—**Mader, D.R.:**
Cryptosporidiosis in Reptiles. *J Small Exotic Animal Med.*, 1993 2(3): 141-142.

—**Mader, D.R.:**
Common Reptilian Bacteria. *Vivarium*, May 1993 4(6): 27-29.

—**Maixner, J.M. et al:**
Effects of Feeding on Serum Uric Acid in Captive reptiles. *J of Zoo Animal Medicine*, 18 (2-3): 62-65.

—**Suedmeyer, W.K.:**
Hypocalcemia and Hyperphosphatemia in a Green Iguana, *Iguana iguana*, with Concurrent Elevation of Serum Glutamic Oxalic Transaminase. *Bulletin of the Association of Reptilian and Amphibian Veterinarians*, 1995 5(3): 5-8.

—**Willete-Frahm, M.:**
Select Protozoal Diseases in Amphians and Reptiles. *Bulletin of the Association of Reptilian and Amphibian Veterinarians*, 1995 5(1): 19-26.

—**Wissman, M.; Parsons, B:**
Dermatophytosis of Green Iguanas. *Reptiles*, July 1995: 78-80.

—**Wright, K.:**
Use of Oral Allopurinol and Saline Dialysis in Management of Hyperuricemia in a Chilean Tortoise. *Bulletin of the Association of Reptilian and Amphibian Veterinarians*, 1992 2(1): 7.

—**Young, L. A. et al;**
Pharmacokinetic of Enrofloxacin in Juvenile Burmese Pythons *Python molurus bivittatus. Proceedings of Association of Reptilian and Amphibian Veterinarians*, 1994: 97-98.

INFECTIOUS DISEASES

by: Todd Driggers, DVM*
Foothills Mobile Exotic DVM
3301 E. Hiddenview Drive
Phoenix, Arizona 85044
Frank Austin DVM, PhD
Diagnostic Laboratory Services
Mississippi State University
College of Veterinary Medicine
Box 9825
Mississippi State, MS 39762

* Address all correspondence to Dr. Todd Driggers, Foothills Mobile Exotic DVM, 3301 E. Hiddenview Dr., Phoenix, AZ 85044

Dr. Todd Driggers is the exotic animal veterinarian at Foothills Mobile Exotic in Phoenix, Arizona and a 1994 graduate of Purdue University. He places special emphasis on diseases and disease prevention of reptiles. He is a member of The Association of Reptilian and Amphibian Veterinarians, American Federation of Herpetoculturists, Association of Avian Veterinarians, and the Association of Zoological Veterinarians.

INTRODUCTION

Considering the great diversity of reptile species and environments, a correspondingly large number of microbial pathogens can be expected to produce disease. Many infectious diseases in reptiles have been described and many others undoubtedly await characterization. In each order of reptiles, examples of viral, bacterial, and fungal microbial pathogens have been reported in the scientific literature. Several microbial pathogens unique to specific reptiles and others that produce disease in a wide array of animals, including man, have been studied at the comparative, evolutionary, and epidemiologic levels. The study of reptile microbial pathogens and the diseases they produce has afforded rich opportunities and unique insight in primal host-pathogen interactions.

Viruses are complex molecular particles with a genome consisting of nucleic acid (either DNA or RNA) surrounded by protein, and sometimes including host-derived lipids and carbohydrates, which can cause infection and disease by redirecting host cell synthetic machinery towards the production of new infectious particles. Thus, viruses can only replicate inside living cells. Bacteria are single celled prokaryotic (without a membrane-bound nucleus) organisms classified in the Phylum Schizomycota. On a very basic clinical level, bacteria can also be divided into Gram-negative and Gram-positive cell wall types through differential staining. Mycobacteria have cell walls that contain waxes and other unique molecules which confer acid-fast staining properties separating them from conventional bacteria. Mycoplasmas are the smallest free-living organisms and lack a cell wall. Most pathogenic bacteria can be grown on artificial laboratory media. However, *Chlamydia* are specialized Gram-negative obligate intracellular bacteria that require living cells for propagation. Fungi are single or multi-celled eukaryotic (true nucleus) plants that have cell walls and lack chlorophyll. Common examples of fungi include yeast, molds, smuts, rusts, mushrooms, and toadstools. Algal organisms are single celled or colonial aquatic eukaryotes that have plant type chlorophyll contained within specialized membranes. Examples of common algae include pond scum and seaweed. Microbial organisms are identified by determining their position in taxonomic classification schemes similar to that of plants and animals. Viruses, although not living organisms, are classified in a similar manner to that of other pathogens. Many different diagnostic tests have been scientifically developed to identify microbial pathogens in man and the domestic animals. Many of these tests have been used and adapted to characterize and identify reptile pathogens.

The diagnostic tests for reptile viruses are limited and the majority of published reports rely on transmission electron microscopy of infected tissue for agent imaging and presumptive identification. Thus many reports in the scientific literature describe Herpes-like or Adeno-like viruses associated with disease conditions. Further characterization, using many other advanced techniques, is required before a definitive diagnosis of a specific virus is achieved. A few reptilian viruses have been isolated using cell cultures for propagation; however, these techniques were carried out at the research level and are not generally available for diagnostic purposes. Unless laboratories maintain reptilian cell cultures, viral diagnostic techniques are limited to electron microscopic characterization of viral morphology. No studies have been reported on attempts to culture reptile viruses in cell lines derived from different species.

Diagnostic tests for bacteria and fungi originating from reptiles are adapted from those used in human and veterinary microbiology. Veterinary microbiology laboratories routinely process specimens from reptiles as the techniques used, excepting incubation temperature, are identical to those for other animals. Many veterinary diagnostic laboratories require that a licensed veterinarian submit the specimen(s) and receive the results for report to the owner/client. Most human laboratories will not accept specimens of animal origin.

Most veterinarians, including the author, apply the mammalian medicine they have learned in veterinary school and through experience to the reptilian species. Conventional medicine is necessary as a learning tool for the growth of reptile medicine. Good conventional mammalian medicine has laid the foundation for knowing what we know about identifying infectious diseases of the species in this class. With nearly 6000 species of reptiles, identifying every pathogen in all the susceptible species will provide hundreds of years of doctoral research. One must know the normal for the species being dealt with in order to differentiate the abnormal. With this in mind, a basic review of common infectious diseases of reptiles will follow.

VIRAL PATHOGENS FOUND IN REPTILES

Viral pathogens isolated in reptiles is a young growing field in reptile medicine. Viral diseases are under-diagnosed in both antemortem and postmortem exams due to "Red Herring" diseases of wild-caught reptiles such as internal parasites and bacterial diseases. Histopathology, electron microscopy, cell culture, and other methods of viral identification are often forgone due to lack of recognition of clinical signs and uncharacterized clinical pictures on the part of the veterinarian and the herpetoculturist. Non-dermal antemortem diagnoses are rare, as few diagnostic tests are available.

VIRAL DISEASES OF SNAKES
Herpesvirus Infection of Boa Constrictors (*Boa constrictor*).

In a clutch of 16 snakes, nine stillborn snakes were given birth to and 6 neonates less than one year died (Hauser, Mettler, Rubel, 1983). Light microscopy revealed amphophilic intranuclear inclusions predominately in the liver. Inclusions were also found in the pancreas and the adrenal gland

This 5 month old Red-tail boa (*Boa constrictor constrictor*) is showing characteristic neurological signs of "star gazing". This neurological clinical sign is consistent with Inclusion Body Disease (IBD) in boids. Other diseases must also be considered such as amoebic encephalitis and bacterial meningitis. Good physical and fecal examinations may help to differentiate. Response to treatment with antibiotics and antiprotozoals are speculative treatments to gauge clinical responses. If there is no clinical response to treatment then IBD should be further investigated. Liver, kidney and esophageal biopsies may be diagnostic. Photo courtesy of Dr. Todd Driggers.

Boas may act as a carrier for IBD to pythons. Boa in foreground. Photo courtesy of Dr. Todd Driggers.

of one snake and in the renal parenchyma of another. Electron microscopy revealed intranuclear inclusions (mostly nucleocapsids) arranged in a crystalline array. Both enveloped and unenveloped particles were found in the cytoplasm.

In this study vertical transmission occurred from the adult female boa. Liver biopsies may be helpful in asymptomatic adult carriers, but can not be routinely recommended at this time due to the apparent low prevalence of this disease. Preventative measures should be to reduce husbandry-related stress as much as possible as herpesviruses becomes active during stressful periods. The route of transmission is not known.

Adenovirus-associated Hepatic Necrosis in a Boa Constrictor (*Boa constrictor*)

Necropsy done on a 4-kg boa constrictor revealed enlarged liver (hepatomegaly) with rounded borders and multifocal diffuse pale areas (Jacobson, Gaskin, 1985). A morphological diagnosis of hepatic necrosis with inflammatory cell infiltration was made based on the histopathologic assessment. Large basophilic inclusions (intranuclear) resulted in ballooning of the nuclei and margination of the chromatin material. Adenovirus was identified by the electron microscopy. Koch's postulate was fulfilled after a neonate boa constrictor was injected with the virus and found

dead in the cage 14 days later. The virus was isolated by culture on viper heart cells grown at 25 degrees Celsius. A similar virus has been found in Rosy Boas (*Lichanura trivirgata*). The route of transmission of this virus have not been determined.

Paramyxovirus in Snakes

This viral disease most commonly occurs in viperid snakes and may decimate entire collections (Jacobson et al, 1981,1992). The virus is transmitted through respiratory secretions and affects the respiratory system and the CNS. The clinical signs of affected snakes mimic that of generalized stomatitis and respiratory disease. Caseous debris in the mouth, excessive mucous production, and respiratory distress are common. Head tremors and opisthotonos are less common but occur in CNS diseases.

Necropsy reveals caseous debris in all or most of the respiratory tract as secondary bacterial infections are the rule. Histologically the lungs are edematous with a mixed inflammatory cell population in the thickened interstitium. Intraluminal caseous debris is common and Gram-negative pathogens are generally present. The affected respiratory epithelium is hypertrophied with intracytoplasmic eosinophilic inclusions. Electron microscopy and tissue culture have identified the virus to be in the paramyxoviridae family.

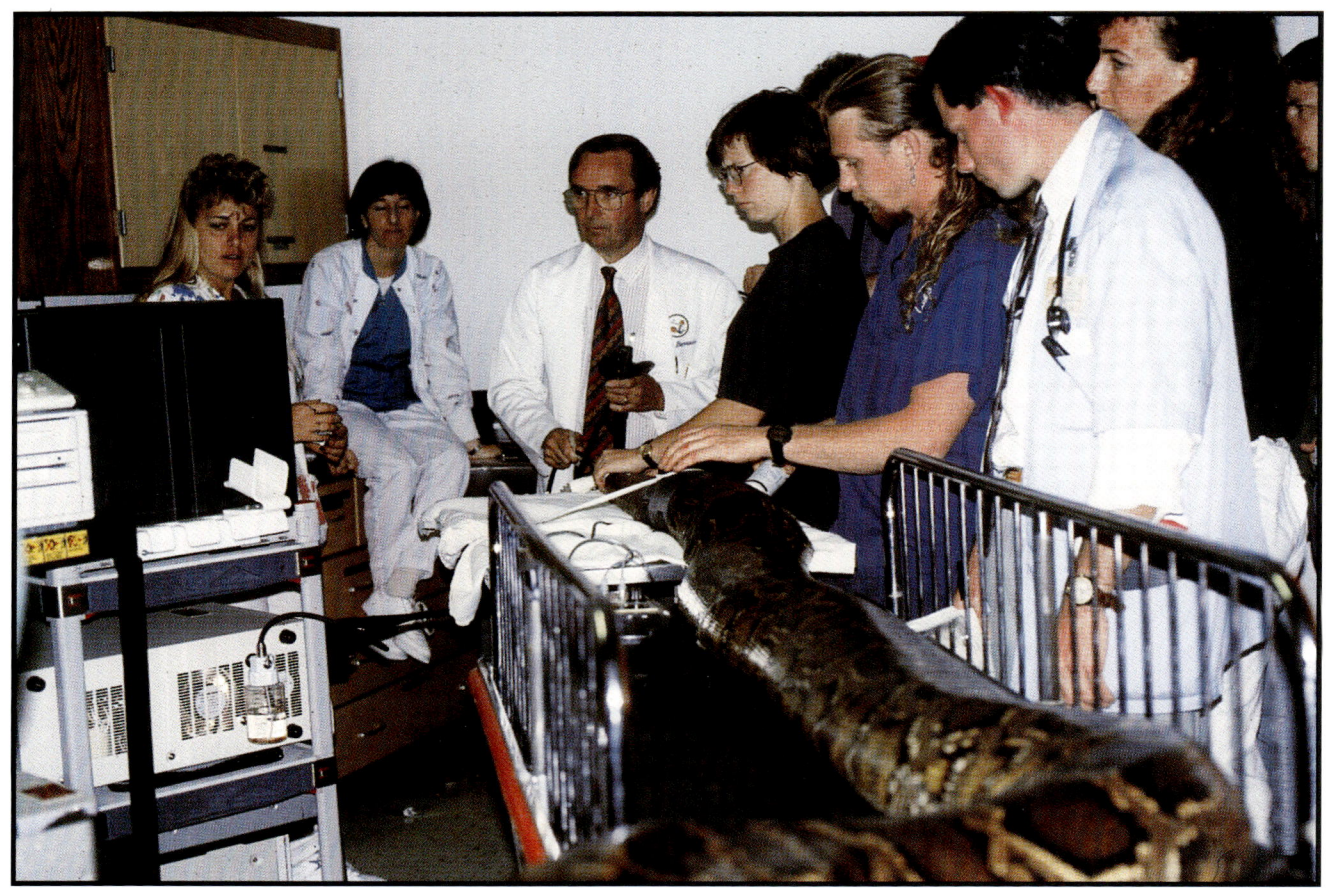

Endoscopic biopsy of the white-tan raised nodules in the esophagus will aid in confirming IBD. Characteristic eosinophilic inclusions are considered diagnostic for the virus. Photo courtesy of Dr. Todd Driggers.

Antemortem diagnosis of PMV should be based on the hemagglutination inhibition (HI) test that was developed at the University of Florida. A positive titer or suspect (1:20 or higher) should be used to confirm carrier status or active infection. Paired HI titers (acute and convalescent) are necessary for confirmation. HI for OPMV should be done before any viper comes out of quarantine.

"Inclusion Body Disease"

Retrovirus has been seen in members of the family Boidae (Schumacher, 1992, 1994). Boas and pythons usually exhibit two different clinical syndromes. The snake mite (*Ophionyssus natricus*) may be a vector of the virus but this is only speculative at this time.

The clinical signs in boas are regurgitation which may later advance to head tremors, disorientation, and possible blindness. Pythons develop clinical signs related to the CNS: head tremors, disorientation "star gazing" and lack of ability to right themselves. With progression of the disease (over several months) clinical signs become worse resulting in anorexia and eventual death. As with many viruses, immune suppression occurs making them susceptible to secondary bacterial infections. Stomatitis and pneumonia may

result. The in boas, the disease seems to progress more slowly which suggests they may be more adapted to the virus or possibly the reservoir host.

IBD should be strongly considered in snakes that are exhibiting any of the above clinical signs. The index of suspicion for IBD should increase if client husbandry is acceptable. Pythons that are in the same cage as boas or with heavy mite infestations are at higher risk of developing the disease. Antemortem diagnosis should be based on clinical signs and biopsy of the liver (in boas). Intracytoplasmic eosinophilic inclusions may be seen on liver biopsy. If flexible endoscopy is available biopsies can be taken from carrier snakes may have isophageal lesions. The lesions are usually raised white nodules but may also have hemorrhage associated with them. Histopathology may yield the characteristic inclusion is usually diagnostic or may be used as a quarantine screening tool. Post mortem diagnosis should be confirmed by electron microscopy. Histopathologically, pythons will demonstrate inclusions in the neurons of the CNS. Boas develop inclusions in the kidneys, pancreas, liver, and the brain. Further research is being done to develop serologic test for "Inclusion Body Disease" at the University of Florida. The virus is being further classified.

VIRAL DISEASES OF CHELONIANS

Gray-patch Disease

Gray-patch disease is an apparent herpesvirus that causes small, circular papular lesions in the skin of captive-hatched juvenile Green Sea Turtles (*Chelonia mydas*) (Rebell, Rywlin, Haines, 1975). The disease occurs more frequently during the stressed times of summer heat where water temperature reaches 86° F or higher (Haines, Kleese, 1990). Overcrowding and poor water quality also contribute to the disease process. The lesions affect the epidermal cells and contain basophilic intranuclear inclusions. Electron microscopy most closely identifies the virus as herpes.

Lung, Eye, and Trachea (LET)

LET is also a herpesvirus that occurs in the epithelial cells of Green Sea Turtles (Jacobson et al, 1986). Turtles one year of age and older are the most susceptible to the virus. The clinical onset appears over a 2-3 week period and results in morbidity or death in weeks to months. Clinical signs consist of caseated material over the globe, harsh lung sounds, and gaping at the water's surface. Amphophilic intranuclear inclusions are seen the tracheal mucosal epithelial cells. The virus has been isolated and identified.

Herpesvirus Stomatitis in Tortoises

Several species of tortoises with oral abscesses and ulcerations have been found to have herpesvirus. Suboptimal environment, husbandry, and overcrowding play a part of the disease process. Affected species have been the Desert Tortoise (*Xerobates agassizii*) (Harper, Hominid, Heusclele, 1982), Argentine tortoise (*Geochelone chilensis*) (Jacobson et al, 1985), and the Spur-thighed tortoises (*Testudo graeca*) (Cooper, Gschmeissner, Bone, 1988). Light microscopic examination revealed eosinophilic intranuclear inclusions. Viral particles consistent with herpesvirus were identified on EM. Topical acyclovir ointment 5% may be helpful at controlling the clinical signs.

Herpesvirus Hepatitis in Freshwater Turtles

Herpesvirus has been found in the post mortem examination of Map (*Graptemys* spp.) (Jacobson, Gaskin, Wahlquist, 1977), Pacific Pond (*Clemmys marmorata*) (Frye et al, 1977), and painted turtles (*Chrysemys picta*) (Cox, Rapley, Barker, 1980). The virus is thought to transmitted by the fecal-oral route. It is unclear as to the incubation period of the virus as no clinical signs have been noted. Necropsy reveals enlarged liver (hepatomegaly)

Overcrowding with any species of reptile will exacerbate the spreading of infectious diseases. Photo courtesy of Dr. Todd Driggers.

with areas of necrosis. Histologically intranuclear eosinophilic inclusions may be seen in the lungs, liver, kidneys, spleen, and the pancreas.

Papilloma-Like Virus in Side-Neck Turtles (*Platemys platycephala*)

Small circular coalescing papular skin lesions were seen in newly imported Bolivian side-neck turtles (Jacobson, Gaskin, Clubb, 1982). The biopsied skin lesions were evaluated under electron and light microscopy. Light microscopy revealed a hyperkeratotic, acanthotic, hyperplastic epidermis. EM revealed intranuclear crystalline arrays of viral particles that were consistent with papillomavirus.

Iridovirus in a Hermann's Tortoise (*Testudo hermanni*)

This tortoise died with no clinical signs of illness. Necropsy revealed gray spots throughout the liver (Geldstab, Bestetti, 1982). The spleen was congested and contained small white foci on the cut surface. Histology revealed basophilic intracytoplasmic inclusions in hepatocytes next to necrotic areas and in the epithelial cells of the intestine. The virus size, shape, and characteristics most closely resembled viral particles in the iridoviridae family.

Fibropapillomatosis

Fibropapillomatosis is a disease process whereby the unidentified virus causes tumors to be produced on the skin (head, neck, flippers, plastron, and the carapace) and internally (Jacobson et al, 1991). These tumors affect the ability of the turtles to move, forage, and see. The result is weak, emaciated turtles. Histologically, eosinophilic intranuclear inclusions are seen in the affected epidermal cells. Both the dermis and epidermis are affected by hyperplastic changes. Electron microscopy revealed 110 to 120 nm viral particles that may resemble those in the family Herpesviridae. Treatment should be wide surgical excision of external lesions.

VIRAL DISEASES IN LIZARDS

Poxvirus in Tegus

Poxvirus has been seen in a captive tegu (*Tupinambis teguexin*) (Stauber, Gogolewski, 1990). The route of transmission is unclear. The lesions were described as multiple brown-colored papules on the skin. Large eosinophilic intracytoplasmic inclusions were seen in the epidermal cells upon histological examination. The lesions healed spontaneously in three to four months.

Adenovirus in a Monitor (*Varanus exanthematicus*)

Adenovirus inclusions were seen in the liver of an imported Savannah monitor. The monitor began spontaneously hemorrhaging from the mouth and cloaca. On necropsy the lizard had a necrotizing viral hepatitis characterized by lightly basophilic inclusions. The inclusions were also seen in the biliary epithelial cells. An ulceration in the small intestine was cultured positive for salmonellosis with histological evidence of a septicemia/viremia.

Similarly, another Savannah monitor died with no clinical signs. Histology revealed multifocal areas of hepatic necrosis. Degenerating hepatocytes contained basophilic intranuclear inclusions. The myocardium also contained multiple necrotic areas. Some endothelial tissue contained inclusions as well (Jacobson, Kollias, 1986).

A bearded dragon (*Pogona barbatus*) was reported to have period inappetence before dying. Histology revealed coagulative necrosis of the liver. Inclusions found in the hepatocytes were eosinophilic and intranuclear.

Adenovirus has been seen in a 6-month-old Jackson's chameleon (Jacobson, Gardiner, 1990). Histology revealed proliferation of the mucosal epithelium of the trachea and esophagus where eosinophilic intranuclear inclusions were found. The mucosa had a mononuclear cell infiltrate throughout. Although no EM was performed on the inclusions, morphologically they were most consistent with adenovirus.

Papilloma virus in Lacertid Lizards

Papilloma in the European emerald lizard (*Lacerta viridis*) is reported to be associated with bites inflicted during the breeding season. Females get papillomas at the tail base and the males get papillomas at the base of the neck according to the authors. Males bite other males at the neck base and bite females at the tail base during the breeding season. Light microscopy revealed hyperkeratosis and hyperplasia of the epidermal cells. Viral particles consistent with herpesvirus, papovavirus, and reovirus were identified. (Cooper et al, 1982)

VIRAL DISEASES OF CROCODYLIA

Poxvirus in Caiman

Captive raised Spectacled caiman were examined and determined to have circular gray-white skin lesions distributed over the entire body surface (Jacobson et al, 1979). Most lesions were in the head area. The number and location of lesions each caiman had varied. Some had glossal and hard palate lesions. Histopathology revealed hypertrophied epithelial cell with eosinophilic intracytoplasmic inclusions.

Adenovirus in the Nile Crocodile

Two eight month old Nile crocodiles (*Crocodylus niloticus*) died with no ante-mortem clinical signs. Necropsy revealed a necrotizing hepatitis and enteritis (Jacobson, Gardiner, Foggin, 1984). Light microscopy revealed basophilic intranuclear inclusions in the hepatocytes and crypt epithelial cells. Electron microscopy revealed viral particles of adenovirus (based on location, size, and morphology).

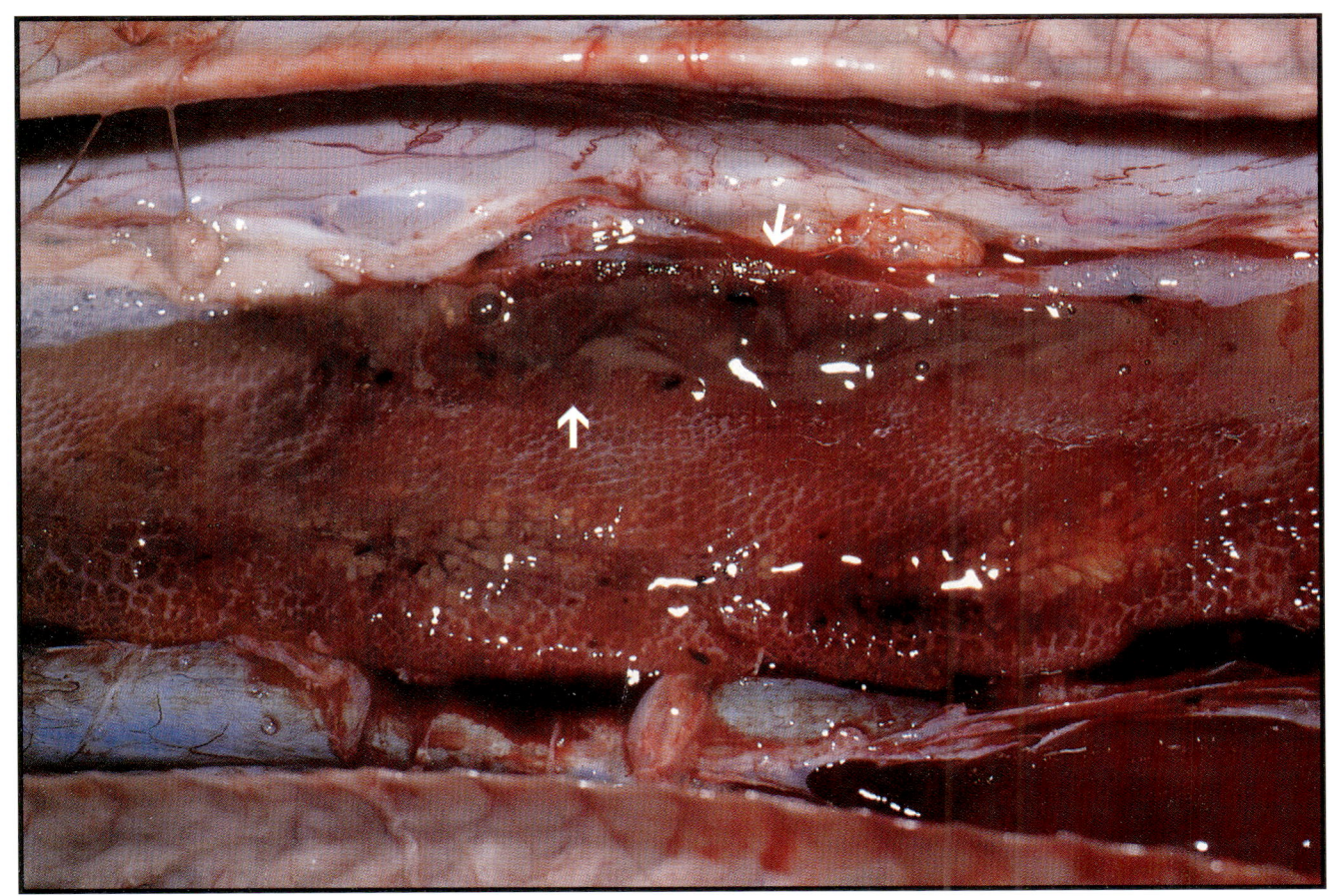

Note the brownish-tinged gelatinous fluid in this large python. She was gravid and died egg bound with evidence of septicemia. *E. coli* was the implicated bacterium. Photos courtesy of Dr. Todd Driggers.

↓ Note the red/white lesions on the snakes oviducts.

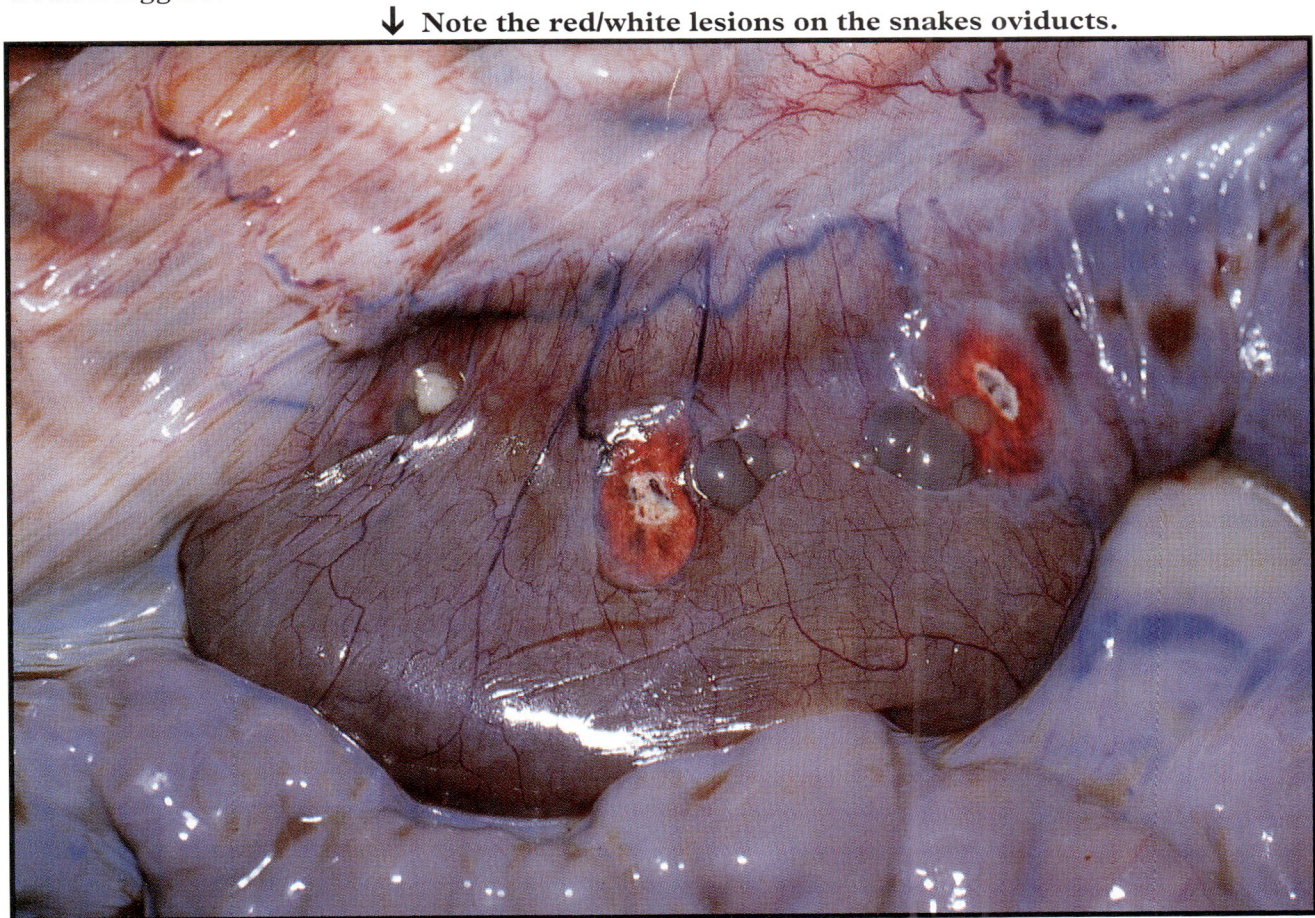

Diagnosing Viral Diseases in Reptiles

In general, ante-mortem diagnosis of viral diseases is very difficult in reptiles. From the relatively small number of papers written on viral diseases in reptiles it is obvious that many reptiles do not get necropsied and the findings submitted for publishing. However, if and when reptiles do not respond to appropriately used (based on culture and sensitivity, proper dose, duration and route) antibiotics or antifungals, a viral disease should be suspected. Biopsies should be performed either surgically or preferably ultrasound guided. If available, the electron microscope can be used on fecals, tissue fluids, and biopsy specimens. Few serologic test have been designed for reptile viruses. Hemagglutination Inhibition tests have been designed for snakes suspected of having paramyxovirus.

Necropsy is invaluable and essential to diagnosing reptile viruses for the particular case and for the benefit of advancing knowledge of reptile medicine. Both histopathology and EM are good techniques for finding viral inclusions or particles. Viral isolation should be the gold standard. Many universities have very good diagnostic facilities to utilize and will employ their techniques better than the general veterinary practitioner. Specimen handling and submission will be handled later in the chapter.

Following are some specific guidelines provided by Dr. Frank Austin of the Diagnostic Laboratory of Mississippi State University, College of Veterinary Medicine.

Because of the nature of viruses and *Chlamydia* and their great variation in pathogenesis, a couple of generalities may be made concerning collection of samples for laboratory examination:

—Both of these agents can best be recovered during the acute phase of the disease, at which time, the agent often may be recovered from blood, exudates, visceral organs, or feces.

—After the acute phase, or with the appearance of circulating antibodies, recovery of these agents is seldom accomplished; consequently, diagnosis must then be determined by serologic techniques.

Freeze all samples immediately on dry ice or liquid nitrogen; freezing of viral samples at minus 20°C is not sufficient to inhibit inactivation of viruses. Collect all samples in individual sealable containers, e.g. whirl-pack bags. All samples shipped on dry ice must be sealed to avoid inactivation of virus by decreased pH. Collect samples during the acute phase of the disease. Collect post-mortem samples within 6 hours of death. Ship all samples frozen on dry ice in Styrofoam dry ice containers. Antemortem samples are usually limited to biopsies, nasal swabs, tracheal washings, and feces. The swabs should be placed in 3-5 mls of isotonic buffered saline (e.g. Lactated Ringer's Solution) in unbreakable, sterile plastic tubes and frozen. Tracheal washes should also be placed in unbreakable, sterile plastic tubes and frozen. Feces should be placed in individual sterile sealable plastic bags (e.g., whirlpacks) and frozen. Package all samples individually and freeze on dry ice. Sample visible lesions with adjacent normal tissue. Sampling for viral serology collect acute and convalescent serum samples 10-14 days apart. Serum must be harvested from a clot before freezing and shipping. Under no circumstances should whole blood be frozen. Allow the clot to form overnight at room temperature; harvest using a needle on a syringe and transfer to a new sterile tube. Sterile serum can be shipped without freezing or refrigeration if transport time is short.

There are three major methods for recovery of viruses from clinical material:
—cell or tissue cultures,
—embryonated eggs, and
—animal inoculation.

These techniques require, in most laboratories, 24 hours to 14 days for recovery of a virus. Once a virus has been isolated, it may be identified by fluorescent antibody techniques, electron microscopy or other methods. Cell cultures are the most routinely applied method for virus isolation. Cell cultures may be derived from almost any organ not contaminated by natural bacterial flora. The cultures, are generally utilized from fetal lungs, spleen, kidney, adrenal or thyroid tissues. The cell cultures used for viral diagnostics should be from the homologous species, that is, use reptile cell cultures for isolation of reptilian viruses. All cell cultures utilized for viral diagnostics must be examined for bacterial and viral contamination and their ability to support the replication of the common viruses being sought. Embryonated chicken eggs have limited use in most diagnostic laboratories and be from specific pathogen free flocks to insure reliable results since contamination with avian leukosis viruses or mycoplasma will interfere with viral culture. Also, various agents require different routes of inoculation and different embryo ages prior to infection or inoculation. The use of animal inoculation is limited primarily by the cost of maintenance of animals for use.

Fluorescent antibody techniques can be used to identify specific viral antigens in clinical material or infected cell cultures or to identify specific viral antibodies in suspect serum. There are two basic techniques of fluorescent antibody testing in use: 1) the direct fluorescent antibody technique and 2) the indirect fluorescent antibody technique.

Note the red tinge to the intact plastron indicative of septicemia. There are also obvious joint swellings. The turtle was relucted to move before being euthanized. Mycobacteria were identified cytologically and the culture grew *M. chelonei*. Photo courtesy of Dr. Todd Driggers.

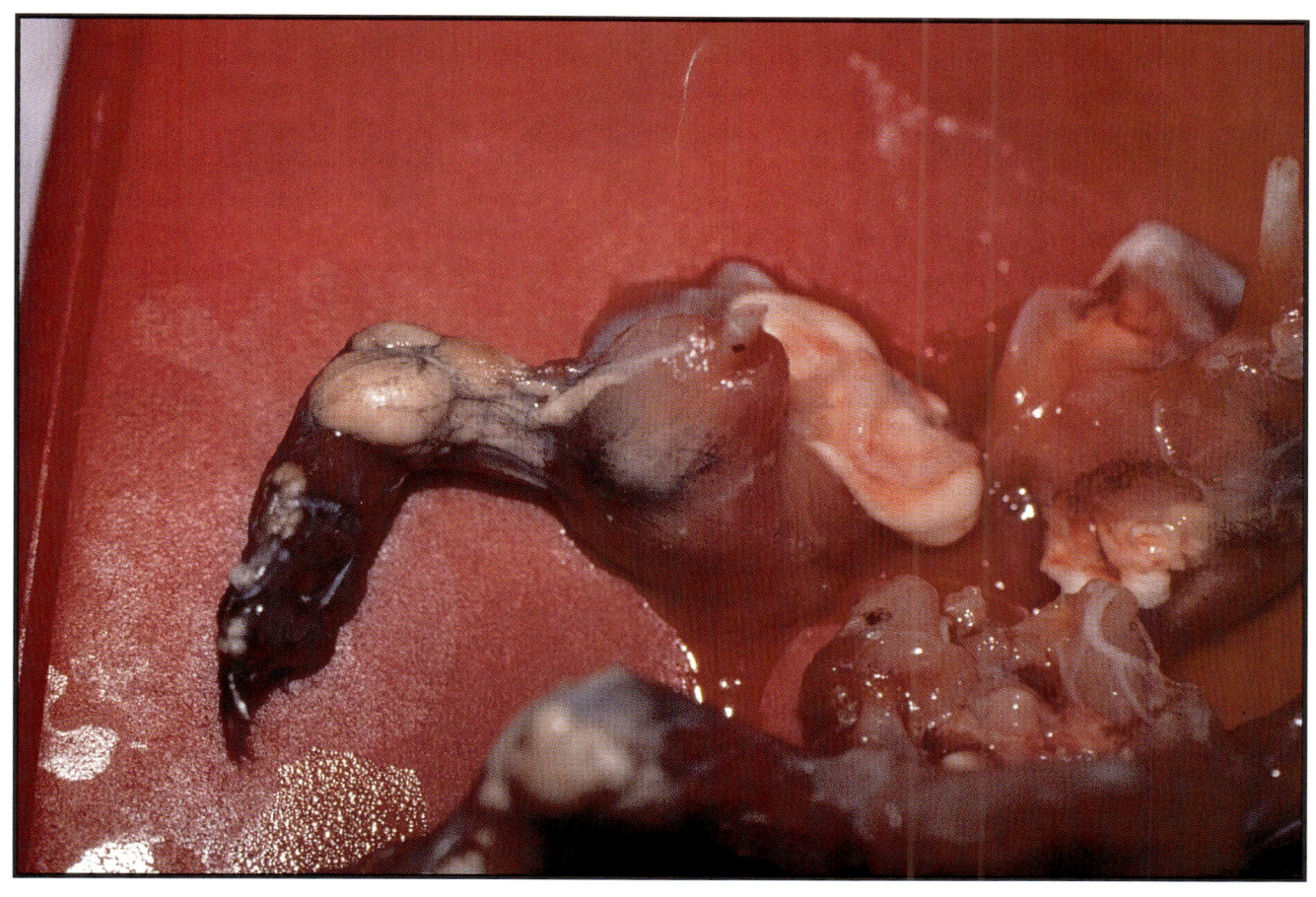

Direct fluorescent antibody technique involves the use of specific antiserum to identify viral antigens in infected cells. Indirect fluorescent antibody technique can be-utilized to identify viral antigens in cells or to identify viral antibodies in serum. To identify viral antigens, an untagged specific antiserum is reacted with the viral antigen and then a tagged anti-antiserum is permitted to react with the virus-antibody complex (if present). To identify specific antibodies in serum, a cell infected with a known virus is reacted with a serum from an animal suspected of being infected with that virus. This system is then reacted with tagged anti-antiserum. For example: The basic premise of FA techniques is that the homologous Ag~Ab reaction forms a permanent bond and the tagged antibodies will not elute during the rinsing processes.

There are three techniques of electron microscopy applicable to viral diagnostics:
—thin-section electron microscopy,
—immunoelectron microscopy, and
—negative contrast electron microscopy (l~CEM) .

Negative contrast electron microscopy involves the separation of viruses from their milieu and performing a negative stain to permit direct visualization of the particles. This technique is used routinely and can he applied to clinical material and infected cell cultures. Immunoelectron microscopy is similar to FA techniques in that a specific antibody coats the viruses and can be visualized following negative staining. This permits serologic identification of viruses, but has limited application in veterinary virology due to the limited number of viruses and vaccines. Thin-section electron microscopy involves a technique similar to histopathology techniques, but due to the time required for preparation and sample size, it is of little or no value as a diagnostic tool.

Serodiagnosis is the diagnosis of a disease by identifying specific antibodies in the serum of a suspect animal. There are two approaches to serodiagnosis:
—Qualitative serodiagnosis which consists of demonstrating the presence or absence of specific antibody in a serum sample and equating the presence with infection, past or present and
—Quantitative serodiagnosis which requires the quantitation of specific antibody in a sample.

Quantitative results are generally reported as either significant level of antibody (which is protective) or insignificant (the animal is susceptible). If paired serum samples are submitted, the results may be reported as positive seroconversion which is definitive evidence of an infection during the time the samples were collected. Seroconversion may be a 4-fold or greater increase or decrease in titer between the acute and convalescent samples.

The various tests utilized for serodiagnosis are:
—serum (virus) neutralization (SN),
—hemagglutination-inhibition (HI),
—immunodiffusion (ID), and
—immunofluorescence (FA).

The SN test requires cell cultures for performance and involves the neutralization of viral infectivity, and, hence, no cell death. The HI test requires that the virus be able to agglutinate erythrocytes and involves the inhibition of the erythrocyte agglutination by specific viral antibodies. The ID test is simply the development of a line of precipitate formed by the interaction of homologous antigen and antibody in an agar matrix.

Isolation of viruses from clinical material is the standard method of viral diagnosis. The major disadvantage is the time required to culture a virus. In all instances, the time required for culture is greater than the time required to determine if the sample(s) is virus negative by other means. Another disadvantage is the difficulty in identifying mixed or multiple virus infections. Generally, one virus will replicate faster, or better, than the other(s) and the end results appear as if only one virus was present. Also, simple production of cytopathic effect (CPE) is not sufficient to identify a particular virus; therefore, other techniques must be utilized to identify an isolate, i.e., FAT, EM. The chief advantage to the FAT is speed; generally much less than 24 hours is necessary to perform this test. Also, the FAT will readily identify mixed viral infections in cell cultures or clinical materials. It is not necessary to have viable virus present for the FAT since the viral antigenicity is not affected by inactivation. The major disadvantage of the FAT is the lack of reagents, e.g., specific, tagged antisera for identification of virus or specifically infected substrates to quantitate antibodies. However, autolytic or necrotic tissue samples may interfere with the FAT resulting in false positive reactions, and improper selection of the tissue may result in a false negative reactions.. The outstanding advantage of negative contrast electron microscopy is the speed and ability to identify mixed viral infections. The major disadvantages are the general requirement for a fluid specimen (feces, nasal swab, urine) and that virus identification is only a morphologic identification (e.g., a virus is identified only as a Reovirus, not as Reovirus Type 3). The disadvantage to serodiagnosis is the necessity to obtain paired serum samples for most diagnoses.

Treatment of Viral Diseases

Very few antivirals exist for treatment of diseases in mammalian and reptile medicine. Treatment of reptiles with viruses entails good supportive care and treatment of secondary bacterial/fungal infections. The author increases the cage temperature 5-8 degrees F above the upper end of the preferred optimal temperature zone. The logic behind this is that reptile viruses are adapted to the normal

Overcrowding, increased humidity, suboptimal temperatures and inadequate husbandry all contribute to the spreading of infectious disease. Mycoplasmosis is very contagious in both wild populations of tortoises and in captivity. Affected tortoises should never be released into the wild as wild tortoises could be decimated. Such has been the case with the Desert tortoise (*Xerobates agasizzi*). Photo courtesy of Dr. Mike Kiedrowski.

temperature at which the reptile is kept. An artificial fever is induced. Little is known about the routes that most of these viral pathogens are contacted. Fecal/oral route is thought to be the most common route. Strict isolation of animals with viral pathogens is necessary to avoid the possibility of transmission. Common sense dictates that water living reptiles should have separate filtration mechanisms. Likewise separate cleaning instruments and agents should be used when cleaning enclosures of infected reptiles. The reader is advised to refer to the chapter on Disinfection and Antisepsis.

BACTERIAL PATHOGENS IN REPTILES

One must know the normal in order to recognize the abnormal. Few studies have been done on the normal, making interpretation of laboratory results vary depending on the level of experience of the veterinarian. Conventional wisdom with reptiles is that potential pathogen equals disease. This is not necessarily the case. The more that is learned about reptile medicine the more realized that pathogen plus clinical signs equals disease. Disease results when the pathogen or po-

tential pathogen has powers that are able to overcome or avoid the host's immune system. Disease may result from a very pathogenic bacteria or a high dose of a moderately pathogenic bacteria, or the bacteria gain access to an area in which the body is unaccustomed (e.g. *E. coli* in the lungs). Bacteria also cause disease when the host is immunocompromised. Immunocompromised reptiles are common to see in private practice as proper husbandry is not always practiced by the owner.

As previously stated, there are several groups that bacteria can be classified into based upon their individual staining techniques and unique physical properties. Gram-positive bacteria (G+), gram-negatives (G-), aerobic, anaerobic, etc. Aerobic, Gram-positive bacteria are generally minimally pathogenic to reptiles unless the given reptile is immunocompromised. Aerobic, Gram-negative bacteria are generally considered more pathogenic in reptiles. Many reptile veterinarians feel that anaerobic bacteria (which can be either G- or G+) are common pathogens in reptiles. Anaerobic (low oxygen requirement) bacteria are not cultured for routinely in reptile or small animal medicine. Aerobic, Gram-positive bacteria should only be treated when the reptile has a pure culture or Gram stain suggesting clinical significance, or when the con-

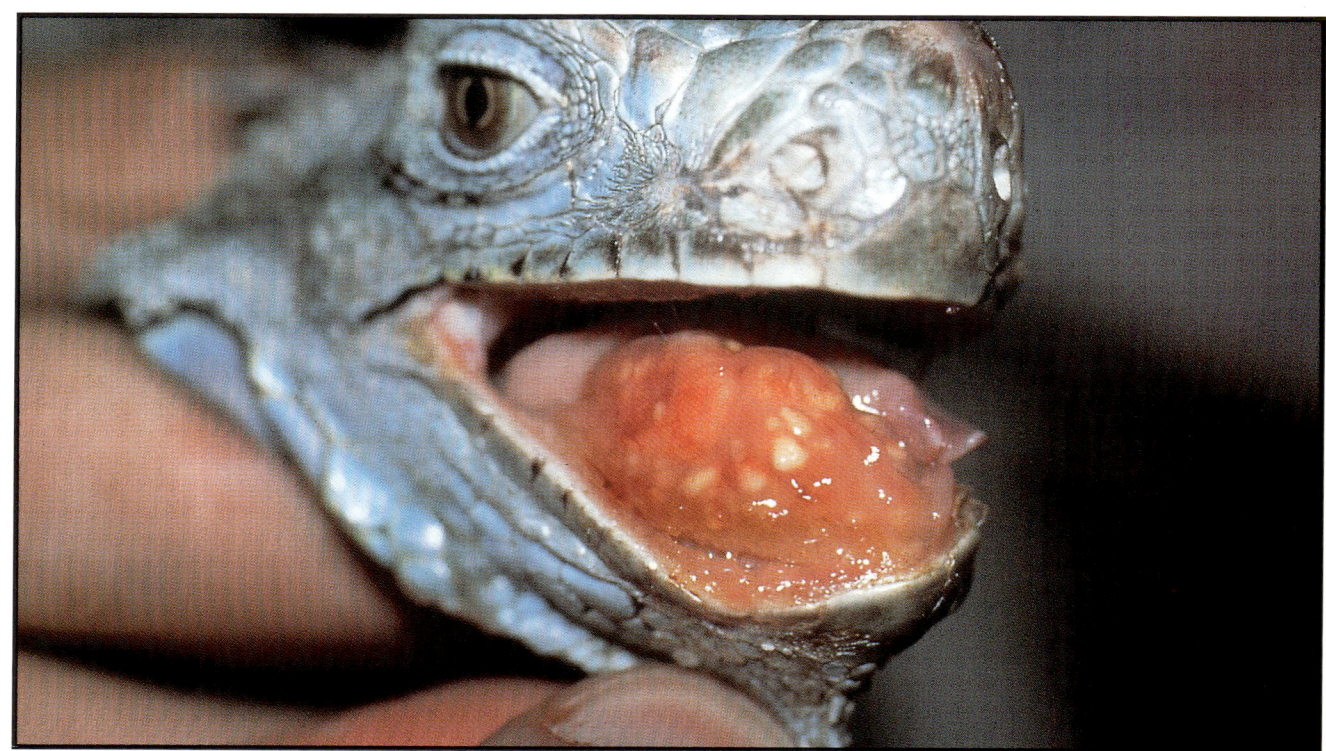

A severe bacterial stomatitis in an immunosuppressed Green iguana (*Iguana iguana*). Aggressive abscess management (lancing macroabscess) and antimicrobial therapy along with increasing the temperature to 95 degrees F in the cage allowed for a full recovery. Photo courtesy of Dr. Todd Driggers.

dition is not responding to therapy for a Gram-negative pathogen and has clinical signs of being ill. Knowledge on pathogenicity of Gram-positive bacteria should be based on what is known in mammalian and human medicine. Aerobic, Gram-negative and anaerobic bacteria will be discussed further in the chapter.

AEROMONAS

Aeromonas spp. are opportunistic bacteria and are normal oral flora in low numbers. Heavy growths on culture may be seen with clinical signs of mouth infections (stomatitis), respiratory disease, or septicemia. Snake mites, *Ophionyssus natricus*, are known vectors for this bacteria. Aggressive antibiotic treatment, wound flushing, husbandry changes, and supportive care are necessary to effect a cure. Antibiotics alone don't always work.

ESCHERICHIA COLI

E. coli is normal intestinal flora for many reptiles. With poor husbandry and cage sanitation this bacteria can be associated with stomatitis, dermal, and respiratory infections. Immunocompromised patients may get severe diarrhea and dehydrate rapidly. Appropriate antimicrobial treatment, husbandry changes, and fluid therapy are necessary to effect a cure.

MYCOBACTERIA

These bacteria are Gram-negative, acid-fast bacteria which exist in the soil, water, and other places. Mycobacteria are commonly encountered by us as humans and by other animals daily. Because most of our immune systems (cell-mediated) are functional we do not acquire the active disease. Reptiles, humans, and other animals acquire the disease when their immune systems are suppressed. Poor husbandry is implicated in many cases. The species-dependent preferred optimal temperature zone (POTZ) is often suboptimal and coupled with poor sanitation. Clinical signs include joint swellings, respiratory distress, diarrhea, osteomyelitis, severe depression, anorexia, and cachexia. The acid-fast bacteria can be cultured or identified cytologically by aspirates, skin scrapings, or smears. The slide can be stained with a Romanowsky stain for rapid identification. Bacteria will contrast with background stained fluid and appear as negatively-stained rods. The acid-fast stain turns the bacteria pink in color. Culturing the bacteria is the gold standard. Bacterial species *M. chelonei*, *M. marinum*, and *M. thamnopheos* have been isolated in reptiles thus far. These are sometimes referred to as atypical mycobacteria since they represent species other than those responsible for causing tuberculosis and leprosy in humans and animals.

MYCOPLASMA

This bacterium is a common pathogen in captive and wild-caught species of tortoises which develop nasal discharges. Clinical signs are anorexia, lack of hibernation, nasal discharge, reddened nostrils and choana, open-mouth breathing, and increased upper respiratory noises. The bacteria has been found in multiple species of tortoises including the Greek tortoise (*Testudo graeca*), Hermann's tortoise (*Testudo hermanni*), Gopher tortoise (*Gopherus polyphemus*), Leopard tortoise (*Geochelone pardalis*), Spur-thighed tortoise (*Geochelone sulcata*), Radiated tortoise (*Geochelone radiata*), Indian star tortoises (*Geochelone elegans*) and the Desert tortoise (*Xerobates agassizii*). This bacteria is difficult to culture but can be identified serologically with tests available at the University of Florida. Clinical disease is associated with captive tortoises kept in temperature and humidity extremes. The treatment of choice is correcting the inappropriate aspects of husbandry and administering injectable enrofloxacin at 5 mg/kg q48 for 10 treatments. Nasal flushes with saline (10 parts) diluted enrofloxacin (1 part) should be done daily for 1 month or until clinical signs stop. Care should be taken to avoid splashing or flush running into the tortoise's eyes as the solution is extremely irritating. Serologically-positive tortoises should be isolated from other tortoises as they should be considered a constant potential infectious source for captive and free-ranging tortoises. Furthermore, no serologically positive tortoise or those showing clinical signs should be released as native populations of tortoises can be decimated by such acts. Many tortoise societies around the nation will act as a refuge for affected tortoises or owners should consider euthanasia (in lieu of releasing). Treatment regimens may have to be administered once or twice yearly most typically.

KLEBSIELLA

Reptile bacterial species of *Klebsiella* are often isolated in oral flora of normal reptiles. Clinical signs of stomatitis, pneumonia, and hypopyon may cause an index of suspicion for this bacteria before culture results are back. Appropriate antibiotic treatment and husbandry changes are effective in early stages of the disease.

PROVIDENCIA

This bacteria is considered normal oral flora in many reptiles. Unless overwhelming numbers are present with accompanying clinical signs, treatment is unnecessary.

PSEUDOMONAS

This bacteria is also normal oral and intestinal flora in some reptiles in low numbers. When cultured out in high numbers, treatment should be considered. This bacteria tends to have a classic sweet smell with a characteristic green color. As with most bacterial infections in reptiles, immune suppression secondary to poor husbandry is an important aspect. Reptiles should be kept within their preferred optimal temperature range, have the ability to thermoregulate and photoregulate, be fed nutritionally complete (diverse) diets, and kept in clean, well ventilated cages.

SALMONELLA

Salmonella is considered a pathogen in most animal species. In reptiles it is considered at least opportunistically pathogenic. It was once regarded as a common zoonotic disease transmitted from hatchling red-eared sliders that were once sold at pet stores to family members. Iguanas and other reptiles are cultured routinely for this bacterium. The author obtains positive cultures at least half of the time in clinically normal newly purchased animals and 80 percent of the time in clinically ill poor doers. Fecal cultures for screening purposes should be done on a pooled sample of stool collected over 3-5 days. Skin lesions, oral abscesses, and diarrhea can be collected and submitted directly if *Salmonella* is suspected. Fecal cultures on clinically healthy reptiles should be done when there are young children in the family or immunocompromised family members. If the culture is positive for *Salmonella* in this situation the author recommends finding a different home for the reptile. The author does not advocate euthanizing *Salmonella*-positive animals that are otherwise healthy. Strict hygiene should be practiced with every animal with respect to cleaning of cages, food preparation, and handling, particularly with *Salmonella*-positive animals.

Treating *Salmonella*-positive animals is a controversial subject with many veterinarians due to the potential for the development of resistant strains. The author treats only if the reptile is clinically ill and the owners understand and accept the risk of developing salmonellosis themselves. Oral gentamicin, amikacin, and enrofloxacin can be used at 5 mg/kg doses SID for intestinal salmonellosis. *Salmonella* septicemia should be treated parenterally with enrofloxacin at 5 mg/kg SID or Amikacin at 5 mg/kg SID (only with aggressive fluid therapy and biochemically sound kidneys).

SERRATIA

This bacterium is normal oral flora in low numbers in healthy snakes. It is a common skin pathogen resulting in caseated abscesses. Sharp objects in the cage or abrasions (from constant rubbing) will result in breakage of the skin barrier. Surgical debridement, flushing, and appropriate antimicrobial treatment are necessary for a cure.

SPIROCHETES

This motile snake-like bacterium are probably more a common pathogen than previously thought. Spirochetes are difficult to culture which results in erroneous conclusions with respect to the pathogen truly causing the disease. The bacteria tend to cause stomatitis in agamid lizards which results in the gingiva and subgingiva separating away from the mandible and maxilla. Caseated abscesses may also be seen in cases of spirochetal stomatitis, but may be due to a secondary bacterial infection. Oral swabs of the gingiva/subgingiva should be taken and rolled onto a slide. Romanowsky (e.g. Diff-Quik®) or Wright's stain will stain all other bacteria. Spirochetes do not stain well and contrast well in the basophilic saliva or mucus on the slide. The characteristic "S" shape is diagnostic as specialized media and isolation is difficult and expensive. These bacteria respond very well to enrofloxacin at 5 mg/kg q24-48. The prognosis is poor for the lizard that has severe gingival and mandibular separation but surgery may be attempted.

CULTURING AND CYTOLOGICAL ANALYSIS

Diagnosis of particular bacterial infections is dependent on a culture and sensitivity of the affected lesions. Proper collection of the culture is the key to attaining meaningful results.

Culturing from random areas or merely on the surface of a lesion gives little information of what the true infection may be. The author prefers culturing the capsule in which the abscess was encased collected as aseptically as possible. If no abscesses are present, an inflamed area should be incised with a scalpel blade and cultured from the cut surface or from a biopsy sample. A tracheal wash should be done if respiratory infections are suspected. A sterile catheter is guided down the trachea and 0.5-1% volume of body weight of sterile saline is flushed into the air sac/lung (sedation/anesthesia may be necessary). After rolling the reptile around, a syringe is used to aspirate the contaminated fluid. Cytological evaluation (looking for inflammatory cells, fungi, and parasite larvae or ovum), Gram stains, and culture and sensitivity can be performed on the attained fluid. Alternatively, cultures can be attained by inserting a mini-tip culturette into the glottis (moe subject to oral contamination). Fecal cultures should be done on the feces itself not the cloaca. A colonic wash is necessary unless stool is readily available. Again, the author routinely swabs all oral lesions and loose stools in all reptiles for both cytological and culture.

Gram staining the affected lesion is important and gives immediate information not only on classifying the particular bacteria but on the homogeneous nature and the population density of a particular bacteria. Gram staining a lesion is helpful when trying to decide if subtle lesions (e.g. mildly inflamed gums) are true pathology or variations of normal. Gram-negative bacteria stain pinkish and Gram-positive stain purple. The author also prefers to stain (Romanowsky or Wright's) a cytology preparation of the area. The information gained in five minutes on these cytology preparations is invaluable. Information about parasites, protozoa, inflammatory reactions, cellular responses, fungi (usually deeply basophilic may be budding), Gram-positive bacteria (stain basophilic), Gram-negative bacteria (*faintly* tan to eosinophilic), certain morphologically distinct bacteria such a spirochetes (snake-like), anaerobes (*Clostridia* stain basophilic and have an "eye of a needle" appearance), and negatively-staining mycobacteria (best seen in mucus or some other extracellular basophilic background material) can be gained without waiting for culture results or responses to treatment.

Utilize a laboratory that routinely runs cultures on reptiles. Growing bacteria on culture media is done the same way as for most veterinary patients with the exception of temperature. The author prefers to culture the bacteria or fungus at the same temperature at which the reptile has been kept. If this temperature is unknown clinical impressions of the owner's husbandry system is used to extrapolate a temperature range. Culturing at the same temperature used for most veterinary patients (37 °C) will lead to erroneous results (overgrowth or no growth).

FUNGAL PATHOGENS FOUND IN REPTILES

Fungal pathogens will be discussed as a whole rather than by order since there is much similarity in the fungi that affect snakes, lizards, chelonians, and crocodilians. Fungal infections in all animals can first be divided into superficial, intermediate and systemic disorders.

SUPERFICIAL MYCOSES
Dermatophytosis

Dermatophytosis (a.k.a. ringworm) is a disorder caused by three genera of fungi: *Microsporum*, *Trichophyton* and *Epidermophyton*. Although dermatophytosis is relatively common in mammals, it is conspicuously rare (or underdiagnosed) in reptiles. It is most commonly reported in iguanas.

Note the green-tinged purulent material exuding from the gingiva of this Parson's chameleon. The purulent material was cultured and was sensitive to ceftazidime. Photo courtesy of Dr. Todd Driggers.

Dermatophytes can only live on the superficial dead layers of the skin and cannot penetrate living tissue or survive in areas of severe inflammation. Dermatophytosis may be diagnosed by Wood's lamp evaluation (not particularly helpful in reptiles), microscopic examination of scales using special stains, fungal culture or skin biopsy but cannot be confirmed by visual examination alone. Fungal cultures on dermatophyte test medium (DTM) are relatively easy to use but the fungi occasionally take up to 2 weeks to grow. The best forms of treatment include antiseptic washes with safe and gentle antiseptics, such as chlorhexidine (avoid any contact with eyes and ears). For very focal lesions, topical antifungal agents such as miconazole can be considered. Ketoconazole can be considered for the most stubborn cases and doses are reported in the pharmacology chapter. Environmental decontamination is the most difficult component of dermatophyte eradication. Some dermatophyte spores can persist in the environment for over one year. Disinfectants that contain chlorine, iodine or quaternary ammonium compounds are suitable for cleansing cages and other paraphernalia.

Yeasts

Yeast infections can plague reptiles as they do other animals. The most common offender is *Candida* but other species might also be troublesome. It is generally appreciated that most yeast infections predominantly affect animals that have been immune compromised due to poor husbandry practices, concurrent disease or other stressors. The yeast tend to affect tissues that tend to remain moist, such as the mouth, eyes, cloaca and genitalia but have also been implicated in pneumonia and hepatic necrosis. The diagnosis can be made by appropriate culture, cytological preparation or biopsy. Treatment must address any underlying problems or the condition is bound to recur. Acidifying solutions such as dilute vinegar and water and anti-yeast medications such as nystatin are the basics of therapy.

INTERMEDIATE MYCOSES

These fungi, for the most part, are common environmental microbes usually contracted by penetration of the skin with foreign objects (e.g., thorns, sticks, bite wounds etc.). They are usually harmless but may produce disease under certain circumstances, such as incompetence of the immune system due to deficiency, suppression, or debilitating diseases. These intermediate mycoses can be classified based on causative organism (e.g., aspergillosis), taxonomic relationship (e.g., phycomycosis) or histopathological appearance (e.g., hyalohyphomycosis). For example, phycomycosis is caused by several fungi of the order Mucorales (e.g., *Rhizopus*, *Mucor*, *Absidia*, *Mortierella*) and Entomophthorales (*Conidiobolus*, *Basidiobolus*). They may enter the system through injury to skin or via the digestive tract. To compli-

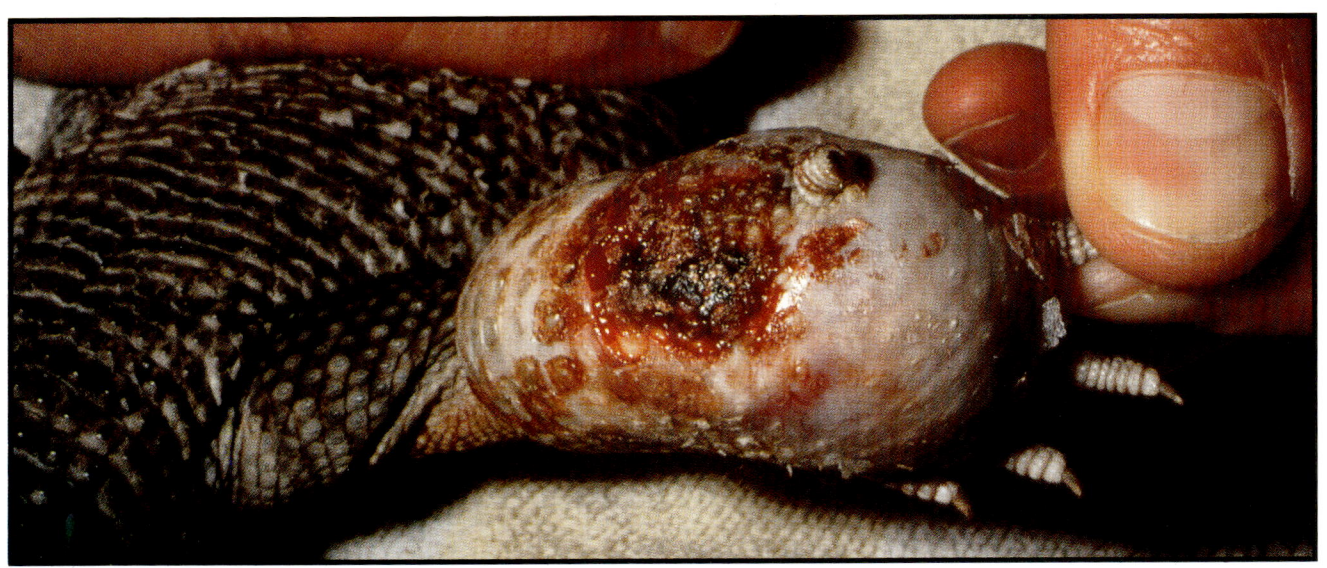

This large abscessed foot on a 2-year-old Savannah monitor (*Varanus exanthematicus*) caused necrosis of the entire foot. Amputation to the stifle was performed and the lizard was managed aggressively with antibiotics. *Serratia* was cultured from the wound. Photo courtesy of Dr. Todd Driggers.

cate matters further, a number of patients previously thought to have phycomycosis have instead been affected by a species of *Pythium*, thus really having (for lack of a better term) pythiosis. The most common fungal offenders in reptiles seem to be *Aspergillus*, *Paecilomyces*, *Dermatophyton*, *Beauvaria* and *Trichoderma*. Protothecosis causes similar conditions but is caused by algae; pythiosis is due to *Pythium* species which are members of the protista, not fungi.

Diagnosis is by direct microscopic examination of infected material, fungal culture, and biopsy. Direct examination may reveal fungal hyphae and spores. Fungal culture produces colonies with characteristic micro- and macro-aleurospores. Biopsies often produce characteristic patterns of fungal involvement. The treatment of choice is often surgical excision of affected regions since most antifungal medications have little effect on these microbes.

SYSTEMIC MYCOSES

Systemic fungal infections are normally acquired by inhaling infectious spores and are therefore not considered contagious. Systemic mycoses typically are characterized by a primary respiratory infection, with spread to other organs including the skin. Three fungi, *Blastomyces dermatitidis*, *Coccidioides immitis* and *Histoplasma capsulatum*, exist in a hyphal or spore stage in nature and grow as budding yeasts in tissues. *Cryptococcus neoformans* exists in only one form, as a budding yeast. In most cases, animals that contract the infection often resolve it on their own without incident. Only the exceptional ani-

mal, usually one with a less than optimal immune system, manifest the full clinical disease. Diagnosis is made by cytological preparation, fungal culture and biopsies for histopathological examination. Culture is potentially dangerous since it produces spores which are immediately contagious to laboratory personnel. Treatment can be instituted with ketoconazole or itraconazole as per recommendations in the pharmacology chapter.

Note the mandibular separation in this agamid lizard. The lesion was cultured by the referring veterinarian and no consistent bacteria were revealed. A cytological specimen taken from the affected area revealed spirochetosis. These bacteria have a snake-like appearence. The author is unsure of where this bacterial infection was contracted. Mites, crickets, and bird feces are possible sources. Photo courtesy of Dr. Todd Driggers.

SELECTION, HANDLING, AND SUBMISSION FOR DIAGNOSTIC MICROBIOLOGY

A primary goal of diagnostic microbiology is to quickly and accurately provide knowledge of the presence or absence of viruses, bacteria, or fungi involved in infectious diseases. This knowledge has direct diagnostic, prognostic, therapeutic, and epidemiologic value. Some complicating factors in achieving this knowledge include improper specimen collection, handling, and or submission. A concerted effort is required to ensure rapid and accurate reporting of results as well as reduce costs. Specimens for viral, bacterial, and fungal diseases may have common or vastly different requirements depending on the procedures requested. Moreover, most specimens are consumed in processing precluding the possibility of further testing. These factors highlight the importance of appropriate specimens in diagnostic microbiology. Some general guidelines are provided below to facilitate high quality testing and assure accurate results.

Selecting the proper specimen and collecting an adequate amount for bacterial examination are essential. commerce swab-transport medium products are economical, convenient, and commonly used to prevent desiccation and hence loss of bacterial viability. However, less than 10% of the original bacterial inoculum is recoverable from swabs. Marked qualitative differences in bacterial recovery, particularly anaerobes, have been demonstrated between swabs and sealed syringe aspirates. A sterile syringe can be used as an anaerobic transport device by expelling the air and plugging the tip. Tissues submitted for bacteriology should contain a representative lesion and some normal tissue. Swabs and aspirates should be collected from the site of active infection.

Specimens should be sent to the laboratory as rapidly as possible. Rapid transport minimizes overgrowth by contaminants which can elaborate powerful growth inhibitory bacteriocins and cause a loss of fastidious bacterial viability. Transport of specimens in enrichment broth is not recommended for this reason. Various transport media and specific instruction regarding its use are available through many laboratories.

Submission of specimens requires an evaluation request form. Several important sections on the request form (signalment, date, clinical history, tentative diagnoses, description of specimens, and examinations requested) bear heavily on the decisions which affect workup. These sections are informational keys which allow discriminate trimming of analytical procedures and elimination of unimportant assays. A concerted effort is required to reduce costs and assure rapid and accurate reporting of results.

RECOMMENDED READING:

SNAKES - VIRUSES

—**Ahne, W W; Neubert, J; Thomson, I:**
Reptilian viruses: isolation of myxovirus-like particles from the snake *Elaphe oxycephala*. J Vet Med, 1987; 34: 607-612.

—**Axthelm, M K:**
Clinicopathologic and virologic observations of a probable viral disease affecting boid snakes. Proc Annu Meet Am Assoc Zoo Vet, 1985; pp. 108.

—**Carneiro, SM; Tanaka, H; Kisielius, JJ; Sesso, A:**
Occurrence of retrovirus-like particles in various cellular and intercellular compartments of the venom glands from *Bothrops jararacussu*. Res Vet Sci, 1992; 53: 399-401.

—**Cupp, EW; et al.:**
Entomological studies at an enzootic Venezuelan equine encephalitis virus focus in Guatemala, 1977-1980. Am J Trpo Med Hyg, 1986; 35(4): 851-859.

—**Hauser, B., Mettler, F., Rubel, A.**
Herpesvirus- like infection in two young boas. J Comp Path, 1983; 93:515- 519.

—**Heldstab, A; Bestetti, G:**
Virus associated gastrointestinal diseases in snakes. J Zoo An Med, 1984; 15: 118-128.

—**Jacobson, ER; Gaskin JM; Flanagan J P; Odum A:**
Antibody responses of western diamondback rattlesnakes (*Crotalus atrox*) to inactivated ophidian paramyxovirus vaccines. J Zoo Wildl Med 1991; 22(2): 184-190.

—**Jacobson ER; Gaskin, J M; Wells, S; Bowler, K; Schumacher J:**
Epizootic of ophidian paramyxovirus in a zoological collection: pathological, microbiological, and serological findings. J Zoo Wildl Med, 1992; 23(3): 318-327.

—**Jacobson, ER; Gaskin, JM:**
Adenovirus-like infection in a boa constrictor. JAVMA, 1985; 187: 1226-1227.

—**Jacobson, ER; Gaskin, JM:**
Paramyxo-like virus infection of snakes: a review. Proc Annu Meet Am Assoc Zoo Vet, 1987; pp. 462-467.

—**Jacobson, ER:**
Viruses and viral associated diseases of reptiles. Acta Zool Pathol Antverp, 1986; pp. 73-90.

—**Jacobson, ER; Gaskin, JM; Page, D; Iverson, W; Johnson, JW:**
Illness associated with paramyxo-like virus infection in a zoologic collection of snakes. JAVMA, 1981; 179: 1227-1230.

—**Muller, M; Zangger, N; Jakob, HP:**
Paramyxovirus infection in snakes. In: Viruses of lower vertebrates. Springer-Verlag, 1989, 114-119.

—**Schumacher, J; Jacobson, E R; Burns, R; Tramontin, R R:**
Adenovirus-like infection in two rosy boas (*Lichanura trivirgata*). J Zoo Wildl Med, 1994; 25(3): 461-465.

—**Schumacher, J; Jacobson, E R; Homer, B L; Gaskin, J M:**
Inclusion body disease in boid snakes. J Zoo Wildl Med, 1992; 25(4): 511 -524.

SNAKES - BACTERIA

—**Chiodini, RJ; Sundberg, JP:**
Salmonellosis in reptiles: a review. Am J Epidemiol, 1981; 113: 494-499.

—**Draper, CS; et al.:**
Patterns of Oral Bacterial Infection in Captive Snakes. J A V M A, 1981; 179(11): 1223-1226.

—**Hall, MLM; Rowe, B:**
Salmonella arizona in the United Kingdom form 1966 to 1990. Epidemiol Infect, 1992; 108: 59-65.

—**HiII, M; Wagner, R A; Yu, V L:**
A prospective study of upper airway flora in healthy boid snakes and snakes with pneumonia. J. Zoo Wildl. Med, 1990; 21: 318-325.

—**Jacobson, E R; Gaskin, J M; Mansell, J:**
Chlamydial infection in puff adders (*Bitis arietans*). J Zoo Wildl Med, 1989; 20(3): 364-369.

—**MacNeill, AC; Dorward, W J:**
Salmonella prevalence in a captive population of herptiles. J Zoo An Med, 1986; 17: 110-114.

—**Quesenberry, KE; el al.:**
Ulcerative stomatitis and subcutaneous granulomas caused by *Mycobacterium chelonei* in a Boa Constrictor. J A V M A, 1986; 189(9): 1131- 1132.

SNAKES - FUNGI

—**Collette, B E; Curry, O H:**
Mycotic keratitis in a reticulated python. JAVMA, 1978; 173: 1117-1118.

—**Crispens, C G, Jr; Marion, K R:**
Algal Infection in a Corn Snake (*Elaphe guttata guttata*). Lab An Sci, 1975; 25(6): 788-789.

—**Jacobson, E R:**
Chromomycosis and fibrosarcoma in a mangrove snake. J A V M A, 1984; 185: 1428-1430.

—**Jessup, D A; Seely, J C:**
Zygomycete fungus infection in two captive snakes: gopher snake (*Pituophis melanoleucus*); copperhead (*Agkistrodon contortrix*) J Zoo An Med, 1981; 12: 54-59.

—**McNamara, T S; Cook, R A; Behler, J L; Ajello, L; Padhye, A A:**
Cryptococcosis in a common anaconda (*Eunectes murinus*). J Zoo Wildl Med, 1994; 25(1): 128-132.

—**Reddacliff, L; Cunningham, M; Hartley, W J:**
Systemic Infection with a Yeast-like Organism in Captive Banded Rock Rattlesnakes (*Crotalus lepidus klauberi*). J Wildl Dis, (1993) 29(1): 145-149.

—**Sindler, BB; et al.:**
Phycomycosis in a red milk snake (*Lampropeltis triangulum syspila*). VM/SAC,1978; 73: 64-65.

—**Timm, K I; Sonn, R J; Hultgren, B D:**
Coccidioidomycosis in a Sonoran gopher snake, *Pituophis melanoleucus affinis*. J Med Vet Mycol, 1988; 26: 101-104.

TURTLES-VIRUSES

—**Balazs, G H:**
Fibropapillomatosis in Hawaiian green turtles. Mar Turt Newsl, 1986; 39: 1-3

—**Cooper, J E; Gschmeissner, S; Bone, R D:**
Herpes-like virus particles in necrotic stomatitis of tortoises. Vet Rec, 1988; 123: 554-557.

—**Cox, WR; Rapley, WA; Barker, IK:**
Herpesvirus-like infection in a painted turtle (*Chrysemys picta*). J Wildl Dis, 1980; 16: 445-449.

—**Heldstab, A; Bestetti, G:**
Spontaneous viral hepatitis in a spur-tailed Mediterranean land tortoise (*Testudo hermanni*). J Zoo An Med, 1982; 13: 113-120.

—**Jackson, OF:**
Respiratory virus antibodies in chelonians. J Small Anim Pract, 1983; 24: 31.

—**Jacobson, ER; Buergelt, C; Williams, B; Harris, R K:**
Herpesvirus in cutaneous fibropapillomas of the green turtle *Chelonia mydas*. Dis Aquat Org, 1991; 12: 1-6.

—**Jacobson, E R:**
Causes of mortality and diseases in tortoises: a review. J Zoo Wildl Med, 1994; 25(1): 2-17.

—**Jacobson, E R; Clubb, S; Gaskin, J M; Gardiner, C:**
Herpesvirus-like infection in Argentine tortoises. J A V M A, 1985; 181: 122I-1229.

—**Jacobson, E R; Gaskin, J M; Roelke, M; Greimer, E C; Allen, J:**
Conjunctivitis, tracheitis, and pneumonia associated with herpesvirus infection in green sea turtles. J A V M A, l986; 189: 1020-1023.

—**Rebell, G; Rywlin, A; Haines, H:**
A herpesvirus-type agent associated with skin lesions of green sea turtles in aquaculture. Am J Vet Res, l975; 36: 1221-1224.

—**Smith, A L; Anderson, C R:**
Susceptibility of two turtle species to eastern equine encephalitis virus. J Wildl Dis, 1980; 16(4): 615-617.

TURTLES - BACTERIA

—**Brown, MB; et al.:**
Mycoplasma agassizii causes upper respiratory tract disease in the Desert Tortoise. Infect Immun, 1994; 62: 4580-4586.

—**Cohen, ML; Potter, M; Pollard, R; Feldman, RA:**
Turtle-associated salmonellosis in the United States: effect of public health action, 1970 to 1976. J A M A, 1980; 243: 1247-9.

—**Dessi, S; Sanna, C; Paghi, L:**
Human salmonellosis transmitted by a domestic turtle. Euro J Epidemio, 1992; 8(1): 120-121.

—**Glazebrook, J S; Campbell, R S F; Thomas, AT:**
Studies on an ulcerative stomatitis - obstructive rhinitis - pneumonia disease complex in hatchling and juvenile sea turtles *Chelonia mydas* and *Caretta caretta*. Dis Aquat Org, 1993; 16(2): 133-147.

—**Jacobson, E R; Gardiner, C H; Barten, S L; Burr, D H; Bourgeois, A L:**
Flavobacterium meningosepticum infections of a Barbour's map turtle (*Graptemys barbouri*). J Zoo Wildl Med 1989; 20(4): 474-477.

—**Jang, S S; Biberstein, E L:**
Observations on the occurrence of *Pasteurella testudinis* in clinical specimens from animals. J Vet Diagn Invest, 1991; 3: 174-176.

—**Masters, AM; Ellis, TM; Carson, J M; Sutherland, SS; Gregory, SS:**
Dermatophilus chelonae sp. nov., Isolated from Chelonids in Australia. Internat J Sys Bacteriol Jan. 1995. p. 50-56

—**Nagel, P; Serrilella, A; Layden, TJ:**
Edwardsiella tarda gastroenteritis associated with a pet turtle. Gastroenterology, 1982; 82: 1436-1437.

—**Schumacher, I M; Brown, M B; Jacobson, E R; Collins, B R; Klein, P A:**
Detection of antibodies to a pathogenic *Mycoplasma* in Desert Tortoises (*Gopherus agassizii*) with upper respiratory tract disease. J Clin Micro, 1993; 31(6): 1454-1460.

—**Shane, SM; Gilbert, R; Harrington, KS:**
Salmonella colonization in commercial pet turtles (*Pseudemys scripta elegans*). Epidemiol Infect, 1990; 105: 307-316.

—**Vanrompay, D; De Meurichy, W; Ducatelle, R; Haesebrouck, F:**
Pneumonia in Moorish tortoises (*Testudo graeca*) associated with avian serovar A *Chlamydia psittaci*. Vet Rec, 1994; 135: 284-285.

TURTLES- FUNGI

—**Georg, L K; Wjttiamson, W M; Tilden, E B; Getty, R E:**
Mycotic pulmonary disease of captive giant tortoises due to *Beauvaria bassiana* and *Paecilomyces fumoso-roseus*. Sabouraudia, 1962; 2: 80-86.

—**Heard, D J; Canlor, G H; Jacobson, E R; Purich, B; Ajello, L; Padhye, A A:**
Hyalohyphomycosis caused by *Paecilomyces lilacinus* in an Aldabra tortoise. J A V M A, 1986; 189: 1143- 1145.

—**Sison, TM; Padilla, MA; Vizmanos, MC; Follosco, M:**
Isolation and identification of fungi found in necrotic skin lesions of captive marine turtles. Phil J Vet Med, 1990; 27(2): 35-36.

LIZARDS - VIRUSUS

—**Cooper, JE; et al.:**
Viral particles in a papilloma from a Green Lizard (*Lacerta viridis*). Lab Anim, (1982) 16: 12-13.

—**Frye, F L; Munn, R J; Gardner, M; Barten, S L; Hadfy, L B:**
Adenovirus-like hepatitis in a group of related Rankin's dragon lizards (*Pogona henrylawsoni*). J Zoo Wildl Med, 1994; 25(1): 167-171.

—**Jacobson, E R; Telford, S R:**
Chlamydial and poxvirus infections of circulating monocytes of a Flap-necked Chameleon (*Chamaeleo dilepis*). J Wildl Dis, 1990; 26(4): 572-577.

—**Jacobson, E R; Kollias, G V:**
Adenovirus-like Infection in a Savannah Monitor. J Zoo An Med, 1986; 17: 149-151.

—**Jacobson, E R; Gardiner, C H:**
Adeno-like virus in esophageal and tracheal mucosa of a Jackson's chameleon (*Chamaeleo jacksoni*). Vet Pathol 1990; 27: 2l0-212.

—**Julian, A F; Durham, PJK:**
Adenoviral hepatitis in a female bearded dragon, *Amphibolurus barbatus*. New Zealand Vet J, 1985; 30: 59-60.

—**Stauber, E; Gogolewski, R:**
Poxvirus dermatitis in a tegu lizard (*Tupinambis teguixin*) J Zoo Wildl Med, 1990; 21(2): 228-230.

—**Telford, S R; Jacobson E R:**
Lizard erythrocytic virus in East African chameleons. J Wildl Dis, 1993; 29(1): 57-63.

LIZARDS - BACTERIA
—**Anver, MR; Park, JS; Rush, HG:**
Dermatophilosis in the marble lizard (*Calotes mystaceus*). Lab Anim Sci, l976; 26: 817-823.

—**Bonney, C H; et al.:**
Klebsiella pneumoniae infection with secondary hypopyon in tokay gecko lizards. J A V M A, 1978; 173: 1115-1116.

—**CDC.**
Reptile-associated salmonellosis - selected states, 1994-1995. MMWR, 1995; 44 (17): 347-350.

—**Chineme, C N; Addo, P B:**
Pathologic changes in lizards (*Agama agama*) experimentally infected with *Dermatophilus congolensis*. J Wild Dis 1980; 16(3): 407-412.

—**Dalton, C; Hoffman, R; Pape, J:**
Iguana-associated salmonellosis in children. Pediatr Infect Dis J, 1995; 14: 319-20.

—**Friend, S C E; Russell, E G:**
Mycobacterium intracellulare infection in a water monitor. J Wildl Dis, 1979; 15: 229-233.

—**Plowman, CA; et al.:**
Septicemia and chronic abscesses in iguanas (*Cyclura cornuta* and *Iguana iguana*) associated with a *Neisseria* species. J Z A M, 1987; 18(2-3): 86- 93.

—**Ramos, AB; Don, MT; Muchlinski, AE:**
The effect of bacteria infection on mean selected body temperature in the common Agama, *Agama agama*: A dose-response study. Comp Biochem Physiol, 1993; 105A(3): 479-454.

—**Troyer, K:**
Transfer of fermentative microbes between generations in herbivorous lizard. Science, 1982; 216: 540-542.

LIZARDS - FUNGI
—**Wissman, MA; Parsons, B:**
Dermatophytosis of green iguanas (*Iguana iguana*). J Sm Exotic An Med, 1993; 2(3): 137-140.

—**CROCODILIANS - VIRUSES**
—**Buenviaje, GN; Ladds, PW; Melville, L:**
Poxvirus infection in two crocodiles. Aust Vet J, 1992; 169(1): 284-285.

—**Jacobson, ER; Gardiner, C H; Foggin, C M:**
Adenovirus-like infection in two Nile crocodiles. J A V M A, 1984; 185: 1421-1422.

CROCODILIANS - BACTERIA
—**Huchzermeyer, F W; Gerdes, G H; Foggin, C M; Huchzermeyer,K D A; Limper, L C:**
Hepatitis in farmed hatchling nile crocodiles (*Crocodylus niloticus*) due to chlamydial infection. Tydskr S Afr vet Ver, 1994; 65(1): 20-22.

—**Jasmin, A M; Baucom, JN:**
Erysipelothrix insidiosa infections in the Caiman (*Caiman crocodilus*) and the American crocodile (*Crocodilus acutus*), Am J Vet Clin Pathol, 1968; 2: 93-95.

—**Manolis, SC; Webb, GJW; Pinch,D; Melville, L; Hollis, G:**
Salmonella in captive crocodiles (*Crocodylus johnstoni* and *C. porosus*). Aust Vet J, 1991; 68(3): 102-105.

—**Ladds, PW; Mangunwirjo, H; Sebayang, D; Daniels, PW:**
Diseases in young farmed crocodiles in Irian Jaya. Vet Rec, 1995; 136: 121-124.

CROCODILIANS - FUNGI
—**Foreyt, WJ; et al.:**
Trichoderma spp. infection in the Alligator (*Alligator mississippiensis*). J Hepetol, 1985; 19: 530-531.

—**Fromtling, RA; Jensen, JM; Robinson, BE; Bu1mm, GS:**
Fatal mycotic pulmonary disease of captive American alligators. Vet Path, 1979; 16: 428-431.

—**Fromtling, RA; Kosanke, SD; Jensen, JM; Bu1mer, GS:**
Fatal *Beauveria bassiana* infection in a captive American alligator. J A V M A, 1979; 175: 934-936.

—**Hibberd, EMA; Harrower, KM:**
Mycoses in crocodiles. The Mycologist, 1993; 7(1): 32-37.

—**Jasmin, JM; Carroll, JM; Baucom, JN:**
Pulmonary aspergi!losis of the American alligator (*Alligator mississippiensis*), Amer J Vet Clin Pathol, 1968; 2: 93-95.

—**Silberman, MS; Blue, J; Mahaffey, E:**
Phycomycoses resulting in the death of crocodilians in a common pool. Proc Am Assoc Zoo Vet, 1977; 101-l02.

DIAGNOSTIC IMAGING: ULTRASONOGRAPHY

Janice S. Grumbles, D.V.M.[1]
and David C. Rostal, Ph.D.[1]
[1]Department of Biology; Georgia Southern University;
P.O. Box 8042
Statesboro, Georgia 30460

Dr. Janice Grumbles received her D.V.M. from Texas A&M University in 1983 and a B.S. in Biomedical Science from Texas A&M University. She has been involved in the research and clinical study of reptiles and other exotic animals for the last seven years. She collaborated on the application and validation of ultrasonography and other low risk techniques to the study of the reproductive biology of endangered chelonian species. She is a research associate in the Department of Biology at Georgia Southern University, Statesboro, Georgia. Currently, she is studying the reproductive biology and ecology of the eastern indigo snake (Drymarchon corais couperi).

Dr. David Rostal received his Ph.D. in Zoology from Texas A&M University. His research focused on the reproductive biology of the Kemp's ridley sea turtle, Lepidochelys kempi. This research incorporated the application and validation of non-invasive and low-risk techniques such as ultrasonography. He was a post-doctoral research fellow at the Center for Reproduction of Endangered Species, San Diego Zoo. Dr. Rostal is presently an Assistant Professor of Biology at Georgia Southern University, Statesboro, Georgia. His research concentrates on the reproductive biology of reptiles and amphibians and has direct application to conservation of endangered species. This work includes the leatherback turtle (Dermochelys coriacea), the black turtle (Chelonia agassizi), the Galapagos tortoise (Geochelone elephantopus), the desert tortoise (Gopherus agassizii), the gopher tortoise (Gopherus polyphemus), the eastern indigo snake (Drymarchon corais couperi), the flatwoods salamander (Ambystoma cingulatum), the striped newt (Notophthalmus peristriatus), and the gopher frog (Rana capito capito).

INTRODUCTION

Diagnostic ultrasound has become commonplace in human medicine since its introduction in the late 1940s. Everyone is acquainted with ultrasound images of human babies *in utero*. The use of veterinary ultrasonography has also become common, especially in large animal obstetrics. Ultrasonography provides a safe (no radiation), non-invasive method for visualizing the internal anatomy of many species. Furthermore, no biohazard has been reported from the routine use of diagnostic levels of ultrasound. Protective shields or apparel are not required. Ultrasound provides instantaneous results; the structures can be viewed as they appear at that moment and "cross-sections" can be viewed.

Ultrasonography allows for the accurate measurement of width and depth of structures by using internal calipers and varying the orientation of the transducer. Ultrasonography can be used for many purposes (du Boulay and Wilson, 1988; Hildebrandt and Göritz, 1995; Horn and Visser, 1989; Kuchling, 1989; Kuchling and Bradshaw, 1993; Morris and Alberts, 1996; Robeck et al., 1990; Rostal, et al. 1989a, 1989b, 1990, 1991a, 1991b, 1994a, 1994b, 1996; Sainsbury and Gili, 1991; Vac et al., 1992), including:

—monitoring reproductive function (e.g., detection of eggs (ovulation), monitoring follicular changes, diagnosing ovarian irregularities, evaluation of egg fertility in some species and, presence of tumors or pathology in some organs);

—sex determination in some monomorphic species;

—diagnosing certain diseases by anatomic changes, and;

—assisting other diagnostic procedures, such as ultrasound guided biopsy

The development of non-invasive and low risk techniques for studying seasonal and cyclic ovarian events is particularly important to the captive maintenance and breeding programs of endangered reptiles. Radiology has been used successfully for detection of eggs and determination of clutch size in a variety of freshwater turtles and tortoises (Frye, 1981; Gibbons and Greene, 1979; Turner et al., 1986) as well as other reptile species such as the tuatara (*Sphenodon punctatus*, Newman and Watson, 1985). Laparoscopy has been available for studying ovarian morphology of sea turtles (Limpus and Reed, 1985; Wood et al., 1983). Laparoscopy, however, does involve risk of trauma and infection to the turtle. Safety and low-risk make ultrasonography especially valuable to studying reptilian reproduction (Figure 1). However, interpretation can be difficult without a working knowledge of ultrasound principles, artifacts, and transectional anatomy of structures.

BASIC PRINCIPLES OF ULTRASOUND

Ultrasound is a pulse of high frequency sound (above the normal hearing range of the human ear; >20,000 Hertz). Piezoelectric (pressure-electric) crystals, housed within an ultrasound transducer, emit these ultrasonic sound waves when subjected to an electric (AC) current. This pulsed electrical deformation of the crystals produces small sound waves that impart kinetic energy to tissue molecules when applied to the body surface with a coupling agent. Reflected sound echoes return to the same transducer causing a slight deformation of the crystals that generate an electric current. This electronic transformation is displayed on an ultrasound screen as an image of the tissue interfaces formed by a series of gray dots.

Different tissues either propagate or reflect the sound waves to varying degrees. The reflected echo portion will appear as shades of gray, from black to white. Liquids do not reflect sound waves (i.e., are anechoic) so the image of a fluid-containing structure (full urinary bladder) appears black on the ultrasound screen. On the other hand, dense tissues (bone) reflect the sound waves (i.e., are hyperechoic) so the image appears white on the screen. Other tissues vary in the amount of sound waves they reflect and are seen in various shades of gray. The variation in the gray scale display will depend upon the ultrasound unit's capability. The two-dimensional (B-mode) image seen on the screen is similar to looking at a slice (cross-section) of tissue since the sound beam that passes through the tissue is quite thin. The section that is viewed can be changed by moving or redirecting the angle of the transducer.

Ultrasound waves travel through the body until a tissue is encountered. Some waves are reflected and return to the transducer crystals while some waves continue to reach deeper structures. The time delays between the propagation of the wave and the returning echo are used to calculate the distance between the crystals and the tissue. As sound waves move through soft tissue, they lose energy by absorption and scattering. These two factors are usually dependent so that lower sound frequency will penetrate farther into soft tissue than high frequency sound. Higher frequency sound produces greater tissue detail due to better image resolution.

Of course, there are many layers of tissue in the body and a tissue interface occurs whenever tissues of different densities (and acoustic impedance) are adjacent. Acoustic impedance is a measure of the resistance of the tissue to propagation of the sound waves. The amount of beam reflected back to the transducer is directly proportional to the difference in acoustic impedance at the tissue interface. The acoustic impedance of soft tissue is 1.63×10^5; air is 0.0004×10^5; and bone is 7.8×10^5. Since, air and bone differ so greatly from soft tissue in acoustic impedance, most of the sound beams are reflected when striking bone or gas. This reflectance causes a white image on the screen and tissue interfaces deeper than bone or gas are not visible. Therefore, if a transducer is placed so that it interfaces bone, no structures will be viewed

Figure 1: Photo of ultrasound equipment set-up at a leatherback sea turtle (*Dermochelys coriacea*) nesting beach at Playa Grande, Costa Rica. The ovaries of this female leatherback were scanned after the female began to oviposition (lay eggs). This did not cause any disruption of her nesting behavior.

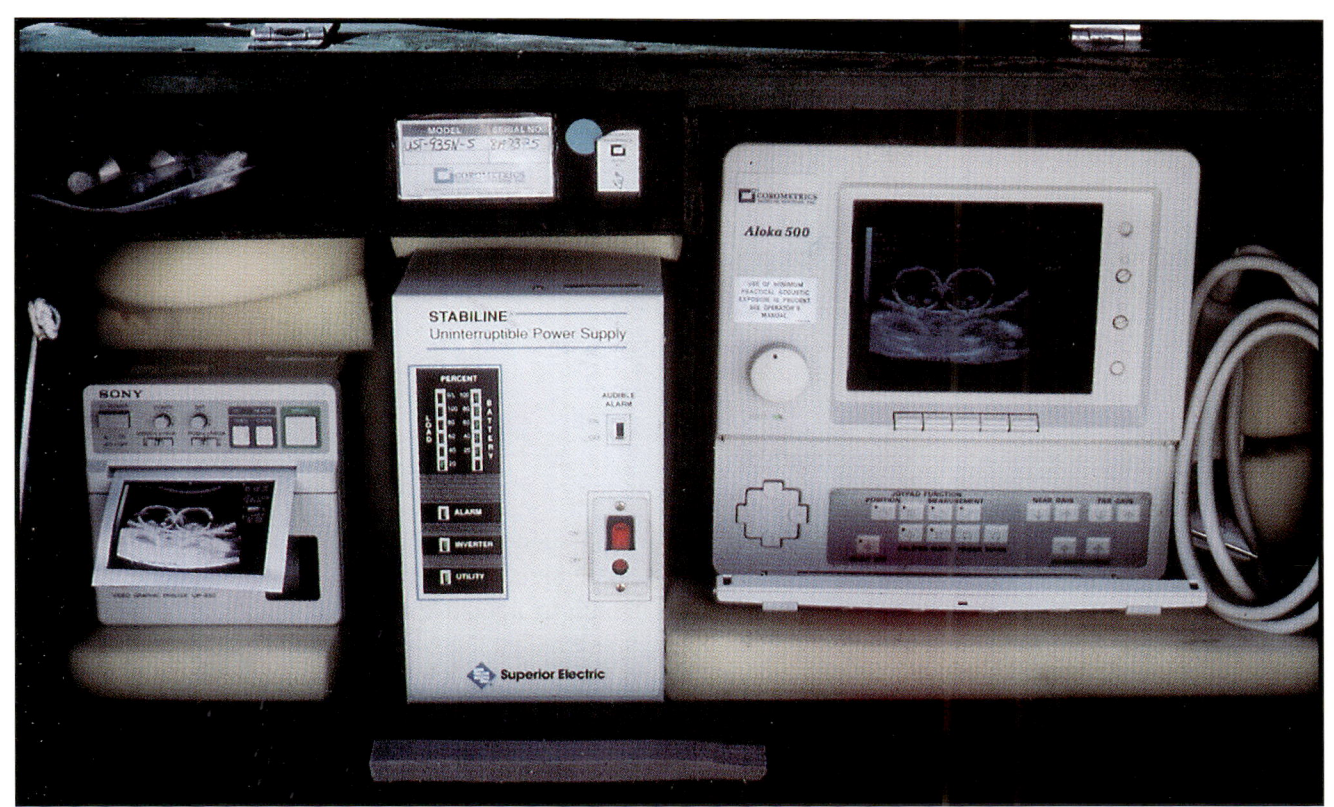

Figure 2A: Basic ultrasound equipment set-up. On the right is the computer console with a viewing monitor and an attached transducer. On the far left is a thermal printer which provides a hard copy of the scanned image. In the center is an uninterruptible power source which is necessary if the power source is a portable generator.

Figure 2 B: Ultrasound setup at a Kemp's ridley sea turtle (*Lepidochelys kempi*) nesting beach at Playa Rancho Nuevo, Mexico. The equipment was transported in the rear of the truck. This female Kemp's ridley was scanned upon completion of her nesting. She was placed in dorsal recumbency on a rubber tire and held with minimal restraint. The entire procedure required no more than 15 minutes before the female was allowed to return to the ocean.

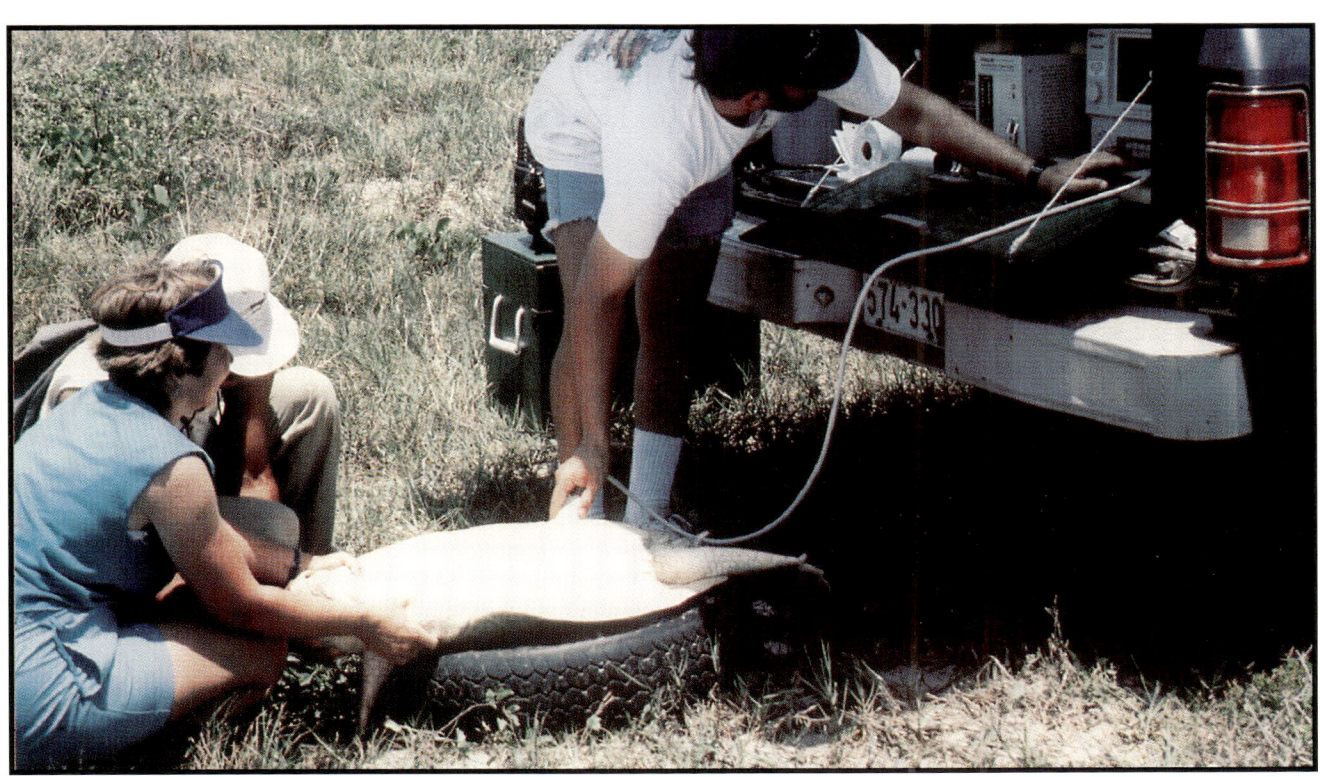

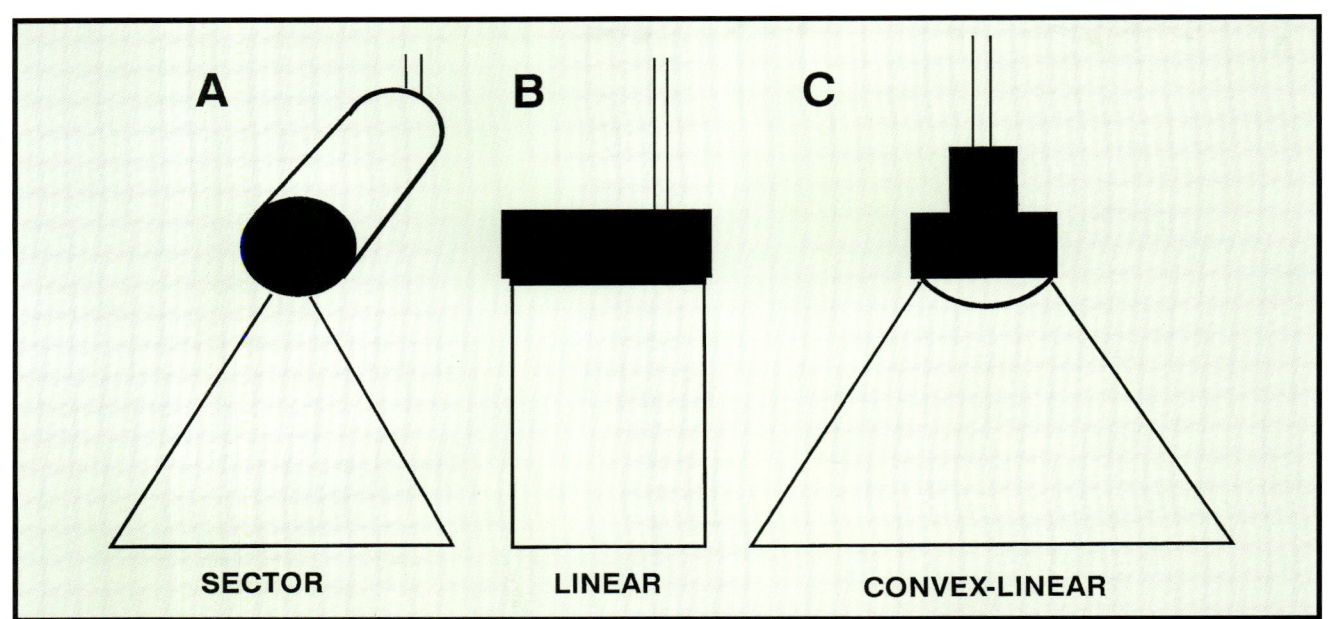

Figure 3: Diagram showing the variation in ultrasound transducer (probe) arrays. A). Sector array transducer with a small contact area "footprint" and the resulting pie shaped scan; B). Linear array transducer with a large contact area "footprint" and the resulting rectangular shaped scan; C). Convex-linear transducer with an intermediate contact area "footprint" and the resulting "hybrid" scan.

beyond the bone. The same is true for the gas-filled intestine or lung; you will not be able to view deeper soft tissue structures.

ULTRASOUND EQUIPMENT

Ultrasound equipment has these basic components: the transducer; the console which is a computer processor that has a pulser, timer, receiver with an amplifier, a digital scan converter, and a monitor for echo display; and some device for image recording (Figure 2A). A system suitable for reptiles must be portable and rugged (Figure 1; 2B).

TRANSDUCERS

The image production and clarity of an ultrasound machine are determined by the frequency (the number of vibrations produced by the crystal per second) of the sound waves produced by the transducer. Most ultrasound transducers have a frequency range of 3-10 megahertz (Mhz). The 3.5 Mhz - 5 Mhz (lower frequency) transducers will penetrate deeper into the body than the 7.5 Mhz - 10 Mhz (high frequency) transducers. The higher frequency transducers provide better resolution (image quality), but, the depth of penetration is lost. The greater tissue penetration of lower frequency transducers will be necessary for scanning large reptiles. The reptiles you intend to ultrasound will determine the transducer frequency you need to use. Some ultrasound machines have interchangeable transducers (probes) and this en-

ables you to vary the frequency and penetration/detail of that machine.

There are 3 types of ultrasound scanners based upon their transducer array: sector, linear-array, and convex-linear array. This transducer array refers to the number and arrangement of piezoelectric crystals. Increases in the number of crystals enhance the resolution of the image. Sector scanners have a round transducer that produces a "slice of pie" shaped image and are taken directly from the human medical market for veterinary use. Sector scanners require less skin surface contact and this can be beneficial when scanning smaller animals (Figure 3a; 4a). In linear-array scanners, the sound waves are emitted perpendicularly from a rectangular transducer along the row of crystals and the waves produced travel parallel to each other in a linear pattern. This produces a rectangular image and the width of the image corresponds to the functional portion of the transducer. These transducers can require a large area of skin contact if the transducer is long (Figure 3b; 4b). The convex-linear scanner is a hybrid of the sector and linear-array scanners. The transducer is semi-circular in shape with the crystals in a linear array. This produces a larger image with a smaller "footprint" (transducer configuration). This transducer provides a wider image with a smaller transducer size thus, combining the advantages of both sector and linear transducers (Figure 3c; 4c). Generally, linear array transducers produce better image resolution than sector array or convex-linear transducers, however, convex-linear image resolution is intermediate (Figure 4).

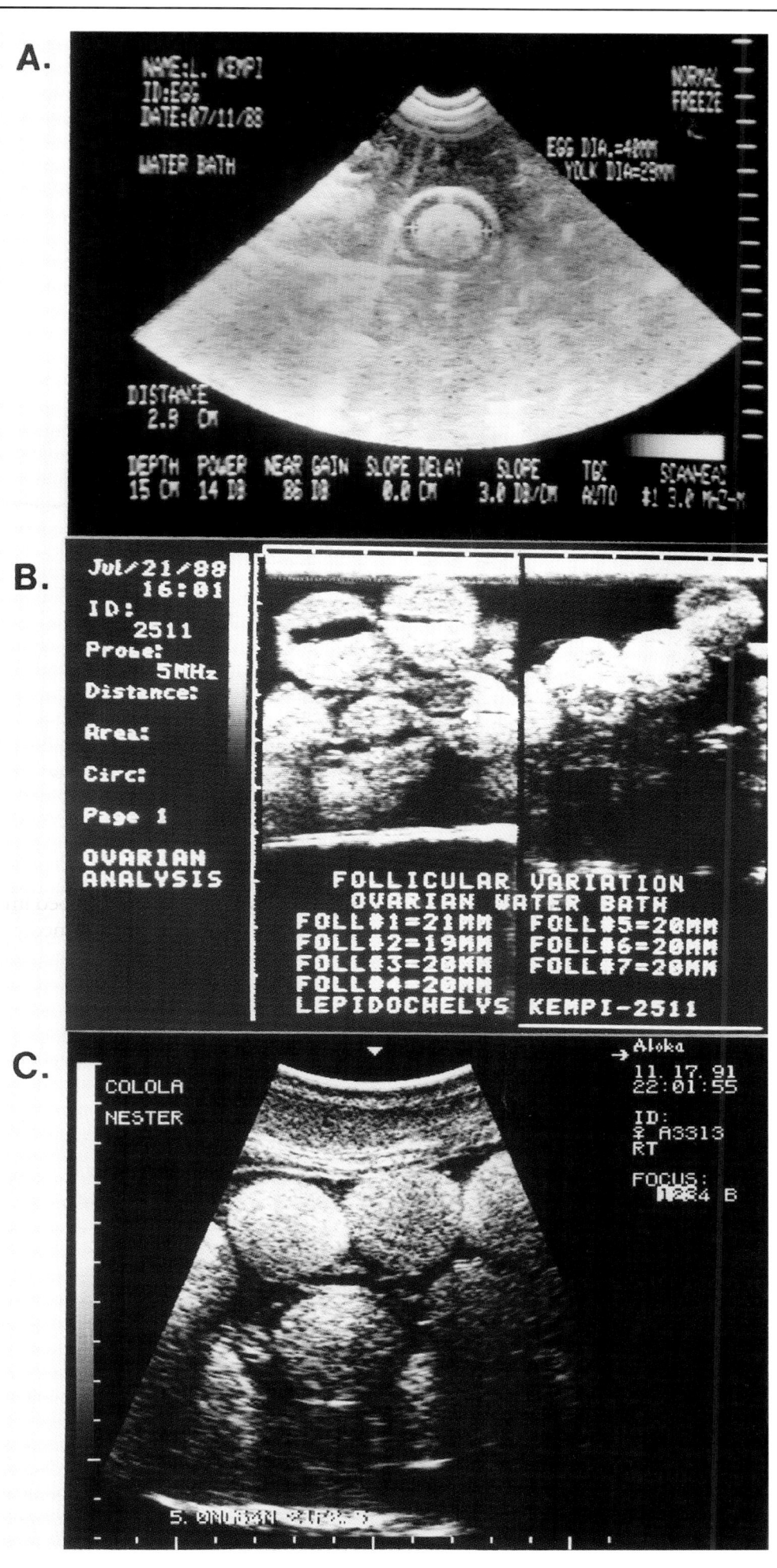

Figure 4: Ultrasound images produced by the three different transducer arrays. A. Sector array scan of an egg from a Kemp's ridley sea turtle, *Lepidochelys kempi*. Note the pie-shaped image production.

B. Linear array scan of atretic ovarian follicles from a Kemp's ridley sea turtle, *Lepidochelys kempi*. The monitor shows split image production. One image was frozen and the second image made before the hard copy was made. Note the rectangular image production.

C. Convex-linear scan of vitellogenic follicles in the ovary of a black sea turtle, *Chelonia agassizi*. Note that the contact point (top of the scan) is intermediate in size between the sector and linear array images.

DISPLAY

THREE MODES OF DISPLAY ARE AVAILABLE AND ARE BEST DESCRIBED IN CHART FORM.

Mode of Display	Description
A-mode = Amplitude mode	A-mode imaging is one-dimensional and displays returning echo amplitude versus distance.
B-mode = Brightness mode	B-mode imaging produces an accurate two-dimensional display of dots where the brightness of the dots is proportional to the intensity of the returning echoes. Real-time, B-mode is a form of B-mode imaging used to record movement. The transducer is moved over an area and echoes are recorded and renewed continuously. The resulting real-time or moving image is comparable to a movie taken with sound waves rather than light waves. This image can be frozen and photographed or recorded on videotape or thermal paper. Real-time, B-mode ultrasound machines are the most common type of machine used for diagnostic ultrasonography. The images shown in this chapter are from real-time, B-mode scans.
M-mode = Motion mode	M-mode imaging is one-dimensional and uses dots like B-mode but the transducer is held in place over moving organs and the display is printed on an oscilloscope or moving strip of light sensitive paper. This mode is used primarily to measure cardiac wall motion and valve function without an actual image of the heart being produced.

DISPLAY IMAGE RECORDING

A hard copy can be made of real-time, B-mode images. Images may be saved on Polaroid film, video tape, or thermographic paper. Internal calipers of the ultrasound machine can be used to measure structures and these measurements can be saved on hard copy. A saved image can be used for permanent record keeping; for measurement and monitoring of size changes; and for self-education.

ULTRASOUND TECHNIQUES IN REPTILES

TRANSDUCER SELECTION

The choice of transducer(s) must be appropriate to the animals being studied. The proper frequency transducer is needed as well as a transducer that will fit the area available for scanning (have the proper footprint). The available area can be quite small in a turtle because the ultrasound cannot penetrate the bone of the shell. For example, if you want to monitor the reproductive status of a small tortoise you would NOT want a low frequency (3.5 Mhz) linear scanner. This transducer would penetrate the turtle too deeply (20 cm), distort the structures visualized, and the transducer footprint would be too large to fit the location available for scanning (the available acoustic window). Acoustic windows are those tissues which attenuate little of the sound waves, thus allowing

more sound to pass beyond to deeper structures. New techniques have been described using miniaturized, high-frequency probes which allow transintestinal or trans-cloacal examination (Hildebrandt and Göritz, 1995) of reptiles.

Ultrasound is poorly propagated in a gaseous medium (the sound waves are reflected and will not penetrate deeper structures). Therefore, no air should be present between the transducer and the area to be scanned. This air interface is removed by the application of a coupling agent (aqueous gel) to the transducer surface. Furthermore, the area may need to be cleaned of soil or debris that will either scratch the transducer surface or appear as artifacts in the ultrasound images. Reduction of movement in the animal to be scanned is also important to ensure proper localization and identification of structures. Chemical restraint of the animal should not be needed. At most, immobilization of the animal by minimal physical restraint is all that is required (Figures 2b, 5, 6, 17). The species and the organs to be scanned determine the positioning of the transducer. Keep in mind that gas (lungs, gas-filled intestines) and bone reflect ultrasound waves and the organs beyond them will not be visualized. Organs of interest should be scanned in two planes at 90 degree angles to each other.

Table 1 lists suggested transducer selections for some reptiles with some recommended locations for scanning organs. The preferred transducer for most small reptiles is 7.5 Mhz with a small footprint (transducer surface size). Organs of larger reptiles can be better visualized with a 5.0 Mhz

Figure 5: Ultrasound imaging using the water bath procedure. The rear portion of this *Kinosternon* sp. is submerged in a pan of water. Note that a relatively large convex-linear transducer is directed toward the inguinal region of the turtle while the hind leg is held away from the body. This water bath technique allows the use of a larger transducer in this small available acoustic window.

transducer. Large testudines need a 5.0 Mhz transducer with a small footprint to fit in the available acoustic windows. Lizards and snakes can be scanned with a 5.0 Mhz or 7.5 Mhz transducer with any array. These reptiles can be scanned almost anywhere on the body by acoustic gel coupling, water bath, or standoff methods. Water bath scanning is accomplished by submerging the portion of the body to be scanned in water and directing the transducer into the acoustic window (Figure 5). No coupling gel is required as fluids (in this case the water) propagate ultrasound waves. The transducer does not have to be in direct contact with the body during the water bath proce-

Figure 6: Placement of a sector array transducer in the inguinal region (the area just cranial to the hind limb) of a Kemp's ridley sea turtle, *Lepidochelys kempi*. The transducer is then reoriented to image different organs and different images of the same organ. The turtle is being held in dorsal recumbency.

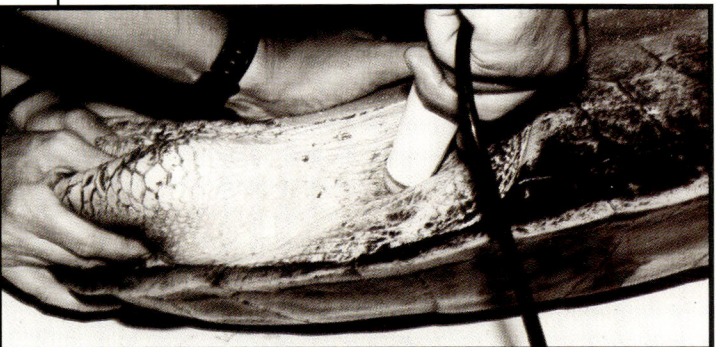

dure. The alternative technique for scanning smaller animals is using a aqueous standoff. This is a fluid-filled "bag" which is placed between the body surface and the transducer and propagates the ultrasound waves. This allows use of a larger footprint transducer in a smaller acoustic window. Crocodilians, dependent upon their size, require a 3.5 Mhz or 5.0 Mhz transducer. Any of the coupling methods should be applicable when using the ventral aspect of the body.

There are obvious species differences in morphology and anatomy which regulate which organs can be visualized and what acoustic windows are available. Gas (air in the lungs or intestinal tract) and bone prevent sound waves from traveling to

Figure 7: The reproductive tract from a dead female sea turtle, displaying large, vitellogenic follicles (2.0 cm in diameter) in both ovaries. The structures that are arranged like grape-clusters are the ovaries of this turtle. The larger tubular structures are the oviducts. The central sac-like structure is an empty urinary bladder. Note that both ovaries are fairly uniform in size and structure. This turtle was found dead and these tissues were salvaged for anatomical studies. (Reprinted with permission from the Journal of Zoo and Wildlife Medicine)

deeper structures and areas where these occur are not acoustic windows. Areas where liquid (full urinary bladder) occur do propagate ultrasound well and conduct sound waves to deeper structures. These fluid-filled organs are excellent acoustic windows. In general, urinary bladders are good acoustic windows; however, in some tortoise species they become sound reflectors when the bladder has lots of urates.

ULTRASOUND IMAGING IN TESTUDINES

Testudines have keratin and bone shells that cover most of their body leaving only a minimal area exposed for use as acoustic windows. The inguinal region (area just in front of the hind limb; Figures 5,6); the axillary region (area behind the front limb); and the cervical region (area between the neck and front limb) on both sides can be used to visualize the heart, gastrointestinal tract, ovaries, oviducts with eggs, parts of the liver, and urinary bladder. The ability to visualize these various organs will be regulated by the footprint and frequency of your transducer compared to the size of the testudine (and thus the size of the acoustic window). Water bath use will facilitate the visualization of organs in very small testudines as the size of the transducer footprint and frequency will be less crucial to the imaging (Figure 5). The resolution may be affected, however, by these factors with a water bath submergence. There is little problem with the size of the footprint in large testudines but transducer frequency must be lower. Some testudines such as pancake and soft shell turtles can be scanned transdermally because of the reduced bone in their carapaces and plastrons. Also, certain male sea turtles will have reduced keratinization of their central plastron during the mating season (Wibbels et al., 1991) producing an acoustic window to the heart in these animals.

Ovaries can be monitored for seasonal patterns in follicular growth, maturation, and regression with serial scans during the reproductive season. In female testudines, identification of ovarian follicles is limited to greater than five millimeters in diameter. In some species it is possible to accurately determine not only follicle size but also estimate total number of follicles (Kuchling, 1989; Kuchling and Bradshaw, 1993) and to identify oviductal eggs (Kuchling, 1989; Kuchling and Bradshaw, 1993; Robeck et al., 1990; Rostal et al., 1989a,b; 1990; 1991a,b; 1994a,b, 1996). In many turtles, such as sea turtles, each ovary may contain from 50 to 200+ large vitellogenic follicles and each turtle may lay multiple clutches per season ranging from 50 to 200 eggs per clutch depending on the species (Moll, 1979). Thus, accurate estimation of the number of follicles or eggs *in situ* is not possible in sea turtles. However, in sea turtles it has been demonstrated that both ovaries display a homogeneous pattern of follicular development (Rostal et al., 1990, 1991a; Figure 7). Therefore, viewing a portion of each ovary yields an accurate estimation of the character of both ovaries. Vitellogenic follicles are highly echoic (appear white; Figures 8,9). In fact, when the follicles are highly vitellogenic the follicle is so echoic that it reflects ultrasound waves. This reflection of the sound waves produces an acoustic shadow (black image) beyond the follicle (Figure 8). Care must be taken to differentiate follicles from loops of intestine. Changing the orientation of the transducer will differentiate a circular structure (follicle) from a linear structure (intestinal loop).

Figure 8: Ultrasound image of three pre-ovulatory (follicles in the ovary before release into the oviduct) vitellogenic follicles of a Kemp's ridley sea turtle, *Lepidochelys kempi*. The follicles are hyperechoic (appear white) due to the large amount of yolk they contain. The central follicle was measured using the internal calipers and the image preserved on thermographic paper. Notice the black area below the central follicle; this image is called acoustic shadowing. This indicates that the sound waves did not propagate through this follicle due to the yolk density.

The presence of eggs in the oviduct can be detected (Figures 10, 11). With this technique, it is possible to determine which females have enlarging ovarian follicles and are likely to breed in a particular season. The determination of the number of eggs present in the oviduct depends upon the species. The yolks and egg shell are highly echoic (white) while the liquid albumen layer is anechoic and appears as a black region separating the

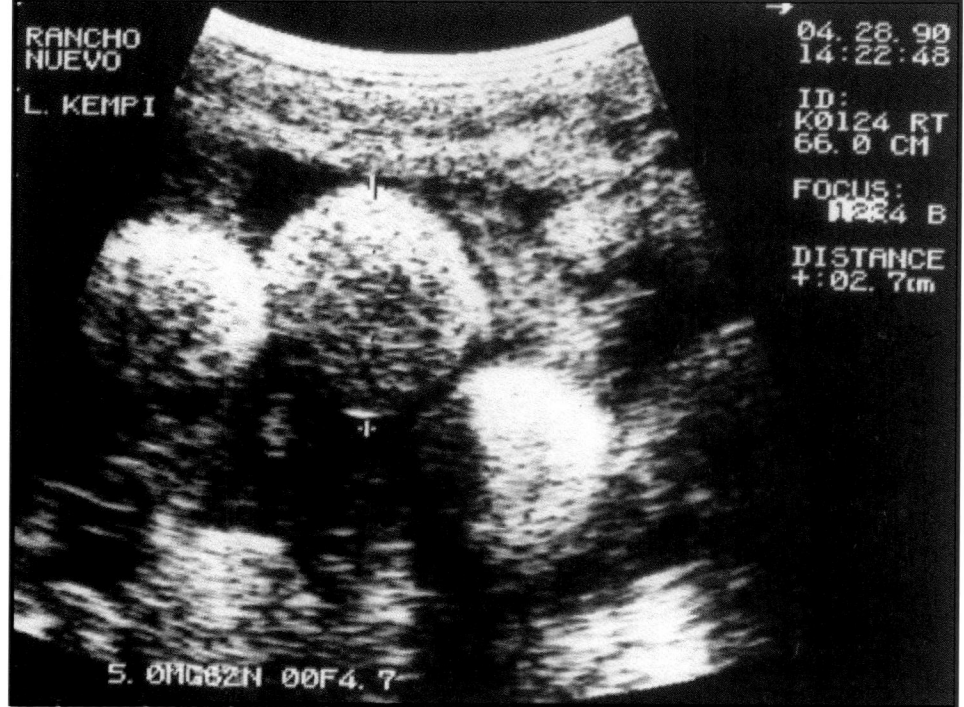

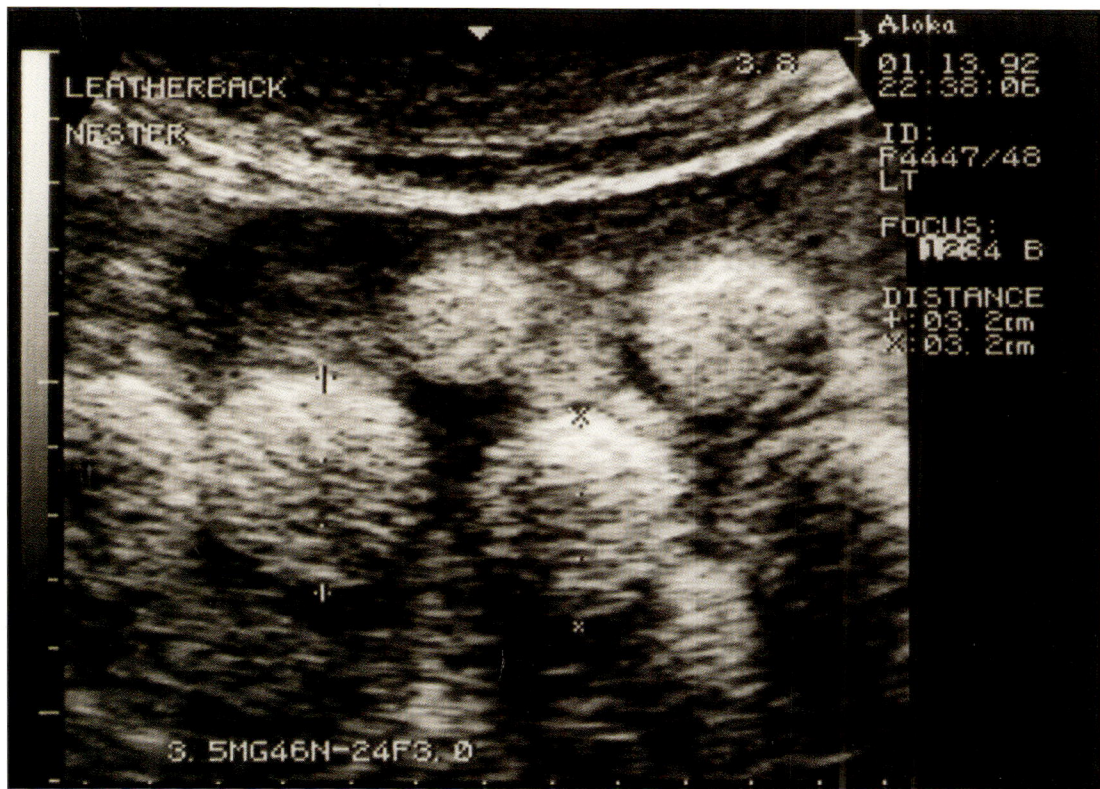

Figure 9: Ultrasound image of an ovary containing multiple large pre-ovulatory vitellogenic follicles. The abundance of this stage of follicles indicates that this turtle is early in her nesting cycle (i.e., she should produce more eggs in this season). This image is from a leatherback sea turtle, *Dermochelys coriacea*.

Figure 10: Ultrasound image of two oviductal eggs (eggs in the oviduct) of a leatherback sea turtle, *Dermochelys coriacea*. Note the echoic yolk (white central area), the anechoic albumen layer (black area) around the yolk, and the highly echoic calcified shell. Notice that the entire yolk, albumen layer, and shell can be easily imaged in this turtle. This is possible because sea turtle eggs are leathery rather than highly calcified.

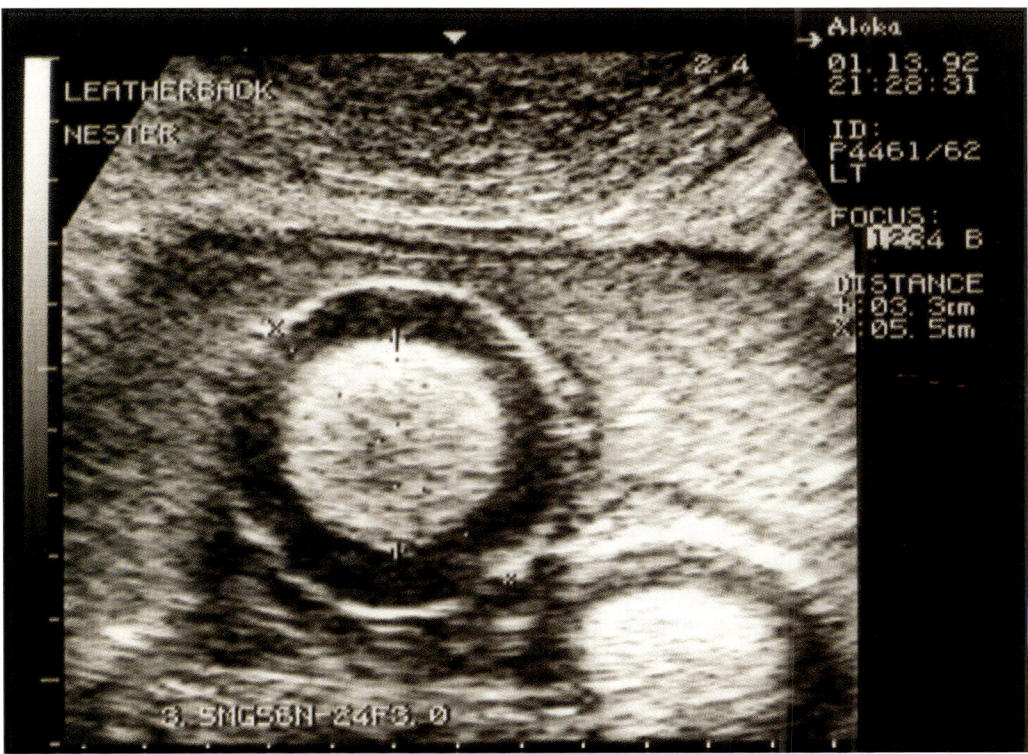

yolk from the shell (Figure 10, 11). The degree of egg shell calcification determines how echoic the shell layer appears. In species (such as sea turtles) which produce leathery shells (Figure 10) ultrasound waves pass easily. Some species, such as tortoises, produce hard shells and the sound waves are reflected and produce an acoustic shadow beyond the egg; Figure 11). In some sea turtle species which have leathery shells, the egg viability may be determined prior to ovipositioning (nesting; Rostal et al., 1991b). The number of eggs in a clutch and the degree of egg shell calcification determine whether the number of eggs can be counted *in situ*. If the egg shells are membranous but numerous, like sea turtles, they can not be counted due to the large numbers of eggs. Whereas,

Figure 12: This is a water bath imaging of the reproductive tract of a dead sea turtle used to validate our ultrasound techniques and identifications. Notice that the image produced by the oviduct is echoic, and tubular in appearance. It is often impossible to differentiate empty oviduct from loops of intestine.

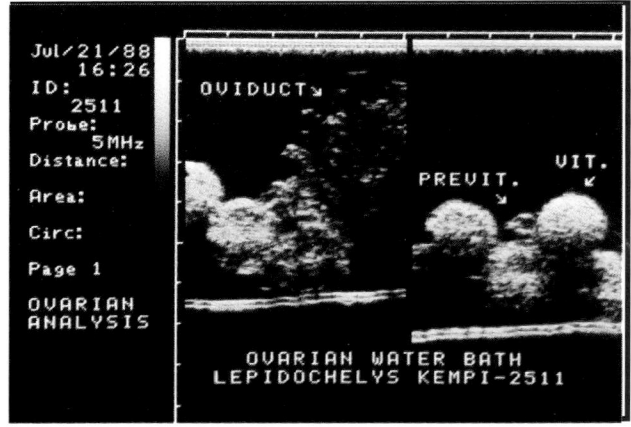

Figure 13: Ultrasound image of follicles in early atresia from a Kemp's ridley sea turtle, *Lepidochelys kempi*. Note the anechoic (dark) core of the follicles. This appearance occurs because the central yolk is becoming liquefied.

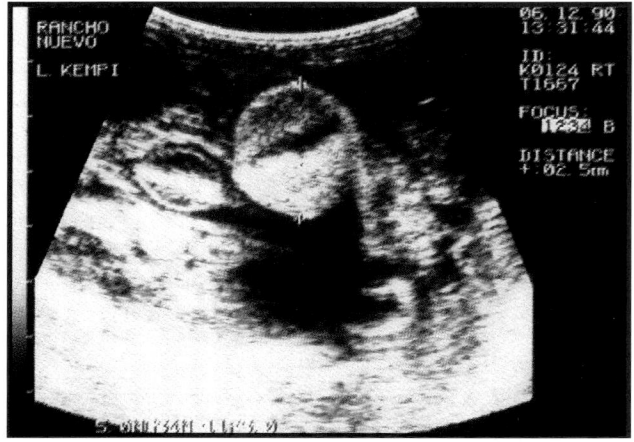

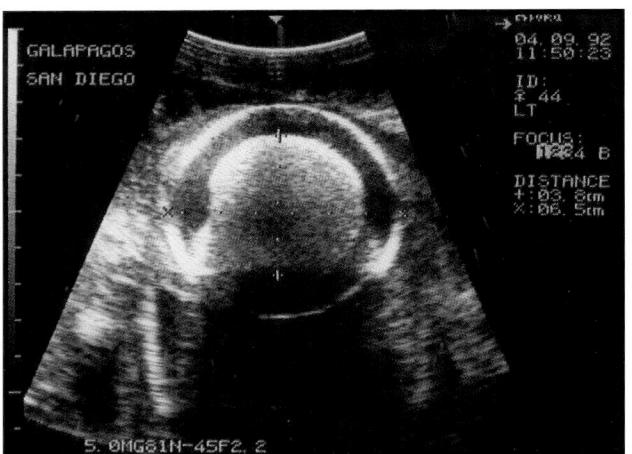

Figure 11: Ultrasound image of an hard shelled oviductal egg in a Galapagos tortoise, *Geochelone elephantopus*. Note the attenuation of the ultrasound waves producing an acoustic shadow at the lower half of the egg due to the heavily calcified shell. Notice, also, that the lower portion of the egg is not clearly seen due to this attenuation.

if the eggs are fewer but the egg shells are highly calcified, like Galapagos tortoises, *Geochelone elephantopus*; Figure 11), eggs are imaged in both oviducts but are often missed or cross-counted due to the sound wave reflectance. Oviducts which are empty (do not contain eggs) are not discernible from ingesta-filled intestines (Figures 12, 15, 16).

Atresia is the process of reabsorbing the large vitellogenic follicles that were not ovulated that season. Atretic follicles appear first as normal follicles with a small anechoic (dark) center where the proteinaceous material has started to be reabsorbed (Figure 13). As atresia continues, the anechoic region increases in size (Figure 14). During a normal nesting season a limited number of atretic follicles are observed.

After final oviposition of the season, ultrasonography images of the ovaries show depletion (Figures 15, 16). At this time one can see various other organs, i.e. intestine, that were previously obscured by the enlarged ovaries and oviduct (Figures 15, 16). Females that do not ovulate normally rarely show completely depleted ovaries, but rather retain a large number of follicles that become atretic. Male testes are not easily imaged and will be difficult to identify. Detecting seasonal variations in testicular tissue is not possible.

The urinary bladder can be visualized when it is full of urine (anechoic, i.e. black; Figure 15) and it is also possible to visualize urates (echoic) in the bladder. The liver (echoic with speckling) is occasionally visible but not reliably. Changing the position of the animal (head down, tilted to one

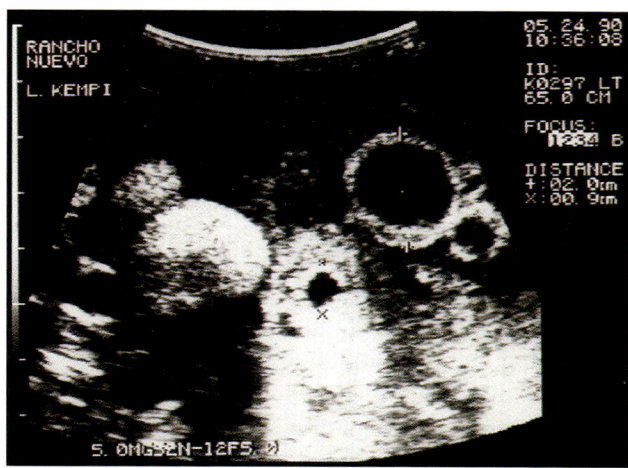

Fig. 14: Ultrasound image of three follicles in late atresia from a Kemp's ridley sea turtle, *Lepidochelys kempi*. These follicles (in the right half of the image) posess a central anechoic (black) area with a hyperechoic wall.

side or the other) as well as the position of the transducer helps facilitate the visualization of different organs. Blood vessels are anechoic structures (fluid-filled) with slightly echoic walls (Figure 16). Identification of landmarks such as the omentum boundary of each ovary (Figure 16) and the urinary bladder (Figure 15) will help in organ identification.

ULTRASOUND IMAGING IN SQUAMATES (LIZARDS AND SNAKES)

The selection of transducer frequency and footprint is not as critical in squamates as in testudines. Many squamates have numerous ribs which protect a large portion of the body, are close together, and thus limit the acoustic window. Scanning the squamate from the ventral aspect of the body should eliminate this problem. Direct body contact, water bath submergence (Figure 17), or standoff use will allow visualization of most organs in most squamates. Specialized intra-cloacal probes may also prove valuable in reproductive imaging studies. Heloderms have osteoderms (bony plates) in their skin which may reflect some ultrasound waves; however, this was not found to be a problem in either beaded lizards (*Heloderma horridum*) or Gila monsters (*Heloderma suspectum*- Wright et al., 1995; Morris and Alberts, 1996). Restraint may be difficult in large squamates but should not require sedation.

Liver, spleen, pancreas, gastrointestinal tract, kidneys, and fat bodies were imaged in varanid lizards by Sainsbury and Gili (1991). These authors were unable to visualize the reproductive tract in all but the female varanid that contained eggs. The only gender identification was of the one fe-

male. The inability to image the reproductive tract in the other varanids was most likely either due to scanning male varanids where testes are difficult to image or scanning female varanids during the quiescent portion of their reproductive cycle. Furthermore, we have observed that poorly maintained or unhealthy female reptiles do not develop robust, vitellogenic ovarian follicles. Other stuides have visualized and imaged follicular development in white throated minitors (*Varanus albigularia*), Gila monsters (*Heloderma suspectum*), beaded liz-

Fig.15: Ultrasound image of a female black sea turtle, *Chelonia agassizi*, which has completed nesting for the season. Note the fluid filled urinary bladder (anechoic structure in the upper left aspect of the image) and intestinal loops (round anechoic structures with central echoic contents). No follicles are visible in this image.

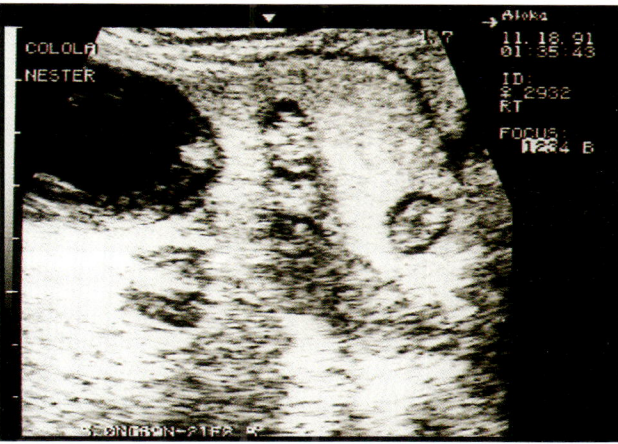

Fig. 16: Ultrasound image of a female leatherback sea turtle, *Dermochelys coriacea*, showing lack of vitellogenic follicles in the ovary. The only reproductive structure imaged is one small, atretic follicle (echoic structure with an anechoic core) on the left. The longitudinal cross sections are intestine that had previously been obscured by the presence of the enlarged ovary and oviduct. Note the ovarian boundary at the top of the image, the thin tubular appearance of this boundary is produced by the vasculature in this structure.

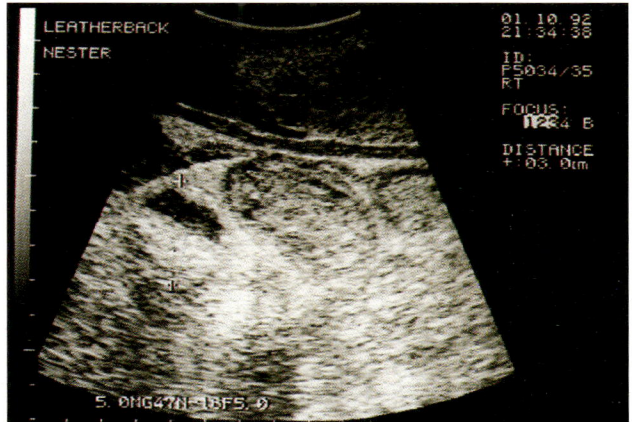

TABLE 1: GENERAL GUIDE TO ULTRASOUND USE IN REPTILES

SPECIES	TRANSDUCER FREQUENCY/ TYPE	ORGANS TO BE SCANNED	TRANSDUCER PLACEMENT
Sea Turtles	3.5 & 5.0 MHz/Sector; Linear, short or Convex- Linear	Ovaries, Oviduct w/Eggs, Intestinal tract, Urinary bladder	Inguinal region in front of hind limb
		Heart	Cervical area between neck & front limb
Galapagos and Aldabra Tortoises	3.5 & 5.0 MHz/Sector; Linear, short or Convex- Linear	Ovaries, Oviduct w/Eggs, Intestinal tract, Urinary bladder	Inguinal region in front of hind limb
		Heart	Cervical area between neck & front limb
Small Tortoises and Freshwater Turtles	7.5 MHz/Sector; Convex Linear 5.0 MHz Linear in water bath	Ovaries, Oviduct w/Eggs, Intestinal tract, Urinary bladder	Inguinal region in front of hind limb
Squamates : Lizards and Snakes	5.0 MHz, 7.5 MHz Sector, Linear, or Convex-Linear	Most organs	Most body surfaces, except where bone & air interfere
Crocodylians	5.0 MHz Sector, Linear, or Convex-Linear	Most organs	Most body surfaces, except where bone & air interfere

Fig. 17: Water bath technique for ultrasound imaging of a rat snake, *Elaphe* sp. This snake had leathery eggs in the oviduct and these eggs are evidenced by the bulge you see in this photo.

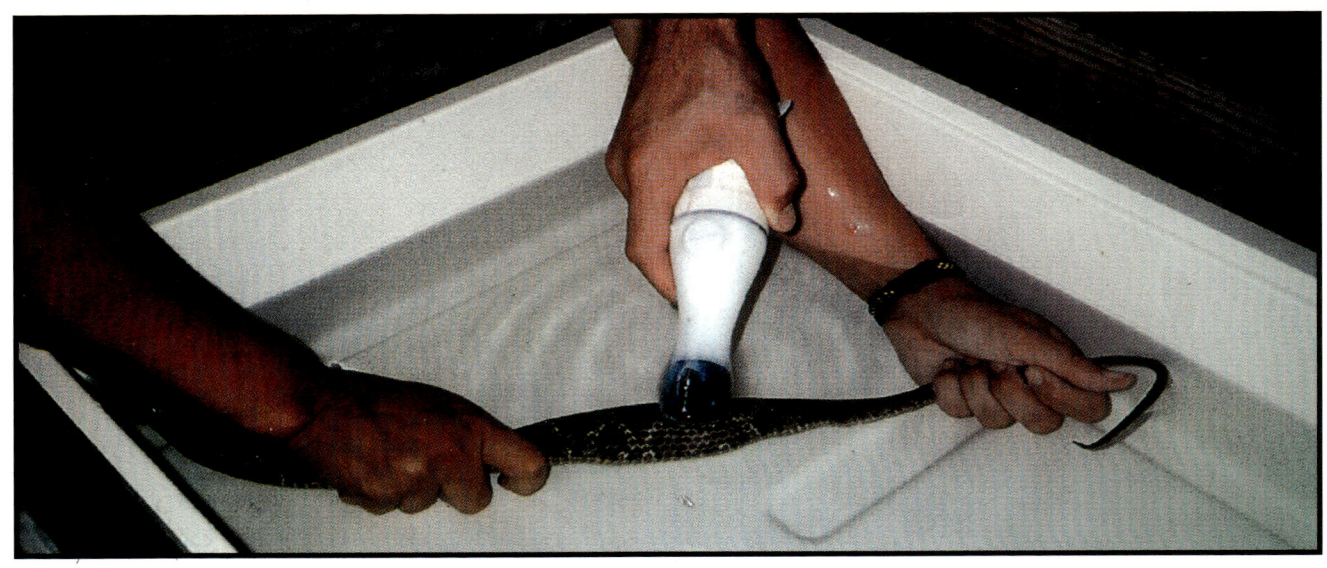

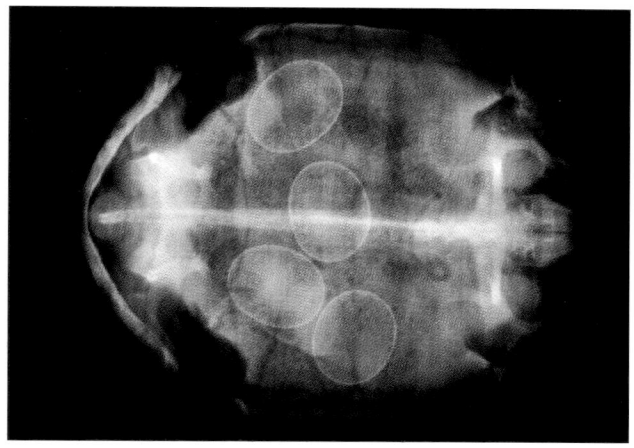

Figure 18: A radiographic image of a female desert tortoise, *Gopherus agassizii*, showing oviductal eggs. The eggs are well calcified and can be easily identified and counted.

ards (*Heloderma horridum*) and Komodo dragons (*Varanus komodoensis*; Morris and Alberts, 1996 and pers. comm.; Wright et al, 1995).

Liver images are echoic with a granular appearance. The pancreas appears echoic but less so than the liver. The gastrointestinal tract is also less echoic than the liver but the identification of the walls of the tract are important to its identification. Blood vessels are anechoic structures (fluid-filled) with slightly echoic walls. Species differences will determine whether a urinary bladder is present to image.

ULTRASOUND IMAGING IN CROCODYLIA

Direct contact with the body or water bath submergence should make imagery of organs possible in most crocodilians. Osteoderms are present in crocodilians and may limit the acoustic window availability. Osteoderms are usually confined to the back and sides of crocodilians so ultrasonography should be possible using the ventral portion of the body. The ventral and lateral aspects of the abdomen have been used to image ovaries in *Caiman latirostris* (Vac et al., 1992) and *Crocodylus johnstoni* (T. Tucker, pers. comm.) The osteoderms in these two species sometimes produced blurred imaging but were not so calcified as to reflect all the ultrasound waves. Some species (e.g. *Melanosuchus niger*, *Paleosuchus trigonatus*, and *Osteolaemus tetraspis*) which possess an abundance of heavily ossified dermal bone may be more difficult to image. The size of the crocodilian will determine the transducer frequency that is required for an individual, however, both 3.5 Mhz and 5.0 Mhz transducers have been used in crocodilians with snout to vent lengths of 85-100 centimeters. Restraint may be a concern with the larger crocodilians.

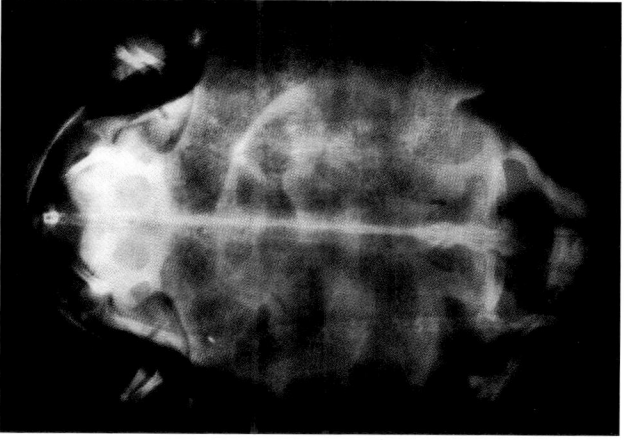

Figure 19: A radiographic image of a female desert tortoise, *Gopherus agassizii*, that does not appear to have oviductal eggs. The main structure visualized is the gastrointestinal tract. However, ultrasound imaging revealed that this tortoise contained 6 oviductal eggs. These eggs were not calcified enough to image by radiography.

APPLICATIONS OF ULTRASOUND IMAGING IN REPTILES

Ultrasonography can be used for health and reproductive assessment in reptiles. We have used ultrasonography to monitor the seasonal cyclicity of wild and captive female sea turtles and tortoises (Kemp's ridley - *Lepidochelys kempi*, Rostal, et al., 1989b, 1990, 1991a; black turtle - *Chelonia agassizi*, Byles et al., 1995; Rostal et al., 1990); Olive ridley - *Lepidochelys olivacea*, Rostal et al., 1991b; Leatherback turtle, *Dermochelys coriacea*, Rostal et al., 1994, 1996); desert tortoises - *Gopherus agassizii*, Rostal, et al., 1994a; and Galapagos tortoises - *Geochelone elephantopus* spp., Robeck et al., 1990; Rostal et al., 1989a) by monitoring follicular growth and egg development throughout the reproductive season. Ultrasonography has been used to monitor follicular development in the broad-nosed caiman, *Caiman latirostris* (Vac, et al., 1992) and monitors (Horn and Visser, 1989)as well as follicular development and ovulation in the Australian freshwater crocodile, *Crocodylus johnstoni* (T. Tucker, pers. comm.); *Chelodina oblonga* (Kuchling, 1989) and the Western swamp tortoise, *Pseudemydura umbrina* (Kuchling and Bradshaw, 1993)

Ultrasonography allows imaging of:
—the development of eggs *in situ*,
—the progression of ovarian atresia as observed *in situ*,
—the appearance of a gravid ovary (full of vitellogenic follicles) versus a depleted ovary and
—the determination of egg viability in some turtles.

Ultrasound provides a safe, non-invasive method for studying the ovarian physiology of testudines. Ultrasonography provides a non-invasive technique by which the general ovarian condition of a particular female can be determined and the presence of eggs in the oviduct detected. With this technique, it is possible to determine which females have enlarging ovarian follicles and are likely to breed in a particular season. It is also possible to monitor those females which contain eggs and need to be watched for nesting, egg retrieval or possible complications during oviposition. Radiography can be used in connection with ultrasonography especially when an exact number of eggs is to be determined prior to ovipositioning (Figure 18). Radiographs will not always image eggs in the oviduct that are not highly calcified, whereas, ultrasound will image these structures (Figure 19).

We have used ultrasound to identify pathologic changes in a sea turtle oviduct. Once one becomes familiar with the normal appearance of different tissues and organs, the identification of pathologic changes will be possible. Ultrasound can also be used to guide biopsies. Ultrasound is safe, rapid, simple, and non-invasive and does not require chemical restraint. Ultrasound equipment is quite expensive and does require skill to operate and interpret images correctly. However, ultrasonography can provide invaluable information especially in the study of reproductive physiology.

REFERENCES

—du Boulay, GH; Wilson, OL:
Diagnosis of pregnancy and disease by ultrasound in exotic species. Symp Zool Soc Lond, 1988; 60: 135-150.

—Byles, R; Alvarado, J; Rostal, D:
Preliminary analysis of post-nesting movements of the black turtle (*Chelonia agassizi*) from Michoacan, Mexico. In, Proceedings of the Twelfth Annual Workshop on Sea Turtle Conservation and Biology, JI Richardson; TH Richardson (Compilers). NOAA Technical Memorandum, 1995, NMFS-SEFSC-361 : 12-13.

—Frye, FL:
Biomedical and surgical aspects of captive reptile husbandry. Krieger Publishing Co., Melbourne, Fl, 1981.

—Gibbons, JW; Greene, JL:
X-ray photography: A technique to determine reproductive patterns of freshwater turtles. Herpetologica, 1979; 35 : 86-89.

—Hildebrandt, TR; Göritz, F:
Ultrasonography as a tool in propagation of zoo animals. In, Proceedings of American Assoc Zoo Veterinarians, 1995; 239-242.

—Horn, H: Visser, G:
Review of reproduction of monitor lizards in captivity. In, International Zoo Yearbook, 1989; 28: 140-150.

—Kuchling, G:
Assessment of ovarian follicles and oviductal eggs by ultrasound scanning in live freshwater turtles, *Chelodina oblonga*. Herpetologica, 1989; 45 : 89-94.

—Kuchling, G; Bradshaw, SD:
Ovarian cycle and egg production of the Western swamp tortoise *Pseudemydura umbrina* (Testudines: Chelidae) in the wild and in captivity. J Zool, London, 1993; 229: 405-419.

—Limpus, CJ; Reed, PC:
The green turtle, *Chelonia mydas*, in Queensland: A preliminary description of the population structure in a coral feeding ground. In, Biology of Australasian Frogs and Reptiles, G. Grigg, R. Shine, and H. Ehmann (Eds). Royal Zoological Society of New South Wales, 1985, pp. 47-52.

—Moll, EO:
Reproductive cycles and adaptations. In, Turtles: Perspectives and Research, M. Harless and H. Morlock (Eds). John Wiley and Sons, New York, 1979, pp. 305-331.

—Morris, PJ; Alberts, A:
Determination of sex in white-throated monitors (*Varanus albigularis*), Gila monsters (*Heloderma suspectum*), and beaded lizards (*H. horridum*) using two dimensional ultrasound imaging. J Zoo Wildl Med, 1996; 27:371-377.

—Newman, DG; Watson, PR:
The contribution of radiography to the study of the reproductive ecology of the Tuatara, *Sphenodon punctatus*. In, Biology of Australasian Frogs and Reptiles, G Grigg, R Shine, and H Ehmann (Eds). Royal Zoological Society of New South Wales, 1985, pp. 7-10.

—Robeck, TR; Rostal, DC; Burchfield, PM; et al.:
Ultrasound imaging of reproductive structures and eggs in Galapagos tortoises, *Geochelone elephantopus* spp. Zoo Biol, 1990; 9: 349-359.

—Rostal, D; Grumbles, J; Owens, D:
Physiological evidence of higher fecundity in wild Kemp's ridleys: Implications to population estimates. In, Proceedings of the Eleventh Annual Workshop on Sea Turtle Conservation and Biology, M Salmon; J Wyneken (Compilers). NOAA Technical Memorandum, 1991a; NMFS-SEFSC-302 : 180.

—Rostal, D; Kalb, H; Grumbles, J; et al.:
Application of ultrasonography to sea turtle reproduction. In, Proceedings of the Eleventh

Annual Workshop on Sea Turtle Conservation and Biology, M Salmon; J Wyneken (Compilers). NOAA Technical Memorandum, 1991b; NMFS-SEFSC-302 : 181.

—Rostal, DC; Lance, VA; Grumbles, JS; et al.:
Seasonal reproductive cycle of the desert tortoise (*Gopherus agassizii*) in the eastern Mojave desert. Herp Monographs, 1994a; 8 : 72-82.

—Rostal, DC; Paladino, FV; Patterson, RM; et al:
Observations on the reproductive physiology of the leatherback sea turtle (*Dermochelys coriacea*). In, Proceedings of the Fourteenth Annual Symposium on Sea Turtle Biology and Conservation, KA Bjorndal; DA Johnson, PJ Eliazar (Compilers). NOAA Technical Memorandum, 1994b, NMFS-SEFSC-351: 128.

—Rostal, DC; Paladino, FV; Patterson, RM, et al.:
Reproductive physiology of the leatherback sea turtle (*Dermochelys coriacea*) at las Baulas de Guanacaste National Park, Costa Rica. Chelonian Conserv Biol, 1996, 2:230-236.

—Rostal, DC; Robeck, TR; Burchfield, PM:
Reproductive physiology of Galapagos tortoises (*Geochelone elephantopus*) at the Gladys Porter Zoo. In, AAZPA Annual Conference Proceedings, 1989a, pp. 473-479.

—Rostal, DC; Robeck, TR; Owens, DW; et al.:
Ultrasound imaging of ovaries and eggs in Kemp's ridley sea turtles (*Lepidochelys kempi*). J Zoo Wildl Med, 1990; 21: 27-35.

—Rostal, D; Robeck, T; Owens, D; et al.:
Ultrasonic imaging of ovaries and eggs in sea turtles. In, Proceedings of the Ninth Annual Workshop on Sea Turtle Conservation and Biology, SA Eckert; KL Eckert; TH Richardson (Compilers). NOAA Technical Memorandum, 1989b; NMFS-SEFC-232: 257-259.

—Sainsbury, AW; Gili, C:
Ultrasonographic anatomy and scanning technique of the coelomic organs of the Bosc monitor (*Varanus exanthematicus*). J Zoo Wildl Med, 1991; 22(4) : 421-433.

—Turner, FB; Hayden, P; Burge, BL; et al.:
Egg production by the desert tortoise (*Gopherus agassizii*) in California. Herpetologica, 1986; 42 :93-104.

—Vac, MH; Verdade, LM; Meirelles, CF; et al.:
Ultrasound evaluation of the follicle development in adult female broad-nosed caiman (*Caiman latirostris*). In, Proceedings of the 11th Working Meeting of the Crocodile Specialist Group 1992, pp. 176-183.

—Wibbels, T; Owens, DW; Rostal, DC:
Soft plastra of adult male sea turtles: An apparent secondary sexual characteristic. Herp Rev, 1991; 22 : 47-49.

—Wood, JR; Wood, FE; Critchley, KH; et al.:
Laparoscopy of the green sea turtle, *Chelonia mydas*. Brit J Herp, 1983; 6 : 323-327.

—Wright, K; Pugh, C; Walker, L:
Ultrasonographic sexing of helodermatid lizards. In, Proceedings American Association of Zoo Veterinarians, 1995; 239-242.

HUMAN PARASITIC DISEASES ORIGINATING FROM REPTILE CONSUMPTION OR CONTACT

Huh Sun, M.D., Ph.D.,[*]
Associate Professor of Parasitology
College of Medicine
Hallym University
Chunchon 200-702
Korea

[*]E-mail correspondence: shuh@sun.hallym.ac.kr.

Dr. Huh graduated from Seoul National University College of Medicine in 1982 and was awarded his Ph.D. from Alumnus University in 1990. Since 1988, he has been an Instructor, Assistant Professor and Associate Professor in the College of Medicine, Hallym University, Korea. Dr. Huh worked for one year as a Research Associate in the Institute of Pathology, Case Western Reserve University, Cleveland, Ohio, USA. He has been a member of the Korean Society for Parasitology since 1982; has served on the Editorial Board of the Korean Journal of Parasitology since 1991.

Dr. Huh specializes in the study of human parasitic diseases related to reptiles and amphibians, especially sparganosis and neodiplostomiasis. He has published papers on clinical studies, histopathology, and serology related with those worms. Currently, Dr. Huh's research includes a sero-epidemiological survey, molecular work for sparganosis

INTRODUCTION

There are a few human parasitic diseases associated with reptiles. From the reptile groups (such as squamates, crocodilians, and chelonians), only snakes are important as a source of human infections of parasitic diseases. Most infections are associated with the habit of eating raw or undercooked snake in some areas in the world. Sparganosis is also caused by the practice in some parts of the world of making poultices from snakes. The following list briefly describes some of the parasitic diseases humans can acquire from snakes:

—Sparganosis. A plerocercoid larval infection. Infections in humans can be caused through the application of raw-snake poultices to open wounds; it can also be caused by the practice of eating raw snake and by drinking water which contains the cyclops intermediate host.

—*Mesocestoides lineatus.* An adult cestode of canines

(dogs, foxes, and wolves); snakes are its paratenic host. Humans can become infected with *M. lineatus* by eating raw snake that harbors tetrathyridium of the parasite.

—Neodiplostomiasis. An endemic intestinal trematodiasis in Korea. Humans can become infected with neodiplostomiasis by eating raw snake or frog. This parasite can cause gastrointestinal symptoms, such as abdominal pain.

—*Alaria marcinae.* In the U.S., mesocercarial infection of *A. marcinae* was reported; the infection was caused by a human who ate undercooked raccoon (Beaver et al., 1977). Later, Shoop et al. (1981) verified that snakes harbor the mesocercariae of *A. marcinae.*

—*Fibribricola cratera.* Experimental human infection with metacercariae of *F. cratera* recovered from snake was successfully established.

—*Gnathostoma spinigerum.* A nematode of felines and canines. When humans are infected with its third-stage larva, they can suffer from meningoencephalitis.

—Pentastomiasis. An arthropod infection due to several species of pentastomid parasites. Believed to originate from ingestion of raw snakes or improperly cooked meat.

This chapter describes human disease caused by sparganosis, *Mesocestoides lineatus* infection, and neodiplostomiasis. No reported human cases of infection with *A. marcinae, F. cratera* or *G. spinigerum* have been confirmed to have been caused by the victims' eating of raw snake. However, the possibility of human infection from eating raw snake remains, since snakes have been found to harbor larval forms of those parasites.

Pentastomiasis is another parasitic infection, which is believed to originate from ingestion of raw snakes or improperly cooked meat. Since it is an arthropod infection, I will mention only briefly

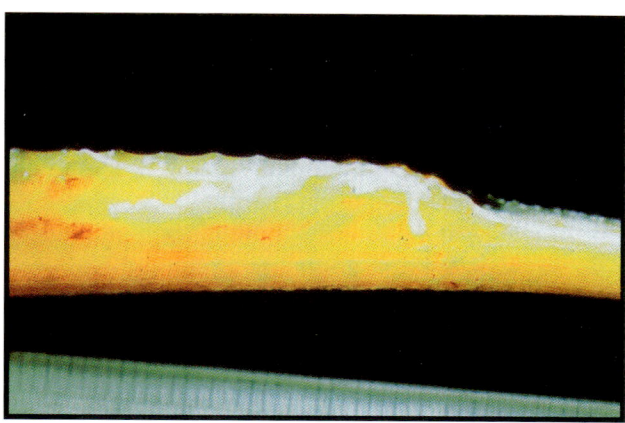

Fig. 1. Sparganum in the muscle of a snake (*Rhabdophis tigrina*). The slender, white-colored worm was shown after peeling the skin off the snake.

the cause of human infections and clinical manifestations at the end of this chapter.

SPARGANOSIS

Sparganosis refers to infection with the migrating larvae (spargana) of pseudophyllidean tapeworms, such as *Diphyllobothrium* sp. or *Spirometra* sp. The term sparganum (plural spargana) refers to the larval stage of these cestodes and is typically used when the exact genus of the adult is not known. When discussing reptiles, sparganosis usually refers to a plerocercoid larval infection of *Spirometra* sp.; larval infections of *Diphyllobothrium* do not occur in reptiles. *Spirometra* sp. can be found world-wide in felines and canines as an intestinal cestode. However, sparganosis is endemic in humans only in those countries where the habit of eating raw snake or frog persists, or where the habit of making poultices with the flesh of snakes or frogs exists. A larval infection can cause serious and fatal problems when the brain or spinal cord is in-

Fig. 2. Section of sparganum in mouse muscle. Calcium corpuscles are blue-colored. Alcian blue (pH 2.5) stain. X 40.

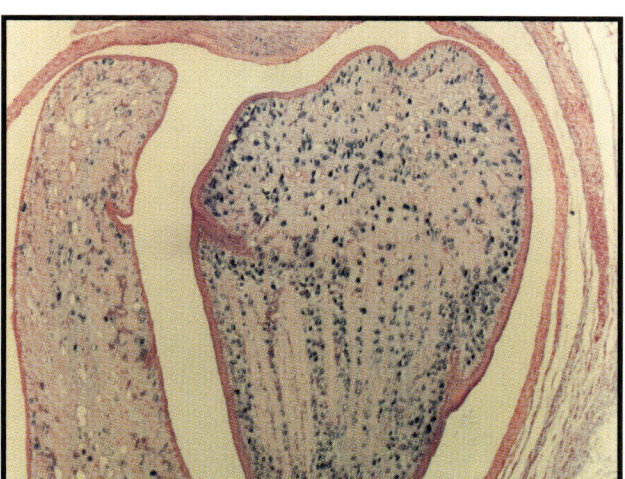

volved. In rare cases, the adult form of the tapeworm can dwell in the intestines of humans.

MORPHOLOGY AND LIFE CYCLE

MORPHOLOGY OF SPARGANA
The size of this larval worm varies according to the host. In general, the larval worm is long and slender, 1.0-20.0 cm x 0.2-0.5 cm. In humans, worms usually grow thicker than in snakes. In laboratory mice, worms can be maintained until the death of the infected animals at the end of the mice normal lifespan (Mueller, 1974).

The worm consists of a scolex, neck, and strobila. The neck and strobila are white (Fig. 1); the scolex is yellow and is thicker than the strobila. The anteriormost part of the scolex is invaginated. The worm can grow only if its scolex is intact. The growing point of the worm is located in the anterior-most portion of scolex, within 0.5 mm from the anterior end (Sohn et al., 1993a).

Although the surface of the worm is smooth, in its stationary state, the worm folds itself so that it is flexible. It can elongate itself more than three to four times its stationary state. When a worm is removed from snake or human tissue, the worm moves in a zigzag manner. Its activity is accelerated when it is placed in a saline solution at 37° C.

Histological findings of sparganum show that it consists of tegument, parenchymal cells, loose connective tissue, muscles, excretory canals, and a calcium corpuscle. Tegument is the site of metabolism, absorption of nutrients, secretion, and protection. The role of the calcium corpuscle is not clear, but it is believed to be an organ for metabolism or nerve transmission (Fig. 2).

TAXONOMY
Currently, there are two identified species of *Spirometra* sp.: *Spirometra erinacei* and *S. mansonoides*. The following is the taxonomic position of Spirometra sp.

Kingdom: Animalia
Phylum: Platyhelminthes
Class: Cestoidea
Subclass: Eucestoda
Order: Pseudophyllidea
Family: Diphyllobothriidae
Genus: *Spirometra*
Species: *S. erinacei* (*S. erinaceieuropaei, S. mansoni*)
S. mansonoides

Mueller (Mueller, 1974 and 1975; Schmidt, 1986a) distinguished the *S. mansonoides* from *S. erinacei*. In this research, Mueller pointed out that the consistent difference between *S. erinacei* and

S. mansonoides was the shape of the uterus of the mature proglottid. Mueller identified a C-formed outer loop in *S. mansonoides*. He also identified the appearance of a lateral expulsion chamber by stricture of the anterior transverse limb. In contrast, he showed that the uterus of *S. erinacei* is filled and twisted (Fig. 3).

However, Iwata (1936 & 1972) believed that nomination of various kinds of *Spirometra* sp. is the result of the difference in shape according to the developmental stage of the worm. Iwata stated that only one *Spirometra* sp. existed, and that, according to the rule of priority, that *Spirometra* should be called *S. erinacei* (Iwata, 1936 & 1972; Yamaguchi, 1959).

Currently, the *Spirometra* in the eastern and southern areas of North America is called *S. mansonoides*. In other areas, it is called *S. erinacei* (*S. erinaceieuropaei*, *S. mansoni*) in the literature (Noya et al., 1992). Data of isozyme patterns by isoelectric focusing suggest that the *S. erinacei* from Japan and Australia are closely related, if not identical, but that *S. mansonoides* is genetically distinct from *S. erinacei* (Fukumoto, 1992).

LIFE CYCLE AND MORPHOLOGY OF *S. ERINACEI* (FIG. 4)

Spirometra sp. is an intestinal parasite of felines, canines, or other carnivorous mammals, such as *Felis geoffroy, F. yagouarondi, Dusycyon gymnocercus,* and *Cerdocyon thous* (Schmidt, 1986b). In general, *Spirometra* plerocercoids can develop into adult worms only in *Felis* sp. or in canines. In other animals, *Spirometra* remains a plerocercoid. In humans, the worm generally remains in plerocercoid larval form; i.e. sparganum. Very rarely, the plerocercoid can develop into an adult worm in the small intestines of a human host. By the mid-nineteen-eighties, only seven cases of

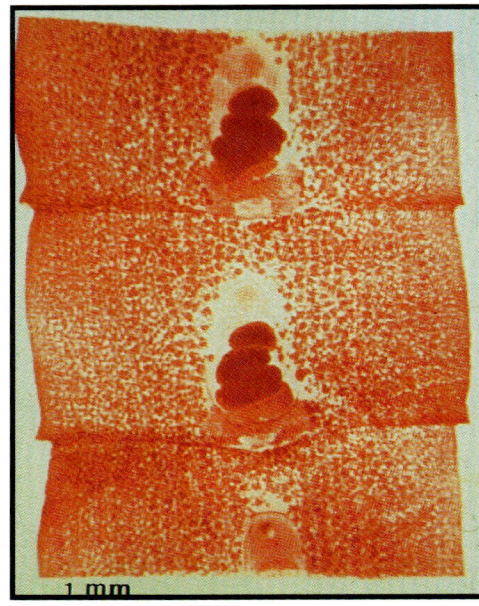

Fig. 3. Mature proglottid of *S. erinacei*, which shows filled-up uterus. Acetocarmine stain.

1 mm

adult worm infections in humans had been reported (Lee et al., 1984).

The life cycle of sparganum can be explained from the life cycle of the adult *Spirometra* sp. In feline hosts, the eggs are passed out in the stool. Coracidium infections subsequently develop from eggs in water sources (Fig. 5). Egg-hatched coracidium enter cyclops, which are the first intermediate host of the parasite. The coracidium in the cyclops then develop into procercoids. Tadpoles are the second intermediate host of the parasite. When tadpoles take in infected cyclops, the plerocercoids develop in the tadpoles. Later, after the infected tadpole becames a frog, it can be eaten by a snake or carnivorous mammal, thus spreading the infection to the snake or mammal host. Ecologically, snakes are important hosts and can spread infections to human. In this case, the snake is called a paratenic host or transport host.

Fig. 4. . Life cycle of *S. erinacei*. Dogs or cats (A) pass the egg (B) through feces into the soil. When the egg is incubated in water, the egg becomes a coracidium (C). When the coracidium is eaten by a cyclops, the coracidium becomes a procercoid larva (D). When the infected cyclops is eaten by a tadpole, the procercoid larva becomes a plerocercoid larva (sparganum, E). The tadpole becomes frog (F), which is a prey animal of snakes (G). The snake is a paratenic host in this case. When a dog or cat (H) eats the snake or frog, the larva becomes adult. Humans (I) can be infected with sparganum after ingesting larva-infected raw snake or frog, or by drinking contaminated water. Very rarely, the adult sparganum worm grows in human small intestines.

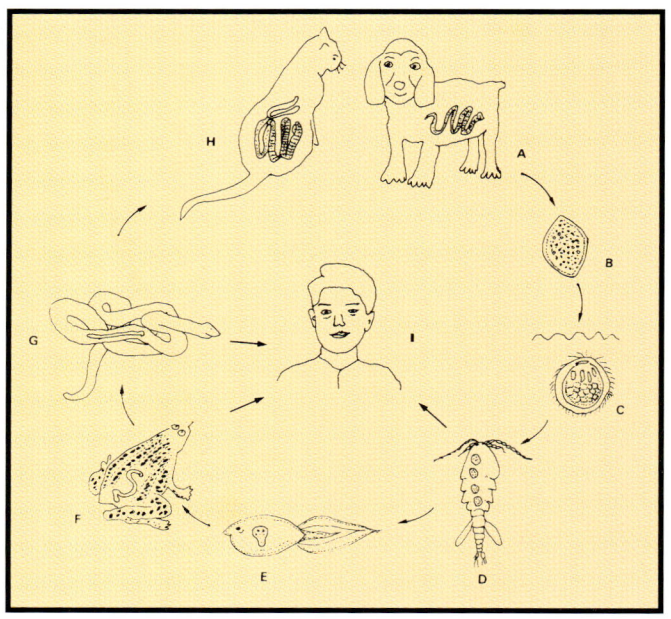

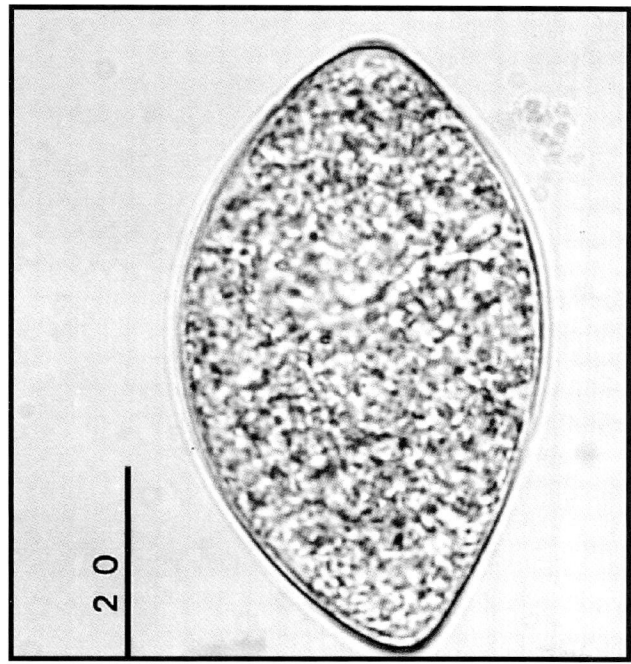

Fig. 5. Egg of *S. erinacei* from an experimental cat. Bar unit: μm (courtesy of Dr. Woon-Mok Sohn).

In a laboratory experiment, parasite embryos were exposed to different temperatures throughout the incubation period. The embryos hatched in:

6-9 days	at 35° C
12-14 days	at 28° C
8-14 days	at 29° C
10-14 days	at 23° C

At hatching, the sizes of the larva coracidium were 38.3-48.5 μm (mean 43.8 μm) X 31.9-45.9 μm (mean 36.9 μm).

Coracidium is eaten by cyclops and exists in the body cavity of cyclops, the first intermediate host. Many cyclops have been known as the first intermediate host in experimental infections (Li, 1929; Kobayashi, 1931; Lee et al., 1990, Fig. 6):

Cyclops affinis
Cyclops phaleratus
Cyclops magnus
Cyclops vicinus
Cyclops bicuspidatus
Cyclops serrulatus (Eucyclops serrulatus)
Cyclops albidus
Cyclops oithonoides
Cyclops leuckarti (Mesocyclops leuckarti)
Cyclops diaphanus,
Cyclops sigatus
Cyclops phlexopedum
Cyclops soli
Cyclops fimbriatus
Cyclops viridis for *S. erinacei*

Three other cyclops species are known hosts for *S. mansonoides*: *Cyclops leuckarti, Cyclops viridis,* and *Cyclops vicuspididatus* (Mueller, 1938).

When eggs of *S. erinacei* were used in laboratory life-cycle experiments, coracidiums become procercoid after their entry into the cyclops. The sizes of the procercoids varies from 56-142 μm X 20-72 μm. Thirteen days postinfection (PI), the procercoids reach maximum mean size: 107.4- 64.6 μm. At five days PI, the calcium corpuscle and the spine appears. The procercoids can begin to infect tadpoles 10- 20 days PI; and infectivity of procercoids to tadpoles is 13-22%. Finally, 30 days PI, the procercoid degenerates.

Tadpoles harbor the plerocercoids in their mesenteries 20 days PI. At that time, plerocercoids include numerous calcium corpuscles, and the minute spine at the anterior end of the procercoids has disappeared. At 32 days PI, plerocercoids in tadpoles grow to lengths up to 2.40-5.50 mm X 0.35-0.55 mm.

Recovery rate of plerocercoids from experimentally infected mice is 6.3 % during 10-20 days PI, when mice were infected with procercoids 17-19 days old. When mice were infected from tadpoles with plerocercoids aged 15-30 days, the recovery rate is 59-84%. When felines and canines are infected with the plerocercoid from tadpoles, eggs are found in the host stools 15-16 days PI.

Parasite eggs are measured as 35-36 μm X 65-69 μm. Adult worms recovered from dogs were 110 cm X 0.8 cm 6 weeks PI. The scolex measures 1.88 mm X 0.46 mm with two lateral bothria. Mature proglottid measures 0.94-2.33 mm X 6.03-9.99 mm. The uterine tubules coils 3 to 5 times. Gravid proglottids contain numerous eggs. A genital pore opens on the ventral midline near the anterior margin of gravid proglottids. Distal to the genital pore, the vagina opens like a slit. The uterine pore is distal to the vaginal pore near the proximal end of the uterine tubules. Mehlis glands and ovary are distal to uterine tubule. On the sagittal section of the gravid proglottid, the genital pore opens separately from the vaginal pore and a cirrus sac is surrounded by the seminal vesicle. Considering the period of the development of each stage, the whole life cycle from egg to egg passage of adult requires 48- 67 days (Lee et al., 1990).

EPIDEMIOLOGY

In Amoy, China, 1882, Manson recovered spargana from the tissue of a native body during an autopsy. Following that autopsy, spargana worms have been identified and reported throughout the world (Beaver et al., 1984a). The most common endemic area of sparganum is Korea and Japan. Since humans in those coun-

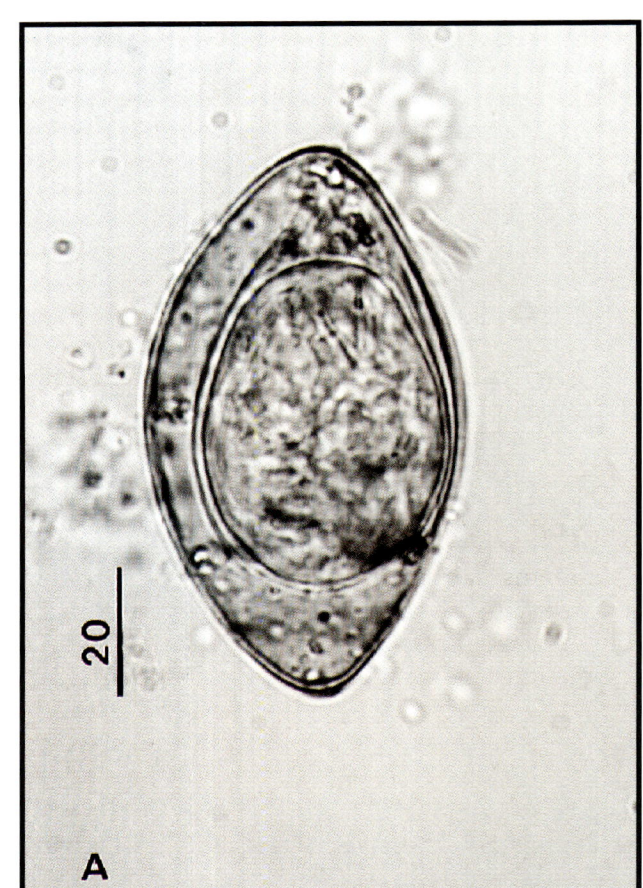

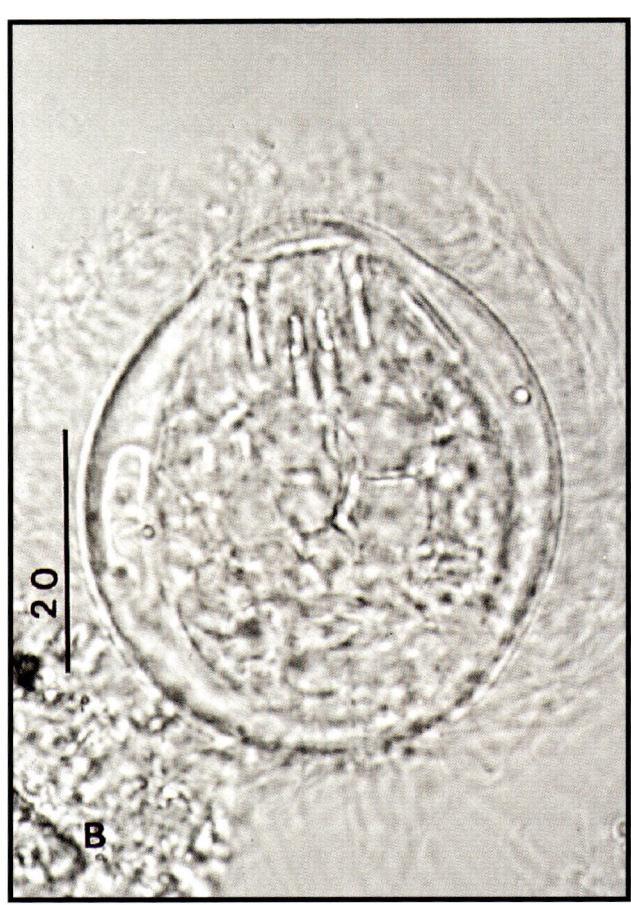

Fig. 6. A-D. Developmental stages of *S. erinacei*. Developing egg (A), coracidium (B), procercoid larvae in the cyclops (*Eucyclops* sp. C), and plerocercoid larva from tadpole (D). Bar unit: μm (courtesy of Dr. Woon-Mok Sohn, Inje University, Korea).

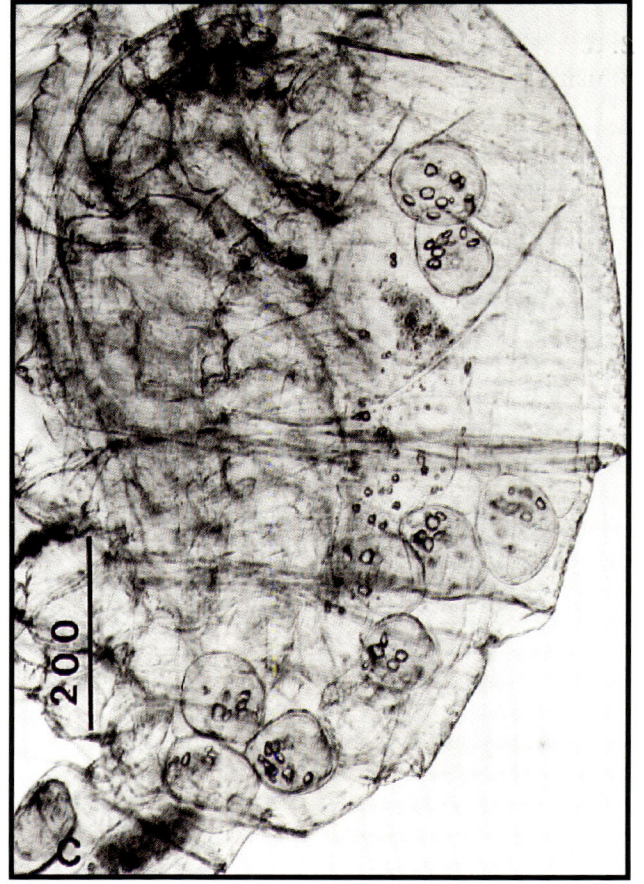

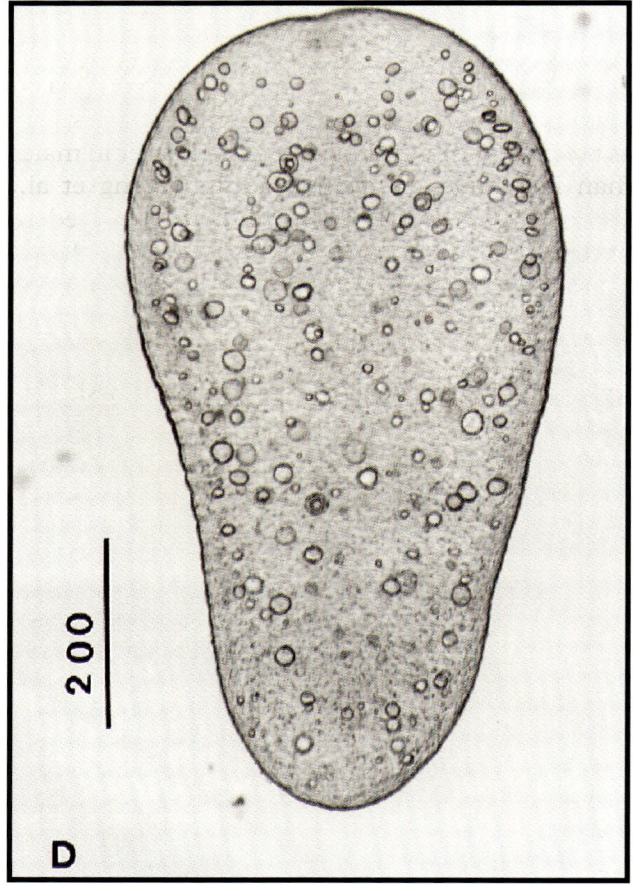

tries eat raw snake as a nutritious food, several hundred cases have been reported in those two countries alone. Sparganosis has also been reported in the following countries as listed here:
—China, Taiwan, Hong Kong (Ko, 1991)
—Philippines (Eduardo, 1991); Vietnam, Laos (Fontan et al., 1975)
—Thailand, India, Australia, East Timor (Munckhof et al., 1994)
—Java, Sumatura, Canary Island (Korean man, Mendez-Medina et al., 1983); Tanzania (Schmidt et al., 1972)
—Italy, Russia; Holland
—Malagasy, Mexico (Landero, 1991)
—Puerto Rico, Panama, Ecuador (Kron et al., 1991)
—Belize (British Honduras), Guyana, Uruguay, Colombia, Paraguay (Beaver et al, 1981); Brazil, Venezuela, Argentina (from Peru, de-Roodts, 1993); Chile (Torres et al., 1982)
—USA and Canada (imported case, Ali-Khan et al., 1973).

In the USA, more than 70 cases of sparganosis has been reported, mostly in the southeastern regions. In Guangxi, southern China, people of the Jiang tribe also eat raw snake.

The development of the serological diagnosis using enzyme-linked immunosorbent assay (ELISA) and radiological imaging would allow a greater number of sparganosis cases—especially cerebral sparganosis—to be detected.

In Korea, the standardized positive rate for anti-sparganum antibody in 850 normal adults was 1.7%. There were areas (Kangwon-do and Chollanam-do) where the positive rate was as high as 8%. The positive rate is ten times higher in males than in females in normal adults (Kong et al., 1994a). ELISA-positive persons are believed to have dormant infections. It is also believed that sparganum can survive in the host tissue for the natural life expectancy of the host.

Reservoir hosts of spargana are amphibians, reptiles, birds, and mammals such as black bears (*Ursus americanus*), African green monkeys (*Cerocoithecus aethiops*), and foxes. Since spargana can survive in swine (Smith et al., 1982), humans can become infected with sparganum by eating raw or undercooked pork. Secondary intermediate hosts or paratenic hosts in Korea include these snakes:
—*Elaphe schrenkii*
—*Elaphe dione*
—*Elaphe rufodorsata*
—*Rhadophis tigrina*
—*Dinodon rufozonatum rufozonatum*
—*Zamenis spinalis*
—*Agkistrodon halys*

The frog, *Rana nigromaculata*, is also known as a second intermediate or paratenic host in Korea. Korean mammalian hosts (Cho et al., 1973) are:
—*Lutreola sibiricus*
—*Charronia flavigula koreana*
—*Nyctereutes koreensis*
—*Vulpes vulpes*
—*Vulpes lupus*
—*Erinaceus amurensis koreens*
—*Sus scrofa domesticus*

Final hosts of *Spirometra* sp. are felines, canines, and other carnivorous mammals; such as *Felis geoffroy*, *F. yagouarondi*, *Dusycyon gymnocercus*, *Cerdocyon thous*, and bobcat.

SOURCES OF INFECTION

Humans can become infected with spargana through:
1. ingestion of raw or undercooked snake, frog, other animals that harbor the plerocercoid larvae
2. ingestion of water which contains cyclops infected with the procercoid larva
3. local application, in the form of a poultice, of the infected flesh of the reservoir host (such as a snake or frog) to the eye, skin, or vagina

In Korea, China, and Japan, ingestion of raw snake or frog is the most common source of infection of *Spirometra*. Of 45 cases in Korea, probable causes of infection were (in descending order of importance- Cho et al., 1975):
1. eating raw snake or frog (Fig. 7)
2. drinking untreated water
3. using eyedrops with frog muscle emulsions
4. eating other raw flesh of other kinds

In Korea, patients with sparganosis ate raw snakes for the following reasons, which are listed in descending order of popularity.
1. for potentiation of masculine activity
2. for therapy of tuberculosis, syphilis and joint pain
3. belief of special nutrition
4. gastronomic delicacy
5. for survival during combat training and field training

In southeast Asia, poultices made from the flesh of snakes or frogs are the most common source of infection. In America, Europe, and Australia, ingestion of cyclops in water is the most common source of sparganum infections.

PARASITE LONGEVITY

Mueller (1938) said that one of most distinct features of spargana is their great longevity. The worm can survive in subcutaneous tissues for the natural life expectancy of a mouse host. In studies of infected monkeys, no senility of worms was

Fig. 7. Soldiers who eat raw snake during their survival training period.

shown for several years. It is believed that sparganum can survive for a period of 20 years, and possibly as long as the natural lifespan of humans. In one case study, a 41-year-old man who was diagnosed with cerebral sparganosis had eaten raw frog and snake 20 years before the diagnosis (Chang et al., 1987).

CLINICAL MANIFESTATION, PATHOLOGICAL FINDINGS, AND PATHOGENESIS

Clinical manifestations of sparganosis depend on the site of infection. The most common sites are subcutaneous tissue and fascia of abdominal wall, thoracic wall, lower limbs, neck and scrotum. Other possible sites of infection are: body cavities, eyes, breasts, central nervous system, spinal canal, urinary bladder, urinary tract, and submucosa of intestinal wall. The next several paragraphs describe clinical manifestations of sparganosis at different sites of infection.

CLINICAL MANIFESTATIONS

Subcutaneous or Fascial Sparganosis

The clinical manifestation of a subcutaneous or fascial infestation is a palpable mass that is migrating, fixed, indolent, or reddening. Itching is another manifestation of infection. Subcutaneous sparganosis can be complicated by the formation of abscesses or by subcutaneous hemorrhage. Histopathological findings of subcutaneous sparganosis are described following this list of sites of infection.

Scrotal sparganosis

Manifestations of scrotal sparganosis are similar to those of other subcutaneous sparganosis. However, because of its location, it is more liable to be complicated by hemorrhage, and the patient will likely experience more severe discomfort. Scrotal sparganosis can be incidentally found without a palpable mass or any complaints during other operations.

Ocular sparganosis

The clinical manifestations of ocular sparganosis are: a migratory mass in the vision field, conjunctivitis, eyelid mass, ptosis, exopthalmosis, restricted eye movement, and ocular pain (Shin et al., 1980; Kittiponghansa et al., 1988).

Abdominal Cavity Infections

If the person is infected by sparganosis in the abdominal cavity, clinical manifestations are: peritonitis, acute abdomen due to hemorrhage, and epigastric discomfort with palpable mass.

Oral Sparganosis

Although submucosal infection is rare, retropharyngeal abscesses have been reported.

Infections of the Urinary Tract

In some patients, vesical sparganosis is caused by eosinophilic cystitis. Such a patient presents with a mass in the urinary bladder, along with peripheral eosinophila. The characteristic sinuous necrosis, which represents the worm tract, was noted with massive diffuse infiltration of eosinophils in the wall of the bladder (Oh et al., 1993). Infection of the urethral orifice manifests as a regional mass with hematuria, dysuria, and the subsequent appearance of worms at the urethral orifice.

Intramural Jejunal Sparganosis

Intramural sparganosis of jejunum manifests as an intestinal obstruction (Cho et al., 1987).

Spinal Cord Sparganosis

Infection at this site manifests as acute chest pain, paraplegia, loss of sensation below the involved spinal level, and urinary incontinence (Park et al., 1983; Cho et al., 1992).

Cerebral Sparganosis

The most serious—even fatal—form of sparganosis is cerebral sparganosis. Clinical findings are headache, generalized seizure, hemiparesis, dysarthria, tonic/clonic seizure, hemianopsia, focal seizure, or mental retardation (Chang et al., 1987; Lee et al., 1987). The histological findings of cerebral sparganosis are described below, after the discussion of subcutaneous sparganosis.

HISTOPATHOLOGICAL FINDINGS OF SUBCUTANEOUS SPARGANOSIS

Histopathological findings of subcutaneous sparganosis are fairly characteristic. Grossly, the lesion is composed of an elongated tract—like a cavity—with or without the worm. Tissue reaction is localized around the worm. Along the tract of the moving parasite, the host tissue is destroyed. As the host tissue is destroyed, it becames necrotic, with nuclear debris, fibrin deposits, and inflammatory cells. The lesion is not encapsulated.

The cavity made by the moving worm is quite characteristic. It differs from microbial abscesses in three ways. First, the lumen of the cavity is generally empty, sometimes includes a small amount of serous fluid or blood. Second, the inner margin of the cavity is serrated, indicating the previously expanded portions of worm. After the movement of the worm to another place, the cavity becomes partially collapsed. Third, the wall of the cavity shows distinctive zonal phenomena in layers. First, there is a thin, innermost layer composed of fibrin, necrotic debris, and eosinophils. The next layer is composed of a band of macrophages and

fibroblasts. A sprinkling of lymphocytes can be seen in this layer. The outer layer is a broad zone which expands into the surrounding fibroadipose muscular tissue. This broad zone consists of granulation tissue and lymphocytic infiltration.

Macrophages occasionally harbor the cytoplasmic calcium corpuscles which are apparently derived from the worm. This shows that the degenerating parasite body is absorbed by the host. It is possible that the worm separates its posterior portion from its anterior portion when its scolex moves to another location. Charcot-Leyden crystals are rarely seen in lesions (Chi et al., 1980, Figs. 8 & 9).

In the experimental sparganosis of mice, numerous eosinophils, neutrophils, lymphocytes, and plasma cells infiltrated focally around the worms two weeks after infection. Those cells surrounded the worms to form a layer of inflammatory reaction four weeks PI. Also, histiocytes and fibroblasts began to appear around the inflammatory cells four weeks PI. At ten weeks PI, worms are encircled by thin, fibrous layers. Six months PI, worms are surrounded by either fibrous tissue or active inflammatory cells. The inflammation is more severe in the tracts left by the worm rather than around the worm itself (Hong et al., 1989).

HISTOLOGICAL FINDINGS OF CEREBRAL SPARGANOSIS

Histological findings of cerebral sparganosis are characterized as a central, irregular, cystic structure that contains an irregular, degenerating worm and fibrin exudate. The cystic wall consists of collagenous fibrous tissue. This tissue is surrounded by an infiltrate of lymphocytes and plasma cells, and by edematous brain tissue gliosis (Chang et al., 1987; Anders et al., 1984, Figs. 10-11). When the worm migrates to another area, the remaining lesion has a tunnel-like appearance, and consists of granulation tissue and the calcium corpuscles (Lee et al., 1987).

Experimental sparganosis of feline brains revealed gross features in the acute phase (two weeks PI): hemorrhagic defects in the parenchyma, and living worms in the parenchyma of the frontal or temporal lobes. Around worms in the white matter, microscopic findings consisted of exudate, capillary proliferation, infiltration of polymorphonuclear leukocytes, lymphocytes, and microglia. Around the tracts, microscopic findings consisted of vascular congestion, edema, pyknosis, and hemosiderin-laden macrophages. In the tracts, microscopic findings consisted of exudate, astrocytes, inflammatory cells, and macrophages (Fig. 11).

In the chronic phase (1 or 3 months PI), gross findings were multiple hemorrhagic defects in the

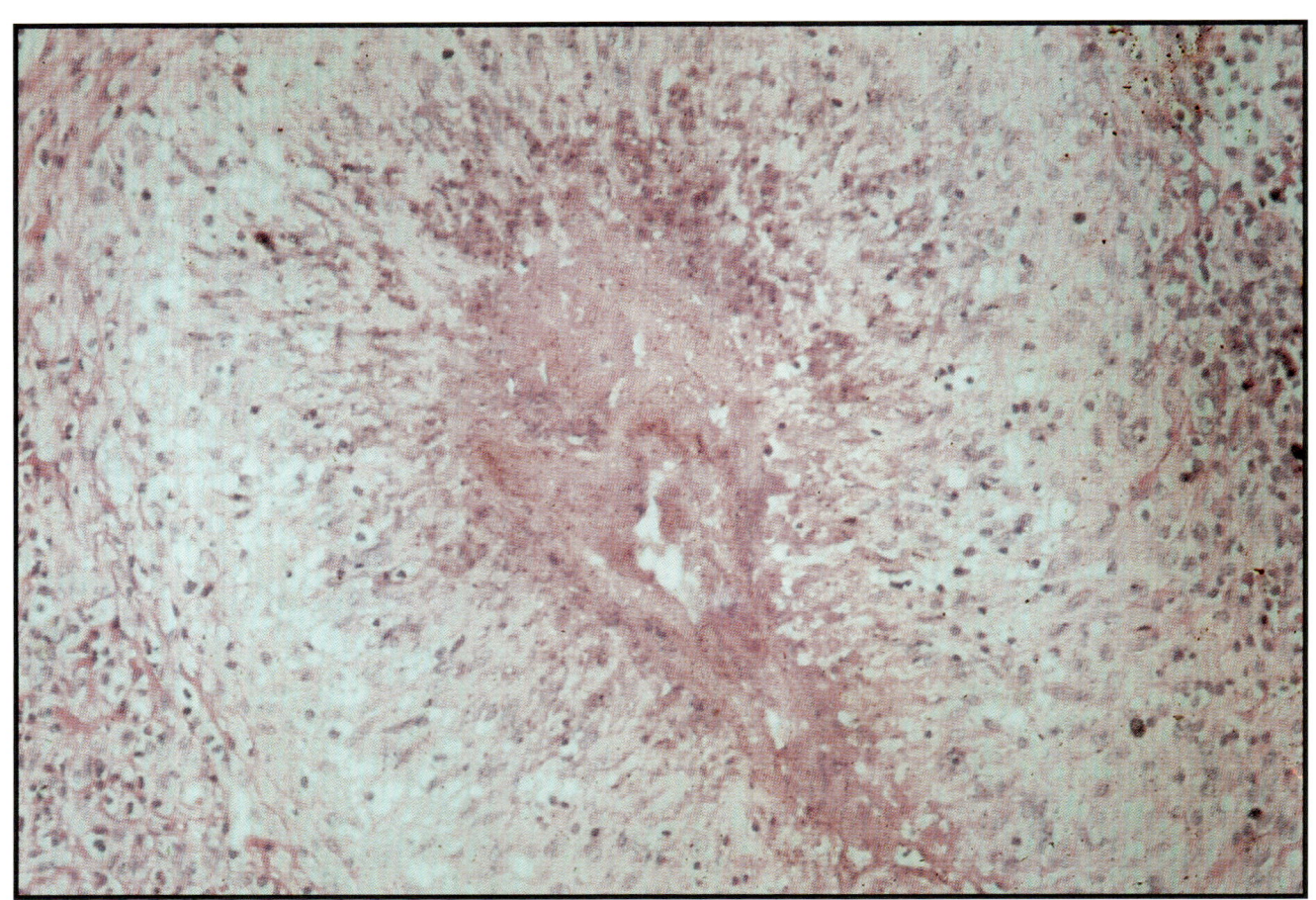

Fig. 8. Histopathological change of tissue infected with sparganum. Degenerated worm is at the center. Around the degenerated worm, the thin, innermost layer is composed of fibrin, necrotic debris, and eosinophils. The next layer is composed of a band of macrophages and fibroblast. The outer layer is a broad zone which expands into the surrounding fibroadipose muscular tissue, and consists of granulation tissue and lymphocytic infiltration. H & E, X 100 (courtesy of Dr. Je G. Chi, Seoul National University, Korea).

Fig. 9. Sparganum recovered from resected soft tissue (courtesy of Dr. Je G. Chi, Seoul National University, Korea).

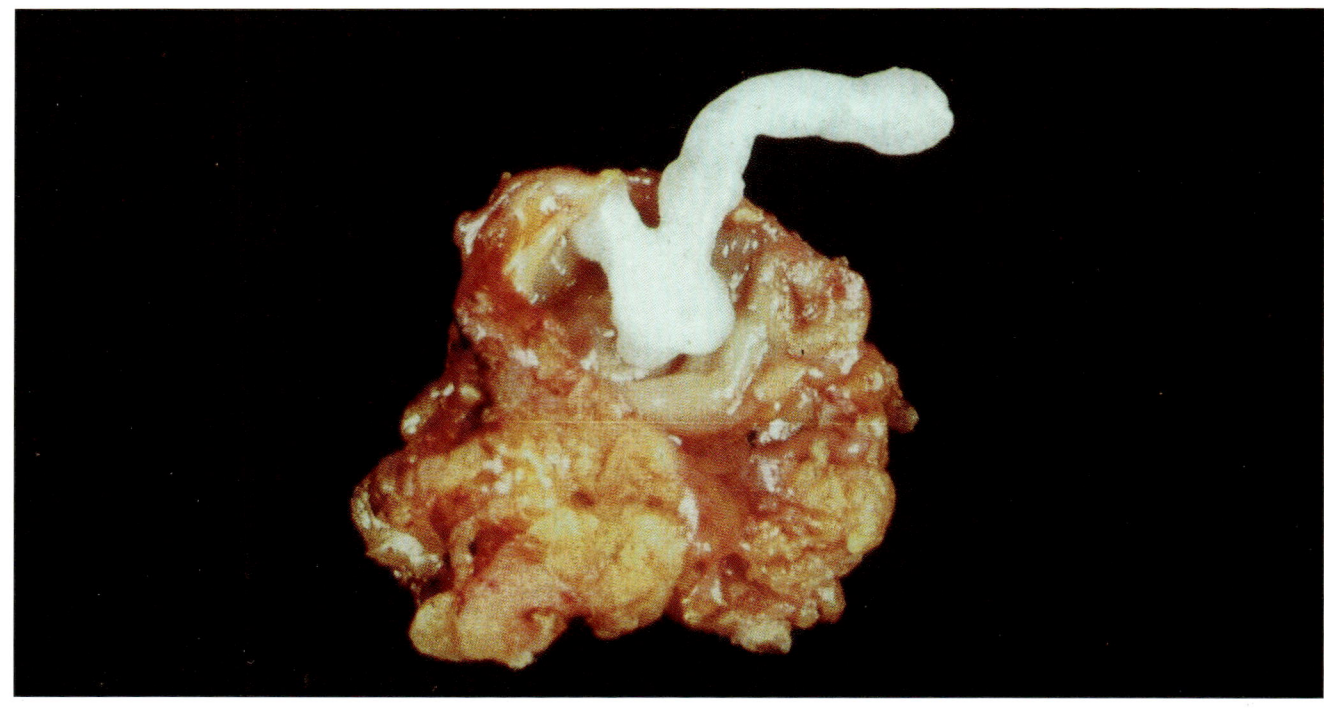

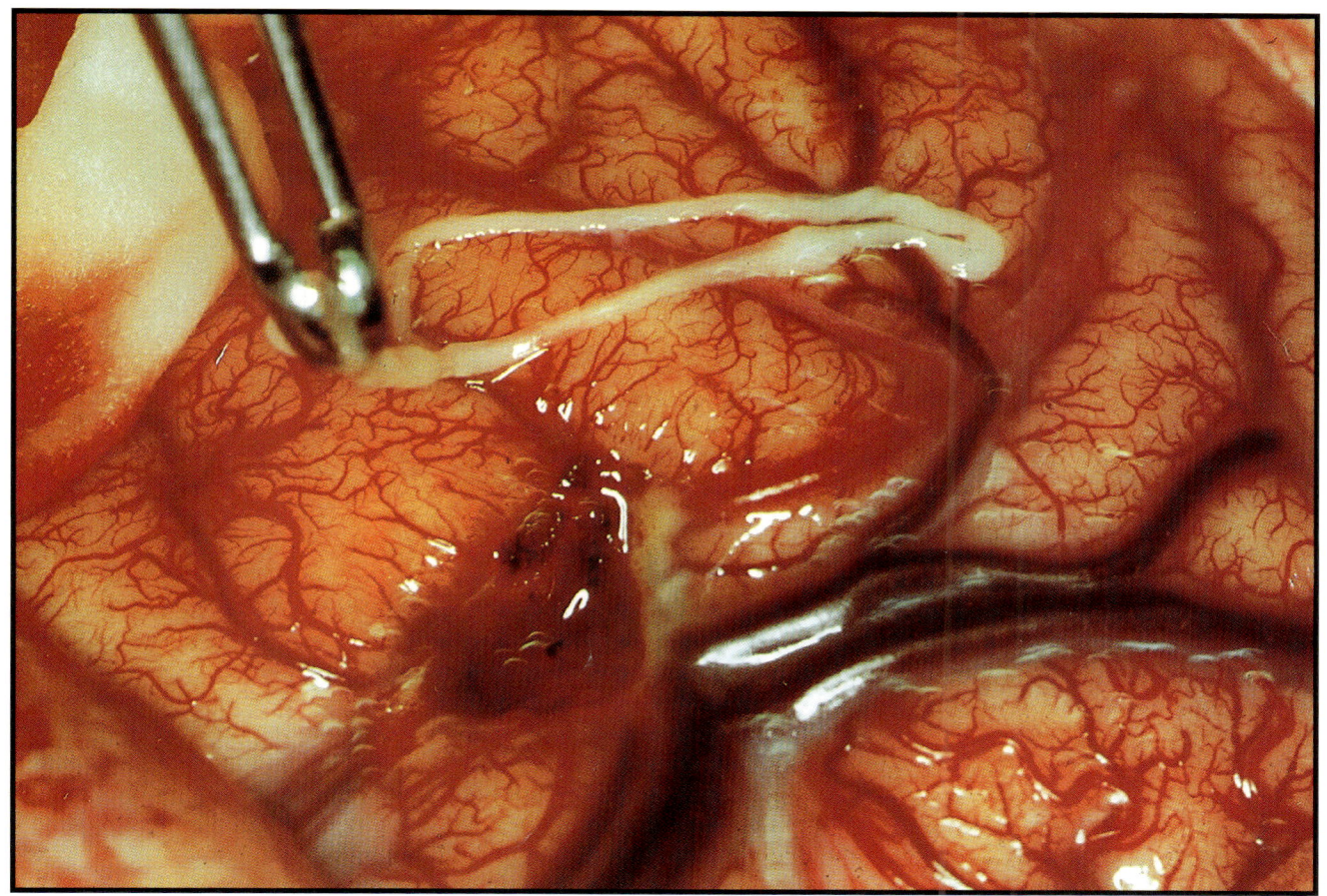

Fig. 10. Sparganum on the surface of the brain during an operation (courtesy of Dr. Je G. Chi, Seoul National University, Korea).

white matter of the frontal lobe, cerebellum, and brain stem. Microscopic findings consisted of exudate, RBCs, inflammatory cells, and hemosiderin-laden macrophages in the tracts; thin, collagen fibers surrounding a dead worm; and hemorrhage, inflammatory cells, and gliosis around the worms (Huh et al., 1993b).

PATHOGENESIS AND IMMUNOLOGY

How do spargana migrate, and how does the parasite evade the immune mechanism of the host? There is no proteolytic gland in the scolex of the sparganum. However, proteolytic enzymes are present in the scolex, and only alkaline phosphatase activity was demonstrated by Kwa (1972a & b). Since then, several kinds of enzymes have been identified as involved in the penetration of and immune reaction to sparganum.

Plerocercoid neutral extracts contain acid thiol proteinase activity against azocoll, actin, and myosin (Nakamura, 1984). Fukase et al. (1985) isolated 19/21 kDa protein that has amidolytic activity with N-alpha-benzoyl-DL-argininie-para-nitroanilide. This activity is maximum at pH 7.0; the activity was decreased significantly in the presence of thiol proteinase inhibitor and pepstatin. Recently, 28 kDa cysteine proteinase was purified and characterized.

This enzyme cleaved the collagen chains into three identical products, and it showed only minor activity toward hemoglobin. Antibody from the infected person recognized the cysteine proteinase (Song et al., 1993). Antigenic 31 and 36 kDa proteins from the excretory-secretory products (ESP) exhibit specific activity of protease. This phenomenum supports the evidence of secretion of cysteine protease from sparganum (Cho et al., 1992).

Three additional novel proteases were isolated from ESP. These three proteases are different in their characteristics from cysteine proteinase of the sparganum. The trypsin-like proteinase of 198 and 104 kDa degraded collagen completely within 24 hours. The chymotrypsin-like 36 kDa enzyme cleaved human-recombinant interferon-gamma and bovine myelin basic protein. All three enzymes have a role in penetrating the tissue and in evading the immune reaction of the host. In addition, all three enzymes elicited strong antibody response in the infected persons (Kong et al. , 1994b).

When IgG is incubated with spargana, it is cleaved into Fab and Fc fragments. Fab/Fc fragments are also hydrolyzed. The enzyme responsible for both cleavage and hydrolization, 27 (±0.8) kDa, is purified from worm extract or ESP. The partial amino-acid sequence of this enzyme was Leu-Pro-Asp-Ser-

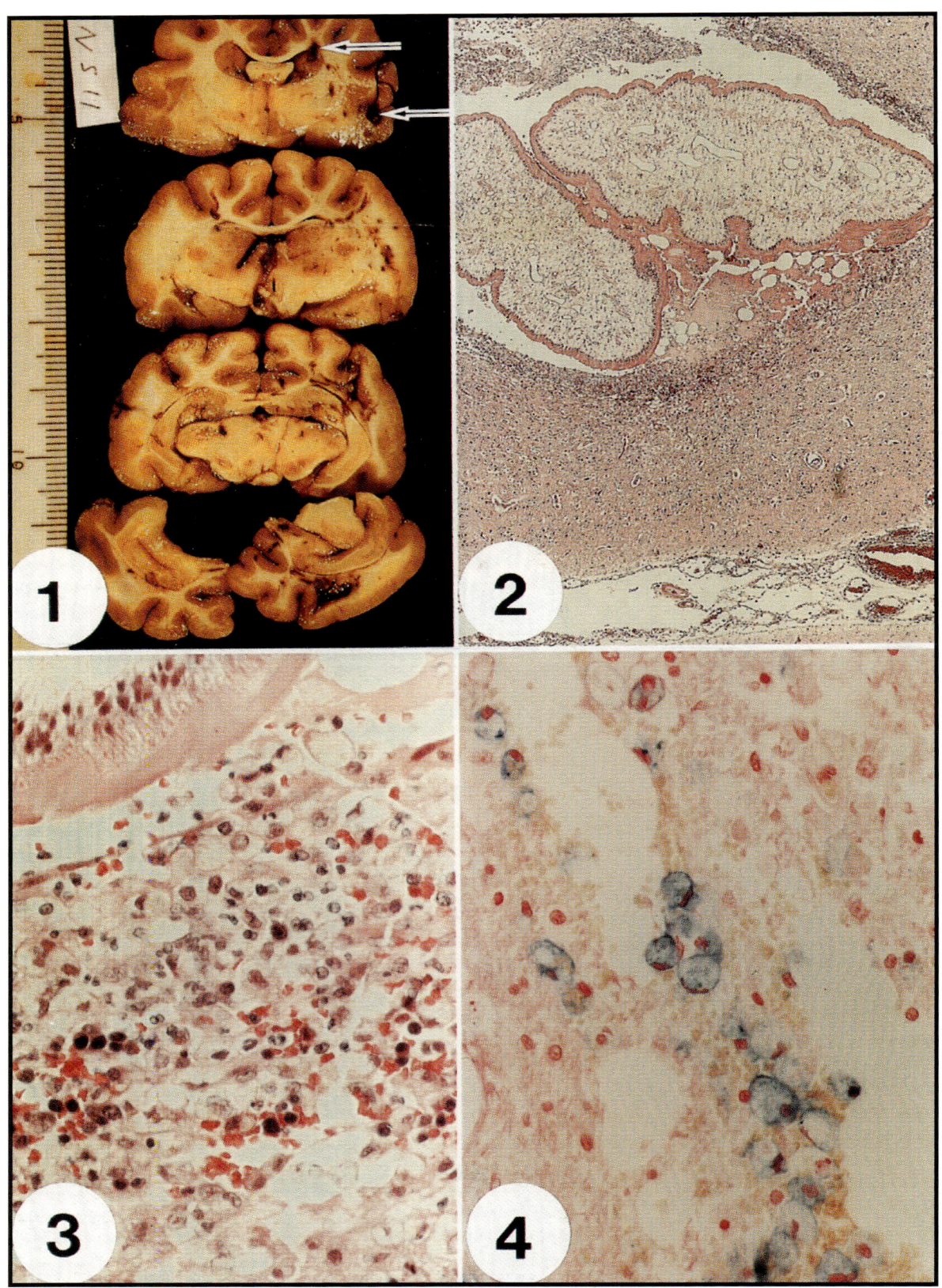

Fig. 11. Histopathological findings from a cat brain, two weeks post-inoculation to cerebrum. 1: Multiple hemorrhagic lesion (arrows) of the brain parenchyma were found in the frontal and temporal lobes. 2: The hemispheric white matter around the living worm, 3 mm deep to the right posterior sigmoid gyrus, showed a defect in the parenchyma, with exudate, capillary congestion, hemorrhage, and cell infiltration. H & E, X 40. 3: A magnified view of previous figures (2) showing numerous, extravasated RBCs, polymorphonuclear leukocytes, lymphocytes, and macrophages around the intact tegument of a worm (left upper). H & E, X 400. 4: High-power view of the margin of an empty worm tract, showing slight edema, scattered pyknotic neurons, and numerous hemosiderin laden macrophages (blue cytoplasm). Prussian blue stain, X 400 (Huh et al., 1993b).

Val-Asn-Trp-Flu-Gly-Ala-Val-Thr-Ala-Val. This partial sequence showed 80% homology to human cathepsin S. Hence, cleavage of immunoglobulin by an excreted-secreted, cathepsin S-like, allergenic protease is also proposed as one of the mechanisms by which sparganum evades the host immune system (Kong et al., 1994c).

The protein, 53 kDa was purified from spargana. The protein revealed weak activity and exhibited IgE response in the patient sera. This enzyme was suggested as a pro- or preproenzyme, processed to a proenzyme, then further processed to a mature form. Another explanation is that, due to its large size, it is dimer of the two enzymes (Kong et al., 1996). Monoclonal antibody that was reacting to 36 and 29 kDa cysteine protease in the ESP was localized at the tegumental syncythium and tegumental cells. Kim et al. (1992) suggested that the potent antigenic proteins of 36 and 29 kDa were produced at the tegumental cell and then transported to the syncythium.

Until now, six different proteases were characterized:
—a 21 kDa cysteine protease (Fukase et al., 1985)
—a 27 kDa cathepsin S like cysteine protease (Song et al., 1993; Kong et al., 1994b)
—a 36 kDa chymase, a 104 kDa trypticase, and a 198 kDa trypticase (Kong et al., 1994b)
—a 53 kDa cysteine protease

Of those proteases, the cysteine protease of 21, 27, and 53 kDa were reactive with IgE, but were weakly reactive with IgG when compared to 36, 104 and 198 kDa neutral protease. Later enzymes are potent antigens in enzyme-linked immunosorbent assays for the serological diagnosis of sparganosis.

In experimental mice, sparganum-specific IgG in serum begins to increase from four weeks PI. Sparganum-specific IgG levels reached a plateau after three months PI (Hong et al., 1989). In experimental intracranial sparganosis of felines, the specific IgG in the cerebrospinal fluid and in serum also begins to increase from four weeks PI. It continues to increases untill three months PI (Wang et al., 1990). It is estimated that the serologic reaction by IgG might be detected from four weeks PI in infected humans also.

GROWTH HORMONE (GH)-LIKE ACTION OF SPARGANUM IN EXPERIMENTAL ANIMALS

Sparganum-infected mice gain weight. This aspect of the host-parasite relationship is very interesting. The mechanism by which sparganum promotes the growth of the host is through the secretion of a plerocercoid growth factor (PGF), which is associated with increased somatostatin production, suppressed pituitary gland secretion, and suppressed blood GH levels. PGF has a different character than that of GH. GH enhances lean growth, with a net loss of fat; PGF stimulates growth, with fattening. Rodents infected with sparganum exhibit increased fat mass; elevated serum triglycerides, cholesterol, and total lipids; and enhanced activity of plasma lipoprotein lipase, hepatic acetyl CoA carboxylase, and fatty acid synthesase (Salem et al., 1986; Tsuboi et al., 1986). Also, in mice, sparganum stimulates cell division in epiphyseal cartilage by enhancing the serum somatostatin activity in its host (Shiwaku et al., 1986).

SPARGANUM PROLIFERUM

Sparganum proliferum is a proliferating form of sparganum. A total of 12 cases of sparganum proliferum infection has been reported (Nakamura, 1990). It is still not known whether this proliferating form is an aberrant form of nonproliferating sparganosis or a new group of proliferating larvae of pseudophyllidean tapeworms (Noya et al., 1992).

DIAGNOSIS

SURGERY

Definitive diagnosis of sparganosis (including subcutaneous sparganosis) is confirmed by surgical biopsy or excisional surgery of the involved tissue, Diagnosis is confirmed by identifying the worm or the worm tract with the histological findings described previously in this discussion. Diagnosis can be assisted by knowing whether or not the patient has a history of eating raw snakes or frogs, drinking mountain water (which may contain procercoid-infected cyclops), or using poultices made from raw snake or frog. The value of preoperative diagnosis in subcutaneous tissue is limited, since currently there is no drug effective in treating sparganosis.

RADIOLOGICAL DIAGNOSIS

It is difficult to differentiate subcutaneous sparganosis from other soft tissue masses (such as lipoma or other granulomata) with simple radiography because granulation by sparganum is shown as radiolucent lesions. However, ultrasonography can be used to help differentiate the lesions. It is also possible to predict the sparganosis if there is a long, radiolucent tract under the long and slender radioopaque mass. The exudate near the sparganum will make a contrast in the image (Park et al., 1993).

Computerized tomography (CT), combined with serologic diagnosis, is essential for correctly diagnosing intracranial sparganosis. The most common and characteristic triad of findings in 34 patients were:
—white-matter hypodensity with adjacent ventricular dilatation (88%)
—irregular or nodular enhancing lesion (88%)
—small punctuate calcification (76%)

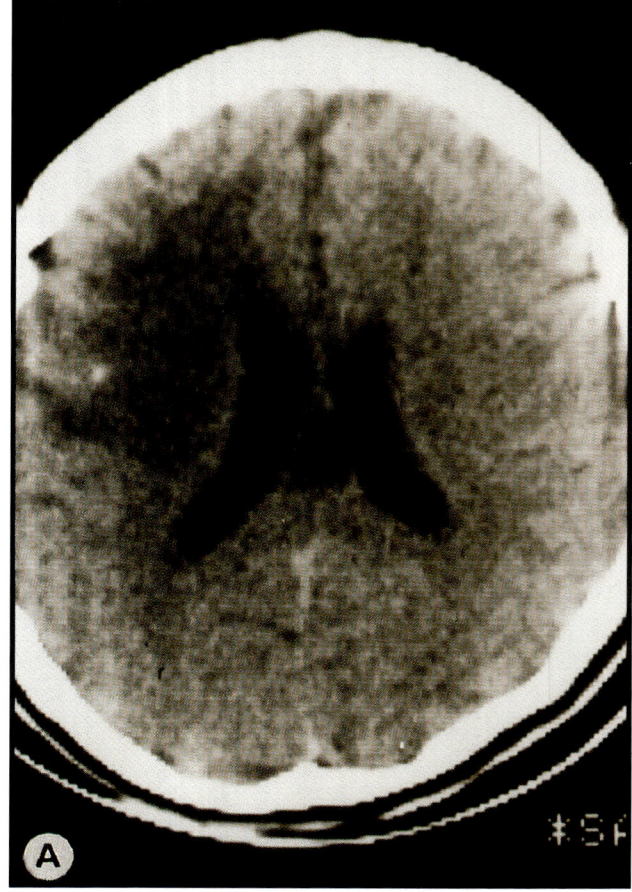 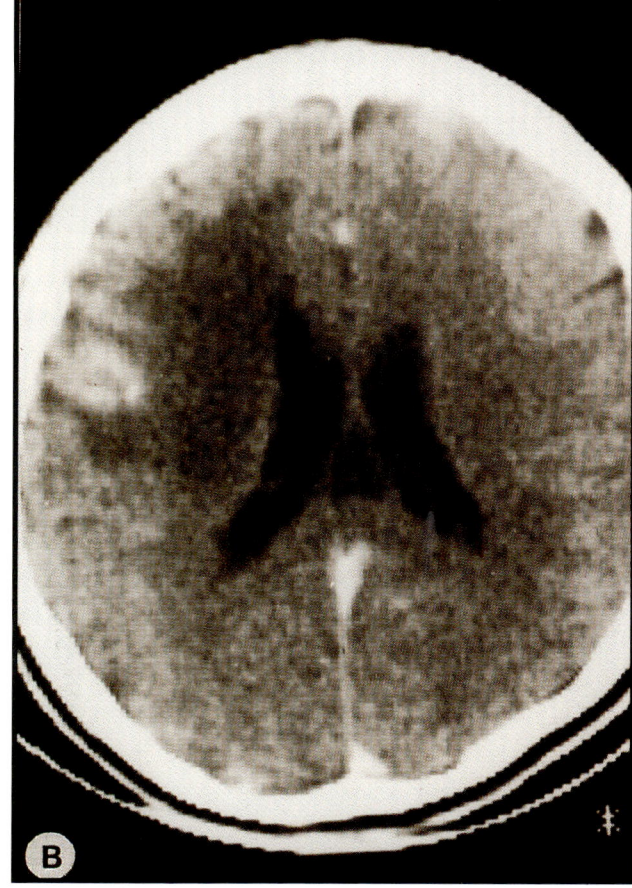

Fig. 12 A & B. CT features of cerebral sparganosis. Nonenhanced brain CT (A) in a 35-year-old man with hemiparesis and seizures for 5 years. This CT shows an ill-defined area of low density in the right parietal lobe and a tiny calcification therein. A contrast-enhanced CT scan (B) of the same patient shows an ill-defined localized contrast enhancement in the cortical area of the right frontal lobe. At surgery, live sparganum was removed (courtesy of Dr. Kee-Hyun Chang, Seoul National University, Korea).

This triad appears to be specific and was noted in 62% of the cases.

It is not possible with a single CT scan to determine whether a worm is alive or dead. If sequential CT scans indicate that the location of the enhancing nodule has changed or that the other CT findings have worsened, the worm is probably alive, and the patient is a candidate for surgery. CT findings are well correlated with pathological findings after craniotomy, as described in the previous section (Chang et al., 1987 & 1992).

White-matter degenerations are slightly hypointense on T1-weighted images and are hyperintense on T2-weighted images. When magnetic resonance (MR) findings are compared with those of CT, the white-matter degenerations are seen as areas of low attenuation in CT. Better contrast between normal white matter and white-matter degeneration was seen with MR. The parasitic granuloma is isodense to brain parenchyma on images obtained with all MR pulse sequences. As with CT, in follow-up examinations, changes in the location or shape of the enhancing lesions suggests migra-tion of the worm. However, although MR shows better contrast of tissues, sometimes MR misses the calcification that is seen in CT. When attempting to diagnose sparganoisis, consider using MR and CT as complementary scans (Moon, 1993, Figs. 12-13).

SEROLOGIC DIAGNOSIS

Although the usefulness of preoperative diagnosis is limited, serologic diagnosis still has value.

1. First, some areas (such as Korea) experience higher incidences of sparganosis, where the population eats or used to eat raw snake or frog (Cho et al., 1975). Also, patients who suffer neurological disease (such as epilepsy) are very good subjects for the field screening (Kong et al., 1994a). A serological approach is reasonable for patients in either area or group.

2. Patients who have had sparganum worms removed through surgery must be checked to make sure they are free of infection by one or more remaining worms. In one case, 12 worms were removed in a sequence of surgeries from a single patient (Lee et al., 1967).

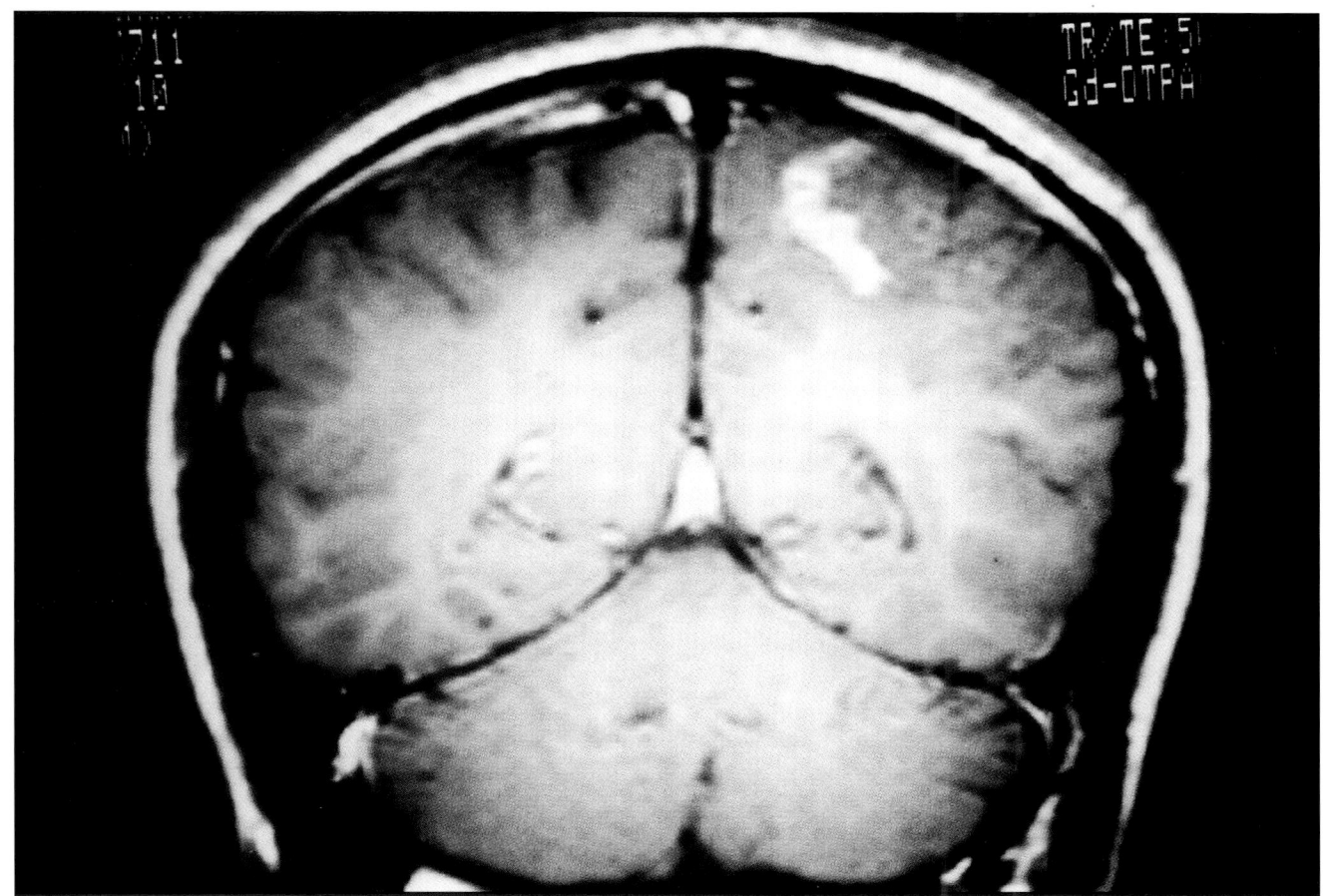

Fig. 13. MR image of cerebral sparganosis. Contrast-enhanced coronal T1-weighted MR image of 40-year-old man reveals a curvilinear enhancing lesion with a somewhat beaded appearance in the left parietal lobe. At surgery, a degenerated worm was found (courtesy of Dr. Kee-Hyun Chang, Seoul National University, Korea).

3. In surgical pathology, a specimen without a worm present is sometimes difficult to differentiate from other parasitic diseases or other granulomatous diseases. In those cases, serologic results can help to differentiate sparganum from other diseases (Kim et al., 1984).

4. It is difficult to diagnose sparganosis when the worm is in the cranial cavity or in the spine. The mass must be differentiated from other infectious, fungal, hemorrhagic or neoplastic lesions. Preoperative diagnosis alters the operation procedure and area, since an approach to the central nervous system is sometimes dangerous—especially when the lesion is in the brain stem. In accordance with radiological findings, serological methods are very useful for the preoperative diagnosis (Chang et al., 1987).

Enzyme-linked immunosorbent assay (ELISA) was developed and adapted for the patients in Korea. Korean physicians now use ELISA as a routine screening method to check for sparganum-specific IgG in intracranial masses. Its sensitivity was 95.6% and its specificity was 89.0% (Kong et al., 1991). In the interpretation of the results, the cross-reaction between *Taenia saginata* infection, paragonimiasis or *Taenia solium* metacestode infection (cysticercosis) should be considered. In a comparison of the test results from both normal and epileptic populations in Korea, tests of the normal population produced a positive rate of 1.9%, while tests of epileptic patients produced a positive rate of 2.3%. Odds ratio of the antibody was 1.32, which indicated an ambiguous etiologic factor for epilepsy (Kong et al. 1994a).

When the antigenic protein band reacted with a patient's sera, out of 30 identified protein bands in the worm extract, 29 (=31) and 36 kDa were the strongest. They frequently reacted with specific antibody in the sera (Choi et al., 1988). Antigenic proteins of 31 (previously 29) and 36 kDa in crude extract of sparganum were purified by affinity chromatography using either monoclonal antibody or gelatin as ligand. When 31 and 36 kDa is applied instead of crude antigen, the specificity increases from 89.0% to 95.6% (Cho et al., 1990; Kong et al., 1991). ELISA using that purified antigen is specific enough to differentiate human sparganosis from gnathostomiass, angiostrongyliasis, and trichinellosis (Morakote et al., 1993). ELISA is stable and simple to perform; currently, it is the best available serologic diagnostic tool.

TREATMENT

Currently, sparganosis cannot be treated except by surgical removal of the worm or lesion. With subcutaneous sparganosis, surgical results are excellent. A laminectomy is required to remove a worm in the spine. A craniotomy is required to remove a worm in the cranial cavity, and prognosis is good if there is no sequele or complications from the operation.

Although praziquantel is highly effective in destroying spargana in vitro, damaged larvae still have infectivity to mice (Sohn et al., 1993a). Praziquantel is not effective in mice (Lee et al., 1986a). Also, praziquantel was administered without success to treat human sparganosis (Chai et al., 1988). Praziquantel is much more effective in successfully treating the adult form of the parasite, *Spirometra*, while having little effect on spargana.

The greatest problem in treating sparganoisis is the possibility of the dormant existence of another worm in the body (Lee et al., 1967). ELISA should be used to check for the specific antibody during the follow-up period of a sparganosis patient. If the antibody level does not decrease six months to one year after the operation, it is possible that another dormant infection exists.

Treatment of proliferating sparganum is the same as that for non-proliferating sparganosis. A single dose of 10 mg/kg praziquantel can deworm a patient for adult forms of the worm (*Spirometra*) in the small intestine while having little or no effect on the spargana.

PREVENTION

Prevention of sparganosis is easily achieved by refraining from:
—eating raw snake or frog
—using a poultice made with raw snake or frog
—drinking untreated or unboiled water from springs or mountain sources.

It is difficult to control sparganosis in the final host, such as felines or canines. Also, it is not possible to control cyclops in water sources. The life cycle of *Spirometra* sp. is well-established in nature; thus, controlling the ingestion of spargana or procercoid larvae is the only measure for preventing human infection with this long-lived larval worm.

MESOCESTOIDES LINEATUS INFECTION

Mesocestoides lineatus, first found in canines, is a rare cestode that infects humans. Until recently, no complete life cycle had been identified. To date, only 25 human cases of *M. lineatus* have been reported.

MORPHOLOGY AND LIFE CYCLE

Adult worms measure up to 136 cm in length and 2 mm in width. Individual, free, gravid proglottids range 2.10-2.25 mm in length and 1.25-1.43 mm in width. The worm has a neck, and the worm's scolex has four suckers without hooklets. Mature proglottids measure 0.75-1.80 x 1.10-1.05 mm.

The parauterine organ of the worm measures 0.40-0.60 mm x 0.41 x 0.735 mm. The parauterine organ is located posterior to the uterus on the midline and measures 0.25-0.28 mm x 0.24-0.25 mm. Ovaries are bilobed, and the posterior of the cestode measures 80-130 μm in length. Testes pre- or post-ovarian, 42 to 54 in number, measure 35-89 μm x 3-68 μm. The cirrus is oval, preequatorial, and measures 120-170 μm x 75-100 μm. Eggs are oval with thin walls, and they measure 28-34 μm x 20-29 μm. Eggs contain the hexcanthoembryo (Fig. 14-15).

No complete life cycle is known for *M. lineatus*. A unique larval form, the tetrathyeidium, is commonly found in mammalian, avian, and reptile intermediate hosts, and it is readily infective to predatory definitive hosts. However, the eggs of *M. lineatus* do not infect vertebrates. Therefore, some other creature must be the first intermediate host for the worm. It is this first intermediate host which has not yet been identified.

Webster (1949) postulated that the first intermediate host of *Mesocestoides* is a terrestrial carnivorous arthropod. It is known that the second and paratenic hosts include 20 species of mammals, 15 species of avians, and 34 species of rep-

Fig. 14. Mature and gravid proglottids and eggs of *Mesocestoides lineatus*. A: Mature proglottid, ventral view. B: Gravid proglottid, ventral view. C: Mature egg observed before fixation. (redrawn from Kumada et al., 1972).

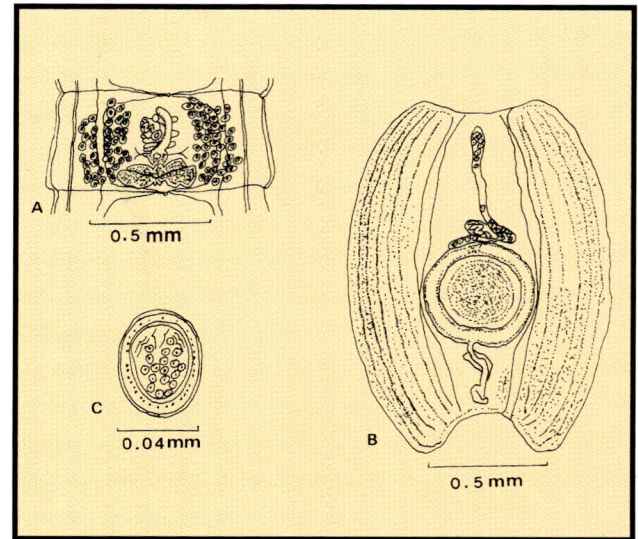

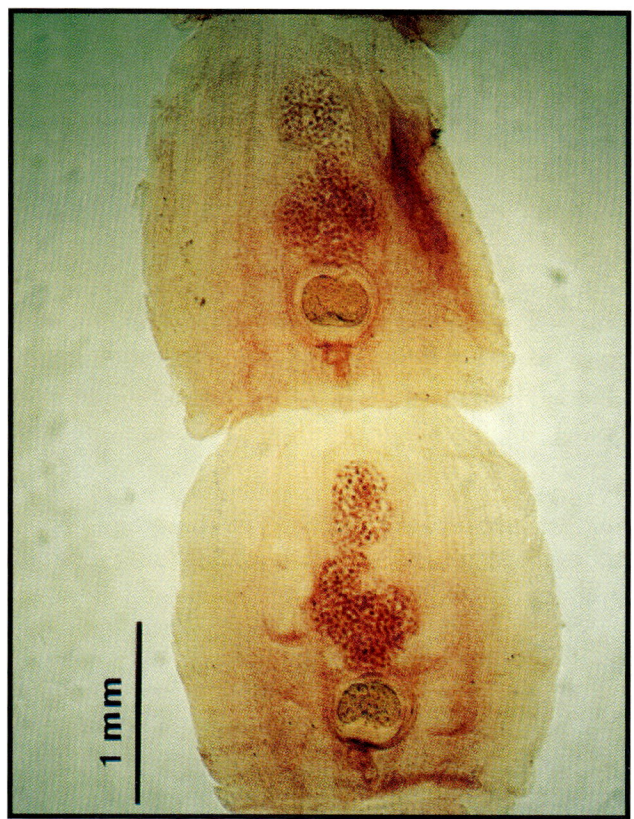

Fig. 15. Gravid proglottid of *M. lineatus* from a 45-year-old poultry-farm worker, Aceto-carmine stain (courtesy of Dr. Keeseon S. Eom, Chungbuk National University, Korea).

tiles (Witenberg, 1934; McAllister et al., 1991; Kumada et al., 1972; Cho et al., 1982). The second and paratenic hosts also include 2 species of amphibian (MaAllister et al., 1990). Final hosts for the cestode are canines: dogs, foxes, and wolves. Human can also be infected with *Mesocestoides* when they eat raw flesh of an animal that harbors the tetrathyridia. Eggs are expelled from the infected person or infected final animal host.

TAXONOMY

Kingdom: Animalia
Phylum: Platyhelminthes
Class: Cestoidea
Subclass: Eucestoda
Order: Cyclophyllidea
Family: Mesocestoididae
Subfamily: Mesocestoidinae
Genus: *Mesocestoides*
Species: *M. lineatus*

M. variabilis is regarded as synonym of *M. lineatus* (Schmidt, 1986b).

EPIDEMIOLOGY

Twenty-five human cases of *M. lineatus* have been reported (see Table 1).

In many eastern countries, it is the custom to eat raw snake to recover from an illness. Many reports in Japan suggest that snakes (such as *Elaphe quadrivirgata* or *Agkistrodon halys*) are the source of infection of this worm. In Korea, *Agkistrodon blomhoffi brevicauda* and chickens were reported as the sources of infection for the two cases. In Ruwanda and Burundi, partridges were regarded as possible sources of the infection.

CLINICAL MANIFESTATION

Persons infected with *Mesocestoides* present with abdominal pain, abdominal fullness, general fatigue, the discharge of sesame seed-like worms in the stools, and eosinophilia (Choi et al., 1967; Eom et al., 1992; Ohtomo et al., 1983). In Japan, patients also experienced persistent diarrhea, nausea, weight loss, dizziness, vomiting, amblyopia, and the feeling of abdominal fullness (Kagei et al., 1974). Proglottids can be recovered from the stool of infected children who are asymptomatic of infection (Fain et al., 1954; Hutchison et al., 1980; Gleason et al., 1973; Gutierrez et al., 1978).

DIAGNOSIS

Diagnosis of *Mesocestoides* can be easily made by an examination of the stool, or by identification of proglottid in the stool.

TREATMENT

A single dose, orally administered, of praziquantel 10 mg/kg is recommended.

PREVENTION

This infection can be avoided by refraining from eating raw reptiles and raw avians (such as chicken, guinea hens, and partridges).

NEODIPLOSTOMIASIS

Neodiplostomiasis is a unique intestinal trematode that infects humans. It is the first strigeid trematode that has been detected in its adult stage in humans. Humans can become infected with *Neodiplostomum seoulense* by ingesting raw snake or

Table 1 Reported Human Cases of *M. lineatus*

No. of Cases	Reported in	Reference
2	Korea	Eom *et al.*, 1992
14	Japan	Ohtomo *et al.*, 1983; Nagase *et al.*, 1983
1	China	Fan, 1988
6	USA	Beaver *et al.*, 1984b; Schultz *et al.*, 1992
1	Greenland	Chandler, 1942
1	Ruwanda Burund	Fan *et al.*, 1954

frog. *N. seoulense* was first named *Fibricola seoulensis*, but was renamed in 1995 to *N. seoulense*. Refer to the taxonomy discussion, later, for information about the characteristics that contributed to the renaming of this fluke.

All 27 human infections that have been reported have occurred in Korea. However, human infections of a similar strigeid fluke, *Fibricola cratera*, have been reported in the United States, where metacercaria are present in snakes. It has been proven experimentally that humans can be infected with this fluke (Shoop, 1989a). Further work is required before it will be known if there are any strigeid metacercariae in snakes or frogs.

MORPHOLOGY AND LIFE CYCLE

The adult body of *N. seoulense* is conspicuously bisegmented and spoon-shaped. It is 1.5 mm long and 0.7 mm wide on average; it has a well-developed ventral concavity in the forebody. The elongated, ellipsoid hindbody is slighter than the forebody. The oral sucker is slightly longer than it is wide. The ventral sucker is transversely elongated. Pharynx and esophagus are very short.

The tribocytic organ, a glandular structure, is somewhat circular or elliptical, and is located about one-third down the length of the forebody, and it lies posterior to the border of the ventral sucker. It occupies the ventral fossa of the spoon-shaped forebody. The glands and tegument of the tribocytic organ are histochemically composed of neutral mucopolysaccharide and tegument. The secretions of the organ are positive for alkaline phosphatase. It has been suggested that the tribocytic organ may play a role as a digestive and absorptive organ (Huh et al., 1990; Kim et al., 1993). Transmission electron-microscopic examination shows that the organ's gland cells possess many granules (Huh et al., 1993a).

Caeca extend to near the posterior end of the body. Vitelline follicles distribute throughout the entire body. The density of the vitelline follicles is high in the fluke's forebody; the density decreases in the hindbody.

The ovary is transversely oval and is situated laterally at the intersegmental portion of the body. The uterine tubule descends ventrally from the anterior border of the anterior testis to the genital atrium, and displays a subterminal aperture. Gravid female flukes will have 1 to 10 eggs in the uterus. Eggs are golden yellow or brown in color, 86-99 μm in length, and 55-63 μm in width.

Testes are transversely elongated, symmetrical, and arranged in tandem. They lie ventrally next to the intestinal trunks in the anterior two-thirds of the hindbody. Testes are butterfly-shaped. The posterior testis is larger and more symmetric than the anterior

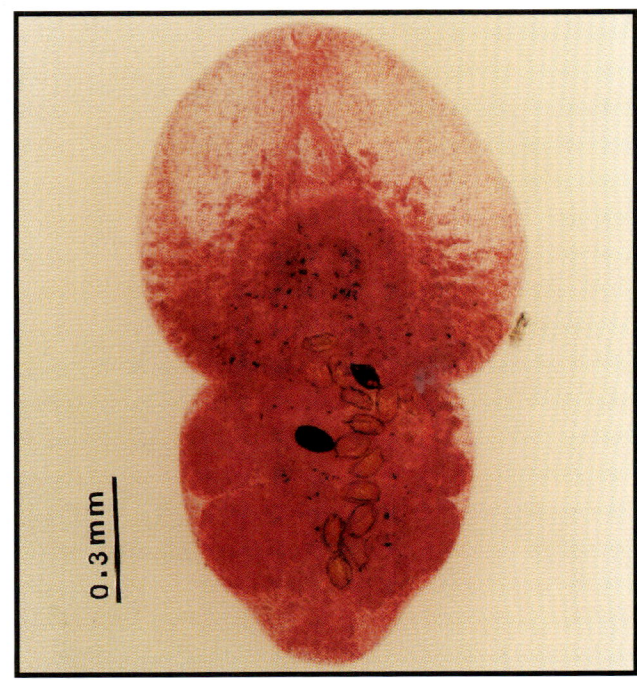

Fig. 16. Adult of *Neodiplostomum seoulense*, recovered from an experimental rat. Acetocarmine stain.

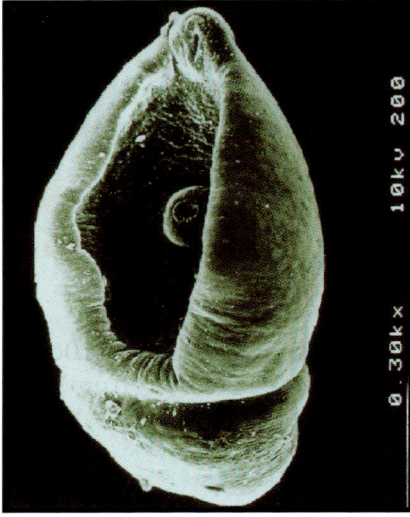

Fig 17. Scanning electron-microscopic findings of *N. seoulense* recovered from experimental rat three days PI (courtesy of Dr. Jong-Yil Chai, Seoul National University, Korea).

testis. The posterior testis has marked median constriction (Seo, 1990, Fig. 16).

Scanning electron-microscopic findings show that the surface of the tegument is covered with cobblestonelike cytoplasmic processes in the forebody, and fingerlike processes in the hindbody (Seo et al. 1984; Lee et al., 1985b, Fig. 17). The outer surface of the tegument is covered with a trilaminated plasma membrane. The electron-dense cytoplasmic layer was 2.5 μm wide in the anterior part. This layer contained numerous vacuoles, mitochondria, and granular material in its matrix (Sohn et al., 1993b, Fig 18).

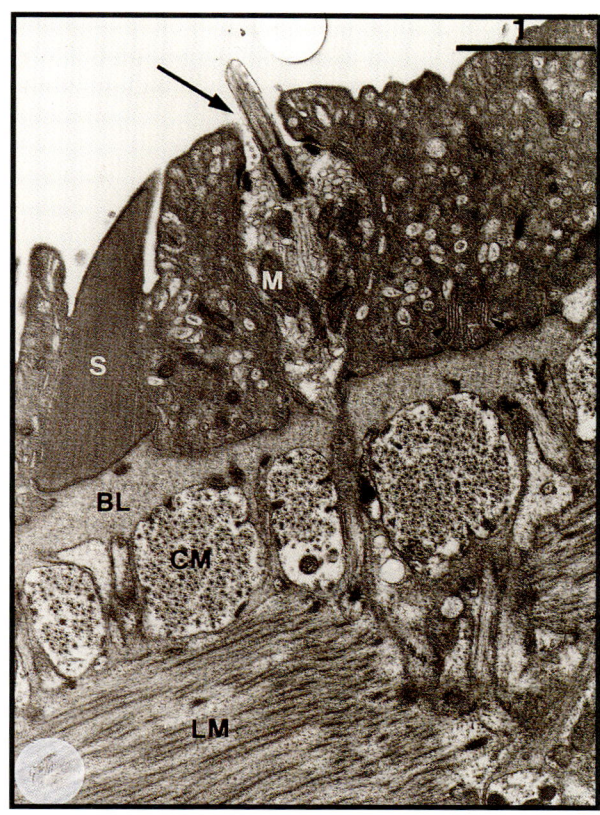

Fig. 18. Transmission electron-microscopic findings of tegument of *N. seoulense*. The tegument on the anterior body of a four-day-old worm showing spine (S), sensory vesicle (arrow), basement layer (BL), processes of basement layer (arrow head), and muscle layer (CM is circular muscle; LM is longitudinal muscle). Bar unit: mm (courtesy of Dr. Woon-Mok Sohn, Inje University, Korea).

The nervous system of *N. seoulense* consists of three pairs of longitudinal nerve trunks. The longitudinal nerve trunks are interconnected with transverse commissures and numerous circular commissures. Considerable numbers of nerve trunks are interconnected with longitudinal nerve trunks lying on the surface of the flukes (Cheon et al., 1993).

MIRACIDIUM (FIG.19)

The miracidium of this fluke is elongated and cylindrical. It measures 119.4 μm (106.6-123.0 μm) in length and 34.3 μm (29.5-41.0 μm) in width. Cilia are mounted uniformly on flat epidermal cells and cover the body surface. The terebratorium is protrusible and measures 16.7 μm long and 8.2 μm wide. There are 22 ciliated epidermal plates in four tiers: 6 plates in the first tier; 9 in the second tier; 4 in the third; and 3 plates in the fourth. The large, crescent-shaped eyespots are present at the junctional level of the first and second tier of the epidermal plates. There are eight sensory papillae. Six of those papillae are located at the center of the posterior margins; the other two papillae are located at the middle interface of the epidermal plates in the first tier.

CERCARIA (FIG. 19)

The body of the cercaria is elongated, ovoid, 93.2 μm (80.6-121.0 μm) long, and 45.0 μm (33.6-57.1 μm) wide. The oral sucker bears no prepharynx, and it leads to a short esophagus, which bifurcates into ceca. The ceca terminate at the level of the posterior margin of the ventral sucker. The ventral sucker's lip is aspinous. Two pairs of penetrating gland cells are pear-shaped; they are located lateral to the ventral sucker. Ducts arising from the penetrating gland cells run anteriorly and bulges in the oral sucker, opening anterolaterally to the ventral opening. The tail is bifurcated. There are ten flame cells. The excretory bladder is small and Y-shaped. The excretory canal passes along the axis of the tail stem, and is bifurcated at the junction of the tail stem and furcae. The excretory canal branches open halfway to the ventral margin of each furca.

METACERCARIAE (FIG. 19)

The metacercariae of *N. seoulense* is recognizable—with normal eyesight—grossly as white dots in the muscle fascia of frogs or in mesentry of snakes. The metacercaria is encapsulated in the host tissue and is round to oval in shape. The diameter of the metacercaria measures 0.303 mm (0.232-0.385 mm) in frog muscle, and 0.326 mm (0.213-0.338 mm) in snakes. The oral sucker is subterminal and pyriform. The pharynx is longitudinal and oval. The esophagus forks behind the posterior end of the pharynx and reaches the posterior end of body. The ventral sucker is oval, and its size is less than that of the oral sucker.

The tribocytic organ is round, prominent, and medially grooved behind the posterior margin of the ventral sucker. The excretory aperture opens subterminally. The excretory bladder is seen at the posterior end of the body and looks like a pair of horns. The paranephric plexus is composed of three longitudinal excretory vessels: one on the median line, and two lateral to the caeca. Those three longitudinal vessels are anastomosed by four complete transverse commissures with the ventral sucker and pharynx (Hong et al., 1994, Fig. 20).

TAXONOMY

Kingdom: Animalia
Phylum: Platyhelminthes
Class: Trematoda
Subclass: Digenea
Order: Prosostomata
Suborder: Strigeata
Superfamily: Strigeoidea
Family: Neodiplostomidae
Subfamily: Neodiplostominae
Genus: *Neodiplostomum*
Species: *N. seoulense*

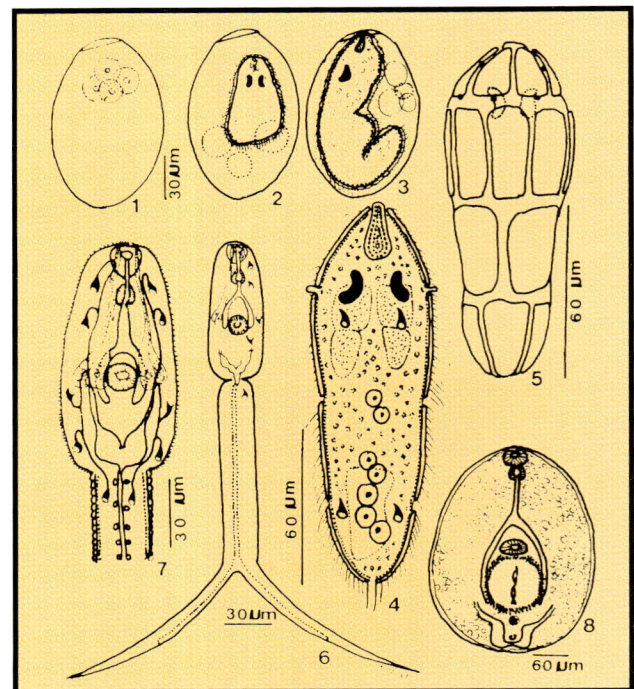

Fig. 19. Morphology of miracidium, cercariae, metacercariae of *N. seoulense*. 1-3: Egg and developing miracidium. 4: Miracidium. 5: Epithelial plates of miracidium. 6: Cercaria. 7: Cercarial body. 8: Metacercaria (Seo, 1990).

N. seoulense was originally named *Fibricola seoulensis* (Seo et al., 1964). In 1994, the name was revised to *N. seoulensis* because of characteristics such as the four transverse commissures in the metacercarial stage, the symmetrical anterior testis in the hindbody of the adult stage, and the symmetrical vitellaria in both the forebody and hindbody in the adult stage (Hong et al., 1994). The name was amended again to *N. seoulense*, according to Latin grammar (Hong et al., 1995). The family, Neodiplostomidae, and the subfamily, Neodiplostominae, were erected by Shoop (1989b).

LIFE CYCLE

The complete life cycle (see Figure 21) of *N. seoulense* has been explored in the laboratory. Natural intermediate and final hosts were also verified (Seo et al., 1988). The natural first intermediate host is *Hippeutis cantori* (Seo et al., 1988). Experimental infection of miracidium in *H. cantori* results the shedding of the furcocercous cercariae from 13 days PI. When eggs (collected from an adult fluke) are incubated at 28° C for 8-9 days, the hatching rate of miracidium from egg shells is over 90% (Lee et al., 1986b). The hatching rate of the eggs collected from fecal pellets of experimental rats is about 50%.

Tadpoles of *Rana nigromaculata* were found to be susceptible to experimental infection with cercariae. The number of metacercariae found in naturally-infected *R. nigromaculata* was 2.3-119.4. In experimentally infected tadpoles, the metacercariae became infective to the final host 21 days or more PI. The metacercariae were located as free organisms in the body cavity of the tadpoles.

When rats were infected with metacercariae, they begin to excrete eggs six days PI (Hong, 1982). The recovery rate of adult flukes is 42.6- 60.9% in rats, one week PI. The recovery rate of adult flukes is 23.5-63.5% in mice, three to ten days PI (Hong, 1982). According to Cho et al. (1983), the recovery rate from rats is 53.1%, the recover rate from mice is 40.0%, and the recovery rate from guinea pigs is 8.7%. Hong et al. (1983) reported the overall recovery rate of six experimental animals: rats, 40.0%; mice 33.9%; cats, 20.9%; dogs, 1.4 %; rabbits, 0.05%; chickens, 0%. In cats and dogs, mature flukes are rare one or two weeks PI. Only 22.7% of recovered flukes are mature in dogs; no mature flukes are found in cats. Humans are another final host for this fluke.

EPIDEMIOLOGY

N. seoulense is the first example in humans of an adult fluke infection by a strigeid trematode. Hu-

Fig. 20. Excretory system of the excysted metacercariae of *N. seoulense*. Excretory aperture opens subterminally. Excretory bladder is seen at the posterior end of the body in the form of a pair of horns. The paranephric plexus was composed of three longitudinal excretory vessels: one on the median line, and two lateral to the caeca. Those three longitudinal vessels were anastomosed by four complete transverse commissures with the ventral sucker and pharynx. OS: Os. LL: Lateral longitudinal vessel. ML: Median longitudinal vessel. T1-4: Transverse commissures. VS: Ventral sucker. T: Tribocytic organ (Hong et al., 1994).

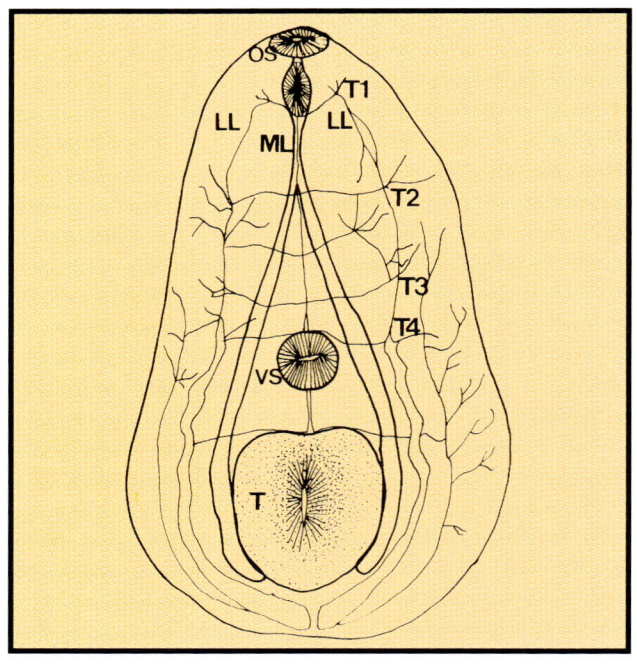

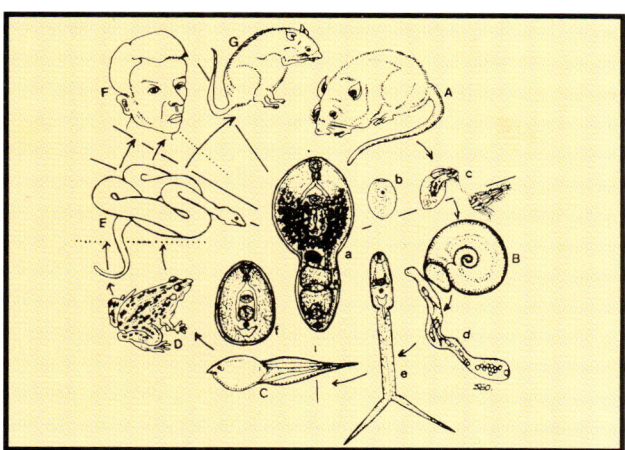

Fig. 21. Life cycle of *N. seoulense*. A: *Rattus norvegicus*. B: *Hippeutis cantori*. C: Tadpole. D: *Rana nigromaculata*. E: snake host. F: Man. G: *Apodemus* sp. a: Adult; b: Egg; c: Miracidium; d: Sporocyst; e: Cercaria; f: Metacercaria (Seo, 1990).

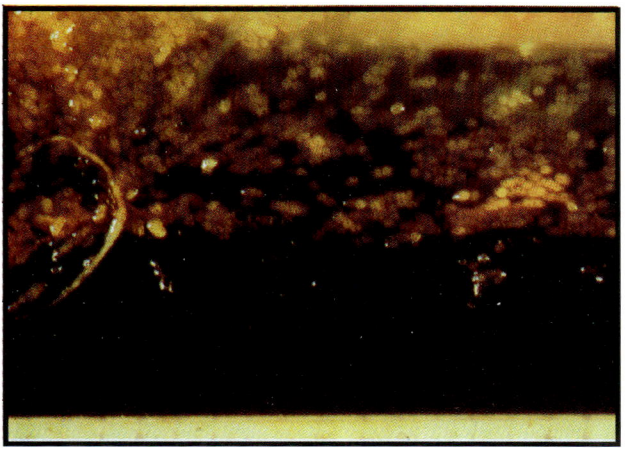

Fig. 22. Metacercariae of *N. seoulense* in the mesentry of a snake, *Rhabdophis tigrina*. Metacercariae can be seen by the naked eyes as tiny white dots.

Fig. 23 Intestine of a mouse infected with *N. seoulense* shows the worm located at the intervillous space. Crypt hyperplasia and villous atrophy was shown. Alcian blue (pH 2.5) stain, X 100.

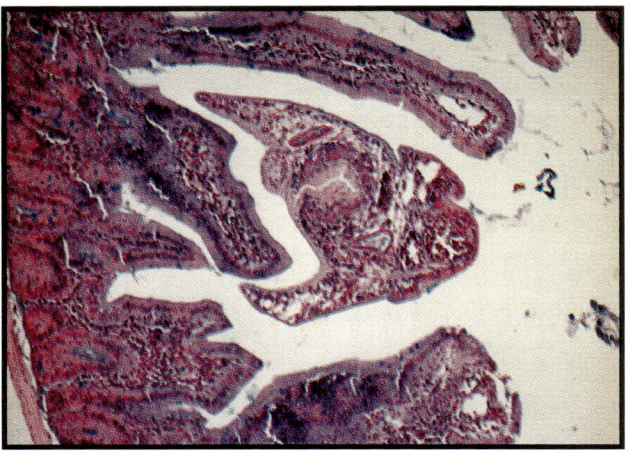

mans acquire the infection by ingesting raw snake or frog. After the first report of a human infection (Seo et al., 1982), 26 more cases have been reported (Hong et al., 1984 & 1986; Huh et al., 1994). With the exception of the first case, all subsequent cases were infections of soldiers.

The first case was treated with Bithionol 40 mg. The other cases were treated with praziquantel 10-20 mg/kg. Nineteen cases were confirmed by stool examination. With four exceptions, all infected patients had a history of eating of raw snake or frog. However, the four excepted patients were not asked about the history of eating of raw frog. It is believed that, in those four cases, the patients ate raw frog instead of snake (Hong et al., 1986). Cases of infection in soldiers are due to the ingestion of raw snake or frog during survival training or to idiosyncratic eating habits.

After the first description of flukes recovered from the rat, *Rattus norvegicus*, in Seoul, it was reported that 57 out of 107 house rats captured in Korea were found to be infected with *N. seoulense* (Seo et al., 1981).

The second intermediate or paratenic hosts for *N. seoulense* are the frog *R. nigromaculata*, and several species of snake. A total of 220 tadpoles from 6 local areas in Korea were examined. These tadpoles tested positive—from 3.3% to 100% by area—for the metacercariae. The number of metacercariae found in the infected tadpoles ranged from 1 to 584. Most of the metacercariae were found in the abdominal cavities of the tadpoles (Hong et al., 1982). Eighty-five *R. nigromaculata* frogs were also tested. Of those 85 frogs, 94.1% were found to have the metacercariae of *N. seoulense* in the skeletal muscles of their hind legs.

The following snakes are known as paratenic hosts: *Rhabdophis tigrina (Natrix tigrina lateralis), Elaphe rufodorsata, Elaphe dione, Dinodon rufozonatum rufozonatum,* and *Agkistrodon blomhoffii brevicaudus.* Of *R. tigrina*, 88.4% of metacercariae were found in the stomach wall and mesentry near the stomach. The number of metacercariae found in infected *R. tigrina* ranged from 1 to 584 (Hong et al., 1982; Cho et al., 1983). (Fig. 22)

Hippeutis (Helicorbis) cantori is a fresh-water snail that lives in rice pads. Out of 1,410 *H. cantori* snails collected from rice pads, less than 1% were infected with furcocercous cercariae identical to those of *N. seoulense* obtained from experimental infection.

CLINICAL MANIFESTATION, PATHOLOGICAL FINDINGS, AND PATHOGENESIS

Except for the first case of human infection by *N. seoulense*, infected soldiers did not complain of any specific gastrointestinal symptoms, such as abdominal pain or diarrhea. This is probably due to chronic infections, since the infections in those 26 cases were found incidentally, during routine stool examinations. In the first case, a 25 year-old man complained of fever, abdominal pain, and severe diarrhea five days after he ingested uncooked viscera along with the roasted muscle of two unidentified snakes. The man was treated with Bithionol, and 79 flukes were recovered. It is presumed that the recognizable clinical symptoms occur in humans in the early stage of a heavy infection.

When mice were infected with 1,000 metacercariae of *N. seoulense*, they began to die 11 days PI. By 16 days PI, all infected, experimental mice were dead. Occult blood from the mice feces was detected 10 days PI. Diarrhea begins to appear after 9 days PI. Histopathological changes were villous atrophy, crypt hyperplasia, inflammatory cell infiltration, and stromal edema. Huh et al. (1988) and Lee et al (1985c) suggest that the cause of death is malnutrition and severe fluid loss due to malabsorption (Fig. 23).

Antigenic components of *N. seoulense* have been studied. When rats were infected with *N. seoulense*, specific IgG in serum increases from 10 days PI and is sustained untill 70 days PI. According to the western blot analysis with crude fluke extract, sera of 20 and 30 days PI react with the 25 kDa band, and sera of 60 and 70 days PI react with the 15 kDa band. However, patient sera reacts with the 12 kDa band.

Potent antigenic components of flukes to infected sera were seminal vesicle and testes (Kho, 1992). In the host reaction to *N. seoulense* infection, the number of mast cells in the duodenum increases from seven days PI, and peaks 21 days PI in Sprague-Dawley rats. This change is well correlated with the expulsion of flukes from infected rats (Kho et al., 1990).

DIAGNOSIS

Specific diagnosis can be made by identifying the eggs in the stool of an infected host. The size of the egg is 86 μm-99 μm in length and 55 μm-63 μm in width. It is golden yellow or brown in color, thin-shelled, bilaterally asymmetric in shape, and slightly flattened on one side. The well-demarcated operculum is obliquely located to the equatorial plane of the eggs (Fig. 24).

TREATMENT

As with other intestinal trematodiases, praziquantel 10mg/kg is recommended in the treatment of *N. seoulense* (Hong et al., 1986). A dosage of 5 mg/kg is also effective in treating infections in rats (Lee et al., 1985a). The morphological changes of *N. seoulense* in mice treated with praziquantel 10 mg/kg are characterized as dilatation of forebody, vacuolization of tegument and parenchyme, and narrowing of the intestinal lumen. Scanning electron-microscopic examinations show the bleb for-

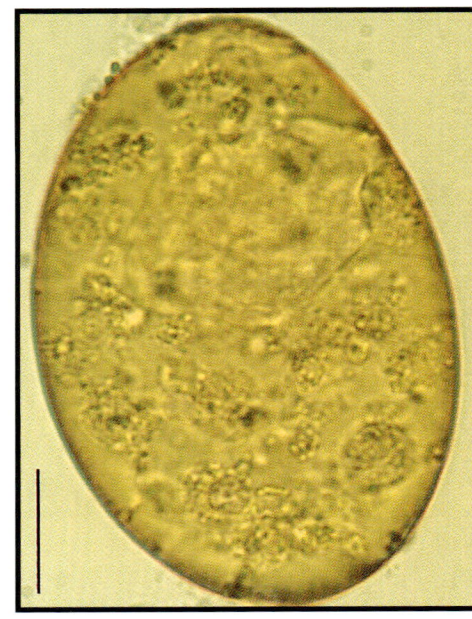

Fig. 24. Egg of *N. seoulense*. bar =20 μm.

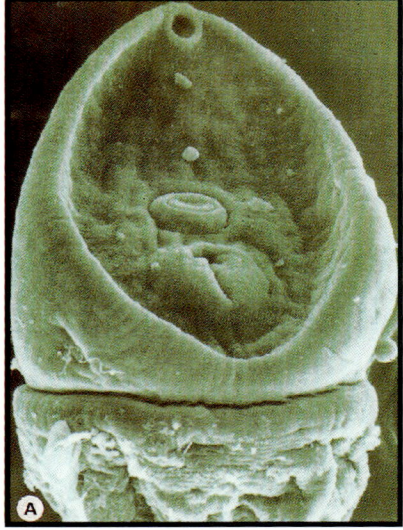

Fig. 25. A: Forebody of *N. seoulense*, seven days PI, from an experimental rat before treatment. The oral sucker, ventral sucker, and tribocytic organ are seen in the groove of forebody.

B: Forebody of the worm was recovered from the rat intestine six hours after

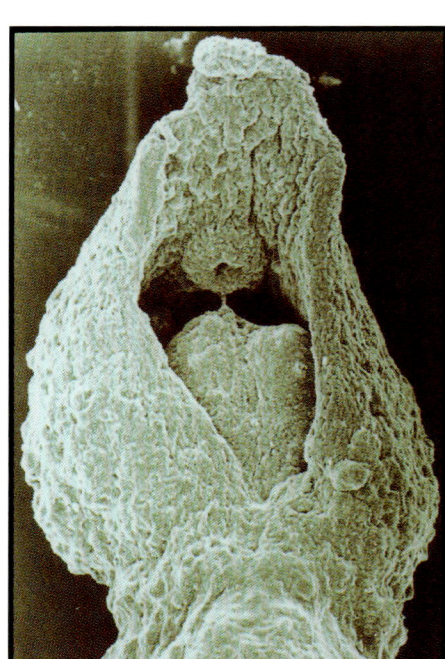

praziquantel treatment 10mg/ml p.o. The rupture and severe destruction of the whole tegument are shown after treatment (Courtesy of Dr. Jong-Yil Chai, Seoul National University, Korea).

mation, followed by rupture and destruction of whole tegument (Seo et al., 1985, Fig. 25).

PREVENTION

The only way to prevent an infection by *N. seoulense* is to avoid eating raw snake or frog.

PENTASTOMIASIS

Pentastomiasis is a zoonotic parasitic infections of man, first described by Pruner in 1847. The causative organism are pentastomes (pentastomids), so called because of the presence of a median subterminal mousse and two pairs of anterior hooks, which gave the appearance of 5 openings. The body is elongated, tongue-like, cylindrical or moniliform with many pseudosegments. They are annulated but non-segmented vermiform blood-sucking endoparasites classified as phylum Arthropoda, subphylum Mandibulata, class Pentastomida. The developmental stages include embryo, nymph, and adult.

Of medical interest are two families of pentastomes namely Linguatulidae and Procephalidae, of which species of the genera *Linguatula* and *Armillifer* (*Procephalus*) are parasites of man. The four species of those genera infecting human are *Linguatula serrata*, a cosmopolitan species, *Armillifer armillatus* and *A. grandis* in Africa and *Armillifer moniliformis* in Asia. Pentastomiasis has been reported from man as larval infection or rarely as an infection with adult pentastomes.

Larvae or nymphs have been recovered from liver, spleen, mesentery, peritoneum, intestinal lumen, lungs, eyes, upper respiratory tract, lymph nodes, and brain (Beaver et al., 1984c). Usually the encapsulated larvae produce no symptoms and are discovered at autopsy. In the lung infecion, it can cause respiratory symptoms. In rare cases it can cause intestinal obstruction. Coughing, hoarseness, dysphagia, anosmia, headache and epistaxis appeared in the nasopharyngeal nymph infection of *L. serrata* (Buslau et al., 1990). In France, there was a fatal case of septicemia due to lung involvement with *A. grandis* (Tiendrebeogo et al., 1982). There was also a generalized and lethal case of *A. grandis* infection in Cote-d'Ivoir (Ivory Coast). Most commonly parasitized organs were lung and brain (Cagnard et al, 1979). The diagnosis can be made by radiography and confirmation made after surgery or autopsy. Visceral pentastomiasis was usually found incidentally during the autopsy. There is no specific treatment except surgery. Prevention is possible by avoidance of eating raw snake or undercooked meat.

REFERENCES

—**Anders K; Foley K; Stern E et al.:** Intracranial sparganosis: An uncommon infection-case report. J Neurosurg 1984; 60: 1282-1286

—**Ali-khan Z; Irving RT; Wingall N et al.:** Imported sparganosis in Canada. Can Med Assoc J, 1973; 108: 590.

—**Beaver PC; Jung RC; Cupp EW:** Clinical Parasitology 9th ed. Lea & Febiger, Philadelphia, USA , 1984a, pp 499-502.

—**Beaver PC; Jung RC; Cupp EW:** Clinical Parasitology 9th ed., Lea and Febiger, Philadelphia, USA, 1984b, pp 507-508.

—**Beaver PC; Jung RC; Cupp EW:** Clinical Parasitology 9th ed., Lea and Febiger, Philadelphia, USA, 1984c, pp568-573.

—**Beaver PC; Little MD; Tucker CF et al.:** Mesocercaria in the skin of man in Louisiana. Am J Trop Med Hyg, 1977; 26: 422-426.

—**Beaver PC; Roan FA:** Proliferating larval cestodes in a man in Paraguay. A case report and review. Am J Trop Med Hyg, 1981; 30: 625-637.

—**Buslau M; Kuhne U; Marsch WC:** Dermatological signs of nasopharyngeal linguatulosis (halzoun, Marrara syndrome)-the possible role of major basic protein. Dermatologica, 1990; 181: 327-329.

—**Cagnard V; Nicolas-Randegger J; Dago-Akairbi A et al.:** Generalized and lethal pentastomiasis due to *Amillifer grandis*(Hett, 1915). Bull Soc Pathol Exot Filiales, 1979; 72: 345-352.

—**Chai JY; Yu JR; Lee SH:** Ineffectiveness of praziquantel for human sparganosis. Seoul J Med, 1988; 29: 397-399.

—**Chandler AC:** First record of a case of human infection with tapeworms of the genus *Mesocestoides*. Am J Trop Med, 1942; 22: 493-597.

—**Chang KH; Chi JG; Cho SY et al.:** Cerebral sparganosis: analysis of 34 cases with emphasis on CT features. Neuroradiology, 1992; 34: 1-8.

—**Chang KH; Cho SY; Chi JG et al.:** Cerebral sparganosis: CT characteristics. Radiology, 1987;165:505-510.

—**Cheon EW; Kim CH:** The nervous system of *Fibricola seoulensis* by acetylcholinesterase histochemistry. Korean J Parasitol, 1993; 31:321-329.

—**Chi JG; Chi HS; Lee SH:** Histopathological study on human sparganosis. Korean J. Parasitol, 1980; 18:15-23.

—**Cho DY; Huh JD; Hwang YS et al.:** Sparganosis in the spinal canal with partial block: an uncommon infection. Neuroradiology, 1992: 34: 241-244.

—**Cho KJ; Lee HS; Chi JG:**
Intramural sparganosis manifested as intestinal obstruction—a case report. J Korean Med Sci, 1987; 2: 137-139.

—**Cho SY, Cho BH, Kang SY:**
Trematode parasites of Korean terrestrial snakes. Chung-Ang J Med, 1983; 8: 13-27.

—**Cho SY; Bae JH; Seo BS et al.:**
Some aspects of human sparganosis in Korea. Korean J Parasitol, 1975; 13: 60-77.

—**Cho SY; Chung YB; Kong Y:**
Component proteins and protease activities in excretory-secretory products of sparganum. Korean J Parasitol, 1992; 30: 277-230.

—**Cho SY; Hwang KI; Seo BS:**
On the sparganum mansoni infections in some Korean terrestrial snakes. Korean J Parasitol, 1973; 11: 87-94.

—**Cho SY; Kang SY; Kong Y:**
Purification of antigenic protein of sparganum by immunoaffinity chromatography using monoclonal antibody. Korean J Parasitol, 1990; 28: 135-142.

—**Cho SY; Song KW; Lee SH et al.:**
Cestode parasites of terrestrial snakes in Korea. Chung-Ang J Med, 1982; 7: 321-333.

—**Choi SH; Kang SY; Kong Y et al.:**
Antigenic protein fractions reacting with sera of sparganosis patients. Korean J Parasitol, 1988; 26:163-167.

—**Choi WY; Im BC; Choi HS:**
The first human infection with tapeworms of the genus *Mesocestoides* in Korea. Korean J Parasitol, 1967; 5: 60-64.

—**de-Roodts AR; Suarez G; Ruzic A et al.:**
A case of human sparganosis in Argentina. Medcina B Aires. 1993; 53: 235-238.

—**Eduardo SL:**
Food-borne parasitic zoonoses in the Philippines. Southeast Asian J Trop Med Pub Health. 1991; 22 (suppl.): 16-22.

—**Eom KS; Kim SH; Rim HJ:**
Second case of human infection with *Mesocestoides lineatus* in Korea. Korean J Parasitol, 1992; 30: 147-150.

—**Fain A; Henri V:**
Note à propos d'un cas d'infestation humaine par un *Mesocestoides* à Astrida (Ruanda-Burundi). Ann Soc Belge Med Trop, 1954; 34: 893-900.

—**Fan SQ:**
First case of *Mesocestoides lineatus* infection in China. Chinese J Parasitol and Parasitic Dis, 1988; 6: 310.

—**Fontan R; Beauchamp F; Beaver PC:**
New helminthiases in Laos II. Platyhelminths. Bull Soc Pathol Exot Filiales, 1975; 68: 566-573.

—**Fukase T; Matsuda Y; Akihama S; Itagaki H:**
Purification and some properties of cysteine protease of *Spirometra erinacei* plerocercoid (Cestoda; Diphyllobothriidae). Jpn J Parasitol, 1985; 34: 351-360.

—**Fukumoto S; Tsuboi T; Hirai K:**
Comparision of isozyme patterns between *Spirometra erinacei* and *Spirometra mansonoides* by isoelectric focusing. J Parasitol, 1992; 78: 735-738.

—**Gleason NN; Kornblum R; Walzer P:**
Mesocestoides (Cestoda) in a child in New Jersey treated with Niclosamide (Yomesan). Am J Trop Med Hyg, 1973; 22: 757-761.

—**Gutierrez Y; Buchino JJ; Schubert WK:**
Mesocestoides (Cestoda) infection in children in the United States. J Pediatrics, 1978; 93: 245-247.

—**Hong SJ; Lee SH; Seo BS et al.:**
Studies on intestinal trematodes in Korea IX. Recovery rate and development of *Fibricola seoulensis* in experimental animals. Korean J Parasitol, 1983; 21: 224-223.

—**Hong ST, Cho TW, Hong SJ et al.:**
Fifteen human cases of *Fibricola seoulensis* infection in Korea. Korean J Parasitol, 1984; 22: 61-65.

—**Hong ST:**
Studies on intestinal trematodes in Korea VII. Growth, Development and recovery of *Fibricola seoulensis* from experimentally infected rats and mice. Korean J Parasitol, 1982; 20: 112-121.

—**Hong ST; Chai JY; Lee SH:**
Ten human cases of *Fibricola seoulensis* infection and mixed one with *Stellantchasmus* and *Metagonimus*. Korean J Parasitol, 1986; 24: 94-96.

—**Hong ST; Hong SJ; Lee SH et al.:**
Studies on intestinal trematodes in Korea VI. On the metacercaria and the second intermediate host of *Fibricola seoulensis*. Korean J Parasitol, 1982; 20: 101-111.

—**Hong ST; Kim KJ; Huh S et al.:**
The changes of histopathology and serum anti-sparganum IgG in experimental sparganosis of mice. Korean J Parasitol, 1989; 27: 261-269.

—**Hong ST; Shoop WL:**
Neodiplostomum seoulensis N. comb (Trematoda: Neodiplostomidae). J Parasitol, 1994; 80: 660-663.

—**Hong ST; Shoop WL;**
Neodiplostomum seoulense, the amended name for *Neodiplostomum seoulensis*. Korean J Parasitol, 1995; 33: 399.

—**Huh S; Chai JY; Hong SY et al.:**
Clinical and histopathological findings in

mice heavily infected with *Fibricola seoulensis*. Korean J Parasitol, 1988; 26; 45-53.

—**Huh S; Lee SH; Seo BS:**
Histochemical findings of the tribocytic organ and tegument of *Fibricola seoulensis*. Korean J Parasitol, 1990; 28: 155-160.

—**Huh S; Lee SU; Huh SC:**
A follow-up examination of intestinal parasitic infections of the army soldiers in Whachon-gun, Korea. Korean J Parasitol, 1994; 32: 61-63.

—**Huh S; Song HB:**
Transmission electron microscopic findings of the tribocytic organ of *Fibricola seoulensis*. Korean J Parasitol, 1993a; 31:315-320.

—**Huh S; Wang KC; Hong ST et al.:**
Histopathological findings of the cat brain in experimental sparganosis. Path Res Pract, 1993b; 189: 181-1186.

—**Hutchison WF; Martin JB:**
Mesocestoides (Cestoda) in a child in Mississippi treated with paromycin sulfate (humatin). Am J Trop Med Hyg, 1980; 29: 478-479.

—**Iwata S:**
Diphyllobothrium mansonoides Mueller is the synonym of *D. erinacei* (Rudolphi). Zool Mag (Japan), 1936; 48: 665-669.

—**Iwata S:**
Experimental and morphological studies of Manson's tapeworm *Diphyllobothrium erinacei* (Rudolphi)- Special reference with its scientific name and relationship with *Sparganum proliferum* Ijima. Progress of Medical Parasitology in Japan, 1972; 4: 536-590.

—**Kagei N; Kihata M:**
The 10th case of human infection with *Mesocestoides lineatus* (Cestoda: Cyclophyllidaea) in Japan. Jpn J Parasitol, 1974; 23:383-390.

—**Kho WG:**
Analysis of antigenic proteins of *Fibricola seoulensis*. Ph.D. thesis to Seoul National University. 1992.

—**Kho WG; Chai JY; Chun CH et al.:**
Mucosal mast cell responses to experimental *Fibricola seoulensis* infection in rats. Seoul J Med, 1990; 31:191-199.

—**Kim H; Kim SI; Cho SY:**
Serological diagnosis of human sparganosis by means of micro-ELISA. Korean J Parasitol, 1984; 22:222-228.

—**Kim HJ; Kim CW:**
Localization and isozyme pattern of phosphatase in *Fibricola seoulensis*. Korean J Parasitol, 1993; 31;356-361.

—**Kim LS; Kong Y; Kang SY:**
Immunohistochemical localization of 36 and 29 KDa proteins in sparganum. Korean J Parasitol, 1992; 30: 25-31.

—**Kittiponghansa S; Tesana S; Ritch R:**
Ocular sparganosis: a cause of subconjuctival tumor and deafness. Trop Med Parasitol, 1988; 39: 247-248.

—**Ko RC:**
Current status of food-borne parasitic zoonoses in Hong Kong. Southeast Asian J Trop Med Pub Health. 1991; 22 (suppl.): 42-47.

—**Kobayashi E:**
Studies on the development of *Diphyllobothrium mansoni* Cobbold, 1882 (Joyeux, 1927) V. The first intermediate host. Taiwan Igakkai Zasshi, 1931; 30: 286-311.

—**Kong Y; Cho SY; Kang WS:**
Sparganum infection in normal adult population and epileptic patients in Korea: A seroepidemiologic observation. Korean J Parasitol, 1994a: 85-92.

—**Kong Y; Chung YB; Cho SY et al.:**
Characterization of three neutral protease of *Spirometra mansoni* plerocercoid. Parasitology, 1994b; 108: 359-368.

—**Kong Y; Chung YB; Cho SY et al.:**
Cleavage of immunoglobulin G by excretory-secretory cathepsin S-like protease of *Spirometra mansoni* plerocercoid. Parasitology, 1994c: 109; 611-621.

—**Kong Y; Kang SY; Cho SY:**
Single step purification of potent antigenic protein from sparganum by gelatin-affinity chromatography. Korean J Parasitol, 1991; 29: 1-7.

—**Kong Y; Kang SY; Kim SH et al:**
A neutral cyteine protease of *Spirometra mansoni* plerocercoid invoking IgE response. Parasitology, 1997; 114: (in press)

—**Kron MA; Guderian R; Guevara A et al.:**
Abdominal sparganosis in Ecuador: a case report. Am J Trop Med Hyg, 1991; 44: 146-50.

—**Kumada N; Mizuno S; Kato Y et al.:**
Eighth record of a human case of *Mesocestoides lineatus* (Cestoda: Cyclophyllidea) in Japan. Jpn J Parasitol, 1972; 212:336-245.

—**Kwa BH:**
Studies on the sparganum of *Spirometra erinacei*-I. The histology and histochemistry of the scolex. Intern J Parasitol, 1972a; 2:23-28.

—**Kwa BH:**
Studies on the sparganum of *Spirometra erinacei*-II. Proteolytic enzymes in the scolex. Intern J Parasitol, 1972b; 2:29-33.

—**Landero A; Hernandez F; Absolo MA et al.:**
Cerebral sparganosis caused by *Spirometra mansonoides*. Case report. J Neurosurg, 1991; 75: 472-474.

—**Lee HB; Lee KW; Lee SB et al.:**
Clinical observation on cerebral sparganosis. J Korean Neurol Assoc, 1987;5:64-69.

—**Lee SH; Chai JY; Seo BS et al.:**
Two cases of human infection by adult of *Spirometra erinacei*. Korean J Parasitol, 1984; 22: 66-71.

—**Lee SH; Chai JY; Seo BS:**
Studies on intestinal trematodes in Korea XVII. Effect of praziquantel in the tegument of *Fibricola seoulensis* infection in albino rats. Korean J Parasitol, 1985a; 23: 41-46.

—**Lee SH; Chai JY; Sohn WM et al.:**
In vitro and in vivo effects of praziquantel on sparganosis. Seoul J Med, 1986a; 27:135-142.

—**Lee SH; Hong SJ; Chai JY et al.:**
Studies on intestinal trematodes in Korea XV. Tegumental ultrastructure of *Fibricola seoulensis* according to developmental stages. Seoul J Med, 1985b; 26: 35-40.

—**Lee SH; Lee HJ; Hong ST et al.:**
The effect of temperature and salinity on maturation and hatching of *Fibricola seoulensis* eggs. Korean J Parasitol, 1986b; 24: 115-120.

—**Lee SH; We JS; Sohn WM et al.:**
Experimental life history of *Spirometra erinacei*. Korean J Parasitol, 1990; 28: 161-173.

—**Lee SH; Yoo BH; Hong ST et al.:**
A histopathological study on the intestine of mice and rats experimentally infected by *Fibricola seoulensis*. Korean J Parasitol, 1985c; 23: 58-72.

—**Lee SK; Lee JT; Kim KH et al.:**
A case of sparganosis. J Pusan Med College, 1967; 7:87-92.

—**Li CH:**
The life history of *Diphyllobothrium decipiens* and *D. erinacei*. Am J Hyg, 1929; 10: 527-555.

—**McAllister CT; Conn DB:**
Occurrence of tetrathyridia of *Mesocestoides* sp. (Cestoidea: Cyclophyllidea) in North American anurans (Amphibia). J Wildl Dis, 1990; 26:540-543.

—**McAllister CT; Conn DB; Freed PS et al.:**
A new host and locality record for *Mesocestoides* sp. tetrathyridia (Cestoidea: Cyclophyllidea) with a summary of the genus from snakes of the world. J Parasitol, 1991;77:329-331.

—**Mendez-Medina R; Cataneda-Suardiaz J; Ravina-Cabrena MD et al.:**
Subcutaneous sparganosis-A new case report. Morfologia Normal y Patologica B, 1983; 7:285-292.

—**Moon WK; Chang KH; Cho SY et al.:**
Cerebral sparganosis: MR imaging versus CT features. Radiology, 1993; 188: 751-757.

—**Morakote M; Kong Y:**
Antigenic specificity of 36 and 31 kDa proteins of *Spirometra erinacei* plerocercoid in tissue invading nematodiasis. Korean J Parasitol, 1993; 31:167-1671.

—**Mueller JF:**
On the occurrence of *Spirometra mansonoides* in South America. J Parasitol, 1975; 61: 774-775.

—**Mueller JF:**
The biology of *Spirometra*. J Parasitol, 1974; 60: 3-14.

—**Mueller JF:**
The life history of *Diphyllobothrium mansonoides* Mueller, 1935, and some considerations with regards to sparganosis in the United States. Am J Trop Med, 1938; 18:41-66.

—**Munkhof WJ; Grayson ML; Susil BJ:**
Cerebral sparganosis in an East Timorese refugee. Med J Aust, 1994; 161: 263-264.

—**Nagase K; Kani A, Totani T et al.:**
Report of a human case of *Mesocestoides lineatus* in Japan. Jpn J Parasitol, 1983; 32 (suppl.): 18.

—**Nakamura T; Hara M; Matsuoka M et al.:**
Human proliferating sparganosis. A new Japanese case. Am J Pathol, 1990; 94: 224-228.

—**Nakamura T; Nakajima M; Yanagisawa T:**
Activity of acid thiol proteinase from *Diphyllobothrium erinacei* plerocercoid. (III) Effects on structural proteins from host muscle. Jpn J Parasitol, 1984; 33 (suppl.): 24

—**Noya BA; Torres JR; Noya O:**
Maintenance of *Sparganum proliferum* in vitro and in experimental animals. Intern J Parasitol, 1992; 22: 835-838.

—**Oh SJ; Chi JG; Lee SE:**
Eosinophilic cystitis caused by vesical sparganosis: a case report. J Urol, 1993; 149: 581-583.

—**Ohtomo H; Hioki A; Ito A et al.:**
Therapeutic effect of paromycin sulfate on the 13th case of *Mesocestoides lineatus* infection found in Japan. Jpn J Antibiot, 1983; 36:632-637.

—**Park CK; Ha YS; Hu CW et al.:**
A case of sparganosis in the intradural space of the thoracolumbar spine. J Korean Neurosurg Assoc, 1983; 12: 739-743.

—**Park KS; Lee Y; Chung SY et al.:**
Soft tissue sparganosis. J Korean Radiol Soc, 1993; 29: 1288-1294.

—**Salem MAM; Phares CK:**
Some biochemical effects of the growth hormone analogue produced by plerocercoids of the tapeworm *Spirometra mansonoides* on carbohydrate metabolism of adipose tissue from

normal, diabetic, and hypohysectomized rats. J Parasitol, 1986; 72: 498-506.

—**Schmidt H; Watschinger H:**
Sparganosis in the Masai land. Acta Trop, 1972; 29: 218-230.

—**Schmidt GD:**
CRC Handbook of tapeworm identification. CRC Press Inc., Coca Raton, Florida, USA, 1986a pp. 93-95.

—**Schmidt GD:**
CRC handbook of tapeworm identification. CRC Press Inc., Boca Raton, Florida, USA, 1986b, pp 202-204.

—**Schultz ; Roberto RR; Rutherford GW et al.:**
Mesocestoides (Cestode) infection in a California child. Pediatric Infec Dis J, 1992; 11: 332-334.

—**Seo BS:**
Fibricola seoulensis, Seo, Rim and Lee, 1964 (Trematoda) and fibricoliasis in man. Seoul J Med, 1990; 31: 61-96.

—**Seo BS; Cha IJ; Chai JY et al.:**
Studies on intestinal trematodes in Korea XIX. Light and scanning electron microscopy of *Fibricola seoulensis* collected from albino rats treated with praziquantel. Korean J Parasitol, 1985; 23: 47-57.

—**Seo BS; Cho SY; Hong ST et al.:**
Studies on parasitic helminths of Korea V. Survey on intestinal trematodes on house rats. Korean J Parasitol, 1981; 19:131-136.

—**Seo BS; Lee SH; Chai JY et al.:**
Studies on intestinal trematodes in Korea X. Scanning electron microscopic observation on the tegument of *Fibricola seoulensis*. Korean J Parasitol, 1984; 22:21-29.

—**Seo BS; Lee SH; Chai JY et al.:**
The life cycle and larval development of *Fibricola seoulensis* (Trematoda: Diplostomidae). Korean J Parasitol, 1988; 26:179-188.

—**Seo BS; Lee SH; Hong ST et al.:**
Studies on intestinal trematodes in Korea V. A human case infection by *Fibricola seoulensis* (Trematoda: Diplostomatidae). Korean J Parasitol, 1982; 20: 93-99.

—**Seo BS; Rim HJ; Lee CW:**
Studies on the parasitic helminths of Korea I. Trematodes of rodents. Korean J Parasitol, 1964; 2: 20-26.

—**Shin DE; Min KH; Chai JY:**
A case of subconjuctival sparganosis. J Korean Ophth Soc, 1980; 21:1449-1452.

—**Shiwaku K; Hirai K; Tsuboi T et al.:**
Enhancement of serum somatomedin activity and cartilage mitotic activity in snell normal and dwarf mice infected with *Spirometra erinacei* plerocercoids. Jpn J Parasitol, 1986; 35:411-417.

—**Shoop WL:**
Experimental human infection with *Fibricola cratera* (Trematoda: Neodiplostomidae). Korean J Parasitol, 1989a; 27: 249-152.

—**Shoop WL:**
Systemic analysis of the Diplostomidae and Strigeidae (Trematoda). J Parasitol, 1989b; 75: 21-32.

—**Shoop WL; Corkum KC:**
Epidemiology of *Alaria marcinae* mesocercariae in Louisiana. J Parasitol, 1981; 67: 928-931.

—**Smith HM Jr; Davidson WR; Nettles VF et al.:**
Parasitism among wild swine in southwestern United States. J Am Vet Med Assoc, 1982; 181: 1281-1284.

—**Sohn WM; Hong ST; Chai JY et al.:**
Infectivity of the sparganum treated by praziquantel, gamma-irradiation and mechanical cutting. Korean J Parasitol, 1993a; 31:135-139.

—**Sohn WM; Lee SH:**
Transmission electron microscopic ultrastructure of the tegument of *Fibricola seoulensis*. Korean J Parasitol, 1993b; 31: 301-313.

—**Song CY; Chappell CL:**
Purification and partial characterization of cysteine proteinase from *Spirometra mansoni* plerocercoids. J Parasitol, 1993; 79:517-524.

—**Tiendrebeogo H; Levy D; Schmidt D:**
Human pentastomiasis in Abidjan. A report on 29 cases. Rev Fr Mal Respir, 1982; 10: 351-358.

—**Torres P; Figueroa L:**
Infection by *Spirometra mansoni* (Cestoda, Pseudophyllidea) in the south of Chile. Bol Chil Parasitol, 1982; 37: 72-73.

—**Tsuboi T; Hirai K:**
Lipid metabolism in golden hamster infected with plerocercoid of *Spirometra erinacei* (Cestoda: Pseudophyllidea). Parasitology; 1986; 93: 143-151.

—**Wang KC; Huh S; Hong ST et al.:**
The fate of spargana inoculated into the cat brain and sequential changes of anti-sparganum IgG antibody levels in the cerebrospinal fluid. Korean J Parasitol, 1990; 28: 1-10.

—**Webster JD:**
Fragmental studies on the life history of the cestode *Mescocestoides latus*. J parasitol, 1949; 35; 83-90.

—**Witenberg G**
Studies of the cestode genus *Mesocestoides*. Arch Zool Ital, 1934; 20: 467-509.

—**Yamaguchi S:**
Systema helminthum. Vol II. The cestodes of vertebrates. 1959, Interscience Pub Co., New York, USA, pp 358-361.

DERMATOLOGIC (SKIN) DISORDERS

Dr. C.J Harvey-Clark
University Director of Animal Care
Dalhousie University
Halifax, Nova Scotia, Canada

Dr. Chris Harvey-Clark has had a lifelong interest in herpetology and veterinary aspects of reptiles. After earning a B.Sc. in marine biology at the University of Victoria, he completed a Doctor of Veterinary Medicine degree at the Western College of Veterinary Medicine in Saskatoon, Saskatchewan, Canada. Following graduation, he worked with a variety of small, exotic and wild animal species. He has worked in the field of laboratory animal medicine for the last eight years.

ANATOMY AND PHYSIOLOGY OF REPTILIAN SKIN

A complete covering of keratinized epidermis is a common feature in all four reptilian orders, excepting a few turtle genera lacking epidermal laminae such as the leatherback family Dermochelyidae. Characteristic features of typical reptilian skin include a thick outer keratinized epidermis, reduced integumental glands, and the presence of bony plates (osteoderms) in the dermis of many crocodilian and chelonian species.

The development of a thick keratinized integument in the evolution of reptiles from amphibian-like ancestors represented a major step in adaptive radiation of life forms on earth. In contrast to the amphibian dependence on water habitat, reptiles with a desiccation resistant integument have been able to adapt to a wide variety of niches, to the extent that many modern desert forms such as the desert tortoises can survive without drinking and derive their water entirely from eating vegetation. However it is important to recognise that the skin of many species of reptiles is highly permeable and that even within a species permeability may vary with age, environmental conditions, health, endocrine and reproductive hormonal status and stage of ecdysis. Some squamata such as the dog-faced watersnake *Cerberus rhynchops* can derive all body water by cutaneous absorption (Seymour 1982) while some desert tortoises have negligible passive cutaneous water flux.

Reptile skin is quite heterogeneous in composition and in some species has different barrier and permeability properties depending on topographic location on the body. Squamates often have more impervious ventral versus dorsal integument, for instance.

Reptilian skin consists of two major layers, epidermis and dermis. In the squamata (lizards and snakes) the epidermis and dermis is folded into scales .Snakes and turtles have scutes , polygonal scales on the belly (with a traction/locomotion function in snakes) or on the carapace and plastron of turtles where their function is protective . On the outer surface of the scale is a very thin layer with fine serrations, beneath which is a layer consisting of the protein keratin, which is produced from one or two underlying cell layers called the germinal epithelium. This layer, which periodically proliferates to produce a new skin layer in the shedding process, sits on an anchoring basement membrane of connective tissue. Reptilian epidermis contains 2 types of keratin based on light microscopic diffraction properties, alpha keratin which is hair-like and imparts flexibility, and beta keratin which is feather-like and imparts strength and hardness to cutaneous structures such as scales (Porter 1972) . These two types of keratin are arranged both vertically and horizontally in differential distribution to create skin structures with differing functional properties. For instance the typical overlapping scales found on a snakes head have a thicker outer beta keratin layer and a very thin underlying alpha keratin layer. The large tuberculate scales of crocodilians and some chelonia consist entirely of thick, hard beta keratin overlying dermal bone while the hinge regions between scales consists entirely of flexible alpha keratin (Lillywhite et al 1982). The hinge regions between scales and junctions between scutes are points in the integument where flexion occurs ,where two types of keratin meet and where cutaneous disease processes often first become discernible. For instance many species of parasitic mites appear to prefer the interscalar skin, and plastron lesions of aquatic turtles (so called "shell rot") often begin at the margin of a scute.

Incorporated in the outer epidermis (also termed the outer epithelial generation) between

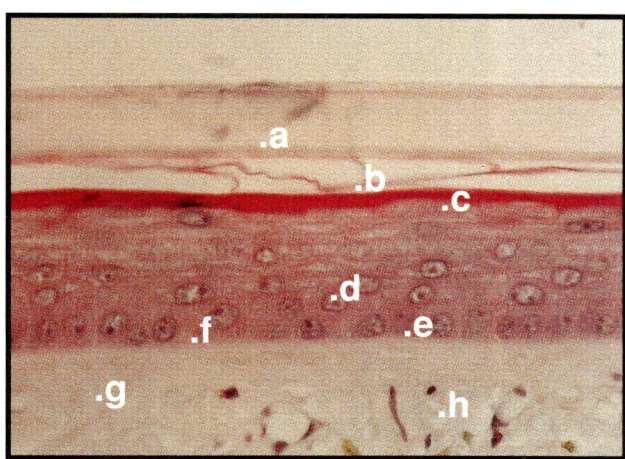

Figure 1:
Snake skin during shedding. Hematoxylin and Eosin (H&E) x 400. This illustration shows snake skin just after the cleavage zone has separated the outer and inner epidermal generations. Legend:
a= shed skin, the outer epidermal generation,
b= cleavage zone,
c= outer keratinized surface (stratum corneum)
d= zone of proliferating cells,
e= germinal epithelial layer,
f= basement membrane,
g= dermis,
h= chromatophores.

the alpha and beta keratin is the mesos layer, which is rich in polar and nonpolar lipids . This layer appears to have a role in forming a permeability barrier to the movement of water and possibly other substances through reptile skin (Roberts et al 1980)

Beneath the germinal epithelium layer lies the dermis, which is relatively thin and avascular. Sitting in the top layers of the dermis just under the germinal epithelium is a layer which contains pigment cell groupings termed chromatophores and glandular structures, the latter connected by ducts to the skin surface. The dermis is in turn connected to the underlying muscle tissue by loose connective tissue (Porter 1972).

Dermal origin bone is present in the carapace, plastron, ribs (gastralia) and lateral struts connecting these structures in chelonia, and does not match the pattern of overlying keratinized scutes. In crocodilia, in addition to dermal bone in the heavily cornified armor scales over the

back and dorsal aspects of limbs, tail and head, dermal bone is also found in the upper eyelid in the form of a protective palpebral bone (Porter 1972).When the protective epidermal laminae with their germinal epithelium are damaged , the underlying dermal bone of chelonia proliferates to close open shell lesions , but this is a prolonged process which may take years to complete.

Integumental specialisation has reached an apex in the reptilia. Keratinisation provides a durable physical protective barrier against abrasion, desiccation and ultraviolet radiation.

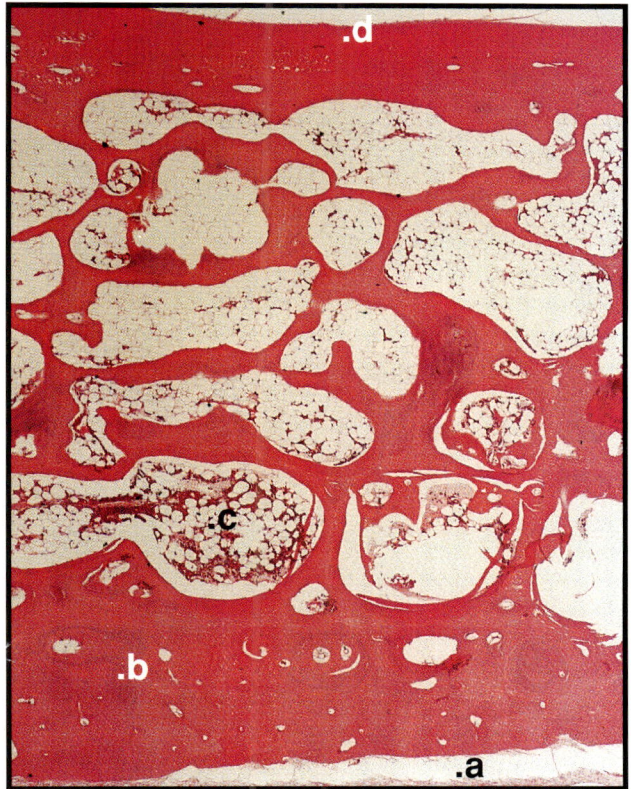

Figure 2:
H&E-stained, full-thickness, cross-section of a shell biopsy from a box turtle, x 20. The keratinized scute separated during histological preparation, leaving the underlying dermal bone. (a) Dermis and connective tissue underlying scute, (b) Haversian canals in dermal bone, (c) bone marrow spicules, (d) coelomic side of dermal bone.

Beaks of turtles,rattlesnake rattles, spines of horned lizards , claws, plaques and spiny crests of lizards are all scale derivatives (Kent 1992). The skin in some species forms flaps and folds which have highly specialised uses, for instance the dewlap of iguanas which has a display and thermoregulatory function, or the lateral body flaps of the flying gecko *Ptychozoon lionotum*, which are extended during jumps to allow a gliding form of aerial locomotion.

GAS, FLUID, AND HEAT EXCHANGE

Reptilian skin is a physiologically active surface capable in some species of major gas , fluid and heat exchange. Nonpulmonary gas exchange via the skin is important in certain species of turtles (*Chelydra, Trionyx*) and in sea snakes. In most terrestrial reptiles cutaneous oxygen exchange comprises a relatively minor component of the total requirements but in some aquatic species such as the trionychid turtles it is the major route of oxygen uptake. The skin is an important route of CO2 loss in most species, approximately 20 percent of total flux in the boa constrictor *Constrictor constrictor* and 75 percent in the sea snake *Pelamis platurus*. (Seymour, 1982).

Absorption of water through the skin is possible in the majority of reptiles and microclimate differences in humidity with resulting effects on hydration status influence survival in many aestivating wild species (Costanzo 1989). Water loss is greatest during shedding , and the permeability of skin in most reptiles is greatest just after shedding. As a rule, non-hydrated epidermis is capable of far lower water flux than hydrated epidermis, likely an adaptation to desiccation (Lillywhite 1982) Based on studies of shed skin, the primary barrier to water movement is the presence of neutral and polar lipids in the mesos layer of the outer skin in squamate epidermis (Roberts and Lillywhite,1980).

SENSORY PHYSIOLOGY

Skin and related structures play a major role in sensory physiology of reptiles for detection of prey , avoidance of predators and a variety of other uses. Cutaneous structures can form highly specialised sensory organs such as the heat sensitive pits seen in some species of snakes, for instance the Crotalid vipers . Crocodilian scales on the side, back, belly and tail incorporate a small depression containing a sensory capsule, which likely functions as a movement detection mechanism in low visibility water analogous to the lateral line of fish (Porter 1972).

Reptile skin is often brilliantly coloured and has the ability to change colour, either rapidly or over the course of days in many species. The integument plays a role as a sign stimulus for cueing warning, social and sexual signals. Many reptiles are brightly coloured and have chameleonic ability due to the presence of a variety of pigment bearing cells termed chromatophores located in the superficial dermis. These cells include guanophores, melanophores, xanthophores and iridophores with various chromatic and reflective properties. The shape and orientation of scales relative to pigment cells may have effect on thermoregulation (Lillywhite 1982). Certain lizard species have the ability to change colour rapidly by the movement of melanosomes (pigment granule organelles) into and out of dermal melanophore processes. In some snake species such as the small terrestrial island boas cyclic 24 hour colour changes in response to day length and activity level have been documented and likely have predation and cryptic value (Hedges et al 1989).

GLANDS

The glandular integument in some reptile species has pheromonal properties. Skin glands in reptiles are dermal derivatives and have

Figure 3 :
Dorsal skin from a Florida water snake, H and E x100. This illustration shows a cross-section through a scale, overlying muscle tissue. The keratinized epidermis is relatively thin on the outside of the scale (a) and thicker on the underside of the scale (b). Note the abundant chromatophores (c), dermis (d), and underlying muscle (e).

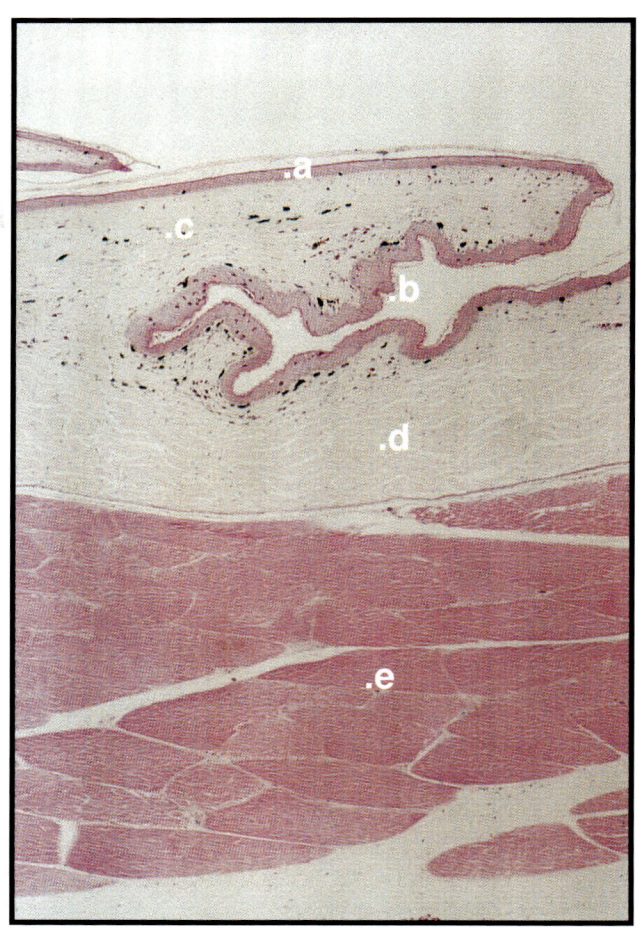

chemosensory, social and recognition functions. This includes crocodilian musk glands, femoral and precloacal pores of lizards, chin (or mental) glands in tortoises and the dorsonuchal glands in some snake species (Alberts et al 1994). Occasionally the ducts of mental glands of some terrestrial tortoises may become plugged, and require treatment with topical hot packs and saline flushing to restore patency. Femoral pores in species such as iguanas are more evident in the male and produce a sweet smelling secretion which flouresces under UV light, and which likely has a scent marking function. "Sebaceous" or epidermal inclusion cysts are a relatively common pathologic finding related to skin glands in some lizard species such as iguanas and are most common on the tail and extremities.

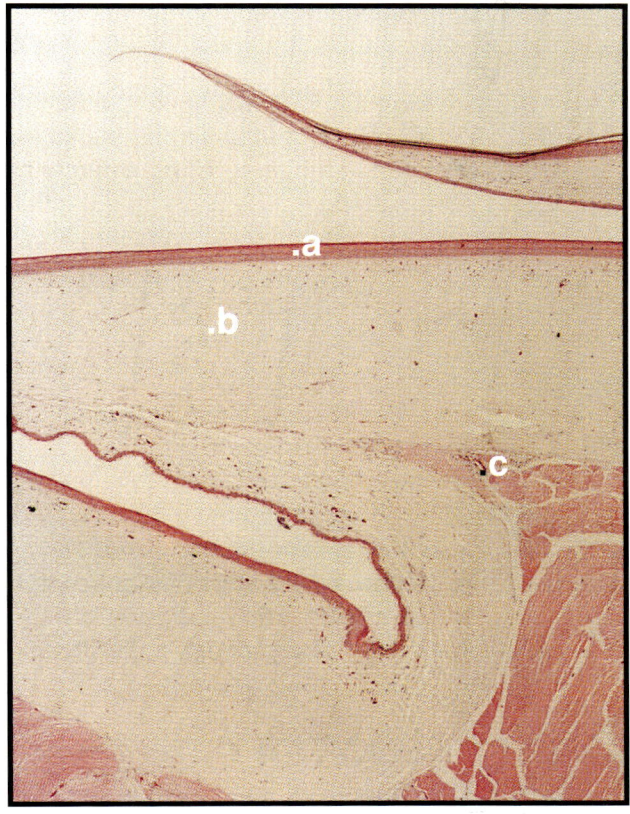

Figure 4 :
Ventral skin from the same snake shown in Figure 3, illustrating locomotory adaptations. The scales are much larger locomotory scutes with a thicker epidermis (a) and dermis (b), closer association of locomotor muscles to scutes (c), and lack of chromatophores.

SHEDDING/ECDYSIS

Squamate epidermal cells have synchronous cell proliferation and are organised in epidermal generations which permit successive and periodic complete shedding in snakes and a few lizard species (such as alligator lizards). Thyroid hormones stimulate shed in lizards and inhibit shed in snakes (Lillywhite et al 1982). The physiology and anatomy of ecdysis in snakes has been reviewed elsewhere (Jacobson 1977). Chelonia, crocodilia and most lizards shed their scales individually or in patches of multiple scales periodically, avoiding the vulnerability and physiological cost of complete ecdysis. As a rule most terrestrial chelonia shed scutes in small fragments while aquatic species shed the covering of the entire scute as one piece. A relatively high frequency of shed may be a necessary adaptation for the retention of intricately detailed foot structures important for climbing, as is seen in the gekkonid lizards. Conversely many xeric habitat lizard species such as *Dipsosaurus dorsalis* and *Uma notata* have a relatively low frequency of shed, perhaps to minimise water loss during the permeable period after shedding.

The physiology and histologic changes associated with shedding has been described in detail and consist of at least 6 distinct phases (Lillywhite et al 1982). Initially the germinal epithelium of the epidermis proliferates to form a new epithelial generation, which causes a thickening and build up of new keratin rich cells above the germinal epithelium and below the keratinized skin , termed the intermediate zone. This layer forms the new inner epidermal generation and , after ecdysis, the new skin is formed when these cells elaborate keratin. This stage is recognisable grossly as the skin and spectacle takes on an opaque, dulled or rainbow appearance and is usually 5 to 10 days in duration in most healthy snakes. In the second phase, the inner epithelial generation becomes keratinized and a cleavage zone forms between the outer and inner epithelial generation. This phase is accompanied by a clearing of the skin opacity, and occurs one to five days prior to shed in snakes. Finally, the cleavage zone separates and shedding occurs, exposing the inner epithelial generation which over the next few days hardens and decreases in permeability, becoming the new skin.

Shedding may be accompanied by temporary behaviour changes such as shyness and hiding, skittishness, aggression and anorexia. Typical behaviour at shed often consists of rubbing rostral scales, defecation during shed and drinking after shedding. Many squamate species have transparent eyeshields or spectacles which are shed with the intact skin, including some skink species , many gecko species, night lizards and all snakes. Snakes will frequently shed the cover-

Figure 5:
Carapace of a mature female box turtle, *Terrapene carolina*, showing the gradual wearing off and replacement of an outer shell scute. This process of gradual wearing exposing the underlying scute is seen in chelonians with predominantly terrestrial habits and in crocodilians. Aquatic turtles tend to shed the entire scute on an annual basis.

ing of the tongue separately during ecdysis , which when found in the enclosure may be misinterpreted as a parasite.

Frequency of shed is proportional to rate of growth and is increased in young animals,and many egg laying snake species will shed in the two week period prior to oviposition. Following shed the skin enters a resting phase until the initiation of the next ecdysis, and the shed to shed interval is regulated by the duration of this phase. Failure to shed may be the result of a variety of interacting disease processes of nutritional, endocrine,environmental or infectious origin

Shedding and reproductive behaviour may be closely (possibly pheromonally) coordinated in some species of snake.

It is important to recognise that shedding represents a considerable physiological stress for reptiles that protein loss and changes in sensory systems occur and that water should be available for drinking and soaking during this period. As a rule, handling should be avoided during ecdysis. Water also represents potential harbourage for reptilian pathogens such as *Pseudomonas* and must be kept scrupulously clean.

The healing process in reptilian (snake) skin has been described elsewhere (Smith et al 1988a,b,c), is essentially similar to the process seen in mammals and will be further discussed below. There are reports of scale loss syndromes and "spontaneous" skin rupture in snakes but the pathogenesis of these lesions is not defined, although cachexia, catabolic metabolism and inadequate nutrition would appear to play a role (Frye, 1991),(Jacobson 1992). Stress from a variety of sources is likely to be contributory (Lance, 1990).

DERMATOLOGIC DIAGNOSTICS IN REPTILE MEDICINE

Because reptilian skin has a limited number of responses to infectious and traumatic insult, with few exceptions the appearance and distribution of lesions does not tend to be pathognomonic for any particular condition. Diagnostic workup incorporating microbial culture and sensitivity, hematology, serum chemistry, skin biopsy and other clinical investigative testing is often necessary. The organisms causing cutaneous disease are frequently identical to organisms found in the animals environment and behave as facultative pathogens, emphasizing the need for environmental assessment as part of the clinical workup. The range of organisms causing cutaneous disease is wide and antibiotic resistance is common in the gram negative enteric organisms, which cause the majority of infectious skin conditions. *Pseudomonas maltophila* resistant to aminoglycoside and quinolone antibiotics has been cultured recently in snake skin infections (Harvey-Clark 1995). The presence of zoonotic *Salmonella, Mycobacteria, Pentastoma* and *Rickettsia* ,the latter in ticks of reptiles underlines the need for caution during handling of reptilian diagnostic materials, and protective lab coats and gloves should be worn during sample collection and processing.

Recent reports indicate that iguana associated salmonellosis is an emerging zoonotic problem, particularly in children (Dalton et al 1995). The U.S. Centers for Disease Control have recently stated that approximately 5 percent of the 2 million cases of salmonellosis reported annually could be linked to reptiles (MMWR 1995).

Mycobacterial disease should always be considered in the differential diagnosis of chronic cutaneous lesions which fail to respond to antibiotic treatment. *Ophionyssus* mites of snakes are extremely common and have caused a papular dermatitis in children and adults after close contact with an infected python (Schultz 1975).

Clinical diagnostic facilities should include the ability to collect material by sterile needle aspiration or open biopsy and to transport samples for aerobic and anaerobic bacterial culture and fungal culture. Anaerobic culture particularly of squamate skin abscesses and granulomas is advisable because of the prevalence of anaerobes in these cases (Stewart 1990). Light microscopic examination of fresh wet mounts and lactophenol cotton blue, gram stain and dip-quick stain in clinic are valuable tools in deciding on antibacterial and antifungal therapy during initial examination . It is important to examine fresh wet mounts particularly in lizards because fixed specimens and histology may fail to reveal some organisms such as Trichomonads (see Bacterial, Fungal and Viral Diseases affecting the Integument of Lizards). Clinical bacteriology of reptiles is well summarised by Boyer 1994. 70 percent alcohol, 10 percent neutral buffered formalin and Bouins solution for biopsy samples and parasites should be available. In snakes and lizards full thickness skin biopsies can be collected using a scalpel with physical restraint and local anesthesia by 2 percent

Figure 6:
Surgical shell biopsy in the box turtle shown in Figure 11. After sedation and sterile surgical preparation of the shell, a full thickness biopsy is collected using a dental burr.

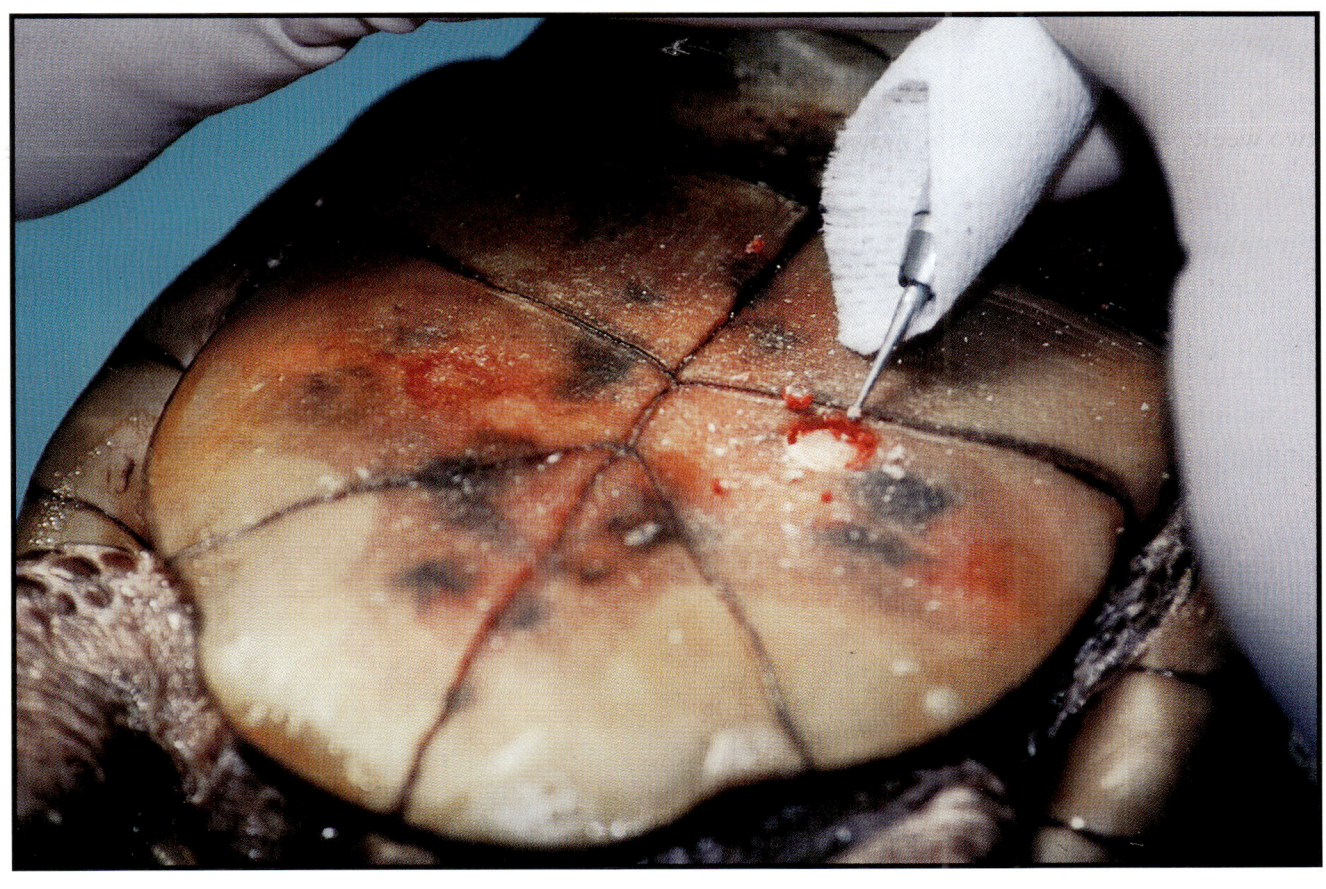

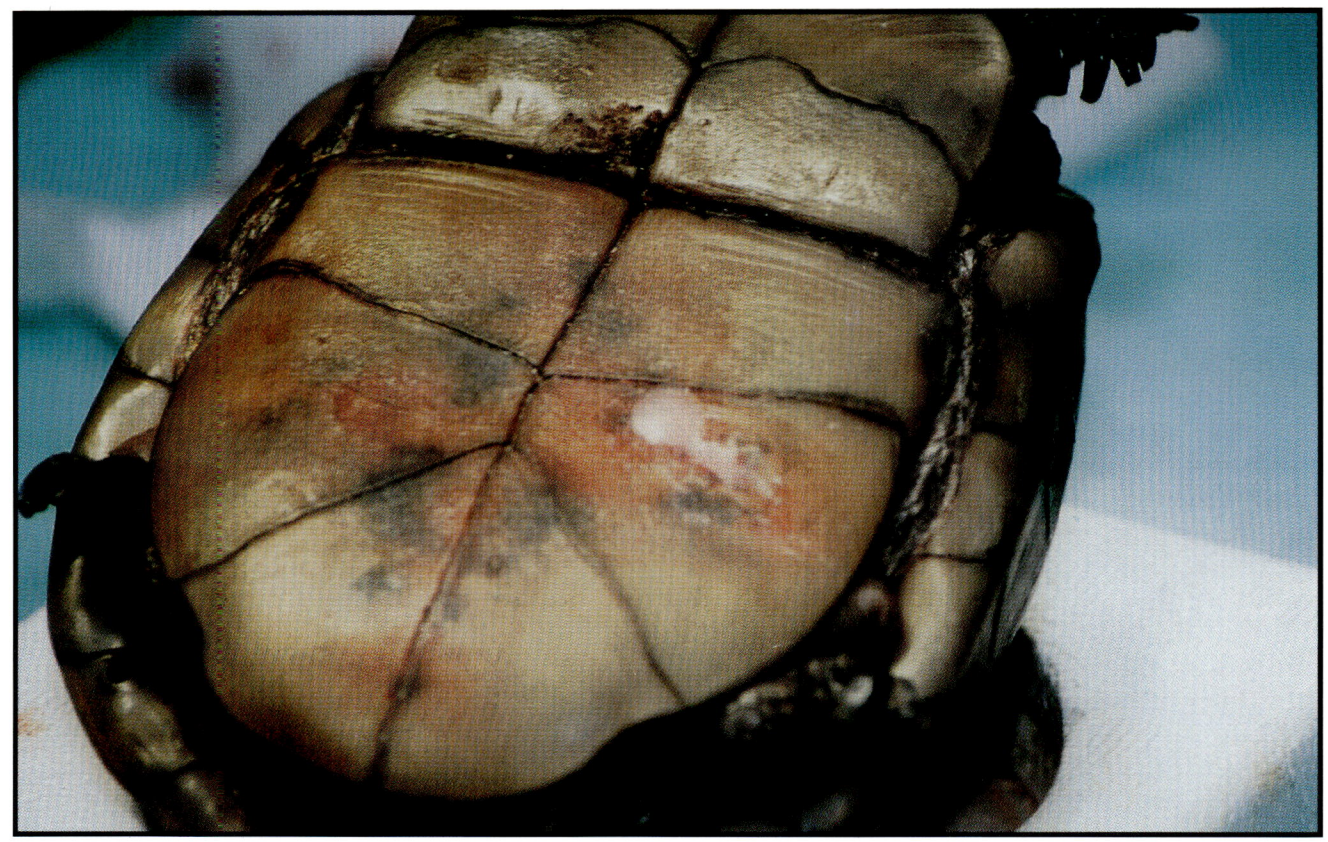

Figure 7:
Completed shell biopsy with a circular dental acrylic patch in place over the collection site.

lidocaine infiltration. After sterile preparation , a wedge resection technique is employed , which creates a deficit which is easier to close than that left by a circular biopsy punch. The biopsy can be divided for histology and microbiology or 2 small biopsies collected. Following biopsy, tissues can be minced with a scalpel blade into fine fragments or ground in a sterile tissue grinder prior to culture , which will enhance recovery of pathogens. Turtle shell biopsies, excisional biopsies of tumours and debridement and closure of large skin lesions usually require general anesthesia, reviewed elsewhere (Boyer 1992a) ,(Bennett 1991). Shell biopsies require permanent repair. The cost,permanent lesion created, potential information gained and need to perform this procedure in long-lived chelonians should be carefully considered on a case basis. Figure 6 shows shell biopsy technique.

THERAPEUTIC CONSIDERATIONS

Physical and chemical injuries, nutritional and ecdysis problems, and secondary cutaneous infectious disease commonly originate with deficits in husbandry. Education through the provision of care and husbandry instructional materials is an important tool for reducing the magnitude of the prob-

lem. There are a number of excellent resources for this type of material (Boyer 1992b).

Husbandry and environmental conditions need to be assessed and corrected as a first step in developing a treatment plan in reptile medicine. It is both worthwhile and necessary to view the vivarium to fully appreciate the role of environment in the development of skin conditions. Onset of skin diseases may be acute or chronic and likewise may take a prolonged period to resolve, particularly in chelonian shell conditions. Conversely, some fulminant skin conditions may occur concurrently with septicemia and require rapid, aggressive treatment. It may be necessary for owners to administer treatments at home, hence time spent in education will positively affect the outcome of home treatment. Ongoing environmental monitoring of water quality parameters and quantitative environmental bacteriology can be useful in determining the degree of environmental microbial burden and efficacy of cleaning procedures, particularly in intensive rearing, commercial breeding establishments, oceanaria and zoo facilities.

In the initial workup of discrete cutaneous lesions and masses such as tumours, abscesses and granulomas, curative surgical excision or drainage with impression smears,gram stain and culture of exudate or aspirate is often the most suc-

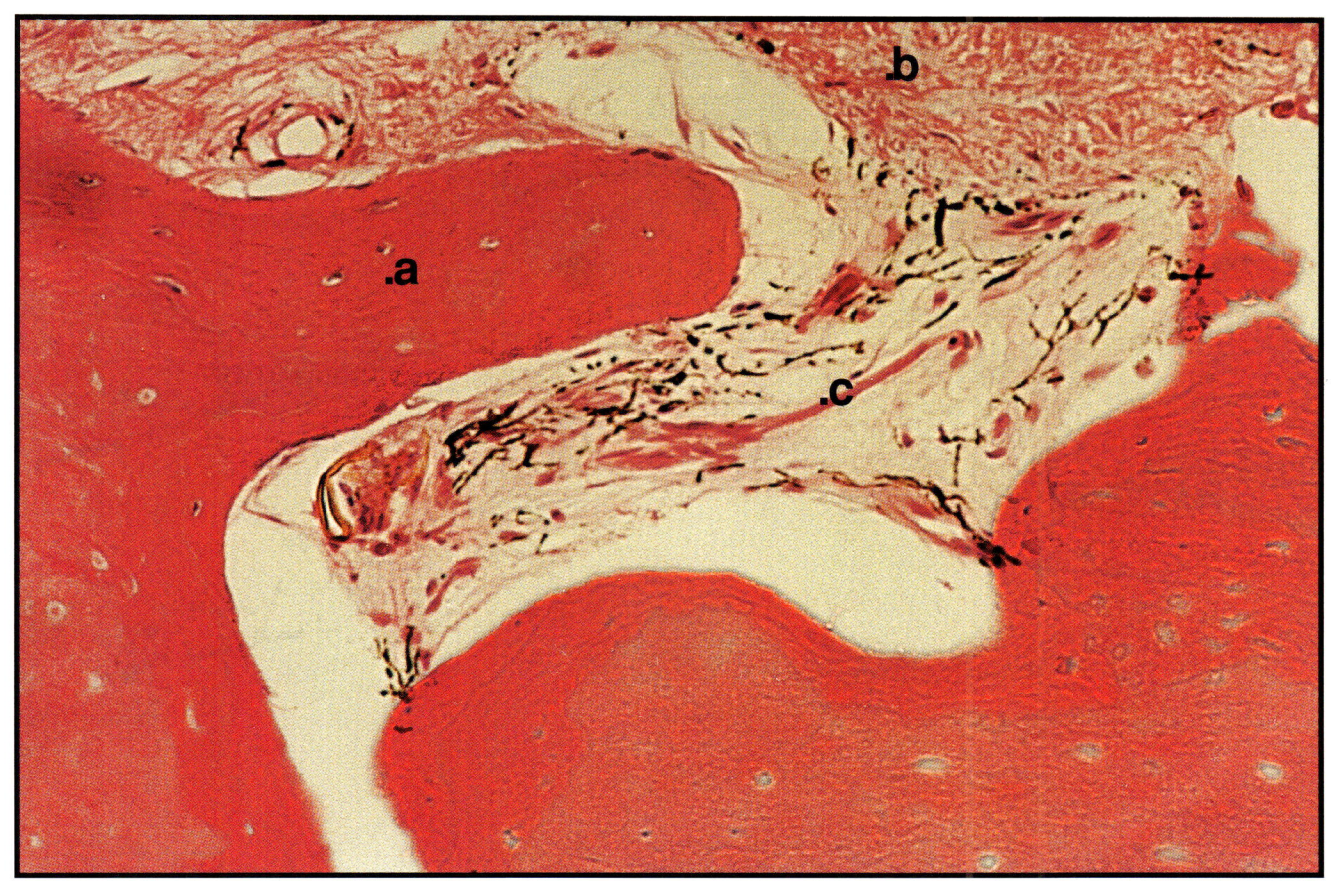

Figure 8:
H- and E-section of biopsy sample from turtle in Figure 11 x 200, showing pigmented branching septate fungal elements invading dermal bone: (a) dermal bone, (b) dermis, and (c) branching brown pigmented septate hyphae.

cessful approach. Spillage of exudates should be minimized during surgery by employing capsular excision techniques . In many reptile species there is little redundant skin and the excision of moderate sized cutaneous lesions may create deficits that are difficult to close. Wherever possible skin incisions for biopsy should be made on lateral or dorsal areas to avoid wound maceration and colonisation, commonly encountered in ventral areas. Where ventral incisions are essential, spraying the closed wound with several layers of polyurethane wound spray (OpSite, Smith and Nephew) or micronised aluminum spray (Alluspray, Austin) (McCutcheon, K., pers comm) will create a physical barrier to decrease the entry of contaminant bacteria. The provision of nonparticulate absorptive warm substrates such as disposable diapers over heating coil warmed heat diffusion plates will also assist wound healing. Incisions should be made along natural tension lines such as the lateral scale-ventral scute margin to minimise suture line tension, and transverse incisions avoided. Where feasible, primary closure of uncontaminated wounds is preferred to treatment as open wounds because of the high risk of bacterial/fun-

gal colonization of open wounds in reptile patients. Most biopsies can be closed with fine 4-0 or 5-0 monofilament and the sutures placed in intrascalar spaces. Pigmentary changes such as darkening of surrounding epidermis is common around healed surgical sites (particularly in Squamata) and owners should be informed of this possible consequence prior to performing surgery. The successful use of cryosurgery on well defined pedunculated masses in reptiles has been described(Baxter et al 1988).

Multifocal infectious lesions such as multiple cutaneous abbesses which are too numerous to excise may respond to systemic antibiotic therapy. Generally parenteral bactericidal antibiotics are preferable to oral bacteriostatic agents, with the choice of antibiotics dictated by published reptilian pharmacokinetic information (Bush 1992) and culture / antibacterial minimum inhibitory concentration data. Initial empirical treatment prior to the receipt of c and s results in life threatening infections is justifiable and hydration by oral or intracoelomic administration of fluids should be assured prior to starting a course of treatment, particularly with nephrotoxic antibiotics. Drug dosage should consider the relative size of the reptile and the metabolic activity of tissues, guidelines on allometric scaling are available (Beynon et al 1992) Principles of antimicrobial chemotherapy in reptilia have been reviewed elsewhere (Jacobson 1988) .

In addition to surgical excision, lesion drainage and systemic antibiotics , elevation of environmental temperature to the high end of preferred optimal temperature (25 to 34 degrees centigrade for most species) and the provision of a dry basking area for aquatic species has recognised beneficial effects in accelerating wound healing (Smith et al 1988b).

The circulation of systemic antibiotics and uptake of locally applied antibiotics will be enhanced as well as humoral and cell mediated immunity. Disinfectant soaking of reptiles with superficial dermatitis in warmed dilute antibacterial / antifungal solutions (such as tamed iodine Betadine or chlorhexidine gluconate) also has beneficial debridement and antibacterial effects.

Large open wounds and wounds on ventral surfaces undergoing continuous abrasion require more complete protection. The majority of active snakes and lizards eventually displace conventional surface dressings. Cyanoacrylate glue (Crazy Glue) applied around the periphery of a conventional bandage adheres it to an aquatic chelonian shell in water for 24-48 hours. Regular applications of topical ointments or spray- on occlusive dressings are useful adjuncts in these cases and permit epithelialisation and wound contraction while protecting the wound. Micronised aluminum spray (Alluspray, Austin) and polyurethane spray (Opsite, Smith and Nephew) can be applied in several layers to form a physical protective barrier over open wounds which will be subsequently shed during ecdysis. A study has demonstrated optimal open wound healing in garter snakes with the use of occlusive polyurethane wound sprays as opposed to other topical treatments (Smith et al 1988c). Bioactive wound dressings may also be employed. Reptilian wounds have been treated using antibacterial ointment under nonlubricated condoms, demonstrating that methods for the treatment of open wounds are only limited by the ingenuity of the veterinarian (Frye 1992).

The rational use of topical antiinflammatory medications with a corticosteroid component remains controversial in reptilian dermatologic practice. The systemic side effects of chronically applied topical corticosteroid products are profound in mammalian species and have not been elucidated in reptiles. Because of the ubiquitous presence of adventitious pathogens in the environment of captive reptiles , any medication with potential local or systemic immunomodulatory effects should be used with caution.

Although reptiles and particularly tortoises have evolved the skin as a permeability barrier, the transcutaneous route remains one of the least invasive means for treating dehydration in reptilia. Good husbandry practice includes the use of warm soaks in isotonic fluids for rehydration after recovery from hibernation in snakes and turtles. The "bovril bath' or Gatorade bath continues to be a means of restoring hydration and protein loss in debilitated turtles. The addition of a mild detergent / wetting agent to warm sprays or soaks will enhance the penetration of transcutaneous fluids in squamates, with the constraint that less hydrated epidermis tends to be more resistant to fluid uptake .

SKIN DISEASES AND CONDITIONS

SKIN DISEASE RELATED TO NUTRIENTS

The reingestion of shed skin is a normal phenomenon in a variety of lizard species such as geckoes and likely represents an adaptation for conservation of the protein found in keratinized material (Bustard et al 1965). ´This phenomenon has also been reported in a variety of snake species such as kingsnakes *Lampropeltis getulus getulus* and vine snakes *Uromacer oxyrhynchus.*

Inadequate dietary calcium, calcium/phosphorus imbalance, lack of Vitamin D or UV exposure, or a combination of these factors leads to soft shells in chelonia, deformed ventral curved plastral scutes, dished marginal scutes due to metabolic bone disease. Oral and in severe cases injectable calcium supplementation, and the use of salmon derived calcitonin in severe cases can help to correct nutritional osteodystrophy (Boyer 1992b), provided proper diet, temperature, light and UV sources are provided.

Well cared for captive born tortoises may develop carapace plates with exaggerated doming and deep grooves between plates. Nutrition is suspected to contribute to this condition , possibly overfeeding of high protein diets early in life. Doming has also been reported in wild leopard tortoises (*Geochelone pardalis)* in South Africa (Rall et al 1993) .

A syndrome of shell necrosis on the carapace, plastron, and forelimb scutes has been described in wild desert tortoise (*Gopherus agasizii)* . The plastron is most severely affected and flaking lesions start at seams between scutes, with portions of the shell becoming grey-white, occasionally orange, and lesions spreading in irregular fashion towards the center of each scute.((Jacobson et al 1994) The etiology of this syndrome is unclear but the authors believe it may be nutritional , related to change in plant micronutrient composition following drought periods.

Blepharitis,palpebral edema and hyperkeratosis of skin and other squamous mucosae in turtles is highly suggestive of vitamin A deficiency. This condition may be treated with injectable Vitamin A 2000 IU/kg im followed with oral multivitamin (including Vitamin A) supplementation until lesions resolve. Some chelonians (such as redfooted tortoise, *Geochelone carbonaria*) under normal conditions have somewhat inflamed looking eyes which can be mistaken for early symptoms of Vitamin A deficiency.

Vitamin A overdosage (a single dose of 5000 IU/kg im) has been associated with dry flaking skin progressing to necrotizing dermatitis in chelonians (Frye 1989). Iatrogenic hypervitaminosis A has also been implicated in the etiology of repeated and excessive shedding in snakes (Beynon et al 1992) Because most parenteral fat soluble vitamin preparations are long lasting, extreme care should be taken in dose calculation and repeated use of these products, in order to avoid overdosage.

HERITABLE AND DEVELOPMENTAL CUTANEOUS CONDITIONS

Common anomalies include absence of,misformed or extra carapace and scute plates in chelonia, possibly related in some cases to excessively high or poorly controlled incubation temperature . Scaleless snakes and snakes with backward pointing scales are occasionally found both in captive breeding situations and as healthy adults in the wild. Interest in the production of amelanistic and other colour variant snakes has resulted in an extensive literature on melanism and patterning in reptilia,particularly squamates. The topic of developmental conditions has been extensively reviewed (Frye 1991)

CUTANEOUS TRAUMATIC LESIONS

TEMPERATURE RELATED TRAUMA

The use of in-cage heat lamps,ultraviolet lamps, hot rocks and electric heating pads to provide temperature gradients in the reptilian environment is the most common cause of cutaneous thermal injury. Stress from excessive heat may also precipitate certain types of cutaneous syndromes- high water temperatures in excess of 39 degrees centigrade have been implicated in initiating the herpesvirus grey patch disease of green turtles (Jacobson 1991).

Burns are often seen on the ventrum in lizards and on the back and neck in snakes . Semiterrestrial turtles entering the pet trade may have old shell injuries from burns sustained during forest fires . Necrosis of thermal burns may be followed in a few days by bacterial colonization, often by resistant Pseudomonads, a common and potentially fatal complication. Wound bacterial culture and sensitivity testing, regular debridement, appropriate systemic antibiotic treatment and following the exudative phase, use of sterile occlusive dressings or spray -on dressings is advisable. Wounds which are too extensive to be primarily closed must be managed as open wounds with debridement, nutritional support and protection of the woundbed with occlusive, bioactive or spray-on dressings.Passive water and protein loss through large uncovered wounds may significantly increase morbidity and should be prevented. In localised burn cases pseudomonacidal topical ointments such as silver sulfadiazine 2% should be regularly applied. Maintenance at the high end of the optimal temperature range has demonstrated beneficial effects in accelerated wound healing (Smith et al 1988b).

Frostbite injury to skin and underlying tissues in large, escape-prone reptiles is not uncommon in snowbelt areas. A Galapagos tortoise (*Geochelone elephantopus*) which became lodged against a metal exterior door during a period of outdoor temperatures in the minus 30 degree centigrade range developed dry gangrene of the right forelimb which necessitated amputation (G Glover, pers comm 1995) .

BITE AND SCRATCH WOUNDS

Reptiles as a rule are asocial and hence intra- and interspecific aggression is a common problem in group housing situations. Subcutaneous hematomas secondary to bite wounds have been described in lizards (Wallach 1983). Bite wounds are common in aquatic turtles,iguanas, monitor lizards and crocodilians particularly while competing for food in group housing , and between territorial species like skinks, chameleons and softshell turtles . Male squamata frequently fight if housed together during the breeding season, and some species such as iguanas commonly sieze the nape of the female dur-

Figure 9:
Cutaneous developmental anomaly: abnormal pattern of vertebral scutes in a juvenile box turtle.

ing courtship, reulting in infected wounds to this area. The author has seen numerous cases of infected wounds in the vicinity of the nape and back of the head in group housed aquatic turtles such as *Pseudemys scripta*, usually during breeding season and generally in the smaller specimens under group housed conditions. It is also common to find infected neck lacerations in female iguanas in group housing situations; the male seizes the neck in his jaws during courtship and the ability of the female to escape may be hampered by the enclosure size and layout. Correcting the social and environmental factors contributing to bite and scratch wounds should be a primary part of the treatment plan (Warwick, 1990).

Deep bite wounds are characteristically both contaminated and devitalised due to crushing and maceration. Rational management is based on the assumption that the wound is infected, so primary care consists of culture and sensitivity (C and S) ,followed by immediate treatment with gram negative bactericidal antibiotics and supportive care where appropriate such as parenteral fluids. Following stabilisation , debridement and open management as described for burn wounds, with an assessment of damage to underlying organs utilizing radiography, endoscopy and exploratory surgery if necessary is justified . After minimal debride-

ment some fresh,cleanly incised non-macerated wounds can be successfully closed primarily with monofilament nylon suture , but more extensive contaminated wounds should be managed as open wounds.

Snakes being fed live prey are frequently bitten by rodents , sometimes severely. On occasion clinically normal reptiles may fail to respond to live feeder animals, or debilitated reptiles may be offered live food as an inducement to feed. Anorexic snakes may in turn be too debilitated to respond to a hungry rodent gnawing through skin to expose bone or viscera. Prognosis is often poor in the affected snake because of pre-existing abnormalities, however even healthy snakes have been injured by live rodents, particularly larger aggressive species such as rats. The provision of food for live feeder rodents left in the cage with snakes may prevent some injuries inflicted by the rodents due to hunger. However supervision during feeding live prey or preferably the use of dead prey will prevent this problem.

Severely damaged turtle shells may be complicated by extensive tissue damage, bleeding , maceration, avulsed, absent and avascular dermal bone and soil contamination. Dog or racoon bites and auto injury appear to be the commonest causes. Initially severe injuries are managed as open wounds with daily cleansing and debridement. Shell fragments can be temporarily stabilized with bridges of 5 minute waterproof epoxy glue impregnated gauze or fiberglass strips which bridge but do not occlude open wounds, permitting drainage and wound access. Permanent repair should be delayed until infection is controlled, wounds are granulating and the patient is stable, generally from 5 days to two months or more in severe cases. In aquatic turtles which have an absolute requirement for submergence in order to feed, temporary waterproof occlusive dressings can be fashioned to protect the wound during this period using transparent polymer occlusive dressings (Tegaderm) attached with cyanoacrylate glue, which last up to 2 weeks and permit periodic debridement. The addition of 1 ppm chlorine in the aquatic system will help to control wound contaminant organisms. When the coelomic cavity is exposed due to a shell defect, after debridement it should be sealed with a temporary occlusive patch such as a transparent occlusive adhesive wound dressing, or plastic wrap to prevent contamination, fluid loss and dehydration. Systemic antibiotics are essential if body cavities are open and peritoneal lavage and drainage may be necessary.

Several techniques for chelonian shell repair have been described using various readily available materials (Bennett 1989). Using standard sterile technique shell edges are disinfected with topical chlorhexidine and cleaned with acetone, large shell deficits are filled with calcium hydroxide dental root paste , over which a patch is applied using dental acrylic, hoof repair material or epoxy impregnated fiberglass patch material. Psittacine beak repair kits (Henry Schein Inc) permit the shell colour to be closely matched in display specimens or where cosmetic results are essential. Large deficits heal exceptionally slowly and the patch must remain in place a minimum of 1 to 2 years in most cases. Periodic patch removal, debridement and replacement may be required to accommodate growth . It is important to avoid the inclusion of inert patch material such as acrylic or fiberglass between healing shell edges which impedes the process of creeping substitution. If interposed in a healing shell lesion these materials may induce foreign body response , chronic nonunion and provide harbourage for bacteria and debris.

Scratch wounds are relatively common in lizards, particularly species such as the iguana where the young animals engage in 'stacking" behaviour around heat sources and accidentally scratch each other. Often these wounds become secondarily infected (see below under infectious diseases of lizards).

MISCELLANEOUS TRAUMATIC SKIN CONDITIONS

Degloving or scale damage lesions secondary to capture using pole snares and snake tongs may be treated as open wounds. Electrocution related injuries in squamates which have encountered exposed wires can be treated as burn wounds. Foreign body reactions in combination with bacterial and fungal infection in lizard and snake species occur predominantly in the perioral and ventral areas. These may present as granulomatous areas , result from encountering cactus spines, wood splinters, fiberglass and other foreign material , and require surgical excision. Etiological diagnosis frequently requires histology in the case of foreign bodies.

Prolapse of the cloaca and hemipenes may be seen in all 4 reptile orders. Obesity in lizards and turtles may predispose this condition, as well as repeated breeding or oviposition attempts. Resolving the predisposing problem (egg retention, impacted hemipenal plugs, parasite infestation, coelomic, gastrointestinal or urogenital foreign bodies and liths etc) is the most successful approach. Symptomatic treatment involving protection and debridement/topical therapy of damaged tissue and reducing / retaining the prolapse generally with a purse string suture is also necessary. Repeated prolapse indicates a more definitive repair such as celiotomy with cloacapexy is necessary, and that the underlying cause requires resolution.

BEHAVIORAL SKIN LESIONS

Abraded rostral scales are a common problem in Squamata and may result from a broad range of causes, so a generic approach is seldom successful. Some of the common identified causes include: excess environmental temperature or failure to supply the necessary temperature gradient,visually transparent boundaries leading to rubbing on window glass,repeated escape attempts from an aggressive cagemate, newly caught specimens which may seek to constantly escape, aggressive or hungry species striking glass repeatedly, failure to supply a shy species with a refuge or hide box, mate seeking during the breeding season, gravid females searching for a nest site, thwarted migratory instincts, species with large home ranges, and questing predators housed in close quarters . Open rostral abrasions frequently become the portal for deep seated cranial bone infection which may be very resistant to treatment.

Predicting and correcting the predisposing situation before rostral rubbing becomes a problem, particularly through the provision of adequate sized enclosures, refuge areas, padding and visual barriers is the most effective approach. Established minor rostral lesions usually respond to topical antibiotics providing predisposing conditions are corrected, with more extensive lesions requiring biopsy, culture and sensitivity, debridement and often prolonged systemic treatment.

Failure to supply slightly abrasive substrates may result in dysecdysis and in overgrowth of toenails in lizards and turtles and beaks in turtle.

RETAINED SHED/FAILURE TO SHED

Much of North America has extreme seasonal change in climate with winter indoor humidity levels below 40 percent, leading to retention of part or all of the skin following shedding in squamata. Where dry particulate bedding materials are employed, or clean water for soaking is not provided in the primary enclosure, dysecdysis is also common. Periodic swims in warm water and humidified air help prevent dysecdysis. Hide boxes containing clean damp materials such as sphagnum moss or dampened foam rubber can help to provide a humid microenvironment. Rough bark or astroturf to facilitate rubbing the skin also helps. If dysecdysis occurs, warm water soaking will usually loosen the skin sufficiently for shedding, or to permit assisted ecdysis. Placing snakes and lizards in a pillow case with a clean damp terrycloth towel on a warm (30 centigrade) substrate will result in a successful shed within 24 hours in most cases. If the spectacle is retained following a shed , it may be cautiously removed with fine forceps following softening and soaking locally or by using the pillowcase method described. Some snakes repeatedly retain spectacles, particularly if they have an old eye, spectacle or periocular injury. Caution must be exercised during the removal of retained spectacles as the inadvertent removal of the entire thickness of the spectacle will result in exposure keratitis and loss of the eye.

Avascular necrosis of digits or portions of the tail leading to dry gangrene from retained skin rings is seen in lizards, particularly iguanas and tegus. Geckoes , skinks and chameleons may experience similar problems when extremities retain a covering of old skin. This can be complicated by bacterial and fungal infection. Soaking and physical skin removal accompanied with topical antibiotics/antifungals will resolve these lesions unless avascular necrosis has occurred ,

which may necessitate amputation and prolonged treatment. Retained skin rings are also seen in snakes, generally caudal to the cloaca and causing avascular necrosis of the distal tail. These are treated in similar fashion to the lesions seen in lizards. Where an extremity is affected, checking vascularity with a needle stick may prevent the needless amputation of viable tissue.

A syndrome of constant skin shedding in snakes with shortened inter-shed intervals has been described (Cooper et al 1981) and postulated as being due to either primary hyperthyroidism or pituitary dysfunction. There is no doubt many cutaneous problems in reptiles have an endocrine component and the clinical elucidation and publication of these cases is needed to clarify incidence and pathogenesis.

Dysecdysis may also mirror general poor health and cachectic state in Squamata with serious systemic disease and should be viewed in conjunction with other symptoms and history.

CUTANEOUS MANIFESTATIONS OF SYSTEMIC DISEASE

Systemic infection and septicemia may be accompanied by cutaneous signs such as multiple small petechial hemorrhages, evident in areas of light coloured scalation and under light or thin scutes. This symptom indicates a fulminating disease process and requires aggressive investigation and treatment when apparent.

Reptiles with upper respiratory infections may suffer from occluded nares, leading to extension of invasive infections of the maxillary bones and turbinates, with cutaneous involvement.

Firm cutaneous swellings in the vicinity of joints may be due to severe inflammatory response to the presence of uric acid crystals. The development of gout tophi may result from renal insult such as the excessive use of nephrotoxic drugs, episodes of dehydration with hyperuricemia or excessive dietary protein. The finding of crystalline uric acid material at necropsy or radiographically is diagnostic. Oral allopurinol and saline dialysis have been used in the treatment of gout in a Chilean tortoise (*Geochelone chiliensis*) (Wright ,1992)

Excessively deep, accentuated lines between growth rings on the scutes of terrestrial chelonia have been associated with chronic systemic disease such as renal failure (Frye 1991) In addition to subcutaneous periarticular gout lesions , renal disease may be accompanied by subcutaneous water retention and shedding difficulties. The development of edema of the tissues deep to the ventral scales is seen in certain cases of renal disease in snakes . Turtles with chronic kidney disease may develop soft shells due to renal osteodystrophy. In the terminal phase of renal disease turtles may develop subcutaneous edema in the extremities as well as swelling, edema and seepage of fluid in the inter-scute spaces.

Severe liver disease in reptiles may lead to changes in oncotic pressure due to hypoproteinemia resulting in cutaneous symptoms. This author has observed ventral edema with jaundice of subcutaneous tissues and oral mucosa in an indigo snake *Drymarchon corais* with severe end-stage liver disease secondary to amebiasis. Subcutaneous edema has been described in two map turtles (*Graptemys pseudogeographica, Graptemys barbouri*) with hepatic necrosis secondary to herpesvirus-like infection (Jacobson et al 1982b)

Dehydration is commonly encountered in reptiles as part of a variety of systemic syndromes and is usually manifested as dry, wrinkled skin and occasionally as a slightly "collapsed" looking eye. Delayed shedding in an otherwise healthy snake may create a dehydrated appearance due to wrinkled skin, particularly in the head area.

Cutaneous deposition of ceroid pigment causing ulcerated granulomatous skin lesions accompanying similar granulomatous lesions in viscera and has been noted in caimans (Frye 1991).

A syndrome associated with obstipation, necrosis of the GI tract and infection of the female reproductive tract has been reported in the burmese python. This progressive condition starts as a few flaking scales but progresses to involve the entire body surface. Histology reveals that the stratum corneum is thinned, and the disease process can be reversed if the primary disease process is treated. (Jacobson et al 1986b).

BLISTER DISEASE

Colubrids such as the water snakes (*Natrix* spp) and garter snake family seem to be particularly prone to blister disease. When high humidity or water saturated absorbent substrates such as wet newspaper are present, small coalescing fluid filled vesicles may form along ventral scales in snakes and some lizard species. Cooler temperatures and lack of air circulation in the primary enclosure also predispose to blister disease. In turn, opportunistic bacterial pathogens can invade vesicles as they

rupture,leading to scale loss and local infection, often accompanied by serious, life threatening systemic disease such as septicemia and pneumonia . Although the pathophysiologic mechanism is not understood vesicle formation may be related to passive water movement through snake skin which is accelerated at some phases of the shed cycle. Treatment consists of provision of clean, dry, warm substrate, debridement, topical and systemic antibiotic treatment based on C and S results when infection occurs, disinfectant soaks and the provision of radiant heat to dry the lesion.

INFECTIOUS CUTANEOUS DISEASES IN CHELONIA

DISEASES OF THE SHELL

BACTERIA

Recent clinical isolates from reptilian cutaneous infections with their antimicrobial sensitivities are available in the literature (Harvey-Clark 1995). Discoloured necrotizing lesions of the carapace and plastron in aquatic turtles may be associated with food and feces contamination of water, inappropriate water temperatures and lack of adequate dry basking sites. The term SCUD (septicemic cutaneous ulcerative disease) is applied when both skin and shell lesions are present due to *Citrobacter freundii* (and possibly *Serratia* coinfection)(Wallach 1983).Accompanying cutaneous processes may be infection / abscessation of viscera accompanied by debility and anorexia. Thromboembolic events related to other septicemic Gram negative enteric organisms very likely cause similar shell lesions with a similar pathogenesis. Aerobic gram negative bacteria have also been found as a cause of peracute necrotizing shell lesions in softshell turtles(Frye et al 1984a). Removal, isolation and initial treatment with potent gram negative bactericidal antibiotics together with debridement and daily soaks in dilute warm chlorhexidine or tamed iodine solutions are advisable. Even with aggressive rehydration, alimentation and the use of parenteral antibiotics based on C and S results this condition is commonly fatal.

The keratin digesting bacterium *Beneckea chitinivora* which is commonly found in crustacean exoskeleton has been associated with chronic blackened focal erosions on the plastron and carapace in aquatic turtles. Employing live or frozen crustaceans as feeders or tank mates should be avoided, due to mechanical carriage of the bacteria on the exoskeleton of these species. Very little debility is associated with infection and isolation, debridement, daily soaking in tamed iodine disinfectant and heat lamp basking in a dry environment will halt lesions. Healing of open shell lesions is prolonged as a rule.

Turtles differ in their susceptibility to bacterial shell infections due to B.chitinivora, for instance under certain circumstances the Eastern Painted Turtle, *Chrysemys picta* , rapidly develops shell lesions while other species (Red Eared Slider, *Pseudemys scripta)* may carry shell-damaging bacteria into a group housed situation without themselves having visible shell lesions.

Control of these slow-to-heal shell infections involves quarantine of new turtles, avoiding the mixing of turtle species and the use of disinfectant dips to decrease mechanical carriage of bacteria.

Compared to the terrestrial tortoises, aquatic and semiaquatic chelonians such as pond turtles, sliders, wood turtles and box turtles appear to be more susceptible to mixed bacterial and bacterial/fungal infection of the shell not attributable to SCUD or *Beneckea*. This may be due to environmental factors such as ambient temperature, environmental bacterial load and particularly mechanical injury from surfaces in the environment such as rough concrete . Pockets of infection deep to the keratinized lamellae of the ventral scutes may involve only the lamellae (superficial infection) or may involve the underlying dermal bone (deep infection) and are most typically located in the plastral region . Deep shell infection with osteomyelitis of dermal bone can extend to the coelomic cavity and requires early aggressive treatment to achieve a good prognosis. The infected area is usually recognised due to foci of black or red-yellow discolouration and softening of the shell, and may be dry or discharging a serosanguinous to purulent exudate.Lesions progress to multiple coalescing craters. Following sedation, it is necessary to deroof the softened and necrotic area with a dental burr, remove all necrotic material with a dental pick to achieve drainage,and apply topical antibiotic treatment (for superficial infection) or topical and systemic antibiotics (for deep infection). Material for bacterial culture and sensitivity testing should be collected at this time. Fungal organisms are frequently present in mixed shell infections requiring the use of antifungal topical and systemic treatment. Regular debridement and enforced dry periods along with ventral radiant heat (from a heated substrate) in the upper end of the optimal temperature range accelerates healing of ventral scutes. Shell scarring is common in deep infections, which require months to granulate and heal. This condition is prevalent in sliders and painted turtles kept in cooler water without adequate amounts of basking space or water filtration/purification. Cooler water may depress metabolism, leading to failure to feed adequately, with subsequent malnutrition , immune suppression and exacerbation of shell and skin lesions.

FUNGAL SHELL DISEASES

The veterinary literature indicates that saprophytic fungi are not common primary etiologic agents in shell lesions, although in unusual species such as Florida softshell turtles (*Abalone ferox*) necrotizing shell lesions associated with *Mucor* have been described (Jacobson et al

Figure 10:
Abscess of the epidermal laminae and dermal bone in the plastron of a painted turtle, *Chrysemys picta*. Note the yellow necrotic centre surrounded by a red circular zone of inflammation. This type of solitary lesion is well-suited to deroofing, surgical debridement and topical antibiotics.

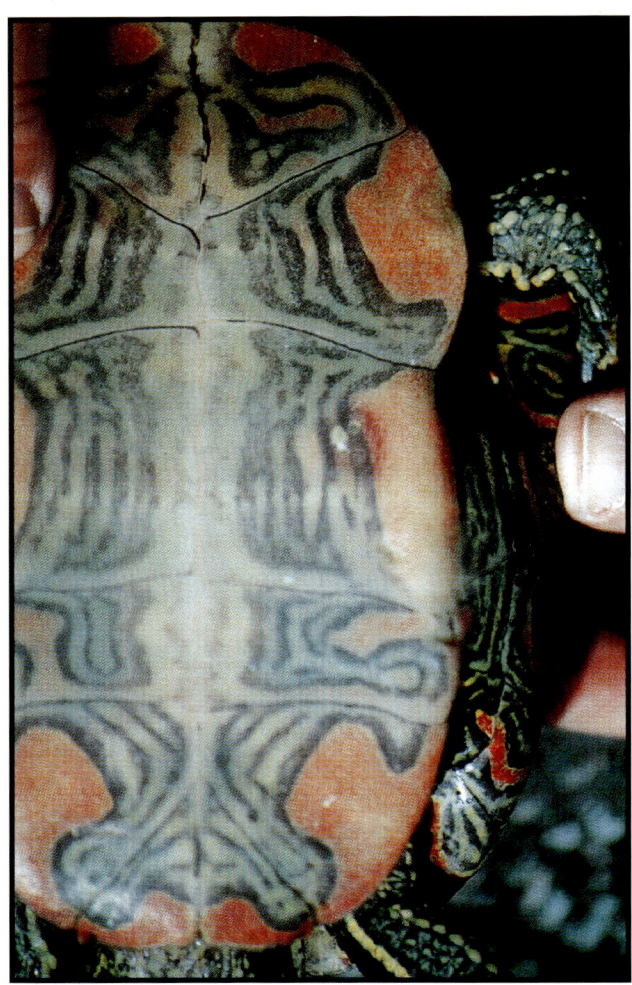

1980). In this case carapace and skin lesions were small white coalescing ulcerations which. had characteristic nonseptate branching hyphae on lactophenol cotton blue stained scrapings and responded to malachite green soaks at .15 mg/l. More commonly fungal agents contribute to secondary shell infections in debilitated animals and in animals with deep penetrating injuries to the carapace, particulary when in contact with soil or dirt. Turtles which are sick, frightenned or socially subordinate may spend more time than normal submerged in water and decreased time in dry basking becoming prone to waterborne fungal and bacterial infection . Certain foodstuffs such as tomatoes if left to spoil in the animals environment have been associated with harbourage of fungal agents causing cutaneous mycoses (Ruiz 1980).

SHELL DISEASES DUE TO PARASITES

Thrombosis and infarction of the shell, sometimes accompanied by limb edema may be due

Figure 11:
Pigmented plastron lesions in a box turtle, *Terrapene carolina*. These lesions developed over several months and spread in a cruciate pattern from the junction of the femoral scutes.

to adults or eggs of spirorchid flukes released in the vascular system of aquatic turtles, which occlude superficial vessels . Positive diagnosis of this syndrome requires demonstration of helminths or ova in shell biopsies. Praziquental 8-20 mg/kg im repeated at 14 days is trematodicidal (Jacobson 1987) . Free living soil dwelling invertebrates capable of digesting keratin have caused shell damage in hibernating chelonia kept in outdoor housing in contact with earth (Frye 1991)

INFECTIOUS SKIN DISEASES OF CHELONIA

As with shell infection, the environment of aquatic turtles has a major effect on the development of infectious skin diseases.Such factors as water pH, hardness, salinity, temperature, the use of separate feeding tanks to minimise bacterial contamination of the primary enclosure, frequency of water changing, use of water conditioning and filtration all influence the onset and recovery from skin diseases of aquatic chelonia. Abrasive and sharp surfaces in the enclosure and substrate and adequate space for all animals to bask in a warm relatively dry location profoundly influence healing (Flanagan 1992). Brackish water species (such as the Diamondback terrapin, *Malaclemys terrapin*) require the addition of sea salt to tank water to duplicate the osmolarity of their estuary/ salt marsh habitat and develop skin conditions if this is not provided. Aquatic turtles experience a variety of signs including axillary and perineal inflammation ,pseudomembrane formation, conjunctivitis skin and nailbed colonisation leading to loss of claws when the environmental burden of gram negative bacteria becomes excessive. Common organisms include *Pseudomonas, Aeromonas hydrophila, Citrobacter, Morganella, Providencia* and other Gram negative aerobes) secondary to fecal contamination of water. Improved water quality, basking lights, water conditioners and aquarium salt,enforced drying time out of water and daily tamed iodine or chlorhexidine scrubs and soaks help resolve the symptoms of superficial dermatitis. Subcutaneous granulomatous abbesses in aquatic turtles have been associated with *Serratia* in experimental infections,may take several months to develop, and may in turn predispose to septicemia (Jackson et al 1970). Unilateral, occasionally bilateral subcutaneous bulges in aquatic and terrestrial turtles in the tympanic region are usually due to abscessation of the middle ear and are not usually associated with equilibrium loss at presentation . These lesions respond well to open drainage and topical flushing, generally systemic antibiotics are not required. Bacterial isolates from these lesions are typically Gram negative coliform organisms such as Citrobacter, Escherichia coli, Pseudomonas spp., Enterobacter , and anaerobes have been isolated in terrestrial chelonia (Stewart 1990). Rarely primary cutaneous granulomas in aquatic turtles are related to mycobacterial infection and can disseminate to viscera (Rhodin et al 1977).

Tortoises may suffer from mycoses of the extremities when kept in damp conditions . Aquatic chelonia rarely present with primary mycotic dermatitis but this should be considered in the differential diagnosis of discrete cutaneous granuloma. Tortoises appear to be more prone to geophilic mycoses ; isolated cases of geotrichosis have been reported in the Galapagos tortoise (*Geochelone elephantopus*)(Ruiz 1980) but deep cutaneous mycoses are usually recognised postmortem versus antemortem. Mycotic hyphae and yeast forms (*Candida* spp.) in mixed infections with bacteria are frequently seen when scraping open skin lesions of aquatic turtles and are also seen in fossorial tortoises. Jacobson 1994p reported multiple hyperkeratotic skin lesions in captive desert tortoises from which no isolate was made but which had light microscopic biopsy characteristics of Dermatophilus. A combination of tamed iodine soaks and antifungal ointments (tolnaftate, miconazole, ketoconazole) over several weeks together with improved husbandry (dry environment, warmth, clean water) was the approach to treatment.

Viruses are uncommon agents of cutaneous diseases in chelonia and virus diseases are considered poorly treatable , however the continued introduction of wild caught animals into the zoo and pet trade means that new viral diseases may be recognised in the future. In control of viral diseases, for which there is currently a lack of vaccines or known effective chemotherapy, emphasis should be placed on proper quarantine and sanitation procedures to prevent the introduction and spread of disease, and good followup procedures such as necropsy of unexplained mortalities.

Grey Patch Disease is an epizootic disease seen in baby green sea turtles *Chelonia mydas* under aquaculture conditions. It is caused by a herpes-like virus and is precipitated by stressors such as crowding, water pollution and particularly high water temperatures or rapid changes in water temperature. Lesions involve the skin of the limbs, neck and head including eyelids and conjunctiva, starting as small papules and

Figure 12:
Necrotising mycotic dermatitis affecting the caudal aspect of the upper legs of a diamond-back terrapin, *Malaclemys terrapin*.

expanding to ulcerated plaques. Depending on coinfection and environmental conditions up to 90 percent of turtles will be affected with fatality rates from 2 to 30 percent. (Haines et al 1977)

Circular white papular coalescing skin lesions progressing to severe necrosis have been described on the head and in the tympanic region of five Bolivian Sidenecked Turtles *Platemys platycephala* . These were associated with papillomavirus - like particles on electron microscopy. Secondary skin infection in the area of the lesions cultured a variety of bacteria and fungi including *Pseudomonas* , *E coli*, *Proteus* and *Fusarium*. (Jacobson et al 1982a)

CHELONIA SKIN PARASITES

Chelonia, particularly wild caught aquatic species, may harbour leeches , and tortoises commonly have ticks in the axilla and pericloacal area when wild caught. Ticks and mites can cause debilitating anemia and transmit hemoparasites and affected animals should undergo hematologic assessment. Leeches in aquatic chelonia may be invisible if in the cloaca or pharynx so wild caught specimens should be carefully examined. Leeches can be removed by traction or by application of topical cautery or ivermectin directly to the leech (use with caution as chelonia are very sensitive to this compound). Subcutaneous maggot infestation of wild and outdoor housed pet turtles and tortoises through unbroken skin in the pericloacal region and elsewhere on the skin is prevalent in the southern US and can be treated by surgical removal, saline infusion of sites and prevented through the use of fly screening around outdoor housing areas (Gould et al 1991).

SERPENTES-INFECTIOUS CUTANEOUS DISEASES

BACTERIAL SKIN DISEASE IN SNAKES

Prospective bacteriologic studies in snakes indicate that in at least one zoological collection upper airway flora in asymptomatic animals routinely contain agents which are considered pathogenic in reptiles such as coagulase positive *Staphylococcus aureus* and aerobic gram negative rods (Hilf et al 1990). It appears that the relative quantity of flora in the oropharynx is a better indicator of potential disease state in reptiles, and the same may hold true for external facultative bacterial pathogens causing cutaneous disease.

Because of the lack of lysosomal enzymes in the leukocytes of reptiles, pyogranulomas are common in snakes as opposed to abbesses, which are associated with relatively few agents.

The most common cause of cutaneous infections is gram negative aerobic rods , in many cases secondary to skin injury . Granulomata may be single and discrete or multiple and may contain pure or mixed flora including *Pseudomonas , Escherichia coli, Proteus, Providencia*, (Jacobson 1992), *Serratia* (Jackson et al 1970), *Salmonella* (Hoff et al 1988), other gram negative enterics, and anaerobes (Stewart 1990) including fusiform bacteria. Occasional gram positive isolates are seen,often in mixed infection with gram negative and fungal organisms, such as alpha *Streptococcus* spp. and *Corynebacterium* spp (Jacobson 1980a).

For this reason it is advisable to perform aerobic and anaerobic culture on subcutaneous lesions and to consider using an anaerobic antibiotic such as metronidazole in nonresponsive cases if initial treatment was based solely on aerobic bacteriology (Stewart 1990). Well circumscribed subcutaneous abbesses may be removed cosmetically through a surgical incision at the junction of lateral and ventral scales. In many cases the use of blunt dissection will permit the removal of intact abbesses without spillage of contents and with successful primary closure.

As with other reptilian dermatoses, mycobacteria are rarely found, and may present as firm circumscribed swellings in the neck area accompanied by visceral involvement (Hoff et al 1988). In some instances deep coelomic infections such as mycobacterial hepatic granulomas may form draining fistulous tracts to the skin. The prognosis for successful treatment in these cases is poor.

There are a number of apparently discrete clinical entities in the lay literature of dermatoses of reptiles, such as necrotising dermatitis of the dorsal tail region in constrictors (so-called "tail rot"). Many of these relate to traumatic as opposed to specific infectious etiologies, with subsequent opportunistic infection. "Scale rot" is a diffuse ventral skin infection affecting epidermis and dermis in constrictor and other snakes characterised by redness, serous or purulent exudate , loss of individual scales exposing underlying tissue and wound colonization with a variety of flora, especially pseudomonads . Common in larger specimens under poor sanitary conditions, particularly when accompanied by high humidity, low temperature , or a history of chronic stress, for instance in venomous snakes which are milked frequently, the condition may be rapidly fatal due to accompanying septicemia. In its early stages this condition responds well to warm disinfectant baths,correction of housing to warm dry conditions and spray-on occlusive dressings to cover open lesions and discourage bacterial colonisation. In extensive, life-threatening infections the early use of systemic antibiotics based on C and S results is advisable in enzootic and fulminant forms of this condition.

Superficial dermatitis in pythons over most of the skin surface due to *Pseudomonas flourescens* has been controlled with acidified water in the enclosure for bathing and drinking, and gram negative bactericidal antibiotics.

Pseudomonas aeruginosa is a prevalent isolate from cases of ulcerative stomatitis in snakes, and in some cases subsequently causes subspectacular abbesses due to ascending infection via the lacrimal duct. Pseudomonas may be cultured from the cloaca and oropharynx of clinically normal reptiles in captivity, hence the pathogenicity of pseudomonads and other coliform organisms in mouth rot is controversial. Nutrition, temperature , oral trauma ,hygeine and other factors are very likely to be synergistic in the development of this condition.

Reptile burn wounds commonly become colonised with bacteria, pyoderma and secondary osteomyelitis due to *Pseudomonas* infection following burn wounds has been described in snakes (Hoff et al 1988) and carries a poor prognosis.

FUNGAL DISEASE

Low environmental temperatures, the presence of soil or hay, poor sanitation and damp substrates with fecal contamination favour the environmental viability of fungal agents in the vivarium. Superficial dermatitis and cutaneous granulomas of fungal origin are relatively com-

Figure 13:
Florida kingsnake, *Lampropeltis getula floridana*, with a subcutaneous abscess of six months duration extending approximately 10 cm on the lateral aspect of the midbody. Exploratory surgery revealed multiple encapsulated spherical abscesses, which were removed intact and yielded a pure culture of *Escherichia coli*.

mon in squamata, in some cases accompanied by oral fungal granulomas. A wide variety of fungal species have been isolated including *Fusarium, Trichoderma and Penicillium* (Jacobson 1980a)) , *Geotrichum* (McKenzie et al 1976) and species of the phycomycete group (Williams et al 1979). Typical lesions are seen in the vent and tail area and ventral scales as a brown to yellow-gold thickened crust-like flaky buildup on lateral or ventral scales which can be loosened by disinfectant soaking and may slough, exposing subcutaneous tissues. On occasion the head and deep bony structures may be involved (Jessup et al 1981). Chronic ulcerative and granulomatous lesions in the pericloacal , cervical and oral regions of snakes due to phycomycosis has been described (Kaplan et al 1983). Diagnosis of fungal skin infection is based on scrapings ,fungal culture and biopsy histology. If the lesion is a localized granuloma it may be surgically excised, however lesions may be diffuse, extensive and require warm tamed iodine soaks and topical antifungal treatment (tolnaftate ,miconazole or ketoconazole topical) with the use of debridement and occlusive dressing to encourage granulation. Systemic antifungal drugs can be used however there is little pharmacokinetic or clinical information on their use in reptilia. Pharmacokinetic data for ketoconazole in the gopher tortoise indicates 15 mg/kg once daily by mouth will achieve therapeutic blood levels (Page et al 1991) however the dosage is not established for other species.

PARASITIC DISEASE

Recently trichomonad species associated with subspectacular and subcutaneous abessation has been described (Miller et al 1995). Subcutaneous granuloma, abscess and open draining tracts may be associated with helminthiasis (*Macdonaldius, Oswaldofilaria, Foleyella*) in wild caught snakes. The filarial nematodes of snakes can cause severe necrotic dermal lesions due to blood vessel and lymphatic occlusion and are transmitted through the bite of argasid ticks (Fowler 1986).

A more unusual source of multifocal pustular lesions over the dorsal and lateral body scales of a variety of snakes are spiruroid nematodes of the Dracunculus family. The unusual pustular dermatitis has been treated with elevated environmental temperatures (30 degrees centigrade for two days followed by 37 degrees centigrade for two days) as well as with oral ivermectin 200 ug/kg twice at 10 day intervals (Jacobson et al 1986a).

Ventral and lateral subcutaneous swellings due to plerocercoids of unidentified tapeworm species have been observed in wild caught garter snakes and ribbon snakes. Trematode

Figure 14:
Burmese python, *Python molurus bivittatus*, with subspectacular and subepidermal abscessation, which yielded trichomonads. Photo courtesy of Dr. Harry A. Miller.

mesocercaria have been implicated in ventral subcutaneous swelling in the cloacal region of a water snake (Chiodini 1986).Pentastomes such as *Armillifer armillatus* ,*Kiricephalus and Porocephalus crotali* (Marcus 1976) are occasionally found in subcutaneous sites or exiting the body wall during aberrant migrations, and can be surgically removed. There are no documented effective drugs for treating pentastomes and these parasites have zoonotic potential, so the risks of retaining infected snakes should be thoroughly appreciated.

Wild caught snakes are commonly infested with mites and ticks,which are also are frequently seen in unsealed wood construction habitats, offering harbourage for the parasites and difficult to sanitise. The snake mite *Ophionyssus natricis* is common in a wide variety of snake species and is identified as tiny black dots round the eyes and in the gular groove area, as well as living in crevices in the host environment. Chronic debility from blood loss, transmission of hemoparasites and *Aeromonas hydrophila* septicemia are associated with mite infestation (Camin 1948). The development of multiple cutaneous lumps in areas of interscalar skin in boids secondary to mite infestation has

been observed (McCutcheon, pers comm) and may represent a cutaneous hypersensitivity reaction to salivary secretions of mites.These lesions reportedly regressed after Vapona strip treatment of mite infested reptile quarters.

Control of mites is achieved through environmental cleaning, surface sealing and insecticidal treatment of the snake and habitat. Many insecticides are highly toxic to reptiles and other lower vertebrates and should be used with caution.Microencapsulated pyrethrin flea products directly applied to ribbon snakes (*Thamnophis sauritus*) resulted in acute death, and the use of dichlorvos impregnated pest strips in reptile rooms has been associated with anorexia and death in a variety of snake species . The antiparasitic drug ivermectin is effective against mites at 200 micrograms per kilogram bodyweight im or orally weekly for three weeks but is toxic in chelonia (Teare et al 1983), particularly tortoise species, as well as some snake and lizard species (Boyer 1992b).and is not licensed for use in reptiles. Trichlorphon spray 0.15% in water Q7D for 4 weeks , together with sealing of crevices and surfaces (Boyer et al 1992) has been effective in control of mites. Ticks can be removed through careful traction or application of vaseline or alcohol. Use of chemotherapeutants alone for mite control is seldom effective; the removal of potential harbourage areas (unsealed wood, cracks in floor) is critical in eliminating these persistent parasites. Lightly wiping affected reptiles with a cloth covered in olive oil has also been a successful and relatively complication free method for removal of mites.

BACTERIA, FUNGI AND VIRUS DISEASES AFFECTING THE INTEGUMENT OF LIZARDS

The spectrum and manifestations of cutaneous disease in lizards are similar to that seen in snakes. Superficial dermatitis due to cool conditions and poor sanitation is often first manifested in ventral pericloacal skin and skin fold areas. Aerobic gram negative organisms frequently are isolated from abbesses and granulomas of the skin. Common isolates include *Pseudomonas, Aeromonas, Citrobacter, Escherichia coli, Proteus ,Salmonella, Arizona, Serratia*, anaerobes and occasionally *Neisseria* (Plowman et al 1987). The range of potential pathogens and therapeutic approach is similar to that seen in snakes, emphasizing the need for culture and sensitivity data due to the prevalence of resistant organisms. The isolation of potentially zoonotic Salmonella from cutaneous lesions in lizards, particularly mandibular and other subcutaneous abbesses in iguanas , is common. Cutaneous and subcutaneous abbesses of lizards are frequently found to contain *Fusobacterium* and other anaerobes in mixed infection (Stewart 1990).Gram positive organisms are found in subcutaneous abbesses of lizards and *Streptococcus, Peptostreptococcus*, and *Corynebacterium pyogenes* have been cultured, although they are less common.(see Jacobson in Ackerman). Abbesses and granulomas are commonly found on the head, mandible and extremities of iguanas and chameleons secondary to territorial aggression and may be chronic with a tumour-like gross appearance. Though generally asymptomatic, salmonella infected iguanas may have a variety of symptoms including cutaneous symptoms such as pericloacal skin inflammation, abessation of the mandibular ramus, and subcutaneous pyogranulomatous abbesses.

Fungal skin lesions are relatively common and etiologies include phycomycetes, *Trichophyton, Chrysosporium* and *Aspergillus*. Juvenile green iguanas which have been overcrowded in transport or which have been "stacking" around a heat source may develop black dry focal necrosis over the head, trunk, limbs, tail and abdomen due to secondary invasion of skin scratches. Ubiquitous geophilic fungi such as *Geotrichum* (Wissman et al 1993) have been implicated in these lesions. San Estaban Chuckwallas (*Sauromalus varius*) with burn-like lesions to the head , thorax and extremities suffered epidermal ulceration, hyperkeratosis and later systemic infection with *Aspergillus* species(Tappe et al 1984)

Hyperkeratotic skin lesions and golden-brown fungating wartlike granulomas on the head, body and limbs of lizards may be due to *Dermatophilus congolensis*.Australian bearded lizards *Amphibolourus barbatus* showing these lesions died despite treatment (Montali et al 1975). These lesions should not be confused with sebaceous or epidermal inclusion cysts in iguanas which are usually found on the limbs and tail, may be pigmented and respond well to surgical excision.

Viral skin disease has been reported in lacertid lizards associated with a papilloma virus. Lesions seen in colony housed European Green lizard *Lacerta viridis* included multiple grey raised spherical papillomatous masses up to 2 cm in diameter found in the neck region in males and the dorsal tail base in females. Bite wound contamination is the likely mode of spread as these sites correspond to areas bitten during courtship and aggression (Raynaud et al 1976).

PARASITIC SKIN DISEASE

Vesicular cutaneous lesions containing trophozoites of a species of trichomonad together with subspectacular lesions have been recently reported in geckoes (lined gecko,*Gecko vetalus,* Tokay gecko *Gekko gekko*, and leopard gecko , *Eublepharis macularius*) . Live trichomonads were readily identified in fresh wet mounts from needle aspirates of subcutaneous vesicles and from fluid in the subspectacular space . Surgical drainage, topical disinfectants and oral metronidazole 40 mg/kg has resulted in regression of lesions(Miller et al 1994).

Subcutaneous filarial nematode infestation, which is unsightly but rarely causes morbidity is seen in wild caught individuals of some species such as geckoes and chameleons, and is readily resolved by surgical removal of the parasite. Arthropod parasites are significant particularly in wild caught lizards. Mats of free living trombiculid mites found in the axillary and ventral inguinal fold region and in the vicinity of the tympanic membrane of lizards may be visible as tiny red spots, or in groups forming a red mat. Constant scratching is observed in affected lizards and in severe infestations these areas may become secondarily ulcerated and infected. Chiggers, ticks and mites cause significant morbidity in some lizard species such as the chuckwalla, *Sauromalus obesus* including anemia, cutaneous inflammation , dermatitis and granuloma formation in some species such as the chuckwalla (Mader et al 1986),(Goldberg et al 1991).Behavioral changes such as scratching and debility may be observed in affected animals, and ectoparasiticides such as carbaryl powder, ivermectin or olive wipes are effective, with the caveats already mentioned. Some lizard species, such as Solomon island skinks,*Corucia zebrata* have died as a result of ivermectin treatment. There have been reports of death losses in chameleons treated with dichlorvos (Vapona) and this product should be used with caution in chameleon species. Black, patchy necrosis on the skin of recently imported juvenile iguanas due to red mites (*Hirstiella* spp.) responds well to ivermectin 200 ug/kg po. These mites have a characteristic triangular pointed abdomen under magnification. However the presence of grossly apparent black skin patches in young recently imported iguanas is indicative only of an inflammatory process and is not pathognomonic for this condition.

INFECTIOUS CUTANEOUS DISEASE IN CROCODILIANS

Captive crocodilians face similar environmental and water quality problems contributing to cutaneous disease as aquatic turtles. Skin disease originating in feces and food contaminated water is not unusual in pet crocodilians such as caimans, and in densely housed zoo and farmed crocodilians . *Aeromonas hydrophila* or *Pseudomonas* is frequently isolated from necrotizing cutaneous lesions, subdominant animals are often more severely afflicted and pneumonia, hypopyon or visceral abessation may be part of the syndrome.

Although the conventional dermatophytes affecting domestic animals are not commonly isolated from reptiles, fungal "bumblefoot" lesions of the footpad and nailbed associated with Trichophyton have been reported in crocodilians housed in cement pools (Migaki et al 1984).

Poxvirus induced skin lesions have been observed in captive caimans (Caiman sclerops) and

Figure 15:
Subcutaneous fluctuant vesicles involving the trunk and limbs of a leopard gecko, *Eublepharis macularius*. Aspiration of the mass revealed trophozoites of a *Trichomonas* species. Photo courtesy of Dr. Harry A. Miller.

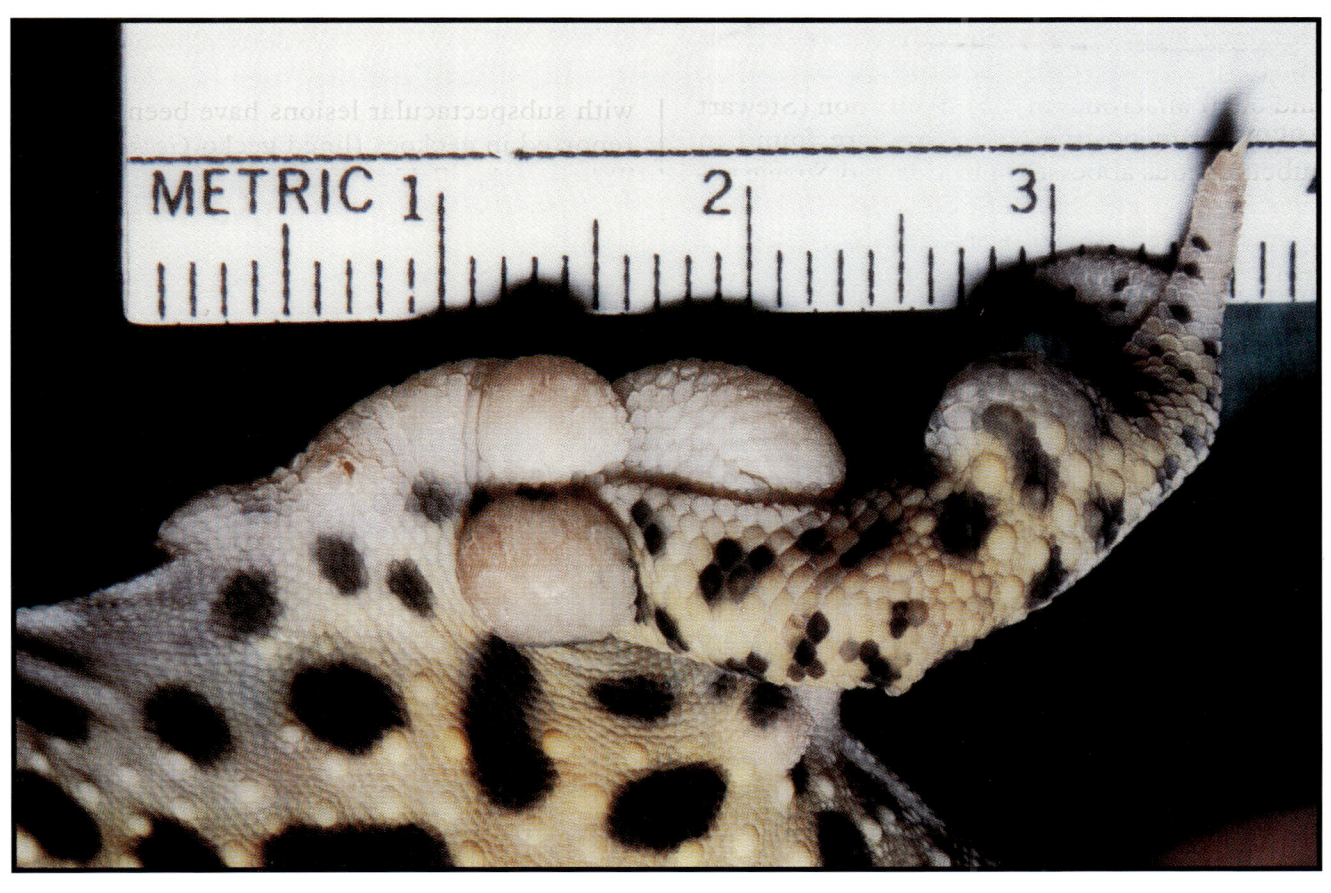

Figure 16:
Lined gecko, *Gekko vittatus*, showing unilateral subspectacular absessation. Following fine-needle aspiration of 0.3 cc. fluid containing trophozoites of a trichomonad, the eye was normal in function and appearance. Photo and case courtesy of Dr. Harry A. Miller.

in farmed Nile Crocodiles (Crocodylus nyloticus). The lesions are located over the body including the oral cavity and palpebrae, except the tail, and result in erosive grey-white circular areas and in some cases severe sloughing of digits (Jacobson et al 1979),(Horner 1988) .

Aquatic leeches can be found in the nasal cavity, axilla and cloacal regions of wild caught crocodilians . The nematode parasite Paratrichosoma has reportedly caused raised linear lesions of the ventral scales in crocodilians (Jacobson 1992).

CUTANEOUS NEOPLASIA IN REPTILIA

Older reptiles frequently present with tumour-like conditions of the skin which on workup may in fact have infectious etiologies, despite a tumour-like gross appearance. Individual cases of a wide variety of primary cutaneous tumours and metastatic or locally invasive visceral tumours have been reported, chiefly in older specimens with the largest number of cases described in the Serpentes. With the exception of chelonian and lacertid papillomatosis in wild populations, there have been no studies demonstrating prevalence of pattern or tumour type in reptilia. Tumour types found in reptilia have been extensively reviewed elsewhere (Machotka 1984).

Primary cutaneous neoplasia is relatively uncommon in pet reptilia although there are a variety of papillomatous conditions chiefly described in wild lizard and turtle species , some of suspected viral etiology . These usually present as multiple discrete wart -like cutaneous masses distributed widely over the body surface.

Squamous cell carcinoma of cutaneous origin is relatively uncommon in reptiles but has been reported in turtles, lizards and snakes, tends to be invasive and carries a poor prognosis (Machotka 1984) .

Tumours of cutaneous pigment cells such as chromatophoromas and melanomas have been reported, particularly in brightly pigmented colubrids (Montali et al 1980).These tumours are frequently metastatic and carry poor prognosis.

Captive corn snakes (*Elaphe guttata*),with single discrete subcutaneous lumps may have lipomas, which can be surgically removed.

Figure 17:
Trophozoites of trichomonads in an aspirate from subspectacular lesion in lined gecko in Figure 16, x 1250. Flocculent fluid aspirated from this lesion was examined by light microscopy and found to contain trichomonads and macrophages. Photo courtesy of Dr. Thomas M. Craig.

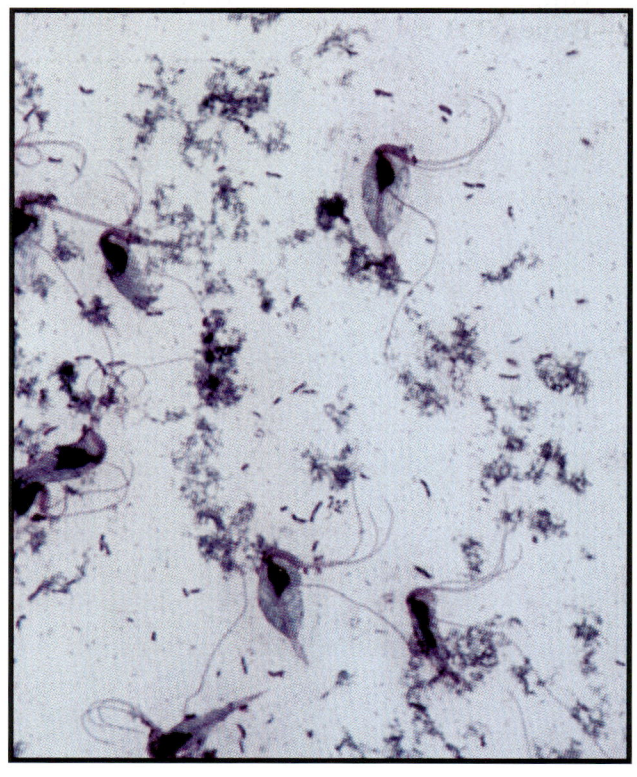

REFERENCES

—**Alberts, AC ; Rostal,DC ; Lance VA:**
Studies on the chemistry and social significance of chin gland secretions in the desert tortoise, *Gopherus agassizii*. Herpetological Monographs,1994; 8:116-124.

—**Baxter, JS; Meek,R :**
Cryosurgery in the treatment of skin disorders in reptiles. Brit Herpetological Journal,1988; 1:227.

—**Bennett,RA :**
A review of anesthesia and chemical restraint in reptiles. J Zoo Wildl Med 1991; 22: 282-303

—**Bennett, RA:**
Reptilian surgery Parts I and II. Comp Cont Ed Prac Vet, 1989, 11:10-20, 122-134.

—**Beynon, PH; Lawton, MPC; Cooper JE. Eds:**
Manual of Reptiles.1992 Gloucestershire. British Small Animal Veterinary Association, pp.73-79, 195.

—**Boyer, DM:**
Adverse reaction to ivermectin in the prehensile tailed skink, *Corucia zebrata*. Bull Ass Rept Amphib Vets, 1992; 2(2):6-7.

—**Boyer,TH:**
Clinical Reptilian Microbiology. In, Current Veterinary Therapy XII Small Animal Practice, Kirk RW (Ed). WB Saunders Co, Phila, PA, 1994,pp. 1353-1357.

—**Boyer,TH :**
Clinical anesthesia of reptiles. Bull Ass Rept Amphib Vets 1992a, 2(2) :10-13.

—**Boyer, TH :**
A practitioners guide to reptilian husbandry and care. AAHA Professional Library Series, Lakewood, Colorado,1992b

—**Boyer, DM; Boyer, TH:**
Trichlorfon spray for snake mites (*Ophionyssus natricis*). Bull Assoc Rept Amphib Vets 1992, 2(1) : 2-3.

—**Burgdorfer, W:**
Q fever. In, Diseases of animals transmitted to man, 6th Edition. Hubbert WT McCulloch WF and PR Schnurrenburger (Eds) Charles C Thomas, Springfield, 1975

—**Bush, M :**
An update on antibiotic therapy in reptiles. In, Current Veterinary Therapy XI Small Animal Practice, Kirk RW and Bonagura JD (Eds). WB Saunders Co, Phila, PA, 1992, pp. 1214—1215

—**Bustard, H; Maderson,PF:**
The eating of shed material in squamate reptiles. Herpetologica 1965; 21: 306-308.

—**Camin, JH :**
Mite transmission of a hemorrhagic septicemia in snakes. J Parasit, 1948, 34:345-354.

—**Chiodini, RJ ;Sundberg JP :**
Mesocercaria in the tail of a water snake. JAVMA,1986, 177(10): 908.

—**Cooper, JE; Jackson OF:**
Diseases of the Reptilia. Academic Press, London,1981,pp 399-401.

—**Costanzo, JP :**
Effects of humidity, temperature, and submegence behavior on survivorship and energy use in hibernating garter snakes, *Thamnophis sirtalis*. Can J Zool, 1989; 67:2486-2492.

—**Dalton, C ;Hoffman, R ;Pape,J:**
Iguana associated salmonellosis in children. Pediatr Inf Dis, 1995; 14:319-320.

—**Flanagan JP:**
Husbandry,handling and nutrition of turtles. In, The care and use of amphibians reptiles and fish in research, Schaeffer, DO; Kleinow, KM and Krulisch, L (Eds): Scientists Center for Animal Welfare, Betheda, Md, 1992, pp 92-97.

—**Fowler, ME:**
Zoo and wild animal medicine(2nd Ed). WB Saunders Co,Phila,PA, 1986, p 1174.

—**Frye,FL :**
Use of a condom as an occlusive bandage in snakes. J Small Exotic Animal Med 1992;2(1) : 13-14.

—**Frye, FL:**
Biomedical and surgical aspects of captive reptile husbandry.Krieger Publ Co, Malabar, Fla, 1991, pp393-417.

—**Frye, FL:**
Vitamin A sources, hypovitaminosis A and iatrogenic hypervitaminosis A in captive chelonians. In Current Veterinary Therapy X Small Animal Practice,Kirk, RW Ed,WB Saunders Co, Phila, PA, 1989, p791.

—**Frye, FL;Gilespie, DS; Fowler, ME :**
Peracute necrotising dermatitis in a softshell turtle. J Zoo Anim Med, 1984a, 15:73-77.

—**Frye, FL; Lane, JR:**
Hemangioendothelioma in a boa constrictor. J Zoo Anim Med,1984b,15: 78-83.

—**Seymour, RS:**
Physiological adaptations to aquatic life. In, Biology of the Reptila, Vol.13 Physiology D. Gans, CG and Pough, FH (Eds), Academic Press, London, 1982, pp 35-40.

—**Goldberg, SR; Bursey, CR :**
Integumental lesions caused by ectopara-

sites in a wild population of the side blotched lizard (*Uta stansburiana*). J Wildl Dis, 1991, 27(1): 68-73.

—**Gould, WJ; Georgi, ME:**
Myiasis in two box turtles. JAVMA, 1991, 199(8) :1067-1068.

—**Haines, H; Kleese, WC:**
Effect of water temperature on a herpesvirus infection of sea turtles. Infect Immunol, 1977, 15: 756-759.

—**Harvey-Clark, CJ:**
Common dermatologic problems in pet reptilia. Sem Av Ex Pet Med 1995, 4(4): 205-219

—**Hedges, SB; Hass, CA; Maugel, TK:**
Physiological color change in snakes. J Herpetol 1989, 23(4) 450-455.

—**Hilf, M; Wagener, RA; Yu, VI:**
A prospective study of upper airway flora in healthy boid snakes and snakes with pneumonia. J Zoo Wildl Med 1990, 21 (3):318-325.

—**Hoff, GL; Frye, FL; Jacobson, ER :**
Diseases of Amphibians and Reptiles. Plenum Press, NY, NY, 1988, pp 1-25, 37-83.

—**Horner, RF:**
Poxvirus in farmed nile crocodiles. Vet Rec 1988, 122 (19) : 459-62.

—**Jackson, CG; Fulton, M :**
A turtle epizootic apparently of microbial origin. J Wildl Ds 1970, 6: 446-448.

Jacobson, ER; Wronski, TJ; Schumacher, J; Reggiardo, C; Berry, KH.
Cutaneous dyskeratosis in free ranging desert tortoises, *Gopherus agassizii*, in the Colorado Desert of Southern California. J Zoo Wild Med 1994; 25(1):68-81.

—**Jacobson, ER:**
Causes of Mortality and Diseases in Tortoises: A Review. J Zoo Wildl Med. 1994, 25:2-17.

—**Jacobson, ER:.**
Reptile dermatology. In, Current Veterinary Therapy XI Small Animal Practice. Kirk RW and Bonagura JD (Eds): WB Saunders Co, Phila, PA, 1992, pp 1205-1206.

—**Jacobson, ER:**
Diseases of the integumentary system of reptiles. In, Dermatology for the Small animal Practitioner : exotics feline canine. Nesbitt, GH; Ackerman, LJ (Eds). Veterinary Learning Systems Co, Trenton, 1991

—**Jacobson, ER :**
Use of chemotherapeutics in reptile medicine. In, Contemporary Issues in Small Animal Practice 9: Exotic Animals.

Jacobson ER and Kolias GV (Eds), Churchill Livingstone NY, NY, 1988, pp 35-48.

—**Jacobson, ER :**
Reptiles. Vet Clin N Am: Sm Anim Prac, 1987, 17(5): 1203-1225.

—**Jacobson, ER; Greiner, EC ; Clubb, S; Harvey-Clark, CJ:**
Pustular dermatitis caused by subcutaneous dracunculiasis. JAVMA, 1986a, 189(9): 1133-1134.

—**Jacobson, ER; Ingling, AL;**
Pyloroduodenal resection in a Burmese Python. JAVMA, 1986b, 169: 985-987.

—**Jacobson, ER; Gaskin, JM M; Clubb, SL:**
Papilloma-like virus infection in Bolivian side-neck turtles. JAVMA, 1982a, 181(11):1325-1328.

—**Jacobson, ER; Gaskin, JM; Wahlquist, H:**
Herpesvirus-like infection in map turtles. JAVMA, 1982b, 181(11) 1322-1324.

—**Jacobson, ER ; Calderwood, MB;, Clubb, SL:**
Mucormycosis in hatchling Florida Softshell turtles. JAVMA, 1980, 177( ):835.

—**Jacobson, ER :**
Necrotizing mycotic dermatitis in snakes: clinical and pathological features. JAVMA, 1980a, 177 (9) :838-841

—**Jacobson, ER :**
Histology, endocrinology and husbandry of ecdysis in snakes (a review). VMSAC, 1977, 72:275.

—**Jackson, CG; Fulton, M :**
A turtle epizootic apparently of microbial
—origin. J Wildl Dis 1970, 6: 446-448.

—**Jessup, DA; Seeley, JC:**
Zygomycete fungus infection in two captive snakes : gopher snake (*Pituophis melanoleucus*) and copperhead (*Agkistrodron contortrix*). J Zoo Anim Med 1981, 12 :54-59.

—**Kaplan, W; Chandler, FW; Padhye, AA et al:**
A zygomycotic infection in captive snakes. Sabouraudia, 1983, 21:85-91.

—**Kent, GC:**
Comparative anatomy of the vertebrates. 7th Ed. Mosby, Toronto, 1992, p 175.

—**Lance, VA:**
Stress in reptiles. In, Progress in Endocrinology. Eple, A; Scranes, CG; Stetson, MH (Eds), Wiley-Liss, NY, NY, 1990, pp 461-466.

—**Lillywhite, HB; Maderson, PFA :**
Skin Structure and permeability. In,

Gans,C; Pough FH (Eds.) Biology of the Reptila, Volume 12, Physiology C. Academic Press, London, 1982, pp397-442.

—**Machotka, SV:**
Neoplasia in Reptiles.In Diseases of Amphibians and Reptiles. Hoff, GL;Frye,FL; Jacobson, ER (Eds), Plenum Press, NY, NY, 1984, pp 543-579.

—**Mader, DR; Houston, RS; Frye, FL :**
Hirstiella trombidiformis infestation in a colony of chuckwallas. JAVMA 1986, 189 (9): 1138-1139.

—**Marcus,LM :**
Parasitic diseases of captive reptiles. In Current Veterinary Therapy V Small Animal Practice, Kirk, RW (Ed), WB Saunders Co, Phila, PA, 1976, pp 632-638.

—**McKenzie,RA; Green, PE :**
Mycotic dermatitis in captive carpet snakes (*Morelia spilotes variegata*). J Wildl Dis 1976, 12:405-408.

—**Migaki, G; Jacobson, ER; Casey, HW :**
Fungal diseases in reptiles. In, Diseases of Amphibians and Reptiles. Hoff, GL; Frye, FL; Jacobson, ER (Eds). Plenum Press, NY, NY, 1984, pp 183-204.

—**Miller, HA; Frye, FL; and Craig, TM :**
Trichomonas associated with ocular and subcutaneous lesions in geckos. Proceedings of the Annual Meeting of the American Association of Zoo Veterinarians, Pittsburgh, PA, 1994.

—**Montali, RJ; Migaki, G (eds):**
The comparative pathology of zoo animals. The Symposia of the National Zoological Park. Smithsonian Inst Press, Washington, DC,1980, pp.585-612.

—**Montali, RJ; Smith, EE; Davenport, M et al :**
Dermatophilosis in Australian bearded lizards. JAVMA 1975, 167:553-555.

—**MMWR**
Morbidity and Mortality Weekly Report, CDC.May 5 1995 Vol 44 No 17.

—**Page, CD; Mantino, M;Derendorf, H et al:**
Multiple dose pharmacokinetics of ketoconazole administered to gopher tortoises (*Gopherus polyphemus*). J Zoo Wildl Med 1991, 22:191

—**Plowman, CA; Montali, RJ; Phillips, LG et al :**
Septicemia and chronic abscesses in iguanas (*Cyclura cornuta* and *Iguana iguana*) associated with *Neisseria* species. J Zoo Anim Med 1987, 18:86-93.

—**Porter, KR :**
Herpetology. WB Saunders Co Phila,PA, 1972,pp 115-128.

—**Rall, M ; Fairall, N:**
Diets and food preferences of two South African tortoises *Geochelone pardalis* and *Psammobates oculifer*. S Afr J Wildl Res 1993, 23(3) 63-70.

—**Raynaud, MMA; Adrian, M :**
Lesions cutanees a structure papillomateuse associees a des virus chez le lizard (*Lacerta viridis* Laur) CR Acad Sci Paris 283D, 1976, 845-847.

—**Rhodin, AGJ; Anver, MR :**
Mycobacteriosis in turtles: cutaneous and hepatosplenic involvement in a *Phrynops hilari*. J Wildl Dis 1977, 13: 180-183.

—**Roberts, JB; Lillywhite, HB :**
Lipid barrier to water exchange in reptile epidermis. Science 1980, 207:1077-1079.

—**Rosskopf, WJ :**
Ivermectin as a treatment for snake mites. Bull Assoc Rept Amphib Vets 1992, 2(1) 7-8.

—**Ruiz, JM; Arteaga, E; Martinez,J et al:**
Cutaneous and renal *Geotrichosis* in a giant tortoise (*Geochelone elephantopus*). Sabouraudia 1980, 18:51-59.

—**Schultz,H :**
Human infestation by *Ophionyssus natricis* snake mite. Br J Derm 1975,93: 695-697.

—**Smith, DA ;Barker, IK :**
Healing of cutaneous wounds in the common garter snake (*Thamnophis sirtalis*). Can J Vet Res 1988a, 52:111-119.

—**Smith, DA; Barker, IK ;Allen, OB:**
The effect of ambient temperature and type of wound on healing of cutaneous wounds in the common garter snake (*Thamnophis sirtalis*). Can J Vet Res 1988b, 52: 120-128.

—**Smith, DA; Barker, IK; Allen, OB:**
The effect of topical medications on healing of cutaneous wounds in the common garter snake (*Thamnophis sirtalis*). Can J Vet Res 1988c, 52:129-133.

—**Stewart, JS:**
Anaerobic bacterial infections in reptiles. J Zoo Wildl Med 1990, 21(2) : 180-184.

—**Tappe,JP;Chandler,FW;Liu,S-K; Dolensk,E:**
Aspergillosis in two San Esteban chuckwallas. JAVMA 1984, 185 (11): 1425-1428

—**Teare,J;Bush,M :**
Toxicity and efficacy of ivermectin in chelonians. JAVMA 1983,183(11):1195-1197.

—**Tracy, RC:**
Biophysical modeling. In, Reptilian Physi-

ology and Ecology. Gans, C (Ed) Biology of the Reptilia Vol 12. Academic Press, NY, NY, 1982, pp 275-321.

—**Wallach, JD; Boever WJ:**
Diseases of Exotic Animals, Medical and Surgical management. WB Saunders, Phila, PA, 1983, p1032.

—**Wallach, JD :**
The pathogenesis and etiology of ulcerative shell disease in turtles. J Zoo Anim Med 1975, 6:11.

—**Warwick, C :**
Reptilian ethology in captivity: observations of some problems and an evaluation of their aetiology. Appl Anim Behav Sci 1990, 26:1-13.

—**Williams, LW; Jacobson, ER; Gelatt, KN et al :**
Phycomycosis in a western Massasauga rattlesnake (*Sistrurus catenatus*) with infection of the telencephalon, orbit and facial structures. VMSAC 1989, August 1181-1184.

—**Wissman, MA; Parsons, B:**
Dermatophytosis of green iguanas (*Iguana iguana*). J Small Exot Anim Med 1993, (2)3:137-140.

—**Wright, K:**
Use of oral allopurinol and saline dialysis in management of hyperuricemia in a Chilean tortoise. Bull Assoc Rept Amphib Vets 1992, 2(1) :7

DIAGNOSTIC IMAGING: RADIOGRAPHY

Willard Nelson DVM
Exotic Pet and Bird Clinic
903 Fifth Avenue, Suite 101
Kirkland, WA 98033

Dr. Willard Nelson is a graduate of the University of Illinois College of Veterinary Medicine and operates the Exotic Pet and Bird Clinic in Kirkland, Washington. He has spent 28 years treating domestic and non-domestic pets, zoo animals and wildlife.

INTRODUCTION

The human eye and other senses are not equipped to visualize the structures below the skin of patients. Imaging is the technology of using equipment to create visual pictures or "images" of patients or parts of patients which can be viewed with the human eye. This allows interpretations to be made of the condition of the deep structures of a patient in order to arrive at a diagnosis.

RADIOLOGY

Radiology involves the imaging techniques and equipment used to pass electromagnetic radiant energy through a patient and produce films which can be viewed with transmitted light. The common term for the process is "x-ray" and the resulting films are often referred to as "x-rays". The "X" in "x-ray" came from the fact that early researchers did not know what the rays were that seemed to penetrate the impenetrable, used "X" to designate "unknown" and named them "x-rays."

EQUIPMENT

For most reptiles, the x-ray machines found in a typical veterinary clinic will be adequate. The limiting factor is the ability of the equipment to penetrate the maximum thickness of the patient to obtain the appropriate view. With a medium-sized veterinary generator and modern, high-speed films and cassettes, even giant tortoises and crocodilians can be

Snake radiograph depicting obstipation. The arrow indicates the site.

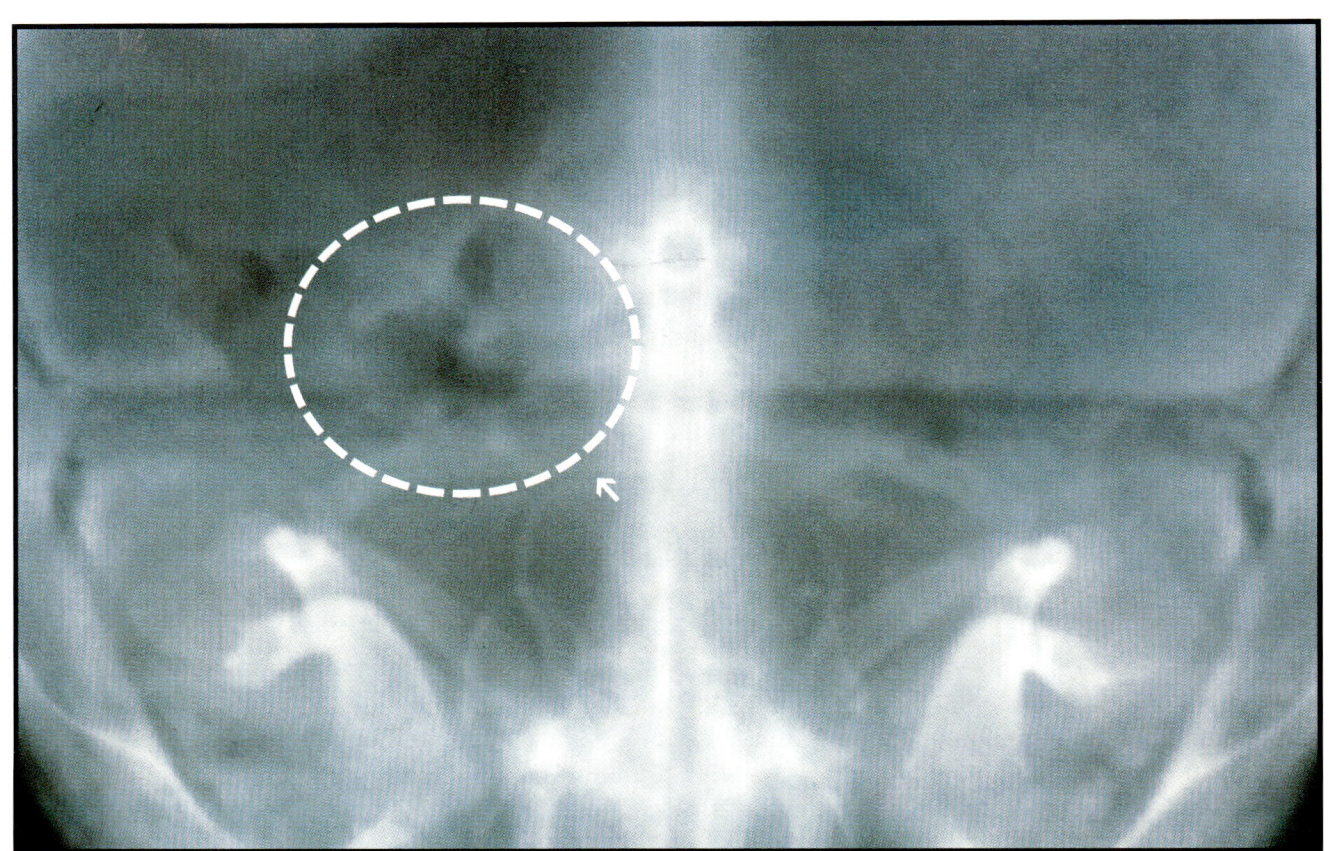

Radiograph of a turtle with shell necrosis, showing extent of damage below the surface. Arrow indicate the affected area.

radiographed. The typical views are planned to pass through the thinner dimension of a patient with the rare exception of such special views as the anterior-posterior view of terrapins in the case of suspected lung conditions.

The radiographic films in use today are described by the general color to which they are designed to be most sensitive. The films are supplied in light proof packages and are handled in the dark or under suitable radiographic/photographic darkroom "safelights". The films are placed one at a time in light proof carriers for use. These carriers are called cassettes, and are constructed in such a way as to place the film tightly between two specially designed "screens" which emit light when excited by radiation which has passed through the patient. Different screens emit different "colors" under the influence of radiation, and the screens and films are selected to have matching colors. Blue based films are generally "faster", that is more responsive to the quantity of the radiation than red based films and screens. After exposure with the patient between the film and the generator, the films are "developed" much like photographic film, providing an image which is available for viewing and which can be stored for subsequent viewing, comparing to subsequent films and for use in review by additional doctors. Markers are used to identify each film as to the landmarks such

as left and right and to assure that every radiograph produced will be accurately identified with the patient identity, the date taken, the clinic or hospital performing the service, and other information deemed valuable to the interpretation and storage of the radiograph. Additional equipment used to position the different reptiles for different views will be described with those views below.

SAFETY

Electromagnetic energy of the type used to produce radiographs does so because it penetrates living tissue. In addition, it has the ability to ionize molecules which it strikes in potentially damaging ways. Few of the waves of energy passing through a patient actually collide with atoms in such a way as to produce dangerous ionizing side effects, but steps are taken to keep the potential for damage to a minimum by:

1. Keeping the exposure as low as possible by proper knowledge of the equipment and techniques involved, using optimum exposures to get the job done the first time and thus minimize the need for retakes.
2. Protecting nearby living animals by the utilization of proper barriers to radiation such as walls thick enough to stop radiation and lead gloves and aprons in the rare instances where the operator must manually restrain the patient.

TECHNIQUES

The view selected needs to include the area of the body suspected of being diseased and must align the tissues and organs in such a way as to provide maximum information about the suspect organ or part of the body. In most cases, two views are planned, and more than two views is not unusual. The views are named using the part of the body the radiation enters followed by the part of the body the radiation exits. While back to front is a reasonable description, medical/anatomic terms are commonly used. Thus a "back to front" view, with radiation entering the back and exiting the front is described as dorsoventral. The anatomic terms can be found in anatomy texts and medical dictionaries.

The patient is positioned between the generator of the radiation and the recording system, generally radiographic based light sensitive film in such a way as to provide the selected direction of radiation through the body and the appropriate portion of the patient's body as well.

The patient must be positioned in such a way that they cannot move out of the planned position for the study, and also in such a way that the patient does not wave its limbs about in an attempt to escape. Such motions will cause blurring of the completed radiograph film because the distance moved by the body part during the fraction of a second exposure will appear as a blur.

The radiation generator is adjusted according to a prearranged table of values for that particular machine depending on two main factors: Tissue/body thickness (or radiodensity) and type of rays desired to produce maximum diagnostic information. Machines vary somewhat, but the usual adjustments are made

1. to the kilovoltage (thousands of volts) applied across the elements (anode and cathode) of the generator tube and

2. to the current that is allowed to flow between the elements of the tube, referred to in milliamperes or MA, and

3. the duration of time in fractions of a second for which the tube will carry the above mentioned kilovoltage and current. The last two, current in MA and time in seconds, are combined on some charts as MAS, meaning milliampere-seconds. Thus, 50 MA for one second would amount to 50 MAS, and 50 milliamperes for 1/10 second would amount to 5 MAS (50 X 1/10). The timer is connected to a switch for the technician to use to initiate the discharge of current through the generator tube when all is

Iguana with spiral fracture of right humerus, lateral view, close up. Arrow indicates the ends of the fractured bone.

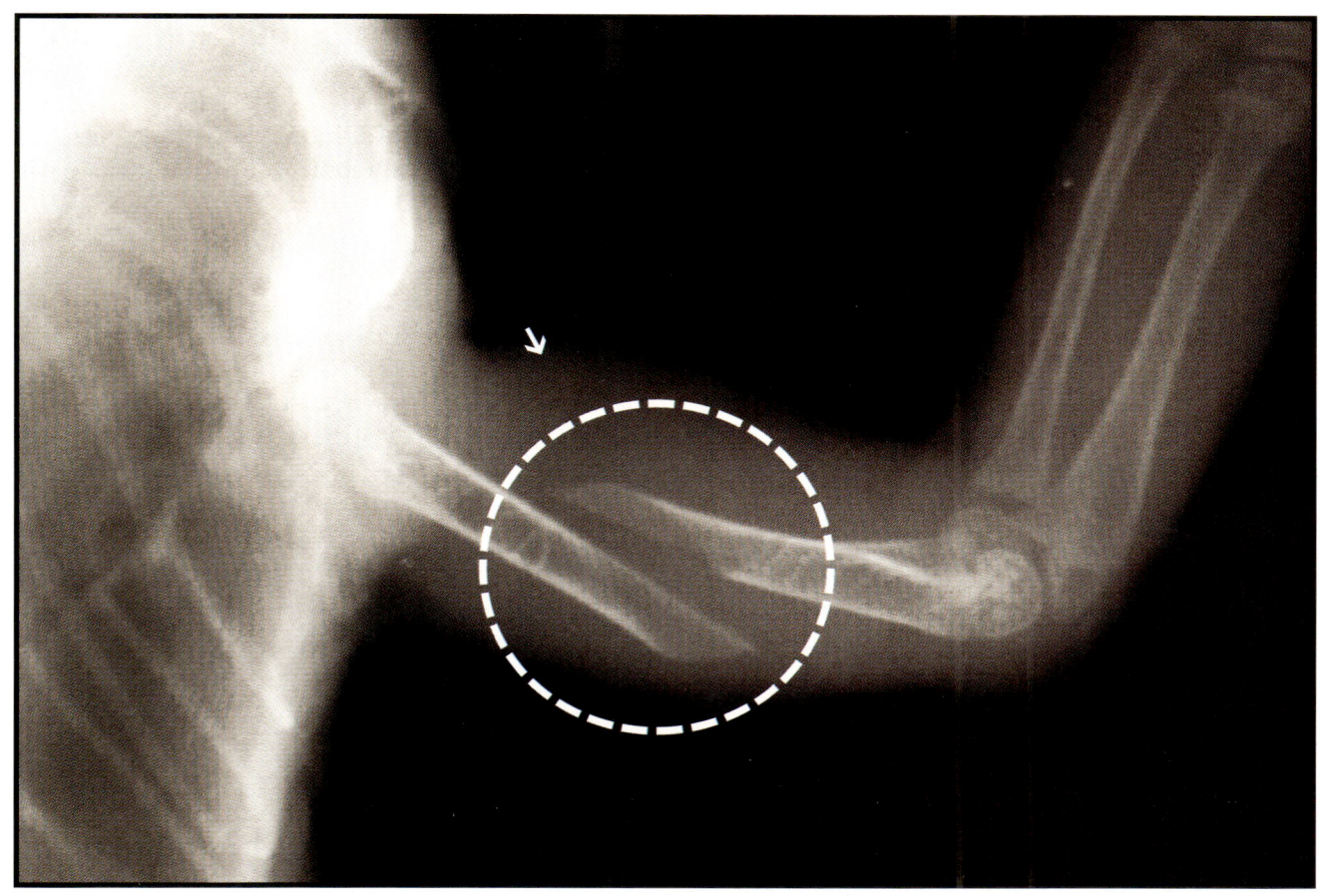

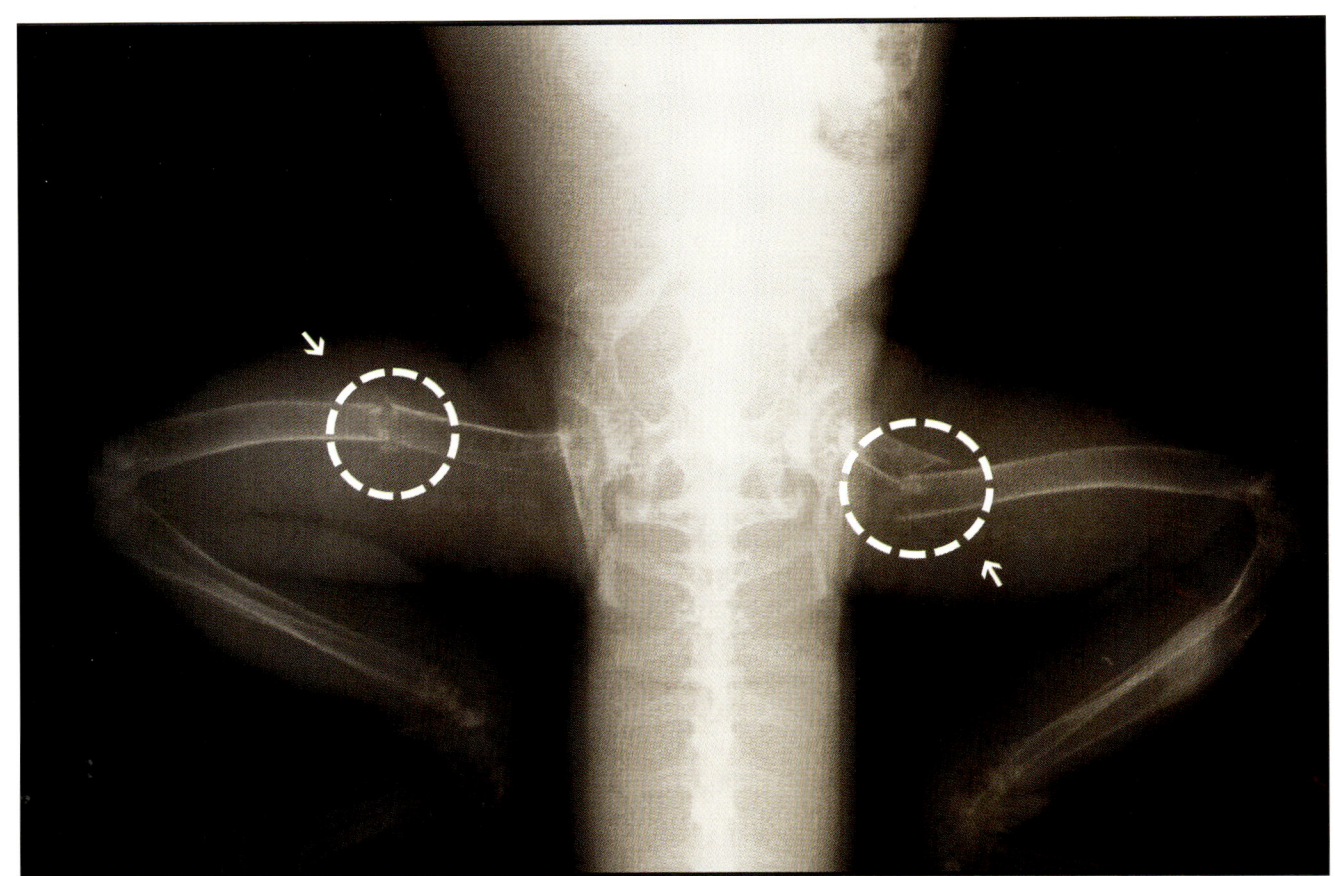

Iguana with multiple femoral fractures (arrows).

ready. The switch is constructed in such a way that if all is not perfect during the discharge, releasing the switch will interrupt the discharge for safety reasons.

TYPICAL TECHNIQUES SUITABLE FOR RADIOLOGY OF REPTILE PATIENTS:

Film/cassette selection and exposure (x-ray generator machine control settings) are accomplished using a clinic's radiographic technique chart, such as the ones provided in this chapter.

Patient restraint in the proper position to achieve a diagnostic view ordinarily involves two or more standard views. They are named by combining the terms of two topographic terms. The first term is the portion of the patient into which the rays enter at approximately 90 degrees. This is usually the part of the patient nearest the x-ray generator tube. The second part of the name is the portion of the patient from which the radiation exits the patient. The second part often describes the part of the patient touching the x-ray film cassette. The most common views are described as: dorsoventral, abbreviated "DV"; ventrodorsal, abbreviated "VD", lateral; anterioposterior, abbreviated "AP" and axial, otherwise known as craniocaudal, most often used in chelonians.

For DV radiographs, the patient is positioned so that the radiation enters the dorsal aspect of the patient and exits ventrally. Usually this means that the generator tube faces downward, the patient is positioned with the dorsal (back) up toward the tube and the ventral part down on the table close to the cassette/film. The opposite orientation is VD. For lateral radiographs, the radiation enters one side of the patient and exits the other. usually this means that the patient is lying on its side close to the cassette/film. For AP radiographs, the radiation enters the anterior portion of the patient and exits the posterior. For axial radiographs, the radiation passes along the long axis of the patient. Its most common application is in chelonians, where they are positioned so that radiation enters at the head end and exits at the caudal end. The patient is usually positioned head up facing the generator tube.

Because of the variability of size of different reptiles, it is often necessary to make careful adjustments to kV and mAS. One should keep the mAS as short as possible in order to avoid movement blur. By using high mA exposures and short exposure times, a lower kVp is possible and this is important when radiographing reptiles.

Film selection is important; LoDose film often gives the greatest detail in small lizards but many x-ray machines in private veterinary practices cannot deliver less than 50kV which are necessary for optimal resolution. The focal film distance can also be varied; as close as 70 cm with most films and 91 cm with LoDose films.

CHELONIANS

Small turtles can be secured to radiolucent plastic sheets with radiolucent tape and positioned as desired on the flat cassette for dorsoventral views. Larger terrapins might need to be anesthetized in order to provide sufficient restraint to keep them from moving out of position or moving their body during exposure. Velcro™ and other restraint means can be applied to hold the patient securely and safely during the time needed to complete the positioning and discharge the generator.

Lateral views are accomplished with the equipment described by placing the patient and restraint radiolucent plastic board at a ninety degree angle to the original position in such a way as to send the radiation through one side and out the other.

It is standard practice to take lateral views with the patient's right side down toward the cassette, that is in such a way as to send the radiation into the left side and out of the right side.

A third view often called for in patients which show signs of respiratory disease or patients who do not float in a balanced manner in water is the axial view. This view is accomplished with the patient restraint board lined up with the patient's posterior part nearest the film and the anterior part nearest the generator. In chelonians, the rays should pass through the very center of the patient from the entry to the shell to the exit. A variation of this is to position the patient so that the radiation passes through the dorsal 1/3 portion of the body cavity, parallel to the center line described above. This position is to view the dorsally located lungs in such a way as to provide information which might be lost in a purely centerline alignment.

LIZARDS

Small lizards can be taped to a radiolucent plastic restraint board with radiolucent tape and positioned for the usual DV and lateral views with relative ease. Large lizards should be considered for anesthesia in order to position them properly, to reduce motion, and prevent patients or operators being injured by the animal's own strong muscular contractions while fighting the heavy restraints which are required to immobilize large, strong lizards. Also, since nutritional osteodystrophy / metabolic bone disease is so common in lizards, it is advisable to reduce kV settings in suspected cases. If this is not taken into account, the likely result will be overexposure of the film and little bone detail available for scrutiny.

SNAKES

Although some snakes will lie still on a cassette, more assertive restraint is usually required. If insufficiently restrained, the result is typically a blurred radiograph of questionable diagnostic value. Plastic tubes of various sizes can be used for restraint.

A small, passive snake can often be restrained on a sheet of rigid plastic with masking tape. The tape will need to be gently and carefully removed afterwards to avoid damage to the skin. Larger and more vigorous snakes will require bandage tape; special surgical tape removers are available commercially.

Radiographing a snake coiled on a cassette is unlikely to provide any diagnostic detail. Since many parts of the snake seem anatomically identical, it is advisable to mark gradations on the snake with a radiopaque marker unless the problem is visually evident. If the gradations are spaced at 10 cm intervals and marked appropriately, it becomes a relatively simple task to precisely identify the problem area when interpreting the films. If contrast studies of the digestive system are needed, it is often necessary to use drugs such as metoclopramide to hasten passen through the intestines to get a timely diagnosis.

CROCODILIANS

Because of their size and temperament, radiographing crocodilians requires proper restraint and facilities for radiographically penetrating thick tissues. After securing the muzle in a closed position with duct tape, they can be further restrained with rope or more tape. The large crocodilians need to be taped or tied to a ladder. The portion of the body to be imaged must be positioned in such a way as to allow radiation to pass through the patient without undue interference from the ladder (or other restraint board). Portable radiology equipment may be required to radiograph a large crocodilian in an outdoor setting.

FILM PROCESSING

Radiographic films are processed or developed by techniques quite similar to photographic developing. The developer chemical causes the silver halides which have been exposed by radiation to change into metallic silver which is black. Those silver halides not affected by radiation do not convert to metallic silver, and are cleared from the emulsion during he second process, clearing and fixing. Fixing firms the metallic silver in the emulsion for stability. A typical film is developed for 5 minutes at 68 degrees Fahrenheit and fixed for 10 minutes at the same temperature. The films are then reviewed for diagnostic quality with a special

Iguana taped to plastic and positioned laterally on 14 x 17 inch cassette. Note the lead blocker in the foreground, allowing the cassette to be used for 2 views. This is accomplished by shifting the blocker after the first exposure and positioning the patient on the half which was blocked during the first exposure.

686

TABLE 1.

SAMPLE RADIOGRAPHY TECHNIQUE CHART USING RARE EARTH SCREENS WITH GREEN SENSITIVE FILM.

Reptile	View	Size	MAS	KVP
Lizards	Lateral & DV	small (1 pound)	7.5	40
		medium (4-5 pounds)	10	45
Snakes	Lateral & DV	small (1 pound)	7.5	40
		medium (8 pounds)	7.5	40
		large (50 pounds)	120	40
Chelonians	DV	large (10 pounds)	10	60
	Axial	large (10 pounds)	10	75

TABLE 2.

SAMPLE RADIOGRAPHY TECHNIQUE CHART USING KODAK LANEX SINGLE SCREEN CASSETTES WITH SINGLE EMULSION, BLUE-SENSITIVE FILM.

Reptile	View	Size	MAS	KVP
Lizards	Lateral & DV	tiny (50 grams)	12	45
		small (120 grams)	7.5	50
		medium (450 grams)	12	40
Snakes	Lateral & DV	medium (6 pounds)	7.5	40
Chelonians	DV	small (118 grams)	7.5	50
	Axial	small (118 grams)	7.5	60
	DV	medium (330 grams)	6	60
	Axial	medium (330 grams)	6	80
	DV	large (700 grams)	6	60
	Axial	large (700 grams)	6	80

light and hung up to dry. Only then is it safe to expose the radiographs to light by removing them from the dark room.

INTERPRETATION

Where radiation has passed easily through the patient, the dry radiograph is black and not transparent. On the contrary, where radiodense patient tissues do not allow radiation to reach the silver halides in the film emulsion, the processing results in clear film which is translucent. When viewed by placing the radiographic film against a light source, the exposed portions are dark and the portions where tissues are radiodense are light. Many variations occur on the resulting film, depending on the variations of the radiodensity of the tissues of the patient. Interpretation is based on a thorough knowledge of the normal radiographic anatomy of patients in all of their sizes, views and other variables in order to be able to recognize those conditions which are abnormal.

A standardized approach is necessary to gain the most out of radiographic evaluation. Experienced clinicians often take a step-by-step approach when evaluating any radiographic film
—Examine the film for proper contrast. Were the film type, exposure settings, focal film distance and cassette used appropriate for optimal resolution?
—Evaluate all major organs systems for position, shape, size, density
—Evaluate all skeletal structures for shape, density, alterations and relationship to muscle and internal organs

For example, when a bone, which is normally dark, is broken, the image often shows a clear outline of the shape of the resulting fragments and the space between them. If softer and less radiodense tissues are abnormal, it can require considerable training, experience and time to arrive at a conclusion based on radiographs. It is not unusual to repeat the process using different positions, generator settings, and/or film/cassette combinations.

The most common radiographic abnormality in lizards is poor skeletal density. All of the member of the Sauria suborder require high levels of calcium in their diet and exposure to ultraviolet light to activate vitamin D3. The second most common radiographic abnormality is fracture of one or more bones.

Urinary tract "stones" or urolithiasis is most commonly seen in chelonians and most appro-

Corn snake being radiographed in a plastic tube. Note the lead blocker.

priately diagnosed by radiography. The bladder of chelonians is large and bi-lobed and uroliths appear more commonly in the left lobe.

In addition, there are contrast radiographic techniques involving the use of radiolucent dyes which produce intense film darkening and which can be seen clearly in dark outline as they pass through body cavities, vessels, etc. The most common contrast study performed is with a barium meal. The barium sulfate suspesion is given by esophageal tube and followed immediately by a volume of air, the amounts being determined by the size of the snake. This gives an effective "double-contrast" on which to make assessment. In snakes, which typically have a long "passage" time through the digestive tract, drugs such as metoclopramide may be given to hasten the passage time so that follow up radiographs can be taken in hours rather than days.

REFERENCES AND RECOMMENDED READING
—**Frye, FL;**
  Biomedical and Surgical Aspects of Captive Reptile Husbandry. Krieger, 1991.
—**Mader, DR:**
  Reptile Medicine and Surgery. Saunders, Philadelphia, 1995, 512pp.
—**Morgan, JP; Silverman, S; Zontine, WJ:**
  Techniques of Veterinary Radiology. Veterinary Radiology Associates, 1975.
—**Nyland & Mattoon.**
  Veterinary Diagnostic Ultrasound. Saunders, Philadelphia, 1995.

PARASITOLOGY

Ellis C. Greiner, Ph.D.*
Department of Pathobiology
College of Veterinary Medicine
University of Florida
Gainesville, Florida 32611 USA
and
Juergen Schumacher, Dr.med.vet.
Wildlife and Zoological Medicine Service
Department of Small Animal Clinical Sciences
College of Veterinary Medicine
University of Florida
Gainesville, Florida 32611 USA

*Send correspondence to: Dr. Ellis C. Greiner, Department of Pathobiology, College of Veterinary Medicine, University of Florida, Gainesville, Florida 32611

Dr. Ellis C. Greiner obtained his BS in zoology from Montana State University in 1966, an MS from the University of Nebraska in 1969 and a Ph.D. from the University of Nebraska in 1971. His graduate work was in parasitology. Upon graduation he taught at Iowa State University from 1972 to 1974. He was then a Research Associate in the International Reference Centre for Avian Malaria Parasites in St. John's, Newfoundland from 1974 to 1978. He then joined the faculty of the College of Veterinary Medicine at the University of Florida where is presently a Professor and Service Chief of the Clinical Microbiology and Parasitology Service. He has published extensively in a broad range of parasitic topics.

Dr. Juergen Schumacher graduated from the College of Veterinary Medicine, Free-University of West-Berlin, Germany in 1988. From 1989 to 1991 he performed his thesis research at the College of Veterinary Medicine, University of Florida. From 1991 to 1993 Dr. Schumacher completed a residency in Anesthesiology at the College of Veterinary Medicine, University of Florida. From 1993 to 1991 Dr. Schumacher was a resident in Wildlife and Zoological Medicine at the College of Veterinary Medicine, University of Florida.

INTRODUCTION

Reptiles have become popular animals in the pet trade during the past 10 years. Increasing numbers of snakes, lizards and chelonians are commonly kept as pets and are presented to the veterinary practitioner for diagnosis and treatment. In addition reptiles are also kept for biomedical research. Diagnosing and treating sick animals is a prerequisite in the management of reptiles kept under these conditions. In order to satisfy the increasing pet market, more reptiles are either imported from their endemic range or produced in large captive collections.

In order to successfully breed reptiles in captivity a thorough understanding of their biology, husbandry and medical management is essential. This will include knowledge of proper environmental requirements as well as routine health screening within the collection. As important as the health within the collection are proper quarantine procedures for newly aquired animals either from other collections or from the wild. While proper quarantine procedures are covered elsewhere within this book, it is essential to have a good knowledge of proper preventive medicine measures to inhibit pathogenic organisms from being introduced into the collection.

Since many reptiles enjoy increasing popularity as pet animals, the veterinarian specializing in reptile medicine is commonly confronted with individual animals originating from the pet trade or directly from the wild for diagnosis and treatment. A good working knowledge about the husbandry, biology and a variety of infectious and non-infectious diseases is necessary to successfully treat the reptilian patient. While an increasing number of publications, either in form of journal articles or books has became available recently to meet this demand, it is obvious that there is still much to learn about reptile medicine and surgery. While there is relatively little published on bacterial, fungal and viral organisms as disease causing agents in reptiles, many papers are available describing the presence of parasites in reptiles. Parasites are often found incidently upon routine fecal examinations. Physical examinations and full necropsies indicate that parasites play a role as pathogens in individual reptiles or in groups of reptiles.

While there may be thousands of parasites named from reptiles, the significance of most of these parasites to their reptilian hosts is unknown. Parasites normally encountered in reptiles range from single celled forms (coccidians, hemogragarines, malarial parasites, hemoflagellates, gut flagellates and ciliates) to multicellular organisms (flukes, tapeworms, spiny headed worms, round worms, pentastomes, mites and ticks).

The purpose of this chapter is not to review all parasites which have been described in the literature as extensive information is covered in some excellent reviews (Jacobson, 1983, 1986, 1993, and Frank 1981), but to discuss the most commonly encountered parasites and provide information on the diagnosis and treatment of parasitic diseases in reptiles. This chapter will follow the taxonomy of the major groups of parasites to avoid redundancy.

PROTOZOA

Protozoa (single celled parasites) are a diverse group of parasites that may be found in any soft tissue within the body. Protozoa are most commonly found within the intestinal tract and associated organs. Many of these are non-pathogenic. Others may cause clinically significant disease and have been associated with major losses within captive populations of reptiles (Keymer, 1981).

Mastigophorans: Flagellates are commonly found within the intestinal tract of reptiles and usually are not considered major pathogens in reptiles. These are tiny organisms (<15 μm) whose trophozoites move via flagella. These have been summarized and illustrated by simple line drawings (Barnard and Upton 1994). The size and shape of the cell and the number and arrangement of the flagella are characteristics used in the identification of flagellates. They may play a role as disease causing organisms if they are present in such high numbers that they predispose the host to secondary infections or other pathogenic organisms create an atmosphere to allow flagellates to be present in such high numbers that they may invade adjacent organs. If flagellates are found in the liver, kidney and gallbladder they have to be considered as pathogens. *Leptomonas* sp. have been associated with enteritis in chameleons. *Hexamita parva* is a pathogen for a variety of aquatic turtles as well as for tortoises and has been known to cause severe nephritis and mortality in infected animals (Zwart, 1975). In some cases the gallbladder of snakes is infected. In chronic infections *Hexamita* spp. may be found in the kidney and liver with only few individuals present within the intestinal tract. Clinically, anorexia, lethargy and excretion of mucoid feces and urine may be seen. The gallbladder will be enlarged in snakes which may be visible on the ventral scales. Pathological findings include swollen and pale kidneys with dilated tubuli which are filled with these flagellates. Glomerulonephritis and proliferation of epithelial cells are common findings. In some snakes fibrotic changes of the liver and proliferation of epithelial cells of the gallbladder are present. Detection of these flagellates within the urine will confirm the diagnosis. Treatment of choice is the administration of metronidazole (100 mg/kg PO, repeat in 2 weeks).

Monocercomonas is another genus of flagellate which commonly lives in snake and lizard intestines. Most of the infections do not cause apparent disease. However, some infected animals become inactive, lose condition, and may have diarrhea. If anorexia persists, death may ensue. While no consistent change in the histology of the gut has been recognized, edema sometimes is seen upon necropsy. These parasites may spread into the lungs, oviducts and stomach as well. On occasion, lymphocytic infiltrate develops in the lamina propria which may cause a separation of the epithelium from the lamina propria. The causes of benign infections to become pathogenic are unknown (Zwart, Teunis and Cornelissen 1982). These infections may be treated with metronidazole as suggested for *Hexamita*.

Sarcodinans: These are amoebae which move by formation of pseudopodia in the trophozoites and are transmitted by cysts passed in the feces. *Entamoeba invadens* is one of the most significant parasitic diseases in reptiles. This organism has been associated with major outbreaks in private and zoologic collections and high mortality. *Entamoeba invadens* resembles morphologically *Entamoeba histolytica* but has a different temperature optimum of 27° - 29° C. It is not transmissible to mammals. Lesions are predominantly located in the large intestine with ulcerations and thickening of the intestinal wall. Bacterial infections will complicate the picture. Severe adhesions are commonly seen in adjacent organs like liver and kidneys. Affected livers are edematous and the capsule is thickened. A rapid distribution of the parasite through the circulatory system will cause necrosis of affected organs and often death of an infected animal within short periods of time. Clinically, all reptiles are susceptible to these amoebae and symptoms include anorexia, weight loss, blood in feces, increased water consumption and lethargy. Central nervous system disease signs are often seen in final stages of the disease. A diagnosis of *Entamoeba invadens* will be very difficult. If an iron hematoxylin stain can be done on fecal smears or histologic secions, the vescicular nucleus will be more prominent than with other stains. The trophozoites range in size from 10 to 40 μm and the cysts are 11 - 20 μm and have 4 nuclei. In acute stages, a fecal sample and detection of trophozoites may be possible. Culture of the organism is the most reliable method but a specialized laboratory will be necessary. Fecal samples should be obtained at least three times a few days apart. In some cases a biopsy and histological evaluation may be successful. Therapy is difficult at best. A variety of agents are available, often for human use but the problem is that human therapy is usually initiated in the acute phase with no extraintestinal organisms. This phase is usually overlooked in reptiles and therefore therapy is more complicated. Treatment of choice at present is metronidazole (100 - 200 mg/kg PO, repeat in 2 weeks). In addition, metronidazole tablets may be inserted into the cloaca. Most infections are complicated by secondary bacterial infections, mostly Gram-negative organisms. Therefore administration of a broad spectrum antimicrobial, effective against most commonly seen pathogen in reptiles such as ceftazidime or enrofloxacin is indicated. An interesting hypothesis was presented by Telford (1971) in which he suggested reptiles affected by *E. invadens* had been moved into new geographic locations and became infected with strains of the amoebae for which the hosts were naive and thus highly susceptable. Thus exotic snakes and chelonians may be at risk whenever they are relocated and precautions must be taken to prevent outbreaks as have been reported recently (Donaldson et al 1975 and Jacobson et al 1983).

Ciliates: Protozoans which have cilia on their trophozoites are ciliates. Two genera are the primary ciliates in reptiles. These are *Balantidium* and *Nyctotherus*. These are not considered pathogenic to their reptilian hosts. If treatment is necessary, doxycycline (10 mg/kg PO SID for 10 days) is recommended.

Coccidians: These are members of the old "sporozoaans" which pass oocysts in the feces of the definitive hosts. The morphology of the oocysts is used for identification to genus, but only after they have fully developed. Oocysts of *Eimeria* and *Isospora* are passed undeveloped and require 2 - 5 days in an oxygenated environment to become sporulated and infectious. Once this occurs, the oocyst of *Eimeria* is subdivided internally into 4 units (=sporocysts) which each contain two bodies (=sporozoites) and those of

Isospora have 2 sporocysts, each with 4 sporozoites. Oocysts of *Sarcocystis* and *Cryptosporidium* pass fully developed and infectious. *Sarcocystis* oocysts rupture releasing two sporocysts each with 4 sporozoites and these measure 10 - 15 μm in length. Oocysts of *Cryptospordium* also contain 4 sporozoites but they are so small that they are difficult to see by light microscopy (4 - 8 μm in diameter). All stages of these parasites develop intracellularly. Only *Sarcocystis* spp. have indirect life cycles relying on a predator-prey relationship for perpetuation.

Eimeria spp. may be associated with clinical disease in juvenile animals whereas adult reptiles will be carriers. In snakes, proliferation of epithelial cells of the gall bladder and hepatomegaly can be seen. Clinically, lethargy and weight loss are commonly seen. A diagnosis can be made by detection of numerous oocysts in feces. *Sarcocystis* spp. have been reported in muscles of turtles, lizards, and snakes which function as intermediate hosts for these species. *Sarcocystis* sp. tissue stages and oocysts were found in a bull snake that had become emaciated, anorexic, and finally died (Duszak and Cunningham 1995). *Cryptosporidium* has been reported in a variety of snake species and lizards (Brownstein, 1972). This parasite was recently seen in a desert tortoise, but the infection was not associated with pathologic changes. Infection will cause hypertrophic gastritis, detected by vizualization and palpation of the enlargement of the stomach in severe cases. The gastric lumen is decreased and regurgitation is commonly seen. Anorexia, weight loss and secondary bacterial infections are seen clinically. A diagnosis can be made by obtaining stomach biopsies for histologic evaluation. *Cryptosporidium* spp. have become a major concern for snake collections because these infections usually result in high mortality. There is no known treatment at present.

Haemogregarines: These are fairly common inhabitants of reptile red blood cells, they have indirect cycles, and are considered non-pathogenic. The most common genus is *Haemogregarina*. The gametocyte of this parasite is usually as long as the host cell and sometimes folds over on itself, there are no pigment granules in the cyctoplasm and the cytoplasm usually stains faintly.

Haemosporidans: These are often referred to as malarial parasites. Two primary genera will be encountered commonly in lizards and occasionally in other reptiles. A comprehensive review of these blood parasites and others in reptiles summarized by Telford 1984. The primary genera are *Plasmodium* and *Haemoproteus*. The former has both schizonts and gametocytes in the erythrocytes and the latter has only gametocytes in the erythrocytes. All of these have malarial pigment which appears as refractile yellow to black dots in the cytoplasm of the parasite. Most of these are considered non-pathogenic. There are indications that subtle changes in host physiology may occur in response to certain lizard malarias in that infected lizards produce fewer eggs than non-infected lizards (Schall, 1990).

HELMINTHS

Trematodes: Digenetic trematodes are more important pathogens to reptiles than are the monogenetic and aspidogastrid flukes. All digenetic flukes have life cycles that require at least a molluscan intermediate host and sometimes a second intermediate host before infecting the definitive host. There are many species of flukes in reptiles and some may be severe pathogens. Hundreds of trematodes of the genus *Styphlodora* have been found within renal tubules and the ureters of pythons. Some species of this genus are acquired by eating fish containing metacercariae. Adult flukes seen in the oral cavity of snakes may be species of several genera including *Ochetosoma*, *Stomatotrema*, and *Pneumatophilus* whereas the flukes in the mouth of alligators are *Odhneriotrema*. These usually can be manually removed from the oral mucosa. Aquatic turtles have interesting fluke communities within them. Most of these reside in the intestinal tract, but some species also reside in the liver, gall bladder, urinary bladder, and circulatory system. The species in the blood vasculature (Spirorchiidae) are important because the eggs have to cross through tissues to exit the host via the digestive system. In their passage through normal tissue, they cause traumatic damage and also stimulate the formation of granulomas around eggs which become encapsulated. A useful reference on trematodes is by Schell 1985. Treatment will include administration of praziquantel (8 mg/kg PO). Repeat treatment in 2 and 4 weeks.

Cestodes: Mature cestodes live within the lumen of the small intestines. The indirect life cycle of cestodes require at least one and sometimes two intermediate hosts. Therefore, transmission from one reptile to another in captivity is uncommon for such genera as *Spirometra* (called spargana) and *Mesocestoides* (called tetrathyridea). Reptiles are the host for mature cestodes as well as for the larval stages. Clini-

cally, cestodes very rarely cause significant disease, depending on the number of mature worms present. Two useful references for tapeworms are Schmidt 1984 and Khalil et al 1994.

Proteocephalid tapeworms: These are most commonly encountered in snakes and lizards. The life cycle includes two intermediate hosts. The majority of cestodes reported in reptiles belong to this group. More than 70 species have been described within the genus *Ophiotaenia*, which primarily infects snakes, rarely aquatic turtles and lizards. Other genera include *Proteocephalus* (lizards), and *Crepidobothrium* (boids). Pathological changes are dependent on the intensity of infection and include intestinal necrosis, loss of epithelium and roundcell infiltrates within the tunica muscularis. Diagnosis can be made by the presence of typical eggs within fecal material or the identification of adult parasites. Treatment will include either niclosamide (200 mg/kg PO repeat in 14 days), bunamidine hydrochloride (50 mg/kg PO) repeated in 14 days, or praziquantel (8 mg/kg IM or PO repeat in 2 and 4 weeks).

Pseudophyllidean tapeworms: Members of the order Pseudophyllidea may reach 80 cm in length. The life cycle includes two intermediate hosts. After infection with infective larvae, the adult cestode will be present after a few days in a susceptible host (snakes and lizards). *Duthiersia* and *Scyphocephalus* are exclusively found in monitor lizards while *Bothridium* is most often seen in boid snakes and a variety of other snake species. Clinically, weight loss is most commonly seen and pathological findings include ulceration of intestinal mucosa, edema, and hemorrhages where cestodes are attached to the mucosa. A diagnosis can be made by identification of eggs within the feces. Eggs are operculated and similar to trematode eggs, except they will rise on fecal flotation. Final identification can be made by culturing eggs for several days on moist strips of filter paper with one end in water to allow the paper to act as a wick and the development of the ciliated coracidium. Treatment will include the same drugs as Proteocephalidae infections.

Cyclophyllidean tapeworms: Most tapeworms of veterinary concern are in this group. Relatively few species of this group occur in lizards as Nematotaenia, Diochetos, and Panceriella. Species of one genus (Oochoristica) infect snakes, lizards, and turtles.

Nematodes: Over a 1000 species of nematodes have been described from reptiles. They may vary in size from a few millimeters to 30 cm and are most commonly found in the intes-

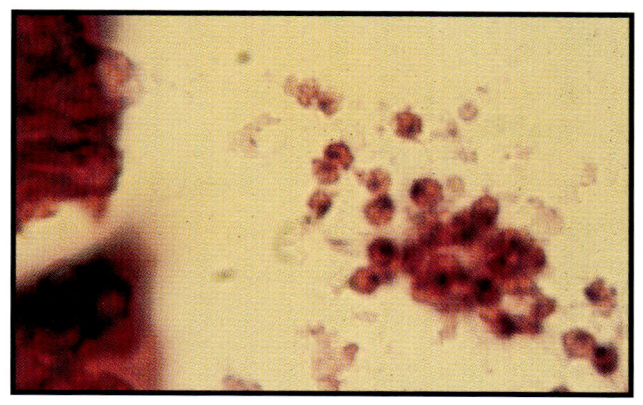

Monocercomonas - trophozoites from tree boa intestine cross section, 3 x 2 μm.

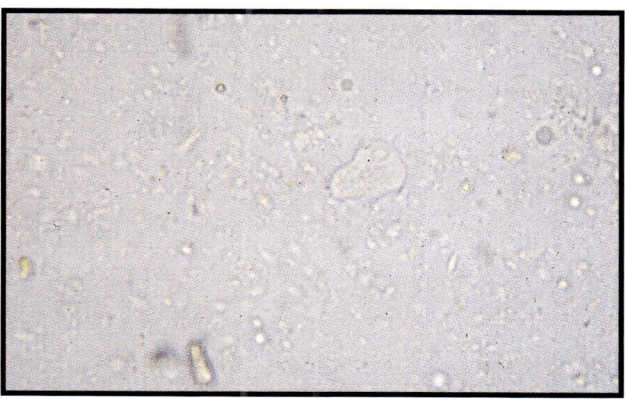

Entamoeba - trophozoite from green iguana, 22 x 11 μm

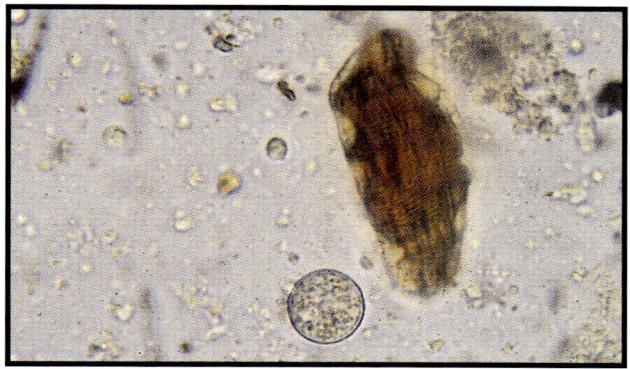

Entamoeba - cyst from green iguana, 19 x 19 μm.

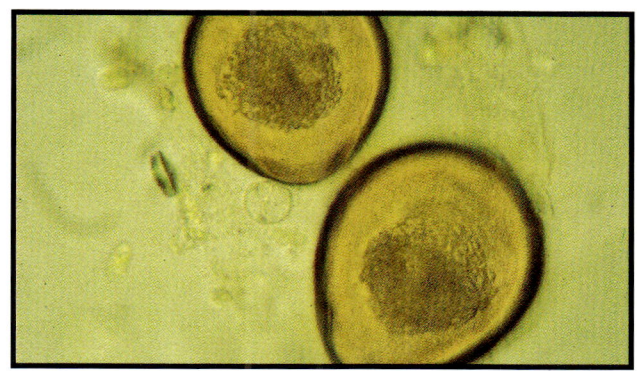

Unknown ciliate (*Balantidum* cyst), from leopard gecko, 80 x 72 μm.

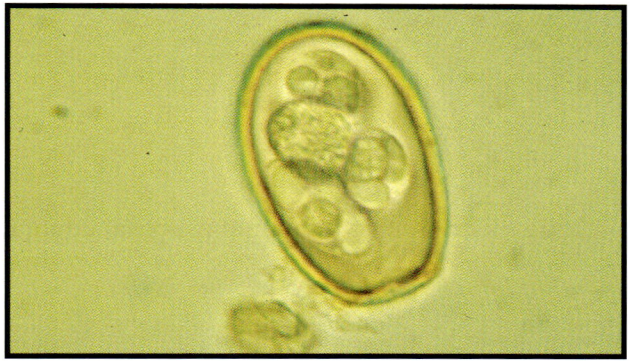

Eimeria - sporulated oocysts from Columbian boa, 33 x 22 μm.

Sarcocystis - sporocyst from viper, 13 x 9 μm.

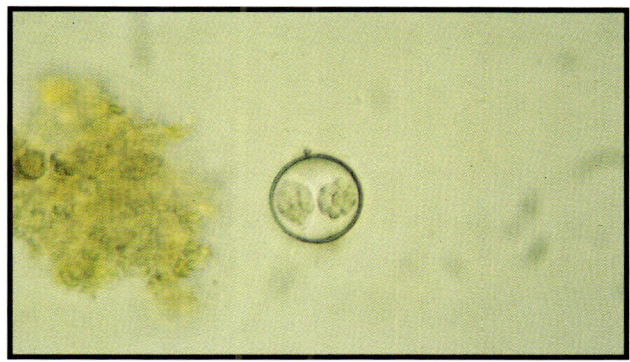

Isospora amphiboluri - sporulated oocysts from bearded dragon, 26 x 26 μm.

Cryptosporidium - oocysts from corn snake (stained red with acid fast procedure), 5 μm.

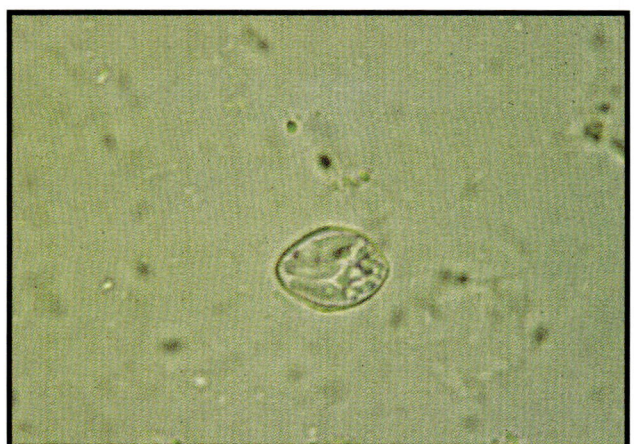

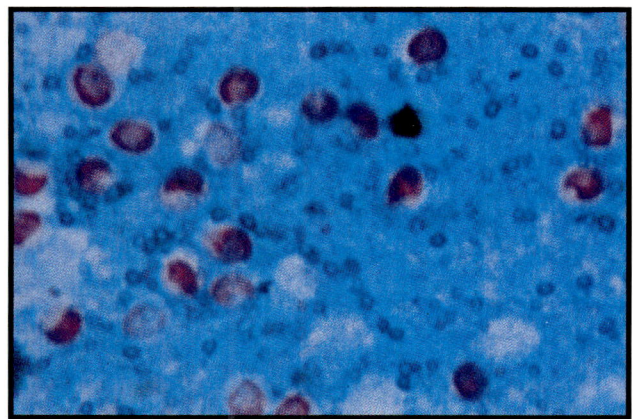

Learedius - eggs from green turtle, 297 mm total length.

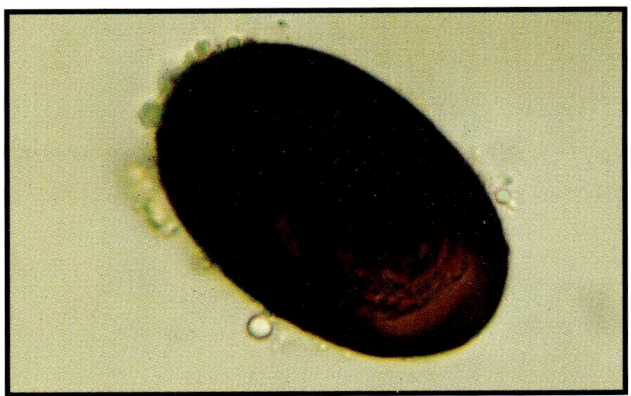

Neospirorchis - egg from green turtle, 57 x 35 µm.

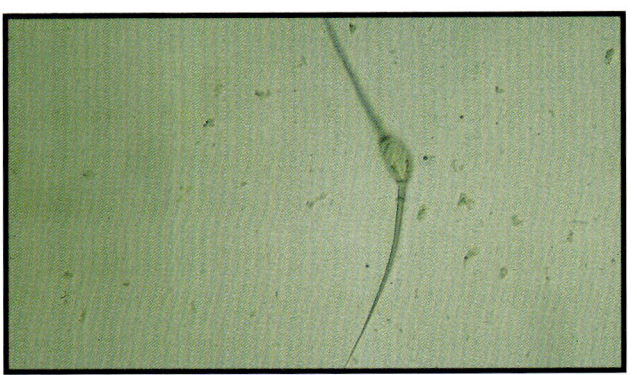

Pronocephalid - egg from green turtle, 384 x 15 µm.

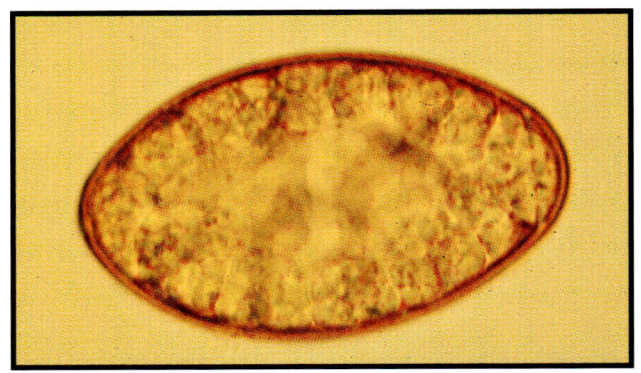

Unknown fluke - egg from green turtle, 81 x 50 µm.

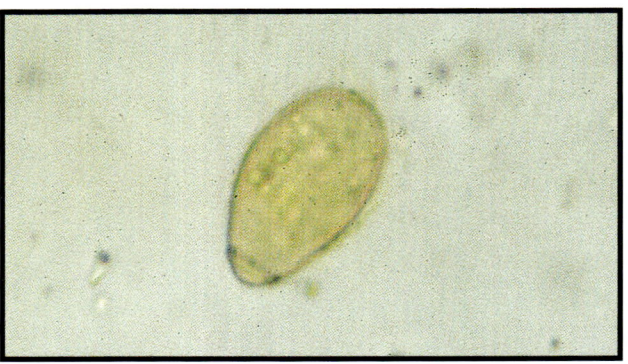

Unknown fluke - egg from crocodile, 72 x 60 µm.

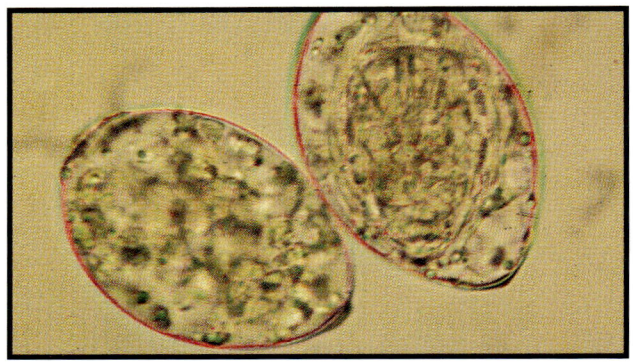

Bothridium - eggs from Burmese python, 71 x 47 mm.

Unknown tapeworm (*Kapsulotaenia* ?) - egg from python, hexacanth larva measures 31 x 28 µm.

Unknown tapeworm - egg cluster from boa, 125 x 95 µm.

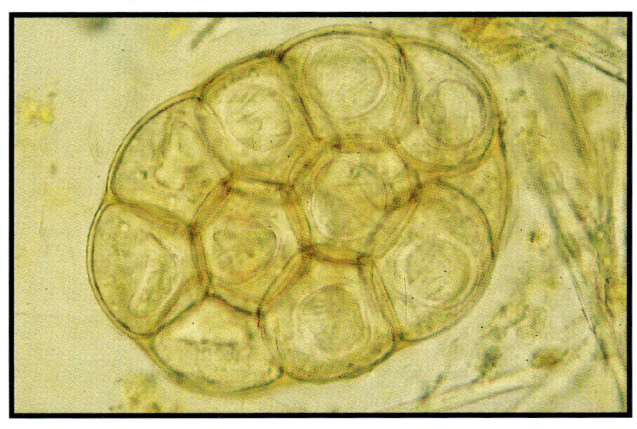

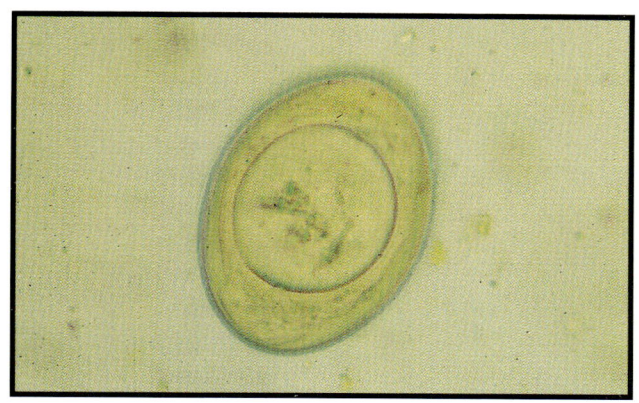

Hymenolepis nana - egg from python, (actually rodent tapeworm) 50 x 38 µm.

Hymenolepis diminuta - egg from python, (actually rodent tapeworm) 77 x 72 µm.

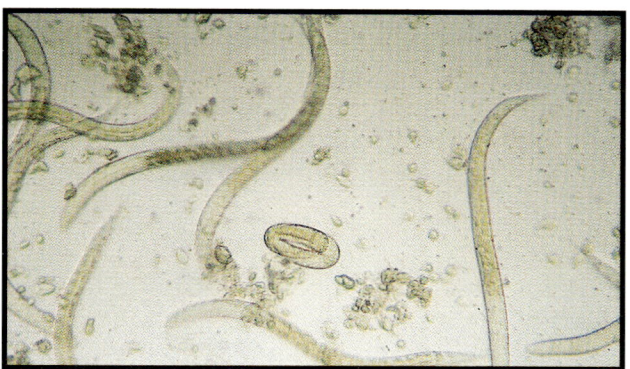

Rhabdias - larvated eggs and larvae from a kingsnake, egg about 60 µm.

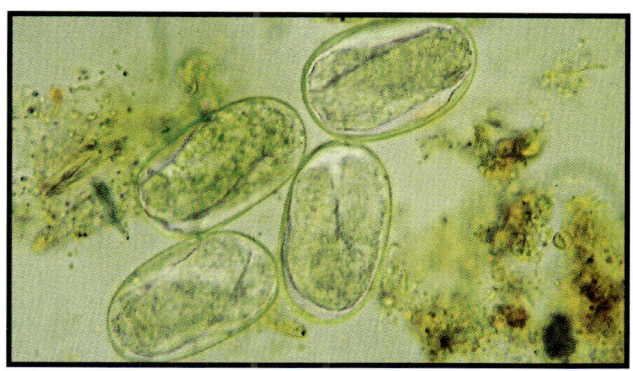

Rhabdias - larvated eggs from red rat snake, 60 x 33 µm.

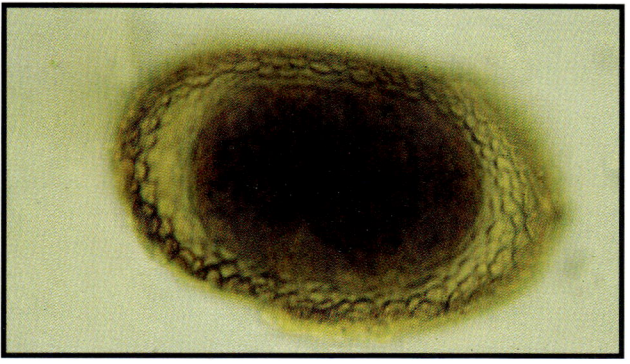

Sulcascaris - egg from hinge backed turtle, 112 x 72 mm.

Ophidascaris - from green tree python, 90 x 64 mm.

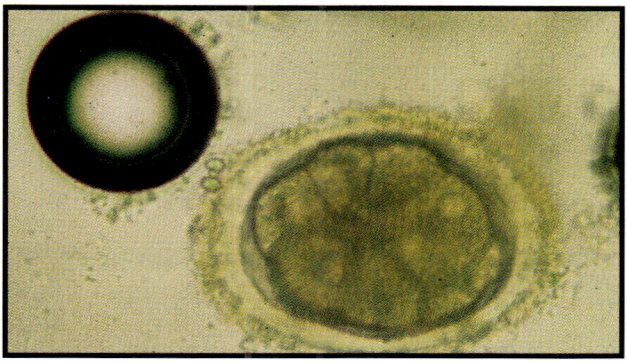

Dujardinascaris - from American alligator, 75 x 70 mm.

Unknown pinworm - same egg as Fig. 13 from gopher tortoise (focus on egg surface), 137 x 64 mm.

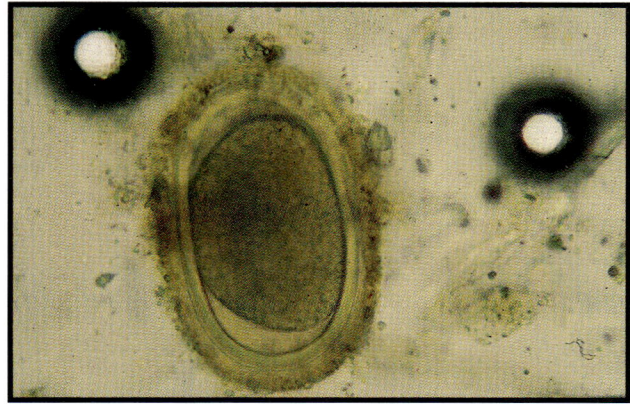

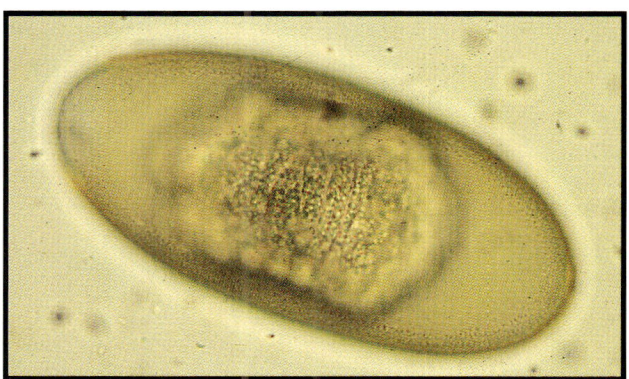

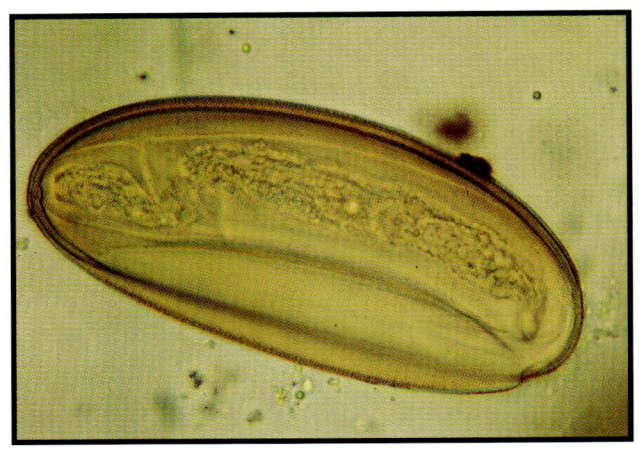

Aleuris - egg from rhino iguana, 157 x 71 µm.

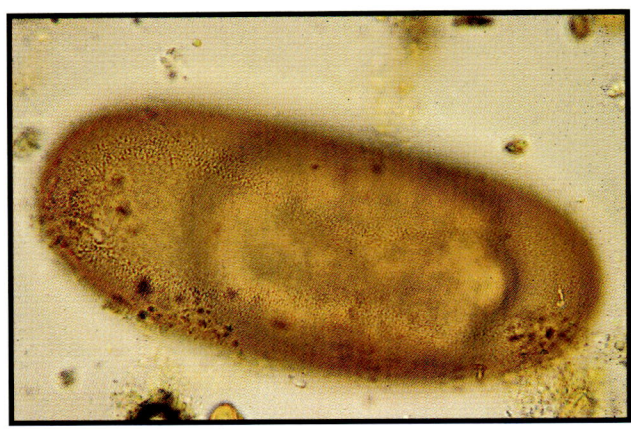

Ozolaimus - egg from green iguana (focus on surface - note fenestrations) 181 x 68 µm.

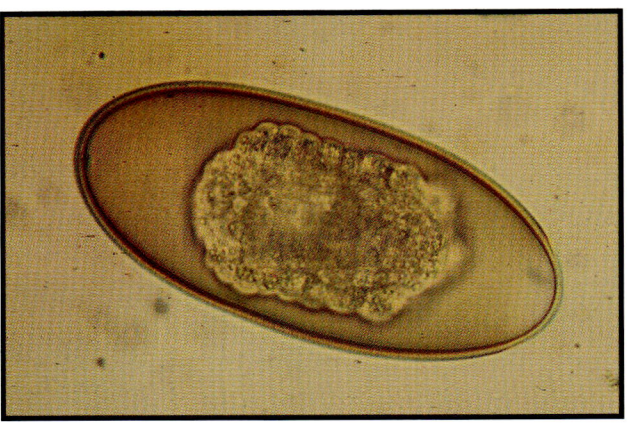

Unknown pinworm - egg from gopher tortoise (focus on egg), 137 x 64 µm.

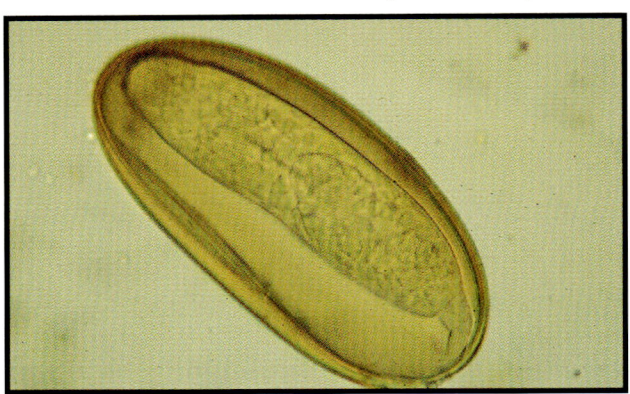

Ozolaimus - egg from green iguana (usually there are three distinct sizes of eggs in green iguanas matching 3 species of this pinworm), 148 x 68 µm.

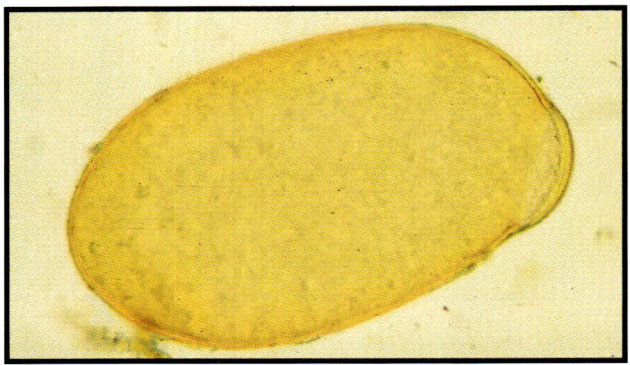

Unknown pinworm, egg from aldabra tortoise, 145 x 80 µm.

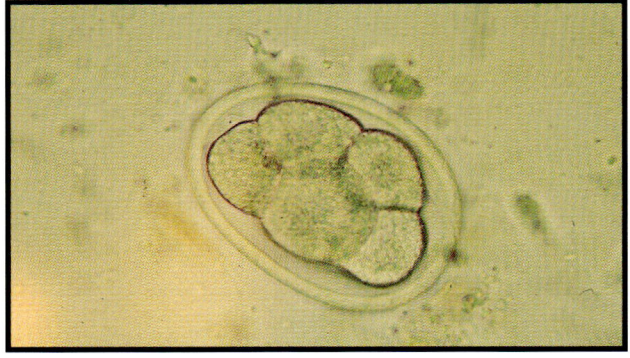

Falcaustra - from ornate terrapin, 77 x 57 µm.

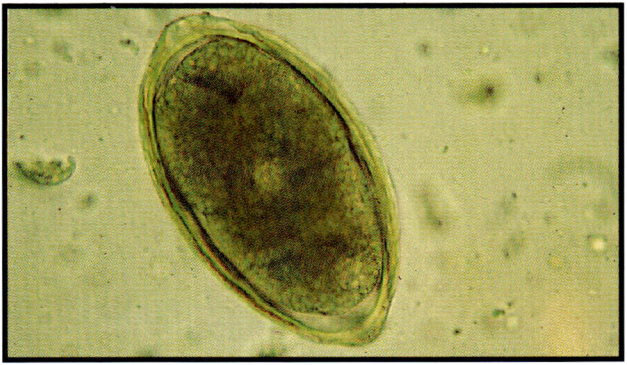

Cruzia - egg from ornate terrapin, 117 x 66 µm.

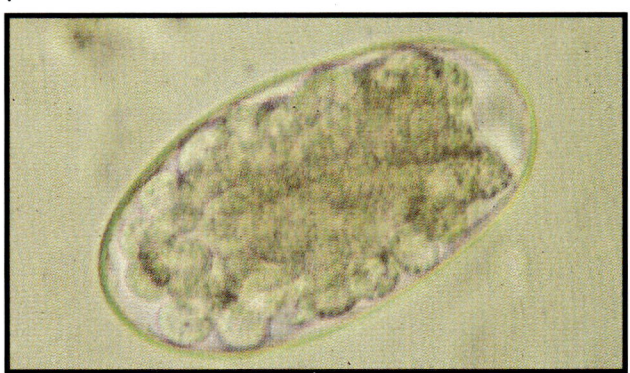

Kalicephalus - egg from red tailed boa, 79 x 43 µm.

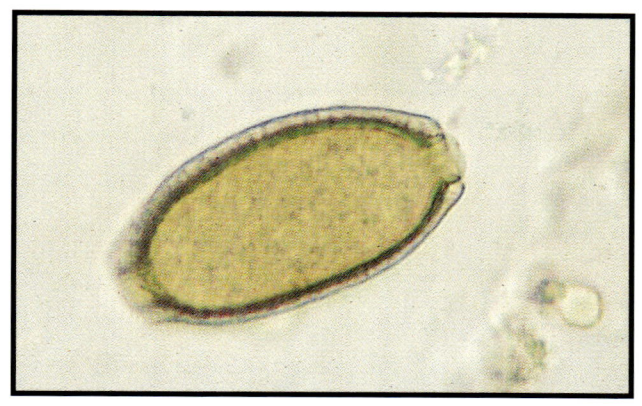

Capillaria - egg from red tailed boa, 53 x 28 μm.

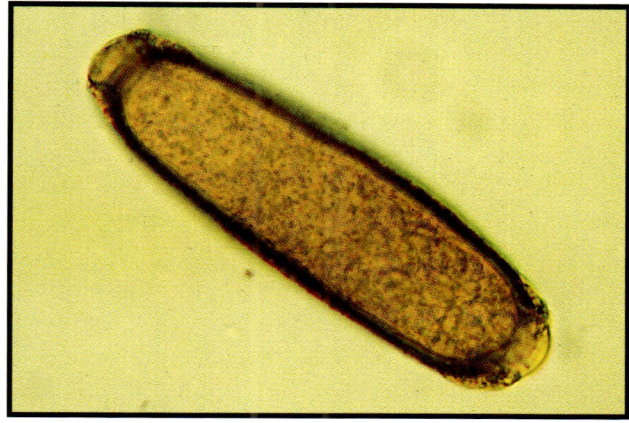

Capillaria - egg from python, 110 x 33 μm.

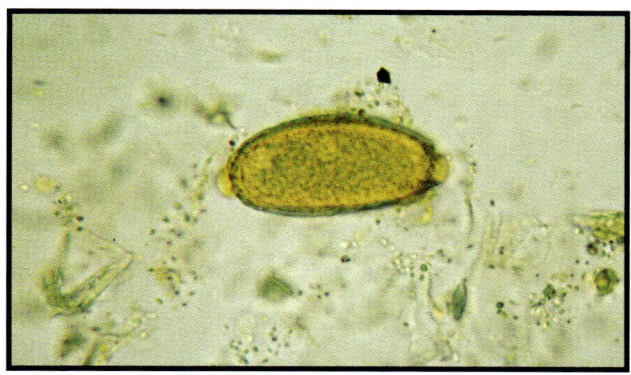

Capillaria - egg from red rat snake, 62 x 28 μm.

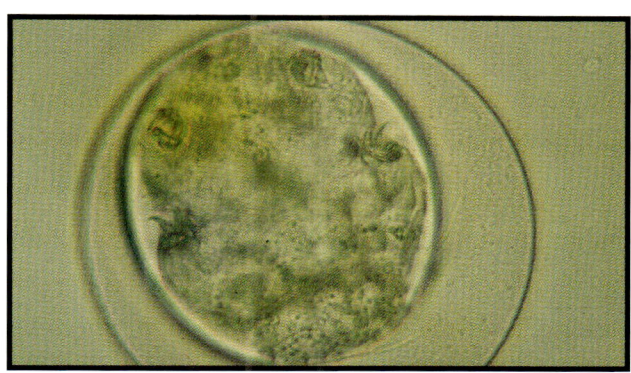

Kiricephalus - egg from indigo snake, 134 x 131 μm.

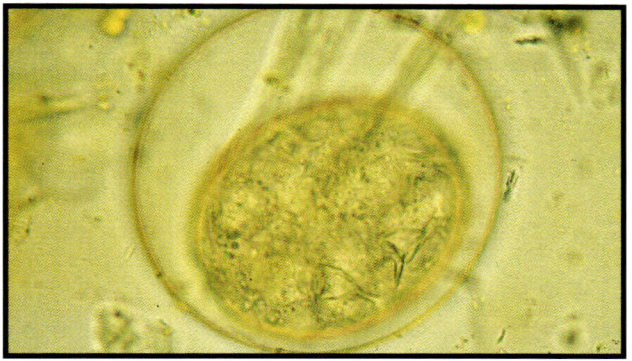

Unknown pentastome - egg from boa, 128 x 119 μm.

Unknown pentastome - egg of same species as in above, but surface projections missing, 80 x 66 μm.

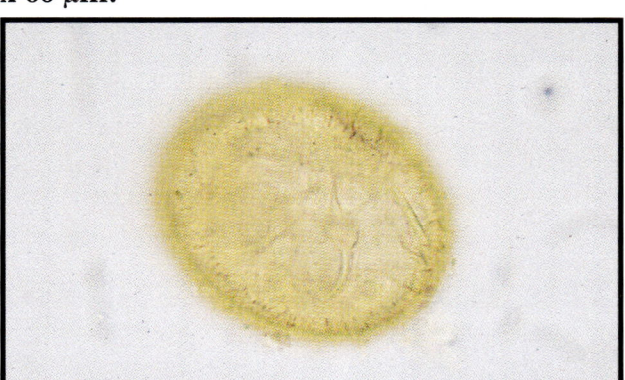

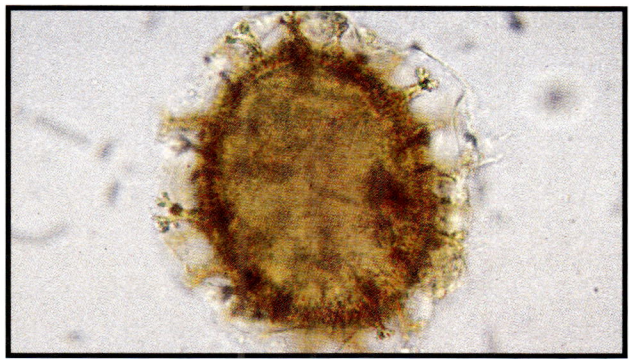

Unknown pentastome - egg from blue-tailed monitor, 108 x 88 μm.

Unidentified mite - egg of mouse mite from python feces, 198 x 46 mm.

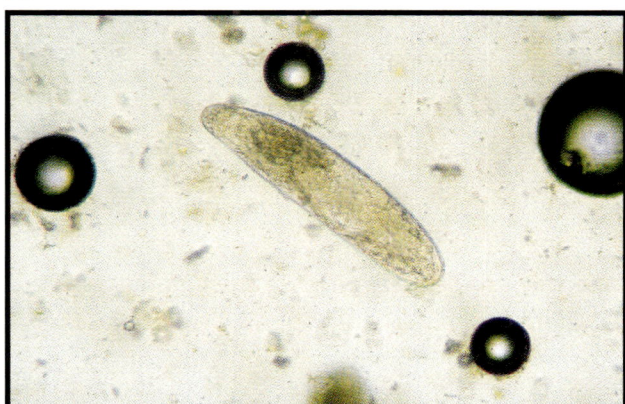

tinal tract. In some cases they are also seen in blood vessels and most visceral organs. They are capable of causing severe pathological changes in the host. They may have a direct (pinworms and strongylate nematodes) or indirect life cycle (ascarids, spiruroids and filaroids). A useful and informative reference on nematodes is Anderson 1992.

Rhabditoid nematodes: These are small nematodes and they are characterized by the fact that they have free-living and parasitic generations. Only adult females are parasitic as the males are present in the free-living generation. *Rhabdias* spp. live in the lungs of snakes. Signs of infection include respiratory disease characterized by irregular breathing patterns, and production of excessive mucous which will contain larvated eggs and larvae. *Strongyloides* spp. are found in the intestinal tract of snakes. Anorexia, weight loss and edema of the gingiva are also common. In addition, secondary bacterial infections are commonly seen. A diagnosis is made by detection of larvated eggs and larvae in oral mucous, lung washes and fecal material. Treatment will include intramuscular administration of levamisole (10 mg/kg, repeat in 2 weeks) or fenbendazole (50 -100 mg/kg PO, repeat in 14 days).

Strongyloid nematodes: Clinically the most significant strongylid are members of the genus *Kalicephalus*. *Kalicephalus* species are relatively small and are found in the gastro-intestinal tract from the esophagus to the duodenum. Very rarely are they found within the stomach. Clinical signs depend on the number of nematodes infecting the host animal. Necrotizing hemorrhagic areas are found in the esophagus and the intestine which are entry ports of secondary bacterial organisms. A diagnosis is made upon fecal examination and detection of thin-walled eggs containing up to 64 blastomeres. Larvae are rarely seen within fecal material. Fenbendazole (50-100 mg/kg PO, repeat in 2 weeks) is the treatment of choice.

Oxyuroid nematodes: They are commonly found in herbivorous reptiles, more rarely in carnivorous species where they inhabit the large intestine in large numbers. Pinworms are small nematodes, represented by over 100 species in multiple genera, which are found in large numbers within the caecum and the rectum. They have a direct life cycle, therefore transmission in captivity is commonly seen. Pinworms are more or less host specific. Clinically, no characteristic symptoms are present. Anorexia may be seen in heavily infected animals. Pinworm eggs of tortoises are variable with some being

symmetrical and others asymmetrical, some have fenestrations on their shells, and some have a polar cap that may be eccentric. They are easily found upon fecal flotation. Treatment, if desirable, will include fenbendazole (50-100 mg/kg PO, repeat in 2 weeks), especially prior to hibernation in some reptile species.

Ascaroid nematodes: They are relatively large nematodes measuring up to 10 cm in length. They may infect all reptile species but are most commonly found in chelonians and boid snakes. Genera infecting reptiles include *Dujardinascaris* (alligators), *Ophidascaris* and *Polydelphis* (pythons) and *Sulcascaris* (chelonians). The over 50 members of this group of nematodes affect both captive and free-ranging animals and will cause pathologic changes. There are no typical clinical symptoms but anorexia, regurgitation and weight loss are commonly seen in individuals with many worms. Pathologic changes are found within the stomach and the intestine, characterized by ulcerations and thickening of the stomach wall. In some animals, migrating larvae are found within visceral organs and the aorta. In severe cases a pronounced gastro-enteritis with granulomatous changes of the stomach and intestinal wall can be seen. In some cases perforation of the wall and a severe peritonitis with subsequent septicemia will develop. A diagnosis is made upon detection of thick and rough-walled eggs within fecal material or after a stomach wash. Therapy will include oral administration of fenbendazole (50-100 mg/kg, repeat in 2 weeks) or albendazole (50 mg/kg PO).

Filarioid nematodes: Filarial nematodes found in reptiles are all members of the family Onchocercidae and they are found in extraintestinal sites as adults.

Some of the reptile inhabiting genera include *Oswaldofilaria* (lizards, caimans in muscles, vasculature or subcutaneous), *Foleyella* (lizards - subcutaneous and intramuscular), and *Macdonaldius* (lizards and snakes - peritoneal cavity and blood vessels). Microfilariae are acquired when taking a blood meal and transmission occurs after appropriate development in the vector, such as ticks and mosquitoes. Clinical signs will include gangrenous changes which may affect the whole skin caused by occlusion of the abdominal artery by this nematode. Pathologically, filarial nematodes may be found at a variety of sites within the body. Typically a thrombosis of affected vessels will be present. A diagnosis can be made upon microscopic examination of a blood smear and demonstration of microfilariae. If ectoparasites are present on the host, such as ticks, they may be examined for the presence of larval nematodes. There is no effective treatment known at present, although it has been recommended that elevation of the environmental temperature to 35°-37° C for up to 48 hours will cause death of adult worms.

Trichuroid nematodes: *Capillaria* spp. are widespread in reptiles. These hairlike worms are mainly in the intestines. No species are known to be pathogenic in reptiles. The eggs have bipolar plugs, a rough or pitted egg shell and rise on fecal flotation.

Acanthocephalans: The worms have an eversible spiny proboscis. The proboscis is inserted into the mucosa and thus anchors the worm in place. The arrangement, number and size of the hooks on the proboscis and the configuration of the proboscis are important characteristics used in acanthocephalan identification. Therefore it is essential to remove the worm from the gut wall without rupturing the body wall or the proboscis will not evert when placed in tap water for several hours. The most common genus of acanthocephalans in reptiles are species of *Neoechinorhynchus* in fresh water turtles. Acanthocephalans are parasites found in all vertebrate classes. Most species measure 1 to 3 cm in size. Adult forms are found within the intestinal tract. Encapsulated larvae are often found within tissues and the intestinal wall. Pathologic findings include inflammation and necrosis of intestinal mucosa. Immature forms present in high numbers may cause abnormal peristaltic and intestinal passage of digesta. Anorexia will be the consequence. A diagnosis can be made upon identification of eggs in feces containing a larva with hooks at one end and the egg shell is composed of many irregular layers. Larvae can only be diagnosed if they are present subcutaneously and can be palpated and after surgical removal. There is no known effective treatment at present.

PENTASTOMIDS:

Adult pentastomes are predominantly found in the lungs of reptiles and very rarely in mammals and birds. Some authorities place these in the phylum Arthropoda and others place them in a separate phylum. Snakes are often infected with this wormlike parasite which is white to yellowish in coloration. Sometimes they are only found within the upper airway. They range in size between 0.5 cm and 14 cm in length. Genera found in snakes include *Armillifer, Kiricephalus, Sebekia,* and *Porocephalus.* Clinically, signs of the respiratory system, including respiratory sounds and nasal discharge are seen.

Direct detection of eggs containing a larva with sclerotized mouth and 2 pairs of claws within the mucous or by fecal flotation will confirm the diagnosis. In suspicious cases, endoscopic examination of the upper airway, the airsacs and the lung and direct visualization of the parasites will confirm a diagnosis. Since there are no safe parasiticides available, surgical removal of the parasite is recommended. Due to the zoonotic potential of some pentastomids, care has to be taken when handling infected animals.

ARTHROPODA:

Arthropods play only a minor role in parasitic diseases of reptiles. The main problem is their role in the transmission of arboviruses. The problem for the herpetologist are mites and ticks which may cause severe anemia and secondary bacterial infections of affected tissues. Larvae of certain flies are capable of causing myiasis.

Mites: A variety of different mites are found on the skin and occasionally within the upper respiratory tract of reptiles. Although a variety of mites belonging to different families have been reported on reptiles, most commonly the snake mite (*Ophionyssus natricis*) is encountered in collections of reptiles. The natural hosts are snakes, but in their absence, this species may also be found on lizards. This mite is distributed world wide and may become a serious problem in captive reptiles. Chiggers also use snakes as hosts. Treatment is very difficult and strict hygiene protocols have to be followed in order to eliminate this parasite. Clinically, infected snakes will have rough scales and may have shedding problems. Petechia may be seen where the mites are attached. In severe cases, anemia may be seen. Often mites are located between the spectacle and the periocular scales, other regions include axillary regions, the cloaca and skin folds beneath the mandible. In addition to direct damage by the mite causing skin disease, secondary bacterial and/or fungal infections develop and it has been shown that mites are capable of transmitting bacterial diseases predominantly gram - negative organisms. Mite eggs are deposited throughout the cage most commonly between rocks and wooden substrates. In severe cases mites may be seen directly, whereas in mild infections they may be difficult to diagnose. Often they may be seen in the water bowl after infested reptiles soak for prolonged periods of time. Treatment will include discarding all items from the tank like wood, rocks and plants as well as the substrate. Snakes may be treated with ivermectin (0.2 mg/kg IM, PO, repeat in 2 weeks). Vapona strips may be used for up to 4 days. In mild cases, the use of olive oil has been proven to be effective. The reptile is covered in oil and care has to be taken to apply oil also to hard to reach regions like the cloacal region and the eyes. In cases were secondary bacterial infections are present the use of a broad spectrum antimicrobial is recommended.

Ticks: Ticks have been diagnosed in virtually all reptilian orders. Only if severe infestation is present are they associated with clinical disease. Tortoises are often imported into the United States with reptilian *Amblyomma* spp. attached, however usually only males will be present as the females have completed feeding and dropped off. Gopher tortoises in Florida often are infested with *Amblyomma tuberculatum*. Commonly, a dermatitis with secondary bacterial infections can be seen and they may cause anemia in severe cases. They have been shown to be a vector for a variety of viral and protozoan diseases. Treatment will include in mild cases manual removal or the use of DDVP strips. If ticks are manually removed care has to be taken not to leave the mouth pieces within the skin which may stimulate abscess formation. If DDVP strips are used they have to be in the cage for at least one week since ticks appear to be more resistant to DDVP than mites.

Myiasis (the infestation of living tissue with fly larvae) is most commonly seen in chelonians and they are found predominantly around the cloacal region or within wounds. Large tortoises in captivity may become infested with larvae of *Cistudinomyia citudinis*. Some species are capable of penetrating intact skin, but more often open wounds are fly struck. In severe cases larvae may be found in large subcutaneous areas. Manual removal of the larvae, flushing the wound with diluted betadine solution and treatment with broad spectrum antimicrobials, as well as removal of the animal from new exposure to flies are effective treatment measures.

Leeches: Leeches are usually restricted to aquatic turtles and crocodilians. While in mild cases no or little clinical signs are present, in severe cases they may cause anemia and dermatitis with abscess formation. Most often, species of *Placobdella* (fresh water) and *Ozobranchus* (marine) are seen. Some function as vectors for hemoparasites such as *Haemogregarina*. Treatment will include either careful manual removal of the leeches or placement of freshwater turtles in hypertonic salt solutions and marine turtles temporarily in fresh water.

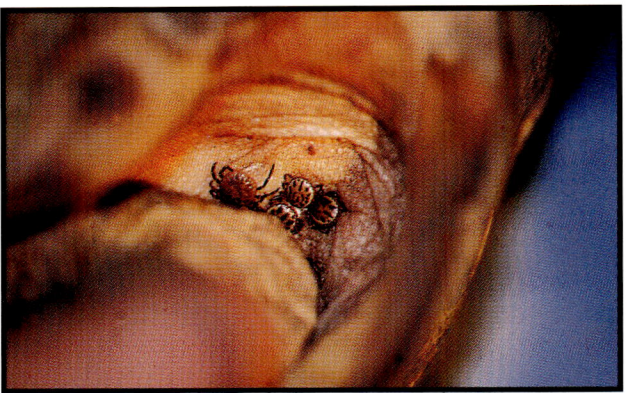

Amblyomma tuberculatum - **recently acquired adults in axillary region of gopher tortoise.**

Amblyomma tuberculatum - **two nearly replete females in axillary region of gopher tortoise.**

Mites on tail of green iguana.

DIAGNOSIS

A major problem in the diagnosis of reptilian parasites is that eggs and/or cysts of the parasites have not been matched to the adults needed to make an identification. In the case of the helminths, when they are collected at necropsy, it is important to collect feces and correlate the eggs with the adults. Some of the eggs and protozoans identified to genus and others determined to parasite group are illustrated.

SAMPLE COLLECTION

It is recommended to examine newly acquired

reptiles for the presence of parasitic diseases to prevent introduction of these organisms into an established collection. While in quarantine, it is advisable to thoroughly inspect the skin for ectoparasites and examine multiple fecal samples for the presence of parasites. Most antiparasitic agents have a broad range of effectiveness and exact identification of the parasite species is often not necessary for proper treatment of the infected reptile. In addition, many reptiles are imported from the wild and many new parasites are seen in these animals. Identification of the major group of parasites is in some cases sufficient for proper treatment. For exact identification, the expertise of a parasitologist specializing in reptiles is a necessity. Although many parasites are host specific, some are capable of infecting related species, like ascaroid nematodes in boid snakes. *Entamoeba invadens* in opposite shows no host specifity and is capable of causing severe infections in virtually all reptile species. *Eimeria* spp. are an example of a parasites having direct life cycles and being host specific.

It is recommended to examine multiple fecal samples in all new arrivals as well as in regular intervals within the collection. Fecal flotations are best done in sodium nitrate if only one medium is being used as it is the most universal medium available. Fluke eggs do not float and thus they need be detected by fecal sedimentation. It is recommended to examine only fresh fecal samples or to use cloacal washes since contamination with nematodes from the cage substrate may lead to a wrong diagnosis. For detection of hemoparasites, a blood sample has to be collected, smears made, and stained. Skin scrapings and biopsies may be necessary for detection of some mites. A stomach wash can easily be obtained from most reptiles by inserting a mouth gag made from an empty syringe case into the mouth and passing a rubber tube into the stomach. Sterile saline will be administered and aspirated until a sufficient sample has been obtained. This may then be examined microscopically or submitted for culture. A cloacal wash is probably the best method to ensure a fresh sample is obtained and evaluated. Gastroscopy and endoscopic techniques are a valuable tool for obtaining diagnostic specimen such as biopsies and cultures, but may also be used for manual removal of parasites, e.g. pentastomids from the lungs or airsacs.

REFERENCES

—**Anderson, RC:**
Nematode parasites of vertebrates. Their development and transmission. CAB International. Wallinford, England. 1992. 578 pp.

—**Brownstein, DG; Standberg, JD; Montali, JD; et al:**
Cryptosporidium in snakes with hypertrophic gastritis. Veterinary Pathology, 1972. 14: 606.

—**Daszak, P; Cunningham, A:**
A report of intestinal sarcocystosis in the bullsanke (*Pituophis melanoleucas sayi*) and a re-evaluation of *Sarcocystis* sp. from snakes of the genus *Pituophis*. Journal of Wildlife Diseases, 1995. 31:400-406.

—**Donaldson, M; Heyneman, D; Dempster, R; Garcia, L:**
Epizootic of fatal amebiasis among exhibited snakes: epidemiologic, pathologic, and chemotherapeutic considerations. American Journal of Veterinary Research, 1975. 36:807-817.

—**Frank, W.**
Endoparasites. In: Diseases of Reptilia. Vol. 1. JL Cooper: OF Jackson (Eds). Academic Press, London, England. 1981.

—**Jacobson, ER:**
Parasitic diseases in reptiles. In: Current Veterinary Therapy VIII. Small Animal Practice. WB Saunders Co. Philadelphia, Pennsylvania. 1983.

—**Jacobson, ER; Clubb, S; Greiner, EC:**
Amebiasis in red-footed tortoises. Journal of the American Veterinary Medical Association, 1983. 183: 1192-1194.

—**Jacobson ER.:**
Parasitic diseases of reptiles. In: Fowler M.E. (ed): Zoo and Wild Animal Medicine. Philadelphia, W.B. Saunders, 1986. pp. 162-181

—**Jacobson ER:**
Snakes. In: The Veterinary Clinics of North America: Small Animal Practice, Exotic Pet Medicine. Quesenberry K.E. and Hillyer E.V. (Eds.). I, 1993. Vol. 23 pp.1179-1212

—**Keymer, IF:**
Protozoa. In: Diseases of Reptilia. JE Cooper and OF Jackson (Eds). Vol. 1. Academic Press, London, England. 1981.

—**Khalil, LF; Jones, A:**
Bray, RA: Keys to the cestode parasites of vertebrates. CAB International. Wallingford, England. 1994. 751 pp.

—**Schall, JJ:**
Virulence of lizard malaria: the evolutionary ecology of an ancient parasite-host association. Parasitology, 1990. 100: 835-852

—**Schell, SC:**
Tremmatodes of North America north of Mexico. University of Idaho Press. Moscow, Idaho. 1985. 263 pp.

—**Schmidt, GD:**
CRC Handbook of tapeworm identification. CRC Press, Boca Raton, Florida. 1984. 675 pp.

—**Telford, SR Jr:**
Parasitic diseases of reptiles. Journal of the American Veterinary Medical Association, 1971. 159: 1644 -1652.

—**Telford, SR Jr:**
Haemoparasites of reptiles. In, Diseases of Reptiles and Amphibians, GL Hoff; FL Frye; ER Jacobson (Eds). Plenum Publishing Corp. New York. 1984. pp. 385-517.

—**Zwart, P; Truyens, EHA:**
Hexamitiasis in tortoises. Veterinary Parasitology, 1975. 1:175- 183

—**Zwart, P; Teunis, SFM;**
Cornelissen, JMM: Monocercomoniasis in reptiles. Comptes Rendus Premier Coloque international de Pathologie des Reptiles et des Amphibians. Angers, France. 1982. pp.73 - 76.

DIAGNOSTIC PROCEDURES: HEMATOLOGY

James Watson BVSc (hons) MACVSc
Veterinary Pathologist
Animal Health Laboratory
Department of Primary Industries and Fisheries
PO Box 46, Kings Meadows, 7249
Tasmania, Australia

James Watson is a veterinary clinical pathologist with an interest in exotic species, including reptiles in particular and wildlife in general. Since graduating from the University of Melbourne and undertaking postgraduate training at Murdoch University, James has, apart from a brief flirtation with the private sector, been working with the Department of Primary Industries and Fisheries in Tasmania, Australia.

INTRODUCTION

Reptilian hematology is something of a young science and while useful information exists, much remains to be learned. The significance of changes seen in disease states in particular awaits further study. The information presented in this chapter summarises many different studies separated by method, species and time, and attempts to provide an overview that will be useful both in those species studied as well as those that have received little or no attention.

SAMPLE COLLECTION

Site, method and volume of sample collection will vary considerably depending on the species being examined. Suitable techniques in a small tortoise are likely to be at best impractical and at worst life threatening in a large crocodilian.

Although EDTA is widely considered the preferred anticoagulant for hematology due to superior preservation and staining of cells, problems may arise in reptiles. In some species, especially chelonians, EDTA may cause hemolysis, leaving the sample dark and tarry in appearance. This problem has been noted also in birds (Hawkey et al, 1989).

For this reason, heparin is preferred as an anticoagulant in reptiles. This is not actually the compromise that it may appear to be at first sight, as comparisons of paired EDTA and heparinised samples in this author's laboratory have revealed similar, and sometimes superior, staining results for the latter in a number of reptile species. In any case, a fresh smear made at collection is preferred, and avoids the problem. An additional advantage is found in smaller reptiles where sample volumes will be correspondingly small, as the use of heparin allows a single sample to be collected for both hematology and biochemistry.

Size of needle and syringe need to be appropriate to the size of the animal to be sampled. In smaller animals, collection from the hub of a needle into pediatric or micro tubes is a useful technique. Flushing of the collection gear with heparin is useful in slow collections and is advised if problems with clotted samples are encountered. In all species, preparation of the site to be sampled by cleaning with alcohol, or other suitable disinfectant, should be mandatory.

CROCODILIANS

The problems of blood collection in crocodiles and alligators generally centre on restraint rather than site selection, and in larger individuals bleeding rapidly becomes both impractical and dangerous and should not be undertaken lightly.

The ventral coccygeal vein is the preferred site for sampling (Samour et al, 1984). The vessel runs in a canal formed by the ventral spines of the coccygeal vertebrae, and a rather long needle is generally required to reach it. The animal should be restrained on its back and the needle inserted in the midline at about 25% of the tail length behind the cloaca, angled about 35 - 45 degrees cranially (Figure 1). It is generally necessary to feel the way with the tip of the needle until a gap between the ventral spines is found and the needle inserted to full depth. It should be noted that lymph vessels also run in these canals, and caution is required to avoid sample contamination with lymph.

Collection is also possible from the dorsal cervical sinuses in most species. These are paired

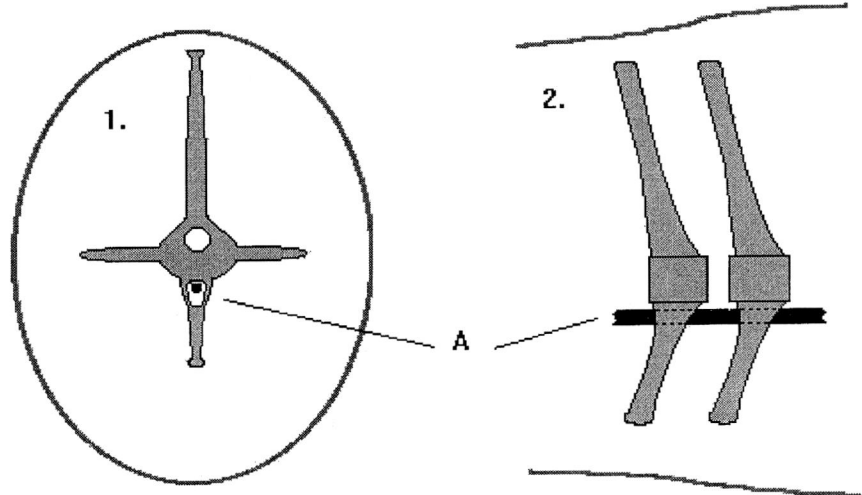

Figure 1: Location of the ventral coccygeal vein (A) in lizards and crocodilians. 1. Cross section and 2. longitudinal section of tail.

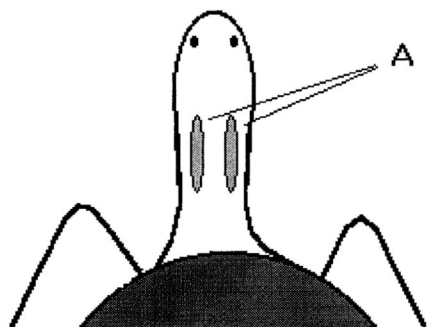

Figure 2: Location of the dorsal cervical sinuses (A)

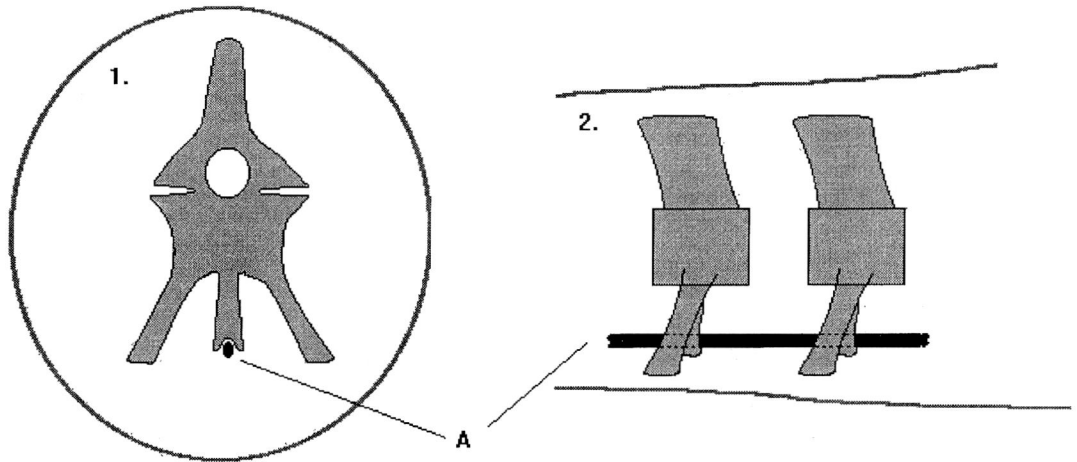

Figure 3: Location of the ventral coccygeal vein (A) in snakes. 1. Cross section and 2. longitudinal section of tail

structures either side of the midline immediately behind the occiput (Figure 2). The neck should be straight and extended, and the head flexed slightly ventrally. The needle is inserted perpendicularly and advanced until the sinus is entered. Great care must be taken with placement and depth of the needle (Heard et al, 1988).

LIZARDS

The ventral coccygeal vein is the preferred site in this group (Samour et al, 1984), and the approach is similar to that described for crocodilians (Figure 1). In male lizards it is possible to inadvertently puncture the hemipenes if the needle is inserted too far cranially - it is preferable to err on the side of caution and collect from further down the tail if in any doubt.

SNAKES

Again the ventral coccygeal vein is the preferred site (Samour et al, 1984), but in this group the anatomy surrounding the vein differs from that found in crocodilians and lizards. In snakes the vein, rather than running in a deep canal, runs in a groove on the ends of ventrally projecting bony spines (Figure 3). It is generally easier to obtain a sample as there are no surrounding spines to be negotiated. The technique is otherwise similar, and the same problem of lymph vessels may also be encountered.

CHELONIANS

A number of sites are possible in this group, and the best choice varies with the species. In small long-necked tortoises, the jugular vein is an excellent site (Haigh, 1991). The animal is held in a head down position and the neck extended. The jugular vein can generally be visualised near the line of colour change in the skin. Gently moving the neck may assist visualisation, and sample collection is generally straightforward. Care should be taken not to collapse the vein with excessive pressure on the syringe.

The dorsal coccygeal vein is a useful site in most chelonians (Samour et al, 1984). The coccygeal vertebrae in this group lack dorsal projections, and the vein runs fairly superficially. The tail is extended, and the needle inserted perpendicularly at about one third of the tail length from the body (Figure 4). The needle should be carefully advanced down to the bone, and withdrawn slightly if blood does not flow.

If head and tail cannot be extracted, generally in larger land tortoises, the brachial vein may be used (McCracken, 1993). The needle should be inserted into the groove below the prominent tendon inside the elbow, just above the joint, and carefully advanced until the vessel is found.

Collection is possible from the dorsal cervical sinuses in most chelonians, and has been recommended in small marine turtles (Bennett, 1986). The technique is as described for crocodilians (Figure 4).

CARDIAC PUNCTURE.

Cardiac puncture is a potential collection site in all reptiles (Frye, 1991), but should probably be regarded as a site of last resort, although the complication rate appears to be lower than might be expected. Generally the heart should be located

Figure 4: Location of dorsal coccygeal vein (A) in chelonians. Cross section of tail.

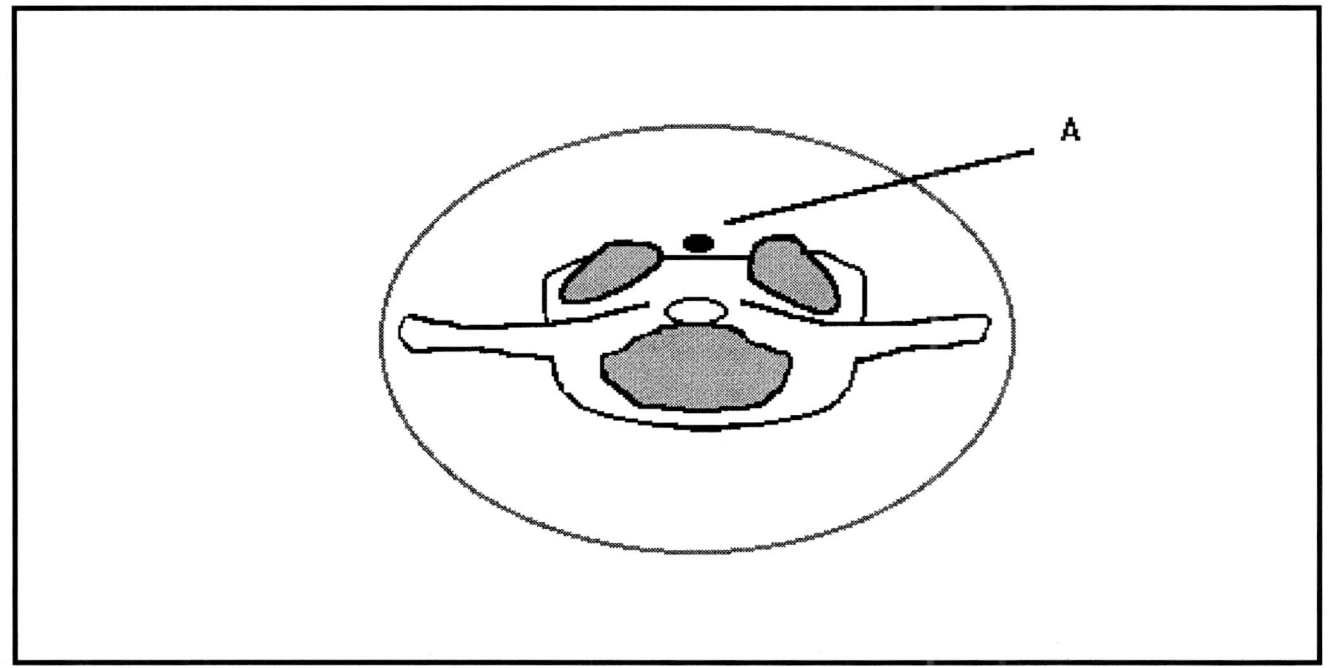

TABLE 1:

COMPARATIVE SIZES OF REPTILIAN ERYTHROCYTES (SYPEK AND BORYSENKO, 1988)

Group	Length	Width	Nucleus: Length	Width	Nuclear/ Cytoplasmic ratio
Testudines (Turtles/ tortoises)	18.5-20	10-12	5-6.5	4-5	0.08-0.15
Rhynchocephalia (Tuatara)	19-25	13-16	8-9	5-6	0.015
Sauria (Lizards)	13-22	5-13.5	5.5-8	2.5-4.5	0.11-0.215
Ophidia (Snakes)	15-19	8-11	5-8	3-4	0.09-0.22
Crocodylia (including alligators)	16-17	9-10	5-6	3.5-4	0.13-0.135

by finding the apex beat. In chelonians this will prove somewhat difficult. In this case a small hole must be drilled ventrally, in the midline, between the pectoral and abdominal plates, allowing a needle to be inserted. It is important to seal the hole after sampling.

BLOOD CELLS

Like birds, and unlike mammals, reptiles possess nucleated erythrocytes and thrombocytes (platelets), presenting a similar set of problems in cell counting and identification. Detailed morphological studies of these cell types have been published (Sypek et al 1988)

ERYTHROCYTES

These cells are ovoid with central ovoid nuclei. The nuclei have densely packed chromatin and stain darkly (Figure 6). The size of erythrocytes varies considerably among reptilian species (Table 1). Immature erythrocytes are commonly seen. These cells tend to be larger, with more basophilic cytoplasm. The nuclei are slightly larger, and more open in appearance with visible chromatin clumping rather than the more amorphously dense nucleus of the mature cell. These cells may be vacuolated in snakes. The numbers of these cells present varies considerably, making assigning a normal figure problematic, but 10 - 15% is not uncommon. Occasional less mature erythrocyte precursors will also be seen - these cells are generally rounder, and show increasingly basophilic cytoplasm and decreasing nuclear density in the less mature forms. These cells must be distinguished from other types, particularly lymphocytes (see below). Rarely, mitotic erythrocyte precursors will be seen in normal animals. Depending on smear quality, considerable numbers of "stripped" erythrocytes will be noted. These bare nuclei may represent cells

disrupted in the smearing process, or degenerating cells in an ageing sample.

THROMBOCYTES

Reptilian thrombocytes (Figure 6) are small ovoid cells with dense rounded nuclei. The cytoplasm is generally clear but may contain a few azurophilic granules. The cell membrane will often have irregular projections. As the thrombocytes become progressively more activated, these projections enlarge, vacuoles appear and the cells tend to clump together. Activated thrombocytes are seen in some disease conditions, but more frequently reflect sample handling, particularly traumatic venipuncture. Thrombocytes may be confused with lymphocytes (see below) and must be distinguished from bare erythrocyte nuclei.

LEUKOCYTES

The literature on reptilian leukocytes abounds with confusing and sometimes contradictory sys-

Figure 5:
Preparation of blood smears.

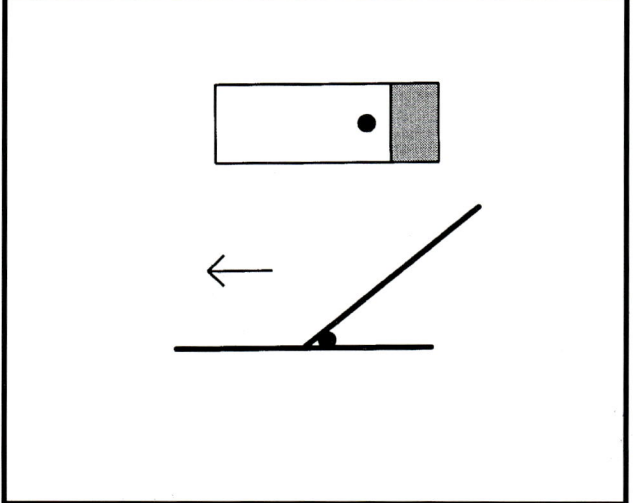

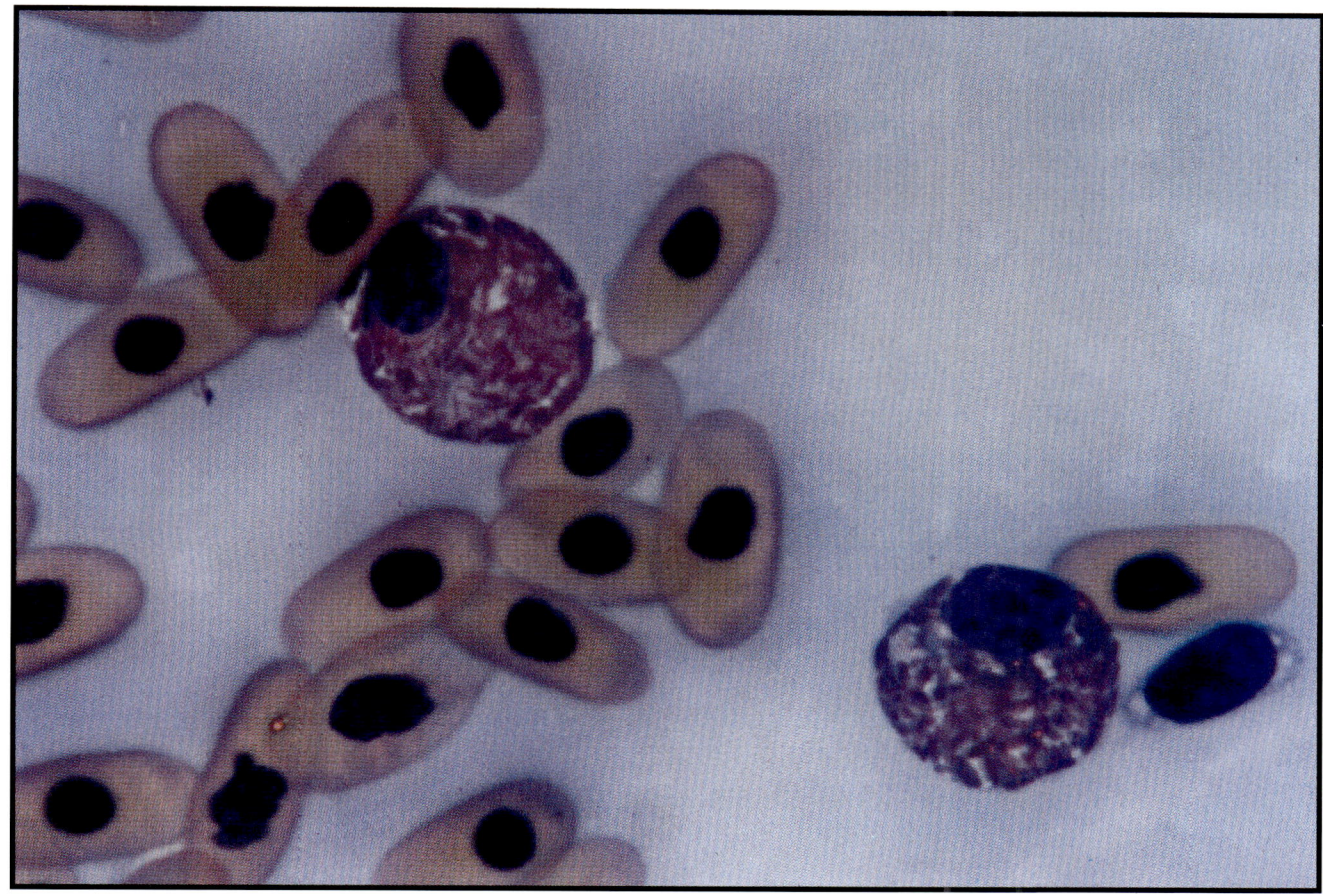

Figure 6: Heterophils. Estuarine crocodile (*C. porosus*).

tems of classification and nomenclature. More recent studies have helped to clarify the situation, but reading on this subject is still apt to cause confusion. All species have identifiable lymphocytes and basophils - the confusion centres on the remainder. Chelonians and crocodilians have two distinct acidophilic granulocytes. These have been described as "Type I and Type II granulocytes" (Canfield, 1985), and also as "Type I and Type II eosinophils". Ultrastructural and cytochemical evidence supports the more conventional nomenclature of heterophil and eosinophil respectively.

Most of the Squamata appear to have a single acidophil granulocyte, usually referred to as a heterophil, although a second type is seen in some lizards. This group also has an unusual cell type generally referred to as an azurophil, or azurophilic monocyte, that combines some morphological features of both granulocyte and monocyte lineages. All reptiles have basophilic granulocytes. These have been referred to as "Type III granulocytes", but are more generally identified as basophils. The sizes of the various cell types vary considerably between different reptiles.

HETEROPHILS

Heterophils contain densely packed acidophilic cytoplasmic granules. These are generally rod shaped, but tend to be more irregular in snakes. The nucleus is generally peripherally located and while ovoid in most reptiles, is multilobulated in many lizard species (Canfield 1988). The cytoplasm, when visible at all, is generally pale, perhaps slightly basophilic. The cytoplasm is most often obscured by the granules. In aged or poorly handled samples, ruptured cells are not uncommon, and free granules may be seen. Heterophils may also degranulate in such samples, and will appear vacuolated and foamy when the smear is examined. Cytochemical and ultrastructural studies generally support the identification of this cell type with the avian heterophil, but like this cell, some of the enzymatic spectrum of the mammalian neutrophil is not present (Montali, 1988). The heterophils seen in some mammalian species, in contrast, do correspond functionally to neutrophils.

EOSINOPHILS

Reptilian eosinophils tend to have rounder and less densely packed granules than heterophils. The granules may stain more intensely orange in these cells, but this is not a reliable finding, being affected by smear age and type of anticoagulant used. More reliable is the cytoplasm, which is more often visible in these cells and is also more basophilic than the heterophils. In most species having

707

both cell types, the differences in morphology, while subtle, will allow reliable differentiation with practice. In addition, eosinophils are almost always present in lower numbers than heterophils. The use of a high power objective (ie 100x) when examining smears is recommended at least until confidence is established. Cytochemical studies in several species (Haigh, 1991; Watson, 1996) support the identification of this cell type with the better-studied mammalian eosinophil. In those reptiles lacking eosinophils, it is generally held that the one acidophilic granulocyte performs the functions of both cell types, although there is little detailed objective evidence to confirm this.

BASOPHILS

These cells are round with round to oval peripheral nuclei, although nuclear detail is frequently obscured by the large intensely basophilic granules that are densely packed into the cytoplasm. Degranulation of these cells is common, and while they may appear as obvious degranulated cells, more often they are seen as irregular blue/purple smudges or blobs, with cellular detail obscure. It is possible that such degranulated cells in fact represent the "neutrophils" that have occasionally been described as an additional leukocyte type in reptiles.

MONOCYTES AND AZUROPHILS

Reptilian monocytes have variable but generally ovoid nuclei, and while slight indentations are seen, the typical mammalian bilobed appearance in uncommon. The cytoplasm will appear at low power to be blue/grey in appearance, but detailed examination reveals a fine granular nature with small azurophilic granules being a common finding, particularly in larger, more activated cells. Azurophils as a type are not well defined, and the general appearance is of small monocytes with variable increases in granulation of the cytoplasm. In most reptilian species, a spectrum of cells can be found varying in appearance from typical monocytes through to typical azurophils. The numbers of each type vary, with "monocytes" dominating in crocodilians and chelonians and "azurophils" more common in the Squamata. It appears most likely that "azurophils" are in fact morphological variants of monocytes, and are probably normal monocytes for those species in which they have been described.

LYMPHOCYTES

These are usually the smallest leukocyte type found in reptilian blood, and are round cells with round, dense nuclei and scant cytoplasm. Sometimes a few fine azurophilic granules will be seen in the cytoplasm. Activated forms will be seen in

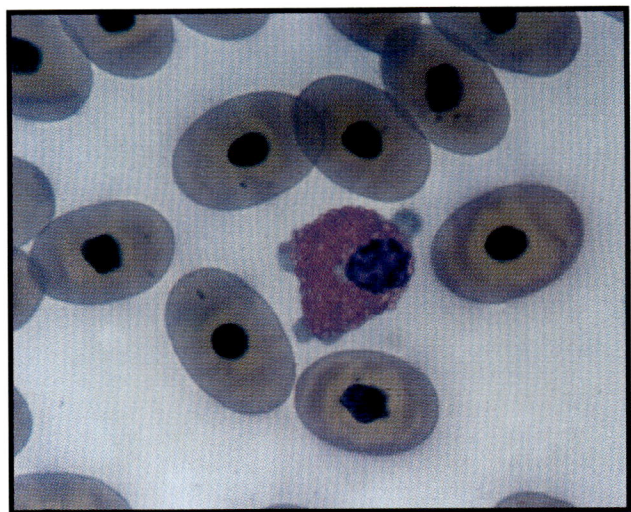

Figure 7: Eosinophil. Long-necked tortoise (*C. longicollis*).

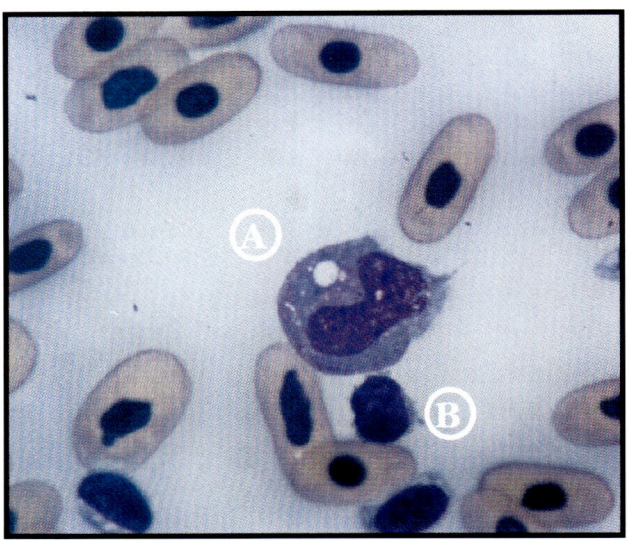

Figure 8: Monocyte (A) and lymphocyte (B). Estuarine crocodile (*C. porosus*).

Figure 9: Lymphocyte (A) and thrombocytes (B). Estuarine crocodile (*C. porosus*).

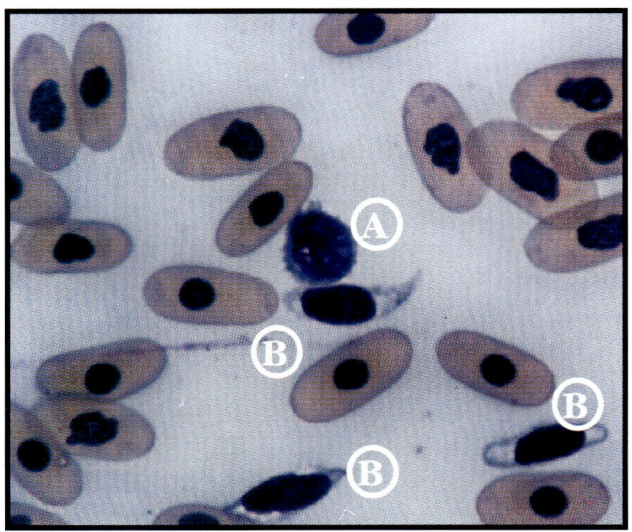

708

TABLE 2:

REFERENCE DATA FOR REPRESENTATIVE SPECIES

Index	Estuarine Crocodile[a]	Long-necked tortoise[b]	Diamond Python[c]	Shingleback Lizard[d]
Hematocrit L/L	0.14	0.18-0.28	0.19-0.30	0.18-0.34
Hemoglobin g/L	43.6-101	45.3-75.7		5.2-8.7
Red Cells 10^{12}/L	0.37-1.03	0.4-0.6	0.73-1.45	0.7-1.3
MCV fL	2088-3630	355-503		
MCH pg	743-1197	94-142		
MCHC g/L	285-410	183-383		
Total White Cells 10^9/L	1.14-10.8	1.9-11.9	3.0-18.3	1.8-5.5
Heterophils 10^9/L	0.19-3.99	0.4-5.2	0.5-5.2	30-74%
Eosinophils 10^9/L	0.0-0.52	0.02-2.8		0-6%
Basophils 10^9/L	0.07-6.66	0.2-1.3	0.01-1.2	0-10%
Lymphocytes 10^9/L	0.18-3.15	0.4-4.6	0.7-11.1	2-14%
Monocytes/Azurophils 10^9/L	0.02-1.04	0.07-1.7	0.7-6.0	16-46%
Thrombocytes 10^9/L	1.77-10.4		7.9-43.8	13.2-29.0

[a] Watson, 1996; [b] Haigh, 1993; [c] Hulst, 1992; [d] Canfield and Shea, 1988

some disease states. These cells are larger and have more obvious and more basophilic cytoplasm.

Lymphocytes are usually the cell type that presents the greatest difficulties in identification. They can be distinguished from thrombocytes as they are larger, have less cytoplasm and a larger and less dense nucleus. The tendency of thrombocytes to clump and elongate into ovoid forms is not seen in lymphocytes. The azurophilic granules of lymphocytes, if present, are finer and usually more numerous than the two to three seen in thrombocytes. Immature erythrocytes generally have more abundant cytoplasm that is distinctly basophilic. The coarse clumping pattern of erythrocyte nuclear chromatin is also quite distinctive.

METHODS

PACKED CELL VOLUME

Packed Cell Volume (PCV) or hematocrit can be obtained by the microhematocrit method. Derived hematocrit figures from automated hematology analysers will not be accurate.

Plasma protein is often measured on microhematocrit samples using a refractometer. This method should not be used in reptiles. The correlation between refraction and plasma protein levels is based on human or canine serum, and when compared with accurate protein levels reptilian plasma shows very poor correlation, making this method unsuitable (Haigh, 1991).

PREPARATION OF SMEARS

Preparing blood films can be frustrating for the novice, but with a little practice good results can be obtained. A number of techniques have been described but the one described below is probably the simplest. It is important to remember two major points:

—reptilian blood cells are fragile compared to their mammalian counterparts - greater care must be exercised.

—reptilian cells deteriorate rapidly after collection, so that making a smear as early as possible is important in obtaining accurate results.

1. Place a small drop of blood on a new, clean slide.
2. Hold another slide at ~45°, and back it up onto the drop, so the blood spreads out (Figure 5).
3. Push the spreader slide away from the drop in a smooth motion.
   —Don't push down, let the spreader "float".
   —Keep the motion smooth - don't accelerate.
   —Don't let the spreader lift off before the blood is spread.
4. Rapidly air dry the slide - ie, wave it about a lot. This step is really important.

DIFFERENTIAL COUNT

Standard Romanowsky-type hematology stains are acceptable for reptilian blood samples. The stained smear is examined in the usual way at the feathered edge, or monolayer area, and the differential count is obtained by counting at least 100 leukocytes and calculating the percentage of each type observed.

CELL COUNTS

The nucleated erythrocytes and thrombocytes of reptiles (and birds) confuse the now commonly used automated cell counters, since these machines assume that anything with a nucleus is a leukocyte. Reasonable white cell counts can nonetheless be obtained using a manual hemocytometer. The cell count is performed using an "eosinophil" method.

[a] Eosinophil Unopette, Becton Dickinson.

A pre-measured disposable system[a] is recommended for ease of use, but manual methods adding stains (such as 1% aqueous phloxine) to standard diluents are also possible.

Using the disposable pipetting system, the manufacturer's directions are followed to process the blood and load a hemocytometer chamber. The cells taking up the stain are counted, and a calculation performed (this varies depending on the volume of the chamber used) to arrive at a total acidophil count (heterophils and eosinophils). The total percentage of these cells is then obtained from the differential count, and the figure corrected to provide a total white cell count.

(Acidophil count) / (Acidophil %) = White cell count

It is also possible to obtain red cell and platelet counts, although these determinations are not often performed. Automated cell counters (or manual methods) will provide a total nucleated cell count (TNCC). A differential erythrocyte/thrombocyte percentage is then obtained from 1000 cells. This figure is used to divide the TNCC into erythrocyte and thrombocyte counts. Ideally, the total figure is first corrected by subtracting the white cell count but in practice this step is trivial as the figures usually differ by three orders of magnitude.

White cell counts can be estimated from a good blood film. If the average number of leukocytes seen in ten evenly distributed high-power (x40) fields is doubled, the figure obtained can be used as an estimated white cell count (x10⁹/L). The weakness in this method is the rarity of seeing a truly even distribution of cells across a smear - clumping is frequently present to some degree, and will invalidate this method.

CHANGES SEEN IN DISEASE

ERYTHROCYTES

ANEMIA

Anemia, or decreased red cell mass, is a relatively common problem in reptiles. Anemia is classified as regenerative or non-regenerative on the basis of the presence of immature erythrocytes in the circulation. Regenerative anemias are most often due to hemorrhage or ectoparasite infestations. Non-regenerative anemias are most often due to malnutrition or the bone marrow suppressive effects of chronic disease. Malnutrition may also cause abnormally shaped red cells to appear in circulation.

There are number of non-disease factors that may induce an apparent anemia. There is a seasonal shift

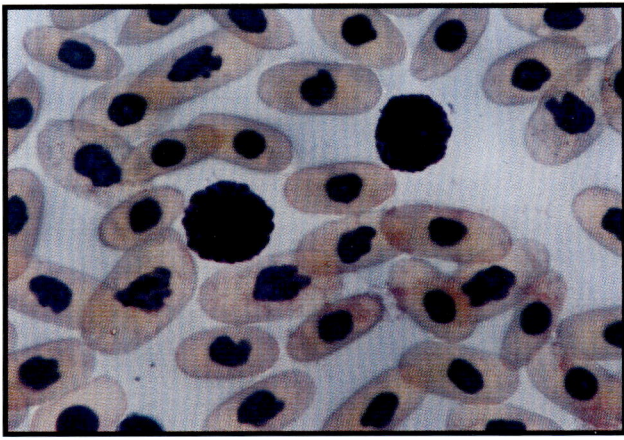

Figure 10: Basophils. Estuarine crocodile (*C. porosus*).

in red cell values, with winter, and particularly hibernation leading to reduced red cell mass. This is presumably due to alterations in metabolic rate. In some species, juveniles, and/or females may have lower red cell values compared to other animals under the same conditions (McCracken, 1993). As noted under sample collection, blood samples may be diluted by lymph, particularly from tail veins. This will lead to an apparent anemia.

POLYCYTHEMIA

Polycythemia, or increased red cell mass is almost always a relative polycythemia due to dehydration. If the change persists after correction of dehydration, causes of an absolute polycythemia must be considered, including excess erythropoetin production and red cell neoplasia, but these conditions have not yet been described in reptiles.

LEUKOCYTES

The patterns of response to various diseases and other factors are described below in general terms. The normal proportions of different cell types vary

Figure 11: Activated thrombocyte (A) and irregular erythrocyte nuclei (B). Long-necked tortoise (C. longicollis).

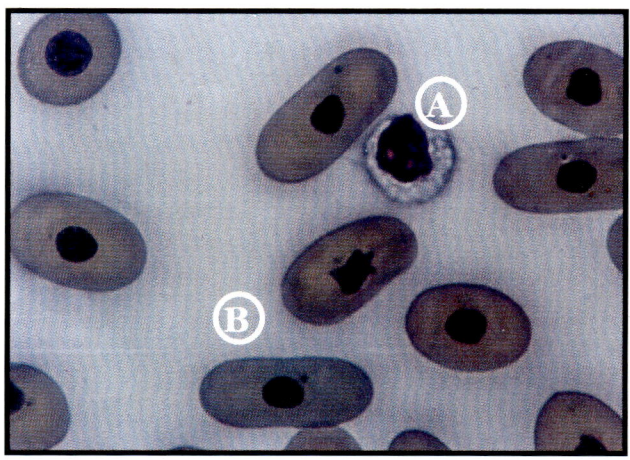

considerably between different groups of reptiles (Table 2) and this must of course be recognised when interpreting patterns of change in hematological results.

SEASONAL CHANGES

A variety of seasonal changes are observed in leukocytes, although these tend to be less marked and less reliable than the erythrocyte changes. Heterophil numbers tend to be highest in summer and lowest in winter/hibernation while eosinophils show the opposite pattern. Reports of changes in basophil numbers are conflicting, and a clear picture has yet to emerge. Lymphocytes also show a summer peak and a winter/hibernation trough, while monocytes (azurophils) show little seasonal variation.

INFLAMMATORY AND INFECTIOUS DISEASES

Heterophils and monocytes (azurophils) are the cells most involved in the inflammatory response. While increased circulating numbers of these cells are often seen, this is not an entirely reliable finding as the numbers may change quite dynamically. In practise, morphological changes are more reliable guide to the presence of inflammatory and infectious diseases. Heterophils may show cytoplasmic vacuolation and increased numbers of abnormal or dark/basophilic granules. These are often described as toxic heterophils. In those species normally having multilobular nuclei, unlobed, or band, forms may be seen in inflammatory disease. Monocytes may show similar changes, and have also been described as toxic. In addition, reactive monocytes will often have irregular cytoplasmic membranes with projections, large granules and may contain phagocytosed bacteria and debris. These cells have been reported to dominate the inflammatory response in some species: particularly snakes and to some extent lizards (McCracken, 1993). Increased lymphocyte numbers have been associated with viral infections.

PARASITIC DISEASES

As might be expected, eosinophilia is the change most often associated with parasitic infestations, and has been reported in hematogenous, intestinal and external parasite diseases. Basophilia has been seen in cases of blood-borne parasitism. It is important to note that neither of these changes is entirely reliable - parasitic disease, even in severe cases, may be seen in the absence of either of these findings. Increased lymphocyte numbers are often seen in parasitic diseases.

NEOPLASIA

There are scattered reports of leukemias (neoplasia of blood cells) in reptiles in the literature (Goldberg et al, 1991). The majority of these cases were in snakes, with some lizards and one in a turtle. The systems used to classify these disease are not always compatible between reports, but a variety of both myeloid and lymphoid forms have been described.

OTHER CHANGES

Lymphocyte numbers may be depressed in malnourished or anorexic reptiles. Temporary increases in circulating lymphocyte numbers may occur just before mating, and also ecdysis (shedding) in snakes.

THROMBOCYTES

While reptilian thrombocytes are assumed to have a similar role to that of mammalian platelets in coagulation, they appear to additional capabilities. Reactive thrombocytes, showing irregular outline and vacuolation, may be seen in anemias, but this must not be confused with similar changes due to sample handling, including delayed processing. Multinucleate thrombocytes, and irregular nuclei have been reported to occur in severe infectious conditions, and in addition reptilian thrombocytes are reported to have some phagocytic capabilities.

PARASITES

Blood cell parasites are a not uncommon finding in reptilian blood films and a wide variety of forms have been seen, generally in fairly low numbers. While the identification of these parasites is not always straightforward, and in many cases presumptive, *Hemoproteus* sp. and *Hemogregarina* sp. are the commonest identifications made. Extracellular parasites including trypanosomes and microfilaria are also occasionally seen. While fascinating for the observer, little evidence has been obtained to suggest these parasites are a significant cause of morbidity in their hosts.

REFERENCE RANGES

Obtaining meaningful reference range data for many reptilian species remains a problem. While many reports exist in the literature, the vast majority of these represent only a handful of, and often single, animals, of undefined health status. In order to have confidence that a stated reference range will actually encompass the majority of healthy individuals of that species, results are needed from a large number of healthy animals. Statistical treatments of this problem often suggest sampling in the order of 200 individuals - clearly an optimistic assumption with most reptilian species, particularly captive populations. With care, useful ranges can be obtained from smaller groups, but it must always be remembered that such ranges are far more loosely defined than the solid "normal ranges" we may be more conventionally used to.

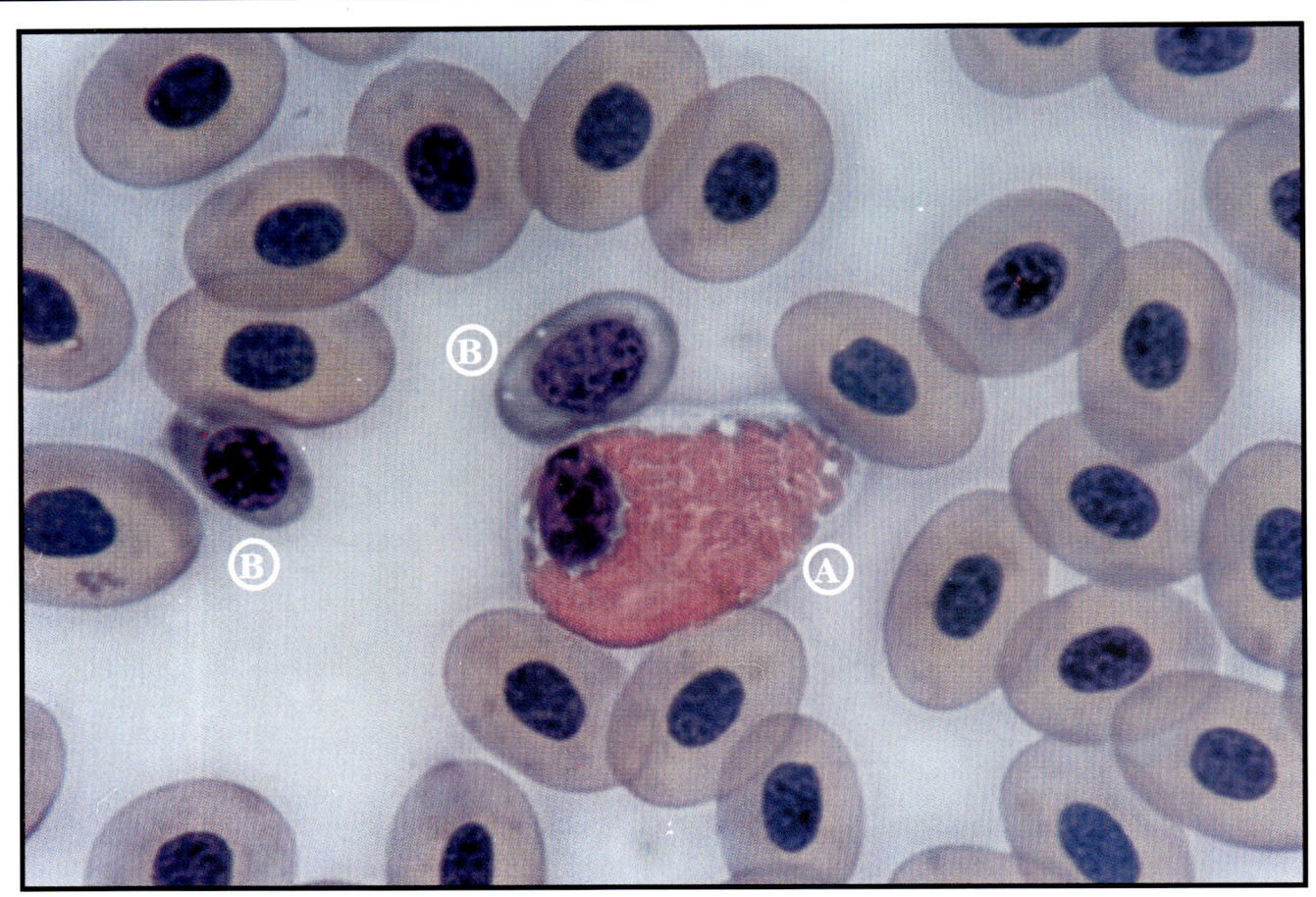

Figure 12:Heterophil (A), immature erythrocytes (B). Gould's monitor lizard.

Figure 13:Eosinophil. Gould's monitor lizard.

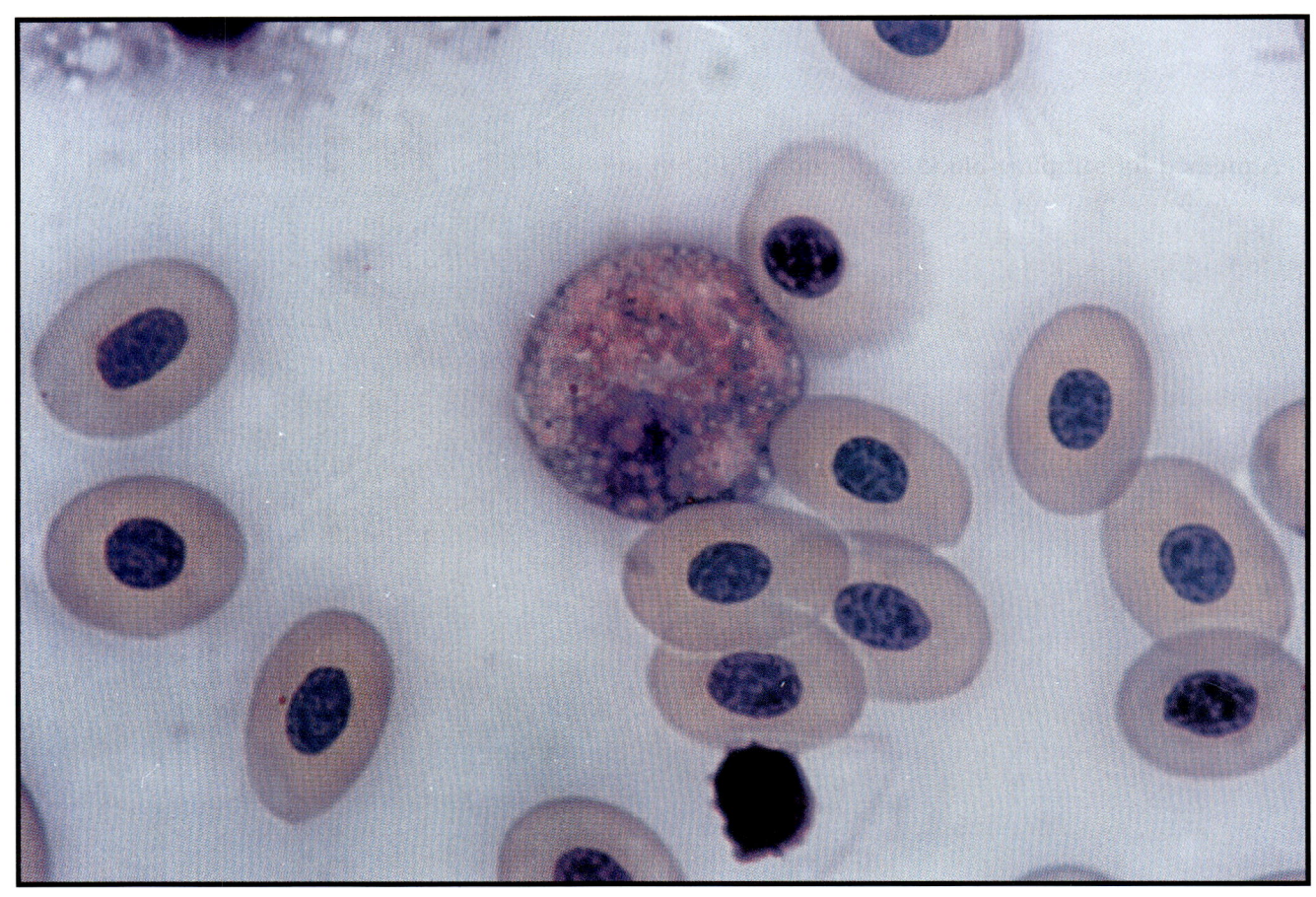

Another problem is often encountered in reporting of reference ranges - the assumption of normal distribution. It has often been stated that two standard deviations above and below the mean of a dataset will give a reference range, or more precisely encompass 95% of the population sampled. This is true if the data are normally distributed. Unfortunately many biological parameters are not so distributed. Past reports have often applied this technique blindly, without testing for normal distribution. This leads at best to erroneous results, and at worst to ridiculous ones, such as ranges that include negative cell counts. Given the very small sample numbers generally available for reptilian species, often the only valid technique is to report the observed range, after cautiously eliminating obvious outliers.

As statistically reliable data do not exist for many species, and a very large number of observations of varying quality do, I have attempted to provide representative data for the major divisions of reptilian species. With due care, these ranges can provide guidance in interpreting test results in other related species where data is lacking. These results are summarised in Table 2.

REFERENCES AND FURTHER READING

—Alleman, A R, Jacobson, E R and Raskin, R E:
Morphological and cytochemical characteristics of blood cells from the desert tortoise (*Gopherus agassizii*). *Am J Vet Res*, 1992; 53: 1645-1651.

—Bennett, J:
A method for sampling blood from hatchling Loggerhead Turtles. *Herp Review*, 1986; 17(2):43.

—Bush, M and Smeller, J:
Blood collection and injection techniques in snakes. *Vet Med/Sm An Clinician*, 1987; 73: 211-214.

—Canfield, P J:
Characterisation of the blood cells of Australian crocodiles (*Crocodilus porosus* Schneider and *C. johnstoni*, Krefft). *Anat. Histol Embryol*, 1985; 14:269-288.

—Canfield, P J and Shea, G M:
Morphological observations on the erythrocytes, leukocytes and thrombocytes of Blue Tongue Lizards (Lactertilia: Scincidae, *Tiliqua*). *Anat. Histol. Embryol*, 1988; 17:328-342.

—Duguy, R:
Numbers of blood cells and their variation. In, Biology of the Reptilia, vol 3 Morphology, Gans, C and Parsons, T (Eds). Academic Press, New York., 1970, pp. 93-109.

—Frye, F L. Haematology:
In, Biomedical and Surgical Aspects of Captive Reptile Husbandry. Vet. Med. Publ. Co, Edwardsville, Kansas, 1981, pp. 61 - 103.

—Goldberg, S R and Holshuh, H J:
A case of leukemia in the Desert Spiny Lizard (*Sceloporus magister*). *J Wildlife Dis*, 1991; 27(3): 521-525.

—Haigh, S A:
Characterisation of the blood cells and the establishment of haematological and biochemical reference intervals for the Eastern Longneck Tortoise (*Chelodina longicollis*). Thesis, Diploma in Veterinary Studies (Wildlife Medicine and Husbandry, University of Sydney), 1991.

—Hawkey, C M and Dennett, T B:
A Colour Atlas of Comparative Veterinary Haematology. Wolfe Medical Publications Ltd, London, 1989.

—Heard, D J et al:
Bacteremia and septic arthritis in a West African dwarf crocodile. *JAVMA*, 1988; 192: 1453-1454.

—Hulst, F:
Studies on the haematology and biochemistry of the Diamond Python, *Morelia spilota spilota*. Thesis, Masters in Veterinary Studies (Wildlife Medicine and Husbandry), University of Sydney, 1992.

—McCracken, H:
Avian and reptilian hematology and biochemistry. In, Proceedings 207: Clinical Pathology. Post Graduate Committee in Veterinary Science, University of Sydney.1993, pp 243-305.

—Montali, R J:
Comparative pathology of inflammation in the higher vertebrates (reptiles, birds and mammals). *J. Comp. Path*, 1988; 99:1-26.

—Olson, G A et al:
Technics for blood collection and intravascular infusion of reptiles.*Lab. Anim. Sci*, 1975; 25(6):783-786.

—Saint Girons, M C:
Morphology of the circulating blood cells. In, Biology of the Reptilia Vol 3, Gans, C and Parsons, T S (Eds), Academic Press, New York, 1970, pp. 73-91.

—Samour, H J et al:
Blood sampling techniques in reptiles. *Vet. Rec*, 1984; 114:472-476.

—Sypek, J and Borysenko, M.
Reptiles. In, Vertebrate Blood Cells, Rowley, A F and Ratcliffe, N A (Eds). Cambridge University Press, New York, 1988, pp. 211-256.

—Watson, J W:
Hematology and biochemistry of the estuarine crocodile (*Crocodylus porosus*). Manuscript in preparation. 1996.

SURGERY

Michael Kiedrowski, DVM
Mountain View Animal Hospital
9812 N. 7th Street
Phoenix, AZ 85020-1763

Dr. Michael Kiedrowski received his B.S. in Zoology in 1985 from Northern Arizona University. He received his D.V.M. degree in 1989 from Colorado State University. He currently practices small and exotic animal medicine in Phoenix Arizona

INTRODUCTION

When first approached to write this chapter I thought of all the interesting and challenging surgeries I have performed, became excited and quickly agreed to contribute. Several weeks later while traveling to another hospital to teach another veterinarian how to "spay" an iguana, I realized that what reptile surgeons share is not a special skill, but a special frame of mind.

While reptile medicine has advanced into its own specialized art form, it is hard to believe that reptile surgery has not followed suit. While it is true that the surgical success rates in most forms of medicine have improved greatly over the last 40-50 years, these successes can be attributed to advances in technology, patient evaluation, instrumentation, suture materials, anesthesia, antibiotics, and other pharmaceuticals, rather than any advance in surgical skill taken as purely an art form. The surgical artists of yesterday were or are as gifted as the surgeons of today, but modern knowledge and technology continues to increase our success rates to measures incomprehensible 50 years ago.

With knowledge and technology readily available to any practitioner the only limiting factors become experience, skill, and art. While art is immeasurable, experience and skill are there to be accomplished, mastered, and used to build a foundation for the future.

SPECIALIZED MATERIAL/ INSTRUMENTS

The majority of instruments required for reptile surgeries are the exact same instruments utilized in everyday practice. Consideration of the size of the patient should be taken into account when selecting instruments. Large patients usually can be operated on with standard small animal surgical instruments, while the much smaller patient surgeries may be aided by some less frequently used instruments. Many of these instruments may be found among dental instruments, ophthalmology instruments or may be home-made.

Standard endotracheal tubes (cuffed and uncuffed) may be used for larger patients while very small patients may require attaching an old endotracheal tube attachment end to the needle hub end of a cut off IV line, butterfly catheter, or tom cat catheter for an adequate size. Patients considered too small to intubate may be maintained by a mask fashioned from an old syringe case with part of a rubber glove used to form a diaphragm (Bennett, 1991). (Figure 1)

Ophthalmologic instruments are designed for small patient use. Eyelid retractors may be used to maintain surgical openings. (Bennett, 1989b, Frye, 1981) Iris scissors allow for fine dissection where metzenbaum scissors are too bulky. Ophthalmology needle holders may be beneficial in small tight areas. (Figure 2)

Dental instruments provide a variety of probes and dissection instruments. The most useful instruments I have found are some of the small "spatula" type instruments. (Figure 2) These are tremendously helpful in opening difficult chelonian beaks as well as in abscess debridement and scraping abscess capsules. (Frye, 1981)

Fig. 1. Equipment. A. Anesthesia masks made from syringe cases; B. Endotracheal tubes made from urinary catheters; C. Standard endotracheal tubes. Photo courtesy of Dr. Michael Kiedrowski.

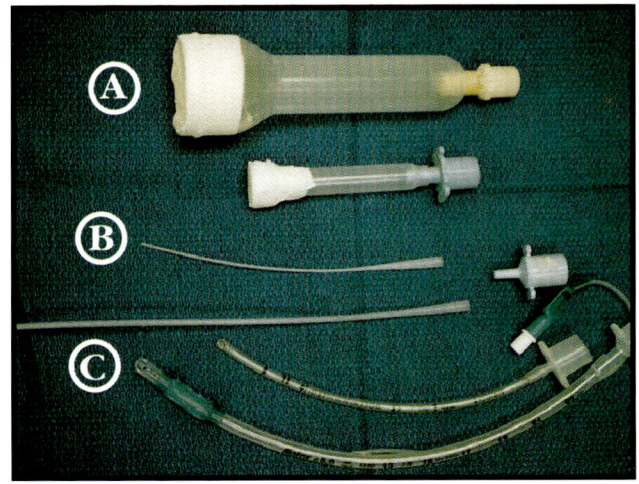

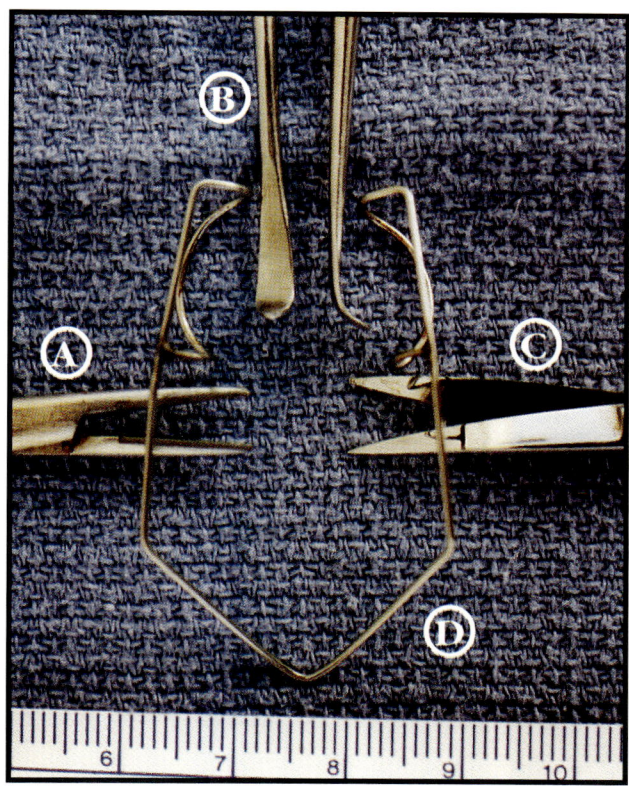

Fig. 2. Ophthalmology and dental instruments. A. Needle holders; B. Dental spatula; C.Iris scissors; D. Eyelid retractors. Photo courtesy of Dr. Michael Kiedrowski.

A dremel tool is useful in grinding beaks, filing nails, and incising/cutting into chelonian shells (Frye, 1981, Mader, 1991). An epoxy and fiberglass repair kit may be required to patch chelonian shells or close surgical sites (Bennett, 1991, Frye, 1981, Mader, 1991). A mechanic's pick-up tool may be useful in retrieving intestinal foreign bodies. (Figure 3)

ANTIBIOTIC THERAPY

Antibiotics are used when dealing with infected areas or when surgical contamination is suspected. (Bennett, 1989b) Antibiotic choices should be based on culture and sensitivity whenever possible. Since most bacterial infections in reptiles are caused by gram negative bacteria, aminoglycosides antibiotics such as amikacin are recommended. (Bennett, 1989b) It has also been shown that up to 54% of reptile cultures contain anaerobic bacteria which do not respond to the aminoglycoside antibiotics. (Stewart, 1990) Enrofloxacin is effective against some anerobes including *Bacteroides* and *Clostridium* as well as gram- bacteria. When antibiotics are necessary the author recommends either enrofloxacin or a combination of amikacin with metronidazole, tetracycline, or chloramphenicol to increase anaerobic effectiveness. (Stewart, 1990)

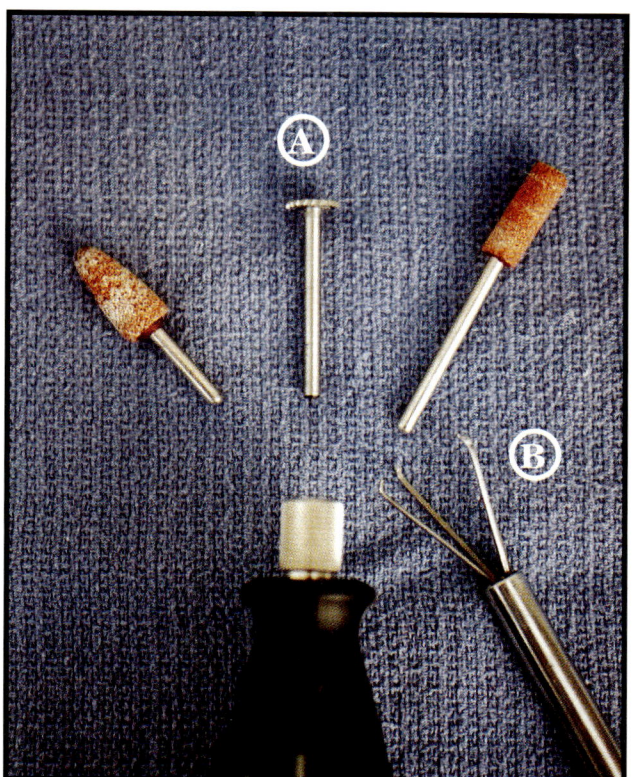

Fig. 3. Assorted tools. A. Dremel tool with tips for cutting and griding; B. Mechanics pick-up tool. Photo courtesy of Dr. Michael Kiedrowski.

GENERAL SURGICAL APPROACHES

SNAKES
Of all the reptiles, the surgical approach to the snake is probably the most consistent due to their repetitive design. The most common approach to subcutaneous lumps and bumps is by direct cut down over the desired area with a longitudinal anterior-posterior incision. This allows for the removal of small abscesses, subcutaneous parasites, and small biopsies. Since the skin is designed to stretch during feeding, there is very little tissue tension at the closure site.

Approaching the coelomic cavity can best be accomplished with an anterior-posterior longitudinal incision between the scale rows. In pythons and snakes with small ventral scutes the incision is made between the second and third lateral scales rows (Finnegan and Kirpensteijn,1991). In most colubrids and snakes with large ventral scutes the incision is made between the first lateral scale row and the ventral scutes. (Bennett, 1989b, Frye, 1981) (Figure 4A & B)

This will place the surgeon just ventral to the ribs resulting in good coelomic cavity exposure, which allows for ease of incision expansion anterior and posterior, avoid the ventral midline blood vessel, and allows for a more lateral skin suture line that does not generally "snag" during locomotion.

I do not recommend lateral dorsoventral incisions between the ribs due to their limited exposure and transsectional blood, nerve, and muscle tissue damage. With ventral middling incisions one must avoid a more extensive blood supply and skin closure may result in skin suture "snagging" during locomotion in the recovery and healing periods prior to suture removal. (Bennett, 1989b)

LIZARDS

Similar to snakes and most of the common mammals we work with, the least traumatizing surgical approaches to lizards are anterior-posterior and proximal-distal. Limb incisions are best made proximal-distal on the anterior surface slightly dorsal or ventral to midline. (Figure 5) This approach avoids the majority of the blood and nerve supplies located posterior and ventral to the long bones similar to the dog and cat. It also avoids the large muscle bellies found centered on the anterior side of the long bones allowing the surgeon to dissect between muscle plains for deeper, less traumatic exposure.

Digit incisions should be made proximal-distal along the long axis of the digit. For abscesses and masses, cut directly down through the outstretched skin covering the mass. (Frye, 1981) For deeper approaches I prefer an incision along the anterior edge where the ventral scutes meet the smaller lateral scales. (Figure 6)

In practice, abdominal or coelomic incisions have typically been a matter of the individual surgeon's preference. Ventral midline is the general "standard" approach used in dogs and cats by most veterinarians in small mammal practice.

Fig. 4a,b A. Note that the ventral scutes of the boa (A) do not completely cover the ventral surface. In the Pine snake (B), the ventral scutes wrap around to the lateral surface.

Fig. 4b B. Boa or python approach (A); small snake approach (B). Photos courtesy of Dr. Michael Kiedrowski.

Fig. 5 Lizard limb bones are approached anteriorly and dorsally. Photo courtesy of Dr. Michael Kiedrowski.

Fig. 6. Lizard toes are approached adjacent to the ventral scutes. Photo courtesy of Dr. Michael Kiedrowski.

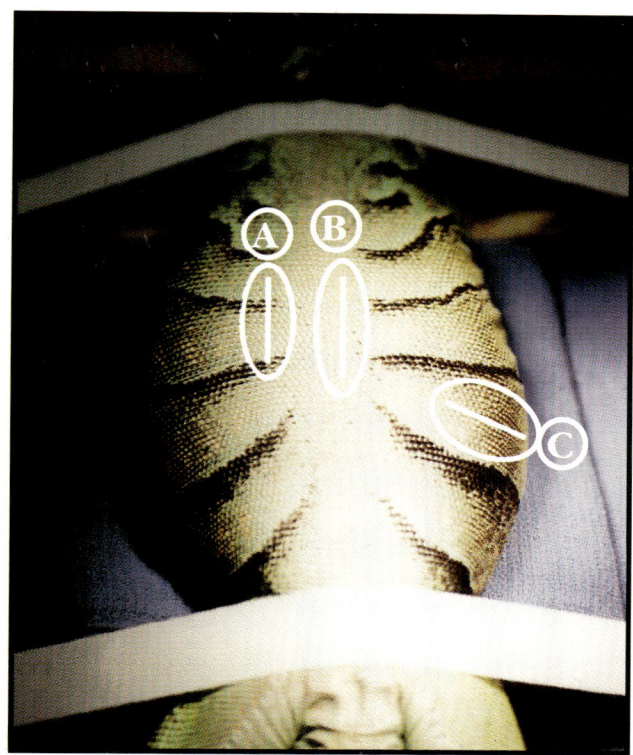

Fig. 7. Approaches to the lizard coelomic cavity. A. paramedian; B. midline; C. paralumbar. Photo courtesy of Dr. Michael Kiedrowski.

The presence of a large venous sinus located ventral abdominal midline makes this approach much more difficult in a lizard (Bennett, 1989b, Orosz et al, 1992). Ventral midline incisions should be started very superficially, the ventral abdominal vein located and retracted before proceeding to deepen or extend any incision. Ventral paramedian incisions avoid the large ventral vein and give good cavity exposure. (Barten, 1991; Boyer, 1991; Frye, 1983, Wissman, 1992) Abdominal muscles are small and thin compared to mammalian patients

Fig. 8. Turtle limb incisions are anterior and dorsal, similar to lizards. Photo courtesy of Dr. Michael Kiedrowski.

resulting in minimal bleeding and tissue trauma. Left paramedian incisions appear to give better abdominal exposure due to an abdominal fat pad attached right of center in the pelvis. This fat pad is very easily retracted in either direction (or flipped caudally) so right paramedian incisions should not be avoided if this approach coincides with the surgeon's normal surgical approach. Paralumbar approaches have also been reported (Bennett, 1989b; Frye, 1981) but are not recommended due to muscle trauma. (Figure 7)

CHELONIANS

Limb and extremity incisions vary with turtles and tortoises. In turtles and "thin skinned" chelonians, limb incisions should be proximal-distal on the anterior surface slightly dorsal, similar to lizards. (Figure 8) This allows for the avoidance of the blood and nerve supplies located posterior to the long bones. In tortoises and "thick skinned" or plated limbs the best approach is dorsal and slightly caudal still in the proximal-distal line. (Figure 9) This places the surgeon just posterior to the large anterior plates, incising through the thinner, more pliable skin. The advantages are ease of incision, a greater ease of skin suture passage, and a decrease in post operative scale sloughing due to the already poor blood supply of the large anterior scales.

Coelomic approaches should be based on the type of internal procedure anticipated and the exposure required. One approach is through the skin located anterior to the hind limbs (Gould et al, 1992; Mader, 1991). (Figure 10) This incision works well for smaller, well defined problems such as a single retained egg or small gastrointestinal foreign bodies as long as the object is smaller than the limb opening. The incision should be anterior-posterior in direction and centered in the limb opening. The bladder can be more readily avoided if the patient is tipped slightly away from the surgeon during the incision process.

The second approach is through the plastron (ventral shell). This approach should not be attempted without a surgical plan for closure such as a fiberglass and epoxy repair kit. This approach allows for better visualization of the coelomic cavity and a larger opening size. Gravity will retract the bladder from the incision in the normal surgical position (dorsal recumbency).

The blood supply to the plastron comes along the ventral midline and fans out through the coelomic membrane penetrating to the periosteal membrane of the plastron bone. Blood also supplies the plastron bone through its thin marrow network. Since cutting the bone will interrupt marrow blood flow it is important to retain as much

Fig. 9. Tortoise limbs are approached posteriorly and dorsally, avoiding the anterior scutes. Photo courtesy of Dr. Michael Kiedrowski.

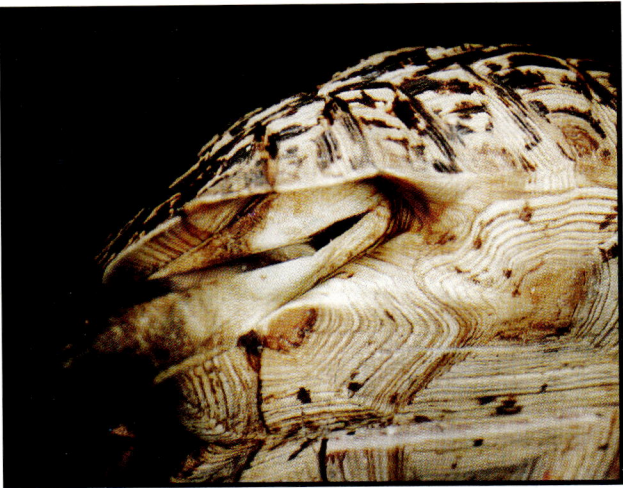

Fig. 10. Chelonian coelomic approach in front of hind limb. Photo courtesy of Dr. Michael Kiedrowski.

tured and the beveled arch incision allows for compression of the fracture/incision site. The site is covered with a fiberglass/epoxy patch.

When cutting plastral bone and when using epoxy resin, copious saline flushes are required to avoid thermal tissue damage. (Mader, 1991) Epoxy must be kept out of the edge of the defect or healing is inhibited. (Bennett, 1989b; Mader, 1991)

Fig. 11. Central square approach through the chelonian shell. Photo courtesy of Dr. Michael Kiedrowski.

periosteal flow as possible. While the approach generally remains constant (paramidline centered posterior to the latitudinal axis), this blood flow and the two ventral venous sinuses (Frye, 1981) result in two approach techniques.

The first technique is cutting a square or rectangular piece of plastral bone (Figure 11) leaving the periosteal and coelomic membranes intact. The bony "plate" is then dissected free of its membranes and removed to be stored in saline. (Frye, 1994; Mader, 1991) The membrane is incised, the ventral venous sinus are retracted and the cavity entered. Closure involves suturing the membrane, replacing the plastral bone, and an epoxy/fiberglass patch. (Frye, 1981; Mader, 1991) Complete healing may take as long as two years. (Mader, 1991)

The second technique is to cut the plastron in a 1/2 circle or ellipse with the straight edge adjacent to ventral midline (Figure 12) This avoids the ventral venous sinuses. (Figure 13) The straight paramidline cut is slightly expanded in a "v" trough configuration and the arch cut is angled under the surgical bone plate resulting in a beveled edge. (Mader, 1991) The membranes are left intact. The arch incision membrane is cut and the bony plate "door" is opened on a "hinge" of periosteal and coelomic membranes maintaining the vascular supply. In closure the arch membrane is not su-

718

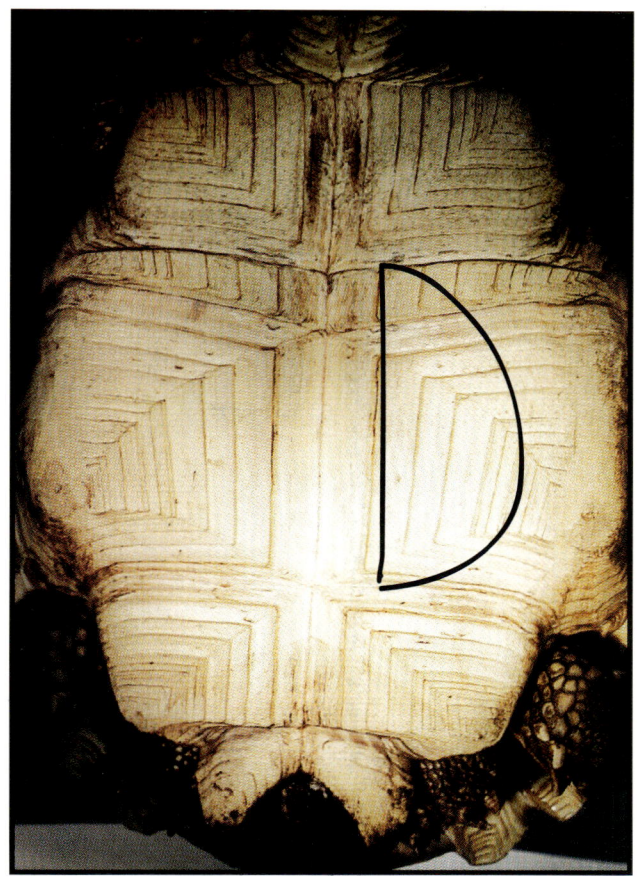

Fig. 12. Paramidline arch approach through the chelonian shell. Photo courtesy of Dr. Michael Kiedrowski.

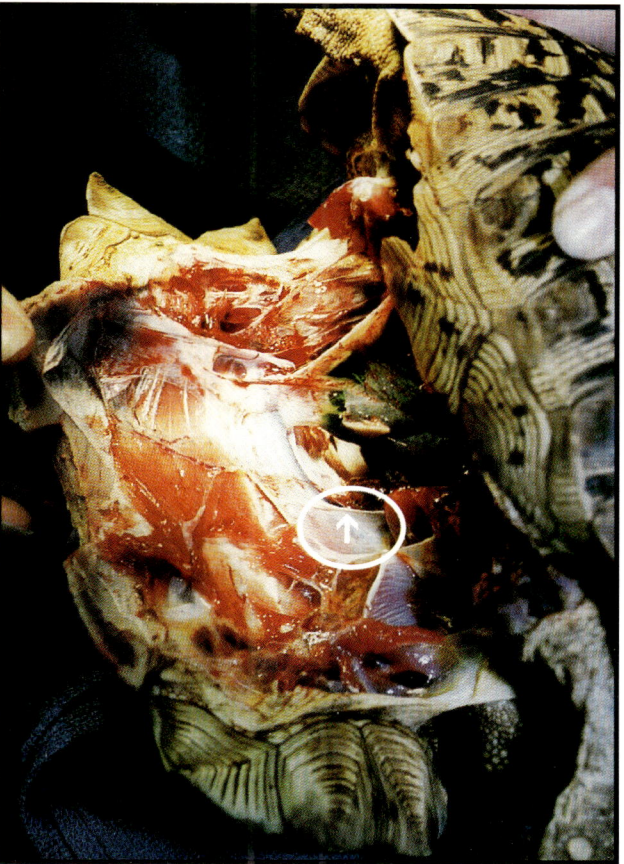

Fig. 13. One of the ventral venous sinuses is visible in the ventral coelomic membrane (arrow). Photo courtesy of Dr. Michael Kiedrowski.

COMMON SURGERIES

SNAKES

Anesthetic induction with isoflurane in an induction chamber works well for snakes. (Figure14) Isoflurane is the first choice for debilitated patients. (Bennett, 1991, Raiti, 1995; Werner, 1987) The induction chamber offsets the disadvantage of patient restraint.(Bennett, 1991) Old endotracheal tube adapters may be fitted to small plastic containers for small snakes and large trash cans for large pythons. The snake should be intubated or maintained on a mask following induction. It usually takes 15-30 minutes for induction adequate for intubation.

Surgical site preparation is accomplished with standard hospital surgical scrubs and soaps, such as povidone iodine or Nolvasan, taking into account the type of tissue being prepared for surgery. Alcohol is not recommended for open wounds, mucous membranes, and hemipenes.

EGG BINDING/RETENTION

For single eggs proximal to the cloacal orifice invasive surgery is often not necessary. Opening the cloacal orifice with a vaginal speculum or a large pair of kelly clamps will allow for visualization of the three cloacal tracts. (Klingenberg, 1991) The gastrointenstinal tract is located ventrally. The two oviducts are located dorsally right and left of the GI tract. An otoscopic cone can be passed up each oviduct searching for the offending egg. Alligator forceps or hemostats can often be used to grasp and remove the egg. When the egg has adhered to the oviduct, cannot be visualized, or multiple eggs are present, a salpingotomy is recommended. (Klingenberg, 1991)

For surgical removal the incision is centered over the offending egg in the case of single egg retention. With multiple eggs the oviduct can be moved or stretched approximately 4-5 egg lengths anteriorly/posteriorly resulting in a skin incision centered between 8 eggs. If an oophorectomy is to be performed an incision is made 75% of the distance from snout to vent. (McCracken, 1991) The incision is started between the smaller lateral scales and the large ventral scutes. (Figure 15) The author (though controversial), prefers to continue the incision with scissors which follows a path between scales rather than cutting through them resulting in a more cosmetic and less traumatic closure.(Frye, 1981)

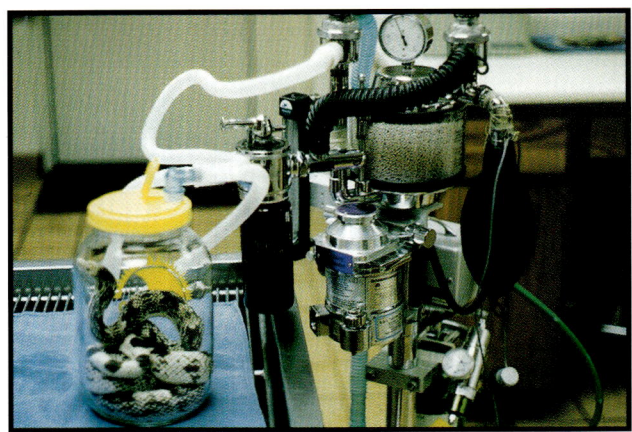

Fig. 14. Anesthesia with an induction chamber made from an iced-tea jar. Photo courtesy of Dr. Michael Kiedrowski.

The ventral edge of the rib cage is then identified and the incision is continued along this ventral rib edge. The incision is continued through several layers of axial muscles, through the coelomic membrane, and commonly through a membrane similar to the greater omentum containing numerous fat bodies. An egg within the oviduct should be identified and the oviduct, (including several eggs), should be easily exteriorized from the body cavity. (Figure 16) An incision is made over the egg for removal. (Figure 17 & 18) Delicate manipulation of the eggs anterior and posterior may allow for multiple egg extractions from this one oviduct incision site. When the eggs have adhered to the oviduct, numerous incisions into the oviduct must be made for egg removal. Center these multiple incisions between eggs slightly over one egg end to allow 2 eggs to be removed from each incision.

Numerous saline flushes should be performed throughout the procedure to maintain tissue health. The oviduct is closed longitudinally with small (4-0/5-0 for a kingsnake, 2-0/3-0 for a large python) monofilament absorbable suture material. The author prefers chromic gut and has never had complications, but PDS, Dexon or Maxon are recommended as well. The use of chromic gut in reptiles is controversial due to the lack of proteolytic enzymes required for degradation. (Bennett, 1989) The coelomic membrane is sutured to itself or the ventral edge of the rib cage. The axial muscles are sutured to themselves as one layer, (small snakes), or several layers (large pythons), with monofilament absorbable suture. The skin is closed with monofilament non-absorbable suture material such as PROLENE or ETHILON in an appositional or slightly exerting closure because reptile skin tends to invert. (Frye, 1974; Frye, 1981) The author recommends a horizontal mattress pattern with the knots placed dorsally to decrease

Fig. 15 Incision into a Florida Kingsnake between lateral scales and ventral scutes. Photo courtesy of Dr. Michael Kiedrowski.

locomotive suture "snagging" in the recovery and healing period. (Finnegan and Kirpensteijn, 1991)

Post operative feeding consisting of small meals, fed not to "stretch" the suture line, may begin the next day. Suture removal is scheduled in 30-45 days. (Frye, 1994) Water is limited to a small dish for 7-10 days following surgery because swimming delays wound healing. (Bennett, 1989)

INTESTINAL FOREIGN BODIES

For intestinal foreign bodies a similar surgical approach as egg binding with a single eggs is taken. The incision is centered over the offending object adjacent to the ventral scutes. Once the coelomic cavity has been entered, the foreign body should be visualized within the gastrointestinal tract. Pror to exteriorizing the gastrointestinal tract and foreign body, the author strongly recommends passing alligator forceps or a mechanic's pick-up tool down/up the nearest orifice in an attempt at internal manipulation of the foreign body with external removal through the orifice. (Figure 19) Removal of the object is often successful. If the foreign body cannot be removed through the mouth or cloaca, the GI tract and foreign body are exte-

Fig. 16. The oviduct and egg is exteriorized. Photo courtesy of Rodger Klingenberg.

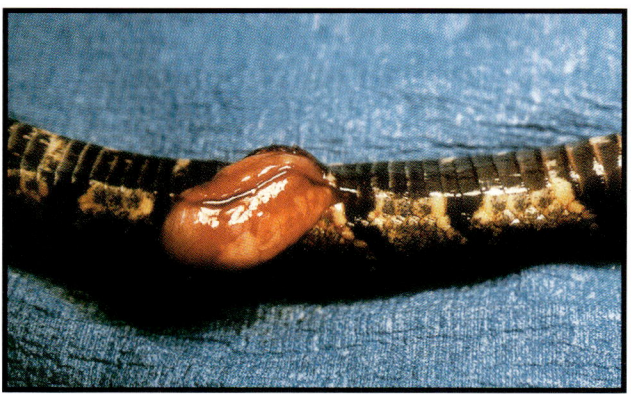

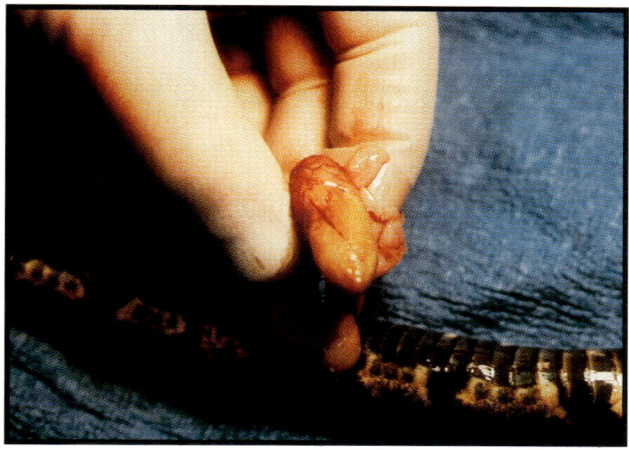

Fig. 17 The egg is removed by incision into the oviduct. Photo courtesy of Rodger Klingenberg.

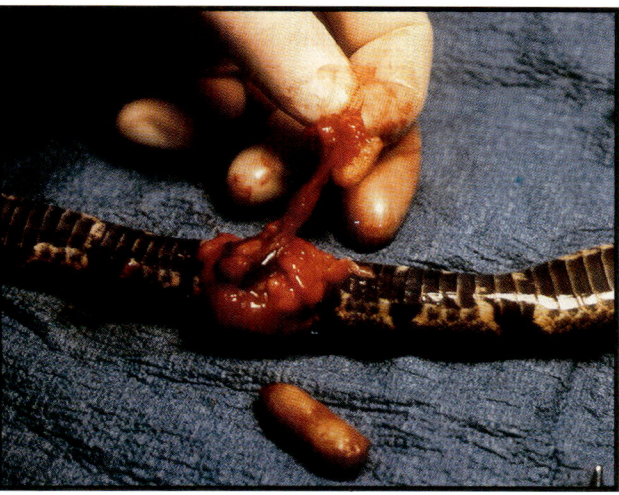

Fig. 18. The resulting small, paper-thin oviduct is closed with a monofilament absorbable suture material. Photo courtesy of Rodger Klingenberg.

Fig. 19. The intestinal tract has been opened in this photo to allow visualization of the mechanic's pick-up tool grasping an intestinal foreign body. Photo courtesy of Dr. Michael Kiedrowski.

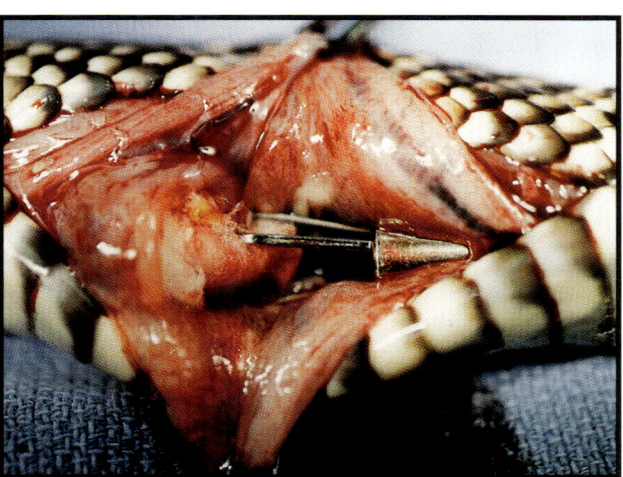

riorized and a longitudinal incision is made on the opposite side of the longitudinal (mesenteric) blood supply. (Figure 20)

The intestinal tract is closed with a monofilament, absorbable suture material such as PDS or DEXON. Chromic gut should be avoided in GI closures. (Bennett, 1989b) Copious saline lavage is recommended to decrease contamination. (Bennett, 1989b)

Abdominal closure is the same as in egg binding. Post operative care involves withholding food for 10 days then beginning feeding small meals fed at a rate to not "stretch" the surgical site for 30 days. Pre and post operative antibiotics such as enrofloxacin or amikacin (combination) are strongly recommended due to potential contamination of the coelomic cavity (Finnegan and Kirpensteijn, 1991; Raiti, 1995).

AMPUTATION OF HEMIPENIS

Hemipenes may be removed under general anesthesia or with localized anesthesia with 2% Iodocaine hydrochloride. (Raiti, 1995) The hemipenis is prepped and scrubbed for surgery with standard soaps and scrubs excluding alcohol.

In large snakes and lizards a circumferential incision is started at the base of the hemipenis with a scalpel and continued into the lumen of the hemipenis, if a lumen exists, many reptile hemipenes do not have an internal lumer. Only 1/2 or 180 degrees of the hemipenis is transected. The external mucous membrane side and the internal lumen side of the hemipenis are identified. Visually it looks like a tube within a tube with the lumen side often retracting into the lumen itself. The lumen membrane edge is sutured to the external mucosal edge with a small monofilament absorbable suture material resulting in continued lumen patency. The circumferential incision is then continued the remaining 180 degrees for complete transection. The resulting surgical edges are apposed and closed as before.

In smaller snakes and lizards a horizontal mattress suture is placed at the base of the hemipenis. The hemipenis is amputated by simple excision. (Raiti, 1995)

Post operative antibiotics such as enrofloxacin or amikacin (combination) are recommended. (Raiti, 1995)

LIZARDS

Anesthetic induction with intramuscular ketamine works well. Dosages range from 20-130 mg/kg body weight. (Bennett, 1991; Cooper and Jackson, 1981; Frye, 1981) The author recommends 40 mg/kg in compromised patients and

55mg/kg in uncompromised patients. Intubation and gas (Isoflurane) is recommended for maintenance. Induction time is 5-10 minutes with Ketamine. Large lizards with autonomous tails, (such as iguanas) should be placed in a dark room after injection to decrease the chance of the tail going through cage bars, or struggle during the induction disorientation period which may result in tail loss.

Similar to snakes, the surgical site preparation is accomplished with standard hospital surgical scrubs and soaps such as povidone iodine, chlorhexidine (e.g., Nolvasan®) or alcohol taking into account the type of tissue being prepared for surgery.

REPRODUCTIVE/GASTROINTESTINAL/UROLITHS

For procedures of this type the patient is placed in dorsal recumbency and the left paramidline area is prepared for surgery. The skin is incised in a longitudinal anterior-posterior fashion centered between the last rib and the pelvis. The incision is deepened through the abdominal musculature, and through the coelomic membrane entering the coelomic cavity. Commonly, a large abdominal fat pad is encountered. (Figure 21) This fat pad is attached to a base within the pelvic inlet. It may be retracted laterally within the abdominal cavity or exteriorised and "flipped" caudally, depending upon its size and the desired exposure. (Figure 22)

Reproductive problems are commonly corrected by removal of the ovaries (oophorectomy) or removal of the ovaries and oviducts (ovariosalpingectomy). In pre-ovulatory egg binding, large follicle-filled ovaries are as gently exteriorized as possible. Complete exteriorization is not always possible. Exterior and lateral displacement of the ovary will result in visualization of the vessels forming the ovarian blood supply. (Figure 23) The vessels are ligated with monofilament absorbable suture material, the author preferring chromic gut. The second ovary is then as exteriorized as much as possible and the procedure repeated. The coelomic cavity is closed leaving the oviducts intact.

In post-ovulatory egg binding, large egg-filled oviducts are first encountered. The eggs are arranged in a linear fashion within an oviduct when exteriorized as opposed to the "cluster" arrangement of the follicles of pre-ovulatory egg binding. The oviducts are removed prior to ovary removal. To acomplish this, the first oviduct and eggs are exteriorized and the oviducts blood supply identified. (Figure 24) The oviduct is ligated anterior to the most rostral egg, and caudal to the most posterior egg with a monofilament absorbable suture material. The oviduct vessels are ligated in a simi-

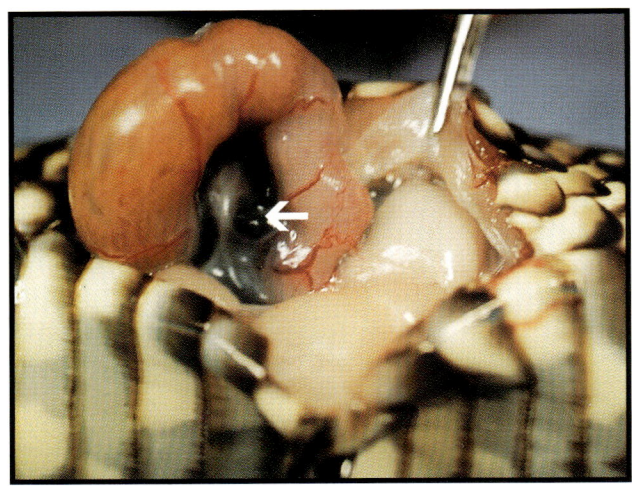

Fig. 20, The intestinal tract is exteriorized to allow visualization of the mesenteric blood supply (arrow). Photo courtesy of Dr. Michael Kiedrowski.

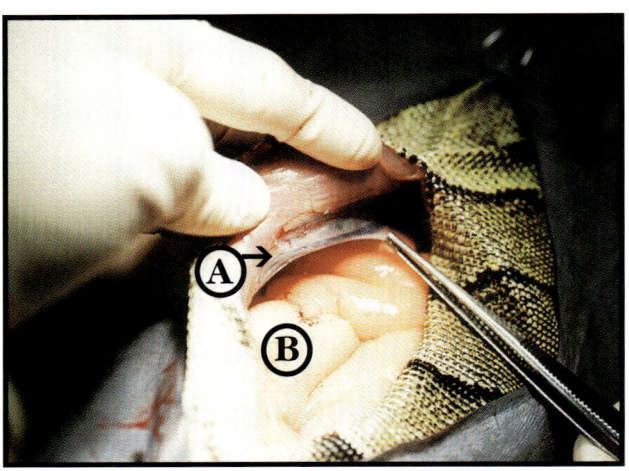

Fig. 21. In this left paramedian coelomic approach in an iguana, the ventral venous sinus (A) and the abdominal fat pad (B) are visible when entering the cavity. Photo courtesy of Dr. Michael Kiedrowski.

Fig. 22. The abdominal fat pad is flipped caudally for cavity exposure. Photo courtesy of Dr. Michael Kiedrowski.

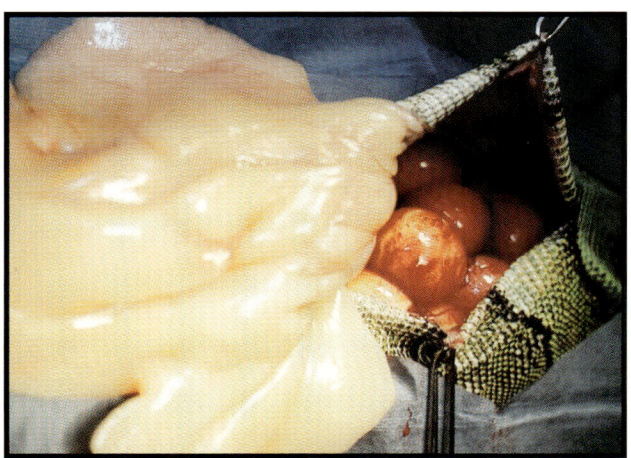

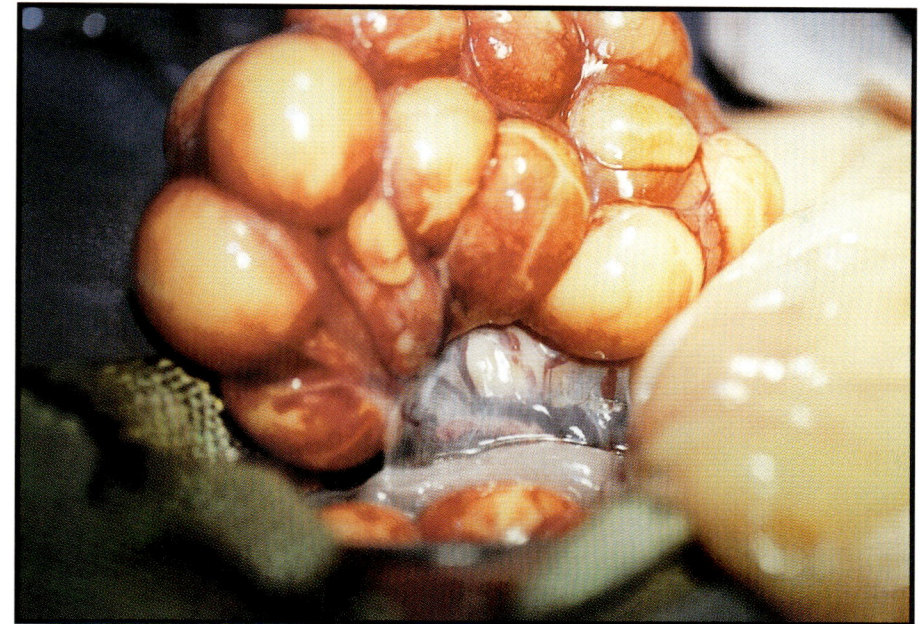

Fig. 23. In pre-ovulatory egg binding, each large ovary is partially exteriorized and retracted laterally to expose its blood supply. Photo courtesy of Dr. Michael Kiedrowski.

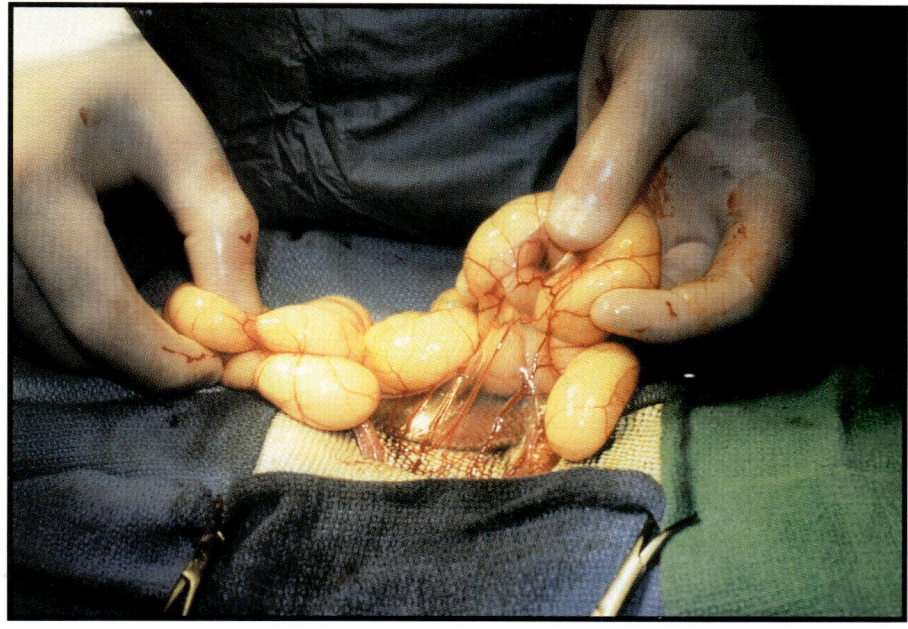

Fig. 24. In post-ovulatory egg binding, the large egg-filled oviducts are exteriorized easily to expose their blood supply. Photo courtesy of Dr. Todd Driggers.

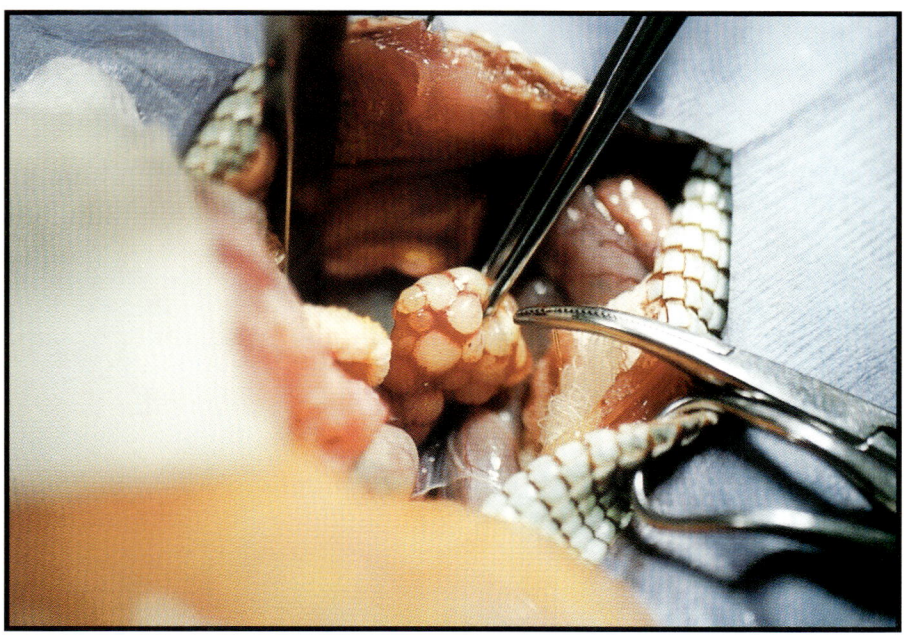

Fig. 25. In post-ovulatory egg binding, after oviduct/egg removal, the small ovaries are retracted for ligation and removal. Photo courtesy of Dr. Michael Kiedrowski.

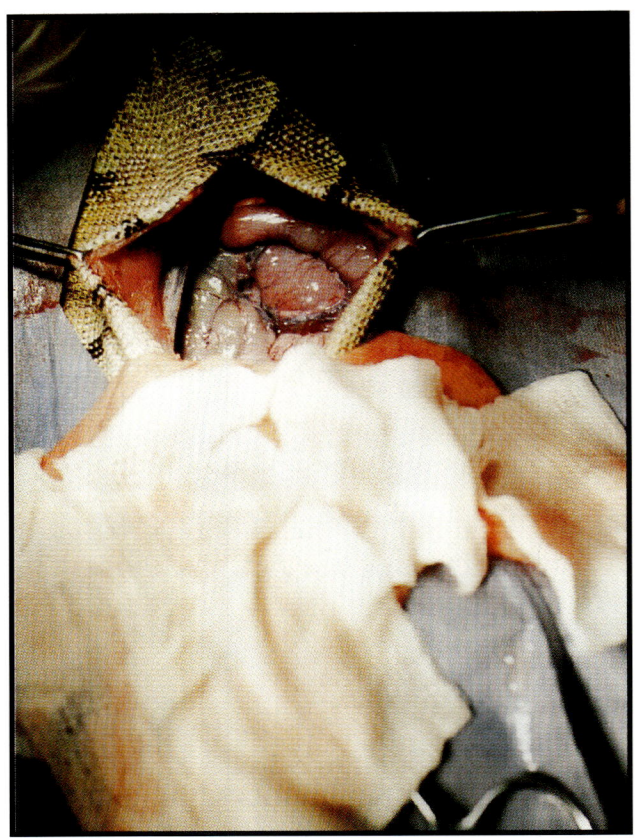

Fig. 26. Once the fat pad is flipped caudally, the gastrointestinal tract is clearly visible. Photo courtesy of Dr. Michael Kiedrowski.

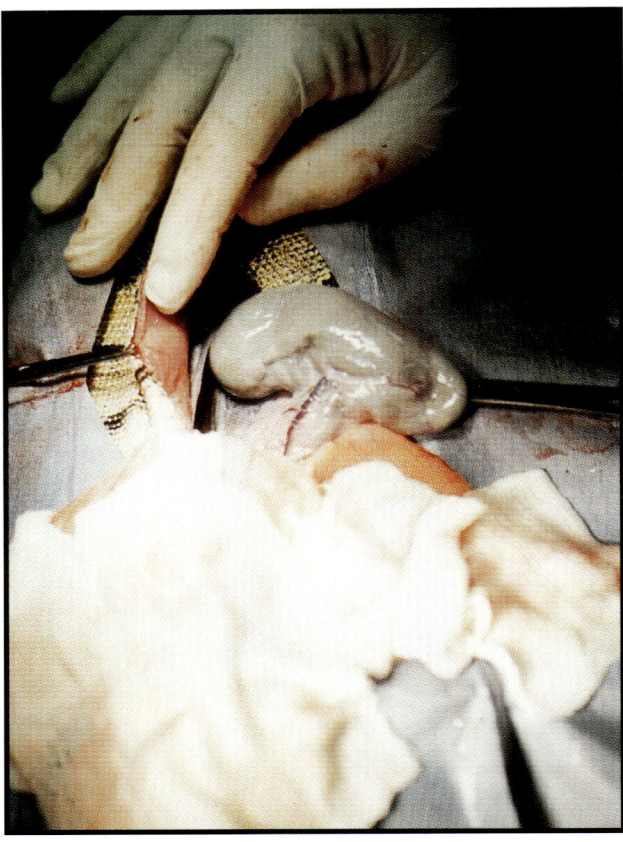

Fig. 27. The stomach is exteriorized for removal of a foreign body. Photo courtesy of Dr. Michael Kiedrowski.

lar fashion. The second egg-filled oviduct is exteriorized and the procedure is repeated.

The ovaries are then identified along the dorsal wall of the coelomic cavity, adjacent to a dorsal venous sinus. If a membrane exists between the surgeon and the ovary, gentle retraction of the gastrointestinal tract should eliminate the interfering membrane. The ovaries are lifted slightly and retracted laterally to allow identification of the ovarian blood supply. (Figure 25) In a two kilogram green iguana these vessels are approximately four millimeters in length. The vessels are ligated with monofilament absorbable suture material and the ovary is removed. The gastrointestinal tract may have to be manipulated a second time to give clear visualization of the second ovary. The ovary removal procedure is then repeated and the coelomic cavity is closed.

The gastrointestinal tract and gastrointestinal foreign bodies can be identified after retraction of the coelomic fat pad by visualization and palpation. (Figure 26) The author strongly recommends passing a blunt instrument orally or rectally to attempt contact with the foreign body. If the foreign body can be contacted, alligator forceps or a mechanic's pick-up tool may be passed. Internal manipulation, coupled with the use of the forceps may be successful in remov-

ing the foreign object orally or through the cloaca.

Foreign objects that cannot be removed through the esophagus or cloaca require that an incision be made into the gastrointestinal tract. Before making an incision, the GI tract is exteriorized if possible. (Figure 27) The GI tract is entered with a longitudinal incision directly over or slightly rostral to the foreign body on the opposite side of the mesenteric blood supply. After the foreign body has been removed, the gastrointestinal incision is closed in a longitudinal fashion with monofilament absorbable suture material. (The author prefers PDS). Chromic gut is not recommended. (Bennett, 1989b) Finally, the coelomic cavity is closed. Pre or post operative antibiotics such as enrofloxacin or amikacin (combination) are strongly recommended due to the potential for coelomic contamination.

Bladder stones (uroliths) are easily visualized within the thin transparent bladder after the coelomic fat pad has been retracted or exteriorized (Frye, 1983, Ryer, 1983). The bladder is exteriorized as gently as possible. (Figure 28) Then, the bladder wall is incised and the stone removed. (Figure 29) The bladder wall is closed with small monofilament absorbable suture material in a two layer closure. (Bennett, 1989b) First the bladder

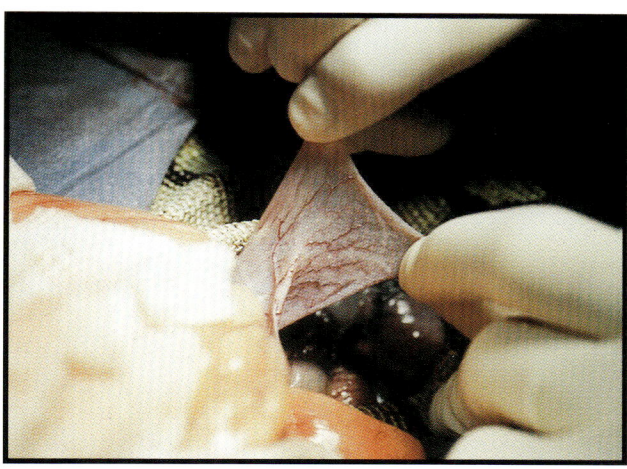

Fig. 28 The thin wall of the bladder is exteriorized. Photo courtesy of Dr. Michael Kiedrowski.

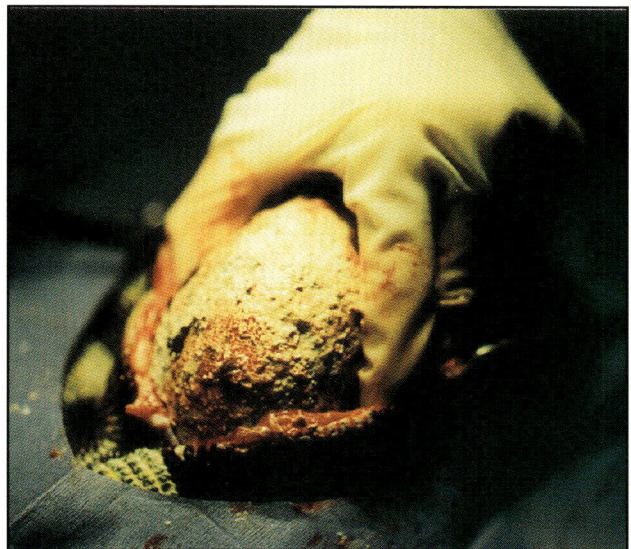

Fig. 29. A large urolith (stone) is removed from the bladder of a green iguana. Photo courtesy of Dr. Michael Kiedrowski.

Fig. 30. The muscle, fascia and subcuticular tissue are sutured as one layer. Photo courtesy of Dr. Michael Kiedrowski.

wall is sutured in an appositional closure, then the first bladder incision is oversewn with an inverting technique. Finally, saline flushes of the coelomic cavity should be performed if the surgeon experienced any urine spillage during the cystotomy. The coelomic cavity is now closed. Pre and post operative antibiotics such as enrofloxacin or amikacin (combination) are strongly recommended.

The coelomic cavity is closed in two layers. First the abdominal muscles are apposed and sutured in a continuous technique with a monofilament absorbable suture material. The author prefers chromic gut. (Figure 30) The holding layer of the abdominal muscle wall is a fibrous layer located just below the skin. Including this fibrous layer in the suture passage will increase tissue compression and decrease the chance of dehiscence. The skin is apposed in an appositional or everting technique with a monofilament non absorbable suture material. The author prefers Ethilon or Prolene in a horizontal mattress pattern with slight eversion. (Figure 31) Post operative care includes removal of any bathing size water dish for 2-3 days since swimming delays wound healing. (Bennett, 1989) Sutures are removed in 30-40 days.

ABSCESSES

The majority of lizard abscesses are caused by inadequate thermoregulation or cagemate aggression. Care should be taken to correct husbandry problems to decrease abscess reoccurrences. Many lizard abscesses can be debrided without general anesthesia, utilizing only manual restraint. Anesthesia is required for deep abscesses or abscesses on larger lizards. First, the abscess surface is cleaned with surgical scrubs and soaps such as povidone iodine or chlorhexidine (e.g., Nolvasan®) prior to incision or excision.

Digit abscesses are incised directly over the affected area or are approached proximal-distal between the lateral scales and the ventral scutes. After exposing the caseous abscess material, an abscess culture is taken to aid in determining appropriate antibiotic therapy. Then, the abscess material is removed and the abscess capsule scraped for debridement. (Figure 32) The author uses several of the "spatula" style dental instruments for this purpose. The remaining abscess tract is flushed with an antiseptic solution and an antibiotic ointment such as furacin may be infused (Barten, 1991; Frye, 1981). The incision site is left open for granulation tissue closure. (Bennett, 1989b)

Abscesses on other parts of the body are approached more directly. (Figure 33) The skin and outer capsule of the abscess is removed and an abscess culture is taken. The remaining abscess tissure and capsule is debrided and the wound is left open for granulation tissue to form. (Bennett, 1989b) (Figure 34) Debrided abscess wounds on the tail and limbs may be bandaged for wound protection at the surgeon's discretion.

Post-operative antibiotics such as enrofloxacin or amikacin (combination) are recommended. Bandages are changed every three to seven days. The author recommends that non-digit abscesses be debrided a second time seven to ten days post surgery. Soaking water dishes should be removed during the granulation period unless their presence is absolutely necessary. Epithelialization is usually complete in two to four weeks depending on wound size.

FRACTURE REPAIR

Before attempting to repair any fracture the health and integrity of the bone is evaluated by husbandry, physical exam, and radiology. Many fractures are due to osteoporosis associated with poor husbandry practices and are poor surgical candidates. The husbandry practices will have to be corrected for proper healing to occur.

Osteoporosis patient fractures are repaired with splints and other external fixation methods (Barten, 1991; Stahl, 1995). Distal limb fractures such as radial or humeral fractures may be splinted away from the body or the splint may be incorporated in part of a body or tail wrap. (Figure 35) Fractures of the humerus or femur may be splinted with the base of the splint encompassing the body to prevent the splint from slipping distally. The limb should be splinted in a flexed position, and not wrapped to the body or tail. This allows for straight bone alignment, reducing angulation at the fracture site. (Figure 36)

Surgical repair is recommended for the non-osteoporosis patient. The fracture site is approached with a longitudinal proximal-distal incision on the anterior side of the limb. The incision should be made slightly dorsal to midline in order to avoid the large muscle bellies and the majority of the vascular supply. Itramedulllary bone pins may be placed antegrade or retrograde with points of exit dependent upon the bone involved. In the case of the humerus or femur the pin is exited through the lateral edge of the scapulohumeral (shoulder) or the coxofemoral (hip) joint respectively. In the case of the radius and tibia the pin exits through the radiocarpal (wrist) and the hock (heel) joints respectively. Circlage wire may be used to incorporate bone fragments into the fracture repair. Bone plates may be used in large lizards where applicable.

To start closure the muscles are apposed with a monofilament absorbable suture material such as chromic gut or PDS. The skin is closed with a

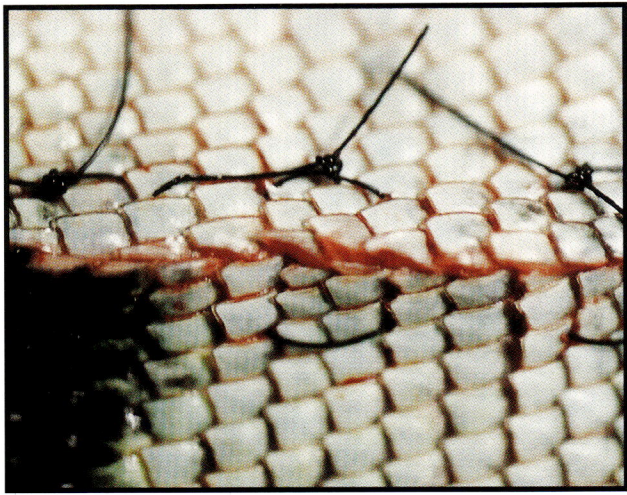

Fig. 31. The skin is closed with a horizontal mattress pattern causing slight eversion. Photo courtesy of Dr. Michael Kiedrowski.

Fig. 32. Caseous abscess material has been expressed from a toe incision adjacent to the ventral scutes. Photo courtesy of Dr. Michael Kiedrowski.

Fig. 33. The abscess in the foot of this Savanna monitor needs to be debrided. Photo courtesy of Dr. Michael Kiedrowski.

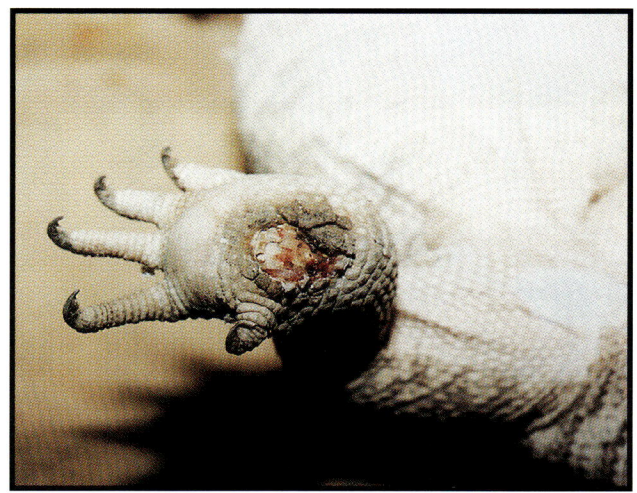

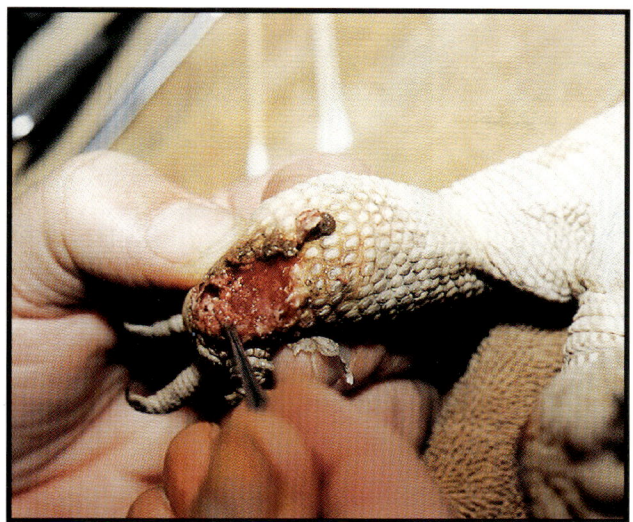

Fig. 34. The debrided Savanna monitor abscess will be left open to close by granulation. Photo courtesy of Dr. Michael Kiedrowski.

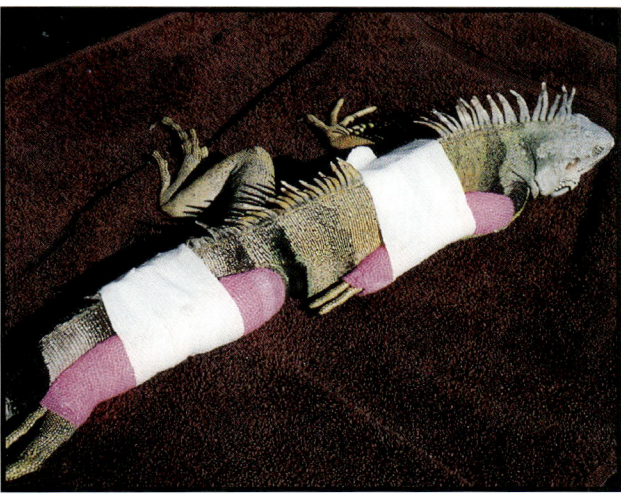

Fig. 35. Distal limb fractures respond well to splints taped to the body or tail. Photo courtesy of Dr. Michael Kiedrowski.

Fig. 36. Proximal limb fractures respond well to angled splints allowed to move free of body wrap. Photo courtesy of Dr. Michael Kiedrowski.

monofilament nonabsorbable suture material such as ETHILON or PROLENE in an appositional or everting suture pattern since reptile skin tends to invert. (Frye, 1974)

Post operative wraps and splints may be required. Pre and post operative antibiotics such as enrofloxacin or amikacin (combination) are strongly recommended. Soaking water dishes should be removed to maintain the incision, splints and bandages in a dry condition. Sutures are removed in thirty to forty-five days. Pins are removed in six to eight weeks following radiographs to confirm fracture healing.

CLOACAL PROLAPSE

The majority of lizard clocal prolapses are due to intestinal parasites, substrate irritation, reproductive disorders, or metabolic disorders especially disorders of calcium metabolism. Care should be taken to correct the predisposing factors as well as the prolapse. In small lizards the prolapse may be reduced without anesthesia using only manual restraint. In large lizards anesthesia is beneficial for restraint and for relaxation of the cloacal orifice.

The prolapse cloaca is gently cleaned prior to reduction. Isotonic (0.9%) or hypertonic (2%) saline is used to decrease tissue edema (swelling). The cloaca is reduced by manipulation with blunt instruments and by placing a soft rubber tube through the cloaca and into the colon. The cloacal vent is closed over the tube by encircling the tail and cloacal vent with tape. (Figure 37) An alternate method utilizes a purse-string of monofilament non absorbable suture material closing the cloacal vent around the tube. Pre and post operative antibiotics are strongly recommended. The patient is not given food for 48-72 hours. The suture or tape and soft rubber tube is removed in 72 hours.

AMPUTATION OF HEMIPENIS

A prolapsed hemipenis in lizards often results in necrosis due to dehydration and blood supply interuption. (Figure 38) Amputation is identical to small snake hemipenis amputation.

AMPUTATION OF TAIL

When performing tail amputations, lizards with tail autonomy are treated differently than lizards without. Lizards with tail autonomy are designed to loose their tails at a bony fracture plane in the center of a tail vertebrae. Anesthesia may not be required in small lizards or in tail tip amputations. To perform this procedure, the tail is gripped firmly with both hands with the intended amputation site between the hands. The tail is bent sharply in the lateral direction, causing a fracture within the tail vertebrae. Next, the amputated piece is rotated to separate muscle segments and complete amputation. The initial result leaves exposed muscle, bone, and minimal hemorrhage. Only pressure is used to stop any hemorrhage. Primary closure of the exposed tail end will reduce regeneration. (Bennett, 1989b) For optimal regrowth, no dressings, disinfectants, anticoagulants, or chemicals are applied. Systemic antibiotics are used if infection is a concern.

Non autonomous tail amputations require general anesthesia first. After anesthesia has been administered a tourniquet is applied to the tail proximal to the amputation site. In small lizards the tail is amputated by complete scalpel excision. Larger lizards are excised in a stepwise fashion. First, the dorsal and ventral blood supplies are isolated and ligated. Then, the exposed vertebra is disarticulated and removed. In large lizards, the exposed muscle tissue is apposed and sutured with monofilament absorbable suture material prior to skin closure with a monofilament non-absorbable suture material. In small lizards, only the skin is closed.

TURTLES AND TORTOISES

Anesthetic induction with intramuscular ketamine works adequately in most chelonians. Dosage ranges from 20-60mg/kg in box turtles (Boyer, 1992) and water turtles to 100mg/kg in tortoises. Induction by gas alone can be prolonged lasting over 1 hour. (Bennett, 1991) Intubation and gas anesthesia for maintenance with isoflurane is recommended for long surgical procedures. (Bennett, 1991)

Surgical site preparation is accomplished with standard hospital surgical scrubs and soaps, such as povidone iodine, Nolvasan, and alcohol. Extreme care must be taken to monitor and assist breathing if maintaining the patient in the dorsal recumbency position.

REPRODUCTIVE

For this class of surgeries, the patient is placed in dorsal recumbency. Anesthesia and respirations must be monitored closely. To begin, a sterile marker is used to draw a one-half ellipse with the strait edge paramidline. (Figure 39) The Dremel saw is used to cut the plastron bone. During cutting, an assistant uses a saline stream/drip to cool the incision site and the dremmel blade preventing thermal damage. The entire incision line is cut at a forty-five degree angle undermining the plastron fragment. (Figure 40) The incision is deepened to the periosteal and coelomic membranes being careful to maintain membrane integrity.

The paramidline straight incision is deepened

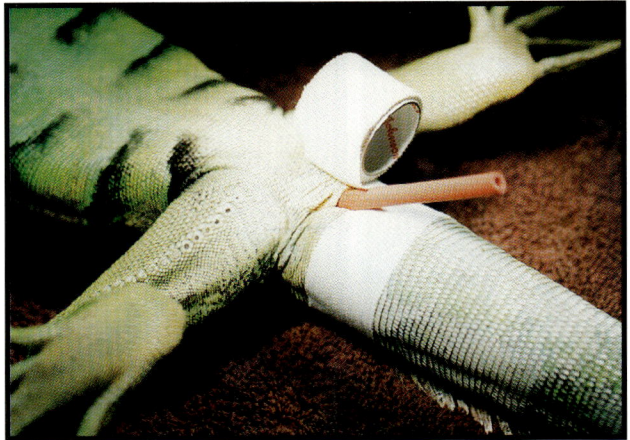

Fig. 37. A soft red rubber tube is placed through the cloaca and taped into place along with taping the vent closed. Photo courtesy of Dr. Michael Kiedrowski.

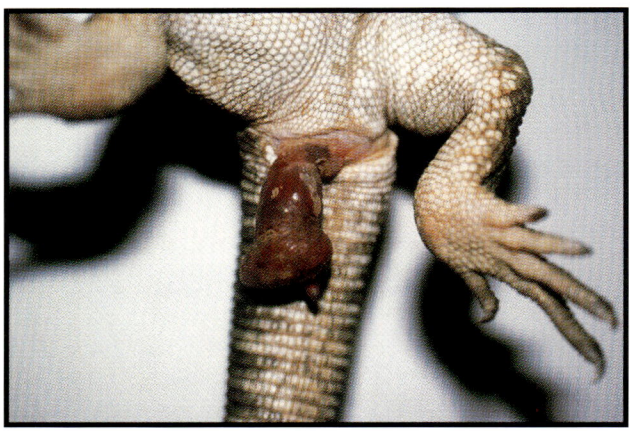

Fig. 38. This prolapsed hemipenis in a varanid lizard was eventually amputated. Photo courtesy of Dr. Todd Driggers.

into a "V" shaped groove by cutting the fragment edge back at the opposite forty-five degree angle. (Figure 41) The arc edge membranes are cut and plastron door is opened along the straight paramidline "V" shaped hinge. (Figure 42)

The reproductive tract should be visible upon entering the coelomic cavity. If the reproductive tract cannot be visualized, gentle manipulation and retraction of the gastrointestinal tract can be used to aid in visualization. The oviduct and eggs are exteriorized. Next, the oviduct is incised over the egg on the opposite side of the oviduct blood supply in a longitudinal fashion. The egg is removed through the oviduct incision. Eggs anterior and posterior to the oviduct incision may be removed by manipulating them through the oviduct and out the single oviduct incision. The oviduct is closed with a monofilament absorbable suture material in a linear fashion and the oviduct is returned to the coelomic cavity. The second oviduct may be exteriorized and the procedure repeated.

Fig. 39. A half-ellipse is drawn on the shell marking the anticipated surgical approach. Photo courtesy of Dr. Michael Kiedrowski.

Fig. 40. A Dremel saw is used to cut the shell at a 45-degree angle bevel. Photo courtesy of Dr. Michael Kiedrowski.

Fig. 41. The straight cut edge is back cut 45-degrees resulting in a "V" trough configuration. Photo courtesy of Dr. Michael Kiedrowski.

Fig. 42. The plastron "door" is opened on a hinge of muscle, coelomic membrane and periosteal membranes. The ventral venous sinus is visible. Photo courtesy of Dr. Michael Kiedrowski.

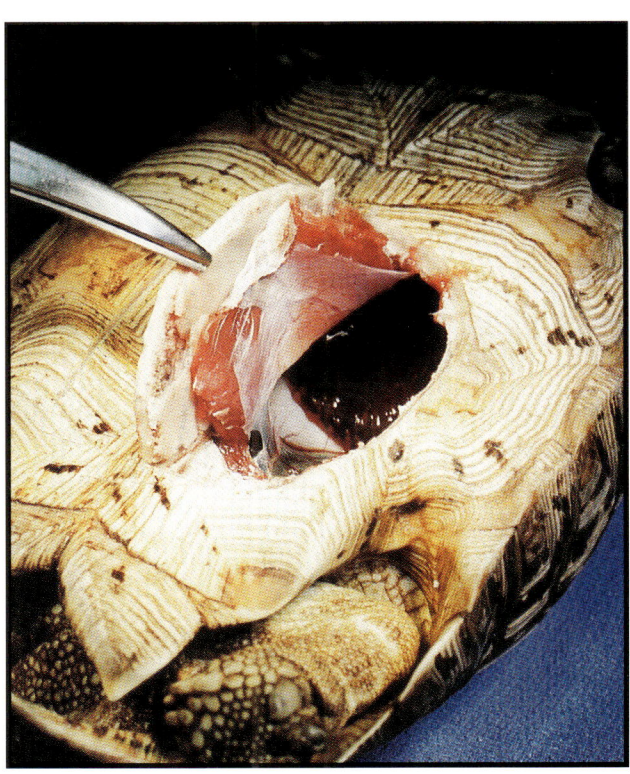

Fig. 43a-d.
A. The plastron "door" is closed; B. Epoxy resin is applied keeping exposed edges clean; C. A fiberglass patch is applied, and; D. Epoxy resin is spread over the fiberglass patch. Figures courtesy of Dr. Michael Kiedrowski.

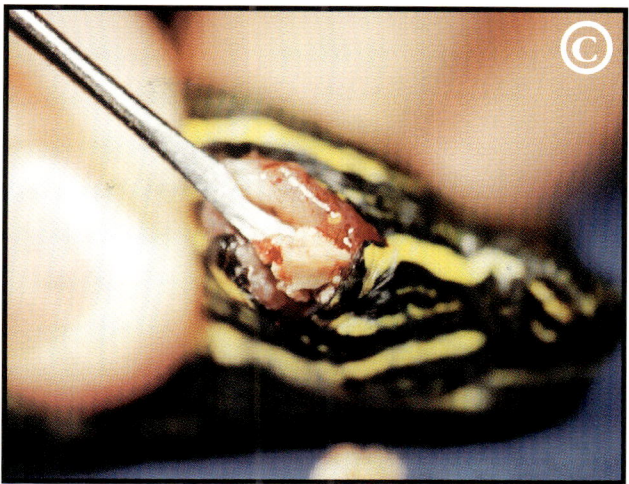
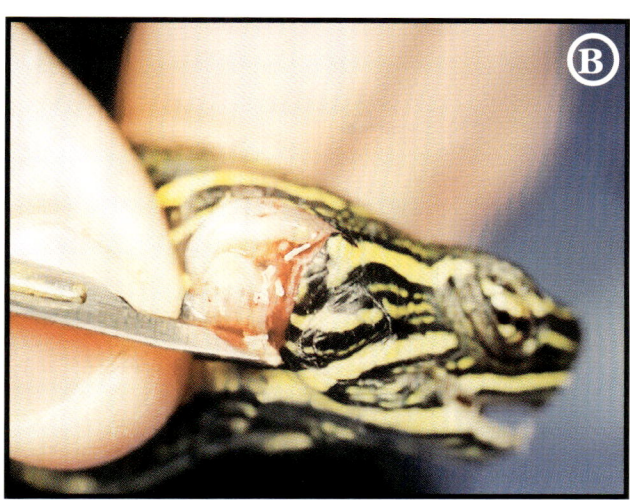
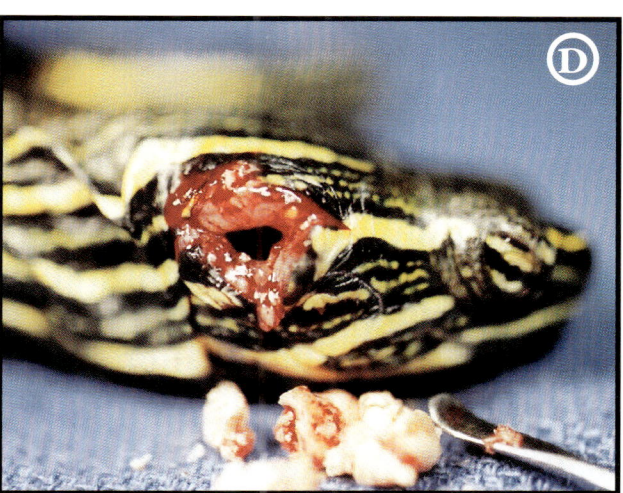

Fig. 44a-d
A. Ear abscess in a Western painted turtle; B. The skin incision reveals the abscess capsule; C. The abscess capsule is opened and abscess material is removed. D. The resulting hole will be filled with antibiotic ointment and left to heal on its own. Photos courtesy of Dr. Michael Kiedrowski.

UROLITHS

The urinary bladder is located in the caudal coelomic cavity. The thin bladder wall may be transparent enough to visualize an offending urolith (bladder stone). Partial exteriorization of the bladder may be possible. The ventral surface of the bladder is pulled through the coelomic incision. Three to four retention sutures are placed around the intended bladder incision site to keep the bladder incision exteriorized. The bladder is incised between the retention sutures resulting in a "bowl" formation of the bladder opened outside the coelomic cavity. The urolith is removed. Uroliths larger than the coelomic opening may be broken down inside the bladder and removed in pieces. The bladder is closed in two layers. An appositional layer is oversewn with an inverting layer. Monofilament absorbable suture material is used. The bladder is returned to the coelomic cavity. Copious coelomic lavage is recommended. (Bennett, 1989b)

Pre and post operative antibiotics such as enrofloxacin are strongly recommended.

The coelomic cavity is closed by closing the plastron fragment "door". (Figure 43A-D) The angled plastron incision edges result in compression of the bone edges upon closure. A fiberglass and epoxy resin patch is placed over the plastron door fragment sealing the door closed. Care must be taken to prevent excess epoxy resin from contacting the exposed bone edge surfaces. (Bennett, 1989b) The epoxy resin patch must be lavaged with saline or water to prevent thermal tissue damage during the epoxy hardening process. In growing chelonians the patch will have to be removed or "released" by grinding along the growth lines 2-6 months post op. Aquatic turtles should be kept dry except to feed for three to four weeks.

ABSCESSES

Abscesses are often caused by inadequate husbandry practices. Correction of husbandry prob-

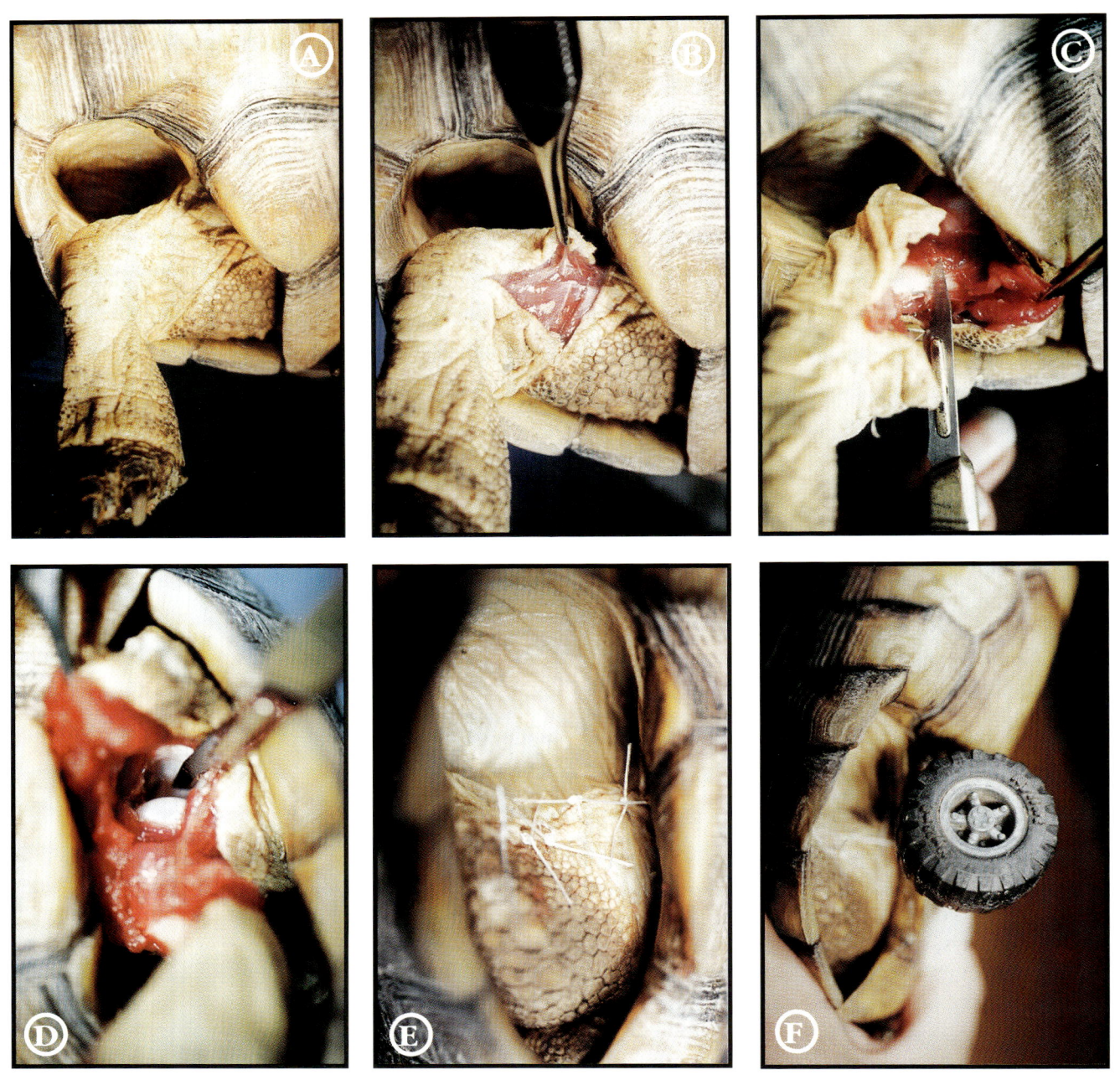

Fig. 45a-f
Hind limb amputation in the tortoise. A. The patient is placed in dorsal recumbency. B. The skin incision is made distal to the large scales. C. Muscle is cut deep to bone and scraped along the bone to the joint. D. The coxofemoral joint is disarticulated. E. The skin is closed. F. The axle of a prostehtic wheel is epoxied to the plastron. Photos courtesy of Dr. Michael Kiedrowski.

lems will speed healing and decrease reoccurrences of abscesses. Superficial, subcutaneous, and ear abscesses can often be debrided without anesthesia using only manual restraint. Large or deep abscesses may require complete anesthesia. A culture should be taken upon entering an abscess capsule to aid in antibiotic selection.

Superficial and subcutaneous abscesses are incised directly over the abscess and its capsule. The outer surface of the capsule is removed then the abscess material is removed. The remaining capsule wall is debrided. Antibiotic or antiseptic lushes like povidone iodine solution may be used to clear

any remaining abscess material. An antibiotic ointment like furacin may be applied to the resultant "hole". The wound is left open to heal by granulation. Pre and post operative antibiotics such as enrofloxacin are recommended.

Ear abscesses are incised directly over the offending abscess. The caseous abscess material is removed and the abscess capsule is gently debrided. (Figure 44A-D) The author prefers to use a cotton tipped applicator for debridement. Antibiotic or antiseptic flushes like povidone iodine solution are used to flush the abscess capsule clear of debris, and to flush the euastacean tube which may contain purulent material acting as a nidus of infection. (Boyer, 1992; Divers, 1995; Jacobsen, 1981) An antibiotic ointment is infused into the remaining empty capsule. The incision is left open to heal by granulation. Pre and post operative antibiotics such as enrofloxacin are recommended. (6,9) Because ear abscesses may be the result of Vitamin A deficiency, an injection of Vitamin A (Aquesol® A or Injacom® 100) is recommended. (Boyer, 1992)

LIMB AMPUTATIONS

In tortoises and terrestrial chelonians the limb is amputated by disarticulation at the most proximal joint available. (Divers, 1995b) The resulting stump should have little to no contact with the ground to decrease long term trauma. The patient is maintained in dorsal recumbency. A circumferential incision is made slightly distal to the scapulonumeral (shoulder) or coxofemoral (hip) joint to allow adequate skin for closure. Muscle bodies are transected and blood vessels are ligated until the bone distal to the disarticulation site is exposed. Blunt dissection is used to disect proximally until the joint is exposed. The joint is disarticulated. The remaining muscle and skin are trimmed until adequate closure can be approximated. The muscle bodies are apposed with absorbable monofilament suture material. The skin is closed with non-absorbable monofilament suture material. A wheel prosthesis may be epoxied to the plastron to assist in locomotion. (Figure 45A-F) (Divers, 1995) Pre and post operative antibiotics such as enrofloxacin are recommended. Sutures are removed in 45-50 days.

In turtles and aquatic chelonians the limb is amputated by disarticulation at the most distal joint available leaving a stump for use. The surgical procedure is similar to tortoises except the skin has more elasticity. No prosthetics are required. Pre- and post-operative antibiotics are recommended. The patient should be kept dry for one to two days post operatively, then only allowed in the water to feed ten to fifteen minutes twice daily. The turtle is returned to its aquatic lifestyle in three to four weeks when the sutures are removed.

REFERENCES:

—**Barten, S.L. 1991.**
"Clinical Problems of Iguanas." Reptile and Amphibian Magazine. Jan/Feb:40-45.
—**Bennett, R.A. 1989.**
"Reptilian Surgery Part I. Basic Principles." Compendium of Continuing Education. 11(1):10-17.
—**Bennett, R.A. 1989b.**
"Reptilian Surgery Part II. Management of Surgical Diseases." Compendium of Continuing Education. 11(2):122-132.
—**Bennett, R.A. 1991.**
"A Review of Anesthesia and Chemical Restraint in Reptiles." Journal of Zoo and Wildlife Medicine. 22(3):282-303.
—**Boyer, T.H. 1991.**
"Common Problems and Treatment of Green Iguanas (*Iguana iguana*)." Bulletin of the Association of Amphibian and Reptilian Veterinarians. 1(1):8-11.
—**Boyer, T.H. 1992.**
"Common Problems of Box Turtles (*Terrapene* ssp) in Captivity." Bulletin of the Association of Reptilian and Amphibian Veterinarians. 2(1):9-13.
—**Cooper, J.E., and O.F. Jackson. 1981.**
Anesthesia and Surgery in Diseases of the Reptilia. New York: Academic Press. Pp 535-549
—**Divers, S. 1995.**
"Veterinary Corner." Reptilian Magazine. 3(3):37-38.
—**Divers, S. 1995b.**
"Ear Abscesses in Chelonians. The Reptilian Abscess An Introduction." Reptilian Magazine. 3(1):40-42.
—**Frye, F.L.1974.**
"Surgery in Captive Reptiles." Pp.640-641 in Current Veterinary Therapy V., R.W Kirk (ed). Philadelphia: WB Saunders Co
—**Frye, F.L. 1981.**
Biomedical and Surgical Aspects of Captive Reptile Husbandry. Edwardsville, KS. Veterinary Medical Publishing Company. Pp 141-242, 247-250.
—**Frye, F.L. 1983.**
"Urinary Calculosis and Cystotomy in a Lizard." Veterinary Medicine/Small Animal Clinician. March 1983:421-433.
—**Frye, F.L.1994.**
"Colo-rectal Atresia and Its Surgical Repair in a Juvenile Amelanistic Burmese Python (*Python molurus bivittatus*)." Journal of Small and Exotic Animal Medicine. 2(4):149-150.
—**Finnegan, M. and J. Kirpensteijn. 1991.**
"Distocia Associated with Oviductal Volvulus and Rupture in a Burmese Python." Journal of Small and Exotic Animal Medicine. 1(2):90-93.
—**Gould, W.J., A.E. Yeager, and J.C. Glennon. 1992.**
"Surgical Correction of an Intestinal Obstruction in a Turtle." JAVMA. 200(5):705-706.

—Jacobsen, E.R. 1981.
"Diseases of Reptiles Part II. Infectious Diseases." Exotic Animal Medicine in Practice Vol 1: 130-134 Reprinted from Compendium of Continuing Education.3(3)

—Klingenberg, R.J. 1991.
"Egg Binding in Colubrid Snakes." Vivarium. 3(2):32-35.

—McCracken, H.E. 1991.
"The Topographical Anatomy of Snakes and its Clinical Application, a Preliminary Report." Proceedings of the American Association of Zoo Veterinarans. 1991:112-118.

—Mader, D. 1991.
"Surgery in Turtles and Tortoises." Vivarium. 4(2):9-11.

—Orosz, S.E. et al. 1992.
"Follical Aspiration for the Treatment of Pre-Ovulatory Egg Binding in a Green Iguana." Journal of Small and Exotic Medicine. 1(4):161-165.

—Raiti, P. 1995.
"Veterinary Care of the Common Kingsnake, *Lampropeltis getula*." Association of Reptilian and Amphibian Veterinarians. 5(1):11-18.

—Ryer, K.A. 1983.
"Urinary Calculi in a Green Iguana." Veterinary Medicine/Small Animal Clinician. Apr:607.

—Stahl, S.J. 1995.
"Fracture Repair in Iguanas, In My Experience." Association of Reptilian and Amphibian Veterinarians. 5(1):4.

—Stewart, J.S. 1990.
"Anaerobic Bacterial Infections in Reptiles." Journal of Zoo and Wildlife Medicine. 21(2):180-184.

—Werner, R.E. 1987.
"Isoflurane Anesthesia: A Guide for Practitioners." Compendium of Continuing Education. 9(5):603-606.

—Wissman, M. 1992.
"Cesarean Section in a *Cyclura*." Journal of Small Exotic Animal Medicine. 1(3):139-141.

OCULAR DISORDERS IN REPTILES

Chantal Dupont D.V.M. M.S.
Christopher J. Murphy* D.V.M., Ph.D.
Department of Surgical Sciences
School of Veterinary Medicine
University of Wisconsin-Madison
Madison Wisconsin

* Address all correspondence to Dr. Christopher Murphy, Department of Surgical Sciences, School of Veterinary Medicine, University of Wisconsin, Madison, Wisconsin 53706

Dr. Chantal Dupont has had a long-standing interest in exotic animal ophthalmology. She trained at St. Hyacinthe in Montreal and obtained her DVM and MS degrees from that institution. She completed her Master's degree on the eyes of birds of prey and then completed an internship in Small Animal Medicine and Surgery.

Dr. Chris Murphy is a board-certified member of the American College of Veterinary Ophthalmologists and has been actively involved in exotic animal ophthalmology throughout his career. He has spoken and published widely on the ocular disorders of non-traditional vertebrate species. He is currently an Associate Professor of Ophthalmology at the School of Veterinary Medicine, University of Wisconsin, Madison.

INTRODUCTION

Ocular disorders are frequently observed in reptiles and can be primary or can develop secondary to a systemic disorder. Unlike mammals, but similar to other poikelotherms maintained in captivity, many ocular problems in captive reptiles are related to poor husbandry practices that reflect a lack of awareness of the animal's nutritional and environmental needs.

The reptilian eye shares many similarities with the mammalian eye but also possesses some interesting and unique features. Four of the five orders of reptiles share very similar ocular anatomy. Chelonians, crocodilians, lizards and the tuatara share many ocular similarities. Snakes, however, have lost the typical reptilian pattern during a fossorial period of their history, only to re-evolve with certain significant differences (Walls, 1942). Some of the anatomical differences between reptiles and mammalian species, as well as the most common ocular disorders of reptiles will be illustrated in the following report.

CLINICAL ANATOMY

OCULAR ADNEXA

The eyelids are well developed in most species and the lower lid is more moveable than the upper. In some lizards, certain scales of the lower eyelid are lacking or have become transparent to allow limited vision when the lids are closed (Duke-Elder, 1958). In some geckos, the skink (*Ablepharus* sp.) and all snakes, the lids are fused over the cornea and form a clear spectacle (Fig 1). In snakes and some lizards, the spectacle has been shown to contain many fine vessels which form different patterns of organization depending on the species (Mead, 1976) (Fig 2). These vessels can become rapidly engorged with irritation or inflammation. These vessels also play a role in the wound healing processes of the spectacle (Kumareson S, Paul-Murphy J et al, University of Wisconsin, 1995- pers comm). The upper eyelid of crocodilians contains a bony tarsus which makes it capable of powerful closure. Perhaps the most remarkable eyelids are the chameleon's, which are constricted around the cornea and move with the highly mo-

Fig. 1. Gross morphology of the ophidian (Gaboon viper- *Bitis* sp.) globe. The spectacle forms from the embryonic fusion of the superior and inferior eyelids. In this photograph, it can be seen that a cleft is formed where the spectacle meets the overlying scales. The spectacle is separated from the underlying cornea by the subspectacular space which is filled with tears in life. Also note the nearly spherical lens. (Photograph courtesy Dr. Richard Dubielzig, University of Wisconsin-Madison)

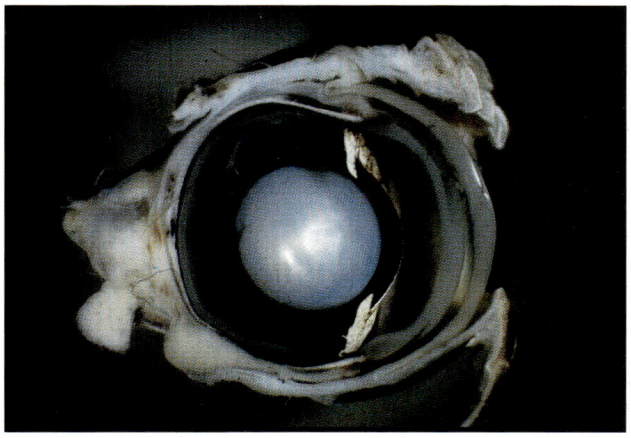

bile globe (Fig. 3). Crocodilians, chelonians and most species of lizards possess a third eyelid. The latter is absent in snakes.

Most lizards possess a Harderian gland, located ventromedially, and a lacrimal gland, located dorsotemporally to the globe (Underwood 1970). Geckos and chameleons only have the Harderian gland. Chelonians possess both a Harderian and a lacrimal gland, which are large, especially in marine turtles. In chelonians, the lacrimal glands also function as an extrarenal salt gland. Crocodilians, in addition to the Harderian and lacrimal glands, possess accessory glands in the conjunctiva. A well developed Harderian gland is found in snakes and the tuatara but a lacrimal gland is absent in these species.

Chelonians do not have a nasolacrimal duct. Their tears are lost by evaporation, absorption by the conjunctiva or spillage from the conjunctival sac. In the other reptiles, the nasolacrimal duct leaves the medial canthus of the eye and enters the roof of the mouth to end just behind or at the base of the vomero-nasal organ of Jacobson (Duke-Elder, 1958). These ducts can become distended if their outflow is obstructed (Fig 4).

GLOBE AND INTRAOCULAR STRUCTURES

The globe is almost spherical, with the antero-posterior axis being the shortest. The rectus muscles are poorly developed, except in lizards, and the retractor bulbi muscle is well developed in most species but is absent in snakes. Movement of the globe is therefore limited, except in chameleons. The sclera is thin and supported anteriorly by a sheet of cartilage. A ring of scleral ossicles is present anterior and superficial to the scleral cartilage which provides shape and support to the globe. The number of scleral ossicles varies between species and is usually between 6-17. In crocodilians, the scleral ossicles are absent but instead, the scleral cartilage extends anteriorly, almost to the ora serrata. In snakes, the sclera is entirely fibrous, lacking scleral cartilage and ossicles (Walls 1942). There is only a thin cartilaginous septum which separates the globes and which cannot offer much resistance to a neoplastic or infectious process extending from one eye to the other.

The cornea is thin and is comprised of an anterior epithelium, stroma, Descemet's membrane and the posterior epithelium (endothelium). Bowman's layer is absent in reptiles. Some geckos are also said to lack Descemet's membrane and endothelium (Walls, 1942, Duke-Elder, 1958).

The iris is thin and possesses well developed striated muscle fibers. The ciliary musculature is also striated and well developed ciliary processes

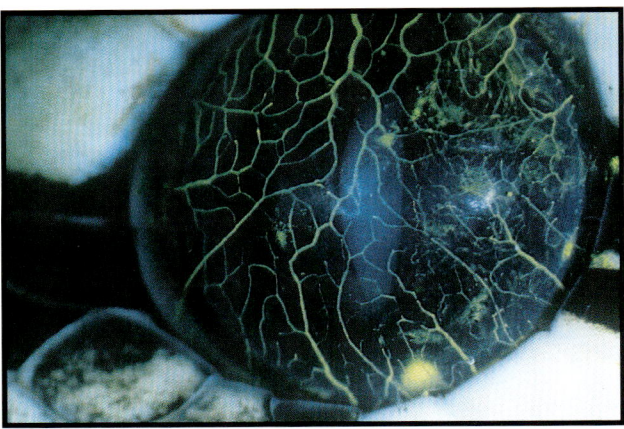

Fig. 2. The microvasculature of the ophidian (ball python- *Python regius*) spectacle. The microvasculature is evident in this anatomic specimen which had been injected with latex. The vasculature of the spectacle can be quite reactive, becoming engorged in association with inflammation.

Fig. 3. Eye and adnexa of a chameleon (*Chamaeleo melleri*). Note the "turret like" arrangement of the lids which move along with the highly mobile globe.

Fig. 4. Outline of the lacrimal duct in a blood python (*Python curtus*). This duct carries tears from the subspectacular space to the region of the vomeronasal organ. Fluorescein had been injected into the subspectacular space which subsequently outlined the duct's course along the roof of the snake's mouth.

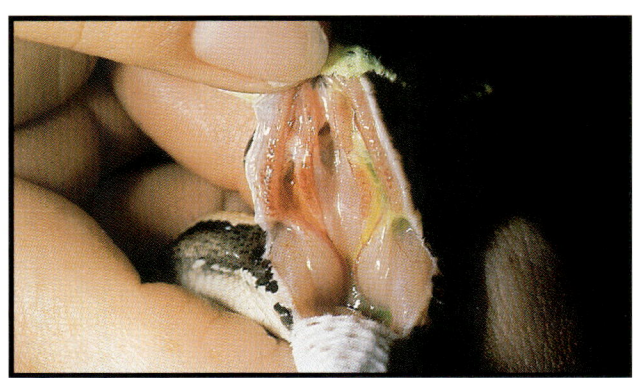

Fig. 5. Horizontal section of the globe of a green iguana (*Iguana iguana*). Note the conus papillaris which protrudes into the vitreous from a base associated with the optic nerve. (Photograph courtesy Dr. Richard Dubielzig, University of Wisconsin-Madison).

are found only in chelonians, crocodilians and snakes. An annular pad, consisting of radially oriented fibers is present at the equatorial region of the lens in many reptiles. It is best developed in lizards and is lacking in snakes. During accommodation in lizards, contraction of the ciliary muscle causes forward and inward movement of the ciliary body, which compresses the lens and reduces its focal length. Aquatic turtles have a well developed iridal musculature which assists in deforming the anterior lens surface. In snakes, accommodation is achieved by forward movement of the lens due to pressure exerted on the vitreous by the ciliary muscle (Walls, 1942, Duke-Elder, 1958). Amphibious reptiles are presented with the task of having to compensate for the refractive loss of the cornea upon submersion in water (thus surrounding the spectacle with media that is of similar refractive index and negating the ability of the spectacle to bend light rays). The loss of the refractive power of the spectacle is compensated in *Thamnophis melanogaster* by posession of an extensive (>100Diopters) range of accommodation while a related species (*T. couchii*) increases its visual resolution underwater by constricting its pupil. Still other *Thamnophis* species did not compensate for the refractive loss of the spectacle when submerged underwater and had poor visual resolution underwater (Schaeffel and de Queiroz 1990). The iridocorneal angle of reptiles generally resembles that of mammals but is not as well developed (Duke-Elder, 1958).

The retina is avascular and nourished by the choroidal vasculature and by the conus papillaris. The latter is a vascular structure derived from the hyaloid vasculature, which arises from the optic nerve head and projects into the vitreous (Fig 5). In snakes, retinal nutrition is also contributed to by a branching array of vessels, the membrana vasculosa retinae, which runs in the posterior vitreous from the periphery of the retina to the optic nerve. The retina contains both rods and cones, their relative proportion representative of the diurnal or nocturnal habits of the different species. Cones predominate in the chelonian retina. Crocodilians possess a tapetum formed by the accumulation of guanine crystals in the retinal pigment epithelium. A well developed fovea is present in lizards.

OPHTHALMOLOGIC EXAMINATION

The ophthalmologic evaluation of a reptile is similar, in many aspects, to the evaluation of a mammal. An adequate source of light and magnification are essential. Although this is best accomplished by a slit-lamp biomicroscope, the 25+ or 40+ diopter lenses of a direct ophthalmoscope are adequate in many instances (Millichamp, 1986). We would also recommend using an optivisor or hand held magnifying lens in the evaluation of periocular structures as well as the anterior segment of the eye. Once the animal is properly restrained, the eyes and adnexa can be evaluated in an orderly fashion. The ocular adnexa and anterior segment of the eye can usually be easily evaluated as opposed to the posterior segment. Similar to birds, most reptiles possess striated iridal and ciliary muscles which enable rapid and extensive constriction of the pupil. Mydriasis can be achieved with general anesthesia, which relaxes the striated iridal musculature, or with the use of a curariform agent applied topically or by intracameral injection. A detailed investigation of the use of curariform agents for mydriasis in reptiles is lacking. Injection of curares into the subspectacular space in snakes has not been effective in inducing mydriasis (Millichamp, 1983). In contrast to other reptiles, the crocodilian pupil is reported to be briskly reactive both to light and drugs (Duke-Elder, 1958).

CONGENITAL AND DEVELOPMENTAL DISORDERS

Various congenital and developmental disorders have been documented in reptiles. These abnormalities are uncommon and can be limited to the eyes and adnexa or be accompanied by other head or skeletal anomalies. These anomalies can be linked to genetic factors or, in many instances, be related to inappropriate environmental conditions during gestation or incubation.

Microphthalmia is the most commonly reported disorder, and seems most common in snakes. It has been described unilaterally or bilaterally, alone or in combination with cranial dysgenesis (Millichamp, 1983). Ensley et al (1978), report microphthalmia in red-headed rat snakes hatchlings in which the eggs had been manually opened because of failure to hatch. Unilateral and bilateral microphthalmia was found in seven out of 16 dead young. Histologically, the eyes were small but otherwise normal, except for the absence of lenses. Millichamp et al, report other cases of microphthalmia in a Nile crocodile (*Crocodylus niloticus*), Indian gharial (*Gavialis gangeticus*), Burmese python and boa constrictor (*Boa constrictor*), the latter associated with cranial dysgenesis. We have observed cases of microphthalmia in California Gopher snakes (*Pituophis catenifer sayi*) as a single entity and in a California King Snake (*Lampropeltis sp.*) that occurred in conjunction with distention of the subspectacular space (Fig 6).

Anophthalmia is extremely rare and can be mistaken with microphthalmia without histologic evidence of the absence of ocular structures. It has been reported either unilaterally or bilaterally in a diamondback terrapin (*Malaclemys terrapin*) with rudimentary eyelids, a red-eared slider turtle (*Trachemys scripta elegans*) and in a colony of northern pine snakes (*Pituophis melanoleucus melanoleucus*), with an established genetically-linked lack of eyes. Finally, it has been demonstrated in a Burmese python (*Python molurus bivittatus*) where histology demonstrated a small area of pigmented retina as the only vestige of ocular tissue (Frye, 1991).

Cyclopia has been described in a clutch of Burmese pythons (*Python molurus bivittataus*), associated with subcutaneous emphysema and in a green sea turtle, associated with microencephaly.

Dermalization of the spectacle and cornea has been seen in an inbred line of longitudinally striped phase gopher snakes (*Pituophis catenifer sayi*) and has been genetically linked (Frye

Fig. 6. Microphthalmia associated with distention of the subspectacular space (pseudobuphthalmos) in a northern California Kingsnake. 6a. Clinical appearance of snake at 4 weeks of age.

1994). One parent was affected as well as approximately 25% of the offspring (Fig 7).

Even though blind or visually compromised, reptiles with congenital anomalies frequently do surprisingly well and learn to accept food from their keeper.

Fig. 6b. "Subspectaculagram": radiograph taken after injection of contrast material into the subspectacular space. Note that the microphthalmic globe is evident as a filling defect adjacent to the medial orbital wall.

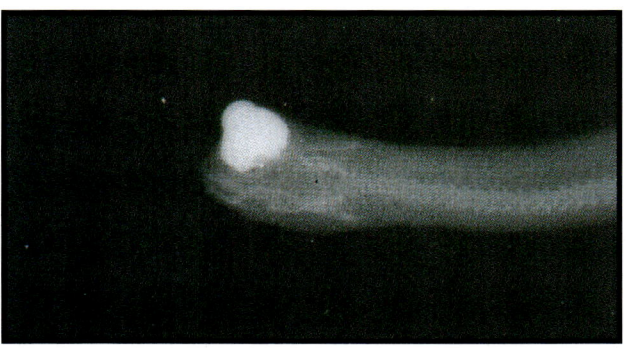

Fig. 6c. Clinical appearance of microphthalmic globe after the spectacle had been removed during enucleation.

Fig. 7. Dermalization of the spectacle in a gopher snake. The dark pigmentation in the center of this dermalized spectacle creates a false image of a pupil (pseudopupil).

NON-INFECTIOUS DISEASES

Perhaps one of the most commonly recognized ocular disorders in aquatic or semiaquatic turtles is hypovitaminosis A (Frye, 1991, Millichamp, 1991, Millichamp, 1983). Turtles of any age can be affected but this condition occurs most often in juvenile turtles fed a diet rich in animal proteins and deficient in either beta carotene or preformed vitamin A, such as meat and insects. The first noticeable clinical sign is a mild to moderate eyelid and orbital edema. As the disease progresses, the eyelids become swollen to the point of causing blindness (Fig 8). Because most chelonians are sight-feeders, the affected turtles will stop eating and progressively weaken. The pathogenesis is squamous metaplasia of the orbital glands and their ducts with the accumulation of desquamated material which blocks the ducts and cause the glands

Fig. 8. Hypovitaminosis A in an aquatic turtle. Note that the eyes are swollen shut which interferes with feeding.

to increase in size. Secondary bacterial or fungal infection can also be present. Squamous metaplasia of the renal, pancreatic, gastrointestinal and respiratory epithelium contributes to the animal's demise in untreated cases (Zwart, 1967). Treatment in the early stage includes correcting the diet to include vitamin A, either by feeding a commercial trout pellet or adding small amounts of cod liver oil to the diet. Vitamin A is injected at a dose of 1000 to 1500 units IM, at weekly intervals until the edema subsides, for at least three treatments. Topical antibiotics or antifungals are used as needed. Animals that do not eat need to be force fed grounded trout pellets. It is very rare for tortoises to develop hypovitaminosis A and treatment of tortoises with vitamin A can cause serious epidermal disease! (Frye 1991)

Chemical-induced keratitis or blepharitis occur when reptiles are exposed to liquid or gaseous toxic substances (Frye, 1994). Terrarium or aquarium disinfectants as well as anti parasitical sprays or powders have to be used judiciously and by following an expert's recommendations. Treatment is symptomatic and includes washing the chemical off the reptile and using broad spectrum antibiotic ointments with or without corticosteroids.

Opacification of the third eyelid by unidentified deposits is reported in aging captive alligators (Millichamp, 1983). The nature of these deposits could possibly represent calcium or other salt deposits in the third eyelid.

By far the most commonly observed ocular problems in snakes involve the spectacle. The spectacle absorbs wear and tear from contact with objects in the environment and then, like a disposable contact lens, it is replaced with a pristine newly formed spectacle at each ecdysis (shedding). It is therefore normal to observe a variety of scratches and small mildly opaque patches on the superficial surface of the spectacle immediately prior to ecdysis. Occasionally, small dents in the spectacle surface are seen which may disappear after ecdysis though, if the germinal layer is permanently deformed, an indentation of the spectacle may be permanent. Retained spectacles occur frequently in snakes. It is typically related to management problems such as insufficient humidity and temperature, improper diet or not providing adequate 'furniture' for the snake to rub against in the process of ecdysis. It can also be associated with any systemic illness. It is not uncommon for a snake to be presented for a retained spectacle only to find out that it is suffering from a systemic disease such as pneumonia. The outer layer of the spectacle is normally shed at each molting cycle but in this condition, one to several layers of the outer spectacle may accumulate over several molt cycles

(Fig 9). Mites or ticks can predispose an animal to this problem because these parasites feed through the thin, non-keratinized skin in the recess between the spectacle and periocular scales (see Fig 1), causing hemorrhage, scarring and accumulation of debris at the edge of the spectacle (Millichamp, 1991).

An attempt can be made to remove the retained spectacle by moistening it with olive oil or acetylcysteine (Mucomyst) and using fine forceps. Another relatively atraumatic technique is to use scotch tape : apply it to the retained spectacle and gently apply traction. If the spectacle does not come off with gentle force, more aggressive efforts should be avoided as avulsion of the newly formed spectacle and its underlying germinal epithelium can cause corneal damage and the eye may be lost. It is far better not to remove a tightly adherent spectacle and wait until the next shed. Correcting any underlying disorder and increasing the humidity in the terrarium is essential. 'Swimming" the snake for an hour, several times a week can be very beneficial. The snake should be placed in a shallow container with warm water and observed for distress as snakes can drown if made to swim excessively in deep containers especially if they are compromised by an underlying systemic disease such as pneumonia.

Pseudobuphthalmos occurs commonly in snakes and lizards which possess spectacles (Millichamp, 1991, Frye, 1991, Millichamp, 1983, Ensley et al 1978). A blockage of the nasolacrimal duct with the accumulation of a clear fluid secreted by the Harderian gland and distention of the subspectacular space occurs (Figs 6 & 10). This may be confused with buphthalmos or true enlargement of the globe associated with glaucoma. This blockage can be congenital, secondary to scarring or inflammation. It can also arise from occlusion caused by tumors or granulomas, or secondary to an ascending infection from the oral cavity. It is also occasionally seen as a transient phenomenon associated with the ecdysis cycle. Care should be taken in recommending aggressive treatment of this condition for some of these cases will resolve spontaneously after undergoing subsequent molts. Additionally, many of these animals appear to be comfortable and function adequately even if the condition is bilateral. For this reason, in the absence of a clearly defined underlying cause, it is recommended to allow the animal to undergoing several sheds prior to pursuing surgical options.

Surgical resection of a wedge of the spectacle is not advised as a definitive treatment for this condition as it will probably recur after the spectacle wound has healed. A surgical site of drainage can be created from the subspectacular space into the oral cavity. This can be performed after resection of a 30° wedge of the spectacle and introducing a needle from the

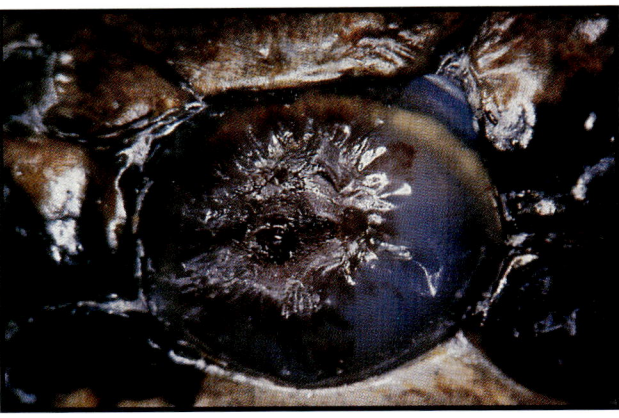

Fig. 9. Retained spectacle in a 12 year old Burmese python (*Python molurus bivittatus*). Note the distention and proliferation of the spectacular vasculature which has occurred secondarily.

conjunctival sac into the mouth as described by Millichamp et al (1986). Drainage may also be provided by retrograde cannulation of the lacrimal duct from the oral cavity. This is performed by identifying the duct in the roof of the mouth (this may be clearly distended with clear fluid or assistance in visualization can be obtained by injecting a small quantity of fluorescein into the subspectacular space using a 30 ga needle, Fig 4), cannulating the drainage duct with fine polyethylene tubing and entering the subspectacular space. The tubing is then secured into the roof of the mouth using fine non-absorbable suture (Fig 11). Systemic antibiotics should be administered as several snakes have been observed that developed ascending infections with resultant subspectacular abscess formation following this surgery.

Non-inflammatory opacities of the cornea are occasionally observed in lizards and chelonians. In chelonians, we have most often observed such opacities in middle aged to older tortoises and clinically they appear to represent a degenerative change characterized by cholesterol deposition (Fig 12). They are slowly progressive and may be unilateral or bilateral. They are typically an incidental finding. In rare cases, a degree of ocular discomfort can develop in association with punctate epithelial defects overlying the region of corneal deposits. Generally, however, they are not associated with any significant clinical symptoms. Whether they occur in association with a hyperlipidemia is unknown. In lizards, we have observed bilateral corneal opacities in Thai water dragons (*Physignathus cocincinus*) that appear similar to corneal dystrophic disorders in mammals (Fig 13). Evaluation of blood parameters have been normal in these individuals. A true corneal dystrophy is heritable but the heritability of this disorder in lizards is unknown.

Fig. 10. Distention of the sub-brillar space (pseudobuphthalmos) in a Tokay Gekko (Gekko gecko) secondary to stomatitis (mouthrot).

Fig. 10a and b. Clinical appearance of the deformation of the brille occurring due to distention of the sub-brillar space. The globe itself is of normal size.

Fig. 10c. The cause of the impaired flow of tears , and thus the distention of the sub-brillar space, is bacterial stomatitis (mouthrot).

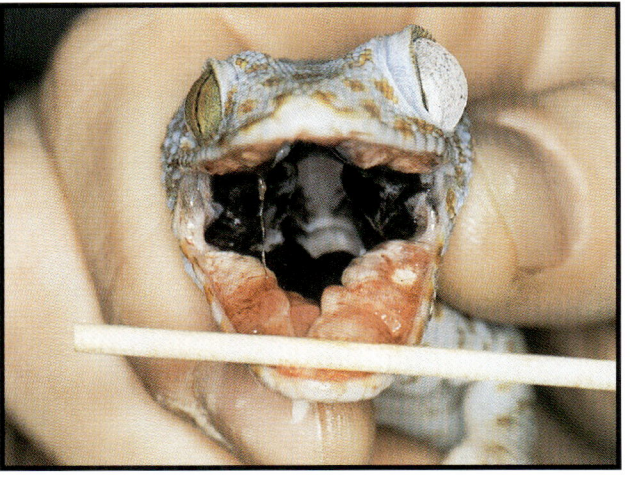

LENS

Nuclear sclerosis is observed in older reptiles. This normal aging process of the lens has no visual consequences for the animal and requires no intervention. Cataracts are encountered sporadically in reptiles and can be unilateral or bilateral (Fig 14). They have been reported in a number of species at various ages, sometimes being present at birth. Acquired cataracts have been described in various snakes, alligators and tortoises following trauma or uveitis related to capture, transport, overcrowding and poor hygiene or nutrition (Millichamp, 1983). Cataracts that developed during hibernation have been described in captive European tortoises (Lawton, 1989).

Chelonians have extremely soft lenses which makes removal of the lens through a fine diameter needle possible. Successful cataract surgery has been performed on several California desert tortoises (*Gopherus agassizi*) using a 23-25 ga needle to aspirate lens material with the anterior chamber being maintained via a separate infusion needle introduced through the limbus.

GLOBE AS A WHOLE AND POSTERIOR SEGMENT

Diseases of the posterior segment have only rarely been reported, most likely because of their small pupils and the difficulty in examining the posterior part of the eye. Millichamp, 1983, reports patchy chorioretinitis in adult alligators. The tapetum showed areas of depigmentation and pigment clumping. Degeneration of all retinal layers was found at necropsy of an adult reticulated python (*Python reticulatus*) which died suddenly, apparently from a cerebrovascular embolus. Nematode larvae were found densely packed into the choroid of a red-eared slider, without any evidence of ocular involvement (Schmidt, 1981). We have observed chorioretinitis and conus papillitis (with hemorrhage of the conus papillaris in some cases) in Tokay geckos (*Gekko gecko*) that have bacterial septicemia.

Ocular neoplasia has occasionally been reported. Fibromas, papillomas and fibropapillomas are reported in juvenile green sea turtles (*Chelonia mydas*) from Florida (Brooks, 1994). Sites of origin included the eyelids, the conjunctiva, the limbus or the cornea. In some turtles, these were locally invasive, leading to blindness and systemic debilitation. These are thought to be of infectious origin. Surgical removal of the tumors is recommended in cases with minimal systemic disease.

Proptosis or prolapse of the globe from the bony orbit can result after trauma (Frye, 1991). The eye should be kept moist until assistance is reached. If the injury is recent and the globe has not sustained marked damage, an attempt can be made to replace it. Enucleation is recommended for a globe that cannot be salvaged.

We have observed several cases of transient exophthalmos in snakes (two boas and one python) of undetermined cause which resolves over a 2-3 month period of time. Slowly progressive exophthalmos has been seen in a Rhino Iguana (*Cyclura cornta*) that became associated with exposure keratopathy. Ultrasound and CT evaluations suggested the cause to be due to an arteriovenous malformation.

Post hibernation blindness has been encountered in tortoises of the genus *Testudo* (Lawton, 1989). The reptiles had been exposed to unusually cold temperatures during hibernation. Ocular changes observed included cataracts, vitreal haziness, retinopathies and central nervous damage. In some animals, the blindness was temporary but in others, it was permanent. More commonly observed in tortoises is a post-hibernation conjunctival discharge which resolves over a several week period as the animal warms up and becomes more active. This is occasionally associated with a secondary bacterial infection which may necessitate treatment with topical antibiotic solution.

INFECTIOUS DISEASES

PARASITISM

Mites and ticks are often found in wild caught species. They can lodge themselves in the scales surrounding the eyes and cause a dermatitis or blepharitis or, interfere with the shedding of the spectacle because of scarring or debris accumulation. The recess formed at the junction of the spectacle and periocular scales is often a chosen site for the parasites since blood is easily accessible through the thin and non-keratinized skin.

Millichamp et al, report leeches of the genus *Ozobranchus* affecting the conjunctiva in green sea turtles and nematode larvae in the choroid of a red-eared slider (*Trachemys scripta elegans*).

Ticks, leeches and other large external parasites can usually be removed manually. A careful exam of the whole reptile and disinfection of the environment are warranted. Treatment of mites is best accomplished by systemic administration of ivermectin.

VIRAL INFECTIONS

Jacobson et al, report pox-like skin lesions in three captive juvenile spectacled caimans (*Caiman sclerops*) in Florida. Small gray, white papular lesions were scattered over the skin and particularly prominent on the palpebrae, phalanges and integument overlying the mandibles and maxillae. In two

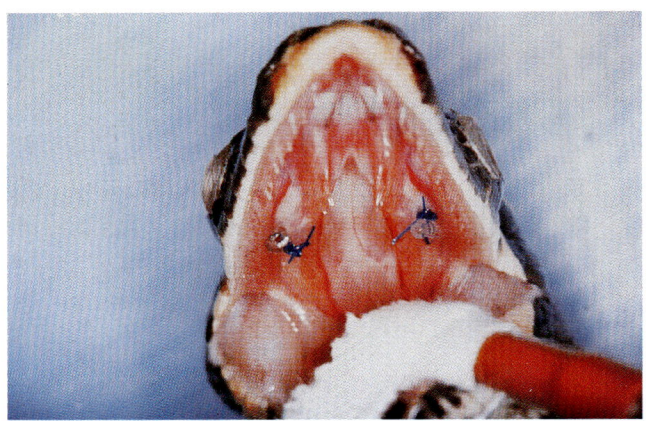

Fig. 11. Retrograde cannulation of the subspectacular space in a young blood python (*Python curtus*). A clutch of blood pythons were observed which had congenital pseudo-buphthalmos. The duct was identified by injection of fluorescein into the subspectacular space (see fig 4), a fine incision made and fine diameter polyethylene tubing introduced in a retrograde fashion into the subspectacular space. The oral end of the tubing was sutured in place with fine diameter prolene suture.

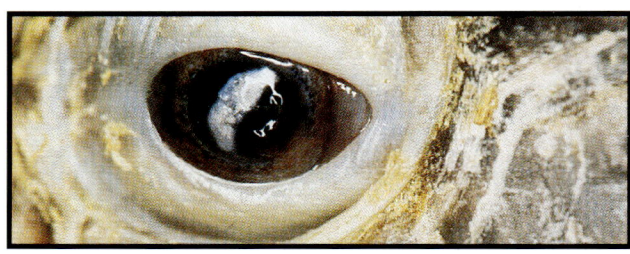

Fig. 12. Corneal opacity in an 11 year old Hermann's tortoise (*Testudo hermanni*). The cause of these lesions in tortoises is unknown. Their clinical appearance is similar to a cholesterol degeneration observed in mammals. They are often central or paracentral in the cornea suggesting that perhaps exposure may play a role in their development.

Fig. 13. Bilateral corneal opacities in a Thai water dragon (*Physignathus cocincinus*). These lesions are bilateral, non-painful, slowly progressive, unassociated with a systemic disease and non-ulcerative. Their heritability is unknown.

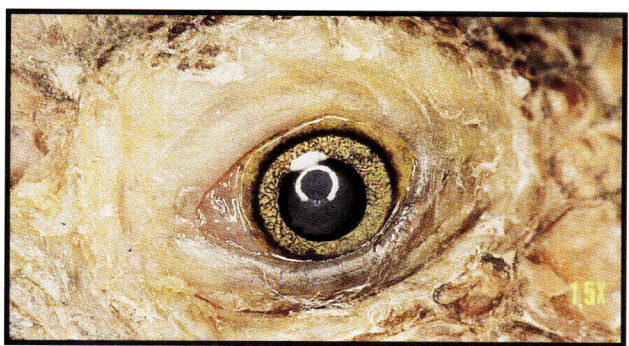

Fig. 14. Complete cataract in a mature California desert tortoise (*Gopherus agassizi*). Cataracts can be successfully removed in chelonians employing fine diameter needles due to the extreme softness of the lens.

Fig. 15. Bacterial conjunctivitis in *Anolis carolinensis*. Several lizards were presented that had bacterial infections in association with fine sand foreign bodies (fine sand was used as the flooring substrate) in the conjunctival sac. Cytology documented rods and cocci to be present. Flushing of the conjunctival sac to remove particulate matter and broad spectrum topical antibiotics (polymyxin-neomycin-gramicidin solution applied 3x daily) brought about complete resolution.

Fig. 16. Bacterial conjunctivitis in a box turtle (*Terrapene carolina*). *Pasteurella testudinii* was isolated. An underlying cause for this bacterial infection was not identified. A large accumulation of casseated material was removed from the conjunctival sac which had contributed to the ocular discomfort of this animal.

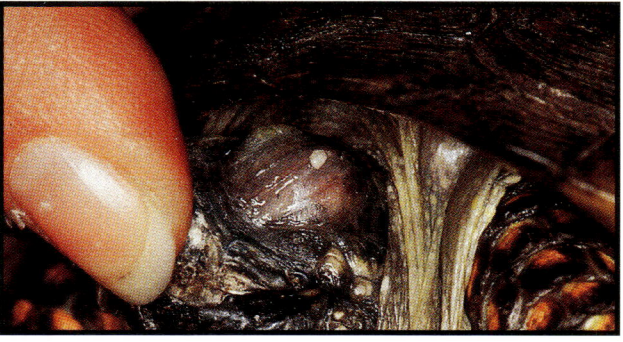

animals, the lesions regressed and disappeared over a month's time with no treatment but the third animal developed conjunctivitis and chemosis and was euthanized. Histopathologic evaluation revealed the lesions to be confined to the skin. Many epithelial cells contained eosinophilic intracytoplasmic inclusions compatible with Poxvirus.

Herpesvirus infection has been described in juvenile green sea turtles (*Chelonia mydas*) at Cayman Turtle Farm in British West Indies. The disease is respiratory in nature and macroscopically the eyes are often covered with a caseous conjunctival exudate, there is periglottal necrosis, tracheitis with intraluminal caseous and laminated necrotic debris and severe pneumonia. Intranuclear viral particles were found in periglottal and tracheal epithelial cells and were identified as herpesvirus. A mixed population of primarily gram-negative microorganisms was also isolated from the tracheal and glottal lesions (Jacobson, 1986). A Herpesvirus-like infection was also described in Argentine tortoises (*Geochelone chilensis*) (Jacobson, 1985). These tortoises were imported along with red-foot tortoises (*Geochelone carbonaria*) and started dying one month after arrival at the import station. Signs of nasal and ocular discharge, regurgitation, anorexia, lethargy and necrotizing stomatitis were noted. The red-footed tortoises remained healthy. Eosinophilic intranuclear inclusions were seen within oral mucosal epithelial cells, typical of herpesvirus. Treatment with Gentamicin (5mg/kg IM) every 48 hours and vitamin mixture IM in one group of tortoises did not change the clinical course of the disease over a week period.

BACTERIAL AND FLAGELLATE INFECTIONS

Bacterial infections have frequently been encountered in reptiles and can involve almost any ocular or adnexal structure. Gram negative organisms are commonly isolated. These infections can result from trauma, penetrating wounds, foreign bodies, bites of ectoparasites or from hematogenous spread of a systemic infection.

Bacterial conjunctivitis is often observed in lizards and chelonians (Figs 15 & 16). The causative organisms are varied. *Aeromonas* (Cooper et al 1980) and *Pseudomonas* (Millicamp et al, 1983) have been reported in association with conjunctivitis in lizards. We have observed bacterial conjunctivitis in association with fine sand particles in lizards. The sand had been used as the flooring substrate for the animals. Culture and conjunctival cytology are invaluable aids in determining the organism involved and thus the appropriate antibiotic regimen to initiate.

The subspectacular space is a common site for infection in snakes and lizards with spectacles. Infectious agents may reach this site hematogenously, via a penetrating injury or ascension from the oral cavity via the nasolacrimal duct. A 30 degree wedge resection of a portion of the spectacle will allow draining of the infected fluid and permit sampling for cultures. *Pseudomonas* sp., *Proteus* sp., and *Providencia rettgeri*, commonly isolated from oral infections, may be recovered from the subspectacular fluid (Gelatt 1994). Flagellates are sometimes also recovered but their role in the development of subspectacular infection is unknown (Fig 17). An ocular ultrasound may be useful in localizing the fluid and in evaluating the intraocular structures. Some cases resolve spontaneously but others require surgical intervention. The subspectacular space may be drained by removing a 30 degree wedge section of the spectacle (Gelatt, 1994, Millichamp, 1986) and flushing the caseous debris out from the subspectacular space (Fig 18). Antibiotics can then be instilled daily using a blunt tipped cannula for 1-2 weeks as the spectacle defect heals. During this period of treatment the spectacle will often become edematous and opaque. This resolves in the weeks following completion of therapy. Careful examination of the mouth and treatment of ulcerative and necrotic stomatitis with systemic antibiotics is essential to a successful outcome.

Abscesses and pyogranulomatous lesions have been found on the eyelids, the conjunctiva, the retrobulbar space, the subspectacular space, periorbital or intraocular. They are commonly seen in tortoises and lizards (Fig 19). Abscesses in reptiles usually contain thick, caseous material and need to be surgically curetted in most instances. Following removal of the caseated material, the surgical wound is flushed with betadine or nolvasan and the animal is often placed on systemic antibiotics. The wound is flushed daily until closure. The eye is sometimes lost secondary to pressure from the abscess or from exophthalmia and exposure. Abscess-like, but non purulent, lesions comprised of an accumulation of cellular debris within the conjunctival sac have been seen in chelonians following hibernation (Frye, 1991).

Anterior uveitis and hypopyon are usually secondary to a systemic infection. *Klebsiella pneumonia* has been isolated from lungs of Tokay geckos (Bonney, 1978). One of the geckos demonstrated ocular symptoms of unilateral buphthalmos and hypopyon. Surgical removal of the hypopyon was performed via a limbal incision through the spectacle and cornea but the gecko died of pneumonia shortly after the surgery. Hypopyon in a red-footed tortoise (*Geochelone carbonaria*) is also described

Fig. 17. Subspectacular abscess in a Gaboon viper (*Bitis* sp.). Note the extreme distention of the subspectacular space with inspisated purulent material. Flagellates were found in association with the purulent material. (Photograph courtesy of Richard Dubielzig DVM, University of Wisconsin-Madison).

Fig. 18. Resection of a wedge of spectacle for treatment of a subspectacular abscess in a fox snake (*Elaphe vulpina*). After removal of the wedge the purulent material is flushed out using a blunt tipped cannula and topical antibiotics administered. A careful physical exam must be done as subspectacular abscesses are often associated with stomatitis.

Fig. 19. Curetting of a periocular abscess in a California desert tortoise (*Gopherus agassizi*). After making a stab incision with a scalpel, the inspisated purulent material is removed and the wound flushed with betadine. Systemic antibiotic therapy is initiated and the wound is flushed daily with betadine until the wound is closed.

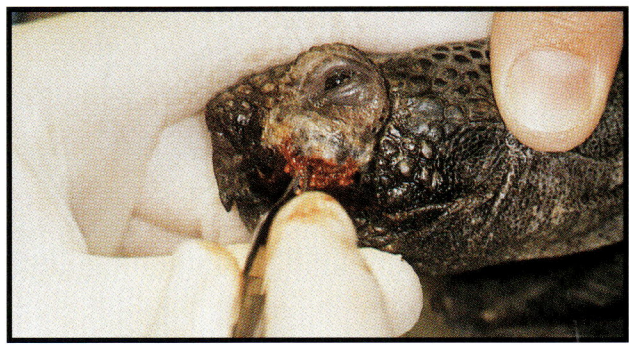

secondary to pneumonia (Tomson, 1976).

Panophthalmitis is an infection involving all the ocular structures. There is usually prominent swelling and discoloration of the eye (Frye, 1991). If left untreated, the globe will either enlarge and be prone to trauma, or shrink down. Enucleation and use of systemic antibiotics are usually required.

Hyphema or blood in the anterior chamber of the eye is rarely seen in reptiles (Frye, 1991). It may be caused by trauma to the globe, helminth parasites, coagulopathies or an intraocular bleeding neoplasm. If no history of trauma is given, a thorough examination of the reptile is warranted.

FUNGAL INFECTIONS

Fungal infections affecting the ocular structures have been described in chelonians, lizards and snakes. Spread from a necrotizing skin infection to the eyelids or spectacle is usually seen. Identified predisposing factors include trauma and poor environmental conditions. Diagnosis is usually by identification of hyphae on cytologic or histopathologic specimens. Culture and identification of the agent has been unsuccessful in several cases. Treatment begins by correcting the environmental factors.

Mycotic keratitis has been described in a Reticulated python (Collette, 1978). Conjunctivitis and corneal opacities had first been noticed and had not responded to topical antibiotic and steroid ointment and systemic antibiotics. At shedding, the spectacle was retained and the eye was still cloudy. A small mass was then palpated under the spectacle, enlarged and enucleation was elected. Spores and mycelia with branching filaments and septation were identified in the corneal epithelium and stroma. These structures were also identified in the sclera, ciliary body, choroid and retina. A rainbow boa (*Epicrates cenchria maurus*) also had fungal infection and was enucleated (Zwart, 1973). Enucleation in snakes does not seem to interfere with normal shedding.

REFERENCES

—**Bonney, CH; Hartfield, DA; Schmidt, RE:**
Klebsiella pneumoniae infection with secondary hypopyon in Tokay Gecko Lizards. J Amer Vet Med Assoc, 1978; 173(9): 1115-1116.

—**Brooks, DE; Ginn, PE; Miller, TR, et al:**
Ocular fibropapillomas of Green Turtles (*Chelonia mydas*). Vet Pathol, 1994; 31: 335-339.

—**Collette BE; Curry, OH.**
Mycotic keratitis in a reticulated python. J Amer Vet Med Assoc. 1978. 173: 1117-1118.

—**Cooper JE, McClelland MH, Needham JR. 1980.**
An eye infection in laboratory lizards associated with *Aeromonas* sp. Lab Anim. 14: 149-151.

—**Duke-Elder, S:**
The eye in evolution. In, System of ophthalmology. St-Louis, CV Mosby, 1958.

—**Ensley PK; Anderson MP; Bacon JP. 1978.**
Ophthalmic disorders in three snakes. J Zoo An Med, 9: 57-59.

—**Frye, FL:**
Ophthalmic conditions. In, Reptile care. An atlas of diseases and treatments. Vol.2. T.F.H. Publications Inc., Neptune City NJ, 1991, pp. 331-344.

—**Frye, FL; Gillespie, DS:**
Tracing the etiology of ocular opacities. Vet Med, November 1994: 1385-1387.

—**Gelatt, KN; Gelatt, JP:**
Surgery of the nasolacrimal and tear system. In, Handbook of small animal ophthalmic surgery. Vol. 1. Pergamon, Trowbridge, 1994, pp. 125-143.

—**Jacobson, ER; Clubb, S; Gaskin, JM et al:**
Herpesvirus-like infection in Argentine tortoises. J Amer Vet Med Assoc, 1985; 187(11): 1227-1229.

—**Jacobson, ER; Gaskin, JM; Roelke, M et al:**
Conjunctivitis, tracheitis, and pneumonia associated with herpesvirus infection in green sea turtles. J Amer Vet Med Assoc, 1986; 189(9): 1020-1023.

—**Jacobson, ER; Popp, JA; Shields, RP et al:**
Poxlike skin lesions in captive caimans. J Amer Vet MedAssoc, 1979; 175(9): 937-940.

—**Lawton, MPC; Stoakes, LC:**
Post hibernation blindness in Tortoises. Proc. Third Int. Colloquium Path. Reptiles and Amphibians, 1989; 97-98.

—**Mead, AW:**
Vascularity of the reptilian spectacle. Invest Ophthalmol, 1976; 15(7): 587-591.

—**Millichamp, NJ:**
Exotic animal ophthalmology. In, Veterinary ophthalmology, KN Gelatt (Ed). Lea and Febiger, Philadelphia, 1991, pp. 680-705.

—**Millichamp, NJ; Jacobson, ER:**
Ophthalmic diseases of reptiles. In, Current veterinary therapy IX, small animal practice, WB Saunders company, Philadelphia, 1986, pp. 621-624.

—**Millichamp, NJ; Jacobson, ER; Dziezyc, J:**
Conjunctivoralostomy for treatment of an occluded lacrimal duct in a blood python. J Amer Vet Med Assoc, 1986; 189(9): 1136-1138.

—**Millichamp, NJ; Jacobson, ER; Wolf, ED:**
Diseases of the eye and ocular adnexae in reptiles. J Amer Vet Med Assoc, 1983; 183(11): 1205-1212.

—**Schaeffel, F, de Queiroz A.**
Alternative Mechanisms of enhanced underwater vision in the garter snakes *Thamnophis melanogaster* and *T. couchii.* Copeia, 1990 (1); 50-58.

—**Tomson, FN; McDonald, SE; Wolf, ED:**
Hypopyon in a tortoise. J Amer Vet Med Assoc, 1976; 169: 942.

—**Underwood G. The Eye. In :**
Biology of the Reptilia . Morphology B Vol 2. Gans, C; Parsons, T; eds. Academic Press New York. 1970. pp 1-97.

—**Walls, GL:**
The vertebrate eye and its adaptive radiation. Bloomfield Hills, MI, Cranbrook Institute of Science, 1942.

—**Zwart, P; Verwer, MAJ; DeVries, GA et al:**
Fungal infection of the eyes of the snake *Epicrates cenchria maurus*: Enucleation under halothane narcosis. J Small Anim Pract, 1973; 14: 773-779.

REPRODUCTIVE DISORDERS

Ms. Sharon Redrobe
BSc (Hons) BVetMed MRCVS
Associate in Laboratory and Exotic Animal Medicine
Department of Veterinary Clinical Studies
Royal (Dick) School of Veterinary Studies
Edinburgh University
Summerhall Square
Edinburgh
EH9 1QH
United Kingdom

Sharon Redrobe attended the Royal Veterinary College, London University, UK where she gained a First Class Honours degree in Basic Medical Sciences with Physiology and served as Student Union President before graduating veterinary medicine with distinction in her elective subject (Zoo and Exotic Animal Medicine). After a brief period as an assistant at a Small Animal Hospital, she took up a Lecturer position at Edinburgh University where she is jointly responsible for laboratory animal care in the University, writing and presenting exotic animal lecture courses for veterinary undergraduates and running a first opinion and referral exotic animal clinic from the Royal (Dick) School of Veterinary Studies, Edinburgh University. She is also the assistant veterinarian for Edinburgh Zoo, whose reptile department has successfully bred and maintained many rare species. Recently, Sharon was invited to be a founder member of the European chapter of the ARAV.

INTRODUCTION

An important aim of the captive husbandry of reptile species must be successful reproduction. Reproductive disorders in reptiles are relatively uncommon when compared to other clinical conditions (Frye 1991). Although reptiles show various types of senescence (death at mating, gradual senescence, negligible senescence) depending upon species, reproductive senility has not been demonstrated conclusively in any aging reptile populations (Patnaik 1994).

There are approximately 6547 species of reptiles, many of which have not been subjected to scientific study of their reproductive systems nor have many disorders been recognized in all species. Thus a chapter on reproductive disorders of reptiles will naturally be biased towards those species commonly kept in captivity. This chapter will divide the class reptilia into snakes, lizards, turtles and crocodilians and so will of necessity include broad generalizations about each group. The reproductive disorders of certain more common captive species will be highlighted.

CLINICAL EXAMINATION.

A full history (anamnesis) and clinical examination should always be obtained even when the animal presents with what seems to be an 'obvious' reproductive disorder to ensure that no concurrent disease is also present and to determine external factors which may have an influence on the disorder. Most reptile disorders, including reproductive ones, are due to poor husbandry practices (Raiti 1994). The history should include the cage size, levels and instrumentation of temperature, humidity and lighting, substrate type, diet, frequency of feeding, cleaning, defecation and ecdysis (shedding), presence of cagemates, source of animal (wild/captive bred), age, weight, prior diseases and any routine treatments. The maintenance of cage cards by the client is to be encouraged to allow more accurate anamnesis. A full clinical examination should include passive observation of the animal at rest, then a careful evaluation by palpation, auscultation of heart, lungs and gastrointestinal tract, examination of nostrils, eyes, mouth, ears/tympanic membrane, cloaca, appendages and skin/scales/shell, and measurement of the weight and dimensions of the patient. (see Table page 193)

DIAGNOSTIC TECHNIQUES

The following diagnostic techniques may be usefully employed in the investigation of a reproductive disorder, and in determining the extent to which supportive therapy may be required. It is vital to the health of the patient that concurrent diseases are also diagnosed and treated, especially where these are life-threatening or form part of the etiology of the reproductive disorder.

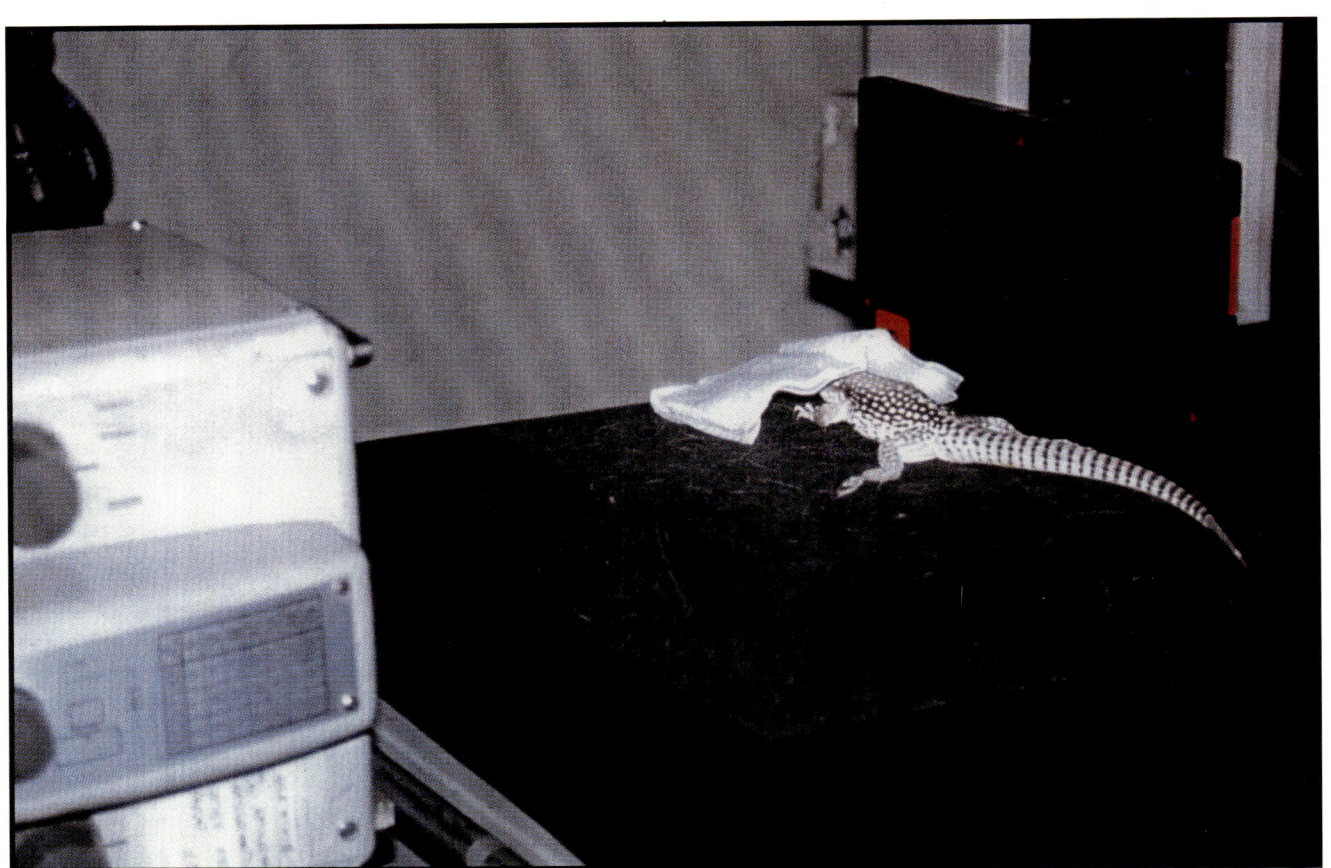

Figure 1. Positioning a lizard for a lateral radiograph. A horizontal beam is preferred, enabling the lizard to be radiographed in a standing position so that the internal organs will be in the natural anatomical positions.

History Relevant to Reproductive Disorders (and associated diseases)	Concurrent diseases important in reproductive disorders
History of stress (dystocia)	metabolic bone disease
poor husbandry (dystocia, salpingitis, abnormal ovarian function)	renal disease
change in behavior (dystocia, pseudopregnancy)	hepatic disease
poor handling technique (aseptic ovarian inflammation, follicular rupture. egg fracture)	cloacal disorders
trauma/fighting/repeated mating (egg rupture/peritonitis, paraphimosis)	soft tissue calcification (see Fig. 3)
sexing with probe (lacerated hemipenes)	

BLOOD ANALYSIS

Hematology and biochemistry can prove valuable in assessing the reptile patient with a reproductive disorder. Dehydration, suggested by a high packed cell volume, creatinine and blood urea nitrogen and uric acid must be corrected to stabilize the patient. A low blood glucose indicates starvation or septicemia. Female reptiles can produce a marked periovulatory hypercalcemia which has no pathological significance (Anderson 1992) but serves as a useful marker of that stage of the reproductive cycle. A high white cell count and their level of toxic degeneration provides a measure of the severity of infection. Blood biochemistry enables the elucidation of various organ involvement in the disease.

BACTERIOLOGY

Culture of infected parts of the reproductive tract e.g. intra-operatively, by aspiration of infected ova, allows identification of the pathological organisms and sensitivity testing allows the selection of appropriate antibiotic therapy.

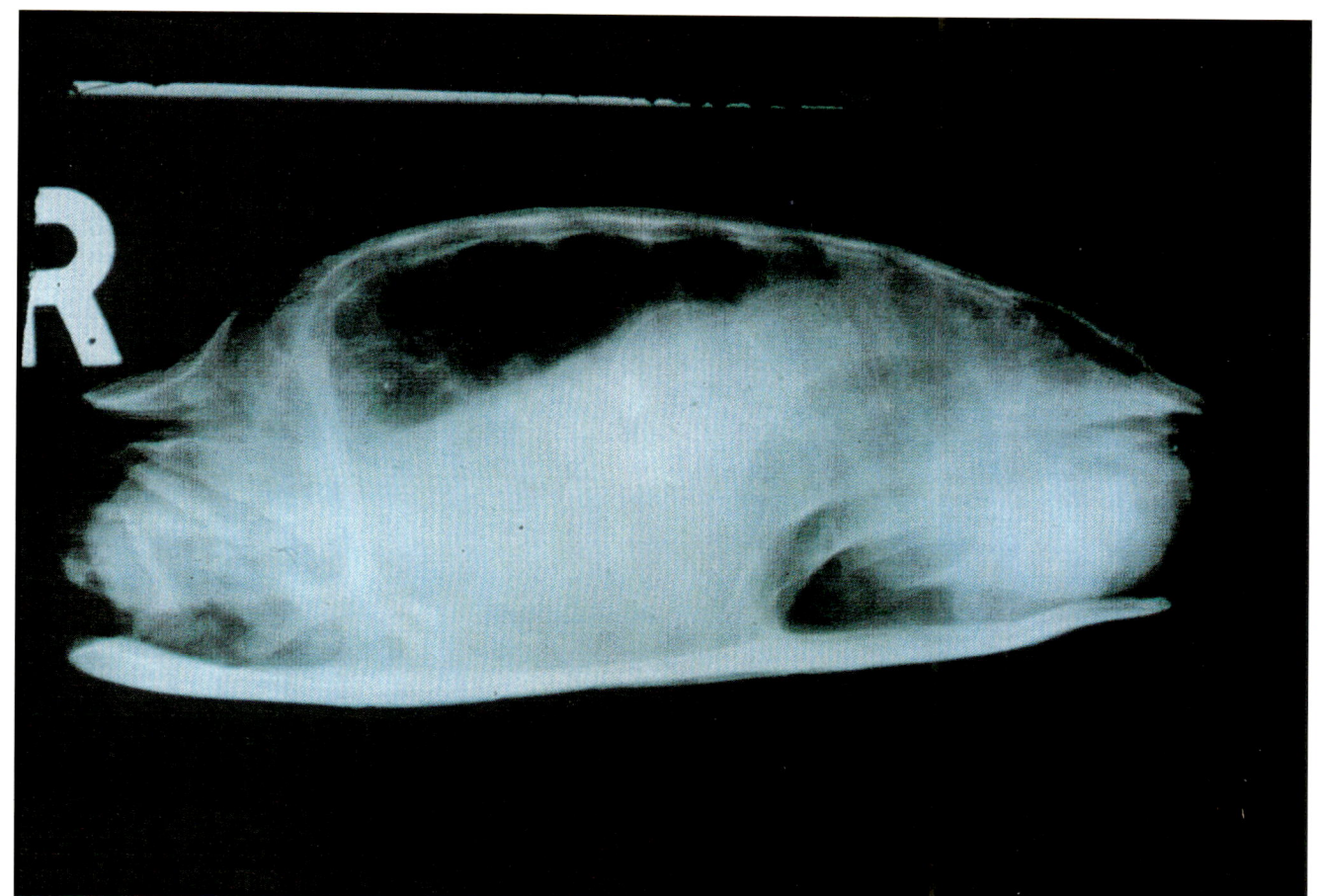

Figure 2. A lateral whole body radiograph of a gravid Hermann's tortoise (*Testudo hermanni*). The outline of eggs may be seen in the caudal coelom.

DIAGNOSTIC IMAGING

The two most common methods, radiography and ultrasonography, will be described. The radiographic features of certain conditions will be described under the relevant section. Magnetic resonance imaging (MRI) and computerized tomography (CT) scans would be useful in the diagnosis of certain conditions but these tests are not yet widely available and so will not be described. Transillumination of thin skinned, smaller species allows the identification of eggs/ masses within the coelom. Laparoscopy allows direct visualization of the reproductive tract however to date little has been published describing the normal and abnormal laparoscopic appearance of the reptile reproductive tract.

Radiography

Most reptiles have been shown to be refractory to diagnostic (mild) doses of radiation (Atland et al 1951, Blair et al 1967, Brooks 1962) and have even been shown to be relatively resistant to larger doses of radiation that would produce harmful effects in higher vertebrates (Cosgrove 1965, 1971; Turner and Lannow 1968). Thus the beneficial effects of diagnostic radiography generally outweigh the potential risk, even in the gravid female.

Positioning is important in interpreting the radiographs and allowing normal anatomical relationships to be maintained. Generally only two views are required; the dorsoventral and the lateral views. Chelonia may be radiographed in a dorsoventral projection by placing the animal directly onto the film cassette and using a vertical beam. The lateral view is best achieved by placing the animal on a raised platform and using a horizontal beam. As most species lack a diaphragm, attempting to position the animal in lateral recumbency merely displaces the coelomic contents into the lung fields. Placing the gravid animal at an angle to the vertical or inverting it may induce egg peritonitis (see section 'Egg peritonitis'). Lizards and crocodilians are similarly positioned, using a horizontal beam for the lateral projection prevents displacement of the coelomic organs even in those species with a functional diaphragm. The same techniques and positioning are used for the snake, however extra care must be taken to ensure the animal does not roll into a more lateral position when the dorsoventral radiograph is required. It is of marginal use to radiograph the coiled snake on a cassette as the organ relationships are altered and this method is not recommended. It is prudent to mark the length of the snake with appropriately placed lead markers along its length if more than one film is required to radiograph its whole length. In this way the position of any radiographic features can be more accurately gauged. Most patients do not require sedation or anesthesia for radiography and can be restrained by hand or using sandbags, tape or ties.

Ultrasonography of the Reproductive Tract

The advent of ultrasonography has made possible the non-invasive, relatively safe assessment of the reproductive tract in many species of reptile. Ultrasonography is the major imaging tool for obstetrical work in reptiles, being useful in infertility assessment, determination of the number of follicles and relating the timing of ovulation to oviposition (Stoskopf 1989).

The use of radiography only allows visualization of shelled eggs and laparoscopy does not facilitate the counting and measuring of enlarged follicles and oviductal eggs (Limpus and Reed 1985). Ultrasonography allows the assessment and counting of follicles and oviductal eggs, and the comparison between the number of oviductal eggs and the number laid in the investigation of dystocia (Kuchling 1989). Ultrasonographic examination usually requires no anesthesia and is associated with less risk of trauma and infections that are associated with laparoscopy. The shell and underlying bony plates of the chelonia restrict the positioning of the transducer to the 'acoustic windows' of the inguinal, pre-femoral, axillary and cervical regions where the probe may be in contact with soft tissue. In the chelonia, the ovaries are paired elongated organs attached to the peritoneum on either side of the dorsal midline anterior to the pelvic girdle. The expanded stroma of the ovaries ensures that enlarged follicles may be imaged by ultrasonography as positioned between other organs e.g. oviducts, intestinal loops. When ovulated, the oviductal egg may be visualized surrounded by the dark hypoechoic albumin. As the shell is deposited, the dense white hyperechoic margin of yolk is seen surrounded by the dense fibrous layers of egg shell increasing the echogenicity of the egg (Kuchling 1989). Recent work in Kemps' Ridley sea turtle found that the resolution using a linear scanner was better than a sector scanner at distinguishing follicles (Rostal et al 1990). A 5 MHz probe may be used with larger species and provides excellent resolution. The 7.5 and 10 MHz sized sector probes are useful in small animals e.g.. Californian desert tortoise (Pennick et al 1991), (Fig. 5, 13) Hermann's tortoise. A 3.5 MHz probe is more effective for large species such as

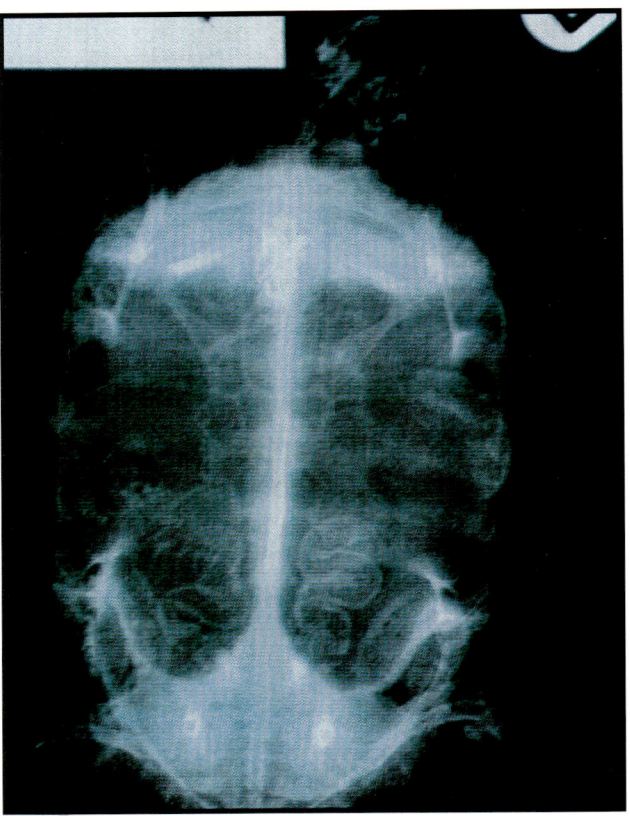

Figure 3. A dorsoventral view of a tortoise with calcified oviducts.

the sea turtles where greater penetration of the beam is required. If the animal and scanner are immersed in a water bath, transmission is satisfactory up to a distance of 2-3cm (Kuchling 1989). The ultrasonographic detection of follicles is limited to those greater than 5mm in diameter (Rostal et al 1990). The accurate estimation of the number of follicles or eggs is not possible in those species which mature large numbers of follicles. In most species the character of the ovaries can be assessed, eggs may be detected in the oviduct, maturing and ovulating follicles may be monitored to allowing timing of matings to be estimated. The pregnancy may be monitored and related to nesting behavior and the correct timing of oviposition.

The testes are located cranial and ventral to the kidneys. They appear uniformly echogenic and slightly more hypoechoic when compared with the adjacent kidneys in chelonia (Penninck et al 1991).

The basic technique in the lizards, snakes and crocodilians is as described above but in the Squamata the whole of the ventral surface of the animal can be scanned. Ultrasonography of the Bosc monitor has been described (Sainsbury and Gili 1991) using a 5 Mhz linear probe. The non-gravid reproductive tract was not identified, although eggs could be seen in the gravid female.

DISORDERS OF THE FEMALE REPRODUCTIVE SYSTEM

It is important to be familiar with the normal female anatomy and reproductive cycle in order to correctly recognize the disorders of the female reptile patient (See 'Reproduction' Chapter). Hence a description of the diagnosis of pregnancy and a brief description of ovulation are included in this section.

DIAGNOSIS OF PREGNANCY

Generally, a female reptile is suspected to be gravid (pregnant) if she shows an increase in weight and girth. Radiography enables assessment of calcification, position, number and size of the eggs. The dorsoventral view is particularly useful in the assessment of egg size and pelvic diameter. (See Fig. 4) Pregnancy can also be detected in ovoviviparous species using this method. As the soft, leathery shells of some species are not very radiopaque, contrast may be used. Air injected into the cloaca provides radiographic contrast to allow visualization of egg masses (Millichamp et al 1983). Ultrasonography is however a safer (at least for the operator) and non-invasive method of pregnancy detection.

Snake, lizard, crocodilians

These species have visible abdominal masses, or they are identifiable on palpation. When radiographing long snakes which require two or more radiographic films, it is wise to label the snake along its length with lead markers. The position of the eggs may then be more accurately gauged. Ultrasonography is a useful tool in these species. A standoff may be required in the smaller species; this is a special piece of rubber material which allows the ultrasound to penetrate whilst distancing the transducer from the skin surface, to allow visualization of the more superficial structures. It is sometimes difficult to examine larger species and maintain a good contact using gel. The animal can be examined immersed in water, allowing the beam to penetrate to various depths more easily at the same time ensuring the exclusion of air from the contact point.

Chelonia

Palpation by 'ballotment' is useful; the animal is held vertically, head up, and the fingers are inserted into the rear limb fossae. By gently rocking the animal side to side, eggs may be felt against the fingers in the caudal coelom. Care must be taken as there is a risk of fracturing the eggs by rough technique (see egg peritonitis).* The bony carapace and plastron limit the areas accessible for ultrasonography, as the beam cannot penetrate

*Calcified eggs are easily identified on a dorso-ventral radiograph (see Fig. 4)

PREDISPOSING FACTORS FOR DYSTOCIA

Factors	Comments
Lack of suitable nesting place and substrate	Many terrestrial species dig holes for the deposition of their eggs. Aquatic species e.g. terrapins, turtles and crocodilians should be provided with a suitable area of dry land for egg laying. The dry area should be maintained at the correct incubation temperature or the female will not be stimulated to lay there, and the eggs may be produced in the (warmer) water or dystocia may develop. Zwart (1985) suggested that psychogenic dystocia may occur, where one dominant female of a group may lay eggs and inhibits the subordinates from laying.
Poor husbandry	Overfeeding and lack of exercise, resulting in poor muscular condition, has been suggested as contributing to primary inertia of the genital tract (Grain and Evans 1984). A low temperature, lack of seclusion, improper diet, unclean cage, abnormal photoperiod, movement stress or change in environment towards the end of gestation have all be implicated in the etiology of some forms of dystocia.
Mineral imbalances, especially calcium	Calcium deficiency may lead to atony of the oviduct. Hyperparathyroidism, in which the parathyroid glands overproduce a hormone which regulates the calcium level in the blood, can be caused by renal disease or an imbalanced diet. It leads to deposits of calcium in the oviductal muscle and so interferes with its proper function. Low serum calcium levels are not considered to be a factor in dystocia of snakes due to their intake of whole animals (Millichamp et al 1983, Barten 1985).

Infections of the oviducts	Infections are generally considered to be secondary to dystocia. In one reported case, however, Zwart (1992) identified *Monocercomonas* sp. in the oviduct of a boa constrictor (*Boa constrictor constrictor*). Some fetuses had died and were retained in the infected section but were alive in the healthy part and were passed normally. Bacterial septicemia has also been associated with egg retention (Cooper 1981, Russo 1987).
Abnormalities of the eggshell	(From Zwart, 1992) i) Focal absence of the calcified outer layer of the shell in *Epicrates* spp. ii) Double thickness of the calcified portion of the egg in *Testudo hermanni*. iii) calcium masses which resembled the size and shape of an egg in a Aldebran giant tortoise (*Megachelys gigantea*) iv) two or more eggs joined at the shell producing a line of eggs in a Hermann's tortoise (*Testudo hermanni*). v) very large/misshapen eggs unable to pass through the pelvis
Infertile eggs	Infertile eggs may be resorbed or passed without difficulty, but they may on occasion cause dystocia. The ova may remain unfertilized despite copulation occurring. The male may be sterile due to incorrect environmental conditions, extreme age or poor nutrition (Crews and Garrick 1980; Laszlo 1983) or the introductions and copulations may have taken place at the wrong time (Laszlo 1983). An infertile ovum may be retained and serve as a nidus for infection, requiring surgical removal (Brown and Martin 1990).
Miscellaneous	Other causes of dystocia include; dead fetuses, trauma, attempting to pass more than one egg simultaneously, endocrine abnormalities, repeated copulation causing egg fracture.

bone. The rear limb fossae are the site for ultrasonographic examination of the caudal coelom. The use of ultrasonography is also limited by the physical size of the transducer head which cannot be placed into the fossa in smaller species, although the use of improvised stand-offs (plastic gloves filled with water), or the immersion of the transducer and animal, may sometimes facilitate its usefulness.

DYSTOCIA

Dystocia is a delay in the normal deposition of the young or eggs. This is perhaps the most common reproductive disorder of reptiles (Frye 1991) with the highest incidence reported in chelonians (Frye 1974; Glassford and Brown 1977). In reptiles, prostaglandins stimulate oviducal contractions and these contractions may be overridden by neuronal control (Guillette et al 1991). It has been suggested that, as reptiles have evolved, modern-day oviparous reptiles have developed a functional cervix (Guillette et al 1991), rather than the more primitive animals which lack a cervix so allowing the eggs/young to move unhindered from the ovary to the cloaca. Thus egg/fetus passage may be blocked by higher mechanisms in the modern reptiles and dystocia occurs. However, it is generally considered that whilst dystocia in mammals is usually caused by primary uterine inertia or hypocalcemia, in reptiles the cause is most often malformed or excessively large eggs (Frye 1994).

CLINICAL SIGNS

These include anorexia, regurgitation, straining (this may cease after a period of time), paresis (especially of the hind legs), respiratory distress, edema of the cranial extremities and cloacal discharge (often foul smelling) (Bennet 1989, Millchamp et al 1983, Frye 1974)

a) Snakes

These species may appear normal and healthy until weeks or even months after the end of the gestation period. In some cases, anorexia may be the only sign of illness. The animal may have laid fewer eggs than expected/ predicted from tests, or began movements consistent with oviposition and contractions observed earlier which then ceased (Brown and Martin 1990)

b) Lizards/Crocodilians

These species may become restless or increase their hiding behavior. Anorexia, lethargy and weight loss are common.

c) Chelonia/Crocodilia

Aquatic species appear restless, swimming in circles, repeatedly stretching out the hind limbs and may swim leaning to one side. A hemor-

Table 1. Drugs used in Reproductive Manipulation

Drug	Dosage (mg/ Kg)	Route(s)	Frequency in hours	Reference
Reproductive Manipulation (general)				
medroxyprogesterone acetate	20	i/m		Bennett 1989
Calphosan	0.2 - 0.5 ml/ Kg		30 to 120 minutes prior to AVT	Lloyd 1991
arginine vasotocin (AVT)	0.01 - 1.0 mcg/ Kg	i/v (i/m or i/c)	after calcium injection	Lloyd 1991
oxytocin	1 - 2 IU/ 100g	i/m	lower doses in larger animals	Frye 1994
calcium gluconate	1 - 2 ml/ 100g of 1% 10 - 50	i/m		Scott 1992 Jenkins 1991
Snake				
Calcium borogluconate (1%)	10 ml/ Kg	i/m s/c		Grain and Evans 1984
oxytocin	1 - 10 iu 10	i/m	every 12 hours	Grain and Evans 1984 Reichling 1988
lizard				
calcium gluconate	1 ml/ Kg of 20%	i/m	24 for 5 days	Lawton 1991
oxytocin	3-6 iu/ Kg	i/m	once only following calcium treatment	Lawton 1991
chelonia				
calcium gluconate	100	i/m i/v (slowly) in divided doses	24	Mautino and Page 1993
oxytocin	2 iu/ 100g 1 iu/ Kg	i/m	24	Mautino and Page 1993 Jackson 1991

rhagic cloacal discharge may be noted (Mautino and Page 1993). After an extended period of dystocia, these symptoms may be replaced by lethargy and weight loss.

DIAGNOSIS

Determining that the female is gravid is described under 'pregnancy diagnosis' and is obviously the first step in diagnosing dystocia. The history may include a change in temperature or photoperiod which may have stimulated gametogenesis and mating behavior. Generally, only one or two eggs in a clutch are retained (Reichling 1988), and so the patient with dystocia will have recently laid eggs or deposited young. Eggs retained for longer than the normal gestation period often become increasingly calcified and so are more opaque on radiography. Deformity or oversize of the egg(s) can be diagnosed from radiographs or other diagnostic imaging techniques. On occasion, the identification of an abdominal mass may be difficult and differential diagnoses including fecal impaction, foreign body, ureteral calculus, ectopic or infertile ovum, granuloma, abscess and neoplasia (Russo 1987). Radiographic contrast studies of the oviducts will reveal retained uncalcified eggs (Russo 1987).

TREATMENT (Table1)

If the size and shape of the egg will allow normal passage through the pelvis, it is preferable to encourage the eggs to be passed via the cloaca. Manipulation of the eggs or fetuses after lubrication of the cloacal and uterine openings can relieve the dystocia (Millichamp et al 1983, Grain and Evans 1984, Frye 1974). This should not be attempted after the administration of oxytocin as the stimulated uterine contractions prevent the movements of the eggs or fetuses by manipulation (Grain and Evans 1984). Calcium and oxytocin injections are recommended by many authors (see table) to induce oviductal contractions. Recent studies have shown that vasotocin is over ten times more effective, and acts more rapidly to produce smooth muscle contraction in the oviduct, than oxytocin (Lloyd 1991). After medical therapy, the reptile should be confined to a warm and secluded cage and provided with the species specific environmental requirements for the deposition of young. Warm water baths may induce gravid reptiles to deliver the offspring (Frye 1994 (b)). In species that produce soft and leathery eggs, percutaneous ovocentesis can collapse the eggs as the contents are aspirated. The percutaneous removal of the egg contents has been previously described (Reichling 1988) and avoids the higher mortality rate associated with surgery. After disinfection of the skin, a large (16-18G) needle attached to a 5 - 10 cc volume syringe is inserted percutaneously laterally (to avoid viscera) into the egg to a depth of 1-1.25cm to avoid exiting the other side of the egg. Enough contents are aspirated to collapse the egg (this can be palpated during the aspiration). Each egg is aspirated once only to reduce the possibility of leakage and peritonitis. Normally, the eggshells will then be passed within 24 hours. Oxytocin or vasotocin may be administered if the egg shells are not passed within 48 hours. Surgery (see section on 'Salpingotomy') is indicated in all cases which prove refractory to medical therapy.

a) Snake

In snakes, parturition generally occurs 7-14 days after ecdysis. The contents of retained eggs remain fluid for approximately 14 days after the parturition date, or for one month after the most recent ecdysis. Eggs retained in excess of this period feel hard on palpation rather than firm and slightly resilient (Reichling 1988). Dystocia is most commonly associated with infection, abnormal eggs or uterine inertia (Lawton 1991). A warm water enema given into the cloaca can aid digital manipulation of the egg towards the cloaca (Brown and Martin 1990). Often a relative calcium deficiency exists in gravid reptiles even though they are maintained on an adequate diet. The effects of calcium administration are seen even when blood calcium levels are normal at the time of treatment (Millichamp et al 1983, Holt 1981). Repeated calcium injections (0.5ml/Kg daily i/m for five days) can restore a minor deficit and increase the propulsive muscular activity of the oviduct. After this 'priming' dosing, oxytocin (3iu i/m) or vasotocin may be given to induce oviductal contraction. Initial treatment of oxytocin together with calcium is to be avoided as it may cause the stimulated oviduct to clamp around the retained egg(s). Percutaneous ovocentesis may be successfully attempted.

b) Lizards

Dystocia is a common reproductive disorder in iguanas and is frequently associated with an inadequate diet (Anderson 1992). It is possible for fe-

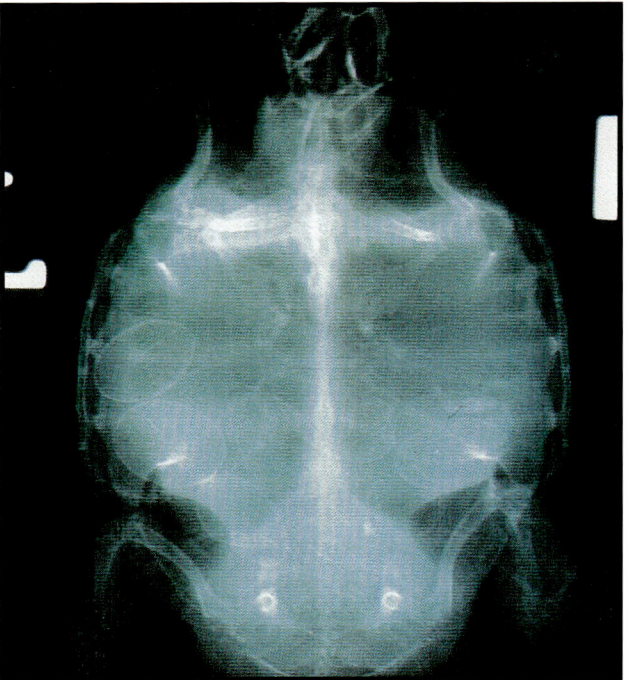

Figure 4. A dorsoventral view of a tortoise with collapsed eggs visible. This animal presented with egg peritonitis.

male iguanas to retain partially mature eggs for several weeks, this does not require treatment. Intervention is indicated if only a few eggs are laid, the inter-egg laying interval is longer than previous occasions or when compared to normals for that species, nesting behavior is not followed by egg laying, the animal becomes anorexic or depressed or calcified eggs are noted in the oviducts. In the early stages of dystocia, the animal may appear clinically normal. Extreme care must be exercised when handling the gravid female as the eggs fill a large part of the coelomic cavity and can be ruptured by rough han-

Figure 5. Intra-operative picture of egg removal via the rear limb fossa from a turtle. The illustration shows aspiration of the egg contents before removal of the egg.

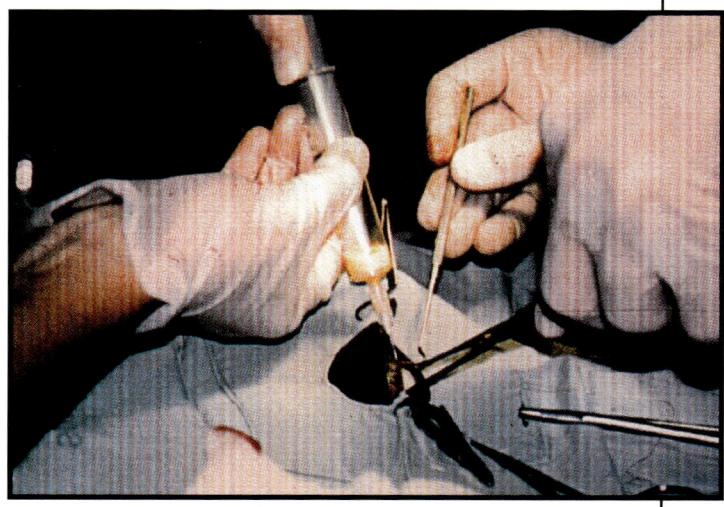

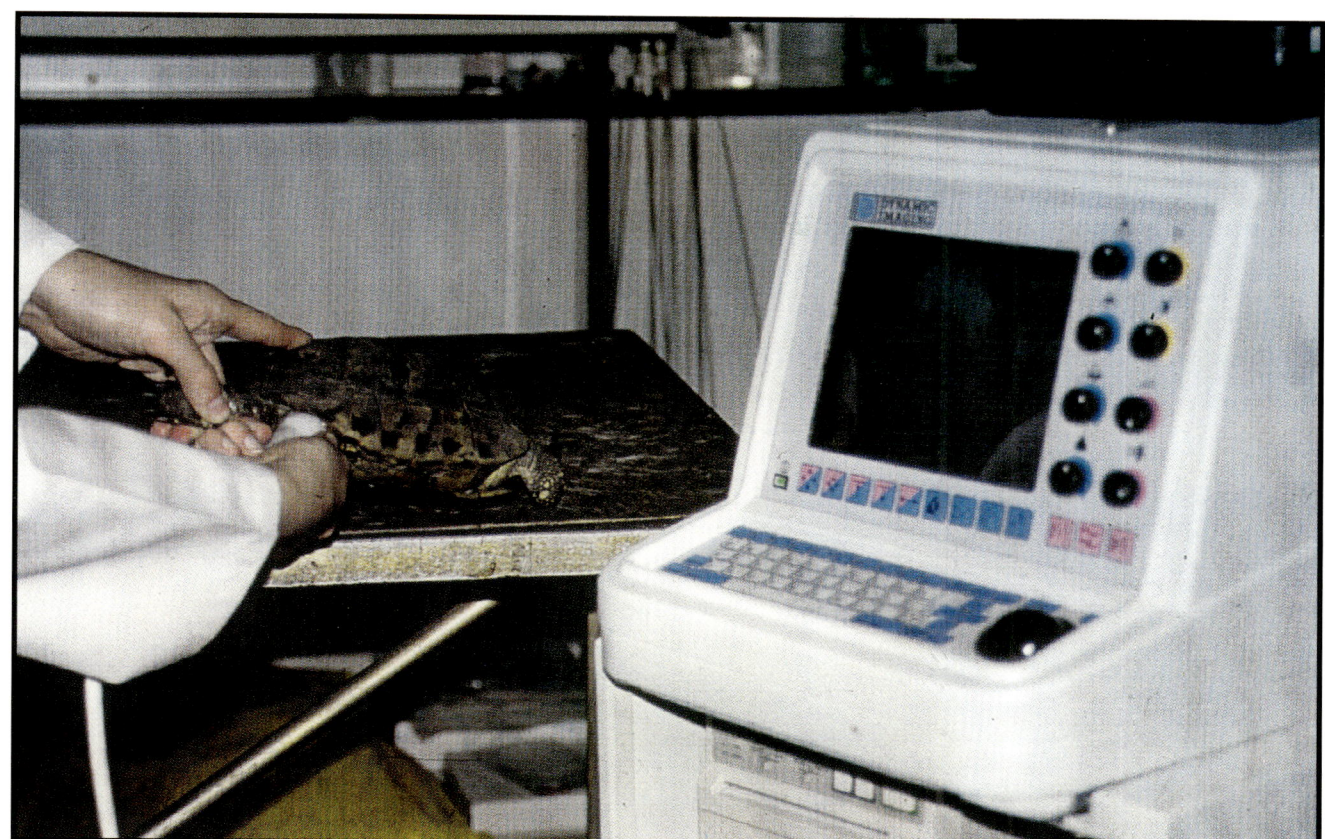

Figure 6. Ultrasonography of a female tortoise (*Testudo hermanni*). The transducer is positioned in the rear limb fossa to obtain a view of the ovaries and follicles.

dling leading to egg peritonitis. Retained eggs are not usually absorbed but may result in the death of the animal from starvation, hypocalcemia, other metabolic disturbances, and pressure on the kidneys and other vital organs (Boyer 1991). Treatment involves the administration of calcium and oxytocin or arginine vasotocin (AVT). Large clutches may require weekly dosing until all eggs are deposited. Geckos (*Hoplodactylus maculatus*) have been experimentally induced to give birth during late pregnancy by the administration of high doses of arginine vasotocin (150ug/g) or a combined treatment of dichloroisoproterenol and prostaglandin F2 alpha (2mug/g dichloroisoproterenol then 200ug/g prostaglandin 20 minutes later) (Cree and Guillette 1991). Manual expression is usually unsuccessful in these species.

c) Chelonia

Treatment is based on the analysis of the radiographs. If the dystocia is not due to obstruction, the administration of calcium gluconate and 5% dextrose may stimulate oviposition (Mautino and Page 1993). The female should also be placed on an appropriate substrate, in the appropriate environmental conditions for that species to encourage oviposition.

EGG YOLK PERITONITIS

Egg yolk is extremely irritating to the coelomic cavity and produces a severe inflammatory reaction. It is rare for eggs to be lost from the reproductive tract into the peritoneal cavity but it may occur as a sequel to surgical egg removal for dystocia if the egg ruptures during its removal from the oviduct, or in situ egg rupture from rough handling or copulation of the heavily gravid female. In chelonians it has been associated with the animal being turned on its back during oviposition, and the presence of cystic calculi traumatizing the developing eggs (Rosskopf and Woerpel 1982). It has been suggested that the ovaries must be removed following hysterectomy to prevent the release of eggs into the peritoneal cavity (Marcus 1981; Frye 1974) but others indicate that ovarian removal is not necessary (Frye 1981; Grain and Evans 1984). Egg yolk peritonitis may be diagnosed from the history of pregnancy and/or surgery for egg removal. Radiography will reveal broken egg shells, fluid densities and extraluminal gas within the coelom. The condition is characterized by fibrin deposition (forming adhesions between coelomic organs) and serosal thickening. The treatment is the surgical removal of the yolk material and copious coelomic lavage with warm sterile saline or reptile Ringers solution with 2-4mg of dexamethasone added per 100ml to reduce the inflammatory reaction (Frye

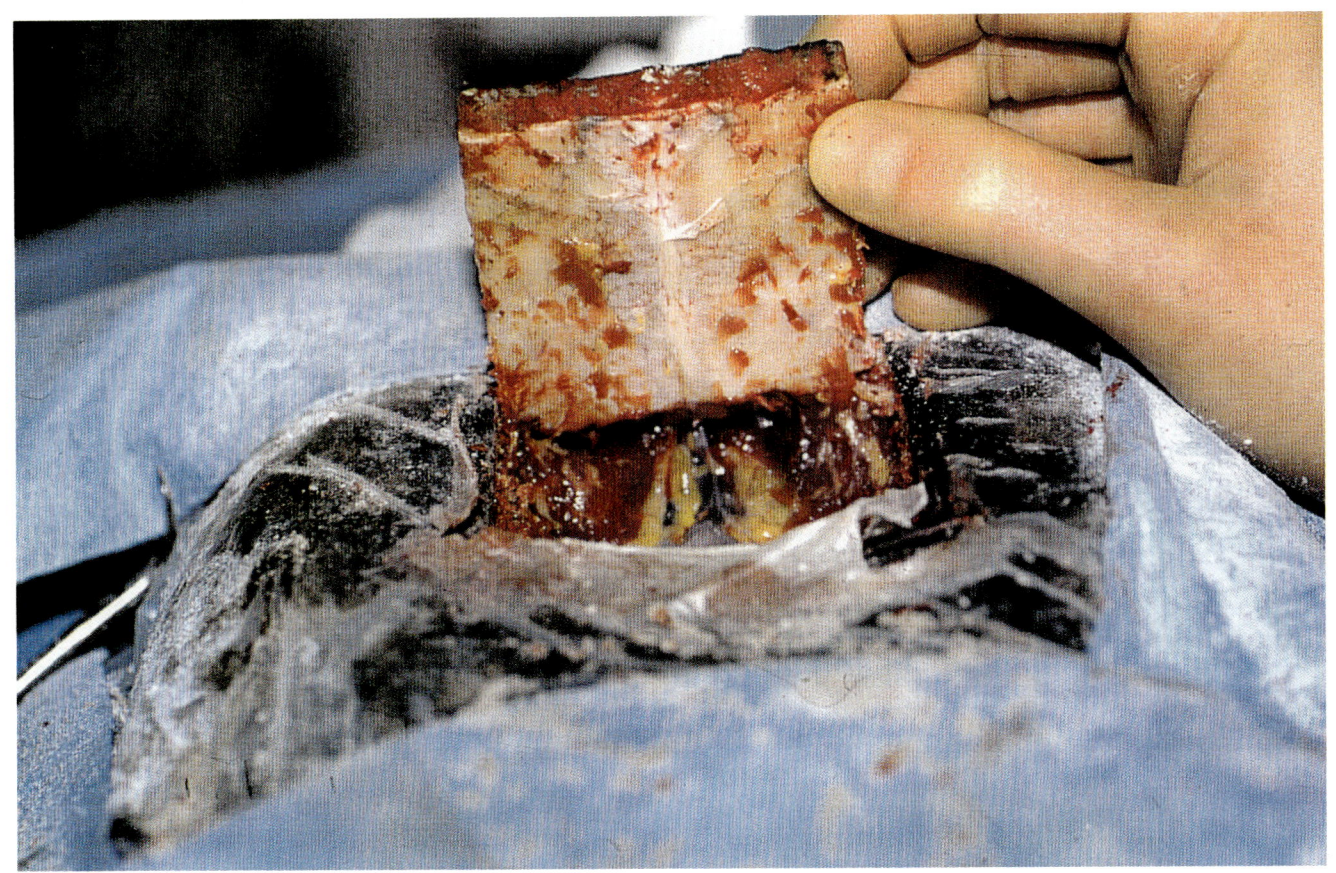

Celiotomy in a Mediterranean tortoise: raising of the plastron flap after cutting three edges of the flap using a bone saw. The intact peritoneum is seen below the bone flap.

Celiotomy in a Mediterranean tortoise: the egg within the oviduct is exteriorised. An incision has been made in the oviduct and stay sutures have been placed at the edge of the incision. These sutures aid identification of the edges to facilitate closure once the egg has been removed.

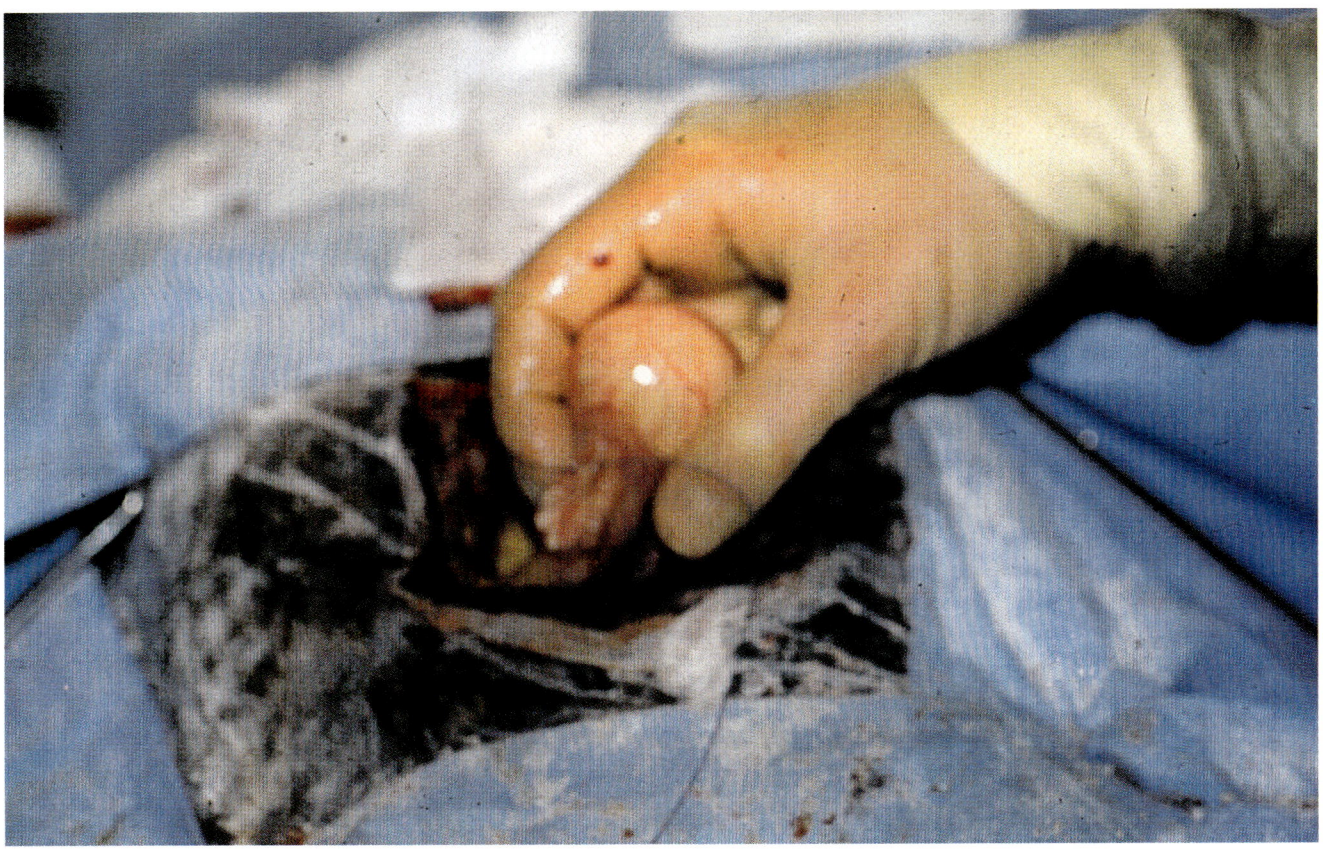

1974). Lavage aids the removal of debris and washes out the pleuroperitoneal cavity. This treatment is carried out as an emergency procedure and the prognosis is grave.

UTERINE PROLAPSE

This is a rare condition in reptiles but has been reported (Frye 1974, 1981). It may be caused by the collapse of ova within the oviduct (Frye 1974). The shell of the collapsed egg may then penetrate the oviduct and the resultant irritation produces constant tenesmus (straining) leading to cloacal and oviductal prolapse. The replacement procedure is the same as for the male copulatory organ. If replacement is not possible, a salpingohysterectomy or amputation is recommended (Frye 1974).

Oviductal and/or cloacal prolapse occurs most commonly in chelonia (Frye 1991). Other causes include bacterial, mycotic or protozoal infections, or helminthiasis. The treatment of large prolapses includes celiotomy to visualize and replace the prolapsed organ(s) and to place colopexy sutures to retain the organ within the coelom. A percutaneous colopexy method has been described (see later).

SUPERFETATION-INANITION

This condition affects ovoviviparous lizards, especially the spotted chameleon (*Chamaeleo pardalis*). The mature weight of a female is 25-40g yet this may increase to over 100g when she is gravid. The affected female will become severely cachectic and may die. On post-mortem examination the organs are atrophic, the body fat deposits, muscle tissue, liver and kidneys are almost absent and gelatinous in appearance. This is thought to be a result of the large fetal number/size overloading the female's metabolism as most of the energy is diverted to the fetuses. The only treatment is cesarean section and ovariohysterectomy to remove the drain on maternal resources. The prognosis is poor.

SALPINGITIS

Irritation or inflammation of the mucosal lining of the oviducts can lead to the production of egg albumin. This proteinaceous material may be passed unaided out of the cloaca as caseous yellow-brown plugs, or may form inspissated masses within the salpinx (Zwart 1992). The masses may be located on ultrasonography. Surgical removal is the treatment of choice. A delay in treatment may result in peritonitis. Salpingitis may be caused

Figure 7. Position of a red-eared slider (*T. scripta elegans*) for craniocaudal radiograph using a horizontal beam.

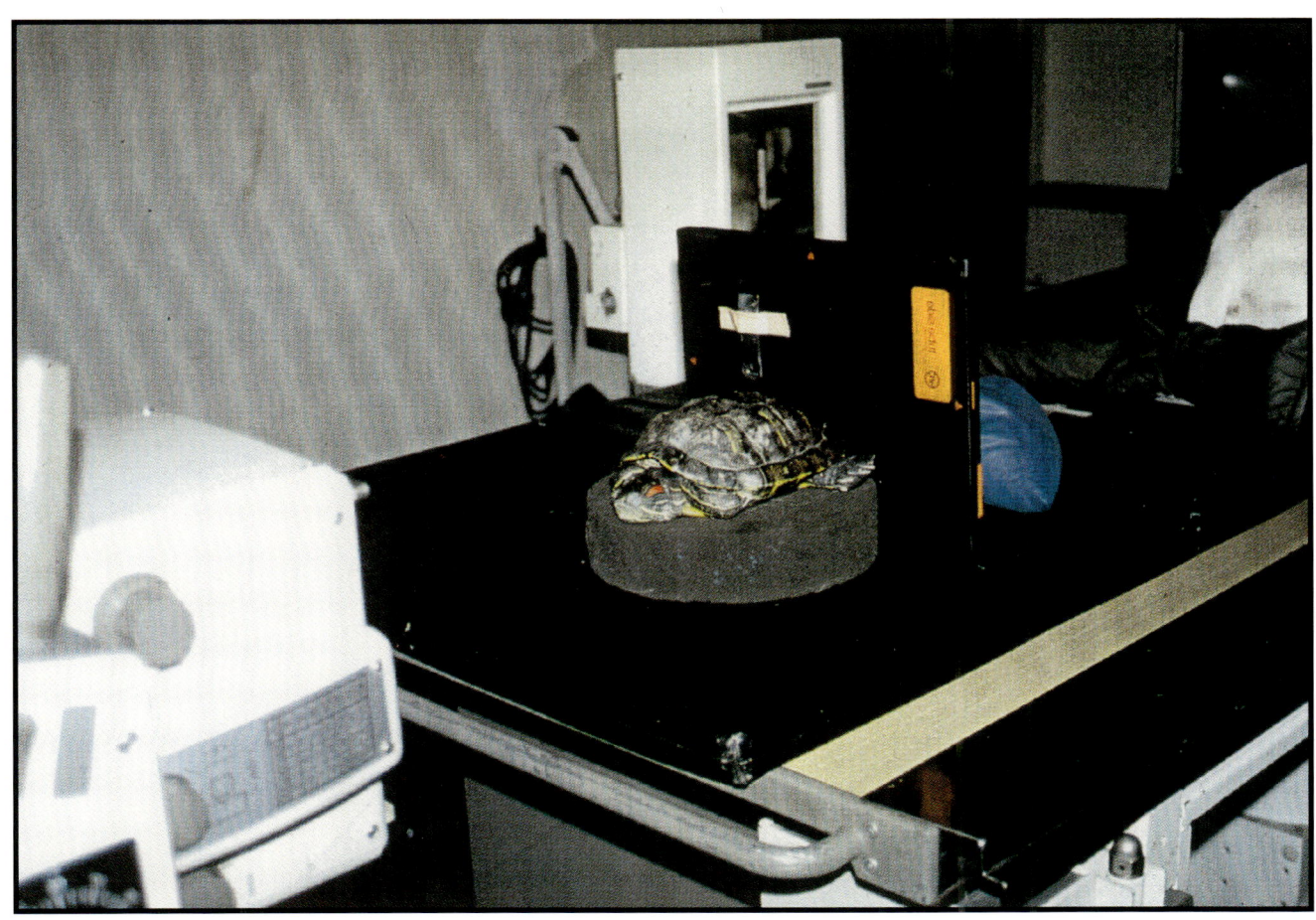

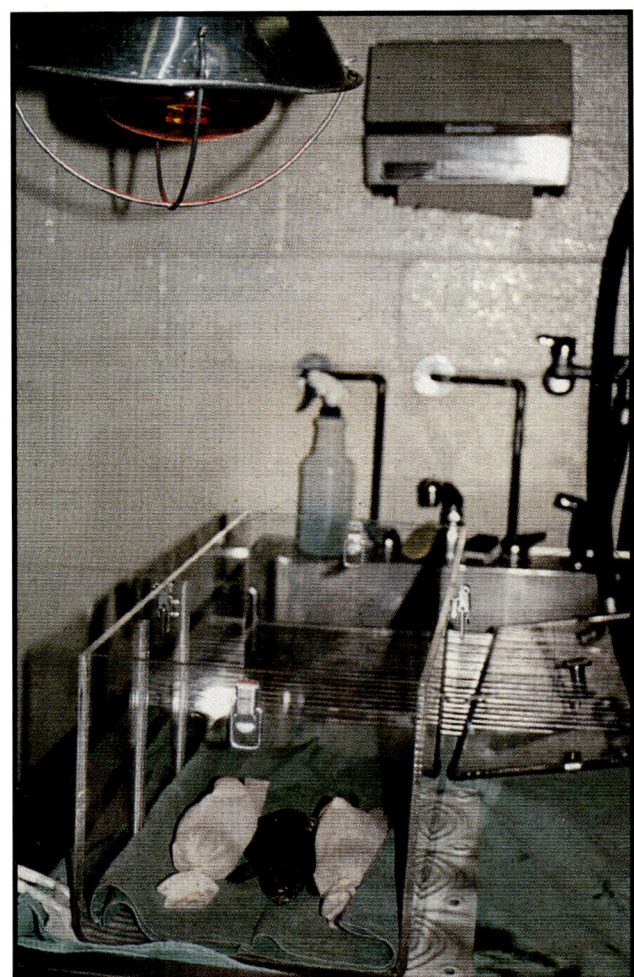

Figure 8. A simple setup for the post-operative recovery of a reptile. The animal is within a chamber with warm water bags either side and a heating pad beneath. An infrared lamp provides additional heat.

by a number of factors including bacterial infections or dystocia. Bacterial infection with *Edwardsiella tarda* causing salpingitis has been reported in alligators (Wallach et al 1966).

GRANULOMATOUS OOPHORITIS

This has been reported as a post-mortem finding in a red-eared turtle (*Trachemys scripta elegans*) (Kaufmann 1968). A number a dead turtles were submitted for routine post-mortem. The gross appearance of the ovaries showed 4-5 misshapen follicles filled with inspissated yolk. The histopathology showed a granulomatous response and *Citrobacter* was cultured from the yolk mass.

INTRA-OVAL NECROSIS (SPONTANEOUS ABORTION)

This condition only becomes of clinical interest if the ova are retained within the oviduct (see section 'Dystocia'). It may also be of interest when the female has been diagnosed as pregnant previously and does not then produce any

eggs or offspring at the end of gestation. The dead ova may be completely resorbed with no ill effects to the female. The possible etiology includes infection, trauma and inadequate environmental conditions.

OVARIAN DYSFUNCTION

The normal ovaries of the Squamata contain a large number of small oocytes grouped in nests throughout the ovary. Some of the oocytes develop into mature follicles in the ovaries in the weeks or months preceding mating. The increase in oocyte size is caused by the accumulation of yolk. The yolk consists of vitelline proteins produced by the liver. The production of vitelline is initiated by the pituitary secreting a gonadotrophin (follicle stimulating hormone-FSH). This FSH stimulates the ovaries to produce estrogens which in turn stimulate vitelline production by the liver. The transport of the vitellines is regulated by estrogens whereas the oocyte uptake of the proteins is regulated by FSH. As the follicles grow in size and change in type of vitelline that they contain, they are called first primary then secondary vitellinogenic follicles. The normal reptilian reproductive cycle is greatly influenced by environmental factors. A high light intensity is important in the activation of the pituitary and hence FSH production. Other influential factors include the condition and age of the animal, a suitable environment, an appropriate temperature and humidity and the availability of food. Once the egg follicles are mature, they are released in to the salpinx where they are fertilized. The post-ovulatory follicles then become corpora lutea. These structures produce steroids including progesterone, and are more persistent in the viviparous than the oviparous Squamata. The continuation of pregnancy is only partly dependent upon progesterone and the pituitary hormones also play an important role. The level of plasma progesterone drops sharply at parturition and it is thought that this increases the uterine sensitivity to oxytocin and arginine-vasotocin, which produce contractions of the uterine smooth muscle. The eggs or live young are then expelled.

FOLLICLE RESORPTION

This abnormality has been reported as occurring in the primary previtellogenic phase (Betz 1963, Guraya 1965) and associated with secondary vitellinogenic follicles (Zwart et al 1990). This process rarely produces clinical signs; one case in a Pacific boa (*Candoia carinata*) has been reported (Zwart 1992). The animal showed local thickening of the body in the position of the overies over two years. Surgery revealed each ovary to have three and four follicles in the process of resorption. Histologically, the follicle was infiltrated by lymphocytes and blood vessels. In these cases, calcium may be deposited in the remnant of the vitelline and can be seen on radiographs. Eventually fibrous scar tissue replaces the resorbed follicle.

PSEUDOPREGNANCY

This was first described in reptiles as a condition where fertilization occurs but further development is arrested and the eggs are resorbed (Zwart, Cooper Ippen 1989). This condition has since been recorded in a number of snakes species and is especially common in the Madagascan boa (*Sanzinia madagascariensis*) (Zwart 1992). An apparently normal pregnancy begins after mating however the females behavior reverts to that of a non-pregnant female shortly before parturition. Post-mortem of two affected females revealed egg follicle resorption was occurring but there were no eggs in the oviduct (Zwart 1992).

ERRATIC FOLLICULAR DEVELOPMENT

Normal follicular development is highly dependent on environmental factors. Erratic follicular development has been noted in garter snakes (*Thamnophis radix* var. *haydeni*). The animals were kept at a constant photoperiod of 12/12 hours of light/dark and maintained at constant temperatures over two years (Zwart 1992). In the same ovaries, primary and secondary vitellinogenic follicles were developing, whilst others were resorbing. The secondary follicles contained the pale vitelline characteristic of primary follicles. No young were bred under these conditions.

ASEPTIC OVARIAN INFLAMMATION

This condition occurs frequently in older individuals, with concurrent follicle resorption (Zwart et al 1990). It is presumed to be initiated by a leakage of vitelline from the follicle into the surrounding mesenchyma. The irritating vitelline induces degeneration of the fat and inflammation of the parenchyma. The inflammation spreads in the fatty tissue and leads to widespread, diffuse scarring throughout the whole ovary. A case was noted in a Round Island boa (*Casarea dussumieri*). The diffuse scarring probably makes the ovary non-functional. The etiology may be the rupture of the follicles following rough palpation of the ovaries, leading to irritation of the surrounding tissues (Zwart 1990).

Figure 9. A dorsoventral radiograph of a gravid lizard. Note the eggs visible in the caudal coelom.

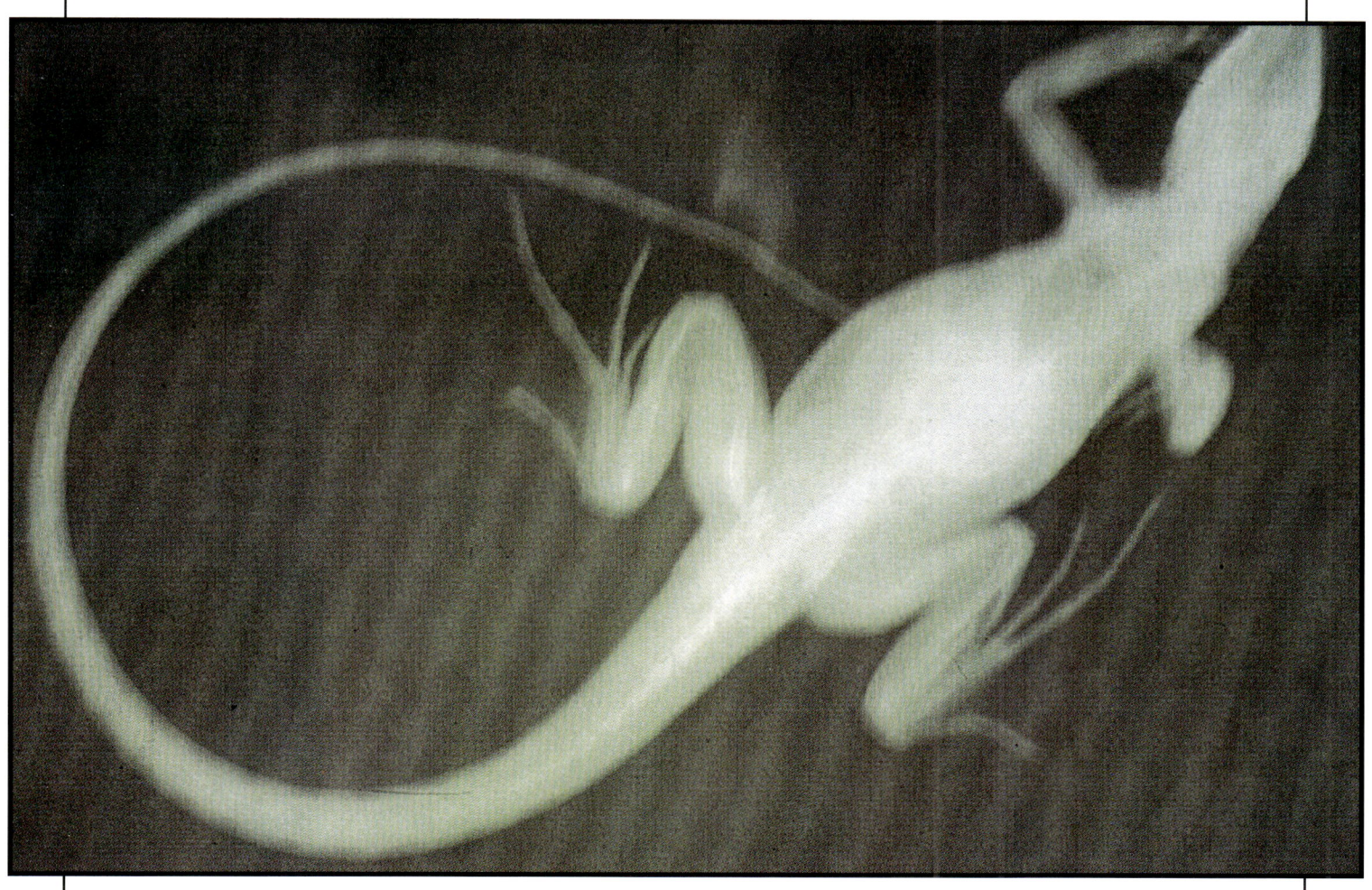

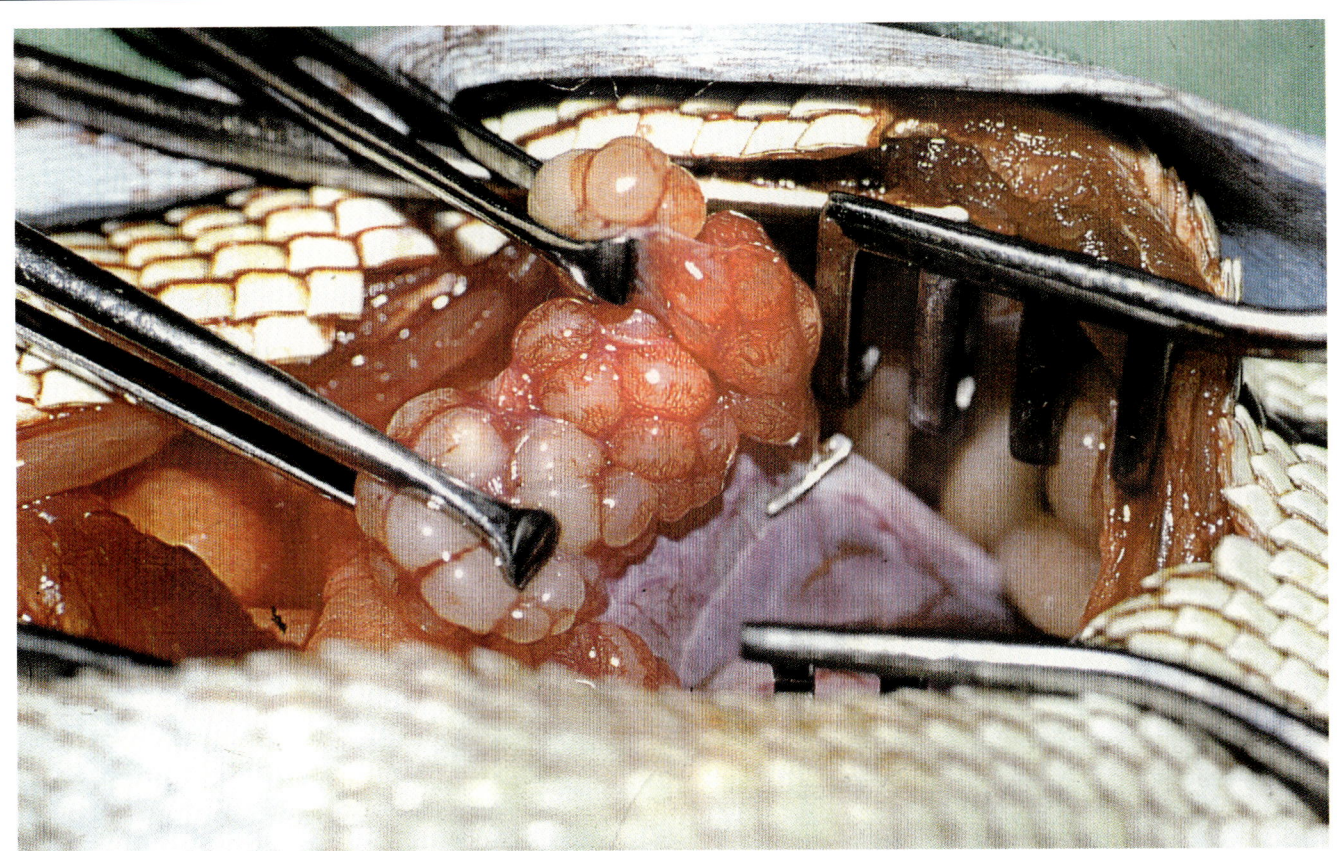

Ovariectomy of a green Iguana *(Iguana iguana)*: a single ovary is grasped by the forceps. Note the metal vascular clip on the cranial edge of the ovarian ligament. Further clips are placed to double ligate each vessel as the ligament is transected allowing removal of the ovary.

Ovariectomy of a green Iguana *(Iguana iguana)*: a single excised ovary. Note the enlarged vitelline (yolked) follicles. This animal presented with anorexia and a diagnosis of preovulatory follicular stasis was made.

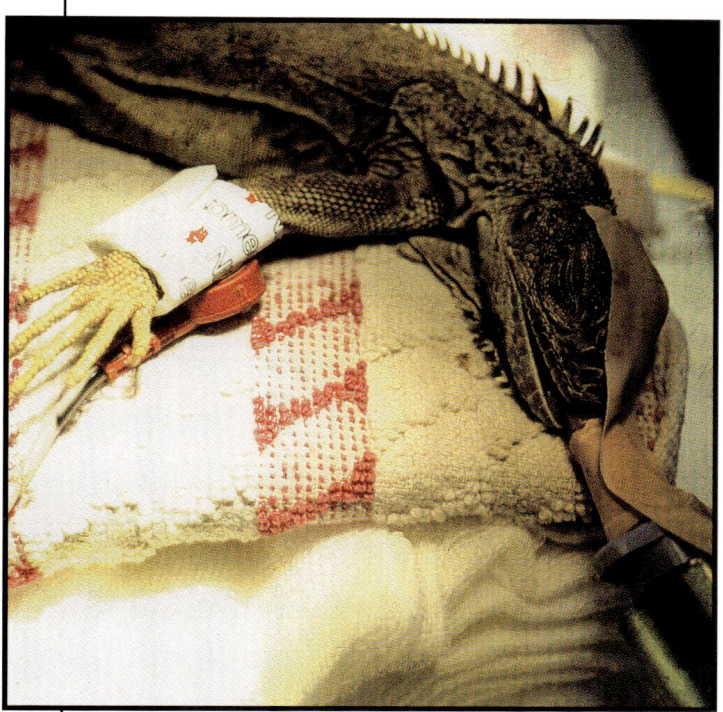

Figure 10. Gaseous anesthesia of a green iguana. A 20-gauge over-the-top catheter is used as an endotracheal tube attached to an Ayre's T piece circuit. Note the ECG lead on the forearm connected via a human ECG pediatric adhesive pad.

ACUTE FOLLICULAR RUPTURE

One reported case occurred in prairie rattlesnake which died suddenly following severe spasm of the abdominal musculature (Zwart 1992). Post-mortem examination revealed all developed follicles to have ruptured on both ovaries.

PRE-OVULATORY FOLLICULAR STASIS IN IGUANAS

This is a common problem in clinical practice. The iguana presents with lethargy, anorexia, weight loss, firm odorless droppings and elevated serum calcium and levels (Orosz et al 1992). On examination and palpation the animal may be cachectic with an enlarged abdomen. Palpation of the abdomen will reveal multiple oval masses approximately 2cm in diameter. Radiography of the abdomen will reveal multiple round soft tissue masses in the cranial abdomen. The caudal abdomen will show a loss of serosal detail. Ultrasonography of the pre-ovulatory follicle will show a finely textured hypoechoic central architecture with a bright hyperechoic central dot. Ultrasonography is particularly useful in those cases where the ova are small in size and difficult to see on radiography. Care must be taken to differentiate uncalcified eggs from bowel loops.

Medical treatment in the form of supportive therapy has been successful. The female may re-quire forced feeding or the insertion of a pharyngostomy tube to maintain nutritional intake. Prophylactic antibiosis has been suggested. Supportive therapy may be required for several months, during which time the eggs are resorbed (or more rarely ovulate). The long period of supportive therapy has lead others to suggest surgical treatment.

Follicle aspiration during celiotomy has proved successful (Orosz et al 1992). In the case reported, each ovary contained over 20 yolked follicles, some of which had become hardened. The follicles were aspirated through a 16G needle inserted in the stigma. Prior to closure of the abdomen, it was lavaged with 200ml of warm saline containing 5,000,000 IU of sodium penicillin. The serum calcium levels dropped nine days post-op and effectively normalized 2 months later. There is the risk of residual yolk becoming a site of infection and inflammation and postoperative ultrasonography of the ovaries to evaluate their status would be prudent.

For the treatments above, future breeding is theoretically possible but has not been reported, and the problem may recur. Ovariohysterectomy may be performed to remove the retained pre-ovulatory follicles (Barten 1992) if they are inspissated, the animal is severely compromised by the masses, or the owner prefers the surgical option to the prolonged medical care. This procedure prevents further breeding of course and recurrence of the problem.

Hormonal manipulation of ovulation is commonly performed in mammals. Although the hypothalamic-pituitary gonadal axis is relatively well understood in mammals, it is still not clearly known in reptiles. In mammals, the gonadotrophins stimulate the gonads to produce sperm, mature ova and increase the rate of steroidogenesis. Pumps that released chicken gonadotrophin were implanted into female iguanas and resulted in ovulation six to eight weeks later (Phillips et al 1985). Medroxyprogesterone acetate can be used to suppress ovulation and future egg laying (Bennett 1989). It is possible that hormonal manipulation may be used in the treatment of follicular retention in reptiles in the future.

DISORDERS OF THE MALE REPRODUCTIVE TRACT

PLUGGING OF THE RETRACTED AND INVERTED HEMIPENES

The normal copulatory activity of the male snake or lizard may be disturbed by the presence of a plug in the sac of the retracted hemipenis

(Zwart 1992). The male will approach the female but moves away without copulating. The plug consists of accumulations of desquamated cornified epithelial cells, but their origin remains unknown. Diagnosis is by observation of the plug when the cloacal scale is lifted. Generally the tip can be grasped with a pair of fine forceps and the plug withdrawn cranially, sometimes assisted by manually 'milking' the plug forwards. The sac is then filled with an antibiotic ointment.

COPULATORY ORGAN PROLAPSE

The male reptile copulatory organ varies according to the order. The squamate reptiles (lizards and snakes) have paired hemipenes which lie inverted within the tail. Chelonians have a single penis as do the crocodilians. Prolapse of the organ is usually a sequel to infection, enforced separation during copulation, iatrogenic damage caused by probing, or trauma including bites from others. More unusual causes include constipation and neurologic dysfunction (Frye 1981; Rosskopf et al 1982). Male tortoises may suffer penile prolapse as a result of neurologic deficiency in the retractor apparatus or cloacal sphincter or impaction of urate material in the cloaca (Mautino and Page 1993).

The primary cause should be identified and

The suture is removed after 3-4 weeks (Millichamp 1985). If the organ has become damaged or cannot be replaced, surgery is indicated.

If the organ is severely lacerated or suffers repeated prolapsing, amputation may be performed as most reptiles possess a hemipenis which does not contain a closed urethra. The prognosis is fair.

SURGERY FOR REPRODUCTIVE DISORDERS

Research into pain perception and analgesia in reptiles has been limited to date. However, anatomic, physiologic and biochemical studies suggest that pain perception in reptiles is analogous to that in mammals and so currently established analgesic protocols should be used in these species when subjected to invasive or potentially painful procedures (Stoskopf 1994) (see Table 2). Anesthesia may be induced and maintained using gaseous or injectable agents (see Table 3). Most reptiles can be intubated using the usual mammalian range of endotracheal tubes, or plastic intravenous catheters which may be used for the smaller species. Passive mask induction using gaseous anesthetic is contraindicated in reptiles, especially aquatic species, as long periods

Table 2. Drugs used for Analgesia

Drug	dosage	route(s)	frequency	reference
Analgesia				
flunixin	0.5 - 1.0	i/m	24 - 72	Heard 1993
morphine	0.5 - 2.0	s/c i/m	12 - 48	
meperidine	5.0 - 10.0	i/m	12 - 24	
oxymorphone	0.05 - 0.2	s/c i/m	12 - 48	
buprenorphine	0.005 - 0.02	i/m	24 - 48	

treated. Replacement of the organ should be attempted as soon as possible. The edematous organ can be coated with glycerin or other hygroscopic fluid to reduce the swelling (Rosskopf and Woerpel 1982) or a cold compress applied (Zwart 1992). The organ should then be cleaned, lubricated with an antibiotic ointment and gently replaced. An episiotomy-like relieving incision may be required to facilitate the replacement of the swollen organ (Frye 1994 (b)). A purse string suture (using 4/0 absorbable suture) may be placed around the cloaca to prevent re-prolapse but to still allow voiding. Placing a suitably sized object in the vent e.g. thermometer for smaller species, syringe cases for the larger animals, allows the suture to be placed firmly but leaving the vent patent.

of apnea are common, and deep anesthesia cannot be achieved nor maintained. It is therefore wise to intubate all anaesthetized subjects so that intermittent positive pressure ventilation may be used to induce and/or maintain reptile anesthesia and to ensure adequate ventilation is maintained. Whilst the reptile is anaesthetized it should be maintained at its preferred optimum temperature, preferably monitored by a rectal thermometer. The use of adhesive transparent sterile drapes facilitate the anesthetic monitoring of the patient, especially in the smaller patient where cloth drapes are cumbersome and difficult to anchor. The skin should be aseptically prepared using proprietary povidone-iodine solution or alcohol to reduce contamination of the surgical site.

Table 3. Drugs used for Chemical Restraint

Drug	Dosage (mg/Kg)	Route(s)	Reference	Comments
General				
acepromazine	0.1 - 0.5	i/m	Bennet 1994	one hour pior to induction to decrease dos of induction agent or as a tranquiliser
teletamine/zolaz epam (Telazol)*	4 - 5	i/m	Bennet 1994	Animal very sensitive to stimuli. Useful for induction/sedation Do not use within 10 days of ivermectin treatment
	10 - 30	i/m i/v	Frye 1994	
alphaxolone/alp hadolone (Saffan)*	6 - 9 9 - 15	i/v i/m	Lawton 1992	Do not use within 10 days of DMSO treatment (Frye 1994)
ketamine*	20 -100	s/c i/m i/v s/c i/m	Lawton 1992	effects vary with species and individual. >110 mg/Kg respiratory arrest
	22 - 44 (sedation) 55 - 88 (anaesth.)	i/m i/v	Bennett 1994	Recovery 24-96 hours Dilute with saline if used i/v
	20 - 60		Frye 1994	
thiopentone	20 - 40 (use 2.5% solution)	i/v i/p	Lawton 1992	long, unpredicable induction time. Long recovery period
succinylcholine	3 - 5	i/m	Bennett 1994	Neuromuscular blocker- use as restraint or adjuct to GA Recovery 7-9 hours
	0.5 - 1.5	i/m	Frye 1994	narrow margin of safety, artifical respiration often required
isoflurane*	4 - 5% in 3-4l O2, induction 1.5 - 4% maintenanc e	inhalation	Bennett 1994	Induction 6 - 20 minutes Recovery 30 - 60 minutes
Anaesthesia (crocodylia)				
telazol	4 - 8	i/m	Heard 1993	
succinylcholine	0.5 - 2.0 3 - 5	i/m	Heard 1993 Bennett 1994	
isoflurane	5% induction 2% maintenanc e	inhalation	Heard 1993	
Anaesthesia (chelonia)				
succinylcholine	0.5 - 1.5	i/m i/v	Heard 1993	
propofol *	14	i/v	Lawton 1992	
Anaesthesia (lizards)				
ketamine	20 - 40	i/m	Heard 1993	
telazol	1.0 - 4.0	i/m	Heard 1993	
propofol *	10	i/v	Lawton 1992	
Anaesthesia (snakes)				
ketamine	20-40	i/m	Heard 1993	

*Authors preferred agents

763

CELIOTOMY

Entrance to the coelom is required to perform many surgical procedures including cesarean section (Chiodini and Sundberg 1980), salpingotomy to remove retained eggs (Millichamp et al 1983), treatment of egg peritonitis (Bennett 1989), ovariohysterectomy (Frye 1991), follicle aspiration (Orosz et al 1992), vasectomy (Lawrence 1982) and celioscopy for sex determination and to evaluate the activity of the ovaries.

a) Snakes

The incision may be made between the last two ventral rows of lateral scales (Millichamp 1988), paramedian through the ventral scales or at the junction of the ventral and lateral scales (Millichamp et al 1983). The skin edges are reflected and the subcutaneous tissues are bluntly dissected down to the abdominal muscles. The muscles and coelomic membrane are incised, avoiding the large midline ventral abdominal vein and its branches. The incision may be retracted using an Barraquer eyelid ophthalmology speculum. Dissection must avoid entering the air sac. The coelomic fat bodies are bluntly dissected to expose the viscera.

b) Lizards and Crocodilians

A paramedian incision is made, avoiding the large ventral abdominal vein running in the midline. Incisions should be made between scales wherever possible. The crocodilians possess ventral scales with bony plates which are difficult to incise. Additionally, the thick ventral scales may take up to six months to heal (Millichamp 1988). In large lizards and crocodilians, an H-shaped incision will increase the surgical exposure. Surgical adhesives should be applied to the repaired incision to maintain a waterproof closure. Wound infections may be avoided by regular changes of the water and the provision of basking areas to encourage the animal to keep the wound dry. There is a risk of dehydration if the animal is denied access to bathing water although crocodilians have been kept out of water for two to four weeks post-operatively with no ill effects (Pleuger 1950).

c) Chelonians

The celiomic cavity is usually accessed through the plastron to achieve good exposure. The pelvic bones should be avoided, the position of these may be located with radiography. The animal is restrained in dorsal recumbency and a rectangular or square incision is made into the plastron, usually into the

Figure 11. Gaseous anesthesia of a turtle. A 20-guage over-the-top catheter is used as an endotracheal tube attached to an Ayre's T piece. A gag should be used to prevent the jaws clamping onto and kinking the tube. The trachea in chelonia bifurcates after a very short distances. A short (e.g., 16mm) catheter should therefore be used to avoid intubating one bronchus and thus only ventilating one lung.

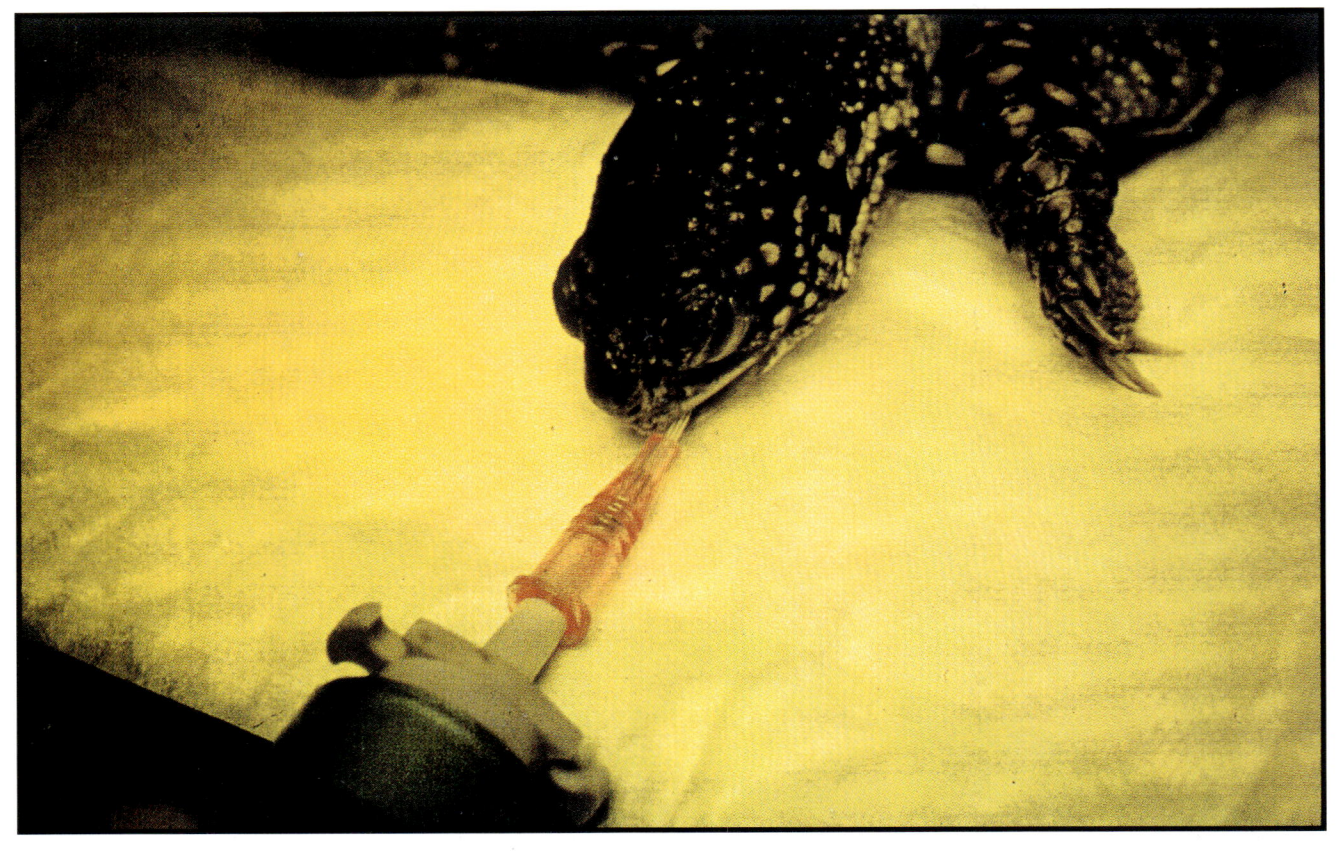

Figure 12. Male and female red-eared slider turtles. Note that the female on the right is larger, has a shorter tail and her vent opens closer to the plastron edge than the male. The longer claws of the male can also be seen.

femoral and abdominal shields, using a drill, high speed burr or orthopedic saw. Saline solution may be used to cool the site and remove debris. Care should be taken not to create too much heat or bone necrosis may result. All debris should be removed before the coelomic cavity is incised. The plastron flap is carefully dissected away from the underlying fascia and coelomic membrane and elevated using a periosteal elevator or scalpel handle. It is advantageous to leave attached to one edge of the plastron flap; preserving the blood supply in this way will speed healing. The reflected plastron flap should be in saline soaked gauze, to which prophylactic antibiotic may be added. The incision into the musculature may be a midline incision or a flap. The latter allows better exposure of the viscera. Only three sides should be excised to maintain a blood supply to the flap. The pleuroperitoneum may be incised as a separate layer from the muscles (Rosskopf, Woerpel and Pitts 1983) although this may prove difficult. The paired midline sinuses located either side of the midline should be avoided, but may be ligated if necessary (Frye 1981). Closure is achieved by using a simple continuous suture with absorbable suture material for the coelomic membrane. The plastron flap is replaced, the gaps filled with bone wax, and held in place with wire sutures placed

through pre-drilled holes (Lawton and Stoakes 1992). The shell must then be made watertight. Rapidly curing epoxy resin and fiberglass cloth may be placed over the repaired shell, with successive layers increasing the strength of the repair (Frye 1974, Holt and Schchman 1981, Bennet 1989). More specialized veterinary products such as Technovite® or Ellman®'s Beak Repair Kits (Lawton and Stoakes 1992) are recommended as they produce less heat and harden rapidly. In terrapins the area may be covered with silicone-glue to ensure the area is watertight (Zwart 1992). It is important to ensure that no material is trapped between the edges of the shell as this will delay healing and may produce bony sequestrums. Prophylactic antibiotic ointment may be inserted into the gaps before the application of the resin (Lawton and Stoakes 1992). Replacement and repair of the covering may be required in subsequent years as the chelonian shell may take years to heal completely. Hibernation following shell repair is not advised in *Testudo* spp. as the resultant reduction in metabolic rate may delay healing.

In species with a reduced plastron e.g. *Chelydra* spp. and *Trionyx* spp., the rear limb fossa may be used to gain access to the coelomic cavity. This technique has been described in a bastard turtle (*Lepidochelys olivacea*). This technique should only be used for salpingotomy and egg removal if radiography/ultrasonography have confirmed that the space between the carapace and plastron is sufficient to allow removal of the intact egg(s) (see egg yolk peritonitis). The incision is made in the skin between the cranial edge of the femur and the caudal edge of the plastron. The fat layer is then dissected to reveal the oblique abdominal muscle, then transversus muscle and the coelomic membrane sequentially. Closure is achieved in layers using an absorbable suture material.

Complications of all types of celiotomy include hemorrhage from the subcutaneous abdominal vein, post surgical wound contamination and wound dehiscence (Millichamp 1988 book). If possible aquatic species should be kept out of water for at least two weeks to allow initial wound healing, thus preventing water seeping into the coelom resulting in infection. The animals may be soaked in clean water twice daily to encourage drinking and prevent dehydration. A pharyngostomy tube may be required to ensure adequate nutrition of aquatic species during this period. A short course of a prophylactic broad spectrum antibiotic may be given. Isotonic dextrose-saline solution may be given as a single dose of 5 ml/Kg intraperitoneally immediately post-operatively (Millichamp et al 1983). Skin sutures are removed three to six weeks post surgery.

SALPINGOTOMY

a) Snake

A routine celiotomy is performed and the oviduct located. The oviduct is incised over one of the eggs and the egg removed. The remaining eggs may be massaged down to this incision and removed. If the eggs are adherent to the duct, as may happen in snakes, multiple incisions in the oviduct may be required (Millichamp et al 1983). In very large snakes, multiple celiotomies may be required to remove all the eggs. The oviduct is sutured with a simple continuous pattern or slightly inverting pattern (Millichamp et al 1983) using 3/0 or 4/0 non-traumatic suture material. The injection of oxytocin shortly before suturing produces oviductal contraction and a thicker layer of musculature which facilitates closure (Zwart 1992). One author reports salpingotomy in a number of snake species without surgical closure of the oviduct, and the animals subsequently bred successfully (Walker 1994).

b) Chelonia

If the celiotomy is performed via the plastron, then the oviduct may be located and incised over the egg , proceeding as for the snake. Access to the coelom via the rear limb fossa requires the exteriorization of the oviduct before its incision to retrieve the eggs. removal of more then one egg is

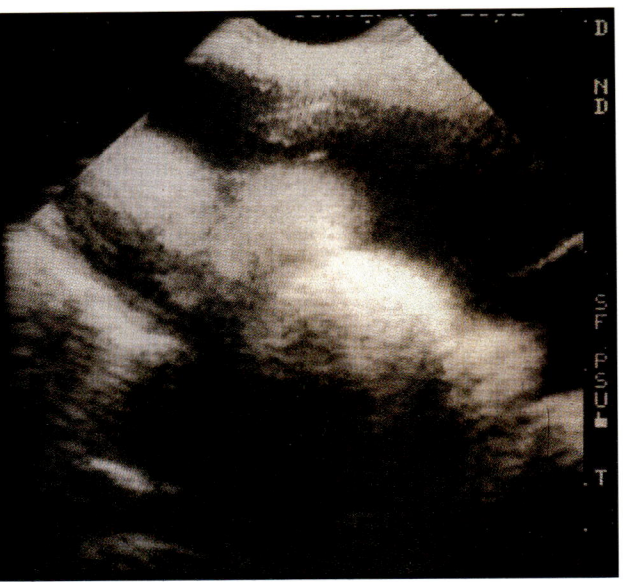

Figure 13. Ultrasound image of ovarian follicles in an adult female red-eared slider turtle. A 10mHz sector probe was used in the inguinal acoustic window. Three large follicles can easily be seen in the caudal coelom.

difficult as the whole oviduct cannot be visualized in situ, or the contents milked down towards the incision. radiography must first be undertaken to assess the number and position, as well as size of the eggs to ensure that this method will be successful.

c) Lizard

The salpingotomy procedure is similar to that of the snake described above. Successful salpingotomy in two chameleon species (*Chamaeleo lateralis* and *Chamaeleo pardalis*) has been reported (Walker 1994). In both cases the oviducts were not surgically repaired, and the *Chamaeleo pardalis* produced eggs naturally the following year (personal communication).

If any eggs are ruptured on removal from the oviduct, the pleuroperitoneum must be copiously lavaged with warm saline and antibiosis initiated (see egg yolk peritonitis).

OVARIOHYSTERECTOMY

A celiotomy is performed in the usual manner. The ovaries are readily recognized if retained eggs are present. Each ovary is elevated from the incision in turn if possible. The mesovarium containing the ovarian blood supply is easily visualized, clamped and ligated and excised. The presence of eggs (pre- or post-ovulatory) stretches the mesovarium facilitating elevation of the ovary. The oviduct is clamped, ligated as distally as possible and the ovaries and oviducts removed.

When ligating the ovarian vessels in a Green Iguana (*Iguana iguana*) one should note that the adrenal gland on the left side is positioned within

Gonadal Neoplasia in Reptiles

Neoplasm	Scientific/Common Name	Reference
ovarian adenocarcinoma	*Python sebae*/python	Bland - Sutton 1885
ovarian carcinoma	*Pelomedusa subrufa*/helmeted turtle	Scott 1928
ovarian adenocarcinoma arising in teratoma	*Iguana iguana*/iguana	Harshberger 1974
granulosa cell tumor	*Eunectes murinus*/ anaconda	Effon et al 1977
granulosa cell tumor	*Thamnophis sirtalis*/Eastern garter snake	Onderka and Zwart 1978
granulosa-theca cell	*Trimeresuirus albolabai*/green tree viper	Effon et al 1977
ovarian fibroma	*Achrochardus piscivorous*/ water moccasin; *A. javanicus*/ elephant trunk snake	Harshberger 1974 Ippen 1972
ovarian hemangioma	*Sistrurus catenatus*/eastern massasauga	Effron 1977
testicular interstitial cell carcinoma	*Gopherus agassizi*/ desert tortoise	Frye, Dybadal and Harshbarger 1988
ovarian dysgerminoma	*Trachemys scripta elegans*/red eared slider turtle	Frye et al 1988
seminoma	*Naja nigricollis*/ cobra	Frye 1991
proximal oviductal tubular adenoma	*Lampropeltis triangulum*/ milksnake	Frye 1991

the ovarian ligament. Its excision with the ovary is to be avoided. The use of vascular clips (see Figure) greatly facilitates the procedure as rapid ligation of the vessels is possible leading to a reduced operating time.

AMPUTATION OF THE MALE COPULATORY ORGAN

Amputation may be performed as most reptiles possess a hemipenis which does not contain a closed urethra. The hemipenis is extended until healthy tissue is revealed. Transfixing sutures are placed near the base of the organ to aid extraction. A ligature is placed around the organ and the traumatized portion excised. The entire accessible length of the organ may be removed as its function has been severely compromised and there may be no benefit to removing only the damaged tip (Frye 1991). The mucosa is sutured in a continuous pattern to cover

the stump. Antibiotic ointment may be instilled into the cloaca post-operatively.

VASECTOMY

Vasectomy of the snake has been described (Lawrence 1982, Zwart et al 1979). This operation may be required when a mixed sex group is to be maintained for display purposes but no further breeding is wanted. The animal is anaesthetized and prepared for surgery in the usual manner. The snake is restrained in dorsal recumbency. It is important to ensure that the site of the surgical incision is correct, which may prove difficult in those species in which the anatomical topography has not been documented. Various authors have reported the locations of the surgical incision in a number of species to be three quarters of the distance between the snout and the cloaca (*Thamnophis sirtalis radix*, Zwart et al 1979; *Natrix sipedon*, Bagdon 1953;

Table 4. Fluid therapy.

Fluid	Rate	Reference
isotonic dextrose saline	5.6 ml / Kg i/p	Millichamp et al 1983
lactated ringers/ Hartmann's	4 % bodyweight/ day 1-3% bodyweight/ day	Lawrence 1987 Jenkins 1991
hypotonic parenteral fluids (1 part lactated Ringers, 2 parts 2.5% dextrose in 0.45% NaCl)	1-3% bodyweight	Jenkins 1991

Reptile Ringers solution (Frye 1974, Fleisey 1968)
To 1000cc sterile water for injection add;
 	
sodium   128.00 meq
   potassium   2.60
   calcium   2.00
   magnesium   2.00
   chloride   112.00
   bicarbonate   20.00
 	
(vitamins (injectable) and glucose (injectable) may also be added.)		

Table 5. Drugs used for Antibiotic Therapy

Drug	Family	Dosage (mg/ Kg)	Route(s)	Frequency	Reference
Gentamicin	lizards	2.5	s/c i/m	72	Barten 1993
(ensure adequate hydration)	snake	2.5	i/m	72 (7-9 doses)	Jacobson 1993
	chelonian	5	i/m	72 (7 - 14 days)	Mautino and Page 1993
	crocodilian	1.75	i/m	96	Frye 1994
	all reptiles	10 2.5	i/m s/c i/m s/c	48 72	Frye 1994
enrofloxacin	lizards	5	s/c i/m	24 - 48	Barten 1993
	snake	5	i/m	48 (10 doses)	Jacobson 1993
	chelonian	2.5 - 5	i/m	24	Mautino and Page 1993
	all reptiles	7.5 - 10	oral i/m	24	Frye 1994
Care: maintain hydration with gentacin therapy or renal failure may result					

Trimeresurus gramineus, Enhydrina schistosa, Natrix natrix, Bellairs 1969; *Bitis* spp, Lawrence 1982). A paramedian incsion is made into the ventral coelom and the fat body and testis identified. Deflection of the fat body reveals the tightly coiled white vasa deferentia on either side of the intestine. A long section (at least 2 cm where possible) is removed from both vasa and the transected ends ligated with a suitable suture material e.g. 6/0 monofilament nylon. The abdomen is closed in the usual manner. It is wise to submit the excised sections for confirmation by histology. Live sperm have been demonstrated in the caudal remnant of the vasa deferentia three months after vasectomy (Zwart et al 1979) and a fertile mating has occurred fourteen days after vasectomy (Lawrence 1982). Thus it is important to separate the male from potential mates for at least three months post-operatively to prevent fertile matings.

PERCUTANEOUS COLOPEXY

The distal colon may be transfixed to the abdominal wall percutaneously, so avoiding a more invasive celiotomy to perform the colopexy. A probe e.g. glass rod, is inserted into the cloaca and pressed against the lateral body wall. A transfixing suture is placed through the skin and colon wall (located by palpation of the probe) on the lateral aspect of the animal. Three or four sutures are placed on each side to fix the colon to the body wall. These sutures may be removed after two to three weeks.

POST OPERATIVE CARE

The post-anesthetic recovery time in reptiles can

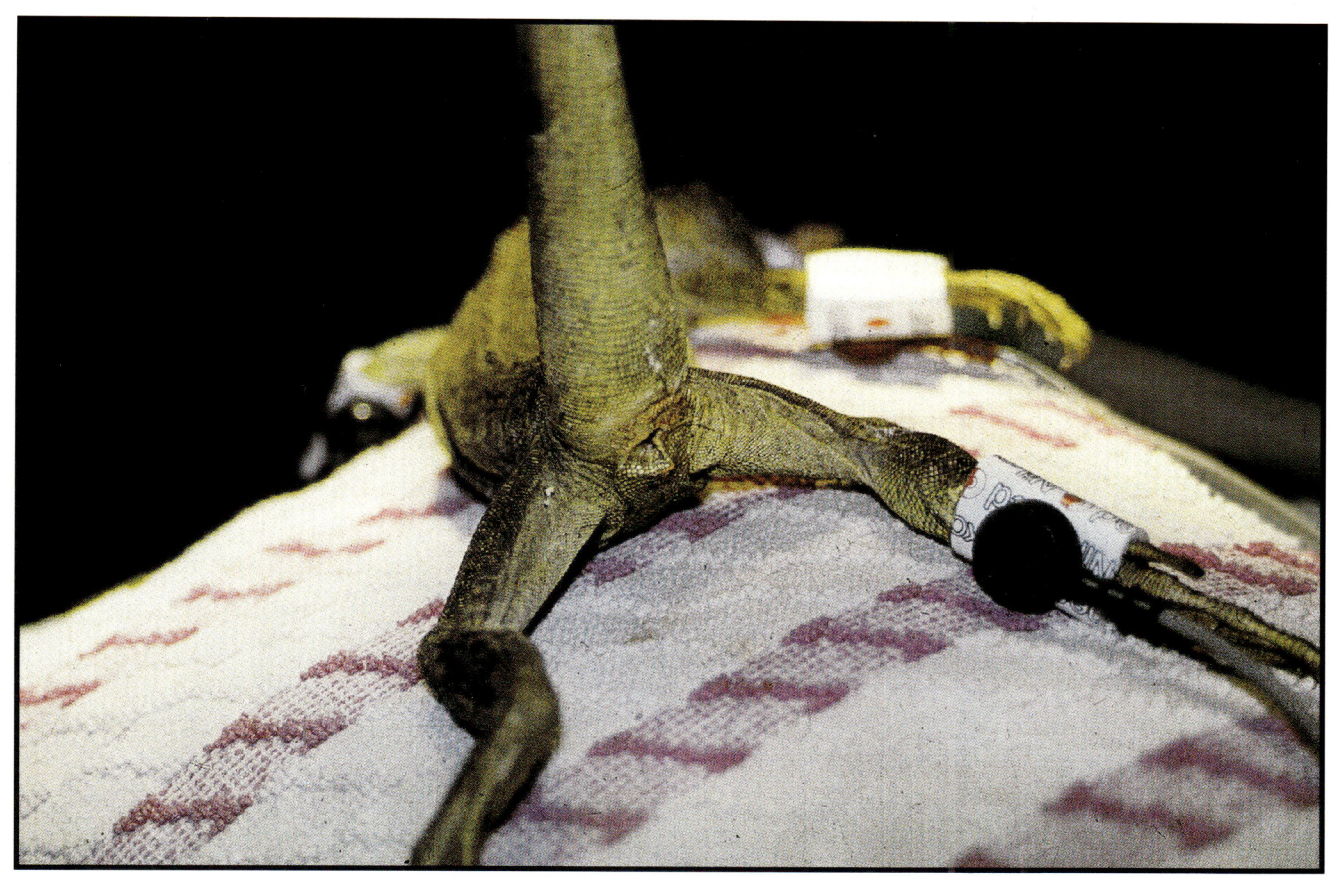

Figure 14. Post-operative view of the vent in a juvenile green iguana. A cloacal prolapse has been replaced and retained with a purse-string suture.

Figure 15. An adult female red-eared slider. Captive indoor females can be induced to lay in a warm bowl of peat if they have been acclimatized to it. this female was placed in the bowl daily for 45-60 minutes after mating had been observed. She later laid two clutches in the peat. The lack of an adequate environment to encourage egg deposition is a common cuase of dystocia in captive reptiles.

be prolonged. The animal should be maintained at the high end of its preferred optimal temperature zone to increase the metabolism of the anesthetic agent(s) used. A dark, quiet area for recovery is preferred. Parenteral fluid therapy may be required to maintain hydration during the recovery period (see Table 4). As many reptiles become anorectic following surgery, force feeding or tube feeding may be required. Antibiotic therapy should be initiated if an infected lesion is present, broad spectrum therapy may be used prior to the results of microbiological culture and sensitivity (see Table 5).

MISCELLANEOUS

GONADAL ANOMALIES

A number of authors have described individual reptiles which possess both male and female gonadal structures. A male Greek tortoise (*Testudo graeca*) was described as having an ovotestis, a normal testis and two oviducts (Fantham 1905). A turtle (*Emys europaea*) possessed one testis and one ovotestis and a penis (Matthey 1927). Paired gonads possessing both male and female elements and blind ending oviducts were described in a *Chrysemys marginata* (Risley 1941). A diamond-backed terrapin (*Malaclemys terrapin*) identified as female was found to have testicular structures within the ovary (Risley 1934). It is believed that true hermaphrodism in male reptiles is due to the persistence of the bisexual phase that occurs in the early embryonic development of the testis (Forbes 1938, Risley 1933) and this may in part explain why most hermaphrodite reptiles are functional males. However, a 'female' hermaphrodite has been reported (Frye 1991). This adult Boa (*Boa constrictor constrictor*) possessed reduced paracloacal spurs, and a normal female reproductive tract apart from small non functioning testis associated with the ovaries. The presence or absence of hemipenes was not ascertained.

TRANSOVARIAN INFECTION

Salmonella and *Arizona* spp. have been demonstrated to be passed by transovarian infection in reptiles (Frye 1974). This may result in embryonic death, but the main implication is the risk to human health. These bacteria can infect man via the infected hatchlings.

TUMORS

Neoplasia is not rare in lower vertebrates and the tumor types usually resembling those noted in mammals. As many captive reptiles live to a greater age than their wild counterparts, older animals develop neoplasia and often multiple primary neoplasms are found (Frye 1994). Care must be taken when interpreting the histological section of gonad as many

reptiles show seasonally cyclic testicular and ovarian quiescence or atrophy followed by recrudescence (Frye 1994). A variety of tumors affecting the reproductive tract of reptiles have been reported (see table). Benign tumors include seminoma (*Naja nigricollis*) and proximal oviductal tubular adenoma (*Lampropeltis triangulum*) (Frye 1991). Malignant tumors include testicular interstitial cell carcinoma (*Gopherus agassizi*) (Frye, Dybadal and Harshbarger 1988) and ovarian dysgerminoma in two turtles (*Trachemys scripta elegans*) (Frye et al 1988). Although dysgerminoma is considered a rare tumor of reptiles, two unrelated turtles in the same household were found with the condition, suggesting a common source for tumor induction, possibly environmental. It has been suggested that improper captive conditions may contribute to the unusually high number of testicular interstitial cell adenomata and hyperplasia observed in reptiles (Frye 1994). Diagnosis and surgical treatment of benign and malignant spontaneous tumors and leukemias include radiography and other forms of non-invasive imaging, fine-needle aspiration and excisional biopsy of the mass concerned, exfoliative cytology, bone marrow biopsy and hematology. Treatments include conventional sharp excision, radiofrequency, laser ablation and cryosurgical techniques (Frye 1994).

INDUCING REPRODUCTION

Progesterone has been shown to stimulate sexual and copulatory behavior in male whip tail lizards (*Cnemidophorus inornatus*), and the green anole lizard (*Anolis carolinensis*) (Young et al 1991, Witt et al 1994).

The production of sperm (spermatogenesis) and sex steroids (steroidogenesis) has been experimentally induced by treating male Garden lizard (*Calotes versicolor*) with exogenous gonadotrophins (Sonar and Patil 1994).

Crocodiles do not breed well in captivity, difficulties ranging from inappropriate egg deposition (in the water), poor incubation and infertile eggs. Yohimbine treatment (30 mg, twice daily, seven days) of male Nile crocodiles (*Crocodylus niloticus*) significantly increased the reproductive period and the fertility percentage of eggs laid by the females in the group (Murpurgo et al 1992).

POLLUTANTS AND FERTILITY

Many environmental pollutants have estrogenic activity in animals. These chemicals are found in many pesticides and industrial chemicals and may accumulate in the body. The effect these common pollutants may have on the reproductive success of wildlife, particularly of endangered species, has recently been the subject of much debate (Hose and Guillette 1995). Recent research has shown that plasma vitellogenin may be induced in male reptiles and amphibians by oestrogenic compounds (Palmer and Palmer 1995), and the detection of this protein in male reptiles may serve as a useful gauge of the exposure of the wild population to oestrogenic pollutants.

REFERENCES

—**Altland, JPD et al.**
Some Effects of X- Radiation in Turtles. *Exp. Zool.* 1951;118:1-19

—**Anderson NL.**
Husbandry and Clinical Evaluation of *Iguana iguana. Compend. Contin. Ed. Pract. Vet,* 1991;13:1265-1269

—**Anderson NL.**
Diseases of Iguana iguana. *Compend. Contin. Ed. Pract. Vet,* 1992;14: 1335-1343

—**Barten SL.**
Oviductal rupture in a burmese python (*Python molurus bivittatus*) treated with oxytocin for egg retention. *J Zoo Anim Med.,* 1985; 16: 141-143

—**Barten SL.**
Pyoslapingitis reported in Frye 1991. 1991; p377

—**Barten SL.**
The medical care of iguanas and other common pet lizards. Vet Clinics N.America; Exotic Pets 1. Quesenberry KE, Hillyer EV (Eds). 1993, 23(6).1213-1249

—**Boyer TH.**
Common Problems and Treatment of the green Iguana, *Iguana iguana. Bulletin of the Association of reptilian and Amphibian Veterinarians,* 1991; 1: 8-11

—**Brooks GH.**
Resistance of the ground Skink, *Lygosoma laterale*, to Gamma radiation. *Herpetologica* 1962; 18:128-129

—**Bellairs A.**
The Life of Reptiles. London, Weidenfield and Nicolson, 1969, p266

—**Bennet RA.**
Reptilian Surgery Part 1 Basic principles. *Compend. Contin. Educ Pract Vet..,* 1989; 11 (1): 10- 21

—**Bennet RA.**
Reptilian Surgery Part 2 Management of Surgical Diseases. *Compend Contin. Educ Pract Vet.* 1989; 11(2): 122- 133

—**Betz A.**
The ovarian histology of the diamond-backed water snake, *Natrix rhombifera*, during the reproductive cycle. *Journal of Morphology,* 1963; 133: 245

—**Bryadon DE.**
Anatomical record, 1953; 117:145

—**Brown CW Martin RA.**
Dystocia in snakes. *Compend. Cont. Educ. Pract. Vet.,* 1990; 12(3): 361-368

—**Chiodini RJ, Sundberg JP.**
Caesarian delivery in the snake. *Vet. Med(SAC),* 1980; 75:1605

—**Cooper JE.**
Bacteria. In Diseases of the Reptilia, JE Cooper, OF Jackson (Eds); Vol 1. New York, Acad Press. 1981, p165-191

—**Cosgrove GE.**
The Radiosensitivity of Snakes and Box Turtles. *Radiation Res.,* 1965; 25: 706- 712

—**Cosgrove GE.**
Reptilian Radiobiology. *JAVMA,* 1971; 159: 1678-1684

—**Crews D, Garrick LD.**
Methods of Inducing Reprduction in Captive Reptiles. In; eproductive Biology and Diseases of Captive Reptiles, SSAR Contributions to Herpetology 1. Ed JB Murphy and JT Collins, 1980.

—**Fantham HB.**
On Hermaphroditism and Vestigial Structures in the reproductive Organs of *Testudo graeca. Ann and Mag. Nat. Hist.,* 1905; (NS7)16:120-126

—**Frye FL.**
Clinical obstetric and gynecological disorders in reptiles. *Proc. AAHA,* 1974; 41:497-499

—**Frye FL.**
Biomedical and surgical aspects of captive reptiles husbandry. Ed 2. Malabar, FL, Kreiger Publishing, 1991.

—**Frye FL.**
Biomedical and surgical aspects of captive reptiles husbandry. Edwardsville. Vet Med Pub Co, 1981

—**Frye FL.**
Histologic Charcteristics of Spontaneous testicular Interstitial Cell hyperplasia and hypertrophy in Breeding reptiles: A Report of Three Cases. *Acta Zool et Path* Antwerp, 1986; 79:91-100

—**Frye FL, Dybdal NO, Harshbarger JC.**
Testicular tumour in a desert tortoise (*Gopherus agassizi*). *J Zoo Anim Med.,* 1988; 19(1-1):55-58

—**Frye FL.**
Diagnosis and surgical treatment of reptilian neoplasms with a compilation of cases 1966-1993. *In Vivo,* (a) 1994; 8:885-892

—**Frye FL.**
Reptile clinicians handbook. Kreiger Publishing Company, Inc, . (b) 1994

—**Glassford JF, Brown K.**
Treatment of egg retention in a turtle. *VM/SAC*, 1977; 72(10): 1641-1645.

—**Grain E, Evans JE.**
Egg Retention in Four Snakes. *JAVMA*, 1984; 185(6):679-681

—**Guraya S.S.**
A histochemical study of follicular atresia in the snake ovary. *Journal of Morphology*, 1965; 135: 151

—**Heard DY.**
Principles and Techniques of anaesthesia and analgesia for exotic practice. Vet Clinics N.America; exotic pets 1. Quesenberry KE, Hillyer EV (Eds)., 1993; 23(6): 1301-1327

—**Holt PE.**
Healing of a surgically induced shell wound in a tortoise. *Vet. Rec.*, 1981; 108:102

—**Jackson OF, Fasal MD.**
Radiology in tortoises, terrapins and turtles as an aid to diagnosis. *JSAP*, 1981; 22:705-716

—**Jackson OF.**
Chelonia. In Manual of Exotic Pets. PH Beynon, JE Cooper (Eds). BSAVA Publications, UK, 1991.

—**Jacobson ER.**
Snakes. *Vet Clinics N.America*; Exotic Pets 1. Quesenberry KE, Hillyer EV (Eds), 1993; 23(6): 1179-1212

—**Jenkins J.**
Medical management of reptile patients. *Compend Contin Educ Pract Vet.*, 1991; 13 (6): 980-988

—**Kaufmann AF.**
Granulomatous oophoritis in a turtle. *JAVMA*, 1968; 153 (7): 860-862

—**Kuchling G.**
Assessment of ovarian follicles and oviductal eggs by ultrasound scanning in live fresh water turtles (*Chelodina oblonga*). *Herpetologica*, 1989; 45(1):89-94

—**Laszlo J.**
Further Notes on reproductive Patterns of Amphibians and reptiles in Relation to Captive Breeding. *Int. Zoo Yearbook*, 1983; 23: 166-174

—**Lawrence K.**
Vasectomy of a puff adder (*Bitis arietans*). Vet Rec, 1982; 110: 542

—**Lawton MPC.**
Anaesthesia. In Manual of Reptiles, PH Beynon, MPC Lawton, JE Cooper (Eds). BSAVA Pub. UK., 1992, pp 170-183

—**Lawton MPC, Stoakes L.**
Surgery. In; Manual of reptiles, Eds PH Beynon, MPC Lawton, JE Cooper. BSAVA Pub. UK, 1992, pp184-193

—**Limpus CJ, Reed PC.**
The green turtle (*Chelonia mydas*) in Queensland: a preliminary description of the population structure in a coral reef feeding ground. In G Grigg, R Shine, H Ehmann (Eds), Biology of Australasian Frogs and reptiles. Royal Zoological Society of New South Wales, 1985, pp 47-52

—**Lloyd M.**
Proc IV Int Coll Pathol Med Reptiles and Amphib, Bad Nauheim, Germany, 27-29 September, 1991, pp299-306

—**Machotka SV, Wisser J, Ippen R, Nawab E.**
Report of dysgerminoma in the ovaries of a snapping turtle (*Chelydra serpentina*) with discussion of ovarian neoplasms reported in reptilians and women. *In Vivo*, 1992, 6:349-354

—**Matthey R.**
Intersexualite chez une tortue (*Emys europaea*). *Compt. Rend. Soc. Biol.* France, 1927; 97:369-371

—**Mautino M, Page CD.**
Biology and medicine of turltes and tortoises. In; Vet Clinics N.America; exotic pets 1. Quesenberry KE, Hillyer EV (Eds), 1993, 23(6). 1251-1270

—**Millichamp NJ, Lawrence K, Jacobson ER, Jackson OF.**
Egg Retention in Snakes. *JAVMA*, 1983; 183: 1213-1218

—**Millichamp P.**
Surgical techniques in reptiles. In Exotic Animals Jacobson ER, Kollias GV (Eds). Churchill Livingstone, 1988, pp49-74

—**Obaldia N, Brenes MR, Alvarez OS, Gale NB.**
Polycystic ovarian mesothelioma in an american crocodile (Crocodylus acutus). *J Zool Wildl. Med*, 1990: 21(2); 231-233

—**Orosz SE, Toal RT, Korenek NL, Teubner VA.**
Follicle aspiration for the treatment of preovulatory egg binding in a green iguana. *J Small Ex. Anim. Med*, 1992; 1(4): 161-165

—**Penninck DG, Stewart JS, Paul-Murphy J, Pion P.**
Ultrasonography of the californian desert tortoise (*Xerobates agassizi*): anatomy and application. *Vet radiography*, 1991; 32(3):112-116

—**Reichling SB.**
A Simple technique for the Treatment of Dystocia in Snakes. *Companion Animal Practice-Herpetology*, 1988; 2 (7): 42-44

—**Risley PI.**
An ovarian Cystadenoma and Its Influence upon Sex Differentiation in an Immature dia-

mond backed terrapin. *Anat. rec*, 1934; 60(Suppl):68

—**Risley PI.**
Some observations on Hermaphroditism in turtles. *J. Morph.*, 1941; 68:101-102

—**Rosskopf WJ, Woerpel R.**
Treatment of an egg bound turtle. *Mod. Vet Pract*, 1983; 64(8):664-645

—**Rosskopf WJ, Woerpel R. Pitts BJ.**
Paraphimosis in a California desert tortoise. *California Vet*, 1982; 36(1): 29-30

—**Rostal DC, Robeck TR, Owens DW, Kraemer DC.**
Ultrasound imaging of ovaries and eggs in Kemp's ridley sea turltes (Lepidochelys kempi). *J. Zoo. Wldl. Med*, 1990; 21(1):27-35

—**Russo EA.**
Diagnosis and treatment of lumps and bumps in snakes. *Compend. Cont. Educ. Pract. Vet*, 1987; 9(8): 795-806

—**Sainsbury AW, Gili C.**
Ultrasonographic anatomy and scanning technique of the coelomic organs of the bosc monitor (*Varanus exanthematicus*). *J Zool Wildl Med*, 1991; 22(4):421-433

—**Scott P.**
Nutritional Diseases. In Manual of Reptiles, Eds PH Beynon, MPC Lawton, JE Cooper. BSAVA Pub. UK, 1992, pp 138-152

—**Stoskopf MK.**
Clinical imaging in zoological medicine: A review. *J Zool Wildl. Med*, 1989; 20(4): 396-412

—**Turner FB, Lannom JR Jr.**
Radiation Doses Sustained by Lizards in a Continuously Irradiated Natural Enclosure. *Ecology*, 1968; 49:548-551

—**Wallach CJ, White Fh, Gore HL.**
Isolation of *Edwardsiella tarda* from a sea lion and two alligators. *JAVMA*, 1966; 149: 881.

—**Walker N.**
Caesarian Section in Chameleons. *Vet. Rec*, 1994; May 7. p508

—**Zwart P, Dorrestein GM Stades FC Broer BH.**
J Zoo Animal Med, 1979; 10 :17

—**Zwart P.**
Erkrankungen der weiblichen Geschlechtorgane. In: Handbuch der Zootierkrankheiten. Band I, reptilien. Eds R. Ippen, H-D. Schroder and K. Elze. Akademie-Verlag, Berlin, 1985.

—**Zwart P. Cooper JE, Ippen R.**
Pathology of the ovaries of Squamata with special emphasis on vitelline-protein induced ovaritis. Verhandlungsbericht des 32nd Internationalen Symposiums uber die Erkrankungen der Zoo und Wildtiere. Akademie-Verlag, Berlin, 1990.

—**Zwart P.**
Urogenital sytem. Chapter 11. In: Manual of reptiles. BSAVA Publications UK. Eds Beynon P.H., Lawton MPC, Cooper JE (Eds)., 1992.

Horned Viper (*Cerastes cerastes*) feeding. Photo courtesy of Karl. H. Switak.

NUTRITION AND NUTRITIONAL DISORDERS

Stuart K. Ware, Ph.D.
Associate Professor
Departments of Clinical Sciences, Physiology & Biophysics
University of Kentucky
Lexington, Kentucky 40536

Stuart Ware is a physiologist at the University of Kentucky. He holds an undergraduate degree from the University of Utah and a Ph.D. degree from Iowa State University. From 1988-92 Stuart was a post-doctoral fellow at Kentucky doing research on the relationship between dietary lipids and cardiovascular function. He is currently an Associate Professor of Clinical Sciences and Physiology at the U.K. Medical Center.

INTRODUCTION

The class Reptilia is composed of more than 6,000 living species classified into four orders: Squamata (snakes and lizards), Chelonia (turtles), Crocodylia (crocodiles, alligators, and caimans), and Rhyncocephalia (the lizard-like tuatara, a single species native to the New Zealand area). The majority (by far) of living species of reptiles are lizards and snakes. Most in the US consider all animals in the order Chelonia to be turtles, but sometimes use the term tortoise to refer to strictly land-dwelling reptiles within that order (especially species of the family Testudinidae, the familiar land tortoises). The term terrapin is used infrequently in the US to refer to turtles of the family Emydidae, also called pond turtles; in Europe the term terrapin is commonly used to include all freshwater turtles.

Reptiles evolved from amphibians toward the close of the Paleozoic Era approximately 300 million years ago. During the following Mesozoic Era reptiles underwent a swift adaptive radiation and became the dominant animals on earth, remaining the most abundant of vertebrates until about 75 million years ago. Reptiles were the first vertebrates fully acclimated to life in dry places, and most extant reptiles are terrestrial. Significant in this adaptation to land was the evolution of an integument impermeable to water, and the development of the cleidoic egg that did not need to be laid in water. As a result, reptiles could take advantage of the large areas of dry land not accessible to the amphibians. Today, reptiles remain a significant part of the faunas of both tropical and temperate regions, but are less abundant than fishes, birds, or mammals. There are many extinct members of the class Reptilia, including the well-known dinosaurs, pterodactyls, and ichthyosaurs. Reptiles are ancestral to both birds and mammals. For further information on reptile phylogeny see Hildebrand (1995) and Young (1962).

Reptiles are lung breathers, have a dry waterproof skin with horny scales, may shed their outer skin regularly (ecdysis), and are born live or hatch from waterproof shelled eggs laid on land. Reptiles are ectothermic (i.e., poikilothermic, cold-blooded), using external rather than internal sources to provide heat for their bodies, and they typically regulate their body temperature by behavioral means, such as basking in the sun for warmth and burrowing underground or submerging in water to cool themselves. Many reptiles will bask in the sun following feeding, and a heat lamp of some sort may need to be provided to captive reptiles for this purpose. Basking increases the body temperature allowing, among other things, the temperature-sensitive digestive enzymes to more efficiently digest the meal. The thermal physiology of ectotherms contrasts with that of endotherms (birds and mammals) which use various physiological mechanisms coupled to an internal heat source (the metabolism of foodstuffs) to regulate their body temperatures. This is an oversimplification however because it is recognized that reptiles can increase the flow of blood to the skin during solar warming to carry the absorbed heat into the body core, then later divert flow away from the skin to conserve the internal heat and thus reduce the rate of cooling. Furthermore, some snakes

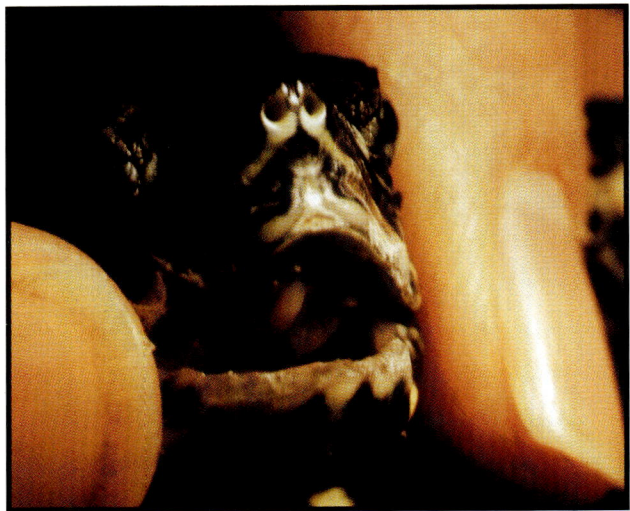

Fig. 2. Hypovitaminosis A. Note the heavily keratinized palate. Photo courtesy of Dr. Willard Nelson.

have been observed to increase their body temperature through muscular contractions while brooding their eggs. An excellent source of information on the comparative aspects of animal temperature regulation can be found in the book by Schmidt-Nielsen (1990).

With regards to the external heat source, some reptiles are heliothermic, meaning that they get their heat from basking, whereas others are thigmothermic, signifying that they get their heat from direct contact with warm objects. These different ways of obtaining heat should be taken into account when providing a heat source to captive reptiles, taking precautions, of course, to prevent thermal injuries.

Despite the fact that nutrition plays a fundamental role in the health status of all reptiles, there are relatively few nutritional studies that have been performed with these animals, and thus we know very little regarding their nutritional requirements. However, it is usually assumed by most workers (until proven differently) that the nutritional requirements of reptiles include the same nutrients, vitamins, and minerals which are required of mammals. Nutritional problems are common in captive reptiles, and most of these difficulties derive from the fact that the animals are not in their natural environments but rather often subjected to crowded, unsanitary conditions and inappropriate diets. Unfortunately, scant attention is all too frequently given to the dietary needs of captive reptiles, often resulting in various nutritional disorders that may ultimately require veterinary intervention. Nutritional deficiencies (especially of protein) may compromise immune function are thus frequently associated with secondary infections and delayed wound healing. Although not the focus of this chapter, almost nothing is known of nutritional disorders of reptiles in the wild.

DIGESTIVE PHYSIOLOGY

Reptiles (like all animals) require food to provide the energy and raw materials necessary to maintain the myriad physiological processes of body cells, and to provide the components necessary for growth and reproduction. All the energy and most of the raw materials and other components are supplied by complex organic compounds (primarily carbohydrates, proteins, and fats) derived from eating plants and animals; some of the required minerals and salts may be obtained in drinking water. It is important to recognize that a diet which furnishes adequate energy (calories) can nevertheless be totally incapable of providing the raw materials necessary for maintenance, growth, and reproduction. In other words, all reptiles have specific nutritional needs that exceed their rather simple requirements for energy. These needs include specific requirements for fats, vitamins, minerals (electrolytes), and proteins to provide the essential amino acids. Additionally, stress, trauma, and sepsis and surgery may increase the need for these nutrients by causing an increased metabolic rate. Symbiotic microorganisms in some reptiles can provide for a few of these specific needs. Some species of reptiles must eat a varied diet to obtain their nutritional requirements; others may get along fine on a single food type.

Foods and feeding mechanisms comprise a very diverse topic in animal physiology, but at the cellular and biochemical levels of nutrition, heterogeneity gives way to unity. This is probably reflective of an ancient evolution of the basic biochemistry of the procaryotic cell, followed by only discreet changes during the long evolutionary history of metazoans. Unlike some animals that can obtain their food as small particles, fluids, or dissolved organic matter, reptiles obtain their food as large particles and masses.

Fig. 1. Iguana presenting with swollen mandibles. Radiographic studies are warranted. Photo courtesy of Dr. Willard Nelson.

Teeth may be present for some degree of mastication in some species, but swallowing food whole or in large chunks is the usual pattern for reptiles. A so-called gizzard may be present (it is actually a part of the stomach) to aid digestion mechanically in some species, and it is not uncommon for reptiles to swallow small stones, called gastroliths, into the stomach for this purpose (this rarely causes problems).

As in higher vertebrates, the digestive system of reptiles is composed of a buccal cavity, esophagus, stomach, small intestine, and large intestine and colon. In some herbivorous species there is a significant sacculated cecum attached to the large intestine, and herbivores usually have a longer intestinal tract than do carnivores. The colon empties into the cloaca, a complex three-chambered structure that also receives the urogenital ducts. Also present are the liver, gall bladder, and pancreas, the exocrine secretions of which empty into the duodenum. The gall bladder may be located at some distance from the liver in some reptiles.

The process of chemical (enzymatic) digestion begins in the stomach with proteins, but most chemical digestion, and virtually all absorption, occurs in the intestine. Salivary secretions are used primarily for lubrication, not digestion (with the exception of venoms which may be proteolytic). Reptiles, like most animals, lack enzymes that digest the structural polysaccharides that constitute a major part of plant materials. However, although no reptiles are ruminants, most herbivorous reptiles likely benefit from symbiotic microorganisms in their postgastric intestinal tract that can digest cellulose and other structural carbohydrates. The

Fig. 4.
Mandibular osteodystrophy secondary to Metabolic Bone Disease (MBD). Note the characteristic *bilateral* swellings which help differentiate abscesses from true MBD. Photo courtesy of Dr. Todd Driggers

Fig. 3.
These mottled legs are resolving pathologic fractures in an iguana with Metabolic Bone Disease (MBD), recovering with calcium supplementation. Recovery will require 1-6 months. Photo courtesy of Dr. Todd Driggers.

green marine turtle has been reported to be able to digest 90% of the cellulose that it eats from sea grasses (Bjorndal, 1979), and the common iguana also benefits from microbial fermentation in the hindgut (Troyer, 1982). Volatile organic acids resulting from cellulose fermentation may constitute a significant portion of the energy budget of these animals, and the symbionts also manufacture numerous vitamins that can be utilized by the reptilian host, especially those of the B group.

Herbivorous and omnivorous lizards and tortoises may eat large amounts of low-fiber food that are then fermented by the microflora in their digestive tract. This can result in intestinal gas production and abdominal swelling, especially when their diet is changed quickly from one high in fiber to one rich in metabolizable carbohydrates. In tortoises, the bloating often results in limb extension and tissue swelling at the limb fossae. Bloating (tympany) may be treated with drugs such as simethicone administered by stomach tube to lyse the gas bubbles, and by the use of drugs such as neostigmine to stimulate intestinal motility. A change in diet may then be necessary to prevent the recurrence of tympany. Oral antibiotics can destroy the intestinal microflora of reptiles. Unflavored yoghurt, Probiocin (Pioneer Microbial Products), and Bene-Bac Pet Gel (Borden) may be given to repopulate the intestinal tract with these beneficial microorganisms. For additional information regarding symbiont-aided digestion consult Howard (1967).

The efficiency of digestion in reptiles (expressed as the ratio of energy assimilated to that ingested) averages between 80-85%, which is about the same as for other vertebrates. It is usually higher in carnivores, somewhat less in herbivores, and is diet-dependent. Once absorbed, the cellular biochemical pathways in reptiles for interconversion, and storage and catabolism of the amino acids, fatty acids, and simple sugars are similar to those of higher vertebrates. In general, digestion in reptiles requires about 72 to 96 hours, and absorption and assimilation of the digestive products may require another 24 to 48 hours.

Body temperature is important to digestive physiology (Skoczylas, 1970). Digestive enzymes have temperature optima, and, if allowed, reptiles will behaviorally regulate their body temperatures at a preferred level that may make the digestive processes more efficient. These preferred body temperatures (PBTs), also called eccritic temperatures, have been reported for a number of reptiles (see Jackson et al, 1981). Some examples of PBTs (in °C): box turtle, 27.2; alligator, 32.9; chuckwalla, 37.9; copperhead, 26; American five-lined skink, 30.6; Gila monster, 28.7; garter snake, 29.3; and boa constrictor, 32.2 as juveniles and 23.1 as adults. For temperate species of reptiles, the preferred temperatures usually range between 22 and 31 °C. Tropical species require a warmer (and more humid) environment. One worker reported that most reptiles prefer a temperature range between 27 and 30 °C, and that it decreases to 22-25 °C at night. Gastric emptying time has been demonstrated to be inversely correlated to temperature, being doubled in a python when the temperature was reduced from 22 to 18° C. It should be obvious that a source of heat must be made available to captive reptiles so that they can maintain a body temperature adequate for an efficient digestion.

Some naturally obtain their heat by basking in the sun (an incandescent light may serve for this purpose), whereas others may get their heat by direct contact with warm objects.

FOODS AND FEEDING

In general, snakes and crocodilians are carnivores whereas chelonians and lizards may be either carnivores, herbivores, omnivores, or insectivores. Tortoises are typically herbivorous. The food intake of herbivorous species is usually greater than that of carnivorous species; preferably herbivores should be fed daily or at least several times weekly. Supplemental vitamins and minerals are especially important to animals that eat plant food, and small amounts of animal protein can often be added to their diets as well. Some reptiles are highly specialized with regards to diet, such as some lizards that eat only ants or hard-shelled molluscs. The majority of captive reptiles likely receive a diet much different from their wild counterparts, not only in the food items eaten, but also with the frequency and time of feeding. Providing an assortment of foods to captive reptiles may be important, particularly to herbivorous and insectivorous species.

All snakes are carnivorous, but diet may differ with species. Some snakes (e.g., pythons, boas, rat and gopher snakes, vipers, milksnakes, kingsnakes) prefer live, warm-blooded prey, although most such snakes can be persuaded to accept dead animals. Many snakes (if not most) will eat small mammals and/or birds, and some (e.g., cobras, brown and garter snakes, kingsnakes, indigo and vine snakes, racers, ribbon snakes) will also eat

Uromastyx **lizard eating. Photo courtesy of Dr. Todd Driggers.**

other snakes, lizards (e.g., racers, vine and ribbon snakes, kingsnakes, coachwhips, brown and indigo snakes, boas, pythons, corn snakes), amphibians (e.g., garter, ribbon, water, corn, indigo, copperhead, hog-nosed, and grass and ring-neck snakes), fish (e.g., garter, grass, ribbon, indigo, and water and sea snakes), and insects (e.g., black-headed, blind, crowned, ground, hook-nosed, and red-bellied and green snakes, and the young of several snake species). An exception is the egg-eating snake *Dasypeltis scabra*, but even this snake will occasionally eat small mammals and birds, and there are other snakes with a preference for eggs in addition to their other fare (e.g., indigo, rat, ribbon, and water moccasin and brown tree snakes). Rattlesnakes are sometimes kept in captivity and prefer small mammals, birds, other snakes, and lizards. Snakes swallow their prey *in toto*.

Alligators, crocodiles, and caimans prefer to eat meat, dead rodents, birds, and fish and amphibians. Young animals may accept large insects. In the wild, crocodilians usually eat whatever they can catch, including carrion, and young animals usually eat large numbers of invertebrates (Magnusson et al, 1987). An exception is the gavial (gharial) which prefers fish, but it will occasionally eat other animals. A vitamin and mineral supplement is useful in these animals, particularly for those fed on raw meat rather than whole animals. Feeding bony meat is better than feeding boneless meat chunks.

Lizards are a diverse group with regards to their preferred foods, but the majority are insectivorous. Horned lizards in the wild eat ants and termites, but they will usually also eat crickets and mealworms in captivity, and they usually require large amounts of such food (Bauer, 1986). Green iguanas are mostly herbivorous (especially as adults) dining on flowers and leaves, but will accept vegetables, fresh fruits, insects, eggs, and will readily eat frozen mixed vegetables, and small amounts of dog and cat food. Gila monsters, tegus, and Mexican beaded lizards do well on raw eggs, chopped meat, small rodents and birds, and occasional fruit. Small skinks, anoles, and chameleons get along well by eating insects such as crickets, flies, and locusts (a variety often being required, and in large amounts). Geckos are mostly insectivorous, and also like fruit puree (the larger ones will also eat mouse pups). Collared lizards eat insects, small rodents, vegetables, and flowers, and will also eat other lizards. The large carnivorous monitors eat enormous amounts of dead rodents, chickens, and meat and eggs. Marine iguanas eat marine algae and kelp, fish, and occasionally shelled molluscs and arthropods. The chuckwalla prefers fruits and vegetables, but will eat insects, boiled eggs, and chopped meat and small rodents.

A block of alfalfa makes a tasty treat for herbivorous reptiles. Photo courtesy of Dr. Todd Driggers.

Swift and fence lizards prefer insects and eggs. When chopped meat is used to feed reptiles, it should be mixed with a source of calcium. Among lizards, herbivores tend to be larger than insectivores, but most of the very large lizards (such as the monitors) are carnivorous (Sokol, 1967).

Most tortoises are herbivores and eat a wide range of plant foods including flowers, succulents, and fresh fruit, and usually like to eat invertebrates such as crickets and worms. They will also eat frozen mixed vegetables, and dog and cat food (one should feed only small amounts of dog and cat food to reptiles because of the large amounts of vitamins A and D and protein contained therein). Tortoises should get a relatively high percentage of roughage from fiber such as that found in alfalfa leaves, coarse grass, and pelleted dried alfalfa. Most aquatic and semi-aquatic turtles are primarily carnivorous but become more herbivorous as they approach adulthood, eating earthworms, small fish, and, when older, green leafy vegetation. Trout Chow (Ralston-Purina), which provides a good nutritionally balanced diet, can be fed to turtles, as can pelleted turtle foods, but they should also receive some natural foods. Commercial turtle

Mixed vegetables make a fine meal for iguanas. Photo courtesy of Dr. Todd Driggers.

foods made of dried insects should not be used because of their poor nutritional qualities. ReptoMin (TetraWerke) is another artificial food that is palatable and nutritionally balanced, and it is specially formulated for reptiles. All chelonians have a high requirement for calcium, phosphorus, and vitamin D, and these nutrients may need to be given as food supplements (Kass et al, 1982). The food preferences of most turtles kept in captivity are known. Alligator and common snapping, soft-shelled, and bog turtles prefer meat, fish, and various invertebrates including insects; box turtles prefer meat, invertebrates, flowers, fruits, and vegetables. The desert, gopher, leopard, and Greek and pancake tortoises favor flowers, fruits, and vegetables; the cooter, false map, map, mud, musk, painted, pond, side-necked, and spotted and red-eared slider turtles prefer meat, fish, invertebrates, and pond weeds and algae. The mata mata favors fish; the wood turtle prefers meats and invertebrates. Aquatic turtles eat with their head submerged and, unlike tortoises, should not be fed on land.

Information on the feeding preferences of specific reptiles is available and should be consulted by those maintaining reptiles in captivity but uncertain of their preferred foods (Frye, 1991a, b; Frye, 1981; Mattison, 1992; Rossi, 1992; Rossi et al, 1995; Vogel, 1964). However, as food preferences often vary from one locale to another in species with a wide natural distribution, some experimentation may be worthwhile. It is worth noting that food of poor quality must be provided in larger amounts than food of better quality as more of the former is required to supply the necessary nutrients and energy. The preferred foods of selected reptiles have been summarized in Table 1; however, this does not mean that the animals will not occasionally accept other foods.

Young reptiles may differ in their food preferences from adults. This can be true with regards to food size (young animals may require smaller pieces, and smaller portions), frequency (young animals usually take food more frequently), and type.

References are available regarding the rearing of specific food items for reptiles such as mealworms, whiteworms, silkworms, wax worms, crickets, earthworms, fruit flies, houseflies, and rodents (Frye, 1991a, 1991b; Frye, 1987; Galtsoff, 1959; Mattison, 1992; Singh, 1977; Vogel, 1964). Many of these invertebrates are easily raised at home and are readily eaten by many reptiles. Mealworms (larvae of the grain beetle *Tenebrio molitor*) should preferably be fed as soft larvae rather than as hard-shelled adult beetles, and silkworms (larvae of the mulberry silk moth *Bombyx mori*) should be fed before they spin their silken cocoons. Although silkworms contain more calcium than do mealworms,

An example of a homemade diet for an iguana, composed of chopped vegetables. Photo courtesy of Dr. Todd Driggers.

neither insect has a good calcium to phosphorus ratio. This can be remedied by adding calcium to their growing medium, and by dusting them with calcium carbonate prior to using as food. Fruit flies can be fed to reptiles such as infant chameleons and geckos that are too small to eat other insects. Because wild insects often serve as hosts for parasites, some of which can infect reptiles, a home culture of insects can avoid transmission of disease. Wild-caught crickets, locusts, grasshoppers, and roaches and snails are especially prone to foster parasites, and they should not be fed to reptiles. Monarch butterfly larvae and Sphinx moth larvae (tomato horn worms) contain alkaloid substances that are toxic to reptiles.

Grasses may be grown at home by hydroponic cultivation and used to feed herbivorous and omnivorous reptiles. One advantage of this is that the fodder can be assuredly pesticide free. Seeds and pulses (e.g., peas, beans, lentils) sprouted at home make excellent nutrient sources for many reptiles. Pulses and alfalfa are good sources of protein, vitamins, minerals (including calcium), and complex carbohydrates for energy. They can be produced inexpensively and year-round.

Plants that should not be fed to reptiles because of their toxic contents include (but are not limited to): azalea, baneberry, bluebonnet, buttercup, common privet, crocus bulbs, daffodil, delphinium, eggplant foliage, eucalyptus, hyacinth, ivy, jimson weed, larkspur, laurel, milk weed, morning glory, nightshades, oak tree leaves and acorns, oleander, peony, philodendrons, poinsettia, uncooked rhubarb, rhododendron, sweetpea stems, tomato plant, trillium, tulip, vetch, water hemlock, and wild parsnip and wisteria.

FEEDING FREQUENCY

Among the various reptiles, a wide assortment of feeding patterns are observed. Some carnivores seek their prey actively by foraging (e.g., box tortoises, pond turtles); others lie in wait and capture prey when they approach (e.g., snapping turtles, mata mata turtle). Some reptiles rely on sight for locating prey (such as those that employ a "sit and wait" type of predation); others use smell or a combination of the two (e.g., snakes). Some snakes prefer to eat in the dark (such as constrictors), and hide boxes may need to be provided for them in which to eat. Whatever the strategy, understanding the behavioral activity used by specific reptiles in feeding is important because they may refuse to eat if prevented from utilizing their normal feeding strategy.

With regards to feeding frequency, some large, languid snakes do not eat more often than once every four to six weeks, but a three month fast is usually cause for veterinary intervention in any snake. Gravid pythons may fast for 6-8 weeks, and gravid boas may not eat for up to 9 months (Ross et al, 1990). With medium to large snakes, a meal every one to two weeks is probably sufficient. Snakes that are more energetic may need food every few days because activity imposes a metabolic cost, and this is also true of other reptiles. Insectivorous reptiles should be fed daily, and aquatic turtles should be given food every other day. Generally speaking, the larger a reptile, the less often it needs to be fed. However this is substantially dependent upon activity and temperature; as either or both of these increase, food intake must also rise.

Exposure to sunlight often results in an increase in activity and the need for more food. In general, active reptiles should be fed several times weekly, and in some cases possibly even daily. Tortoises and aquatic turtles may eat daily if the temperature is adequate for normal activity, and most lizards, including iguanas, feed daily. Small species of turtles and lizards may be fed daily on an *ad lib* basis, whereas larger lizards and chelonians may be fed 1-3 times weekly. The correct amount of food may have to be arrived at empirically. Mature crocodilians can be fed 1-2 times per week, but younger ones may need feeding 3-4 times weekly. After eating, basking may be important for digestion. Young reptiles that are rapidly growing, and animals undergoing reproduction, should be fed more often than others.

An inappropriate temperature, photoperiod, or humidity may disturb the regular feeding pattern. Handling the animal too often can also interfere with the normal pattern of eating. Fasting may be prolonged without causing serious effects if the water consumption is adequate for normal kidney function. Reptiles have been reported to fast for as long as 3 years without serious effect, but this likely represents the maximum.

Many temperate species of captive reptiles will naturally enter into a state of hibernation, or torpidity, usually beginning in the fall and continuing until spring. During this time, the metabolic rate will be greatly reduced and feeding discontinued (the lowered metabolic rate being fueled by stored foodstuffs, especially fat). A low environmental temperature may trigger the entrance into this dormant state, and the animal should be healthy prior to entering into this phase. A diet rich in readily digestible nutrients (e.g., squash, apples, melons, sweet corn, sprouts, alfalfa pellets, and rip figs for herbivorous reptiles) given for several weeks prior to hibernation will increase the amount of stored energy, and this may be particularly desirable for chelonians that may hibernate for six of every 12 months. If readily digestible carbohydrates are to be fed, they should be introduced into the diet gradually to avoid the tympany that can result from microfloral fermentation in the digestive tract. Food should be withheld for several days immediately prior to hibernating so that the digestive tract will be empty. If dormancy is intentionally induced by reducing the temperature (to about 10° C), it is important that full hibernation be attained; a state of partial dormancy usually results in a brisk utilization of stored energy reserves causing the animal to tolerate the hibernation poorly, if at all. The stored foods are primarily fat (located in fat bodies), with smaller amounts of glycogen in liver and muscle.

Upon emerging from hibernation, animals will usually be feeding robustly within two weeks. Lawrence (1987) investigated the phenomenon of post-hibernational anorexia (PHA) in a tortoise. Typically animals emerging from hibernation will feed when triggered to do so by a rise in blood sugar. However, an occasional reptile will not show this rise in blood glucose, and will instead become anoretic. Treatment to raise the blood sugar level (from below 1.0 up to 3.2 mmol/liter), and to lower the blood urea level, may be successful in eliminating the PHA.

COMMERCIAL FOODS AND SUPPLEMENTS

Frequently, pelleted commercial chows formulated for animals other than reptiles are used as reptile food. Those prepared for guinea pigs and rabbits can be used *ad lib* with reptiles, but those formulated for horses, goats, monkeys, and cats and dogs should be used for feeding reptiles in small amounts only because of the concentrated levels of protein and vitamins that they contain. Other commercial foods that can be used with reptiles (e.g., ReptoMin, Trout Chow) are discussed in other sections of this chapter.

There are a number of vitamin supplements that can be used with reptiles. Some consist of only a few vitamins and/or minerals, whereas others may contain a whole range of such nutrients and are referred to as multi-vitamins or multi-vitamins with minerals. Most contain varying amounts of vitamins A, C, E, and D, as well as calcium and phosphorus. These supplements can come as either tablets, powder, or liquids and can be mixed with or sprinkled on food, or placed inside food nuggets. Examples of supplements include Nutrobal (Vetark), with a Ca/P ratio of 46:1 and high doses of vitamin D and calcium, and ACE-High (Vetark), with a Ca/P ratio of 2:1 and high doses of vitamins A, C, and E, and may be given daily at a dose of about 0.1 g/kg. There are also other such supplements, such as Vionate and Vitetrin (Squibb), and SA-37 (Intervet). For aquatic animals, water-soluble preparations may be useful, such as Abidec (Parke-Davis) and Vitament (Beecham); the powder supplements added to the food may be washed away if the animal is not fed on land. If vitamin D is a concern, one needs to make sure that the supplement used contains vitamin D3, the biologically active form of the vitamin in reptiles. Dosages of the various vitamins and minerals are still difficult to recommend, and experimentation may be necessary. Additional vitamin and mineral supplements are considered in further sections of this chapter.

In general, turtles and tortoises are quite subject to vitamin and mineral deficiencies, especially of vitamins A and D, and of a calcium/phosphorus imbalance. It is thus recommended that a vitamin and mineral supplement be added to their food, and that extra calcium be given in the form of calcium carbonate. Some commercial pelleted foods are available containing these nutrients. In general, basking lizards should also receive a vitamin and mineral supplement. Snakes, as a rule, do not require supplementation with vitamins and minerals unless they have a diet composed chiefly of fish and insects. Some authors advocate the use of supplements with most or all captive reptiles, but caution against their overuse. Others frown upon the use of supplements unless specifically indicated (particularly with most snakes).

NUTRITIONAL ASSESSMENT

Evaluation of the diet of a given reptile may need to be done to establish if it is receiving either inadequate or excessive nutrients. A diet analysis and clinical examination may be the most practical way to approach this. However, given that many reptiles are highly discriminating with regards to the food they will eat, it must be recognized that the diet offered and the diet eaten may be markedly distinct. Additionally, to evaluate the long-term nutritional intake of an animal, the dietary appraisal must reflect the habitual nutrient intake rather than the intake immediately preceding the survey. Once the identity and quantity of foods consumed are known, a computer program may be used to determine the amount of each specific nutrient ingested. Eventually however the nutrients consumed must be compared to an estimate of the requirements, and this may be troublesome as so few nutrient requirements of reptiles are known. Information on the natural foods for that species may provide some clues.

Nutritional values may be assessed by comparison to such values taken from a healthy reference population. However, values obtained from a population typically form a normal statistical distribution making it unclear as to what actual reference value to make the comparison. Frequently, the 5th and 95th percentiles are chosen, but in reality it may be improper to denote a single measure which falls outside those percentiles as abnormal because it is possible that such a value could have occurred purely by chance. Cutoff points, unlike reference limits, may be set at values for which functional impairment or signs of deficiency arise, if such information is available. However, given the inherent biological variation which occurs in nature, there will likely be some overlap of normal and abnormal members of the population, leaving the investigator with a quandary difficult or impossible to resolve. With borderline values it is prudent to avoid a hasty interpretation and instead to consider diagnostic alternatives.

WATER REQUIREMENTS AND DEHYDRATION

Water is often considered the most important nutrient in animal nutrition. This stems from the fact that most animals will succumb to lack of water long before they will die from lack of food. Because of the great ability of many reptiles to conserve body water, some are able to exist under arid conditions for prolonged periods without water. The Palestine saw-scaled viper has been kept in an arid environment devoid of water for 665 days without compromising its health (Goode, 1983).

Before providing water to captive reptiles, attention to the natural habits used by the animal to obtain water may be prudent. Some will readily drink from a shallow receptacle; others will lap up water in the form of droplets on foliage, such as

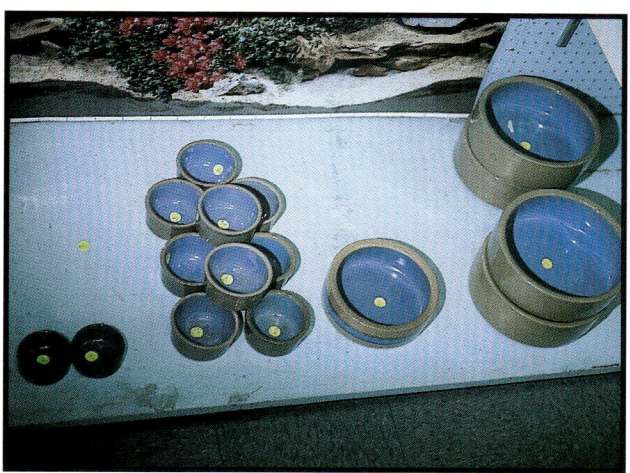
Variety of ceramic water bowls. Photo courtesy of Dr. Todd Driggers.

the various species of *Anolis*, chameleons, and other reptiles native to tropical rain forests. A spray bottle may be used several times daily to provide misted water to these animals. Others, such as many snakes, may immerse themselves in the container requiring the water to be replaced frequently. Some animals obtain most of their water from the food which they eat (e.g., horned lizards and tortoises), but the majority of these animals will learn to drink from a container.

If the reptile will not accept water from a container, droplets applied to the lips by pipette may work. This is occasionally necessary with lizards and snakes, and chameleons will usually learn to lick water from a pipette. If the water is not presented in the proper way, many reptiles may simply refuse to drink. Interestingly, some lizards, such as the desert horned lizards, obtain their water from that which condenses on their skin as dew, so misting water onto the skin of these animals may be useful (Gans et al, 1982; Schwenk et al, 1987).

Dehydration is often simply the result of an unfamiliarity with the natural water-drinking habits of the species. With dehydration, the kidneys may no longer be capable of adequately riding the circulating blood of nitrogenous wastes resulting in an accumulation of these chemicals. The major excretory products resulting from protein metabolism in most reptiles are uric acid salts (uric acid plus the ions of sodium, potassium, and ammonium), but in aquatic and semi-aquatic species ammonia and urea may form in significant amounts. Furthermore, the blood volume decreases during dehydration which may ultimately cause circulatory collapse and death.

The signs of water deprivation may include a wrinkling of the integument, a dry flaky skin, lassitude, anorexia, loss of skin and subcutaneous turgor, and hemoconcentration. Uric acid salts may precipitate out of solution as they become concentrated, causing the formation of urate crystals in the tissues. The renal tubules may become obstructed by such crystals. Thus, it is vital to provide water to all captive reptiles, even to those who normally live in arid, desert-like environments.

Reptiles showing clinical signs of water deprivation should be rehydrated. Placing water in the mouth of the animal at regular intervals may be sufficient, but with severe dehydration an oral, intracoelomic, or subcutaneous (s.c.) infusion of an electrolyte solution may be necessary (e.g., sterile isotonic saline or lactated Ringer's solution at about 2 ml/100 g body weight daily). The electrolyte solution can also be administered through a stomach tube, but in most cases it is given by intracoelomic injection. Entrolyte (Beecham) is an electrolyte replacement that is readily absorbed from the gastrointestinal tract. GatorAde (Stokely Van Camp) can be used if diluted 1/1 with water prior to use.

Frye (1991a) has reported that phosphoric acid added to the drinking water (enough to reduce the pH to 5.0-5.5) will suppress the growth of *Pseudomonas* sp. and *Aeromonas* sp., two genera of serious reptile pathogens, and without imparting a bad taste to the water. Iodination and chlorination of the water will restrain the growth of other pathogens.

FAT-SOLUBLE VITAMINS

Vitamins are required for life but not synthesized by the body, or at least not usually in sufficient quantities. Although many of them are directly involved in the cellular biochemical pathways releasing energy from foodstuffs (especially those of the B complex), vitamins are not themselves used as energy sources, nor are they assimilated into tissue structures. Vitamins are frequently classed according to their solubility in water and fat. Vitamins given parenterally may be better absorbed and provide a better response in reptiles than those given orally (Fischer, 1957).

VITAMIN A

Aquatic and semi-aquatic turtles (particularly when young) often show signs of acute vitamin A (retinol) deficiency, especially when fed an all-meat, or pet shop turtle food, diet (Frye, 1989). Such a deficiency has also been reported in lacertid lizards. Chronic hypovitaminosis-A probably occurs more frequently in captive reptiles than is usually recognized; it may even be the most frequently encountered vitamin deficiency (Elkan et al, 1967; Frye, 1984).

A deficiency of vitamin A is most often manifested in changes in epithelial tissues, especially respiratory and ocular tissues, and vitamin A maintains the integrity of such tissues (Fowler, 1980).

TABLE 1.

FOODS PREFERRED BY SELECTED REPTILES.

Reptile	Preferred Foods
CROCODILIANS	all vertebrates, carrion, insects
TUATARA	small mice, insects
SNAKES	
boas, pythons	mammals, birds, lizards
garter	mammals, snakes, amphibians, fish
gopher	mammals, birds
green	lizards, insects
indigo, ribbon	all vertebrates, eggs
kingsnake	all vertebrates
racer	all vertebrates (except fish)
rat	mammals, birds, eggs
rattlesnake	all vertebrates (except fish and amphibians)
ring-necked	amphibians, snails & slugs
vine	snakes, lizards
water	amphibians, fish, earthworms
LIZARDS	
anole, Old World chameleon, legless, banded rock chuckwalla	insects
collared	fruits, vegetables mammals, lizards, insects, fruits, flowers
gecko	mammals, insects, fruit puree
Gila monster	mammals, birds, eggs
glass, lacerta	mammals, birds, insects
horned, moloch	ants, termites
iguana (common)	insects, eggs, fruits, vegetables
iguana (desert)	insects, fruits, vegetables
skink (small)	insects, snails
skink (large), tegu	mammals, birds, insects, eggs, fruits, vegetables
spiny, spiny-tailed	mammals, insects
TURTLES	
alligator, common snapping, Blanding's, soft-shelled	meat, fish, insects
box	meat, insects, flowers, fruits, vegs
cooter, painted, pond, spotted, red-eared, mud, musk	meat, fish, insects, pond weeds & algae
desert, gopher, Chaco, radiated tortoise	flowers, fruits, vegetables

With hypovitaminosis-A, the epithelium loses its normal shape and function, resulting in respiratory difficulties, swollen and inflamed eyelids (blepharitis), and a decrease in many glandular secretions (such as mucus) because of epithelial metaplasia (a change in epithelial cell type). A reduced resistance to infections may occur because the mucous epithelia are more susceptible to invasion by microorganisms. There is also a generalized edema caused by liver failure, an overgrowth of horny mouthparts, lesions of the thyroid gland, and fatty infiltration of the liver (hepatic lipidosis). The epithelial tissues show a change from cuboidal- or columnar-shaped cells to squamous-shaped cells (squamous metaplasia), and hyperkeratosis (an overgrowth of the horny layer of the skin).

Therapy for hypovitaminosis-A consists of either oral or injectable forms of vitamin A, guarding to not give excessive amounts that can be toxic. An intramuscular injection of 5,000 units of vitamin A, repeated once a week later, may be sufficient; it has also been recommended at a dosage of 40 IU/100 g body weight. Alternatively, the vitamin may be given by stomach tube. The vitamin should then be added to the diet. Watercress, Swiss chard, fresh fish, fresh pond weeds and grasses, and liver are good sources of vitamin A or carotene (the vitamin precursor). Placing a few drops of cod-liver oil on food items can also supply this vitamin (as well as vitamin D3). Jectadine (Beecham) contains vitamins A, D3, and E and is useful in treating turtles with hypovitaminosis-A. The oral administration of ABDEC Drops (Parke-Davis) may also be employed. Supplementation with vitamin A at 100,000 IU/kg has been reported to promote ecdysis and possibly the rate of healing of skin lesions (Zwart, 1986), but overdosage is a distinct possibility at this level of supplementation, which may cause bony growths on the surfaces of bones and hepatomegaly. Hypervitaminosis-A is often the result of the overuse of vitamin A-containing products, especially those which are injected. In chelonians, this iatrogenic condition presents as a dry scaly skin that eventually becomes erythematous and necrotic, and sloughs to expose the underlying tissues. Large areas of the superficial integument may separate from the dermis. Infections and the loss of fluids may then occur. If supplemental vitamin A is clearly needed in a given animal, it is probably best to use an oral vitamin A-containing supplement rather than to inject the vitamin and chance an overdose.

VITAMIN E

Steatitis can be caused by a lack of vitamin E, or tocopherol (Dierenfeld, 1989; Wallach, 1968). The condition is seen most commonly in animals fed a diet of oily or fatty fish, including tuna, mackerel, and mullet and smelt (such as crocodilians and chelonians). It has also been identified in snakes fed on obese rodents that were reared on diets of polyunsaturated fatty acids. Steatitis is characterized by yellow or brownish pigmented nodular lesions in the fatty tissues of the body cavities, visceral organs, and subcutaneous tissues (the pigment is called ceroid). There are also adhesions between visceral organs causing the development of large tissue masses, fatty infiltration and necrosis of the liver, lesions of the skin and oral epithelium (such as lingual ulcerations owing to changes in the fat pad at the tongue base), incoordination, and necrosis and sloughing of the skin because of ischemia. The fatty tissues may be found to be firm

TABLE 2.

VITAMIN AND MINERAL DEFICIENCY SIGNS AND TREATMENTS.

Vitamin or Mineral	Deficiency Signs	Treatments
A	respiratory infections, wheezing, swollen and inflamed eyelids, edema, epithelial changes	Oral/im vitamin A, Change in diet
E	steatitis, white muscle disease, fatty tissue lesions, anorexia, visceral adhesions	Oral/im vitamin E, Selenium, Change in diet
K	bleeding of gums, spontaneous hemorrhages	Oral/im vitamin K, Varied diet.
D	soft & misshapen bones, bone fractures, tremors, metabolic bone disease	Oral vitamin D, Oral/im calcium, Change in diet
thiamin	neuropathy, paralysis, muscular twitches & atrophy, anorexia, sunken eyes.	Oral/im vit B, Change in diet
biotin	muscular weakness & tremors, lethargy, anorexia	Oral B supplement, Change in diet
riboflavin	paralysis	Oral/im vit B
C	stomatitis, gum bleeding, splitting of the skin	Oral/im vitamin C
calcium	see vitamin D	im Ca gluconate, Oral Ca lactate, Oral vitamin D3. Change in diet
iodine	hypothyroidism, goiter, anorexia, lethargy, edema	Oral iodide salts Change in diet.
selenium	see vitamin E	see vitamin E

on palpation. Often the only presenting sign is a progressive anorexia; in other cases the animals will continue to eat until death.

It is thought that steatitis results from the chronic ingestion of polyunsaturated or rancid fatty acids, the subsequent peroxidation of which ultimately results in a granulomatous inflammatory response in adipose tissue. Vitamin E functions as an anti-oxidant and may thus prevent or reduce this peroxidation.

To prevent the development of steatitis, supplemental vitamin E should be given to reptiles who have an oily-fish diet, and ideally their intake of unsaturated fats reduced by replacing some of the fish in their diet with other animals. Oral or parenteral doses of up to 800 IU of vitamin E given 1-3 times weekly, or 100 IU/daily, have been recommended to treat the condition. A 1.8 kg iguana was effectively treated with 0.025-0.50 mg sodium selenate combined with 50-100 mg vitamin E (Farnsworth et al, 1986), and it is now usually recommended that treatment consist of both exogenous vitamin E (as alpha or mixed tocopherols) and selenium. Individual doses are often arrived at empirically. Jectadine (Beecham) given at 0.2 ml/kg i.m. has been used to treat steatitis, and there are also other commercial sources of vitamin E. Because the toxicity of vitamin E is low, there is little danger in giving too much. To prevent hypovitaminosis-E, a varied diet should be provided. Routine dietary supplementation should be at about 15-25 IU vitamin E/day. Vitamins A and E have been used by some to increase the immune response of reptiles.

Muscle lesions consistent with white muscle disease have been observed in some reptiles, and the possible relationship of this myopathy to vitamin E and the mineral selenium (which act synergistically) is under study. A deficiency of either vitamin E or selenium may result in similar clinical signs, especially in muscle tissue (Rost et al, 1984; Van Vleet, 1985). A combined deficiency is usually encountered in captive reptiles. The muscles usually affected are the skeletal and cardiac muscles; smooth muscle tissue is involved less often. The muscle fibers exhibit swelling, disruption, and eventual replacement by fibrous connective tissue. The muscle fibers take on a "moth eaten" appearance, and there is a reduction in the number of cross-striations and nuclei per cell. A biopsy is usually required to confirm the diagnosis of myopathy and cardiomyopathy.

VITAMIN K

Vitamin K (phylloquinone) deficiency is relatively rare but has been reported in reptiles, especially crocodilians. It is usually the result of chronic antibiotic therapy that decimates the normal intestinal microflora that produce this vitamin. It sometimes occurs idiopathically, and it usually appears as a spontaneous hemorrhage, like bleeding of the gums and bleeding from tooth sockets when teeth are lost.

Injectable vitamin K (0.5 mg/kg) can be used to stop the bleeding, followed by oral vitamin K. Commercial preparations are available for this purpose, such as Konakion (Roche) and Synkamin (Parke-Davis) given i.m. at 0.5 mg/kg. To prevent a deficiency, the diet of captive reptiles may be supplemented with vitamin K. A varied diet may reduce the incidence of this disorder.

VITAMIN D

Vitamin D will be discussed later in the section on Metabolic Bone Disease. The active form of the vitamin is produced from photooxidation of 7-dehydrocholesterol in the skin (under the influence of ultraviolet radiation) to produce vitamin D3 (cholecalciferol), followed by chemical modification in hepatic and renal tissues to 1,25-dihydroxycholecalciferol, which is the active form of the vitamin (i.e., 1,25-dihydroxy D3). If the animal is not exposed to natural sunlight, or to artificial light of the appropriate wavelength and intensity, vitamin D should be included in the diet to prevent the development of metabolic bone disease. Hypovitaminosis-D results in a reduction in blood calcium levels, an increase in para-thyroid hormone secretion, and mobilization of calcium from bone. This makes the bones weak and susceptible to fractures. An oral dose of vitamin D should be used to treat this deficiency (at 50-100 IU/kg 3 times weekly). Commercial supplements containing vitamin D, calcium, and phosphorus are available to avert and to treat disorders of bone formation, such as Pet Cal (Beecham). If calcium is lacking in the diet, vitamin D should not be given without also giving calcium or else the vitamin may cause endogenous bone calcium to be exploited to the detriment of the animal. A weekly intake of about 100 IU D/kg body weight should be sufficient to prevent disorders with bone formation.

Artificial lighting is not usually of the proper wavelength to effect the biochemical production of D3 from 7-dehydrocholesterol. There are, however, lighting units that can reportedly provide an almost natural type of light, including Vitalite (Durotest), Chroma Series (General Electric), and TL12 (Phillips), but some units may need to be replaced after about six months of use (even if they are still working) as they may lose part of their spectrum. Furthermore, the light may need to be located near the cage in order to provide the necessary intensity of illumination; a ceiling light would likely be ineffective. Some authors have questioned the efficacy of artificial full-spectrum lights in eliciting a significant production of endogenous vitamin D, but most agree that they stimulate feeding and improve the attitude of some reptiles, especially those that are diurnal.

The action of vitamin D is to prime the digestive tract for the absorption of calcium and phosphorus, for the mobilization of bone calcium and phosphorus, and for reabsorption of calcium by the renal tubules so that it is not lost in the urine. A decreased blood calcium level is usually found when vitamin D is lacking.

Hypervitaminosis-D can occur with excessive oral supplementation, especially when ultraviolet light is also being used. Severe problems in a lizard were provoked with a dose of 200,000 IU/kg, and even 100 IU/kg has caused problems in iguanas. Blood calcium levels are elevated, and calcification of blood vessels may occur and be noted on radiographs. Other soft tissues containing smooth muscle may also become mineralized, resulting in radiodense images (e.g., radiodense pulmonary fields). Anorexia, and renal tubular necrosis with calcium deposition, are also observed, and any preexisting skeletal demineralization is usually made worse. Diets known to induce this mineralization of soft tissues include dog and cat foods that may contain too much vitamin D. The most regular and only clinically important form of arteriosclerosis in reptiles is calcification of arterial walls, likely caused by hypervitaminosis-D. For further information on vitamin D see Barnes et al (1978), Gehrmann (1987), Tsoukas et al (1984), and Wallach (1966).

WATER-SOLUBLE VITAMINS

THIAMIN

Fish may contain an enzyme (thiaminase) that destroys vitamin B1 (thiamin). Thus, reptiles eating primarily fish, such as many aquatic reptiles, may develop a thiamin deficiency unless supplemented with this vitamin. Fish that contain particularly high amounts of this enzyme include fresh water smelt, milkfish, green snapper, and cod and gray mullet, but it is also found in others, like minnows and goldfish. Hypovitaminosis-B1 has also been observed in lizards that fed on certain house plants containing phytothiaminase. Thiamin deficiency symptoms are largely neurological and include peripheral neuropathy, muscular twitches and tremors, tonic paralysis, muscular atrophy, anorexia, pulmonary edema, and a sinking of the eyes into the orbits. This vitamin deficiency should be considered whenever there is a continual loss of body weight despite an adequate intake of fish. Treatment may consist of thiamin hydrochloride injected three times weekly at a dosage of 10-15 mg/kg (or once at 80 mg/kg), thiamin added to the food (e.g., it is recommended that at least 33 mg of thiamine be added per kg of smelt in the diet), vitamin drops placed in the water, and adding non-fish items to the diet. Non-fish foods (such as dead rodents) may be disguised as fish by applying fish slime to their bodies. It has been reported that if fish are heated to 80° C for five minutes just prior to feeding, the thiaminase is destroyed and the problem abrogated (Mattison, 1992). It has been recommended however that 20 mg B1 be added to each kg of fish after cooling and before using as food.

The microflora in the intestinal tracts of reptiles can synthesize many B-complex vitamins, including thiamin. These vitamins are then absorbed from the intestinal contents. Antibiotic therapy may induce a thiamin deficiency by killing the intestinal microflora. The microflora can be reintroduced by feeding yoghurt or other *Lactobacillus* culture products.

BIOTIN

Despite the fact that avian egg yolks contain high levels of B vitamins, raw egg white contains a substance (avidin) that will induce a deficiency of biotin (another B vitamin). Heat destroys the avidin. Signs of a biotin deficiency include anorexia, muscle tremors, and a diffuse muscular weakness frequently interpreted as lethargy. Biotin deficiency is seen most commonly in tegus, monitor lizards, and Gila monsters and other lizards fed a diet of mostly raw unfertile hen's eggs. In nature these oviphagous reptiles would likely eat other items in addition to eggs, and the eggs consumed would most often contain biotin-rich embryonated tissues. Treatment consists of augmenting the diet with raw meat, small mammals, and a B-complex vitamin supplement.

VITAMIN C

A deficiency of vitamin C (ascorbic acid) has been observed in captive snakes and lizards. This often occurs because their prey species (such as rats and mice) are not fed just before being offered as food (the vitamin C exists in the intestinal tract of the prey). Thus a deficiency of this vitamin may often be prevented by using very recently fed rodents and birds as food items for reptiles, and by inserting exogenous vitamin C into dead prey animals before using them as food. Animals deficient in vitamin C will show clinical signs associated with a reduced synthesis of collagen (Chatterjee, 1967), such as poor wound healing. Snakes deficient in this vitamin may show an acute splitting of the skin, which may need to be corrected surgically. Spontaneous gingival bleeding may also occur. Infectious ulcerative stomatitis (also called "mouth rot") may also be associated

with a deficiency of this vitamin, and some workers have advocated the use of vitamin C as one element of its treatment (10-30 mg daily for ten days), as well as for maintaining healthy mucous membranes.

Treatment of vitamin C deficiency involves providing supplemental oral ascorbic acid (up to several grams for large reptiles has been recommended, as has doses of 25 mg/kg), or daily i.m. injections of 10-20 mg/kg. It has been demonstrated that reptiles can usually synthesize adequate amounts of vitamin C in their renal tissues, but kidney dysfunction may compromise this ability (Vosburgh et al, 1982). Vitamin C is also synthesized by bacteria in the colon of reptiles, but disruption of the intestinal flora by the chronic administration of antibiotics can compromise this source (as well as many of the B vitamins and vitamin K). There have been no reports of hypervitaminosis-C in reptiles.

OTHERS

Mattison (1992) reports that hypovitaminosis-B2 (riboflavin) causes paralysis of the hind legs of lizards (especially iguanids, agamids, and similar), and that this can be avoided by using a multi-vitamin supplement, such as Vitamin B Complex (Parke-Davis) given i.m. at 0.5 ml/kg (this can also be used for other B-complex vitamin deficiencies). Parentrovite (Beecham) given at 0.2 ml/kg i.m. could also be used.

Researchers have been unable to effect deficiency signs of niacin even after a totally niacin-deficient diet was fed to bull snakes for 132 days (Bartkiewicz et al, 1982). Whether a deficiency of vitamin B12 (cobalamin) occurs as a clinical entity in reptiles is not clear. Large oral doses may be used with some success to stimulate feeding in anoretic animals. Deficiencies of pyridoxine (B6), pantothenic acid, folic acid, and other members of the vitamin B-complex group may arise in reptiles, but they have not been characterized.

Deficiencies of specific individual vitamins may be readily identifiable in reptiles. However, it is rare that a single deficiency occurs alone. It is usually prudent therefore to give a multi-vitamin and mineral supplement whenever a specific nutritional deficiency is noted.

SALTS, MINERALS AND GLUCOSE

SODIUM CHLORIDE

Reptiles are not able to produce urine hyperosmotic to their blood. However, salt glands, usually situated in the nasal passages or orbits of the eyes, have evolved in some reptiles (especially marine and desert-dwelling species) as a means to conserve water by excreting hyperosmotic concentrations of sodium, chloride, and potassium ions obtained from the diet (Dunson, 1969; Dunson et al, 1967; Norris et al, 1964; Templeton, 1964). Salt glands in marine species are even able to effect a net gain in body water when the animals are drinking pure seawater! Because most diets fed to captive reptiles contain some sodium chloride, the need for supplemental salt in the diet is usually confined to marine species kept in fresh water (they continue to excrete salt when kept in fresh water even though they have no significant salt load), and even then only a small amount is needed because of their reduced salt intake. It has also been suggested that desert reptiles may occasionally need salt supplementation (particularly those with noticeable salt crystals around the nostrils). Most reptiles however get enough sodium chloride in their regular diet. Desert tortoises (which do not have salt glands) excrete excess dietary potassium in the form of potassium urates. Because uric acid is almost one-third nitrogen, tortoises fed a plant diet high in potassium will have a difficult time maintaining a positive nitrogen balance (Oftedal et al, 1994).

IODINE

Owing to diet, some reptiles, especially tortoises, may become deficient in iodine. This deficiency may lead to hypothyroidism unless the element is given as a supplement or their diet is changed. Oral supplementation can occur by adding iodized salt to the diet, or by the feeding of bread dressed with a sodium iodide solution several times weekly. Drinking water can also be supplemented with iodide, but it, like NaI-dressed foods, may be bitter and thus rejected. If so, powdered kelp tablets may be used, or iodinated casein. Giant land tortoises may require especially high levels of iodine in their diets because their natural diet is so rich in this mineral, and feeding them NaI-dressed bread regularly has been recommended (Frye et al, 1974). The dosage is not critical; a few mg/week is usually sufficient. Many vitamin and mineral supplements contain adequate iodine levels to be used prophylactically.

Some animals may develop hypothyroidism if fed large amounts of goitrogenic vegetables (e.g., cabbage, kale, Brussels sprouts, broccoli, spinach, soybean sprouts). If such plants must be used, addition of extra iodide to the diet should help to reduce the undesirable effect of these vegetables on the thyroid. Hypothyroidism (myxedema) is seen as loss of appetite, lethargy, goiter, and generalized edema. It is most often found in terrestrial chelonians, especially giant land tortoises. In aquatic and semi-aquatic turtles, a goiter may not be seen in the living animal. Histologically, the underactive thyroid appears as irregularly shaped follicles containing scanty colloid surrounded by a columnar epithelium. A normal thyroid shows regular shaped follicles containing abundant colloid surrounded by a cuboidal epithelium. Treatment may consist of supplementation with thyroxine (T4), diet correction, and/or iodide supplementation. Sodium iodide can be given for prevention. Surgical removal of the goiter is usually not recommended.

OTHER MINERALS

Commercial trace mineral salt mixes are available when the diet does not contain sufficient amounts of cobalt, magnesium, manganese, copper, zinc, and iron and other minerals. It is likely that most of these trace minerals are required by reptiles (especially herbivorous species), but deficiency diseases for them have not been reported. Calcium and phosphorus minerals are considered later in the section on Metabolic Bone Disease. A dietary excess of calcium alone is not absorbed from the intestinal tract. However, when it occurs with an excess of vitamin D3, such as when moderate or large amounts of commercial dog and cat food are fed to reptiles, the calcium can be absorbed resulting in widespread soft tissue mineralization, especially in those tissues containing smooth muscle. Female animals are usually less affected than their male counterparts because of their use of calcium in the formation of egg shells.

GLUCOSE

Stress has been associated with hypovitaminosis-C. It has also been associated with hypoglycemia and reduced levels of hepatic glycogen, especially in crocodilians raised in crowded conditions. During a feeding frenzy, hypoglycemic shock may occur (dilated non-light responsive pupils, muscle tremors, weakness, and incoordination and possible drowning). This tends to occur most often during the winter and spring when blood levels of glucose are at seasonal lows. Oral or parenteral glucose at 3 g/kg has been advocated, to be repeated every 2-3 days as needed (Wallach, 1971). Removal of the stressful conditions that caused the low blood sugar is also important. Normal glucose levels in crocodilians range from 2.8-5.6 mmol/liter, with values in the lower part of the range occurring during the October to May time period. A persistent hyperglycemia may indicate diabetes mellitus, but transiently high blood sugar levels can also be caused by stress (Britton et al, 1939). Spontaneous diabetes mellitus is rare in reptiles, being manifested by lethargy, weakness, anorexia, and glucosuria.

A summary of the various vitamin and mineral deficiencies is given in Table 2.

NUTRITIONALLY-RELATED MEDICAL CONDITIONS

PICA

Pica is the general term used to indicate the craving for unnatural foods and substances. Some reptiles appear to ingest soil (geophagy) and/or rocks (lithophagy) during the process of feeding (Kramer, 1973; Peaker, 1969; Rhodin, 1974). Some of this may be unforeseen, but it has been suggested that rocks may serve as gizzard stones aiding in mechanical digestion. They may also serve in the control of buoyancy in aquatic and semi-aquatic reptiles. It has been proposed that ingested soil may provide some essential dietary minerals, and that the intake of rocks and soil is thus intentional (Skorepa, 1966; Sokol, 1971).

Bowel impaction may result from eating stones and soil, and can often be successfully treated with a simple cathartic, with colonic irrigation, or by employing a warm water soak (Frye, 1981). Occasionally, surgery may be necessary to remove an intestinal obstruction. Substances such as wood chips, sawdust, small stones, gravel, and sand can cause serious intestinal obstruction, and often these items are used as cage litter for reptiles.

Some young reptiles have been observed ingesting fresh feces from older conspecific animals, but such consumption is not common. The possibility for horizontal transmission of pathogens with such behavior is obvious. The conduct may be related to the acquisition of symbiotic microbes necessary for the processing of complex carbohydrates and the production of vitamins (Troyer, 1984, 1982).

Autooviphagy (the eating of ones own eggs) has been observed in snakes and geckos. Cannibalism occurs in many reptiles such as snakes, lizards, and crocodilians and turtles and is often triggered by a "feeding frenzy" that may occur when confined animals are given food.

Ingesting the molted skin is not unusual for some snakes and lizards (Bustard et al, 1965). This keratophagy (dermatophagy) may represent a recycling of sulfur-rich amino acids found in the epidermal proteins.

Sea turtles often eat calcareous corals and coral reef sponges that may contain silica and other materials toxic to most vertebrates (Meylan, 1988). However, the turtles appear to remain healthy.

ANOREXIA AND STARVATION

Anorexia is one of the most common problems experienced with captive reptiles. It can be caused by a very large number of factors, including a temperature that is too low. Many reptiles require a temperature of at least 25° C before they will feed and, in general, young reptiles need a slightly higher temperature than adults. An inappropriate humidity level may be a cause for anorexia (most reptiles do well in the range of 30 to 70%, which may require a humidifier during the winter), as

---

TABLE 3

CAUSES AND SIGNS OF SELECTED NUTRITIONALLY-RELATED CONDITIONS

Condition	Causes	Signs
anorexia	excess handling of animal, improper temperature or lighting, ecdysis, hibernation, infections, parasites, stress, trauma, stomatitis, improper diet, lack of vitamins, hypothyroidism, diabetes mellitus, hypervitaminosis-D, gout, pregnancy	weight loss, sunken eyes, prominent bones, muscle wasting, lassitude
bloating	too much low-fiber food, constipation	abdominal swelling
dehydration	improper presentation of water, lack of available drinking water, may accompany anorexia	skin wrinkling, lassitude, appetite loss
metabolic bone disease	lack of dietary calcium, too much dietary phosphorus, lack of vitamin D, hyperparathyroidism, chronic renal disease	bone fractures, skeletal deformities, swollen and weak limbs
edema	hypovitaminosis-A, deficiency of iodine, goitrogenic diet	generalized swelling of tissues
articular gout	dehyration, high protein diet, chronic renal disease	swollen and painful joints
obesity	excessive caloric intake	enlarged fat deposits, swollen tail
constipation	intestinal obstruction	bloating
vomiting	constipation, ulcers, stress, handling of animal after eating, low temperature, food gorging, intestinal obstruction, toxins, intestinal parasites & bacteria	dehydration, inanition
diarrhea	intestinal parasites & bacteria, low temperature, pancreatitis	dehydration, inanition

may an improper photoperiod (15 light/9 dark has been recommended for some temperate species of reptiles), but a constantly lighted environment should never be provided because of the stress it imposes. The addition of full-spectrum fluorescent light may stimulate feeding in some reptiles, and exposure to unfiltered sunlight may be a powerful stimulant to the appetite in anorectic animals (especially turtles and lizards that have been deprived of natural sunlight and warmth). Sunlight may even cause overt aggressive behavior in previously unaggressive animals. See Regal (1980) for additional information.

Anorexia can also be caused by internal parasites, infections (such as "mouth rot"), excess handling of the animal, trauma associated with capture and the stress of a new surroundings, during preparation for ecdysis, and during periods of psychosocial stress caused by factors such as overcrowding. Providing a hide box may be helpful for shy species. Furthermore, anorexia may be owing to a monotonous diet, hibernation (e.g., alligators in the vivarium may cease to feed for six weeks to three months without hardship), inadequate ventilation, diabetes mellitus, hypothyroidism, vitamin deficiency (E, B1, biotin), or lack of knowledge regarding the proper diet for a given reptile species. As a matter of fact, the most common reason for anorexia is because an incorrect diet is being offered. Even the temperature of the food may be important. A complete evaluation of the environment and maintenance practices for the animal may be required to identify the cause of the anorexia. Once identified however the reason is usually quite easily corrected; the challenge lies in recognizing the basis for the anorexia.

Sometimes an animal reluctant to eat may be persuaded to do so by presenting it with a large variety of food. If the food chosen is not easily obtainable, the animal often can be weaned onto something more convenient by offering the foods together and gradually reducing the proportion of the former. Scents may be important in feeding. A snake that will eat only lizards or toads may be manipulated into eating mice after rubbing the lizard or toad over the rodents skin, or by feeding the two prey items together.

When feeding whole dead animals (especially other reptiles) that may contain external or internal parasites, the prey animal should be deeply frozen for at least 96 hours to kill the suspected pathogens, then thawed and warmed before using as food. This will usually kill fleas, ticks, and mites and worms, but some bacteria and protozoans will likely survive.

Most reptiles can survive for many weeks without eating. However, as the energy stores are reduced with chronic starvation, clinical signs begin to become evident. These signs include a subnormal weight, sunken eyes, a prominent bony skeleton, muscle wasting because of protein deficiency, a shrunken or wrinkled skin, and secondary infections and stunted growth. On autopsy, one may observe a small liver, a deficiency of fat in the body cavities, and muscle atrophy. As the caloric intake is reduced, the metabolic rate decreases as compensation (Belkin, 1965). However, because a finite metabolic rate is necessary to sustain life, this reduction can only prolong the inevitable if the energy intake is not reestablished.

Tube-feeding (gastric gavage) with a warm slurry of a high-calorie nutritional supplement may be necessary for animals that will not eat. There are several commercially available products that can be used for this purpose, including Nutrical (EVSCO), Vivonex (Norwich Eaton), and Hycal (Beecham) and Pet Kalorie (Haver-Lockhart). You can make your own supplement by adding raw egg yolks to homogenized liver and a multi-vitamin and mineral supplement, and there are other recommended formulations as well (see Frye, 1981; Holt, 1981). A syringe fitted with a length of soft rubber or plastic tubing, an appropriately sized endotracheal tube, or an intravenous or small urinary catheter of the proper diameter, can be used to administer the food directly into the animals stomach. The tubing should be lubricated with egg yolk before trying to pass it through the throat and into the stomach. Do not force the tube if it doesn't slide down easily, and be careful not to place it into the trachea. If need be, the location of the tube can be determined radiographically. About 10-15 ml of nutritional supplement per 100 g body weight per day given in divided doses has been recommended. To prevent regurgitation the material should not be given too quickly. Force feeding herbivorous reptiles readily fermentable carbohydrates can result in serious cases of tympany.

It has been reported that when royal pythons refuse to eat, long-term tube-feeding may become necessary, often for the rest of the animals life. It has also been reported that large oral doses of vitamin B12 may stimulate feeding in reptiles that are anorectic. The drug metronidazole (Flagyl - Searle) given to anorectic snakes will often cause them to eat. A single dose of 15-25 mg/kg delivered directly into the stomach by tube (as a slurry or suspension) is recommended. The mechanism by which

Green tree python with a g-tube. Photo courtesy of Dr. Todd Driggers.

this antiprotozoan drug works to stimulate feeding is not known.

In some cases, force-feeding the natural food may need to be done. This can be accomplished by gently pushing the food item down the esophagus using a rounded glass rod or similar item. In snakes, the food must be pushed down to about one-third the length of the body in order to enter the stomach. In general, force-feeding turtles, crocodilians, and lizards is more difficult than snakes. Hand feeding a natural diet to reptiles that will not eat may also work, but the meals should be small and frequent for the first few days. If a nutritional supplement is used, attempts to hand-feed a natural diet should follow as soon as possible. Food can simply be placed in the mouth and the animal replaced into its cage. Some reptiles will not adjust well to captivity, requiring hand-feeding indefinitely.

Starvation is frequently accompanied by dehydration and an imbalance of serum electrolytes (Jarchow, 1988). It has been suggested that tube-feeding or force-feeding of the emaciated reptile be postponed until after the administration of fluids of 2-3% of body weight for several days to correct the electrolyte imbalance and dehydration. Hartmann's solution or a 5% dextrose solution with 0.3% potassium has been recommended for this purpose, but there are various other electrolyte solutions that may be used as well.

METABOLIC BONE DISEASE

Disorders of calcium metabolism may comprise the single most important area of captive reptile nutrition, and they are certainly the most regularly encountered mineral-related nutritional problems. Because the majority of nutritional problems

Examples of gavage tubes. Photo courtesy of Dr. Lowell Ackerman.

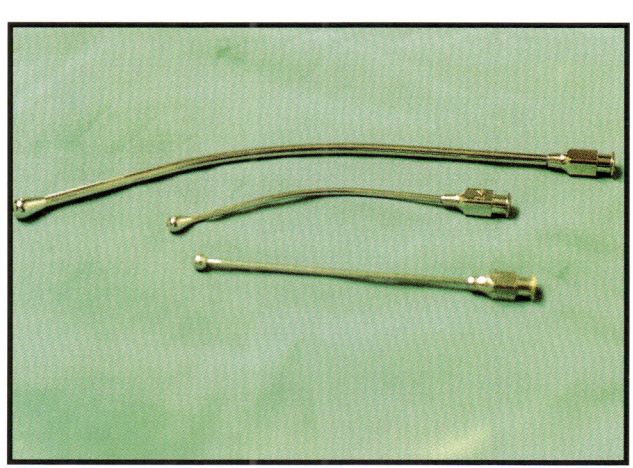

become apparent during growth, bone disease often occurs where young animals are being reared (such as with crocodile farming). Even though reptiles continue to grow their entire lives (i.e., have indeterminate growth), they grow most rapidly during their first several years.

Metabolic bone diseases may be divided into three types: those characterized by porosis, those distinguished by malacia, and those characterized by petrosis (Smith et al, 1972). With osteoporosis the bone mass is reduced because of defects in bone formation or because of intense resorption of bone, but the existing bone is properly calcified, and there is no excessive osteoid production (osteoid is unmineralized bone matrix produced by osteoblasts).

Desert Tortoise with normal shell morphology. Photo courtesy of Dr. Bernard A. Mangone.

Osteomalacia occurs when the osteoid fails to calcify into true bone, and this malady forms the primary feature of the disease rickets. Osteopetrosis is distinguished by excessive mineralized bone that results in thickened yet fragile bones.

Metabolic bone disease has been called fibrous osteodystrophy, secondary nutritional hyperparathyroidism, nutritional osteodystrophy, osteomalacia, rickets, cage paralysis, osteogenesis imperfecta, osteoporosis, juvenile osteoporosis, osteodystrophia fibrosa cystica, and other terms. These diseases have a similar pathogenesis, being induced by endogenous parathyroid hormone (PTH), calcitonin dysfunctions, and/or problems with vitamin D, calcium, and phosphorus, which upset the balance that exists between calcium in the bone and that in the body fluids. Metabolic bone disease is the preferred term of some authors.

Rickets is an osteomalacic disorder of the young animal distinguished by the failure of the bone osteoid to mineralize to mature bone. Soft, easily deformed and fractured bones result, with a widening of the metaphyseal plates, a thickening of the epiphyses, and a flaring of the articular cartilages. Swellings ("rachitic rosettes") may be seen where the bony and chondral ribs articulate. Rickets is caused by an insufficient intake (or production) of vitamin D, and the ensuing inability to absorb calcium. Serum calcium levels are usually low.

Fibrous osteodystrophy is a frequent disease seen in captive reptiles, especially in herbivorous and omnivorous lizards like iguanids, and is the most common metabolic bone disease (Wallach et al, 1968). It is characterized by osteomalacia; however, the disease differs from true osteomalacia and rickets in that bone resorption eventually occurs, the resorption being caused by excessive levels of PTH acting on the matrix of the bone. To compensate for the loss of bone substance, osteoblastic activity is increased replacing the demineralized bone with osteoid, thus weakening the bone. Both osteomalacia and rickets can progress to fibrous osteodystrophy. The high levels of circulating PTH can result from primary hyperparathyroidism (usually owing to benign parathyroid tumor; Frye et al, 1975), but are more commonly caused by nutritional secondary hyperparathyroidism in response to hypocalcemia or, commonly, hyperphosphatemia.

Nutritional secondary hyperparathyroidism frequently occurs when the diet is chronically deficient in calcium or excessive in phosphorus, or when vitamin D is lacking (without vitamin D, calcium cannot be absorbed from the digestive tract or mobilized from bone). Radiographs will show bone with a normal sized medullary cavity, but surrounded by thickened cortical bone of a markedly spongy nature and diminished radiodensity. These decalcified bones are soft, deformed easily, and highly susceptible to fracture, even from normal weight-bearing. In chelonians, the bony shell can be deformed. Because of the peculiarities of shell growth, treated chelonians may grow rapidly and assume a spherical shape. Some may become so misshapen that their feet may not be able to come into firm contact with the ground. The first sign of a calcium deficiency is often muscle tremors.

Renal-associated osteodystrophy ("renal rickets") is caused by chronic renal disease and the accompanying inability to excrete phosphorus. The elevated phosphorus of the body fluids then elicits secretion of PTH that, in turn, invokes the resorption of bone matrix by osteoclasts. Blood urea nitrogen (BUN) levels are often elevated as well, indicating renal disease. Most cases are caused by a chronic loss of renal function owing to an interstitial or pyelonephritis. Dialysis is of only temporary help.

Desert tortoise with abnormal shell morphology due to metabolic bone disease. The diet of this animal as a juvenile was guinea pig chow. Photo courtesy of Dr. Bernard A. Mangone.

The calcium/phosphorus ratio is extremely important in reptile nutrition, especially in chelonians, lizards, and crocodilians, and diets with too low a ratio are the usual cause of metabolic bone disease. This low ratio often occurs because the captive diet may contain inadequate sources of calcium, and/or too much soluble phosphorus in relation to the available calcium. When the phosphorus intake is excessive it becomes difficult to get enough calcium in the diet to maintain a desirable Ca/P ratio. In addition, the diet is often deficient in vitamin D. Problems become most evident when the rapid growth of young animals outstrips the available calcium and phosphorus. The optimum dietary Ca/P ratio lies between 1-2/1 (the higher ratios being required by juveniles and breeding females), but with some diets can approach 1/40. A ratio too low can result in an increased secretion of PTH to mobilize calcium from bone, and low ratios can be made worse in reptiles with a vitamin D deficiency. Most captive diets need some supplementation with calcium (without phosphorus), especially the diets of carnivores fed muscle meat (Collins, 1971). Muscle meat by itself (lacking bones) is not nutritionally balanced as it lacks calcium and fat-soluble vitamins. It has been recommended that 900 mg of calcium carbonate be added to each 100 g of red meat, and 1.5 g to each 100 g of fish.

Nutritionally-induced metabolic bone disease (fibrous osteodystrophy) is arguably the most common disease of iguanas, but it can affect all reptiles, and is also frequently seen in aquatic and semi-aquatic turtles. Affected reptiles present as lethargic, often to the extent that the hind limbs (which may be markedly swollen) do not move, and muscle atrophy may be apparent. Spontaneous fractures can also occur; those of the appendicular skeleton and spine are common. The mandibles of lizards and crocodilians are often distorted

Desert tortoise with nutritional hyperparathyroidism. Note mandibular prognathism. Photo courtesy of Dr. Bernard A. Mangone.

and swollen, and there are gross deformities of the plastron and carapace of chelonians. The hypocalcemia which accompanies this disorder may then cause muscle tetany, tremors, and cardiac failure. Demineralization of bone may be apparent on radiographs. Treatment involves reversing the hypocalcemia by giving a solution of 1% calcium gluconate at a dose of 1-2 ml/100 gram body weight followed by diet correction and/or oral supplements. A dose of 500 mg/kg given intramuscular has also been advocated. Adding calcium to the drinking water may also be useful, four grams of calcium lactate being placed in one liter of water. The use of ultraviolet light to produce the proper levels of vitamin D3 may be recommended for long term maintenance (Boivin et al, 1990).

Reptiles feeding largely upon mealworms, crickets, earthworms, lean meat, liver, and chicken and fish; vegetables including lettuce, cucumber, and cabbage; fruits such as bananas (which can also cause constipation in chelonians), grapes, pears, and apples and tomatoes, may develop an undesirable calcium/phosphorus ratio. There are a number of plants rich in calcium and relatively low in phosphorus (e.g., alfalfa, clover, dandelion, beets, pea pods, some pelleted commercial chows, soybean leaves, turnip and broccoli tops, oranges, carrots, watercress) that can serve to correct a nutritional imbalance of these ions if introduced into the diet gradually. Broccoli tops and watercress are particularly desirable, because they not only contain a high ratio of Ca/P, but also have large absolute amounts of calcium. Using whole adult rats and mice as food is also good. It is possible to raise mealworms using a vitamin/mineral supplement so that their Ca/P ratio is greatly improved, and to dust them (and other invertebrates) with calcium carbonate prior to use as food; if so, such food would then be more appropriate. References on how to increase the calcium content of various invertebrate foods used to feed reptiles are available (Allen et al, 1982; Strzelewicz et al, 1985).

To summarize, metabolic bone diseases may result in bone fractures; decalcified, thickened bone; skeletal deformities like kyphoscoliosis; soft and deformed mandibles; soft, misshapen, and lumpy shells (chelonians); and swollen and weak limbs. Sometimes it becomes difficult for the animal to use its legs to move about. Radiographs may show a poorly defined skeleton; in fact, calcium present in the digestive tract may be more evident than the animals own skeleton. Most nutritional bone disorders are due to diets low in calcium or in the Ca/P ratio. Therapy to stop the advancement of the disease may include subcutaneous and intramuscular injections of 10% calcium gluconate (1-2 ml/kg), oral vitamin D3 (50-100 IU/kg 3 times/

Desert tortoise with nutritional hyperparathyroidism. Note protruding eyes due to shell deformity and inflammation. Photo courtesy of Dr. Bernard A. Mangone.

week), calcium lactate added to the drinking water (3-4 g/liter), and a change to an appropriate diet. Pure calcium carbonate may be found unpalatable, but powdered cuttlefish bone, and egg shell and commercial supplements may be accepted. Because iodine may be required to get the animal into a positive calcium balance, a mineral supplement containing iodine (or a KI solution) should also be given. Cod-liver oil is a good source of vitamin D3 (84 IU/ml), but it can become rancid. Canned dog and cat foods are good protein sources, and are usually supplemented with the appropriate level of calcium, but the high levels of protein will cause a too-rapid growth, so only small amounts of these foods should be used with reptiles. Commercial vitamin supplements can also be used, such as Nutrobal given at 0.1 g/kg/day until the problem is corrected, or Vionate administered at 1 g/kg/day. Although the progression of the disease may be halted, it is unlikely that any skeletal deformities already existing will be reversed.

Ingestion of too much calcium is rare, but when it occurs it stimulates the ultimobranchial bodies and the parafollicular C cells of the thyroid to secrete calcitonin. This hormone prevents the resorption of calcium from bone and causes the ion to be excreted in the urine (i.e., it is antagonistic to PTH, reducing plasma calcium levels).

Many of the metabolic bone diseases discussed earlier are, as already pointed out, frequently lumped together under the terms nutritional osteodystrophy or nutritional (secondary) hyperparathyroidism. There are several good sources of information on metabolic bone diseases of reptiles (Capen et al, 1983; Fowler, 1993; Jackson et al, 1981; Wallach, 1971; Wallach et al, 1982; Zwart et al, 1969).

NITROGEN EXCRETION AND GOUT

When carbohydrates and fats are oxidized in the body, water and carbon dioxide are the end-products. Protein and nucleic acid metabolism also gives rise to H_2O and CO_2, but nitrogen-containing end-products are also produced. The primary nitrogenous waste products excreted by reptiles are correlated to the habitat of the animal: ammonia in aquatic species, and uric acid salts and urea in semi-aquatic and terrestrial forms. In general, lizards and snakes excrete mostly uric acid salts. Aquatic turtles excrete almost no uric acid, whereas this compound dominates in the most terrestrial species. Crocodilians excrete mostly ammonia (Cragg et al, 1961; Moyle, 1949). Reptiles are often spoken of as being predominantly ammonotelic, ureotelic, or uricotelic depending upon their major nitrogen-containing waste product (Dessauer, 1970; Schmidt-Nielsen, 1990). Most terrestrial reptiles are functionally uricotelic. A good discussion of the physiology of desert reptiles can be found in the book written by Schmidt-Nielsen (1964).

Ammonia is highly toxic and highly soluble and thus needs to be flushed rapidly from the body. The high rate of urine production required for this usually causes no problem as aquatic species which produce ammonia generally have unlimited access to drinking water. Urea is less toxic than ammonia, and uric acid has a low solubility in water. Therefore, animals who do not always have ready access to drinking water have evolved a biochemistry based primarily on uric acid excretion that allows them to conserve water. The extreme is seen

Profile of a desert tortoise with metabolic bone disease. Note pointing of snout. Photo courtesy of Dr. Bernard A. Mangone.

in many arid, desert-dwelling reptiles who excrete uric acid almost exclusively, it being much less water-soluble than urea. Porter (1972) discusses the evolution of uric acid excretion as being requisite for the protracted development of the reptilian embryo in the cleidoic egg. The uric acid is stored inertly as a crystal precipitate within the allantois, reducing the amount of urine that would otherwise need to accumulate during development in the closed egg.

Well-hydrated animals can readily clear uric acid from the blood, but given its low water solubility it may accumulate as crystals within body tissues whenever its concentration in the blood increases. Theoretically, this may occur if the animal becomes water-deprived or suffers renal failure (both of which reduce the renal clearance of uric acid salts), or if the animal is given a high protein diet (which produces a larger uric acid load to contend with). Renal failure can result from the use of any of several nephrotoxic drugs that damage the renal tubules and glomeruli (Montali et al, 1978). It has been claimed that dehydration is likely the chief factor predisposing to urate crystal formation in reptiles (Jackson et al, 1981). However, a high protein diet is also considered to be a significant cause of crystal formation, a condition often observed in commercially farmed alligators where the uric acid levels have been observed to increase as much as 17-fold (Coulson et al, 1964). Additionally, the ingestion of proteins rich in the amino acid serine may cause renal damage and uric acid accumulation (hyperuricemia). It thus almost goes without saying that a protein-rich diet may rapidly become a problem in the dehydrated animal. Prevention of hyperuricemia (sometimes called "renal constipation") is afforded by providing a well-balanced diet (protein-rich dried and canned dog and cat foods should be used sparingly), and by making plenty of fresh water available at all times (Wallach, 1971).

Gout is the disorder which occurs when uric acid crystals become deposited in tissues (Appleby et al, 1967). Visceral gout results from crystal formation in the viscera, including the pericardial sac, heart, lung, and liver and kidneys. The microcrystals of uric acid may consolidate to form large, starburst-shaped structures called tophi that can be seen with a microscope in affected tissues. Tophi are actually granulomatous tissue lesions formed as a result of an inflammatory reaction to the uric acid crystals. The tophi may subsequently become mineralized with calcium salts. Visceral gout is relatively common in captive reptiles, and it can be fatal. Signs may include a decreased appetite and lethargy, but sometimes the animal may just be found dead with no prior indication of the disorder. Chalky-white urates may be located throughout the viscera, imparting a pale yellow color to the tissues.

Less common in reptiles is articular and periarticular gout, where the uric acid crystals and tophi accumulate in and around the joints, respectively. This type of gout is often associated with an abnormally high intake of animal protein by herbivorous reptiles. The signs include swollen joints, pain, and an aversion to movement. The tophi can be seen radiographically if they are calcified, but the urates are usually radiolucent. Chalky-white or yellow-white deposits from pinpoint size up to several centimeters in diameter may be found in the joints (or in the viscera in the case of visceral gout).

The kidneys are often damaged in gout, the urates being deposited in various renal tissues and even blocking the renal tubules. Renal disease may initially cause the hyperuricemia due to a decreased clearance of uric acid, or it may be caused by some other factor (such as dehydration). Whatever the cause, an accumulation of urate crystals in the renal tissues may follow causing (further) renal dysfunction and even less uric acid excretion, eliciting a vicious metabolic cycle.

Treatment for gout consists of reducing the protein intake and rehydrating the animal. Allopurinol (at 15-20 mg/kg) may be used together with colchicine (Jackson et al, 1981), but the effectiveness of this drug treatment is uncertain. If the animal has been receiving a nephrotoxic drug, such as some aminoglycoside and sulfonamide-containing antimicrobials, it should be withdrawn. Surgical removal of the urates may be necessary in some cases. Efficacy of treatment of this disorder can be determined radiographically. A deficiency of vitamin A can cause renal tubular degeneration, predisposing some reptiles to gout (Humphries, 1978).

Diseases which appear clinically related to articular gout are articular and periarticular pseudogout, or false gout (Jackson et al, 1981). In this uncommon condition, caused by a disorder of calcium metabolism, there is involvement and swelling of joints and possibly the tissues around joints, but the deposition is not of uric acid but rather of calcium hydroxyapatite crystals. It is important to note that crystals of hydroxyapatite, like calcified tophi, are radiopaque. A cream-colored gritty material may be found at necropsy.

OBESITY

Most nutritional difficulties in captive reptiles appear to be associated with malnutrition and vitamin and mineral deficiencies. However, many reptiles suffer from too much caloric intake relative to their requirements. Captive animals, unlike their wild counterparts, expend little energy in obtaining food, so there is a real threat that they will eat more than they should (and it is often under such growth-promoting circumstances that dietary inadequacies are

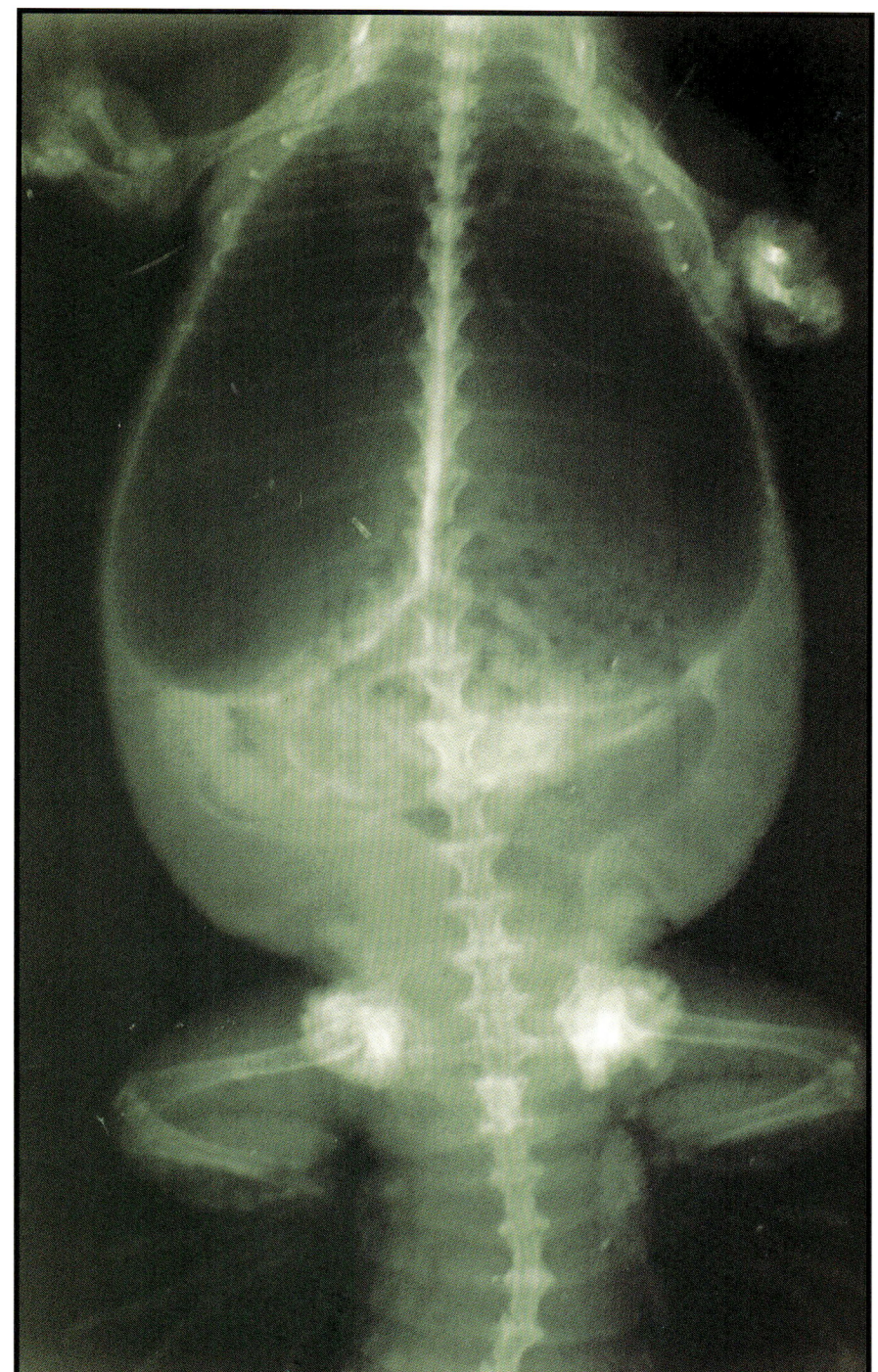

Radiograph of a lizard with gout. Radiograph courtesy of Dr. Todd Driggers. Photo courtesy of Dr. Lowell Ackerman.

relatively little subcutaneous fat in reptiles. With obesity, large amounts of adipose tissue may accumulate in coelomic, intermuscular, and fascial and subcutaneous sites. There is also fatty infiltration of the liver and other visceral organs, and skeletal abnormalities may occur in chelonians. To prevent obesity, the frequency and amount of feeding must be closely matched to the metabolic needs of the animal (taking into consideration growth, activity, and reproduction). Daily feeding is recommended for highly active animals, but some large reptiles should be fed much less often. Reducing the food intake may be necessary until the obese animal returns to its normal body weight. For additional information on lipid storage and use in reptiles see Derikson (1976) and Loumbourdis (1987).

HEPATIC LIPIDOSIS

Hepatic lipidosis is a disorder characterized by an abnormal accumulation of lipid in the cytoplasm of liver cells (hepatocytes). Although affecting the parenchymal cells, which are often swollen as a result, the endothelial, Kupffer, and biliary duct cells are not altered. The affected liver appears as a swollen organ with a pale yellow or tan color (the liver of some reptiles may be heavily pigmented due to the deposition of melanin), and, due to the lower density of accumulated lipid, will float in water. The cellular changes may occur because normal hepatocytes are presented with an increased fat load, or because injured cells are unable to metabolize lipid properly. This disorder is relatively common in captive reptiles, and seems to occur most often as a result of obesity (too many food calories relative to metabolic needs). The obesity imposes an increased fat load on the liver. Pathways for fat metabolism may be damaged with injury to the hepatocytes, and lipid may accumulate in the cells as fat production exceeds use and export. This may occur when liver cells are damaged by bacterial toxins. The liver is

revealed). The more highly active reptiles expend more energy in their daily activities and, even with daily feedings, do not become obese (e.g., garter snakes, racers, vine snakes, anoles, basilisks, geckos, chameleons, aquatic freshwater turtles).

A high caloric intake may result in obesity, and the enlarged fat deposits may interfere with organ function, such as with lung expansion. These fat deposits can often be seen around the neck and upper limbs, and a swollen tail may also be a sign of obesity. Normally, fat is stored in the abdominal cavity in adipose tissue masses called fat bodies; there is particularly vulnerable to fatty change because that is where most fats are synthesized and metabolized, but fatty accumulations can also occur in other organs, such as the heart and kidneys.

Fat is absorbed into the body fluids from the intestine primarily in the form of chylomicrons, which are triacylglycerol-rich lipoproteins. The chylomicrons are then metabolized in the adipose tissues, with the triacylglycerols being stored there. Glucose absorbed from the intestine (beyond that which can be stored as glycogen in liver and muscle) is converted into triacylglycerols in the hepatocytes, added to protein to form very low density lipoproteins (VLDLs), and secreted into the blood. The VLDLs from the liver are then metabolized by adipose tissues, and the triacylglycerols stored there. Absorbed glucose can also be taken up by adipocytes and stored as triacylglycerols. When needed for energy, the triacylglycerols stored in adipose tissue cells can be hydrolyzed to fatty acids and released into the blood for use by other tissues.

Hepatic lipidosis may occur as the result of an excessive release of fatty acids from adipose tissue stores in comparison to their oxidation for energy. Lipidosis can also occur with a reduction in the synthesis of hepatic VLDLs due to a decrease in liver protein synthesis. The accumulation of lipid in the liver may also be secondary to the metabolic derangements of diabetes mellitus. With hepatic lipidosis, the use of carbohydrates for energy is impeded, and there is an incomplete oxidation of fatty acids which may result in the release of ketoacids from the liver. Lipidosis is often a progressive and fatal disorder.

CONSTIPATION, VOMITING AND DIARRHEA

The rate of digestion and passage of food through the digestive tract is greatly dependent upon the content of the food, body temperature, and activity level of the animal. Stools passed may differ significantly in their frequency, consistency, and content, and it is difficult to judge when a given animal is truly constipated. Constipation seems especially to affect terrestrial chelonians. Factors that can lead to constipation include limited access to drinking water, little or no exercise, ingestion of cage litter, and lack of dietary roughage. Fluid absorption from retained feces often causes them to become hard masses which are then difficult or impossible to move with normal peristalsis. Radiography may be used to detect constipation where gas-filled, dilated loops of intestine may be present cranial to the obstruction. Treatment may include a tepid bath, the use of a small amount of mineral oil or a magnesium oxide suspension, and giving doctyl sodium sulfosuccinate (DSS) diluted 1/20 in warm water (Paul-Murphy et al, 1987). The DSS is administered by stomach tube or given as an enema into the copradeum (but not the urodeum or common proctodeum). A small amount of oral simethicone solution (e.g., Mylicon - Stuart) can be used to break the gas bubbles.

Vomiting in reptiles can be caused by constipation. Digestion may proceed too slowly at low temperatures, resulting in food putrefication and vomiting, and handling the animal too soon after feeding can also cause vomiting (especially in snakes and lizards). The vomit reflex is particularly active in snakes. Complete digestion takes 72-96 hours, and handling the animal should not occur for at least 48 hours after feeding to avoid postprandial vomiting. Indeed, these two factors (low temperature and handling) may be the most common reasons for vomiting in reptiles. Vomiting may also be caused by an obstructive lesion of the digestive tract, located either inside the tract (e.g., ingested foreign body, inspissated stool) or outside it (e.g., abscess, granuloma, tumor). It may also be caused by intestinal stasis induced by chemicals, including toxins. Intussusception can cause vomiting, and this condition may occur whenever the gut becomes hypermotile. Intestinal bacteria and parasites can also cause vomiting, particularly cryptosporidiosis in snakes, so stool samples should be examined for the presence of pathogens and their ova. If the vomited material is blood-tinged, gastric erosion and ulcers should be suspected. Fiberoptic endoscopy, with or without gastric biopsy, and radiography, may be used to uncover the etiology of persistent vomition. In some cases, simple gorging on food may be the reason for the regurgitation. Chronic vomiting in chelonians carries an unfavorable prognosis.

Diarrhea is an uncommon problem in captive reptiles. In cases of diarrhea, the stools should be examined for pathogens (protozoan and metazoan parasites, and bacteria and mycotic pathogens). If negative for pathogens, any of several anti-diarrheal medications can be given as treatment, such as Kaopectate (Upjohn) and Pectolin (EVSCO). Low temperatures can also cause diarrhea, as can pancreatitis (the autodigestion of pancreatic tissue). Loose stools can be caused by a diet rich in hydrated foods, and adding pelleted ground alfalfa to the diet may firm the stools. Fusion of the intestinal villi may occur in food contaminated with polychlorobiphenols (PCBs) and similar chemicals resulting in a reduced surface area for absorption. This causes diarrhea and malnutrition. The extent of the diarrhea appears related to the number of villi affected. With chronic diarrhea, the animal may become dehydrated and also suffer electrolyte imbalances, both of which may require veterinary intervention. Horizontal transmission of any pathogens that may be responsible for the vomiting and/or diarrhea must be prevented.

TABLE 4. Scientific names for various reptiles mentioned in this chapter.

Common Name	Scientific Name
agama lizard	*Agama* sp.
American alligator	*Alligator mississippiensis*
alligator snapping turtle	*Macrochelys temminck-ii*
anole lizard	*Anolis* sp.
banded rock lizard	*Petrosaurus mearnsi*
black-headed snake	*Tantilla* sp.
Blanding's turtle	*Emydoidea blandingi*
blind snake	*Rhamphotyphlops* sp.
boas, (common)	*Boa constrictor* ssp.
bog turtle	*Clemmys muhlenbergi*
box turtle	*Terrapene* sp.
brown tree snake	*Boiga irregularis*
bull snake	*Pituophis melanoleucus* spp.
Chaco tortoise	*Chelonoides chilensis*
chameleons, (old world)	*Chamaeleo* sp.; *Brooksia* sp.
chuckwalla lizard	*Sauromalus obesus; S. varius*
coachwhip snake	*Masticophis* sp.
collared lizard	*Crotaphytus* sp.
cooter turtle	*Chrysemys* sp.
copperhead snake	*Agkistrodon contortrix*
crocodiles	*Crocodylus* sp.
crowned snake	*Tantilla* sp.
desert tortoise	*Gopherus agassizi*
false map turtle	*Graptemys pseudogeographica*
fence lizard	*Sceloporus* sp.
garter snake	*Thamnophis* sp.
gecko	*Chondrodactylus* sp.; *Coelonyx* sp.; *Eublepharis* sp.; *Gekko* sp.; *Gehyra* sp.; *Gonatodes* sp.; *Hemidactylus* sp.; *Phelsuma* sp.; *Phyllodactylus* sp.; *Pytodactylus* sp.; *Shaerodactylus* sp.; *Tarentola* sp.
Gila monster	*Heloderma suspectum*
glass lizard	*Ophisaurus ventralis*
gopher snake	*Pituophis melanoleucus* ssp.
gopher tortoise	*Gopherus polyphemus*
Greek tortoise	*Testudo graeca*
green snake	*Liopeltis* sp.
hog-nosed snake	*Heterodon platyrhinos* ssp.; *H. nasicus; H. simus; Lioheterodon madagascariensis*
hook-nosed snake	*Glyalopion* sp.; *Ficimia streckeri*
iguana, (common)	*Iguana iguana*
iguana, (desert)	*Dipsosaurus dorsalis*
indigo snake	*Drymarchon corais* ssp.
kingsnake	*Lampropeltis* sp.
lacerta lizard	*Lacerta* sp.
legless lizard	*Anniella pulcra*
leopard tortoise	*Geochelone pardalis* ssp.
map turtle	*Graptemys geographica* ssp.
mata mata turtle	*Chelys fimbriata*
Mexican beaded lizard	*Heloderma horridum*
milksnake	*Lampropeltis triangulum*
moloch lizard	*Moloch horridus*
monitor lizard	*Varanus* sp.
mud turtle	*Kinosternon* sp.
musk turtle	*Sternotherus* sp.
painted turtle	*Chrysemys picta* ssp.
pancake tortoise	*Malacochersus torneri; M. procteri*
pond turtle	*Clemmys* sp.
racer snake	*Coluber constrictor* ssp.
radiated tortoise	*Geochelone radiata*
rat snake	*Elaphe* sp.; *Spilotes* sp.; *Zaocys dhumnades*
rattlesnake	*Crotalus* sp.
red-eared turtle	*Trachemys scripta elegans*
ribbon snake	*Thamnophis* sp.
slide-necked turtle	*Chelodina longicollis*
skink, (large)	*Chalcides* sp.; *Corucia* sp.; *Egernia* sp.; *Mabuya* sp.; *Tiliqua* sp.; *Trachydosaurus* sp.
skink, (small)	*Eumeces* sp.; *Scincella* sp.; *Scincus* sp.; *Lerista* sp.
slider turtle	*Trachemys* sp.
snapping turtle, (common)	*Chelydra serpentia*
soft-shelled turtle	*Trionyx* sp.
spiny lizard	*Sceloporus magister*
spiny-tailed lizard	*Uromastix* sp.
spotted turtle	*Clemmys guttata*
swift lizard	*Sceloporus* sp.
tegu lizard	*Tupinambis nigropunctatus; T. tequixin; T. rufescens*
tuatara	*Sphenodon punctatus*
vine snake	*Oxybelis* sp.; *Thelotornis* sp.; *Uromacer* sp.
water moccasin snake	*Agkistrodon piscivorus*
water snake	*Natrix* sp.; *Nerodia* sp.; *Endydris* sp.
wood turtle	*Clemmys insculpta*

REFERENCES

—**Allen, ME; Oftedal, OY:**
Calcium and phosphorus levels in live prey. Proc NE Section of Amer. Assoc. Zoos, Parks, and Aquar., 1982; pp.120-128.

—**Appleby, EC; Siller, WG:**
Some cases of gout in reptiles. J Path Bact, 1967; 80: 427-430.

—**Barnes, MJ; Lawson, DEM:**
Biochemistry of bone in relation to the function of vitamin D. In: Vitamin D. DEM Lawson (ed). Academic Press, New York, 1978, pp. 267-302.

—**Bartkiewicz, SE; et al:**
A preliminary study of niacin needs of the bull snake, *(Pituophis melanoleucus sayi)*. J Zoo Anim Med, 1982; 13(2): 55-58.

—**Bauer, BE:**
Longevity of horned lizards of the genus *Phrynosoma*. Bull Maryland Herp Soc, 1986; 23: 149-151.

—**Belkin, DA:**
Reduction of metabolic rate in response to starvation in the turtle, *Sternotherus minor*. Copeia, 1965; 1965(3): 367-368.

—**Bjorndal, KA:**
Cellulose digestion and volatile fatty acid production in the green turtle, *Chelonia mydas*. Comp Biochem Physiol, 1979; 63A: 127-133.

—**Boivin, GP; Stauber, E:**
Nutritional osteodystrophy in iguanas. Canine Prac, 1990; 15: 37.

—**Britton, SW; Klein, RF:**
Emotional hyperglycemia and hyperthermia in tropical mammals and reptiles. Am J Physiol, 1939; 125: 730-734.

—**Bustard, HR; Maderson, PF:**
The eating of shed material in squamate reptiles. Herpetologica, 1965; 21: 306-308.

—**Capen, CC; Marten, SL:**
Calcium-regulating hormones and diseases of the parathyroid glands. In: Textbook of Veterinary Internal Medicine. 2nd ed, SJ Ettinger (ed), WB Saunders, Philadelphia, 1983, pp. 1561-1565.

—**Chatterjee, GC:**
Effects of ascorbic acid deficiency in animals. In: The Vitamins. WH Sebrell and RE Harris (eds), 2nd ed, Vol 1, Academic Press, New York, 1967, pp. 407-457.

—**Collins, D:**
Quantities of calcium carbonate needed to balance calcium-phosphorus ratios of various meats. J Zoo Anim Med, 1971; 2(1): 25.

—**Coulson, RA; Hernandez, T:**
Biochemistry of the Alligator: A Study of the Metabolism in Slow Motion. Louisiana State Univ Press, Baton Rouge, 1964.

—**Cragg, MM; Balinsky, JB; Baldwin, E:**
A comparative study of nitrogen excretion in some amphibia and reptiles. Comp Biochem Physiol, 1961; 3: 227-235.

—**Derikson, WK:**
Lipid storage and utilization in reptiles. Am Zool, 1976; 16: 711-723.

—**Dessauer, HC:**
Blood chemistry of reptiles: physiology and evolutionary aspects. In: Biology of the Reptilia. C Gans and TS Parsons (eds), vol III, Academic Press, New York, 1970, pp. 1-72.

—**Dierenfeld, ES:**
Vitamin E deficiency in zoo reptiles, birds, and ungulates. J Zoo Wildlife Med, 1989; 20:3-11.

—**Dunson, WA:**
Electrolyte excretion by the salt glands of the galapagos marine iguana. Am J Physiol, 1969; 216:995-1002.

—**Dunson, WA; Taub, AM:**
Extra-renal salt excretion in sea snakes *(Laticauda)*. Am J Physiol, 1967; 213: 975-982.

—**Elkan, E; Zwart, P:**
The ocular disease of young terrapins caused by vitamin A deficiency. Vet Path, 1967; 4: 201-203.

—**Farnsworth, RJ; et al:**
A vitamin E-selenium responsive condition in a green iguana. J Zoo Anim Med, 1986; 17: 42-45.

—**Fischer, LE:**
Absorption of vitamin supplements in lizards. J Am Vet Med Assoc, 1957; 130: 412.

—**Fowler, ME:**
Metabolic bone disease. In: Zoo and Wild Animal Medicine. 2nd ed, ME Fowler (ed), WB Saunders, Philadelphia, 1993.

—**Fowler, ME:**
Comparison of respiratory infection and hypovitaminosis-A in desert tortoises. In: Pathology of Zoo Animals. RJ Montali and G Migaki (eds), Smithsonian Institution, Washington, DC, 1980, pp. 93-97.

—**Frye, FL:**
Biomedical and Surgical Aspects of Captive Reptile Husbandry. 2nd ed, Krieger, Malabar, Florida, 1991a.

—**Frye, FL:**
Reptile Care: An Atlas of Diseases and Treatments. 2 vols, TFH, Neptune City, New Jersey, 1991b.

—**Frye, FL:**
Vitamin A sources, hypovitaminosis-A, and iatrogenic hypervitaminosis-A in captive chelonians. In: Current Veterinary Therapy, Vol

X, RW Kirk (ed), WB Saunders, Philadelphia, 1989, pp. 791-796.

—Frye, FL:
Care and feeding of some invertebrates kept as pets or study animals. Proc CVMA 99th Ann Mtng Sci Seminar, 1987, pp. 271-304.

—Frye, FL:
Nutritional disorders in reptiles. In: Diseases of Amphibians and Reptiles. GL Hoff, FL Frye, ER Jacobson (eds), Plenum, New York, 1984, pp. 633-660.

—Frye, FL:
Biomedical and Surgical Aspects of Captive Reptile Husbandry. Veterinary Medicine, Edwardsville, Kansas, 1981.

—Frye, FL; Carney, JD:
Parathyroid adenoma in a tortoise. Vet Med Sm Anim Clin, 1975; 70: 582-584.

—Frye, FL; Dutra, FR:
Hypothyroidism in turtles and tortoises. Vet Med Sm Anim Clin, 1974; 69: 990-993.

—Galtsoff, PS:
Culture Methods for Invertebrate Animals. Am Assoc Adv Sci, Dover Press, New York, 1959.

—Gans, C; et al:
The water-collecting mechanism of *Moloch horridus* re-examined. Amph Rept, 1982; 3: 57-64.

—Gehrmann, WH:
Ultraviolet irradiances of various lamps used in animal husbandry. Zoo Biol, 1987; 6: 117-127.

—Goode, M:
Echis colorata (Palestine Saw-Scaled Viper): water economy. Herp Rev, 1983; 14(4): 120.

—Hildebrand, M:
Analysis of Vertebrate Structure. 4th ed, Wiley, New York, 1995.

—Holt, PE:
Drugs and dosages. In: Diseases of the reptilia. Vol 2. JE Cooper & OF Jackson (eds), Academic Press, New York, 1981.

—Howard, BH:
Ruminants and other vertebrates with microbial symbiotes. In: Symbiosis. Vol 2, SM Henry (ed), Academic Press, New York, 1967, pp. 317-385.

—Humphries, P:
Non-infectious diseases. In: Zoo and Wild Animal Medicine. ME Fowler (ed), WB Saunders, Philadelphia, 1978.

—Jackson, OF; Cooper, JE:
Nutritional diseases. In: Diseases of the Reptilia. Vol 2, JE Cooper and OF Jackson (eds), Academic Press, New York, 1981, pp. 409-428.

—Jarchow, JL:
Hospital care of the reptile patient. In: Exotic Animals. ER Jacobson (ed), Churchill Livingstone, New York, 1988.

—Kass, RG; et al:
A study of calcium requirements of the red-eared slider turtle *(Pseudemys scripta elegans)*. J Zoo Anim Med, 1982; 13(2): 62-65.

—Kramer, DC:
Geophagy in *Terrapene ornata ornata* Agassiz. J Herp, 1973; 7(2): 138-139.

—Lawrence, K:
Post hibernational anorexia in captive mediterranean tortoises (*Testudo graeca* and *T. hermanni*). Vet Rec, 1987; 120: 87.

—Loumbourdis, NS:
Lipid storage and utilization in the lizard *Agama stellio stellio*. J Herp, 1987; 21(3): 237-239.

—Magnusson, WE; et al:
Diets of amazonian crocodilians. J Herp, 1987; 21(2): 85-95.

—Mattison, C:
The Care of Reptiles and Amphibians in Captivity. 3rd ed, Blandford, London, 1992.

—Meylan, A:
Spongivory in hawksbill turtles. A diet of glass. Science, 1988; 239: 393-395.

—Montali, JR; et al:
The pathology of nephrotoxicity of gentamicin in snakes: a model for reptilian gout. Vet Path, 1978; 16: 108-115.

—Moyle, V:
Nitrogenous excretion in chelonian reptiles. Biochem J, 1949; 44: 581-589.

—Norris, KS; Dawson, WR:
Observations on the water economy and electrolyte excretion of chuckwallas (Lacertilia, *Sauromalus*). Copeia, 1964; 1964(4): 638-646.

—Oftedal, OT; et al:
Nutrition, urates, and desert survival: potassium and the desert tortoise *(Gopherus agassizii)*. Proc Am Assoc Zoo Vet, 1994; Oct: 308-313.

—Paul-Murphy, J; et al:
Necrosis of esophageal and gastric mucosa in snakes given oral doctyl sodium sulfosuccinate. Proc Am Assoc Zoo Vet, 1987; pp. 474-477.

—Peaker, M:
Active acquisition of stomach stones in the american alligator, *Alligator mississippiensis* Daudin. Brit J Herp, 1969; 4: 103-104.

—Porter, KR:
Herpetology. WB Saunders, Philadelphia, 1972.

—Regal, PJ:
Temperature and light requirements of captive reptiles. In: Reproductive Biology and

Diseases of Captive Reptiles. JB Murphy and JT Collins (eds), Soc Study Amphib Rept, 1980, pp. 79-89.

—Rhodin, AGJ:
Pathological lithophagy in *Testudo horsfieldi*. J Herp, 1974; 8: 385-386.

—Ross, RA; Marzec, G:
The Reproductive Husbandry of Pythons and Boas. Institute for Herpetological Research, Stanford, California, 1990.

—Rossi, J:
Snakes of the United States and Canada: Keeping Them Healthy in Captivity. Vol I (Eastern Area), Krieger, Malabar, Florida, 1992.

—Rossi, JV; Rossi, R:
Snakes of the United States and Canada: Keeping Them Healthy in Captivity. Vol II (Western Area), Krieger, Malabar, Florida, 1995.

—Rost, DR; Young, MC:
Diagnosing white-muscle disease. Vet Med Small Anim Clin, 1984; 80: 1286-1287.

—Schmidt-Nielsen, K:
Animal Physiology: Adaptation and Environment. 4th ed, Cambridge Univ Press, New York, 1990.

—Schmidt-Nielsen, K:
Desert Animals. Oxford Univ Press, New York, 1964.

—Schwenk, K; Greene, HW:
Water collection and drinking in *Phrynocephalus helioscopus*: a possible condensation mechanism. J Herp, 1987; 21: 134-139.

—Singh, P:
Artificial Diets for Insects, Mites and Spiders. Plenum, New York, 1977.

—Skoczylas, R:
Influence of temperature on gastric digestion in the grass snake *Natrix natrix* L. Comp Biochem Physiol, 1970; 33: 793-804.

—Skorepa, AC:
The deliberate consumption of stones by the Ornate Box Turtle, *Terrapene ornata* Agassiz. J Ohio Herp Soc, 1966; 5: 108.

—Smith, HA; et al:
Veterinary Pathology. 4th ed, Lea & Febiger, Philadelphia, 1972.

—Sokol, OM:
Lithophagy and geophagy in reptiles. J Herp, 1971; 5: 69-71.

—Sokol, OM:
Herbivory in lizards. Evolution, 1967; 21: 192-194.

—Strzelewicz, MA; et al:
Feeding insectivores: increasing the calcium content of wax moth *(Galleria mellonella)* larvae. J Zoo Anim Med, 1985; 16(1): 25-27.

—Templeton, JR:
Nasal salt excretion in terrestrial lizards. Comp Biochem Physiol, 1964; 11: 223-229.

—Troyer, K:
Behavioral acquisition of the hindgut fermentation system by hatchling *Iguana iguana*. Behav Ecol Sociobiol, 1984; 14: 189-193.

—Troyer, K:
Transfer of fermentative microbes between generations in a herbivorous lizard. Science, 1982; 216: 540-542.

—Tsoukas, CD; et al:
1,25-dihydroxyvitamin D3; a novel immunoregulatory hormone. Science, 1984; 1438-1440.

—Van Vleet, JF:
Comparative pathology of selenium and vitamin E deficiency and excess. Comp Path Bull, 1985; 17(4): 1-4.

—Vogel, Z:
Reptiles and Amphibians: Their Care and Behavior. Studio Vista, Highgate Hill, London, 1964.

—Vosburgh, KM; Brady, PS; Ullrey, DE:
Ascorbic acid requirements of garter snakes: plains (*Thamnophis radix*) and eastern (*T. sirtalis sirtalis*). J Zoo Anim Med, 1982; 13: 38-42.

—Wallach, JD:
Environmental and nutritional diseases of captive reptiles. J Am Vet Med Assoc, 1971; 159: 1632-1643.

—Wallach, JD:
Steatitis in captive crocodilians. J Am Vet Med Assoc, 1968; 153: 845-847.

—Wallach, JD:
Hypervitaminosis D in green iguanas. J Am Vet Med Assoc, 1966; 149.

—Wallach, JD; Hoff, GL:
Metabolic and nutritional diseases of reptiles. In: Noninfectious Diseases of Wildlife. GL Hoff, JW Davis (eds), Iowa State Univ Press, Ames, 1982.

—Wallach, JD; Hoessle, C:
Fibrous osteodystrophy in green iguanas. J Am Vet Med Assoc, 1968; 153: 863-865.

—Young, JZ:
The Life of Vertebrates. 2nd ed, Oxford Univ Press, Fair Lawn, New Jersey, 1962.

—Zwart, P:
Infectious diseases of reptiles. In: Zoo and Wild Animal Medicine. 2nd ed, ME Fowler (ed), WB Saunders, Philadelphia, 1986.

—Zwart, P; Van de Watering, CC:
Disturbances of bone formation in the common iguana (*Iguana iguana* L.): pathology and etiology. Acta Zoo et Path Anat, 1969; 48: 333-356.

PHARMACOLOGY, PHARMACODYNAMICS AND DRUG DOSING

Gretchen E. Kaufman DVM
Assistant Director, Tufts Wildlife Clinic
Tufts University School of Veterinary Medicine
200 Westboro Road
North Grafton, MA 01536

Dr. Gretchen E. Kaufman graduated from Tufts University School of Veterinary Medicine in May, 1986. From 1986-1987, she worked in a small animal practice in the greater metropolitan Boston area. In July of 1987, she moved to California to begin a 2-year residency in zoological medicine at the University of California at Davis. On completion of the residency, she returned to Tufts University to create and run the Exotic Animal Medicine Service in the Small Animal Teaching Hospital. In August of 1995, she assumed the position of Assistant Director of the Tufts Wildlife Clinic.

INTRODUCTION

Drug therapy in reptiles is still in its infancy. One major stumbling block is the great diversity among species in the class of reptiles. Many species have developed unique adaptations to their environmental niche which influence their handling of drugs differently. Often, these special characteristics are not well understood nor are the fundamental pharmacodynamic processes such as drug metabolism, liver enzyme systems, renal clearance, protein binding, bioavailability, etc. In the face of this void, veterinarians and herpetologists often are forced to follow their experience, the experience of others, and use common sense and general knowledge to adequately treat an ill animal.

It is best to begin developing rational drug therapy by understanding the individual in question as well as possible: knowing its diet and frequency of eating, its activity patterns, sex and reproductive status, age, humidity and temperature requirements. All of these factors will influence the uptake, behavior, distribution and elimination of any drug. Lifestyle and temperament considerations may dictate frequency of handling and route of administration under some circumstances. Stress, although difficult to assess in most reptiles, can play a major role in the response to disease. Minimizing stress, while administering appropriate therapy will produce the best results.

Particularly important for the reptile is body temperature. To predict the activity of a drug, one must know and adhere to the preferred optimal body temperature of that species. This is the temperature at which the animal should be functioning most efficiently. Variation from this temperature will produce unpredictable results including treatment failure. It is vital to record the body temperature/environmental temperature during treatment, and to note the temperature of animals used in pharmacokinetic studies.

Ideally, pharmacokinetic information should be available for drugs such as antibiotics commonly used in a variety of reptile species. Most of the available pharmacokinetically derived drug doses are listed and referenced in the formulary at the back of this chapter. The availability of such data is usually the exception and not the rule. All too often, drug dosages are derived through experience only, or extrapolated from other very unrelated species such as dogs or humans. A reptile veterinarian is repeatedly faced with treating a species with a particular medication for the very first time. Concerns over toxicity or effectiveness are real when confronting such a problem.

ALLOMETRIC SCALING

The tool of allometric scaling to derive drug dosages comes in very handy when attempting to predict an accurate therapy for the first time or in a novel species. Allometric scaling is a mathematical description of various physiological parameters across species of variable size. It has been found that many basic parameters such as oxygen consumption, cardiac output, and metabolic energy requirements follow these mathematical rules. It is an exponential relationship, not a linear relationship based on body mass. It has been suggested that the behavior of many drugs can be predicted from one species to the other, utilizing the principles of allometric scaling. This is especially true of drugs which follow first order kinetics, have similar protein binding characteristics, and are eliminated either through the kidney or biliary systems. The theory and derivation of this concept have been well documented and this phenomenon has been established for many drugs (Mordenti, 1985, 1986).

Sedgwick has suggested that drug uptake, distribution and elimination is often parallel to resting metabolic rate. By using the mathematical formulas for resting metabolic energy requirements (minimum energy cost, MEC) as a reflection of metabolic rate, one can compare different animals and extrapolate an appropriate drug dose from a subject where the dose and rate of administration is well established (Sedgwick, 1988). Animals are conveniently arranged into 5 simple groups based on a common mean core body temperature: reptiles, marsupial mammals, placental mammals, non-passerine birds, and passerine birds. The basic formula varies in the constant (K) for each of these five groups:

$$MEC = K \times BWkg0.75 \qquad where$$

K = 10 Reptiles
K = 49 Marsupial mammals
K = 70 Placental mammals
K = 78 Non-passerine birds
K = 129 Passerine birds

Sedgwick has developed a technique to establish a formulary of Universal MEC Doses which could then be applied to any animal falling into these 5 groups. Use of this formulary allows one to predict a dosage and rate of administration for any individual. "Universal MEC doses" are included for many drugs listed in the formulary in the back of this chapter. Practitioners are encouraged to add to this formulary on their own as their experience dictates. A worksheet is included which will assist in calculating Universal MEC doses for new drugs.

For the purposes of illustration, one might investigate the use of cisapride as a gastrointestinal stimulant for use in a case of functional intestinal ileus in a 2 kilogram tortoise following a prolonged period of anorexia. **Cisapride** is a relatively new drug prescribed for esophageal reflux in humans. It is related to metaclopramide, but unlike metaclopramide it possesses general gastrointestinal stimulant properties, including enhanced colonic and cecal motility. It also results in much fewer sympathetic (antidopaminergic) side effects (AHFS, 1995; Barone, 1994). By knowing the dose and rate of administration of cisapride in a human child one can compare the child's metabolic rate (in the form of caloric requirements) with that of the subject's and derive a reasonable dosage regimen for the use of cisapride in the tortoise. In this instance the MEC of the known "model" animal is calculated first:

A 20kg child has a MEC of $70 \times 20^{0.75} = 662$ kcal

The recommended dose of cisapride in children is 0.2 mg/kg every 6 or 8 hours (Molinari, 1994; Barone, 1994). The single dose for the child is calculated next.

The 20kg child should receive 0.2 mg/kg x 20 kg = 4 mg per dose

The Universal MEC dose is then calculated by dividing the calculated single dose (4 mg) by the known model's MEC (662).

The **Universal MEC dose of Cisapride** is 4/662 = **0.006**

To determine the rate of administration, a frequency coefficient is calculated by dividing the frequency interval by the model animal's MEC/body weight in kilograms. In this case the frequency interval of 4 times daily is divided by 662/20kg.

The **frequency interval for Cisapride** is 4/(662/20) = **0.12**

These two numbers for Cisapride can then be used to calculate an appropriate dose for any animal: a Universal MEC dose of 0.006 and a frequency coefficient of 0.12. In the case of a 2kg tortoise, the patients MEC is calculated using the basic formula:

MEC of the tortoise patient = $10 \times 2^{0.75} = 16.8$

To obtain this patients dose, one would then multiply the Universal MEC dose of Cisapride by the patients MEC (0.006 x 16.8 = 0.1mg) and multiply the frequency coefficient by the patients MEC/bodyweight in kg (0.12 x 8.4 = 1).

The tortoise patient's dose regimen is **0.1 mg once daily**

For purposes of comparison, the dose rate for the tortoise is 0.05 mg/kg once daily, while the child received 0.2 mg/kg 4 times daily. This reflects the slower metabolic rate of the tortoise when compared to the child.

Metabolic scaling can also be used to derive more practical and accurate drug dosing among closely related animals which vary greatly in size. An ex-

ALLOMETRIC SCALING WORKSHEET

REQUIRED DATA

Drug:_____

Source:_____

Model Animal _____ Body Weight (kg) _____ Dose_____

Model Animal MEC $= K \times BW_{kg}^{0.75} =$ _____ Single Dose_____mg

mg/kg x mg

UNIVERSAL MEC DOSE CALCULATION

Divide known single dose (mg) by Model Animal MEC

UNIVERSAL MEC DOSE=_____

FREQUENCY COEFFICIENT CALCULATION

Divide frequency (per 24h) by [Model Animal MEC/Bodyweight(kg)]

FREQUENCY COEFFICIENT = _____

To calculate a patient's dose:

1) Multiply patient's MEC by Universal MEC dose = mg/treatment
2) Multiply patient's (MEC/body weight in kg) by Frequency coefficient = # times/day

ample of this is the use of **ceftazadime** to treat bacterial infections in snakes. A preliminary pharmacokinetic study (Lawrence, 1984) has produced a dose of 20 mg/kg every 72 hours using a variety of snakes ranging in size from 0.29 to 5.26 kg. One additional python was used weighing 13 kg. When using this drug to treat a very large python, one might logically conclude that the larger snake would require less drug per kg bodyweight than the smaller snake and should require a longer time between injections. In this case the smaller snake is used as the "model" animal with a body weight of 2 kg dosed at 20 mg/kg every 72 hours (3 days). The Universal MEC dose is 2.4 with a frequency coefficient of 0.044. A 30 kg python (MEC=128) would then receive 307 mg, that is 10.24 mg/kg every five days. Considering the fact that ceftazadime is also very expensive, this permits the practical use of a very effective medication in large snakes.

Use of the nephrotoxic aminoglycosides in large snakes should also follow metabolic scaling to avoid tragic consequences of inadvertent overdosing that may occur with calculations based strictly on body weight. Dosing gentamicin with this technique in an 80kg anaconda results in a dosage rate of 0.23 mg/kg every 4 days instead of the standard dose for a much smaller snake of 2.5 mg/kg every 72 hours (Bush, 1978).

METHODS OF ADMINISTRATION

Drug therapy in reptiles is often governed by the available forms of the drug and the most convenient routes of administration. There are limiting factors due to species lifestyle differences, ease of handling, bioavailability, etc. For example, the frog-eyed gecko (*Teratoscincus scincus*) will often

Fig. 1. Intramuscular injection site in snakes. Illustration by Barbara Bonner, DVM.

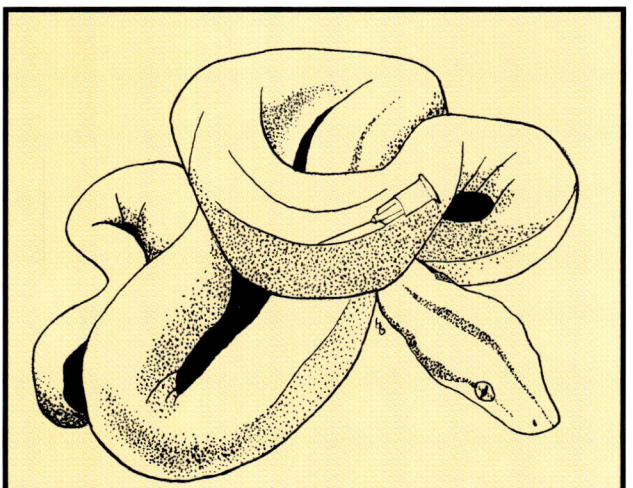

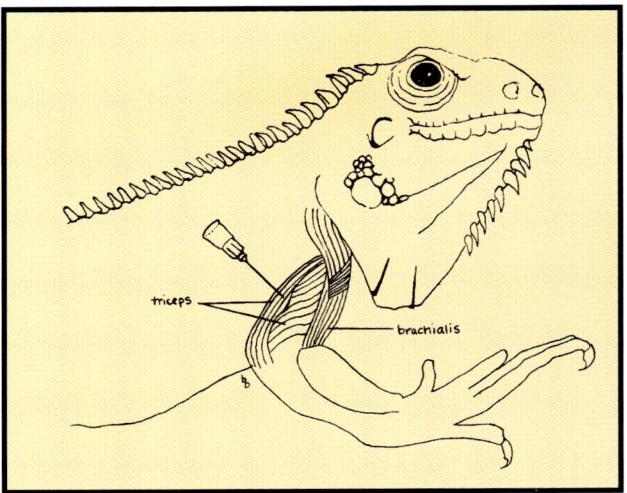

Fig. 2 a. Intramuscular injection site in lizards and crocodiles. Illustration by Barbara Bonner, DVM.

shed its skin, full thickness, if handled repeatedly and overly stressed. This and other species that are extremely sensitive to physical handling may benefit most from medication through food.

Oral routes of administration can be utilized through medicating in food or directly by gavage. This technique is apparently innocuous and easy in mammals but can present several problems in some groups of reptiles. The bioavailability of a daily administered oral medication should be questioned in an animal that normally eats once or twice

**Fig. 2b
Intramuscular injection site in lizards and crocodiles. Illustration by Barbara Bonner, DVM.**

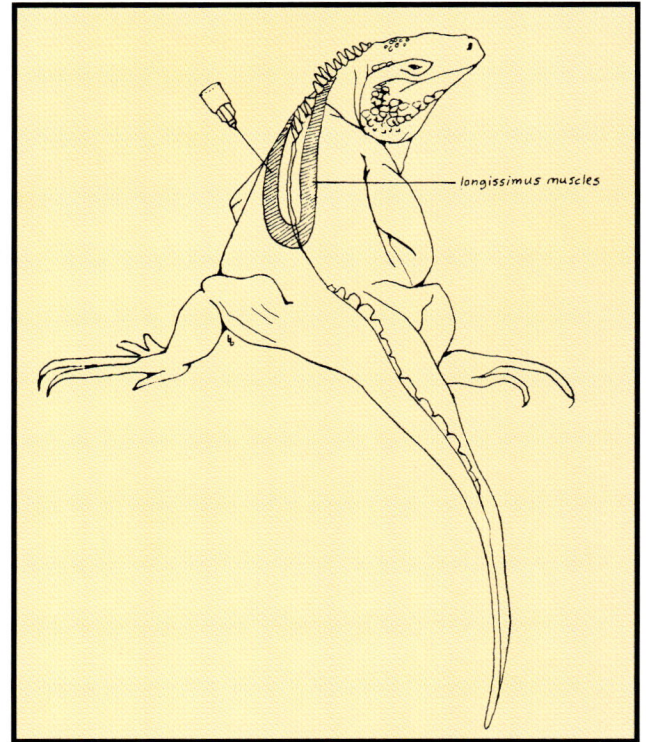

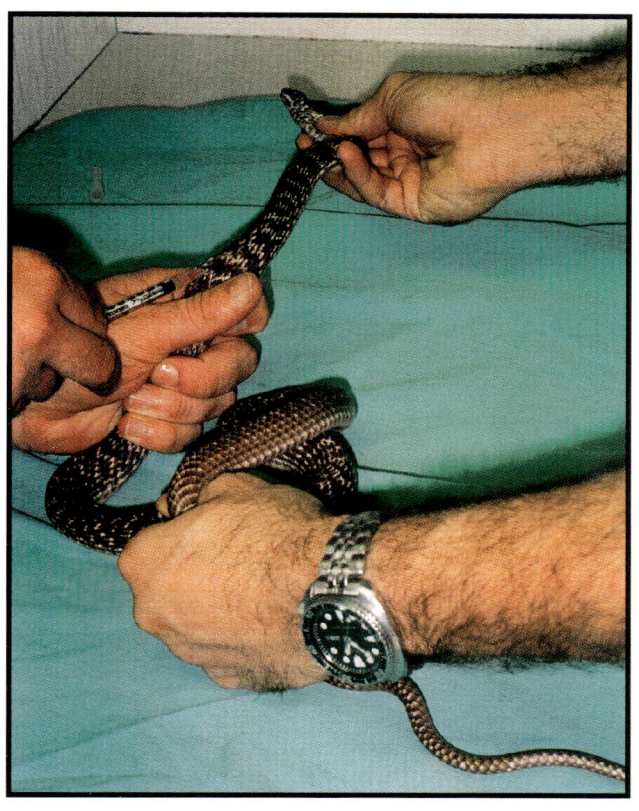

Dr. Todd Driggers administers an intramuscular injection to this coachwhip snake. Photo courtesy of Dr. Lowell Ackerman.

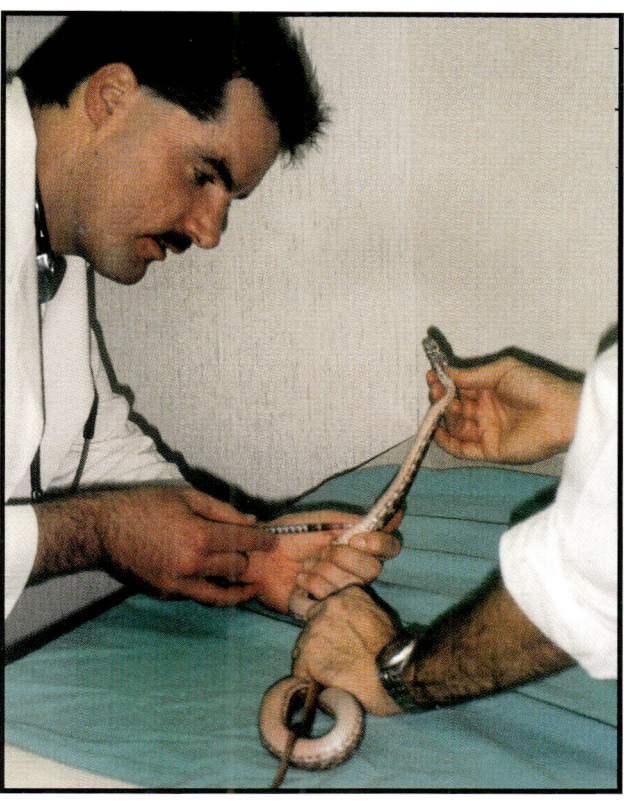

Dr. Todd Driggers demonstrates intravenous administration of drugs into this coachwhip snake. Photo courtesy of Dr. Lowell Ackerman.

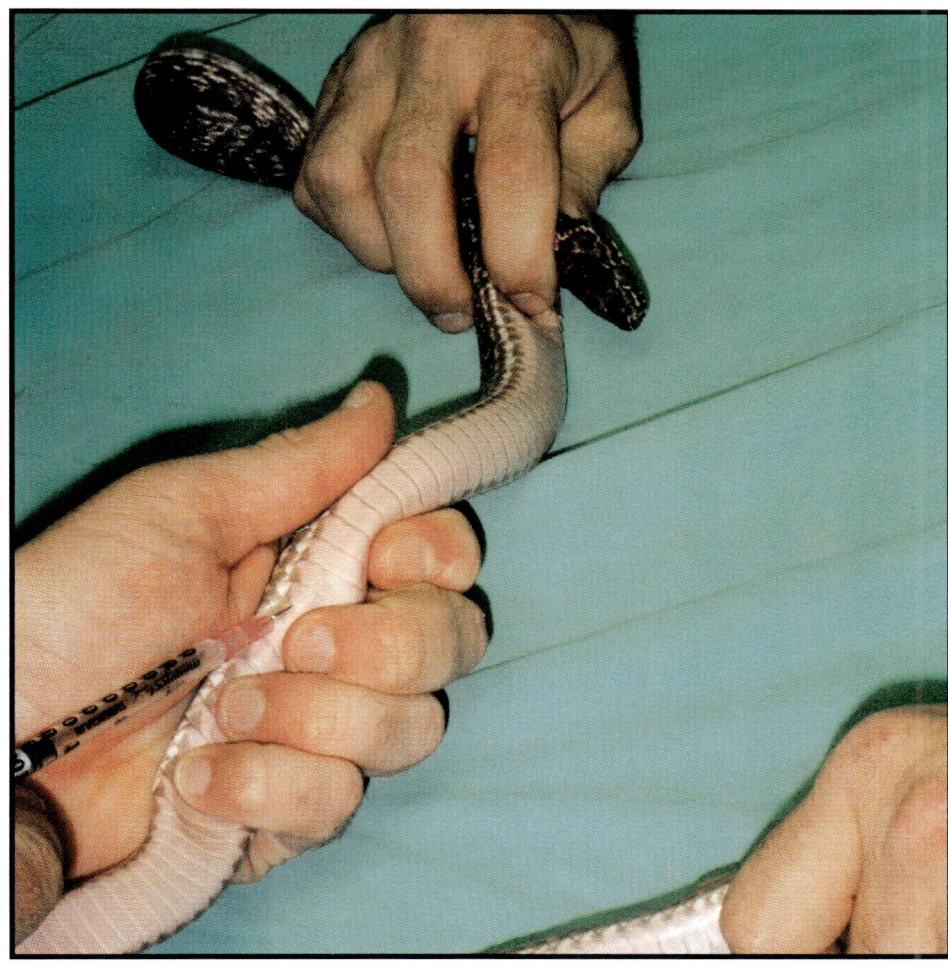

Dr. Todd Driggers demonstrates an intracoelomic injection into this coachwhip snake. Photo courtesy of Dr. Lowell Ackerman.

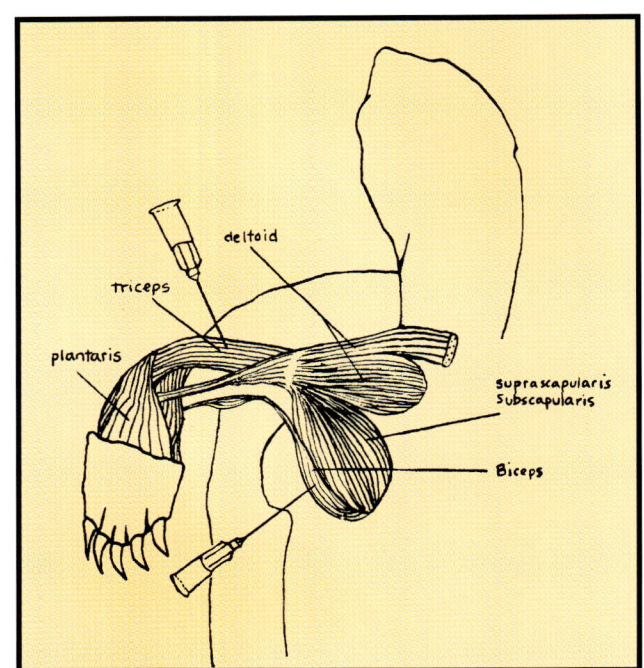

Fig. 3.
Intramuscular injection site in chelonions. Illustration by Barbara Bonner, DVM, adapted from Ashley, LM: Laboratory Anatomy of the Turtle, Wm. C. Brown Co. Publishers, Dubuque, Iowa, 1962.

in a month (e.g. a snake). The gastrointestinal tract may not be functioning optimally in between meals to allow for predictable absorption of drugs. In

Fig. 4.
Intraosseous injection site in lizards. Illustration by Barbara Bonner, DVM, adapted from Oldham, JC: Laboratory Anatomy of the Iguana, Wm. C. Brown Co. Publishers, Dubuque, Iowa, 1975.

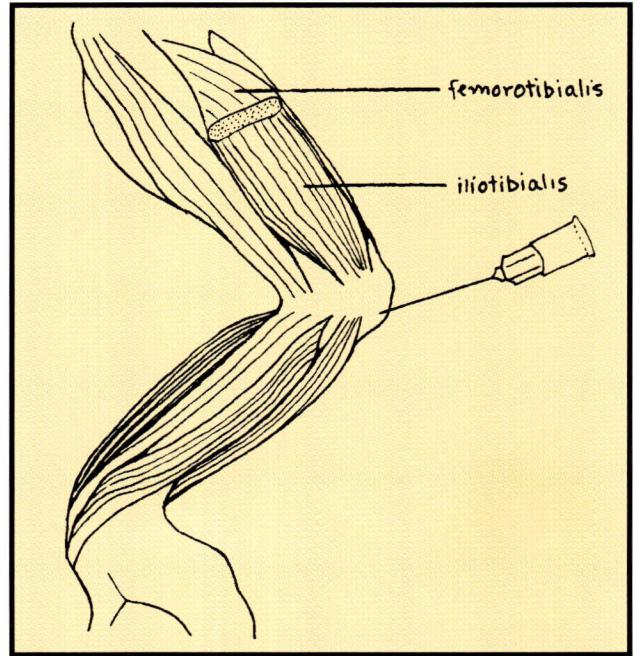

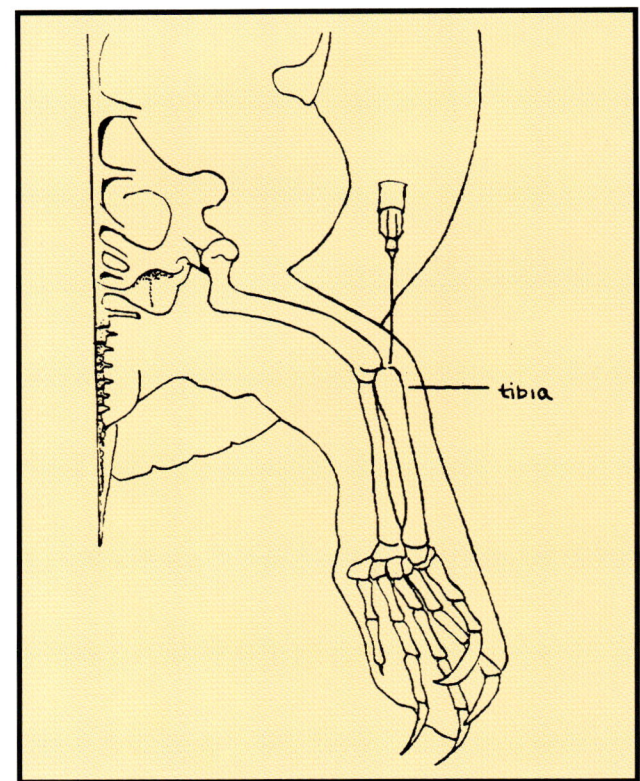

Fig. 5.
Intraosseous injection site in chelonions. Illustration by Barbara Bonner, DVM, adapted from Ashley, LM: Laboratory Anatomy of the Turtle, Wm. C. Brown Co. Publishers, Dubuque, Iowa, 1962.

addition, the snake does not appreciate daily gavage procedures which may result in significant stress and/or damage to the mouth or esophagus from repeated intubation. The obstinant tortoise may also not appreciate or permit repeated gavage. Oral administration of drugs directly or with food should be most successful in animals that normally eat on a daily or every other day schedule.

In general, *subcutaneous* and *intramuscular* administration are the easiest routes to consider for medicating most species since this requires mini-

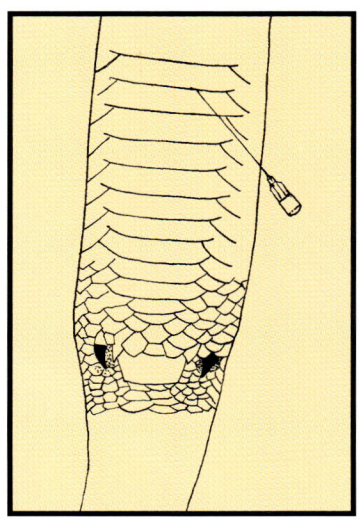

Fig. 6
Intracoelomic injection site in snakes. Illustration by Barbara Bonner, DVM.

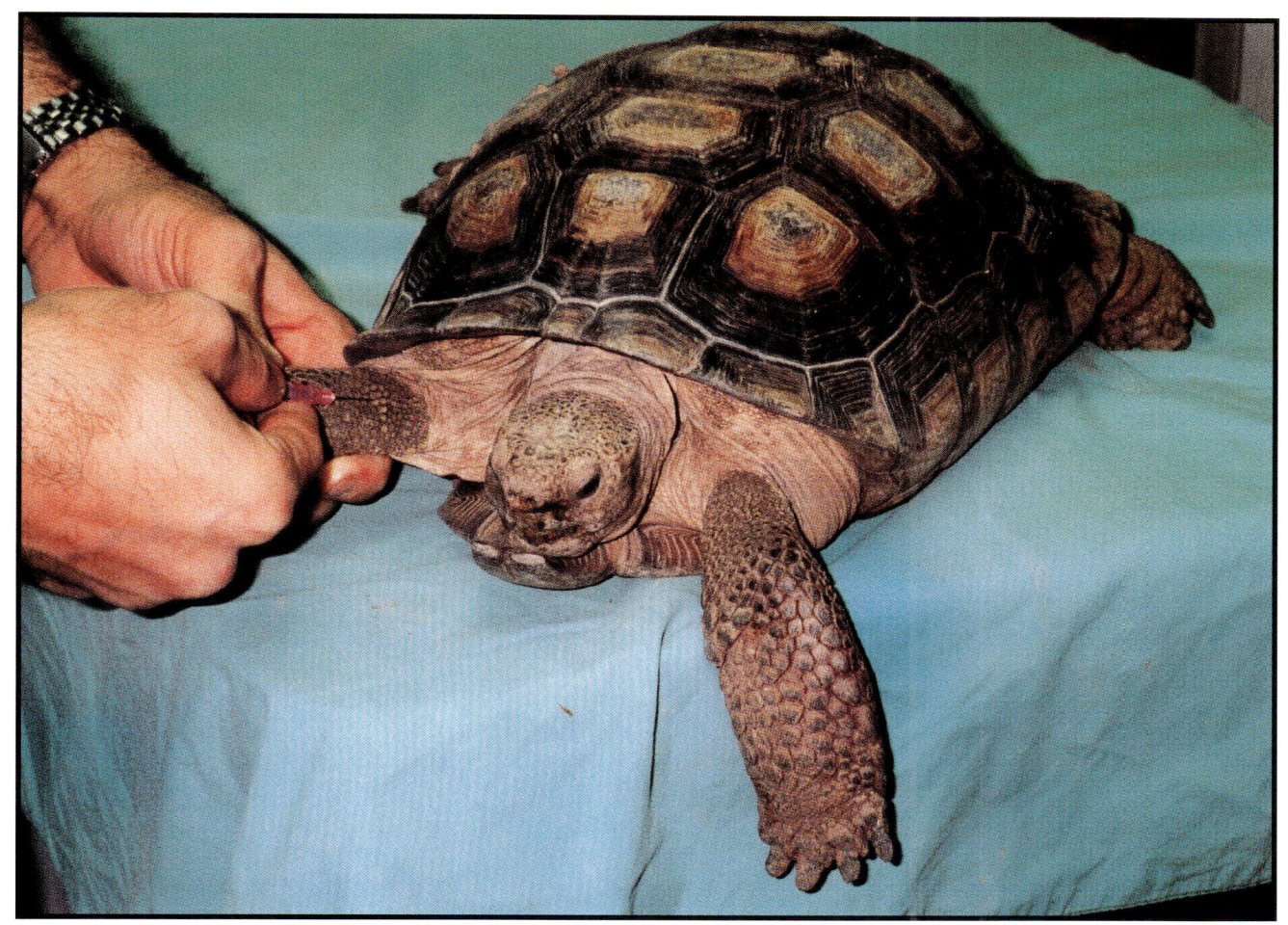

Dr. Bernard Mangone gives an intramuscular injection to a desert tortoise. Photo courtesy of Dr. Lowell Ackerman.

Dr. Bernard Mangone demonstrates another intramuscular injection site in a desert tortoise. Photo courtesy of Dr. Lowell Ackerman.

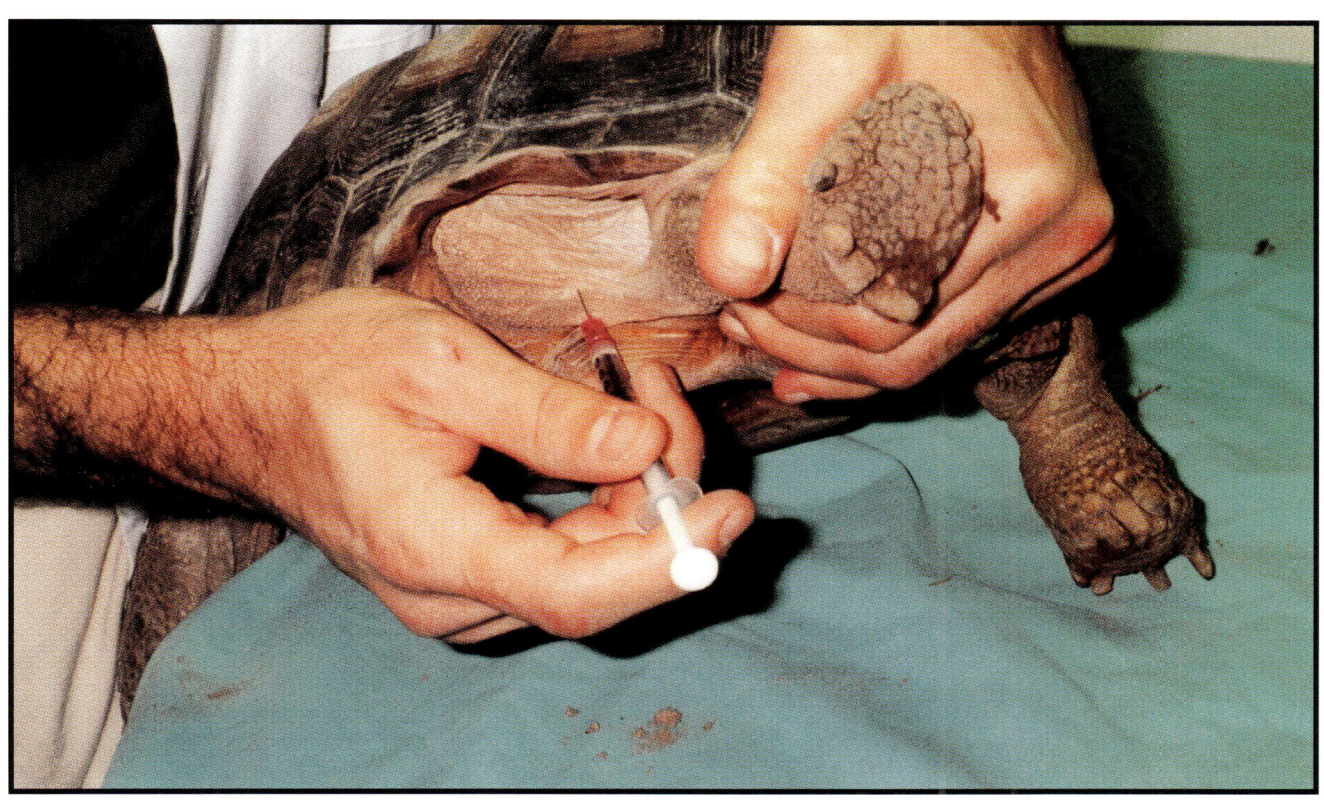

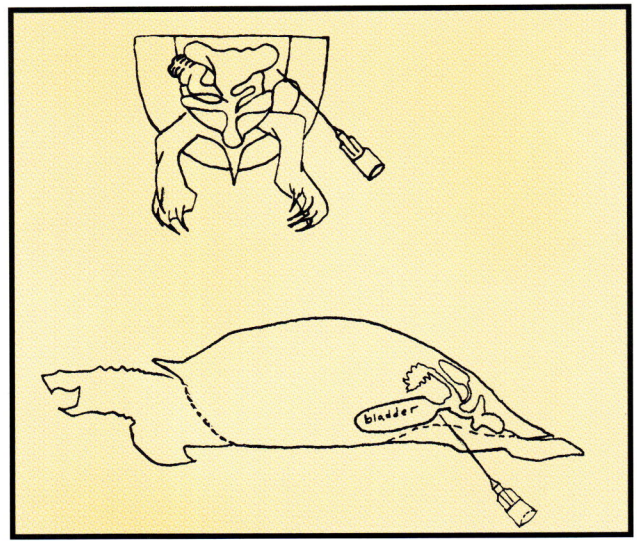

Fig. 7.
Intracoelomic injection site in chelonions. Illustration by Barbara Bonner, DVM, adapted from Ashley, LM: Laboratory Anatomy of the Turtle, Wm. C. Brown Co. Publishers, Dubuque, Iowa, 1962.

mal restraint and the animal is assured of receiving the full dose. Suggested injection sites are illustrated below. It is recommended that medications be given in the front half of the body to avoid possible circulatory effects of the renal-portal system. There is still a great deal of argument over the effect of the renal-portal system on the distribution of drugs in reptiles. It is theorized that when drugs are given in the caudal aspects of the body, shunting of blood through the renal-portal system may cause rapid elimination of the drug through

Fig. 8.
Intravenous injection site in lizards. Illustration by Barbara Bonner, DVM.

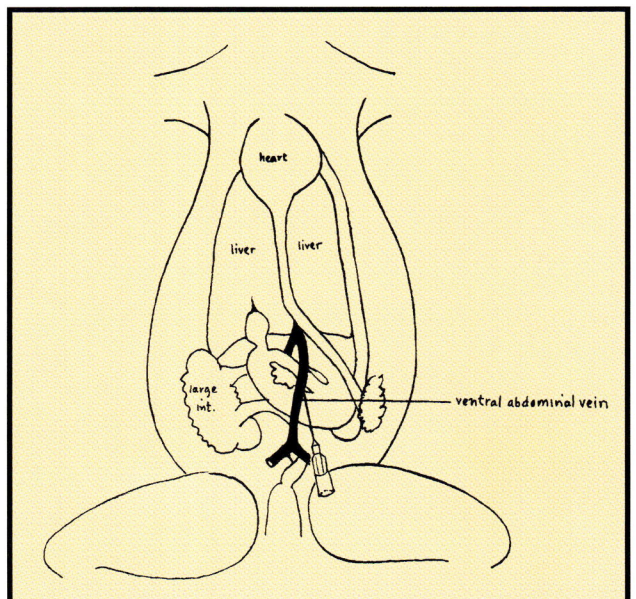

the kidneys before the appropriate levels are distributed throughout the body and may amplify the effect of nephrotoxic drugs presented to the kidney at an exceptionally high level. Recent studies of this phenomenon suggest that the renal-portal system may not significantly affect therapeutic blood levels of antibiotics, however this recent finding has not been thoroughly examined especially in situations of dehydration and disease (Holz, 1994).

Intravenous access in many species is difficult or may not be within the skill of the average practitioner or herpetologist. Some of the access points are illustrated below (diagram). In emergency situations, intravenous access should be attempted followed by possible catheter placement but may require surgical manipulation to be successful.

Fig. 9.
Subcutaneous injection site in lizards. Illustration by Barbara Bonner, DVM.

Intracoelomic fluid therapy and drug administration is often a good, fairly rapid approach and can be safe if done properly. The biggest risk involves accidental injection of the air sac space rather than the desired coelomic space. Knowledge of the anatomy and appropriate positioning of the animal are essential. Common intracoelomic sites are illustrated.

Intraosseous administration of fluids and drugs is an under utilized technique which may allow rapid intravenous access without the trouble of locating a usable vein. Procedures for placing intraosseous catheters in birds and small mammals should be followed (Ritchie, 1990; Lamberski, 1992).

Cloacal administration of drugs has recently been investigated. Tortoises were given fenbendazole per cloaca for the treatment of oxyurids (Innis, 1995). The local effect of the medication appeared to be more effective than with orally administered fenbendazole. Many reptiles are capable of absorbing water through the cloaca and distal colon. Although blood levels in this case were not measured, the possibility of administering other medications and achieving systemic conc

THERAPEUTIC OPTIONS

A thorough understanding of the patient and an accurate assessment of it's present physiological and clinical status is imperative before choosing the appropriate therapy. Accurate assessment of the animals body temperature, fluid status, and nutritional status must be made and taken into account.

FLUID SUPPORT

Fluid support is a fundamental therapy in reptiles as it is in other animals. Correction of fluid imbalances and restoration and maintenance of the circulatory system are critical. Assessment of fluid balance is essentially subjective but is based on history (prolonged anorexia, vomiting or diarrhea, lack of access to water, history of incomplete sheds, etc.), clinical appearance (skin turgor, mucous membranes, and fullness of the eyes) and laboratory tests. Several methods can be used to assess needs; the actual requirements of such a varied group are not well understood. Reptiles in general are felt to have higher intracellular fluid volumes, but lower plasma, extracellular and interstitial fluid volumes than mammals (Jarchow, 1988). This is quite variable between different types of reptiles as one might suspect (freshwater, saltwater, terrestrial, desert, etc.) Calculations can be based on an estimated daily fluid requirement of 1-3% of body weight (kilograms). Alternatively, Sedgwick has suggested that daily fluid requirements may be based on the animals MEC (see above), where the MEC equals the daily fluid requirement in milliliters (Sedgwick, pc).

There are also no hard and fast rules about the composition of the fluids to be administered. The readily available isotonic fluid solutions (0.9% NaCl, lactated Ringers solution, etc.) can be used safely to support a reptile patient. Jarchow has suggested using a slightly hypotonic mixture to promote intracellular diffusion by combining two parts 2.5% dextrose in 0.45 % NaCl with 1 part Ringer's solution (Jarchow, 1988).

The route of administration of fluids will be dictated by the clinical situation presented. Mild dehydration, resulting in dysechdysis for example, can often be managed by soaking the animal in water for a period of time each day and/or increasing the humidity in the environ-

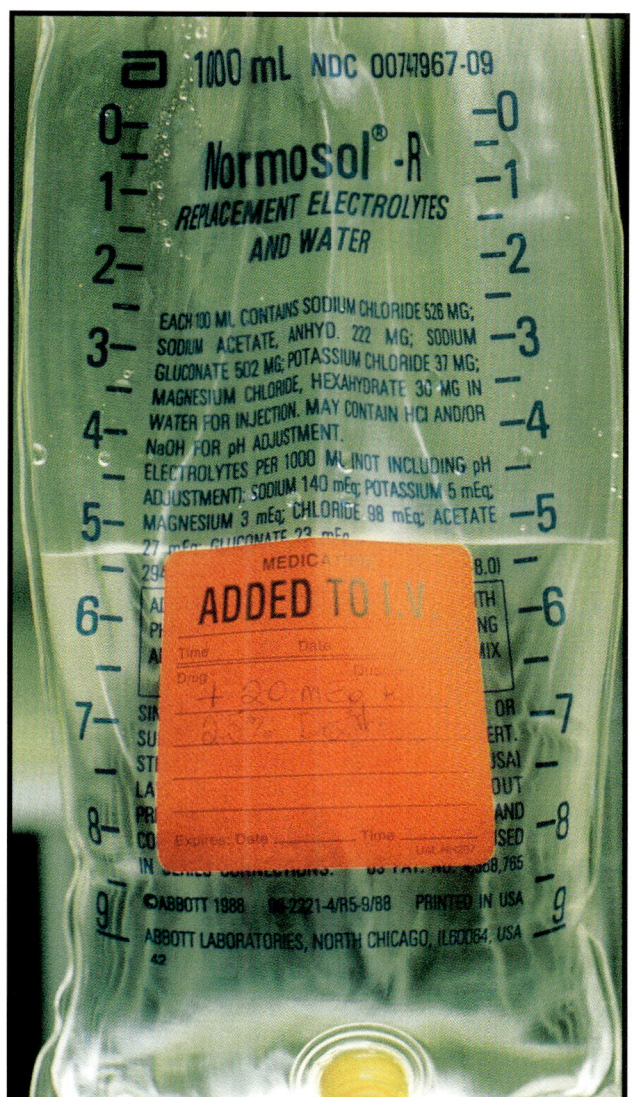

Fluid therapy is an excellent way to replace fluid volume and electrolytes. Photo courtesy of Dr. Lowell Ackerman.

ment. Clinically ill and dehydrated animals will need active rehydration and support through subcutaneous, intracoelomic, intravenous or intraosseous techniques depending on the rate at which rehydration must occur. Relatively large volumes of subcutaneous fluids can be given to turtles, tortoises and lizards fairly easily. Snakes however offer very little subcutaneous space for large volume administration and are more easily managed through intracoelomic therapy. Care must be taken not to inject into the air sac space (see illustrations of preferred sites). Intracoelomic fluids should be absorbed rapidly and are a good choice for severely dehydrated animals.

Intravenous or intraosseous therapy may be required in animals in cardiovascular collapse whether due to severe dehydration, prolonged illness, or acute distress. This is the only technique that will bring about immediate vascular volume expansion.

ANTIMICROBIALS

Antibiotics and antifungal medications are used frequently in reptiles and their use is based on several factors. First of all, the identity of the pathogenic organism must be determined by culture. Secondly, sensitivity testing of the isolated organism will provide a range of possible effective antibiotics. The techniques of culturing reptile pathogens is different from the routine methods used on mammals and birds. One should make sure that the laboratory performing the culture is aware of these differences. Cultures should be incubated at both room temperature (22-25°C) and at 37°C as well as at a reduced oxygen tension (Frye, personal communication, 1989; Needham, 1985).

Thirdly, the available route of administration may influence the drug choice. For example, the majority of medications used in mammals and/or birds in the oral form have not been tested for bioavailability in reptiles, and therefore may be ineffective. Other medications may be available only in intravenous form and may be impractical to administer repeatedly to most reptile patients.

TOPICAL MEDICATIONS

There are many effective topical antibacterial and antifungal agents available which can be useful in treating superficial skin infections of reptiles. Common problems such as infectious stomatitis, superficial rat bites, superficial fungal or bacterial dermatitis and minor wounds can be effectively handled with the use of topical agents. The most commonly used topical preparations are over-the-counter triple antibiotic ointments and silversulfadiazine or sulfadine cream. These preparations are generally effective against common reptile pathogens such as *Pseudomonas* and *Aeromonas* spp. Silversulfadiazine is especially effective against these bacteria and also possesses antifungal properties (Swaim and Lee, 1987). It is highly recommended for treatment of thermal burns, but can also be used for other cutaneous infections. No toxicity has been recorded in reptiles.

Povidone iodine and chlorhexidine solutions (0.05%) and ointments can be used to clean and disinfect wounds. Animals with generalized cutaneous infections can be soaked in very dilute aqueous solutions for up to 1 hour, once or twice daily to help reduce skin contaminants. Dilute povidone iodine baths (0.005%) can be very beneficial in treating superficial conditions. Fungal or algal infections in chelonia can be effectively treated by scrubbing the shell with a stiff surgical scrub brush or toothbrush and aqueous povidone iodine solution. Aquarium preparations of malachite green, gentian violet, potassium permanganate, or salt, coppertox, or formaldehyde solutions in water are

Chlorhexidine is a very effective topical antiseptic. Photo courtesy of Dr. Lowell Ackerman.

also recommended for water turtles (Jacobson et al, 1983; Murphy and Collins, 1983).

Topical antifungal agents that may be useful include 1% tolnaftate cream (Jacobson, 1980), miconazole preparations and some of the newer over-the-counter imidazoles such as clotrimazole ointment or solution.

SYSTEMIC ANTIBIOTICS

The bioavailability of most oral antibiotics have not been studied in reptiles. Therefore their use should be limited to animals with regular feeding patterns, with a healthy gastrointestinal tract and at optimal ambient temperatures. Medicating the water is generally not recommended since many species do not drink on a regular basis or their daily water intake may be reduced during illness. As stated earlier, repeated stomach tubing can be stressful and may be difficult in some species. Due to these considerations, parenteral administration of antibiotics is most often the best choice.

The ***fluoroquinolones*** are the newest family of antibiotics to become available and are very useful against the major reptile pathogens including *Pseudomonas aeruginosa* and many of the mycobacterial species. The major drawback is that they are only minimally active against anaerobes. The human products include norfloxacin, ciprofloxacin, ofloxacin, enoxacin, pefloxacin and others. The veterinary product is enrofloxacin and comes as a tablet or an intramuscular injectable solution. The injectable form of enrofloxacin is very irritating and the manufacturer cautions against repeated injections (Baytril, Haver/Mobay, data sheet). The author has used the injectable for prolonged therapy (2-3 weeks) generally without complications. Rarely sterile injection abscesses may form. An effort should be made to alternate injection sites due to the irritation.

The ***cephalosporins*** include the third generation compound ceftazadime. This antibiotic was developed specifically to be effective against *Pseudomonas* spp. It possesses minimal nephrotoxicity (Lawrence, Muggleton, and Needham, 1984). This drug is available in powder form and must be reconstituted before use. Once reconstituted, the shelf life (refrigerated) is 10 days (Tazidime, Lilly, data sheet). The shelf life may be extended by freezing the reconstituted solution. Individual doses for a two or three week course of therapy for a particular patient may be drawn up into syringes at the time that the vial is reconstituted. These individual syringes can then be frozen until just prior to use (Kollias, personal communication, 1989). Cephalothin, and cephaloridine have also been used in reptiles however culture and sensitivity information should dictate their use since these agents are generally not effective against *Pseudomonas* and *Aeromonas* spp. The cephalosporins do possess good activity against *Klebsiella*, *Enterobacter*, and *Proteus* spp. (Gilman et al, 1990).

Aminoglycosides have historically been used to treat reptiles due to their particular effectiveness against *Pseudomonas* and *Aeromonas* spp. These agents are potentially nephrotoxic to birds, mammals and reptiles (Montali et al, 1979; Jacobson, 1976). Many ill reptiles become moderately to severely dehydrated. Use of aminoglycosides in these patients is very dangerous. Currently, the availability of newer antibiotics equally effective against the common reptile pathogens preclude the routine use of aminoglycosides and avoid potential nephrotoxicity.

Amikacin and gentamicin are the most frequently used aminoglycosides. They possess a good Gram negative spectrum, but a limited Gram positive range, with no activity against anaerobes. Of all the aminoglycosides, amikacin possesses the broadest spectrum and is the least likely to encounter resistance (Gilman et al, 1990). There is a very narrow safety margin with side effects of nephrotoxicity, ototoxicity, cardiotoxicity, and neuromuscular blockade (Jacobson and Kollias, 1988). Toxicity is both dose and frequency related. The toxicity of these agents also depends on the state of hydration of the animal and the resultant functional state of the kidneys. Accurate evaluation of renal function and dehydration are perhaps the most important factors in using these drugs successfully, after the correct dosage has been determined. The state of hydration should always be corrected before initiating systemic therapy with aminoglycosides. It is advised that fluid therapy be maintained throughout the course of antibiotic therapy to help support renal function and reduce the likelihood of toxicity. Finally, the animal may be fasted to reduce the nitrogen load (uric acid production) on the system (Jacobson and Kollias, 1988).

Chloramphenicol is another antibiotic historically used to treat infections in reptiles. It is a broad spectrum, bacteriostatic antibiotic effective against many Gram positive and Gram negative aerobic and anaerobic bacteria. It is often an effective agent against *Salmonella* spp. (Clark et al, 1985; Booth and MacDonald, 1988). The half-life of this drug is quite variable among different species of reptiles (Clark et al, 1985). No side effects have been reported in reptiles (Jacobson and Kollias, 1988). Unfortunately, *Pseudomonas* is sometimes resistant to chloramphenicol.

Trimethoprim-sulfa is a relatively non-toxic broad spectrum antibiotic. It is unfortunately only available in oral form in the United States. A parenteral form may be obtained through a compounding pharmacist. This drug is not always effective against *Pseudomonas* spp., especially *Pseudomonas aeruginosa*, and sensitivity testing should be performed prior to use (Gilman et al, 1990).

Other antibiotics which should be considered for treating reptile infections include carbenicillin and piperacillin. Both drugs have excellent activity against *Pseudomonas* spp. The recommended dose of carbenicillin requires large volumes to be given. Resistent strains may develop rapidly with carbenicillin. (Lawrence et al, 1984 Lawrence et al, 1986). Metronidazole is an excellent choice for the treatment of anaerobic infections.

The use of antibiotics in combination may be required to increase the spectrum, decrease the development of resistance, and for synergistic or additive effects which would allow reduced dosages and thus reduce any potential toxicity. Combining an aminoglycoside plus a penicillin or cephalosporin can broaden the effective antibiotic spectrum and can be useful in treating mixed infections. Empirical therapy with aminoglycosides alone will not be effective against infections involving Gram positive or anaerobic organisms (Stewart, 1990). It is suggested that empirical treatments for conditions such as pneumonia cover the possibility of anaerobic involvement and include a scheme such as amikacin plus ampicillin. The use of gentamicin plus carbenicillin is controversial. The advantages cited are questionable and may in fact be detrimental (Jacobson and Kollias, 1988).

Systemic fungal diseases are difficult to treat in any animal. The exact circumstances surrounding the development of this type of infection should be investigated since fungal diseases are often secondary to some type of immunocompromise or suboptimal environmental conditions. Improper environmental conditions relating to temperature, humidity, and hygiene are often implicated (Jacobson, 1980). The family of imidazole antifungal agents offer a variety of therapeutic options. Historically ketoconazole has been the most commonly used systemic antifungal agent. However, itraconazole and fluconazole are being used more and more due to their greater efficacy and reduced toxicity . All of the imidazoles are only available in an oral form. An alternative drug, Amphotericin B must be used intravenously or it can be nebulized in respiratory infections (Jacobson and Kollias, 1988). Amphotericin B is potentially nephrotoxic, so care should be taken to monitor renal function when used intravenously. Nystatin can be used for gastrointestinal candidiasis (Jacobson and Kollias, 1988). It is not absorbed from the gastrointestinal tract into the systemic circulation and consequently cannot be used for systemic mycoses. Griseofulvin has not been shown to be effective in reptiles so far (Jacobson and Kollias, 1988).

ANTIPARASITIC TREATMENT

Antiparasitic medications are often used by the practitioner in a variety of situations. Wild-caught specimens are frequently parasitized as are animals kept closely together or those fed live food.

Protozoal infections can be a major cause of anorexia in many reptiles. Normal protozoa may proliferate and develop into a pathogenic population, or primary pathogenic protozoa such as *Entamoeba invadens* are capable of causing severe life threatening disease. Metronidazole is recommended for protozoal infections and is easily administered orally. Toxicity has been seen in indigo snakes and tricolor ring snakes and care should be taken to calculate the dose accurately (Jacobson and Kollias, 1988). Other similar compounds such as dimetridazole have been used, but may no longer be available. Compounds such as emetine, paromomycin with or without diiodohydroxyquin, have been advocated (Murphy and Collins, 1983).

Coccidiosis in reptiles is not unusual and should be treated when clinical signs are apparent. As in mammals, problems with coccidia are most often related to overcrowding and/or poor hygiene practices in the captive environment. Treatment may involve the use of oral sulfadimethoxine, sulfaquinoxaline, or sulfamethazine. Injectable sulfamethoxydiazone has also been used successfully (Jacobson and Kollias, 1988). Chelonia have also been treated with amprolium (Murphy and Collins, 1983).

Cryptosporidial and haemoprotozoal infections are generally thought to be untreatable except with supportive care. Many agents have been tried against cryptosporidia, but so far all have failed to clear the animals of the organism (Cranfield, 1995).

Trematode infections are not unusual in aquatic species, particularly turtles. Treatment with praziquantel has met with variable success. Usually the encysted forms of the trematode are not reached by this drug and repeated testing and treatment is required. Some of the newer mammalian antitrematodal drugs such as clorsulon and albendazole, may be more effective and need to be investigated (Booth and MacDonald, 1988). Suggested scaled doses are given at the end of this chapter.

Cestode infections occur in a wide variety of reptile species, particularly free-living or recently captured animals. Praziquantel is the most effective treatment currently available. Older medications such as bunamide hydrochloride and niclosamide have been used successfully.

Nematode infections are the most common and can be very serious. Suggested therapies include compounds from the benzimidazole group, such as thiabendazole and fenbendazole, piperazine and the avermectins, particularly ivermectin. Toxicity has been seen with the use of ivermectin in chelonia. Experimentally induced toxicity was seen specifically in red-footed tortoises, leopard tortoises, box turtles, and red-eared sliders (Teare and Bush, 1983). Use of this drug should be avoided in all chelonions (Jacobson and Kollias, 1988). Recent experience with milbemycin oxime shows promise for use in chelonions. Red-eared sliders and box turtles were treated successfully without signs of toxicity (Bodri, 1992).

Lungworm infestations with *Rhabdias* spp. may be treated with levamisole (Jacobson and Kollias, 1988). Treatment of lung worm infestations with fenbendazole or ivermectin is effective in mammals and should be considered in reptiles due to the potential toxicity of levamisole.

Pentastomes are rarely diagnosed in animals other than reptiles. However, they have been reported to infect mammals, including humans, as an incidental intermediate host. Because of this, proper precautions should be taken when handling infected animals. They can potentially cause significant disease during their migrations (Hendrix, 1988). There is no effective treatment for all stages, although Jacobson (1988) suggests ivermectin as the most likely drug to attempt to eliminate extraintestinal parasites.

Acanthocephalan infections may also require treatment. Treatment with dithiazanine iodide and levamisol have been suggested by Frye (1981).

Arthropod infestations can be difficult to eradicate. Mites and ticks are often seen in collections or on individual animals that have recently come from a large collection or have been recently captured. Treatments have historically included the use of dichlorvos impregnated strips. These products may be difficult to obtain and are potentially toxic. Recent reports of the insecticide permectrin spray are encouraging and appear to be effective and safe when used properly (Boyer, 1995). Clinical experience has shown that ivermectin appears to be very effective against mites, and can also be effective against ticks when combined with manual removal. Secondary infections, viruses and septicemias may be induced by arthropod infestations and should not be overlooked. Any treatment regimen must involve elimination of the arthropod from the environment as well as on the individual animal. Cages should be thoroughly cleaned, disinfected and may also be treated with an insecticide.

ANALGESICS

Analgesic use in reptiles has been very limited except in the case of surgical anesthesia. There is a distinct lack of research aimed at better understanding pain in lower vertebrates. Personal observations verify the reflexes of pain in reptiles in response to injections or surgical trauma usually expressed as flinches or aversive behaviors. Assessment of pain in more chronic cases may be represented by reluctance to move, anorexia, or general lethargy. These latter situations are much more difficult to assess. It should be assumed that reptiles feel the full spectrum of pain in similar situations of trauma, injury and disease that are well documented in mammals. The practitioner should make an attempt to address such situations and use medications accordingly. Increased experience with analgesic medications will only add to the minimal current understanding of relief of pain in reptiles. Suggested medications for the relief of traumatic or post-operative pain are **butorphanol**

and **flunixin meglumine**. Scaled dosages are recommended and have been used by the author with apparent positive results.

There are a multitude of situations where other medications are called for in reptile clinical cases. Some of the more common miscelaneous indications for drug use are cases of gout and/or renal failure and gastrointestinal motility problems (ileus). Allometric scaling is very often extremely useful in developing rational therapies in these situations.

Treatment of gout or renal failure should include fluid therapy at twice the normal rate to achieve diuresis. In addition, drugs used classically in humans for gout may be helpful in reptiles, although their action has not been confirmed. **Allopurinol** has been used to help reduce hyperuricemia. In humans this drug helps to prevent further accumulation of uric acid by inhibiting the production of uric acid from oxypurines. Use of allopurinol should be closely monitored in patients with renal function impairment (AHFS, 1995). Another drug, **probenecid**, promotes the excretion of uric acid in the kidney by blocking its reabsorption in the tubules (AHFS, 1995). Both of these drugs have been used by the author with some success in snakes using allometric scaling. The Universal MEC doses are listed below.

Treatment of gastrointestinal motility disorders with **cisapride** was discussed earlier in an example for how and when to use allometric scaling. Other drugs that have been suggested for constipation following rehydration include mineral oil, milk of magnesia and dioctyl sodium sulfosuccinate (DSS)(Frye, 1991). DSS is potentially toxic in snakes if administered incorrectly (Paul-Murphy, 1987).

FORMULARY

The following recorded doses are taken from the literature as noted. Dose information based on pharmacokinetic data is indicated with an asterisk (*). The Universal MEC dosages of many of the medications listed are also given. To use the MEC dose simply multiply the subjects MEC by the MEC dose listed and the dose in milligrams will result. To determine the frequency, divide the subjects MEC by their body weight in kilograms and multiply by the Frequency listed and the frequency per day will result.

Dosages for chelonions are based on the entire weight of the animal, including the shell. It has been recommended to use the snake dosage for tortoises, rather than the water turtle dose, unless a tortoise dose is specifically listed. (Bush, 1980)

Medication	Species	Dosage	Comments
Albendazole *MEC dose*	Cattle model	MEC dose 0.64	
Allopurinol *MEC dose*	Human model	MEC dose 0.18 Freq. 0.04	
Amikacin *MEC dose*	Gopher Snake Alligator Gopher tortoise (30°C) Gopher snake model	5 mg/kg IM (loading dose), then 2.5 mg/kg q72h 2.25 mg/kg IM q 72-96h 5 mg/kg IM q48h MEC dose 0.4, 0.2 Freq. 0.024	*Mader, 1985. *Jacobson, 1988. *Caligiuri, 1990. Use for large snakes.
Aminophylline *MEC dose*	Cat model	MEC dose 0.08 Freq. 0.04	
Amphotericine B	None given	5 mg in 150 ml NaCl, nebulized 1h bid x 7d	Jacobson, 1988. Treatment for fungal pneumonia.
Ampicillin *MEC dose*	Rattlesnake Tortoise Dog model	7 mg/kg IM q24h x 3 weeks 20 mg/kg IM q24h x 7-14 days MEC dose 0.665 Freq. 0.09	*Moulton, 1975. Page, 1990.
Butorphanol *MEC dose*	Cat model	MEC dose 0.004 Freq. 0.12	
Calcitonin *MEC dose*	Human model	MEC dose 0.165-0.331 Freq. 0.083	
Calcium edetate *MEC dose*	Avian model	MEC dose 0.333 Freq. 0.019	Treatment for lead poisoning.

Carbenicillin	Snakes
	
	Tortoises
		400 mg/kg IM q. 24 hrs.
		    x 2 weeks
		400 mg/kg IM q 48 hrs.
		    x 2 weeks
			*Lawrence, 1984.
			
			*Lawrence, 1986.

Cefotaxime	Tortoises	20-40 mg/kg IM q24h x 7-14 days	Page, 1990. May be used with aminoglycosides.
Ceftazadime *MEC dose*	Snakes Snake model	20 mg/kg IM q72h x 2-3 weeks MEC dose 2.4 Freq. 0.044	*Lawrence, 1984. Use for large snakes.
Cephaloridine	None given	10 mg/kg IM, SQ q12h x 10 days	Frye, 1991.
Cephalothin *MEC dose*	None given Dog model	20-40 mg/kg IM q12h x 10 days MEC dose 0.5 Freq. 0.076	Frye, 1991.

Medication	Species	Dosage	Comments
Chloramphenicol	Gopher snakes	40 mg/kg SQ q24h x 2 weeks	*Bush, 1976.
	Indigo, Rat and King snakes	50 mg/kg SQ q12h x 2 weeks	*Clark, 1985.
	Boid and Moccasin snakes	50 mg/kg SQ q24h x 2 weeks	*Clark, 1985.
	Rattlesnake	50 mg/kg SQ q48h x 2 weeks	*Clark, 1985.
	Nerodia snake	50 mg/kg SQ q72h x 2 weeks	*Clark, 1985.
	Tortoises	20 mg/kg IM or PO q12h x 7-14 days	*Page, 1990.
Ciprofloxacin *MEC dose*	Human model	MEC dose 0.3 Freq. 0.08	
Cisapride *MEC dose*	Child model	MEC dose 0.006 Freq. 0.1	
Clorsulon *MEC dose*	Cattle model	MEC dose 0.45	
Dimetridazole	Snakes	40 mg/kg PO q24h x 5 days	Jacobson, 1988.
Dithiazanine iodide	None given	20 mg/kg PO q24h x 10 days	Frye, 1981.
Emetine HCL	None given	0.5 mg/kg IM or SQ q12-24h x 10 days	Frye, 1981.
Enrofloxacin	Gopher tortoise	5 mg/kg IM q24-48h	*Prezant, 1994.
	Indian star tortoise	5 mg/kg IM q12-24h	*Raphael, 1994.
	Burmese Python (juvenile)	5 mg/kg IM q48h	*Young, 1994.
Fenbendazole	None given	50-100 mg/kg PO, repeat in 2 weeks	Jacobson, 1988.
MEC dose	Dog model	MEC dose 1.5 Freq. 0.03	
Fluconazole *MEC dose*	Human model	MEC dose 0.24 (loading), 0.12 Freq. 0.04	
Flunixin meglumine *MEC dose*	Horse model	MEC dose 0.074 Freq. 0.068	
Furosamide *MEC dose*	Dog model	MEC dose 0.06-0.12 Freq. 0.06	
Gentamicin	Gopher and Bull snakes	2.5 mg/kg IM q72h x 2-3 weeks	*Bush, 1978 and 1980. **Use snake dose for desert tortoises.**
	Blood pythons	2.5 mg/kg IM, then 1.5 mg/kg q96h	*Hilf, 1991.
	Red eared slider turtle	6 mg/kg IM q72h x 3 weeks	*Raphael, 1985.
	American alligator	1.75 mg/kg IM q96h x 3 weeks	*Jacobson, 1988.
MEC dose	Gopher snake model	MEC dose 0.25 Freq. 0.03	Use for large snakes.

Medication	Species	Dosage	Comments
Itraconazole *MEC dose*	Dog model	MEC dose 0.076 Freq. 0.06	
Ivermectin	All except chelonions	0.2 mg/kg PO or SQ, repeat in 2 weeks	**DO NOT USE in chelonions** (Teare, 1983).
Kanamycin	None given	10-15 mg/kg divided IV, IM q12-24h	Frye, 1991.
Ketoconazole	Gopher tortoise	15 mg/kg PO q24h x 2-4 weeks	*Page, 1991.
Levamisole	Snake	10 mg/kg IP, repeat in 2 weeks	Jacobson, 1988.
Mebendazole	None given	20-25 mg/kg PO, repeat in 2 weeks	Jacobson, 1988.
Megesterol acetate *MEC dose*	Cat model	MEC dose 0.02 Freq. 0.02	
Metaclopramide *MEC dose*	Dog model	MEC dose 0.006-0.015 Freq. 0.09	
Metronidazole	Snakes Indigo snakes King snakes Tortoises	100-275 mg/kg PO, repeat in 2 weeks 40 mg/kg PO, repeat in 2 weeks. 100 mg/kg PO, repeat in 2 weeks. 250 mg/kg PO, repeat in 2 weeks	Jacobson, 1988. **CAUTION in Indigo Snakes and Tricolor ring snakes.** Page, 1990.
MEC dose	Dog model	MEC dose 1.8 Freq. 0.03	
Milbemycin oxime	Ornate box turtles	0.25 mg/kg SQ, repeat in 2 weeks	Bodri, 1992. No toxicity seen in red-eared sliders, gulfcoast box turtles or ornate box turtles.
Nystatin	Python	100,000 units/kg PO q24h x 10 days	Jacobson, 1988.
Oxytetracycline	None given Alligators	6-10 mg/kg IV or IM q24h 10 mg/kg PO q24h	Frye, 1991. Jacobson, 1988.
Paramomycin	None given	33-110 mg/kg PO q24h for up to 4 weeks	Jacobson, 1988.
Penicillin (Potassium G)	None given	10,000-20,000 units/kg IM or SQ q6-8h	Frye, 1991.
Piperacillin	Blood pythons	100 mg/kg IM q48h	*Hilf, 1991.

Medication	Species	Dosage	Comments
Piperazine	Alligators and Crocodiles	50 mg/kg PO, repeat in 2 weeks	Jacobson, 1983.
Praziquantel	Green turtles	7.5 mg/kg PO, repeat in 2 weeks	Jacobson, 1988.
MEC dose	Dog model	MEC dose 0.15-0.3	
Prednisone			
MEC dose	Dog model	MEC dose 0.033 Freq. 0.06	
Probenecid			
MEC dose	Human model	MEC dose 0.148 Freq. 0.08	
Sulfa-diazine	Lizards and Snakes	25 mg/kg PO q24h x 1 week	Jacobson, 1983.
Sulfa-dimethoxine	None given	90 mg/kg PO day 1, then 45 mg/kg PO q24h x 5 days	Jacobson, 1988.
Sulfamerazine	Lizards and Snakes	25 mg/kg PO q24h x 1 week	Jacobson, 1983.
Sulfa-methazine	None given	75 mg/kg PO day 1, then 40 mg/kg PO q24h x 5-7 days	Jacobson, 1988.
Sulfa-methoxydiazone	None given	80 mg/kg SQ or IM day 1, then 40 mg/kg q24h x 4 days	Jacobson, 1988.
Sulfa-quinoxaline	None given	75 mg/kg PO day 1, then 40 mg/kg PO q24h x 5-7 days	Jacobson, 1988.
Tetracycline	None given	10 mg/kg PO q24h x 10-14 days	Jacobson, 1983.
Thiabendazole	None given	50 mg/kg PO, repeat in 2 weeks	Frye, 1981.
Trimethoprim-sulfa	None given Tortoises	15 mg/kg SQ q24h x 10 days 30 mg/kg IM or PO q48h x 7-14 days	Jacobson, 1988. Page, 1990.
MEC dose	Dog model	MEC dose 0.5 Freq. 0.06	
Tylosin	Lizards and Snakes	5 mg/kg IM q24h x 10 days	Jacobson, 1983.
Vitamin A	Tortoises	11,000 IU/kg IM	Page, 1990.
Vitamin B complex	None given	0.5 ml/kg IV, IM, or SQ	Frye, 1981.
Vitamin C	None given	10-20 mg/kg IM q24h	Frye, 1991.
Vitamin D_3	Tortoises	1650 IU/kg IM	Page, 1990.
Vitamin K	None given	0.25-0.75 mg/kg IM	Frye, 1991.

REFERENCES

—**AHFS Drug Information 95.**
American Society of Health Systems Pharmacists, c1995.

—**Barone, JA., et al.**
Cisapride: A gastrointestinal prokinetic drug. The Annals of Pharmacotherapy, 1994; 28(April): 488-500.

—**Bodri, MS, Nolan TJ, Skeeba SJ.**
Safety of milbemycin (A3-A4 oxime) in chelonions. Proceedings of the American Association of Zoo Veterinarians and the American Association of Wildlife Veterinarians, Joint Conference, November 15-19, 1992: 156-157.

—**Booth, NH McDonald LE, (eds.).**
Veterinary Pharmacology and Therapeutics. Iowa State University Press, Ames, Iowa, c1988.

—**Boyer, DM.**
Snake mite (*Ophionyssus natricis*) eradication utilizing permectrin spray. Bulletin of the Association of Reptilian and Amphibian Veterinarians, 1995; 5(1): 4-5.

—**Bush, M, et al.**
Preliminary study of antibiotics in snakes. Annual Proceedings of the American Association of Zoo Veterinarians, 1976: 50pp.

—**Bush, M, et al.**
Biological half-life of gentamicin in gopher snakes. American Journal of Veterinary Research, 1978; 39(1): 171-173.

—**Bush, M.**
Antibiotic therapy in reptiles. IN Kirk, RW, (ed.). Current Veterinary Therapy, Vol. 7. W.B. Saunders, Philadelphia, PA, 1980: 647-649.

—**Caligiuri, R, et al.**
The effects of ambient temperature on amikacin pharmacokinetics in gopher tortoises. Journal of Veterinary Pharmacology and Therapeutics, 1990; 13: 287-291.

—**Cisapride. AHFS**
Drug Information 95. American Society of Health System Pharmacists, Bethesda, MD, c1995: 2027-2029.

—**Clark, CG, Rogers ED, Milton JL.**
Plasma concentrations of chloramphenicol in snakes. American Journal of Veterinary Research, 1985; 46(12): 2654-2657.

—**Cranfield, MR, Graczyk TK.**
An update on ophidian cryptosporidiosis. Proceedings of the American Association of Zoo Veterinarians, the Wildlife Disease Association, and the American Association of Wildlife Veterinarians, Joint Conference, August 12-17, 1995: 225-230.

—**Frye, FL.**
Biomedical and Surgical Aspects of Captive Reptile Husbandry. Veterinary Medicine Publishing Company, Edwardsville, KA, 1981.

—**Gilman, AG, et al. (eds.)**
Goodman and Gilman's The Pharmacological Basis of Therapeutics. 6th ed. Pergamon Press, New York, 1990.

—**Hendrix, CM, Blagburn, BL.**
Reptilian pentastomiasis: a possible emerging zoonosis. Compendium of Continuing Education, 1988; 10(1): 46-51.

—**Hilf, M, et al.**
Pharmacokinetics of piperacillin in blood pythons (*Python curtus*) and in vitro evaluation of efficacy against aerobic Gram-negative bacteria. Journal of Zoo and Wildlife Medicine, 1991; 22(2): 199-203.

—**Hilf, M, Swanson D, Wagner R.**
A new dosing schedule for gentamicin in blood pythons (*Python curtus*): a pharmacokinetic study. Research in Veterinary Science, 1991; 50: 127-130.

—**Holz, P, et al.**
The reptilian renal portal system and its effect on drug kinetics. Proceedings of the American Association of Zoo Veterinarians and the Association of Reptilian and Amphibian Veterinarians, Annual Conference, October 22-27, 1994: 95-96.

—**Innis, C.**
Per-cloacal worming of tortoises. Bulletin of the Association of Reptilian and Amphibian Veterinarians, 1995; 5(2): 4pp.

—**Jacobson, ER.**
Gentamicin-related visceral gout in two boid snakes. VM/SAC, March, 1976: 361-363.

—**Jacobson, ER.**
Necrotizing mycotic dermatitis in snakes: clinical and pathologic features. Journal of the American Veterinary Medical Association, 1980; 177(9): 838-841.

—**Jacobson, E, Kollias GV, Peters LJ.**
Dosages for antibiotics and parasiticides used in exotic animals. The Compendium on Continuing Education, 1983; 5(4): 315-324.

—**Jacobson, ER, Kollias, GV (eds.).**
Exotic Animals. Churchill Livingstone, New York, 1988.

—**Jacobson, ER, et al.**
Serum concentration and disposition kinetics of gentamicin and amikacin in juvenile American alligators. Journal of Zoo Animal Medicine, 1988; 19(4): 188-194.

—**Jarchow, JL.**
Hospital care of the reptile patient. IN Jacobson, ER, Kollias, GV (eds.). Exotic Ani-

mals. Churchill Livingstone, New York, 1988: 19-34.

—**Lamberski, N, Daniel GB.**
Fluid dynamics of intraosseous fluid administration in birds. Journal of Zoo and Wildlife Medicine, 1992; 23(1): 47-54.

—**Lawrence, K, et al.**
A preliminary study on the use of carbenicillin in snakes. Journal of Veterinary Pharmacology and Therapeutics, 1984; 7: 119-124.

—**Lawrence, K, Muggleton PW, Needham JR.**
Preliminary study on the use of ceftazidime, a broad spectrum cephalosporin antibiotic, in snakes. Research in Veterinary Science, 1984; 36: 16-20.

—**Lawrence, K, Palmer GH, Needham JR.**
Use of carbenicillin in two species of tortoise (*Testudo graeca* and *T hermanni*). Research in Veterinary Science, 1986; 40: 413-415.

—**Mader, DR, Conzelman GM, Baggot JD.**
Effects of ambient temperature on the half-life and dosage regimen of amikacin in the gopher snake. Journal of the American Veterinary Medical Association, 1985; 187(11): 1134-1136.

—**Molinari, F, Farrington E.**
Cisapride. Pediatric Nursing, 1994; 20 (2): 202-203.

—**Montali, RJ, Bush M, Smeller JM.**
The pathology of nephrotoxicity of gentamicin in snakes. Veterinary Pathology, 1979; 16: 108-115.

—**Mordenti, J.**
Pharmacokinetic scale-up: accurate prediction of human pharmacokinetic profiles from animal data. Journal of Pharmaceutical Sciences, 1985; 74(10): 1097-1099.

—**Mordenti, J.**
Forecasting cephalosporin and monobactam antibiotic half-lives in humans from data collected in laboratory animals. Antimicrobial Agents and Chemotherapy, 1985; 27(6): 887-891.

—**Mordenti, J.**
Man versus Beast: pharmacokinetic scaling in mammals. Journal of Pharmaceutical Sciences, 1986; 75(11): 1028-1040.

—**Moulton, RG, et al.**
Technique for testing antibiotic plasma levels in ophidia. Utah Herpetological League, 1975; 2: 1-4.

—**Murphy, JB, Collins JT.**
A review of the diseases and treatment of captive turtles. AMS Publishing, Lawrence, KS, c1983.

—**Needham, JR.**
Laboratory aspects of reptilian infections. IN Reptiles: breeding, behavior and veterinary aspects. British Herpetological Society, 1985: 121-124.

—**Page, CD, et al.**
Preliminary pharmacokinetics of ketoconazole in gopher tortoises (*Gopherus polyphemus*). Journal of Veterinary Pharmacology and Therapeutics, 1988; 11: 397-401.

—**Page, CD, Mautino M.**
Clinical management of tortoises. Compendium, 1990; 12(2): 221-228.

—**Page, CD, et al.**
Multiple-dose pharmacokinetics of ketoconazole administered orally to gopher tortoises (*Gopherus polyphemus*). Journal of Zoo and Wildlife Medicine, 1991; 22(2): 191-198.

—**Paul-Murphy, J, et al.**
Necrosis of esophageal and gastric mucosa in snakes given oral dioctyl sodium sulfosuccinate. American Association of Zoo Veterinarians Annual Conference, 1987: 474-475.

—**Prezant, RM, Isaza R, Jacobson ER.**
Plasma concentrations and disposition kinetics of enrofloxacin in gopher tortoises (*Gopherus polyphemus*). Journal of Zoo and Wildlife Medicine, 1994; 25(1): 82-87.

—**Raphael, B, Clark CH, Hudson R.**
Plasma concentration of gentamicin in turtles. Journal of Zoo Animal Medicine, 1985; 16(4): 136-139.

—**Raphael, BL., et al.**
Pharmacokinetics of enrofloxacin after a single intramuscular injection in Indian star tortoises (*Geochelone elegans*). Journal of Zoo and Wildlife Medicine, 1994; 25(1): 88-94.

—**Ritchie, BW, et al.**
A technique for intraosseous cannulation for intravenous therapy in birds. The Compendium of Continuing Education, 1990; 12(1): 55-58.

—**Sedgwick, CJ, Pokras MA.**
Extrapolating rational drug doses and treatment periods by allometric scaling. Proceedings of the American Animal Hospital Association 55th Annual Meeting, 1988: 156-161.

—**Stewart, JS.**
Anaerobic bacterial infections in reptiles. Journal of Zoo and Wildlife Medicine, 1990; 21(2): 180-184.

—**Swaim, SF, Lee HA.**
Topical wound medications: a review. Journal of the American Veterinary Medical Association, 1987; 190(12): 1588-1593.

—**Teare, JA, Bush M.**
Toxicity and efficacy of ivermectin in chelonians. Journal of the American Veterinary Medical Association, 1983; 183(11): 1195-1197.

DIAGNOSTIC PROCEDURE: URINALYSIS

James Watson BVSc (hons) MACVSc
Veterinary Pathologist
Animal Health Laboratory
Department of Primary Industries and Fisheries
PO Box 46, Kings Meadows, 7249
Tasmania, Australia

James Watson is a veterinary clinical pathologist with an interest in exotic species, including reptiles in particular and wildlife in general. Since graduating from the University of Melbourne and undertaking postgraduate training at Murdoch University, James has, apart from a brief flirtation with the private sector, been working with the Department of Primary Industries and Fisheries in Tasmania, Australia.

A urine culture transport kit. Photo courtesy of Dr. Lowell Ackerman.

INTRODUCTION

Urinalysis in reptiles is a neglected subject, but not without some justification. It is difficult to obtain good specimens in most species, for a variety of reasons. Not the least of these is the desert lizard from Australia that achieves zero water loss via the kidney over the summer (Bentley, 1959).

It is important to note that the reptilian kidney does not function identically to the mammalian organ in maintaining fluid homeostasis in the body. While it has the major role in maintaining osmotic stability, it cannot produce urine at a higher osmolarity than blood. Many species have accessory glands that contribute to this function - marine species frequently have salt glands to provide ancillary excretion, and some freshwater species can absorb sodium from their environment. In addition, as noted in the previous chapter, wide fluctuations in osmolarity and electrolyte levels are tolerated by many species.

In uricotelic species the urine fraction of the dropping may be collected, provided the dropping is passed onto a suitable surface so the liquid fraction is not lost. The problem then becomes obtaining a sample that is free from fecal contamination. This is often difficult to achieve.

In aquatic species, the urine is liquid, and fecal contamination is likely to occur in the cloaca before excretion. In any case, excretion is likely to occur in the water, which presents a fairly formidable challenge to sample collection.

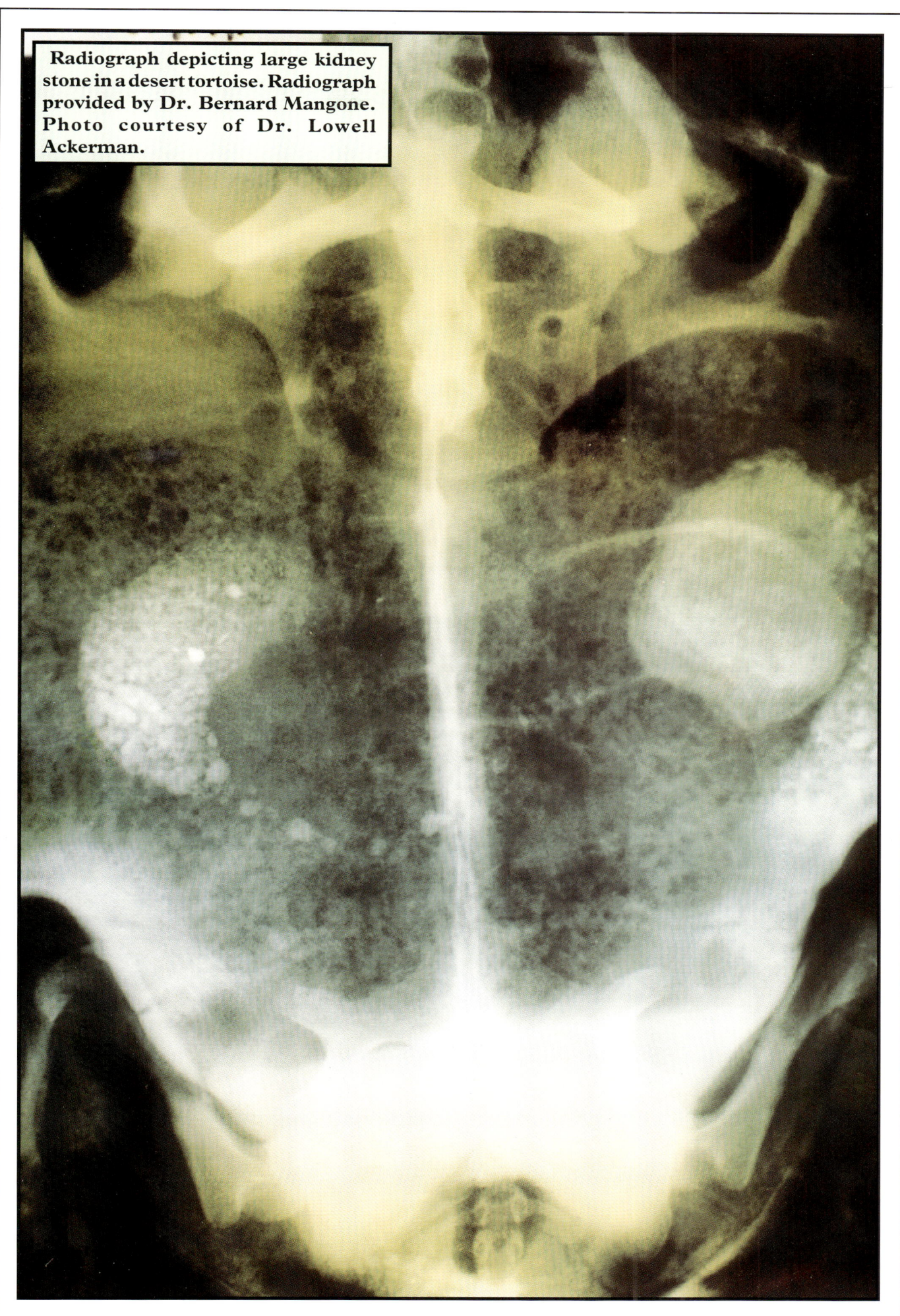

Radiograph depicting large kidney stone in a desert tortoise. Radiograph provided by Dr. Bernard Mangone. Photo courtesy of Dr. Lowell Ackerman.

In the end, if the individual situation and circumstances can be arranged to permit collection of a fresh, uncontaminated sample of urine, then urinalysis can provide some useful clinical information and is worth undertaking. The comments below relate principally to terrestrial uricotelic species, as these are the most likely to allow collection of a useful sample.

APPEARANCE

Urine should normally only be coloured by the urates, forming a chalky white mass accompanied by a variable but generally small amount of liquid. The principle change noted in colour is a yellow/green discolouration due to biliverdinuria. This is associated with liver disease. Excessive fluid suggests polyuria, but careful observation may be required to be certain of this finding. Red/brown discoloration of the urates suggests hematuria or hemoglobinuria.

CHEMICAL ANALYSIS

The dipsticks used for routine mammalian urinalysis can be used, with some caveats, on reptilian urine. Dipstick pads for specific gravity, bacteria, leukocytes and urobilinogen are not appropriate to the situation and should not be used.

pH

The pH of reptilian urine would be expected to show considerable variation given the wide swings in blood pH seen in many species. It is interesting to note that the alligator, which undergoes profound changes in blood pH in response to feeding generally excretes an alkaline urine, due to the excretion of ammonium bicarbonate as a sodium and chloride conservation measure (Dessauer, 1970).

PROTEIN

Should be negative to slight positive only, but note that alkaline urine will cause a false positive reaction. This is because the dipstick pad detects protein by it's interference with a standard pH indicator colour reaction. Excessively alkaline urine overloads the buffer in the pad, giving an artefactual colour change. Proteinuria may indicate glomerular damage.

BLOOD

A reaction for blood clearly suggests hematuria, but may also be caused by hemorrhage from the intestinal or reproductive tracts. Hematuria needs to be differentiated from hemoglobinuria by microscopic examination. Lead poisoning has been associated with hemoglobinuria in birds and should be considered in reptiles also.

Biliverdinuria in an Eastern Massassauga rattlesnake. Photo courtesy of Dr. Todd Driggers.

GLUCOSE

Glucose is expected to be negative in normal animals, although little information exists on renal thresholds for glucose excretion in different species. Some glycosuria is likely to accompany hyperglycemia, but the extent is likely to vary in different species due to the threshold. Persistent glycosuria warrants investigation of blood glucose levels and may indicate diabetes mellitus.

KETONES

Little information exists on ketonuria in reptiles, but a positive reading is worth further investigation. Catabolic, or negative energy balance, states are the most likely cause, but is possible that ketoacidosis may occur in diabetes.

BILIRUBIN

Although the major bile pigment in reptiles is biliverdin, in practice, a low level of bilirubin may be produced, and in liver disease, a reaction for bilirubin may be observed. This will almost invariable accompany biliverdinuria. Biliverdin does not react with the bilirubin pad on urine dipsticks.

MICROSCOPIC EXAMINATION

BLOOD CELLS

Both erythrocytes and leukocytes may be present in small numbers, but more than five to ten cells per high power field are likely to be significant. A positive dipstick reaction for blood with no erythrocytes suggests either hemoglobinuria (see above) or myoglobinuria, in which case plasma creatine kinase (CK) is likely to be elevated.

EPITHELIAL CELLS

Epithelial cells in the urine are likely to come from the cloaca and should not be present in large numbers.

CRYSTALS

Amorphous urates are expected to form the major crystalline component of the urine. Other crystal types may be observed, and can be presumptively identified from their appearance.

BACTERIA

Given the anatomy of the urinary tract, the major concern if bacteria are found will be to ensure they are not contaminants from the feces. The presence of bacteria without significant numbers of white cells should be interpreted as contamination. Bacterial phagocytosis by leukocytes is useful in confirming a genuine infectious problem.

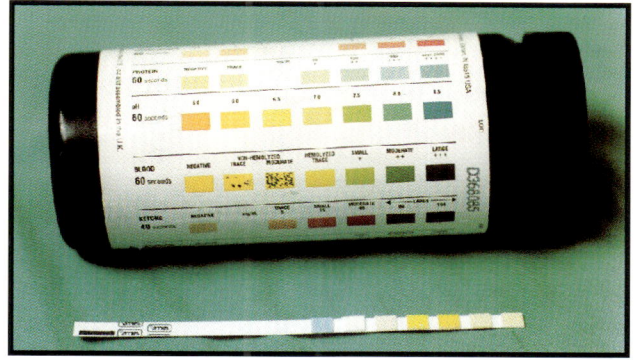

Standard dipstick tests are available for evaluating urine of reptiles. They are the same as those used for mammals. Photo courtesy of Dr. Lowell Ackerman.

Again, this will not always be a urinary tract problem. Calculi in the cloaca, generally composed of urates or gravel, may cause a traumatic bacterial cloacitis. This condition can result in bleeding that may be detected in the urinalysis.

REFERENCES AND FURTHER READING

—**Bentley, P J:**
Studies on the water and electrolyte metabolism of the lizard *Trachydosaurus rugosus* (Gray). *J. Physiol, Lond,* 1959; 145: 37-47.

—**Dessauer, H C:**
Blood chemistry of reptiles: physiological and evolutionary aspects. in, Biology of the Reptilia, Vol 3 Morphology, Gans, C. and Parsons, T (Eds). Academic Press, New York, 1970, pp. 1-72.

—**Duncan, R J, Prasse, K W and Mahaffey, E A:**
Urinary System. in, Veterinary Laboratory Medicine: Clinical Pathology. Iowa State University Press, Ames, Iowa. Third Edition, 1994, pp 162-183.

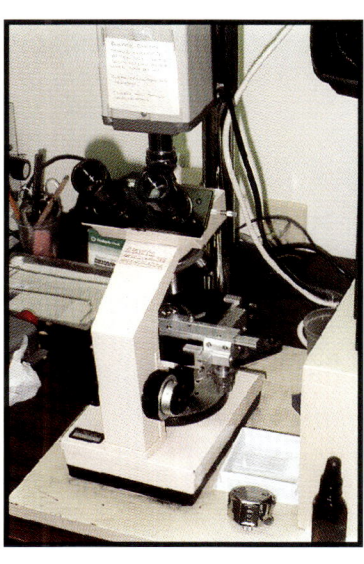

Urine sediment needs to be evaluated microscopically. Photo courtesy of Dr. Lowell Ackerman.

DIAGNOSTIC PROCEDURES: CHEMISTRY

James Watson BVSc (hons) MACVSc
Veterinary Pathologist
Animal Health Laboratory
Department of Primary Industries and Fisheries
PO Box 46, Kings Meadows, 7249
Tasmania, Australia

James Watson is a veterinary clinical pathologist with an interest in exotic species, including reptiles in particular and wildlife in general. Since graduating from the University of Melbourne and undertaking postgraduate training at Murdoch University, James has, apart from a brief flirtation with the private sector, been working with the Department of Primary Industries and Fisheries in Tasmania, Australia.

INTRODUCTION

Biochemistry of reptilian species is, like hematology, an area in which much work remains to be done. Even more so than is the case with hematological determinations, reported values vary considerably in validity as reference data, and are not always directly comparable, due to differences in methodology. None of this is meant to discourage the use of biochemistry in clinical situations - much useful information exists even if the current state of knowledge could be improved, and it is only by applying these techniques that further clinical data will be gained.

Lithium heparin is the preferred sample type for biochemistry. Serum (plain) samples are less desirable as clot formation can be very slow with reptilian samples due to very low intrinsic activity

Blood collection supplies. Photo courtesy of Dr. Lowell Ackerman.

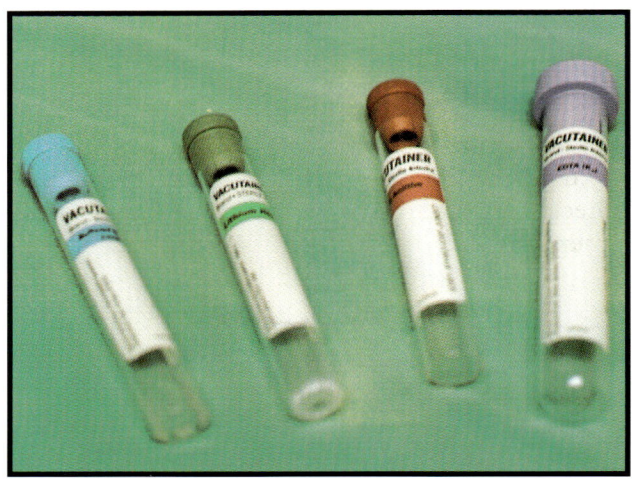

A variety of tubes are available for blood collection, depending on which tests are being performed. Photo courtesy of Dr. Lowell Ackerman.

of the coagulation system. This in turn leads to delayed separation of serum, during which time significant changes can occur in the levels of some analytes (Bolten et al, 1992). In addition, as noted in the previous chapter, lithium heparin samples allow both hematology and biochemistry to performed on the one sample, which in smaller species is a great convenience. Sample collection techniques are covered in the chapter on hematology.

PLASMA COLOUR

Normal plasma or serum of most reptiles should be colourless. In some species of lizards (particularly the Iguanidae and chameleons), high levels of circulating carotenoids can give the plasma a yellow to yellow/green coloration. This is also seen in some species of snakes (*Python* sp., *Bothrops* sp. and *Mastigodryas* sp.), where riboflavin also contributes to the observed colour (Dessauer, 1970).

Green discolouration of the plasma suggests biliverdinemia. The predominant bile pigment produced by the reptilian liver is biliverdin rather than bilirubin. This is due to a lack of the enzyme,

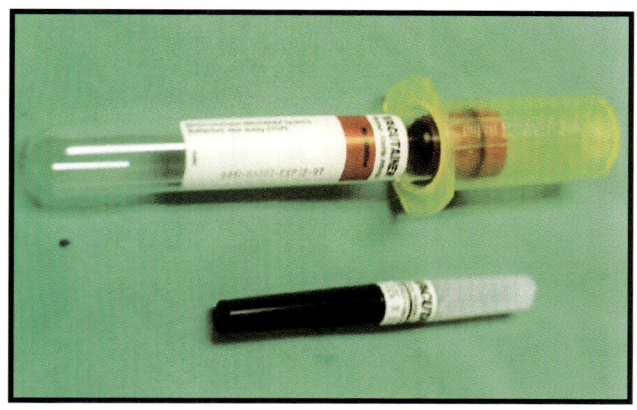

Vacutainers can be used for blood collection but the vacuum inside may be sufficient to collapse small veins. Photo courtesy of Dr. Lowell Ackerman.

biliverdin reductase, that catalyses the conversion of biliverdin to bilirubin in the liver. In practice, a green discolouration is perhaps more often appreciated in the urates rather than the plasma, but nonetheless biliverdinemia is a significant finding and points to hepatic dysfunction.

ENZYMOLOGY

Useable reference ranges have been obtained for a number of enzymes, as shown in the table below. Data linking these levels directly with disease are needed to improve the predictive value of these determinations, as little is known of the expected response to injury. In interpretation of these results, caution must be exercised as the predominant organ of origin of the circulating enzymes, and their half lives in circulation are not well understood. Some work in avian species (Lumeij, 1987) has shown that transposing what is known about these enzymes in mammalian species is not always valid.

That creatine kinase (CK) activity is associated with skeletal muscle is in little doubt on either

Because reptiles have nucleated red blood cells, automated hematological analyzers do not provide reliable results with reptile blood.

practical or theoretical grounds. The site of venipuncture must always be considered in interpreting this enzyme as deeper sites almost invariably have some sample contamination with tissue fluids, leading to an elevated CK value. To illustrate this, compare the normal ranges (Table 1) for the crocodile, sampled from the tail vein (deeply embedded in muscle), with the long-necked tortoise, sampled from the jugular vein (superficial and subcutaneous). The notable difference in the CK level is more or less a function of the depth of the vein sampled. Nonetheless, significant elevations of this enzyme indicate damage to skeletal muscle.

The reported ranges for other enzymes vary considerably between species and have been reported to vary with nutritional condition and also with the reproductive cycle. Enzymes most frequently tested include aspartate aminotransferase (AST), alanine aminotransferase (ALT), gamma glutamyl transferase (GGT), lactate dehydrogenase (LDH) and glutamate dehydrogenase (GLDH). Correlation between elevated levels and disease states are not always consistent, but associations with liver and kidney disease are most frequently reported. Liver disease is probably the most important diagnosis sought from enzyme levels. It has been shown that GLDH is the most liver specific enzyme in both mammals and birds, so it is reasonable to assume as a first hypothesis that high levels of this enzyme indicate liver disease in reptiles. It should also be noted that there are reports of animals with significant liver pathology at necropsy that had no elevation of assumed liver enzymes pre-mortem.

MISCELLANEOUS TESTS OF LIVER FUNCTION

Direct tests of functional liver capacity include dye clearance tests and circulating bile acid levels. Dye clearance studies (bromsulphpthalein, indocyanine green) have not been sufficiently stud-

Centrifuges are needed to derive serum and plasma from blood samples. Photo courtesy of Dr. Lowell Ackerman.

TABLE 1

REFERENCE DATA FOR REPRESENTATIVE SPECIES: ENZYMES

Enzyme	Estuarine Crocodile[a]	Long necked tortoise[b]	Diamond-backed water snake[c]	Green Turtle[d]
CK IU	115-4232	6-568	92-572	
AST IU	30-82	9-134		31-389
ALP IU	7-85	4-56	27-157	13-95
ALT IU	20-58	0-8		1-17
GGT IU		0-5		
LDH IU	42-908	29-452	69-538	48-342

[a] Watson, 1996; [b] Haigh, 1993; [c] McDaniel et al, 1984; [d] Bolten and Bjorndal, 1992

ied in reptiles to be diagnostically useful, and limited work with bile acid determinations in this author's laboratory have failed to yield useful results.

GLUCOSE

Blood glucose levels in reptiles are less tightly controlled than is usually the case in mammals. This reflects both the variable metabolic rate and a relative insulin resistance. Some insulin resistance is expected on first principles in animals that feed irregularly, but this is unlikely to be the sole explanation for this phenomenon in reptiles.

Natural variations in glucose levels generally reflect these factors, with higher levels expected in summer, at elevated temperatures, and post feeding; with lower levels in winter, at low temperatures and following fasting. A number of variations on this general theme occur, with chelonians often showing hypoglycemia at higher temperatures, and snakes showing little post-prandial hyperglycemia. Freshwater turtles show a marked hyperglycemia when diving, reflecting anaerobic metabolism (Dessauer, 1970).

The principal disease associations with glucose are hypoglycemia accompanying anorexia or starvation, and hyperglycemia as a stress response, particularly in snakes and crocodilians. The stress associated hyperglycemia is assumed, on general physiological principles, to be due

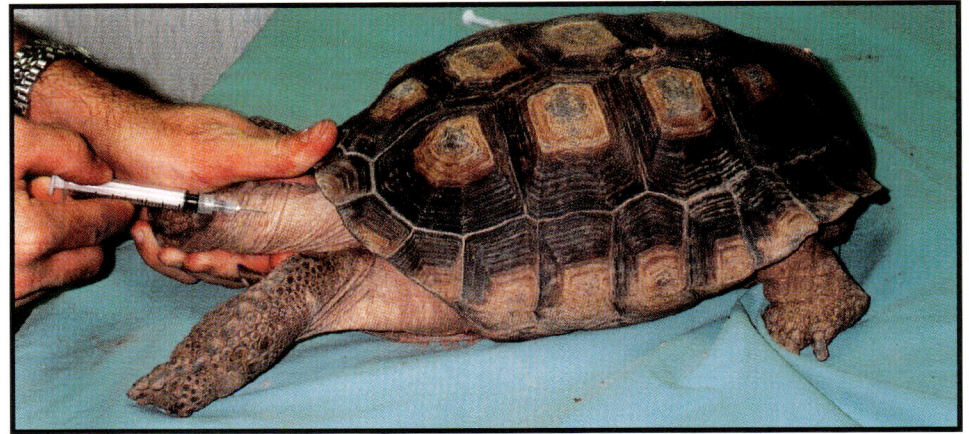

Dr. Bernard Mangone collecting blood by jugular puncture in a desert tortoise. Photo by Dr. Lowell Ackerman.

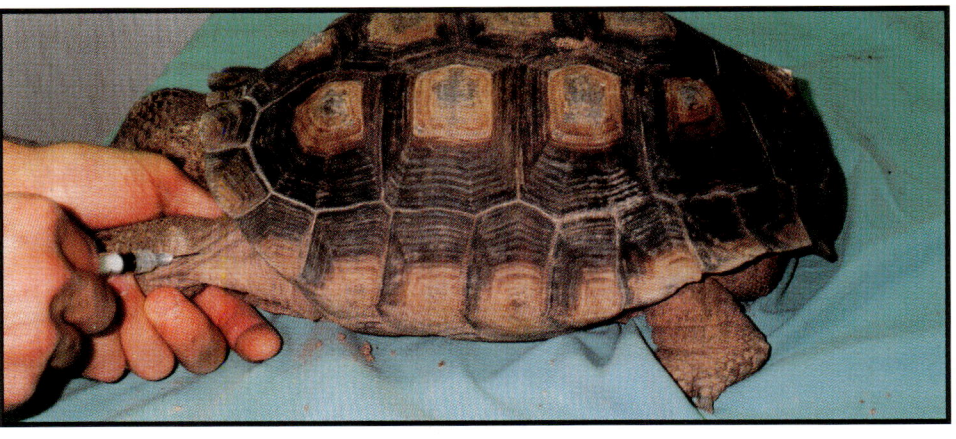

Dr. Bernard Mangone collects blood from a venous sinus of a desert tortoise. Photo courtesy of Dr. Lowell Ackerman.

to release of glucocorticoids and epinephrine. Diabetes mellitus (persistent inappropriate hyperglycemia) has been reported in a single turtle (McCracken, 1993).

ELECTROLYTES AND ACID-BASE

Plasma osmolarity varies between reptile groups, being lowest in freshwater turtles and highest in terrestrial desert species. In all cases, the major osmotic constituents of plasma are sodium, chloride and bicarbonate. Osmolarity

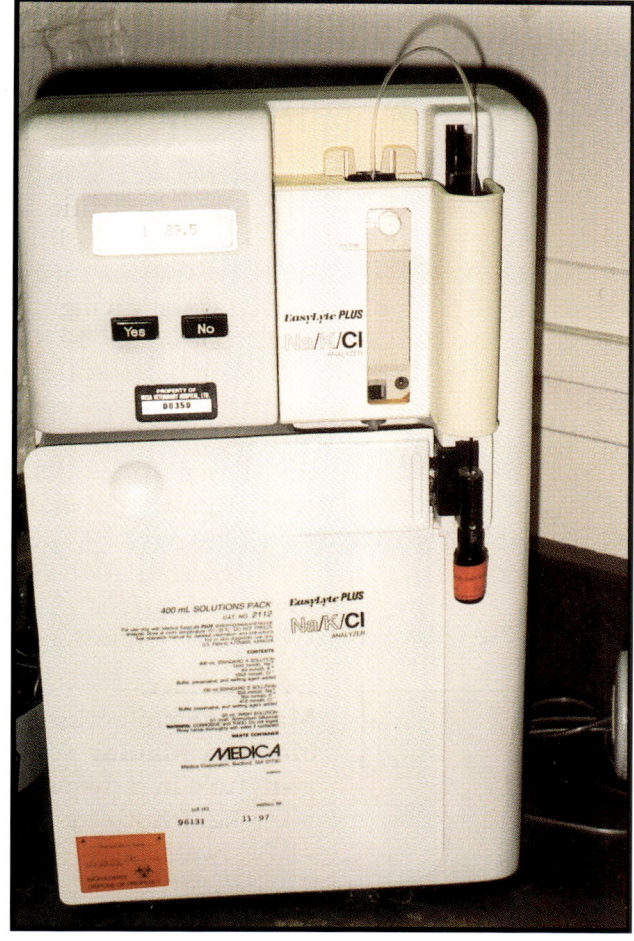

Measuring electrolyte levels is important in assessing ill reptiles. Photo courtesy of Dr. Lowell Ackerman.

Sinoloan milk snake. Photo courtesy of Dr. Todd Driggers.

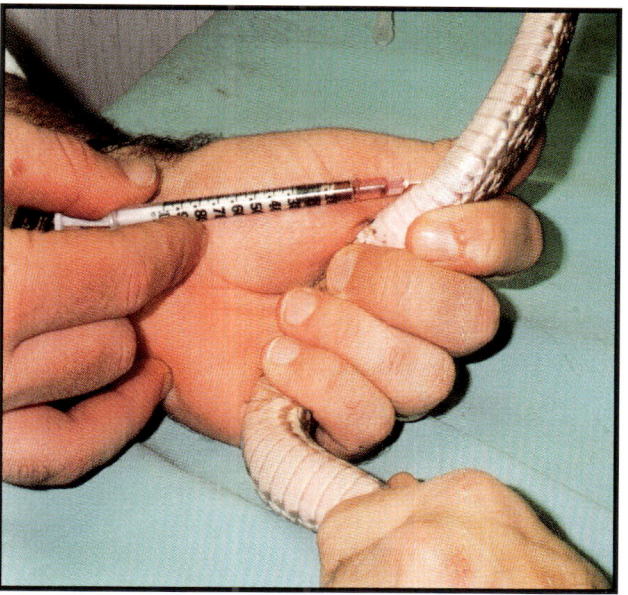

Dr. Todd Driggers collecting blood from a coachwhip snake. Photo by Dr. Lowell Ackerman

is however less regulated than in mammals and reptiles may tolerate considerable variations in plasma osmolarity, generally reflecting their environment. In aquatic species, this is a function of the osmolarity of the surrounding water, and in terrestrial species usually reflects hydration status. Sodium levels as high as 190 mmol/L have been recorded in dehydrated lizards without apparent ill effect. Potassium levels appear to be under tight control and do not vary greatly between species. Elevated potassium levels may be seen in hemolysed samples, and in samples where separation of plasma from cells is delayed.

Reptiles are capable of withstanding acid-base fluctuations over a wider range of pH than is possible for a mammal. Blood pH measurements taken immediately post-capture from estuarine crocodiles have been recorded as low as 6.6

A pair of pine snakes. Photo courtesy of Dr. Todd Driggers.

Chameleon. Photo courtesy of Dr. Todd Driggers.

(Seymour et al, 1985), a truly remarkable figure. In general , samples taken at rest from chelonians tend to have slightly alkaline pH, around 7.8, while from other reptiles will be around 7.4.

Freshwater turtles have a striking tolerance for anoxia, and during prolonged dives rely on anaerobic metabolism. During these dives, blood pH may approach 6.8, and the arterial oxygen tension will be near zero. Blood lactate levels rise correspondingly (Robin et al, 1964).

Feeding in crocodilians induces marked changes in pH, with a pronounced alkalosis, reflecting hypochloridemia as acid is secreted into the stomach, and an elevated bicarbonate level as a compensatory change. This exchange is progressive over about 18 hours, and then reverses itself over a similar period (Coulson et al, 1989).

It is important when conducting blood gas analyses on reptiles that the instrument be set to reflect the body (environmental) temperature of the animal sampled. Failure to do so will lead to markedly inaccurate results.

A machine that can analyze pH and blood gases can be crucial in a severely ill reptile. Photo courtesy of Dr. Lowell Ackerman.

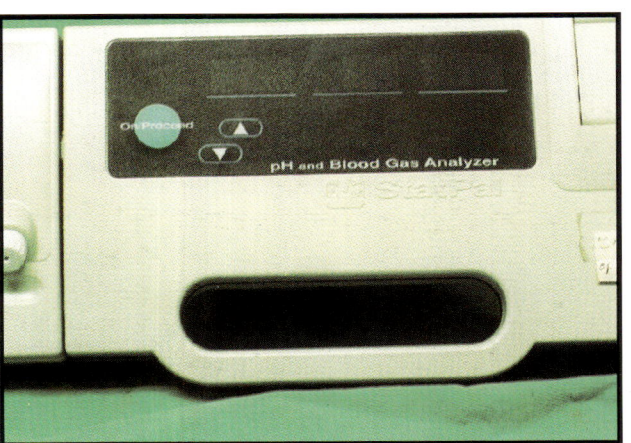

RENAL FUNCTION

Values have been reported for uric acid, urea and creatinine in a variety of reptile species. Of these, uric acid and urea most directly reflect the physiology of reptilian renal function. The balance between these forms of nitrogenous wastes shows considerable variation between species, from terrestrial species that are almost completely uricotelic (ie, secreting nitrogenous wastes as uric acid) as a form of water conservation, to aquatic species in which most nitrogenous wastes are secreted in soluble form (urea and ammonia) with as little as 10% secreted as uric acid.

Both renal and pre-renal factors may cause an elevation of circulating nitrogenous wastes (azotemia). Pre-renal azotemia is most commonly seen as a consequence of dehydration - nitrogenous wastes are not excreted due to decreased renal perfusion. This is a frequent problem in captive reptiles, and can be a particular problem in tropical species kept in insufficiently humid conditions (McCracken, 1993). Dehydration must always be suspected when both azotemia and hyperproteinemia are present (see Proteins, below). Excessive dietary protein intake will cause an elevation of blood uric acid levels. Vitamin A deficiency may also lead to azotemia due to impaired renal tubular function.

Renal azotemia is the failure to excrete nitrogenous wastes due to inadequate renal function. In addition to primary renal diseases, nephrotoxicity due to drug administration is an important cause of functional renal failure. Aminoglycoside antibiotics are the most frequently implicated drugs. It should also be noted that pre-renal azotemia due to dehydration will, if untreated, progress to renal azotemia as prolonged inadequate perfusion of the kidney will cause anoxic damage, as well as allowing intra-tubular crystal deposition.

When assessing azotemia, attention should be paid to both uric acid and urea levels, with consideration given to which compound is expected to dominate the renal physiology of the species in question. Urea levels may be significantly elevated in pregnant viviparous snakes, reflecting the predominance of urea in the nitrogenous wastes produced by the embryo (Dessauer, 1970).

Uric acids levels are of particular value in the diagnosis of gout - the abnormal deposition of uric acid crystals in joints and soft tissues. Early detection of hyperuricemia will allow the institution of effective therapy before the pathological changes are too far advanced. It has been reported (Maixner, 1987) that a sudden jump from merely abnormal (~0.5 mmol/L) to extreme (~6.0 mmol/L) hyperuricemia may be seen as a terminal change in gout - such a finding in general can be interpreted as indicating a poor prognosis.

Iguanas are commonly kept as pets and there is a wealth of biochemical information available for them. Many commercial laboratories that process reptile samples maintain tables of "normal values" for comparison purposes. Photo by R.D. Bartlett.

PROTEINS

In general two methods are reported for serum/plasma protein determinations: biochemical (biuret) and refractometer. Many refractometers have a protein scale in addition to specific gravity. It is important to note that this scale is based on the correlation between the serum/plasma specific gravity and its protein content, and is based on mammalian, usually human, data. As the composition of reptilian blood is known to vary from that of mammalian species, it is to be expected that this correlation may not be valid. In fact, in both reptiles and birds, refractometer protein determinations have been shown to correlate poorly with the more accurate biochemical methods (Haigh, 1991) and should not be used.

Elevated plasma protein levels are a good indicator of dehydration, particularly if polycythemia (increased red cell mass) is present also. Abnormally low protein levels may be seen in malnourished animals, and may also reflect pathological protein loss, most often via the gut or the kidney.

The levels of different protein fractions vary considerably between reptile groups - this is reflected in the differing appearance of their protein electrophoretic traces. Albumin is a major component of plasma in crocodilians and most lizards, accounting for at least 50% of the colloid osmotic pressure, while in turtles it may account for less than 20%. This distribution seems to relate to metabolic rate and environmental temperature,

In-clinic biochemical analyzers can run reptile profiles although they were not designed to do so. Photo courtesy of Dr. Lowell Ackerman.

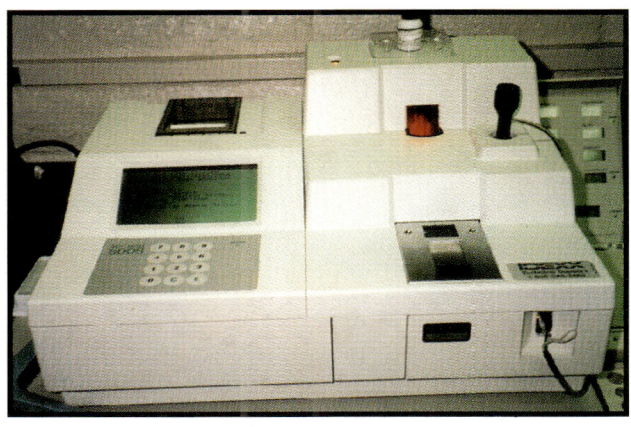

TABLE 2

REFERENCE DATA FOR REPRESENTATIVE SPECIES: GENERAL BIOCHEMISTRY

Test		Estuarine Crocodile[a]	Long necked tortoise[b]	Diamond-backed water snake[c]	Iguana[d] (Mean values)	Green Turtle[e]
Glucose	mmol/L	1.94-7.92	1.0-3.6	0.22-5.39	8.62	4.84-9.29
	mg/dL	35-142	18-65	4.0-97	155	
Urea	mmol/L	0.12-1.32	0.8-17.3	0-1.07	0.36	0.71-13.2
	mg/dL	0.34-3.70	2.24-48.5	0.3.0	1.0	2-37
Uric Acid	mmol/L	0.042-0.935	0.194-0.114		0.299	0.030-0.209
	mg/dL	0.70-15.6	0.32-1.91		5	0.5-3.5
Creatinine	μmol/L	0-96	13.3-29.3	17.7-159		26.5-79.6
	mg/dL	0-1.09	0.15-0.33	0.2-1.8		0.3-0.9
Cholesterol	mmol/L	0.09-5.37	0.1-3.5			1.9-9.49
	mg/dL	3.46-206	3.85-135			73-365
Calcium	mmol/L	2.33-3.42	2.3-3.1	5.0-8.0	2.7	0.4-3.05
	mg/dL	9.32-13.7	9.2-12.4	20-32	10.8	1.6-12.2
Phosphorus	mmol/L	0.59-2.79	0.4-0.9	0.7-2.5	2.0	1.23-3.33
	mg/dL	1.83-8.63	1.24-2.79	2.17-7.74	6.19	3.8-10.9
Magnesium	mmol/L	0.96-1.55	1.4-2.1	0.9-1.5	0.9	
	mg/dL	2.34-3.78	3.4-5.1	2.2-3.7	2.2	
Protein	g/L	52.0-75.9	42-60	43-76	44	26-69
Albumin	g/L	2.1-18.6	16-22			6-21
Sodium	mmol/L			154-175	157	157-183
Potassium	mmol/L			2.8-6.4	3.5	4.1-6.9
Chloride	mmol/L	97-129	82-117	117-131	118	100-130

[a] Watson, 1996; [b] Haigh, 1993; [c] McDaniel et al, 1984; [d] Dessauer, 1970; [e] Bolten and Bjorndal, 1992

with higher levels of albumin typically seen in those species with higher metabolic rates, and/or ambient temperatures. The remaining protein components of plasma include identifiable transferrins, coagulation proteins (including fibrinogen) and antibodies, but the levels and electrophoretic mobility of these components vary widely between species.

BIOCHEMICAL CHANGES IN ESTRUS

A number of striking changes in blood chemistry occur in reproductively active females. These have been best described in snakes and lizards where the changes correspond to the period of yolk formation and peak at ovulation. Both calcium and magnesium levels will be markedly elevated, although it appears the ionic component is relatively unchanged - the rise is due to an increase in the protein bound fraction. Inorganic phosphorus is also significantly increased. Plasma protein levels are also elevated, reflecting an increased level of vitellin in the plasma.

REFERENCE RANGES

As reference data have been published for too wide a range of species to contemplate listing them all, and as the reliability of these data are somewhat varied, I have selected values for a number of representative species for which good data exist. The use of these ranges is discussed more fully in the chapter (Hematology). Where appropriate, both molar and mass units are given.

Burmese pythons, one wild type and one albino. A fair collection of biochemical statistics is available for these animals. Photo courtesy of Dr. Todd Driggers.

REFERENCES AND FURTHER READING

—**Bolten, A B et al:**
Effects of anticoagulant and autoanalyser on blood biochemical values of loggerhead sea turtles (*Caretta caretta*). *Am J Vet Res,* 1992; 53: 2224-2227.

—**Coulson, R A, Hedbert, J D and Coulson, T D:**
Biochemistry and physiology of alligator metabolism *in vivo. Amer. Zool,* 1989; 29: 921-934.

—**Dessauer, H C:**
Blood chemistry of reptiles: physiological and evolutionary aspects. In, Biology of the Reptilia, Vol 3 Morphology, Gans, C. and Parsons, T (Eds). Academic Press, New York, 1970, pp. 1-72.

—**Haigh, S A:**
Characterisation of the blood cells and the establishment of haematological and biochemical reference intervals for the Eastern Long Neck Tortoise (*Chelodina longicollis*). Thesis, Diploma in Veterinary Studies (Wildlife Medicine and Husbandry, University of Sydney, 1991.

—**Kopplin, R P et al:**
Serum profile of the iguanid lizard (*Dipsosaurus dorsalis*). *J. Zoo. An. Med,* 1983; 14: 30-32.

—**Lumeij, J T and Westerhof, I:**
Blood chemistry for the diagnosis of hepatobiliary disease in birds. *The Veterinary Quarterly,* 1987; 9: 255-261.

—**Maixner, J M et al:**
Effects of feeding on serum uric acid in captive reptiles. *J. Zoo. An. Med,* 1987; 18(2-3): 62-65.

—**Mazzotti, F J and Dunson, W A:**
Osmoregulation in crocodilians. *Amer. Zool,* 1989; 29: 903-920.

—**McCracken, H:**
Avian and reptilian hematology and biochemistry. In, Proceedings 207: Clinical Pathology. Post Graduate Committee in Veterinary Science, University of Sydney. 1993, pp 243-305.

—**McDaniel, R C:**
Serum chemistry of the Diamond-Backed Water Snake (*Nerodia rhombifera rhombifera*) in Arkansas. J. Wildl. Dis, 1984; 20(1):44-46.

—**Robin, E D et al:**
Prolonged anaerobiosis in a vertebrate: anaerobic metabolism in the freshwater turtle. *J. Cell. Comp. Physiol,* 1964; 63: 287-297.

—**Seymour, R S et al:**
Blood gas tensions and acid-base regulation in the saltwater corocodile *Crocodylus porosus,* at rest and after exhaustive excercise. *J. Exp. Biol,* 1985; 118: 143-159.

—**Smeller, J M et al:**
Effect of feeding on plasma uric acid levels in snakes. *Am. J. Vet. Res,* 1978; 39(9): 1556-7.

—**Watson, J W:**
Hematology and biochemistry of the estuarine crocodile (*Crocodylus porosus*). Manuscript in preparation. 1996.

ENVIRONMENTAL HEALTH AND SAFETY CONCERNS

Mark F. Miller
Herpetology Network
P.O. Box 52261
Philadelphia PA 19115-7261 USA

Mark F. Miller created the Herpetology On-line Network in 1982 [operating on 215-698-1905]. He is one of the founding staff of the PetsForum on CompuServe, currently serves as President of the Philadelphia Herpetological Society and functions as a consultant to zoos, herpetoculturists, conservation organizations, the pet industry, and governments. He may be reached via email at MMiller@tjuvm.tju.edu or 70176.1153@compuserve.com on the internet.

INTRODUCTION

Reptiles, like all organisms, have evolved in particular habitats and specific environmental niches, and usually require similar conditions to thrive in captive enclosures. Some reptiles are considered relatively easy or difficult to maintain based (in part) on how closely their natural habitat needs to be recreated in captivity. When the basic conditions they require are not provided or safely recreated, they will succumb to a variety of problems, diseases, injuries, and maladaptive syndromes — many leading directly to their demise if not identified and corrected quickly. This chapter will address aspects of health and safety related to the captive environment of reptiles.

CONSTRUCTION/ MATERIAL HAZARDS

Reptile enclosures need to be securely constructed and absolutely escape-proof. They should be free of mechanical hazards that could injure, lacerate, entrap, abraid, or impale the prospective inhabitants.

Commercial fiberglass, plastic, or wood enclosures are commonly available and usually acceptable for a wide range of reptiles. Custom enclosures are often superior because they can be tailored to the nature of taxon being contained. Aborial lizards such as the Old World chameleons (family Chamaeleonidae) prefer tall, well ventilated enclosures, for example. Colubrid snakes do well in enclosures designed with sufficient surface area but do not require as much height. Many commercial herpeticulturists use plastic shoe or sweater boxes in heated racks to take advantage of the snakes reduced space requirements.

Wild Desert Tortoise Habitat. Photo courtesy of Dr. Bernard A. Mangone.

Wild desert tortoise, as found, at the base of creosote bush, near Tucson. Photo courtesy of Dr. Bernard A. Mangone.

Wild Tortoise burrow. Photo courtesy of Dr. Bernard A. Mangone.

Banded Gila Monster in the wild near Safford Arizona. Photo courtesy of Dr. Bernard A. Mangone.

Desert Tortoise Habitat, near Tucson Arizona. Photo courtesy of Dr. Bernard A. Mangone.

Collared lizard in its normal habitat. Photo courtesy of Dr. Todd Driggers.

All designs employed must have a secure closure and preferably a safety lock or pin. Hinged doors or lids can use spring-loaded catches to automatically latch upon closure. Weights on top of enclosures are to be avoided as they do not prevent escapes. Enclosures for venomous, potentially dangerous, or environmentally injurious species should be key locked and contained within an isolated and locked room. Acrylic plastic is preferred over glass for dangerous snakes. Large monitor lizards can be contained with 1/4 inch thick tempered glass in secure frames (they will scratch acrylic plastic.) Personal and public safety should not be overlooked or dismissed.

Cage or enclosure designs that employ branches, shelves, or other climbing materials must have these accessories securely mounted to prevent injury to the reptile as it transfers its weight to it. Appropriate design must be created with the specie in mind. Heavy boids require flooring capable of holding up to 100 pounds or more.

Ventilation may be provided via smooth plastic or metal grills or covered with smooth fiberglass or nylon screening. A backup of sturdy material can be placed behind smooth air vents in case the animal tears the protective screen. Selection of material should be determined based on the type of reptile to be contained. Rostral abrasions can often be avoided by placing vents away from top or bottom edges of enclosures. In some cases offset baffles can be employed to prevent direct access to vent holes (or to protect keepers from the fangs of venomous snakes.)

Substrate selections should be carefully evaluated. Some species prefer a fine or soft bedding material (most snakes, softshell turtles, fossorial species, etc.) while a rough gravel can cause abrasions or ingestion hazards.

CHEMICAL HAZARDS

There are also potential dangers from chemical hazards that may be related to the enclosure materials or contents.

Enclosures constructed with silicone should use only those products labeled for use in aquariums. Some industrial silicone sealers designed for home/plumbing use have mildew inhibitors that could be toxic to sensitive reptiles.

Most of the urethane and epoxy coatings (for wood enclosures) are generally considered to be safe when completely dry and cured. For extra protection, there are a couple polyurethane products designed for children's furniture that are safest (but expensive.)

If the interior of an enclosure requires paint, murals, or color —the least incompatible paint is acrylic artist color. Obtainable from any art sup-

Cricket housing system. Photo courtesy of Dr. Todd Driggers.

ply store (usually in tubes) in a wide variety of mixable colors. When dry these colors are highly water-resistant and relatively safe for any vertical surface.

Particle board and other constructed wood panels may have irritating gasses that originate from the binder or glue within them. In most applications, simply sealing the material with urethane or epoxy coatings (on all edges and faces) makes them usable for all but the most sensitive or valuable specimens.

The floor of enclosure should be waterproof — plastic, fiberglass, laminated wood, glass, slate, tile, sealed concrete and related materials are acceptable.

Substrates of oily/aromatic woods such as cedar should be avoided as the components of the wood are very irritating and have been associated with various failures.

Wood for semi-aquatic enclosures should be true driftwood —where all the water soluble compounds have already been extracted by weeks or months of time underwater. Toney (1992) suggests that wood can be boiled in a strong salt solution for several hours, followed by soaking in fresh water for one to two weeks, to make it safe for aquarium use. While some reptiles are not affected by the "tea" colored, acidic extract that uncured wood produces —there are many variables in wood and species kept so it is best to use caution in this area.

Cleaning and disinfection is best accomplished with the reptiles removed to a temporary holding container, and their primary enclosure cleaned with a hypochlorite or quaternary ammonium compound. The latter is less toxic but not quite as effective (Davison, 1990.)

All disinfectants, including ammonia solutions, alcohols, ampholytes, and pine fluids, are to be considered potentially toxic to sensitive reptiles. All traces of the cleaning solution should be rinsed completely and the enclosure dried and ventilated before the reptile is returned.

Insecticides, especially those containing organophosphates, are toxic to reptiles. Even the "no-pest" strips that some hobbyists use to control mites, can be dangerous to use near reptiles. There are a few non-toxic mite treatments, most notably Ectoparasite Eradicator® (a zoo product) or Rep-Rinse® (consumer product). Veterinarians can usually provide low-toxicity alternatives as well.

BIOLOGICAL HAZARDS

Captive reptiles also need protection from biological hazards that may be introduced into their environment. New acquisitions must be quarantined to prevent pathogens or parasites from infecting the existing collection. Depending on the species, its origin, and the veterinarian's recommendation/testing —the quarantine period can range from 60 days (Samour, 1989) to 90 days or more.

Paramyxovirus infections in captive reptiles are often transmitted from other reptiles in the collection. Extended quarantine periods are the best protection from this widespread airborne pathogen that causes a very high mortality. Paramyxovirus-like particles have been documented in Testudinidae, Teiidae, Boidae, Colubridae, Elapidae, Viperidae, and Crotalidae (Ahne, 1994.)

Cryptosporidium (a fecal or water transmitted micropathogen) occasionally appears as a contaminant in municipal water systems because it is not killed by the usual chlorination water treatments. This organism has been implicated in reptile disease and it might be desirable to use a water filter (at least 1 micron absolute filter) to remove the oocysts of cryptosporidium from reptile supply water.

Fully aquatic snakes such as file snakes (*Acrochordus* species) have presented considerable difficulty for those keeping them, with skin lesions being common (Banks 1989) and often culturing bacterial pathogens of intestinal flora. Water sterilizing equipment is one approach (along with antibacterial treatment) employed to reduce skin infections that probably originate from the specimen itself. This is one of the reasons that aquatic snakes are considered difficult to maintain in captivity (Reitinger & Lee 1978).

Protozoans such as *Entamoeba invadens* have been know to infect snakes with amoebiasis transmitted via aquatic turtles that were added to a reptile collection (Jes 1989.) Strict isolation should be employed to prevent cross contamination.

Some zoos use ultraviolet light and HEPA viral filters to clean air entering reptile chambers (Baker 1985)

Plants used in vivaria with omnivorous or herbivorous reptiles should ideally be limited to plants native to the habitat of the species being contained. If this is not possible, then limiting the plants to those known to be edible is essential. Some reptiles such as the box turtle (*Terrapene c. carolina*) eat poisonous mushrooms, whereas ordinary apple or apricot seeds could poison a small bearded dragon (*Pogona* species.) Lists of "poisonous" plants are of limited use since they are usually based on human toxicology.

ELECTRICAL/THERMAL HAZARDS

All animal enclosures that utilize electrical power should be equipped with a ground fault interrupter (GFI) to protect the keeper and the kept from electrocution in the event of a loss of the return ground path. This inexpensive device (about US$10) is installed in a grounded electrical box and all enclosure or vivaria accessories are connected to it via the usual electrical plugs.

Wires entering the interior of an enclosure should be protected from chewing, water, abrasion, heat, and chemical degradation from urea/feces. They can be protected within a flexible stainless steel or synthetic cord protector (from hardware/farm supply stores) or rerouted to the outside of the enclosure. Fans require mechanical isolation via screening or remote mounting via ductwork.

Water leakage should be expected and no electrical contacts should exist in direct contact with the interior floor of the enclosure.

Incandescent lamps account for a great deal of burns to captive reptiles and even a few reptile-related house fires. They must be mounted securely outside the enclosure, behind a protective screen with sufficient ventilation and protection to all combustible materials. Test the temperature at the nearest point that the reptile can approach the light. It should never exceed 110°F. Reduce the wattage or increase the distance from the reptile to lower the temperature.

Heating reptile cages is best accomplished by placing a small heater at one side of an enclosure to provide a temperature gradient. Fiberglass "pig blankets" like those made by Kane and Osborne are effective and safe. Never try to maintain a tropical species in a very cold room by using enclosure heaters alone. Enclosure heaters are intended to provide approximately 25 degree F boost to one section of a cage. They are not intended to heat all the air in the room.

If a design employs a digital device to control lighting/heating, check to see how it reacts to a power failure/power restoration cycle. Without a battery backup, some digital controllers (BSR modules for example) resume at full power —with the potential for disaster after an unattended power failure. A manually adjustable, proportional controller (such as Microclimate DL Series) is preferable.

Aquatic reptiles such as turtles and crocodilians can easily damage a glass aquarium heater. These devices, if used, must be mounted remotely or shielded from contact with the reptile. The submersible units can be installed into a remote filter unit or via an inline tank to prevent breakage. Large amounts of water are best heated with several lower-wattage units rather than one large unit. This provides some margin of safely in case one heater becomes defective.

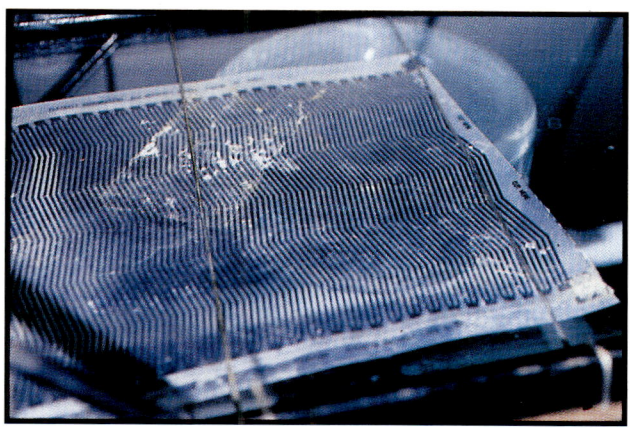

Heat tape. Photo courtesy of Dr. Todd Driggers.

Heating systems are subject to failures causing overheating. Temperature alarms are useful if the enclosure is monitored. Using redundant thermostats offers a greater degree of protection in any event. See Ross & Marzec (1990) for a description of a two-thermostat heating system for incubators.

It should be noted that the electromagnetic fields produced by resistive electric heaters, lights, pumps, and other appliances have not been studied to determine the effect on constant, close proximity to reptiles. There exists the possibility that reproductive fitness might be compromised by such fields. Work in this area should be encouraged.

RADIATION HAZARDS

Excess UV radiation from the keeper's desire to emulate sunlight can provide a hazard to reptilian (and human) eyes and skin (Sliney 1983.) Use only light sources designed for home use, vivaria use, or labeled for use in reptile enclosures. Avoid any sunlamp, medical, or industrial light sources, especially those that have unknown emissions or produce light less than 290 nm. Especially dangerous are the older UV systems that frequently appear at flea markets and lamps designed for use with timers/eye protection. Some protection from the harmful, short wavelengths may be provided by using cellulose triacetate film as a filter (Worrest & Kimeldorf, 1976).

In many cases, lizards can be provided with their UV requirements from natural sunlight through the newer, UV transmitting plastics (like Bioglass TM) or their requirement for UV reduced by adding Calcium/vitamin D3 to their diet. Artificial lights do not simulate the intensity of the natural light/UVB from the sun, although they may provide a useful portion of the frequency emission.

HUMIDTY CONSIDERATIONS

Most reptiles seem to do well at 50-70% relative humidity but arid, desert dwelling species may languish in high humidity as some tropicals will quickly dissicate in low humidity enclosures. Individual accommodations should be prepared for the species contained. A knowledge of a specie's microhabitat is useful. Gila monsters (*Heloderma suspectum*) for example, are residents of burrows and underground retreats where a higher humidity is encountered and associating them with the arid climate above would be inaccurate.

Humidity can be controlled with a ducted commercial humidifier in large enclosures (or rooms) or individual enclosures can be controlled with drip systems, rain chambers, or simply by changing the surface area of the water container(s). Water bowls in small or medium sized enclosures can be moved over the heater to increase humidity.

In very humid areas (South Florida for example) enclosures for low-humidity specimens would need to be de-humidified using a compressor powered commercial unit. Depending on the temperature, air conditioning might also be employed.

Snakes usually shed their skin in one piece when they are well hydrated and the ambient humidity is sufficient. Snakes that require a higher humidity can be provided with a plastic chamber (with one or two small openings) containing moist sphagnam moss. Large boids and tortoises can be equipped with humidity chamber via a walk-through door constructed of vertical segments of overlapping flexible transparent plastic, within or connected to their primary enclosure. An automated misting system can be installed within the humidity chamber.

STRESS CONSIDERATIONS

The behavior, social, psychological considerations must be accommodated for captive reptiles to remain healthy and safe. Hiding places should be incorporated for those species that require them. Limiting specimens to individual or small breeding groups is safer than large numbers of animals caged together. Wild-caught crocodiles, for example, need considerable space (dry and water surface) for males to establish their dominance and territory or they will rarely fertilize eggs (Marais & Morgan, 1990.)

With few exceptions, reptiles have a low tolerance for continued, non-essential handling. Excessive handling, moving, or disturbance can easily cause stress. For a good review of maladaption fundamentals the reader is referred to Cowan (1980)

Inside view of a terrarium. Photo courtesy of Dr. Todd Driggers.

Small terrarium housing a ground iguana. Photo courtesy of Dr. Todd Driggers.

REFERENCES AND RECOMMENDED READING

—**Ahne, W. 1994.**
Paramyxovirus infections of reptiles. (presentation) Second World Congress of Herpetology, 29 Dec 93 - 06 Jan 94, Adelaide, South Australia.

—**Banks, CB. 1989.**
Management of fully aquatic snakes. *Int. Zoo Yb.* 28: 155-163

—**Baker, AG. 1985.**
High Tech Herpetology: An update on the Fresno Zoo's computerized environmental chambers. 9th International Herpetological Symposium on Captive Propagation & Husbandry. p.74

—**Cowan, DF. 1980.**
Adaptation, maladaption and disease. SSAR Contributions to Herpetology Number 1. Reproductive Biology and Diseases of Captive Reptiles. Co-editors: James Murphy and Joseph Collins.

—**Davidson, G. 1990.**
Choosing the right disinfectant. Snake Breeder. Aug 1990. Snake Keeper Publishing. England.

—**Jes, H. 1989.**
Treatment of amoebiasis in turtles. In International Zoo Yearbook, Vol. 28: 60-61. Zoo. Soc. London

—**Marais, J., Morgan, DR. 1990.**
Reptile Husbandry. Proceedings of the First Herpetological Association of Africa Reptile Husbandry Symposium. J. Herp. Asso. Africa. 38: November 1990

—**Reitinger, F. & Lee, J.K.S. 1978.**
Common Snakes of South East Asia and Hong Kong. Hong Kong. Heinemann.

—**Ross, RA., Marzec, G. 1990.**
The Reproductive Husbandry of Pythons and Boas. p. 99. Institute for Herpetological Research, Standord CA.

—**Samour, JH., Parsons, RC., Pugsley, SL., Ryan, AL. 1989.**
Observations of parasitic infections in captive reptiles. Clinical and husbandry considerations related to helminthiasis in captive serpentes and sauria. *Herpetopathlogia*, 1 (2):37-39. 1989.

—**Sliney, DH. 1983.**
Biohazards of ultraviolet, visible and infrared radiation. *J. Occupational Med.* 25(3):203-206.

—**Toney, J. 1992.**
Wood in the aquarium. *The aquarium.* Vol. 34, No. 12, p. 21. Calgary Aquarium Society, Alberta Canada.

—**Worrest, RC; Kimeldorf. 1976.**
Distortions in amphibian development induced by ultraviolet-B enhancement of a simulated solar spectrum. *Photochemistry and Photobiology.* 24:377-382

ANESTHESIA

Khursheed Mama, D.V.M., Diplomate ACVA
Department of Clinical Sciences
College of Veterinary Medicine
Colorado State University
Fort Collins, CO 80523

Dr. Khursheed Mama received both her Bachelor of Science and her Doctor of Veterinary Medicine degrees from Washington State University. She then did an internship at the Ontario Veterinary College in Guelph, Canada and her residency in veterinary anesthesiology at the University of California, Davis. A board-certified veterinary anesthesiologist, Dr. Mama was a lecturer in veterinary anesthesiology at the University of California, Davis College of Veterinary Medicine and recently accepted a position as an Assistant Professor in Anesthesiology at Colorado State University, College of Veterinary Medicine, in Fort Collins Colorado.

Anesthetized desert tortoise about to be prepared for surgery of the inguinal area. Photo courtesy of Dr. Bernard A. Mangone.

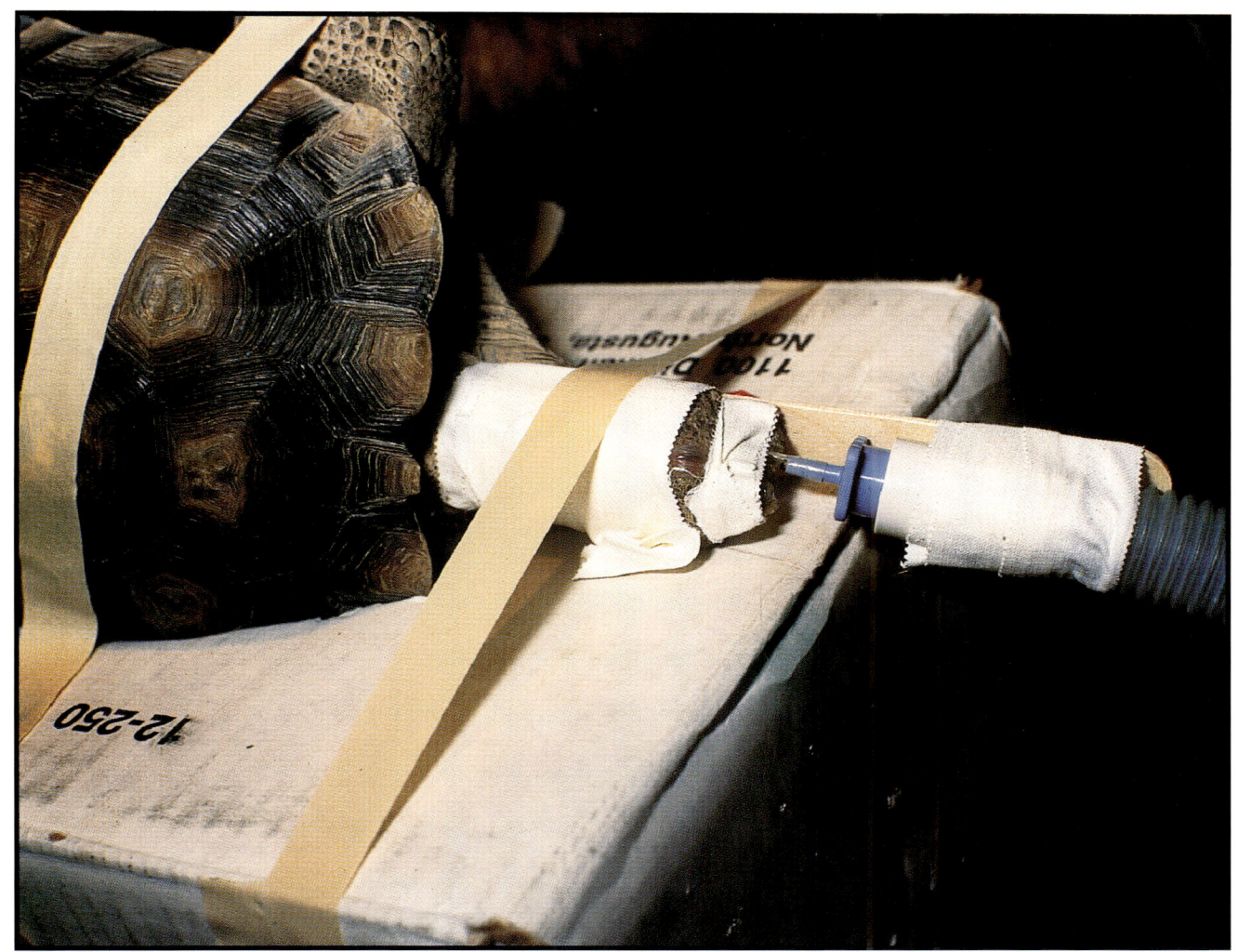

Anesthetized desert tortoise showing method for keeping E.T. tube in place. Photo courtesy of Dr. Bernard A. Mangone.

INTRODUCTION

General anesthesia is commonly used in reptiles to facilitate physical examination, conduct certain diagnostic procedures and to provide satisfactory conditions for surgery. The diversity of management considerations associated with this class of vertebrates makes their anesthetic management a challenging task. This chapter reviews anatomic, physiological and other considerations important to principles of careful anesthetic management of reptiles. Particular focus is on actions of commonly used anesthetic agents and techniques of physiological support and anesthetic monitoring techniques.

PREANESTHETIC EVALUATION

The preanesthetic period includes an assessment of the physical status of the animal to be anesthetized (preanesthetic evaluation) and the formulation of an anesthetic plan. The objective is to facilitate the most effective and safest possible anesthetic.

The preanesthetic evaluation includes the gathering of a careful history of the individual including information of any recent and/or concurrent illnesses and where possible a physical examination. Appropriate diagnostic tests are also conducted as indicated to augment the history and physical examination. This evaluation characterizes the state of the animals well-being and is used as a basis for any necessary improvements in the animals preanesthetic condition.

In order to properly examine a patient, physical restraint usually is necessary. Handling technique is important for patient and handler safety and guidelines vary according to individual needs (Cooper, 1987; Cunnigham et al, 1992; McDonald, 1976). Briefly, chelonians (turtles, tortoises, terrapins) are generally held by grasping the rear portion of the carapace, venomous and nonvenomous snakes maybe handled with tongs or plastic tubes (a snake stick is generally recommended if the individual is of a venomous variety). Lizards are gently supported from below the body and handled from above the shoulders. Crocodilians are restrained using the shoulders and

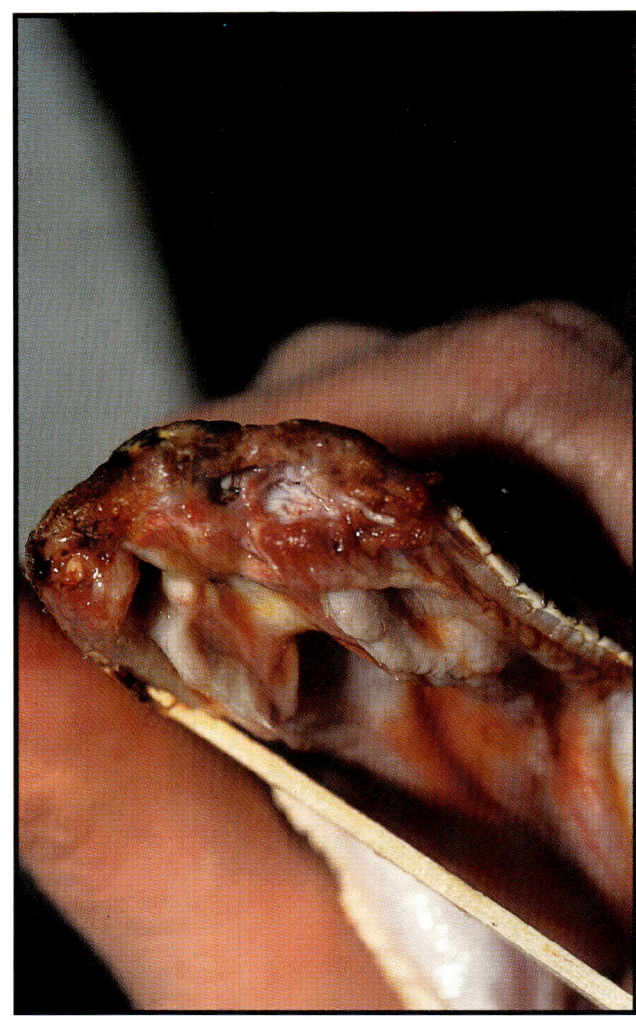

Rhinoplasty in a boa constrictor. Procedure performed by J.L. Jarchow DVM. This snake was a nose rubber and traumatized its nares. There was also exposure gingivitis secondary to mouth breathing along with osteomyelitis of the maxilla. Here is the boa prior to surgery, showing severe gingival inflammation and exposure of maxilla. Photo courtesy of Dr. Bernard A. Mangone.

tail, while the jaw is held closed. When physical restraint is not feasible as with larger crocodilians, venomous and/or large snakes and biting terrapins or turtles, chemical restraint may become necessary prior to physical examination.

Physical examination is conducted to assess the animal s state of well-being and forms a basis for improving the animals condition before or during general anesthesia. Assessment emphasis is on the cardiovascular and respiratory systems, but information regarding the hepatic, renal and central nervous systems is also desirable. Body weight should be recorded and hydration status evaluated during examination of the patient. Dehydration often accompanies emaciation. Comparing current body weight to a previously recorded value may be helpful to

assess state of hydration in addition to evaluation of skin elasticity (loose skin suggests loss of body condition) and position of the eye (Boyer, 1993). Reptiles are ectothermic and have little ability to internally regulate body temperature. This stresses the importance of appropriate ambient conditions and animal behaviors (heat or shade seeking) to maintain body temperature within optimal ranges. Basal metabolic rate is directly influenced by changes in body temperature in reptiles as in mammals. The Q10 describes the change in metabolic rate for a given species over a 10° C change in body temperature (Rupp et al, 1986). Values for Q10 (between 2 and 3) are similar for reptiles and mammals (Bartholomew, 1982; Rupp et al, 1986). However, the activity temperature range (body temperature at which a free ranging animal engages in its normal routine) of reptiles is greater (cycles may be diurnal or seasonal) than for mammals (Pough et al, 1982; Wallach, 1971). Hence heart rate should be considered relative to the animals body temperature and should be used as a guideline for support of normal metabolic function under anesthesia in an individual animal.

Guidelines for cardiac auscultation are described, but may have limited value due to the lack of clearly audible heart sounds in some reptilian species (Frye et al, 1988). Difficulties with heart auscultation are most likely a reflection of the three chambered reptilian heart (except crocodilians where four chambers are more clearly defined), the variation in orientation and location of the heart within the coelomic cavity and the tissues through which sound must be transmitted in the different species (Frye et al, 1988; Porter, 1972). Use of the ultrasonic Doppler flow probe for evaluation of heart sounds is described in the section on monitoring. The heart is located at the level of the axillae near the ventral midline in quadruped lizards and crocodilians, at the junction of the cranial third and caudal two-thirds of the body in snakes where it is easily palpated and between the limbs within the shell above the plastron in chelonians.

Respiratory system evaluation is similarly confounded by the diverse anatomy and unique physiology of reptiles compared to mammals (Porter, 1972; Wood et al, 1976). The ability to obtain meaningful preanesthetic respiratory rates is complicated by arrhythmic breathing patterns and the ability of some reptilian species to breath hold for considerable periods of time. For example, green iguanas *(Iguana iguana)* can breath hold for up to 4.5 hours (Moberly, 1968). Many aquatic turtles breath

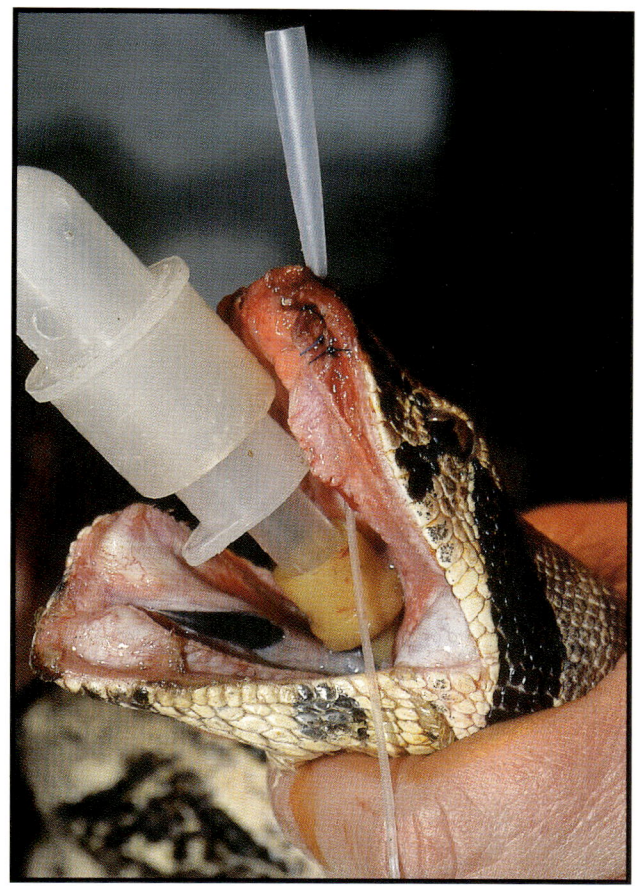

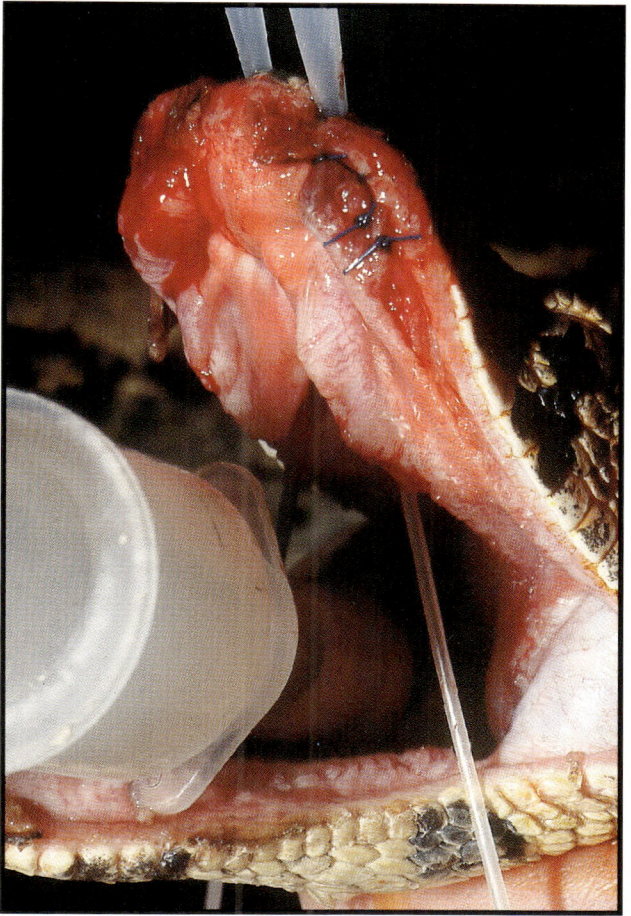

Snake with one tomcat catheter placed in the nares. Photo courtesy of Dr. Bernard A. Mangone.

The tomcat catheters are placed in both nares. Photo courtesy of Dr. Bernard A. Mangone.

hold for extended periods of time utilizing a range of adaptive mechanisms and additionally converting to anaerobic metabolism during this period (Jackson et al, 1974; Wood et al, 1976). The ventilatory response to changes in arterial carbon dioxide tension ($PaCO_2$) is variable but in general, reptiles are less sensitive to increases in $PaCO_2$ compared to mammals (Wood et al, 1976).

In addition to physiologic differences from mammalian species, anatomy of the upper and lower respiratory tracts reflect stages of evolution from amphibians to higher vertebrates. The larynx is supported by paired arytenoid cartilages and an incomplete cricoid ring and is located at the base of the tongue. In this location it is most rostral and easily accessible in snakes. It is partially obscured by soft tissue structures (e.g. the tongue) and more caudally located in chelonians. A fold of tissue cranial to the glottis, homologous with the mammalian epiglottis may be present in some lizards and crocodilians. In crocodilians this structure is termed the basihyal valve. The glottis in reptiles remains closed at rest (Bennett, 1991; Boyer, 1993; Heard, 1993). Tracheal length varies and

is species dependent. In snakes with a single lung only the right bronchus is developed. Tracheal rings are incomplete in snakes and lizards and complete in turtles, tortoises and crocodilians. Respiratory tissue is found on the dorsal tracheal surface of some snakes and is thought to facilitate ventilation during ingestion of prey (Davies, 1981). The pleural and peritoneal cavities are continuous in reptiles due to the absence of a true diaphragm. However, a membranous separation partially divides the two cavities in chelonians and crocodilians (Porter, 1972). The liver of crocodilians is attached to this connective tissue and additionally connected by diaphragmaticus muscles to the pelvic girdle. Despite the lack of separation of body cavities, muscular contractions expand and contract the pleuroperitoneal cavity creating changes in pressure which aids or results in respiratory gas movement. Lung structure ranges from a primitive single sac-like structure in the lizard like tuatara to the more partitioned lung of crocodilians. The left lung becomes more vestigial with elongation of body length as evidenced in the majority of snakes. Air sacs are present in some snakes and lizards and may function to

Post-surgical view with both nares opened and tomcat catheters sutured into place. The ends of the tomcat catheters in the choana are cut short enough that they do not contact the glottis. Photo courtesy of Dr. Bernard A. Mangone.

increase respiratory capacity. Non-respiratory functions of these structures may include maintenance of buoyancy in aquatic species or behavioral displays.

Hepatic and renal function are difficult to assess on physical examination. Adequate function is necessary as these organs are at least in part responsible for metabolism and excretion of many anesthetic drugs. An additional influence on the disposition of drugs is the presence of the renal portal circulation in all reptile species (Bennett, 1991; Williams, 1992). Blood from the caudal third (including the limbs) of the animal drains to the renal arterial supply. This increases the likelihood of more rapid excretion of drugs injected in the musculature of the hind limbs. Nephrotoxicity is another potential complication of caudal injections.

Palpation of the coelomic cavity is difficult due to the presence of ribs in some animals and shells in others. Other diagnostic procedures such as serum chemistry and radiography may be used to aid in diagnosis of abnormalities (Jackson et al

1992; Page, et al, 1990). Unlike mammals, reptiles are unable to concentrate urine to conserve water. Uric acid which is highly insoluble is therefore the most commonly excreted nitrogenous waste of terrestrial reptiles (Minnich, 1982; Porter, 1972). Marine and aquatic reptiles excrete a higher proportion of the more water soluble nitrogenous wastes, ammonia and urea (Minnich, 1982; Porter, 1972). Cephalic-salt secreting glands play a significant role in sodium regulation and maintenance of serum osmolality (Davies, 1981; Minnich, 1982; Porter, 1972).

Ideally, laboratory data should be obtained prior to anesthesia and surgery. However, patient size, inaccessibility of peripheral veins and difficulty restraining some animals without drugs limits the ability to routinely obtain this information. Additionally, normal variability with changes in ambient conditions, time of sample collection, patient activity, post-prandial duration and size further complicates interpretation of these values (Al-Badry et al, 1983; Hutton, 1961). Normal ranges (in primarily captive reptiles) for hematologic and serum chemistry values are summarized elsewhere (Beynon, 1992; Frye, 1994). Generally hematocrit and plasma protein values are lower in reptiles than in mammals with reported values ranging from 19-26 % and 4.5 - 5.5 g/dl respectively (Al-Badry et al, 1983; Frye, 1994). As in birds and unlike mammals the red blood cells are nucleated. Serum electrolyte concentrations are significantly impacted by environment. For example, terrestrial and desert reptiles often have higher normal values for serum sodium than aquatic counterparts. Blood glucose values are slightly lower than those in mammals.

ANESTHETIC TECHNIQUES

General anesthesia should provide amnesia, analgesia, muscle relaxation and patient immobility. The availability of newer drugs and improved monitoring techniques have led to complex anesthetic protocols for human patients in which a number of individual agents are administered to target one or more of the above components rather than administration of a single drug. The outcome is patient comfort with less physiological insult, ie, a safer anesthetic. Unfortunately, due to the marked differences in reptilian physiology, this technique cannot be extrapolated directly to reptiles and traditional, single drug techniques are still routinely used despite potential adverse effects. This situation is compounded by the inability to consistently restrain many reptiles and/or gain venous access prior to anesthesia because it may impose added life-threatening risk of injury to the handler and/or stress to the animal. Typically an anesthetic protocol may be divided into four phases; premedication, anesthetic induction, maintenance of general anesthesia and recovery from anesthesia. This section will briefly review some of these anesthetic techniques, including their advantages and potential adverse effects in different reptilian species. The reader is referred to recent publications (Bennett, 1991; Lawton, 1992) for more extensive review of specific drugs and drug dosage.

INJECTABLE ANESTHETICS

Many injectable agents have been used in reptiles for sedation, restraint and general anesthesia (Bennett, 1991; Frye, 1981; Lawton, 1992). A number of routes of administration have been used to administer these drugs. Intraperitoneal (ip)

Intubated and anesthetized desert tortoise. Photo courtesy of Dr. Bernard A. Mangone.

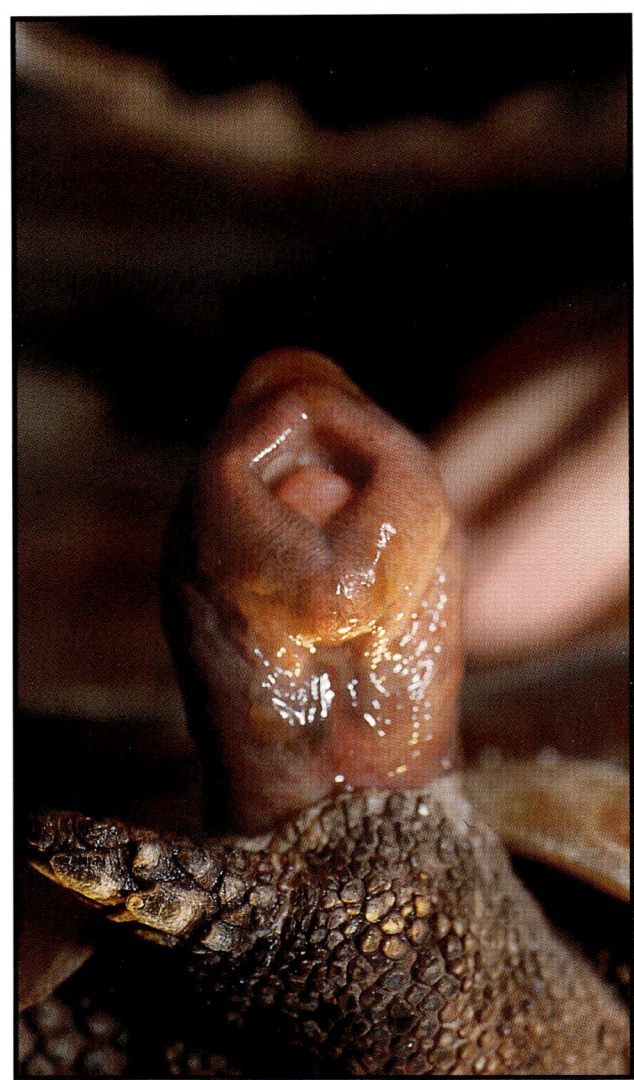

Exposed penis of an anesthetized adult male desert tortoise. Photo courtesy of Dr. Bernard A. Mangone.

injections are easily administered in animals that may be restrained, but may cause local tissue irritation (eg, thiobarbiturates) and unpredictable systemic effects. With intramuscular (im) and subcutaneous (sc) injections, drug uptake (affecting anesthetic onset and peak effect) is variable and duration may be unpredictable. The inability to accurately assess body weight in turn results in inaccurate and inconsistent drug dose which may further add to the variability of anesthetic conditions. Additionally, drugs with an acidic pH (eg. ketamine) often sting when given im or sc and may cause adverse behavioral reactions in some animals. While the intravenous (iv) route provides the most consistent onset of drug action and generally shorter duration of action (as less agent is necessary to obtain the desired effect) difficulty in obtaining and maintaining venous access in some reptile species often limits its use. Perivascular tissue necrosis has been reported with extravascular administration of some drugs such as the thiobarbiturates (Dripps et al, 1988). Injections made in the caudal third of the animal regardless of route may show more variation in effect due to the renal-portal circulation of reptiles. Temperature related changes in metabolic rate affect drug uptake, distribution, metabolism and excretion. These features account for the wide dose ranges and variation in effect of the many drugs reported in the literature. Additionally anesthetic characteristics of the individual drugs differ among reptiles and between reptiles and the clinically more familiar mammalian species making it difficult to uniformly assess anesthetic depth.

The dissociative anesthetics ketamine and tiletamine produce a state in mammals characterized as catalepsy. Following injection the animal loses its ability to right itself and shows no response to noxious stimuli (Beck, 1976; Custer et al, 1980; Glenn et al, 1972). However, reflex activity (laryngeal, pharyngeal, palpebral etc) is usually maintained and the eyes often remain open. Involuntary muscle movement is dose dependent; muscle relaxation may be enhanced with concurrent use of phenothiazines or benzodiazepines [Telazol is a mixture of the dissociative (tiletamine) and benzodiazepine (zolazepam) drugs]. In humans peculiar sensory experiences often occur during anesthetic induction and recovery. These drugs are useful as sedatives and anesthetic induction agents prior to intubation in many reptile species. In mammals blood pressure and heart rate are usually depressed only slightly or increased and respiration is little affected by effective anesthetic dose. Similar dose dependent cardiovascular and respiratory effects following ketamine are reported for reptiles (Arena et al, 1988; Custer et al, 1980; Glenn et al, 1972; Schumacher et al, 1992). Increases in heart rate are reported at lower drug doses and may be associated with a transient increase in motor activity seen following drug administration. Respiratory rate is decreased following drug injection but some animals become apneic with higher doses. Decreases in heart rate often accompany the apneic periods and intervention (ventilation with an oxygen rich inspired gas) is recommended at this stage. Doses range from 20 mg/kg to over 100 mg/kg given im or ip depending on the species and desired effect (Bennett, 1991; Boyer, 1993; Harding, 1977; Lawton, 1992; Wood et al, 1982). The onset of ketamine effect following intramuscular or intraperitoneal administration averages about 30 minutes. The duration of anesthesia is far more variable, but generally follows dose. Complete recovery may range from hours to days depending upon conditions. The volume of ketamine necessary to restrain larger reptiles (eg. crocodilians) limits its usefulness.

Telazol, a drug of increased potency has effects similar to those of ketamine and has been used in these animals at doses ranging from 4 to 8 mg/kg to provide immobilization prior to intubation (Heard, 1993).

Unlike the dissociative drugs, the barbiturates are depressant anesthetics. The thiobarbiturate, thiopental, the oxybarbiturate, pentobarbital and the methylated oxybarbiturate methohexital have been used in reptiles (Calderwood, 1971; Frye, 1981; Wood et al, 1982). They are generally administered iv or ip to produce anesthesia, but im and sc use is also reported. Oral administration of pentobarbital in alligators (Calderwood, 1971) and crocodiles (Jacobson, 1984) is also reported. The anesthetic dose-response is variable and onset and duration unpredictable. Adverse outcomes including respiratory and cardiac arrest are also reported. In the green sea turtle (*Chelonia mydas*) for example, approximately 20 mg/kg sodium thiopental administered iv resulted in anesthetic induction of the majority of animals in 5 to 10 mins and complete recovery in 6 hours (Wood et al, 1982). Other turtles in the same study failed to become deeply anesthetized even with additional increments of thiopental and anesthetic related mortality was observed in three turtles (maximum cumulative dose of 25.2 mg/kg). Adverse outcomes similar to the above example following barbiturate administration coupled with the advent of safer anesthetic techniques limits their routine use in reptiles.

Other depressant anesthetics such as the alkyl phenol propofol and the steroid anesthetic, saffan have been used in reptiles and more in depth descriptions of their use are available elsewhere (Calderwood et al, 1979; Lawton, 1992; Lawrence, 1983). Although propofol offers many advantages due to its rapid onset and short duration, it is an expensive alternative and administration must be by the intravenous route. Saffan is not currently available in the United States.

Etorphine, a potent opioid which has been used in the past to restrain large reptiles is presently difficult to obtain in the United States (Bennett, 1991; Frye, 1981; Jacobson, 1984). Little information is available on the use of other opioids in reptiles although morphine, meperidine and oxymorphone have reportedly been used (Heard, 1993; Kanui et al, 1992). These drugs should be considered adjunct drugs and potential analgesics, but not true anesthetics. Similarly, local anesthetics such as lidocaine may be used topically to supplement other restraint and anesthetic regimes (Bennett, 1991; Boyer, 1993).

INHALED ANESTHETICS

Although the use of inhaled anesthetics neces-sitates the use of specialized equipment (including induction chambers, face masks, anesthetic machines, vaporizers and endotracheal tubes), they have been, and continue to be, frequently used in the anesthetic management of a wide range of reptile species (Frye, 1981; Custer et al, 1980; Fagella et al, 1987; Shaw et al, 1992). Diethyl-ether, methoxyflurane, halothane, isoflurane and more recently sevoflurane have been used in reptiles. The use of diethyl-ether is complicated by its flammability. General use of methoxyflurane has declined greatly with the advent of newer inhalants with lower blood/gas solubilities (resulting in more rapid anesthetic induction and recovery), decreased percent metabolized (compared to 50% metabolism of methoxyflurane in humans) and fewer toxic side effects. Inhaled anesthetics with low blood/gas solubilities are desirable especially in reptiles as agent solubility is increased at lower body temperatures prolonging the anesthetic induction and length of anesthetic recovery. The order of increasing blood/gas solubility (at 37°C in human beings) for currently used inhaled anesthetics is desflurane (0.42), sevoflurane (0.6), isoflurane (1.4), halothane (2.3) (Steffey, 1995). Nitrous oxide which is sometimes used as an adjunct to the potent inhaled anesthetics has a blood gas solubility of 0.47. An additional benefit of using inhalants is the minimal effect of metabolism on the termination of effect of these drugs. Biotransformation accounts for up to 25% of recovered halothane, 3% of sevoflurane, 0.17% of isoflurane and 0.02% of desflurane (Steffey, 1995). Organ toxicity which is in part related to the amount of drug metabolized is therefore also lower with the newer inhaled anesthetic agents. Administration of a safe anesthetic dose is unaffected by body weight and although no specific guidelines (eg. minimum alveolar concentration) for their use have been described in reptiles, the characteristics of anesthesia produced by inhaled anesthetics are fairly uniform across species (Steffey, 1995). Vaporizer dial settings for anesthetic induction and maintenance in reptiles with halothane and isoflurane are similar to those reported in mammals (Dripps et al 1988; Fagella et al, 1987; Shaw et al, 1992; Steffey, 1995). For example, anesthesia was induced in marine and freshwater turtles with a vaporizer dial setting of 4% isoflurane (Shaw et al, 1992). Concentrations between 1.5 and 1.7 % were needed for maintenance. Mechanical ventilation was used in these animals during the maintenance and recovery periods. Although anesthetic requirements are likely not markedly different from those for mammals, the time to achieve an appropriate anesthetic depth varies significantly from mammals. In the above example it took 60 to 90 mins to reach a surgical plane of anesthesia (defined by absence of a withdrawal reflex and weak to absent palpebral reflex). Although this duration is influenced in part by the relatively large size of the anesthetic circuit (compared to the animal s minute volume) and oxygen flow rates used in this study, the trend to a longer anesthetic induction is plausible and supported by other studies (Custer et al, 1980; Fagella et al, 1987) and personal clinical experience. Similarly recovery times are also longer than those of mammals even when animals are mechanically ventilated and body temperature is maintained normal during this period.

MUSCLE RELAXANTS (NEUROMUSCULAR BLOCKING DRUGS)

The use of neuromuscular blocking drugs in reptiles poses an interesting ethical question. In no other species of animal would their sole use be condoned in todays environment of strict guidelines for the humane treatment of animals. The justification for their continued use in reptiles in most instances has been personnel safety and use of this technique to restrain animals for non- noxious procedures (eg, sexing, tagging and transportion). Others have claimed this as an alternative to the stress of manual restraint (Bennett, 1991; Spiegel et al, 1984). Paralysis in the absence of other drugs to alter consciousness is said to be a very frightening and stressful experience in people with some long term consequences even in the absence of a noxious stimulus. It is difficult to extrapolate this directly to reptiles where the knowledge that this shouldn't be happening to them is likely not a factor. While I do not categorically oppose their singular use, because of our broader knowledge of their actions in other species their use alone must be considered and justified on the basis of individual circumstance.

In addition to the humane considerations, the drugs commonly used for muscle relaxation produce adverse side affects which may be detrimental to the patient. The most obvious of these is the inability to breathe. While some reptiles may be more tolerant of this due to some of their physiologic adaptations, it is possible that some of the unexplained deaths following these drugs were a direct result of hypoxemia resulting from apnea. Hence it is recommended that animals be mechanically ventilated during use of these drugs. Cardiovascular effects including an increase in cardiac arhythmogenicity and vasodilation are observed with this class of drugs in mammalian species. Muscle pain is also reported in people following use of succinylcholine and is likely due to the early fasciculations caused by this depolarizing muscle relaxant. Coarse twitches involving large muscle

groups have been reported following succinylcholine administration to a caiman crocodile (Klide et al, 1973). In chelonians a prolonged rigid extended posture is observed prior to relaxation which generally occurs 20-30 mins following drug administration (Boyer, 1993). This is likely due to a different form of muscle innervation in which stimulation with a depolarizing agent results in muscle contraction (Harvey et al, 1983). Similar postural responses are observed in birds following depolarizing agents. Succinylcholine and gallamine triethiodide (a non-depolarizing muscle relaxant) are used in reptiles but are reported to have a variable muscle relaxing effects in different species (Bennett, 1991; Jacobsen, 1984; Spiegel et al, 1984). Succinylcholine has been administered at a dose of 0.5 to greater than 1.0 mg/ kg im or ip to crocodilians and chelonians. (Boyer, 1993; Frye, 1994; Spiegel et al, 1984). Gallamine has been successfully used at doses of 0.4 to 1.25 mg/kg in crocodilians (Morgan-Davies, 1980).

HYPOTHERMIA

Due to the poikilothermic physiology of reptiles, cold environmental temperatures slow metabolic rate and render the patient immobile. Historically, this technique was commonly used to provide immobilization for surgical procedures (Parker, 1939; Frye, 1981). More recently it has been suggested that sensory neural conduction while slowed may still be present in the hypothermic reptile (Hutchinson et al, 1970; Rosenberg, 1978), but motor responses are impaired preventing escape behavior (Frye, 1981). The question of whether a noxious stimulus is perceived during hypothermia in reptiles has still not been conclusively answered. In human beings hypothermia is used to facilitate a range of surgical procedures. By slowing down metabolism (and so the rate of oxygen consumption), it offers benefit in preservation of organ function during low or no flow states as with partial or complete arterio-venous occlusion during cerebral or cardiac surgery. Additionally a 5-7% decrease in anesthetic requirements (per °C decrease in body temperature from 37 °C) is reported (Regan et al, 1967; Rupp et al, 1986; Antoginini, 1993).

Despite the potential benefits of hypothermia, associated physiologic changes may be detrimental to non-hibernating mammals who maintain body temperature within a narrow range. Damage to the skin depending on the cooling technique used, compromise of immune function and vessel wall integrity, changes in blood viscosity and coagulation are potential complications. Additionally the threshold for myocardial arrhythmogenicity is decreased and acid base and electrolyte changes are commonly seen (Reitz et al, 1989; Rupp et al,

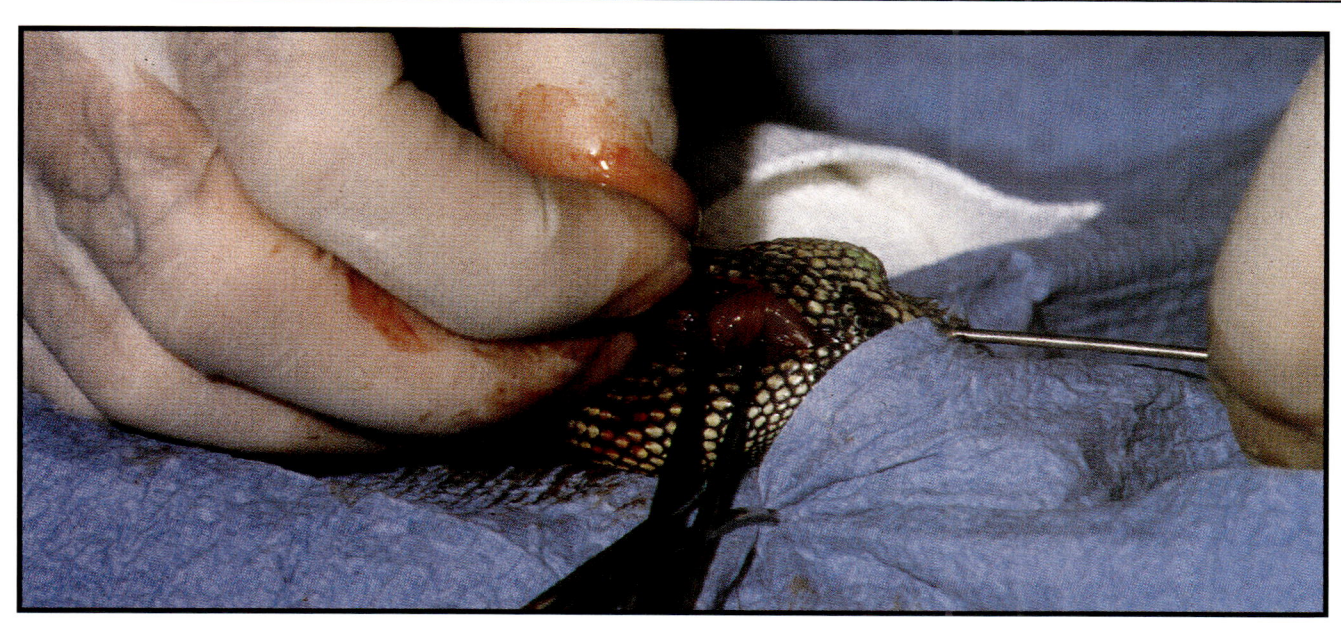

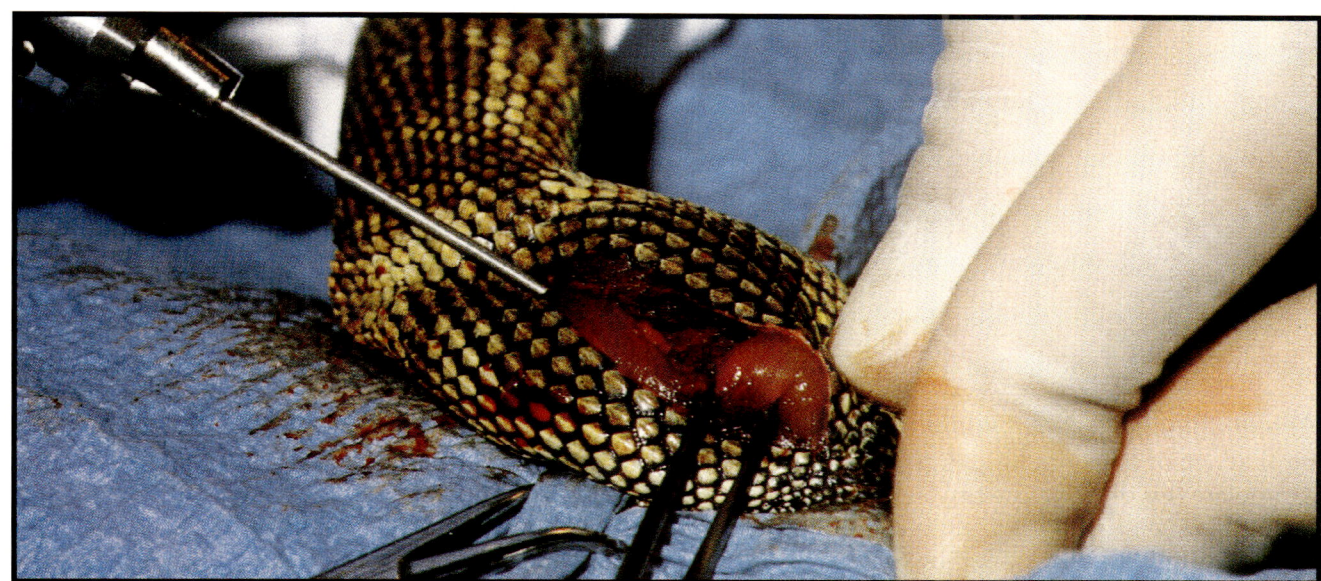

Pinning of a broken femur in an adult male iguana. Photos courtesy of Dr. Bernard A. Mangone.

1986). Reptiles may better tolerate hypothermia from a physiologic standpoint as they are adapted to wider body temperature ranges. In one report of induced hypothermia in alligators *(Alligator mississippiensis)* a 10 °C change in body temperature (30 to 20 °C) caused minimal changes in measured variables except heart rate, $PaCO_2$ and pHa (Douse et al, 1991). Others report permanent damage in the form of axonal degeneration following hypothermia in snakes (Northcutt et al, 1974). Gradual cooling appears to be less detrimental than rapid cooling, but most physiologic changes occur early in the cooling process. With the current information available, although I do not advocate the use of hypothermia as a sole means by which to immobilize reptiles for noxious procedures, moderate hypothermia may have some role in restraint and tissue preservation of these vertebrates.

INSTRUMENTATION, SUPPORT AND MONITORING

Given the unique physiology and varied environments in which anesthesia is performed in reptiles, recommendations must be adaptable to circumstances. However, general principles of patient support and monitoring during anesthesia are applicable.

Due to the physiologic influence of body temperature, efforts should be made to maintain optimal temperature for each patient during general anesthesia. Most reptiles have an optimal temperature between 75-85 °F (24.5-29.5°C). This may be monitored continuously with a cloacal or esophageal temperature probe or intermittently using a

Figure 1.
Use of a cloacal temperature probe in a lizard.

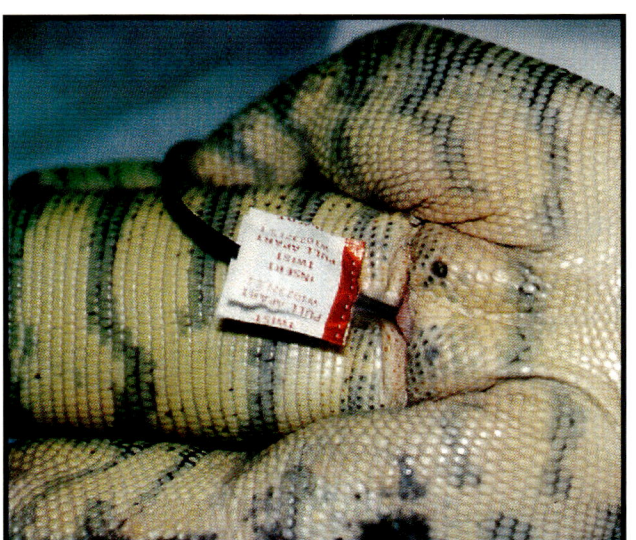

digital thermometer positioned in the cloaca (Fig 1). The decrease in metabolic rate induced by general anesthesia, surface cooling associated with aseptic preparation of the surgical site and loss of heat from open body cavities is likely to result in a decrease in body temperature over time. Hence supplemental heat in the form of circulating water blankets, radiant heat lamps and/or simply warmed intravenous fluids should be used as necessary throughout general anesthesia and during recovery from anesthesia. Care must be taken to protect the animal from direct contact to warming devices so as not to create thermal skin burns.

Heart rate will change in direct relation to changes in body temperature and anesthetic depth. As in mammals, heart rate and rhythm may be easily monitored with an electrocardiogram (ECG). The ECG leads are attached to the body using clips, needles or patch electrodes (Fig 2).

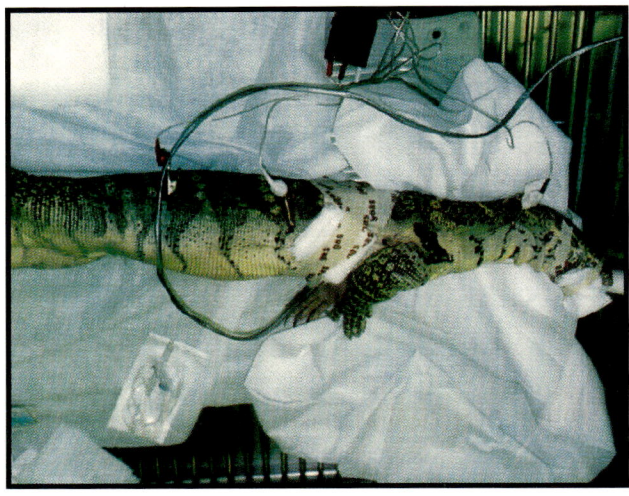

Figure 2.
An anesthetized lizard instrumented with ECG leads and a Doppler crystal.

Alternatively, an esophageal ECG lead may be used (Fig 3). Recall however that ECG's record electrical but not mechanical activity. Mechanical activity may be monitored indirectly with the use of an ultrasonic Doppler probe placed directly over the heart (except in animals with a shell; eg, turtles and tortoises) (Figs 2 & 3). Blood flow through the heart chambers is audible with each contractile cycle. In reptiles with a shell and others, the Doppler flow crystal may be placed over the femoral artery or carotid artery. The Doppler crystal may occasionally record sound over a peripheral (distal limb) artery and with the use of a pressure cuff positioned proximal to the doppler crystal on an extremity, trends in blood pressure can be recorded. Caution is stressed however as the usefulness and accuracy of this indirect (noninvasive) technique for blood pressure measurement in rep-

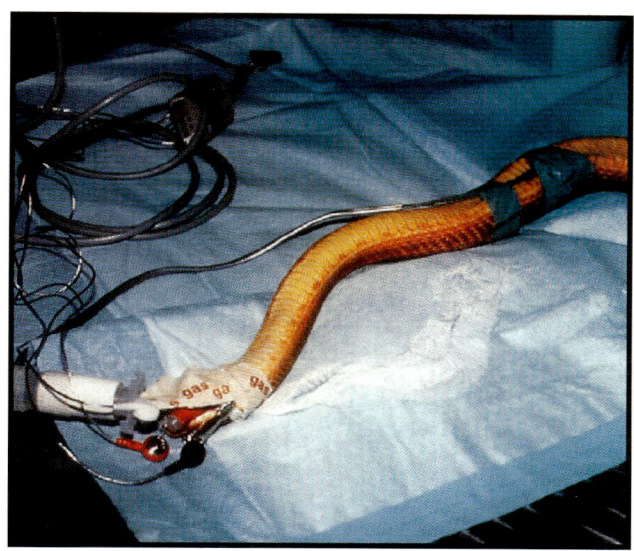

Figure 3.
An anesthetized snake instrumented with a Doppler crystal and esophageal ECG lead.

tiles has not yet been validated. Direct arterial blood pressure may be recorded from either the carotid or femoral artery in reptilian species following surgical cannulation of these vessels. However, the invasive nature of this form of monitoring limits its use clinically. Normal values for direct arterial blood pressure have been reported in experimental animals. Mean arterial pressure recorded from the femoral artery of chronically instrumented resting alligators *(Alligator mississippiensis)* at 30°C was 35 mmHg (Douse, et al, 1991). Systolic and diastolic pressures recorded from the carotid artery in three unanesthetized green turtles (*Chelonia mydas*) were 38 and 30 mmHg respectively (Butler et al, 1984). Systolic blood pressure measured from the carotid artery in 4 anesthetized (isoflurane or isoflurane/nitrous oxide) Kemp's ridley sea turtles (*Lepidochelys kempii*) averaged 31 mmHg (Moon et al, 1995). A mean value of 46 mmHg was measured in awake turtles by Moon et al, 1995.

Monitoring and support of respiration may range from a simple observation of respiratory rate and breath character to controlled mechanical ventilation and blood gas analysis and is based on available equipment and personal preference. Maintenance of anesthesia with inhalation anesthetics can result in wide swings of anesthetic depth given the arrhythmic breathing pattern of many reptiles and their ability to remain apneic for extended periods of time. Controlled ventilation will remove some of this ventilation related variability in anesthetic depth and facilitate a more consistent plane of anesthesia. A ventilator may also be used in situations where body position is likely to compromise respiratory function (e.g. dorsal recumbency in chelonians) and when neuromuscular blocking

agents are in use. However, care must be taken not to overinflate the lungs as damage to the air sacs or parenchyma may occur (Boyer, 1993). Normal tidal volumes are reported in spontaneously breathing turtles (*Chelonia mydas*) (Butler et al, 1984) and alligators *(Alligator mississippiensis)* (Douse et al, 1992; Hicks et al, 1992) and may be used as guidelines for mechanical ventilation. Minute ventilation in spontaneously breathing turtles (*Pseudemys scripta elegans*) prior to and after water dives average 32 mls/kg/min to 287 mls/kg/min (Jackson et al, 1974). In the above examples body temperature ranged from 24 - 29 0C. No adverse side effects were seen with positive pressure ventilation to a peak inspiratory pressure of 10 cm H_2O in alligators *(Alligator mississippiensis)* (Douse et al, 1991). Similar peak inspiratory pressures have been used in a wide range of reptile species with respiratory rates of 2-10 b/min (Douse et al, 1991; Fagella et al, 1987; Moon et al, 1995).

Endotracheal intubation techniques are described for a variety of reptiles (Bennett, 1991; Heard, 1993). The ability to directly visualize the rostrally located glottis in snakes makes intubation of this class of squamates simple providing the animal can be adequately restrained (Fig 4). The more caudal location and presence of papillae in some chelonians (eg. sea turtle) and fleshy tongue in some lizards makes visualization and intubation in these animals more difficult. Laryngoscope blades are useful in these species and in crocodilians where the glottis is also more caudally located. In these animals it is sometimes necessary to move the basihyal valve to view the glottis. Intubation may be performed in the awake reptile if adequate restraint and visualization are possible. This is advantageous when an inhaled anesthetic is chosen for anesthetic induction as intubation facilitates mechanical ventilation. However, in mammalian species intubation is associated with marked physiologic responses in lightly anesthetized patients and consideration must be given to the stress such a procedure may similarly cause in reptiles. Sedatives and topical anesthetics may be used to facilitate a stress free intubation. As the glottis in reptiles remains closed except during breathing, considerable time may be spent attempting to intubate a reptile. Topical anesthetics such as 2% lidocaine are useful as they help prevent glottic constriction and allow gentle passage of the endotracheal tube. Cuffed and uncuffed endotracheal tubes may be used. In small snakes and lizards over the needle catheters may serve as endotracheal tubes. Care should be taken in all species, but especially in those with complete tracheal rings not to cause trauma from overinflation of the tracheal tube cuff. Tube length should be measured to prevent

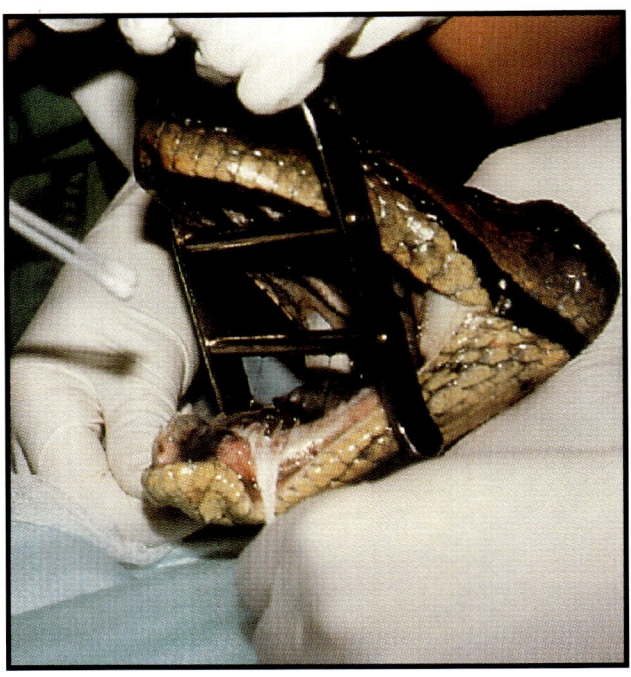

Figure 4a,b.
Tracheal intubation of a large snake.
Above: Use of a mouth speculum to facilitate access to the oral cavity for tracheal intubation. Below: Placement of the endotracheal tube within the glottic opening.

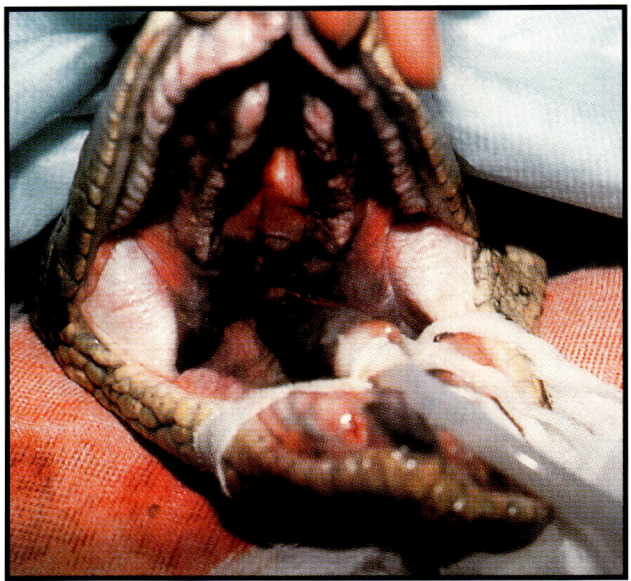

endobronchial positioning. The endotracheal tube should be secured once in a suitable position and care taken not to disrupt it during transport of the animal. Even with a tube in place inspiratory and expiratory tidal movement should be monitored whether the animal is spontaneously breathing or ventilated as tubes may kink or become occluded with airway secretions.

Perioperative respiratory function and acid base status may also be monitored using blood gas analysis if animals are appropriately instrumented and the necessary analyzer is available. Ideally samples should be taken at a consistent body temperature and from the same arterial site. Since red blood cells are nucleated, samples should be analyzed promptly to prevent variability due to continued oxygen utilization. Resting arterial pH, $PaCO_2$ and PaO_2 vary with body temperature (Rupp et al, 1986; Douse et al, 1992). The PaO_2 is also affected by the percent oxygen inspired, the stage of the ventilatory cycle and the degree of cardiac and non-cardiac shunting present at the time of sampling. Appropriate interventions may be made if values reflect significant differences from previously recorded normal values (Table 1). These may include changing body temperature, the fraction of inspired oxygen, ventilatory patterns and supporting acid base balance with the use of intravenous fluids and electrolyte solutions.

Guidelines for the type and rate of intravenous fluid administration during anesthesia are not well defined for reptiles. In mammals, the ionic composition of intravenous fluids used during anesthesia resembles that of serum. Lactated ringers and Plasmalyte-148 are commonly used balanced electrolyte solutions for fluid replacement. These solutions have been used in reptiles where reported values for sodium, potassium, chloride, and bicarbonate are similar to those of mammals (Frye, 1994; Minnich, 1982). Some desert and aquatic reptiles are exceptions. In healthy mammals perioperative fluid administration rates of 5-10 ml/kg/hr are recommended to compensate for normal fluid (urinary, gastrointestinal, cutaneous and respiratory) and minor surgical losses. Although the sources of water loss in reptiles are similar to mammals they show more variation with changes in habitat, activity level and temperature and a single overall guideline for fluid administration rate may not be practical. Total body water (TBW) is about 70% of body weight in reptiles (McDonald, 1976; Minnich, 1982) and is divided into the intracellular compartment (ICF) composing about 55% and the extracellular compartment (ECF) composing about 15 %. Plasma represents about 3-5% of total body water. These compartments determine the eventual distribution of intravenously administered fluids. In mammals fluids administered intravenously rapidly redistribute to the ECF (about 30% of TBW) and then ICF. The speed of redistribution of fluids from the vascular compartment to other compartments in reptiles is unknown and rapid administration of large volumes may be detrimental. In dehydrated animals guidelines again come from clinical experience managing higher order vertebrates. Clinical assessment of percent dehydration is made and this value is then multiplied by the body weight in kilograms to arrive at an estimation of fluid volume (in liters) to be administered. Although the shell of chelonians is considered live tissue, it represents about 30% of body weight and overestimation of fluid requirements may occur if the above formula is used with this group of animals. A prior recommendation for maximal fluid administration of no more than 5% of body weight at a rate of no greater than 1 ml/min is reported for tortoises (Page et al, 1990).

Administration of intravenous fluids is facilitated by the placement of an indwelling catheter. Sites and techniques for venipuncture and catheter placement vary with species and in depth guidelines are given elsewhere (Mader, 1992, Richter et al, 1977; Samour et al, 1984). Briefly, a catheter may be placed percutaneously in the caudal tail vein (Fig 5) or via a cut-down in the cephalic vein located on the craniomedial aspect of the antebrachium of lizards. A small cut down may also be used to place a catheter in the vein running along the ventral midline of the abdomen in these species. The jugular vein is the most common catheterization site in chelonians (Fig 6). Usually a small cut-down to the vein is necessary.

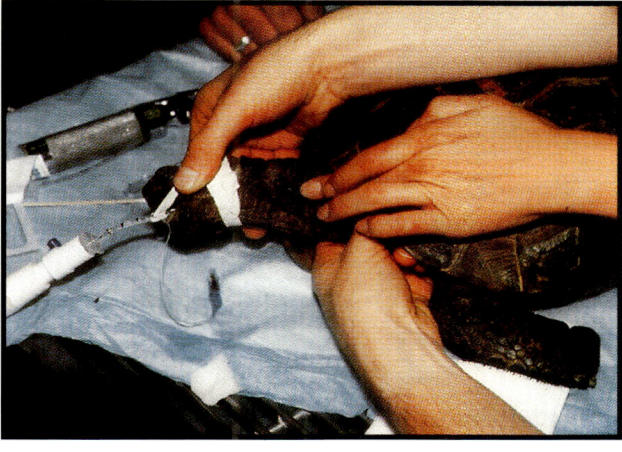

Figure 6.
A turtle with a jugular venous catheter in place.

Catheterization of snakes is more difficult and requires a surgical approach to the jugular vein (the right is larger than left) located medial to the ribs (Fig 7). When catheterization is impractical, fluids may be administered subcutaneously, in the pleuroperitoneal cavity or via the bone marrow following placement of a bone marrow needle. The femur and tibia have been used clinically as sites for placement of a bone marrow needle in iguanas. Absorption from the former sites will be slower and more variable than through the intravenous route. Caution with the latter technique is necessary in malnourished animals where pathologic fractures are a potential complication.

Monitoring anesthetic depth is confounded by the variable states of arousal of these patients and the effect of temperature on anesthetic depth, neural conduction and the ability of the animal to respond to noxious stimuli. Cardiovascular and respiratory responses to changes in anesthetic depth are not consistent (although elevations in heart rate at a consistent body tem-

Figure 5.
Placement of an intravenous catheter in the caudal tail vein of a lizard.

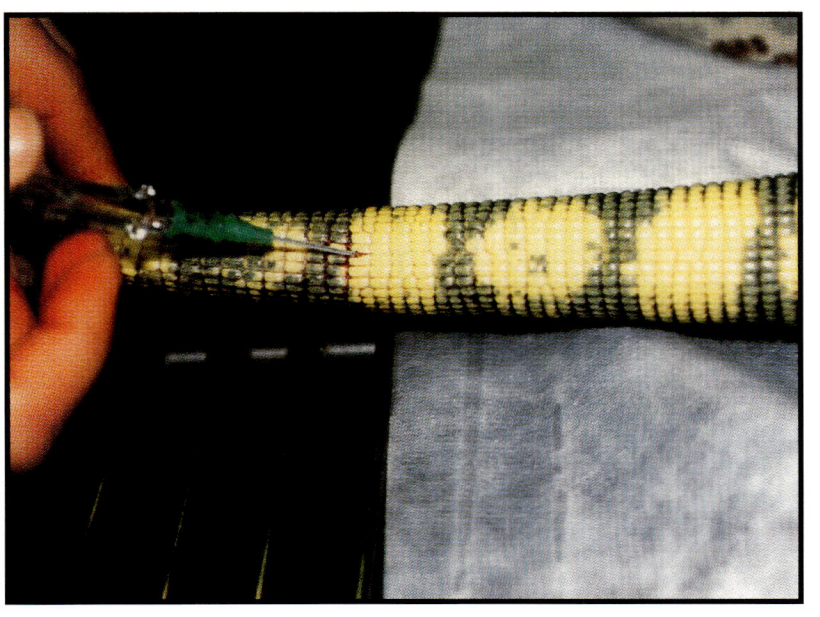

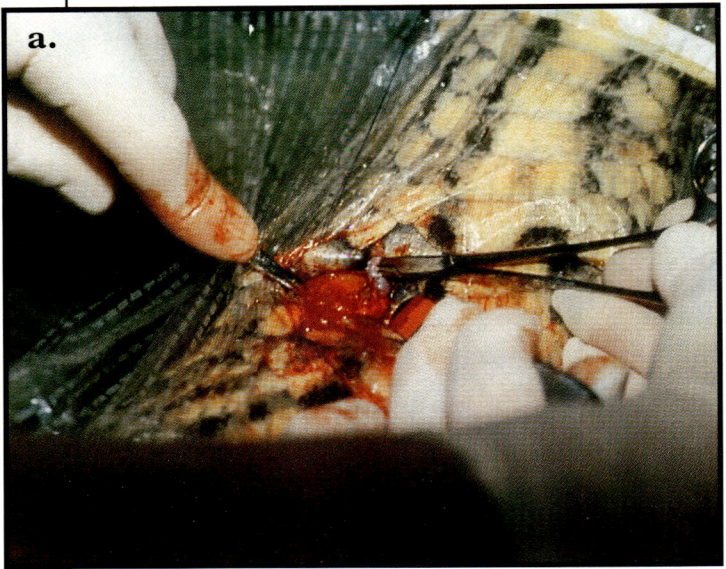

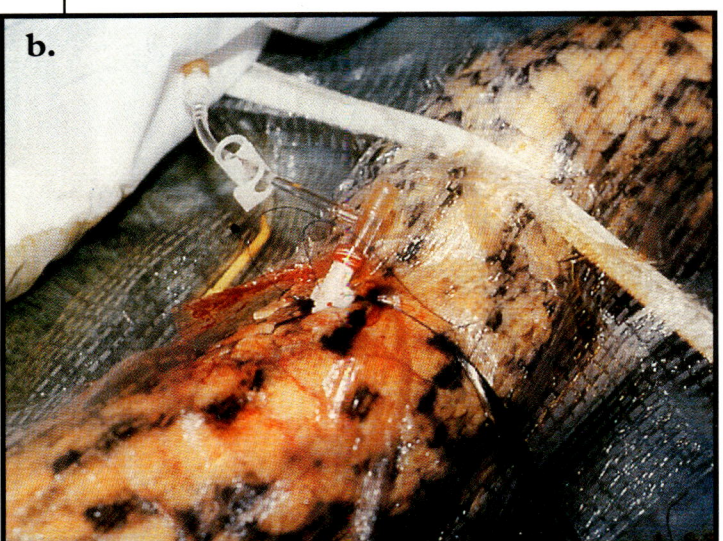

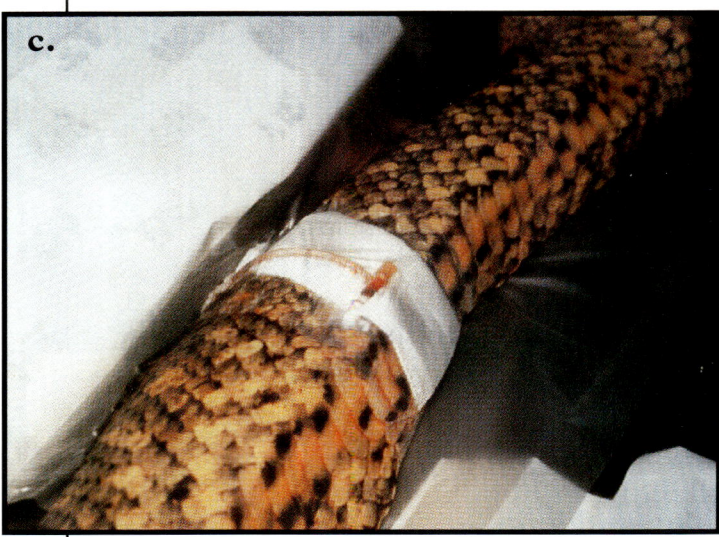

Figure 7a,b,c.
Placement of a jugular catheter in a snake.
a: Isolation of the right jugular vein (via a surgical cut down).
b: Aseptic placement of the catheter.
c: Securing the catheter in position.

perature indicate a lightly anesthetized patient) and variations in response may be seen depending on the anesthetic technique used. Despite this, general guidelines have been established based on experience and techniques used in other species. The reader is encouraged to use these as a starting point from which to further develop skill as an anesthetist. Gross purposeful movement in response to surgical stimulation is the most obvious indicator of an inadequately anesthetized animal, but not a desirable technique for a number of reasons related to both the animal s well being and compromise of surgical technique. Hence evaluation of reflexes that change with different planes of anesthesia are recommended. The loss of the ability of the animal to right itself is an early indicator of a deepening plane of anesthesia. In snakes relaxation generally occurs from a cranial to caudal direction. Lack of response to a tail (snakes) or toe (lizards, chelonians) pinch, loss of the head withdrawal reflex (chelonians) are other guidelines to judge anesthetic depth. The loss of the corneal reflex in lizards and chelonians and loss of the tongue flick reflex in snakes (lack of eyelids precludes use of corneal reflex) may reflect an animal that is too deeply anesthetized. The return of these reflexes and regular spontaneous ventilation are useful as indicators of anesthetic recovery.

RECOVERY

Marked variation in duration of anesthesia is reported in reptiles. This variation is probably related to a number of factors including the drug used, dose administered, route of administration, body temperature (which affects metabolic rate and solubility of inhalation anesthetics), acid base balance (influence on free versus bound drug), variations in regional blood flow (for example, shunting blood away from the lung) and metabolic rate (which in turn affects drug metabolism and excretion). If the length of recovery can be explained it is reasonable to continue support and monitoring begun during the anesthetic phase. The more critical the patient, the more intensive the care provided during this phase. At a minimum, body temperature should be kept within the optimum range and ventilation supported until the animal shows return of normal reflexes and behaviors. Care should be taken not to replace a partially recovered animal in an unsuitable location. This might include an area with water (where an uncoordinated animal may become submerged) or poor ambient temperature regulation (if the animal is unable to compensate with altered behavior) or an enclosure with other animals (that may traumatize the recovering animal). Appropriate management of the patient during this phase is important to the eventual outcome and hence should not be forgotten.

SUMMARY

Although there are many unanswered questions, anesthesia in reptiles may be safely managed. Basic principles are followed with attention to unique anatomic and physiologic characteristics. Responses to anesthetic drugs may differ markedly from mammalian species and should be accounted for. Outcome may be positively influenced with appropriate support and monitoring during anesthesia and careful attention to the patient during anesthetic recovery.

ACKNOWLEDGEMENTS

The author appreciates manuscript review and constructive comments by Drs. Darryl J. Heard, Peter J. Pascoe, Lyndsay Phillips and Eugene P. Steffey. Thanks to Jeanne Moje and John Patz for their technical assistance.

REFERENCES AND RECOMMENDED READING

—**Al-Badry, KS:**
Hematological and Biochemical Parameters in Active and Hibernating Sand Vipers. Comp Biochm Physiol, 1983, 74A: 137-141.

—**Antognini, JF:**
Hypothermia Eliminates Isoflurane Requirements at 20° C. Anesthesiology, 1993, 78(6): 1152-1156.

—**Arena, PC; Richardson, KC; Cullen, LK:**
Anaesthesia in Two Species of Large Australian Skink. Veterinary Record, 1988, 123: 155-158.

—**Bartholomew, GA:**
Physiological Control of Body Temperature. In, Biology of the Reptilia, Vol 12, Carl Gans (Ed). Academic Press, New York, NY, 1982, pp. 167-211.

—**Beck, CC:**
Vetalar (ketamine hydrochloride) A Unique Cataleptoid Anesthetic Agent for Multispecies Usage. J Zoo Anim Med, 1976, 7(3): 11-38.

—**Bennett, RA:**
A Review of Anesthesia and Chemical Restraint in Reptiles. Journal of Zoo and Wildlife Medicine, 1991, 22(3): 282-303.

—**Beynon, PH (Ed), Lawton, MPC; Cooper, JE**
(Scientific eds). Appendix Three: Haematological and Biochemical Data. In, Manual of Reptiles, British Small Animal Veterinary Association, Gloucestershire, England, 1992, pp. 219-220.

—**Boyer, TH:**
Clinical Anesthesia of Reptiles. In, A Practitioner's Guide to Reptilian Husbandry & Care. AAHA 1993, pp. 73-85.

—**Butler, PJ; Milsom, WK; Woakes, AJ:**
Respiratory, Cardiovascular and Metabolic Adjustments During Steady State Swimming in the Green Turtle, Chelonia mydas. J Comp Physiol B, 1984, 154: 167-174.

—**Calderwood, HW:**
Anesthesia for Reptiles. JAVMA, 1971, 159(11): 1618-25.

—**Calderwood, HW; Jacobsen, EJ:**
Preliminary Report on the Use of Saffan on Reptiles. In, American Ass of Zoo Vet, 1979, pp. 23-26.

—**Cooper, JE:**
Veterinary Work with Non-Domesticated Pets IV: Lower Vertebrates. Br Vet J, 1987, 143(3): 193-201.

—**Cunningham, AA; Gili, C:**
Management in Captivity. In, Manual of Reptiles, PH Beynon (Ed), MPC Lawton; JE Cooper (Scientific eds). British Small Animal Veterinary Association, Gloucestershire, England, 1992, pp. 14-31.

—**Custer, RS; Bush, M:**
Physiologic and Acid-Base Measures of Gopher Snakes during Ketamine or Halothane-Nitrous Oxide Anesthesia. JAVMA, 1980, 177(9): 870-874.

—**Davies, PMC:**
Anatomy and Physiology. In, Diseases of the Reptilia, Vol. 1, JE Cooper and OF Jackson (Eds). Academic Press, New York, NY, 1981, pp. 9-73.

—**Douse, MA; Mitchell, GS:**
Effects of vagotomy on ventilatory responses to CO2 in alligators. Respiration Physiology, 1992, 87: 63-76.

—**Douse, MA; Mitchell, GS:**
Time course of temperature effects on arterial acid-base status in *Alligator mississippiensis*. Respiration Physiology, 1991, 83: 87-102.

—**Dripps, RD; Eckenhoff, JE; Vandam, LD:**
Intravenous Anesthetics. In, Introduction to Anesthesia: The Principles of Safe Practice, 7th Edition. W. B. Saunders Company, Philadelphia, PA, 1988, pp. 141-155.

—**Dripps, RD; Eckenhoff, JE; Vandam, LD:**
Fundamentals of Inhalation Anesthesia. In, Introduction to Anesthesia: The Principles of Safe Practice, 7th Edition. W. B. Saunders Company, Philadelphia, PA, 1988, pp. 103-132.

—**Faggella, AM; Raffe, MR:**
The Use of Isoflurane Anesthesia in a Water Monitor Lizard and a Rhino Iguana. Com-

panion Animal Practice - Exotic Medicine, July 1987, pp. 52-53.

—Frye, FL:
Anesthesia. In, Biomedical and Surgical Aspects of Captive Reptile Husbandry. Veterinary Medical Publishing Company, Edwardsville, Kansas, 1981, pp. 241-246.

—Frye, FL; Himsel, CA:
The Proper Method for Stethoscopy in Reptiles. Veterinary Medicine. December 1988, pp. 1250-1252.

—Frye, FL:
Clinical Laboratory Sample Collection and Processing. In, Reptile Clinician's Handbook. Krieger Publishing Company, Malabar, FL, 1994, pp. 71-132.

—Frye, FL:
Clinical Methods. In, Reptile Clinician's Handbook. Krieger Publishing Company, Malabar, FL, 1994, pp. 133-159.

—Glenn, JL; Straight, R; Snyder, CC:
Clinical Use of Ketamine Hydrochloride as an Anesthetic Agent for Snakes. Am J Vet Res, 1972, 33(9): 1901-1903.

—Harding, KA:
The Use of Ketamine Anaesthesia To Milk Two Tropical Rattlesnakes (*Crotalus durissus terrificus*). Vet Rec, 1977, 100: 289-290.

—Harvey, AL; Marshall, IG:
Muscle. In, Physiology Biochemistry Domestic Fowl, Vol. 4, Academic Press, London, England, 1983, pp. 219-233.

—Heard, DJ:
Principles and Techniques of Anesthesia and Analgesia for Exotic Practice. Exotic Pet Medicine I, November 1993, 23(6): 1301-1327.

—Hicks, JW; White, FN:
Pulmonary Gas Exchange During Intermittent Ventilation in the American Alligator. Respiration Physiology, 1992, 88: 23-36.

—Hutchinson, NA; Koles, ZJ; Smith, RS:
Conduction Velocity in Myelinated Nerve Fibres of xenopus laevis. J Physiol, 1970, 208: 279-289.

—Hutton, KE:
Blood Volume, Corpuscular Constants, and Shell Weight in Turtles. Am J Phsiol, 1961, 200(5): 1004-1006.

—Jackson, DC; Silverblatt, H:
Respiration and Acid-base Status of Turtles Following Experimental Dives. American Journal of Physiology, April 1974, 226(4): 903-909.

—Jackson, OF, Sainsbury, AW:
Radiological and Related Investigations. In, Manual of Reptiles, PH Beynon (Ed), MPC Lawton; JE Cooper (Scientific eds). British Small Animal Veterinary Association, Gloucestershire, England, 1992, pp. 63-79.

—Jacobsen, ER:
Immobilization, Blood Sampling, Necropsy Techniques and Diseases of Crocodilians: A Review. J Zoo An Med, 1984, 15: 38-45.

—Kanui, TI; Hole, K:
Morphine and Pethidine Antinociception in the Crocodile. J Vet Pharmacol Therap, 1992, 15: 101-103.

—Klide, AM; Klein, LV:
Chemical Restraint of Three Reptilean Species. J Zoo Anim Med, 1973, 4(1): 8-11.

—Lawrence, K; Jackson OF:
Alphaxalone/alphadolone Anaesthesia in Reptiles. The Veterinary Record, 1983, 112: 26-28.

—Lawton, MPC:
Anaesthesia. In, Manual of Reptiles, PH Beynon (Ed), MPC Lawton; JE Cooper (Scientific eds). British Small Animal Veterinary Association, Gloucestershire, England, 1992, pp. 170-183.

—Mader, DR:
Intravenous Catheters. Reptile Medicine TNAVC 1992 Proceedings Manual, pp. 699-700.

—McDonald, HS:
Methods for the Physiological Study of Reptiles. In, Biology of the Reptilia, Vol. 5, C Gans (Ed), WR Dawson (Co-ed). Academic Press, New York, NY, 1976, pp. 19-126.

—Minnich, JE:
The Use of Water. In, Biology of the Reptilia, Vol. 12, Physiology C, C Gans (Ed), FH Pough (Co-ed). Academic Press, New York, NY, 1982, pp. 325-395.

—Moberly, WR:
The Metabolic Responses of the Common Iguana, iguana iguana, to Walking and Diving. Comp Biochem Physiol, 1968, 27: 21-32.

—Moon, PF; Stabenau, EK:
Anesthetic and Post-anesthetic Management of Kemp's Ridley Sea Turtles. (Accepted for publication, JAVMA, 1995).

—Morgan-Davies, AM:
Immobilization of the Nile-crocodile (*Crocodylus niloticus*) with Gallamine Triethiodide. J Zoo An Med, 1980, 11: 85-87.

—Northcutt, RG:
Retinal Projections in the Northern Water Snake *Natrix sipedon sipedon*. J Morph, 142: 117-135.

—Page, CD; Mautino, M:
Clinical Management of Tortoises. The Com-

pendium Small Animal, February 1990, 12(2): 221-228.

—**Parker, GH:**
General Anesthesia by Cooling. Proc Soc Expl Biol Med, 1939, 42(1): 186-187.

—**Porter, KR:**
Herpetology. W.B. Saunders Company, Philadelphia, 1972, pp. 160-192.

—**Pough, FH; Gans, C:**
The Vocabulary of Reptilian Thermoregulation. In, Biology of the Reptilia, Vol. 12. Carl Gans (Ed). Academic Press, New York, NY, 1982, pp. 17-23.

—**Regan, MJ; Eger, EI:**
Effect of Hypthermia in Dogs on Anesthestizing and Apneic Doses of Inhalation Agents: Determination of Anesthestic Index (Apnea/MAC). Anesthesiology, 1967, 28: 689-700.

—**Reitz, BA; Ream, AK:**
Uses of Hypothermia in Cardiovascular Surgery. In, Acute Cardiovascular Management: Anesthesia and Intensive Care, Ream and Fogdall (Ed). Lippincott, Philadelphia, PA, 1982, pp. 830-851.

—**Richter, AG; Olsen J; Fletcher K; et al:**
Techniques for Collecting Blood from Galapagos Tortoises and Box Turtles. VM/SAC Exotic Species, August 1977, pp. 1376-1378.

—**Rosenburg, ME:**
Thermal Relations of Nervous Conduction in the Tortoise. Comp Biochem Physio, 1978, 60A: 57-63.

—**Rossi, GT; Britt, RH:**
Effects of Hypothermia on the Cat Brain-Stem Auditory Evoked Response. Electroencephalography and clinical Neurophsyiology, 1984, 57: 143-155.

—**Rupp, SA; Severinghaus, JW:**
Hypothermia. In, Anesthesia, 2nd edition, R.D. Miller (Ed). Churchill Livingstone, New York, NY, 1986, pp. 1995-2022.

—**Samour, HJ; Risley, D; March, T; et al:**
Blood Sampling Techniques in Reptiles. The Veterinary Record, 1984, 114: 472-476.

—**Schumacher, J; Lillywhite, HB; Norman, W; et al:**
The Effects of Ketamine on Cardiopulmonary Function in Snakes. 1992, Proceedings Joint Meeting AAZV/AAWV, p. 173.

—**Shaw, SL; Leone-Kabler, S; Lutz, P; et al:**
Isoflurane: A Safe and Effective Anesthetic for Marine and Freshwater Turtles. In, Under Our Wing, IWRC Proceedings 1992, pp. 112-119.

—**Spiegel, RA; Lane, TJ; Larsen, RE; et al:**
Diazepam and Succinylcholine Chloride for Restraint of the American Alligator. JAVMA, 1984, 185(11): 1335-1336.

—**Steffey, EP:**
Inhalation Anesthetics. In, Veterinary Pharmacology and Therapeutics, 7th Edition, HR Adams (Ed). Iowa State University Press, Ames, Iowa, 1995, pp. 179-208.

—**Wallach, JD:**
Environmental and Nutritional Diseases of Captive Reptiles. JAVMA, 1971, 159(11): 1632-1643.

—**Williams, DL:**
Cardiovascular System. In, Manual of Reptiles, PH Beynon (Ed), MPC Lawton; JE Cooper (Scientific eds). British Small Animal Veterinary Association, Gloucestershire, England, 1992, pp. 80-87.

—**Wood, FE; Critchley, KH; Wood, JR:**
Anesthesia in the Green Sea Turtle, *Chelonia mydas*. *Am J Vet Res*, 1982, 43(10): 1882-1883.

—**Wood, SC; Lenfant, CJM:**
Respiration: Mechanics, Control and Gas Exchange. In, Biology of the Reptilia, Vol. 5, C Gans (Ed); WR Dawson (Co-ed). Academic Press, New York, NY, 1976, pp. 225-274.

NECROPSY (POSTMORTEM EXAMINATION)

Brad Bolon DVM, MS, PhD[*]
Pathology Associates International Corporation (an SAIC Company)
National Center for Toxicological Research,
P.O. Box 26
Jefferson, Arkansas 72079

Brad Bolon, D.V.M., M.S., Ph.D. is a board-certified veterinary pathologist. Dr. Bolon is extensively trained in toxicologic neuropathology; exotic animal pathology (reptiles and fish) is an avocation.

[*]Address correspondence to: Dr. Brad Bolon, Wyeth-Ayerst Research Division of Molecular Genetics, CN 8000, Rm. 2005, Princeton, NJ 08543-8000; E-mail: bolonb@war.wyeth.com

INTRODUCTION

A postmortem examination (or necropsy) is a critical tool in diagnosing diseases in reptiles. Gross lesions observed at necropsy and additional findings from ancillary tests (e.g., clinical pathology, histopathology, microbiology, toxicology) may provide insight regarding the pathogenesis (course) and etiology (cause) of the condition. In addition, in large groups of reptiles such as farms and zoological collections, a necropsy will provide valuable information to guide therapy of other ill animals and to prevent future disease outbreaks. The usefulness of the postmortem examination in formulating prevention and treatment programs depends on carcass quality, so the necropsy should be performed as soon as practicable after death.

This chapter describes materials and a necropsy protocol needed to consistently acquire diagnostic pathology specimens of high quality from dead reptiles. A detailed clinical history and, if feasible,

Necropsy specimen from a collared lizard. Note the wide folds of mucosa. Hematoxylin and Eosin, 100 x magnification. Specimen provided by Dr. Todd Driggers. Photo courtesy of Dr. Lowell Ackerman.

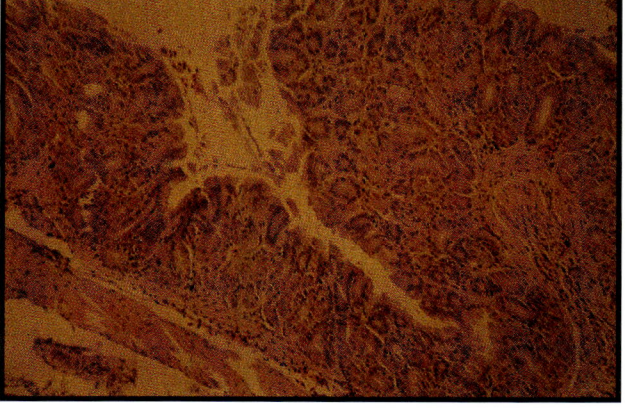

terminal physical examination should be obtained for the ill reptile prior to the necropsy.

Next, a thorough postmortem examination is performed in an orderly sequence to discover gross lesions and to obtain samples for ancillary analyses. Basic tenets of interpretation are also considered in this chapter, but this skill requires considerable practice and, in most cases, some knowledge of class- and species-specific anatomic features and patterns of disease. Throughout the chapter, a snake disease has been used to illustrate relevant concepts of the necropsy procedure.

DIAGNOSTIC PATHOLOGY SPECIMENS TO BE ACQUIRED AT NECROPSY

Three types of diagnostic samples may be acquired at necropsy. First, tissue lesions may be seen, including discolored or enlarged organs, masses, ulcers, or abnormal scales. In short, a tissue's appearance is different than expected. Blocks of tissue may be fixed for light or electron microscopy, cultured for microbial pathogens (see chapter on infectious diseases) or quick-frozen for microbiology, toxicology or special microscopic techniques (e.g., immunohistochemistry). Fluids including blood, cerebrospinal fluid (CSF), cyst contents, discharges, or effusions into a body cavity may also be gathered, yielding cells for cytological examination (see chapter on diagnostic cytology) or liquid for chemistry tests (see chapter on diagnostic biochemistry) or microbiological culture. Finally, excreta may be used for chemical, cytological (for cells or parasites), or microbiological (for bacterial, fungal, or viral) assays. As described below, a single sample may be divided between multiple tests.

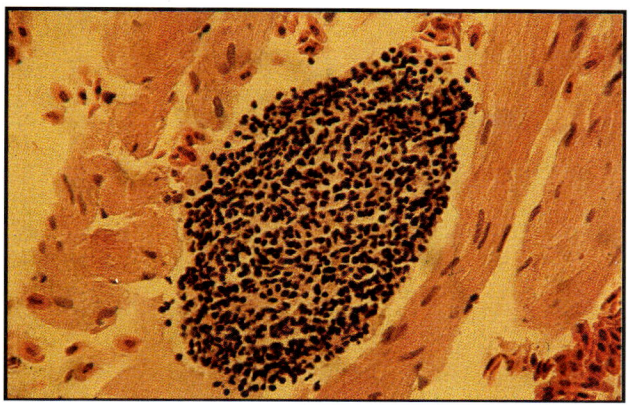

Nodular collection of inflammatory cells in the connective tissue of a collared lizard. Hematoxylin and Eosin, 400 x magnification. Specimen provided by Dr. Todd Driggers. Photo courtesy of Dr. Lowell Ackerman.

PREPARATION FOR THE POSTMORTEM EXAMINATION

HISTORY AND PHYSICAL EXAMINATION

A thorough clinical history must be obtained prior to initiating the necropsy. A good history may direct the prosector to specific organ systems and diagnostic tests that will help to reduce the necropsy time as well as the expense of performing unnecessary analyses. Information that should be acquired for the ill or dead reptile includes:

1. **Signalment**: What species? How old? Source (wild caught or captive bred)? How long with the current keeper?
2. **Husbandry**: What diet is fed, and how often is it given? What bedding and housing unit are used? How often is the unit cleaned, and with what solutions? What are the ambient atmospheric conditions in the housing unit?
3. **Medical History**: What are the clinical signs (e.g., altered behavior or feeding habits, soft tissue mass, etc.)? How long have they been present? Have there been prior episodes of the same or a different disease? What are the results of recent medical tests? Have there been past attempts at therapy, and were they successful?

If the reptile is from a collection, additional "herd health" parameters must also be considered. This information should include:

1. **Herd Husbandry**: How many animals in the collection? Are different species housed in the same room? If so, are the same cleaning tools and solutions used on all cages? Are new animals acquired from outside the collection? If so, from what source and how often? What length is the quarantine period?
2. **Herd Medical History**: Are the clinical signs in the dead reptile consistent with those ob-

served during past disease outbreaks in the collection? If so, what lesions were observed in animals from the past episodes?

If possible, the reptile should be observed by the prosector prior to the necropsy. This physical examination allows the practitioner to confirm or add to the history, thus gaining insight regarding potential sites of tissue lesions. In addition, this practice ensures better diagnostic results since necropsies performed with live reptiles that are currently exhibiting signs of disease minimize the artifactual distortion of lesions resulting from autolysis (postmortem decomposition). After the physical examination is completed, the reptile may be killed with an overdose of anesthetic (see chapter on humane euthanasia).

Using the clinical history and physical examination, the prosector should develop a list of differential diagnoses that could account for the clinical signs. The differential list will suggest an approach to the necropsy as well as one or more diagnostic tests and samples that will be needed to confirm or rule out specific diseases. For example, a snake with regurgitation as the principal clinical sign and a thickened tubular viscus as the chief finding during the physical examination likely has lesions of the stomach and/or intestines. Thus, the necropsy in this snake would initially focus on a thorough investigation of the gastrointestinal tract and its contents before other organ systems are assessed. This "systems" approach maximizes the value of the necropsy as well as the quality of the samples gained from the likely sites of disease.

PRESERVATION OF DEAD REPTILES FOR NECROPSY

While a gross postmortem examination may be performed upon autolyzed carcasses, good tissue

Necropsy specimen from a collared lizard. Note the finger-like folds of mucosa. Hematoxylin and Eosin, 100 x magnification. Specimen provided by Dr. Todd Driggers. Photo courtesy of Dr. Lowell Ackerman.

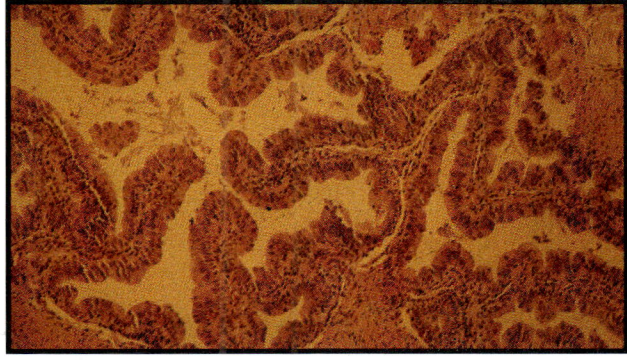

preservation is required to ensure that tissue specimens will be useable for further tests such as histopathology and microbiology. The longer the delay before necropsy and fixation of tissues, the more advanced will be the decomposition of tissues. Thus, the necropsy should be performed as soon as possible after death, ideally to begin immediately after the physical examination and euthanasia have been concluded.

If the necropsy will be delayed, the carcass of a dead reptile may be refrigerated or placed on ice. This storage environment will retard tissue decomposition for six to twelve hours. However, spread of enteric bacteria into viscera may occur through the walls of the digestive tract, thus obscuring the presence of potential pathogens such as bacteria, fungi, protozoa, and viruses. **Under no circumstances should the carcass be frozen.** Freezing renders the tissues unsuitable for many diagnostic procedures, notably histopathology.

NECROPSY SUPPLIES

A number of instruments are used during the reptile necropsy, the sizes of which will depend upon the size of the carcass. A basic necropsy kit will include one or two sharp, straight or curved knives with stainless steel blades and handles of hard plastic or wood. A steel and sharpening stone with appropriate lubricant (e.g. oil) may be useful for honing the knives if more than one thick-skinned reptile (e.g., crocodilian) is to be necropsied. Other instruments will include scissors (a set for heavy dissecting and a set for fine cutting), one or more sets of forceps or hemostats, rongeurs or tin snips (for cutting through bones and the shells of small turtles), scalpel blades and handles, and a saw or cleaver (for cutting thick bones and the shells of large turtles). Some sterile instruments should be available to collect tissues or fluids for microbial culture. The sterile equipment should include a pair of sharp scissors, forceps, and scalpel blades; a wire inoculating loop may also be used. A mobile working surface of hard wood or plastic is helpful for cutting tissues; a square cutting board with sides approximately 50 cm in length is helpful for field necropsies. Finally, a box of glass microscope slides should be available for preparing cytological specimens (see chapter on diagnostic cytology). These instruments should be dedicated for use in necropsies.

The prosector should wear personal protective gear to prevent the transmission of zoonotic diseases such as salmonellosis. At minimum, rubber or latex gloves should be worn. For larger reptiles, a laboratory coat, safety goggles, disposable plastic aprons, and rubber boots are often advisable.

Containers of fixatives should be available prior to beginning the necropsy. For routine purposes, neutral buffered 10% formalin (pH 7.4) is used. Other fixatives such as Bouin's or Zenker's may be useful, but the histology laboratory that will process the tissues should be consulted before using these fixatives. Samples to be submitted for transmission electron microscopy may be fixed by immersion in 2.5% glutaraldehyde or 4% paraformaldehyde in phosphate buffered saline (pH, 7.4).

Ventral surface of a lizard demonstrating the midline incision used to enter the coelomic cavity. [An identical approach is used for crocodilians.]

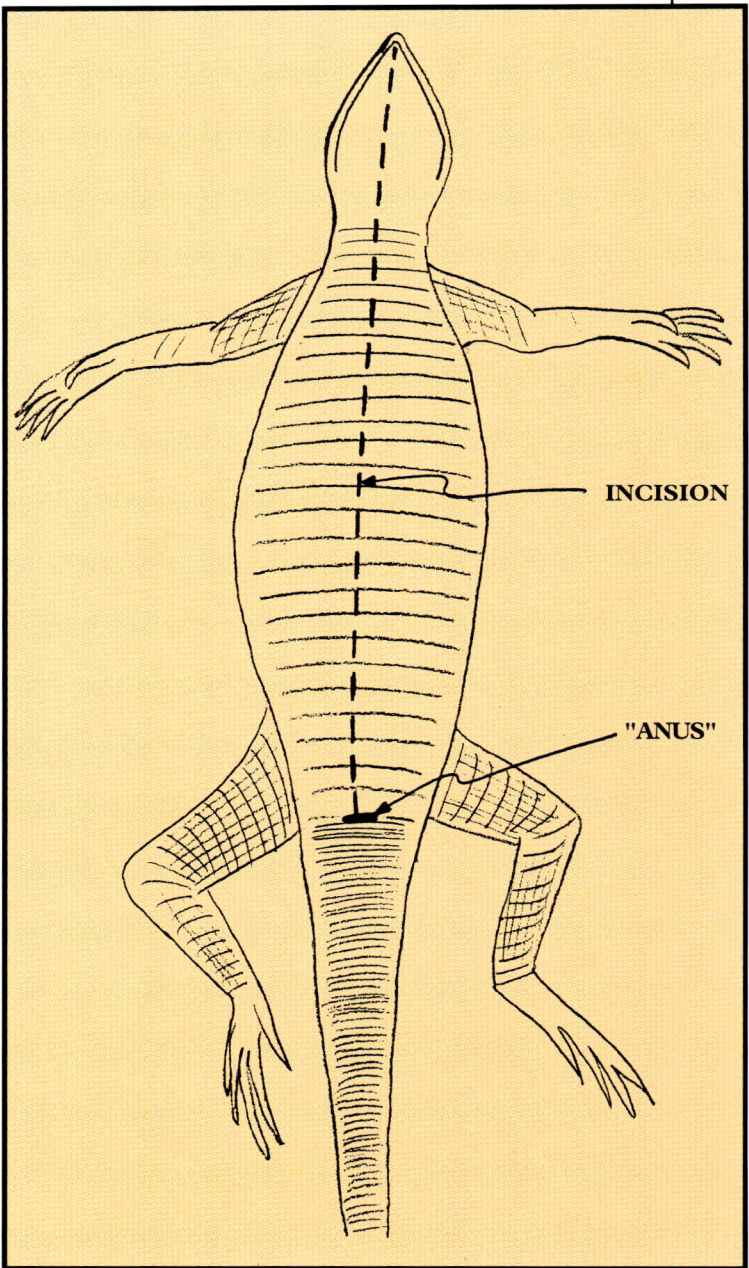

Culture materials should also be available prior to beginning the necropsy. Sterile metal instruments or a wire inoculating loop are used to acquire tissue samples; a flame (e.g., Bunsen burner) and alcohol should be available to sterilize tools between samples. A flat metal spatula may be necessary to sear contaminated surfaces prior to sampling. Sterile needles and syringes, cotton swabs, culture plates, specimen cups or test tubes filled with transport medium should be available for bacterial, fungal, and viral cultures of fluids or small pieces of tissue. Larger blocks of tissue may be frozen rapidly by immersion in isopentane cooled with carbon dioxide or liquid nitrogen and then stored in sterile specimen cups. The diagnostic laboratory should be consulted regarding the type and quantity of sample needed for specific classes of pathogens prior to submitting samples.

Disinfectants should be available for cleaning soiled equipment. Soap and water are acceptable for removing visible tissue remnants from the necropsy instruments. Subsequently, instruments should be immersed briefly in bleach or a similar germicide to kill residual pathogens.

NECROPSY PROCEDURE FOR REPTILES

The protocol outlined below is recommended for most reptiles. It ensures that all external and internal organs will be examined and that acceptable diagnostic specimens will be taken. The necropsy should be done in a consistent and systematic sequence. Tissues should be gathered in an order that will minimize autolysis to diagnostic features of tissue architecture. Ideally, labile tissues which undergo rapid postmortem decomposition (e.g.,eyes, gastrointestinal lining) should be removed and fixed first, followed by more stable tissues (e.g., bone, liver, lung, skin, spleen). In practice, a "systems" approach is often used in which the results of the clinical history and physical examination determine which organs will receive the earliest and most thorough evaluation. If a "systems" approach is used to organize the necropsy, the sequence set forth in the protocol below will have to be adjusted. The prosector must then remember to collect samples from the other organ systems. If the practitioner is unfamiliar with the anatomy of the reptile that is to be dissected, a text of reptile anatomy should be consulted prior to necropsy. All organs should be removed and examined at necropsy, and representative specimens should be fixed by immersion in formalin. Samples that lack distinguishing gross features (e.g., different parts of the gastrointestinal tract, multiple cu-

taneous ulcers) should be uniquely marked to ensure that appropriate regions are processed for histopathological analysis. Identification may be made by placing different tissues in labeled bags inside a single container, or by putting them in separate labeled vials. An additional alternative is to notch the specimen border (e.g., where one notch is esophagus, two notches for stomach, etc.). When saving lesions, take samples from the lesion margin and divide them in half with a cut placed perpendicular to the border of the abnormal focus; this practice will allow comparison of abnormal tissue to the adjacent normal components. Immerse one half of the lesion in fixative for histopathology, and freeze the other for potential microbial culture. A complete description of each gross lesion should be recorded. A major feature is location, including the affected organ and the specific area of the organ that is altered; for example, in the regurgitating snake a cross section of stomach wall would reveal mucosal thickening. Other important features of lesions will include the size, shape, color, consistency (soft or firm), and a semi-quantitative estimate of severity (minimal, mild, moderate, marked). In certain systemic diseases, lesions may occur in multiple organs, so an assessment of the number and distribution of abnormal foci is appropriate. Lesions may be photographed, especially to record their specific location and size (by use of a ruler or scale in the frame) as well as any unusual characteristics.

EXTERNAL EXAMINATION.

1. Record external identifying features such as tattoos and unusual markings as well as the body weight and length (tip of nose to base of tail).
2. Examine all external surfaces for lesions such as discoloration or absence of scales, ulcers, wounds, and external or subcutaneous masses.
3. Palpate the trunk and extremities to check for dehydration (loss of skin turgor), muscular atrophy, skeletal deformity, fluid accumulation (in the subcutis or the coelom), or enlargement of viscera. [A radiograph may be useful for demonstrating skeletal defects, the presence of ascites (fluid in the coelomic cavity), or abnormal size or density of viscera.] Bilaterally sym-

NOTE
Cold reptiles are sluggish, so first verify that the animal to be necropsied is actually dead. A postmortem examination rapidly becomes exciting if a chilled pit viper is "resurrected" by handling during the external examination or by the first incision during the internal examination!

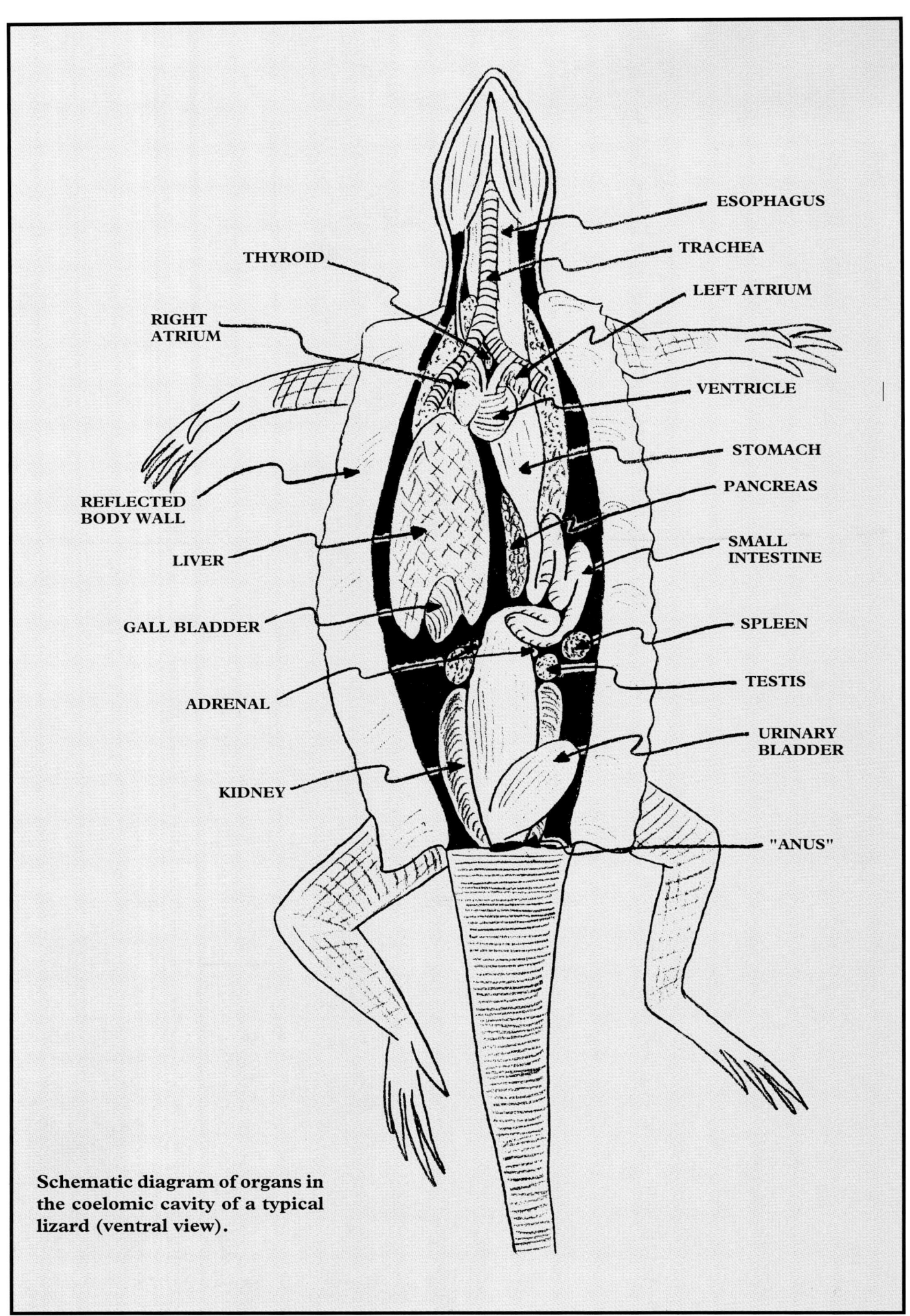

ESOPHAGUS

TRACHEA

THYROID

LEFT ATRIUM

RIGHT
ATRIUM

VENTRICLE

STOMACH

PANCREAS

REFLECTED
BODY WALL

SMALL
INTESTINE

LIVER

GALL BLADDER

SPLEEN

TESTIS

ADRENAL

URINARY
BLADDER

KIDNEY

"ANUS"

**Schematic diagram of organs in
the coelomic cavity of a typical
lizard (ventral view).**

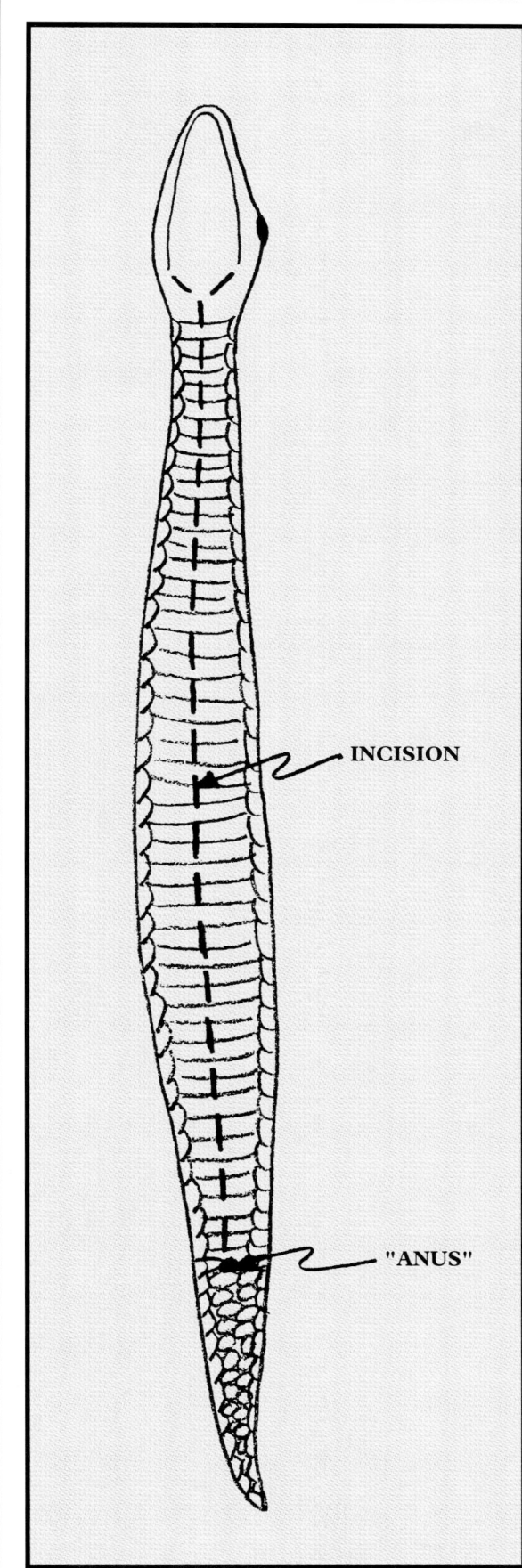

Ventral surface of a snake demonstrating the midline incision used to enter the coelomic cavity.

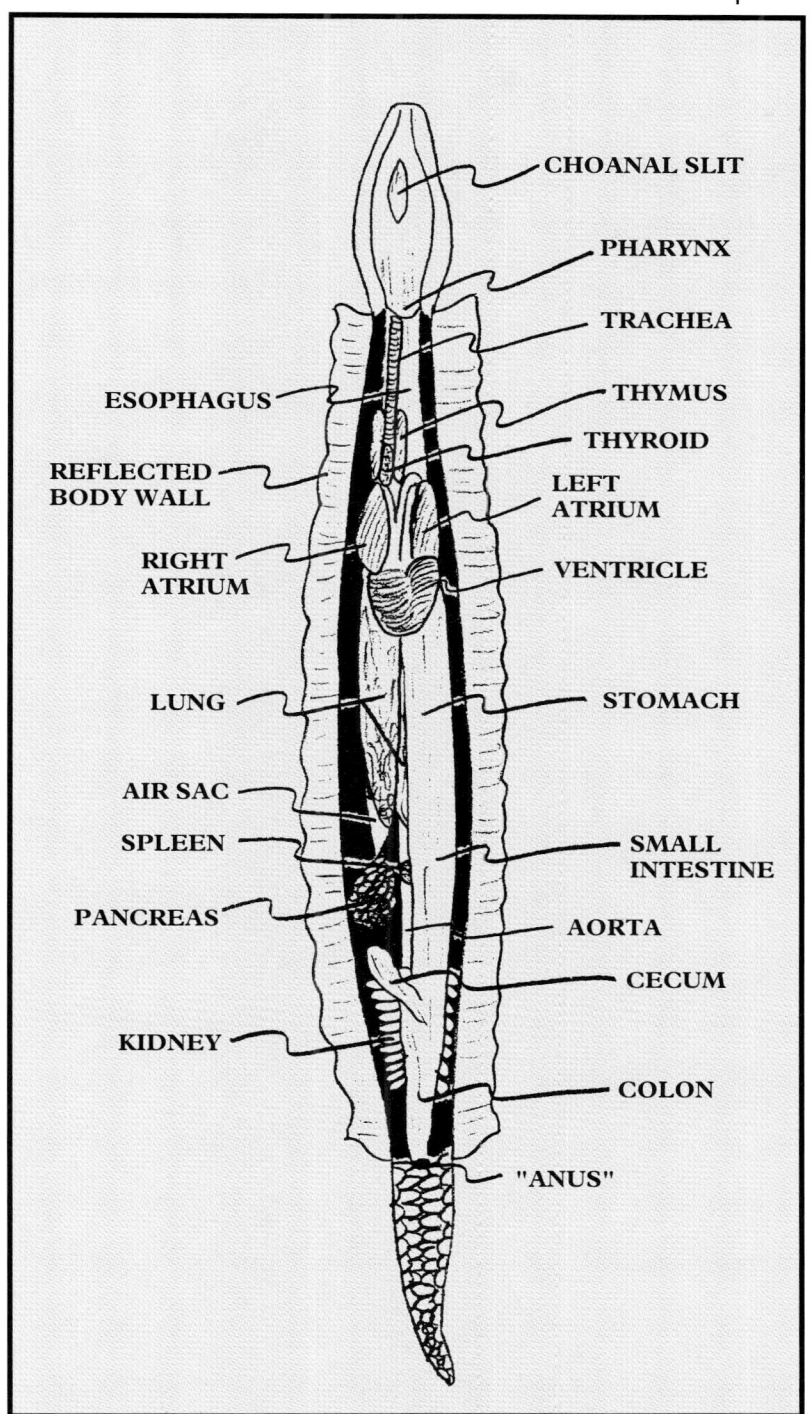

Schematic diagram of organs in the coelomic cavity of a typical snake (ventral view).

metrical structures such as eyes and limbs should be assessed for unilateral abnormalities.

4. Examine the eyes and body orifices (nares, oral cavity, anus) for discolored or ulcerated tissue, exudates, or parasites. Examine the lining of the oral cavity as well.

5. If external lesions are present, rapid cytological techniques are warranted (see chapter on diagnostic cytology). Cutaneous abnormalities such as discolored or deformed scales should be assessed using a skin scraping or a squash preparation. Exudates from ulcers or external orifices first should be sampled with sterile instruments

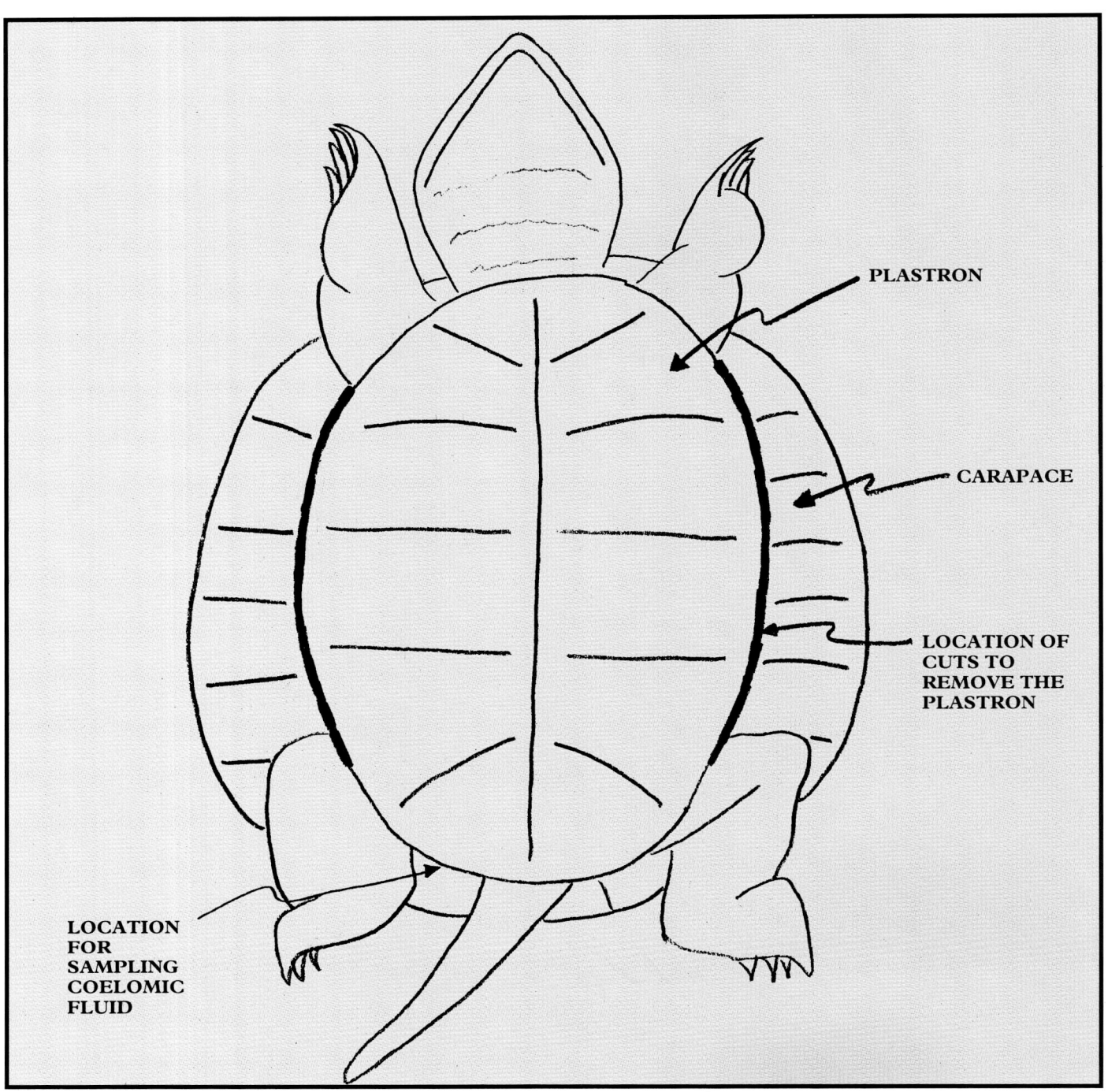

PLASTRON

CARAPACE

LOCATION OF CUTS TO REMOVE THE PLASTRON

LOCATION FOR SAMPLING COELOMIC FLUID

Ventral surface of a tortoise demonstrating the two cuts used to remove the plastron (lower shell) from the carapace (upper shell) to enter the coelomic cavity. If necessary, and *before the plastron is cut,* the cavity may be entered to collect sterile fluid for microbiological testing by piercing the skin between a hind limb and the tail.

for potential microbial cultures, and the remaining material should be examined cytologically. In like manner, fluid from a palpable subcutaneous mass may be removed by inserting a sterile needle to gather material for cytological and microbiological analyses.

6. Acquire samples of all cutaneous and subcutaneous lesions, particularly from those located on the dorsal surface (which will be inaccessible during the remainder of the necropsy). Divide samples in two. Immerse one half in fixative for histopathology, and where appropriate freeze the other for potential microbial culture.

INTERNAL EXAMINATION.

Care should be taken to keep the necropsy log sheets clean during the procedure. This may be accomplished by using an interim "cheat sheet" from which the preliminary findings are transcribed to clean paper, by the use of protective plastic sheets to cover log sheets, or by the use of an assistant to record findings.

7. After the external examination, remove the eyes. This step is easily performed with the carcass in ventral recumbency (belly down). Grasp the conjunctiva gently with a forceps and apply mild traction while freeing the globe with a pair of

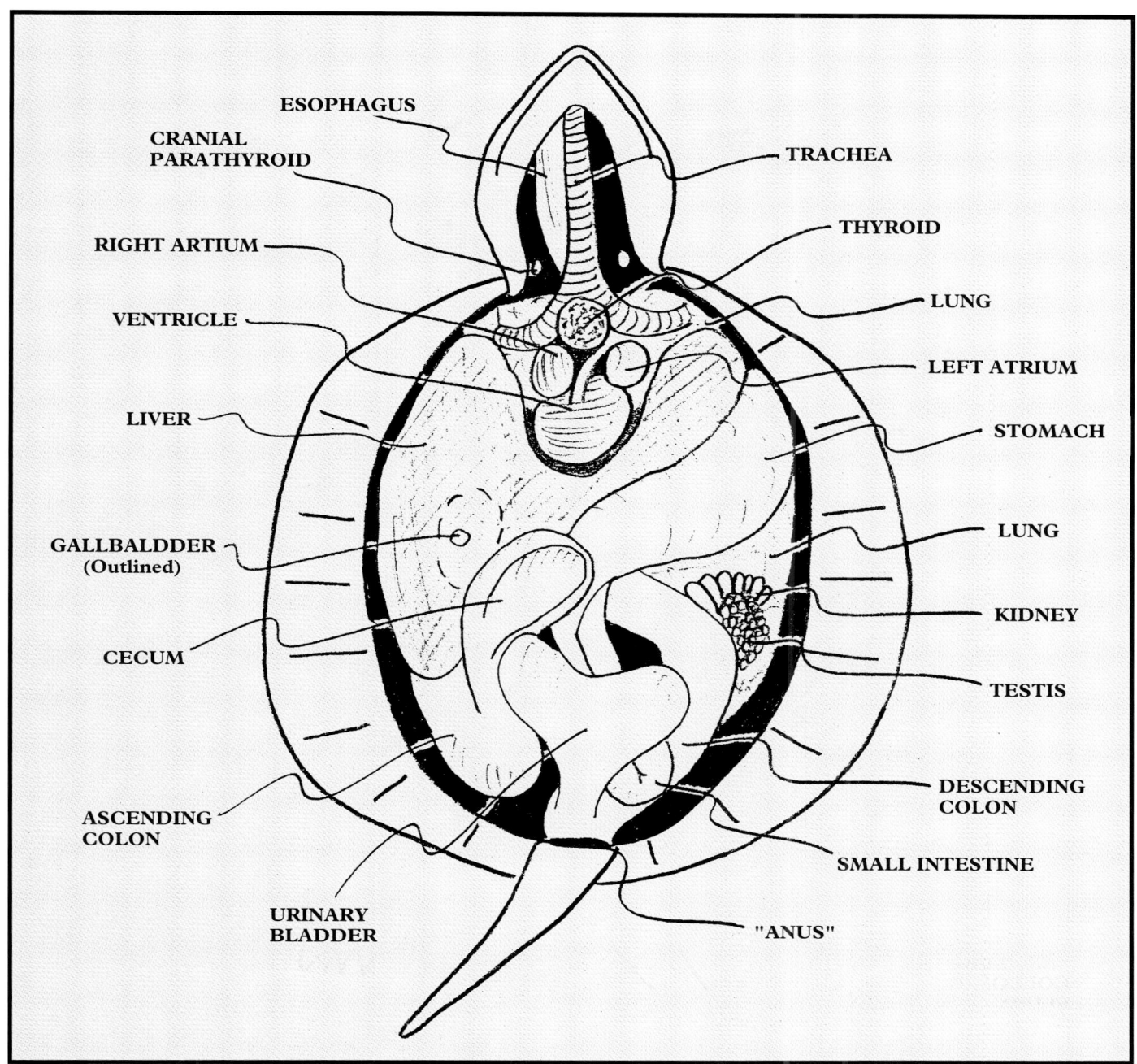

Schematic diagram (ventral view) of the organs first observed when the plastron of a typical tortoise is removed.

fine scissors or scalpel blade. At least one eye should be fixed intact for histopathological analysis; if acceptable to the histology laboratory, fixation in Bouin's fixative for up to 48 hours followed by transfer to and transport in 70% alcohol will likely provide better fixation of the retina than will formalin. The remaining eye may be opened to evaluate internal ocular structures.

8. Next, place the reptile in dorsal recumbency (belly up). For all reptiles but chelonians, cleanse the skin surface over the ventral abdomen with 70% alcohol, taking care to remove visible sources of dirt and matter. Make a small (2-5 cm) slit in the skin of the ventral midline and search for fluid in the coelomic cavity. If liquid is present, obtain a sample using a sterile needle and a three ml syringe; after aspirating the fluid, express all air from the syringe barrel and replace the cap on the needle.

9. Extend the incision cranially to the mandibular symphysis (chin) and caudally to the pelvis, and carefully reflect the skin and muscles of the ventral thoracic and abdominal walls. For chelonians, the slit to enter the coelomic cavity is made in the left caudal abdomen just cranial and medial to the left leg. After examining the cavity, the ventral shell (plastron) is removed by cutting its attachments to the dorsal shell (carapace) with a saw, hand ax, or tin snips. For all species of reptiles, care should be taken to avoid contaminating the coelomic lining and visceral surfaces while

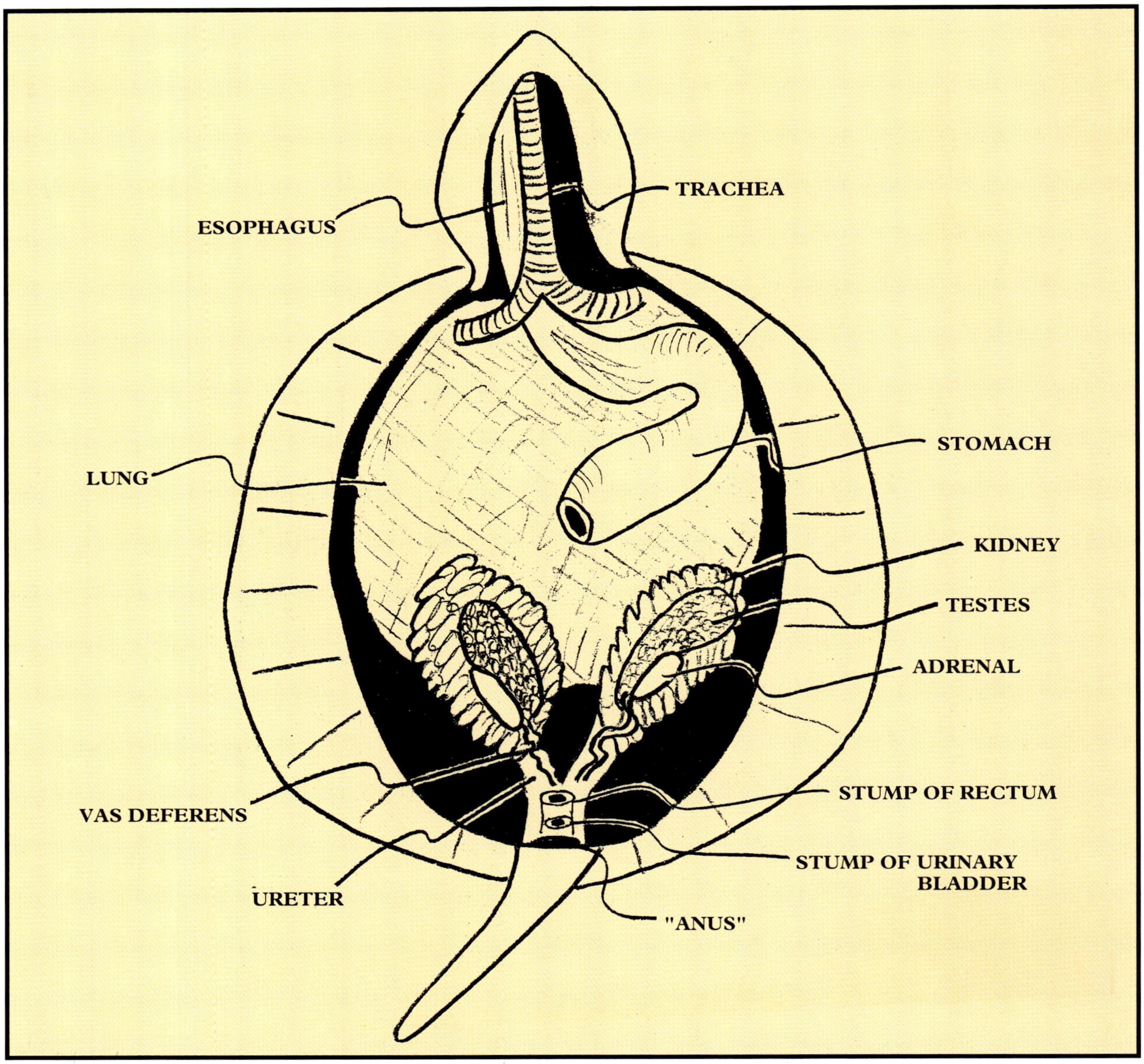

Schematic diagram of organs, ventral view, with the following labels:

ESOPHAGUS

TRACHEA

LUNG

STOMACH

KIDNEY

TESTES

ADRENAL

STUMP OF RECTUM

VAS DEFERENS

STUMP OF URINARY BLADDER

URETER

"ANUS"

Schematic diagram (ventral view) of organs that are attached to the inner surface of a typical tortoise's carapace. These are exposed by removing the organs (shown on p. 307) that are seen first when the plastron has been removed.

Plastron cut on a desert tortoise at the beginning of necropsy. Photo courtesy of Dr. Bernard A. Mangone.

removing the ventral body wall. The limbs may be disarticulated and reflected at this point if they are in the way.

10. Examine the coelomic lining for discoloration, adhesions between viscera, and the presence of large quantities of fluid (particularly if it is cloudy or opaque). Record the volume, color, and consistency of this liquid. Normal surfaces will be smooth and glistening, and only a small quantity (< 1 ml) of clear fluid may be present. Note the distribution and abundance of fat between the organs. Normal fat is white or tan to green. A fat sample (several cm³) should be frozen for potential toxicological analysis.

11. If warranted, acquire additional samples for microbial culture. All fluid and surface swab

Necropsy specimen of a desert tortoise with a ruptured bladder and large (arrow) cystolith in the coelomic cavity. Photo courtesy of Dr. Bernard A. Mangone.

samples for microbial culture must be taken before further manipulation of the viscera and carcass. Fluid specimens are obtained with a sterile needle and syringe or a sterile cotton swab. Adhesions and discolored areas of the coelomic walls and viscera (e.g., liver, spleen) may be sampled by excising tissue wedges (approximately four to eight cm^3) using sterile forceps and scissors and transferring them to sterile specimen cups. If the organ surface was contaminated during reflection of the body wall, it may be heat-sterilized for approximately five seconds with a heated flat spatula; the underlying tissue is then stabbed with a flame-sterilized wire loop.

12. Parasites found in the coelomic cavity (e.g., *Armillifer* sp.) should be retained in saline for subsequent identification.

13. Evaluate the position, size, shape, and color of all internal organs. Note and record any abnormalities before disturbing them. Solid organs such as the liver and spleen are normally dark brown to dark red and firm, lungs are pink and spongy, and the walls of the digestive tract are tan and firm. With autolysis, all tissues become dull red to dark green to black, and organ walls become friable.

14. Break or saw through a bone (e.g., femur, rib, sternum) to collect bone marrow. The marrow should be exposed to allow rapid fixation. Normal marrow is red or tan and gelatinous. Excessive fluid in the marrow may be indicative of malnutrition.

15. The thymus and thyroid/parathyroid complex should be removed from the ventral surface of the trachea. The thymus is a fatty white tissue in young animals but may be absent in older ones. The thyroids are dark brown to red and small. Their position varies with the species from the cranial trachea to the heart, so a careful examination will be required to locate them.

16. The viscera may now be removed by detaching the esophagus and trachea near the mandibular symphysis and peeling all organs away from the vertebral column. In chelonians, the lungs are intimately attached to the carapace, so they may remain attached at this stage of the necropsy. Examine the contents of the cloaca before freeing it from the anus. Remove samples from the cloaca for further analyses by

A tear in the apex of the urinary bladder is evident in this desert tortoise. Note the white crystals of urinary precipitate attached to the borders of the tear. Photo courtesy of Dr. Bernard A. Mangone.

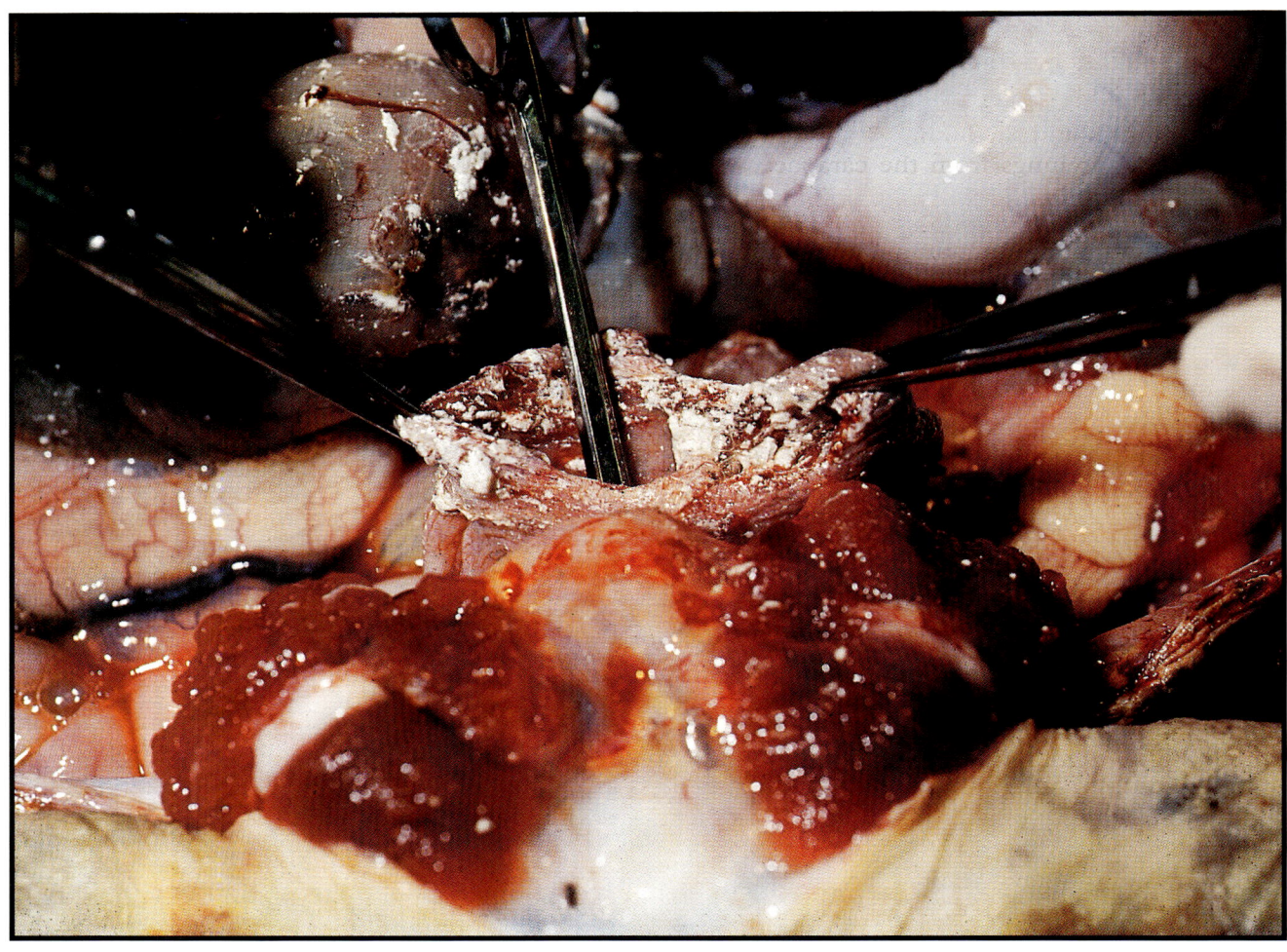

piercing the wall of the organ with a needle (to obtain fluid) or scalpel blade (to gather solids) before severing its anchoring tissues.

17. Separate the gastrointestinal tract from the remaining organs. Beginning at the cranial end, open the tract. Be careful to note lesions of the lining, particularly mucosal discoloration, thickening or ulceration or the presence of parasites. Scrape, squash, or touch preparations of lesions (for example, the stomach lining from the regurgitating snake) should be taken on glass slides for cytological evaluation. Visible parasites should be retained in saline for identification. A fecal sample from the cloaca should be retained for direct and sedimentation evaluations for parasite ova. Sections of all portions of the digestive tract should be uniquely identified and immersed in formalin; these portions should be flushed with formalin or opened before immersion to ensure adequate fixation. Separate pieces of tissue should be used for the fresh cytological and fixed histopathological specimens, and care should be taken not to abrade the mucosa of the portions removed for histopathology. At this point, discard the unused tissue and contents and clean the necropsy surface and instruments to avoid contaminating other organs.

18. Examine the remainder of the major viscera, including heart, kidneys, liver, lungs, pancreas, reproductive tract, spleen. Open the heart and major airways of the lungs to evaluate both the parenchyma and the lining. In chelonians, removal of the lungs from the carapace at this stage will automatically open the airways. If foci of abnormal coloration or texture or generalized tissue enlargement are observed (especially in the liver or spleen), touch preparations should be made. After removal and prior to fixation, the tissue is divided in two through the lesion using a sterile scalpel blade or clean necropsy knife. One cut surface is gently blotted on a paper towel to remove excess blood and tissue fluid, and the blotted surface is touched to several glass slides. After acquiring the touch preparation, the two halves of the mass can be immersed in fixative for histopathological analysis. Samples of solid organs should be no more than 0.5 cm to 1 cm thick when placed in fixative. Normal lung should float in the fixative. Alternatively, the untouched side (a block of tissue that is four to eight cm³) may be submitted frozen and submitted subsequently for microbiological or toxicological analysis; samples of solid organs such as kidney, liver, and spleen are particularly desirable for this purpose. Once samples are taken

for microbiological analysis, a series of parallel cuts should be made in the parenchyma of these organs.

19. The musculoskeletal system should be evaluated. In the carcass, examine the ventral surface of the vertebral column and the bones of the pelvis for displaced fractures. One or more joints should be opened, particularly if they are swollen. The joint capsule should be pierced with a clean knife, and the nature and quantity of the joint fluid should be noted. Normal fluid is scant, viscous, and clear. Increased amounts of discolored material may indicate the presence of an infection, so the fluid should be sampled with a sterile swab for possible microbiological culture. A bone including an articular surface (e.g., femur) should be fixed for histopathological analysis. Samples of skeletal muscle and the attached sciatic nerve may be obtained from the lateral surface of the proxi-

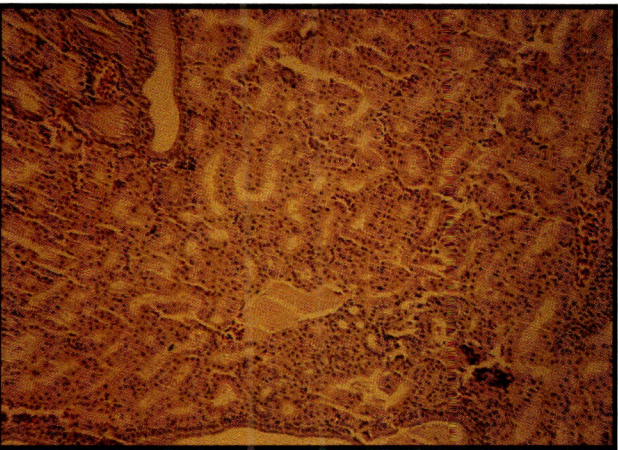

Necropsy specimen from the kidney of a collared lizard. Note the short cuboidal epithelial cells outlining central lumina. Hematoxylin and eosin, 100x magnification. Specimen provided by Dr. Todd Driggers. Photo courtesy of Dr. Lowell Ackerman.

mal hindlimb. Normal muscle is red to dark brown and firm.

20. If possible, open the calvaria and remove the brain. A pair of scissors may be suitable for this purpose in small reptiles with thin skulls (e.g., lizards, snakes), while a saw or hand ax may be necessary in larger animals (crocodilians). Evaluate the color of the meninges (the membranes covering the brain) and the color of the CSF. Red meninges or cloudy CSF may indicate an infectious process; a sterile swab should be inserted in an untouched recess to obtain a specimen for microbiological culture. The exposed brain will be soft and should be fixed *in situ* and removed later if the animal has been

dead for some time. The firmer brains of fresh carcasses may be removed and examined at the time of necropsy. A series of partial coronal (transverse) sections should be made through the dorsal surface of the brain. The cut surfaces should be examined for fluid-filled cysts before it is immersed in fixative. If present, the cystic fluid is sampled with a sterile swab. If necessary, the spinal cord may be exposed using rongeurs to remove the bony vertebrae. The spinal cord may be approached ventrally (from inside the carcass) or dorsally (by reflecting the dorsal skin and muscles to expose the vertebral arches). In many cases, the effort involved to expose and sample the reptile spinal cord is excessive. Therefore, this organ usually is examined only if the "systems" approach warrants it.

HANDLING, TRANSPORT, AND PROCESSING OF DIAGNOSTIC PATHOLOGY SPECIMENS

In general, specimens from the reptile postmortem examination are submitted for cytological, histopathological, microbiological, and/or toxicological analyses. Due to their expense, the clinical history and gross findings are used to select the appropriate tests. Additional samples may be retained in formalin or the freezer if further testing is required. Specimens are usually submitted to a commercial veterinary diagnostic laboratory. The laboratory should be contacted before acquisition of the samples to ensure that appropriate techniques are used for collecting, handling, and shipping the material. Ideally, the same facility may be used for all diagnostic tests and for any subsequent necropsies.

Cytological preparations such as needle aspirates and touch preparations should be air-dried.

The dried cells are then fixed for from one to five minutes in 100% methanol. Ideally, cytology specimens should be shipped separately from formalin-filled vials because formaldehyde vapors in the enclosed package can drastically alter the staining characteristics of cytological preparations (Meyer, 1987). Alternatively, cytological materials may be placed in an air-tight container sealed within a zip-locked plastic bag so that cytology and histopathology specimens from the same case may be shipped in one package.

Adequate fixation is critical to histopathological analysis. When fixing solid organs such as liver and spleen, blocks of tissue may be several centimeters long in two dimensions but must be no more than 0.5 cm to 1 cm thick in the third to allow for adequate penetration of the fixative. For a given container, 90% of the volume should be filled with the fixative, and only 10% should be taken by tissues. The fixative should be changed once within the first 24 hours after necropsy to ensure adequate fixation. Organs have been completely fixed when there is no zone of raw, red tissue in the center of the sample. Once the samples are fixed (48 hours to several days), the tissues can be shipped to the histology laboratory in a container filled with just enough fixative to cover them.

Frozen tissues, swabs and fluid-filled syringes for microbiology or toxicology may be shipped to the laboratory on dry ice by express mail. Materials should be placed in an air-tight container sealed within a zip-locked plastic bag. Regulations for shipping potentially biohazardous material should be obtained from the laboratory prior to shipment.

REFERENCE

—**Meyer, DJ:**
The management of cytology specimens. *Compend Contin Educ Pract Vet*, 1987; 9:10-16.

HUMANE EUTHANASIA

Luette Forrest, DVM
University of California, Irvine
University Laboratory Animal Resources
Irvine, CA 92717-1310

Luette Forrest D.V.M., Assistant Veterinarian University of California, Irvine received her veterinary degree at Michigan State University in 1980. Since then, she has been in clinical practice and basic research in rodents, Xenopus, and cell culture. Most of her research work has been in the department of physiology at the University of California, Irvine. Her current position is as a laboratory animal veterinarian. The facility includes various amphibians and reptiles, including turtles, lizards, and alligators. Dr. Forrest has previously published on Type I diabetes research in the BB rat.

INTRODUCTION

Before the discussion on "how's" of euthanasia begins, it would serve to reflect on the "why's" of the euthanasia. In a clear case of animal suffering; it is without question warranted and ethical. In other situations involving healthy animals, consider all other feasible options that minimize unnecessary loss of animal life, especially in endangered or threatened species. With the advent of electronic mail, it is possible to reach a wide audience of fellow herpetologists. Perhaps, through the use of electronic medium, tissue or other data collection and dissemination can be performed for fellow herpetologists.

The term "humane" is defined: marked by compassion, sympathy, or consideration for other human beings or animals. Euthanasia derives from the Greek word for literally "good death". (Websters). Some of the criteria for what constitutes a "good death" are as follows (AVMA panel on Euthanasia):

1. Handling prior to euthanasia in such a way as to

Rosy boas. Photo courtesy of Dr. Todd Driggers.

When an animal succumbs to an infectious disease, remember to properly disinfect the environment. Photo courtesy of Dr. Todd Driggers.

avoid stress and anxiety to the animal. Minimal handling is the best way to avoid stress. When practical, leave the animal in its regular environment. Animals handled by experienced people are less likely to be anxious.

2. Rapid unconsciousness. An unconscious animal cannot experience pain because the cerebral cortex is not functioning.

3. Subsequent loss of cardiac, respiratory and neurolgic function.

4. Verification of death prior to disposal of remains. Reptilian physiology being what it is, this is not always a straightforward task.

Due to the wide variety of species and situations encountered in herpetology, there is no single "best" method of euthanasia. Some considerations to take into account are:

1. Safety of the personnel. In cases of large or venomous reptiles, this is obvious, but it should take precedence above all else. Proper restraint by experienced people is essential in these cases. Newly caught individuals tend to be more aggressive. Safety of the personnel includes chemical considerations. For example, the use of inhalant anesthetics constitutes an occupational hazard. Inhalant anesthetics should only be used in a fume hood or other area where waste gases are scavenged. Another example: ether is extremely flammable and no longer advocated for any animal use.

2. Training of personnel. Veterinarians and other

scientifically educated personnel have knowledge of and access to techniques and drugs unavailable to others who may need to euthanize reptiles. When choosing the best method of euthanasia, you should weigh the level of experience of each person involved. Whenever possible, work with an experienced individual. Unesthetic or unsuccessful attempts at euthanasia are extremely stressful for all involved.

3. Distress and discomfort to the animal before and during euthanasia.

4. Minimal time to unconsciousness. Items three and four need to be considered in tandem. In some cases, you might have to trade-off the rapidity of time to unconsciousness if that will cause less overall stress to the animal.

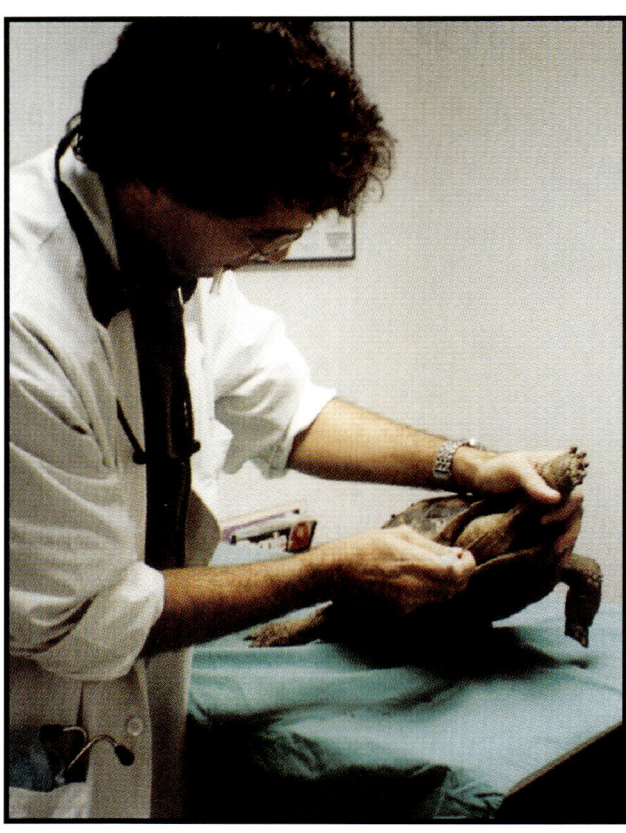

Dr. Bernard Mangone prepares for an injection into this desert tortoise. Photo courtesy of Dr. Lowell Ackerman.

5. Species involved. Techniques vary based on size, ease and safety of handling, as well as certain physiologic characteristics.

6. Field or indoors. When working in the field, the method must be portable and practical.

7. Use of specimen or tissue after death. In some cases; it is paramount the animal be left in good physical condition; in others, the tissue should not be contaminated with chemicals.

8. Cost and time. Generally, these should be lesser considerations. Cost of any acceptable method is not unreasonable.

METHODS OF EUTHANASIA

The recommended methods of euthanasia in this chapter are consistent with the AVMA panel recommendations of acceptable methods. (Mention of other methods approved in Canada and Europe are noted as such.) Unless otherwise stated, the information in this section derives directly from the AVMA guide, which is both current and concise. Some euthanasia methods are inhumane and should not be used.

CHEMICAL METHODS

Chemical methods of euthanasia include injectible, inhalant, and anaesthetic chemical agents.

INJECTABLE CHEMICAL AGENTS

Intravenous administration of euthanasia chemicals is the preferred route of injection in terms of rapidity. In most reptiles, this is technically difficult. For reptiles, you may administer the drug into the heart or body cavity (reptiles have no diaphragm) as well as in the muscle or underneath the skin.

Barbiturates. These drugs are sedatives and the most common choice of injectable agents. Barbiturates are controlled substances, and available only to approved individuals, either in medicine or research; records must be kept of their disposition.

One widely used barbiturate derivative is sodium pentobarbital; it is the active ingredient in many commercially available euthanasia solutions. The recommended does for reptile euthanasia is 60mg/kg(ILAR), which is lower than the mammalian dose of 100 mg/kg. However, since the endpoint is death, it is better to be generous when weight is an unknown.

T 61. This is an acceptable agent in Europe and Canada.(Canadian Council, Zwart et al, 1989), but unavailable in the United States. This drug should only be used intravenously, as there is differential absorption of ingredients when given by other routes.

Procaine. There is a reference to procaine hydrochloride as an euthanasia agent, used in a dose of 500 mg/kg (Livesay, 1958). Chemical suppliers of procaine hydrochloride sell only to organizations. Although not approved by the AVMA panel, this may be a reasonable choice in field collection where you cannot obtain controlled substances. I have used Benzocaine (a procaine analog) as a submersible anesthetic in frogs, and it seems to work rapidly in this situation.

Urethane, Chloralose. These agents are approved by the Canadian Council for Experimental Animals, but not by the AVMA. Chloralose (chloral hydrate) is used as a saturated solution, given at 1-10 ml. Urethane is dosed at a 10-20% solution, also 1-10

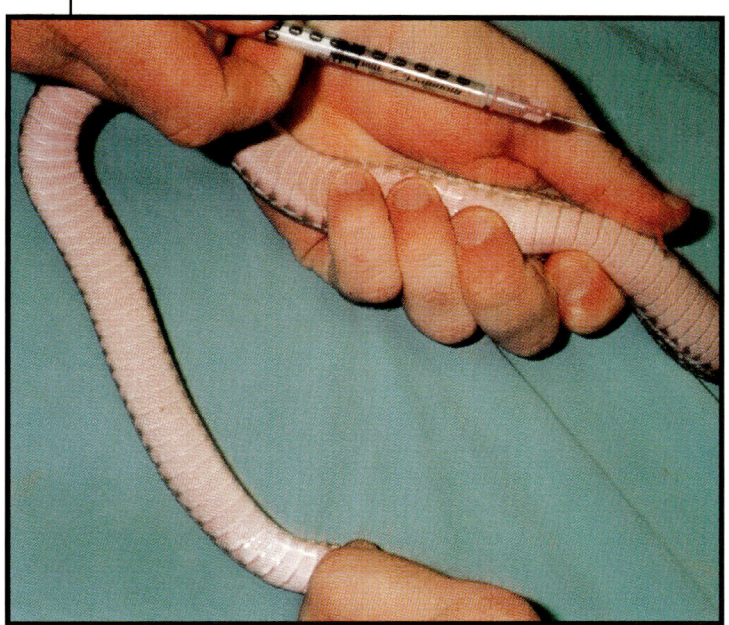

Dr. Todd Driggers prepares for an injection into this coachwhip snake. Photo courtesy of Dr. Lowell Ackerman.

ml. Both are given into the body cavity. Urethane is a carcinogen, and proper handling is required.

Warning

Urethane is a carcinogen. To avoid contamination or exposure, use proper handling and storage techniques when using this chemical.

INHALANT CHEMICAL AGENTS

When euthanizing reptiles by inhalants, keep in mind the well-developed capability in some reptiles to undergo anaerobic metabolism There are documented studies of various reptiles ability to tolerate anoxia. Chelonians in particular have well-developed anoxic capacity, some surviving over 24 hrs. in nitrogen (Gans, 1976). Other reptile species listed survived less than 2 hours in this condition. Alligators, crocodiles, and some others have hemoglobin, which is more efficient at delivering oxygen (Komiyama, 1995). An anecdotal report mentions a Western rattlesnake placed in a jar with an ether soaked jar for an hour that was "sluggish but not anesthetized" (Sedgewick, 1980). When using this method, therefore, ensure death by allowing the animal to remain in the agent for a prolonged period that can be several hours (Cooper, 1989). If there is any doubt that the animal is indeed dead, follow up with a physical method (crushing of skull) of euthanasia once the animal is rendered unconscious.

For small reptiles, it is convenient to use a desiccator jar (Figure 1). Place the agent of choice on a piece of cotton or paper in the bottom of the jar, place the grid, and allow the chamber to equilibrate for a few minutes prior to animal being placed. This system is especially useful in the case of dry-ice euthanasia, where the dry ice may cause burning of the animal's skin. You can also attach gas tanks and/or anesthetic machines to plastic chambers (Figure 2). Many veterinary clinics use this type of chamber to anesthetize fractious cats.

ANESTHETIC AGENTS

Recommendations for all anesthetic agents are essentially the same. On anesthetic machines, adjust the setting to the maximum of the vaporizer. In the majority of situations, time to unconsciousness is within minutes. The AVMA lists in order of preference:

—Halothane
—enflurane
—isoflurane
—methoxyflurane
—ether

Fig. 1. Example of a desiccation jar. Dry ice is placed in the bottom and the animal is on top of the perforated disc. Photo courtesy of Dr. Luette Forrest.

CARBON DIOXIDE

This gas is heavier than air, nonflammable, nonexplosive, and poses little toxic risk to personnel. Carbon dioxide can be used to euthanize animals used for food, and the gas does not affect tissue ar-

Warnings

Anesthetic agents can cause physical harm. To avoid inhalation, use proper safety gear, and use anesthetic agents only in an area properly equipped with fume hoods or some other vapor scavenger system.

Ether is EXTREMELY flammable, and should be avoided for safety reasons.

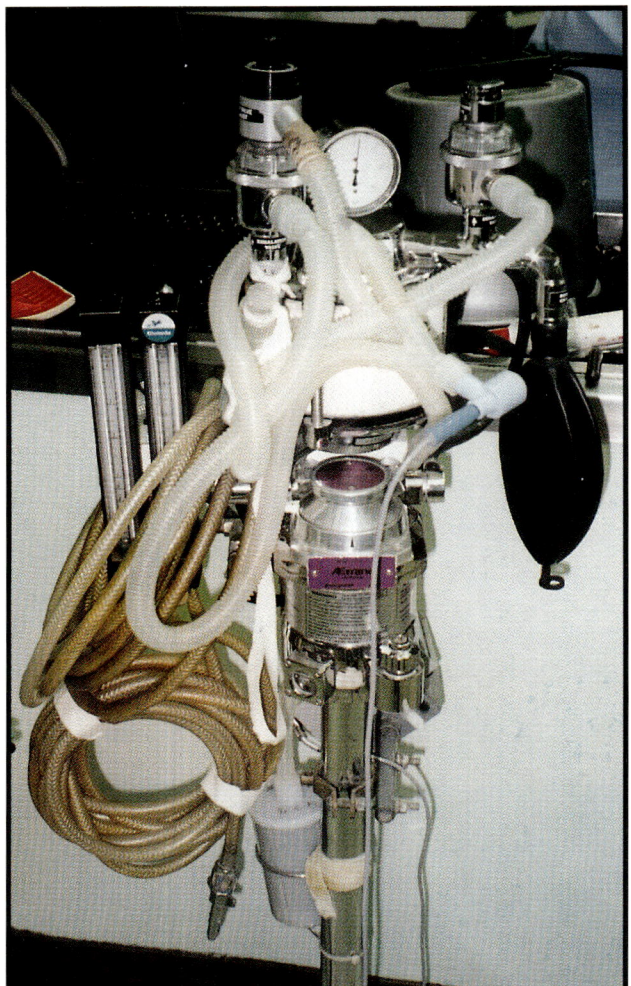

Inhalation anesthesia can be used for euthanasia, but halothane would be a better choice than the isoflurane in this unit. Photo courtesy of Dr. Lowell Ackerman.

chitecture. It is available to laypersons in the form of gas cylinders or dry ice.

When dry ice is properly stored, it will last several days; it can be used for field work. Euthanasia from carbon dioxide occurs due to the depressant and anesthetic effects of the gas. Death occurs within 5 minutes of inhalation in cats and day-old chickens. Euthanize only terrestrial species by this agent.

UNACCEPTABLE CHEMICAL METHODS OF EUTHANASIA

There are many chemical agents that are not acceptable as methods of euthanasia. These include succinylcholine, cyanide, strychnine, chloroform, potassium chloride, magnesium chloride, and trichloroethylene. Nitrogen and helium cause death by anoxia alone and are also not acceptable.

PHYSICAL METHODS OF EUTHANASIA

These methods are options to be used in some situations. If correctly done by experienced individuals, these methods can be very rapid. If not done properly, these methods can cause injury to both human and animal. This section will derive in large

Fig. 2. A tank of carbon dioxide attached to a plastic container. Photo courtesy of Dr. Luette Forrest.

part from the manuscript published by J.E. Cooper, Euthanasia of Amphibians and Reptiles.

The objective of physical euthanasia is to damage the central nervous system enough to kill the animal instantly. However, the physiology of some reptiles, including turtles, is resistant to measures such as decapitation or exsanguination (due to hypoxia resistance). Heads of some decapitated reptiles show signs of consciousness for up to fifty minutes, including movement in response to touch, defense behavior patterns, and pupillary reflexes (Klauber, 1956). Prior sedation or induction of torpor by refrigeration may greatly facilitate physical euthanasia. However, it is important to note that reptiles which have been cooled are not less susceptible to pain.

Some type of trauma must be delivered to the brain in order for physical methods to cause rapid death. The trauma can be created by concussion (striking the head with a heavy object or, in the larger species, by shooting). Some turtles have a significant bony crest on the skull, which may hamper this technique. For all species, the point of aim should be just behind the eyes. In some reptiles, there are parts of the skull in this location, referred to as windows, where the bone is a single layer. Some species have considerable bony areas, and in some cases, bullets or bolts may deflect, leaving the animal wounded instead of killed.

SPECIAL CONSIDERATIONS

Chelonians. Turtles and tortoises have many "death-resistant" features. One of the problems with euthanizing chelonians using physical methods is retraction of the head. Dr. Cooper advises the following methods to prevent retraction of the head:

—Land tortoises: Place the animal in shallow, tepid, water.

—Large marine species: Setting the turtle head-upwards on frame angled at 45 degrees may cause some extension of head.

—Soft-shelled species: Turning the animal on its back may cause the head to protrude as the animal attempts to right itself.

As an additional precaution, exsanguination should follow the head injury. Penetrating captive bolts must be placed on the correct part of the skull. Nonpenetrating captive bolts are not recommended for euthanasia (AVMA).

Crocodilians. It is imperative that you restrain both the jaws and tail of a crocodilian during euthanasia. You can restrain small specimens by placing a rope over the jaw and applying pressure on the tail. For small speciments, a small rifle or penetrating captive-bolt pistol is effective. Only experts should handle larger animals, and heavy caliber rifles should be used on these specimens.

FREEZING (HYPOTHERMIA)

Although mentioned in several references as a euthanasia method, Both the AVMA and the Cooper manuscript advise against this method. Freezing and the formation of ice crystals are likely to cause pain and distress in the animal. In addition, there is a well-documented freeze-tolerance capacity in exothermic animals (Storey, 1992). Some reptiles can endure freezing for weeks.

HYPERTHERMIA (HOT WATER)

This method is inhumane and is not recommended.

SUMMARY

There is little concrete information available on euthanasia of reptiles. Much research could be carried out in this area. However, there are some specific recommendations that can be made:
1. Barbituate injection is the method of choice when circumstances allow.
2. Inhalant anesthetic is the next preferred method.
3. Carbon dioxide is a good choice for laypersons or field collectors, as it is readily available, safe, and nondamaging to tissue.
4. Physical methods should be reserved for experienced personnel that are not squeamish. Torpor or sedation should precede this method if practicable.

REFERENCES AND RECOMMENDED READING

—**American Society of Ichthyologists and Herpetologists, Herpetologist League.**
Society for the use of live amphibians and reptiles in field research. *J Herpetology* 1987: 21(Suppl 4):1-14.

—**American Veterinary Medical Association Report on the AVMA panel on euthanasia.**
J Am. Vet. Med. Ass., 1993; 202 (2) : 229-249.

—**Committee on Pain and Distress in Laboratory Animal, ILAR, Commission on Life Sciences, National Research Council:**
Recognition of Pain and Distress in Laboratory Animals, National Academy Press, Washington, DC, 1992.

—**Cooper JE, Ewbank R, Platt C, et al.,**
Euthanasia of amphibians and reptiles. London: UFAW/WSPA, 1989.

—**Gans C, Dawson W:**
Biology of the Reptilia Volume 5. Academic Press, London 1976 556 pp.

—**Guide to the Care and use of Experimental Animals.**
Canadian Council on Animal Care Volume 2, 1984.

—**Komiyama NH, Miyazaki G, Tame J, Nagai K:**
Transplanting a unique allosteric effect from crocodile into human haemoglobin. *Nature* 1995:373(6511):244-6.

—**Livesay RL:**
Procaine Hydrochloride as a killing agent for reptiles and amphibians. *Herpetologica* 1958:13:280.

—**Sedgewick C:**
Anesthesia of Reptiles. Kirk's Current Veterinary Therapy VII W.B. Saunders Philadelphia PA 1980 1360 pp.

—**Storey KB; Storey JM:**
Natural freeze tolerance in ectothermic vertebrates. *Annu. Rev. Physiol.* 1992: 54:619-37.

—**Zwart P, de Vries HR, Cooper Je, Het correct doden van vissen, amfibien, reptielen en vogels.**
Tijdschrift voor Diergeneeskunde 1989:114:557-565.

DIAGNOSTIC PROCEDURES: CYTOLOGY

Brad Bolon DVM, MS, PhD*
and
Trudy Hagstrom CMT
Pathology Associates International
  Corporation (an SAIC Company),
National Center for Toxicological Research,
P.O. Box 26
Jefferson, Arkansas 72079

*Address correspondence to: Dr. Brad Bolon, Wyeth-Ayerst Research, Division of Molecular Genetics, CN 8000 Rm. 2005, Princeton, NJ 08543-8000; E-mail bolonb@war.wyeth.com

Brad Bolon, D.V.M., M.S., Ph.D. is a board-certified veterinary pathologist. He is extensively trained in toxicologic neuropathology; exotic animal pathology (reptiles and fish) is an avocation.

Trudy Hagstrom, M.A. is a certified medical technologist with over fifteen years' experience in preparing and evaluating cytological specimens.

INTRODUCTION

Cytology is the discipline in which the numbers, types, and/or structural features of cells are examined microscopically to obtain insight regarding a patient's health. As with other species, microscopic examination of *ante mortem* specimens from ill reptiles provides crucial diagnostic

Mycoplasma-positive desert tortoise with severe mucous nasal discharge. The discharge can be effectively evaluated by impression-smear cytology. Photo courtesy of Dr. Bernard A. Mangone.

TABLE 1

COMMON CLINICAL INDICATIONS FOR CYTOLOGICAL EVALUATION

Specimen	Specific Sign(s)	Type of Sample
Fluid		
Blood	Anemia, Fever	Smear, Concentration Prep
Cerebrospinal Fluid (CSF)	Altered Behavior, Ataxia, Seizures	Concentration Prep
Cyst Contents	Palpable Fluid-filled Mass	Concentration Prep
Effusion	Coelomic Enlargement	Smear, Concentration Prep
Lavage (Organ Wash)	Regurgitation (stomach) Diarrhea (colon) Respiratory Distress (lung)	Smear, Concentration Prep
Synovial Fluid	Swollen Joint	Concentration Prep
Tissue		
Bone Marrow	Anemia	Needle Aspirate, Touch Prep
Discolored Organ	Abnormal Color (at surgery or necropsy)	Needle Aspirate, Touch Prep
Enlarged Organ	Palpable Enlargement	Needle Aspirate, Touch Prep
Mass	Palpable Mass	Needle Aspirate, Touch Prep
Ulcer	Visible Skin or Mucosal Penetration	Scrape, Touch Prep, Wet Mount
Scale Abnormality	Crusted or Twisted Scale	Wet Mount
Excreta		
	Regurgitation (stomach) Diarrhea (colon) Edema (Kidney)	Smear, Concentration Prep, Wet Mount

information. A variety of materials may be assessed by routine cytological techniques. The usefulness of cytological specimens in formulating husbandry and disease management programs depends on sample quality and the practitioner's interpretive expertise. This chapter describes appropriate methods to obtain and process cytologic specimens from reptiles. Basic tenets of interpretation are also considered, but this skill requires considerable practice and, in most cases, some knowledge of reptile class- and species-specific patterns of disease.

TYPES OF SPECIMENS

Common cytological specimens and the reasons for acquiring them are illustrated in Table 1. These samples may be collected along with materials for other diagnostic tests such as histopathology, electron microscopy, microbiology, or serum chemistry analysis. In many instances, a single specimen can be divided between two or more tests. The present chapter describes a plan for acquiring cytological specimens from a variety of tissues and fluids. While sampling methods will be referenced (to sources in this volume and elsewhere), this chapter concentrates on the reasons for selecting a particular cytological specimen and the appropriate means for handling, shipping, and processing such materials.

In general, diagnostic cytology may be performed using cells from three classes of specimens. The most common source for cells is a fluid, such as blood, cerebrospinal fluid (CSF), contents of a cyst, a discharge (e.g., nasal), or effusion into a body cavity. For diagnostic purposes, the cell-rich liquid aspirated from a tubular organ (e.g., cloaca, lung, nasal cavity) during lavage is also considered a "body fluid". A second major source for cytological materials are tissue lesions such as discolored or enlarged organs, masses, ulcers, or abnormal scales—in short, from tissues that appear different than expected. Finally, cells in excreta may be useful indicators of disease. Collection procedures usually result in recovery of sufficient cells to permit the preparation of multiple slides,

Green iguana 10 days after opening the tympanum to drain an abscess. Procedure performed by Terry Campbell DVM, PhD. Photo courtesy of Dr. Bernard A. Mangone.

which should be air-dried and retained in the event that special procedures (e.g., to demonstrate microbes) are necessary.

COLLECTION OF CYTOLOGICAL SPECIMENS

FLUIDS

To prevent additional stress to an ill reptile, the practitioner must employ specific knowledge from the literature or personal experience regarding appropriate collection site(s) for various biological fluids. These sites vary greatly among reptilian classes and species. If the skin must be penetrated during collection (e.g., for blood, CSF, body cavity effusion, or joint fluid), the scales at the puncture site should be swabbed with an organic iodine followed by 70% alcohol and allowed to dry before sampling. Anesthesia may be required to obtain certain samples (e.g., CSF, lung washes) from many species.

Animal handling techniques and collection sites for acquiring biological fluids from reptiles have been well described (reviewed in Jacobson, 1993). Multiple sites (each with its own advantages or disadvantages) may be available for blood collection depending on the size and cooperation of the individual animal (see Chapters in this volume on hematology and biochemistry; also Frye, 1991; Willette-Frahm, 1995). Peripheral veins (especially the ventral coccygeal vein) are readily accessible locations in most reptiles (Samour et al., 1984). Drops of blood squeezed from closely trimmed toenails or collected from capillary tubes placed in the orbital sinus (located in the eye socket medial to the globe) also yield acceptable samples in chelonians and lizards, while cardiac puncture may be used in crocodilians and snakes. Blood is drawn from the veins and heart using a 22 to 25 gauge, 1 inch needle or butterfly catheter attached to a 3 to 6 ml syringe. Collection of CSF from reptiles is difficult at best. The CSF reservoir of chelonians and crocodilians may be tapped dorsally via the atlantooccipital joint using a 25 gauge needle attached to a 3 ml syringe, but penetration of the overlying supravertebral blood vessels usually results in contamination of the CSF sample with peripheral blood. Interlocking of the fragile vertebrae in snakes and lizards prevents acquisition of CSF in most cases. Fluids may be removed from cysts or body cavities (e.g., coelom, swollen joint) by introducing a needle (22 to 25 gauge) through the chamber wall. Placement of a needle in a palpable cyst is performed while gently compressing the mass in order to stabilize the fluid-filled cav-

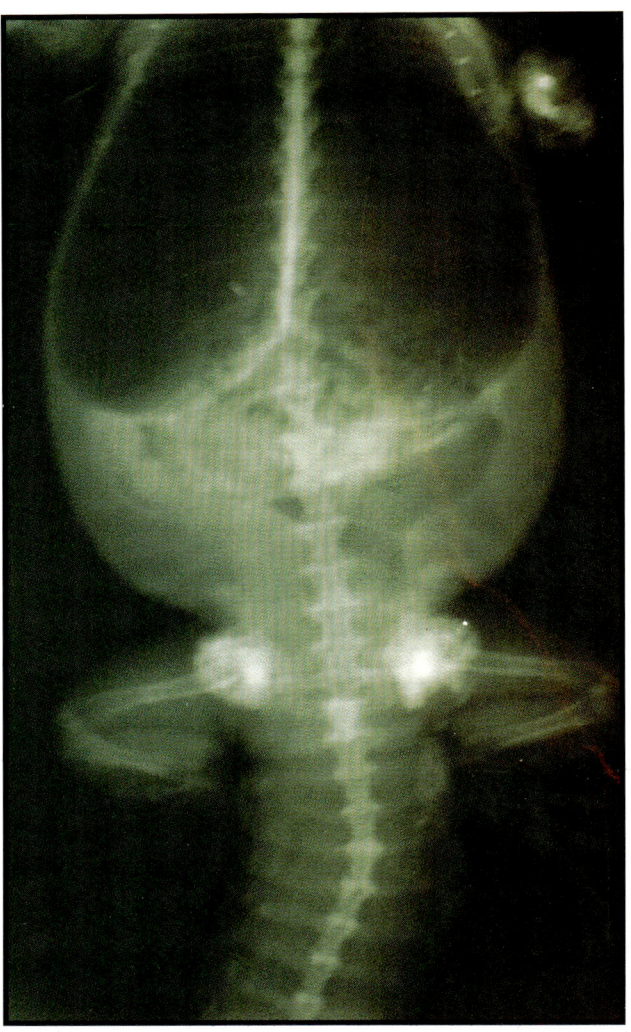

Radiograph of a lizard with gout. Note the bilateral opacities in the coxofemoral (hip) joints. Radiograph provided by Dr. Todd Driggers. Photo courtesy of Dr. Lowell Ackerman.

ity; this technique may also be used to acquire uncontaminated urine samples from reptiles (chiefly chelonians) that have large urinary bladders. When entering a body cavity, the needle is directed through the body wall at a shallow angle and for only a short distance to avoid trauma to viscera (and contamination of the specimen with parenchymal cells). The needle point is then redirected toward the dependent (lowest) part of the cavity or, alternatively, passed through the wall of a fluid-filled organ (e.g., urinary bladder) to gather the fluid sample. Discharges from body orifices (e.g., nares) may be sampled directly by touching a clean (dust- and grease-free) glass slide to the fluid or by transferring several drops from the mucosa to a glass slide using a sterile swab. Finally, organ washes are obtained by introduction of sterile saline (pH 7.4) into a tubular organ (e.g., cloaca, lung, nasal cavity) through a flexible sterile catheter attached to a syringe (3 ml). The length of the catheter is approximated by measuring the depth of the organ passages based on either clinical experience or, preferably, measurements taken from the patient's body or a regional radiograph. A small quantity of saline (0.25 to 3 ml, using greater volumes in larger reptiles) is injected and aspirated several times using a syringe before being removed

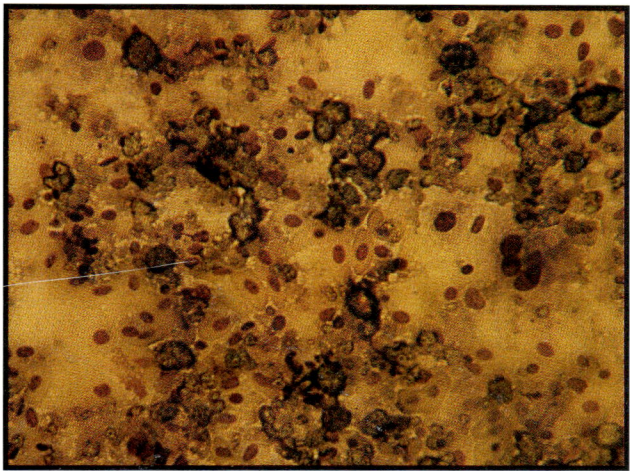

Fine-needle aspirate from a lizard with gout. Note the tophi (urate crystals), erythrocytes and large mononuclear cells. Sample provided by Dr. Todd Driggers. Photo courtesy of Dr. Lowell Ackerman.

for analysis. The tip of the catheter can be repositioned so that multiple luminal regions of the organ may be sampled with a single wash. Alternatively, the syringe can be filled with fresh saline before the catheter is relocated so that different sites can be evaluated individually. When collecting a wash, the location of the organ must be known prior to introduction of the catheter to prevent penetration of the organ wall (if the catheter is too long) or inadvertent sampling of the wrong site (if the catheter is improperly positioned). For example, lung position varies significantly among groups of reptiles, and for snakes even between members of the same family (Jacobson, 1993). Organ location in a given species is verified either by using published reports, radiographs, or through the practitioner's prior experience.

LESIONS

Cytological specimens can be obtained readily from lesions affecting either body surfaces or solid tissues. Surface defects are usually masses, ulcers, or diseased scales; changes to internal tissues may include alterations in color or texture, generalized organ enlargement (organomegaly), or the presence of a discrete mass. Sampling methods for these lesions include needle aspirates, touch preparations (touch preps), scrapes, or wet mounts. These diagnostic procedures are extremely valuable because such techniques are easily learned,

and the samples from tissue lesions are rapidly and easily acquired, processed, and interpreted. Several methods may be appropriate for any given condition, so the choice of sampling procedure will depend upon the preferences of the practitioner and the cytologist.

Needle aspirates are generally acquired from palpable masses prior to their removal, or from enlarged viscera that may be palpated through the body wall. The skin over the mass or organ is disinfected with an organic iodine and 70% alcohol, and a 20 to 25 gauge, 1 inch needle attached to a 3-12 ml syringe is inserted into the lesion. Full negative pressure (produced by drawing the plunger back by 3 to 5 ml) to aspirate cells is applied by rapidly retracting the syringe plunger; additional regions of the mass may be sampled while the plunger is still retracted by redirecting the needle (without removing it from the mass). When sampling is completed, the plunger is gently released before withdrawing the needle from the skin so that cells and tissue fluid remain in the needle shaft. Finally, the syringe is removed from the needle and filled with air (3 to 5 ml). After reattaching the needle, aspirated cells are expelled onto a clean (dust- and grease-free) glass slide by rapid depression of the plunger. When a viscus has been biopsied in this fashion, the animal should be monitored for clinical signs of internal hemorrhaging. Needle aspiration may also be used in crocodilians, large lizards, and some chelonians to remove bone marrow from the greater trochanter of the femur (Frye, 1991). The procedure is performed under anesthesia. A rigid trochar containing a stylet is required to bore a channel through the bone for insertion of the biopsy needle. After the bony cortex is penetrated, the stylet is withdrawn and an 18 to 25 gauge needle attached to a 3 ml syringe is inserted in its place. The point of the biopsy needle should be advanced well into the marrow cavity, while the tip of the trochar should remain near the endosteal surface. Cells are aspirated using gentle negative pressure (to prevent rupture of the fragile blood cell precursors) and then expelled immediately onto a clean glass slide (to prevent clotting in the needle).

Touch preparations are usually prepared from excised masses or enlarged or discolored tissues. The areas to be sampled must be carefully selected so that the cytological specimens will be representative of the lesion. In general, collect solid (viable) tissue from the lesion periphery and avoid friable (necrotic) and hemorrhagic regions which often occupy the center of large masses. The best imprints are made by making repeated touch preparations from small pieces of tissue. After removal at surgery or necropsy and *prior to fixation*, the mass or tissue is divided into small blocks with

Normal profile of a desert tortoise. Photo courtesy of Dr. Bernard Mangone.

cut surfaces of 0.5 to 1.0 cm^2 using a new scalpel or razor blade. Each piece to be sampled is grasped with forceps (on the side opposite the cut surface), and the cut surface is gently blotted several times on a paper towel to remove excess blood and tissue fluid. The blotted surface is touched multiple times to one or more glass slides; avoid excessive compression of tissue blocks during blotting to reduce morphological artefacts resulting from pressure damage to cells. Depending on the size of the tissue, it may be touched from five to 20 times on each slide. Imprints should not overlap. Touch preparations may also be made from ulcers on the skin or digestive tract using a comparable "blot and touch" technique. Finally, large clumps of bone marrow (including bone marrow cores) may be extracted from the femur and blotted on a slide surface, which often yields a higher number of intact blood cell precursors relative to the few cells available from the typical marrow aspirate. Bone marrow cores are acquired surgically by twisting a 13 to 16 gauge bone marrow biopsy needle into the femoral marrow cavity. The resulting sample is touched to a piece of sterile gauze to remove excess blood prior to preparation of the slides. Because bone marrow cores are cylindrical, the touch preparation from these specimens can also be made by grasping one end of the blotted core with a fine pair of forceps (ridged tips, not "rat-toothed") and then rolling it along a glass slide. After acquiring the touch preparation, pieces of the mass or bone marrow sample can be immersed in fixative for histopathological assessment. Alternatively, untouched blocks may be submitted for microbiological cultures.

Scrapings are generally obtained from lesions on the skin (or shell) or mucous membranes. A new scalpel blade is drawn (sideways) across the selected surface so that the skin or mucosa is su-perficially abraded but the epithelial surface is not actually penetrated. Exfoliated cells, scales, and mucus which collect along the edge of the scalpel can be gently removed and applied to a glass slide. When scraping a dry lesion on the skin or shell, a thin film of mineral oil may be applied to the edge of the scalpel to trap exfoliated cells. Thick aggregates of scraped material can be spread by placing them in a drop of saline (pH 7.4) that is centered on the slide to create a wet mount. Aggregated cells may be separated by gently stirring the saline drop using a needle point. Scales, scabs, and other large items (e.g., ectoparasites) that can be removed from a body surface may also be examined as wet mount preparations. Additional spreading can be obtained for extremely thick preparations containing keratin and mucus by including a short digestion step (1-5 minutes, using longer times for more tenacious material) with dilute (1-2%) potassium hydroxide. Alternatively, a coverslip may be added to create a "squash preparation". The coverslip is applied with gentle pressure and a twisting motion, which results in a 90° rotation (one quarter turn) of the coverslip relative to its original orientation. A good squash preparation is characterized by a uniformly thin layer of material with a feathered edge.

EXCRETA

Evaluation of solid elements (blood or inflammatory cells, parasite eggs) in feces and urine provides valuable diagnostic information. Fecal analysis procedures to detect parasite ova have been well described (see parasitology chapter in this volume). Methods for collection of uncontaminated urine specimens from chelonians and for cloacal washes have been described above in the section on FLUIDS. A mixture of feces and urine may be collected from crocodilians, lizards, and snakes during or immediately after voiding, but interpretation is difficult due to the intermingling of these excretions and contamination by environmental materials.

HANDLING, TRANSPORT, AND PROCESSING OF CYTOLOGICAL SPECIMENS

FLUIDS

Handling procedures for liquid samples are dependent on the nature of the fluid. Whole blood and protein-rich exudates are often collected in vials containing an anticoagulant. Such agents are neither needed nor preferred if the sole use for the fluid is to create a smear; instead, smears are made immediately after the fluid is collected. If needed to prevent clotting for other tests (e.g., clinical chemistry assays), the preferred anticoagulant for reptiles is heparin. Use of ethylenediaminetetraacetic acid (EDTA) alters the structural features of reptilian blood cells and hemoparasites (Willette-Frahm, 1995) and leads to hemolysis in certain chelonians (Jacobson, 1987). Blood vials containing an anticoagulant are inverted several times immediately after collection to prevent clotting. Slides are made as soon as possible and then waved briefly through the air to dry them; this action prevents hemolysis of the fragile blood cells. Other fluids, such as urine and organ washes, can be collected in clean glass vials that lack special coatings. Where possible, diagnostic specimens should be processed immediately. However, refrigeration (4-8°C) of samples for up to 24 hours preserves acceptable morphology of many cellular elements. The best results are obtained if the refrigeration period is less than 4 hours. Blood cells will hemolyze if refrigerated for long periods. Blood cell morphology is also destroyed by freezing.

Cells in fluids may be examined microscopically in two fashions, smears and concentration (sediment) preparations. Smears are made from peripheral blood to obtain differential cell counts and reveal hemoparasites. Smears may also be prepared from cellular fluids with plasma-like consistency (particularly effusions). To prepare a smear, a drop of fresh blood is placed centrally at one end of a clean glass microscope slide that has been placed on a flat counter top. The edge of a second slide is touched to the first at an angle of 30° to 45° and drawn into the drop. After the fluid spreads along the edge, the second slide is rapidly but smoothly pushed along the surface of the first slide away from the drop. This action requires practice to obtain single layer smears. The speed at which the second slide is moved in producng the smear will depend on the viscosity of the fluid—the thicker the specimen, the slower the slide is moved. Preparation of blood smears using coverslips rather than slides as a means of spreading the fluid may reduce the number of ruptured cells (Willette-Frahm, 1995). Concentration preparations are used to consolidate the suspended solids in many fluids. Typical specimens for this procedure include CSF, cyst contents, exudates, urine, and organ washes; the buffy coat (leukocyte) fraction of centrifuged whole blood is also a sediment. Sediment is harvested by centrifuging an aliquot of freshly harvested fluid for up to 15 minutes at room temperature (15-25°C) and approximately 1000 x g. After air drying, unstained blood smears and some sediment preps may be stored in racks for extended periods at room temperature. Staining of blood smears is better if they are fixed immediately in fresh 100% percent (absolute) methanol immediately after drying (i.e., before storage). Alternatively, dried specimens may be stained and coverslipped prior to storage. Certain sediments (e.g., cloacal washes, urine) should be stained and assessed immediately.

LESIONS

After application to glass slides, cells from needle aspirates and touch preparations are air-dried at room temperature. Dried specimens are usually stained and coverslipped for immediate evaluation, but they may be stored in racks for extended periods at room temperature without staining. Scrapes and wet mounts are evaluated immediately, after which they are usually discarded. Thus, application of coverslips to these latter samples is optional.

EXCRETA

Evaluation of cells in feces and urine may provide valuable diagnostic information. Freshly collected material is applied to a clean glass slide, coverslipped, and evaluated immediately. Solid elements may be concentrated by centrifugation if desired.

Emerald Tree Boa _(Corallus caninus)_ Photo courtesy of Dr. Todd Driggers.

STAINING

Samples are air-dried and fixed for from several seconds up to 20 minutes in 100% percent methanol before staining; one minute is usually adequate. If slides will be submitted to a diagnostic laboratory, obtain the fixation procedure (if any) that is suggested for use with reptilian specimens (see below). The usual stain used to color nucleated cells in reptile cytology specimens is a Romanowsky stain (Needham, 1981). Romanowsky stains are

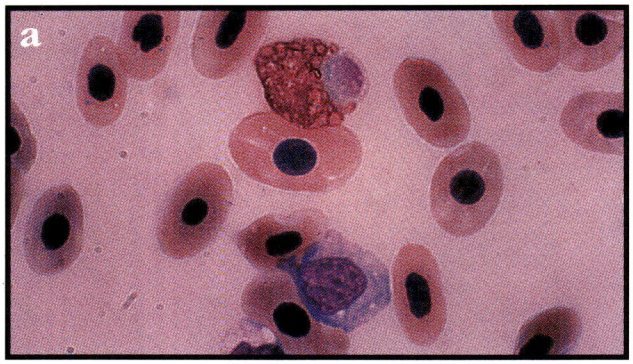
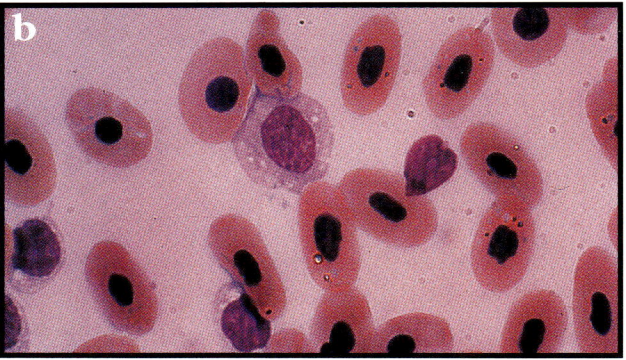

Blood smear from a green sea turtle (*Chelonia mydas*) demonstrating normal morphology of circulating blood cells. a. Several erythrocytes (oval cells with central dark nuclei and homogenous eosinophilic cytoplasm), a heterophil (round cell with an eccentric pale blue nucleus and numerous cytoplasmic granules), and a monocyte (large round cell with eccentric red nucleus and abundant blue cytoplasm). b. Erythrocytes, a centrally located monocyte, and three lymphocytes (small round cells with scant rims of blue cytoplasm, located at lower left). The isolated leukocyte nucleus (located just right of center) emphasizes the fragility of reptilian blood cells. The morphology of blood cells in other species is similar (see Frye, 1991). Giemsa, x630. Photo courtesy of Dr. E.R. Jacobson.

combinations of acidic and basic dyes dissolved in methanol. For most cytological samples, the practitioner should select one type of Romanowsky stain, such as Giemsa, and then use the same brand of stain because the dye composition varies considerably between suppliers; furthermore, differences in mixing dye batches indicates that staining must be optimized for each new lot of stain. Specimens are covered with freshly prepared Giemsa stain (10% in distilled water, buffered to pH 7.0) for 45 to 90 minutes and then washed in buffer until cell structures become prominent. Tap water may be substituted for distilled water, but some morphological deterioration may be noted in the cells. After staining, slides are air-dried in by stacking them in vertical racks or leaning them at a steep angle (80° from horizontal) against a vertical surface. An organic mounting medium (e.g., Permount®) is used to permanently attach the coverslip. The use of commercial "quick" stain kits (e.g., Diff-quik®, American Scientific Products, Inc., McGaw Park, IL) may be acceptable for screening studies in clinical emergencies or for field work but should be avoided for definitive studies because they alter certain features of cell and parasite morphology. In particular, the staining intensity of small organelles may be reduced, and cytoplasmic vacuoles may result.

Special staining procedures may be required to establish cell identity (Mateo et al., 1984), to evaluate cell function (Mateo et al., 1984), or to provide for a definitive diagnosis of certain pathogens. Each additional method will necessitate one or more extra slides. Such techniques (e.g., gram and acid-fast stains for bacteria, silver stains for fungi) are usually performed by veterinary diagnostic laboratories. However, one variant of the Giemsa stain may be readily performed by the practitioner to accentuate hemoparasites. Using this method, hemoglobin is removed from erythrocytes by immersion of the smear in distilled water until the red color fades (Needham, 1981). Giemsa is then applied for at least 30 minutes. This practice is not recommended for routine studies because it destroys many features of blood cell morphology and disrupts hemoparasite structures that are required for taxonomic classification.

INTERPRETATION OF CYTOLOGICAL SPECIMENS

STRATEGY

Slides should be evaluated using a light microscope equipped with, at minimum, one low (4x or 10x) and two high (40x and 63x or 100x) power objectives. Initial assessment should be performed at low power to observe the general features such as numbers (low or high) and types (e.g., inflammatory, neoplastic, microbial) of cells. The entire slide should be scanned. Subsequent evaluations are performed at high magnification to evaluate cell structure. Excellent references exist for normal reptile blood cells (Frye, 1991), blood parasites (Telford, 1984, 1994, 1995), and gastrointestinal parasites (Jacobson, 1986). However, while cytological features for a variety of other conditions have been described in many species, microscopic criteria for diagnosing most diseases in rep-

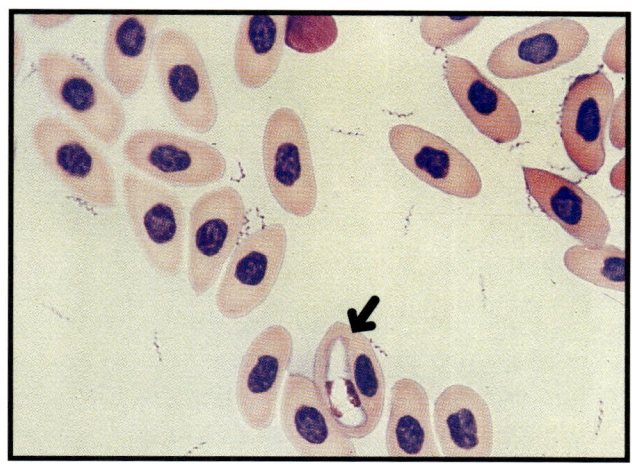

Blood smear from an (Iguana iguana), demonstrating both a hemoparasite and circulating bacteria. The cytoplasm of one erythrocyte (lower central) contains a clear, crescentic *Hemogregarina* sp. organism (arrow). Numerous twisted *Spirillum* sp. bacteria are located between erythrocytes. Giemsa, x630. Photo courtesy of Dr. E.R. Jacobson.

tiles have seldom been reported. Therefore, the success of diagnostic cytology in reptiles will depend heavily on the practitioner's experience and, where possible, the availability of samples (either fresh or archived) from healthy animals of the same species for comparison.

BASIC CRITERIA

Features to be examined in cytological specimens include the type(s) and numbers of cells, nuclear and cytoplasmic characteristics, and the presence of intracellular or extracellular pathogens. The importance of these criteria varies with the nature of the cytological specimen. For example, whole blood and bone marrow will include many cell types at several stages of differentiation. Important information may include alterations in cell number, such as an increase in circulating inflammatory cells, as well as the presence of abnormal cells (e.g., tumor metastases) or pathogens (bacteria, hemoparasites). Cytological interpretation of blood smears is addressed in the hematology chapter of this volume. In contrast, touch preparations from solid tissues may contain one or a few cell types, including normal cells. An experienced practitioner may obtain a presumptive diagnosis from a well selected sample within seconds using these criteria.

Certain cytological patterns are used clinically as presumptive evidence for a given class of disease. The major classes of disease that may be diagnosed in reptiles by cytological examination are inflammation and neoplasia. Inflammation is diagnosed cytologically from peripheral blood, exu-

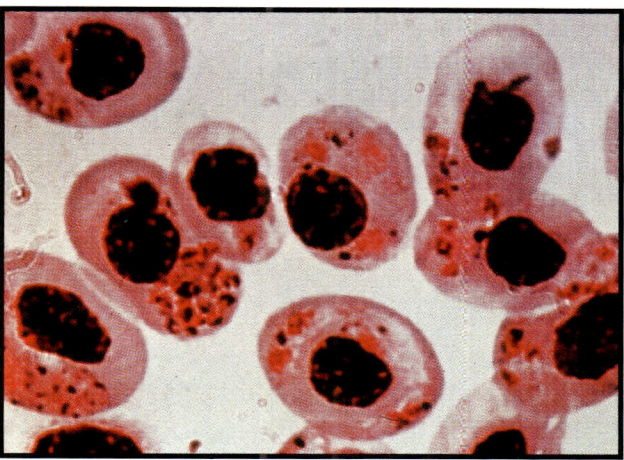

Blood smear from a fence lizard (*Sceloporus occidentalis*) demonstrating numerous grapelike schizonts of the malarial parasite *Plasmodium* sp. in the cytoplasm of erythrocytes. Giemsa, x1000. Photo courtesy of Dr. Sam R. Telford, Jr.

dates, tissue masses, and organ washes. The basic finding in any of these samples will be increased numbers of leukocytes. The hallmark of acute bacterial-induced reactions such as abscesses and effusions is the presence of numerous heterophils; if present, the bacterium is often located in the cytoplasm or attached to the plasma membrane. Additional components may include macrophages, lymphocytes, and plasma cells. Chronic inflammation is characterized by the presence of numerous macrophages in association with lymphocytes and plasma cells. Less commonly, pathogens (bacteria, fungi, or parasites) may be observed in the inflammatory debris associated with chronic infiltrates. Neoplasia is commonly diagnosed from tissue masses or enlarged organs based on the occurrence of a relatively uniform population of abnormal cells. Cytological criteria of neoplasia chiefly consist of atypical nuclear features such as increased nuclear size (resulting in a high nuclear to cytoplasmic ratio), variations in nuclear shape, multiple large nucleoli or many atypical mitotic figures (in which chromosomes form a starbust pattern rather than their usual parallel alignment). Relative to their normal counterparts, tumor cells exhibit extensive pleomorphism (e.g., large differences in cellular size and shape) and have hyperchromic (darker) nuclei and cytoplasm. These features are particularly exaggerated in malignant tumors. The presence of non-inflammatory cell types that do not normally occur at the sample site may also suggest the presence of a metastasis. In concluding that a specimen lacks evidence of neoplasia, the cytologist should recall that many tumors contain large zones of necrosis (in which subtle cellular features are uninterpretable) and that many cancer cells are fragile and may rupture during preparation of the specimen; thus, multiple regions of a suspicious mass should be evaluated. Practitioners should have their cytological diagnoses confirmed using histopathological examination (where possible, using the same tissue specimen) until they become proficient at interpreting cellular features of inflammatory and neoplastic diseases.

Cytological data must be interpreted in conjunction with other clinical findings. For example, certain parasites may be found in the peripheral blood of clinically normal reptiles (Frye, 1991). In addition, the practitioner should be aware of the possibility that contamination of a specimen with peripheral blood may result in the spurious presence of hemoparasites within the material. This finding has been documented in snakes and lizards with "spectacles" where clear or purulent fluid collects in the sub-spectacular space (Millichamp et al., 1983). A comparable phenomenon of spurious parasitism should be ruled out in other samples which may be heavily contaminated with peripheral blood (e.g., bone marrow, CSF).

ARCHIVING CYTOLOGICAL SPECIMENS

Once samples have been interpreted, the practitioner should retain a visual record of the diagnostic features for the given disease. This cytology archive may consist of stained slides, photomicrographs (prints or 35 mm slides), sketches, or written notes; a parallel record of histopathological findings should be retained and cross-referenced to the cytology archive. Slides should be stored vertically in racks (not stacked) in a cool, dry, darkened room. Romanowsky-type stains (including Giemsa) are essentially permanent. In contrast, staining intensity for the rapid staining kits decreases over time even if slides are stored under optimal conditions. Slides should be periodically monitored for the presence of cracks in the mounting medium. Affected slides can be refurbished by immersion in xylene until the coverslip releases, followed by addition of a new coverslip.

Blood smear from a fence lizard (*Sceloporus poinsetti*) showing tortuous *Trypanosoma* sp. (center of slide) near the membrane of a monocyte. Giemsa, x2000. Photo courtesy of Dr. Sam R. Telford, Jr.

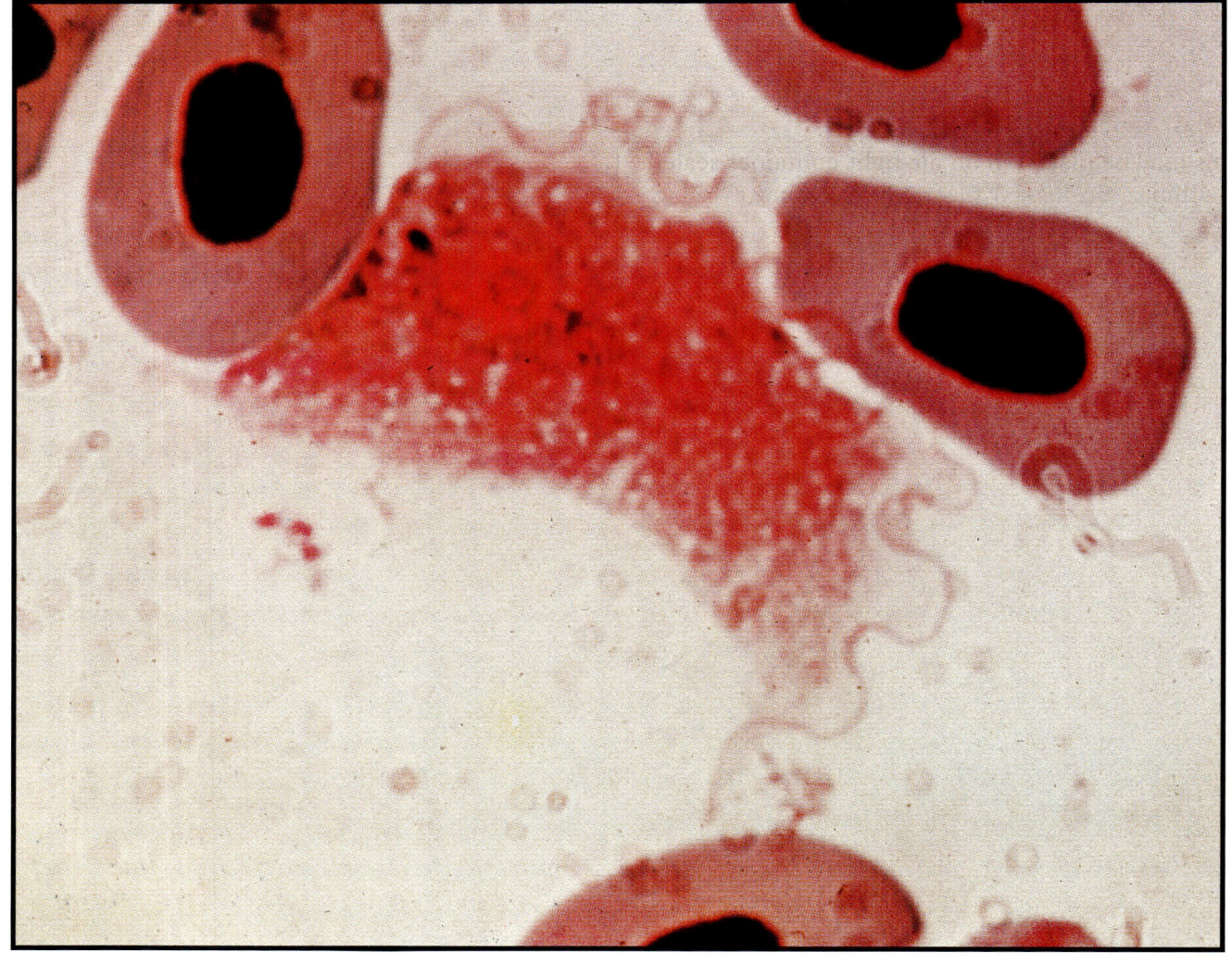

SUBMISSION OF CYTOLOGICAL SPECIMENS TO REFERENCE LABORATORIES

The busy practitioner, particularly one with limited experience in the interpretation of reptile cytology specimens, may prefer to submit samples to a commercial veterinary diagnostic laboratory. Many of these facilities have personnel specifically trained to evaluate cytological samples; however, their expertise is only effective if the sample is submitted properly. Therefore, the practitioner should contact the veterinary diagnostic laboratory before acquisition of the sample to ensure that appropriate techniques are used for collecting, handling, and shipping the cytological material.

Fluids should be placed in heparin (green top) tubes to prevent clot formation. If the sample will be in transit for more than 4-8 hours, a smear should be made using a drop of the uncentrifuged fluid; samples containing few cells may be centrifuged (15 minutes at 1,000xg) to concentrate the solid components before preparing the smear. Smears should be air-dried, as should material obtained from needle aspirates and touch preparations. The dried cells are then fixed for from one to five minutes in 100% methanol. Ideally, cytology specimens should be shipped separately from formalin-filled vials because formaldehyde vapors in the enclosed package can drastically alter the staining characteristics of cytological preparations (Meyer, 1987). Alternatively, cytological materials may be placed in an air-tight container sealed within a zip-locked plastic bag so that cytology and histopathology specimens from the same case may be shipped in one package.

REFERENCES

—**Campbell, TN; Coles, EH:**
Avian clinical pathology. In, Veterinary Clinical Pathology, EH Coles (Ed.). W.B. Saunders Co., Philadelphia, 1986, pp. 279-301.

—**Frye, FL:**
Hematology as applied to clinical reptile medicine. In, Reptile Care: An Atlas of Diseases and Treatments, FL Frye (Ed.). TFH Publications, Neptune City, NJ, 1991, pp. 209-279.

—**Jacobson, ER:**
Blood collection techniques in reptiles: Laboratory investigations. In, Zoo & Wild Animal Medicine: Current Therapy 3, ME Fowler (Ed.). W.B. Saunders Co., Philadelphia, 1993, pp. 144-152.

—**Jacobson, ER:**
Parasitic diseases of reptiles. In, Zoo & Wild Animal Medicine: Current Therapy 2, ME Fowler (Ed.). W.B. Saunders Co., Philadelphia, 1986, pp. 162-181.

—**Jacobson ER:**
Reptiles. In, Veterinary Clinics of North America: Small Animal Practice, J Harkness (Ed.). W.B. Saunders Co., Philadelphia, 1987, pp. 1203-1225.

—**Mateo, MR; Roberts, ED; Enright, FM:**
Morphologic, cytochemical, and functional studies of peripheral blood cells of young healthy American alligators (*Alligator mississippiensis*). *J Am Vet Med Assoc*, 1984; 45:1046-1053.

—**Meyer, DJ:**
The management of cytology specimens. *Compend Contin Educ Pract Vet*, 1987; 9:10-16.

—**Millichamp, N; Jacobson, ER; Wolf, ED:**
Diseases of the eye and ocular adnexa in reptiles. *J Am Vet Med Assoc*, 1983; 183:1205-1212.

—**Needham, JR:**
Microbiology and laboratory techniques. In, Diseases of the Reptilia, Vol. I, JE Cooper, OF Jackson (Eds.). Academic Press, London, 1981, pp. 125-132.

—**Samour, HJ; Risley, D; March, T; et. al.:**
Blood sampling techniques in reptiles. *Vet Rec*, 1984; 114:472-476.

—**Schermer, S:**
The Blood Morphology of Laboratory Animals, 3rd ed. Davis, Philadelphia, 1967, pp. 137-169.

—**Telford, SR Jr.:**
Hemoparasites of reptiles. In, Diseases of Amphibians and Reptiles, GL Hoff, FL Frye, ER Jacobson (Eds.). Plenum Book Co., New York, 1984, pp. 385-517.

—**Telford, SR Jr.:**
The kinetoplastid hemoflagellates of reptiles. In, Parasitic Protozoa, 2nd ed., Vol. 10, JP Kreier (Ed.). Academic Press, New York, 1994, pp. 161-223.

—**Telford, SR Jr.:**
Plasmodia of reptiles. In, Parasitic Protozoa, 2nd ed., Vol. 7, JP Kreier (Ed.). Academic Press, New York, 1994, pp. 1-71.

—**Willette-Frahm, M:**
Blood collection techniques in amphibians and reptiles. In, Kirk's Current Veterinary Therapy XII: Small Animal Practice, JD Bonagura (Ed.). W.B. Saunders Co., Philadelphia, 1995, pp. 1344-1348.

Acknowledgments
The authors thank Drs. Thomas J. Bucci (veterinary pathologist), James D. Fikes (veterinary pathologist), A. Eric Schultze (veterinary clinical pathologist), and Sam R. Telford, Jr. (reptile parasitologist) for editorial comments.

ZOONOSES

Steve Grenard*
Staten Island University Hospital
375 Seguine Avenue
Staten Island, New York 10309
and
Kevin A. Nunan
City University of New York
College of Staten Island
Staten Island, New York

* Address all correspondence to Steve Grenard, Staten Island University Hospital, 375 Seguine Avenue, Staten Island, New York 10309

Steve Grenard is a registered respiratory therapy practitioner specializing in critical respiratory care. He is currently Clinical Coordinator of the Sleep Disorders Laboratory at Staten Island University Hospital in New York. Prior to this he spent three years as a respiratory specialist at the A.G. Holley State Hospital in Lantana, Florida which specialized in the treatment of tuberculosis and related infectious diseases. He has been actively involved in herpetology for more than 30 years. He is the author of Handbook of Alligators and Crocodiles, a text for wildlife management specialists and Medical Herpetology, the first book dedicated solely to the medical aspects of amphibians and reptiles He has also authored or co-authored some 13 textbooks and workbooks on the diagnosis and treatment of respiratory diseases.

Kevin Nunan is a veterinary/animal technician currently studying for his biology degree at the City University of New York. He has been actively involved in the captive care and husbandry of amphibians and reptiles for most of his life with a special interest in zoonotic diseases. He has established, together with Steve Grenard, a world wide web page dedicated to the dissemination of information on the recognition and prevention of zoonotic diseases in amphibians and reptiles.

INTRODUCTION

Zoonoses are diseases communicable to humans from animals; there are about 240 such diseases known world-wide. According to Norman Frank, DVM (personal communication) the most serious and most commonly-encountered communicable zoonotic diseases are obtained from animals which are more closely related to humans, such as other primates and then other mammals. When you consider infections passed from one human to another you are most apt to find the highest incidence of disease and potentially the most serious diseases.

Although a zoonosis such as rabies is extremely serious and frequently fatal without proper treatment, its occurrence among humans is far less than say, Human Immunodeficiency Virus (HIV) infection, which is also fatal. After mammalian zoonoses, diseases obtained from birds occur with the most frequency and then come those from amphibians and reptiles. Thus amphibian and reptile zoonoses, under natural conditions, occur with far less frequency than the zoonotic diseases of birds and mammals. In addition there are no amphibian or reptile diseases which (like rabies, HIV, Ebola or Hantavirus) carry a universally high incidence of mortality. Under unnatural conditions, however, such as close contact with captives, there may be a greater than expected number of zoonotic diseases contracted from amphibians and reptiles and , in addition, some such diseases may be potentially fatal among people who fall into certain risk groups.

All four classes of microbial communicable diseases (viral, bacterial, parasitic and fungal) occur in reptiles and/or amphibians. Amphibians are often inextricably linked with a damp or watery en-

It is important to keep terraria clean and disinfected to minimize the risk of zoonotic infections. Photo courtesy of Dr. Todd Driggers.

vironment. It is important to be aware of the following parasites which could find their way into a captive environment established for these animals:

—*Cyclopsora,*
—*Acanthamoeba,*
—*Microsporida,*
—*Ascaris,*
—*Dientameoba,*
—*Entamoeba,*
—*Blastocystis,*
—*Baylisascaris,*
—*Giardia* and
—*Cryptosporidia.*

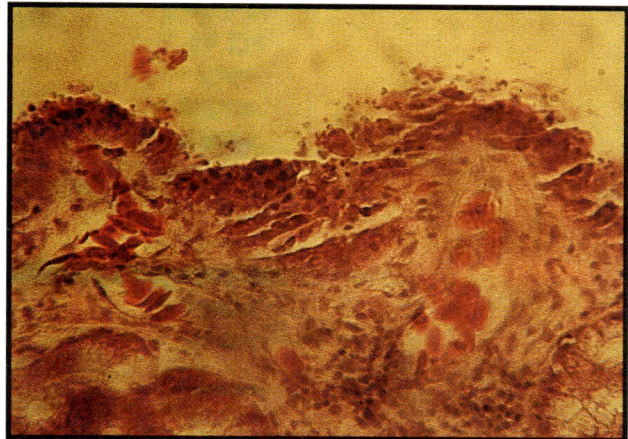

Cryptosporidiosis in a red rat snake. This organism is not likely zoonotic to humans unless immunocompromised. Sample provided by Dr. Todd Driggers. Photo courtesy of Dr. Lowell Ackerman.

In addition, various metazoan parasites such as tapeworms have been linked to the ingestion of improperly cooked frogs' legs. Hepatitis may be present in the damp or watery habitat of many amphibians. At least one case of human hepatitis-A has been linked to the watery milieu of a shipment of frogs imported into the U.S. from Ecuador. Other potentially pathogenic viruses that may be present in such a habitat include astroviruses, rotaviruses and caliciviruses.

Water-borne bacterial organisms include:
—*Salmonella,*
—*Escherichia,*
—*Yersinia entercolitica,*
—*Campylobacter* and
—*Aeromonas.*

While not all pathogens that can potentially infect reptiles cross over to humans, many do. Atypical mycobacterial infections such as *M. marinum* may also occur in reptiles as well as fish and are transmitted to humans through small cuts or breaks in the skin. It results in a painful cutaneous lesion. *Mycobacterium avium*

There is actually very little danger of zoonotic infections from handling snakes such as this kingsnake if proper handwashing/disinfection is performed. Photo courtesy of Dr. Todd Driggers.

intracellulare is highly contagious to immunocompromised humans and is found in a wide variety of fish, amphibians, reptiles, birds and other animals. Diseases produced by Mycobacteria range from a progressing, fulminating process which destroys all tissue in its path to localized granulomas which sometimes occur as space-occupying lesions in the abdominal and thoracic cavities. *Erysipelothrix*, which causes erysipelas in humans and other animals, is widely distributed in nature and has been isolated from reptiles, amphibians and fish. *Candida* yeast infections may also be present in reptiles, particularly where injuries or surface abrasions have occurred. *Candida* is potentially transmissible to susceptible individu-

Iguanas are now a more common cause of human salmonellosis in North America than baby turtles. Photo courtesy of Dr. Todd Driggers.

als, especially immunocompromised humans such as those with HIV infection or those taking chemotherapy for cancer treatment.

Zoonotic diseases transmitted by reptiles are more frequent and tend have higher morbidity levels than those transmitted from amphibians. There are several reasons for this. As delicate aquatic organisms, amphibian pets are less likely to be handled than reptiles. In addition, far more hobbyists keep pet reptiles (snakes, turtles and lizards) compared to the more demanding and difficult to maintain amphibians. If you follow the dictate mentioned by Norman Frank (ibid.), reptiles are of at least one order of magnitude more closely related to humans on the evolutionary scale than amphibians. Thus, as air breathing, thick-skinned terrestrial vertebrates, the microorganisms that occur in them are more likely to succeed in humans than those adapted to amphibians or fish.

SALMONELLOSIS

The presence of *Salmonella* in reptiles has been documented as long ago as 1947 but it wasn't until the more prosperous post-war years and the widespread emergence of these animals as household pets in the 1950s and '60s that reptile-associated salmonellosis gained notoriety as a zoonoses causing statistically significant numbers of infections in humans.

Organisms of the Gram-negative bacterial tribe Salmonelleae characteristically inhabit the intestinal tract of many vertebrates either as diarrhea-producing pathogens or as harmless commensals. There are some 500 serovars which have been identified in reptiles and most of these have never been found in humans. While most are harmless to the infected animals, some cause problems in individu-

Swabbing the oral cavity of a snake for *Salmonella*. Photo courtesy of Dr. Lowell Ackerman.

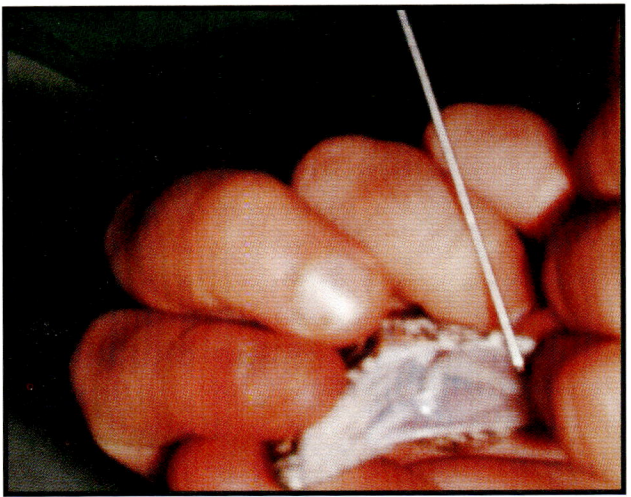

als which are immunocompromised because of stress, improper captive conditions (such as inappropriate temperature and humidity), inadequate diet or concurrent disease.

Turtles and other animal carriers of zoonotic salmonellosis are living reservoirs which cannot be easily or effectively "sterilized." In fact *Salmonella* is part of the normal intestinal flora in turtles and herbivorous lizards so that eradicating such flora may cause digestive problems and death of the animal. Omnivorous and carnivorous reptiles that consume food or prey contaminated with *Salmonella* are constantly reinfected so it is both dangerous and unrealistic to continuously administer antibiotics to such animals. Overmedicating with antibiotics has been shown to increase the ability of bacteria to become resistant to a wide variety of drugs, causing major problems in the medical treatment of human patients; there are resistant strains of some organisms which ultimately are fatal to humans. Such resistance has been directly linked to the

Eggs incubating. Even captive-reared reptiles can carry salmonellae. Photo courtesy of Dr. Todd Driggers.

overuse of antibiotics in both humans and in animals.

In immunocompetent adults, salmonellosis (a.k.a. "food poisoning") may cause gastroenteritis of 24 to 72 hours' duration. The infection is usually self-limiting, requires minimal treatment, and responds well to fluid replacement and anti-diarrheal medications. However, certain subsets of the population which are immunocompromised for any reason are at risk of more serious infection and sepsis from *Salmonella* as from any zoonosis. These groups include:
1. Pregnant women due to risk to the fetus
2. Newborn infants and small children to age 7.
3. Individuals who are immunocompromised due to infection with HIV.

4. Individuals who are immunocompromised due to treatment with various drugs including cyclosporine (given to transplant recipients to prevent rejection), corticosteroids, and other biological response modifying drugs.
5. Individuals on cancer chemotherapy or those receiving radiation treatment.
6. Individuals with diseases affecting antibody production or those receiving treatments which result in bone marrow depression .
7. Individuals with natural or iatrogenic diseases which cause lymphocytopenia.
8. The chronically malnourished.
9. Elderly or frail individuals.

These individuals should avoid contact with reptiles, amphibians and other animals known to cause zoonotic disease. Individuals who have contact with these categories of individuals and animals should wash their hands thoroughly for 30 seconds or more with an antibacterial soap and hot water immediately after handling any animal, its caging materials or detritus.

Clayton Hann (1995: Reptile-Associated Salmonellosis in Pennsylvania - unpublished research paper) defines exposure to reptiles in salmonellosis patients as any one of the following:
1. owning a reptile.
2. having a friend or relative who owns a reptile
3. direct contact (i.e. touching) a reptile in the wild
4. employment in which there are reptiles in close proximity (pet store and zoo workers)

Salmonella continues to cause millions of infections due to contamination of food. Food contamination is especially common in poultry meat and eggs which are improperly cooked. Additionally, foods may be recontaminated in kitchens where cooked product comes in contact with raw product or traces of raw product left on surfaces used to hold both cooked and uncooked food. So while turtle and other reptile-associated salmonellosis cause only a relatively small percentage of the infections in susceptible individuals these individuals (children, the elderly and the immunocompromised) are none-the-less a high profile group that captures much public attention.

SALMONELLA IN TURTLES

In 1962 the Centers for Disease Control published a report in its weekly bulletin by Hershey and Mason that would set the stage for broad-sweeping legislation throughout the United States to ban the interstate transport of turtles and tortoises with a carapace length of 4 inches or less. In 1965 Dr. L. Paul Williams, Jr., recently retired as Oregon's Public Health Veterinarian, co-authored a paper in the Journal of the American Medical Association (192:6-10) titled "Pet turtles as a cause

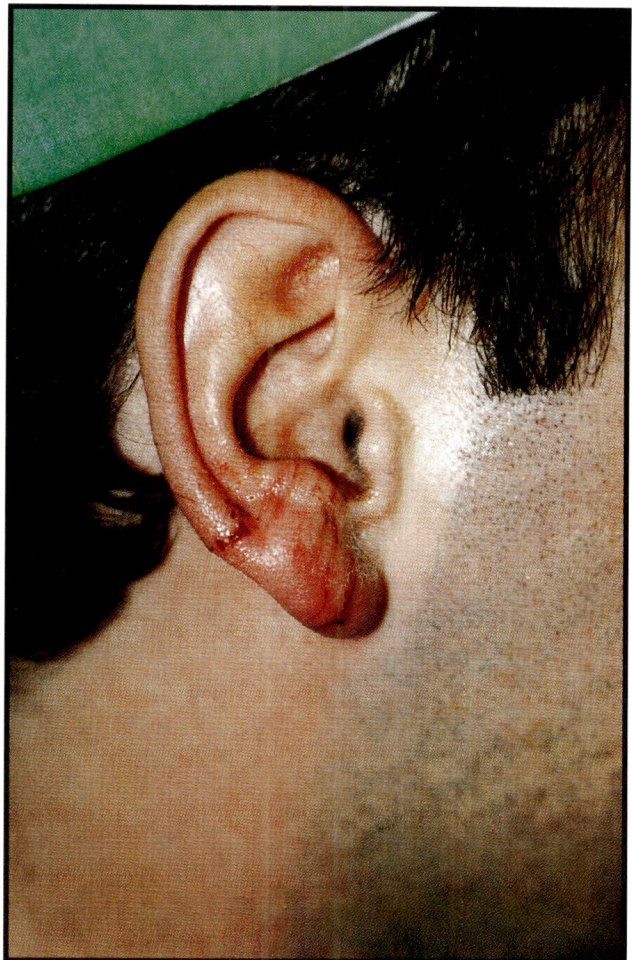

Bite wound from a sexually-mature iguana. Photo courtesy of Dr. Todd Driggers.

of human salmonellosis." This landmark paper started the move toward banning baby turtles.

Gradually, local health agencies started passing such laws around 1971 but a national ban, enforced by the U.S. Food and Drug Administration didn't go into effect until 1975. The 1962 CDC report revealed that *Salmonella hartford* was isolated from the pet turtle of a seven-month-old baby who was gravely ill with gastroenteritis due to this same organism. In the years preceding the 1975 law, millions of these baby turtles were sold in pet shops, tourist attractions, fairs, circuses, carnivals and even by street vendors. Bowls of these "pets" were everywhere, even on food stands.

These turtles were bred in large-scale outdoor turtle farms throughout the southeast in states such as Louisiana, Florida, Alabama and Arkansas. When medical authorities found that thousands of children ill with diarrhea were infected with a species or serotype of *Salmonella* identical to the serotype isolated from the turtle's water bowl or stool sample it became immediately apparent that the turtles were the source of the problem. As a cheap alternative pet for children, these animals were grossly mishandled and ill cared for. Most died within a year or less but not before infecting their young owners with salmonellosis. At the height of the turtle-associated salmonellosis outbreak in infants and young children tens of thousands of kids were infected and a number of infants died before medical intervention could save them.

After the ban on baby turtles went into effect the epidemic of turtle-associated salmonellosis in infants and small children ground to a halt with only sporadic cases occurring. Twenty years later this ban is still in effect in the United States but American turtle farmers are still able to export millions of baby turtles to Europe and elsewhere for the pet and novelty trade. The Federal government conducts a pre-export *Salmonella* surveillance program which helps to diminish the number of baby turtles exported which are actively shedding *Salmonella*. Baby turtles raised in-state and not entering interstate commerce are not banned from sale except where prohibited by local law. Most counties and municipalities have such ordinances.

Sale of and possession of baby turtles is also permissible for scientific study and educational

Remember that homemade diets can become contaminated with *Salmonella* and other microbes. Keep food preparation area clean and disinfected. Photo courtesy of Dr. Todd Driggers.

purposes. In some cases these reasons are used as a ruse and local health and wildlife authorities have been known to detain and question purchasers of baby turtles at reptile swap meets. If the purchaser cannot satisfactorily prove that a baby turtle purchase is truly for scientific or educational purposes the animal could be confiscated immediately and the purchaser would need to provide satisfactory evidence to get it back later.

SALMONELLA IN IGUANAS

More recently, baby green iguanas (*Iguana iguana*) have moved into the position once occupied by baby turtles as an inexpensive, alternative pet for children. And, like the baby turtles, most of these animals are improperly fed and cared for and almost all of these lizards carry various serotypes of *Salmonella* capable of infecting humans. To veterinary, medical and public health experts as well as herpetologists who dealt with the baby turtle situation in the 1960s and 70s, the enormous surge in baby iguana popularity seems like déja vu. It is reliably estimated that in 1994-1995 more than a million baby iguanas were imported into the United States from farming and ranching operations in Central and South America. In addition tens, perhaps hundreds of thousands of fertile iguana eggs have been shipped to ranching operations in the U.S. southeast for hatching.

Various serotypes of *Salmonella* enter the developing lizard cloacally or trans-ovarially from the soil. Baby iguanas also obtain inocula of *Salmonella* by eating the feces of other, older iguanas as well as eating insects which carry the organism. Young iguanas are not obligate vegetarians and will ingest animal (insect) protein given the opportunity to do so. *Salmonella* is part of the animal's normal intestinal flora and may play some role in hind gut fermentation, a necessity in vegetarians. Like the baby turtles of a few decades ago, baby iguanas begin shedding *Salmonella* in their stool immediately after hatching and taking their first meal. Therefore, iguanas that are either captive-bred or captive-born are not any more free of *Salmonella* than wild-caught lizards.

Ranching and farming these popular animals, rather than relying on wild-caught animals, is infinitely more cost effective for the pet industry. In addition, it is possible to preserve wild populations by sustainable cultivation as an alternative to unrestrained overcollecting in the wild. Although a super abundance of *Salmonella* colonies in captive lizards and other reptiles can cause problems requiring veterinary treatment, the only effective way to prevent the spread of this bacteria to humans is through the use of hand washing and other preventive measures discussed elsewhere. Refer to the chapter on reptile rehabilitation for a list of steps to follow when feeding, handling, cleaning habitat, or treating *Salmonella*-infected reptiles.

SOME CASE STUDIES

As an intern with the Pennsylvania Department of Health, Hann studied 97 cases of reptile salmonellosis reported in that state in 1994-1995. Of these, 35 cases were disregarded since no contact could be established with the patient. Of the 62 cases for which information was available, Hann determined that 21 or 34% were in children under the age of 1 year, a further 22 cases or 35% were in children between 1 and 10 years of age.

Some two thirds of the cases reported were in children under age 10. There were practically no differences in distribution among males and females or educational level. Some 57 or 92% of the cases were in white, non-Hispanic persons.

Hann also performed a study of 58 of the 62 cases, isolating serotypes from *Salmonella*-infected persons. From those infected persons, Hann isolated 15 reptile-associated serotypes with the highest prevalence of infection being caused by *Salmonella poona*. Hann concluded that, if *Salmonella poona* was isolated from the patient, there was a 70% chance that the patient or a close friend or relative of the patient owned either an iguana or a turtle.

The following serotypes were identified in the Pennsylvania study:
—*Salmonella Carrau*,
—*Salmonella eilbeck*,
—*Salmonella java*,
—*Salmonella javiana*,
—*Salmonella kintambo*,
—*Salmonella litchfield*,
—*Salmonella marina*,
—*Salmonella monschaui*,
—*Salmonella poona*,
—*Salmonella O:48:Z52:Z (Arizona)*,
—*Salmonella group Y O:48 (Arizona)*,
—*Salmonella subspecies 3 (Arizona)*,
—*Salmonella subspecies 4*,
—*Salmonella tuindorp*,
—*Salmonella urbana* and
—*Salmonella wassenaar*.

According to Hann (ibid) *Salmonella* infection with reptile-associated serotypes produces significant financial impact on victims or their families. Cases studied in Pennsylvania required an average 3.2 day hospital stay. In addition to medical costs, infection is easily spread to other humans and contactees of the primary patient. When the primary patient was a member of a household, this usually resulted in infection among other family members.

Hann attributes the majority of cases to careless handling of reptile enclosures and cleaning of debris such as fecal material. He believes that such operations result in the contamination of other fomites (counter surfaces, sinks, the hands) which serve to spread the infection. He noted that rubber gloves were claimed to be worn by only 25% of the respondents when they engaged in tasks related to the cleaning of reptile cages.

Since 1986, the Oregon Health Department's Center for Disease Prevention and Epidemiology has been studying the incidence of reptile-associated salmonellosis in Oregon. The Oregon CDPE reported 36 documented cases of salmonellosis, 10 of which were reported between 1993 and the first half of 1995. The following six case excerpts appeared in the June 13, 1995 (44:12) edition of the CD Summary, a publication of the Oregon Health Department.

1. *Salmonella* subspecies II was isolated from a 2-month-old Clackamas County infant with diarrhea, and subsequently from the father's white boa constrictor (no other species ID was given). The family dog, parakeets and a pet lizard tested "negative" for the bacterium.

2. In 1986, premature triplets were placed in a neonatal intensive care unit until their conditions stabilized. After several weeks they were moved to intermediate neonatal care where the parents could handle and feed them. Within a few days, one infant developed diarrhea and found to be culture-positive for a rare *Salmonella* subspecies (IIIa). His two siblings soon also became ill; the same organism was recovered from their stools. No other infants on either ward were affected. After an initial investigation by the health department, stool was collected from one of the black rat snakes owned by the father. The specimen grew out *Salmonella* (both IIIa and IIIb).

3. *Salmonella javiana* was recovered from the stool of a 2-year-old female Marion County resident, as well as the resident iguana. Interestingly a stool survey of the household menagerie turned up six other *Salmonella* serotypes (*give, hvittingfoss, welikade, poona, wassenaar* and subspecies II) from four other animals: a turtle, a dog, another iguana and a good sized caiman. The frog and goat tested negative.

4. A rare serotype, *Salmonella kintambo*, was isolated from a 63-year-old Linn County woman with a history of protracted diarrhea. She had not traveled outside of the U.S. and there were no household pets. After extensive and repeated questioning she confessed that her adult son was an exotic reptile fancier. A stool survey of his boa constrictor, iguana, and (big!) monitor lizard (which had the run of the house) proved fruitful. *Salmonella kintambo* and *Salmonella widemarsh* were isolated from the monitor and boa; the iguana carried *Salmonella glostrup*.

Oregon health authorities state that greater susceptibility to more virulent infection with *Salmonella* in infants and small children may be due to:
1. Presence of fewer competing gut flora
2. Lower stomach acidity levels (=higher stomach pH)
3. Small mass requiring a smaller inoculum to cause significant infection

4. Poor hygienic practices (little or no supervised handwashing)
5. Carelessness in cleaning up after pets
6. Propensity to place fingers in mouth, nose and eyes (e.g. thumb/finger sucking)
7. Propensity to eat sweets or sandwiches without handwashing

Oregon officials feel that official statistics grossly underestimate the magnitude of true occurrence of reptile-associated salmonellosis. Household reptiles that have died, been given away or hidden from scrutiny confound the issue of statistical reliability. In addition, the difficulties of sample collection and culture may play a role in this situation. Swabbing the cloaca of a python or large lizard may be difficult for some technicians or veterinarians and droppings recovered from cages are not always culturable. Only 3 or 4 colonies may be picked and eventually serotyped from a culture plate containing several hundred and some serotypes may overgrow others. Many reptiles simultaneously carry two, three or more serotypes so it may be easy to miss linking the reptile's *Salmonella* with that of an infected human.

A report in the Epidemiology Bulletin of the Virginia Department of Health (June, 1995: vol. 95, number 6) presents four case histories of reptile-associated salmonellosis investigated by the Piedmont Health District and the staff of the Bureau of Disease Surveillance and Epidemiologic Studies. On March 8, 1995 an 8-month old Amelia County girl was seen by a pediatrician for fever and diarrhea. A stool culture was obtained and subsequently reported positive for *Salmonella litchfield*. Based on a report by the physician, the Amelia County Health Department investigated and identified the same *Salmonella* serotype in stool samples from both adult family members, one of whom was also suffering from fever and diarrhea.

Although initial suspicions regarding the source of infection focused on foodborne, waterborne or person-to-person transmission, attention eventually turned to the family pet snake, a boa constrictor. The health department submitted samples of the snake's stool for culture and the same rare serotype as that isolated from affected family members was identified. In addition to this Amelia county case, the CDC requested that the Virginia Department of Health investigate three other cases in that state involving *Salmonella marina*. On January 26, 1994 a 6-week-old bottle-fed male infant presented with bloody diarrhea. A stool culture collected on February 2nd revealed *Salmonella marina*. The family owned a reptile (not identified) that was kept in a cage in the living room. When the cage was cleaned, the reptile was kept perched on the mother's shoulder and the infant was reported to thus have frequent contact with the animal. A day later, on January 27th, a three month old formula fed male infant also developed symptoms of non-bloody diarrhea, vomiting and fever. A stool specimen collected six months later, on July 7th, revealed the presence of *Salmonella marina*. In this case the family had a two year old iguana which was kept in the cage and primarily handled by an older sibling who had never displayed any symptoms. On September 15, 1994 a 12-year-old boy presented with bloody diarrhea, fever and abdominal pain. A stool culture yielded *Salmonella marina*. The family owned a cat, a turtle, an iguana and a caiman. Since the iguana was reported to have had frequent loose stools, a culture on the animal was run six months later. It revealed *Salmonella* serotype *Abaetetuba*.

National attention was focused on the re-emergence of reptile-associated salmonellosis when the CDC's Morbidity and Mortality Weekly Report (MMWR) in 1995 (44:347-50) carried the following case histories of reptile-associated salmonellosis:

Connecticut. During January, 1995 a 40-year-old man was hospitalized for acute illness characterized by constipation, lower back pain, fever and chills. He reported having taken ranitidine and an antacid for symptoms of heartburn before onset of mild diarrhea 3 days prior to hospitalization. Blood culture yielded *Salmonella wassenaar*. An MRI scan of the right sacrum suggested osteomyelitis. Ciprofloxacin treatment was initiated for presumed *Salmonella* osteomyelitis and he was discharged after 14 days. All household contacts were asymptomatic.

The family had purchased two iguanas in October, 1994. Although the patient denied handling the iguanas he reported having recently cleaned their aquarium enclosure. Stool samples obtained from both iguanas yielded *Salmonella wassenaar*.

New Jersey. During September, 1994 a 5-month-old girl was hospitalized because of an acute illness including vomiting, lethargy and fever. On admission it was noted she had a bulging fontanelis and stiff neck. Blood cultures and cerebrospinal fluid yielded *Salmonella* serotype *rubislaw*. She was treated with I.V. ceftazidime for *Salmonella* sepsis and meningitis and discharged after 10 days. Other family members were asymptomatic. The infant was routinely fed infant formula. Although the family did not own a reptile, the infant frequently stayed at the home of a baby-sitter where an iguana was kept. Culture of a stool sample from this iguana yielded *Salmonella rubislaw*. The infant was reported to not have touched the iguana; however the animal was frequently handled by the baby-sitter and other members of the family. All members of the baby-sitter's family were asymptomatic but stool cultures from two members, including a child who had frequently played with and fed the infant, were positive for *Salmonella rubislaw*.

(Authors note: This is an interesting finding since the children and other members of families which have kept reptiles for many years rarely if ever get ill, indicating that they may acquire resistance to the *Salmonella* in their animals).

New York. In December, 1994 a 45-year-old man infected with HIV was hospitalized because of weakness, nausea, vomiting and diarrhea. His CD+4 (T-4 lymphocyte) count was decreased. Stool cultures revealed *Salmonella* serotype IIIa 41:Z4ZZ3, subspecies of *S. arizona*. He owned corn snakes and until shortly before his illness had worked in a pet shop where he handled reptiles frequently. *Salmonella* sepsis was diagnosed and he was treated with oral ciprofloxacillin.

North Carolina. During December, 1994 a 2-day-old boy born 8 weeks prematurely developed respiratory difficulties, was diagnosed with pneumothorax and transferred to a referral hospital. Blood obtained at birth for culture has been negative but blood obtained 9-days later because of an elevated white blood count yielded *Salmonella* serotype *kintambo*. He was treated with I.V. ampicillin for *Salmonella* sepsis and was discharged from the hospital after 30-days. Eleven days after the positive culture in this case was collected, *Salmonella kintambo* was also cultured from a blood sample obtained from a 12-day-old acutely ill boy who was born at 28 weeks gestation and had shared a room at the referral hospital with the first infant.

The second infant was treated with I.V. cefotaxime and was discharged after 44 days. Both infants has been in the hospital continuously from birth to onset of illness. The mother of the first infant reported having a diarrheal episode 4-days before she gave birth. She also reported frequently handling a Savannah Monitor lizard the family acquired in September, 1994 and kept in a cage in the kitchen. Culture of a stool sample from the lizard yielded *Salmonella kintambo*. The family of the second infant did not own a reptile.

(Authors note: the implication here is that the second infant acquired *Salmonella* from the first infant and it was carried on the hands/fomites of medical/nursing personnel who cared for both babies).

Ohio. During January, 1994 a 6-week-old boy was hospitalized because of diarrhea, stiff neck and fever. Culture of blood samples and cerebrospinal fluid yielded *Salmonella* serotype *stanley*. The infant was treated with I.V.

cefotaxime for Salmonella sepsis and meningitis and released from the hospital after 56 days. He had been fed only formula and not attended a child care facility. Household contacts were asymptomatic. The family had purchased a 4-inch aquatic turtle in April, 1993. A culture of stool from the turtle yielded *Salmonella stanley*. Although the infant had not had contact with the turtle, other family members did and the turtles water bowl was washed in the kitchen sink.

Pennsylvania. During October, 1994 a 21-day-old girl was hospitalized because of an illness that included vomiting, bloody diarrhea and fever. She received empirical treatment with I.V. ampicillin. Stool culture yielded *Salmonella* serotype *poona*. She was discharged from the hospital after 11 days. Other members of the family were asymptomatic. The infant had been fed infant formula and did not attend a child care facility. The family owned an iguana and a culture of stool from the animal yielded *Salmonella poona*. Although the infant had no contact with the iguana it was handled frequently by her mother and other family members.

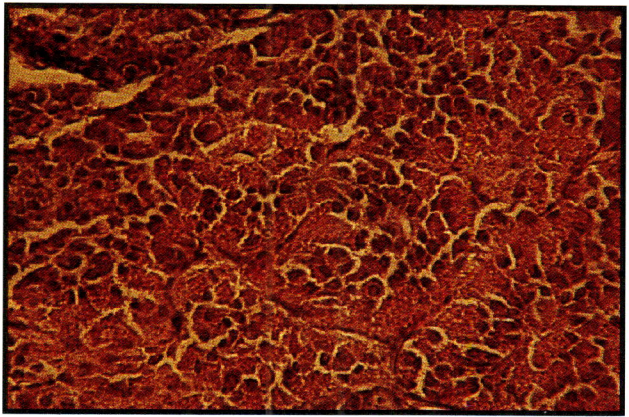

Hepatozoan infection which is not zoonotic to humans. Hematoxylin and Eosin, 100 x magnification. Sample provided by Dr. Todd Driggers. Photo courtesy of Dr. Lowell Ackerman.

Other States. According to the CDC report other states (California, Colorado, Florida, Illinois, Minnesota and Utah) have reported isolation of the same *Salmonella* serotype from household reptiles as found in patients diagnosed with *Salmonella* infections. At least one newborn infant has been reported to have died as a result of a prenatal reptile-associated *Salmonella* infection in the mother. Reptile-associated salmonellosis has been diagnosed in both the handlers and non-handling members of households with reptiles present. Direct contact does not appear to be necessary in order to become infected.

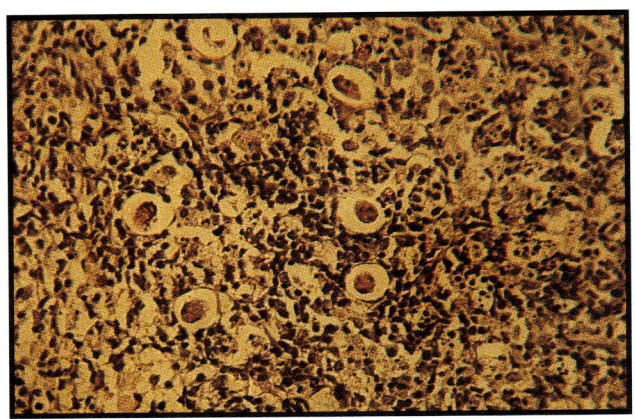

Hepatazoan infection which is not zoonotic to humans. PAS, 100 x magnification. Sample provided by Dr. Todd Driggers. Photo courtesy of Dr. Lowell Ackerman.

OTHER REPTILE-ASSOCIATED BACTERIAL ZOONOSES

Salmonella are not the only potentially zoonotic bacteria harbored by reptiles.

DERMATOPHILOSIS

Dermatophilus congolensis is a Gram-positive filamentous bacterium with a life cycle that involves the release of spores from the filaments and the development of these spores to form germ tubes and new filaments. In humans and animals it causes an exudative dermatitis and hard, crusty scabs. It has been found in cattle, sheep, horses and some 18 other animals including seals, lizards and even in polar bears. Handling of infected animals by humans can result in human disease. It has recently been isolated from a pet Savannah monitor (*Varanus exanthematicus*). In immunocompromised humans it can attack the brain, lungs and kidneys.

LYME DISEASE AND EHRLICHIOSIS

Lizards are also bitten by *Ixodes* ticks which harbor bacterial infections such as *Borrelia* which causes Lyme disease and *Ehrlichia* which causes ehrlichiosis. in humans and other animals. While these diseases may not be zoonoses in the sense a human could not casually become infected from contact with the lizard, the ectoparasite of the lizard could, conceivably, vector the disease to humans. A great deal of care must be taken when treating or removing ticks from such animals.

PARASITIC ZOONOSES

Reptiles such as lizards and snakes may also serve as reservoirs for such parasites as *Leishmania* and *Plasmodium* but disease in humans normally requires infection by the parasites' normal arthropod vector. The snake and lizard pentasomid parasite *Raillietiella* is also capable of infecting humans although the usual means of infection is by ingestion of improperly cooked or raw lizards.

VIRUSES

No viruses are known to be zoonotically transferred from reptiles to humans but a number of potentially communicable viruses have been identified in reptiles including the Western Equine Encephalitis Virus, the Bunyaviruses and the Togaviruses. Again transmission to humans normally requires the presence of the usual arthropod vector. and reptiles may represent an intermediate reservoir for such viruses.

While no documented cases of a zoonotic virus occurs in reptiles, this order may harbor viruses potentially transmissible to humans. Turtles, in particular, have been discovered infected with herpesvirus naturally. Experimentally it has been demonstrated that some water turtles can become infected with hepatitis-B. Both these viruses are extremely contagious in humans and hepatitis-B is frequently fatal even in immunocompetent individuals. Herpesvirus can be extremely debilitating in immunocompromised individuals and some variants can be fatal when they attack the brain or other vital centers.

WOUNDS AND BITES

All animal bites (including human) represent a potential for infection and sepsis. Any wound infection or necrotizing process in a reptile may contain potentially pathogenic organisms. A good example of this is mouth rot in snakes and lizards which may contain *Staphylococcus*, *Shigella*, or *Pseudomonas*, all of which are potentially pathogenic in humans. Infectious sequelae from the bites of reptiles can be considered zoonotic diseases if the microorganisms present in the wound resided in the animal responsible for the bite.

If bit by a reptile, it is extremely important to immediately disinfect and wash the bite with soap. Bites on the hand or foot, fingers or toes, should be literally soaked in a basin of povidone-iodine (Betadine®) solution for an hour or more. Bites on other locations should be dressed with sterile gauze pads soaked in disinfectant and all animal bites should be followed up with medical attention. In addition to prophylactic antibiotics and dressing change protocols it may also be necessary to receive a tetanus booster and other follow-up treatment. Swelling, inflammation, or discoloration around or extending from any animal bite requires an immediate visit to the emergency room or doctor's office.

LIZARDS

Bites by monitors are notoriously infective. Komodo monitor (and other monitor) bites can cause overwhelming sepsis resistant to a broad range of intravenous antibiotics. Hobbyists who keep monitors or other reptiles capable of biting should keep disinfectants and first aid kits handy and thoroughly disinfect and wash out such wounds immediately to help prevent serious infectious sequelae.

CROCODILIANS

Crocodilian bites, in addition to the trauma they can cause, may also become seriously infected. Such bites need immediate disinfection, cleaning and follow-up medical attention.

SNAKES

Most infectious organisms transmitted by snakes to humans occur as a result of their bite. A few species of venomous snake, curiously, have venoms with antiseptic properties. While their bite can be fatal due to the action of their venom such bites rarely become infected.

Pathogenic organisms isolated from the mouths of snakes or from abscesses that appeared at snakebite sites include:
—*Morganella*,
—*Providencia*,
—*Escherichia coli*,
—Group A and D streptococci,
—*Enterobacter*,
—staphylococci,
—*Pseudomonas* and
—*Clostridium*.

The use of dried rattlesnake-flesh capsules as a folk remedy has been linked to severe salmonellosis and death in immunocompromised individuals taking such nostrums.

Snakes which normally are well-mannered and calm when handled can bite unexpectedly during or around feeding sessions. The presence of rodent scent on the hands of a human handler or even rodents in the general vicinity may cause the snake to bite the hand that feeds it when it would never normally be expected to do so. Snakes should not be handled immediately before, during or for at least two days after eating. Also, before handling a snake, make sure you remove all traces of their prey items from the vicinity in order to help prevent an unexpected attack by an ordinarily well acclimated and placid animal. Some snakes consider all approach by humans as a signal that they are going to be fed. Handlers need to use a certain amount of ingenuity in conditioning the animal against biting when approached.

SUMMARY

Reptiles are among the fastest growing and most popular categories of household pet in the United States. It is estimated by pet industry sources that nearly 7.5 million pet reptiles are present in nearly 3% of all U.S. households. These kinds of numbers invariably will result in more cases of reptile-related zoonotic diseases than ever before in human history.

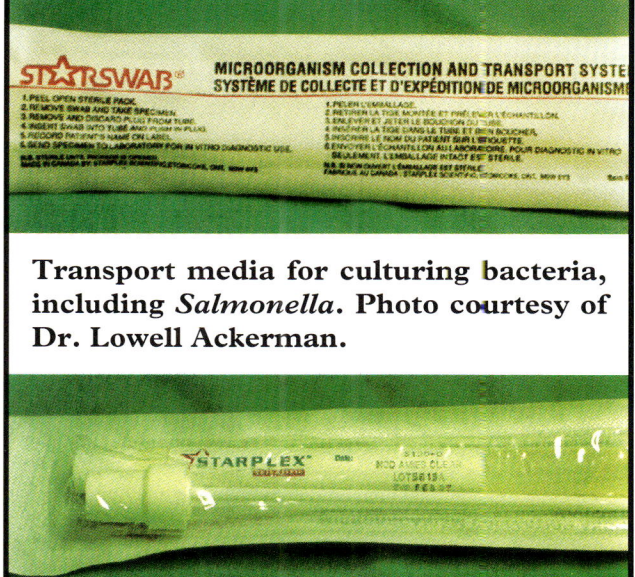

Transport media for culturing bacteria, including *Salmonella*. Photo courtesy of Dr. Lowell Ackerman.

The following points should be kept in mind when dealing with this problem:
1. Many reptiles are asymtomatic carriers of *Salmonella* and other microorganisms potentially pathogenic to humans. While they can be treated and eliminated in some reptiles, they are often part of the normal intestinal flora in animals that use hind gut fermentation.
2. Even if eliminated through veterinary intervention with antibiotics, infection can recur with the animal's next meal.
3. Attempts to eliminate *Salmonella* and other commensals with antibiotics leads to a preponderance of antibiotic-resistant forms which make medical treatment of humans more difficult or impossible.
4. Reptiles may be infected cloacally and transovarially so acquiring newborns/hatchlings provides no guarantee that the animal is pathogen free.
5. Some reptiles, including baby iguanas, also become infected by eating feces of other animals. This is a typical hatchling behavior designed to establish a level of normal intestinal flora.

6. According to Frank (Reptile and Amphibian Magazine, 1990) "education, not legislation" continues to be a problem with the keeping of reptiles and amphibians.

ROUTES OF ZOONOTIC INFECTIOUS TRANSMISSION

There are several routes through which humans can become zoonotically infected.

ORAL (INGESTION)

The most common route of infection is through oral ingestion, usually as a result of eating with hands carrying microorganisms such as bacteria or parasites or their ova. Small children and adults with nervous habits may place fingers in their mouths. Smokers may pass inocula of bacteria onto the tips of cigarettes which they also place in their mouth.

BITES, SORES AND WOUNDS

Salmonella and other microorganisms can infect humans through a bite wound, non-bite cut or abrasion, sore or other wound and enter directly into the bloodstream where a serious septicemia or blood infection can occur. In addition iguanas, other sharply clawed lizards and turtles may cause cuts or abrasions in human handlers which could become infected. Claws are often impacted with or contain traces of fecal material or other contaminated detritus from the animals enclosure. Deep scratches from contaminated claws can result in fatal or near fatal sepsis, especially in immunocompromised individuals.

EYES, NASAL PASSAGES, MOUTHS AND OPEN WOUNDS

Salmonella and other infectious microorganisms can enter humans through splashing of contaminated material into the eyes (through the conjunctiva), nasal passages, mouth or onto a cut or open sore or abrasion.

INHALATION

Infection can also occur through the inhalation (aerosolized droplets) of contaminated solutions or dusts. Raising dust through the handling of some reptile substrates can result in the aerosolization of microscopic particles which, when inhaled, could transmit infection.

PREVENTION

Proper cleansing and hygiene is essential for preventing zoonotic infections. Individuals who are immunocompromised for any reason should avoid contact with amphibians, reptiles and any other animals known to transmit zoonotic infections.

Reptile hobbyists can avoid becoming infected or becoming a common-vehicle (carrier/fomite) of zoonotic infections by taking a few simple precautions:

1. After handling any animal, including reptiles and amphibians, wash hands for at least 30 seconds, using a simulated surgical scrub technique, with hot water and a store-bought antibacterial soap.
2. If washing isn't always possible have a pump spray hand disinfectant/hand wash available. This is especially useful at swap meets or in the field.
3. Rinsing hands in water only is not effective in eliminating most microorganisms including salmonellae.
4. If you have to use kitchen or bathroom (rather than outdoor or basement) sinks and wash-up facilities to clean reptile enclosures, accessories (water bowls, reusable substrate, etc.), be sure and stow all kitchen utensils or personal use articles such as drinking glasses, toothbrushes, toothpaste tubes, combs, razors and so forth.
5. Under no circumstances should you touch food for human consumption after handling any animal or its accessories unless hands are washed as above.
6. Do not touch or otherwise handle any utensils, cookware or serving ware used for human food after handling or touching any animal or its accessories unless hands are washed as above.
7. Do not permit unsupervised handling of any reptile by children under 12 years of age.
8. Wash, disinfect and seek medical attention for any skin-breaking animal bite or clawing, especially if there is swelling, discoloration or inflammation at the site.
9. Keep reptile enclosures, caging, water bowls, substrate and other surfaces as clean as possible.
10. Teach children to wash hands as above after handling any reptile or amphibian and do not permit them to do so unless they first agree and understand why this is necessary.
11. Do not handle any amphibian, reptile or other animal with open cuts, sores or abrasions on one's hands. If handling is necessary use rubber household gloves or disposable medical gloves for this purpose.
12. If in doubt about any medication, treatment or medical condition you or a member of your household may have and its effect on immune status check with your doctor.
13. When handling animals with sharp claws, guard against deep scratches by using protective handgloves and clothing.
14. Individuals immunocompromised for any reason should avoid contact with amphibians, rep-

tiles and other animals known to transmit zoonotic infections.

Zoonotic infections from reptiles and amphibians are entirely preventable. In general zoonoses from these animals are rare and they represent a small fraction of all the infectious diseases which occur. Nevertheless, when they do occur, they often engender very negative publicity for herptiles so all hobbyists should be involved in disseminating information to prevent such infection from occuring.

REFERENCES AND RECOMMENDED READING

—**Ackman, DM et al. 1995**
Night of the Iguana: Iguana-Associated Salmonellosis - New York State. EIS 44th Annual Conference.

—**Cabello, F. et.al.(eds) 1993**
Biology of Salmonella - NATO-ASI Series Number A-245. New York: Plenum Press, Inc.

—**D'aoust, J.Y. et al. 1990.**
Pet turtles: a continuing international threat to public health. *Am J Epidemiol* 132:233-7

—**Frank, Norman 1990**
Deuces and One-eyed Jacks are Wild: The Story of John Haga [turtle farmer]. *Reptile and Amphibian Magazine*, May/June, 1990, p. 53.

—**Grenard, S., Katz, D. 1994**
Medical Herpetology. Pottsville (PA): NG Publishing, Inc.

—**Grenard,S., Nunan, K.A. 1995**
Reptile-Associated Salmonellosis - WWW Information Site. http://www.xmission.com/~gastown/herpmed/salm. htm New York: HerpMed Communications

—**Gyles, CL, Thoen, CO 1986**
Pathogenesis of Bacterial Infections in Animals Ames (IA): Iowa State University Press

—**Hann, C 1995**
The Lizard King: Reptile-associated salmonellosis in Pennsylvania. (unpubl.report) State of Pennsylvania, Department of Health.

—**Kaplan,MK 1995**
If You Have to use the Kitchen Sink. WWW information Site. http://www. xmission.com/~gastown/salm.htm, New York: Herpmed.

—**Oregon, State of 1995.**
Reptile-Associated Salmonellosis in Oregon. CD Summary, Oregon Health Division, Department of Human Resources. 44(12):1-2

—**Shane,SM et al 1990.**
Salmonella colonization in commercial pet turtles [*Pseudemys scripta elegans*] *Epidemiol. Infec.* 105:307-16

—**Virginia, State of 1995**
Reptile-Associated Salmonellosis. Epidemiology Bulletin, State of Virginia, Department of Health 95(6):1-4

—**Williams, LP Jr, Helsdon, HL 1965**
Pet Turtles as a cause of human salmonellosis. *JAMA* 192:6-10.

REPTILE REHABILITATION

Melissa Kaplan
RepEnvirEd
6366 Commerce Blvd #216
Rohnert Park CA 94928

Kaplan's work and practical experience includes six years in wildlife rehabilitation, with emphasis on reptiles; behavior observation in zoo and field settings; and oil-spill bird recovery. Kaplan is a freelance educator, who both presents programs on reptiles and their environment and develops integrated curricula based on animal and plant life. She is the author of many articles on reptile rehabilitation, pet care, and related issues. Currently, Kaplan is completing her masters thesis on the selection, care and use of animals in the classroom. She does extensive consulting, both on- and offline, on reptile care and behavior with emphasis on the green iguana.

INTRODUCTION

Wildlife rehabilitation involves the acute care of sick, injured, or orphaned native species, primarily mammals and birds. Most wildlife rehabilitation facilities receive few reptiles. It is not known at this time whether this is because the general public has less regard for reptiles in distress than for birds and mammals in similar situations, or because reptiles are more successful at hiding from humans.

Most wildlife rehabilitators are lay individuals who have received special training in the care and treatment of wild animals. Training is both on-the-job as well as through certification courses and workshops. Rehabilitators work closely with veterinarians in the diagnosis and treatment of the animals. Rehabilitators often do much of the routine work themselves, such as treating minor lacerations, ulcerative stomatitis, abscess, parasites and shell infections and they can ably assist veterinarians in some of the more complicated procedures.

Reptile rehabilitators work with both native and exotic species of reptiles. This presents certain difficulties in that, for many of the exotic reptiles, it may be difficult to determine the animal's proper habitat (temperature, light, humidity, substrata, furnishings). It may also be a problem to procure proper foods or to construct appropriately nutritious diets should the reptile require force-feeding. Also, once exotic reptiles have been restored to health, they cannot, as with local, native species, be released back into the wild. This forces the rehabilitator to provide or find permanent homes for a wide variety of species.

Many herpetologists and herpetoculturists find themselves managing large permanent or transient

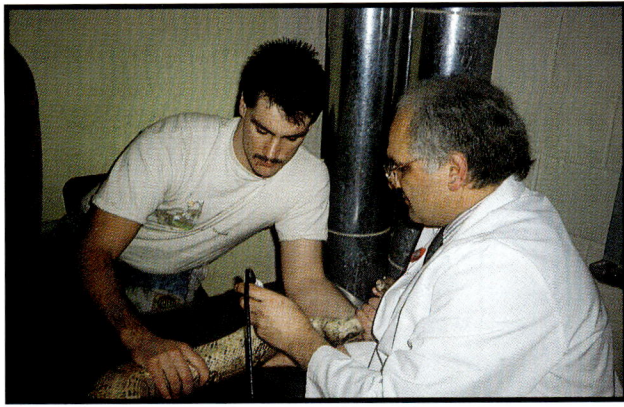

Ultrasound being performed on a boa constrictor. Photo courtesy of Dr. Todd Driggers.

collections of reptiles. In these cases, zoo medicine overlaps with wildlife medicine: the assessment and treatment of the individual overlaps with the use of herd health management (Franzmann, 1986). Treating individuals within a population may cause one to lose sight of problems within the group that may be underlie individual pathologies.

Many of the techniques and treatments used by the wildlife rehabilitator may be used successfully by herpetologists, herpetoculturists and hobbyists in the care of their reptiles. This information will also be of help to the reptile owner when he or she takes reptiles to the vet; it can help facilitate clear, precise communication between veterinarian and client. The vet may also more easily instruct the client in home care procedures, and have confidence that such prescribed home care will be done properly.

WARNING

Do not attempt to perform the more complicated treatments described in this chapter without first being trained in those procedures by an experienced rehabilitator or veterinarian.

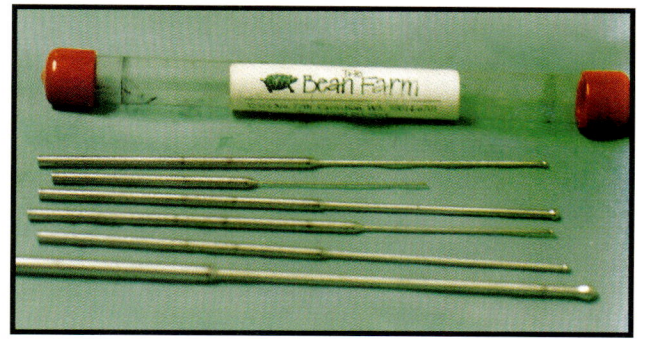

Example of probes used for sexing snakes. Photo courtesy of Dr. Lowell Ackerman.

INITIAL EXAMINATION AND VITAL SIGNS

All healthy animals carry a load of bacteria, viruses, and parasites. Some of these organisms are commensal. Others are infectious organisms that are successfully held at bay by the healthy animal's immune system (Iverson, 1986; McBee, et al., 1986). In the latter case, it is only when the animal is stressed, and the immune system thus compromised, that the disease process begins.

Both wild-caught and farm-raised pet-trade reptiles are subjected to incredible stress from the time they enter the export/import system. Crowded surroundings and improper temperatures, coupled with the lack of food and water, all contribute to the high mortality rate. Of those which survive and are distributed throughout the pet trade, many are dehydrated, emaciated, and experiencing adverse effects of bacterial and parasitic infections (Fowler, 1986a, b). The stress of being in captivity and surrounded by what may be perceived to be hostile

Dr. Bernard Mangone demonstrates the technique used to sex this female coachwhip snake. Photo courtesy of Dr. Lowell Ackerman.

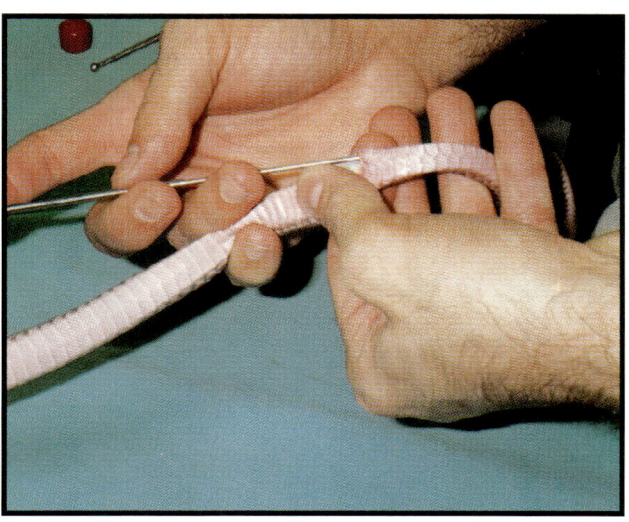

surroundings is also a cause for stress. Thus, even when wild-caught animals are not subjected to the less-than-adequate conditions typically found in the pet trade, those animals may still suffer from the effects of short- and long-term stress (Arena, 1995).

A healthy animal is alert, aware of its surroundings and generally responsive to tactile stimuli; lizards and chelonians will respond to sounds. Pets and long-term captives who are subject to frequent human interaction, including holding, gentle restraint and manipulation may be habituated to human contact. They are thus less likely to respond adversely to gentle stimuli which in turn reduces the stress reactions encountered in reptiles who

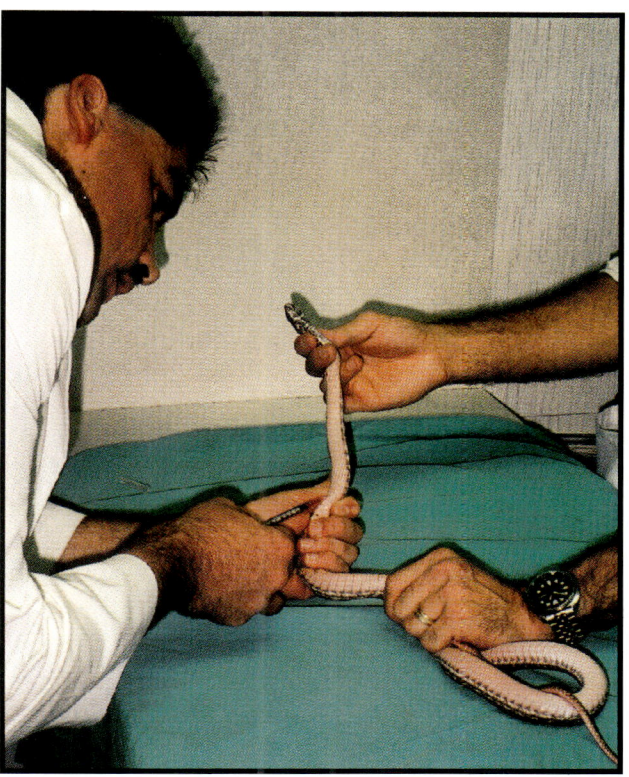

Dr. Todd Driggers collects a blood sample from a coachwhip snake. Photo courtesy of Dr. Lowell Ackerman.

are not used to such interactions. Non-habituated reptiles may be stressed by gentle handling, touching, observation, and the sound of the human voice. Healthy, habituated captive animals feed regularly, with reductions or cessation in feeding consistent with periods of hibernation, aestivation, reproduction, and shedding (Frye, 1991, Barnard, 1995).

Reptiles, like many animals, are adept at hiding signs of distress almost to the end of their lives (Arena, 1995). Unless one is very familiar with a specific animal or a species of animal, it may be difficult to tell when something is wrong. The more subtle signs of illness and injury will be discussed later in this chapter.

Obvious signs of injury include:
—paralysis
—paresis
—unusual limb extension
—limb, tail, or body held at odd angles
—cuts
—major skin defects
—puncture wounds
—dried blood on the reptile, substrate or furnishings.

Obvious signs of illness include:
—loss of appetite
—inanition
—change in feces or urates (appearance and frequency)
—loss of muscle tone
—paresis
—paralysis
—lethargy
—unusually responsive or non-responsive to normal stimuli
—unnatural body posture
—lumps or swellings.

GENERAL EXAMINATION

A general examination of every new reptile should be done before the animal is placed in its housing. Regular examinations of all captive animals should be done at least monthly. Certain situations may necessitate more frequent exams. These situations include pre-and post hibernation, breeding, ante- and post-partum, and shedding.

A healthy captive will be relaxed but alert, and responsive to handling. A wild specimen may be jumpy, responsive to even minimal stimuli. A lethargic, non-responsive animal may be suffering from a number of conditions, including starvation, dehydration, parasites, hypothermia, metabolic bone disease, systemic infections, and acute or chronic stress (Guiltette, 1995).

SPECIAL CONCERNS WITH WILD ANIMALS

Regular exams of animals to be released back into the wild must also take place, but care must be taken not to overly habituate these animals to human contact. Reptiles are not as prone to imprinting and habituation as are many bird and mammal species. However, the continued well-being of the released reptile often depends upon its healthy dislike or avoidance of human contact.

There is a fine line between handling an animal as a pet and as an animal to be kept wild. Rehabilitators do not talk to wildlings and often not even to each other except in whispers or very quiet tones when working in the presence of wildlings. While the animals are handled as gently as needed, they are not cosseted or petted as are pets and non-releasables that are being habituated and perhaps socialized for use in educational contexts. Wildlings should be kept secluded in quiet areas. This helps reduce the likelihood of habituation to noises associated with daily living (in households) and noises associated with facility operation (at rehabilitation centers). This also helps reduce the likelihood of habituation to humans and other domestic and wild animals.

MOVEMENT

When you watch a reptile, you should observe it moving smoothly in the manner of its species. If it is a species that uses its tongue to smell, there should be regular and frequent flicks of the tongue. Limbs should move fluidly. Any weakness, ataxia, or tetany may be due to metabolic bone disease, nutritional deficiencies, or neurological damage (Frye, 1991; Jackson et al., 1992). If the animal favors a limb, that action could indicate a fracture or inflammation of the joint.

Pick the animal up, providing proper support, and feel it sit and move in your hands. You should be able to feel the strength of its muscles as it grips and moves within your hands. Even in animals that are quite small, you should be able to feel the strength of their muscles. A snake should coil or wrap its body around your fingers or arms. A healthy snake, when held with just its tail end wrapped around a finger or wrist, head hanging down, will easily pull its head back up towards your hand. Turned upside down, a healthy snake will easily right itself; failure to do so may indicate neurological damage.

NOSE

The rostrum should be free of lacerations, scabs, and encrustations. (The exception to this is the salt deposits which are typical of iguanid and some agamid lizards.) Breathing should be through the nose, not the mouth. There should be no clicking or wheezing sounds heard when breath is taken and expelled. The head should be held in the normal position for the species; if a head is raised for long periods of time, it may indicate a protozoan infection or a neurological condition. When accompanied by gaping, gasping, or excessive salivation, there may be a respiratory infection.

MOUTH

The mouth should be free of food debris, swellings, encrustations, and excess salivation. Pockets of trapped food may indicate previous infection or metabolic bone disease. Swellings and encrustations indicate bacterial infection. Excess salivation is a common symptom of respiratory infection, but may also accompany advanced cases of stomatitis (mouthrot).

Desert tortoise with nutritional hyperparathyroidism. Note mandibular prognathism. Photo courtesy of Dr. Bernard A. Mangone.

The interior of the mouth should be pink, free of whitish or yellowish plaques in the gums. Pale pink, grayish pink, or bluish tissues in the mouth maybe indicative of dehydration or an underlying systemic infection that is typically accompanied by secondary opportunistic infections such as stomatitis and respiratory infection. In chelonians, an overgrown beak may indicate anorexia or improper diet. The interior should be free of swellings and the Eustachian tube free of pus, the presence of which indicates possible otitis media (middle ear infection).

Some lizards (most notably water dragons, *Physignathus* sp.) and snakes are prone to rostral abrasions and extensive tissue damage due to rubbing their snout against their enclosure. When this goes on for some time, glass and wooden surfaces may do as much damage as wire mesh. As these defects may make it appear that the reptile has been attacked by another animal, it is important to ascertain the origin of the defect when the animal is presented, and treat and house the animal accordingly.

EYES

The eyes of a healthy reptile are clear and bright. The pupils should be responsive to light. In a wild or nervous animal, it is not unusual to see the pupils contract and dilate rapidly while being held or, in many cases, when merely being observed. Eyes that are cloudy (except for snakes in the final stages before shedding), swollen, wet, or crusty with dried fluids suggest an infection, injury, or a foreign body in the eye. Indentations in a snake's eyes may indicate one or more retained spectacles or dehydration. Swollen eyelids in chelonians often indicate a vitamin A deficiency. Healthy chelonians, especially *Testudo* sp., may show an overflow of tears (Jackson, et al., 1992).

Note that many species of lizards will puff out their eyelids many times their normal size during the shedding period. While this may look rather alarming, it helps to loosen the old skin layer and is a normal occurrence.

EARS

In chelonians, the ears should be flat or slightly concave. Swellings or mild bulging of the tympanic membrane may indicate otitis media. In lizards, the tympanic membrane should be flat and without defect.

BODY

The body of a healthy reptile is well fleshed. While some species are normally thin, they are not exceedingly bony in appearance. Wild reptiles may have been injured by prey, predators, humans, equipment operated by humans, or pets, especially dogs and cats. In captivity, lacerations or abrasions may be a sign of fighting amongst cagemates. Lacerations or abrasions may also be a sign of injury caused by attempted escapes or poorly designed enclosures or furnishings.

Hard and soft swellings indicate abscesses due to bacterial infection or parasites. Discolored patches and blisters on back and belly may indicate the animal has been too close to an unshielded heat bulb or has been on a hot rock or heating pad too long. Series of blisters on the belly may indicate blister disease, a bacterial infection caused by damp and generally unclean substrates, or thermal burns. Small dark spots may be signs of a fungal infection or may just be areas of the skin from which scabs have fallen and the scaling has not regenerated, weeping or oozing lesions may be due to *Salmonella* infection.

In lizards and snakes, baggy, or wrinkled skin exceeding that which is normal for the species indicates emaciation and dehydration. In chelonians, emaciation is indicated by deep recesses between the neck and shoulder. While chelonians do shed their skin, excessive sloughing of skin may indicate an underlying illness. In most instances of reptile dysecdysis, the underlying cause may be traced back to inadequate or improper environmental conditions.

The normal coloring of healthy animals in many species may cover a wide range of colors and patterns. Reptile skin contains chromatophores enabling it to change colors. The turning of the normal color to an overall dark gray or brown is generally a sign of stress. The stress may be environmental or psychological (interactions with humans, conspecifics, other animals) (Greenberg, 1995).

The rate of such stress-related color change may happen quite rapidly, with the color darkening, dimming or taking on stress patterns (as the multicolored patches on true chameleons) within a few moments or minutes of physical contact or close observation. Evnironmentally-induced stress color changes, such as that of being kept at improper temperatures, may take longer to occur, gradually progressing over a period of days, covering an ever increasing portion of the body.

Keep in mind basic reptile anatomy when palpating the coelomic cavity. It can be difficult to accurately palpate a snake because of the length over which its elongated and narrow organs are spread. Roughly speaking, the first third of a snake (starting at the head) contains the esophagus, trachea, and heart; the second third the lungs, liver, stomach, and part of the air sac; the final third contains the balance of the gastrointestinal systems, reproductive organs, and cloaca (Jackson et al., 1992).

LEGS AND FEET

The legs should be regularly formed with no puncture wounds, lacerations, or enlarged bumps

Pinning of a broken femur in an adult male iguana. Photo courtesy of Dr. Bernard A. Mangone.

along the limb or at the joints. Feet and toes should be regularly formed and without swellings. The digits should be free of old unshed skin.

It is not uncommon for lizards to lose toes or claws due to injuries and infection in the wild. It is also not uncommon for lizard toes to be amputated for similar reasons in captivity. These generally heal well and have little or no effect on the lizard's ability to function.

VENT

The vent and the folds of skin surrounding the vent should be clean and free of feces. There should be no signs of irritation, swelling, or prolapse of intestinal tissue or hemipenes. If one of these conditions is present, it may indicate illness or parasite infection.

TAIL

The tail should be free of punctures, lacerations, bumps, swellings, or abnormal compressions. It should be firm and should move in the manner of the species. If the tail has recently

autotomized (dropped off in defense of perceived attack, when trapped, or grabbed inappropriately), the exposed tissues should be folding over the end of the stump and healing over with no sign of swelling or inflammation. Tails that are extremely limp, especially in the presence of bumps or crushed areas, may have a compression or crush fracture and the beginning of tissue necrosis.

FECES

Healthy reptile feces are firm enough to hold their shape and are brown in color. In carnivore feces, you might see bits of fur; in insectivore feces, bits of indigestible invertebrate chitin; in herbivore feces, bits of undigested plant matter. Loose, watery, bloody, discolored, or unusually odoriferous feces indicate that further medical investigation is required. These conditions may be related to parasites, such as worms amoebic infections, or to disorders of the digestive system or key organs.

The fluid portion (the urates) of the bowel movement should be clear, laced with white to off-white matter. In snakes and carnivorous and omnivorous lizards, this white matter may solidify into hard, chalky lumps. The clear liquid of the urates may become tinged with red or orange as a result of the feeding of certain brightly colored fruits; however, this discoloration should disappear within 24 hours or so of feeding. If any such discoloration occurs repeatedly or in conjunction with abnormal feces, or any other sign of systemic or organ dysfunction, it should prompt a detailed ex-

The gray scabby areas on this iguana (*Iguana iguana*) are the result of being gnawed on during dominance encounters with another male. The deformed and truncated nuchal and dorsal crest is as a result of the prior owner keeping the iguana in a harness much of the time.

amination, a diagnosis being attained and treatment initiated. Yellow clotting urates may indicate dehydration.

HANDLING

There are many books that provide detailed information on the proper handling and restraint of reptiles for examination. For both wild and captive animals, the handling and restraint used for capture and physical exams can be quite stressful, and the animal's stress may cause misleading results in certain blood chemistry tests (Kreger, 1993a). There is, however, indication that nonreleasable animals can become habituated to regular gentle handling, thus reducing the likelihood of producing skewed biochemistry results (Kreger et al., 1993b).

Reptiles are generally less frightened by slower movements than abrupt, quick ones. While you must often be abrupt and quick to catch an animal, once the animal is in hand and safely restrained, you should use slower, gentler movements. To further reduce stress, there should be minimum of auditory and visual stimuli, especially rapid hand movements, in the examination area.

When necessary, use two or more people to restrain larger specimens. Also use two or more people to handle and restrain those specimens which may be aggressive or unwieldy during examination and treatment.

CHELONIANS

Use extreme care when working a turtle or tortoise head out of the protective shelter of its shell. Often times, you can put gentle pressure on the hind limbs. Pushing the limbs into the body cavity results in the displacement of the forequarters. Once the head is out, you can grasp it between thumb and finger or between two fingers, placing your fingers behind the head along side the neck. Be careful not to apply pressure to the tympanic membranes.

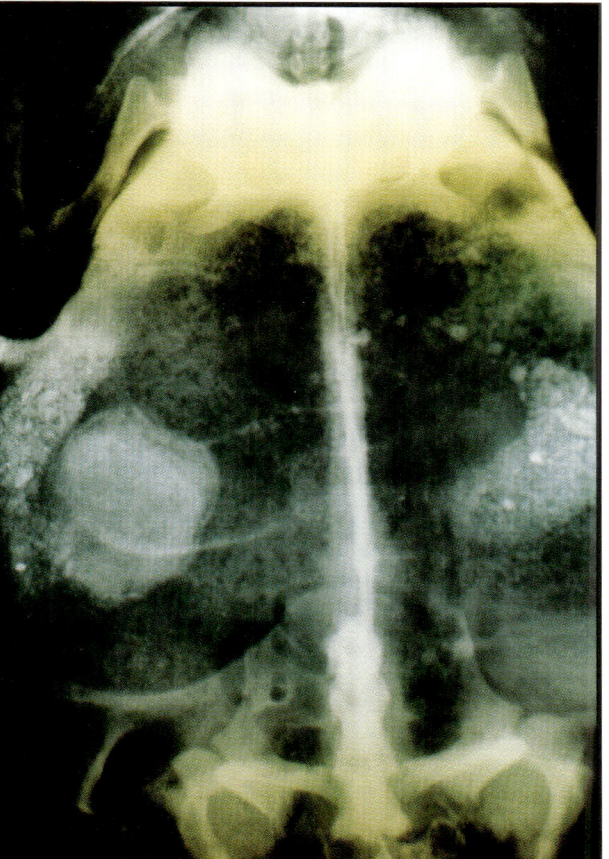

Large kidney stone in a desert tortoise. Photo courtesy of Dr. Lowell Ackerman.

Exercise care when working with box turtles; they can easily snap their shell shut, trapping a finger. Application of gentle pressure on the back or the front of the plastron will force open the opposite section of plastron. To do this, insert a thumb and finger in the opening and gently spread the opening apart, allowing a limb to be extracted. Once the limb is out, holding it will prevent the shell from closing.

Use caution and common sense when holding snapping turtles and turtles with long necks. Hold them at the rear of the carapace; offering a towel or glove for the turtle to bite on often keeps biters occupied. Once such a turtle has hold, it often continues to hold on, which makes it much easier to complete the exam of the rest of the body (Jackson et al., 1992).

LIZARDS

Lizards presented in bags or boxes may initially be restrained—through the bag, if necessary—by grasping the back of the neck and shoulders. This allows for careful uncovering and transferring control of the head from one hand to the other. Once the head is under control, you may pick up the body with your other hand, placing your hand under the lizard's belly and hips. You can restrain thrashing lizards by holding the forelimbs to the sides of their bodies and the hind limbs alongside the tail. Some lizards may be more stressed, and struggle more vigorously, when tightly held. A relaxed supportive hold will enable them to relax. Many will sit still, allowing gentle manipulation. Be careful when picking up, grabbing for, or restraining lizards by the tail; many species have the ability to tail autotomy. While this is not inherently harmful to the lizard, it does place additional stress on what might already be a highly stressed animal. Additional stress can lead to complications in healing and overall recovery.

SNAKES

Snakes are often presented coiled up in a bag or box. If possible, lift a non-venomous snake by supporting the coiled body. This is not only less stressful initially for the snake but it also gives you the opportunity to assess muscle tone and general state of health. The snake should be allowed freedom of movement when possible; you should restrain the head and neck as needed for examination. For aggressive species, control the snake by grasping the neck just behind the head while the snake is still bagged.

SIGNS AND TREATMENT

Many diseases and disorders have signs, or symptoms, in common. Accordingly, it is easy to confuse one disorder with another because two conditions can have the same or similar clinical manifestations. Each time you evaluate a reptile, make sure you consider whether common signs and symptoms are indicative of something other than a simple physical problem. For example, a relatively minor problem, such as a mild case of mouthrot, may be indicative of a systemic infection. This is because "mouth rot" is not a diagnosis, but rather a clinical description. Many different diseases can give rise to mouth lesions which might be described as mouth rot (see chapter on internal medicine for more details). Treating "mouth rot" without knowing the actual cause at best prolongs the recovery period. At worst, it may cause the reptile's overall condition to continue to deteriorate.

Poor environment and diet are the root of most reptile disorders. Treatment that does not also correct what is wrong in the environment or diet may well fail to restore the animal to health (Cunningham et al., 1992; Frye, 1991).

SHOCK

In reptiles, the two most common types of shock are hypovolemic shock and septic shock. Shock is essentially the failure of the body to circulate blood, and thus oxygen, to peripheral tissues. If cells are not nourished or oxygenated, or if waste products are not removed from cells, cell death will occur. Cell death is followed by organ and gastrointestinal failure, increased bacterial proliferation, and fluid loss as mucosal layers are destroyed. This puts additional strain on the heart as it attempts to keep vital systems functioning. One of the major complications in treating shock is that the animal—especially a wild one—can fail quite rapidly from the time it first begins to exhibit signs of shock.

Hypovolemic shock is caused by blood loss from:
—hemorrhaging (internal bleeding)
—bleeding from lacerations, bites, and other wounds
—fluid loss from vomiting
—seepage from burn sites

The animal's body attempts to counteract this loss of fluid by constricting blood vessels. This causes a reduction in capillary pressure. The body attempts to keep up the circulation of blood to the brain and key organs as long as possible. In the short term, this is an effective survival tactic, but if the bleeding or fluid loss is not halted, a cycle of generally irremediable events begins to occur. This cycle includes hypoxia, cell death, and organ failure (White, 1988).

The amount of time it takes to lose the blood or fluid can affect the outcome of the animal's shock. If you are caring for a reptile in shock, you must deal with the underlying cause of the blood loss at the same time you are attempting to reduce the effects of the shock itself. As with mammals, such treatment (White, 1988; Lawton, 1992) includes:
—gently raising the animal's core body temperature to its preferred body temperature (PBT)
—keeping the animal in a quiet, warm environment
—replacing fluids to increase circulatory volume
—possible use of corticosteroids.

Septic shock results from the toxins produced by bacterial infections such as *E. coli*, *Salmonella* sp. and *Pseudomonas* sp. Signs of septic shock include low blood pressure, pale mucosa, hypothermia, rapid heart beat, and muscle weakness. Treatment for septic shock includes:
—gently raising the body temperature by providing a warm environment
—fluid replacement
—possible use of steroids and antibiotics (White, 1988).

USE OF HEAT IN SHOCK THERAPY

Raising a shocky animal's body temperature increases dilation of peripheral vessels and increases blood flow to hypoxic areas. The increased blood flow in turn increases the animal's pulse, blood pressure, and respiration. Nutrients, oxygen, and waste products again begin to cross cell membranes, and some sense of well-being is restored to the animal (White, 1988).

However, while heat is important in the treatment of shock, you must be careful not to use too much heat and not to heat the animal too quickly. Raising the animal's body temperature too fast or too high, or providing heat in an inappropriate manner, can cause cell death and lower blood pressure. Heat should be provided by placing the animal in an environment with an ambient air temperature such that the reptile may be raised to its normal PBT. This can be accomplished by placing the reptile in an incubator or free-standing intensive care unit, or in an enclosure with a properly regulated and monitored heat lamp. Thermometers should be placed inside the tank at the same level as the reptile and they, as well as the reptile, must be monitored on a regular basis. Lo-

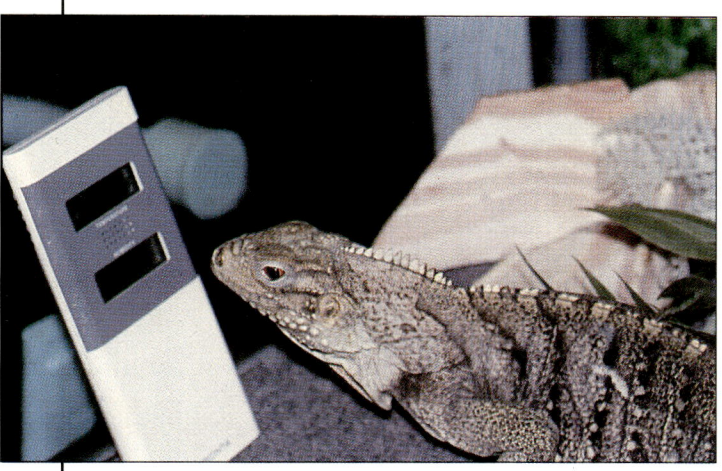

Land iguana terrarium equipped with a thermometer/hygrometer. Photo courtesy of Dr. Todd Driggers.

calized heat sources (such as heating pads) can cause blistering and burns, and tissue necrosis, where the animal's body comes into contact with the heat pad (White, 1988).

DEHYDRATION

Dehydrated reptiles have skin that is often deeply wrinkled at the neck and along the sides of their bodies. The eyes are often sunken or may be wrinkled. When pinched, the skin does not rapidly spring back but remains puckered. Often there is unshed skin on the body, frequently in patches, especially on the head, toes, crests and tails. Dehydrated animals are lethargic and will not eat, and should not be force-fed until rehydration has been started. Dehydration may be caused by diarrhea, heat stress, improper diet, or an inappropriate or absent water delivery system (Raley, 1992; Frye, 1991; Boyer, 1994).

Mild dehydration may be treated by:
—giving an initial soak in lukewarm water
—providing daily mistings
—ensuring access to drinking water in a form suitable for the species

Terrarium that has been misted. Photo courtesy of Dr. Todd Driggers.

If the reptile will drink when soaked, you should soak the animal in an appropriate electrolyte fluid, such as a 1:1 solution of Gatoradeä (an electrolyte replacement sports drink) and water, or an undiluted solution of Pedialyteâ (a children's electrolyte drink). If you soak a reptile in an electrolyte fluid, make sure to rinse the animal with fresh, warm water before returning it to its enclosure. Follow your veterinarian's directions regarding time-frame for the soaking period since it often differs from species to species.

You should provide frequent, plain-water soaks and mistings for animals native to more humid climates and for animals which have chronic or acute constipation. Snakes and lizards may be soaked for 20-30 minutes at a time; weak animals should be physically supported or closely supervised. Chelonians should be soaked for 24 hours in lukewarm water, which is not deeper than the chelonian's chin when the animal's head is retracted into the shell (Boyer, 1994)

To treat moderate dehydration, you must soak the animal for long periods of time, as well as administer fluids orally. Soak for 30-60 minutes, supporting or closely supervising weak animals. Follow your veterinarian's directions closely.

Severe dehydration requires the administration of fluids by injection. For such dehydration, it is best to administer the fluids by intracoelomic injections. However, if you have not been trained in placing the needle so that a vital organ is not punctured, or if you are working alone with a large or more active reptile, you may need to administer the rehydration fluids orally or through subcutaneous injections instead.

The most common fluid administered is lactated Ringer's solution. This is isotonic (it will not cause dehydration by drawing fluids out of the cells) and can be administered orally, subcutaneously, intramuscularly, or intracoelomically. Also, you can add dextrose to the Ringer's solution to increase the number of calories administered to the animal. However, at concentrations above 3% dextrose, the solution becomes hypertonic and will cause dehydration at the cellular level (White, 1988).

Make sure you do not administer too much fluid at one time or too much fluid over a short period of time. Too much fluid over too short a time overloads the vascular system and can kill the animal (White, 1988). For moderate dehydration in small reptiles, administer 25 ml/kg rehydration fluid per day. For moderate dehydration in large reptiles, give 15 ml/kg of fluid per day. For both large and small reptiles, administer the rehydration fluid in two or more divided doses (Barten, 1993; Boyer, 1994). Severely dehydrated reptiles may require as much as 40 ml/kg per day, administered in at

Table 1. REHYDRATION

Route	Dose / Solution
Fluid Therapy Oral	15-25 ml/kg/24 hr[1]
Parenteral	15-25 ml/kg/24 hr[1] 20-40 ml/kg/24 hr[2]
Solutions Parenteral	-Sterile isotonic saline -Lactated Ringer's solution -Two parts 2.5% dextrose in .45% sodium chloride + one part Ringer's solution[2]
Oral, Gavage	-One part each Gatorade® + water[1] -Pedialyte® -Entrolyte®[1] -One qt warm water + 3 t. sugar + 1 t. salt[3]
Gavage	Emeraid II 1.0 ml/40gm[1]

[1] Frye [2] Barten [3] Raley

least two doses. These are just guidelines. Follow your veterinarian's recommendations closely.

For tortoises, intravenous fluid administration should be reserved for only the most severely dehydrated and moribund animals. Page, et al. (1990) report that the fluid volume administered at any one time to a tortoise should not exceed 5% of the animal's body weight. Page also reports that the rate of intravenous fluid administration should not exceed 1 ml/min. Intracoelomic fluids must be limited to only 2-3% of body weight, due to the risk of compression of the lungs or direct perfusion of the bladder—a critical factor in chelonians. Refer to Table 1 for rehydration recommendations of fluids and quantities for lizards and snakes.

In moderate to severe cases of dehydration, start with parenteral administration of mildly hypertonic fluids. This will promote intracellular perfusion of water. You can then progress to subcutaneous and oral fluids as the animal's fluid balance is restored (Barten, 1993).

As the reptile attains normal fluid balance, monitor the animal's drinking water to make sure that the reptile is, in fact, drinking. Always offer drinking water in a manner appropriate to the species. Some reptiles who can learn to lap from a bowl may be initially stimulated to do so by the sight and sound of dripping water. You can create the sight and sound of dripping water in several ways. One method is to place ice cubes on a mesh cage top so that the melted ice drips into a bowl of water situated beneath it on the cage floor. Another method is to place ice cubes on top of a hamster water bottle suspended over the water bowl, so that the water from the melting ice runs down the bottle and nipple to drip into the bowl. For lizards who lap up water droplets, provide artificial leaves and vines, sprayed with water to form droplets for lapping. Because you can easily clean and disinfect artificial leaves and vines that become soiled, artificial plants are preferable to live plants, especially for debilitated reptiles.

EMACIATION

Emaciation itself is simple to diagnose; however, the underlying cause for the animal's failure to eat or maintain weight may be more difficult.

Emaciated snakes look bony and appear triangular in cross-section, with the vertebrae easily felt or visualized. In emaciated lizards, the hips are prominent. In advanced cases of lizard emaciation, the ribs and vertebrae in the back and base of the tail are easily visualized. In both snakes and lizards, the skin may be baggy. Since dehydration often accompanies emaciation, the skin will be dry and inelastic.

Emaciation in chelonians is easily seen in the flesh around the limbs and between the forearms and neck. Deep recesses in these areas signal emaciation. If an underweight chelonian enters hibernation, or a healthy one is not maintained at cool enough or constant temperatures during hibernation, the animal will use up critical calories during hibernation. During hibernation, temperatures above the species-optimum hibernation temperature result in an animal using up precious reserves of fluid, fat, and glycogen (Frye, 1991). In either case, the animal emerges from hibernation in an emaciated, severely weakened and immunbiologically compromised state.

One of the most common reasons for emaciation, loss of appetite, or for reduced food intake, is an environmental temperature that is too low for the reptile. Reptiles have a preferred body temperature (PBT) at which their metabolism and immune systems run most efficiently. To maintain their PBT, reptiles need a range of temperatures. This range, the preferred optimum temperature range (POTR), not only varies between species, but some species may also have seasonal shifts in their POTR. Too often, reptiles are offered just one temperature within their enclosure; this is just as stressful and ultimately unhealthy for them as temperatures that are too hot or too cold (Coo-

per, et al., 1992). Without a proper range in temperatures, the animals are unable to behaviorally control their PBT (Barten, 1996).

Emaciation can also result when two or more animals are housed together. Direct aggression and subtle intimidation may occur between the animals. This can result in one or more of the cagemates not eating or thermoregulating itself. Resolution of aggression and intimidation problems must include alleviating the psychological stress caused by moving one or more of the reptiles into other enclosures (Warwick, 1990).

Gut bacteria, which may have been lost through extended periods of starvation (Frye, 1991), can be reestablished by feeding:
—supplements containing live *Lactobacillus acidophilus* bacteria
—nonfat yogurt containing live bacterial cultures
—Bene-Baca™
—liquified greens (such as alfalfa pellets).

Emaciated reptiles may have to be force-fed until

Three-toed box turtle (*Terrepene carolina triunguis*) is both emaciated and dehydrated. Diet for previous six years reported to be only cantaloupe melon.

they are strong enough to eat on their own, or until they begin to show an interest in eating. There are three types of force-feeding:

—hand-feeding the reptile's regular food
—force-feeding a slurry through an inserted gastric tube
—encouraging lizards to lap the slurry off the tip of a syringe, eyedropper, or spoon.

When treating emaciated animals, it is important to cause the least amount of stress possible. It is also important to feed foods that will not cause further deterioration of their condition. Take into account nutritional value and consult with your veterinarian. For example, lettuce would be a poor choice to feed an emaciated iguana because of its poor nutritional content. When an animal's energies are already depleted, foods that are hard to digest can force the animal to use up precious calories trying to digest that food (White, 1988). For example, trying to force a mouse or rat down a snake may cause a great deal of stress, which in turn burns calories. Whole prey takes more energy to break down than the more easily digested slurries administered by gavage.

When selecting foods for emaciated animals, select easily digestible foods that are high in nutrition; smaller than usual food items are more easily and efficiently digested. Select small, freshly molted insects, mouse pups rather than fuzzies, mice rather than rats, pieces of collard greens rather than whole leaves, shredded rather than chopped vegetables, etc.

EMACIATION PROTOCOL

Emaciated reptiles can be divided into three categories:

—Category 1 are animals who have not eaten in several days, weeks or perhaps months, but who are not significantly underweight. They weigh 90-

Gavage tubes are very important for feeding the convalescent reptile. Photo courtesy of Dr. Lowell Ackerman.

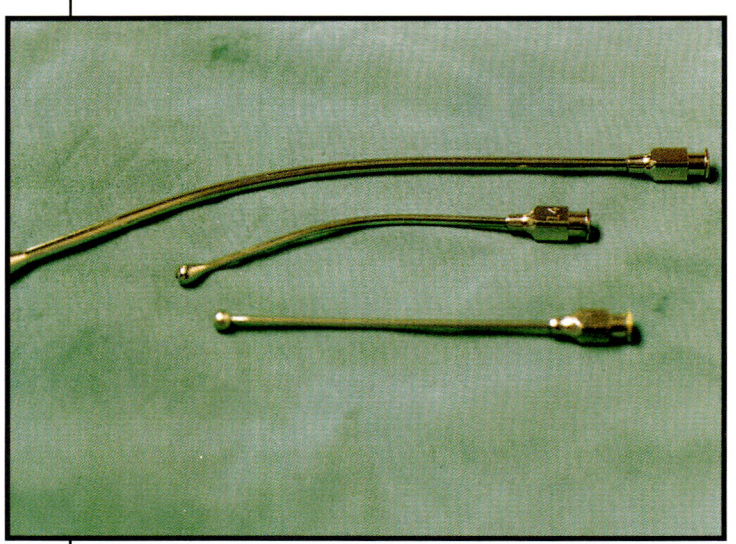

Green tree python with a g-tube. Photo courtesy of Dr. Todd Driggers.

100% of normal weight for the species age or size; they may appear hypoglycemic and may occasionally seizure.

—Category 2 are those who are between 75-90% of the normal body weight for the species age or size.

—Category 3 are those who are at 50-75% of their normal weight, generally skeletal in appearance and extremely lethargic or shocky (White, 1988).

Key points to restoring an animal to the point of self-feeding and digestion of normal foods include:

1. Warm the animal to the PBT for the species.
2. Hydrate using warmed rehydration solutions. Gently warm the gavage tube by running it under hot water. If necessary, lubricate the tube to reduce the friction of the tube against dehydrated or constricted tissue.
3. Administer simple molecular substances to Category 2 and 3 animals; do not administer whole prey or canine- or feline-based slurries until the animal has been in Category 2 and is soon to be reclassified to Category 1.
4. Initially, begin supplying 1.5-2 times the basal metabolic requirement, increasing to 3, 4 or 6 times that amount depending upon the age or condition of the animal.
5. Make changes gradually, weaning from the simple formulas (such as Ensure-based formulas) to the more complex and difficult to digest. Combine small amounts of the latter with greater amounts of the former, gradually reversing the ratio over a period of several days or weeks.

To determine how much food a reptile needs, you must calculate the animal's basal metabolic requirement, or minimal energy cost (MEC). This is the number of calories a day that an animal needs just to maintain basic body functions; it is not the intake required to promote growth or recovery. MEC is based not on body size, but on metabolic requirements. In fact, smaller animals require more calories more often than do larger animals. This

Table 2. BASAL METABOLIC REQUIREMENTS (MEC) IN KCALS

Weight (kg)	Basal* (MEC)	2 x Basal**	3 x Basal**	4 x Basal**	6 x Basal†
0.1	1.78	3.56	5.33	7.11	10.67
0.2	2.99	5.98	8.97	11.96	17.94
0.3	4.05	8.11	2.16	16.21	24.32
0.4	5.03	10.06	15.09	20.12	30.18
0.5	5.95	11.89	17.84	23.78	35.68
0.6	6.82	13.63	20.45	27.27	40.90
0.7	7.65	15.31	22.96	30.61	45.92
0.8	8.46	16.92	25.38	33.84	50.75
0.9	9.24	18.48	27.72	36.96	55.44
1.0	10.00	20.00	30.00	40.00	60.00
2.0	16.82	33.64	50.45	67.27	100.91
3.0	22.80	45.59	68.38	91.18	136.77
4.0	28.28	56.57	84.85	113.14	169.71
5.0	33.44	66.87	100.31	133.75	200.62

Based on White (1983) et al.
*The energy required to maintain basic bodily functions such as circulation, respiration.
**The energy required for normal activity, growth, reproduction.
†The energy required for extremely ill animals.

type of metabolic scaling is also used to calculate drug dosages (Frye, 1991).

MEC is expressed as the number of kilocalories required per day to keep the basic body functions operational. To calculate the MEC, use the following formula (White, 1988; Frye, 1991): Weight$^{.75}$ x 10 = Kcals / 24 hours.

This can be calculated on a regular calculator by cubing the weight in kilograms (weight x weight x weight), calculating the square root, then taking a square root again. The result is the Basel MEC.

When beginning a feeding regimen for an emaciated reptile, use the actual weight of the animal as the starting weight on which the MEC is calculated. Do not use the weight the animal should be for its size or age. As the reptile gains weight, recalculate the MEC, increasing the kilocalorie intake accordingly.

Once you have determined the MEC for basal metabolic function, multiply the kilocalories by a factor of 2 (adult, large, low natural activity), 3 (young, small, high natural activity levels), 4 (young, small, wound healing) or more (based on your veterinarian's recommendations) to determine the total calorie intake required per day. Young and small reptiles require more calories than do older, larger reptiles; and sick reptiles require more than healthy ones. See Table 2 for sample basal requirements already computed for certain weights.

HAND-FEEDING

You can hand-feed lizards and chelonians by offering them small pieces of their usual food items (plant or animal items). Depending upon the animal, you may use fingers or forceps to hold the offered food. You might also need to gently pry open the animal's mouth in order to get the food in. The following tools can be used to gently open the mouths of a variety of animals: rubber kitchen spatulas; chemistry spatulas; wooden, modeling clay tools; and flat, blunt-ended toothpicks, rubber-coated metal children's spoons.

Hand-feeding takes time and patience. You may need to repeat the feedings several times a day. Repeated feedings can ensure the animal gets enough calories not only to sustain basic metabolic processes, but enough calories to enable healing or recovery.

FORCE-FEEDING

All reptiles may be force-fed using the following tools:
—rubber gastric feeding tubes
—ball-tipped stainless steel feeding and dosing needles
—special curve-tipped plastic syringes such as those made by Monoject.

Large snakes and lizards can easily take the gastric tubes. Many lizards will start, and should be encouraged, to lap the formula off the tip of the feeding tube or syringe once a small amount of food has been placed into their mouths or throats. Some lizards, tortoises and box turtles may then easily be started on taking the slurry from a shallow bowl.

Some reptiles, such as monitors and chelonians, can bite hard enough to crimp the rubber gastric tubes, crack plastic syringes, and to damage their teeth or gums on the steel feeding tubes. In such cases, use a dowel of appropriate diameter, drilled with a transverse hole, for the reptile's mouth. The reptile can then bite the softer wood of the dowel, while you put the feeding tube through the hole and insert the tube into the esophagus.

You can also use squares of radiographic film in such situations. After you punch a hole in the center of a square of film, you fold the film in half and place it in the reptile's mouth to wedge it open. While the animal's mouth is wedged open, you then feed the tube through the hole in the film to administer the slurry (Suedmeyer, 1991).

There are many considerations to keep in mind when force-feeding a reptile.

—Insertion of Tubes. To make sure the feeding and gastric tubes are not pushed too far down the animal's throat, measure the tube first against outside of the reptile to be fed. With the tip of the tube at the chest or stomach area, wrap a piece of tape around the tube where it passes the mouth. When the tube is inserted into the reptile's mouth, the tape indicates when the tube has been inserted far enough. A rule of thumb for most reptiles is to insert the tube no more than one-third of the way along the length of the body as measured from the

mouth. In snakes, this will not be far enough to reach into the stomach, but it will be far enough down to forestall regurgitation.

—Lubrication of Tubes. Lubricate the tips of the feeding and gastric tubes with a lubricating jelly. Some sources recommend using raw, beaten egg as a lubrication. However, with the increasing presence of *Salmonella* sp. in factory-produced poultry, this may be risky when working with an already debilitated, at-risk animal (CDC, 1995b).

—Lubrication of Whole Prey. Lubricate the heads of killed rodent prey if you are forcing whole prey into the reptile.

—Force-Feeding Whole Prey. Some people prefer to force-feed whole prey to the reptile. This is generally quite stressful for the animal, and it can be counterproductive (White, 1988). One way to provide whole prey to the reptile without overstressing the animal is to puree the prey in a blender. You can then thin the puree as necessary with a hydrating solution, and then administer the resulting slurry through a gastric tube. You can also use a pinkie pump to puree mouse pups in the feeding syringe itself.

—Location of the Glottis. When starting to insert the tube, be sure that you are able to visualize the glottis. In some snakes and lizards, the open glottis is large enough that a feeding tube can be inserted through it. The result of this is that the lungs can be flooded with formula.

—Overfeeding and Aspiration. Do not overfeed an animal at any one session. Expel formula slowly to prevent it from backing up into the mouth, where it may be aspirated through the glottis into the lungs. If you see formula backing up into the mouth or coming out of the nostrils, stop immediately, and tilt the reptile face-downward to let the formula drip out of the mouth. Afterwards, carefully flush the mouth with water or hydrating solution, and place the reptile back in its enclosure. You will have to closely monitor the animal over the next several days for signs of respiratory infection. Let the animal rest a day before trying to feed it again.

—Withdrawing Gastric Tubes. When withdrawing a rubber gastric tube from the animal's throat, pinch the tube just below the hub of the syringe to prevent suction. To help prevent regurgitation in squamates, keep the animal's head horizontal or slightly elevated for a minute or so after tubing food or fluids. To help prevent regurgitation in chelonians, restrain the head for a minute to prevent the animal from retracting its head right away.

Table 3 contains a list of force-feeding formulas for carnivores, herbivores and omnivores. Insectivores may be fed as for carnivores.

Table 3. FORCE-FEEDING SLURRIES

Nutritional Slurries	Ingredients (admin: 2% bw q 24-48 hrs[1]
Carnivore	Hill's a/d™ thinned with Pedialyte® or 1:1 solution of Gatorade® and water
Omnivore	Equal amounts Hill's a/d™ and baby food vegetable thinned with Pedialyte® or 1:1 solution of Gatorade® and water One part Herbivore slurry (recipe below) mixed with Hill's a/d™ and baby food vegetable thinned with Pedialyte® or 1:1 solution of Gatorade® and water
Herbivore	Soaked alfalfa pellets mixed with baby food squash, baby food fruit, reptile multivitamin and calcium supplement, thinned with Pedialyte® or 1:1 solution of Gatorade® and water One can Ensure® blended with one banana + one Centrum® multivitamin[2]

[1] Barten, 1995. [2] Mader, 1995. All other diets based on avian and mammal recipes (White, 1988)

Table 4 contains a list of key nutritional components of prey and other foods commonly used to create slurries. Slurries are highly digestible and result in odd-looking feces and urates. As the animal is restored to eating foods normal for its species, the animal's feces and urates should return to the form, color, and consistency normal for the species. However, odd colors and consistency may indicate kidney or liver dysfunction in normally feeding reptiles. If in doubt, have fresh samples checked by a veterinarian.

PARASITES

This section briefly describes parasites commonly encountered by reptile rehabilitators, treatment of parasitic infections, and environmental considerations for preventing such parasites. Reptile parasitic infections are described below. Human parasitic infections, caused through contact with reptiles, are described in the chapters dealing with zoonotic and contact disorders.

Imported and wild-caught native reptiles are often infested with internal and external parasites.

A healthy animal can tolerate a certain level of infestation; a sick or stressed animal, however, cannot. Left untreated, a reptile's circulatory system may spread the parasitic organisms throughout the body (Willette-Frahm, et al., 1995). As the parasite population explodes beyond the levels normally tolerated by a healthy animal, the reptile will become increasingly weakened and ill. As with dehydration and emaciation, not only must you deal with the parasites themselves, but you must also correct the underlying cause that enabled the infestation to gain ascendancy. Underlying causes can include: environmental conditions, diet, confinement stress, agonistic behavior by conspecifics, etc..

When diagnosing or treating parasitic infections, pay particular attention to the animal's environment. Not only might the environment need treating to eradicate those organisms which have infiltrated the area, but the environment itself may not be appropriate for that reptile.

When working with reptiles, follow proper cleaning and disinfecting procedures at all times, but most especially when you are treating reptiles for endoparasites. Particular care must be taken not

Table 4. NUTRITIONAL COMPONENTS OF PREY AND SELECTED FOODS

Food Item	% Protein	% Fat	% Calcium	% Phosph.	Energy/ Kcal/gm	Source
Mealworms	22.3	14.9	.26	.23	2.74	3
	20.8	12.0	.03	.27	2.04	3
	54.6	31.4	.07	.71	5.35	2
	52.82	35.42	.06	.53		2
	47.0	35.0	.23	.71		1
Crickets	55.3	30.2	.23	.74		1
Silkworms†	64.7	20.8	.21	.54	5.74	2
Whole egg	12.3	10.9	.052	.22	1.47	1
	12.9	11.5	.054	.21	1.62	3
Day-old chick	15.3	4.4	.44	.40	1.04	1
Mouse, 1-2 day			1.6	1.8		1
7-10 days			1.43	1.29		1
adult	19.8.	8.8	.84	.61	2.07	3
Rat	7.6	1.99	.51	1.35	.69	1
Canned dog food	13.5	6.6	.76	.44	1.3	3
Canned cat food	16.0	16.8	.61	.53	2.42	3
Monkey chow	25.0	5.3	1.15	.79	4.17	3
High protein cereal	35.0	6.2	.66	.751	3.72	3
Baby food - beef	13.6	4.1	.007	.107	.91	3
- vegetable	2.2	.3	.035	.042	.32	3
Junior food - beef	15.1	4.0	.008	.111	.96	3
Alfalfa	15.5	1.7	1.29	.21	3.94	3

[1] Scott, 1992 [2] Frye, 1991 [3] White, 1988
† gut-loaded with mulberry leaves

to accidentally transfer infectious organisms from enclosure to enclosure. The transfer of infectious organisms is often caused by the use of the same cleaning utensils and supplies from enclosure to enclosure. Cleaning utensils and supplies that can transfer infectious organisms include: rags, gloves, sponges, and the water in which the sponges or rags are rinsed.

ENDOPARASITES

There are numerous species of worms and amoebae that regularly infect reptiles on a benign level. Herbivorous lizards and chelonians carry commensal protozoan and nematode organisms. However, those organisms can cause illness in animals which do not carry commensal loads of these organisms. Parasitic organisms affect herbivores and carnivores in different ways, attaching to different sites (Willette-Frahm, et al., 1995) in the reptiles' bodies. Traces of amebic cysts may be found in the feces of healthy animals, but these numbers in no way approach those found in heavily infested reptiles (Iverson, 1982; Bone, 1992).

Internal parasites may cause problems throughout the body. Internal parasites can cause gastrointestinal problems, such as the failure to gain or maintain weight despite normal food intake. Internal parasites can also affect the central nervous system. The following conditions can also be related to parasitic infection: diarrhea, vomiting, anorexia, excessive thirst, feces abnormal in color or consistency, regurgitation of ingesta, listlessness, and general malaise.

Gastrointestinal parasites may inhabit the mouth. These parasites can come from infected prey or from regurgitated prey that has brought parasites up into the mouth from lower down in the intestinal tract. Gastrointestinal parasites live out parts of their life cycle within an intermediate or primary host, taking up residence in and migrating through different organs and systems of the hosts. Reptiles are often infected by such parasites through fish and amphibians that are used by the parasite as intermediate hosts during the parasite's life cycle.

Different medications can be more or less effective in treating different organisms, especially in the treatment of worms and protozoa. Always perform a fecal exam on fresh feces to identify the infecting organism(s) so that you can administer an appropriate medication. Table 5 includes considerations and specific information about different anthelmintics.

Follow these general steps when collecting feces for examination:

1. Collect feces from the animal to be tested in a clean plastic bag or fecal collection kit.
2. Label the bag or kit with the date and with the species name from which the feces were collected.
3. Deliver fecal samples to the vet within four hours of collection. If necessary, you may store feces in the refrigerator for up to 24 hours before taking them to the vet. If you must store feces in a refrigerator in which there is also food, place the bagged sample in a second sealed bag after first washing your hands thoroughly with hot, soapy water. Reptiles do carry zoonotic organisms, and this washing and double-bagging will help reduce the risk of contamination to humans.

At times it may be impossible to get a fecal sample from a reptile. You might also be in a situation in which there is no time to wait until enough food is forced into the animal to produce feces. In this case, your vet may try to collect a sample through the use of a wash. Fluid introduced and subsequently aspirated from the cloacal, mouth, and lungs will include cysts and protozoa for identification. Your vet may also swab the choana.

If groups of animals are housed together, collect several different feces for examination. If any sample tests positive, all the animals in that enclosure should be treated. The presence of one or more apparently healthy animals in an enclosure with an obviously sick animal does not mean that healthy-seeming reptiles are not also infected with the organism. Rather, the healthy-seeming animals may be carrying heavy loads of the parasite but, being healthier to begin with, do not yet show signs of infection.

Rhabdias sp. are commonly found in garter snakes (*Thamnophis* sp.), grass snakes (*Natrix* sp.), and water snakes (*Nerodia* sp.). *Rhabdias* sp. may cause abscesses within the mouth or may migrate to the lungs. Snakes with *Rhabdias* sp. infections may be treated with levamisole at 10 mg/kg SQ (Bone, 1992). If the parasites are being transferred to the snakes through feeder fish, you can also treat the fish by leaving them to swim for 24 hours in a gallon of water mixed with 250 mg of levamisole.

The following list describes considerations and gives information about various anthelmintics. Please also refer to the chapter on pharmacology for more specific information on dosages, indications and contraindications. Do not attempt any treatment without confirming the diagnosis and treatment regimen with your veterinarian. In general, you can treat parasitic infections by administering two or more doses of anthelmintics.

Metronidazole. Generally administered for protozoa.

Fenbendazole. Used for many worms and can be administered to all reptiles.

Ivermectin. Often prescribed for worms. However, at least one study indicates that fenbendazole gets rid of worms when administered at lower doses and less frequency than ivermectin (Klingenberg, 1992). Very small, severely debilitated lizards often get worse after being treated with ivermectin, whereas similar lizards do not experience the same ill effects after being treated with fenbendazole. Never administer ivermectin to chelonians; it is extremely toxic to them (Frye, 1991; Mader, 1995b).

Levamisole. Membrane depolarizing anthelmintics, such as levamisole, have caused flaccid paralysis in weakened reptiles (Wright, 1992).

Piperazine citrate 5 mg/kg. Available at pet stores, and has been reported successful in the treatment of lungworms and roundworms in fish-eaters, such as garter snakes, water snakes, and box turtles.

Ivermectin. Seems to be more effective in treating lungworm and roundworm infections in lizards and in snakes other than garter snakes and water snakes (Klingenberg, 1993).

Thiabendazole. Often used to treat strongyloid infections (Frye, 1991).

Fenbendazole. Used to treat roundworms—a frequent, persistent, and often asymptomatic problem in chelonians (Boyer, 1992). May be more effective and less harmful to lizards than ivermectin. (Refer to the previous information about ivermectin.)

See Table 5 for medications and dosages commonly used in the treatment of endoparasites.

MAGGOTS

In wild anoles, botflies typically lay their eggs under the skin (*Anolis* sp.). The hatched larvae (maggots) feed on the anole from the inside, ultimately killing it. Anoles infected with botfly larvae should be euthanized. With stronger lizards and snakes, you must evaluate the severity of the animal's condition and the maggot infestation. Severely debilitated animals should probably be

Table 5. ENDOPARASITIC DRUGS

Parasite	Drug	Dose mg/kg/ Route		Frequency	Comment	Ref.
Cestodes Tapeworm	Praziquantel	5-8	PO	rep q 2 wks, 1 x		1
	Niclosamide	150	PO	rep in 2 wks		2
Nematodes Hepatic worms	Fenbendazole	25	PO	rep q 2 wks, 2-3 x	Common in garter and water snakes fed earthworms	1
Hookworm	Fenbendazole	25	PO	rep q 1 wk, 2-3 x		1
Lungworm	Fenbendazole	25	PO	rep q 2 wks, 2-3 x	Percutaneous and fecal-oral acquisition	1
Pinworm	Ivermectin†	0.2	PO	rep q 2 wks, 2-3 x		1
	Piperazine citrate	50	PO	rep in 2-3 wks	Fecal-oral acquisition	3
Roundworm	Fenbendazole	25	PO	rep q 2 wks*	-Consider deparasitizing prey -By gavage for turltes and tortoises	1
		100	PO	q 2 d for 3 wks		4
Strongyloides	Fenbendazole	25	PO	rep q 2 wks, 2-3 x		1
	Thiabendazole	20-25	PO	rep in 2 wks		1
Pentastomids	Fenbendazole	25	PO	rep q 2 wks, 2-3 x		2
	Ivermectin†	0.2	PO	rep q 2 wks, 2-3 x		1
Protozoans Amebiasis	Metronidazole	25-50	PO	rep q 2 wks*	-Giant tortoises, boas, colubrids, elapids, vipers and crotalids highly susceptible	1
		40	PO	rep q 2 wks*	-For tricolor kings, indigos and Uracoan rattlers	1
		125	PO	rep q 2 wks*	-For large boids	2
Coccidia	Sulfadimethoxine	50	PO	sid q 3 d; rep in 3 d	Fecal-oral acquisition Supplement with parenteral fluids	1
		90 45	PO IM PO IV	1st day, then sid q 5 d		2
	Sulfadiazine	75 45	PO PO	1st day, then sid q 5 d	May be normal intestinal organism	2
Flagellates	Metronidazole	25-50	PO	rep in 3-4 d if req.		1

[1] Klingenberg, 1993   [2] Frye, 1991   [3] Mattison, 1992   [4] Boyar, 1992
† Ivermectin is lethal when administered to turtles and tortoises.
* Continue to repeat every two weeks until feces tests negative

euthanized. Stronger animals having relatively minor maggot infestations will have a better chance of survival.

Maggots are also frequently found in both wounded wild chelonians and in escaped pet chelonians. The botflies not only burrow under the skin to lay eggs, but they will also invade defects in the skin and shell, laying eggs therein. You can use tweezers to gently pull maggots out of chelonians. Flush large infestations—and large defects suspected of harboring maggots—with sterile water, with dilute chlorhexidine diacetate, or with dilute povidone-iodine. Flushing causes the maggots to come to the surface where they will be easier to remove. Continue flushing wounds suspected of harboring maggots and, if possible, spread the edges of the wound apart to check visually for more maggots.

ECTOPARASITES

Ectoparasites generally consist of mites, ticks, and leeches. This section describes the common infestations of mite and ticks. Refer to the chapters in this book dealing with parasites and skin diseases for more specific information. Leeches are commonly found on wild aquatic turtles. They may be removed with forceps and the wounds then treated topically with dilute povidone-iodine (1.5-2.5%).

Working with pesticides—internal and external products alike—to eradicate ectoparasites always involves some risk to the infected animal. An animal may be oversensitive to a product or to a particular component in a product. In a group of animals being treated, one may suffer while the others remain unaffected. This could be due to an extreme sensitivity or to an unknown underlying physiological condition.

Many herpetoculturists have for years used pest strips inside their reptile enclosures with no apparent ill effect. However, never leave a pest strip in or on an enclosure with an animal. Poikilotherms metabolize substances at rates much different from mammals and birds. It cannot be assumed that what is safe for one animal (such as dog and cat flea collars or cattle wormer) is safe for your reptile.

Treatment for parasitic infections always carries the potential for harm, even death to the reptile. If you have any questions about these or other procedures or products, you should discuss them with an experienced reptile veterinarian. The next several discussions describe mites, ticks, treatments for mite infestations of snakes and lizards, and treatments for tick infestations of chelonians.

MITES

Mites, which are frequently found on wild-caught reptiles (particularly squamates), have several feeding and nonfeeding morphs. Their metamorphosis from one stage to the next is dependent upon ambient temperatures. Because of this, mite eradication is a process that must be repeated at least once.

Mites can be introduced into a group of mite-free reptiles when a mite-infested reptile is brought into contact with the other animals. People can also be unwitting carriers of mites. When people have come into contact with a mite-infested reptile, the mites can remain on the human bodies and clothing long enough to be transferred to a mite-free reptile or enclosure.

Mites can usually be found roaming the body, tucked under the edges of scales, and congregating around the eyes, ears, and any place on the body where the scales are thinner. If you can see the mites from about three feet away, or if, after touching the reptile, your hand comes away with several mites, then you have a severe infestation.

The presence of mites requires immediate environmental intervention as well as treatment of the individual animals. Also, reptiles that are moderately to severely debilitated may require fluids and nutrient supplementation to help restore fluid balance and provide energy for rapid recovery.

SNAKES: LISTERINE/PESTICIDE METHOD

To treat mite infestations, you must treat both the snakes and their enclosures. Bathing in antiseptics, such as Listerine or povidone-iodine is acceptable. The next set of steps explains how to eradicate a mite infestation from snakes while you treat their enclosures (in the procedure following this one).

1. Make a dilute Listerine-and-warm-water bath. Use just enough Listerine to tint the water a light gold. In very rough terms, this is equivalent to adding 1-1.5 pints of Listerine to a bathtub filled one-third with water. The bath should be warm (approximately 80-85 degrees F) to the touch when you test it with your arm.

2. Place the snakes in a dilute Listerine-and-water bath.

3. Leave the snakes soaking while you work on their enclosure(s) as described in the next procedure.

4. Keep the snakes warm by emptying and refilling the tub with the water-Listerine mixture as often as necessary, while you work on the snake enclosure(s). If the snakes are able to escape from the tub or room, you will have to put the snakes in a holding container after they are bathed. Use an easily cleaned carrier or a disposable cardboard box as a holding container, making sure the container is clean and warm. Then keep the snakes in the container in a warm room until you finish setting up the fumigation of their enclosure.

5. If necessary, you can put a small portable room

heater into the bathroom—well away from the tub—to provide additional heat for the snakes.

6. When the fumigated enclosure is ready for the snakes, place the snakes back into the tank and wipe them down with a clean towel.

7. Dab mineral oil on each eye using a cotton-tipped swab. This will suffocate mites that have burrowed into the pits near the eyes or in-between the spectacle and surrounding skin.

Follow these general steps to clean out the snake enclosure:

1. In this first step, you are trying to remove all the loose eggs, mites, and mite feces (the white dust on your snake and in the bottom of the tank) from the enclosure. To do this, first remove and dispose of all the substrate in the enclosure. Vacuum the inside of the enclosure thoroughly, paying special attention to the angles of the walls. If the tank is made of wood, lightly scrape the inside angles with the edge of a blunt knife, then vacuum the enclosure again. If you have a glass or Plexiglas tank, wipe all surfaces down with hot soapy water. Remove all soap residue. For good measure, take the time to thoroughly disinfect glass tanks by swabbing them down with a 1:30 bleach-water solution. Let the solution sit on the surfaces for 10-15 minutes before thoroughly rinsing out the bleach residue.

2. If you have cage furnishings such as branches or rocks, bake them in the oven, set at 250 F (120° C), for two hours (rocks may be boiled, completely submerged, for 20-30 minutes). If they are too big to place in the oven, soak rocks in a bucket, cement mixing tray, or tub in a 1:30 solution of bleach and water for eight hours. Rinse all cage furnishings thoroughly, spraying water into all the crevices, and playing the water over the wood and rock until they are well saturated and flushed. Then let the furnishings sun-dry for at least 24 hours.

3. Wash all bowls with the bleach-water solution, rinse well, then air-dry.

4. If you have heating pads inside the tank, remove them and unplug them. Wipe them down with the bleach-water, let them sit for ten minutes, then rinse them clean, and set them aside. If you have stick-on heating pads, check under them as best you can, or get rid of them entirely. Replace stick-on heating pads with a people-type heating pad or other free-standing heating pad or tape.

5. Disconnect all light fixtures and wipe them down with a damp cloth.

6. Now place a piece of aluminum foil inside the enclosure. Leaving the pesticide strip or flea collar still in its envelope, place the strip or collar on the foil. Squeeze the strip or collar out of its envelope onto the foil, leaving a bit still inside the envelope so that you can slide the strip or collar back

in when done.

7. Close the tank and seal it up as air tight as possible. Cover large screened areas or ventilation holes with paper, taped in place. Tape over the seams and any gaps between the doors and tank. You want to keep as much of the pesticide fumes inside the tank as possible. Leave the seals in place for at least three hours; large enclosures can require an additional hour or more depending upon the porosity of the enclosure materials (wood takes longer to fumigate than glass).

8. When the fumigation is complete, unseal the tank. Dispose of all paper and tape in a plastic bag, seal the bag, and immediately place the bag in the trash. Push the strip or collar back into the foil envelope, place it in a ziplock-type bag, then dispose of it according to manufacturer's recommendations. Leave the tank open and air it out for several hours. If possible, open a window in the room and turn on a fan to help air out the fumes.

9. Put new substrate in the enclosure and add any new furnishings. It is best to use simple substrates, such as paper towels, for the next couple of weeks. These are easy for cleaning purposes and may provide adequate contrast to visualize some larger mites.

10. Replace the water bowl, hide box, etc., into the tank.

In the two to six weeks following the treatment of the snakes and environment, watch the snakes and check the tank carefully. If there is any reappearance of the mites or traces of mites (such as their ashy feces), repeat the above procedures. If you see no reappearance of mites, you may wish to repeat the procedure in 6 weeks just to make sure that you have caught all the eggs.

LIZARDS: POVIDONE-IODINE METHOD

This procedure explains how to treat for mites that infest a lizard which can be soaked.

1. Fill a bath with warm water to a level that is shoulder-deep to the lizard.

2. Now add enough povidone-iodine to the water to make the bath the color of medium tea.

3. If the lizard is a small one, or is a species that does not regularly swim, keep the animal in a dry, warm area until the tank has been treated.

4. Now follow the procedure for fumigating the snake enclosure, described above.

5. While the tank is being fumigated, remove the soaking lizards from the tub or holding area.

6. Saturate a clean soft cloth in undiluted povidone-iodine. Use the cloth to gently wipe down the body.

7. Using a cotton-tipped swab, apply the povidone-iodine around the eyes and nose. Do not put

oil in their eyes as it may cause irritation or inflammation.

8. Let the lizard soak again in a fresh povidone-iodine dilute solution, or keep the lizard in a warm place until the tank is done being fumigated. (The povidone-iodine soak soothes and treats the mite bites.)

Note: For nonsoaking lizards, using a cotton-tipped swab, apply undiluted povidone-iodine to crusty areas after their wipe-down. Then, for several days, daily reapply the undiluted providone-iodine to the crusty areas.

9. When the tank is fumigated, aired-out, and refurnished, place the lizard back into the tank and wipe it down with a clean towel.

10. Repeat the povidone-iodine bath at least every couple of days while the bites heal.

LIZARDS: IVERMECTIN METHOD

Another way to eradicate mites requires the use of a prescription medication, ivermectin. However, ivermectin poses a potential danger to any animal. Ivermectin is most likely to cause severe problems when administered systemically (orally or by injection) to severely debilitated reptiles. Take extreme care when using it topically as well.

You can obtain ivermectin without a prescription in the bovine or equine section of feed stores. If you obtain ivermectin from a feed store, mix .5 cc (5 mg) of injectable ivermectin (10 mg/cc) per quart of water. Shake or stir vigorously and use the resulting solution immediately (Abrahams, 1992).

To bathe a lizard with povidone-iodine, follow the same general steps as for treating a snake with Listerine.

1. First, follow the same steps for creating a dilute povidone-iodine-and-warm-water bath for the lizard, as described above in steps 1-7 for creating a dilute Listerine-and-warm-water bath for snakes.

2. Now follow steps 1 through 5 of the snake-enclosure fumigation procedure (described earlier) to begin cleaning the lizard tank.

3. At this point, instead of using a pest strip or flea collar, soak a cloth in the ivermectin-water solution, or pour the solution into a spray bottle.

4. Now thoroughly wipe down or spray the entire inside of the tank, wiping down the unplugged heating pads and light fixtures.

5. While the ivermectin solution is drying in the tank, soak a clean cloth in the solution and wipe down the lizards.

6. Use a cotton-tipped swab to apply the solution around the lizard's eyes, ears, and nostrils. Be extremely careful to not get any of the solution in the lizard's eyes or nostrils.

7. Put substrates and furnishings back into the tank.

8. Replace the reptile in the tank.

You will need to monitor the lizard carefully over the next several weeks for the reappearance of mites. If necessary, repeat the cleaning and fumigation procedures.

TICKS

Ticks are also frequently found on wild-caught reptiles (particularly squamates and chelonians). Treat any tick parasite with caution. An otherwise healthy or mildly debilitated reptile may be able to handle one or two ticks that may be left in place for a short time. Moderately to severely debilitated animals, especially those suffering from dehydration or shock, must be treated quickly.

To remove and preserve for examination a tick, follow these steps:

1. Apply alcohol to the exposed portion of the tick. This is best done with a swab.

2. Grasp the tick firmly in a pair of tweezers and gently twist to withdraw the tick. In most cases, firm but gentle pressure is preferred to twisting which might cause the head to separate and remain lodged in the skin. Wear gloves or cover your hands with plastic wrap while removing the tick. Exposure to tick contents can be sufficient to transmit a variety of diseases.

An alternative is to apply a drop of ivermectin directly to the tick and leave the tick in place until the skin sheds next. This method is useful when the tick is lodged where removal is otherwise difficult or may cause some injury, such as in a nostril or around the eyes (Rossi, 1996). N.B. Ivermectin is extremely toxic to chelonians. Do not use ivermectin in chelonians under any circumstances.

3. Make sure you extract the mouth parts of the tick. You can tease out any mouth parts left attached to the skin by using a small dental curette or needle. Mouth parts that are not removed can result in an infected site.

4. Drop the tick in a small vial of alcohol.

5. Label the vial with the date and indicate the type of animal from which the tick was removed. Send to diagnostic laboratory for positive identification.

Because of the risk of infectious disease, you should preserve—if possible—the ticks that are removed from an animal.

Turtles and tortoises are often found with ticks. On tortoises and box turtles, the ticks may blend in with the raised scales on the legs. Box turtles and tortoises cannot tolerate long immersion in water higher than their bridge. They should be wiped down with a clean, damp cloth and inspected carefully. The folds of skin around the limbs and neck must be unfolded and checked. Look at the skin closely and feel it with your fingers; often ticks that cannot be seen can be felt. You can soak aquatic turtles in water, then blot off the excess water and inspect the animal. Before placing the chelonian back in its tank, make sure you clean the enclosure as described above, taking care to thoroughly rinse out all chemical and biological residues.

Never use ivermectin with chelonians. It is highly toxic to them and may result in the death of the animal (Frye, 1991; Mader, 1995b).

DISEASE AND DISORDERS

The following conditions are often encountered in wild and captive reptiles. Conditions related to diet and environment are considered together, as it is often difficult—if not impossible—to separate the effects of one from the other.

In the wild, the reptile's environment includes access to basking and hiding areas, food, and mates. All of those factors are predicated on the stability and overall health of the micro- and macro-ecosystem in which the animal lives. Even subtle changes can take their toll. Factors which can affect an environment include: changes in the chemical composition of the soil, contaminated water and rain, introduction of new species, the eradication of species, and the rearrangement of the landscape by humans and livestock.

Wild reptiles who cannot find their usual sources of water will move to other water locations, which are often near human habitation. This can bring about further problems, including an increased risk of poisoning, and the likelihood of meeting the business end of a shovel. Drought, toxins, and habitat destruction also affect not only reptiles, but their plant and animal food sources. Ultimately, both those reptiles who survive in the degraded environment and those who seek better conditions elsewhere are often stressed to the point of illness and parasite overload.

Artificial environments for captive reptiles include these elements: heating, lighting, photoperiod; enclosure layout and size, substrate, furnishings, and the presence or absence of conspecifics. Problems in the artificial environment can cause stress and illness, exacerbate existing poor conditions, or retard recovery. Elements or factors in an artificial environment which can degrade or retard the condition of the reptile include:

—Improper heating devices; inadequate temperatures; constant temperatures; temperatures within too narrow a range.
—Inadequate or inappropriate humidity.
—Periods of darkness (scotophase) or light which are too long or too short.
—Lack of access to ultraviolet A and B wavelengths.
—Insufficient room for natural movement.

—Inappropriate or insufficient substrate for natural movement and habits.
—Lack of privacy; lack of or inadequate boxes in which to hide.
—Exposure to predators, real or perceived (this may include pheromonal cues as well as visual line-of-sight exposure).
—Being housed with dominant conspecifics; dominance may be physical (pheromones) or psychological.
—Exposure to stress-inducing noise and visual stimuli.
—Inadequate nutrition.
—Inadequate or inappropriate water source.

Proper diet includes the feeding of proper foods of the proper size. Feeding prey or plant matter that is too big for the reptile may cause problems that include: anorexia, regurgitation, internal bleeding, and partial transient paralysis. Malnutrition may occur as large items are less-efficiently digested than smaller items. Ultimately, the reptile can starve, if the food is not properly prepared or offered (Frye, 1991; Warwick, 1990).

A proper diet also means that you make sure that prey animals are themselves healthy and well fed. Whenever possible, feed gutloaded prey obtained from quality breeders. Parasites are often introduced to captive reptiles through their prey animals. Always assume that wild-caught prey animals—including insects—are hosts to parasites of some kind. However, store-purchased prey animals can also host parasites, such as pinworms and tapeworms. Prey purchased from stores may also be contaminated inadvertently through inadequate cleaning and and disinfection techniques. Especially for reptiles that are already stressed, sick, or injured, make sure your reptile food producers are reputable and the food sources are clean and healthy.

Water, too, is important. All reptiles need some water. The frequency with which each animal drinks varies from species to species, but all animals require moisture. Some species get most of their metabolic fluids from the foods they eat; but all need to drink or lap droplets. If you do not provide proper foods to those reptiles which rely on foods for fluids, or if you provide an inappropriate water source so that the reptile cannot gain access to the water, the reptile will become dehydrated. As dehydration progresses, the reptile will cease eating. This is because digestive processes require fluids the reptile does not have. Eventually, if the fluid volume continues to drop, the reptile may go into hypovolemic shock.

Rehabilitators sometimes do not have access to good information about the species' requirements. In these cases, rehabilitators may have to try changing several different elements of the artificial environment to find out what is causing stress to the reptile. Initially, there may be a delicate balance between the reptile's natural habits and what is best for the post-surgical or wounded animal. Make sure you accommodate the reptile's natural inclinations as soon as possible (Warwick, 1990; Kreger, 1993a).

ANOREXIA

Anorexia is the refusal to feed or lack of appetite. It is a symptom, not a disease. Anorexia may be caused by a host of pathological and environmental conditions, which may make the underlying cause difficult to diagnose. Conditions which can cause a lack of appetite include:

—a change in environment, including keeper interaction

—an inappropriate environment prior to your acquisition

—lack of a proper hide box

—improper or inadequate heat or lighting

—improper food items or food items that are too big

—handling

—breeding season and gestation

New reptiles, imports, native, wild-caught reptiles, and captive-bred reptiles may not feed due to the stress of the change in environments or to being kept in inappropriate environments prior to acquisition. New, captive reptiles may stress when handled. Some long-term captives and certain species never become acclimated to handling. These animals may stress any time their environment changes, including changes in keeper interaction. Psychological stress may affect an animal's food intake; for example, green iguanas (*Iguana iguana*) frequently stop or drastically reduce their feed when moved to new locations or when their owners leave for a period of time. Some reptiles may reduce or cease feeding during breeding season and gestation. Snakes may refuse to feed on live prey after they have been attacked by prey; some of these snakes easily convert to killed prey, while others may need time and coaxing to convert.

Determining the underlying cause of the anorexia may require some probative questioning and examination of the reptile. Internal injuries, parasites and bacterial infections may cause anorexia. Other, visual indicators include:

Exudates around the eyes may indicate the presence of mites or infection. Bubbling or dripping discharge from the nose or mouth, or excess saliva, may indicate a respiratory infection. Petechiae (focal hemorrhage) or cheesy, white exudates in the mouth may be the early signs of mouthrot.

You may not be able to determine the cause of the anorexia by evaluating the environment, reducing stress, or performing an external physical examination. In those cases, you should begin laboratory work to determine possible internal factors that could be causing the condition (Messonnier, 1995; Wright, 1991).

ARTICULAR GOUT/PSEUDOGOUT

Gout is the swelling and crystallization of the joints and visceral organs. There is no effective way to reduce uric acid production in reptiles and, once gout has started, the condition cannot be reversed. Causes for gout include (Frye, 1991; Mader, 1995):

· dehydration

· ingestion of excessive calcium oxalate

· ingestion of excessive protein without proper hydration

· ingestion of improper protein sources

· hypovitaminosis A

Gout may also be caused iatrogenically through the extensive use of nephrotoxic drugs or when such drugs are administered caudally or without proper fluid supplementation (Lewbart, 1990). There is some indication that keeping reptiles below their POTR may reduce their ability to clear uric acid (a by-product of protein digestion) from the blood. As the uric acid (the white part of the urates you see when reptiles defecate) builds up in the blood, it forms crystals that are then deposited in tissues, joints and organs.

Crystal build-up in joints is called gouty arthritis or articular gout; when found around the joint, it is periarticular gout. Visceral gout is the term used to describe the crystallization of the soft tissues and organs.

Gout in its early stages may be difficult to diagnose in reptiles. To help diagnose the condition, review the animal's captive care, if the history is known. Evaluate the diet, environmental temperatures, availability of water, lighting and the use of nephrotoxic drugs on the animal. Radiographs may show crystallization of the joints or stones in the kidneys or bladder.

Gouty reptiles find it increasingly difficult to move, and they may require assistance in eating and drinking. Based on how gout affects humans, it is presumed to be quite painful for affected reptiles as well. The pain affects the animal's ability to compete (with other animals with which it is housed) for food, heat, and privacy. Gouty reptiles should be housed by themselves, or housed in a large-enough environment with just one or two animals with whom they are compatible.

Treatment for gout is limited. Beyond what is known about gout in humans, there exists very little information about gout in other animals. In advanced cases of gout, veterinarians may go into the joints and clear out the crystals. However, by that time that measure is taken, the disease is generally well-advanced, and the surgery has only a short-term effect at best. If gout is caught in the very early stages, it is possible to treat the condition with medication, but the medication must be administered on an on-going basis. The long-term prognosis for advanced cases of gout is guarded to poor (Mader, 1995); humane euthanasia should be considered when the condition does not respond satisfactorily to treatment.

BURNS

Thermal burns are not uncommon in reptiles, especially lizards and snakes. The most common burns are from hot rocks and overhead lights. Marketing pressures persist which encourage pet owners to provide heat to non-desert reptiles by furnishing enclosures with hot rocks. The rocks are often the only source of heat provided for tropical animals, and this results in the reptiles remaining on the rocks for long periods of time. Overhead heat lights and heating elements are often not shielded to prevent direct contact. Even without coming into direct contact with the light or heating element, the reptile can often get close enough to get blistered and burned.

Treat burns with povidone-iodine dilute baths. If there is necrotic skin, gently debride it and top the wounds with silver sulfadiazine. Repeat the treatment daily, debriding necrotic skin as necessary. As the burn heals, you may need to assist shedding in the area of the burn, so that thin scabs or new skin layers may be shed off with the old skin. Once the wounds are completely closed, you can halt the povidone-iodine baths. Stop the applications of silver sulfadiazine when the reptile's skin is no longer tender. There may be permanent scarring in the burn area.

Dehydration can be a particular problem with burn victims. If the burns extend over a large area of the body or extend into subcutaneous tissues, there may be extensive fluid loss. You may need to administer oral or subcutaneous fluids, as well as systemic antibiotics, to the reptile. Refer to the heading, Dehydration, earlier in this chapter, for specific information about rehydrating reptiles. Support nutritionally if needed. Force feed those animals unable to self-feed. If the animal is partially self-feeding, able to eat small amounts but not enough to sustain the healing process, force feeding may be used to augment the self-feeding.

CONSTIPATION

Reptiles can become constipated in these situations:
—they have been chilled after eating
—are kept at temperatures below their POTR
—they have ingested foreign material, and that material has become impacted.

In the case of reptiles too chilled to digest their foods, digestion will continue again when they are warmed up to their required temperatures. Mild impactions can occur when reptiles ingest cage litters, sand, bark, gravel, strings from artificial grass, or chitinous insects. In these cases, warm baths and gentle massage of the abdominal area may correct the condition. Severe impactions, which cause bloating and anorexia, should be properly diagnosed and treated by a veterinarian; radiographs can help you locate foreign matter lodged in the digestive tract. Avoid home laxative remedies, since those remedies may be too strong for the reptiles. Severe impactions may require surgery to correct the condition.

Reptiles may at times become constipated for no apparent reasons. If this happens to a snake or lizard, follow these steps to try to encourage defecation:
1. Bathe the reptile in warm (not hot) water for 10-15 minutes.
2. Gently massage the animal, for approximately five minutes, with strokes that run from the sternum to the vent.
3. Replace the animal in the warm bath, and allowed it to sit in the bath for another 10-15 minutes.

This is often enough to encourage defecation, either immediately, or within the next 24 hours. Prolonged or repeated occurrences of constipation indicate that something is not right, either environmentally or physiologically. To determine the cause of constipation in these cases, thoroughly check not only the reptile itself, but the animal's housing, including temperatures, substrate, and food items.

DYSECDYSIS

A healthy animal housed in the proper environment will shed properly. With snakes, this means shedding in one, inside-out piece. Most lizards shed in patches. Chelonians shed the skin on their heads, necks, and limbs as well as the keratinous scales. When reptiles exhibit difficulty in shedding, it is a sign that the reptile is ill or that something is wrong with the environmental humidity or water source.

If the humidity is too low, or the reptile does not have access to a bowl or tub for soaking, the reptile's skin becomes too dry. The layer of fluid that builds up between the old and new skin layers is insufficient to meet the demands of shedding. In these cases, the old skin cannot loosen, or it loosens only in patches. If the reptile is ill, it generally will have difficulty shedding properly, even when the proper environmental conditions are provided. In these cases, the reptile must be evaluated clinically to determine and treat the underlying condition causing the illness. Then, while undergoing treatment, the reptile may be assisted in completing the shed.

There are two ways to assist reptiles with shedding when the problem centers around humidity:

—Place a humidity box in the reptile's tank.

—Wrap a freshly bathed reptile in a damp cloth and replace the animal in its tank.

To make a humidity box, fill a plastic-lidded container with sphagnum moss that has been dampened with warm water. In the top of the container, cut an access hole big enough for the reptile to enter and exit. An alternative to the humidity box is to bathe the reptile in a tepid, plain water bath (75-80°F) for 20-30 minutes, then loosely wrap it in a warm, damp terry cloth towel or a pillowcase and place it in the tank; allow the snake or lizard to emerge from the towel at will, removing the towel from the enclosure when it has done so.

Be aware that increases humidity can create an environment that promotes microbial growth. If a permanent increase in humidity is needed, ventilation should be increased as well; a simple method is to drill a series of small holes in opposite side walls of the enclosure. Temporary humidity increases, such as the short-term use in an enclosure of a humidity box or a damp towel, placed in a container or on a plate so as not to dampen the substrate, should not cause any such problems nor necessitate increased ventilation.

Another shedding problem, sometimes encountered with snakes, concerns the spectacles, or eyecaps. When snakes shed, they shed the old skin covering each eye, and you must check the head shed to make sure that the spectacles have indeed come off. Snakes experiencing problems with shedding often retain one or both spectacles. Numerous methods have been described in the veterinary and pet-care literature describing how to remove these eyecaps, including the use of forceps and tweezers. Veterinarians that deal with reptiles frequently see snakes with damaged eyes when laypersons attempt to remove eyecaps themselves. This procedure is best left to veterinarians if the eyecap does not come off itself with the following procedure. Follow these steps to assist a snake in shedding its eyecaps:

1. Bathe the snake in warm water (80-85°F) for 20-30 minutes.
2. Gently place a drop of mineral oil on each eye with a cotton-tipped swab.
3. Replace the snake in its tank.

The mineral oil lubricates the eyecap and the skin around the eye, and should enable the eyecap to fall off within the next 24 hours. If the eyecap remains in place, try the following steps:

1. Wrap transparent acetate (e.g., Scotch®) tape several times around several of your fingers, with the sticky side out.
2. Starting from the side of the eye closest to the rostrum, gently touch the sticky side of the tape to the eye, and rock it slowly across the eye.

This should lift the eyecap off the eye. If those steps do not work, repeat the bath, mineral oil, and tape process. If the eyecap still fails to come off, watch carefully for the next shed to start. When the next shed starts, gently work the snake's skin off its face to ensure that the retained caps come off. If the eyecaps still will not come off, you may need to take the animal to a veterinarian. Retained eyecaps can cause problems with the eyes, and so should be dealt with when they are detected.

EYE INFECTIONS

Infections of the eye may be the result of trauma, such as burns from heat lamps, lacerations and punctures from feeding live prey, or a retained or improperly removed eyecap. Reptiles kept on peat or sand may get particulate matter into their eyes, resulting in lacerations or irritations. Chelonians hibernated in straw may get seeds or small pieces of the straw into their eyes. They may rub their eyes into the substrate or against enclosure walls, thereby exacerbating the problem.

Mild discoloration of the eye, haziness or cloudiness, swelling, and abnormal tearing or keeping one or both eyes closed are all signs of potentially serious problems and may indicated infections, retained shed, head trauma or the presence of a foreign body in the eye. Dry, lusterless eyes, or mucoid discharges from the eye may be the result of impairment of tear production in reptiles. This may be a result of a vitamin-A deficiency, blockage of the tear ducts due to bacterial infection, an increase in intraocular pressure, or trauma. An ophthalmologic examination may be necessary to determine the underlying cause (Lawton, 1992b). Also see chapter on ophthalmologic diseases.

A reptile can develop conjunctivitis but, unlike the same condition in a mammal, it is rare to see a discharge from the animal's eyes. Instead, the conjunctivitis results in a caseous plaque in or on the eye. The conjunctivitis may be due to an infection, trauma, or to a vitamin-A deficiency. Treatment should be aimed at the underlying problem.

If flushing a slightly swollen or tender eye with sterile saline solution does not resolve the swelling or tenderness, the reptile should be seen by a reptile veterinarian. The vet can perform various tests to determine the source of the problem. It is important to note that, if the conjunctivitis is caused by a vitamin-A deficiency, correcting the deficiency will not also resolve the conjunctivitis. You must take the reptile to a vet who can carefully remove the caseous material from the eye. The vet may also remove foreign bodies and plaques, stitch up lacerations, and prescribe topical or systemic antibiotics (Frye, 1991; Lawton, 1992b).

Snakes may develop conjunctivitis in the form of a subspectacular abscess. The condition may be caused by untreated stomatitis or by a systemic infection. Again, veterinary intervention is required to cut into the spectacle and flush the abscess. You should also request a culture to determine the best course of antibiotic therapy (Lawton, 1992b).

GASTROENTERITIS

Gastroenteritis in reptiles is generally caused by *Entamoeba invadens*, which may cause the death of the animal within a relatively short time. Symptoms of gastroenteritis include regurgitation, anorexia, and slimy feces. The vomitus generated by *E. invadens* is often quite odorous, a sign that may be of use if the animal is presented with no known history. Amoebiasis may be diagnosed through a fecal exam and treated with metronidazole.

Note that regurgitation may also occur when a reptile is handled too soon after eating. Gastrointestinal upset may also occur if the reptile is kept in too cool an environment.

CRYPTOSPORIDIOSIS

Cryptosporidium can cause moderate to severe problems when ingested by animals which are immunocompromised (Gittleman, 1995; CDC, 1995a). Infection and death of collections have been increasingly reported in the United States. It has been postulated that reptiles become infected with the parasite after they consume prey which is infected with the organism (Frye 1991).

In recent years, the presence of *Cryptosporidium* in the drinking-water supply has become more widely known. These extremely small cysts pass through the water filtration systems in major municipal water supplies. Those water-management systems can not eradicate this organism, as it is smaller than the size the filtration systems can capture, and it is not affected by chlorine. If you live in an area with known high levels of *Cryptosporidium* (CDC, 1995a), you should consider using boiled water or a reverse osmosis water-filtration system to provide water free of *Cryptosporidium* for reptiles who are severely debilitated. Severely debilitated reptiles are more likely to have a serious reactions to a *Cryptosporidium* infection.

HEMIPENIAL PLUGS

Snakes and lizards may develop hard, waxy plugs composed of seminal fluid and cellular debris in their inverted hemipenes. Most reptiles expel these plugs when defecating. However, some reptiles may periodically or regularly retain the plugs. When this occurs, you must remove the plug manually (Frye, 1991; Stahl, 1994).

The plugs may form unnoticed until such time as they protrude into the vent itself. By that time, repeated defecation has deposited layers of feces onto the ends of the plugs where they protrude from the hemipenes. Remove such a plug by following these steps:

1. Soak the reptile in a 80-85°F bath.
2. Gently rock one of the plugs to loosen it.
3. Once the plug rocks easily, you can gently pull it free from the hemipenes. Note that extraction is easier if a gentle rocking motion is maintained during the removal.
4. Repeat steps 1 through 3 to remove the second plug.

Hemipenial plugs may not always be so benign. Stahl (1994) reports severe infections in chameleons as a result of retained plugs. Two early signs of plug formation are the animal's straining when defecating, and feces appearing just inside the ventral folds. In some reptiles, plugs may reform with some regularity. Reptiles who are found with plugs should be checked regularly thereafter, with any new plugs removed as described above.

HYPOTHERMIA/HYPERTHERMIA

Prolonged exposure to temperatures that are too cold or too hot can have devastating effects on reptiles. Healthy animals may be able to tolerate periods of inappropriate temperatures. Sick animals, or animals exposed to temperatures far outside their POTR may suffer if exposed for longer than 24 hours (Boyer, 1994).

Hypothermic reptiles are cold to the touch, lethargic, and non-responsive. Hypothermic reptiles should not be placed in the high part of their POTR. They should be warmed up gradually. Once they are thermoregulating naturally, they must be watched for several weeks (up to a month for chelonians) to assure that they have not acquired a respiratory infection. When reptiles have reached their PBT, they may regurgitate their last meal. If necessary they should be treated for dehydration and allowed to rest before being fed.

When reptiles have been kept at temperatures above their normal POTR, they may suffer from the effects of hyperthermia. For most reptiles, this is when temperatures reach or exceed 100° F (37.4°C). Signs of hyperthermia include:
—open-mouth breathing (gaping)
—panting
—prolonged periods of time soaking in water (not associated with preshed behavior or mites)
—hiding under the substrate in the coolest part of the tank.

A hyperthermic reptile should be placed in cool (70-75°F) water for a short time to reduce the animal's core body temperature to within its PBT range. Its body or head may need to be supported to prevent it from collapsing in the water. The reptile should be checked for dehydration and rehydrated orally, subcutaneously, or intracoelomically. If brain swelling occurs, you may need to administer prednisolone sodium succinate at 5-10 mg/kg (Boyer, 1994).

INFLAMED/ABSCESSED JOINTS AND LIMBS

Inflammation of joints and limbs may occur as a result of an injury, such as a bite or laceration, or may occur without any apparent reason. The latter are generally the result of a period of stress which takes its toll on the immune system, impairs immune function, and inhibits the body's natural response to infectious organisms. Some swellings in the digits, limbs, back, and tail may be fractures. If you cannot determine whether the swelling is due to a fracture or an abscess, have the reptile x-rayed.

Minor abscesses may be excised, cleaned, and flushed without resorting to general anesthesia. Some abscesses may be resolved without surgery, with only a course of systemic antibiotics. Major abscesses, especially those which compromise one or more joints, should be treated while the animal is under general anesthesia. This prevents unnecessary injury or trauma to the animal as a result of it pulling its limb away as it is being worked on. Many abscesses require follow-up treatment. Follow-up treatment can range from systemic antibiotics, to daily flushing of the site, to reentry to remove additional caseous material.

If the limb has been fully involved and the damage is extensive, it may be best to amputate the entire limb. Lizards fare well when toes are amputated, but both large lizards and chelonians do poorly when partial limbs are amputated. Partial limbs are prone to infection and continuing stump trauma (Lawton, et al., 1992c).

An increasing number of green iguanas (*Iguana iguana*) are presenting with periarticular abscesses from which *Salmonella* has been cultured (Frye, 1995). In the case of persistent infections or where *Salmonella* is suspected, a culture should be done.

INCLUSION BODY DISEASE

Inclusion body disease (IBD) has been increasingly diagnosed in boas and pythons (boids). It affects these two groups of snakes slightly differently but the long-term effects are the same (i.e., the disease is terminal in those animals who exhibit clinical signes of the disease).

Signs of infection in boas include central nervous system disorders (paralysis, inability to right itself, "star-gazing" and inability to strike or constrict). Other signs include chronic regurgitation, extreme weight loss, respiratory infections, and

This abscess at the elbow caused by a bite from a conspecific initially involved the entire arm of this iguana (*Iguana iguana*).

dysecdysis due to the inability to control body movements enough to rub off the old skin. The disease is rapidly fatal in young and juvenile boas, typified by rapid onset of flaccid paralysis. In pythons, the disease progresses much more rapidly than in boas. Along with the above signs (excluding chronic regurgitation), pythons also may develop infectious stomatitis, heightened or exaggerated reflex responses, disorientation (which may be precipitated by the onset of central blindness) and loss of motor coordination.

The virus may be transmited by contact with infectious organisms on animals, by aerosolized secretions and excretions, or by the keeper passing the virus from one snake or enclosure to another during the course of handling or cleaning (when strict quarantine and cleaning procedures are not followed).

There is currently no treatment for the disease and it should be considered fatal and highly contagious. Euthanasia of affected individuals is recommended to help curb further transmission. Even if the snake can be kept alive through supportive measures (hydration and force-feeding), the damage to the nerves, brain, spinal cord and internal organs is so great — and progressive — that life is only prolonged with ever decreasing quality and increasing pain.

Quarantine all new boids for a minimum of 3 months (and preferably 6-12 months) and take precautions when visiting other collections, pet stores, herp expos or sales, and when accepting new snakes or borders who may have been exposed to IBD.

METABOLIC BONE DISEASE

Metabolic bone disease (MBD) is an umbrella term. It covers a number of disorders related to the weakening of the bone or related to impaired systems function that are caused by an imbalance in vitamin D3, calcium, and phosphorus. MBD and calcium metabolism are discussed in detail in the chapter on internal medicine.

Vitamin D3, calcium, and phosphorus interact together to perform a number of functions besides bone growth and maintenance, including muscle contractions and blood coagulation (Wright, 1993). The result is a well-functioning system, with calcium restored to and, in the case of growing animals, added to the bone matrix. Reptiles acquire the three nutrients in these ways:

Vitamin D3 is acquired through diet or is derived from exposure to ultraviolet B.

Calcium is acquired through diet and through matter recycled from the bone matrix.

Phosphorus is acquired through diet.

An imbalance in the nutrients may be caused by:

—too much vitamin D3, calcium (hypercalcemia), or phosphorus
—a lack of vitamin D3, calcium (hypocalcemia), or phosphorus
—failure to provide one or more of those nutrients in a bioavailable form.

Too much phosphorus can throw this process off, as can too much or too little vitamin D3, or too little access to ultraviolet B wavelengths. As pet-owners become more aware of the dangers of calcium deficiency, there is an increased risk that they may add too much calcium to their reptile's diet. It is important to note that hypercalcemia, like hypocalcemia, may also result in death if left untreated.

Many of the foods highly touted for their calcium content also contain calcium oxalates that bind calcium. (These foods include spinach, carrots, collards, chards and other thick leafy greens.) Calcium oxalates render most or all dietary calcium unavailable for maintenance and growth. The calcium oxalates bind to the dietary calcium both in the foods provided to the reptile and to the calcium provided in nutritional supplements.

Signs of MBD may be felt before they can be seen. This makes a careful physical exam important. Signs of metabolic bone disease include:
—hard knobs in the long bones of the legs
—bumps along the vertebral column of the back and tail
—softening or hard swelling of the jaw
—softening of the plastron or carapace
  Visible signs of moderate to severe MBD include:
—jerky gait when walking
—tremors and twitches in the limbs and muscles of the legs and toes when at rest
—shakiness when being held.

Advanced cases of MBD include all the above signs plus anorexia and fractured bones. Severely deficient reptiles tend to be lethargic and may only be able to drag themselves along the ground. Arboreal lizards will end up spending all their time on the ground because they will lack the strength to grip and climb.

You may treat mild cases (where the signs are felt or just barely visible) by providing the proper environment and diet. In the case of diurnal lizards and chelonians, proper environment includes not only the proper temperature ranges and diet, but also daily access to ultraviolet B. UV-B is obtained by exposure to direct unfiltered sunlighted or artificially via specially-made fluorescent bulbs. Only fluorescent full-spectrum lights can provide UV-B; incandescent lights do not provide UV-B. Incadescent bulbs are sometimes misleadingly marketed as "full spectrum" when, in fact, no incandescent bulb can produce ultraviolet B wavelengths.

This 17-month-old iguana (*Iguana iguana*) with sever fibrous osteodystrophy (MBD) was 7 inches (17.7cm) svl and weighed 173 grams.

To treat a moderate to severe case of MBD caused by a deficiency in the nutrients, you must provide the reptile with the proper diet, temperatures, and light wavelengths; as well as provide a more powerful calcium supplement than those found in pet stores. Oral administration of calcium glubionate (1 cc/kg PO bid prn) or injections of calcitonin or calcium gluconate are generally prescribed by veterinarians. Mader (1993) reports faster recovery when Calcimar® (50 IU/kg IM in front leg, repeated once a week for two weeks) is administered to iguanas who have been returned to normal serum calcium levels. Use of calcitonin before normal levels have been established, however, may cause hypocalcemic tetany and death.

There remains much debate at this time as to the necessity and efficacy of natural and artificially-produced ultraviolet B (UV-B) wavelengths in the development of precursors to vitamin D3 and the metabolism of calcium. (Ultraviolet A acts upon appetite and behavior.) Gehrmann (1991) reports anecdotally that not all lizards require UV-B to maintain proper D3-calcium-phosphorus balance. Bernard, et al. (1991) found that green iguanas (*Iguana iguana*) fared much better when exposed to UV-B wavelengths than they did to vitamin D3 injections or supplements added to their food. Both UV-A and UV-B wavelengths are more likely to benefit diurnal lizards and chelonians than not. Because of this, daily periods of access to such wavelengths should be considered a necessary part of the care of diurnal lizards and terrestrial and semiaquatic chelonians (Alberts, 1994).

Recovery from MBD requires proper day and night temperature gradients, a nighttime dark period of sufficient length (based on native habitat), and proper diet. Nutrient-deficient herbivores and omnivores should be fed calcium-rich, nutrient-dense foods such as squashes, green beans, alfalfa (from rabbit food pellets or pulverized hay cubes), parsnips, mustard greens, dandelions, and escarole; and fruits such as figs, papaya, cantaloupe and berries (Barten, 1993; Frye, 1991). The food should be supplemented with additional calcium and a multivitamin formulated for reptiles or birds, or a crushed Centrum® vitamin tablet formulated for humans (Donoghue, 1996, Mader, 1995a). Nutrient-deficient omnivores and carnivores should be fed whole captive bred prey (to reduce risk of zoonotic infection from parasites commonly found in wild prey) that have been raised on nutritious foods or have been gut-loaded with nutritious foods for several days before being fed out.

Calcification of the large blood vessels may occur as a result of excessive amounts of vitamin D3 and calcium. The mineralization may be noted in a radiological evaluation. Once significant minieralization has occurred, there is little that can be done to reverse the process. Treating hypercalcemia early is the best way to prevent additional compromise of tissues.

PARALYSIS

Reptiles may become fully or partially paralyzed; the paralysis may be permanent or transient. Permanent paralysis may be the result of trauma to the spinal column. Such trauma may be exteriorly visible as a swelling, laceration, lesion, or bite on the dorsum. Spinal trauma may have been caused by:

—a broken or severed spinal column
—bacterial and viral infections
—toxins (including pesticide strips)
—parasites
—nutritional disorders.

Traumatic fractures, infections, and lesions may occur with no external sign. Bites from live prey may heal without any apparent complication, only to fester subcutaneously, with the resultant lesion causing paralysis. Bites that cause spinal trauma can also result from attacks by other animals, including mammals, birds and other reptiles. In captivity, spinal trauma can be caused by enclosure doors swinging shut on the animal or the animal's getting stepped on. Nutritional disorders, not surprisingly, stem from the imbalance of calcium, phosphorus, and vitamin D3 or lack of exposure to ultraviolet radiation (UV-B).

Transient paralysis of unknown etiology has been seen in some box turtles. The cases, possibly caused by parasites, have resolved themselves with only supportive therapy given (soaking, encouraging feeding, proper heat and light).

PATHOGENIC INFECTIONS

Domestic, wild-caught, and imported reptiles are often ill with a wide variety of pathogens, including *Coccidia* sp., *Salmonella* sp., and *Pseudomonas* sp. Affected reptiles may be more or less symptomatic, depending upon their nutritional status, hydration, and immune function at the time presented. Weak animals will suffer the effects of in-

Inguinal approach for abdominal surgery in the desert tortoise. Photo courtesy of Dr. Bernard A. Mangone.

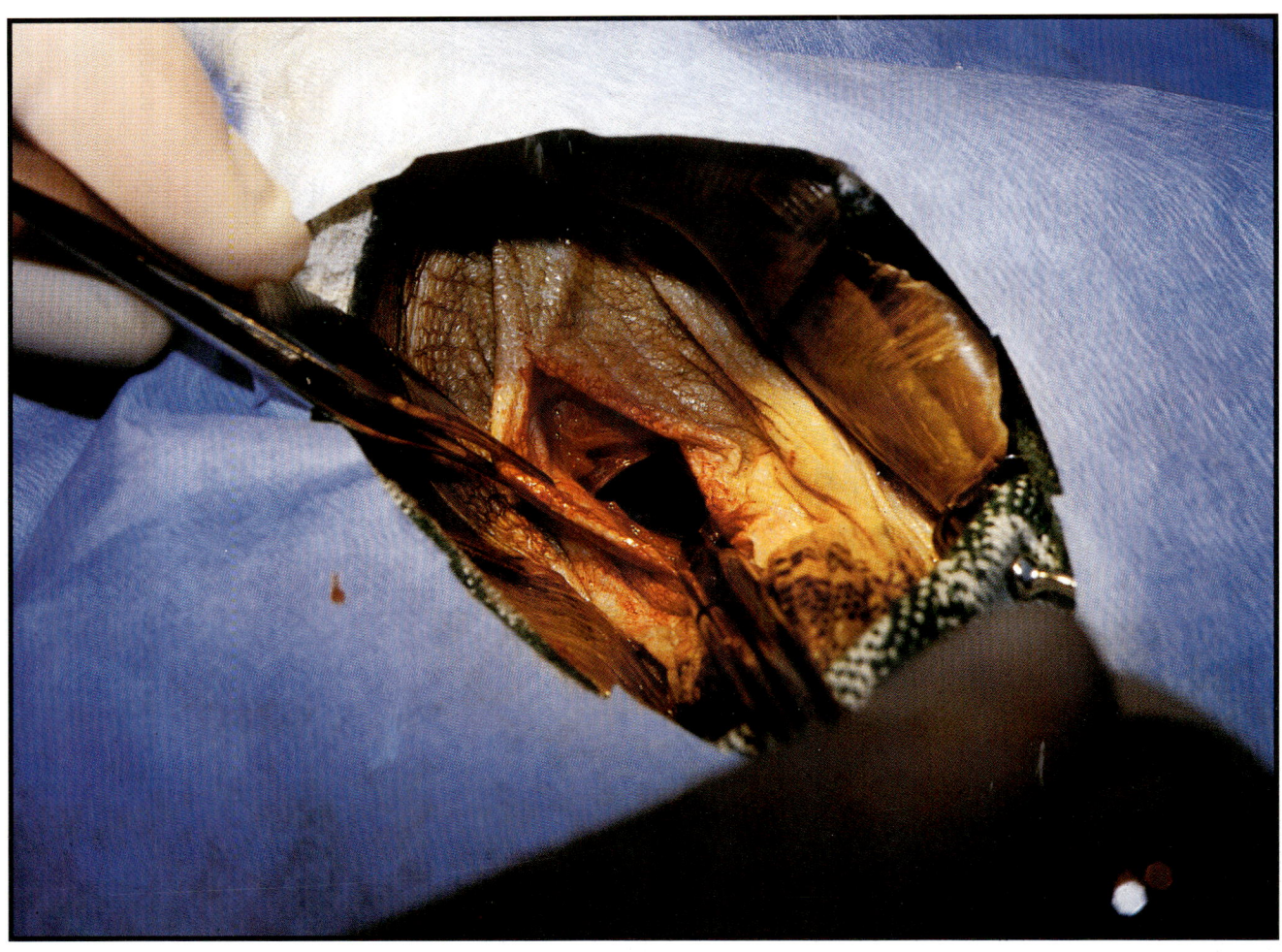

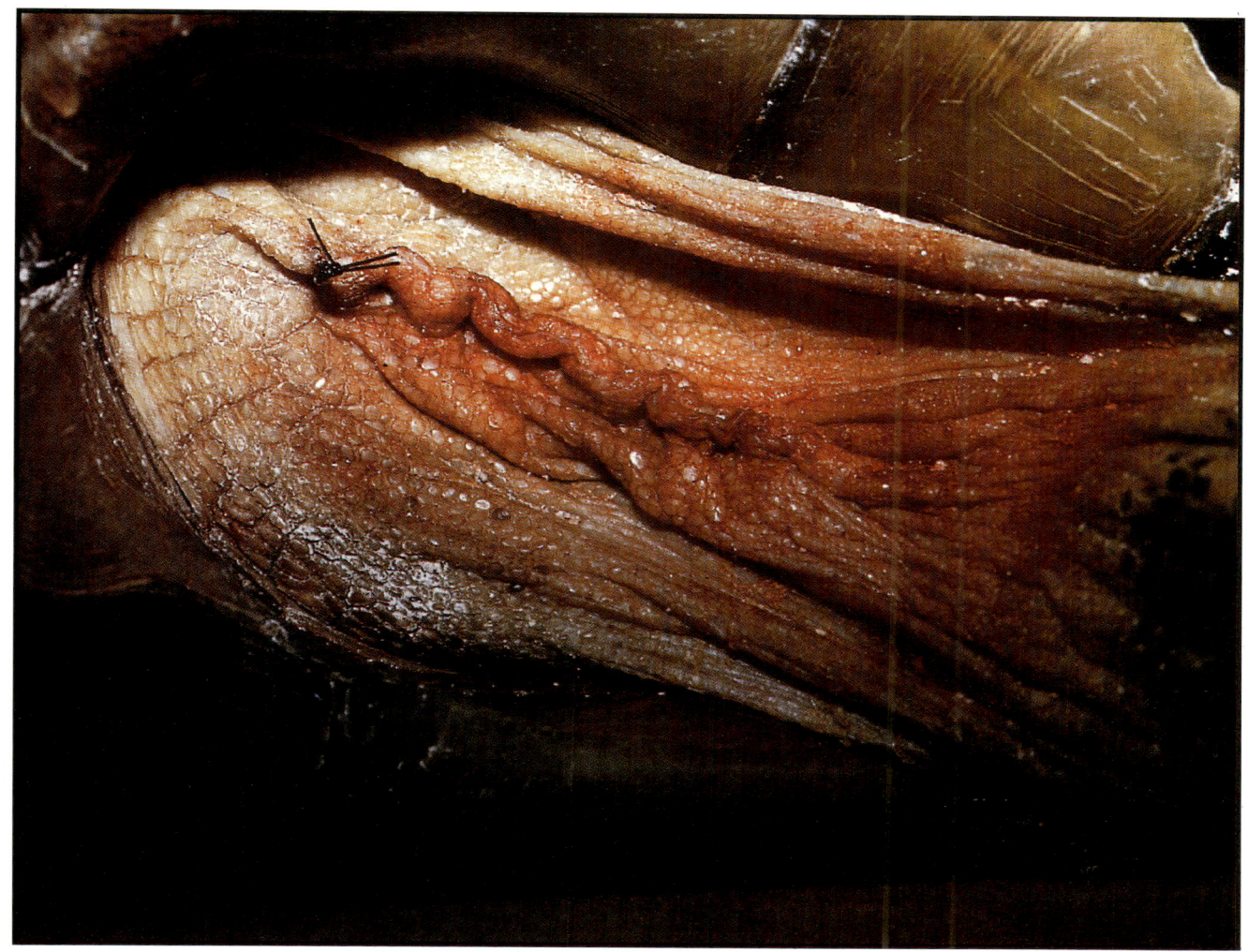

Closed surgical wound from abdominal surgery in a desert tortoise. The suture was 4-0 nylon in a continuous horizontal mattress pattern. Photo courtesy of Dr. Bernard A. Mangone.

fection more so than reptiles who are still relatively healthy. If you suspect that a reptile is diseased, you should immediately begin clinical evaluation and pathology to determine the causative organism and appropriate treatment.

Signs of infection include:
—listlessness
—sunken eyes
—anorexia
—lesions around the mouth (not to be confused with necrotic stomatitis, which is found inside the mouth) and on the body that fail to heal
—abscesses
—pyogranulomatosis
—arthritis.

Abscesses, pyogranulomatosis, septic arthritis and septicemia may be due to *Salmonella sp.* infection (Frye, 1995). Gray, crusty scabs may be due to being gnawed on by conspecifics during dominance or mating. Black, crusty scabby areas may be a fungal infection (Wissman, 1995).

RESPIRATORY INFECTION

Despite their being referred to as lower, or more primitive, animals, reptiles have a remarkable respiratory system that enables them to remain submerged in water for long periods of time. They are able to hibernate under water and deep in the ground for extended periods of time and to generally withstand conditions that would prove fatal to higher orders. Belkin (1963) reports that chelonians have survived an atmosphere of pure nitrogen for up to eight hours; sea snakes routinely remain submerged for 45 minutes, and rattlesnakes have survived more than 24 hours in pure carbon monoxide.

Given their ability to remain alive in such inhospitable environments, it may be surprising that reptiles do get as sick as they do. Reptiles do not have a functional diaphragm. This prevents them from coughing up mucous and lung secretions. For these and other reasons, they are unable to clear their lungs themselves. Snakes and chelonians seem most susceptible to respiratory infections, but any reptile that is not kept in proper conditions may be considered at risk (Frye, 1991). Inadequate temperatures, dirty enclosures, overcrowded enclosures, poor diet, and stress all contribute towards the reptile's susceptibility.

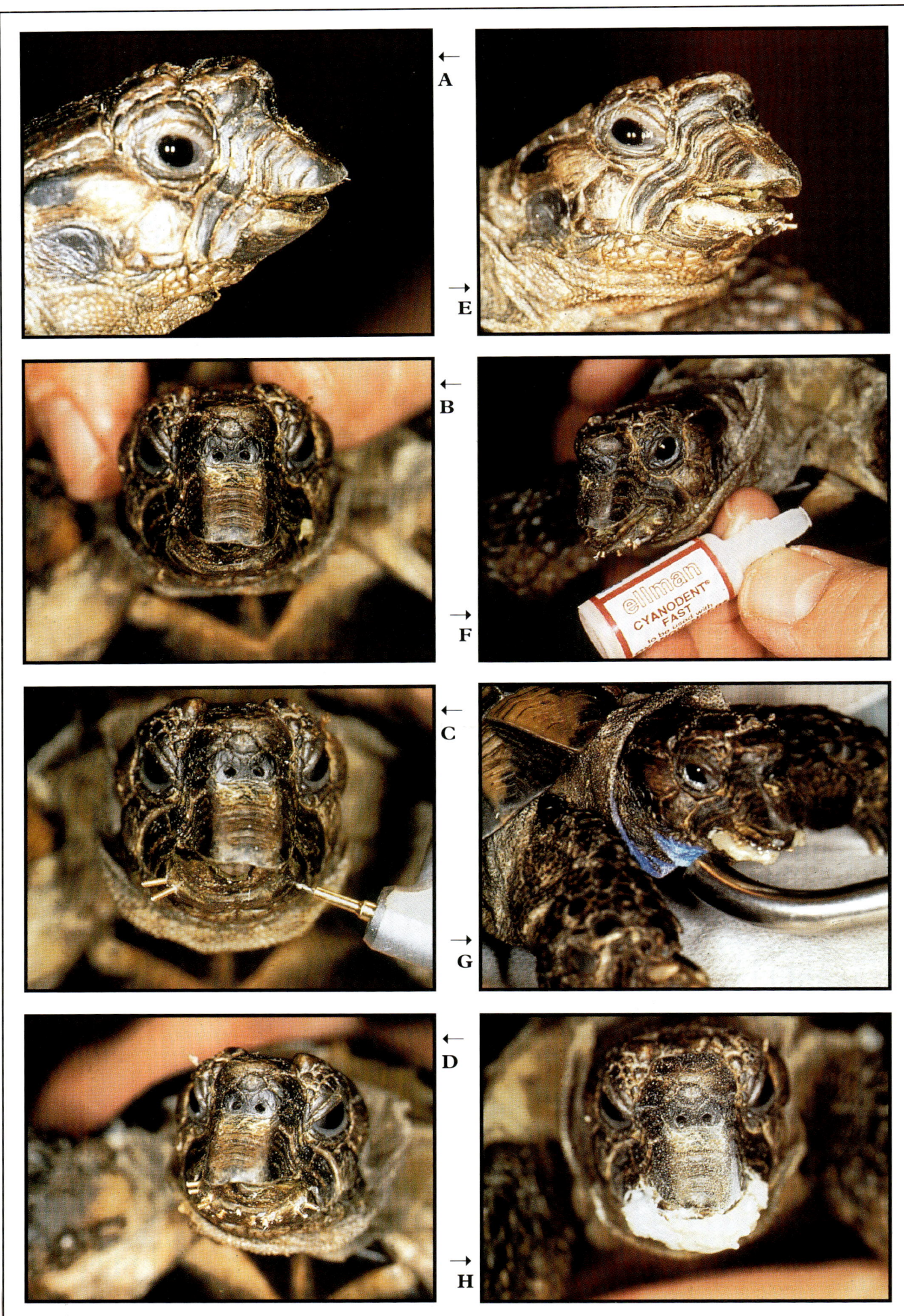

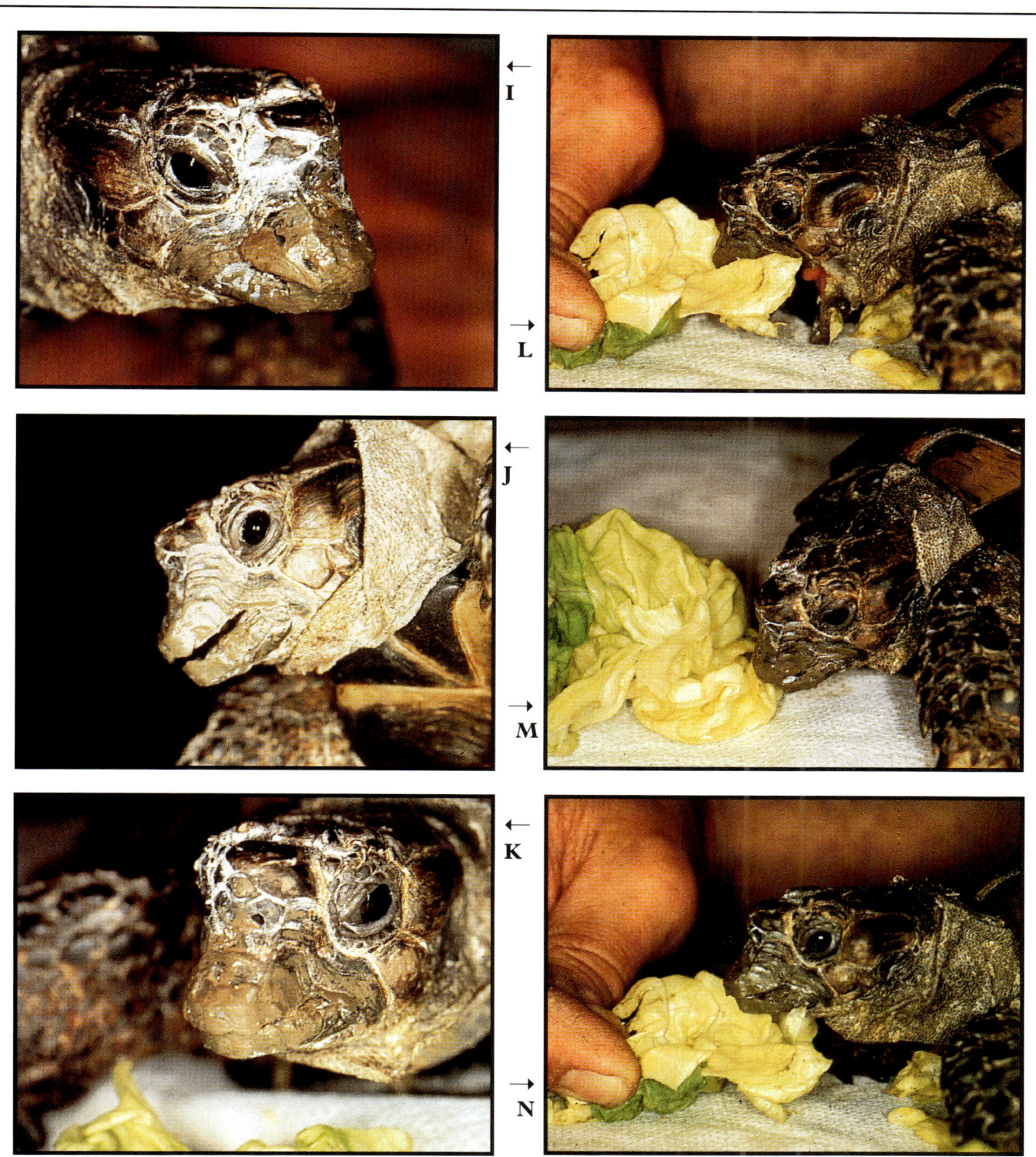

I

L

J

M

K

N

A to N: The story of a poor turtle where the anterior half of the mandible is lacking; the turtle was unable to grasp food. A. Lacking the anterior part of the mandible, the turtle cannot grasp its food. B. Front view - even in a closed position, the mouth seems to stay open permanently. C. Parapulpar pins are inserted for mechanical anchorage. D. Multiple parapulpar pins are already inserted. E. The pins from a side-view. F. ELLMAN's cyanodent is applied for additional chemical bonding with the consecutively applied composite. G. Light-curing dental composite was applied and is hardened with a light-curing lamp. H. The hardened composite material before modeling and polishing. I. The artificial anterior mandible was painted with natural-looking acrylic colors. J. The correct shape of the new mandible allows grasping food again. K. "…Shall I try it?" L. "OK, let's try it!" M. "…What a crispy salad!" N. Grasping and tearing salad leaves was possible again (see parts of torn salad beside the feet). All photos provided by Ellman International.

Symptoms of respiratory infection (Boyer, 1994) include:

—Listlessness.
—Weight loss due to decreased appetite.
—A swollen or bloated body.
—Gaping or open mouth breathing, the latter often accompanied by a clicking or bubbling sound when the infection becomes more severe.
—Labored breathing.
—In snakes: the forks of the tongue may stick together.
—In squamates: excessive saliva; or thick, ropy, or sheeting saliva.
—Aquatic and semi-aquatic turtles: will list to one side when in the water as a result of a congested or collapsed lung. When both lungs are involved, the turtle may have difficulty diving and staying afloat.
—Tortoises and box turtles: may bob their heads more than usual when breathing.
—Chelonians: discharges from the eyes, nose and mouth.

Respiratory infections must be treated both by antibiotics and by correcting any environmental deficiencies. If the condition fails to improve after a course of broad-spectrum antibiotics, request a tracheal or lung washing. This will allow you to obtain sample organisms for culturing, so that the pathogen can be identified, and the best antibiotic treatment can be determined. Supportive therapy includes nutritional support, optimum temperatures, and rehydration and forcefeeding as required.

After treating an animal for infections, you might have to help reestablish the beneficial gut bacteria in the reptile. To do this, feed herbivorous reptiles one of these supplements (Bone, 1992; Frye, 1991):

—liquefied greens
—yogurt containing live bacterial cultures
—a supplement containing *Lactobacillus acidophilus*
—a gut-bacteria replacer such as Bene-Bac™.

ROSTRAL ABRASIONS

Snakes and lizards may abrade their rostrum when trying to escape. Some may develop stereotypic behavior such as the constant rubbing of their snout against the enclosure wall, floor, or furnishings. Still others may be housed with unsuitable rocks or in cramped conditions, which result in frequent bumping and rubbing of the rostrum against surfaces. Abrasions may be mild—just a few layers of skin rubbed away over a small area. In more severe cases, the skin and underlying tissues may literally be worn down to the bone.

Rostral abrasions also occur with animals kept in stressful conditions, such as those housed with aggressive conspecifics, and those housed in plain sight of predators. An inappropriate environment can also cause behavior that results in rostral abrasions. Inappropriate environmental conditions include: enclosures which are too hot, too damp, or too small, or that have no place for hiding or privacy. If environmental conditions are part of the underlying cause for rostral abrasions, you must modify the animal's environment at the same time you initiate treatment for the abrasions. In the case of appropriately sized enclosures, you can cover interior surfaces—especially mesh or screen—with soft towels. You can help reduce visual stress by covering part or all the tank, or by separating the stressed animal from any aggressive or dominant conspecifics. Animals kept in enclosures that are too small must be moved into larger ones. In all cases, you should provide hide boxes or plants in which the animal can hide to help reduce visual stress.

Treatment for rostral abrasions consists of swabbing the abrasion with povidone-iodine or dilute chlorhexidine diacetate. If the abrasion is severe, administer a daily application of the antibiotic, silver sulfadiazine. Silver sulfadiazine also acts as a skin toughener and helps scabby plaques to shed more easily.

SALMONELLA

Salmonella, thought to be a part of the normal intestinal flora of many animals, has been recognized for over twenty years as a problem in reptiles. *Salmonella* in human food supplies has also been a problem, but it is only now being well-publicized. The two are related in that, while all organisms may carry one or more *Salmonella* species, animals which are not well cared for or are kept in crowded, unsanitary, or stressful conditions are more vulnerable to infection from the organism. They are also more likely to spread it to other animals, including humans (Frye, 1991). Salmonellosis as a zoonotic disease is discussed further in the chapter on Zoonosis and under Zoonoses and the Rehabilitator below.

Treatment for *Salmonella* consists of antibiotic therapy with such drugs as trimethoprim-sulfamethoxazole or trimethoprim-sulfadiazine (Frye, 1991). Intensive supportive therapy must also be initiated. Supportive therapy includes: electrolyte and fluid replacement, nonsteroidal anti-inflammatory drugs, and nutritional support in the form of easily digestible nutrients.

Animals which are infected with *Salmonella* or who are suspected of being infected should have several fecal exams. Infected animals may produce false negative results several times before showing a positive. Once a positive test result is obtained, do rechecks over the next several weeks to ensure that the organisms are under control. Cryptic infections may occur where the reptile acts as a carrier, periodically shedding the organism and thus is able to infect others, while remaining asymptomatic itself. The possibility of cryptic infections necessitates proper cleaning and disinfecting procedures at all times.

Isolate affected animals and make sure their enclosures are set up during recovery to facilitate thorough cleaning and disinfecting. Follow strict quarantine and hygiene procedures, making sure you use separate cleaning equipment and supplies (disposable gloves, separate sponges, buckets, etc.) for the affected animals, with another set being reserved for the healthy ones. Healthy animals should be cleaned and fed before you work with the sick ones; this will further reduce the risk of spreading the organism through the entire population. Disinfect equipment, including nondisposable rubber or latex gloves, between each enclosure of sick animals; always disinfect such equipment after each cleaning session.

SKIN BLISTER DISEASE

Blister disease (necrotizing dermatitis) may be caused by a number of different factors, such as gram-negative bacteria, fungi, thermal burns, and parasites.

Blisters may appear on the ventral surface of snakes and lizards due to their being kept in an environment that is too humid or moist, or one that has not been cleaned properly of food, wastes, or spilled water. Symptoms include hard, scaly raised bumps or thin, watery blisters. Left untreated, the condition may worsen, progressing to caseous abscessations that invade deeper subcutaneous tissue and vascular structures. Untreated conditions may ultimately lead to septicemia and death (Frye, 1991).

If a reptile has blister disease, bathe the animal immediately, washing the area with a mild germicidal soap (chlorhexidine diacetate surgical scrub or povidone-iodine surgical scrub) diluted to one quarter strength (Frye, 1991). You may soak the animal several times a week in a 1% solution of chlorhexidine diacetate through the recovery period.

Concurrent with the initiation of the bathing and soaking, you must start antibiotic therapy. Also perform an analysis of the exudates, scrapings, or biopsy to identify the pathogen causing the outbreak and determine the best antibiotic or antifungal with which to treat it. Depending upon the severity of the condition, initiate supportive modalities such as fluid therapy (especially when using nephrotoxic drugs) and nutritional support.

If the crusty, darkened patches occur in young iguanas, it may be a seasonal fungal infection. These seasonal infections are thought to stem from patho-gens entering minute cuts and scratches caused by the overcrowding of iguanas. In these cases, you may treat the necrotic patches with topical or systemic anti-fungal medications (Wissman, 1995).

Parasitic organisms commonly found in aquatic snakes and fish-eating reptiles may cause blister-like nodes. These nodes become apparent when the parasites migrate out to the skin surface as they complete their life cycle. You can remove the parasite with tweezers, flush the site with a chlorhexidine diacetate or povidone-iodine solution, and begin a course of anthelmintic drug treatment.

To reduce the risk of reinfection, keep the animal's enclosure clean and dry. Use nonparticulate substrates until the blisters are completely healed. Follow strict quarantine procedures to reduce the risk of spreading the organisms to others.

STARGAZING

Stargazing is a term used to describe a deceptively innocuous behavior: the head and neck are raised almost straight up, as if the affected animal is gazing at the stars. This condition is common to several diseases that affect the central nervous system. Symptoms that often occur with stargazing are disorientation and the inability of the animal to right itself. Stahl (1995) names several conditions which may cause the symptom of stargazing, including:
—Viral infections, such as paramyxovirus, which is found in viperids and some colubrids and boids, and which attacks the respiratory and neurological systems.
—Inclusion body disease, found in boids, which involves the respiratory, gastrointestinal and neurological systems.
—Bacterial infections, such as meningitis.
—Septic infections that breach the blood-brain barrier.
—Major organ dysfunction, which may cause dysregulation of normal metabolism, and may, in turn, cause neurological disease.
—Extreme temperatures, head injuries, and toxins (as from flea sprays, pest strips, cleaning products, and environmental toxins) which cause neurological disorders.

A thorough examination, including fecal and pathology work-up, must be done to determine the underlying cause. As stargazing is merely a symptom of a deeper, potentially quite serious disease or disorder, the underlying condition itself must be treated.

STOMATITIS

Stomatitis is an opportunistic infection secondary to a serious systemic infection caused by aero-

bic and anaerobic organisms (Frye, 1991). Early symptoms may be subtle, and may include:
—slight petechiae
—a reluctance to feed
—a change in food selection
—increased, thickened, ropy, or sheeting saliva
In cases of sudden and severe onset, you may see the following symptoms:
—acute inflammation of the tissues lining the inside of the mouth
—gingival necrosis
—pockets of caseous yellow, yellowish-gray or white-gray pus in the soft tissues.
In advanced cases, you may see these symptoms:
—osteomyelitis of the jaw and cranial structures
—swollen head
—loose teeth within the necrotic tissue.

Before the appearance of modern antibiotics, diverse substances were used (and are often still recommended by pet stores) to wash out the infected mouth: vinegar, hydrogen peroxide, feminine douche products, iodoform, mouthwashes such as Listerine, and a variety of patent medications. Some of these substances worked to a certain degree, in that they altered the environment of the mouth to make it less desirable to many of the organisms. Some of these products are cytotoxic and, coupled with the fact that they fail to address the underlying, causative infection, have fallen out of use in favor of less destructive preparations and systemic antibiotics.

To treat stomatitis, follow these general steps:
1. Flush the animal's mouth with low-cytotoxic solutions, such as 1% povidone-iodine or 0.25%-0.5% solution of chlorhexidine diacetate (Frye, 1991). Be careful to prevent accidental aspiration or ingestion of detritus. Swab away any loose detritus with a swab dipped in the dilute solution.
2. Debride gently using dulled dental curettes, small bone curettes, needle-nose serrated tweezers, and cotton-tipped swabs. Gentle debridement is necessary to minimize trauma to already sensitive, inflamed tissues.
3. Check the resultant cavity to make sure you have removed all caseous material.
4. Once the plaques are removed, flush the mouth again.
5. Initiate a course of antibiotics for the animal.

During the course of the antibiotic therapy, check the mouth daily for recurring plaques. It is not unusual for the above process to be repeated two or more times during recovery. Particularly severe cases may require more than a single treatment on the first day or two.

If there is copious bleeding upon the removal of the first plaque, stop the procedure. Instead, start the reptile on a 10-day course of antibiotics, such as enrofloxacin, before continuing the curetting.

Enrofloxacin encapsulates the plaque and reduces vascular activity immediately around the site, enabling a less-traumatic removal of the plaque.

Some infections prove resistant despite curetting and treatment with broad-spectrum systemic antibiotics. In these cases, a culture and sensitivity should be done to determine the most efficacious antibiotic. The standard culture sampling techniques of swabbing or washes may yield a confusing mixture of natural and opportunistic buccal and environmental flora. A better method for obtaining a sample for culturing in resistant stomatitis cases is to make an incision into the infected gum and take a small sample of the infected tissue for culturing (Boyar, 1994).

In severe cases of stomatitis, the reptile may be unable to self-feed or drink, and so must be nutritionally supported and hydrated. To reduce stress on inflamed tissues, gavage foods into the animal in the form of slurries. Tables 1 and 3, earlier in this chapter, contain information on hydration and force-feeding (Kaplan et al., 1995).

TREMORS AND PARALYSIS

These signs may be associated with calcium or thiamin deficiency. Thiamin deficiencies may be caused by the feeding of frozen fish to fish-eating snakes, and through long-term use of frozen green vegetables with herbivores and primarily herbivorous reptiles (Frye, 1991). Biotin deficiencies may also cause tremors in lizards, such as monitors and tegus, who are frequently fed raw, unfertilized eggs. Unlike a calcium deficiency, a thiamin deficiency may cause visual impairment. This sign may be one way to tell the difference between the two conditions when an animal is presented with several environmental and dietary factors that could be causing the tremors and paralysis or paresis (Lawton, 1992a). Omnivores and carnivores fed prey that is too large may also suffer transient paralysis.

Parasites, bacterial or viral infections, and trauma to any part of the spine may affect the central nervous system, also resulting in paralysis, paresis, and tetany.

WOUNDS AND POST-SURGICAL SITE MANAGEMENT

The task of cleaning and dressing wounds can be problematical with reptiles. You must sometimes use creative measures when working with animals that have no legs, or which spend much of their time in water.

You can flush bites, lacerations, and opened abscesses with sterile (bacteriostatic) water, dilute (0.5%) chlorhexidine diacetate or povidone-iodine. Topical antibiotics, such as a triple antibiotic ointment and silver sulfadiazine, may be used alone or under a dressing.

Juvenile iguana with a cast being applied. Photo courtesy of Dr. Todd Driggers.

Aquatic turtles must be kept in a dry tank, and put in water only for limited periods each day for feeding and hydration. All reptiles must be observed to make sure they do not soak in their water bowls; a sick or injured lizard can be quite adept at working off saturated dressings using only one foot and its rostrum. Such soaking may also cause infection or prolong the healing, and it must be discouraged by limiting free access to water during recovery.

Bandaging techniques used on lizards and chelonians are similar to those used on mammals and birds. As with fur and feathers, you must be careful to avoid damaging or forcibly removing scales when removing dressings from snakes and lizards. To replace a bandage, secure a gauze dressing first with a paper tape. This light, low-tack adhesive tape is made for sensitive skin and is available in a variety of widths. Once the dressing is secure, you can overwrap the paper tape with regular adhesive tape; this prevents the paper tape from loosening.

Vetrap® is a light, elastic, outer bandaging material that is applied over the tape and gauze dressing. You can use it to cover the dressing to prevent its becoming soiled and is mildly water resistant.

You can also use Vetrap to anchor the dressing by wrapping the Vetrap around the torso and opposing limb. If you use Vetrap to overwrap a bandage on the tail, make sure the edges of the Vetrap extend beyond the edge of the tape on both sides of the dressing.

Creative measures (finger cots and condoms) may be required to affix occlusive bandages to snakes (Frye 1992b). To dress such a wound on a snake, follow these steps:

1. Dress the wound as usual.
2. Select a finger cot or condom, whichever is appropriate, depending upon the girth of the snake.
3. Cut off the sealed end of the finger cot or condom.
4. Pull the resultant tube gently along the length of the body to the wound site. It is best to start at the head and work down, going with the scales. Take extreme care when pulling a tube up from the tail.
5. Seat the tube over the wound site.
6. Wrap each end of the tube with adhesive tape, with the tape half on the skin and half on the tube.

7. Cut the tape. When cutting the tape, cut the end in a semi-circle rather than straight across; this will help prevent the ends from peeling back when the snake moves around (Frye, 1992b).

You can use finger cots and condoms on lizard tails. You can also use liquid and spray bandage products, both on lizards who consistently soak off their bandages, and on a reptile whose defect is so extensive that bandaging is not possible (Frye, 1991).

Once a reptile has been treated, you must be careful to provide a supportive environment to promote rapid, uncomplicated recovery. Make sure you provide temperatures towards the higher end of the reptile's POTR. Also, delay or postpone hibernation completely until the following year. Good nutrition and adequate intake must be maintained; nutritional deficiencies, such as hypoproteinemia and hypocalcemia, will delay the healing process, with the latter affecting the healing of broken or weakened bones (Lawton, et al., 1992c). The environment must be kept as clean as possible during recovery to ensure the least amount of contamination of the wound sites. In this case, it is of paramount importance that you keep the enclosure set-up simple, and easy to clean and disinfect. While you may not be able to provide more-natural substrates because of the medical needs of the animal, you must sill furnish hide boxes to reduce psychological stress.

CONDITIONS SPECIFIC TO CHELONIANS

BROKEN AND CRACKED SHELLS

Turtle and tortoise shells are composed of living tissues, and injuries to the shell should be treated as are wounds to the flesh.

Fresh wounds to the shell can be cleaned in the same way you clean any wound by flushing it with povidone-iodine or chlorhexidine diacetate. Carefully remove any debris from the wound, and check the shell to make sure the wound does not penetrate into the coelomic cavity. If there are no cracks or holes that penetrate into the body cavity, the wound can be left as is, treated daily with the povidone-iodine or chlorhexidine diacetate.

As a rule of thumb, any fracture more than a few hours old should be considered infected (Barten, 1996). If the wounds are extensive or penetrative, always consider that they could be infected. If possible, check the cavity for signs of infection. If there are signs of infection, such as necrotic or foul-smelling tissue or exudates, the infection in the cavity must first be treated before repairing the shell. Use a wet-to-dry bandage until the infection has been resolved (Mader, 1992). Whether or not you see visual signs of infection with such extensive or deep wounds, your veterinarian may want start a course of systemic antibiotics.

Fragmented and fractured shells can be repaired. The process, which uses fiberglass cloth and epoxy resins, is well documented by Frye (1991), Mader (1992), and others. Breaks and cracks can occur as a result of crush injuries sustained when being run over by cars, encounters with farm and maintenance equipment, and attacks by powerful predators. Fragmented and fractured shell injuries must be immediately attended to. Not only do shell defects provide access for bacteria into the body cavity, but chelonians who have lain injured for a while may also have been infested by fly larvae.

It is not uncommon to meet with box turtles (*Terrapene* sp.) who have bilateral punctures on either side of their carapace. This is the result of being captured in the wild by humans who use pincers or large tongs for grabbing. These holes should be checked to see if they penetrate into the body cavity, the turtle treated and the holes plugged as necessary.

DRY SKIN

Dry skin with deep lateral and accordion folds generally indicates dehydration. In this case, you should soak the reptile and administer parenteral or oral fluids as necessary.

Excessively dry skin may be caused by hypervitaminosis A. Vitamin A, in conjunction with vitamins D and E, is often given indiscriminately whenever a chelonian, especially tortoises, has nasal discharges (Frye, 1991). These vitamins are also often administered in hopes of improving the appetites of anorexic or meager eaters. However, when a chelonian receives too much vitamin A, its skin becomes very dry and begins to flake off. Within a few days after the injection, the skin is gone, leaving the underlying muscles exposed and vulnerable to injury and infection.

Dry skin may also occur in terrestrial chelonians who are not soaked regularly. Tortoises (*Testudo* sp.) should be soaked weekly, while box turtles (*Terrapene* sp.) are soaked every 4-5 days. Chinese (*Cuora* sp.) box turtles require more frequent access to water and often will not feed unless given access to shallow water.

EYE INFECTIONS

It is easy to see if a chelonian has an eye infection, because the lids of one or both eyes will be swollen—sometimes completely shut. Infections may be caused by injury, a foreign body, or stress. Swollen lids are a common sign of vitamin-A deficiency. Some tearing is normal in tortoises (*Testudo* sp.) and may not require treatment unless such tearing becomes severe.

In the case of infection or injury, an ophthalmic ointment, such as terramycin, may be prescribed after the eye has been checked and either flushed out or the trauma attended to. The discomfort from the injury or infection may lead to reduced activity and loss of appetite. This is because the impaired vision interferes with the chelonian's ability to navigate within its environment and compete with conspecifics for food. It is best to keep such animals in isolation and support them nutritionally by hand or force-feeding (if necessary) until they are recovered enough to begin to fend for themselves again.

To treat the abscess, lance and drain them, flush them with a dilute solution of povidone-iodine or chlorhexidine diacetate, then check them daily, draining them again as required.

Make sure you check the inside of the mouth, not only for the presence of stomatitis and lesions, but also for infected Eustachian tubes. To do this, gently open the chelonian's mouth, and with the mouth open, put gentle pressure on the ear area. If there is an infection, the exudates will come out of the tubes in the inner cheek area.

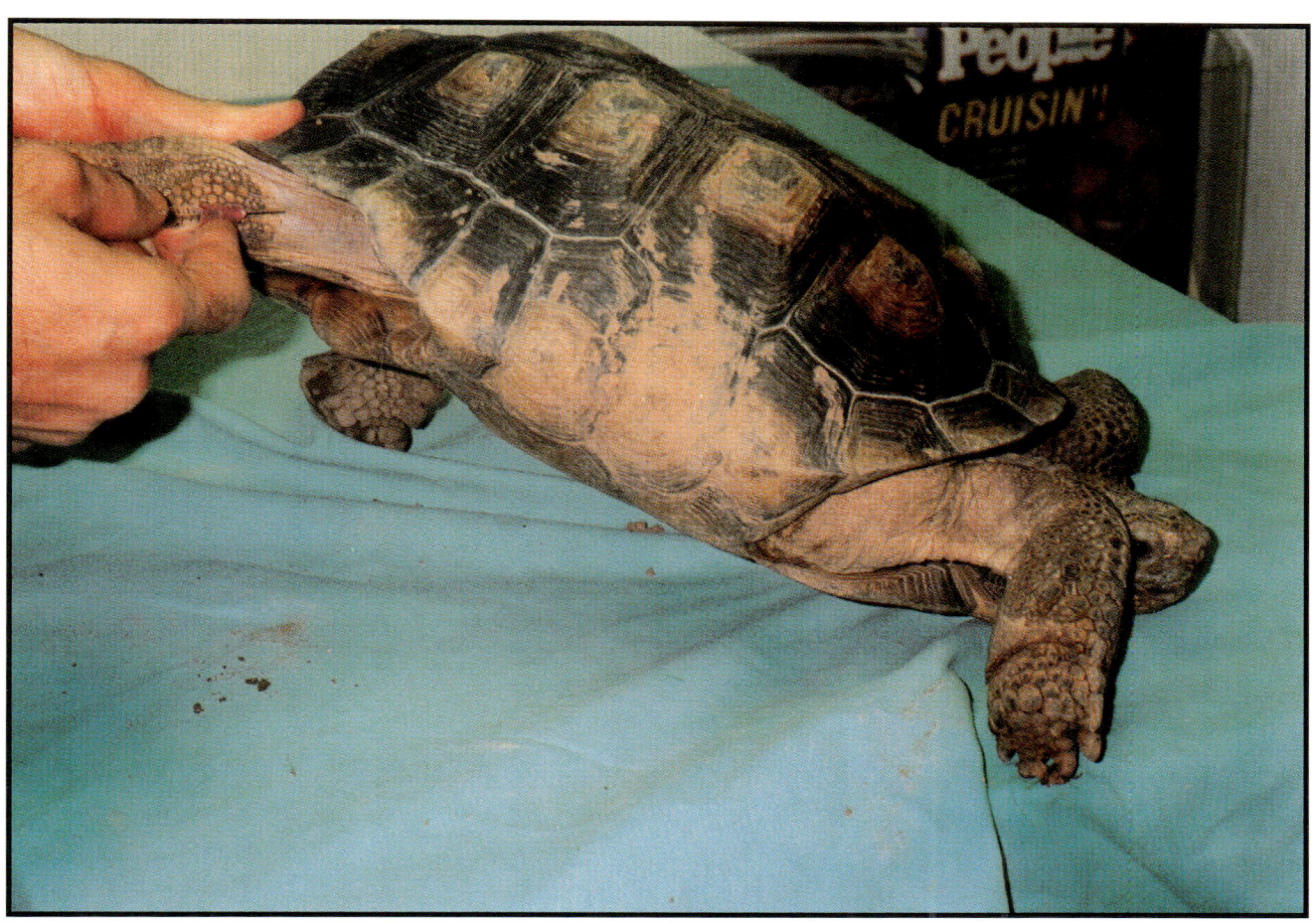

Dr. Bernard Mangone gives this desert tortoise an intramuscular injection. Photo courtesy of Dr. Lowell Ackerman.

Vitamin-A deficiencies may be treated by parenteral or oral administration of vitamin A. Mild deficiencies may be corrected by a change in diet and the administration of small amounts of cod liver oil. Administer cod liver oil by mixing a few drops of it into the chelonian's food.

EAR AND CHEEK ABSCESSES

Facial and mouth abscesses should not be treated lightly; left unattended, the abscess may continue to grow, eroding away tissue and bone. As with eye infections, there are numerous ways for such infections to occur in the ear and cheek.

SHELL INFECTIONS

Fungal and bacterial organisms have been associated with the condition known as shell rot (Frye, 1991). Small scratches or abrasions provide entry for these organisms. As the organisms take hold in the bone beneath the keratinous covering of the carapace or plastron, they begin to erode the bone, and they may penetrate into the body cavity.

The conditions that caused the shell rot to begin with must be addressed concurrent with treatment. Typically, this means cleaning and disinfecting the tank, and keeping the water clean by use of a regularly serviced filtration system and frequent water changes.

To treat shell rot, follow these steps:

1. Soak the turtle in a dilute povidone-iodine bath or place compresses of dilute povidone-iodine over the lesions to soften them.
2. Gently scrape away the areas of infection, using a blunt edged instrument such as a table knife.
3. Swab the scraped areas with povidone-iodine solution or ointment.
4. Keep aquatic turtles in dry tanks during the healing process, providing immersion water only for feeding and drinking.

Fungal and bacterial shell rot typically occurs in aquatic turtles. Pits of varying size and depths have also been found in terrestrial chelonians. These pits are typically the result of the animal being preyed upon by invertebrates while the chelonian is in hibernation. Treatment is the same as for aquatic turtles. After the underlying tissues have been cleaned, you can seal deep erosions with fiberglass cloth and epoxy resin.

Septicemic cutaneous ulcerative disease (SCUD) affects both the shell and the skin, as well as the liver, heart, blood, kidney, and spleen. This disease is most often seen in aquatic turtles kept in unfiltered water that is heavily contaminated with feces.

SKIN BLISTERS

Blistering of the skin may be due to parasites, thermal burns, or a reaction to being housed on cedar chips. Treat burns and cedar-related blisters with povidone-iodine, while making sure you also change the environmental conditions which caused the burns and blisters. If the blisters are caused by parasites, remove the parasites from the skin with tweezers. Then flush the site with dilute povidone-iodine or chlorhexidine diacetate, and evaluate the wound to determine whether or not to use anthelmintics.

STOMATITIS

Simple stomatitis in chelonians may be treated by thorough washing of the buccal cavity with dilute povidone-iodine or chlorhexidine diacetate solution, finished by an application of topical antibiotics. Some veterinarians believe that systemic antibiotic therapy is generally not required in mild cases of stomatitis. It should be remembered, however, that stomatitis is an opportunistic infection; it is merely a symptom of an underlying systemic infection that requires treatment to resolve (Kaplan, et al., 1995).

In severe or resistant stomatitis, cultures should be done to identify the primary and any secondary organisms that may retard recovery.

EUTHANASIA

Euthanizing reptiles presents some difficulties not experienced in other vertebrates. When an animal must be euthanized (for whatever reason), always use the most humane, least stressful and painful method. This discussion gives only general information about euthanasia. Refer to the chapter on reptile euthanasia for more specific information.

Due to the ability of many reptiles—especially aquatic species—to withstand long periods of anoxia, volatile anesthetic gases may be used. Carbon dioxide, however, which provides a rapid and almost instantaneous way of euthanizing mammalian and avian prey, may take too long a time to work on reptiles. The anoxia-withstanding ability of reptiles also makes suffocation difficult, and it is one of the problems associated with sealing animals in plastic bags and freezing them to kill them (Frye, 1991). Cooper and others (1989) believe that hypothermia causes pain as ice crystals form in the skin and tissues; others, such as Frye (1991), dispute this.

For reptiles, intravenous barbiturates are the method of choice. They are effective in rapidly putting the reptile under without posing the risks of nitrous oxide to the handler (Frye, 1991). Intraperitoneal and intramuscular injections are also effective, but they take longer than intravenous injections (Lawton, 1992b). The timeframe can be shortened by keeping the animal at the upper end of its POTR. If the animal is going to be examined postmortem, do not use an intraperitoneal injection. If the animal to be euthanized is aggressive or venomous, you may anesthetize it first, thus making it easier to give the lethal injection.

Decapitation as a painless and immediate cause of death is also under dispute (Cooper, 1989; Frye, 1991). Cooper (1984) reports that the brain remains viable for up to an hour after decapitation, and thus should never be used as the sole method of dispatching the animal. Decapitation can be combined with pithing the brain, the pithing to be done immediately after the head has been decapitated. The reptile can also be anesthetized before decapitation.

ZOONOSES AND THE REHABILITATOR

There are hundreds of organisms that may be transmitted between different species, and humans are not immune to such infection. Parasites themselves can be transmitted, as can any pathogenic organisms they carry. Protozoan and bacterial organisms can be transferred all too easily from the affected animal—and its wastes—to humans. In some instances, direct contact with the affected reptile is not required; anyone who handles the infected animal may transmit the disease to others through direct physical contact or indirect contact, such as food preparation.

For example, during the spring months, many native small lizards play host to the *Ixodes pacificus* tick. This tick carries *Borrelia burgdorferi*, the spirochete responsible for Lyme Disease (Matz, 1993). These ticks respond to movement and so must be killed and preserved immediately upon being extracted.

Imported ball pythons *(Python regius)* have been found harboring *Aponomma latrum*, which has been implicated in the transmission of Q fever. The larvae and nymphs of Q fever can live on mammals and birds (Frank, 1991).

Pentastomids may use humans as intermediate hosts. Wild rodents are frequent carriers of pentastomids and should not be used as a food source for captive reptiles (Hendrix, 1993). The annulate metazoans themselves parasitize the reptilian respiratory system. Human infections with this parasite, transmitted through animal feces, have been documented throughout the world, but especially in Africa and Malaysia. Pentastomes migrate through tissues and organs; this, as well as the calcification of nymphs, may cause problems for humans and other mammals, such as dogs and cats. As yet, there is no good test for pentastomid infection in humans.

SALMONELLOSIS

Studies have found that 85% of turtles, 77% of lizards, and 92% of snakes carry one of the 500 serotypes of *Salmonella* (Grenard, 1994). In a more recent study at North Dakota State University, routine necropsy and bacterial analysis were performed on three long-term captive snakes which suddenly died. Herpetologists at the university found that 88% of their snakes tested positive for *Salmonella* (Grier, et al., 1993). Based on antigen-antibody characteristics, they found twenty-four strains of Salmonella in their snake collection, including eighteen strains in the widespread Arizona group. Some snakes were carrying more than one strain. Herpetologists also found, during retesting, that animals known to be positive for *Salmonella* occasionally tested negative, indicating that animals can have salmonellae without always shedding them.

Most interesting was their finding that *Salmonella* remained viable on shed snake skins that had been in the lab for several years. When a wooden tank was tested six months after the last occupant moved out, viable *Salmonella* organisms were found. Frozen samples proved to be just as active after they were defrosted as they were before they were frozen.

The best way to control the risk of spreading *Salmonella*—and other infectious diseases—is to use common sense and practice proper hygiene. Do not use the same equipment for your animals that you use for yourself. Use different sponges, brushes, food bowls, etc. Wash everything in hot soapy water and then disinfect with chlorhexidine diacetate (four tablespoons to one gallon of water) or a solution of household bleach (one half cup bleach to one gallon of water), or undiluted isopropyl alcohol.

Wash your hands with hot, soapy water after cleaning each enclosure; and wash your hands again at the end of your cleaning. If you wear gloves, use disposable gloves; and put new ones on between every enclosure if working with numerous sick animals. Always begin cleaning and feeding sessions with the healthy animals, finishing with the sick ones. Do not eat or smoke while cleaning your reptile enclosures. If your reptile is new, sick, or stressed, wash your hands after handling it before, eating, smoking, or before coming into contact with young children and others at higher risk for infection.

If you can avoid doing so, do not pour bowls or tubs of water containing fecal material into your kitchen sink, and do not place such containers on counters where you prepare your food. Keep a bottle of diluted bleach (four ounces per gallon of water) or chlorhexidine diacetate by the bathtub and sink to disinfect them after animals have been bathed in them or food and water dishes cleaned in them. *Salmonella* organisms live a long time on inanimate and non-biological surfaces. The organisms may enter your system through a laceration or lesion when you shower or bathe. They may easily get into food by cooking and serving utensils coming into contact with sinks and counters that have not been disinfected or sterilized.

Some individuals are at higher risk for contracting *Salmonella* and other zoonotic diseases, including pregnant women and their unborn babies, infants, toddlers, the frail elderly, and anyone with a compromised or weakened immune system. For additional information, see the chapter on reptile zoonoses.

CONCLUSION

Working with reptiles in any capacity is endlessly fascinating. By combining aspects of behavior, ecology, and medicine, the interactions become increasingly complex. They also add immeasurably to our understanding of how these animals live and how to best keep them healthy in the field and in captivity. As more research is done into the physiological aspects of reptile responses to captive care, we will better be able to determine the underlying causes of illness and stress, improving our ability to treat both medically and environmentally.

TABLE 6. DRUGS MENTIONED IN THE CHAPTER

Drugs Mentioned	Manufacturer	Generic
Baytril	Miles, Inc.	Enrofloxacin
Betadine	The Purdue-Frederick Co.	Povidone-iodine
Betadine Surgical Scrub	The Purdue-Frederick Co.	Povidone-iodine
Calcimar	Roerer Pharmaceutical Co.	Calcitonin
Calcium gluconate	Phoenix Pharmaceutical Inc.	Calcium gluconate
Centrum	Lederle Consumer Health	Vitamins
Flagyl	Lemmon Co.	Metronidazole
Ivomec	Merck & Co.	Ivermectin
Levasole	Pittman-More	Levamisole Phosphate
Neo-Calglucon	Sandoz Pharmaceutical Co.	Calcium gluconate
Nolvasan	Fort Dodge Labs	Chlorhexidine
Nolvasan Surgical Scrub	Ft. Dodge Labs	Chlorhexidine
Panacur	Hoechst-Roussel	Fenbendazole
Pipzine	Aquatronics	Piperazine
Silvadene	Marion Laboratories, Inc.	Silver sulfadiazine
SMZ-TMP	Phoenix Pharmaceutical Inc.	Trimethoprim sulfamethoxazole
Solu-Delta Cortef	Upjohn Co.	Prednisolone sodium succinate
Thiabenzole	Merck & Co.	Thiabendazole
Tribrissin	Coopers Animal Health	Trimethoprim sulfadiazine

REFERENCES

—**Abrahams, R:**
Ivermectin as a spray for treatment of snake mites. *Bull ARAV*, 1992; 1(1): 8.

—**Alberts, A:**
Ultraviolet light and lizards: More than meets the eye. *The Vivarium*, 1994, 5(4):24-25.

—**Almandarz, E:**
Husbandry. In, Zoo and Wild Animal Medicine, ME Fowler (Ed.), W.B. Saunders, Philadelphia, PA, 1986, pp. 136- 139.

—**Arena, PC, Warwick, C:**
Miscellaneous factors affecting health and welfare. In: Warwick, C, Frye, FL, Murphy JB. (Eds). Health and Welfare of Captive Reptiles. Chapman & Hall, London, 1995. pp 262-283.

—**Barnard, SM:**
Reptile Keeper's Handbook. Krieger Publishing Co., Malabar Fl. 1996. 252 pp.

—**Barten, SL:**
Lizards. In: Mader, DR. Reptile Medicine and Surgery. WB Saunders Co., Philadelphia, PA. pp. 47-61.

—**Barten, SL:**
The medical care of iguanas and other common pet lizards. *Vet Clin N Am: Exotic Pet Medicine*, November 1993, 23(6): 1213-1249.

—**Barten, SL:**
Personal communication, 1995.

—**Barten, SL:**
Shell Damage. In, Reptile Medicine and Surgery, DR Mader (Ed.). W.B. Saunders Co., Philadelphia, 1996, pp. 413-417.

—**Belkin, DA:**
Anoxia: Tolerance in reptiles. Science, 1963, 139:492-493.

—**Bennett, RA: Neurology.**
In, Reptile Medicine and Surgery, DR Mader (Ed.). W.B. Saunders Co., Philadelphia, 1996, pp. 141-148.

—**Bernard, JS; Oftendal, OT; Barboza, PS; Allen, ME; Citino, SB; Ullry, DE; Montali, RJ.**
The response of vitamin D deficient green iguanas (*Iguana iguana*) to artificial ultraviolet light. *Proc Am Vet* 1991:147-150.

—**Bone, RD:**
Gastrointestinal System. In, Manual of Reptiles, PH Beynon, MPC Lawton and JE Cooper (Eds). Iowa State University Press, Ames IA, 1992, pp. 103-116.

—**Boyar, TH:**
Vitamin A toxicity. *Bull ARAV*, 1991; 1(1): 3.

—**Boyer, TH:**
Emergency Care of Reptiles. In, Seminars in

Avian and Exotic Pet Medicine, AM Fudge and J Jenkins (Eds.), 1994, 3(4):210-2.

—**Centers for Disease Control and Prevention.** Cryptosporidosis. National Center for Infectious Diseases, Division of Parasitic Diseases, June 1995a. Brochure.

—**Centers for Disease Control and Prevention.** *Salmonella enteritidis* Infection. Division of Bacterial and Mycotic Diseases, June 1995b. Brochure.

—**Cooper, JE; Ewbank, R; Rosenberg, ME:** Euthanasia of tortoises. Veterinary Record, 1984, 114, p. 635.

—**Cooper, JE:** Physiology. In, Zoo and Wild Animal Medicine, ME Fowler (Ed.), W.B. Saunders, Philadelphia, PA, 1986, pp. 132-135.

—**Cooper, JE; Ewbank, R; Platt, C; and Warwick, C:** Euthanasia of Amphibians and Reptiles. (Eds.) Universities Federation for Animal Welfare, Potters Bar, 1989.

—**Cunningham, AA; Gill, C:** Management in Captivity. In, Manual of Reptiles, PH Beynon, MPC Lawton and JE Cooper (Eds). Iowa State University Press, Ames IA, 1992, pp. 14-31.

—**Done, LB:** Postural Abnormalities. In, Reptile Medicine and Surgery, DR Mader (Ed.). W.B. Saunders Co., Philadelphia, 1996, pp. 406-411.

—**Donoghue, S; Langenberg, J:** Nutrition. In, Reptile Medicine and Surgery, DR Mader (Ed.). W.B. Saunders Co., Philadelphia, 1996, pp. 148-174.

—**Evans, HE:** Introduction and Anatomy. In, Zoo and Wild Animal Medicine, ME Fowler (Ed.), W.B. Saunders, Philadelphia, PA, 1986, pp. 108-132.

—**Fowler, ME:** Stress. In, Zoo and Wild Animal Medicine, ME Fowler (Ed.), W.B. Saunders, Philadelphia, PA, 1986a, pp. 34-35.

—**Fowler, ME.** Preventive medicine. In, Zoo and Wild Animal Medicine, ME Fowler (Ed.), W.B. Saunders, Philadelphia, PA, 1986b, pp. 14-17.

—**Frank, NL:** Tick infestations in ball pythons. *Reptile and Amphibian Magazine*, May/June 1992, pp. 41-42

—**Franzmann, AW:** Wildlife medicine. In, Zoo and Wild Animal Medicine, ME Fowler (Ed.), W.B. Saunders, Philadelphia, PA, 1986, pp. 8-11.

—**Frye, FL:** Reptile Care: An atlas of diseases and treatments. T.F.H. Publications, Inc., Neptune City, NJ, 1991, 637 pp.

—**Frye, FL:** Captive Invertebrates: A guide to their care and husbandry. Kreiger Publishing Company, Melbourne, FL, 1992a, 137 pp.

—**Frye, FL:** Use of a condom as an occlusive bandage in snakes. *JSEAM*, 1992b, 2(1):13- 14.

—**Frye, FL:** Salmonellosis in pet reptiles and their owners. *Reptiles*, 1995, 3(1):26-42.

—**Funk, RS:** Herp health hints and husbandry: parasiticide dosages for captive amphibians and reptiles. *Bull Chicago Herpetol. Soc.*, 23(2):30.

—**Gehrmann, William H.** No UV from tungsten filament incandescent light. *ARAV*, 1992, 2(2):5.

—**Gittleman, AL:** Parasites: Alive and well in the U.S.A. Health Counselor, 1995, 7(2):15-18.

—**Greenberg, R:** Ethologically informed design in husbandry and research. In: Warwick, C, Frye, FL, Murphy JB. (Eds). Health and Welfare of Captive Reptiles. Chapman & Hall, London, 1995. pp 239-262.

—**Grier, JW; Bjerke, JS; Nolan, LK:** Snakes and the Salmonella Situation. *Bull. Chicago Herp. Soc.*, 1993, 28(3):53-59.

—**Guillotte, LJ, Cree, A, Rooney, RA:** Biology of stress: Interactions with reproduction, immunology, and intermediary metabolism. In: Warwick, C, Frye, FL, Murphy JB. (Eds). Health and Welfare of Captive Reptiles. Chapman & Hall, London, 1995. pp 32-81.

—**Hendrix, CM:** Reptilian Pentastomiasis: A possible emerging zoonosis. The Compendium Collection, 1993, 3(1):93-98.

—**Iverson, JB:** Adaptations to herbivory in iguanine lizards. In, Iguanas of the World: Their Behavior, Ecology and Conservation, Noyes Publications, Park Ridge, NJ, 1986, pp. 60-76.

—**Jackson, OF; Lawton MPC:** Examination and diagnostic techniques. In, Manual of Reptiles, PH Beynon, MPC Lawton and JE Cooper (Eds). Iowa State University Press, Ames IA, 1992, pp. 32-72.

—**Jacobson, E:** Parasitic Diseases of Reptiles. In, Zoo and Wild Animal Medicine, ME Fowler (Ed.), W.B. Saunders, Philadelphia, PA, 1986, pp. 162- 181.

—**Kaplan, M; Jereb, R:**
Stomatitis. *Journal of International Wildlife Rehabilitation*, 1995, 18(2):13-15, 18,

—**Klingenberg, RJ:**
Understanding Reptile Parasites. Advanced Vivarium Systems, Lakeside, CA, 1993, 81 p.

—**Kreger, MD:**
Zoo-Academic collaborations: Physiological and psychological needs of reptiles and amphibians. *Herpetologica*, 1993a, 49(4): 509-512.

—**Kreger, MD; Mench, JA:**
Physiological and behavioral effects of handling and restraint in the ball python (Python regius) and the blue-tongued skink (*Tiliqua scincoides*). Applied Animal Behaviour Science, 1993b, 38, pp. 323-336.

—**Lawton MPC:**
Miscellaneous. In, Manual of Reptiles, PH Beynon, MPC Lawton and JE Cooper (Eds). Iowa State University Press, Ames IA, 1992a, pp. 153-156.

—**Lawton MPC:**
Ophthalmology. In, Manual of Reptiles, PH Beynon, MPC Lawton and JE Cooper (Eds). Iowa State University Press, Ames IA, 1992b, pp. 157-169.

—**Lawton, MPC; Stoakes, LC:**
Surgery. In, Manual of Reptiles, PH Beynon, MPC Lawton and JE Cooper (Eds). Iowa State University Press, Ames IA, 1992c, pp. 184-193.

—**Lewbart, GA:**
Gout in captive reptiles. *Reptile and Amphibian Magazine*, May/June 1990, pp. 34-37.

—**Mader, D:**
Shell repair in turtles and tortoises. *The Vivarium*, 1992, 4(1):9-12.

—**Mader, D:**
Use of calcitonin in green iguanas, Iguana iguana, with metabolic bone disease. *ARAV*, 1993a, 3(1):5.

—**Mader, DR:**
Common Reptilian Bacteria: What are they and what is their significance. *The Vivarium*, 1993b, 4(6):27-29.

—**Mader, DR:**
Reptile Medicine and Surgery. W.B. Saunders Company, Philadelphia, PA, 1996, 512pp.

—**Mader, D:**
Ivermectin. *Reptiles*, 1995, 2(3):74-76.

—**Mader, D:**
Reptilian Gout. *Reptiles*, 1995, 2(4):40-46.

—**Matz, KS:**
Spring, ticks and lizards. Southwestern Herpetological Society, 1993, 23(8):7.

—**Mattison, C:**
The Care of Reptiles and Amphibians in Captivity. Sterling Publishing Co., New York, NY, 1992, 317 p.

—**McBee RH; McBee VH:**
The hindgut fermentation in the green iguana, Iguana iguana. In, Iguanas of the World: Their Behavior, Ecology and Conservation, Noyes Publications, Park Ridge, NJ, 1986, pp. 77-83.

—**Messonnier, SP:**
Anorexia in snakes. *Reptile and Amphibian Magazine*, 1995, pp. 111- 115.

—**Murray, MJ:**
Pneumonia an dNormal Respiratory Function. In, Reptile Medicine and Surgery, DR Mader (Ed.). W.B. Saunders Co., Philadelphia, 1996, pp. 396-405.

—**Page, CD; Mautino, M:**
Clinical management of tortoises. *Compend Contin Educ Pract Vet*, February 1990, 12(2):221-228.

—**Raley, PL:**
Primer of Wildlife Care and Rehabilitation. Bruckner Nature Center, Troy, OH, 1992, 225 pp.

—**Rossi, JV:**
Dermatology. In, Reptile Medicine and Surgery, DR Mader (Ed.). W.B. Saunders Co., Philadelphia, 1996, pp. 104-117

—**Schumacher, J; Jacobson, ER; Moher, BL; Gaskin, JM:**
Inclusion body Disease in Boid Snakes. *Journal of Zoo and Wildlife Medicine*, 1994; 25(4): 51-54.

—**Scott, PW:**
Nutritional Diseases. In, Manual of Reptiles, PH Beynon, MPC Lawton and JE Cooper (Eds). Iowa State University Press, Ames IA, 1992, pp. 138-152.

—**Snake mite**
(*Ophionyssus natricis*) eradication utilizing Permectrin spray. *Bulletin of the Association of Reptilian and Amphibian Veterinarians*, 1995, 5(1): 4-5.

—**Stahl, SJ:**
Complications with hemipenial plugs in Old World chameleons. *Journal of Small Exotic Animal Medicine*, 1994, 2(4):177.

—**Stahl, SJ:**
Stargazing. The League of Florida Herpetological Societies, July 1995.

—**Suedmeyer, WK:**
Use of chlorhexidine in the treatment of infectious stomatitis. *Bull ARAV* 1991, 2(1): 6.

—**Suedmeyer, WK:**
A simple method for administering oral medication in reptiles. *Journal of Small Exotic Animal Medicine*, 1991, 1(1)43-44.

—**Warwick, C:**

Reptilian ethology in captivity: Observation of some problems and an evaluation of their aetiology. *Applied Animal Behaviour Science,* 1990, 26, pp. 1-13.

—**White, J:**

Basic Wildlife Rehabilitation. International Wildlife Rehabilitation Council, Suisun, FL, 1988, 126 pp.

—**White, J; Emanuelson, S: Emaciation:**

A Protocol for Recovery. In, *IWRC Journal,* Summer 1983, pp. 5-7.

—**Willette-Frahm, M; Wright, K; Thode, B:**

Select protozoal diseases in amphibians and reptiles. *Bulletin of Association of Reptilian and Amphibian Veterinarians,* 5(1):19-29.

—**Wissman, M:**

Dermatophytosis. *Reptiles,* 1995, 3(3):78-80.

—**Wright, KM:**

Husbandry: An essential component of diagnosing disease in reptiles and amphibians. *The Vivarium,* 1991, pp. 23, 25-27.

—**Wright, KM:**

The use of anthelmintics in captive herbivorous reptiles. *The Vivarium,* 1992, 3(6):23-25.

—**Zwart, P:**

Infectious Diseases of Reptiles. In, Zoo and Wild Animal Medicine, ME Fowler (Ed.), W.B. Saunders, Philadelphia, PA, 1986, pp. 155-162.

ANTISEPSIS, DISINFECTION, AND HYGIENE

James C. Cokendolpher,
Adjunct Professor of Biology,
Midwestern State University,
Wichita Falls, Texas 76308

James Cokendolpher received an A.A.S. in Chemical Technology and a B.S. and M.S. in Biology from Midwestern State University. He attended graduate school at Texas Tech University, Lubbock, Texas and became an Adjunct Professor of Biology at Midwestern State University in 1989. From 1991 to 1995, Mr. Cokendolpher was the Pesticide Specialist with the Antimicrobial Complaint System of the National Pesticide Telecommunications Network which was jointly funded by the U.S. Environmental Protection Agency and Texas Tech University Health Sciences Center in Lubbock, Texas.

INTRODUCTION

Hygiene, or the principles and science of the preservation of health and prevention of disease, is a broad field covering sanitation, quarantine, and many other topics. Maintaining sanitary conditions is essential for the long-term maintenance and breeding of captive herptiles. Sanitation goes beyond simple cleaning and must be done in such a manner as not to cause harm to the captive animals through either stress or exposure to harmful chemicals or conditions.

HYGIENE

HOUSING

Housing should provide the captive animal with a safe and secure home. For success, the environmental needs of the animals will have to be met while maintaining cleanliness. While some animals will thrive in an essentially bare cage with newspaper flooring or a log in a pool, most will require more sophisticated and enriched environments. Stress caused by the lack of sufficient hiding places or over-crowding can be detrimental to a herptiles health. The herptile enclosure should be kept as simple as possible while still providing a secure environment. The simpler the design, the easier it will be to maintain a clean environment. Over-crowding must always be avoided.

All terraria should be kept clean. This one houses a brown Cuban anole. Photo courtesy of Dr. Todd Driggers.

Keeping cages free of fecal material is important in limiting the spread of disease. Photo courtesy of Dr. Todd Driggers.

Snake-breeding cage set-up. Photo courtesy of Dr. Todd Driggers.

Each cage should be inspected at least daily for the presence of stools, urinary wastes, and shed skins. These materials along with any soiled cage litter should be removed as soon as possible. Cage inspections can accompany feeding and watering, but waste should not be removed at this time or the food or water may be contaminated.

The Merck Veterinary Manual (Fraser et al, 1991) suggests that both terrestrial and aquatic environments should be disassembled and disinfected every six months. This is a good idea, but the length of time between disassembly will be determined by the environment and the number of animals in that environment. For example, large well-planted natural enclosures with only a few herptile inhabitants may not have to be disassembled; whereas, small crowded cages may have to be broken down once a month, or more. Even if the herptiles are originally free from parasites and the contents of the enclosure are acting as a community (plants and minute invertebrates are recycling herptile waste rapidly), disassembly and disinfection might be needed if pathogens or parasites are introduced via the food or water. Monitoring the general behavior and stools of the inhabitant herptiles will be the guide to environmental health.

AIR

Airborne pathogens are difficult to control in a room with many caged animals. Ultraviolet light is microbiocidal and should help reduce the numbers of infectious agents in the air. Because UV light does not penetrate well, it can not kill microorganisms which are covered with a film of body fluids or other detritus. Likewise, plastics and glass used in the construction of cages reduce the amount of UV light striking the enclosure surfaces. In addition to UV light available from sun-light and minor amounts from full-spectrum lighting, special biocidal lamps are available. Quarantine facilities for large and valuable collections could benefit from positive air pressure (air is carried away from the animal facilities and exhausted into the atmosphere a safe distance from the facility).

Large banks of cages should not be connected by vent holes through which fan-driven air is passed. While fans are useful in circulating air and adjusting humidity levels, rapid air movement can carry disease causing microbes. Screen topped cages which gradually circulate air are preferred over fan-driven systems.

Corn snake in a breeding box. Photo courtesy of Dr. Todd Driggers.

WATER

Water must be clean and fresh. It should be presented in a fashion that is natural to the animal (misting, dripping, pools, etc.). Water used in drip or misting systems should not be collected and reused, unless it can be filtered and decontaminated. Reusing water can lead to problems if any infectious agent is present on areas over which the water runs. Water dishes and soaking pools, if present, should be cleaned routinely and at the appearance of any excreta or dead food items.

Flow-through aquatic systems are less likely to spread pathogens than recirculating systems. The water should be adjusted to the appropriate temperature, mineral content, salinity, and pH before it is placed in the enclosure. If recirculating water systems are all that are available, each pool or tank should have a self-contained system to minimize cross-contamination. A bacteriostatic water filter may be added to recirculating aquatic systems if the inhabitants are not sensitive to silver or other ions used in the system.

Chlorine and chloramine (if present) should be removed from incoming pool water either by aging, boiling, or treatment with sodium thiosulfate (one drop of saturated solution per gallon of water). Whereas chlorinated water can be detrimental to some pool inhabitants (especially aquatic amphibians), chlorinated drinking water appears to be beneficial as it is essentially free of bacteria and protozoa. More studies are needed to confirm the benefits of chlorinated drinking water for herptiles.

FOODS

All foods should be of an appropriate type, quality, and quantity to provide balanced nutrition for the captive herptile. Foods should be stored and prepared in sanitary conditions. The feed, water, and cages of prey animals should also be sanitary. Rodents and insects reared in filthy conditions can result in disease in the captive predatory species.

Because live foods crawl through/over any excreta on the floor or in the food dish of the herptile, it is important to keep these surfaces clean. Likewise, plants and other substrates used as watering vessels should be free of excreta or dead food items. "Musical foods" should not be practiced; i.e., foods offered but not eaten by one animal should not be offered to another animal. Whereas some authors suggest foods from quarantined animals should not be given to non-quarantined; the correct procedure is no rotating foods regardless of the animals quarantine status (i.e., foods refused by non-quar-antined animals should not be given to quarantined animals). The savings on the price of a mouse or rat can not compare to the cost of a veterinarian visit or the death of a herptile.

HERPTILES

By providing a clean home, the animals will not have to crawl or swim through their or penmates excrement or spoiled food. Potable water baths should be provided for terrestrial species which soak. Do not assume that all animals from a desert do not like to soak. Baths are frequently used by many desert animals. Frye (1991) reported that several Gila monsters and Mexican beaded lizards at the San Diego Zoological Garden spent so much time in the water that they turned green from the mass of algae growing on their skin. Keep baths shallow as many terrestrial herptiles do not swim well. A special effort should be taken to verify that molts are completed and that old skin or other detritus are not left attached to the animal.

KEEPER/HANDLER

A special effort must be made to reduce cross-contamination between cages of animals. Handwashing or wearing rubber/latex gloves before and after handling animals will protect both the animals as well as the handler. These procedures are especially important in protecting herptile health if the handler smokes or uses any form of lotions or other skin preparations. Nicotine is one of the most toxic chemicals known (LD_{50} = 1 mg/1 kg in rodents) and the handler should not smoke in the room housing herptiles or their foods. Second-hand smoke can be deadly to low body-weight animals. If rubber/latex gloves are worn they should be changed between patients to protect the health of the animals. Likewise, leather/cloth gloves, nets, snake-hooks, handling cages or containers should be decontaminated after contact with each animal, if there is a possibility of disease transmission.

QUARANTINE

Probably the single most important step in herptile infection control is isolation of all potential sources of pathogens, whether from a single patient or population. A potentially infectious source (newly acquired herptile) should be treated as an infectious source. Thus, quarantine should not just be a period in which the new animal is observed but a period in which the animal is treated as if verified to be infectious.

New arrivals to a collection, whether wild caught or captive born, may have undergone serious stress that predisposes it to disease. Prior to acquisition, the herptile may have been exposed to over-crowding, incorrect environmental conditions (temperature, photoperiod, etc.), or inadequate water or diet. Partially dehydrated and malnourished wild caught animals are especially sensitive to pathogenic viruses, bacteria, and parasites which they may encounter (from other captive herptiles) en route to the market. These animals, as well as those infected in the wild may appear normal upon arrival, but a quarantine period will allow the pathogens or parasites time to incubate and manifest their presence as a disease.

The new herptile, the contents of its cage, and any refuse must not come into contact with other animal unless it is also placed in quarantine. Even if the new animal is on breeding loan and presumably healthy, it is to be regarded with caution. Anything less could result in disaster. Specimens bred to loaned animals should be placed in quarantine prior to being returned to the general population.

Isolating a newly acquired or apparently ill animal, but not its excreta or other body fluids, does little good in halting the spread of pathogens or parasites. At worst, the pseudo-isolation gives the keeper a false sense of accomplishment and might slow the early detection of infection or infestation. Early release of an animal from quarantine because it is eating and active also can result in the spread of disease.

Newly arrived animals or those suspected of being ill should be kept in cages isolated from long-term stock. During this period, checks for parasites or signs of pathogens should be routine. These tests contribute to the health of the animal keeper as well as to the welfare of the animals under observation. Also, note if the animal is eating and defecating normally. Monitor body weight; a loss in weight signifies illness.

The length of quarantine generally recommended is between 30 and 90 days (Frye, 1991; Wright, 1991, 1994; Jacobson, 1994). A minimum of 60 days, and preferably 90 days, seems more appropriate with the long incubation periods of some pathogens and parasites. This period is automatically extended if any illness is detected during the period of strict isolation from resident animals. By the same logic, an ill animal placed in quarantine should remain in isolation until the animal has returned to normal health (three negative fecal examines or cultures, five days apart in the case of parasites), plus additional time spent in isolation (at least 14 days, Wright, 1994) to allow for incubation

of any secondary infections. This period of "post-cure" could start following the first negative culture or examination. If the disease agent can not be identified (such as acute death syndrome of American tortoises) or is viral in nature (especially ophidian paramyxovirus) the animal should remain in quarantine. In such cases, it may be easier to donate the animal to a collection already housing animals with such signs and symptoms rather than maintaining the animal in quarantine indefinitely.

Quarantine will probably not reveal the presence of symbiotic or resident microorganisms. These organisms do not normally cause disease in their natural host or carriers, but may be fatal to other species of herptiles, or even conspecifics from other geographical regions. Animals leaving quarantine to the main collections should still be regarded with caution. Good hygienic practices should continue throughout the facility at all times.

As stressed earlier, musical foods should not be practiced. Nothing should pass to or from one quarantined animal to or from any other in the collection. Porous or other difficult to clean materials (logs, plants, etc.) should either be discarded (preferred method) or retained with the quarantined animal(s) as they pass from quarantine to the long-term stock area. Cages and other items used in quarantine should either be sterilized or disinfected with at least a tuberculocidal disinfectant.

Many authorities will suggest a protocol whereby feeding and cleaning schedules will require the non-quarantined animals to receive attention prior to those in quarantine. The theory is that by doing so, no pathogens are accidentally passed to the general population. The problem is that some microbes which are not pathogenic in the general population can be passed to the potentially immune-compromised quarantined animal, resulting in disease. The correct procedure is to thoroughly wash hands and disinfect all instruments between quarantine and non-quarantine area visits (even better is a second set of instruments to be used only with quarantined animals). If this practice is strictly adhered to no organisms should pass in either direction. If animals or other materials might come into contact with clothing, a protective laboratory coat or apron should be worn and removed before attending the next animal.

Quarantine can be potentially stressful for caged herptiles. While it is easier to maintain sanitation in a bare glass cage, such an environment will stress many herptiles. Densely planted enclosures will be required for some sensitive

Multiple snake-housing system. It is imperative to control disease transmission in this kind of setting. Photo courtesy of Dr. Todd Driggers.

herptiles. Cover, Barnett, and Saunders (1994) stress the importance of cage enrichment for dendrobatid and Neotropical hylid frogs. In their facility (National Aquarium in Baltimore), sick frogs are generally treated in their home tank and are not exposed to the stresses of moving to a special quarantine tank. When patients are moved, they are placed in similarly enriched tanks. The quarantine cage for any herptile should be no less optimal (light, temperature, humidity, retreats, etc.) than environments afforded animals in the main collection, but they must be setup so that even the shiest animal can be monitored. New arrivals are already having to deal with possible stresses encountered prior to acquisition and do not need additional stresses. Placing a social animal in strict isolation can also be detrimental to its health. In such cases, plans should be made for conspecific interactions. Adding several conspecific social animals to a collection at the same time and maintaining them as a community should result in a less stressful quarantine. If the animals were all obtained from the same source, they were probably exposed to the same (if any) in-

fectious agents. Quarantine is also a period for new arrivals to rest and regain vigor before being placed in the general collection.

Births and egg-laying are not uncommon in quarantines of wild caught herptiles. Appropriate environments/substrates should be provided for the offspring. The offspring, although captive-born should remain in quarantine for the full term. They can be isolated from the parent, but should not be placed with long-term captives.

INFECTION CONTROL

Infection control is to, literally, control the transmission of microorganisms (viruses, bacteria, and fungi), which may cause or contribute to infections. Viruses and virus-like particles are normally found inside a host and can not multiply outside of a living cell (although some may remain infective outside of a host for days). However, some bacteria and fungi can replicate outside of the body on contaminated surfaces. All of these microbes are invisible to the naked eye. Therefore, one must be able to anticipate when and where they may be in sufficient numbers to be potentially harmful. Once these sites are identified, they should be decontaminated (cleaned and disinfected, or sterilized, or antisepticized), thus limiting growth and proliferation of the microorganisms to control disease transmission.

CLEANING

While commonly assumed (even by some in the medical and veterinary professions), cleaning is not antisepsis or disinfection. Cleaners/ detergents, antiseptics, and disinfectants are not the same. Cleaning is the process (vacuuming, scrubbing, washing, etc.) by which debris (including some disease-causing agents) is physically removed and must precede antisepsis and disinfection procedures. However, the importance of cleaning should not be downplayed. Cleaning is actually the most important step in a disinfection/antisepsis process since the presence of organic material (dirt, blood, excrement, etc.) can present a physical barrier between the chemical antiseptic/disinfectant and the target microorganisms. If the antimicrobial agent can not reach the microbes, there is little chance that they will be killed. Furthermore, cleaning alone often reduces the numbers of pathogens below the level required for disease transmission.

Cleaning is absolutely necessary because it:
—allows the decontaminate chemicals to physically contact the microbes
—removes large numbers of the microorganisms
—eliminates the risk of organic substances reacting or neutralizing the antimicrobial agents.

Cleaning can be a source of disturbance to captive herptiles. Moving substrates, branches, or other cage furniture has been reported to cause stress leading to death in some shy/nervous animals. None-the-less, some form of cleaning is generally required. Experience will show how much disturbance an animal will tolerate during any cleaning session. Some animals can be removed while the entire cage is cleaned, whereas others will move from one corner to another as the cleaning proceeds. Cages of easily disturbed animals can be cleaned in sections over a period of time: i.e., dishes, floor, walls, and branches on separate days. Larger enclosures will reduce the stress as the animals will be able to retreat further from cleaning activities.

Complete removal of feces or other secretions which might contain pheromones or other markers for intraspecific communication can also alter the behavior of the caged individuals. Snakes kept in "clean" cages were constantly alert or otherwise more "uncomfortable" than individuals in cages where a small amount of fecal matter is left each time the cage is cleaned (Chiszar et al, 1980). Similarly, plethodontid salamanders mark their cages with pheromones in their feces, and salamanders in freshly cleaned cages make more attempts to escape than do salamanders that are housed in cages where they have marked their enclosure (Jaeger, 1986; citations therein). At the Philadelphia Zoo, it has been a common practice to leave a few soiled items in herptiles cages after cleaning (except during disease outbreaks). This procedure has resulted in less behavioral disturbance than observed with totally cleaned cages (Conant, 1971). Fecal ingestion may be necessary to "inoculate" the neonates of some vegetarian reptiles. Understanding the needs of each type of herptile under care will aid you in developing an effective cleaning program.

While the use of wet/dry vacuum cleaners can be useful, care should be exercised. The noise can be disturbing to some animals and should be monitored. Filters on vacuum cleaners are not fine enough to remove viruses or bacterial spores. The use of a vacuum cleaner could potentially produce an aerosol of these agents. Similarly, filters on mobile external water cleaning systems can not remove all pathogens and should not be moved from tank to tank without appropriate decontamination between tanks.

While it is often convenient to clean as one feeds, be careful not to contaminate the food items. It is generally better not to mix tasks; either feed and water or clean the enclosure.

Cleaning also extends to objects used in the treatment or movement of animals (i.e., medical instruments, snake hooks, forceps, etc.). These items can generally be washed in soap/ detergent and water with the aid of a brush. They can also be soaked in a cleaning bath. These baths can be useful in keeping fluids from drying onto surgical instruments and, therefore, allowing them to be more easily cleaned. Some individuals also use an enzymatic cleaner to help remove dried-on body fluids and tissues. Enzymatic cleaners can be used in combination with an ultrasonic bath, but be careful to avoid any splashing of the pathogen-laden solution. Use appropriate personal protective equipment (gloves, face shields, etc.) when cleaning medical devices. Remember that items being cleaned are not disinfected/sterilized and can potentially transfer pathogens to humans who are careless in the handling of these objects during cleaning. When washing sharp objects, especially

A thermometer/hygrometer in the cage of a land iguana. Unsuitable temperature and humidity promote the transmission of disease organisms. Photo courtesy of Dr. Todd Driggers.

medical equipment, be sure to wear puncture resistant gloves.

One of the most important steps in reducing cross-contamination is handwashing. The keeper/handler should wash hands:

—before invasive procedures

—before and after contact with wounds

—before contact with susceptible patients (with catheters or other invasive devices, with depressed host-resistance, and neonates)

—after contact with source that is possibly contaminated (touching animals in quarantine, cleaning cages or bowls)

—between patients or quarantined animals.

All jewelry should be removed before washing. Wet hands and then apply soap or antiseptic. Keep hands lower than elbows so that material will not run down the arms. Vigorously rub fingers, palms, back of hands, wrists, forearms, and clean under nails for at least 10 seconds. Rinse under a stream of running water. Use clean towel (preferably paper) to dry hands. Use paper towel (if available) to turn off the faucet and discard. If water is not available, antiseptic foams or solutions can be used. Hands should then be washed with soap and water as soon as possible. Other details on proper methods of handwashing are found in Garner and Favero (1986).

Safety in using chemicals is important in each step of decontamination (cleaning and antisepsis/disinfection/sterilization). Read the label of the detergent or other cleaning material before use. Some cleaning agents react with antimicrobial products. Thoroughly rinse (with potable water) all cleaning agents from surfaces prior to the application of an antiseptic or disinfectant. Never mix cleaners with disinfectants (especially ammonia and chlorine-based bleach) unless instructed so by the product labels. Doing so could result in the creation of deadly (both to humans and animals) compounds or gases or inactivation of the antimicrobial product.

ANTIMICROBIALS

Any agent that kills or inhibits the growth or replication of microorganisms is considered an antimicrobial. This term covers both physical (ultraviolet light and heat) and chemical agents (antiseptic, disinfectant, and sterilant products).

Antisepsis is the process by which many or all fungi, bacteria, viruses, or other pathogenic microorganisms are controlled in or on *living tissue*, and the chemical used is termed an antiseptic or germicide. Disinfection is the process by which pathogenic microorganisms are reduced, killed, or inactivated on an *inanimate* object or surface (including deceased animals). The product used to accomplish this process is called a disinfectant. Even though antiseptics and disinfectants have similar actions, they are regulated by the government and used in different ways and should not be confused.

Disinfectants and antiseptics are not interchangeable. An antiseptic should not be used to "disinfectant" a cage and a disinfectant should not be used as a rinse or soak for a herptile. While it is true some disinfectants and antiseptics have the same active ingredients, they are generally formulated differently. They are often not in the same concentration or associated with the same inert or other active ingredients. Because disinfectants generally have not been tested for skin contact, health risks are unknown when they are used in such a fashion. Unfortunately, skin testing of antiseptics are conducted on rabbits and rodents and therefore only indicate reactions which might be seen in herptiles. Even so, some testing is better than none. The level of disinfection (i.e., type and numbers of microorganisms killed) is uncertain when an antiseptic is used as a disinfectant as the antiseptic was formulated to work upon living tissues and is generally less concentrated than true disinfectants. Furthermore, because of strict regulations governing the use of drugs, pesticides, and medical devices, using these agents in any manner other than described on the label breaks federal laws (Federal Food, Drug, & Cosmetic Act; Federal Insecticide, Fungicide & Rodenticide Act). While the Food and Drug Administration (FDA) and the Environmental Protection Agency (EPA) will not hunt you down and fine you for misusing a disinfectant or antiseptic, this misuse of the product could be used in litigation over an incident involving either your patient, employees, or other injured individual.

ANTISEPSIS

ANTIMICROBIAL DRUGS = ANTISEPTICS

Antiseptics, broadly defined as antimicrobial products for use on animate organisms, are considered drugs and therefore are regulated by the FDA. The FDA's regulatory authority is provided by the Federal Food, Drug and Cosmetic Act, and antimicrobial products considered under this act include: Antimicrobial soaps, broad-spectrum antimicrobial handwashes, preoperative skin preparations, skin antiseptics, skin wound cleansers, skin wound protectants, and surgical hand scrubs.

In appropriate concentrations (70-92%), alcohols (ethanol, isopropanol) provide the most rapid and greatest reduction in microbial counts on human skin. A vigorous one minute rubbing (with enough alcohol to wet the hands completely) has been shown to be the most effective

Table 1.—
Characteristics of commonly used antiseptics (data from Larson, 1988).

Chemical	Gram + bacteria	Gram - bacteria	Tubercle bacilli (mycobacteria)	Fungi	Viruses	Rapidity of action	Residual activity	Safety/toxicity
Alcohols (ethanol and isopropanol)	Excellent	Excellent	Good	Good	Good	Most rapid	None	Drying, flammable
Chlorhexidine	Excellent	Good	Poor	Fair	Good	Intermediate	Excellent	Ototoxicity, keratitis
Hexachlorophene	Excellent	Poor	Poor	Poor	Poor	Slow to Intermediate	Excellent	Neurotoxicity
Iodine and iodophors	Excellent	Good	Good	Good	Good	Intermediate	Minimal	Absorption from skin with possible toxicity, skin irritation more common
PCMX (Para-chloro-meta-xylenol)	Good	Fair	Fair	Fair	Fair	Intermediate	Good	Unknown
Triclosan (5-chloro-2[2,4-dichlorophenoxyl]phenol Irgasan DP-300)	Good	Good (except for *Pseudomonas*)	Fair	Poor	Unknown	Intermediate	Excellent	Unknown

method for hand antisepsis (Larson, 1988). Alcohol can be used on sites where water is not available. Alcohol is commonly used for cleansing sites for injections or other procedures breaking the skin. Alcohol can also be formulated in combination with iodine or chlorhexidine to form tinctures, which are also effective. The major disadvantage of alcohols is the drying effect. Several products on the market now have emollients added to minimize such damage.

Alcohol-based chlorhexidine solutions are effective as a final-stage skin preparation for invasive procedures. The bacterial action (at least two minute contact time) exceeds that of similar solutions of povidone-iodine, triclosan, hexachlorophene, or PCMX. Numerous studies indicate that chlorhexidine at 0.5-4.0% is safe when used on skin (Larson, 1988; Denton, 1991). Although it is ototoxic to mammals if instilled directly into the middle ear, there is no evidence of absorption through the skin. It is not suggested for use near the periorbital or eyelid areas as ocular damages have been observed in mammals. Effects are unknown in herptiles; suggesting caution. Likewise, chlorhexidine has been shown to be toxic to nerve cells in mammals, and therefore contact with the brain or meninges should be avoided (Denton, 1991). Frye (1994) reported that chlorhexidine diacetate (0.5-1.0% solution) was the preferred reptile wound-irrigating solution. Much weaker solutions of chlorhexidine gluconate (0.01-0.05%) have been found to be effective in burn management and wound irrigation in mammals (Denton, 1991). The role of chlorhexidine (as a rinse and gel) as an effective prevention agent and treatment of oral disease in mammals is well studied. Research on herptile subjects should be undertaken. The effectiveness of chlorhexidine is pH dependent: an increase in pH will increase activity against *Staphylococcus* and *Escherichia* but lower activity against *Pseudomonas* (Denton, 1991). Check the label of the particular product that you are using. A 2% chlorhexidine diacetate solution (Nolvasan® Solution, Fort Dodge Labs., Inc.) diluted for use by some individuals is labeled by the manufacturer as not being effective against *Pseudomonas aeruginosa* or gram-positive cocci.

Hexachlorophene at 1-3% can be used on skin by prescription only. Use on broken skin, mucous membranes, or total body bath are contraindicated. Because of the ineffectiveness of this product against anything other than gram-positive bacteria, coupled with the known neurotoxic hazard, this product is herein not suggested for any use.

Iodine, and to a lesser extent iodophors, are recognized for their skin irritation and damage, as well as possible allergic or toxic effects in sensitive patients. Tincture of iodine (the most effective with 1-2% iodine and potassium iodine in 70% alcohol) is used as a preoperative skin preparation. It is relatively fast acting and safe for humans, but because of the potential for irritation it must be removed after drying. Jackson (1981) stated that tinctures of iodine are unsafe for reptiles and that repeated applications burn. The iodophor most commonly used in human medicine is povidone-iodine. Cover, Barnett, and Saunders (1994) stated that Betadine (povidone-iodine solution) is highly toxic to frogs. Povidone-iodine is used in a 7.5% solution as a surgical hand scrub and as 10% solutions on applicators. Some 2% solutions are also available. The activity of iodine and iodophors are negatively affected by the presence of organic matter.

PCMX (Para-chloro-meta-xylenol) is available in a number of different handwashing products, usually in concentrations of 0.5-4.0%. These products are generally not as effective as other antiseptics.

Triclosan (5-chloro-2[2,4-dichlorophenoxyl] phenol or Irgasan DP-300) can be absorbed across intact human skin, but appears to be non-allergenic and non-mutagenic with short term use. Commonly used in household soaps to inhibit growth of skin bacteria and therefore reduce body odor at 0.3-1.0% concentrations.

In the past, quaternary ammonium compounds (such as benzalkonium chloride - Alkyl dimethyl benzyl ammonium chloride) have been used as antiseptics, but the Centers for Disease Control (Simmons, 1983) have recommended against their use (with humans) because of several outbreaks of infections associated with in-use contamination. Furthermore, they have poor antiseptic qualities and are generally ineffective against *Pseudomonas* and *Mycobacterium*.

Three other agents not listed in Table 1 are used in wound irrigation of reptiles: hydrogen peroxide, sodium hypochlorite, and acetic acid (Frye, 1994). All three are readily available to the home herpticulturist. Hydrogen peroxide solutions typically contain 0.5-3.0% by volume. This is one of the safest antiseptics with the innocuous end products of water and oxygen. The liberation of oxygen not only arrests microbial growth, but the foaming is useful in the mechanical removal of pus and cellular debris from wounds. A 3.0% solution of hydrogen peroxide is effective against a wide variety of bacteria (greater activity against gram-negative than

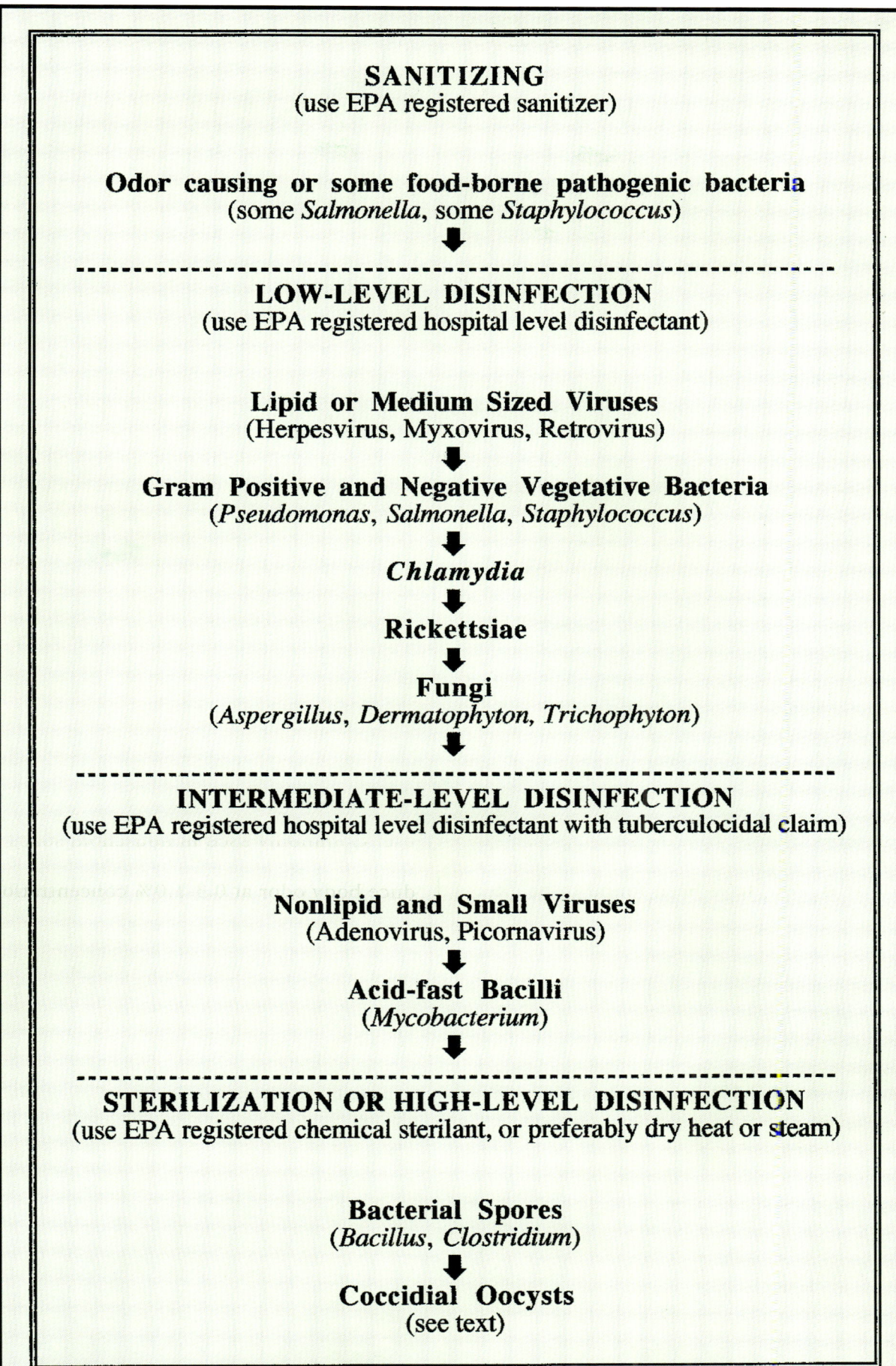

SANITIZING
(use EPA registered sanitizer)

Odor causing or some food-borne pathogenic bacteria
(some *Salmonella*, some *Staphylococcus*)

⬇

LOW-LEVEL DISINFECTION
(use EPA registered hospital level disinfectant)

Lipid or Medium Sized Viruses
(Herpesvirus, Myxovirus, Retrovirus)

⬇

Gram Positive and Negative Vegetative Bacteria
(*Pseudomonas, Salmonella, Staphylococcus*)

⬇

Chlamydia

⬇

Rickettsiae

⬇

Fungi
(*Aspergillus, Dermatophyton, Trichophyton*)

⬇

INTERMEDIATE-LEVEL DISINFECTION
(use EPA registered hospital level disinfectant with tuberculocidal claim)

Nonlipid and Small Viruses
(Adenovirus, Picornavirus)

⬇

Acid-fast Bacilli
(*Mycobacterium*)

⬇

STERILIZATION OR HIGH-LEVEL DISINFECTION
(use EPA registered chemical sterilant, or preferably dry heat or steam)

Bacterial Spores
(*Bacillus, Clostridium*)

⬇

Coccidial Oocysts
(see text)

Table 2.
Order of resistance of microorganisms to disinfection and sterilization and the level of disinfection required (modified from Favero and Bond, 1991; Quinn, 1991). Arrows indicate more resistant organisms. Individual species may vary from the activity listed for that category, see text.

gram-positive), yeasts, and viruses, in a relatively short time. Block (1991) provides a table of the effective time periods needed for lethality of various microorganisms.

Sodium hypochlorite has been used (in humans and animals) since World War I to antisepticize wound infections by the so-called Carrell-Dakin surgical irrigation treatment. Dakin's solution is 0.4-0.5% sodium hypochlorite in water. Because of potential toxicity, this material should not be used on amphibians. Rinsing with a 0.2% solution of sodium hypochlorite stops post-operative bleeding after a minute in human oral operations/extractions (Dychdala, 1991).

Frye (1994) listed acetic acid (vinegar) diluted to a 0.5% solution as a wound-irrigation solution for reptiles. Similar solutions are used on humans and other mammals and may have further uses with herptiles. A 1% solution has been used in surgical dressings and a 5% solution is effective against many bacteria, and has been used to treat otitis externa in mammals caused by bacteria and fungi (*Pseudomonas*, *Candida*, *Malassezia*, or *Aspergillus*; Fraser et al, 1991).

DISINFECTION

ANTIMICROBIAL PESTICIDES = DISINFECTANTS AND COLD STERILANTS

There is a hierarchy in the susceptibility of pathogens to disinfectants. The current scheme was developed by Favero and Bond (1991) to represent the relative levels of chemical resistance of human pathogens It is modified here (Table 2) to include herptile pathogens and agents which control them.

Because disinfectants and related products are to be used in or on inanimate surfaces they are legally defined as antimicrobial pesticides (Federal Insecticide, Fungicide & Rodenticide Act) and are therefore regulated by the EPA. The EPA registers chemicals with a variety of efficacy claims for use on many types of inanimate surfaces. Product types range from those intended to reduce odor-causing bacteria on trash receptacles to products intended to sterilize medical instruments.

In addition to the classification scheme of the EPA (based on product efficacy), there are device and process classifications used by the Centers for Disease Control and Prevention (CDC) and other infection control groups. Because all the terminology can be confusing, equivalent terms are listed in both Tables 2 and 3. Specifically, the EPA categorizes chemicals which can be used to complete a CDC disinfection process. A third set of terms are those used to describe the nature of the items to be disinfected. The EPA product efficacy classification is (from least stringent to most efficacious): sanitizer, limited disinfectant, general disinfectant (= broad spectrum disinfectant), hospital disinfectant (with and without mycobacteria activity), and sterilant. The CDC process classification is

Table 3.—
Classification of devices, processes, and antimicrobial pesticides (modified from Favero and Bond, 1991). See Table 2 for examples of microorganisms that can be controlled.

Device classification	Devices/surfaces	CDC process classification	EPA product classification
(does not touch animal)	Food preparation surfaces	(none)	Sanitizer
Noncritical (touches intact skin)	Stethoscopes, tabletops, cage surfaces	Low-level disinfection	Hospital disinfectant without tuberculocidal activity
Semicritical (touches mucous membranes)	Food and water dishes	Intermediate-level disinfection	Hospital disinfectant with tuberculocidal activity
	or		
	Flexible endoscopes, endotracheal tubes	High-level disinfection	Sterilant (short contact)
Critical (enters sterile tissue or vascular system)	Implants, scalpels, needles other surgical instruments	Sterilization	Sterilant (prolonged contact)

(from least stringent to most stringent): low-level disinfection, intermediate-level disinfection, high-level disinfection, and sterilization. The Spaulding device classification is: noncritical item, semicritical item, and critical item. These terms will be discussed in greater detail below.

Once the cleaning (including rinsing and drying where appropriate) has been accomplished, the next step to consider in the disinfection/sterilization process is the level of microbial kill or inactivation that is required. Selecting the appropriate product requires a knowledge of the organisms which might be present, the degree of risk of infection, as well as the efficacy of the antimicrobial product.

Spaulding (1968) proposed a rational approach to disinfection and sterilization of human patient care items and equipment. His classification is so logical that it has been generally accepted by infection control practitioners in human medicine and should be followed in veterinary medicine. The categories of Spaulding's system are based on the degree of risk of infection involved in the use of the items. These categories are easily applied to herptiles; except that unlike humans, herptiles do eat and drink from the walls and floors. The three categories of items he described are correlated with items to be disinfected, CDC process classification, and EPA product classification in Table 3.

The data in Tables 2 and 3 are only to be used as minimal standards when selecting the appropriate level of disinfection needed. Heat resistant items can always be sterilized in an autoclave or dry-heat sterilizer, regardless of the items classification code. Use of higher level disinfectants than are needed can expose the environment, animals, and individual using the disinfectant to more hazardous chemicals than are required. Read the product label precautionary statements carefully.

Food preparation areas can be treated effectively with an EPA registered sanitizer. Because food and water bowls can be contaminated with difficult to control microorganisms, they should be treated with a disinfectant (see below), not a sanitizer.

Noncritical items come into contact with intact skin but do not touch mucous membranes. Intact skin acts as an effective barrier to most pathogens and sterility is not required. Low-level disinfectants (EPA registered hospital-level disinfectant) are suitable for these items.

Although EPA registered limited and general disinfectants could be used in non-clinic areas they have no proven efficacy against most viruses, fungi, *Pseudomonas*, or more difficult to kill bacteria. They are okay for cleaning/disinfecting homes (i.e., bathrooms, garbage receptacles, etc.) to control influenza, *Staphylococcus*, or *Streptococcus* bacteria, but they have limited use in a clinical area. Since many herptiles drink and feed off the floors and walls of cages, it is safer to consider these items (as well as food and water bowls) to be semicritical items. Many herptile keepers/handlers have treated these surfaces as noncritical items and have used less stringent disinfectants. Research should be undertaken to determine which herptiles are normally susceptible to *Pseudomonas* and mycobacteria via an oral route. The cages and bowls of those animals should then receive intermediate-level disinfection.

Semicritical items come into contact with mucus membranes or non-intact skin. These items should be relatively free of microorganisms, except for bacteria spores. Intact mucos membranes are generally susceptible to acid-fast bacilli (mycobacteria) but not bacterial spores. Cage walls, floors, water and food dishes can be effectively treated with an intermediate-level disinfectant (EPA registered hospital disinfectant with tuberculocidal claims), but semicritical devices like flexible endoscopes and endotracheal tubes should preferably receive high-level disinfection (wet pasteurization or chemical sterilant/high-level disinfectant). High-level disinfected items should be rinsed with sterile water after disinfection so that they will not be contaminated with organisms found in tap water (e.g., *Mycobacterium*, *Pseudomonas*).

Critical items come into contact with normally sterile areas of the body and pose a high risk of infection if they are contaminated with any microorganisms, including bacterial spores. Such items must be kept sterile. Most critical items should be purchased sterile or, if heat stable, sterilized with steam under pressure, or dry-heat. Items that are heat labile can be treated with ethylene oxide or liquid chemical sterilants.

SANITIZERS

This category of products is intended to reduce the number of bacteria and viruses on the inanimate surfaces to levels considered safe as determined by human public health codes or regulations. Nonhalogenated food-contact surface sanitizers must be effective against either *Escherichia coli* or *Staphylococcus aureus* bacteria. Halogenated food-contact surface sanitizers must be effective against either *Salmonella typhi* or *Staphylococcus aureus* bacteria. A non-food contact surface sanitizer must be effective against *Staphylococcus aureus* and either *Klebsiella pneumoniae* or *Enterobacter aerogenes* bacteria.

Sanitizers are used in caring for herptiles in the food preparation area. Surfaces used for such activities should ideally be treated as if the materials were being prepared for human consumption. A 1:250 dilution of household bleach (5.25% sodium hypochlorite) (200 ppm available chlorine: 1 tablespoon of bleach in 1 gallon of water) makes an effective sanitizer for smooth hard surfaces.

DISINFECTANTS

A disinfectant is intended to destroy or inactivate one or more specific bacterial groups depending upon whether the product label claims "limited," "general," or "hospital" disinfection:

—Limited disinfectant = A disinfectant that is EPA registered for use against a specific major group of bacteria (gram-negative or gram-positive bacteria). Efficacy has been demonstrated in laboratory tests against either *Salmonella cholerasuis* or *Staphylococcus aureus*.

—General disinfectant = A disinfectant that is labeled for use against both gram-negative and gram-positive bacteria. Efficacy demonstrated against both *Salmonella cholerasuis* and *Staphylococcus aureus*. Also referred to as a "broad spectrum disinfectant."

—Hospital disinfectant = A disinfectant that is registered for use in hospitals, clinics, or any other medical related facility. Efficacy demonstrated against *Salmonella cholerasuis*, *Staphylococcus aureus*, and *Pseudomonas aeruginosa*. In addition, hospital disinfectants can bear a label claim as a tuberculocide. This is especially important, as the mycobacteria, including *M. tuberculosis*, are more difficult to kill than most other species of bacteria, and all fungi and viruses. Hospital disinfectants can be used for low- or intermediate-level disinfection (based on mycobacteria activity).

Low-level disinfection - hospital disinfectant, which is not registered as effective against *Mycobacterium*: Will kill most vegetative bacteria, fungi, and lipid viruses. Will not kill spores, oocysts, or nonlipid viruses and sometimes less active against *Pseudomonas* and *Mycobacterium* (Table 2). Examples of low-level disinfectants are alcohols, quaternary ammonium compounds, and certain iodophors or phenolics.

—Intermediate-level disinfection - hospital disinfectant registered as effective against *Mycobacterium*: Kills vegetative bacteria, acid-fast bacilli (*Mycobacterium*), fungi, lipid and nonlipid viruses. Does not kill resistant bacteria spores and coccidial oocysts (Table 2). Examples of intermediate-level disinfectants are some alcohols, iodophors, phenolics, and hypochlorite compounds.

—Fungicides are disinfectants intended to destroy fungi, both those of medical importance as well as those that attack inanimate organic matter (foods, building material, cloth, etc.). If the fungi are of human medical importance they will be specifically named on the product label. Virucides are disinfectants intended to destroy or inactivate one or more specific viruses named on the disinfectant's label. I am not aware of any disinfectant that is specifically labeled for protozoa or helminths. Fortunately, these organisms and their eggs are relatively large and can generally be removed from the environment by thorough cleaning.

Disinfectants are available in a variety of products, each with its own special uses and abilities to control microorganisms. As part of the registration of these products, the manufacturer performs specific microbiological and human toxicity experiments. Data from these experiments are used to formulate the labels of the products, which include application rates, temperatures, and contact times. Unfortunately, supportive test data for label claims (statements on the label of the product indicating which organisms they will kill) are only required by the EPA for pathogens of human health. There are herptile pathogens which do not cause disease in humans and therefore are not regulated by the EPA. Look for pathogens listed on the label which are congeneric or similar to those which might be present in the environment you plan to disinfect. While these tests are generally aimed at microorganisms affecting human health, they can serve as guides for herptile care.

There are many disinfectants available for use around herptiles. The choice of products is influenced by the conditions under which the cages and other inanimate objects will be treated. All objects must be thoroughly cleaned before being disinfected. Even if the label of the product being used states the product is a disinfectant-detergent, the surface must be precleaned with the product and then a second application must be made to disinfectant it. Household detergents are cleaners, but do not assume that they can be used as a disinfectant. If the product is a disinfectant, the label will list the organisms that it will control. Read the label of the product carefully noting such things as: method of application, dilutions, contact times, contact temperatures, and precautions.

An autoclave uses heat and pressure to sterilize instruments. Photo courtesy of Dr. Lowell Ackerman.

As with any pesticide, these use directions should be strictly followed. Doubling the concentration will not halve the time the product should remain in contact with the cage surface. In fact, increased concentrations of some pesticides result in an increase in the required contact time.

Probably the best disinfectant available to all herptile keepers is household bleach (5.25% sodium hypochlorite). Bleach solutions are recorded as being effective against both gram-positive and gram-negative bacteria (including *Mycobacterium* spp.), viruses (both lipid and non-lipid), fungi, algae, protozoa, and nematodes (Dychdala, 1991).

Unfortunately, not all bleach products are specifically labeled for use as a tuberculocidal disinfectant. Therefore, use directions are not listed on the label. A 1:10 dilution (5,000 ppm available chlorine: 1.5 cups of bleach in 1 gallon of water) is appropriate for porous surfaces (wood, cloth, concrete, etc.) that cannot effectively be pre-cleaned of organic matter. The 1:10 dilution is typically considered too corrosive for many surfaces. A 1:100 dilution (500 ppm available chlorine: 1/4 cup of bleach in 1 gallon of water) can be used on smooth pre-cleaned surfaces (glass, plastic, metal, etc.). The object to be disinfected should be thoroughly precleaned and then moistened with the solution (spray or sponged) for not less than 10 minutes at room temperatures. After the appropriate time, the cage can be rinsed with potable water and dried. If amphibians or other sensitive animals are to be placed in the cage and the smell of bleach is still strong, it can be neutralized by treatment with a dilute solution of sodium thiosulfate, and then rinsed. While the Centers for Disease Control (1987) recommend a fresh bleach solution should be mixed daily, Rutala (1990) stated that diluted solutions last much longer than one day, up to 30 days when stored in brown opaque containers without air or light contact. Elevated temperatures, presence of organic matter or metals, and ultraviolet irradiation greatly reduce the stability of the bleach solution. Dark, sealed, plastic or glass containers that are kept cool are best for extending storage times. Data from the Professionals in Infection Control and Epidemiology, Inc., reveal that a bleach solution mixed for extended use should be mixed at twice the concentration of those which are used within 24 hours. The concentrations given above are for solutions which will be used within a day.

The above mentioned dilutions are for killing mycobacteria and less resistant organisms (Table 2). If protozoa or nematodes are suspected, more concentrated solutions may need to be used. Jacobson (1994) recommends steam-cleaning followed by disinfection with a 3% sodium hypochlorite solution (30,000 ppm available chlorine) for *Entamoeba invadens*. Although he does not provide a contact time, 20 minutes should be sufficient. Dychdala (1991) reported that dilute solutions (0.08-0.12 ppm available chlorine) took 150 minutes to kill *Entamoeba histolytica* cysts. Cameron (1950) lists a 5.75% solution of calcium hypochlorite as being effective against nematod eggs of horses in feces. Because hypochlorites are easily inactivated by feces, a much weaker solution would be effective on a precleaned surface. Sodium hypochlorite is ineffective against coccidial oocysts (Quinn, 1991).

HIGH-LEVEL DISINFECTION AND STERILIZATION

While sterilants and high-level disinfectants (whether chemical or physical) are used only on inanimate surfaces, they are regulated differently than disinfectants. The chemical agents are registered by the EPA, but because they are required for reprocessing medical equipment they are considered "medical devices." All medical devices (including autoclaves, dry-heat sterilizers, and chemical sterilants) are regulated by the FDA.

True sterilization destroys or inactivates all microorganisms including high numbers of resistant bacterial spores and coccidial oocysts. This can only be accomplished by the use of heat. Chemicals which can kill all microorganisms (except coccidial oocysts and a few other virus like particles that do not occur in herptiles) are referred to as chemical sterilants. When a sterilant is used at contact times shorter than that required for sterilization, it is termed "high-level disinfection." High-level disinfection will destroy most microorganisms, but not all of the resistant bacterial spores.

Household ammonia (5-10% solution, ammonium hydroxide) has been recommended for "sterilization" of substrates in amphibian tanks (Wright, 1994). While this procedure is effective against some microorganisms, it can not "sterilize," regardless of how long it remains in contact with the environmental surface. Quinn (1991) listed ammonium hydroxide as only having limited activity against nonenveloped viruses, acid-fast bacteria, and bacterial spores. But, it is probably the best solution for disinfecting against coccidial oocysts. According to Kheysin (1972), a 25% solution of ammonia was effective against *Eimeria magna* in 30 minutes, but a 10% solution was ineffective for that species. For *Eimeria tenella*, a 1% solution of ammonia killed 100% of the oocysts in 24 hours, 5 % solution was lethal in two hours, and a 10% solution in 45 minutes (Kheysin, 1972; and citations therein). Fraser et al (1991) stated that *Cryptosporidium parvum* oocysts can be killed in the environment with 5% ammonia solution; but they do not provide a contact time. Based on these data, a minimal protocol for disinfecting environmental surfaces possibly contaminated with coccidial oocysts should be either heat sterilized or chemically disinfected: (1) thoroughly clean surfaces with detergent and warm water, (2) moisten surface and keep wet for minimum of 45 minutes with a 10% solution of ammonia (or 5% solution for 2 hours), (3) thoroughly rinse with potable water, (4) disinfect (if needed for other organisms) with hospital level disinfectant with tuber-culocidal label claim or sodium hypochlorite solution and rinse. Failing to rinse the ammonia prior to adding sodium hypochlorite could result in the production of a deadly gas. Quinn (1991) stated some phenolic disinfectants also had activity against coccidial oocysts. Unfortunately, the contact times for the various cresol and phenolic compounds to be effective against coccidial oocysts are 6-48 hours (Kheysin, 1972). Likewise, sodium and potassium hydroxide solutions are effective with contact times in 24-120 hours, but these times are unrealistic for routine disinfection.

Formaldehyde solutions have been used in the past for disinfection and sterilization of inanimate surfaces. Because of the human health risk associated with the use of this chemical, its use is discouraged here.

HIGH-LEVEL DISINFECTION

High-level disinfection can be accomplished by the use of hot water pasteurization (75-100 °C, 30 minutes) or exposure to an EPA registered liquid sterilant for a shorter exposure time than is required for sterilization. Follow the manufacturers labeled directions on times and temperatures for high-level disinfection. Currently, only some of the glutaraldehyde sterilants are labeled for high-level disinfection. The FDA is in the process of reviewing other chemistries for their effectiveness and safety.

COLD STERILIZATION

Cold sterilization can be accomplished by the use of EPA registered sterilants. These chemicals include the gaseous ethylene oxide and three liquids: glutaraldehyde, stabilized hydrogen peroxide, and peroxyacetic acid (= peracetic acid). The following profiles are provided to aid in the selection of a product. For specific use directions consult the label of the product and directions supplied with any specialized chambers or reprocessing devices. Do not attempt to use sterilant products without training. All chemical sterilants are very dangerous and are only used in special chambers or baths. They can not be applied with a sponge, mop, mist or similar application.

HEAT STERILIZATION

Heat stable objects can be treated in a dry-heat sterilizer at 170 °C (340 °F) for 1 hour [160 °C (320 °F) for 2 hours, 141 °C (285 °F) for 3 hours] (Soule, 1983). The dry-heat times and temperatures can not be used with confidence with a home oven, because these devices do not maintain the correct temperatures for the prescribed time periods. None-the-less, home ovens can be used to "sterilize" non-medical instruments, i.e., cage substrates, tongs, snake hooks, etc. Because some resistant bacterial spores can survive many hours in boiling water, hot water pasteurization should not be relied upon for sterilizing surgical instruments, but it can be used to "sterilize" non-medical instruments.

PROS AND CONS OF VARIOUS DISINFECTANTS

Agent	Pros	Cons	Comments
Ethanol (ethyl alcohol) and **isopropanol** (isopropyl alcohol)	(1) Effective against a broad spectrum of microbes, including fungi, bacteria, and some viruses, (2) works rapidly without leaving a residue, (3) does not stain or corrode metal.	(1) Are not sporicidal or effective against coccidial oocysts, (2) are inactivated by the presence of organic material, (3) have no residual activity, (4) difficult to maintain needed contact time (5-10 minutes) for microbe kill due to high evaporation rate, (5) highly flammable and volatile; must be stored in cool well-ventilated area, (6) will dry and irritate skin with frequent contact, (7) cidal activity drops sharply when diluted below 50% or above 90% concentration.	See Lanson and Morton (1991) for further details
Iodophors	(1) Broad spectrum of effectiveness; effective against bacteria (some tinctures are also effective against mycobacteria), and viruses, (2) low acute toxicity to humans, (3) time sustained antimicrobial activity, (4) easily combined with detergents or other surfactants.	(1) Inactivated by presence of organic substances, (2) potentially corrosive to metals, (3) removable stains on some surfaces, (4) must be diluted exactly as directed, small margin for error, (5) povidone-iodine can become contaminated by *Pseudomonas*, (6) povidone-iodine is highly toxic to frogs and tinctures of iodine are unsafe for reptiles.	See Gottardi (1991) for further details.
Phenolics	(1) Effective against a broad spectrum of microorganisms.	(1) Absorbs into porous materials and is not removable, even after complete rinsing, (2) residual film can build up and cause cleaning problems, (3) can cause skin irritation from frequent use, (4) human skin can be depigmented by disinfectants containing *p*-tert-butylphenol or *p*-tert-amylphenol, (5) some formulations are ineffective aganist viruses, (6) not effective against coccidial oocysts in usable time periods, (7) not sporicidal.	See O'Connor and Rubino (1991) for further details.
Quaternary Ammonium Compounds	(1) Wide range of effectiveness, (2) low toxicity, (3) low cost.	(1) *Pseudomonas* is resistant to some and mycobacteria to all quats (some gram-negative bacteria have been found to grow in these compounds), (2) effectiveness limited by presence of organic substances, (3) chemical may be neutralized or absorbed by materials and fibers including cotton and wool, (4) effectiveness of some quats limited by contact with soap and hard water (and other anionic compounds), (5) not effective against coccidial oocysts or bacterial spores.	See Merianos (1991) for further details.

PROS AND CONS OF VARIOUS COLD STERILIZERS

Agent	Pros	Cons	Comments
Hypochlorites (sodium hypochlorite, calcium hypochlorite)	(1) Inexpensive and readily available, (2) effective against a broad spectrum of organisms including viruses, and both gram-positive and gram-negative bacteria (including mycobacteria), (3) low acute toxicity to humans; easy to handle, (4) fast acting.	(1) Corrodes some metals, (2) inactivated by organic substances, (3) not easily combined with detergents and other cleaners, (4) diluted solutions are unstable, (5) ineffective against coccidial oocysts.	See Dychdala (1991) for further details.
Ethylene oxide	(1) An effective sterilant for heat labile instruments, (2) compatible with many materials used in medical equipment, including plastic, rubber, and metal, (3) because sterilized objects are wrapped, they are less likely to be contaminated than objects that are unwrapped and treated by liquid chemical sterilants.	(1) Very toxic to patients, personnel, and the environment, (2) explosive and flammable at high concentrations, (3) carcinogenic, (4) requires special sterilization chamber for use, also requires precise temperature and humidity levels, (5) long cycle times, (6) difficult to monitor the sterilization process/level of effectiveness, (7) expensive.	See Parisi and Young (1991) for further details.
Glutaraldehyde	(1) Effective sterilant and high-level disinfectant for heat labile instruments, (2) compatible with many materials used in medical equipment, including plastic, rubber, and metal, (3) sterilization within a 10 hour period.	(1) May induce respiratory and dermal irritation in those frequently exposed to the fumes or liquid, (2) unstable, use-life of 24 to 30 days, (3) may corrode or stain high-carbon steel (e.g., lower quality, 400-series stainless steel) and leave residue on metals, (4) items can not be wrapped to prevent subsequent contamination prior to use, (5) efficacy can not be biologically monitored, (6) ineffective against coccidial oocysts.	See Scott and Gorman (1991) for further details.
Peroxy compounds (peroxyacetic acid and hydrogen peroxide)	(1) Relatively low acute toxicity (breaks down into acetic acid, water, and oxygen), (2) not strongly limited by presence of organic matter.	(1) Limited availability of registered products, (2) corrosive to soft metals, such as copper, brass, and aluminum, (3) items can not be wrapped to prevent subsequent contamination prior to use, (4) efficacy can not be biologically monitored, (5) peroxyacetic acid is currently available only for use in expensive reprocessing machines, (6) ineffective against coccidial oocysts.	See Block (1991) for further details.

Steam under pressure, as supplied in an autoclave, is a good method for sterilization. Autoclaves are readily available and are probably the best method for treating heat tolerant materials. The length of time required for sterilization depends on temperature and pressure. Follow the instructions provided with the device. Contact times are generally much shorter than other sterilization methods.

PRODUCT USE SAFETY

Common sense and careful reading of a product label/literature will aid the keeper/handler in the selection and use of antimicrobial products. If a label reports that a particular product is an irritant and should not be inhaled or allowed to contact human skin, do not use it on or near your plants or herptiles. Likewise, a product that has a label listing special safety equipment (gloves, goggles, respirator, etc.) for correct application is an indicator that this material should not be used on a living plant or animal. This does not mean that it is not suitable for cages, but rather that the inhabitants must be removed from the cage during application. Following the application, the cage surfaces which were in contact with the disinfectant should be rinsed thoroughly and dried before returning living plants and animals.

Obtaining the Material Safety Data Sheet (MSDS) can alert you to other hazardous ingredients in antimicrobial pesticide products which are not listed on the labels. Although MSDS are designed to inform employees of job-related hazards, home users of a product can obtain a copy of the MSDS from the manufacturer or distributor of the product.

When selecting a disinfectant, it is important to note that some leave a toxic residue which can be absorbed or ingested by herptiles. The denaturants in rubbing alcohols are bitter and difficult to rinse from a surface. Likewise, disinfectants containing phenolic compounds are difficult to rinse and should not be used. Even

Rats kept in unclean conditions can cause disease in predator reptile species. Always check your source. Photo courtesy of Dr. Todd Driggers.

though not stated on all product labels, a good practice is to rinse all objects with potable water after disinfection. Even products which are not known to cause problems in humans might do so in a herptile. Because of the herptile's smaller size and different metabolism, trace amounts of antimicrobial pesticides might be hazardous to them. Like antimicrobial products, many detergents and cleaners leave residues and should be rinsed thoroughly before disinfecting or returning animals to their cages.

Specific toxicity problems are known for some halogens and phenolic compounds. Dychdala (1991) reported that a 10 ppm sodium hypochlorite solution at room temperature killed *Rana pipiens* frogs in four days. *Rana pipiens* were also reported to suffer petechiation and ulceration of the skin when kept in water containing four ppm of chlorine in the form of calcium hypochlorite and that the disease is irreversible and fatal when the concentration is raised to 5 ppm (Marcus, 1981). *Necturus maculosus* salamanders are reported to suffer toxic effects from chlorine in tap water, manifested by excitement, exhaustion, convulsions, paralysis, and death (Marcus, 1981). Five ppm of fluoride in water caused anemia, leukopenia, and gastrointestinal hyperemia and hemorrhage in *Rana pipiens*. Fatalities occurred with concentrations greater than 50 ppm, and mortality increased with the level of fluoride concentration (Marcus, 1981).

Jackson (1981) stated that tinctures of iodine are unsafe for reptiles and that repeated applications burn the patient. Cover, Barnett, and Saunders (1994) stated that povidone-iodine solution is highly toxic to frogs.

Phenol, cresol, and other coal tar derivatives are highly toxic to herptiles and should be avoided (Marcus, 1981). While some authors suggest that these products can be used and rinsed before reoccupation by herptiles, this is unwise, especially if the object disinfected is porous. Phenolic compounds are well known to absorb into porous objects and can not be rinsed from those objects.

If an incident (accidental human or animal exposure) occurs with an antimicrobial pesticide, some helpful information may be obtained from the National Pesticide Telecommunication Network. This national network, located at Oregon State University, is co-funded by the EPA to answer questions from the public and private sectors related to any pesticides via a toll-free number (1-800-447-6349). Incidents involving humans should be directed to a poison control center (telephone number in local telephone directory and available from NPTN) or your local emergency room, depending on the severity of the exposure. Animal exposures should be directed to a local veterinarian or the ASPCA National Animal Poison Control Center, which is the only animal-oriented poison control cen-

Water bowl with a hide box. Photo courtesy of Dr. Todd Driggers.

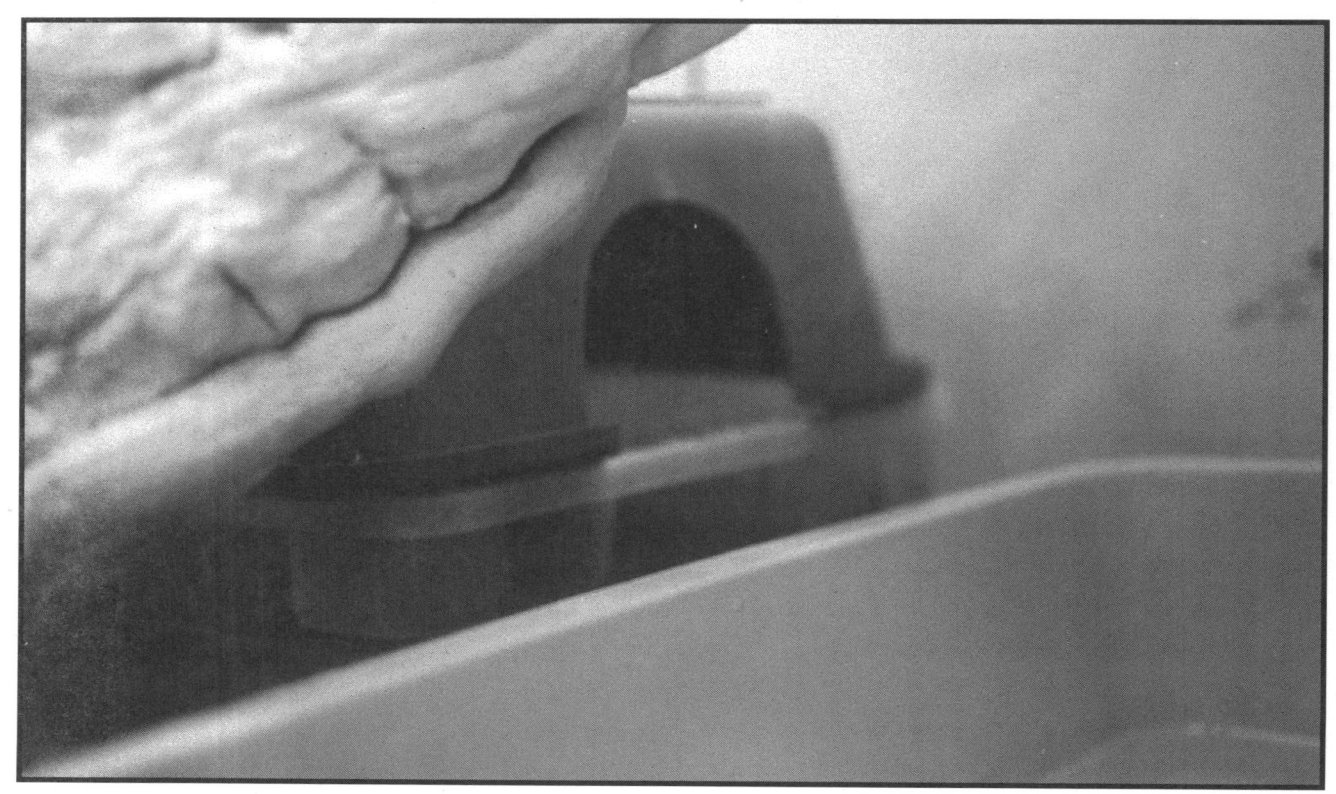

ter in the country. There is a fee for the service with two methods of payment:

— 1-900-680-0000. The charge is $20 for the first five minutes and $2.95 for each additional minute (there is a $20 minimum charge).
— 1-800-548-2423 and 1-888-426-4435. A flat fee of $30 per case is charged, payable only by credit card; included in the $30 charge are follow-up calls until the problem is resolved.

REFERENCES AND RECOMMENDED READING

—Block, SS:
Peroxygen compounds. In, Disinfection, sterilization, and preservation, SS Block (Ed). 4th Ed, Lea & Febiger, Philadelphia, PA, 1991, pp. 167-181.

—Cameron, TWM:
Epidemiology and sanitary measures for the control of nemic parasites of domesticated animals. In, An introduction to nematology, JR Christie (Ed). Rev Ed, BG Chitwood Publisher, Washington?, DC, 1950, Section II, Part II, pp. 302-308.

—Centers for Disease Control. U.S. Department of Health and Human Services:
Recommendations for prevention of HIV transmission in health-care settings. MMWR (Morbidity Mortality Weekly Report), 1987; Suppl. no. 36(2S):3-18.

—Chiszar, DS; Wellborn, S; Wand, MA; Scudder, KM; Smith, HM:
Investigatory behavior in snakes, II: Cage cleaning and the induction of defecation in snakes. Animal Learning & Behavior, 1980; 8(3):505-510.

—Conant, R:
Reptile and amphibian management practices at the Philadelphia Zoo. International Zoo Yearbook, 1971; 11:224-230.

—Cover, JF, Jr; Barnett, SL; Saunders, RL:
Captive management and breeding of dendrobatid and Neotropical hylid frogs at the National Aquarium in Baltimore. In, Captive management and conservation of amphibians and reptiles. JB Murphy, K Adler, JT Collins (Ed), Society for the Study of Amphibians and Reptiles, Ithaca, NY, 1994, pp. 267-273.

—Denton, GW:
Chlorhexidine. In, Disinfection, sterilization, and preservation, SS Block (Ed). 4th Ed, Lea & Febiger, Philadelphia, PA, 1991, pp. 274-289.

—Dychdala, GR:
Chlorine and chlorine compounds. In, Disinfection, sterilization, and preservation, SS Block (Ed). 4th Ed, Lea & Febiger, Philadelphia, PA, 1991, pp. 131-151.

—Favero, MS; Bond, WW:
Sterilization, disinfection, and antisepsis in the hospital. In, Manual of clinical microbiology, EH Lennette, A Balows, WJ Hausler, HJ Shadomy (Ed), 5th Ed, American Society of Microbiologist, Washington, D. C., 1991, pp. 183-200.

—Fraser, CM; Bergeron, JA; Mays, A; Aiello, SE (Ed): 1991.
The Merck veterinary manual. 7th Ed, Merck & Company, Inc., Rahway, NJ, 1832 pp.

—Frye, FL:
Biomedical and surgical aspects of captive reptile husbandry. 2nd Ed. Krieger Publishing Company, Inc., Malabar, FL, 1991; 653 pp.

—Frye, FL; 1994.
Reptile clinician's handbook: A compact clinical and surgical reference. Krieger Publishing Company, Inc., Malabar, FL, 1994; 276 pp.

—Garner, JS; Favero, MS:
Guidelines for handwashing and hospital environmental control, 1985. American Journal of Infection Control, 1986; 14(3):110-126.

—Gottardi, W:
Iodine and iodine compounds. In, Disinfection, sterilization, and preservation, SS Block (Ed). 4th Ed, Lea & Febiger, Philadelphia, PA, 1991, pp. 152-166.

—Jackson, OF:
Clinical aspects of diagnosis and treatment. In, Diseases of the Reptilia. JE Cooper; OF Jackson (Ed). Academic Press, London, 1981, Vol 2, pp. 508-534.

—Jacobson, ER:
Veterinary procedure for the acquisition and release of captive-bred herptofauna. In, Captive management and conservation of amphibians and reptiles. JB Murphy, K Adler, JT Collins (Ed), Society for the Study of Amphibians and Reptiles, Ithaca, NY, 1994, pp. 109-118.

—Jaeger, RG:
Pheromonal markers as territorial advertisement by terrestrial salamanders. In, Chemical signals in vertebrates, D Duvall, D Måller-Schwarze, RM Silverstein (Ed), Plenum, New York, NY, 1986, pp. 191-203.

—Kheysin, YM:
Life cycles of Coccidia of domestic animals. University Park Press, Baltimore, MD, 1972, 264 pp.

—**Larson, E:**
Guideline for use of topical antimicrobial agents. American Journal of Infection Control, 1988; 16(6):253-266.

—**Larson, EL; Morton, HE:**
Alcohols. In, Disinfection, sterilization, and preservation, SS Block (Ed). 4th Ed, Lea & Febiger, Philadelphia, PA, 1991, pp. 191-203.

—**Leland, SE, Jr:**
Antiprotozoan, antihelmintic, and other pest management compounds. In, Disinfection, sterilization, and preservation, SS Block (Ed). 4th Ed, Lea & Febiger, Philadelphia, PA, 1991, pp. 482-492.

—**Marcus, LC:**
Veterinary biology and medicine of captive amphibians and reptiles. Lea & Febiger, Philadelphia, PA, 1981, 239 pp.

—**Merianos, JJ:**
Quaternary ammonium antimicrobial compounds. In, Disinfection, sterilization, and preservation, SS Block (Ed). 4th Ed, Lea & Febiger, Philadelphia, PA, 1991, pp. 225-255.

—**O'Connor, DO; Rubino, JR:**
Phenolic compounds. In, Disinfection, sterilization, and preservation, SS Block (Ed). 4th Ed, Lea & Febiger, Philadelphia, PA, 1991, pp. 204-224.

—**Parisi, AN; Young, WE:**
Sterilization with ethylene oxide and other gases. In, Disinfection, sterilization, and preservation, SS Block (Ed). 4th Ed, Lea & Febiger, Philadelphia, PA, 1991, pp. 580-595.

—**Quinn, PJ:**
Disinfection and disease prevention in veterinary medicine. In, Disinfection, steril-ization, and preservation, SS Block (Ed). 4th Ed, Lea & Febiger, Philadelphia, PA, 1991, pp. 546-868.

—**Russell, AD:**
Chemical sporicidal and sporostatic agents. In, Disinfection, sterilization, and preservation, SS Block (Ed). 4th Ed, Lea & Febiger, Philadelphia, PA, 1991, pp. 365-376.

—**Rutala, WA:**
APIC guideline for selection and use of disinfectants. American Journal of Infection Control, 1990; 18(2):99-117.

—**Scott, EM; Gorman, SP:**
Glutaraldehyde. In, Disinfection, sterilization, and preservation, SS Block (Ed). 4th Ed, Lea & Febiger, Philadelphia, PA, 1991, pp. 596-614.

—**Simmons, BP:**
Guideline for hospital environmental control. American Journal of Infection Control, 1983; 11:97-115.

—**Soule, BM (Ed):**
The APIC curriculum for infection control practice. Kendall/Hunt Publishing Company, Dubuque, IA, 1983, Vol 1, 571 pp.

—**Spaulding, EH:**
Chemical disinfection of medical and surgical materials. In: CA Lawrence, and SS Block (Ed), Disinfection, sterilization, and preservation. Lea & Febiger, Philadelphia, PA, 1968, pp. 517-531.

—**Wright, K:**
Quarantine. Reptile & Amphibian Magazine, 1991; July/August, pp. 34-37.

—**Wright, K:**
Quarantine procedures for amphibians. The Vivarium, 1994; 5(5):32-33.

APPENDICES

Craig Hassapakis
Amphibian & Reptile Conservation
2255 North University Parkway, Suite 15
Provo, UT 84604-7506

APPENDIX 1

ZOOLOGICAL PARKS & AQUARIUMS

Arizona-Sonora Desert Museum, 2021 North Kinney Road, Tucson, Arizona 85743-8918. Telephone: (602) 883-1380, Fax: (602) 883-2500.

Australian Reptile Park, Pacific Highway, PO Box 192, Gosford, New South Wales, Australia. Telephone: 043-284311.

Audubon Park & Zoological Gardens, 1140 Seventh Street, New Orleans, Louisiana 70115. Telephone: (504) 861-2537.

Busch Gardens Zoological Park, Box 9158, Tampa, Florida 33674-9158. Telephone: (813) 988-5171.

Chicago Zoological Park (Brookfield Zoo), Golf Road, Brookfield, Illinois 60513. Telephone: (312) 242-2630.

Clyde Peeling's Reptileland, Box 388, Allenwood, Pennsylvania 17810. Telephone: (717) 538-1869.

Columbus Zoological Gardens, 9990 Riverside Drive, Box 400 Powell, Ohio 43065. Telephone: (614) 889-9471.

Dallas Zoo, 621 East, Clarendon Drive, Dallas, Texas 75203-2996. Telephone: (214) 670-6825, Fax: (214) 670-7450.

Fort Worth Zoological Park, 1989 Colonial Parkway, Fort Worth, Texas 76110-1797. Telephone: (817) 870-7050.

Fresno Zoo, 894 West Belmont Avenue, Fresno, California 93728. Telephone: (209) 488-1549.

International Wildlife Conservation Park (Bronx Zoo), New York Zoological Society, 185th Street & Southern Boulevard, New York, New York 10460-1099. Telephone: (212) 220-5100.

Lincoln Park Zoological Gardens, 2200 North Cannon Drive, Chicago, Illinois 60614. Telephone: (312) 294-4660.

Minnesota Zoological Gardens, 13000 Zoo Boulevard, Apple Valley, Minnesota 55124-8199. Telephone: (612) 432-9010.

Madras Crocodile Bank Trust, Vadanemmeli Village, Perur Post, Mahabalipuram Road, Chingleput Dist. Tamil Nadu, South India 603104.

Nairobi Snake Park, National Museum of Kenya, PO Box 40658 NRB, Nairobi, Kenya. Telephone: 742131.

National Zoological Park, 3000 Connecticut Avenue NW, Washington, DC 20008. Telephone: (202) 673-4717.

Philadelphia Zoological Gardens, Zoological Society of Philadelphia, 34 Street & Girard Avenue, Philadelphia, Pennsylvania 19104. Telephone: (215) 243-1100.

San Diego Zoological Gardens, Box 551, San Diego, California 92112. Telephone: (619) 747-8702.

Seaway Serpentarium, Unit 30, Seaway Mall, 800 Niagara Street N, Welland, Ontario L3C 5Z4, Canada. Telephone: (416) 732-2902, (416) 732-3685. Education.

Snake Park, Port Elizabeth Museum Complex, PO Box 13147, Humewood 6013, South Africa. Telephone: (041) 561051, Fax: (041) 562175.

St. Augustine Alligator Farm, Box 9005, St. Augustine, Florida 32085-9005.

St. Louis Zoological Park, Forest Park, St. Louis, Missouri 63110. Telephone: (314) 781-0900.

Steinhart Aquarium, California Academy of Sciences, Golden Gate Park, San Francisco, California 9418. Telephone: (415) 221-5100.

The Living Desert, 47-900 Portola Avenue, Palm Desert, California 92260. Telephone: (619) 346-5694.

Transvaal Snake Park, PO Box 97, Halfway House, 1685, South Africa. Telephone: (011) 805-3116.

Zoological Society of London, Regent's Park, London, NW1 4RY, Great Britain. Telephone: 01-722-3333.

Zoo Atlanta, 800 Cherokee Avenue SE, Atlanta, Georgia 30315. Telephone: (404) 624-5600.

APPENDIX 2

Source: IUCN/SSC/CBSG

GLOBAL REGIONAL ZOO PROGRAMS AND ORGANIZATIONS

The World Zoo Organization/International Union of Directors of Zoological Gardens (IUDZG)

President: Professor Dr. Gunther Nogge, Aktiengesellschaft Zoologischer Garten Koln, 50706 Kohn, Postfach 680369, Riehler Strasse 173, Germany. Telephone: (49) 221-778-5101, Fax: (49) 221-778-5111.

African Propagation Program (APP)
Arabian Peninsula Captive Breeding Group (APCBG)
Association of Meso-American Zoos (AMAZOO)
Australasian Species Management Program (ASMP)
AZA Species Survival Plan (SSP)—US & Canada
Chinese Association of Zoological Gardens (CAZG)
European Endangered Species Programme (EEP)
Indian Zoo Studbook Programme (IZSP)
Indonesian Zoo Association (PKBSI)
Joint Management of Species Committee (JMSC)—United Kingdom
Society of Brazilian Zoos (SZB)
Southeast Asian Zoo Association (SEAZA)
Species Survival Committee of Japan (SSCJ)
Thailand Zoo Organization (TZO)
Venezuelan Association of Zoological Parks and Aquaria (AVZPA)

Note. The most current list of national and regional zoological association can be found in the International Zoo Yearbook volume 33, pp. 469-471 and used to supplement the appendix above.

APPENDIX 3

EUROPEAN ENDANGERED SPECIES PROGRAMME (EEP)

CURRENT EEPS
Gila Monster (*Heloderma suspectum*)
Beaded Lizard (*Heloderma horridum*)
Cuban Boa (*Epicrates angulifer*)

INTERNATIONAL STUDBOOK
Cuban Boa (*Epicrates angulifer*)
(Coordinated by Ivan Rehak, Praque Zoo).

EUROPEAN STUDBOOKS: 0

APPENDIX 4

AUSTRALIAN SPECIES MANAGEMENT PROGRAMME (ASMP)

PRIORITY PROGRAMS
Philippines Crocodile
Western Swamp Tortoise
Galapagos Giant Tortoise
Striped Legless Lizard

PROGRAMS UNDER DEVELOPMENT
Tuatara (Brother's Island)
Tuatara (Stephen's Island)
Giant Otago Skink
Fijian Crested Iguana
Fijian Banded Iguana

REGIONAL STUDBOOKS
Western Swamp Tortoise
Galapagos Giant Tortoise
Aldabra Giant Tortoise
Giant Otago Skink
Otago Skink
Waimarten Skink
Fijian Crested Iguana

STUDBOOKS UNDER DEVELOPMENT
Tuatara (Brother's Island)
Tuatara (Stephen's Island)
Fijian Banded Iguana
Green Python
Alligator Snapper Turtle

Rainforest Dragons
Knob-Tailed Geckos
Australian Varanids (Small)
Australian Varanids (Large)
Frilled Lizard
Reticulated Gila Monster
Woma
Broad-Headed Snake
Eastern Diamondback Rattlesnake

APPENDIX 5

COMPUTER AND NETWORK COMMUNICATION

MAILING LISTS

Instructions: To subscribe to the mailing lists below send an email message to the list processor or list server listed in "Message to:." In the body of the message type *subscribe*, [space], *title of mailing list*, [space] "your name". For example, in your email message type: *Subscribe herp-l Craig Hassapakis*. Address all questions concerning the particular list to the list's administrator. Post messages to mailing list by sending an email message to the email address in "Post to:." Your message will be copied and posted to all subscribers of the mailing list.

ACN-L.
Message to: majordomo@pinetree.org. List administrator: Peter Unmack. Email: springfish@mail.utexas.edu. Post to: Acn-l@pinetree.org. Subject: Private sector conservation, aquatic biodiversity and conservation.

AFRIHERP-L.
Message to: listproc@wcmc.org.uk. List administrator: Lynn Raw. Email: gdr@iafrica.com. Post to: Afriherp-l@wcmc.org.uk. Subject: African herpetofaunal biodiversity programme (AHBP).

AMPHIBIAN AND REPTILE CONSERVATION.
Message to: listproc@orsp1.adm.binghamton.edu. List administrator: Steve Schafer. Email: steve@orsp1.adm.binghamton.edu. Post to: HERPCONSERV@orsp1.adm.binghamton.edu. Subject: Amphibian and reptile conservation.

CHAMELEON CONSERVATION.
Message to: listproc@orsp1.adm.binghamton.edu. List administrator: Steve Schafer. Email: steve@orsp1.adm.binghamton.edu. Post to: CHAMCONSERV@orsp1.adm.binghamton.edu. Subject: Chameleon conservation.

CITES-L.
Message to: listproc@wcmc.org.uk. List administrator: Lesley Mcguffog. Email: Lesley.Mcguffog @wcmc.org.uk. Post to: CITES-L@wcmc.org.uk. Subject: Wildlife trade and CITES.

CONSLINK.
Message to: listserv@sivm.si.edu. List administrator: Michael Stuewe. Email: nzpem001@sivm.si.edu. Post to: Conslink@sivm.si.edu. Subject: Conservation biology.

CTURTLE.
Message to: listserv@nervm.nerdc.ufl.edu. List administrator located at: Accstr@zoo.ufl.edu. Post to: Cturtle@nervm.nerdc.ufl.edu. Subject: Sea turtle biology, conservation and news.

HERP-L.
Message to: listproc@ucdavis.edu. List administrator: Sean Barry. Email: sjbarry@ucdavis.edu. Post to: HERP-L@ucdavis.edu. Subject: Herpetology

BULLETIN BOARD SERVICES

Herpetology On-Line Network (Herp-Net), PO Box 52261, Philadelphia, Pennsylvania 19115-7261. Fax: (215) 464-3561, CIS: 70176, 1153, BBS: (215) 464-3563 (300-2400 bps), (9600+ 14.4K+ V.32, V.42bis). Email: Mark.Miller@mail.tju.edu

Ophidian Herpetological BBS, (602) 837-7305. 300-2400 bps, 8+N+1 (602) 468-9860

WORLDWIDE WEB PAGES
Note: Websites often change their addresses (URL) frequently. The most current list of websites related to amphibian and reptile conservation can be found on the Amphibian and Reptile Conservation website listed below.

Amphibian and Reptile Conservation
http://www.byu.edu/~arcon/
Aquatic Conservation Network:
http://www.achilles.net/holiday/acn/acnhome.html
AZA Conservation Programs
http://www.aza.org/aza/conservation.html
Biological Resources Division, US Geological Survey
http://www.nbs.gov
Chameleon Conservation Society
http://orsp1.adm.binghamton.edu/~steve/CCS/
Crocodilian Natural History & Conservation
http://www.bio.bris.ac.uk/research/crocs/cnhc.html
Herpetologists Email Directory
http://crystal.harvard.edu:8000/herp/hwd
IUCN Red List of Threatened Animals
For comments and corrections email to: redlist@wcmc.org.uk

Global Biodiversity. Quarterly bulletin published by the Canadian Museum Of Nature.

Herp Quest. A bi-monthly newsletter published by Herp Quest International. Promotes eco-tourism, education and ecological projects for interested volunteers.

Herpetological Conservation. A monograph series published annually by the SSAR. Editor: Stephen Corn.

Herpetological Monographs. A monograph series published by the Herpetologists' League.

Herpetological Natural History. Published semi-annually by International Herpetological Symposium, Incorporated.

Herptofauna News. The semi-annual international reptile and amphibian conservation newsletter published by the Herpetofauna Conservation International Ltd, United Kingdom.

Iguana Times. Newsletter of the International Iguana Society, Incorporated.

Intermountanus. Newsletter published by the Utah Association of Herpetologists.

International Zoo Yearbook. Annual series published by the Zoological Society of London, United Kingdom.

Journal of Herpetology. A quarterly herpetological journal published by SSAR.

Journal of Wildlife Management. Journal published by Wildlife Society.

Legislation & Conservation Alert section IN Herpetological Review. Published by the SSAR.

Lyriocephalus. Journal published by Amphibian & Reptile Research Organization of Sri Lanka.

Oryx. The Journal of the Fauna and Flora Preservation Society published quarterly by Blackwell Scientific Publications, Ltd., United Kingdom.

Re-Introduction News. Newsletter of the IUCN/SSC Re-introduction Specialist Group.

Reptile & Amphibian Magazine. Hobbyist magazine published bi-monthly by Ramus Publishing, Inc.

Reptile Hobbyist. Published monthly by T.F.H. Publications.

Reptiles: Guide to keeping reptiles and amphibians. Published monthly by Fancy Publications, Incorporated.

Russian Journal of Herpetology. Journal published by the Folium Publishing Co., Moscow, Russia and Russian Herpetology Society.

San Diego Herpetological Society Newsletter. Newsletter of the San Diego Herpetological Society.

Species. Newsletter of the IUCN/SSC.

Traffic USA. A quarterly newsletter published on the international trade in wildlife and wildlife products by Traffic USA.

Vivarium. Bi-Monthly magazine published by the American Federation of Herpetoculturists.

Wildlife Law News Quarterly. Center Wildlife Law Newsletter.

Zoo Biology. Published bi-monthly by John Wiley & Sons, Incorporated.

APPENDIX 9

ORGANIZATIONS/ PUBLISHERS

ORGANIZATIONS

African Herpetofaunal Biodiversity Programme (AHBP). Lynn Raw, PO Box 200, Merrivale, 3291, South Africa. Telephone: +27-331-460796, Fax: +27-331-460895, Email: gdr@iafrica.com

Agama International, Incorporated. Route 2, Box 285, Montevallo, Alabama 35115. Lizard farm.

American Association of Zoo Keepers, Incorporated. (AAZK). Administrative Offices, 635, Gage Blvd., Topeka, Kansas 66606-2066. Telephone/fax: (913) 273-1980.

American Zoo and Aquarium Association (AZA). 7970-D Old Georgetown Road, Bethesda, Maryland 20814-2493. Telephone: (301) 907-7777, Fax: (301) 907-2980.

American Federation of Herpetoculturists (AFH). 360 North Midway, Suite 203, Escondido, California 92027. Telephone: (619) 747-4948.

Amphibian and Reptile Conservation (ARC). 2255 North University Parkway Suite 15, Provo, Utah 84604-7506, USA. URL: http://www.byu.edu/~arcon/, Email: ARC@byu.edu

Amphibian & Reptile Research Organization of Sri Lanka (ARROS). Anslem de Silva, c/o Faculty of Medicine, University of Peradeniya, Peradeniya, Sri Lanka. Telephone/fax: 0094 1 732371, Email: Auslem@Med.pdn.ac.lk

Aquatic Conservation Network (ACN). 540 Roosevelt Avenue, Ottawa, Ontario, Canada K2A 1Z8. Telephone: (613) 729-4670, Fax: (613) 729-5613, Email: ag508@freenet.carleton.ca

Association of Reptilian and Amphibian Veterinarians (ARAV). PO Box 605, 1 Smith Bridge Road, Chester Heights, Pennsylvania 19017.

Australasian Species Management Program (ASMP). Reptile Taxon Advisory Group (Reptile TAG), Convenor: Chris Banks, Senior Curator, Melbourne Zoo, PO Box 74, Parkville Victoria 3052. Fax: 03-285-9370.

AZA Conservation Center. 7970-D Old Georgetown Road, Bethesda, Maryland 20814. Telephone: (301) 907-7777, Fax: (301) 907-2980.

Brazilian Association for Turtle Conservation (English translation), Associacao Brasileira Para A Conservacao Das Tartarugas-Pro-Tartaruga. na Av. Goias, n 315, Ed. Itamaraty, sala 701, Centro, Goiania/GO, CEP 74005-010, Telefax (062) 223-9216.

British Herpetological Society (BHS). c/o Zoological Society of London, Regent's Park, London NW1 4RY, United Kingdom.

California Herpetological Advisory Council (CHIAC). Gray Flanagan, 8459 Lakeland Drive, Granite Bay, California 95746. Telephone: (916) 791-3528.

Canadian Amphibian and Reptile Conservation Society. 9 Mississauga Road North, Mississauga, Ontario L5H 2H5, Canada. Last known address. Possibly defunct.

Canadian Museum of Nature. Department CB, Box 3443, Stn. "D", Ottawa, Ontario, Canada K1P 6P4. Telephone: (613) 990-6595, Fax: (613) 990-0318.

Caribbean Conservation Corporation. PO Box 2866, Gainesville, Florida 32602-2866. Telephone: (904) 373-6441, Fax: (904) 375-2449.

Casa De Tortuga. 10455 Circulo de Zapata, Fountain Valley, California 92708. Telephone: (714) 962-0612.

Center for Reproduction of Endangered Wildlife (CREW). Cincinnati Zoo & Botanical Garden, 3400 Vine Street, Cincinnati, Ohio 45220. Telephone: (513) 961-2739, Fax: (513) 569-8213.

Center for the Reproduction of Endangered Species (CRES). Zoological Society of San Diego, PO Box 551, San Diego, California, 92112-0551. Telephone: (619) 557-3955, Fax: (619) 557-3959.

Center for Wildlife Law, Institute of Public Law. University of New Mexico, School of Law, 1117 Stanford NE, Albuquerque, New Mexico 87131. Tel: (505) 277-5006, Fax: (505) 277-7064.

Chameleon Works. 271 Bennett Avenue, Suite #B, Long Beach, California 90803.

Chelonian Research Foundation (CRF). 168 Goodrich Street, Lunenburg, Massachusetts 01462. Telephone: (508) 534-9440, (508) 582-9668, Fax: (508) 840-8184, Email: Rhodin@aol.com

Conservation International (CI). 2501 M Street, Suite 200, Washington, DC 20037.

Convention on International Trade in Endangered Species of Wild Fauna and Flora (CITES). Secretariat CITES, Case Postale 456, CH-1219 Chatelaine/Geneve, Switzerland. Telephone: (4122) 979 9139 40, Fax: (4122) 797 3417, Email: CITES@unep.ch

Desert Tortoise Conservation Center. 4765 West Vegas Drive, PO Box 26569, Las Vegas 89126.

Desert Tortoise Preservation Committee (DTPC). PO Box 453, Ridgecrest, California 93556. Telephone: (714) 884-5906.

Earthwatch. 680 Mount Auburn Street, PO Box 403, Watertown, Massachusetts 02172-9104. Telephone: (617) 926-8200, (617) 926-8532.

El Bagual Ecological Reserve. Alberto Yanosky, Salta 994 (3600) Formosa, Republica Argentina. Telephone/Fax: (54) (717) 25843 Formosa, Telephone: (541) 313-5346 (Buenos Aires), Fax: (541) 313-0530 (Buenos Aires). Tegu farm.

European Endangered Species Programme (EEP). Reptile Taxon Advisory Group (Reptile TAG), Dipl. Ing. Vladislav T. Jirousck, Chairman, Zoo Jihlava, 586 01 Jihlava, Czech Republic. Dr. Ivan Rehak, Zoologicka Zahrada Praha, 171000 Praha 7-Troja, Czech Republic.

Fauna and Flora Preservation Society (FFPS). 1 Kensington Gore, London SW7 2AR, United Kingdom. Telephone: 171 823 8899. Fax: 171 823 9690.

Geckkonidae Breeding Foundation. 443 West 14th Place, Chicago Heights, Illinois 60411. (Last known address).

Gopher Tortoise Council. PO Box 61301, St. Pete, Florida 33784-1301.

Herp Quest International. 326 North Indiana Avenue, Vista, California 92084. Telephone: (619) 941-9336.

Herpetological Conservation. Stephen Corn, Editor, Biological Resources Division (USGS), Aldo Leopold Wilderness Research Institute, 709 East Beckwith Avenue, Missoula, Montana 59807. Herpetofauna Conservation International Ltd. **Triton House, Bramfield Halesworth, Suffolk, IP19 9AE, United Kingdom.**

Herpetofauna Consultants International. PO Box 1, Halesworth, Suffolk IP19 9AW, United Kingdom. Telephone: 098 684 518, Fax: 098 684 579.

Herpetological Conservation Trust. c/o Dr. I.R. Swingland, Durrell Institute of Conservation & Ecology, University of Kent, Canterbury CT2 7NX, United Kingdom. Telephone: 0227 764000.

Herpetologists' League. East Tennessee State University, Department of Biological Sciences, Box 70726, Johnson City, Tennessee 37614-0726. Telephone: (615) 929-6929, Fax: (615) 929-5958.

Iguana Conservation and Research Group. Dr. Peter Vogel, Zoology Department, University of the West Indies, Mona, Kingston 7, Jamaica. Telephone: 92-71-6619.

International Gecko Society. PO Box 370423, San Diego, California 92137.

International Herpetological Symposiums, Incorporated (IHS). Mr. David Hulmes, Secretary, 361 Van Winkle Avenue, Hawthorne, New Jersey 07506. Telephone: (201) 427-0768.

International Iguana Society (IIS). Route 3, Box 328, Big Pine Key, Florida 33043.

International Reptile Breeders Association. Box 85152-279, San Diego, California. Telephone/Fax: (619) 263-6898.

International Species Information System (ISIS). 12101 Johnny Cake Ridge Road, Apple Valley, Minnesota 55124-8151. Telephone: (612) 431-9295, Fax: (612) 432-2757, BBS: (612) 432-9292, Email: ISIS@epx.cis.umn.edu

International Venomous Snake Society (IVSS). PO Box 4493, Apache Junction, Arizona 85278-4498. Telephone: (602) 984-6017.

IUCN (World Conservation Union). rue Mauverney, CH-1196 Gland, Switzerland. Telephone: 22 9990001, Fax: 22 9990002.

IUCN—US (World Conservation Union—US). 1400 16th Street NW, Washington, DC 20036. Telephone: (202) 797-5454. Fax: (202) 797-5461.

Japan Snake Institute. Yabuzuka-honmachi, Nittagun, Gunma 379-23, Japan. Telephone: 0277 (78) 5193, Fax: 0277 (78) 5520.

Jersey Wildlife Preservation Trust (JWPT). Les Augre's Manor, Trinity, Jersey, JE3 5BF, Channel Islands, United Kingdom. Telephone: 0534 864666; Fax: 0534 865161, Email: zooherps@int.net

Madras Crocodile Bank. Post Bag 4, Mamallapuram 603104, Tamil Nadu, South India. Telephone: 091-044 418747, Fax: (091) 44 491 0910.

Mediterranean Association to Save the Sea Turtle (MEDASSET). c/o 24 Park Towers, 2 Brick Street, London, W1Y 7DF, United Kingdom. Telephone/Fax: 071 629 0654. MEDASSET - Greece 1C Licavitou Street, 106 72 Athens, Greece. Telephone/Fax: (30) 1 3613572.

National Center for the Conservation and Management of Amazon Turtles. Vitor Hugo Canterelli, CENAQUA/IBAMA Rua 229 #95, Goiania, Goias, Brazil. Fax: 62-225-0770.

National Herpetological Alliance. PO Box 5143, Chicago, Illinois 60680-5143.

National Wildlife Federation (NWF). 1400 Sixteenth Street NW, Washington, DC 20036-2266. Telephone: (202) 797-5445, Fax: (202) 797-6646.

Nature Conservancy, The (TNC). 1815 North Lynn Street, Arlington, Virginia 22209. Telephone: (703) 841-5300, Fax: (703) 841-1283.

Pet Industry Joint Advisory Council (PIJAC). 1220 19th Street NW, Suite 400, Washington, DC 20036. Telephone: (202) 452-1525, 800-553-7387, Fax: (202) 293-4377.

Pro Iguana Verde Foundation. Apartado 692-1007, San Jose, Costa Rica. Telephone: (506) 31-6756, Fax: (506) 32-1950.

Russian Journal of Herpetology. c/o Museum of Vertebrate Zoology, University of California, Berkeley, California 94720.

Society for Conservation Biology (SCB). University of Wisconsin, Department of Wildlife Ecology, Madison, Wisconsin 53706. Telephone: (608) 263-6827.

Society for the Study of Amphibians and Reptiles (SSAR). Contact: Karen Toepfer, Treasurer, PO Box 626, Hays, Kansas 67601-0626. Telephone: (913) 628-1437, Fax: (913) 625-8890, Email: Aren@ksuvm.ksu.edu

Therion Animal Identity Laboratory. Rensselaer Technology Park, 185 Jordan Road, Troy, New York 12180. Telephone: (518) 286-0016, Fax: (518) 286-0018. Specializing in DNA profile technology.

Traffic USA. c/o World Wildlife Fund for Nature, 1250 24th Street NW, Washington, DC 20037. Telephone: (202) 778-9699, Fax: (202) 775-8287.

United States Fish and Wildlife Service (USFWS). United States Department of Interior, Fish and Wildlife Service, Washington, DC 20240. Telephone: (703) 358-2390, Fax: (703) 358-1735, Email: r9fwe_des.bim@mail.fws.gov

> **Division of Law Enforcement (DLE).** 911 NE 11th Avenue, Portland, Oregon 97232-4181. Telephone: (503) 231-6125.

> **Division of Endangered Species (DES).** ARLSQ 452, Washington, DC 20240. Telephone: (703) 358-2171, Fax: (703) 358-1735.

> **Office of Management Authority (OMA).** 4401 North Fairfax Drive, Room 432, Arlington, Virginia 22203. Telephone: (703) 358-2104, Fax: (703) 358-2280. Permits Branch, Telephone: (703) 358-2104, Fax: (703) 358-2281, 800-358-2104.

> **US Scientific Authority.** 4401 North Fairfax Drive, Arlington, Virginia 22203. Telephone: (703) 358-1708.

Utah Association of Herpetologists (UtAH). 195 West 200 North, Logan, Utah 84321-3905. Telephone: (801) 752-0297, Email: Herpbooks@sisna.com

Wildlife Conservation Society (WCS). 185th Street and Southern Boulevard, Bronx, New York 10460. Telephone: (212) 220-5100, Fax: (212) 220-7114.

Wildlife Society. 5410 Grosvenor Lane, Bethesda, Maryland 20814-2197.

World Conservation Monitoring Centre (WCMC). 219 Huntingdon Road, Cambridge CB3 0DL, United Kingdom. Telephone: (44) 223 277314, Fax: (44) 223 277136, Email: Info@wcmc.org.uk.

> Wildlife Trade Monitoring Unit (WTMU). Telephone: +44 (0) 1223 277314, Fax: +44 (0)1223 277136, Email: Trade@wcmc.org.uk

World Rainforest Movement. 8 Chapel Roe, Chadlington, OX7 3NA, England. Telephone: 0608 676691, Fax: 0608 676743, Email: wrm@gn.apc.org

World Wide Fund for Nature (WWF). 1250 24th Street NW, Washington, DC 20037. Telephone: (202) 293-4800, Fax: (202) 293-9211.

Zoological Society of London. Reagent's Park, London NW 1 4RY, United Kingdom. Telephone: 01-722-3333.

PUBLISHERS

Blackwell Scientific, Incorporated. 238 Main Street, Cambridge, Massachusetts 02142. Telephone: (617) 876-7000, Fax: (617) 876-7022.

Blackwell Scientific Publications Ltd. Osney Mead, Oxford OX2 0EL, United Kingdom. Telephone: 0865 240201, Fax: 0865 721205.

Chapman & Hall. 2-6 Boundary Row, London SE1 8HN, England. Telephone: 071-865-0066, Fax: 071-522-9623.

Fancy Publications, Incorporated. 3 Burroughs, Irvine, California 92718.

Folium Publishing Corporation. 58 Dmitrovskoe shosse, Moscow, 127238 Russia. Telephone: (095)482-5590, Fax: (095)482-5647, E-mail: rjh@folium.msk.su

Fundacion C&M. Maipf 853-4th Floor, 1006 Buenos Aires, Argentina. Fax: (+541) 312-2480 9095.

Elsevier Science Publishing Ltd. Crown House, Linton Road, Barking, Essex IG11 8JU, England. Telephone: 44-81-594-7272, Fax: 44-81-594-5942.

Island Press. Editorial Office, 1718 Connecticut Avenue NW, Suite 300, Washington, DC 20009. Telephone: (202) 232-7933, Fax: (202) 234-1328, Email: ipress@igc.apc.org, URL: http://www.islandpress.com

John Wiley & Sons, Incorporated. 605 Third Avenue, New York, New York 10158-0012. Telephone: (212) 850-6000, Fax: (212) 850-6088.

Slave Ware. PO Box 30744, Seattle, Washington 98102. Fax: (206) 546-2912.

Ramus Publishing, Incorporated. 1168 Route 61 Highway S, Pottsville, Pennsylvania 17901.

Telephone: (717) 622-6050, Fax: (717) 622-5858, Email: awhr04a@prodigy.com

T.F.H. Publications. 1 TFH Plaza, Neptune, New Jersey 07753.

Zoo Book Sales. 403 Parkway Avenue North, Lanesboro, Minnesota 55949-0405. Telephone: (507) 467-8733, Fax: (707) 467-8735, Email: zoobooks@ptel.net

IUCN/SSC SPECIALIST GROUPS

Source: IUCN/SSC

IUCN/Species Survival Commission. Brookfield Zoo, Chicago Zoological Society, 3300 Golf Road, Brookfield, Illinois 65513.

African Reptile & Amphibian. Contact: Lynn Raw, PO Box 200, Merrivale, 3291, South Africa. Chairman of the IUCN/SSC African Reptile and Amphibian Specialist Group and editor of the IUCN/SSC African Reptile and Amphibian Specialist Group Newsletter, Dr. Kim Howell, Department of Zoology & Marine Biology, University of Dar es Salaam, PO Box 35064, Dar es Salaam, Tanzania.

Australasian Reptile and Amphibian. Chairman, Dr. Harold G. Cogger, The Australian Museum, 6 College Street, Sydney NSW 2000, Australia.

China Reptile and Amphibian. Chairman, Professor Er-mi Zhao, Chengdu Institute of Biology, Chinese Academy of Sciences, Chengdu Sichuan Province, Sichuan Province, Chengdu, 610015, China.

Conservation Breeding Specialist Group. (Formerly the Captive Breeding Specialist Group), 12101 Johnny Cake Ridge Road, Apple Valley, Minnesota 55124.

Crocodile Specialist Group. Chairman, Professor Harry Messel, Bond University, Office of the Executive Chancellor, Gold Coast, Queensland, 4229, Australia. Executive office and Crocodile Specialist Group Newsletter, Dr. Perran Ross, Florida Museum of Natural History, Gainesville, Florida 32611.

European Reptile & Amphibian. Mr. Keith F. Corbett, Herpetological Conservation Trust, 655a Christchurch Road, Boscombe, Bournemouth, Dorset, BH1 4AP, United Kingdom.

Madagascar Reptile and Amphibian. Chairman, Mr. Quentin M.C. Bloxam, Jersey Wildlife Preservation Trust, Les Augres Manor, Trinity, JE3 5BF, United Kingdom.

Marine Turtle. Chairman, Dr. Karen Bjorndal, Center for Sea Turtle Research, Department of Zoology, Bartram Hall, University of Florida, Gainesville, Florida 32611. Marine Turtle

Newsletter, Karen Eckert and Scott Eckert, Hubbs-Sea World Research Institute, 2595 Ingraham Street, San Diego, California 92109.

Re-Introduction. c/o Africa Wildlife Foundation, PO Box 48177, Nairobi, Kenya.

South American Reptile and Amphibian. Co-chair, Professor Jorge D. Williams, Director Alterno, Museo de la Plata, Casilla de Correo 745 1900 La Plata, Argentina. Co-chair, Ms. Tristao Berardes, Aline, Deto, Tecnico-Cientifico, Fundacao Biodiversitas, Rua Maria Vaz de Melo 71, Bairra Dona Clara, 31260-110 Belo Horizonte-MG, Brazil.

South Asian Reptile and Amphibian. Dr. Indraneil Das, Centre for Herpetology, Madras Crocodile Bank Trust, Post Bag No. 4, Mamallapuram, Tamil Nadu, South India, 603 104, India.

Tortoise and Freshwater Turtle. Chairman, Dr. John L. Behler, New York Zoological Society, Department of Herpetology, Bronx Zoo, Bronx, New York.

AZA FAUNA INTEREST GROUPS (FIGS)
Source: AZA

Brazil. Natasha Schischakin, Houston Zoological Gardens. John Wortman, Denver Zoological Gardens.

Madagascar. David Anderson, San Francisco Zoo.

Meso-America. Cheryl Asa, St. Louis Zoological Park.

Paraguay. Robert D. Klemm, Sunset Zoological Park.

Southeast Asia. Vacant.

West Indies. Peter J. Tolson, Toledo Zoological Gardens.

Zaire. Rick Barongi, Walt Disney World Company. John Lukas, White Oak Plantation.

AZA SCIENTIFIC ADVISORY GROUPS (SAGS)
Source: AZA

Behavior/Husbandry. Jill D. Mellen, Metro Washington Park Zoo. Kathy Carlstead, National Zoological Park.

Contraception. Cheryl Asa, St. Louis Zoological Park. Ingrid Porton, St. Louis Zoological Park.

Genome Banking. Karen Goodrowe, Metropolitan Toronto Zoo.

Nutrition. Sue Crissey, Chicago Zoological Park.

Re-Introduction. Benjamin Beck, National Zoological Park.

Research Coordinators Committee. Steven Thompson, Lincoln Park Zoological Garden.

Small Population Management. Robert Wiese, Forth Worth Zoological Park.

Systematics. Dr. George Amato, Bronx Zoo/Wildlife Conservation Park.

Veterinary. Eric Miller, St. Louis Zoological Park. Peregrine Wolff, Minnesota Zoological Gardens.

AZA TAXON ADVISORY GROUPS (TAGS)
Source: AZA

Chelonian. John Behler, Bronx Zoo (New York Zoo), New York. Brett Stearns, Institute for Herpetological Research.

Crocodilian. Peter Brazaitis, Central Park Wildlife Conservation Center, 51 Landscape Avenue, Yonkers, New York. R. Andrew Odum, Toledo Zoological Gardens, 2700 Broadway Avenue, Toledo, Ohio 43609.

Lizard. Richard Hudson, Fort Worth Zoological Park, 1989 Colonial Parkway, Fort Worth, Texas 76110-1797.

Snake (Squamates). Jeff Ettling, St. Louis Zoological Park, Forest Park, St. Louis, Missouri 63110. Former: John Mclain, San Antonio Zoo & Aquarium, 3903 North Saint Mary's Street, San Antonio, Texas 78212.

INDEX

Please Note: This Index includes page references for all three volumes of
The Biology, Husbandry and Health Care of Reptiles.

Abscess, 529, 566, **608**, **668**, 671, **672**, **673**, 674, **676**, 725-726, 731-733, **731**, 744, **744**, 901, 913, 923, **923**, 935
Acanthophis pyrrhus, **399**
Achetus domesticus, **418**, **493**
Acid-base, 829-830
Acrantophis dumerili, *247*, *336*
Acrochordus arafurae, **365**
Adenovirus-associated Hepatic Necrosis, 595, 598
Aeromonas, 604, 887
African Rock Python, **378**
African Slender-snouted Crocodile, **90**
African Spurred Tortoise, **250**, **352**
Agama agama, **97**
Agamidae, 469-470
Agkistrodon [Calloselasma] rhodostoma, **379**
Agkistrodon piscivorous, **135**
Ahaetulla prasina, **390**
Aipysurus eydouxi, **202**
Alaria marcinae, 628
Albumin, 62-63, 75, 76, 831
Aldabra Giant Tortoise, **154**, **425**,
  thermoregulatory behavior, 418
Aleuris, **696**
Alligator mississippiensis, **45**, **46**, **54**, **89**, **171**, **310**,
  embryonic development, 46-48
  reproductive cycles, 72, 74,
  stress, 74,
  TSD, 45, 46,
Alligator sinensis, **251**
Alligator Snapper, feeding behavior, 418
Allometric Scaling, 803-806
Allozyme electrophoresis, 136, 137
Amblyomma tubercalutum, **700**, **700**
Ameiva, **471**
American Alligator, **45**, **46**, **54**, **89**, **171**, **310**,
  embryonic development, 46-48,
  reproductive cycles, 72, 74,
  stress, 74
  TSD, 45, 46,
American Crocodile, **252**
American Racer, **370**
American Sand Skink, **242**
Amphisbaenia, 7
Amphisbaenians,
  auditory sensitivity, 191, 192,

ear anatomy, 187-188, 189,
  morphology of nasal passage, 200
Anal spurs, 374
Analgesia, 318-320, 815
Anelytropsidae, 469
Anemia, 710
Anesthesia, 841, 845-854,
  hypothermia, 848-850,
  inhaled, 847-848,
  injectable, 845-847,
  life support, 850-854,
  monitors, 850-854,
  muscle relaxants, 848,
  recovery, 854
Anguidae, 471
Animal Welfare, 282, 290,
  husbandry, 293-298,
  regulations and guidelines, 298-300
  stress, 291-293,
Anniellidae, 471
Annulated Sea Snake, **215**
Anolis capito, **492**
Anolis carolinensis, **158**, **291**, **318**, **743**,
  activity temperature gradient, 158
  reproductive cycles, 73,
Anolis chrysolepis, **133**
Anolis equestris, **469**
Anolis opalinus, reproductive cycles, 73
Anolis sagrei, **296**, **942**
Anolis trachyderma, **501**
Anorexia, 529, 789-791, 919
Antimicrobials, 812-814, 948-949,
  systemic antibiotics, 812-814
  topical, 812,
Antiparasitics, 814-815
Antisepsis, 949-952
Antsingy Leaf Chameleon, **254**
Arafura File Snake, **365**
Argus Monitor, **308**, **498**
Armadillo Spinytail Lizard, **321**
Aruba Island Rattlesnake, **247**
Ascarid, **529**
ASPCA National Animal Poison Control Center, 960-961
Aspidelaps lubricus, **146**
Audition, **see** Hearing